For T
Christmas 1979
Frank and Suyy

BOOKS BY

H. L. MENCKEN

THE AMERICAN LANGUAGE

THE AMERICAN LANGUAGE: Supplement I

THE AMERICAN LANGUAGE: Supplement II

HAPPY DAYS
NEWSPAPER DAYS   } which, taken together, constitute
HEATHEN DAYS   *The Days of H. L. Mencken*

A NEW DICTIONARY OF QUOTATIONS

TREATISE ON THE GODS

CHRISTMAS STORY

A MENCKEN CHRESTOMATHY (with selections from the *Preju-dices* series, *A Book of Burlesques, In Defense of Women, Notes on Democracy, Making a President, A Book of Calumny, Treatise on Right and Wrong,* with pieces from the *American Mercury,* the *Smart Set,* and the Baltimore *Evening Sun,* and some previously unpublished notes)

MINORITY REPORT: H. L. MENCKEN'S NOTEBOOKS

THE BATHTUB HOAX and Other Blasts and Bravos
   from the *Chicago Tribune*

LETTERS OF H. L. MENCKEN,
   selected and annotated by Guy J. Forgue

H. L. MENCKEN ON MUSIC, edited by Louis Cheslock

THE AMERICAN LANGUAGE: a one-volume abridgment
   by Raven I. McDavid, Jr.

These are BORZOI BOOKS, *published in New York by* ALFRED A. KNOPF

THE AMERICAN LANGUAGE

ONE-VOLUME ABRIDGED EDITION

THE

American Language

AN INQUIRY
INTO THE DEVELOPMENT OF ENGLISH
IN THE UNITED STATES

BY

H. L. Mencken

*The Fourth Edition and the Two Supplements, abridged, with
annotations and new material, by*
RAVEN I. McDAVID, Jr.

With the assistance of David W. Maurer

NEW YORK · ALFRED·A·KNOPF
1977

THIS IS A BORZOI BOOK
PUBLISHED BY ALFRED A. KNOPF, INC.

Copyright 1919, 1921, 1923 by Alfred A. Knopf,
Inc.; Copyright renewed 1947, 1949, 1951 by H. L.
Mencken. Copyright 1936, 1945, 1948, © 1963 by
Alfred A. Knopf, Inc. Copyright renewed 1964 by
August Mencken and Mercantile-Safe Deposit &
Trust Company. Copyright renewed 1973, 1976 by
Mercantile-Safe Deposit & Trust Company. All
rights reserved under International and Pan-Amer-
ican Copyright Conventions. Published in the
United States by Alfred A. Knopf, Inc., New York,
and simultaneously in Canada by Random House of
Canada Limited, Toronto. Distributed by
Random House, Inc. New York.
Library of Congress Cataloging in Publication Data
Mencken, Henry Louis, 1880–1956.
The American language.
1. English language in the United States.
2. Names—United States.
I. McDavid, Raven Ioor. II. Title.
[PE2808.M43 1977]   420'.973   76-54715
ISBN 0-394-73315-0
Manufactured in the United States of America
Abridged Edition Published November 11, 1963

Published March 25, 1977
Second Printing, June 1977

Editor's Introduction

I

Mencken always insisted, with what seems to most linguists an excessive modesty, that he was not a scholar himself, but one who pointed out the quarry for scholars to bag. It is, however, something more than a coincidence that linguistic science in North America, and particularly the study of the varieties of English spoken in the Western Hemisphere, has developed remarkably since the first publication of "The American Language" in 1919.[1] Much of this development has been a response to the challenge which Mencken's work provided, through a realization among professional scholars that American English demanded serious and systematic investigation by the best minds, and that the fruits of this investigation might not only be interesting in themselves but have beneficent effects upon American letters and the American educational system. In part these investigations were motivated by the scientific desire to see assumptions documented and theories put to the test; as a result, since World War I the outlines of the history of American English and the affiliations of the most significant geographical and social variants have been sketched with considerable accuracy, and every year the unknown areas grow smaller. But this expansion in knowledge and insight and general interest also reflects the encouragement that Mencken so generously extended to all those, professional scholars and laymen alike, who interested themselves in the nature and origins of the language of the most powerful nation of the free world, in the slow progress of this language toward acceptance as the legitimate vehicle of our scientific discourse and our imaginative expression, and in the details, sometimes gross but more often subtle, by which

[1] In 1945 A. G. Kennedy remarked (*AS*, Vol. XX, Dec. 1945, pp. 245–6) that the number of items on American English published since the appearance of the first edition of The American Language had already far exceeded what had appeared before 1919.

a speaker betrays where he stands in our complex society. A list of those whose concern with linguistics was stimulated by correspondence about "The American Language," or whose research was furthered directly by Mencken himself, would include most of those who have made the study of American English a respectable discipline in its own right. "The English of England," Allen Walker Read's forthcoming historical dictionary of the peculiarly British element in our common language, was encouraged by Mencken from the outset; the field work in Maryland for the Linguistic Atlas was made possible by a conversation in which Mencken directed Hans Kurath to sources of financial support. The direction of my career was shifted from the literature of the English Renaissance to the language of the United States by a reading of "The American Language," a long letter of comment and the prompt and heartening acknowledgment that Mencken always gave beginners; the emphasis of my research in recent years—on the relationships between linguistic patterns in the American English speech community and the complex of social forces in American society—derives from the extensive and pleasant correspondence which I had with Mencken from the resumption of Linguistic Atlas field work in the South after World War II until his stroke in 1948. If this research has done a little toward breaking down the barrier—so bitterly deplored in recent years—between the humanistic and scientific cultures, much of the credit is due to both the example and the encouragement of Mencken.

II

Like many books, "The American Language" had a long history before it reached the form in which it is generally known today: the Fourth Edition of 1936 and the two Supplements of 1945 and 1948. Contrary to a widely held opinion, it did not spring from anti-British and pro-German sentiment during World War I, but from a long period of wide reading and from continued close observation of the varieties of speech current in Baltimore, a city of complex cultural origins and social structure, situated astride a major dialect boundary. So early as 1910, Mencken had written several columns in the Baltimore *Evening Sun* which called attention to some of the significant traits of the national tongue, and especially to the apparent divergence of the two streams of English, British and American. If one may speculate, had World War I not broken out, there would have been further incidental pieces, but almost certainly no systematic discussion. But as a nation of wild-eyed, hypermoral innocents entangled itself in the sticky web of international politics, Mencken—like many other good Americans—found himself officially muzzled because he felt that something more than simple outraged morality had committed us to the Allied cause, and that something more than hanging the Kaiser was needed if we were to end war forever and make the world safe for an American-style middle-class democracy. In lieu of his editorials he devoted himself to the ostensibly harmless drudgery of philological comment, and in 1919 produced the first edition of "The American Language," with the thesis that the divergence of American and English would soon result in mutually unintelligible vernaculars. It sold out rapidly and was followed by a second edition (1921) and a third (1923), with the same organization and the same basic text but with some expansions, many more footnotes and occasional revisions in the light of comments from observers, academic and lay alike. It was popular with the laity, if scorned by the self-styled illuminati, for it spared no sacred cows, plumped for the autonomy of the national idiom and appeared in a vigorous, unacademic style. Many of the surviving authorities of the period—including some who should have known better—have never seen "The American Language" in a later edition, nor forgiven Mencken for what he said at the time, nor bothered to look at the evidence on which Mencken's statements were based.

If philologians wonder at the time that elapsed between the third and fourth editions, social historians do not. The third decade of this century, in the United States at least, was an unparalleled era of buncombe: the vacuous normalcy of Harding, the silent coolness of Coolidge and the great engineering of Hoover, launched with dramatic fanfaronades and ending in a *sauve qui peut*. Here came of age a genuine American literature, with the *American Mercury* of Mencken its most effective voice. Here was a plethora of florid sensations: the Florida real-estate bubble, the Leopold-Loeb trial, the Tennessee "monkey law," the legalized lynching of Sacco and Vanzetti, the crimearchy of Al Capone, the idyl of Peaches Browning, the putative kidnapping of Aimee Semple McPherson and the climactic orgy of boom and bust on Wall Street. Here was more than enough for the most energetic social critic. But this was also the period in which the study of the national tongue began to establish itself in Academe, especially at the University of Michigan. This same period saw the founding of the Linguistic Society of America, of *American Speech*, and of the *International Journal of American Linguistics;* the beginnings of the Linguistic Institutes, of the "Dictionary of American English" and of the Linguistic Atlas project; the publication of Leonard Bloomfield's "Language" and of George Philip Krapp's "The English Language in America." Perhaps even more important than any of these phenomena was the establishment of the basic tradition of American linguistics: hard-boiled objectivity in observing and classifying the evidence and free and generous co-operation in research and in exchange of information. In creating this new climate of opinion Mencken and "The American Language" played an important part.

The return of Mencken to his linguistic interests coincided with a decline in his activity as social satirist during the New Deal and the subsequent American involvement in World War II. It should be no reproach that he never fully understood the gravity of either the domestic economic and social tensions or the foreign menace from the organized bestiality rampant in Germany and Italy. Men who knew more about economics proclaimed the healthiness of deflation and the imminence of a new Republican prosperity, and sought to stabilize the economy by raising taxes in a period of rising unemployment and falling income; men who knew more about diplomacy applauded Hitler and Mussolini for ending unemployment and making trains run on time, expected these new dictators to honor treaties, and justified the betrayal of Czechoslovakia as bringing "peace in our time." There was plenty to poke fun at in the errors and excesses of the New Deal, but there was no longer the common agreement on a system of values that effective social satire demands.

In any event, the Fourth Edition that appeared in 1936 was an almost new work. Not only was the organization drastically changed, but the basic thesis was different. The 1919 version had emphasized the increasing divergence of American and British speechways; that of 1936 proclaimed that the march of events had so shifted the balance of the English-speaking world that future scholars might well study "English" as a dialect of "American." The expansion of the work continued, with a formidable growth in the scholarly apparatus as American linguists contributed not only through citations of their published works but through comments in personal correspondence. Perhaps a trifle more sedate than its predecessor, the 1936 edition is still consistently lively and based on solid objective observations.

There was no revision after 1936. The two Supplements of 1945 and 1948 followed the organization of the Fourth Edition, with indications where the addenda might be hooked on; nevertheless, each Supplement is a readable volume in its own right, a contribution to our knowledge of how we talk and write. The style in the Supplements is somewhat more diffuse and anecdotal than in the Fourth Edition; the examples are more numerous and somewhat less selective; the documentation is much more extensive. The first Supplement covered the territory of the first six chapters of the 1936 version; the second the next five. Left without exegesis were the final chapter, on the future of the language, and the appendix on non-English languages in the United States; left untouched, and ripe for discussion by ambitious and energetic young students, were such matters as "the language of gesture, that of children, the names of political parties, cattle brands, animal calls, and so on," which might have formed other appendices or parts of another Supplement. But Mencken prophetically observed: "At my age a man encounters frequent reminders, some of them disconcerting, that his body is no more than a highly unstable congeries of the compounds of carbon." Eight months after the appearance of Supplement Two he had his first stroke and never wrote again, though at intervals *The New Yorker* published a series of "Postscripts to the American Language"—articles previously composed, amplifying statements made in the three volumes.

In short, "The American Language," uniquely Mencken's, is at the same time a work of serious scholarship that underwent progressive modifications in successive versions, in response to changes in Mencken's viewpoint, to changes in the speech he was describing and to changes in the amount and quality of information available about that speech. Its early bases were sound intuitive judgment and impressionistic and practical observations. But not these alone: even in the first edition there was a demonstrated familiarity with the best current scholarship in the field, as one might expect from the owner of the best private linguistics library in the United States. The scholarly significance of the work increased with each edition, as academic investigators were led to explore hitherto uncontemplated ramifications of the subject; in turn, their explorations were reflected in Mencken's revisions of his earlier statements. The incidental horseplay is in keeping with a lively subject,[2] the endlessly proliferating linguistic behavior of an unregimented and somewhat disorderly people; the frequent discursiveness is in keeping with Mencken's mission *in partibus infidelium,* to demonstrate to the widest possible audience the interest and importance of the subject. His occasional impatience toward more recent developments of phonemic theory and rigorous structural grammar can perhaps be excused. As James Sledd, for instance, has repeatedly declared (and most serious linguists agree), there is as yet no single analysis uniformly valid for all times and occasions; as many other linguists will concede, the pressure to analyze and describe with mathematical rigor, and to convince one's scientific colleagues of the validity of one's scientific methods, has too often resulted in a crabbed, infelicitous style that sometimes merely conceals muddled thinking. And under any circumstance and in any discipline there is a difference in vocation between the pioneer theorist, the student who tests the theories in a particular setting, the writer who prepares a useful pedagogical interpretation and the teacher who expounds it in the classroom. So far, despite some worthy

---

[2] For a notable manifestation of this spirit among the academicians, see *Lg.,* Vol. XI (Apr.–June 1935), p. 98, *n.* 3.

efforts, there has been no work of scientific integrity that adequately explains the principles of modern linguistics to the layman and to the academician in other disciplines. The Mencken of 1910 or 1919 could survey intelligently the entire field of "philology," as it was then called; the Mencken of 1945–8 was overwhelmed by the spate of writings, many of algebraic terseness, released by an exponentially growing discipline.

III

This same spate of writings, further swollen, faced me as editor of the abridged version. A simple bibliography of linguistic publications since World War II would make a volume as fat as the 1919 edition. The extent of the new evidence, however, can be suggested briefly. In commercial lexicography we have had a third edition of the Merriam-Webster New International, and serious rivals to the abridged "Webster's Collegiate" in Random House's "American College Dictionary" (of which an expanded second edition is in preparation), the World Publishing Company's "Webster's New World Dictionary" and the new Barnhart work under various names. Of scholarly lexicons we have in print the "Dictionary of Americanisms," by Mitford M. Mathews, and three volumes of a new "Middle English Dictionary"; editorial work has begun on a second supplement to the Oxford; and dictionaries of Canadian, Jamaican and Newfoundland English are in various stages of preparation. The Linguistic Atlas project has extended into most of the United States and parts of Canada; its principal findings for the Atlantic seaboard have been summarized in Hans Kurath's "Word Geography," Bagby Atwood's "Verb Forms" and Kurath's and my "Pronunciation." Several studies of regional and local vocabulary have appeared, including a study of Texas by Atwood. "Wisconsin Words," by F. G. Cassidy and Audrey Duckert, soon to appear, will be the first systematic step toward the long-awaited dictionary of American regional speech. In bilingualism and onomastics significant research has been undertaken, in the first under the leadership of Einar Haugen and Uriel Weinreich, in the second under the auspices of the American Name Society, which has just observed its tenth anniversary. Bloomfield's "Language" and Sapir's book by the same name are still widely read, but they have been supplemented by H. A. Gleason, Jr.'s, "Introduction to Descriptive Linguistics," Winfred Lehmann's "Historical Linguistics," Charles F. Hockett's "A Course in Modern Linguistics" and John P. Hughes's "The Science of Language," and—on a highly rarefied intellectual plane—by Zellig Harris's "Methods in Structural Linguistics," Noam Chomsky's "Syntactic Structures," Henry Hoenigswald's "Language Change and Linguistic Reconstruction" and Kenneth Pike's "Language in Relation to a Unified Theory of the Structure of Human Behavior." For modern English there are descriptions, often at variance with one another, by Bernard Bloch and George L. Trager, Trager and Henry Lee Smith, Jr., C. C. Fries, Archibald A. Hill, Sledd, Ralph Long and W. Nelson Francis, to mention a few of the most notable. Psychiatrists have probed the relationship between language behavior and personality adjustment, in co-operation with such linguists as Hockett, Trager, Norman A. McQuown and William M. Austin. The American Council of Learned Societies, the College Entrance Examination Board, the Modern Language Association and the National Council of Teachers of English have shown increasing interest in the objective study of American English, both for its own sake and for the potential improvement in the teaching of language and literature.[3] Furthermore, the historian and sociologist of language must reckon with the effects of World War II, the Korean pacification, the Cold War, the death throes of colonialism and the emergence of new nations in Asia and Africa, and the rise of the Soviet Union to the rank of a super power matched only by the United States. Everywhere there has been unprecedentedly rapid and widespread social change, marked by industrialization, urbanization and the spread of mass education. One aspect of the new industrialization, automation, is bringing not only social change and its own accretions to the vocabulary but also the development of new syntactic devices by which prepared tapes may transmit consistent and accurate instructions to machinery. It is not surprising that the American vernacular has undergone drastic changes during this period, sometimes in ways Mencken could never have foreseen.

IV

These continuing changes in the language and in the culture the language reflects, added to the history of "The American Language" as an evolving work, confronted me with an inescapable dilemma in my role as editor of the abridgment. If I considered "The American Language" an inspired text, to be abridged but never altered, I would abdicate my responsibility as a scholar and offer a dated work; if I tried to recognize all the major linguistic discoveries and social changes of the past fifteen years, I would inevitably alter what Mencken had written, sometimes beyond recognition. In the interchange between editor and publisher that accompanies the progress of a book toward print, it was finally and amicably agreed that this book should be simply an abridgment and condensation of Menck-

---

[3] Current American Usage, a study of American grammatical practice at mid-century, sponsored by the NCTE and edited by Margaret M. Bryant, appeared as the manuscript of this book was nearing completion.

en's three volumes, with updating where necessary and editorial commentary at critical points.[4] As the manuscript has taken shape, its rationale has been clearly defined, with each editorial problem being judged on its own merits. For this I am deeply indebted both to Henry Robbins, of Alfred A. Knopf, Inc., the final editor in charge of the manuscript, and to Jess Stein, a long-time friend who is now vice-president of Random House, Inc., of which the Knopf firm constitutes a division.

Most of the new matter will be clearly identifiable by editorial brackets. Transition sentences or parts of sentences using Mencken's material but rephrasing it have usually been left out of brackets. Normally a summary paragraph is not bracketed, if a major part of the phraseology is Mencken's, even though it may be rearranged. For any changes in sentence rhythm I accept responsibility, though I have tried to keep it as much like Mencken's as possible.

The following editorial procedures were used:

1. The "Dictionary of Americanisms," shorter than the "Dictionary of American English" but offering much new evidence on the American innovations in the vocabulary, appeared in 1951, three years after Supplement Two. Where AL4 or a Supplement refers to the DAE, I have consistently checked the DA; if (as often happens) the DA offers an earlier first citation than the DAE, its citation date has been substituted. Sometimes, as with the compounds formed from the word *Indian*, this procedure has meant a shortening of the period from which illustrative citations are drawn: using the DAE, Mencken drew his list of derivatives from the entire Seventeenth Century; using the DA, I have drawn an adequately long list from 1600–25.

2. I have always checked references to the 1934 New International against the 1961 edition, and usually checked references to the GPO Style Manual against the 1959 printing.

3. Insofar as possible, all statements about proper names (illustrating the bubbling of the American Melting Pot) have been based on 1960–1 editions of telephone directories, military rosters, "Who's Who in America" and the like, rather than on the 1930 or 1940 compilations that Mencken used. This later evidence seldom changes a phrase in the commentary itself, but illustrates our culture more fairly as of the date of going to press.

4. The table of principal parts of verbs in Chapter IX, Section 2, was apparently drawn from a variety of sources. Since the Linguistic

---

[4] The other part of the forest, an examination of American speechways through the interrelated disciplines of linguistics, psychology and anthropology, will be the theme of The American Idiom, by David W. Maurer and Raven I. McDavid, Jr., to appear in 1964.

Atlas systematically sampled a large number of verb forms, and the variants from wide areas have been presented in Atwood's "Verb Forms of the Eastern United States" and Virginia McDavid's "Verb Forms of the North-Central States and Upper Midwest," the evidence from these works was used to compile a new list, somewhat shorter (as befits an abridgment) and derived from field observations by trained scholars.

5. Where the sequence of AL4 differs from that of the Supplements, I have had to decide which to follow. For these decisions there have been apparently logical reasons, or at least a plausible basis for rationalization. For example, *dope* and *snoop,* loans from the Dutch first recorded in the Nineteenth Century, are treated both in Chapter III (The Beginnings of American) and in Chapter IV (The Period of Growth); I have condensed the two treatments in Chapter IV. Again, some of the problems of grammatical usage are treated in Chapter V (The Language Today), others in Chapter IX (The Common Speech); I have generally limited Chapter V to the discussion of word formation and treated all problems of usage in Chapter IX. With Chapter VIII, Section 5 (Punctuation, Capitalization and Abbreviation), I have amalgamated the discussion of abbreviations that appeared in Chapter V; to Chapter VI as Section 6 has gone the treatment of gobbledygook and counter words, likewise originally in Chapter V. The original Section 6 (Euphemisms) has been divided into two parts, Euphemisms, now Section 7, and Terms of Abuse, now Section 9, appearing between Forbidden Words and Expletives, now respectively Sections 8 and 10. Finally, the sequences of the nationalities discussed in Chapter X, Section 1 (Surnames) and Section 2 (Given Names), are not the same in AL4 and Supplement Two; here I have compromised.

6. Sometimes there were several occurrences of the same anecdote or observation, notably Witherspoon's comment that the dialects in the United States were fewer and less distinctive than those in the British Isles. I have kept the full quotation where it first occurs, in Chapter I, Section 1 (The Two Streams of English: The Earliest Alarms), and reduced it to an incidental reference in Chapter VII, Section 1 (The Pronunciation of American: Its General Characteristics), and Section 4 (Dialects). As a general principle, I have cut anecdotes and word lists by at least half; this sometimes removes charming notes on American *Kultur,* but there are many such left. Anyone who misses some of his favorite passages may console himself with the knowledge that I have deleted many of mine.

. . .

One caution I should give to friends and foes alike: this is not a "revision" of "The American Language," and never could be. It is simply an attempt to present in briefer form the essence of a three-volume work in which Mencken himself had made many revisions over nearly three decades; what modifications I have made have been required by the recent changes in the language and in the civilization which the language reflects. I have naturally tried to see the changing situation as Mencken himself might have seen it, and after several years of association with "The American Language" the norms of my style have possibly drifted toward the norms of his. But I am not Mencken, and make no pretensions of arrogating to myself his unique contributions to linguistics.

v

No one produces a major work unaided, even as an editor. During the several years this manuscript has been growing, I have put myself in debt to many people. The staff of Alfred A. Knopf, Inc., have been uniformly generous with intelligent advice. Departmental colleagues have offered helpful criticism, and encouragement when the way seemed endless; I note particularly Joseph Friend, W. Powell Jones, Lyon Richardson and Priscilla Tyler, of Western Reserve University, and Walter Blair, Daniel Boorstin, Fred Eggan, Arthur Friedman, Eric Hamp, Norman McQuown, McKim Marriott, Mitford M. Mathews, Arthur Norman, Kenneth Northcott, Julian Pitt-Rivers, Theodore Silverstein, Sol Tax and Dean Napier Wilt of the University of Chicago. William Card, of Chicago Teachers College, verified the Yiddish loans and was generally helpful on the vocabulary of the city. In becoming a competent linguist, I am, like all of my generation, indebted to the inspiration of Edward Sapir, Leonard Bloomfield, Edgar Sturtevant and Charles C. Fries, and to the continued encouragement of George Bolling. In various professional relationships I have continued to learn from such extramural colleagues as Edward Artin, William M. Austin, J Milton Cowan, George P. Faust, W. Nelson Francis, Philip Gove, Einar Haugen, A. A. Hill, Fred Householder, Martin Joos, John Kepke, Donald W. Lee, James B. McMillan, Randolph Quirk, Allen Walker Read, I. Willis Russell, James H. Sledd, Henry Lee Smith, Jr., Hans Sperber, Donald Swanson, George L. Trager, W. Freeman Twaddell and Francis Lee Utley. I am particularly indebted to the fraternity of dialectologists, notably Bernard Bloch, my first formal teacher of linguistics; Hans Kurath, the most generous director a research scholar could have; Albert H. Marckwardt, who has sacrificed much of his own career as a scholar so that linguists and linguistics could gain wider acceptance; Harold Allen, Bagby Atwood, Fred Cassidy, Robert A. Hall, Jr., Marjorie

Kimmerle, Angus McIntosh, William G. Moulton, and Carroll and David Reed. Before becoming a linguist, and since, I have profited from associations with Alfred T. O'Dell, of Furman University, Allan Gilbert and Paull Baum, of Duke University, James G. Harrison, of The Citadel, and William S. Price, now of the University of Tulsa. Wayne Tyler, now of River Falls State College, was a fellow student at the Linguistic Institute of 1937, and introduced me both to linguistic geography and to "The American Language." Francis Nipp, Sumner Ives, Alva Davis and James Downer have been loyal friends and severe critics. In the interchange with my own students, such as Mildred Abbott, Walter Avis, William and Madie Barrett, Thomas Creswell, Dan Desberg, John Hagopian, Clyde Hankey, Mrs. Janet Kimball, William Kirwin, Norman McCullough, Lee Pederson, Roger Shuy, Gerald Udell, William R. Van Riper, Thomas Wetmore, Juanita Williamson and Rex Wilson, I have learned at least as much as I have taught.[5] In my work at the Board on Geographic Names I became acquainted with the practical problems a government agency faces in systematizing the appearance of names on a map. From the American Council of Learned Societies I have had both financial and moral support during my scholarly career, as well as permission to cite unpublished data from the Linguistic Atlas files; from the six hundred informants whom I interviewed for a total of some five thousand hours for the Atlas, I gained invaluable linguistic information and insights into the richness of our cultural heritage.[6] David Maurer, who knows more about criminal argots than any other legitimate citizen, not only prepared the abridgment of the chapter on slang but also shared the burden and heat of the day throughout. Dr. Jerome Kavka both made it possible for me to complete the work by helping me to understand the intricate polyhedron of forces within which I was reared and contributed a deeper understanding of the problems an immigrant faces in becoming acculturated to the American scene. The administrations of the University of New Brunswick and of West Virginia State College provided relaxed working and living conditions during the summers of 1961 and 1962, which made possible more rapid progress than I had dreamed of at the time. My wife, Virginia McDavid, has not only compiled the indexes but made her influence, as a distinguished scholar in her own right, felt throughout. To these, and to

---

[5] I single out for particular mention Carolyn H. and Vernon S. Larsen, who contributed generously of their time and professional skill in the reading of the proofs. In this labor they were assisted by my sons: Glenn Truxtun McDavid, Raven I. McDavid 3d, and Thomas Inglesby McDavid.

[6] In many instances the introductions to these informants were obtained through the wide spectrum of contacts which my father, Raven I. McDavid, developed through a long and active but never adequately fulfilled political career.

others too numerous to mention, I acknowledge indebtedness to be found on every page.

The growth of "The American Language" was aided by an army of private correspondents, whose every contribution Mencken specifically recognized. Since, in most instances, that private correspondence has not continued with me, I have ordinarily not repeated these gratulatory footnotes, but hereby acknowledge their importance *en bloc.* As an abridgment this work has not drawn the same horde of voluntary contributors, but there have been some notable ones, particularly Thomas Pyles, of the University of Florida, author of the most readable book on American English since Supplement Two, John J. Appel, Hermann Barnstorff, Alan E. Comyns, Antonio Cuffari, Albert K. Dawson, Gerard Fay, of the Manchester *Guardian,* Miriam Allen de Ford, Winthrop Holmes, Arthur Jacobs, J. J. Lamberts, Southworth Lancaster, Andrew Levens, William C. McCoy, Jr., Emanuel Raias, S. G. Rich, Robert Roberts, William I. Schreiber, Richard B. Sealock, Edward Stanley and Mrs. Helen Starr. In the interest of setting the record straight when the opportunity permits, I welcome comments and observations, which may be sent to me either through the publisher or directly to the English Department of the University of Chicago. It is this type of response that helped Mencken attain his objective of showing the academic brethren and the public at large that "the study of the national tongue could be interesting—and, more than interesting, important."

RAVEN I. McDAVID, JR.

Chicago
September 12, 1962

Contents

IX. THE COMMON SPEECH

X. PROPER NAMES IN AMERICA

XI. AMERICAN SLANG

XII. THE FUTURE OF THE LANGUAGE

Abbreviations

To SAVE space some of the books and journals referred to frequently are cited by the following catchwords and abbreviations:

ACD   The American College Dictionary, edited by Clarence L. Barnhart; New York, 1947.

AJP   American Journal of Philology.

AL1   The American Language, by H. L. Mencken; 1st ed.; New York, 1919.

AL2   The same; 2nd ed.; New York, 1921.

AL3   The same; 3rd ed.; New York, 1923.

AL4   The same; 4th ed.; New York, 1936.

AS   American Speech

Barrère   Argot and Slang, by A. Barrère; London, 1887.

Bartlett   A Glossary of Words and Phrases Usually Regarded as Peculiar to the United States, by John Russell Bartlett; New York, 1848; 2nd ed., Boston, 1859; 3rd ed., Boston, 1860; 4th ed., Boston, 1877.

Bentley   A Dictionary of Spanish Terms in English, by Harold W. Bentley; New York, 1932.

Berrey and Van den Bark   The American Thesaurus of Slang, by Lester V. Berrey and Melvin Van den Bark; New York, 1942; 5th printing, 1947.

Boucher   Boucher's Glossary of Archaic and Provincial Words; a Supplement to the Dictionaries of the English Language, Particularly Those of Dr. Johnson and Dr. Webster, . . . by the late Rev. Jonathan Boucher, . . . edited jointly by the Rev. Joseph Hunter and Joseph Stevenson; London, Part I, 1832; Part II, 1833.

Bristed   The English Language in America, by Charles Astor Bristed; in Cambridge Essays, Contributed by Members of the University; London, 1855.

Burke   The Literature of Slang, by W. J. Burke; New York, 1939.

Cairns   British Criticisms of American Writings, by William B. Cairns; Madison, Wis., 1918.

CE   College English.

Concise Oxford   The Concise Oxford Dictionary of Current English, adapted by H. W. Fowler and F. G. Fowler; 4th ed., revised by E. McIntosh; Oxford, 1950.

DA   A Dictionary of Americanisms on Historical Principles, edited by Mitford M. Mathews; Chicago, 1951.

DAE   A Dictionary of American English on Historical Principles, edited by W. A. Craigie and James R. Hulbert; 4 vols.; Chicago, 1938–44.

DN   Dialect Notes.

Dunglison   Americanisms, in the *Virginia Literary Museum and Journal of Belles Lettres, Arts, Sciences &c.*, signed Wy and supposed to be by Robley Dunglison; Charlottesville, Va., 1829–30.

EDD   The English Dialect Dictionary, edited by Joseph Wright; 6 vols.; Oxford, 1898–1905.

EDG   The English Dialect Grammar, by Joseph Wright; Oxford, 1905.

EJ   The English Journal.

Farmer   Americanisms Old and New, by John S. Farmer; London, 1889.

Farmer and Henley   Slang and Its Analogues, by John S. Farmer and W. E. Henley; 7 vols.; London, 1890–1904.

Grose   A Classical Dictionary of the Vulgar Tongue, by Francis Grose; London, 1785; new edition edited by Eric Partridge; London, 1931.

Holt   American Place Names, by Alfred H. Holt; New York, 1938.

Horwill   A Dictionary of Modern American Usage, by H. W. Horwill; Oxford, 1935; 2nd ed., 1944.

Humphreys   Glossary appended to The Yankey in England, by David Humphreys; n.p., 1815.

IJAL   International Journal of American Linguistics.

JAF   Journal of American Folklore.

JEGP   Journal of English and Germanic Philology.

Jour. AMA   Journal of the American Medical Association.

Joyce   English As We Speak It in Ireland, by P. W. Joyce; 2nd ed.; London, 1910.

Kennedy   A Bibliography of Writings on the English Language from the Beginnings of Printing to the End of 1922, by Arthur G. Kennedy; Cambridge and New Haven, 1927.

Kenyon and Knott   A Pronouncing Dictionary of American English, by

John Samuel Kenyon and Thomas Albert Knott; Springfield, Mass., 1944.

Krapp The English Language in America, by George Philip Krapp; 2 vols.; New York, 1925.

LA Linguistic Atlas of the United States and Canada; Linguistic Atlas of New England, by Hans Kurath, Miles L. Hanley, Bernard Bloch, Guy S. Lowman, Jr., and Marcus L. Hansen; 3 vols. (bound as 6) and a handbook; Providence, R.I., 1939–43.

Leonard The Doctrine of Correctness in English Usage, 1700–1800, by Sterling Andrus Leonard; Madison, Wis., 1929.

Lg. Language

Maitland The American Slang Dictionary, by James Maitland; Chicago, 1891.

Marryat A Diary in America, by Frederick Marryat; 3 vols.; London, 1839.

Mathews The Beginnings of American English, by M. M. Mathews; Chicago, 1931.

MLN Modern Language Notes.

MP Modern Philology.

OED Oxford English Dictionary: Being a Corrected Re-issue of A New English Dictionary on Historical Principles, founded mainly on the materials collected by the Philological Society and edited by James A. H. Murray, Henry Bradley, W. A. Craigie and C. T. Onions, [1888–1928], 1933.[1]

OED Supplement The Oxford English Dictionary Supplement and Bibliography; Oxford, 1933.

PADS Publications of the American Dialect Society.

Partridge A Dictionary of Slang and Unconventional English, by Eric Partridge, 1937; 4th ed., London, 1951.

Pickering A Vocabulary or Collection of Words and Phrases Which Have Been Supposed to Be Peculiar to the United States of America, by John Pickering; Boston, 1816.

PMLA Publications of the Modern Language Association of America.

QJS Quarterly Journal of Speech.

QJS Ed. Quarterly Journal of Speech Education.

---

[1] Earlier publications often refer to this work as the NED, from its original title; but it seems best to use the abbreviation now current and derived from the title under which the work is issued by the publishers.

Schele de Vere   Americanisms: The English of the New World, by M. Schele de Vere; New York, 1871; 2nd ed., 1872.

Shankle   American Nicknames, by George Earlie Shankle; New York, 1937.

Sherwood   Gazetteer of the State of Georgia, by Adiel Sherwood; 3rd ed., 1857.

Shorter Oxford   The Shorter Oxford Dictionary on Historical Principles, prepared by William Little, H. W. Fowler and J. Coulson, and revised and edited by C. T. Onions; 2 vols.; Oxford, 1933. [A thin-paper edition, bound in one volume, is sold in the United States as the Oxford Universal Dictionary.]

SIL   Studies in Linguistics.

SPE Tract   Society for Pure English Tract

Stewart   Names on the Land, by George R. Stewart; New York, 1945; 2nd ed., 1958.

Supplement I   Supplement I: The American Language, by H. L. Mencken; New York, 1945.

Supplement II   Supplement II: The American Language, by H. L. Mencken; New York, 1948.

Thornton   An American Glossary, by Richard H. Thornton; 2 vols.; Philadelphia, 1912. Vol. III published serially in *Dialect Notes*, 1931–9.

Warfel   Noah Webster, Schoolmaster to America, by Harry R. Warfel; New York, 1936.

Webster 1806   A Compendious Dictionary of the English Language, by Noah Webster; New Haven, 1806.

Webster 1828   An American Dictionary of the English Language, by Noah Webster; New York, 1828.

Webster 1847   An American Dictionary of the English Language, by Noah Webster; revised and enlarged by Chauncey A. Goodrich; Springfield, Mass., 1847; reprinted several times (1852, 1854, etc.).

Webster 1934   Webster's New International Dictionary of the English Language; 2nd ed., edited by William Allan Neilson, Thomas A. Knott and Paul W. Carhart; Springfield, Mass., 1934.

Webster 1961   Webster's Third New International Dictionary of the English Language; editor in chief, Philip Babcock Gove; Springfield, Mass., 1961.

Weekley   An Etymological Dictionary of Modern English, by Ernest Weekley; New York, 1921.

Wentworth   American Dialect Dictionary, by Harold Wentworth; New York, 1944.

Woulfe   Irish Names and Surnames, by Patrick Woulfe; Dublin, 1923.

Wyld   A History of Modern Colloquial English, by Henry Cecil Wyld; London, 1920.

In some cases the authors whose principal works are listed above are also the authors of other works. All references to the latter are in full.

THE AMERICAN LANGUAGE

A NOTE ON THE USE OF BRACKETS

IN GENERAL, the new material added by the editor to this abridged edition has been enclosed in brackets. However, transition sentences or parts of sentences using H. L. Mencken's material but rephrasing it have usually not been bracketed. Nor have paragraphs that merely summarize longer sections in the original work if the phrasing is basically Mencken's.

I

The Two Streams
of English

1: THE EARLIEST ALARMS

The first American colonists had perforce to invent Americanisms, if only to describe the unfamiliar landscape, weather, flora and fauna confronting them. Half a dozen that are still in use are found in Captain John Smith's "Map of Virginia," published in 1612, and there are many more in the works of the New England annalists. By 1621 Alexander Gil was noting in his "Logonomia Anglica" that *maize* and *canoe* were making their way into English.[1] But it was reserved for one Francis Moore, who came out to Georgia with Oglethorpe in 1735, to raise the earliest alarm against this enrichment of English from the New World, and so set the tone that English criticism has maintained ever since. Thus he described Savannah, then a village only two years old:

> It stands upon the flat of a Hill; the Bank of the River (which they in barbarous English call a *bluff*) is steep, and about forty-five foot perpendicular.[2]

John Wesley, another companion of Oglethorpe, provides the Oxford Dictionary's earliest example of *bluff*, in his diary for December 2, 1737, [though M. M. Mathews's "Dictionary of Americanisms" indicates that the word had been in use in South Carolina since 1687]. But Moore was the first to denounce it, and for that pioneering he must hold his honorable

---

[1] British Recognition of American Speech in the Eighteenth Century, by Allen Walker Read, *DN*, Vol. VI, Pt. VI, 1933, p. 313.

[2] A Voyage to Georgia, Begun in the Year 1735; London, 1744, p. 24.

place in this history. In colonial times there was comparatively little incitement to hostility to Americanisms, for few Englishmen came to America to write books about their sufferings, and fewer American books reached London. [Nevertheless, as Allen Walker Read points out,[3] the legend of American speech as something exotic and difficult to understand—reflecting the manners of a new and barbarous society—had been established before the Revolution.] The first call for a glossary of the new patois came from Richard Owen Cambridge, author of the "Scribleriad," in a humorous comment on a letter dealing with Indian warfare on the New York frontier.[4] All of the lexical curiosa Cambridge cited, such as *sachem, take up the hatchet, speechbelt, string of wampum,* and such tribal designations as *Chippeways* (Ojibwas) and *the Six Nations* (Iroquois), had been in the language since the Seventeenth Century, but Cambridge joined them in such a way as to suggest the difficulties an educated Englishman had in understanding the life and language of the New World. Within the next few years the same words appear so frequently in popular English articles about American life that one suspects the British reading public demanded them. One of the New World lexical oddities Englishmen felt obliged to comment on was *cleared,* as applied to land formerly covered with trees. The American delight in *cleared* land amazed the Eighteenth Century Englishman, accustomed to cherish his forests and mock the comparative treelessness of Scotland. [Even John Wilkes, a friend of the Americans, was struck by this American sense of *cleared.*]

Dr. Johnson, as everyone knows, hated all things American, so it is surprising to learn that he admitted to his "Dictionary of the English Language" (1755) an American-born author, Charlotte Lennox, as an authority for the use of two words, one of which, *talent,* had a satellite adjective *talented* that was to be denounced as a vile and intolerable Americanism when it began to be used toward the end of the century.[5] Johnson himself once used an Americanism, *tomahawk,* in the "Idler," [6] but decently disguised it as *tom-ax.* In 1756, a year after his Dictionary was published, he sneered in a review in the *London Magazine* at the "mixture of the American dialect" in Lewis Evans's "Geographical, Historical, Philosophical and Mechanical Essays," [7] calling it "a tract [8] of corruption to which every language widely diffused must always be exposed." "Johnson," says Read, "probably was offended by such of Evans's words as *portage, statehouse,*

---

[3] *Op. cit.,* pp. 313–34.
[4] Cambridge (1717–1802) was a Londoner, educated at Eton and Oxford. After 1751 he lived at Twickenham and was one of the intimates of Horace Walpole.
[5] *Talented* was actually quite sound in

English, but it had dropped out of use. Coleridge argued against it in his Table-Talk so late as July 8, 1832.
[6] No. 40, 1759.
[7] Philadelphia, 1755.
[8] A variant of *trace,* and already becoming obsolete in Johnson's time.

creek, gap, upland, spur (glossed as '*spurs* we call little ridges jetting out from the principal chains of mountains, and are of no long continuing'), *branch, back of* or *fresh* (noun)."

But not all Englishmen of that era were so hostile. If none, in the Eighteenth Century, actually praised American neologisms, some, at least, noted with approval that most educated Americans used very few of them. The *Monthly Review* praised the contents of "Addresses and Recommendations of the States," issued by Congress, as "pieces of fine, energetic writing and masterly eloquence." [9] Franklin usually got a pretty good press, but he had spent so much time in England that he wrote like an Englishman and was himself dubious about most Americanisms. Jefferson, however, was cried down, partly because of his free-thinking, but even more because of his free use of such Americanisms as *to belittle*.[1] Most of the English travelers before 1800 reported that the Americans, at least of the educated class, spoke English with a good accent. Indeed, one of them, Nicholas Cresswell,[2] declared that they spoke it better than the English. But this favorable verdict was mainly grounded on the discovery that there were no marked dialects in America. "Accustomed as he was to the diversity of dialect in his own island," says Read, "the Englishman found a principal subject of comment in the purity and uniformity of English in America." [3]

Whatever faults the Englishman found with American innovations in the vocabulary were lost sight of against the background of more immediate causes for disagreement before and during the American Revolution. The next attack, a few months before Cornwallis was brought to heel at Yorktown, was launched by a Briton living in America and otherwise ardently pro-American. He was John Witherspoon (1723–94), a Scottish clergyman who had come out in 1769 to be president of Princeton *in partibus infidelium*.

Witherspoon took to politics when the war closed his college, and was elected a member of the New Jersey constitutional convention. In a little while he was promoted to the Continental Congress, and in it he sat for six years as its only member from the clergy. He signed both the Declaration of Independence and the Articles of Confederation, and was a member of the Board of War throughout the Revolution. But though his devotion to the American cause was thus beyond question, he was pained by the American language, and when, in 1781, he was invited to contribute a series of papers to the *Pennsylvania Journal and Weekly Advertiser* of Philadelphia,

---

[9] Nov. 1783. See William B. Cairns, British Criticisms of American Writings, 1783–1815; Madison, Wis., 1918, p. 21.

[1] This one, incidentally, was apparently his own invention. The first recorded example comes from his Notes on Virginia,

written in 1781–2. See *Belittle*, by W. J. Burke, *AS*, Vol. VII, Apr. 1932, p. 318.

[2] In his journal for July 19, 1777.

[3] British Recognition of American Speech, p. 322.

he seized the opportunity to denounce it, albeit in the politic terms proper to the time. Beginning with the disarming admission that "the vulgar in America speak much better than the vulgar in England, for a very obvious reason, *viz.*, that being more unsettled, and moving frequently from place to place, they are not so liable to local peculiarities either in accent or phraseology," he proceeded to argue that Americans of education showed a lamentable looseness in their "public and solemn discourses":

> I have heard in this country, in the senate, at the bar, and from the pulpit, and see daily in dissertations from the press, errors in grammar, improprieties and vulgarisms which hardly any person of the same class in point of rank and literature would have fallen into in Great Britain.

Witherspoon's mention of "the senate" was significant, for he must have referred to the Continental Congress, and some of the examples he cited to support his charge must have come from the sacred lips of the Fathers. He divided these "errors in grammar, improprieties and vulgarisms" into eight classes, as follows:

1. Americanisms, or ways of speaking peculiar to this country.
2. Vulgarisms in England and America.
3. Vulgarisms in America only.
4. Local phrases or terms.
5. Common blunders arising from ignorance.
6. Cant phrases.
7. Personal blunders.
8. Technical terms introduced into the language.[4]

By Americanisms,[5] said Witherspoon,

> I understand an use of phrases or terms, or a construction of sentences, even among people of rank and education, different from the use of the same terms or phrases, or the construction of similar sentences in Great Britain. . . . It does not follow in every case that the terms or phrases used are worse in themselves, but merely that they are of American and not of English growth. The word *Americanism*, which I have coined for the purpose, is exactly similar in its formation and significance to the word *Scotticism*.

---

[4] Witherspoon's papers appeared under the heading of The Druid. This list and the foregoing quotation are from No. V, printed on May 9, 1781. This subject was continued in No. VI on May 16, and in No. VII (in two parts) on May 23 and 30. All the papers are reprinted in Mathews.

[5] Witherspoon's specific claim to the invention of *Americanism* has never been challenged.

Witherspoon listed and deplored twelve examples of Americanisms falling within his definition. His first was the use of *either* to indicate more than two, as in "the United States, or *either* of them." This usage seems to have had some countenance in the England of the early Seventeenth Century, but it had gone out by Witherspoon's day, and it has since lost favor in the United States. His second caveat was laid against the American use of *to notify*, as in "The police *notified* the coroner." "In English," he said, somewhat prissily, "we do not *notify* the person of the thing, but *notify* the thing to the person." But *to notify*, in the American sense, was simply archaic English, preserved like so many other archaisms in America, and there is no plausible logical or grammatical objection to it.[6] Witherspoon's third Americanism was *fellow countrymen*, which he denounced as "an evident tautology," and his fourth was the omission of *to be* before the second verb in such constructions as "These things were ordered delivered to the army." His next three were similar omissions, and his remaining five were the use of *or* instead of *nor* following *neither*, the use of *certain* in "a *certain* Thomas Benson" (he argued that "a *certain person called* Thomas Benson" was correct), the use of *incident* in "Such bodies are *incident* to these evils," and the use of *clever* in the sense of worthy and of *mad* in the sense of angry.[7]

It is rather surprising that Witherspoon found so few Americanisms. Among the verbs a large number of novelties had come into American usage since 1750, some revivals of archaic English verbs and others native inventions—*to belittle, to table, to deed, to appreciate* (to increase in value) and so on. Benjamin Franklin, on his return to the United States in 1785, after nine years in France, was impressed so unpleasantly by *to advocate, to notice, to progress* and *to oppose* that on December 26, 1789, he wrote to Noah Webster to ask for help in putting them down, but they seem to have escaped Witherspoon. He also failed to note the changes of meaning in the American use of *creek, shoe, lumber, corn, barn, team, store, rock, cracker* and *partridge*. Nor did he have anything to say about American pronunciation, which had already begun to differ materially from that of Standard English.

Witherspoon's second category of errors consisted of "vulgarisms in England and America" and his third of "vulgarisms in America only." Among the former he listed *an't* (now *ain't*), *can't, don't, couldn't, knowed* for *knew, see* for *saw, this here, drownded, winder* for *window, on 'em* for

---

[6] The OED's first example is dated 1440. After 1652 all the examples cited are American, until 1843, when the usage reappears in England.

[7] The OED traces *mad* in this sense to the Fourteenth Century and says that it is the ordinary word for *angry* in some of the English dialects. But it is much more commonly heard in the United States than in England, and most Englishmen regard it as an Americanism.

of 'em, lay for *lie, thinks* in the first person singular, *has* for *have, as* follow-ing *equally, most highest, had fell, had broke, sat out* for *set out* and *as how.* Most of these are common vulgarisms. The astonishing thing is that Witherspoon reported them in use by "gentlemen and scholars" in America. "There is great plenty," he said, "to be found everywhere in writing and conversation. They need very little explication, and indeed would scarcely deserve to be mentioned in a discourse of this nature were it not for the circumstance . . . that scholars and public persons are at less pains to avoid them here than in Britain." Apparently the American politicians of those days, as Witherspoon knew them, were as careless of their parts of speech as those of today—and no doubt as calculatingly so. *Can't, don't* and *couldn't* are sound in both English and American. [*Ain't,* sent below the salt by generations of schoolma'ams,[8] still survives in the familiar conver-sation of proper Charlestonians as well as among the landed gentry of England.]

Witherspoon's list of "vulgarisms in America only" was just as poorly chosen, and most of the phrases he condemns are in good use today. "I have not done it yet, but I am just *going to*" is perfectly good American idiom. So is "I have been *to* Philadelphia." So is the free use of *spell* to designate a stretch of time or action. The DAE traces the latter, in the form of "a *spell* of weather," to 1705; it was not encountered in England till 1808. In the more general sense, as in "I'll continue a *spell,*" it goes back to 1745, and in the form of "a *spell* of sickness" to 1806.[9]

His fourth list, of "local phrases or terms," shows that, despite his state-ment that the Americans of the time were not "liable to local peculiarities either in accent or phraseology," there were still differences in regional dialect. He offers, unfortunately, but seven examples, so his list is not very illuminating. Three are ascribed to New England, or "the northern parts": the use of *considerable* as a general indicator of quality or quantity, the use of *occasion* as a substitute for *opportunity* and the use of *to improve* in such a sentence as "He *improved* the horse for ten days," meaning he rode it. The DAE says that this use of *considerable* is old in English, and the OED cites an example from Hobbes's "Leviathan" (1651). But the Ameri-cans seem to have employed the adjective much more freely than the English, and may have originated its application to material things, as in *considerable snow* and *considerable money.* Combined with *of,* as in *con-siderable of a shock,* it appears to be clearly American. The other New Englandisms that Witherspoon mentions survive only in rural dialects. He

---

[8] *Schoolma'am* is an Americanism, traced by the DA to 1831; *schoolmarm* to 1841.

[9] The DAE's examples, like those of any historical dictionary, do not always show actual use; all they indicate is the first *printed* use encountered by its searchers.

offers two specimens of "improprieties" from the South and two from the middle colonies. The former are *raw salad* for *salad* and the verb *to tote*, which he spells *tot*. [The condemnation of *raw salad* ("There is no salad boiled") is precious, especially to Southerners for whom *turnip salad* (or *salat*), meaning the cooked green leaves, is a common dish.] *To tote* goes back to the Seventeenth Century and is still in wide use. Witherspoon's two examples from the middle colonies are *chunk*, in the sense of a half-burned piece of wood, and *once in a while* in the sense of occasionally, as in "He will *once in a while* get drunk." *Chunk* is but little used in English, but it is very familiar in American, and in many senses indicating a thick object. *Once in a while* for *occasionally* was apparently a novelty in Witherspoon's day, for the DAE's first example is taken from his denunciation. It is still somewhat rare in English, but in American it has long been perfectly sound idiom.

Witherspoon's fifth category of Americanisms is made up of "common blunders through ignorance," *e.g.*, *eminent* for *imminent*, *ingenious* for *ingenuous*, *successfully* for *successively*, *intelligible* for *intelligent*, *veracity* for *credibility*, *detect* for *dissect*, *scrimitch* for *skirmish*, *duplicit* as an adjective from *duplicity* and *rescind* for *recede*. Most of these must have been rarely encountered among educated persons, even in Witherspoon's day. He says specifically, however, that one of them, the substitution of *veracity* for *credibility*, was "not a blunder in conversation, but in speaking and writing." The example he gives is "I have some doubt of the *veracity* of the fact." But *veracity* has been used as a synonym of *truth* by some of the best English authors, including Samuel Johnson. In fact, the OED's second definition of it is "agreement of statement or report with the actual fact or facts; accordance with truth; correctness, accuracy." *Scrimitch* is obviously only a bad reporting of *scrimmage*, not a man-handling of *skirmish*. In the precise sense of skirmish it goes back in English to the Fifteenth Century. In American it was in common use during the Revolution, and since the Civil War it has been made familiar as a football term, often used figuratively in the general speech. Witherspoon, in fact, had a bad ear, and not only missed many salient Americanisms, but reported others that probably did not exist. He was archetypical of the academic bigwigs of his day, and showed many of the weaknesses that have since marked the American schoolma'am.

Most of his "cant phrases introduced into public speaking or composition" are what we would now call slang, *e.g.*, *to take in* (to swindle), *to bilk*, *to bite* (to swindle), *quite the thing*, *not the thing*, *to bamboozle*, *to sham Abraham*. All of these save the last, a sailor's locution meaning to pretend illness, are in common use, and not one of them originated in America.

His seventh and last category comprises "personal blunders, that is to say, effects of ignorance and want of precision in an author, which are properly his own and not reducible to any of the heads above mentioned." [1] These throw a revealing light upon the sad state of American writing in 1781, but have little to do with the subject of Americanisms. His examples are:

1. The members of a popular government should be continually *availed* of the situation and condition of every part.
2. A degree of dissensions and oppositions under some circumstances, and a political lethargy under others, *impend* ruin to a free state.
3. I should have let your performance sink into *silent disdain*.
4. He is a man of most *accomplished* abilities.
5. I have a *total* objection against this measure.
6. An *axiom* as well established as any Euclid ever demonstrated.

Witherspoon hints that he found these in the political writing of the time. All they show is that when the primeval American politicians tried to imitate the bow-wow manner of their elegant opposite numbers in England, they sometimes came to grief. Number 6, I suspect, was introduced mainly to show off Witherspoon's learning. It must have been a considerable satisfaction for a president of Princeton to be able to inform a non-academic publicist that Euclid "never demonstrated axioms, but took them for granted."

Witherspoon's account of the Americanisms prevailing in his day must be received with some caution, for he was a Scotsman and had never lived in London. Wyld shows in "A History of Modern Colloquial English" that not a few of the words, phrases and pronunciations that he denounced in America were commonly heard in the best London society of the time.

Witherspoon's strictures fell upon deaf ears, at least in the new Republic. He was to get heavy support, in a little while, from the English reviews, but on this side of the ocean the tide was running the other way, and there was a widespread tendency to reject English precedent and authority altogether, in language no less than in government. In the case of the language, several logical considerations supported that disposition, though the chief force was probably only national conceit. For one thing, it was apparent to the more astute politicians of the time that getting rid of English authority in speech, far from making for chaos, would encourage the emer-

---

[1] In his first article, published May 9, 1781, he promised to close his discussion with "technical terms introduced into the language," and at the end of his fourth article, published May 30, he renewed that promise, but The Druid did not proceed any further.

gence of home authority, and so help to establish national solidarity. And for another thing, some of them were farsighted enough to see that the United States, in the course of the years, would inevitably surpass the British Isles in population and wealth, and to realize that its cultural independence would grow at the same pace.

To assure that the new language of the new Republic would be controlled by the best minds and manners, several of the Founding Fathers called for one of the favorite projects of the Eighteenth Century—an Academy to pass on the merits of new words. The most prominent advocate of an Academy was John Adams. He was possibly the writer who, under the pseudonym Aristarcus, suggested in the *Royal American Magazine* (January 1774) the organization of the Fellows of the American Society of Language.[2] In September 1780 Adams wrote two signed letters from Amsterdam to the President of Congress, recommending that Congress set up an Academy, and hoping that after an American Academy had been set up, England would follow suit.

> This I should admire. England will never more have any honor, excepting now and then that of imitating the Americans. I assure you, Sir, I am not altogether in jest. I see a general inclination after English in France, Spain and Holland, and it may extend throughout Europe. The population and commerce of America will force their language into general use.[3]

Despite this ardent advocacy of an Academy "for refining, improving and ascertaining the English language" in America, Adams does not seem to have joined the Philological Society that was organized in New York in 1788, with substantially the same objects. But Noah Webster, the lexicographer, was a member of it, and indeed the boss. It got under way on March 17 and apparently blew up early in 1789, after he had moved to Boston. Its only official acts of any importance, so far as the surviving records show, were to recommend his immortal spelling-book "to the use of schools in the United States, as an accurate well-digested system of principles and rules," and to take part in a "grand procession" in New York in July, "to celebrate the adoption of the Constitution by ten States."[4]

The Philological Society was not the first organization of its sort to be projected in America, nor was the "American Academy for refining, improving and ascertaining the English language" that Adams suggested in 1780, nor the American Society of Language proposed in 1774. So early as

---

[2] The full text is in Mathews.
[3] See Mathews, pp. 41–3; Krapp, Vol. I, p. 7.
[4] See The Philological Society of New York, by Allen Walker Read, *AS*, Vol. IX, Apr. 1934, pp. 133–4; also his The Constitution of the Philological Society of 1788, *AS*, Vol. XVI, Feb. 1941, pp. 71–2.

1721 Hugh Jones, professor of mathematics at William and Mary College, had adumbrated something of the sort in "An Accidence to the English Tongue," the first English grammar produced in America.[5] But nothing came of this, and it was not until the end of the century that any active steps were taken toward getting such a project under way.[6] They resulted in 1806 in the introduction of a bill in Congress incorporating a National Academy or National Institution, one of the purposes of which was to nurse and police the language, but that bill collided with a rising tenderness about states' rights, and soon died in committee, though it was supported by John Adams's son, John Quincy, then a senator from Massachusetts. The projectors, however, did not despair, and in 1820 they organized an American Academy of Language and Belles Lettres in New York, with John Quincy Adams as president. Its objects were thus set forth in the first article of its constitution:

> To collect, interchange and diffuse literary intelligence; to promote the purity and uniformity of the English language; to invite a correspondence with distinguished scholars in other countries speaking this language in connection with ourselves; to cultivate throughout our extensive territory a friendly intercourse among those who feel an interest in the progress of American literature, and, as far as may depend on well meant endeavors, to aid the general cause of learning in the United States.[7]

There was but little indication here of a design to set up American standards. The Academy was quite willing to accept English authority, and its committee on Americanisms was instructed "to collect throughout the United States a list of words and phrases, whether acknowledged corruptions or words of doubtful authority, which are charged upon us as bad English, with a view to take the best practical course for promoting the purity and uniformity of our language."

A formidable party of bigwigs supported the Academy, including James Madison, former President of the United States, John Marshall, Chief Justice of the Supreme Court, Charles Carroll, of Carrollton, John Jay,

---

[5] American Projects for an Academy to Regulate Speech, by Allen Walker Read, *PMLA*, Vol. LI, Dec. 1936, p. 1141.

[6] There were, however, several local academies which occasionally showed some interest in language. One was the American Philosophical Society of Philadelphia, the heir and assign of Franklin's Junto of 1727. Another was the Connecticut Academy of Arts and Sciences of New Haven, of which

Webster was a member. He joined it at some time before 1799 and in 1804 made over to it 50 cents for every 1,000 copies of his spelling-book printed in Connecticut. But both organizations were much more interested in the sciences than in letters.

[7] The constitution of the academy is printed in full in Read's American Projects for an Academy to Regulate Speech, just cited, pp. 1154–6.

Daniel Webster, Henry Clay, William B. Astor, General Winfield Scott and various governors, senators, ambassadors, judges, congressmen and college presidents; but there were also some opponents, and one of them was Noah Webster, though he consented grudgingly to being elected a corresponding member.[8] "Such an institution," he wrote, "would be of little use until the American public should have a dictionary which should be received as a standard work." This standard work, of course, was already in progress in Webster's studio, but it was not to be published until 1828. Before it came out he launched a plan of his own for a sort of joint standing committee of American and English scholars to consider "such points of difference in the practise of the two countries as it is desirable to adjust," but when he appointed Samuel Lee, professor of Arabic at Cambridge, to take charge of it in England, the dons of the two universities refused to have anything to do with it. Jefferson was offered the honorary presidency of the Academy, but refused it. When he was then elected an honorary member he wrote from Monticello, on January 21, 1821:

> There are so many differences between us and England, of soil, climate, culture, productions, laws, religion and government, that we must be left far behind the march of circumstances, were we to hold ourselves rigorously to their standard. . . . Judicious neology can alone give strength and copiousness to language, and enable it to be the vehicle of new ideas.

Of all the early American savants to interest themselves in the language of the country, the one destined to be the most influential was Webster.[9] There was nothing of the traditional pedagogue about him—no sign of caution, policy, mousiness. He launched his numerous reforms and innovations with great boldness, and defended them in a forthright and often raucous manner. Frequently traveling in the interest of his spelling-book,[1] he got involved in political, medical, economic and theological as well as philological disputes. It was almost impossible for him to imagine himself in error, and most of his disquisitions were far more pontifical than argumentative in tone. He had no respect for dignity or authority. Once he even upbraided the sacrosanct Washington—for proposing to send to Scotland for a tutor for the Custis children. When it came to whooping up his spelling-book he was completely shameless, and did not hesitate to demand

---

[8] A full list of the first members—honorary, resident and corresponding—is in The Membership of Proposed American Academies, by Allen Walker Read, *American Literature,* Vol. VII, May 1935, pp. 145 ff.

[9] A penetrating and amusing account is Noah Webster, Schoolmaster to America, by Harry R. Warfel; New York, 1936.

[1] It first appeared in 1783, as the first part of his Grammatical Institute of the English Language, published at Hartford. It was the most successful book ever brought out in America, and is still in print.

encomiums from Washington, Jefferson and Franklin. Franklin responded with a somewhat equivocal letter, and Washington with a frankly evasive one, but the franker Jefferson, though inclined to support the Websterian reforms, did not like Webster, and not only refused to help him but once denounced him as "a mere pedagogue, of very limited understanding and very strong prejudices and party passions." [2]

But Webster was often right, and many of the doctrines he preached so violently, at least about language, gradually won acceptance. When he came upon the scene there was a rising, if still inarticulate, rebellion against the effort to police English from above. "The prevailing view of language in the Eighteenth Century," says Sterling Andrus Leonard, in "The Doctrine of Correctness in English Usage, 1700–1800," [3] "was that English could and must be subjected to a process of classical regularizing. Where actual usage was observed and recorded—even when the theory was promulgated that usage is supreme—this was, in general, done only to reform and denounce the actual idiom." Webster's natural prejudices ran the same way, for he was not only a pedagogue but also a Calvinist, and a foe of democracy. [4] Indeed, all his attacks upon authority were arguments against the other fellow's and in favor of his own. But he was too shrewd to believe that language could really be brought under the yoke. He had observed that it was a living organism with a way of life of its own—with a process of evolution but little determined by purely rational considerations. Thus, when he came to write his own books, he knew that the task before him was predominantly one of reporting rather than of philosophizing, of understanding before admonition. He saw clearly that English was undergoing marked changes in America, both in vocabulary and in pronunciation, and, though he might protest now and then, he was in general willing to accept them. He adopted the pronunciations of educated New Englanders, and offered resistance to American neologisms only when they were what his Puritan soul regarded as "low." When taken to task for admitting into his trial-balloon dictionary (1806) such New World barbarisms as *customable* and *decedent*, he explained that such terms were bound to arise, whatever lexicographers or critics might think. Consequently, a lexi-

---

[2] Letter to James Madison, Aug. 12, 1801.

[3] Madison, Wis., 1929, p. 14. [See also Harold B. Allen, Samuel Johnson and the Authoritarian Principle in Linguistic Criticism, diss. (microfilm), U. of Michigan, 1940; Karl W. Dykema, Historical Development of the Concept of Grammatical Proprieties, *College Composition and Communication*, Vol. V, Dec. 1954, pp. 135–40, and Where Our Grammar Came From, *CE*, Vol. XXII, Apr. 1961, pp. 455–65; James H. Sledd and Gwin J. Kolb, Dr. Johnson's Dictionary: Essays in the Biography of a Book, Chicago, 1955.]

[4] His blistering opinion of democratic government, set forth in a letter to the New York *Spectator* for Aug. 1837, is reprinted by Warfel, pp. 425–7.

cographer ought to include them, to protect the unwary reader.[5] For pronunciation, he insisted on an American standard, based on current cultivated usage rather than that of the university, dictionary or stage; "common practice, even among the unlearned," he declared in the preface to his "Dissertations," "is generally defensible on the principles of analogy and the structure of the language. . . . The most difficult task now to be performed by the advocates of *pure English* is to restrain the influence of men learned in Greek and Latin but ignorant of their own tongue." [6]

Webster's program was outlined in his "Dissertations on the English Language" (1789). The book still makes excellent reading. He was convinced that "several circumstances render a future separation of the American tongue from the English necessary and unavoidable." Among these circumstances were England's involvement in European dynastic wars, the inevitable rise of North America to the center of power in the English-speaking world, and the inevitable divergent changes that occur when a language is spoken in two or more widely separated areas. Webster was no linguist, in the modern sense; indeed, scientific linguistics barely antedates his "Dissertations." Like most of his contemporaries, he leaned overheavily, in his etymological speculations, upon Holy Writ, and argued that mankind must have originally spoken what he called Chaldee, *i.e.*, what is now known as Biblical Aramaic. But he saw a relationship between such apparently disparate languages as Greek, Latin, English, French and Russian and recognized English as a Germanic language, despite its large admixture of Latin and French terms. For the last he credited Horne Tooke's "The Diversions of Purley." [7] Diligent study convinced him that most of the other English writers on language in his day were quacks.[8] "They seem not to consider," he said, "that grammar is formed on language and not language on grammar." Here he might have been preening himself on his own wide acquaintance with languages, at least twenty in all. Even if we concede that his knowledge of most was rather superficial, the number is staggering.[9]

---

[5] Letter to Thomas Dawes, Aug. 5, 1809.

[6] pp. viii–ix.

[7] The first volume was published in 1786.

[8] The best account of their speculations is in Leonard, lately cited.

[9] In his Notes on Early American Work in Linguistics, *Proceedings of the American Philosophical Society*, 1943, p. 26, Franklin Edgerton, Sterling Professor Emeritus of Sanskrit and comparative philology at Yale, speaks disdainfully of

Webster's "Chaldee" etymologies. "Even the relative isolation of American scholarship from Europe," says Edgerton, "hardly excuses such astounding ignorance in Webster, writing forty years after Sir William Jones, twenty after Schlegel, a dozen after Bopp, and half a dozen or more after the first volume of Jacob Grimm." Jones (1746–94) first called attention to the similarity between the grammatical structures of Sanskrit, Greek and Latin. Franz Bopp (1791–1867) published Über das Conjugations-

Webster got little support for what he called his Federal English from the recognized illuminati of the time; indeed, his proposals for a reform of American spelling, set forth in an appendix to his "Dissertations," were denounced roundly by some of them, and the rest were only lukewarm. He dedicated the "Dissertations" to Franklin,[1] but Franklin delayed acknowledging the dedication until the last days of 1789, and then urged Webster to make war upon various Americanisms of recent growth, and perhaps with deliberate irony applauded his "zeal for preserving the purity of our language." A year before the "Dissertations" appeared, Dr. Benjamin Rush anticipated at least some of Webster's ideas in "A Plan of a Federal University,"[2] and they seem to have made some impression on Thomas Jefferson, who was to ratify them formally in 1813; but the rest of the contemporaneous sages held aloof. Webster, however, was not fazed. After Franklin was dead and could not object, he published his letter in the New York *American Mercury*, and exegesized it in fourteen articles, one of which advocated *them* as a plural demonstrative in such phrases as *them horses*.

At this time, probably, Webster was at work upon his first dictionary, which appeared in 1806.[3] It was not cordially received; in fact, before it actually came out it was denounced. Webster, always ready for a row, vigorously defended it. On June 4, 1800, he inserted a puff in the New Haven papers describing it as "a small dictionary for schools" and announcing that enlarged revisions would follow, but it was actually a very comprehensive work for its time and listed 5,000 more words than Johnson's dictionary of 1755. It was full of the author's crotchets and prejudices, and many of its proposed reforms in spelling were so radical and grotesque that even their author later abandoned them, but despite all these deficiencies it showed wide learning and hard common sense, and so opened the way for the large "American Dictionary" of 1828. In all the years since its first publication there has been no working dictionary of

---

system der Sanskritsprache in Vergleichung mit jenem der griechischen, lateinischen, persischen und germanischen Sprache in 1816, and his Analytical Comparison of the Sanskrit, Greek, Latin and Teutonic Languages (in English) in 1820. Jacob Grimm (1785–1863) published the first part of his Deutsche Grammatik in 1819 and the second in 1822. August Wilhelm von Schlegel (1767–1845) began publishing his *Indische Bibliothek* in 1823.

[1] In 1768 Franklin himself had published A Scheme for a New Alphabet and a Reformed Mode of Spelling; it is reprinted in Franklin's Works, ed. by John Bigelow; New York, 1887–8, Vol. IV, pp. 198 *ff.* [See also C. M. Wise, Benjamin Franklin as a Phonetician, *Speech Monographs*, Vol. XV, 1948, pp. 94–120.]

[2] Contributed to the *American Museum* for 1788.

[3] It issued from Sidney's Press at New Haven on Feb. 11, and made a volume of 408 pages, plus a 21-page preface. The original price was $1.50. The full title was A Compendious Dictionary of the English Language.

English, of any value whatsoever, that does not show something of its influence. There are plain tracks of it even in the "Concise Oxford Dictionary" of the brothers Fowler.[4]

At the time, however, this was far from recognized. In 1801 an unidentified Aristarcus delivered an attack on Webster in a series of articles contributed to the *New England Palladium* and reprinted in the *Port Folio* of Philadelphia.[5] The author objected to various real and imaginary Americanisms, among them *spry, lengthy, illy, sauce* (in the sense of a vegetable), *caucus, to wait on* (in the sense of wait for) and the use of *grand* and *elegant* as intensives of all work. Most were not Americanisms, but had been in use in England for many years. Like most of the other Englishmen and Anglomaniacs who wrote against Americanisms in his time, Aristarcus objected on the idiotic ground that they were unnecessary.

The doctrine that English was already complete and needed no enrichment from Yankee sources persisted among Englishmen and Anglomaniacs long after Aristarcus's time. Captain Basil Hall, who ventured into the American wilds in 1827 and 1828 and published an account of his sufferings on his return home,[6] went so far in urging it as to visit Webster in New Haven and tackle him in person.

"But surely," argued Hall, "such innovations are to be deprecated."

"I don't know that," replied old Noah. "If a word becomes universally current in America, where English is spoken, why should it not take its station in the language?"

"Because," replied Hall loftily, "there are words enough already."

2: THE ENGLISH ATTACK

The general tone of English criticism, from the Eighteenth Century to the present, has been one of suspicion, and not infrequently it has been extremely hostile. The periods of remission have usually been evidences of adroit politicking, as when Oxford, in 1907, helped liquidate the Venezuelan unpleasantness by giving Mark Twain an honorary D.C.L. In England all branches of human endeavor are bent to the service of the state, and there is an alliance between society and politics, science and literature that is unmatched anywhere else on earth [outside the Iron Curtain]. Though this alliance, on occasion, may find it profitable to be polite to the Yankee, and even to conciliate him, there remains an active aversion under the surface, born of the incurable rivalry between the two countries,

---

[4] Oxford, 1911; revised several times since.
[5] They were summarized by Leon Howard in Towards a Historical Aspect of American Speech Consciousness, *AS,* Vol. V, Apr. 1930, pp. 301–5.
[6] Travels in North America in the Years 1827–28; 3 vols.; Edinburgh and London, 1829.

and accentuated perhaps by their common tradition and their similar speech. [Nor has the eclipse of British power by the rise of the United States and Russia, or the simultaneous liquidation of much of the one-time Empire (now hopefully renamed the *Commonwealth*, with *British* designedly omitted), cured either English distrust or American brashness.] Americanisms are forcing their way into English all the time, of late at a truly dizzy pace, but they seldom get anything properly describable as a welcome [save from such small sects of iconoclasts as the Angry Young Men], and every now and then the general protest against them rises to a roar. American literature is still regarded in England as somewhat barbaric and below the salt, and the famous sneer of Sydney Smith, though now absurd in all other respects, is yet echoed complacently in many an English review of American books:

> In the four quarters of the globe, who reads an American book? or goes to an American play? or looks at an American picture or statue? What does the world yet owe to American physicians or surgeons? What new substances have their chemists discovered? or what old ones have they analyzed? What new constellations have been discovered by the telescopes of Americans? What have they done in mathematics? Who drinks out of American glasses? or eats from American plates? or wears American coats or gowns? or sleeps in American blankets? Finally, under which of the old tyrannical governments of Europe is every sixth man a slave, whom his fellow creatures may buy and sell and torture? [7]

There is an amusing compilation of some of the earlier diatribes in William B. Cairns's "British Criticism of American Writings, 1783–1815." [8] The attack began in 1787, when the *European Magazine and London Review* fell upon the English of Thomas Jefferson's "Notes on the State of Virginia." The *Gentleman's Magazine* joined the charge in May 1798, with sneers for the "uncouth . . . localities [*sic*]" in the "Yankey dialect" of Noah Webster's "Sentimental and Humorous Essays," and the *Edinburgh* followed in October 1804 with a patronizing article upon John Quincy Adams's "Letters on Silesia." The *Edinburgh* predicted that a "spurious dialect" would prevail, "even at the Court and in the Senate of the United States," and that the Americans would thus "lose the only badge that is still worn of our consanguinity." The appearance of the five volumes of Chief Justice Marshall's "Life of George Washington," from 1804 to 1807, brought forth corrective articles from the *British Critic*, the *Critical*

---

[7] In a review of Adam Seybert's Statistical Annals of the United States, *Edinburgh Review*, Jan.–May 1820.

[8] *University of Wisconsin Studies in Language and Literature*, No. 1, Madison, Wis., 1918.

Review, the *Annual*, the *Monthly* and the *Eclectic*. The *Edinburgh*, in 1808, declared that the Americans made "it a point of conscience to have no aristocratical distinctions—even in their vocabulary." They thought, it went on, "one word as good as another, providing its meaning be clear." The *Monthly Review* in March of the same year denounced "the corruptions and barbarities which are hourly obtaining in the speech of our transatlantic colonies [*sic*]."

The *British Critic*, in April 1808, admitted that the damage was already done—that "the common speech of the United States has departed considerably from the standard adopted in England." The others, however, sought to stay the flood by invective against Marshall, and, later, against his rival biographer, the Rev. Aaron Bancroft. In Bancroft's "Life of George Washington" (1808), according to the *British Critic*, there were offensive "new words, or old words in a new sense . . . at almost every page"; and in Joel Barlow's "The Columbiad" (1807, reprinted in England in 1809) the *Edinburgh* found "a great multitude of words which are radically and entirely new, and as utterly foreign as if they had been adopted from the Hebrew or Chinese," and "the perversion of a still greater number of English words from their proper use or signification." Some of Barlow's novelties were fantastic enough—*to vagrate* and *to ameed* among the verbs, *imkeeled* and *homicidious* among the adjectives, and *coloniarch* among the nouns. But many of the rest were either obsolete words whose use was proper in poetry, or nonce words of obvious meaning and utility. Some of the terms complained of by the *Edinburgh* are in good usage at this moment—*e.g., to utilize, to spade* (the soil), *crass* and *scow*.[9] But to the English reviewers of the time words so unfamiliar were not only deplorable on their own account, but also proofs that the Americans were a sordid and ignoble people.

Most of the leading English writers of the late Eighteenth Century took little interest in American writings, and those who did, like Cowper and Blake, were much more interested in their theological or political content than in their literary merits. Scott liked Charles Brockden Brown's novels, Freneau's "Eutaw Springs" and Irving's "Knickerbocker's History of New York"; Shelley read and admired several of Brown's works. But that is all. Landor proposed to dedicate one of his books to James Madison, but he showed no interest in either American literature or American *Kultur* in general, and when Southey sent him a bitter protest against this dedication, he replied complacently, "I detest the American character as much as you do."

Of the English and Scotch reviews of the time, those most constantly

---

[9] See A Historical Note on American English, by Leon Howard, *AS*, Vol. II, Sept. 1927.

anti-American were the *European Magazine and London Review*, the *Anti-Jacobin Review*, the *Edinburgh*, the *Quarterly* and the *Monthly Mirror*. The *Anti-Jacobin* and the *Quarterly* were not only hostile, but also scurrilous. The *Anti-Jacobin* specialized in reviling George Washington, and the *Quarterly* in spreading scandal about Thomas Jefferson. The former, in 1788, denounced Washington as guilty not only of "the horrid crime of rebellion, which nothing but repentance can efface," but also of the still worse infamy of deism. The latter propagated the fable that Jefferson maintained a harem of Negro mistresses at Monticello, and derived a large revenue from the sale of their (and his) children. Both reviews were implacably contemptuous of American writing, and to their diatribes they commonly added flings at the whole of American civilization. Thus the *Quarterly*:

> No work of distinguished merit in any branch has yet been produced among them. . . . The founders of American society brought to the composition of their nation few seeds of good taste, and no rudiments of liberal science.[1]

The Englishmen who toured America in the post-Revolutionary period were, on the whole, more favorable in their comments than the English and Scotch reviewers. Even after the turn of the century they seem to have been generally friendly; it was only in the years following the War of 1812 that they took over the job of denouncing everything American. They noticed the strange neologisms that had appeared on this side of the water, and sometimes they were shocked by them, but in the main they showed a tolerant spirit, and were pleased to discover that the dialectal differences between the speech of various parts of the country were less marked than those familiar to them in Britain.

Nevertheless, the English travelers of the time noted that American speech was not quite identical with any form of English speech—that it made use of many words not heard in England, and was also developing certain peculiarities of pronunciation and intonation. "There are few natives of the United States," wrote the editor of the London edition of David Ramsay's "History of the American Revolution" in 1791, quoting an unnamed "penetrating observer," "who are altogether free from what may be called *Americanisms*,[2] both in their speech and their writing. In the case of words of rarer use they have framed their own models of pro-

---

[1] "We owe to the *Quarterly*," said N. P. Willis in the preface to Pencillings by the Way (London, 1835), "every spark of ill-feeling that has been kept alive between England and America for the past twenty years."

[2] Read suggests that the "penetrating observer" was probably John Witherspoon, who invented the term *Americanism* in 1781.

nunciation, as having little access to those established among the people from whom they have derived their language." The more naïve travelers were sometimes astonished to discover that familiar objects had acquired new names in America. Thus Richard Parkinson, in "A Tour of America, 1798–1800": [3]

> It was natural for me to enquire what they kept their cows and horses on during the Winter. They told me—their horses on *blades* and their cows on *slops*. . . . [*Blades*] turned out to be blades and tops of Indian corn, and the *slops* were the same that are put into the *swill*-tub in England and given to hogs.

Read lists some of the other novelties remarked by English travelers— *lengthy* and *to advocate* by Henry Wamsey in 1794; [4] *to loan, to enterprise, portage, immigration* and *boatable* by Thomas Twining in 1796; [5] and *fork* (of a road) by Thomas Anburey shortly before 1789. [6] Most of these terms are discussed in other places. *Boatable,* an obvious coinage to designate streams too shallow to be called *navigable,* is traced to 1683, when it was used by William Penn. *To loan,* in the sense of to lend, goes back in England to the Sixteenth Century and probably even beyond, but the OED marks it "now chiefly U.S." It is now in such wide use in the United States that it has appeared in the text of laws, though purists still frown upon it. *To enterprise* seems to have died out. The DAE does not list it, and it is marked "archaic" by the OED, though John Ruskin used it in "Fors Clavigera" so recently as 1871.

It must be conceded that at this time American letters were yet in a somewhat feeble state. John Pickering, so late as 1816, said that "in this country we can hardly be said to have any authors by profession," and Justice Story, three years later, repeated the saying and sought to account for the fact. "So great," said Story, "is the call for talents of all sorts in the active use of professional and other business in America that few of our ablest men have leisure to devote exclusively to literature or the fine arts." In 1813 Jefferson, anticipating both Pickering and Story, had written to John Waldo:

> We have no distinct class of literati in our country. Every man is engaged in some industrious pursuit, and science is but a secondary occupation, always subordinate to the main business of life. Few, therefore, of those which are qualified have leisure to write.

---

[3] London, 1805, Vol. I, pp. 39–40.
[4] An Excursion to the United States of North America in the Summer of 1794; Salisbury (Eng.), 1796, p. 214.
[5] Travels in America One Hundred Years Ago; New York, 1894, p. 167.
[6] Travels Through the Interior Parts of America; London, 1789, Vol. II, p. 197.

This was already something of an exaggeration, for Irving's "Knicker-bocker" had been published in 1809, the *North American Review* had been set up in 1815, and the *Federalist,* the writings of Franklin, Jefferson, Paine and Jonathan Edwards and all the novels of Charles Brockden Brown were behind Pickering as he wrote. But the great burgeoning was still ahead. In 1817 came Bryant's "Thanatopsis"; in 1818, the poems of Samuel Woodworth, including "The Old Oaken Bucket"; in 1819, Irving's "Sketch-Book"; in 1820, Cooper's "Precaution"; in 1821, "The Spy"; in 1822, "Bracebridge Hall"; and in 1823, three Cooper novels. By 1828 Noah Webster was able to say in the preface to his American Dictionary that one of his aims was to call attention to the writings of various American authors.

Difficulties of communication hampered the circulation of native books. "It is much to be regretted," wrote David Ramsay to Noah Webster in 1806, "that there is so little intercourse in a literary way between the States. As soon as a book of general utility comes out in any State it should be for sale in all of them." The most Ramsay could imagine was a sale of 2,000 copies for an American work in America. But even that was apparently beyond the possibilities of the time. It would be a mistake, however, to assume that the Americans eschewed reading altogether. In 1802 the *Scot's Magazine* reported that at a book fair held shortly before in New York, the sales ran to 520,000 volumes, and that a similar fair was projected for Philadelphia. Six years before this the London bookseller Henry Lemoine [7] found that very few books were being printed in the country, and ascribed the fact to the high cost of labor, but he encountered well-stocked bookstores in New York, Philadelphia and Baltimore, and plenty of customers for their importations.

But other visitors were much less impressed by the literary gusto of the young Republic. Henry Wamsey reported that the American libraries were "scanty," that their collections were "almost entirely of modern books," and that they were deficient in "the means of tracing the history of questions, . . . a want which literary people felt very much, and which it will take some years to remedy." And Captain Thomas Hamilton, in his "Men and Manners in America," [8] said flatly that "there is . . . nothing in the United States worthy of the name of library." According to Hamilton, all

---

[7] *Gentleman's Magazine,* Nov. 1796.

[8] Published in Edinburgh in 1833, and reprinted in Philadelphia the same year. The book did not bear Hamilton's name, but was ascribed on the title page to "the author of Cyril Thornton." Hamilton was a friend to Sir Walter Scott and himself a frequent contributor to *Blackwood's.* Cyril Thornton, published in 1827, was a successful novel, and remained in favor for many years. Men and Manners in America was translated into French and twice into German.

the books imported from Europe for public institutions during the fiscal year 1829–30 reached a value of but $10,829.

But whatever the fact here, the Americans were quickly aware of every British aspersion upon their culture, whether in a book or in one of the reviews. If nothing else was read, such things were certainly read, and they came with sufficient frequency, and in terms of sufficient offensiveness, to keep the country in a state of indignation for years. In this holy war upon the primeval damyankee, William Gifford, editor of the *Anti-Jacobin* in 1797–8, and after 1809 the first editor of the *Quarterly*, played an extravagant part,[9] but he was diligently seconded by Sydney Smith, Southey, Thomas Moore and many lesser lights. "If the [English] reviewers get hold of an American publication," said James K. Paulding in "Letters from the South" in 1817, "it is made use of merely as a pretext to calumniate us in some way or other."

Such violent assaults, in the long run, were bound to breed defiance, but while they were at their worst they produced a contrary effect. The native authors became extremely self-conscious and diffident, and the educated classes, in general, were daunted by the torrent of abuse. "The first step of an American entering upon a literary career," said Henry Cabot Lodge, writing of the first quarter of the century,[1] "was to pretend to be an Englishman in order that he might win the approval, not of Englishmen, but of his own countrymen." Cooper, in his first novel, "Precaution" (1820), chose an English scene, imitated English models and obviously hoped to placate the English critics thereby. Irving, too, in his earliest work, showed a considerable discretion, and his "Knickerbocker" was first published anonymously. But this puerile spirit did not last long. The English libels were too vicious to be received lying down; their very fury demanded that they be met with a united and courageous front. In 1828 Cooper undertook a detailed reply to the more common English charges in "Notions of the Americans," but he was still too cautious to sign his name: it appeared as "by a Travelling Bachelor." By 1834, however, he was ready to apologize formally to his countrymen for his early truancy in "Precaution." Irving, even more politic and suffering from Anglomania in a severe form, nevertheless edged himself gradually into the patriot band, and by 1828 he was brave enough to refuse the *Quarterly*'s offer of a hundred guineas for an article on the ground that it was "so persistently hostile to our country" that he could not "draw a pen in its service."

---

[9] Gifford was a killer in general practice, and his onslaughts on Wordsworth, Shelley and Keats are still remembered. He retired from the *Quarterly* in 1824 with a fortune of £25,000—the first magazine editor in history to make it pay.

[1] In his essay, Colonialism in America, in Studies in History; Boston, 1884.

The real counterattack was carried on by lesser men—the elder Timothy Dwight, John Neal, Edward Everett, Charles Jared Ingersoll, James K. Paulding, William Wirt and Robert Walsh, Jr., among them. Neal went to England, became secretary to Jeremy Bentham, forced his way into the reviews and so fought the English on their own ground. Walsh set up the *American Review of History and Politics,* the first American critical quarterly, in 1811, and eight years later published "An Appeal from the Judgments of Great Britain Respecting the United States of America." Everett performed chiefly in the *North American Review* (founded in 1815), to which he contributed many articles and of which he was editor from 1820 to 1824. Wirt published his "Letters of a British Spy" in 1803, and Ingersoll followed with "Inchiquin the Jesuit's Letters on American Literature and Politics" in 1811. In January 1814 the *Quarterly* reviewed "Inchiquin" in a particularly violent manner, and a year later Dwight replied in "Remarks on the Review of Inchiquin's Letters Published in the *Quarterly Review,* Addressed to the Right Honorable George Canning, Esq." Dwight ascribed the *Quarterly* diatribe to Southey. He went on:

> Both the travelers and the literary journalists of [England] have, for reasons which it would be idle to inquire after and useless to allege, thought it proper to caricature the Americans. Their pens have been dipped in gall; and their representations have been, almost merely, a mixture of malevolence and falsehood.

Dwight rehearsed some of the counts in the *Quarterly*'s indictment—that "the president of Yale College tells of a *conflagrative* brand," that *to guess* was on the tongues of all Americans, and so on. His reply was to list, on the authority of Pegge's "Anecdotes of the English Language," 105 vulgarisms common in London—*e.g., chimly* for *chimney, saace* for *sauce, kiver* for *cover* and *hisn* for *his*—to accuse "members of Parliament" of using *diddled* and *gullibility* [2] and to deride the English provincial dialects as "unintelligible gabble."

But it was Paulding who got in the heaviest licks. In all, he wrote five books dealing with the subject. The first, "The Diverting History of John Bull and Brother Jonathan" (1812), was satirical in tone, and made a considerable popular success. Three years later he followed it with a more serious work, "The United States and England," another reply to the *Quarterly* review of "Inchiquin." The "Letters from the South" came out in 1817, and in 1822 "A Sketch of Old England," a sort of *reductio ad absurdum* of the current English books of American travels. He had never

---

[2] At that time both words were neologisms. The OED's first example of *gullibility* is dated 1793. So late as 1818 it was denounced by the Rev. H. J. Todd, one of the improvers of Johnson's Dictionary, as "a low expression, sometimes used for *cullibility*." The OED's first example of *to diddle* is dated 1806.

been to England, and the inference was that many of the English travelers had never been to America. Finally, in 1825, he resorted to broad burlesque in "John Bull in America, or The New Munchausen." Now and then some friendly aid came from the camp of the enemy. After 1824, when the *North American Review* gave warning that if the campaign of abuse went on it would "turn into bitterness the last drops of good-will toward England that exist in the United States," even *Blackwood's* became somewhat conciliatory.

But this letting up did not last. Toward the end of the 30s the English reviews again began to belabor all things American, and especially American books, and during the decade following they had the enthusiastic support of a long line of English travelers, headed by Frances Trollope and Charles Dickens.[3] During the 50s *Harper's Magazine* made frequent protests against the unfairness of the current English notices of new American books. In October 1851, for example, it took the London *Athenaeum* to task for a grossly prejudiced notice of Henry Theodore Tuckerman's "Characteristics of Literature,"[4] and complained that it was "systematically cold to American writers." The month following[5] *Harper's* quoted and denounced a patronizing and idiotic review of Francis Parkman's "History of the Conspiracy of Pontiac."[6] In 1864 Tuckerman struck back in "America and Her Commentators," a well-documented and very effective counterblast, but now so far forgotten that even the Cambridge History of American Literature does not mention it. To this day English reviewers are generally wary of American books, and seldom greet them with anything properly describable as cordiality. In particular, they are frequently denounced on the ground that the Americanisms which spatter them are violations of the only true enlightenment.

3: AMERICAN "BARBARISMS"

The occasional English tolerance for things American was never extended to the American language. Most English books of travel mentioned Americanisms only to revile them.[7] Typical was Captain Hamilton in

---

[3] An excellent account of the reports of these pilgrims, with copious extracts, is in American Social History, by Allan Nevins; New York, 1923. Other useful books on the same theme are As Others See Us, by John Graham Brooks; New York, 1908; and The English Traveler in America, by Jane Louise Mesick; New York, 1922. All three works include bibliographies, and Brooks also lists French and German books.

[4] Published in two series; Philadelphia, 1849 and 1851.

[5] Literary Notices, p. 857.

[6] Two vols.; Boston, 1851.

[7] ["As Struthers Burt has reported, 'There was a most popular English book . . . in which it was only necessary to say that a thing was American to condemn it, or to say that a thing was un-American to praise it'" (Burt's The Other Side; New York, 1928). Quote from The Adjective *American* in England, by Allen Walker Read, *AS*, Vol. XXV, Dec. 1950, pp. 280–9.]

"Men and Manners in America." "The amount of bad grammar in circulation," he said, "is very great; that of barbarisms [*i.e.*, Americanisms] enormous." Worse, these "barbarisms" were not confined to the ignorant, but came almost as copiously from the lips of the learned. Hamilton then described some of the prevalent ones:

> The word *does* is split into two syllables and pronounced *do-es*. *Where*, for some incomprehensible reason, is converted into *whare*, *there* into *thare;* and I remember, on mentioning to an acquaintance that I had called on a gentleman of taste in the arts, he asked "whether he *shew* (showed) me his pictures." Such words as *oratory* and *dilatory* are pronounced with the penult syllable long and accented: *missionary* becomes *missionairy, angel, ângel, danger, dânger*, etc.
>
> But this is not all. The Americans have chosen arbitrarily to change the meaning of certain old and established English words. . . . The word *clever* . . . has here no connexion with talent, and simply means pleasant or amiable. Thus a good-natured blockhead in the American vernacular is a *clever* man. . . . I heard of a gentleman having moved into a *clever* house, of another succeeding to a *clever* sum of money, of a third embarking in a *clever* ship, and making a *clever* voyage with a *clever* cargo; and of the sense attached to the word in these various combinations, I could gain nothing like a satisfactory explanation. . . .
>
> The privilege of barbarizing the King's English is assumed by all ranks and conditions of men. Such words as *slick, kedge* and *boss*, it is true, are rarely used by the better orders; but they assume unlimited liberty in the use of *expect, reckon, guess* and *calculate*, and perpetrate other conversational anomalies with remorseless impunity.

This Briton was as full of moral horror as of grammatical disgust, and put his denunciation upon the loftiest of grounds. He concluded:

> Unless the present progress of change be arrested by an increase of taste and judgment in the more educated classes, there can be no doubt that, in another century, the dialect of the Americans will become utterly unintelligible to an Englishman, and that the nation will be cut off from the advantages arising from their participation in British literature.[8]

Hamilton was one of the most amiable of the English travelers of the first half of the century, and described his adventures in the United States, says Allan Nevins, "in a spirit of picturesque enjoyment rather than of censure. . . . Only rarely do we catch a captious accent in his book." But he nevertheless found American English somewhat disconcerting. In addition to noting the pestiferous prevalence of *to expect, to reckon, to guess*

---

[8] The quotations are from pp. 127–9.

and *to calculate*, he was baffled and somewhat shocked by *coffin ware-house* (it would now be *casketeria!*), *hollow ware*, *spider* (in the sense of a skillet or frying pan) and *firedog. Hollow ware* was not actually an Americanism, despite the fact that it appeared strange to him. But *spider*, in the sense noted, seems to have originated in this country, and the DAE's first example is dated 1790. *Firedog* is still used in England, but the DAE's first example, dated 1792, precedes by three-quarters of a century the first English example so far unearthed. *Fender* may be an Americanism, though this is uncertain. The DAE's first example, dated 1647, antedates the first recorded English example by forty-one years. In the sense of a fire screen the word is undoubtedly American.

Mrs. Frances Trollope reported in her "Domestic Manners of the Americans" (1832) that during her whole stay in the Republic she had seldom "heard a sentence elegantly turned and correctly pronounced from the lips of an American"; there was "always something either in the expression or the accent" that jarred her feelings and shocked her taste. She concluded that "the want of refinement" was the great American curse.

Captain Basil Hall was so upset by some of the novelties he encountered in 1827 and 1828 that he went to see Noah Webster, then seventy years old, to remonstrate. Webster upset him still further by arguing stoutly that "his countrymen had not only a right to adopt new words, but were obliged to modify the language to suit the novelty of the circumstances, geographical and political, in which they were placed." The lexicographer went on to observe judicially that "it is quite impossible to stop the progress of language—it is like the course of the Mississippi, the motion of which, at times, is scarcely perceptible; yet even then it possesses a momentum quite irresistible. Words and expressions will be forced into use, in spite of all the exertions of all the writers in the world." Webster tried to mollify Hall by saying that "there were not fifty words in all which were used in America and not in England"—an underestimate of large proportions—but Hall went away muttering.

Captain Frederick Marryat, in "A Diary in America" (1839), ten years after Hall, observed that "it is remarkable how very debased the language has become in a short period in America," and then proceeded to specifications—*e.g.*, the use of *mean* for *ashamed*, of *clever* in the sense which stumped Captain Hamilton, of *bad* as a deprecant of general utility, of *how?* instead of *what?* as an interrogative, of *considerable* as an adverb, and of such immoral verbs as *to suspicion* and *to opinion*. Once, he said, he heard "one of the first men in America" say, "Sir, if I had done so, I should not only have doubled and trebled but *fourbled* and *fivebled* my money." Unfortunately, it is hard to believe that an American who was so plainly alive to the difference between *should* and *would* would have been unaware of *quadrupled* and *quintupled*. No doubt, then as now, visiting Englishmen were sometimes taken for rides. American speech, Marryat argued, was actually a gallimaufry of all the dialects of England, and the fact that this heterogeneous mixture had been "collected and bound up" in a dictionary by Noah Webster did not suffice to make it a *Kultursprache*. Every Americanism turned out to be either "a provincialism of some English county, or else obsolete English." "The upper class of Americans," he went on, "do not speak or pronounce English according to our standard; they appear to have no exact rule to guide them, probably from the want of any intimate knowledge of Greek or Latin. You seldom hear a derivation from the Greek pronounced correctly, the accent being generally laid upon the wrong syllable. In fact, everyone appears to be independent, and pronounces just as he pleases. But it is not for me to decide the very momentous question as to which nation speaks the best English. The Americans generally improve upon the inventions of others; probably they may have improved upon our language. . . . It must be acknowledged that they have added considerably to our dictionary; but . . . I shall just submit to the reader the occasional variations, or improvements, as they may be, which met my ears during my residence in America, as also the idiomatic peculiarities, and having done so, I must leave him to decide for himself."

Marryat was impressed by the verb *to fix*, which he described as "universal" and as meaning "to do anything." It also got attention from other English travelers, including Godfrey Thomas Vigne, whose "Six Months in America" was printed in 1832, and Charles Dickens, who came in 1842. Vigne said that it had "perhaps as many significations as any word in the Chinese language," and proceeded to list some of them—"to be done, made, mixed, mended, bespoken, hired, ordered, arranged, procured, finished, lent or given."

Like all the other English travelers of his time, Marryat noted the large use of *guess*, *reckon* and *calculate* in America. "Each term," he said, "is said to be peculiar to different States, but I found them used everywhere, one as often as the other." He noted the tendency in America for technical words and phrases to enter into the general speech by metaphor. For example:

> In the West, where steam navigation is so abundant, when they ask you to drink they say, "Stranger, will you *take in wood?*"—the vessels taking in wood to keep the steam up, and the person taking in spirits to keep his steam up.

In a letter written on an Ohio River steamboat on April 15, 1842, Dickens reported that "out of Boston and New York" a nasal drawl was universal, that the prevailing grammar was "more than doubtful" and that the "oddest vulgarisms" were "received idioms." His observations on American speech habits in his "American Notes" (1842) were so derisory that they drew the following from Emerson:

> No such conversations ever occur in this country, in real life, as he relates. He has picked up and noted with eagerness each odd local phrase that he met with, and when he had a story to relate, has joined them together, so that the result is the broadest caricature.[9]

The first traveler to show a genuine liking for all things American seems to have been Lady Emmeline Stuart Wortley, who published "Travels in the United States" in 1851. She met many notables during her stay in 1850, including Agassiz, the historian William H. Prescott and President Zachary Taylor, and gushed over them all. She was naturally astonished to hear that Prescott, despite "The Conquest of Mexico" and "The Conquest of Peru," had never visited either country, but she insisted that he was nevertheless "as delightful as his own delightful books." Taylor gave her a cordial reception at the White House, advised her to visit St. Louis, which he described as "altogether perhaps the most interesting town in the United States," and on her departure "insisted most courteously on conducting us to our carriage, and bareheaded he handed us in, standing on the steps till we drove off."

Lady Emmeline not only refrained from denouncing the speech of Americans; she actually praised their habit, then in full tide, of giving grandiloquent sobriquets to their cities. New Bedford, Mass., she reported, was called the *City of Palaces*. She went on:

> Philadelphia is the *City of Brotherly Love*, or the *Iron City;* Buffalo, the *Queen City of the Lakes;* New Haven, the *City of Elms*, etc. . . . I am afraid matter-of-fact John Bull, if he attempted such a fanciful classification, would make sad work of it. Perhaps we should have Birmingham the *City of Buttons* or *Warming-pans;* Nottingham the *City of Stockings;* Sheffield, the *City of Knives and Forks*, and so forth.[1]

Almost every English traveler between the War of 1812 and the Civil War was puzzled by the strange signs on American shops. Hall couldn't

---

[9] Journal, Nov. 25, 1842. [See also The American Dialect of Charles Dickens, by Louise Pound, *AS*, Vol. XXII, Apr. 1947, pp. 124–30; and Dickens's *Household Words* on American English, by Anne Lohrli, *AS*, Vol. XXXVII, May 1962, pp. 83–94.]

[1] The DA traces *City of Brotherly Love* to 1793 (it is a translation, of course, of the Greek *Philadelphia*), *City of Elms* to 1843, *Queen City* (for Cincinnati) to 1839, *Queen City of the Lakes* (for Buffalo) to 1846.

make out the meaning of *Leather and Finding Store*, though he found *Flour and Feed Store* and *Clothing Store* self-explanatory, albeit unfamiliar. Hamilton failed to gather "the precise import" of *Dry-Goods Store*. But all this was relatively mild stuff, and after 1850 the chief licks at the American dialect were delivered, not by English travelers, most of whom had begun to find it more amusing than indecent, but by English pedants, who did not stir from their cloisters. The climax came in 1863, when the Very Rev. Henry Alford, D.D., Dean of Canterbury, printed his "Plea for the Queen's English." [2] He said:

> Look at the process of deterioration which our Queen's English has undergone at the hands of the Americans. Look at those phrases which so amuse us in their speech and books; at their reckless exaggeration and contempt for congruity; and then compare the character and history of the nation—its blunted sense of moral obligation and duty to man; its open disregard of conventional right when aggrandisement is to be obtained; and I may now say, its reckless and fruitless maintenance of the most cruel and unprincipled war in the history of the world.

Alford here abandoned one of the chief counts in Sydney Smith's famous indictment, and substituted its exact opposite. Smith had denounced slavery, whereas Alford, by a tremendous feat of moral virtuosity, was now denouncing the war to put it down! But Samuel Taylor Coleridge had done almost as well in 1822. The usual English accusation at that time was that the Americans had abandoned English altogether and set up a barbarous jargon in its place. Coleridge took the directly contrary tack. "An American," he said, "by his boasting of the superiority of the Americans generally, but especially in their language, once provoked me to tell him that 'on that head the least said the better, as the Americans presented the extraordinary anomaly of *a people without a language*. That they had mistaken the English language for baggage (which is called *plunder* in America), and had stolen it.' " [3]

---

[2] A second edition followed in 1864, and an eighth was reached by 1880. There was also an American edition. In October 1864, G. Washington Moon, an American resident in England, brought out a counterblast, The Dean's English. This reached a seventh edition by 1884. Moon employed the ingenious device of turning Alford's pedantries upon him. He showed that the dean was a very loose and careless writer, and often violated his own rules. Alford was the first editor of the *Contemporary Review* and brought out a monumental edition of the New Testament in Greek. He was born in 1810, served as dean of Canterbury from 1857 to 1871, and died in the latter year.

[3] Letters, Conversations and Recollections of S. T. Coleridge, ed. by Thomas Allsop; London, 1836. [De Quincey's attitude was of a piece with Coleridge's. See De Quincey's Use of Americanisms, by Robert E. Hollinger, *AS*, Vol. XXIII, Oct.–Dec. 1948, pp. 204–9.]

4: THE ENGLISH ATTITUDE TODAY

Smith, Alford and Coleridge have plenty of heirs and assigns today. The sect of Anglomaniacs in the United States is influential, not only in what passes for society but also in politics, finance, pedagogy and journalism, but the corresponding sect of British Americophiles is small and feeble, though it shows a few respectable names. Seldom is anything specifically American praised in the English press, save some new manifestation of American Anglomania. The realm of Uncle Shylock remains, at bottom, the "brigand confederation" of the *Foreign Quarterly*. In language an Americanism is generally regarded as obnoxious *ipso facto,* and when a pungent new one begins to force its way into English usage the guardians of the national linguistic chastity belabor it. If it makes progress, they often switch to the doctrine that it is really good English, and search for it in Chaucer, or even in the Venerable Bede; [4] but while it is coming in they give it no quarter. What begins as an uproar over a word sometimes ends as a holy war to keep the knavish Yankee from ruining the English *Kultur* and annexing the tattered relics of the Empire. Amusingly enough, phrases denounced as abominable Americanisms are often unknown in the United States but familiar to the habitués of London music halls. And often the denunciations of them are sprinkled with genuine Americanisms, unconsciously picked up.

This war upon Americanisms naturally has its pitched battles and its rest periods between. These rest periods tend to coincide with the times when it is politic, on grounds remote from the philological, to treat the Yankee barbarian with a certain amount of politeness. Such a time came in 1917, and lasted until the first mention of the repayment of war debts, when the genial if oafish Uncle Sam was supplanted by the horrendous Uncle Shylock. It came again in 1943, when American troops began pouring into England in large force, and the fear of invasion, so lively during the first years of World War II, was allayed at last. The Ministry of Information and the Board of Education celebrated this happy deliverance by bringing out jointly a pamphlet by Louis MacNeice, entitled "Meet the U. S. Army." This pamphlet was circulated not only among the English soldiery but also among school children. Its title showed a graceful concession to an American vulgarism that more than one English pedagogue had reviled in the past, and in the text there were many more.

---

[4] "This dichotomy," says Allen Walker Read in British Recognition of American Speech in the Eighteenth Century, *DN,* Vol. VI, Pt. VI, 1933, p. 331, "runs through most British writing on American speech . . . : on the one hand the Americans are denounced for introducing corruptions into the language, and on the other hand those very expressions are eagerly claimed as of British origin to show that the British deserve the credit for them."

The English seldom differentiate between American slang and Americanisms in respectable use; both they label as the American slanguage.[5] An American book is seldom reviewed in England without some reference to its strange and generally unpleasant diction. The *Literary Supplement* of the London *Times* is especially alert to discover Americanisms in the most decorous American authors. Of its 240 lines on the first two volumes of the Dictionary of American Biography, 31 attacked the language of the learned authors. The Manchester *Guardian* and the weeklies of opinion follow dutifully. The *Guardian* began a review of Harry Emerson Fosdick's "As I See Religion" by praising his "telling speech," but ended by deploring sadly his "full-blooded Americanisms which sometimes make even those who do not for a moment question America's right and power to contribute to the speech which we use wince as they read." [6] But in wartime this forthright attitude is considerably ameliorated in all the great organs of British opinion. The somewhat malicious Baltimore *Evening Sun* was able to note in 1940 [7] that even the *Times* had grown "a good deal cagier" than usual "about denouncing certain expressions as horrid Americanisms," and that the *Times* itself had achieved the extraordinary feat of belaboring *to check up on* without "any mention of America." When an anonymous reader took space in the Edinburgh *Scotsman* on November 6, 1941, to denounce *by and large, to contact, to demote* and *O.K.*,[8] it printed an article the same day saying that "it can be argued that these expressions are useful currency; they present definite nuances and inflections and make possible a certain informality of mood or approach which is not otherwise attainable. And they have a certain historical significance and even dignity, in virtue of their association with a restless, changeable and disturbing age." There was no mention of their American origin. The same prudence is visible on lower levels. When Commander Reginald Fletcher, M.P., private secretary to the First Lord of the Admiralty, undertook in 1941 to confute and confuse "the people who say that Germany will be out of oil next week or will crack next month" by hurling at them a derisive "Oh, yeah!" a columnist

---

[5] *Slanguage* dates from the 1880s, in Edward E. Rice's Evangeline, in which a long-suffering father used it to describe the current slang which his daughter was using to sauce him. *Slanguage* is not listed by Partridge, but it is used in England and Ireland.

[6] Weekly edition, Aug. 26, 1932, p. 175. [Of late years the *Guardian Weekly* has become more tolerant, or simply more careless. The change is recorded in Die Amerikanismen im Manchester *Guardian Weekly* (1948–1954): Ein Beitrag zur Funktion der englischen Zeitung in den amerikanisch-britischen Sprachbeziehungen der Gegenwort, by Günter Panten; Munich, 1959 (Mainzer amerikanistische Beiträge, Bd. 2).]

[7] The King's English, editorial page, Feb. 12.

[8] Of *O.K.* he said: "From the slang of the American bargee it has advanced to the favor of the diplomatist." There is, of course, no such thing as an American *bargee;* we call him a *bargeman.* The DA traces *by and large* to 1767, *to demote* to c. 1891, *to contact* to 1929.

in the London *Sunday Mercury* [9] backed gracefully into his denunciation of the infamy:

> I have every respect for the Americans; I think the graphic descriptive vigor of much American prose has an animating effect upon the English language; but the nasal American intonation—and "Oh, yeah!" is a typical example of it—is vile.

In times of peace and security the British critics of American speech seldom pull their punches; they lay about them in a berserk and all-out manner, and commonly couple flings at the American character with their revilings of the American language. "Every few years," says D. W. Brogan, "someone sounds the clarion and fills the fife, calling us on to man the breaches and repel the assailing hordes that threaten the chastity of the pure well of English undefiled. Sometimes the invaders intend to clip off the strong verbs, sometimes they threaten to enrich our language with new and horrid words. Whatever they do, or threaten to do, it must be resisted." [1]

It is a pity that no literary pathologist has ever investigated the ebb and flow of this resistance during the past several generations, as Pickering, Cairns and Read have investigated its manifestations in the era between the Revolution and the Civil War. The first real blast of the modern era was delivered by Alford, who began by describing American as a debased and barbaric form of English, and then proceeded to a denunciation of the "character and history" of the Republic. This was before Gettysburg, when most Englishmen of the dean's class were looking forward to the ruin of the United States, with benefits to British trade, not to mention what then appeared to be British military and naval security. When that hope perished, there ensued a period of uneasy politeness, but with the *Alabama* claims there was a sharp revival of moral indignation, and *Punch* expressed the prevailing English view:

> If the pure well of English is to remain undefiled no Yankee should be allowed henceforth to throw mud into it. It is a form of verbal expectoration that is most profane, most detestable. [2]

By 1870 the rage against the loutish and depraved Americano had gone so far that the *Medical Times and Gazette* (London) alleged quite seriously

---

[9] English Is Good Enough, Nov. 9, 1941.
[1] The Conquering Tongue, London *Spectator*, Feb. 5, 1943, reprinted in *Encore*, Sept. 1943, p. 351. Brogan, professor of political science at Cambridge, spent some time at Harvard and knows the United States well. A large part of his writing is devoted to explaining Americans to Britons and vice versa.

[2] I borrow this quotation from an article by James Thurber in *The New Yorker*, May 13, 1939, p. 49. [See also American English in *Punch*, 1841–1900, by Jane W. Stedman, *AS*, Vol. XXVIII, Oct. 1953, pp. 171–80.]

that the medical journals of the United States were written in a slang too outlandish for any decent English medical man to understand.[3]

Sharpshooting went on through the 70s and 80s, culminating in a violent attack with all arms after Grover Cleveland's Venezuela message of December 17, 1895, but when the possible effects thereof were pondered there appeared a more conciliatory spirit, and during the uneasy years before World War I the Americano began to be cherished as an Anglo-Saxon brother, and not much was heard about the villainousness of either his character or his speech. The war itself brought a return to Bach, and by two routes. First, the American and British troops, coming into contact in France, found that intercommunication was impeded by harsh differences in speechways, and laid those differences to moral deficiencies. Second, the American movie, which invaded England on a large scale at the end of the war, introduced so many Americanisms, especially on the level of slang, that the guardians of the King's English were aroused to protest. But even more influential was the sinister talk of war debts that began in 1920. Uncle Sam became Uncle Shylock, and every fresh Americanism an insult to the English language.

In 1927 an International Conference on English was held in London, but the fact that the call for it came from the American side [4] made it suspect from the start. On June 25, 1927, the *New Statesman* let go with a heavy blast, warning Americans in no weasel terms to keep hands off the mother tongue. "Why," demanded the author, "should we offer to discuss the subject at all with America? . . . For all serious lovers of the English language it is America that is the only dangerous enemy."

During the timorous deliberations of the conference, Henry Seidel Canby, one of the American delegates, permitted himself the blasphemy of speaking of Anglicisms as well as of Americanisms. This slip was denounced with ferocity by the *New Statesman* writer:

> What Dr. Canby meant by it, presumably, was some usage which his own country had not adopted. . . . He claimed for America a right equal to our own to decide what is English and what is not! That is a claim which we cannot too emphatically repudiate. . . . The English language is our own.

---

[3] Jan. 8 and June 4, 1870.

[4] It was issued in Mar. 1922, and was signed by James W. Bright, of Johns Hopkins; Charles H. Grandgent, of Harvard; Robert Underwood Johnson, secretary of the American Academy of Arts and Letters; John Livingston Lowes, of Harvard; John M. Manly, of the University of Chicago; Charles G. Osgood, of Princeton; and Fred Newton Scott, of the University of Michigan. A reply was received in Oct. 1922 from an English committee consisting of the Earl of Balfour, Robert Bridges and Sir Henry Newbolt, but it was not until five years later that the conference was actually held.

The proposal that a permanent Council of English be formed, with 50 American members and 50 from the British Empire, brought the *New Statesman* to the verge of hysterics. It admitted that such a council "might be very useful indeed," but argued that it "ought not to include more than one Scotsman and one Irishman, and should certainly not include even a single American."

The other English journals were rather less fierce in their denunciation of the council and its program, but few of them greeted either with cordiality.[5] Nor was there any more favorable response from colonial newspapers and pedagogues. The Canadian and Australian commentators sneered at it, and J. R. R. Tolkien, of Oxford, who was born in South Africa, wrote in "The Year's Work in English Studies": [6] "Whatever may be the special destiny and peculiar future splendor of the language of the United States, it is still possible to hope that our fate may be kept distinct." Nothing more was heard of the proposed General Council on English, and the hundred immortals were never appointed.

So long ago as 1913 Sir Sidney Low, who had lived in America and had a sound acquaintance with Americanisms, suggested ironically in an article in the *Westminster Gazette* that American be taught in the English schools. He reported that the English businessman was "puzzled by his ignorance of colloquial American" and "painfully hampered" thereby in his handling of American trade. He quoted an extract from an American novel then appearing serially in an English magazine—an extract including such Americanisms as *side-stepper*, *boob*, *bartender* and *kidding*, and many characteristically American extravagances of metaphor. It might be well argued, he said, that this strange dialect was as near to "the tongue that Shakespeare spoke" as "the dialect of Bayswater or Brixton," but that philological fact did not help to its understanding. "You might almost as well expect [the British businessman] to converse freely with a Portuguese railway porter because he tried to stumble through Caesar when he was in the Upper Fourth at school."

At the time Low published his article the invasion of England by Americanisms was just beginning in earnest, and many words and phrases that have since become commonplaces there were still strange and disquieting. Writing in the London *Daily Mail* a year or so later, W. G. Faulkner thought it necessary to explain the meaning of *hobo*, *hoodlum*, *bunco steerer*, *dead beat*, *flume*, *dub*, *rubberneck*, *drummer*, *sucker*, *dive* (in the sense of a thieves' resort), *clean up*, *graft* and *to feature*, and another interpreter added definitions of *holdup*, *quitter*, *rube*, *shack*, *band wagon*,

---

[5] There is an account of their attitude, with quotations, by Kemp Malone, who was an American delegate, in *AS*, Vol. III, Apr. 1928, p. 261.
[6] Vol. VI, 1927.

road agent, cinch, live wire and *scab.* In the early days of the American movie, Faulkner denounced its terminology as "generating and encouraging mental indiscipline." As Hollywood gradually conquered the English cinema palaces, such warnings became more frequent and more angry, and in 1920 the London *Daily News* began a formal agitation of the subject, with the usual pious editorials and irate letters from old subscribers.

When the American talkie began to reinforce the movie, in 1929, there was a fresh outburst of indignation, but this time it had a despairing undertone. Reinforced by the spoken word, Americanisms were coming in faster than they could be challenged and disposed of. "Within the past few years," said Thomas Anderson in the Manchester *Sunday Chronicle* for January 12, 1930, "we have gradually been adopting American habits of speech, American business methods, and the American outlook." To which Jameson Thomas added in the London *Daily Express* for January 21:

> One must admit that we write and speak Americanisms. So long as Yankeeisms came to us insidiously we absorbed them carelessly. They have been a valuable addition to the language, as nimble coppers are a valuable addition to purer currency. But the talkies have presented the American language in one giant meal, and we are revolted.[7]

But this revolt, insofar as it was real, was apparently confined to the aged: the young of the British species continued to gobble down the neologisms of Hollywood and to imitate the Hollywood intonation. During the next few years the English papers printed countless protests against this corruption of the speech of British youth, but apparently to no avail.[8]

Parallel with this alarmed hostility to the jargon of Hollywood, much of it borrowed from the American underworld, there has gone on in England a steady opposition to the more decorous varieties of American. Back in 1919 H. N. Brailsford, who had been in the United States many times and often contributed to American magazines, actually objected to the vocabulary of the precious and Anglomaniacal Woodrow Wilson, then in action at Versailles.[9]

In the Twentieth Century, most Englishmen who attack American speechways have been content to fire long-range shots from the privileged sanctuary of their island fortress. One of the last to invade the United States and reprove the barbarians in their homes was Charles Whibley, who contributed an extremely acidulous article on "The American Language" to the *Bookman* (New York) for January 1908. "To the English traveler

---

[7] Words That We Borrow, Jan. 21, 1930.

[8] [During World War II many English children were sent to the United States for safety. For the effect on their speech see American Accent of British Children, *The New York Times*, Nov. 11, 1946, p. 58.]

[9] London *Daily Herald*, Aug. 20.

in America," he said, "the language which he hears spoken about him is at once a puzzle and a surprise. It is his own, yet not his own. It seems to him a caricature of English, a phantom speech, ghostly yet familiar, such as he might hear in a land of dreams." Whibley objected violently to many characteristic American terms, among them *to locate, to antagonize* and *proposition.* The onslaught provoked even so mild a man as Henry W. Boynton to publish a spirited rejoinder in the *Bookman* for March of the same year. "It offends [the English]," he said, "that we are not thoroughly ashamed of ourselves for not being like them." The controversy was carried on for months, with American patriots on one side and Englishmen and Anglomaniacs on the other.

It is easy to loose such an uproar. In an article for the London *Daily Express* on the progress of Americanisms in England between my visits of 1922 and 1929–30, I ventured to say:

> The Englishman, whether he knows it or not, is talking and writing more and more American. . . . In a few years it will probably be impossible for an Englishman to speak, or even to write, without using Americanisms, whether consciously or unconsciously. The influence of 125,000,000 people, practically all headed in one direction, is simply too great to be resisted by any minority, however resolute.[1]

This article was violently arraigned by volunteer correspondents of the *Express* and by contributors to many other journals. One weekly opened its protest with "That silly little fellow, H. L. Mencken, is at it again," and headed it "The American Moron," and in various other quarters I was accused of a sinister conspiracy against the mother tongue. The chosen gladiator of the *Express* was James Douglas, then editor of its Sunday edition and later director of the London *Express* Newspapers, Ltd. He took the strange line of arguing that the talkies were having virtually no effect on English speech. "It is not true to say," he said, "that 'the Englishman is talking and writing more and more American.' American dialects and slang find us curiously unimitative."[2] But other contributors to the discussion were less complacent.

I was the unwitting cause of another uproar in 1936, when the *Daily Express* reprinted extracts from an article that I had written for the *Yale Review.*[3] I argued that the increasing adoption of American words and phrases in England was natural and inevitable, because England had "nothing to offer in competition with them—that is, nothing so apt or pungent,

---

[1] What America Is Doing to Your Language, Jan. 15.

[2] You Are Wrong about the Mother Tongue, Jan. 18, 1930.

[3] The American Language, Spring 1936. The *Daily Express* extracts appeared on June 5, 1936, and were headed Boloney!

nothing so good." There were the usual protests from indignant English-men, whereupon the *Express* fanned the flames by printing further extracts from my article, including the following:

> Confronted by novelty, whether in object or in situation, the Americans always manage to fetch up a name for it that not only describes it but also illuminates it, whereas the English, since the Elizabethan stimulant oozed out of them, have been content merely to catalogue it.[4]

"Most Americanisms," said one rejoinder, "are merely examples of bad grammar, like *going some place else*. Many others are vulgar and lazy representations of recognized English words." This charge appears very often in English discourses. In 1935 a correspondent signing himself W. G. Bloom informed the London *Daily Telegraph* [5] that "many so-called American colloquialisms" were "only emigrants returning to England." Thus he specified:

> *Too true* is to be found in Shakespeare, and so is *to beat it*. In Cowper *tell the world* appears, and Byron gives us *and all that. Son of a gun*, while savouring of Arizona, is to be found in "The Ingoldsby Legends," and *to bite the dust* is in "The Adventures of Gil Blas."

A year later, when a justice of the High Court rebuked a lawyer for using the American *to bluff* in an argument, one of the London newspapers assured its readers that it was actually sound English, and argued that the game of *poker*, from which it had been borrowed, was English too.[6] A contributor to the London *Morning Post*, in 1936, claimed *beeline* and *comeuppance* for old England, and even questioned the American origin of *cracker*, in the sense of what the English call (or used to call) a biscuit. The facts, unhappily, do not agree with these patriots. *Too true* is not an Americanism, and neither is *and all that*. It is possible that *to tell the world* may be found in Cowper, but Partridge says that its latter-day vogue originated in the United States, and that it was not until 1930 or 1931 that it was "anglicized as a colloquialism." He says that *to beat it* is also of American origin, and does not list *to bite the dust* as an English phrase. The OED's first example of the latter is from William Cullen Bryant's translation of the Iliad, 1870. The history of *son of a gun*, like that of the allied *son of a bitch*, is obscure. *Beeline* and *comeuppance* seem to be indubitable Americanisms. The first is traced by the DA to 1830, and the second by the DAE to 1859. *Cracker* in the sense of a small hard biscuit, *e.g.*, a *soda*

---

[4] This appeared under the heading of More Boloney, June 10, 1936.

[5] Homing Emigrants, Mar. 11, 1935.

[6] The Origin of *Bluff*, *John o' London's Weekly*, Apr. 4, 1936, p. 33.

cracker, is traced to 1739 in America but only to 1810 in England, and the OED marks it "now chiefly in U.S." *Graham cracker* goes back to 1882 and *soda cracker* to 1830; both are Americanisms. [The DA traces *animal cracker* only to 1925, but it is much older.]

The British discussions of the origin of such terms are unfortunately carried on, in the main, by patriots rather than by etymologists. Those who avoid a show of bogus learning and devote themselves frankly to damning the abominable Yankee and his gibberish are much more amusing. They had a field day in 1935 when the 100% British Cunard White Star Line, advertising (in London) the first sailing of the *Queen Mary*, offered prospective passengers *one-way* and *round-trip* tickets instead of *single* and *return* tickets. "Is the *Queen Mary*," asked the Manchester *Guardian* gravely, "to be a British or an American vessel?" [7] There was another pother in 1938, when Sydney F. Markham, M.P., expressed the waggish hope that King George VI and Queen Elizabeth, then about to embark on their American tour, would not come home speaking American instead of English.[8] The subject was tender at the time, for Edward VIII, whom George had succeeded only two years before, had been accused of a traitorous and unmanly liking for Americanisms. But the new king and queen somehow escaped contamination. Such doubts and dubieties, down to Pearl Harbor, produced a great deal of indignant writing about the American language. In 1937 there was a heavy outbreak of it,[9] with Cosmo Hamilton denouncing the "slick Americanisms . . . that belong to the worst illiteracy of a foreign tongue"; William Powell damning "the gibberish of morons" produced by "immigrations of South Europeans, many of whom were backward and illiterate"; [1] and Pamela Frankau taking space in the London *Daily Sketch* [2] to arraign all "victims to the American craze" as enemies of the true, the good and the beautiful.

At the time this moral rebellion against Americanisms was going on in England there were also repercussions in the colonies and dominions, especially in Canada. In January 1937, a C. Egerton Lowe, described as "of Trinity College, London," turned up in Toronto warning that American influence was corrupting the pure English that the Canadians (at all events, in Ontario) formerly spoke. He was denounced in the Detroit *Free Press*,[3] but he found a certain amount of support among those he was seeking to save, until the outbreak of World War II provided more serious work for

---

[7] Dec. 27, 1935.
[8] Associated Press dispatch from London, Nov. 8, 1938.
[9] "The outcry against the pollution of our well of pure English by Americanisms," said a writer in the London *Tatler*, Oct. 6, 1937, "has yet once again become

very clamant."
[1] Americanisms, Glasgow *Daily Record and Mail*, June 30, 1937.
[2] Snob-stuff from U.S.A., Oct. 25, 1937.
[3] Good Morning, by Malcolm W. Bingay, Jan. 21, 1937.

the Dominion. [In the last decade the prestige of English speech in Canada has waned along with the power of England in world affairs. W. W. Brodie, Director of Broadcast English for the Canadian Broadcasting Corporation, has advised Canadians to use their own speech rather than an ersatz British; [4] and in most Canadian universities, Canadian English is perfectly respectable, both to speak and to study.]

In 1925 the English antipathy to American translations of foreign books broke forth into one of the fiercest of its recurring outbursts. The *casus belli* was a version of the Italian plays of Luigi Pirandello in two volumes, one being translated by Arthur Livingston, an American, and the other by Edward Storer, an Englishman. Livingston, professor of Romance languages at Columbia, was an Italian scholar of the highest eminence, and the qualifications of Storer were considerably less conspicuous, but the English reviewers, with few exceptions, denounced Livingston and whooped up Storer. Their chief objection was that, where English and American usage differed, Livingston preferred the locutions of his own country and did not try to write like an Englishman.

Under the pseudonym Simon Pure, a critic (probably Frank Swinnerton) expressed the opinion that English translations of foreign books were frequently offensive to Americans, and for like reasons. In a reply in the *Saturday Review of Literature* for December 26, 1925, Ernest Boyd—himself a translator of wide experience, born in Ireland, educated there and in England, for seven years a member of the British consular service, and resident in New York since 1920—denied that there was hostility to English translations in this country. "English translators," he said, "are accepted at their own—or their publishers'—valuation in America," but American translators "are received with prejudice and criticized with severity" in England. Said Mr. Boyd:

> Dr. Livingston, the American, is taken to task though his Italian scholarship is well authenticated and beyond dispute. Mr. Storer, on the contrary, is an Englishman, and his translations are so defective in places as to show a complete misunderstanding of the text, but no complaints have been raised on that score. . . . British nationality is more important than American scholarship, apparently.

The ensuing debate is still resumed from time to time, with the English champions holding stoutly to the doctrine that there can be but one form of English pure and undefiled, the British variety. Thus Raymond Mortimer in the *Nation and Athenaeum* for July 28, 1929: "It is most unfortunate that American publishers should be able to buy the English as well as

---

[4] [The Well of English; Toronto, 1949.]

the American rights of foreign books. For the result usually is that these books remain permanently closed to the English reader."

During the 1930s the flood of Americanisms pouring in through the talkies and the comic strips was reinforced by a fashion, among English columnists, for imitating Walter Winchell, and, among other journalists, for borrowing the jargons of *Variety* and *Time*. This new menace was attacked by J. B. Firth in the London *Daily Telegraph*, by A. E. Wilson in the London *Star*, by St. John Ervine in the London *Observer* and by various other orthodox literati. Thus Ervine described the English imitators of "American tabloids" as echoing "a hybrid language which is often incomprehensible to many Americans."

But whether comprehensible to Americans or not, it was plainly a success in England, and many Englishmen apparently concluded that the time was too late for halting it. In 1932, Ellis Healey reported in the Birmingham *Gazette* [5] that "a definitely American flavor" had appeared in "the more progressive" English newspapers and even in "the more modern" English magazines; worse, he played with the resigned thought that "in about fifty years" England might be only "a moral colony of America." Naturally enough, there were efforts to track down the agencies chiefly responsible, and in 1935, A. Noxon, headmaster of Highfield College, Leigh, found a convenient goat in the British Broadcasting Corporation. "It is high time," he wrote to the Southend *Standard*,[6] "that protest was made against the increasingly wretched example set by the B.B.C. in broadcasting during the Children's Hour the most horrible American slang for the benefit of children who, naturally imitative, quickly pick up all the atrocities which are broadcast for their benefit (?)."

The objection here, of course, was primarily to American slang, though few of the Britons who wrote to the newspapers differentiated clearly between it and more decorous American speech. Many of them denounced *sidewalk, elevator* and *candy store* quite as vigorously as they denounced *sez you, nerts* and *oh, yeah.*

The English object not only to the American vocabulary, but also to the characteristic American style, which begins to differ appreciably from the normal English style. Once the English guardians of the mother tongue tried to haul American into conformity, but of late they seem to be resigned to its differentiation, and are concerned mainly about the possibility that Standard English may be considerably modified by its influence. So long ago as 1906 H. W. and F. G. Fowler, in "The King's English," decided that "Americanisms are foreign words and should be so treated." They admitted that American had its points of superiority—"*Fall* is better on the

---

[5] The Invasion from U.S.A., Apr. 11.
[6] Broadcasting and American Slang, Oct. 31, 1935.

merits than *autumn*, in every way; it is short, Saxon (like the other three season names), picturesque; it reveals its derivation to everyone who uses it, not to the scholar only, like *autumn*" [7]—but they protested against taking even the most impeccable Americanisms into English. "The English and the American language and literature," they argued, "are both good things, but they are better apart than mixed." In 1910 the Encyclopaedia Britannica (Eleventh Edition) admitted that this falling apart had already gone so far that it was "not uncommon to meet with American newspaper articles of which an untravelled Englishman would hardly be able to understand a sentence." "The fact is," said the London *Times Literary Supplement* for January 21, 1926, in a review of G. P. Krapp's "The English Language in America," "that in spite of the greater frequency of intercourse the two idioms *have* drifted apart; farther apart than is, perhaps, generally recognized. . . . A British visitor in America, if he has any taste for the niceties of language, experiences something of the thrills of contact with a foreign idiom, for he hears and reads many things which are new to him and not a few which are unintelligible." "If the American temperament, despite its general docility, persists in its present attitude towards a standardized language," said Ernest Weekley in "Adjectives—and Other Words" (1930), "spoken American must eventually become as distinct from English as Yiddish is from classical Hebrew." Or, added J. Y. T. Greig, in "Breaking Priscian's Head" (1929), as "Spanish is from Portuguese." One school holds that the United States is not only drifting away from the mother country linguistically, but is fundamentally differentiated from it on wider cultural grounds. "Those who have had to do with Americans," said Geoffrey Grigson in the London *Morning Post* for February 13, 1934, "will not mistake them for our intimate cousins, our near psychic relations."

The late Cecil Chesterton said something to the same general effect in the London *New Witness* so long ago as 1915. "I do not believe," he wrote, "that nations ever quarrel merely because they feel that they do not understand each other. That attitude of mind of itself tends to produce a salutary humility on the one side and a pleasantly adventurous curiosity on the other. What really produces trouble between peoples is when one is certain that it understands the other—and in fact doesn't. And I am perfectly certain that that has been from the first one of the primary causes of trouble between England and America." [8]

---

[7] [Under the noses of Col. McCormick and his successors on the Chicago *Tribune,* the official calendar of the University of Chicago uses *autumn.* But some departments, *e.g.,* Anthropology, use *fall* in their departmental bulletins.]

[8] The article is summarized, with long extracts, in the *Literary Digest* for June 19, 1915, p. 1468.

But not *all* Englishmen, even at the height of the recurrent alarms, were unqualifiedly against all Americanisms. The prevailing tone remains loftily anti-American, but there have lately arisen two more moderate factions, the one contending that American speech is really not the barbaric jargon it is commonly thought to be, and the other arguing boldly that its peculiarities, though maybe uncouth, have their merits. Among the first faction was Sir Charles Strachey, K.C.M.G., a former official of the Foreign and Colonial Offices. On May 2, 1931, he wrote to the London *Times* to protest against the assumption that the argot of Chicago gunmen is the official language of the United States. "American diplomatic correspondence," he said, "is always a model of correct English, and it would be a gross error to suppose that the United States Ambassador calls revenue the *dough* or the *berries* and refers to his Italian colleague as a *wop*." But this Strachey faction was not large, and even the language of American diplomacy generally grates on English nerves.

The revolutionary theory that the American language actually has some merit seems to have been launched by William Archer, a Scotsman, in an article entitled "American Today," printed somewhat prudently, not in England, but in *Scribner's Magazine* for February 1899. "New words," he said, "are begotten by new conditions of life; and as American life is far more fertile of new conditions than ours, the tendency toward neologism cannot but be stronger in America than in England. America has enormously enriched the language, not only with new words, but (since the American mind is, on the whole, quicker and wittier than the English) with apt and luminous colloquial metaphors." Twenty years later Archer returned to the matter, on English soil, in the *Westminster Gazette*.[9] He protested vigorously against the English habit of "pulling a wry face over American expressions, not because they are inherently bad, but simply because they are American. The vague and unformulated idea behind all such petty cavillings," he continued, "is that the English language is in danger of being corrupted by the importation of Americanisms, and that it behooves us to establish a sort of quarantine in order to keep out the detrimental germs. This notion is simply one of the milder phases of the Greater Stupidity."

In May 1920, Richard Aldington made an eloquent plea for American linguistic independence, and praised the development of a characteristically American idiom.[1] "Are Americans," he demanded,

> to write the language which they speak, which is slowly but inevitably separating itself from the language of England, or are they

---

[9] Reprinted in the *Literary Review* of the New York *Evening Post*, July 23, 1921.

[1] *Poetry* (Chicago), May 1920.

to write a devitalized idiom learned painfully from books or from a discreet frequentation of London literary cliques? . . . Another century may see English broken into a number of dialects or even different languages, spoken in Canada, Australia, South Africa, the United States, and England. The result may eventually be similar to the break-up of Latin.

This pro-American party can show some well-known names. Robert Bridges, Poet Laureate and founder of the Society for Pure English, was in sympathy with it, and it won support from Wyndham Lewis, Edward Shanks, Virginia Woolf and Sir John Foster Fraser. In February 1925, H. E. Moore printed an elaborate defense of Americanisms in the *English Review*. He contrasted the academic tightness in Standard English with the greater naturalness of American, and praised some of the salient characters of the latter—its hospitality to neologisms, its fertility in effective metaphor, its "fluid" spelling. "As this divergence of English and American," he said, "has proceeded through strata of English derision and American defiance it has tended to become deliberate and constructive. England and academic America generally have asserted the old criteria. But they have been swept aside by America's egalitarian millions, and established changes have now made any acceptance of literary Southern English impossible." "I have never found it possible," said Shanks in the London *Evening Standard* in 1931,

> to understand why with so many people there should be an automatic objection to anything that can be called an Americanism. An Americanism is an expression adopted by those who speak our common language but who live in the United States. There are more of them than there are of us, and so one would suppose, on democratic principles, that their choice was entitled at least to our serious consideration.

A year later, Sir John Fraser [2] made a vigorous attack upon the dominant anti-American party, and accused it of trying absurdly to halt a process of inevitable change. In *Life and Letters* for April 1934, Wyndham Lewis argued that, even if it was rational, it was too late for the English to stem the advance of American:

> While England was a uniquely powerful empire-state, ruled by an aristocratic caste, its influence upon the speech as upon the psychology of the American ex-colonies was overwhelming. But today that ascendancy has almost entirely vanished. . . . So the situation is this, as

---

[2] London *Sunday Graphic*, Jan. 3, 1932.

far as our common language is concerned: the destiny of England and the United States is more than ever one, but it is now the American influence that is paramount. The tables have effectively been turned in this respect.

At the same time there was sage advice to his fellow countrymen by Alistair Cooke, then of the British Broadcasting Corporation:

> When you hear an expression that seems a little odd to you, don't assume it was invented by a music-hall comedian trying to be smart. It was probably spoken by Lincoln or Paul Jones. . . . And when you hear a strange pronunciation remember you are not hearing a chaotic speech that anyone has deliberately changed. . . . It is the cultivated speech of a New England gentleman of 1934, and it happens in essentials also to be the cultivated speech you would have heard in London over two hundred years ago.[3]

There have been many reinforcements to this pro-American party in later years. "We have to admit," said a staff contributor to the Manchester *Evening News* in 1936,[4] "the intense vitality and colorful expressiveness of the American tongue, no matter what the purists may say. . . . American makes plain English sound a tortuous and poverty-stricken language. It is no idle fancy of the younger generation which seizes on the American idiom to express something which would need a lot more words in English." A few months later Wilfred R. Childe, lecturer in English at Leeds, said much the same thing,[5] and presently there was in progress an earnest if somewhat mild defense of certain Americanisms under fire from chauvinists. Even the Manchester *Guardian*, ordinarily at least 150% British, took a hand in this counterattack when Dr. Henry Albert Wilson, Bishop of Chelmsford, denounced *to release* in his diocesan paper. "Why," asked the *Guardian*, "is *released*, in the sense of a film's being freed for general exhibition, 'an abominable Americanism'? It seems to convey a perfectly plain meaning in a perfectly plain way." [6] The London *Times* went the whole hog (as Abraham Lincoln was fond of saying) in its obituary of John V. A. Weaver, the American poet, in 1938. His books in vulgar American—"In American," "More American" and so on—offered proof, it allowed, that "the American language is a separate and living tongue, capable of beauty and poetry in itself. These vernacular Ameri-

---

[3] Printed as That Dreadful American, *Listener*, Jan. 30, 1935.
[4] To-night, by Tempus, Mar. 24.
[5] Americanisms and Slang, *Catholic Her-ald* (Manchester edition), June 19, 1936.
[6] An English Paper Deplores a Bishop for Deploring, Baltimore *Evening Sun*, editorial page, Nov. 6, 1936.

can poems have something of the same freshness, robustness and beauty of 'The Canterbury Tales.' " [7]

Finally D. W. Brogan went overboard in the grand manner in 1943:

> There is nothing surprising in the constant reinforcement, or, if you like, corruption of English by American. And there is every reason to believe that it has increased, is increasing and will not be diminished. If American could influence English a century ago, when the pre-dominance of the Mother Country in wealth, population and prestige was secure, and when most educated Americans were reverentially colonial in their attitude to English culture, how can it be prevented from influencing English today, when every change has been a change of weight to the American side? That the balance of linguistic power is upset is hard to doubt. Of the 200,000,000 people speaking English, nearly seven-tenths live in the United States, and another tenth in the British Dominions are as much influenced by American as by English English. Nor is this all. As an international language, it is American that the world increasingly learns. . . .
>
> To understand what is happening to the language in whose owner-ship and control we are now only minority shareholders is an object of curiosity worthy of serious persons. It is also an object worthy of less serious persons, for the study of American is rich in delights and surprises.[8]

Five months later the *Times* called for an armistice in the ancient war. "There is urgent need," it said, "for surmounting what someone has called the almost insuperable barrier of a common language. It would never do for Great Britain and America to think they understand, yet miss, the point of each other's remarks just now. Both versions of the common language must be correctly understood by both peoples." It then went on to com-mend a school set up in London to teach Americanisms to British officers and Anglicisms to Americans, and paused to recall, perhaps with a touch of nostalgia, the ill humors of days now past:

> "English as she is spoke" by foreigners has always been a popular touch in comedy. It was an old device when Shakespeare wrote the English of that fine theoretical and practical soldier, the Welsh Fluellen. By the time of the Restoration the Dutch were sharing the honors with the Irish, who lasted until the latter part of the Victorian

---

[7] June 17, 1938. What the *Times* had to say of Weaver's poems in American at the time of their publication in the early 20s—if, indeed, it said anything at all—I do not know.

[8] The Conquering Tongue, London *Spectator*, Feb. 5, 1943, pp. 120–1.

era, when they yielded first place to the French. Then came the Americans. The Briton who could not raise a laugh by pretending to talk American was either a great fool or a very dull dog.[9]

The complaint that Americanisms are inherently unintelligible to civilized Christians is still heard in England, though not as often as in the past. They frequently deal with objects and ideas unfamiliar to the English, and sometimes they use metaphors too bold for the English imagination. In consequence there has been a steady emission of glossaries since the earliest days, some of them on a large scale. The first seems to have been that of the Rev. Jonathan Boucher, probably drawn up before 1800, but not published until 1832, when it appeared in the second edition of his "Glossary of Archaic and Provincial Words."[1] It was followed by that of David Humphreys, one of the Hartford wits, which was printed as an appendix to his play "The Yankey in England" in 1815.[2] The play was apparently designed for an English audience, though there is no record that it was ever played in London. The glossary was added because Humphreys feared that the talk of Doolittle, the Yankey of his title, might be unintelligible without it. Among its 275 items are only 19 Americanisms: *to boost*, 1815;[3] *breadstuffs*, 1793; *to calculate* (to suppose or expect), 1805; *cent*, 1782; *cuss*, 1775; *cussed*; *darned*, 1806; *fortino* or *fortzino* (for aught I know);[4] *forzino* (far as I know), c. 1870;[5] *gal*, 1795; *to guess* (to think or suppose),

---

[9] Two Peoples and One Tongue, June 29, 1943. [The new geniality of the *Times* is shown in When English Goes West, by Mr. Justice Vaisey, June 20, 1961. A judicious appraisal of the two varieties of English, from the point of view of a writer, is found in Which Side of the Atlantic? by Sir Charles P. Snow, *Harper's*, Oct. 1959, pp. 163–6. Sir Charles points out that the metaphorical exuberance of American is counterweighted by a fondness for abstractions, but concludes that one variety is as good as the other for serious literature. Because Sir Charles had a distinguished career as a physicist and government administrator before becoming a novelist, he is suspect in the eyes of caste-conscious literary mandarins on both sides of the Atlantic, and in Mar. 1962 was the target of a vicious if pointless attack by one F. R. Leavis, a literary critic at Cambridge.]

[1] Boucher, who was born in England in 1737, came out to Virginia in 1759 as a private tutor. In 1762 he returned home to take holy orders, but was soon back in Virginia as rector of Hanover parish.

In 1770 he became rector at Annapolis. His Loyalist sentiments got him into difficulties as the Revolution approached, and in 1775 he returned to England, where he died in 1804. After his death his friends began the publication of his Glossary of Archaic and Provincial Words, on which he had been engaged for thirty years. In 1832 the Rev. Joseph Hunter and Joseph Stevenson undertook to continue the work, but it got no further than *Bl*. Boucher's brief glossary of Americanisms appeared in the introduction to this second edition. It listed but 38 words.

[2] It is reprinted in Mathews, pp. 56–63.

[3] The dates are those of the earliest examples in the DAE or DA. That of *to boost* is the date of the play's publication. The word was apparently just coming in at the time.

[4] I suspect that Humphreys invented this monstrosity; the first recorded example comes from his glossary.

[5] Or *farzino*. The DAE throws no light on either form; the DA considers *forzino* a variant of *fortino*.

1732; *gum* (foolish talk, nonsense); *to improve* (to employ), 1640; *lengthy*, 1689; *Sabbaday, c.* 1772; *slim* (sick), 1815;[6] *to spark it* (to engage in what more recently has been called *petting* or *necking*), 1787; *spook*, 1801; *to stump* (to challenge or dare), 1766. Of these nearly half are now obsolete.[7]

The rest of Humphreys's list is a monument to his faulty observation and lack of common sense. Scores of the pronunciations he sets down were at least as common in England as in America, *e.g.*, *biled* for *boiled*, *hoss* for *horse* and *kittle* for *kettle*. Many were in perfectly good usage in both countries and remain so to this day, *e.g.*, *strait* for *straight*, *vittles* for *victuals*, *blud* for *blood* and *fokes* for *folks*. Finally Humphreys was apparently unaware, despite his English wife, that such clipped forms as *cute* for *acute* and *potecary* for *apothecary* were common in England, and that *to argufy* for *to argue* was anything but a novelty. Worse, he failed to list certain actual Americanisms that occurred in his play, *e.g.*, *to pluck up stakes*, 1640 (later, *to pull up stakes*); *as fine as a fiddle*, 1811; and *to rain pitchforks*.[8]

To guess was not actually an Americanism, for Shakespeare, Chaucer, Wycliffe and Gower had used it, but it seems to have dropped out of use in England in the Eighteenth Century, and was either preserved or revived in America. Its constant use by Americans in the sense of *to believe* or *suppose* was remarked by nearly all the early English travelers. Some of them illustrated its use with dialogues, *e.g.*, Henry Bradshaw Fearon, who offered the following in his "Sketches of America": [9]

Q. What is your name?
A. William Henry ——, *I guess.*
Q. Is your wife alive?
A. No, she is dead, *I guess.*
Q. How long have you been married?
A. Thirty years, *I guess.*

Humphreys's glossary was followed in 1816 by John Pickering's "A Vocabulary or Collection of Words and Phrases Which Have Been Supposed to Be Peculiar to the United States of America, to Which is Prefixed an Essay on the Present State of the English Language in the United States," the first really competent treatise on the subject.[1]

---

[6] Here again the first recorded example is from Humphreys himself.

[7] The DA does not list *cussed, darned, gal, to guess* or *gum.*

[8] The DAE's first example is from Humphreys himself.

[9] London, 1818. The subtitle is *A Narrative of a Journey of Five Thousand Miles Through the Eastern and Western States.*

[1] Pickering, the son of Timothy Pickering, Postmaster General, Secretary of War and Secretary of State under Washington, was himself apparently trained for a political career, but he preferred scholarship. Franklin Edgerton, Sterling

Pickering's Vocabulary was prepared in 1815 for a meeting of the American Academy of Arts and Sciences of Boston, of which he was president, and was published in its *Memoirs*,[2] but the circulation was so limited that he reissued it in June of the next year, with extensive additions, as a book. He says in his preface that he began to record Americanisms during a residence in London, as secretary to Rufus King, the American minister, from the end of 1799 to the autumn of 1801. Pickering not only depended upon his own collectanea for its substance; he made drafts upon Witherspoon, and got a great deal of material from the denunciations of Americanisms in the British reviews of the time. On the whole, he was in sympathy with their protests. He gave next to no attention to the loan words from the Indian languages,[3] but confined himself to the new coinages from English material and to the changes in meaning that had overtaken some of the terms of Standard English. Pickering was not greatly concerned about the actual novelties invented in America; in fact, he believed that their production was falling off. "It has been asserted," he said, "that we have discovered a much stronger propensity than the English to add new words to the language, and the little animadversion which, till within a few years, such new-coined words have met with among us seems to support that opinion. The passion for these senseless novelties, however, has for some time past been declining." His dominant fear, it appears, was not of new words, but of old ones preserved in America after their abandonment in English, and of new meanings attached to words still surviving.

Pickering's Vocabulary runs to more than 500 terms, and some of his discussions are of considerable length: he gives nearly five pages to *to advocate*. This verb was frowned upon by Benjamin Franklin, who asked Noah Webster, in a letter of December 26, 1789, to use his authority "in

---

Professor Emeritus of Sanskrit and comparative philology at Yale, says that he was "one of the two greatest general linguists of the first half of the Nineteenth Century in America," the other being Peter Stephen Du Ponceau (1760–1844). Born in Salem, Mass., in 1777, Pickering survived until 1846. Says Edgerton: "He was an excellent classical scholar, and prepared what has been called 'the best Greek-English dictionary before Liddell and Scott.' In 1814 he declined the newly founded Eliot professorship of Greek at Harvard (to which Edward Everett was then appointed); he had previously declined the professorship of Hebrew at the same institution. Even while working on his Greek dictionary he found time to go deeply into the American Indian languages." (*Proceedings of the American Philosophical Association*, July 1943.)

[2] Allen Walker Read says in American Projects for an Academy to Regulate Speech, *PMLA*, Vol. LI, Dec. 1936, p. 1150, that the academy usually devoted itself to "practical matters in geology, agriculture, mathematics and the like": the Pickering paper was something of a novelty for it. [The Vocabulary was in part derivative: see Allen Walker Read, The Collections for Pickering's "Vocabulary," *AS*, Vol. XXII, Dec. 1947, pp. 270–86.]

[3] The only ones he listed were *barbecue, caucus, hominy, moccasin, netop, papoose, samp, squaw* and *succotash*.

reprobating" it, but Webster admitted it to his American Dictionary of 1828—and supported it with a number of examples from high English sources. It was not an American invention, but had been used in England long before. Pickering quoted at length from a discussion of it in the Rev. Henry J. Todd's edition of Johnson's Dictionary, "with numerous corrections and additions," including citations from Milton and Burke. Todd's sneer at imaginary American inventors of the term got under Pickering's skin, despite his general willingness to accept British admonitions docilely:

> Mr. Todd seems to suppose that the Americans "affect to plume themselves on this pretended improvement of our language," and he then, in a tone which the occasion seemed hardly to require, calls upon them as well as their "abetters," to "withdraw their unfounded claim to discovery.". . . The truth is that although most Americans have adopted it, yet some of our writers who have been particularly attentive to their style have (whether there is any merit in this or not, let scholars judge) avoided using it. Nor would they probably have felt themselves warranted in employing this, any more than they would many ancient words (the word *freshet*, for example) because it is to be found in Milton or Burke, unless it were also *in general use at the present day* among Englishmen.

To this, as an afterthought, he added the following in the brief supplement that followed his vocabulary:

> If the Americans have not a right to "plume themselves" on this word as a "discovery," they may justly claim the merit (if there is any in the case) of *reviving* it.

To advocate is now perfectly good English on both sides of the water, though Robert Southey attacked it so late as 1838. So is *to belittle*, though when Thomas Jefferson used it in his "Notes on the State of Virginia," 1781–2, the *European Magazine and London Review* let go with a veritable tirade against it. Pickering sought to get rid of it by pretending that only Jefferson used it seriously. This imbecility was echoed by Robley Dunglison, in his treatise on Americanisms in the *Virginia Literary Museum* (1829). *Belittle*, he opined, was "not an Americanism, but an individualism." Noah Webster, in his American Dictionary of 1828, described it as "rare in America, not used in England," but it was already lodged firmly on this side of the water and was soon making progress on the other, and today it is everywhere accepted.

Pickering's list included a number of terms that are now obsolete, *e.g.*, *to admire* (in the sense of to be pleased),[4] *citess* (a female citizen, bor-

---

[4] Mark Twain used it in Sketches Old and New, 1864, but it is now heard only in rustic speech, and seldom there.

rowed from the French *citoyenne*), *to happify* (to make happy), *to improve* (in the sense of to occupy),[5] *to missionate, redemptioner* [6] and *to squale* ("to throw a stick, or other thing, with violence, and in such a manner that it skims along the ground"). Some of the terms listed were so little used, even in his day, that Noah Webster professed to be unfamiliar with them, *e.g., brash* (brittle and easily split, as of wood),[7] *clitchy* (clammy, sticky, glutinous), *to squale* and *to squat* (to squeeze or press).[8]

But a much larger number of Pickering's terms survive in the speech of today, *e.g., accountability, to Americanize, to appreciate* (to raise in value), *appellate* (of a court), *backwoodsman, balance* (remainder), *bookstore, dutiable, to evoke, fall* (for autumn), *governmental, to heft, immigrant* (as the newcomer is seen from the receiving end), *influential, nationality, to obligate, passag*e (of a legislative act), *census, constitutionality, corn* (maize), *creek* (an inland brook), *to deed* (to convey by deed), *to demoralize, to deputize, to locate, presidential, to progress, to solemnize, squatter, stockholder* and *to systematize*. Many of these were not actually American inventions, but most of them were in greater vogue in this country than in England, and not a few were denounced violently by the English purists of the time, *e.g., appellate, balance, dutiable, influential, to obligate, to demoralize, presidential* and *to progress*. *Appellate*, in the sense in which it is used in Article III, Section 2, of the Constitution, 1788, was employed by Blackstone in the first volume of his "Commentaries on the Laws of England" in 1765, but so late as 1808 the *Annual Review* denounced John Marshall for using it in his "Life of Washington."

Balance, in the sense of remainder, is apparently a genuine Americanism. The DAE's first example is dated 1788. The reviewer of the *Monthly Anthology* (published in Boston, 1803–11) censured Marshall for using *dutiable* in his "Life of Washington" (1804–7), but the DAE shows that it was used in England fifteen years before it was heard in the debates of Congress, 1789. It was, however, so much more frequent in America than in England that it came to be thought of as an Americanism. *Influential* belongs to the same category. It has been traced back to *c.* 1734 in England, and Johnson admitted it to his dictionary, but it was seldom used, and when it began to appear frequently in American writings it was mistaken for an Americanism, and denounced as such. *To obligate* is even older in English:

---

[5] Traced to the Connecticut probate records of 1647.

[6] This word, which arose at the close of the Eighteenth Century, went out with the disappearance of the redemptioners themselves. They were immigrants who paid for their passage to America by binding themselves to serv-ice for a term of years.

[7] The OED traces *brash* in this sense to 1566, but says that it is "now chiefly U.S." It is now used universally by workmen dealing with wood, *e.g.,* carpenters and cabinet-makers.

[8] I take this Webster list from Mathews.

the OED's first example is from one of Robert Smith's sermons (1692). But it began to go out in England as it came into vogue in this country, and the OED lists it as "not now in good use." *To demoralize* was introduced into American, in the form of *demoralizing*, by Webster in 1794, and he entered the infinitive in his dictionary of 1806. It is said to have been his only original contribution to the American vocabulary. The *Edinburgh Review* sneered at it when it appeared, as *demoralization*, in a book by an English lady publicist, Miss Helen Maria Williams (1762–1827), but it continued to flourish in this great Republic. One finds it hard to believe that so logical and necessary a word as *presidential* should have been denounced, but the *Monthly Anthology* called it a "barbarism," and the *North American Review* agreed. "English writers," said Pickering, "have sometimes used it, but only in speaking of American affairs." [The DA cites *presidential year* from 1785 (Richard Henry Lee), *presidential electors* from 1785 and *presidential chair* from 1797 (Alexander Hamilton).] *To progress*, according to the OED, was in common use in England in the Seventeenth Century, but then became obsolete there. It was "retained (or formed anew) in America, where it became very common, *c.* 1790." It was readopted by the English after 1800, but is still "characterized as an Americanism, and is much more used in America than in Great Britain." The DAE's first example is from Franklin's letter of December 26, 1789, to Noah Webster, in which he described it as "most awkward and abominable." In 1876 Richard Grant White was still hot against it, even in the form of *progressive*.

The rest of the words on the Pickering list may be noticed briefly. *Accountability, to evoke, fall, nationality, passage* (of a legislative act), *census, to deputize, to solemnize* and *to systematize* were not American inventions, but most of them were in wider use in this country than in England, and some are still regarded as Americanisms by Englishmen. Of the genuine Americanisms, *to Americanize* has been traced to 1797, *backwoodsman* to 1784 (*backwoods* goes back to 1709), *bookstore* to 1763, *governmental* to 1744, *immigrant* to 1789, *constitutionality* to 1787, *to deed* to 1806 and *to locate* (on land) to 1652. *To Americanize* was listed in Noah Webster's dictionary of 1806, but Pickering, writing in 1815, said that he had never encountered it; it had been used by John Jay in 1797 and by Jefferson in 1801. *To appreciate* (raise in value) is traced to 1778, but when Webster listed it in his dictionary the *Monthly Anthology* alleged that it was "only admitted into genteel company by inadvertence." It seems to be going out, and the DAE's last example is dated *c.* 1889. In the sense of to rise in value (intransitive) it goes back to 1779. The corresponding noun, *appreciation*, was used by John Adams in 1777, and is still sound American. Pickering says that in his time *backwoodsman* was applied "by the people of the commercial towns to those who inhabit the territory westward of the Allegany [*sic*] [9] mountains." The word was commonly used, he adds, "as a term of reproach (and that, only in the familiar style) to designate those people who, being at a distance from the sea and entirely *agricultural*, are considered as either hostile or indifferent to the interests of the commercial states."

Bookstore was one of the new words that followed the transformation of the English *shop* (for a retail establishment) to *store*—a very characteristic Americanism, still often remarked by English travelers. The DAE's first example of this use of *store* is from the *American Weekly Mercury* of March 16, 1721. *Governmental* seems to have appeared in the South in 1774, but by 1796 it had spread to New England. The ever-watchful *Monthly Anthology* denounced it as a barbarism, and Noah Webster excluded it from his dictionary of 1806, but he admitted it to his American Dictionary of 1828, and ascribed it to Alexander Hamilton. Pickering discusses *immigrant*, *immigration* and *to immigrate* at some length. He says that they were first used by Jeremy Belknap (1744–98) in his "History of New Hampshire" (1784–92), but the DAE's first example of *immigrant*, apparently the oldest of the three words, comes from "An American Geography," by one Morse, published in 1789. In the United States it is usual to employ *immigrant* to designate an incoming wanderer and *emigrant* to designate one leaving. In England it is more common to use *emigrant* in both cases, maybe under the influence of the French *émigré*. It is astonishing that *constitutionality* did not appear in England before it was used by Alexander Hamilton in 1787, but such seems to have been the case. The OED's first example of its English use is dated 1801. The DAE classes *constitutional amendment*, *constitutional lawyer* and *constitutional convention* as Americanisms, first recorded, respectively, in 1854, 1830 and 1843. *To deed*, defined by Webster as to give or transfer by deed, is listed by Pickering as "a low word, used colloquially, but rarely, except by illiterate people." "None of our writers," he continued, "would employ it." But James Fenimore Cooper was using it by 1845, and it is now respectable. So with *to locate*, which goes back to 1652 in America, but did not appear in England until 1837.

One of the indubitable Americanisms that was attacked by the English reviewers, but in vain, was *lengthy*. Albert Matthews has traced it to 1689, and by the end of the Eighteenth Century it was in common use in the United States. "This word," says Pickering, "has been very common among us, both in writing and in the language of conversation, but it has been so much ridiculed by Americans as well as Englishmen that in *writing* it is

---

[9] The spelling of this Indian word is variable. The Pennsylvania town, river and college are *Allegheny*, the mountains are the *Alleghanies*, and the New York village and county are *Allegany*.

now generally avoided." [1] Pickering then undertakes to show how, by the use of *diffuse, lengthened, prolonged, extended, extensive* and *prolix, lengthy* might be avoided. He was, of course, wasting his energy. The word not only got firm lodgment in America; it also penetrated England, and in a little while many of the best writers were using it, notably Bentham, Dickens and George Eliot, sometimes as a conscious Americanism but oftener not.

Pickering also discussed the American use of *to* instead of the English *at* or *in* in such phrases as "I have been *to* Philadelphia." Witherspoon had denounced this practice in 1781, but it survived and is today sound American.

The other early glossaries of Americanisms were of much less value than Pickering's painstaking work. On March 18, 1829, Dr. Theodoric Romeyn Beck (1791–1855) read a rather trivial paper on Pickering before the Albany Institute, and it was printed in the *Transactions* of the Institute for 1830. [2] This was followed by a series of articles in the *Virginia Literary Museum and Journal of Belles Lettres, Arts, Sciences, etc.*, on December 16 and 30, 1829, and January 6, 1830, by Dr. Robley Dunglison. [3] "His sport," says Allen Walker Read, "was that of so many a later man: the proving that many so-called Americanisms are distinctly of British origin." But he also made some useful contributions to the subject. He was, for example, the first lexicographer to list the word *blizzard*, and the entry in his glossary is the earliest example yet unearthed. He is also credited with the first example of *to hornswoggle, to mosey* and *sockdolager*.

Another early glossary of Americanisms was that of the Rev. Adiel Sherwood, first published in his "Gazetteer of the State of Georgia" in 1827 and much extended in a third edition of 1837. [4] It is mainly interesting because of its indications of the prevailing vulgar pronunciations of the South in the 1830s, *e.g., arter* for *after, axd* for *asked, becase* for *because, crap* for *crop, hit* for *it, mounting* for *mountain, year* for *here,* but it also shows some other curiosa, *e.g., Baptises* for *Baptists, done said, flitter* for *fritter, to get shet of, hadn't ought, mighty* and *monstrous* as general

---

[1] There was evidence against Pickering here. John Davis, in his Travels of Four Years and a Half in the United States of America, 1798, 1799, 1800, 1801 and 1802 (London, 1802), said "it is frequently used by the classical writers of the New World."

[2] [For other comments on Pickering, see Hennig Cohen, Drayton's Notes on Pickering's List of Americanisms, *AS*, Vol. XXXI, Dec. 1956, pp. 264–70.]

[3] Dunglison, an Englishman educated in Germany, had been brought out by Jefferson in 1824 to be professor of medi-

cine in the University of Virginia. In 1833 he moved to the University of Maryland and in 1836 to Jefferson Medical College, Philadelphia. He was a competent medical man, and Fielding H. Garrison says of him that he "compiled an excellent medical dictionary and wrote an amazing array of textbooks on nearly every subject except surgery." (An Introduction to the History of Medicine; 4th ed.; Philadelphia, 1929, p. 443.)

[4] It was reprinted by Mathews in *DN*, Vol. V, Pt. X, 1927, and also in Mathews.

intensives, *prasbattery* for *presbytery* and *to use* for *to feed*. The DAE's first example of *bodaciously*, in the sense of wholly, is from Sherwood. "It will be seen," he said in his brief introduction, "that many of our provincialisms are borrowed from England."

The first attempt at a comprehensive dictionary of Americanisms was made by John Russell Bartlett [5] in 1848, with his "Glossary of Words and Phrases Usually Regarded as Peculiar to the United States." This glossary, beginning as a volume of 412 pages, was expanded to 524 when it was reissued in 1859, and reached 813 with its fourth and last edition in 1877. From his first edition onward Bartlett supported his entries, whenever possible, with illustrative quotations, but most of them, unfortunately, were not dated. In the preface to his fourth edition he discussed the origin of new Americanisms, and defended his listing of what critics had apparently denounced as ephemeral slang. The novelties of his time, he said, came chiefly from the following sources: first, the jargon of the stock market, rapidly adopted by the whole business community; second, the slang of the "colleges and higher schools"; third, the argot of "politicians, of the stage, of sportsmen, of Western boatmen, of pugilists, of the police, of rowdies and roughs, of thieves, of work-shops, of the circus, of shopkeepers, workmen, etc." Many of these neologisms had only short lives, but Bartlett insisted sensibly that they should be listed nevertheless, if only for the sake of the record. "Sometimes," he said, "these strange words have a known origin, but of the larger number no one knows whence they come. Slang is thus the source whence large additions are made to our language."

"The Glossary of Supposed Americanisms" of Dr. Alfred L. Elwyn, which appeared in 1859, was chiefly devoted to showing that most of the 465 terms it listed were English provincialisms or archaisms, but he also listed a few words and phrases picked up in Pennsylvania. Elwyn, under *ball*, offered one of the early descriptions of baseball. He called it *bat and ball*, said that it was played in his youth, and hazarded the guess that it might be "an imperfect form of cricket," though calling it, in the same breath, "a Yankee invention." M. Schele de Vere's [6] "Americanisms: The English of the New World," which followed in 1871, was not arranged in

---

[5] Bartlett, a Rhode Islander, born in 1805 and surviving until 1886, began life as a bank clerk in Providence and was later a partner in a publishing house in New York, but he attained to a considerable reputation as a bibliographer and antiquarian and also dabbled in ethnology. He should not be confused with John Bartlett (1820–1905), the Boston publisher who, in 1855, brought out a volume of Familiar Quotations that, with revisions by other hands, is still a standard work.

[6] Of Swedish and French parentage, Schele de Vere took his Ph.D. at Bonn in 1841 and came to America soon afterwards. In 1844 he was recommended for the chair of modern languages at the University of Virginia by Longfellow and others, and there he taught till 1895, when he retired to Washington. He was one of the founders of the American Philological Association in 1869, published a number of books on language and served on the staff of the Standard Dictionary, 1893–5. He died in 1898.

vocabulary form, but included a great deal of matter not in previous works, especially a learned and valuable discussion of loan words. For seventeen years afterward no contribution of any importance was made to the subject save Bartlett's fourth edition of 1877. Then, in 1889, John S. Farmer brought out "Americanisms Old and New," a stout volume of 564 double-column pages, listing about 5,000 terms.[7] This contains many dated quotations from American newspapers, mainly of the year 1888. It shows but little dependence upon its predecessors in the field, and is, in the main, a workmanlike and valuable work. His preface made it plain that the impact of Americanisms upon English speechways was already powerful in 1888:

> Even our newspapers, hitherto regarded as models of correct literary style, . . . are lending countenance to what at first sight appears a monstrously crude and almost imbecile jargon; while others, fearful of a direct plunge, modestly introduce the uncouth bantlings with a saving clause. The phrase, "as the Americans say," might in some cases be ordered from the type-foundry as a logotype, so frequently does it do introduction duty.

Whatever Farmer's distaste, as a patriotic Englishman, for this "monstrously crude and almost imbecile jargon," he was too good a philologian to believe that it could be stayed. He believed that the English of England would have to take in much of it, and that the preponderance of population in the United States would eventually force American speechways upon the language as a whole.

After "Americanisms Old and New" came Sylva Clapin's "New Dictionary of Americanisms," a third-rate compilation, but valuable because of the inclusion of a number of Canadian terms. Finally, in 1912, appeared the two volumes of Richard Harwood Thornton's "American Glossary,"[8]

---

[7] Farmer was a busy compiler and lexicographer, and is chiefly remembered for the monumental Slang and Its Analogues: Past and Present, which he began to publish in London in 1890. This ambitious undertaking, which was enriched with dated quotations on the plan of the Oxford Dictionary, ran to seven quarto volumes and was completed in 1904. Beginning with the second volume in 1891, the name of William E. Henley, the poet, was associated with that of Farmer on the title page, and in consequence the work is commonly referred to as Farmer and Henley. In 1905 Farmer brought out a one-volume abridgment for general circulation, with the quotations omitted and no mention of the numerous profane and obscene terms listed in the seven-volume edition.

[8] Thornton was an Englishman, born in Lancashire, Sept. 6, 1845. He passed the Oxford entrance examinations in 1862, but was too poor to go to the university. Instead he got a job with a business house in London and there he remained until 1871. In that year, seeing only poor prospects in London, he immigrated to Canada, and in 1874 came to the United States. In 1876 he entered Columbia Law School at Washington, and was graduated therefrom in 1878. He was then admitted to the bar in Philadelphia, but soon moved to Williamsport, Pa., the home of his wife. In 1884 he went to Portland, Ore., as the first dean of the Oregon Law School, and there, save for several trips to England, he remained until his death on Jan. 7, 1925.

and the lexicography of Americanisms was put on a firm and scientific foundation at last.

When Thornton began work on his "American Glossary" does not seem to be known, but it must have been before 1907, for in that year he was in London, pursuing inquiries toward it. Its format, without doubt, was suggested by that of the OED, which had begun to appear in 1888. Thornton acknowledged in his preface his debt to Bartlett, to Farmer and to Albert Matthews,[9] but the chief burden of assembling his extraordinarily copious materials lay upon his own shoulders. He undertook the herculean task of reading the *Congressional Globe* from the beginning to 1863, and also got together an immense mass of citations from newspapers, magazines and books. He endeavored to unearth dated quotations showing the use of every one of the 3,700 terms he listed, and in many cases he found and presented a large number—in that of *Yankee*, no less than sixty. Nothing on so comprehensive a scale or following so scientific a method had been undertaken before, and Thornton's first two volumes, issued in 1912, remain indispensable to this day. The author could find no publisher for his work in the United States, and had to take it to London. There it was brought out in an edition of 2,000 by a small firm, Francis and Company. Once it was in type Lippincott, the Philadelphia publisher, took 250 sets of the sheets and issued them with his imprint, but they sold only slowly and so late as 1919 the small edition was still not exhausted. It was never reissued. Meanwhile, Thornton kept on accumulating materials, and during World War I he tried to find a publisher willing to bring out a third volume or backers willing to stake it. He was unsuccessful in his lifetime, but in 1931, six years after his death, its publication was begun serially in *Dialect Notes*. The chronic financial difficulties of the Dialect Society got in the way, and the last of the material was not actually worked off until July 1939. The installments were so paged that they could be cut out of *Dialect Notes* and bound together, but there has never been a reprint in book form.

5: THE POSITION OF THE LEARNED

Since the early Eighteenth Century, as we have seen, English hostility to Americanisms has been abetted by a formidable American fifth column, vowed to the strict policing of the national speech habits, with the English example in mind. In 1724 Hugh Jones, professor of mathematics at William and Mary College, expressed the wish that a "Publick Standard were

---

[9] A Boston antiquary, born in 1860, whose diligent and valuable work entered into the OED, the DAE, the DA and other dictionaries, and greatly enriched the files of learned journals. Unhappily, he never collected it. [There is a brief sketch of him by M. M. Mathews in *AS*, Vol. XXXI, Feb. 1956, pp. 55–60.]

fix'd" to "direct Posterity, and prevent Irregularity, and confused Abuses and Corruptions in our Writings and Expressions." [1] The abortive moves to establish a national Academy, as well as various local Academies, had the same object in mind. In 1816 the American Academy of Arts and Sciences, in Boston, received from one of its members, John Pickering, his Vocabulary, whose preface was largely devoted to a defense of the English reviewers. Pickering argued that their animadversions were well founded, and called upon his erring countrymen to "imitate the example of the learned and modest Campbell," [2] who, though he had devoted a great part of a long life to the study of the English language, "yet thought it no disgrace to make an apology for his style," and to remember the similar diffidence of Irenaeus, Bishop of Lugdunum (Lyons) in Gaul, who prefixed a similar apology for his shaky provincial Latin to his "Adversus Haereses." Thus Pickering summed up:

> As a general rule, we should undoubtedly avoid all those words which are noticed by English authors of reputation as expressions with which *they are unacquainted,* for although we might produce some English authority for such words, yet the very circumstances of their being thus noticed by well-educated *Englishmen* is a proof that they are not in use at this day in England, and, of course, ought not to be used elsewhere by those who would speak *correct English.*

Multitudes of American pedagogues still believe that the natural growth of the language is wild and wicked, and that it should be regulated according to rules formulated in England. To this end they undertake periodical crusades against "bad grammar," the American scheme of pronunciation and the general body of Americanisms—in the classroom, by means of hortatory pamphlets and leaflets and over the air. In 1915 the National Council of Teachers of English, following that hopeful American custom which gave the nation Mother's Day, and Safety-First, Paint-Up–Clean-Up and Eat-More-Cheese Weeks, proposed to make the first seven days of November Better-Speech Week. Some of the schoolma'ams, despairing of effecting a wholesale reform, concentrated their efforts upon specific crimes, and among the subsidiary weeks thus launched were *Ain't*-less Week and Final-*G* Week. They also established a Tag Day, and hung derisory tags on youngsters guilty of such indecencies as "I have *got*" and "It's *me.*" [3] This missionary effort was not confined to school children.

---

[1] An Accidence to the English Tongue; London, 1724.

[2] George Campbell (1719–96), a Scottish theologian who published a New Translation of the Gospels in 1728. He is best known, however, for his Philosophy of Rhetoric (1776). Pickering's reference is to the preface to the Gospels.

[3] The Baltimore *Evening Sun,* on Jan. 21, 1925, reported that this was a new project in the Baltimore public schools.

Efforts were also made to perfect the speech of their parents and of the public in general, and even the newspapers were besought to mend their linguistic ways. In 1925, a Los Angeles schoolma'am went about southern California inducing women's clubs to pass a resolution that "editors of newspapers and comic writers [should] eliminate grammatical errors in the comic strips and jokes except for decided character roles." [4] The object of attack here was the grotesque slang that appears from nowhere, has its brief day and then vanishes. But the American pedagogues often seem to be opposed to more decorous Americanisms, and many of them teach a pronunciation that is quite foreign to the country and inculcate grammatical niceties that were concocted during the earnest but innocent days when English grammar was assumed to be a kind of Latin grammar—niceties that have been long since abandoned by the English themselves. The influence of Samuel Johnson is thus still potent in the American public schools.

Until World War II, few American philologians specialized in the native tongue, and nearly all serious investigators were either amateurs or foreigners, sometimes both. The earlier native *Gelehrte* of the language faculty, with the massive exceptions of Webster and Pickering, disdained the subject as beneath their notice, and even Pickering discussed it with distaste. Beginning with Lindley Murray (1745–1826), the more influential of its accepted expositors threw themselves into a mighty effort, not to describe and study the language of their country, but to police and purify it, by the highly artificial standards set up by English pedants of the Eighteenth Century. By a curious irony it fell to Murray's fate to be more influential in England than in America, and one might argue that he was responsible beyond all others for the linguistic lag visible in the mother country to this day, but he also had a great deal of weight at home, and was the *Stammvater* of the dismal pedagogues who still expound "correct English" in our schools and colleges.[5] From these pedagogues the investigation of the living speech of 180,000,000 Americans has seldom got any effective assistance. All the contributions from the English faculty that have gone into the files of *Dialect Notes* and *American Speech* and into such enterprises as the Dictionary of American English and the Linguistic Atlas of the United States and Canada have come from an extremely small

---

[4] *AS*, Vol. I, Jan. 1926, p. 250. [For a recent counterblast to this attitude, see Donald J. Lloyd, Let's Get Rid of Miss Driscoll, *The Education Forum*, Mar. 1954, pp. 341–8.]

[5] Murray was born in Lancaster County, Pa., in 1745. Trained as a lawyer, he went into business and made a comfortable fortune during the Revolution. In 1784 he moved to England, where he died in 1826. His Grammar of the English Language Adapted to the Different Classes of Learners first appeared in 1795. It ran through hundreds of editions. [See Priscilla Tyler, School Grammars to 1850, diss., Western Reserve University, 1952.] In 1804 he published a spelling-book that became a formidable rival to Webster's.

minority, scattered among the general as sparsely as raisins in an orphanage cake. Of course, this lack of professional keenness can be observed in other groups. Of the more than 255,000 physicians and surgeons in the country, probably not 5,000 have added anything to the sum of medical knowledge, and among lawyers the ratio of legal scholars to legal hewers of wood and drawers of water is even smaller. But the percentage of actual students of the American vernacular among American teachers of English seems to be the smallest of all.

The highest varieties of gogues are somewhat less naïve than the ordinary English teachers, but they nevertheless show a reluctance to deal with American as the living language of a numerous and puissant people, making its own rules as it goes along and well worthy of scientific study. [The American Dialect Society has never had more than 500 members, and the circulation of *American Speech* is little larger. The surveys of the Linguistic Atlas were launched by an Austrian-born professor of German, and the DAE was edited by a Scotsman imported for the purpose. Of the dozens of American universities, only a handful have made long-term contributions to such projects, notably Brown, Columbia, Chicago, Michigan, Wisconsin, Minnesota, California, Colorado and Texas. Elsewhere research in American speechways is an individual matter, pursued by a devoted remnant, generally after hours, and at their own expense, except for occasional grants from foundations or from the research funds of institutions better heeled and more enlightened than their own. The Modern Language Association of America has a membership of 10,000, and membership is as indispensable to the professionally ambitious teacher of languages and literature as a United Auto Workers card on the Ford assembly line. Of this number relatively few have shown any interest in the language in which the business of their country—and their association—is conducted. The leadership of the MLA has shown somewhat more interest, both through their publications (*e.g.*, George Hempl, C. H. Grandgent and O. F. Emerson) and through their sponsorship of such publications as George Philip Krapp's "The English Language in America" (1925). Since 1921, the year in which AL2 appeared, the Present-Day English section has been one of the liveliest and most popular at the annual meetings, though papers on American English rarely appear in the *Publications* of the Association. The Linguistic Society of America, organized in 1924, has shown a growing concern with the national tongue,[6] probably as the result of the ac-

[6] [Some of the more important works by American linguists during the last generation are Leonard Bloomfield, Language, New York, 1933; Bernard Bloch and George L. Trager, Outline of Linguistic Analysis, Baltimore, 1942; George L. Trager and Henry Lee Smith, Jr., An Outline of English Structure (*SIL*, Occasional Paper No. 3), Norman, Okla., 1951; Zellig S. Harris, Methods in Structural Linguistics, Chicago, 1951 (reprinted in paperback as Structural Lin-

tivities of its younger members in World War II. In Supplement One it was observed that the LSA was less interested in American English than in Hittite and Old Church Slavonic; but at the Linguistic Institute of 1958, Thomas Sebeok, of Indiana University, complained that no new linguistic theory could gain acceptance unless it dealt with American English. Sebeok's institution, however, is relatively uncorrupted; it sponsors an *International Journal of American Linguistics*, devoted principally to the vestiges of American Indian languages, and its scholars have produced several volumes on Cheremis, an obscure Finno-Ugric tongue in central Russia, but have hardly touched the dialects of the state which produced Theodore Dreiser and George Ade. *Language*, the journal of the Linguistic Society, carries few articles on American English, but reviews almost everything current in the field. *The Journal of English and Germanic Philology* likewise is more hospitable to reviews than to articles dealing with American English; *Studies in Philology, Modern Philology* and the *Philological Quarterly* ignore it almost completely.]

The American Dialect Society was founded in 1889, with Francis J. Child, the authority on English and Scottish ballads, as its first president. It made very slow progress. It started off with but 140 members, and the publication of the first volume of *Dialect Notes*, running to 497 pages, dragged through six years. [In fact, only six volumes of *Dialect Notes* appeared in the 52 years of its existence.] Yet it long offered the only outlet for the work of the few American scholars who took the national language seriously and gave it scientific study.

Of these few, the work of Louise Pound, of Nebraska, was especially productive, for whereas most of the other members of the Society confined their investigations to regional dialects, she and her pupils studied the gen-

guistics, 1960); Kenneth L. Pike, Language in Relation to a Unified Theory of the Structure of Human Behavior, preliminary ed., Glendale, Cal., 1954–60; H. A. Gleason, Jr., An Introduction to Descriptive Linguistics; New York, 1955, 2nd ed., 1960; Roman Jakobson and Morris Halle, Fundamentals of Language (*Janua Linguarum*, No. 1), 's Gravenhage, 1956; Noam Chomsky, Syntactic Structures (*Janua Linguarum*, No. 4), 's Gravenhage, 1957; Martin Joos, ed., Readings in Linguistics: the Development of Descriptive Linguistics Since 1925, Washington, 1957; Archibald A. Hill, Introduction to Linguistic Structures, New York, 1958; Charles F. Hockett, A Course in Modern Linguistics, New York, 1958; John P. Hughes, The Science of Language, New York, 1962; Benjamin L. Whorf, Language, Thought and Reality, Cambridge, Mass., and New York, 1956; Harry Hoijer, ed., Language in Culture, Chicago, 1954. The field is summarized at length in John B. Carroll, The Study of Language, Cambridge, Mass., 1953; more briefly in George L. Trager, The Field of Linguistics (*SIL*, Occasional Paper No. 1), Norman, Okla., 1949; Einar Haugen, Directions in Modern Linguistics, *Lg.*, Vol. XXVII, July-Sept. 1951, pp. 211–22; C. M. Wise and Ruth Hirsch, Directions in Linguistics, *QJS*, Vol. XXXIX, Apr. 1953, pp. 225–31; Archibald A. Hill, Linguistics Since Bloomfield, *QJS*, Vol. XLI, Oct. 1955, pp. 253–60.]

eral speechways of the country.[7] Her first contribution to *Dialect Notes* was published in 1905; thereafter, for twenty years, she or her pupils were represented in almost every issue. In 1925, in association with Kemp Malone, of Johns Hopkins, and Arthur G. Kennedy, of Stanford, she founded *American Speech*,[8] becoming its first editor, and serving in that capacity until 1933. *American Speech*, even more than *Dialect Notes*, has encouraged the study of American; but it has got but little more support from American teachers of English than its predecessor. When Dr. Pound retired in 1933 it was taken over by the Columbia University Press, and William Cabell Greet, of Barnard College, Columbia University, became editor. [Under Greet and the successor managing editors—Elliott V. K. Dobbie, Allen Walker Read, Allan F. Hubbell and James Macris—the number of subscribers has gradually increased, though with a list of barely a thousand, including libraries, it is still published at a loss. Nevertheless, it has managed to draw contributions from a widening circle of serious scholars, without forfeiting its popular appeal.]

The original aim of the American Dialect Society was the publication of an American Dialect Dictionary comparable to the English Dialect Dictionary of Joseph Wright (1898–1900). By 1917 *Dialect Notes* had printed 26,000 examples of American dialect terms and phrases, and had accumulated almost as many more. The publication of a Dialect Dictionary thus suggested itself.[9] Unhappily, it was delayed inordinately by the Dialect Society's recurrent financial crises, and when, in 1941, Harold Wentworth, then of West Virginia University, projected a dialect dictionary of his own, and applied for the use of the Society's files, it was found that they had been lost. Harvard University, having other uses for the space they occupied, had moved them out, and after that they vanished. [In 1942, under the threat of bankruptcy, the Society was reorganized. In 1943 appeared the first publication of the reorganized Society, a circular entitled "Needed Research in American English," in which the whole subject was surveyed for willing investigators. Since then there have been 37 issues of the *Publications*, plus two special issues devoted to conferences on the proposed Dialect Dictionary. The quality of the *Publications* has steadily improved. Thus the Society stands in its second half-century, rejuvenated and indeed

---

[7] She took her degree at Heidelberg under the distinguished Anglicist Johannes Hoops, and soon afterward joined the English faculty of the University of Nebraska [where she served till her retirement in 1945; she remained active till her death in 1958].

[8] [Mencken is conceded to be the real founder of *AS*. See *American Speech* 1925–1945: the founders look back (comments by Mencken, Louise Pound, Kemp Malone and A. G. Kennedy), *AS*, Vol. XX, Dec. 1945, pp. 241–6.]

[9] The American Dialect Dictionary, by Percy W. Long, *AS*, Vol. I, May 1926, pp. 439–42.

reincarnated. It is still small, but its members include all the American philologians who are really interested in American English, and it has more ambitious plans than ever before. The University of Wisconsin has provided space for the archives of the Society under the supervision of Frederic G. Cassidy, who is completing a survey of Wisconsin folk speech as a pilot study toward the long-awaited Dialect Dictionary.

[Meanwhile, two other enterprises have greatly extended our knowledge of the history and geographical distribution of words and pronunciations in North America. The first of these is the Dictionary of American English on Historical Principles (or DAE), published by the University of Chicago Press in 1936–44, under the editorship of Sir William Craigie, one of the editors of the Oxford English Dictionary, and James Hulbert, of Chicago. The other project is a group of surveys of regional speech with the collective name of Linguistic Atlas of the United States and Canada, sponsored by the American Council of Learned Societies and under the general supervision of Hans Kurath, now also editor of the Middle English Dictionary at the University of Michigan.]

According to Sir William,[1] the idea for the DAE first came to him in the summer of 1924 in Chicago, while he was reading proof for the Oxford Dictionary. He observed that for "two or three words beginning with the prefix *un-* the older quotations (from the Seventeenth Century) were from English sources, while the later ones (of the Eighteenth Century) were all American." His curiosity about the antiquity of such words in American usage fetched up against the hard fact that no one had systematically traced the development of the American vocabulary; even Noah Webster, for all his patriotic gesturing, had been content to cite American authors as well as English. Sir William discussed this idea with John M. Manly, then head of the Department of English at Chicago, "who at once took steps to interest the University of Chicago in the project." Sir William was made professor of English in the University, and was provided with a highly competent staff of American assistants; his students collected additional evidence. Unfortunately, the DAE got little help from volunteer outside readers, lay or academic, in contrast with the experience of the Oxford Dictionary, whose file of quotations was largely assembled by volunteers.[2]

---

[1] *EJ*, Vol. XV, Jan. 1926.

[2] [Charles J. Lovell, The *DA* Supplement, *AS*, Vol. XXVIII, May 1953, pp. 80–91.] The expense of getting out the DAE was shared by the General Education Board, the American Council of Learned Societies and the University of Chicago. The print order was for 2,500 copies, of which all but about 100 had been sold before the last volume was delivered. Unhappily, the plates of the earlier sections were destroyed before the work was completed, so a reprint was impossible; [a reissue by photographic offset appeared in 1960 and is in steady demand].

The DAE lists about 26,000 terms and is by no means restricted to those originating in the United States. It also includes many words that, while old in English, have acquired new meanings in this country, or have come into wider use than in England, or have survived here after becoming obsolete there. Nearly all entries are supported by illustrative quotations, with dates, and whenever a word or phrase has a history in England the date of the first OED quotation is noted. Such are the "historical principles" of the title of the work. Of course, the quotations do not show the actual age of the term: all they show is the date of its first appearance in print, or, more accurately, the date of the first appearance discovered by the dictionary's searchers. But this is a defect visible in all "historical" dictionaries, including the OED. It can be remedied more or less by the accumulation of new material, and in the case of the OED an attempt was made to push the histories back in time by a Supplement issued in 1933, five years after the main work was completed. [A Second Supplement is now in preparation.] But in the majority of cases the history of a given word or phrase must remain incomplete, for it would be impossible to read *all* the printed matter in English, and allowance must be made for the fact that a considerable body of it has disappeared altogether, and for the more important fact that many terms have a history before they are recorded in print, and that others are never recorded at all. There is no way to get round these difficulties, and the most a lexicographer can do is to be as diligent as possible. The editors of the DAE did not spare hard work, and the result is an extremely valuable dictionary, despite its defects.

Unhappily, some of the limitations that the editors set for themselves forced the omission of interesting and useful matter. With few exceptions, they did not investigate American slang after 1875 or the American vocabulary in general after 1900. Moreover, they gave relatively little attention to etymology, and avoided the indication of speech levels (always a vexatious business) whenever possible.[3] But for all these lacks the DAE remains an impressive monument to the scholarship of its editors. A close examination turns up occasional evidence that the chief of them was a foreigner, and hence a stranger to the national *Sprachgefühl*, but against that misfortune must be set the fact that he was an expert lexicographer whose personal prestige (especially after he was knighted in 1928) over-

---

[3] [The difficulty of judgments on usage led the editors of Webster's Third New International Dictionary (Springfield, Mass., 1961) to reduce drastically the number of such indications; popular reviews suggest a preference for at least the illusion of preciseness. In Homeostasis in English Usage, *College Compo-* *sition and Communication*, Vol. XIII, Oct. 1962, pp. 18–22, Martin Joos, of the University of Wisconsin, suggests that anything like a precise indication of usage status would require a four-dimensional five-stage system, or 625 designations.]

came much of the prevailing prejudice against the serious study of American speechways.[4]

The limitations of the DAE left the way open for further work. The average reader is bound to be critical of a lexicon of Americanisms, however meritorious, which omits such terms as *blurb, highbrow, jitney, flivver, rubberneck, boob, gob* (sailor) and *leatherneck*, and often shies away from profanity and other loose language. There is, furthermore, the objection to its high cost: $100. To supply something at once more comprehensive, less burdened with historical apparatus, and less expensive, the University of Chicago Press undertook a "Dictionary of Americanisms" (DA) with the competent M. M. Mathews as editor. It includes every sort of Americanism save the most transient slang, and tries to bring the record up to the time of publication. [It provides etymologies, pronunciations and—particularly for things no longer in use—illustrations. Under *A* there are pictures for *airtight stove, allocochick* (Indian shell money), *aparejo* (a kind of pack saddle), *apple parer, arc light, arctics* (high waterproof overshoes), *armbands* (of the type used by eastern Dakota Indians), *ash hopper* and *atlatl* (Aztec throwing stick, for launching spears). The DA was originally published in 1951, in two volumes, priced at $50. A one-volume reprint was issued in 1956 at $12.50, a price even a scholar's purse can stand.]

Meanwhile, Allen Walker Read, another collaborator of Sir William Craigie, continues at work upon his "The English of England" (a historical dictionary of Briticisms), announced in 1939 [and now scheduled to go to press in 1963]. It will be devoted to "words found in England but not in America," *e.g., squirearchy, pub, corn law, bloody* (as an expletive), *woolsack* and *hear, hear*, and will be fortified by dated quotations of the sort made familiar by Thornton, the OED and the DAE. [The Canadian Linguistic Association is sponsoring a "Dictionary of Canadian English on Historical Principles," and scholars at the Memorial University of Newfoundland are recording the speech of that province.] The need for special works confined to relatively small areas in space or time was admirably set forth by Sir William Craigie in Tract No. LVIII of the Society for Pure English. [Before his death, in 1957, he had taken "A Dictionary of the Older Scottish Tongue" through *Judas-crois*.] There is plenty of room yet for intensive studies, *inter alia*, of English in colonial America, of the

---

[4] Like all dictionaries, the DAE drew heavily on its predecessors in the field. In 1930 (*AS*, Vol. V, p. 260) Sir William made specific acknowledgment of the dictionary's debt to Thornton and testified to "the great value of his labors," and in the preface to the first volume (1938) Thornton was given thanks for "frequently" supplying the work with "its earliest instances, as well as the illustration of many colloquialisms and rarer uses."

novelties introduced into the language by the great movement into the West, of American trade argots and, on a large scale, American slang.[5]

[The Linguistic Atlas had been discussed in the Present-Day English section of the Modern Language Association from the very beginning. The first formal proposal was made at the meeting in 1928, but the first constructive move to get support was made independently by Edward Sapir, of Yale, who persuaded his colleague Edgar H. Sturtevant, delegate from the Linguistic Society to the American Council of Learned Societies, to invite the Council to consider a systematic survey of American English. After a series of conferences, Kurath was appointed director of the project, a post which he still holds; since 1946, when he was appointed editor of the Middle English Dictionary and transferred the Atlas archives from Brown to the University of Michigan, he has spent relatively little time on the Atlas. Nevertheless, with his courage and energy, he has not only made monumental contributions to our knowledge of American English but has stimulated his colleagues and students to do likewise.[6]]

The reasons why New England was chosen as the first section for intensive study were stated by Kurath:

> 1. The dialects of New England are primary as compared with those of the more Western areas, such as the Ohio region. . . .
>
> 2. New England has striking geographical dialects; the class dialects are perhaps more distinct than in any other part of the country; there are clear urban and rural dialects; there are large elements of the population that have been only recently assimilated or that are in part still unassimilated.
>
> 3. The fact that we possess more information regarding the linguistic situation in New England than we have for any other area will shorten and simplify the important task of selecting the dialect features that are to be recorded in *all* the communities selected for study.
>
> 4. There is already available a considerable body of reliable information regarding the history of the population. . . . Thus a more scientific choice of representative communities is possible.[7]

---

[5] [A promising beginning in the last field is the Dictionary of American Slang, comp. and ed. by Harold Wentworth and Stuart Berg Flexner; New York, 1960.]

[6] [A biographical sketch of Kurath, with a full bibliography to date, appears in *Orbis*, Vol. IX, Dec. 1960, pp. 597–612.]

[7] [New linguistic atlases continue to appear, the most spectacular recent one being that of the Soviet Union, the first sections of which were published in 1960. The American Atlas derived its principles from the atlases of Germany (Georg Wenker and Ferdinand Wrede), of France (Jules Gilliéron and Edmond Edmont) and of Italy and southern Switzerland (Karl Jaberg and Jacob Jud). A bibliography of linguistic geography is found in the Handbook of the Linguistic Geography of New England, by Kurath,

Field work for the New England Atlas was begun in 1931, with nine investigators, and completed two years later. Editing began almost immediately; the first volume appeared in 1939 and the last in 1943. The completed "Linguistic Atlas of New England" consists of three volumes, each in two parts, and the six immense folios are made up of no less than 734 double-page maps. Along with the first volume, in 1939, there appeared a quarto "Handbook of the Linguistic Geography of New England." The Linguistic Atlas attempts to record dialectal variations, not only in pronunciation but also in vocabulary. Thus Map No. 235 shows that the common round or littleneck clam (*Venus mercenaria*) is usually called a *quahog* along the New England coast, but that in some places it is spoken of as a *round, hard, hard-shell* or *hen* clam.[8] Similarly, the soft or long-neck clam (*Mya arenaria*) is sometimes called a *long*, or *soft-shell*, or *sand*, or *steaming* clam or simply a *clam*. Many other familiar terms show local variations. The common *lightning bug* remains a *lightning bug* until it comes into the Boston *Sprachgebiet*, where it becomes a *firefly*. *June bug*, in wide use to the southward, is seldom encountered in New England, but *fire bug* is recorded.[9] *Faucet* is the usual New England name for the kitchen water tap, but *spigot* seems to be coming in from the southward, and *cock* and *tap* are also recorded. A wooden spigot in a cider barrel is sometimes called a *spile*. The towel used for drying dishes is usually a *dish towel*, but in various places it is a *cup towel*, a *wiping towel*, a *wiper*, a *dish wiper* or a *cup wiper*. The DAE neglects such forms, and as a result the Linguistic Atlas makes a novel and useful contribution to the study of the American vocabulary.

[But the layman has difficulty in using the Atlas because it attempts to provide full and detailed evidence on the pronunciation of every word recorded in the investigation. The field workers used "a finely graded phonetic alphabet based on that of the International Phonetic Association," an alphabet so extensive that nineteen pages of the accompanying handbook are needed to explain it and the minute differences in the ways it is used by the different field workers. In consequence, the lay student is confronted by a maze of strange characters that are frequently unintelligible and sometimes almost maddening. The sounds of American speech—as of any language—are so numerous that it is difficult to represent all of them with complete accuracy by means of printed symbols. They vary not only

---

Marcus L. Hansen, Bernard Bloch and Julia Bloch; Providence, R.I., 1939. The field is surveyed in detail in La Dialectologie, by Sever Pop; 2 vols.; Louvain, 1950. *Orbis*, founded by Pop and edited by him till his death in 1961, surveys dialect research in all languages.]

[8] Variants of *quahog* (from the Pequot *p'quaughhaug*) are *cohog*, *quohog* and *pooquaw*. [The village of *Quogue*, on Long Island, may also derive from this source.]

[9] *Lightning bug*, an Americanism, is traced to 1778.

in every pair of individuals, but also in the same individual at different times.

[Even a simpler version of the IPA (or any other systematic phonetic alphabet) would have presented difficulties. Unlike their opposite numbers in European countries, who introduce phonetic alphabets in elementary schools, American pedagogues have been unwilling to learn the IPA even in its simplest form, much less teach it in their classes. As a result, such a useful work as "A Pronouncing Dictionary of American English," by John S. Kenyon and Thomas A. Knott [1]—the best broad-gauge treatment of American pronunciation to date—is almost unknown outside the ranks of professional linguists.

[The evidence from the New England records was so illuminating that even while they were being edited, field work was begun further south. By 1949, despite the interruptions of World War II, field work was complete along the Atlantic seaboard, and another decade saw the same stage reached in the Great Lakes area, the upper Midwest, Colorado, California and Nevada. In other areas field work is under way, and in some sections editing is well advanced. A detailed survey will be found in Chapter VII.[2]]

These manifestations of interest in the scientific study of American English among American philologians are gratifying, but even now many teachers of English fight shy of American and see in it only a corruption of English. Just as the obfuscations of Eighteenth Century law have been preserved in American law long after their abandonment in England, so the tight rules of the Eighteenth Century purists, with their absurd grammatical niceties, their fanciful etymologies and their silly spelling-pronunciations, tend to be preserved. This pedantry continues to be cherished among the rank and file of American pedagogues, from the kindergarten to the graduate school. In the American colleges and high schools there is no faculty so weak as the English faculty. It is the common catchall for aspirants to the birch who are too lazy or too feeble in intelligence to acquire any sort of exact knowledge, and the professional incompetence of its typical ornament is matched only by his hollow cocksureness. [Nor does the presence of a strong department of linguistics mollify the belletristic Brahmins. At neither Yale nor California, two of the

---

[1] Springfield, Mass., 1944. [The pronunciation key to Webster 1961 is more systematic than that of its predecessors, although it still eschews the IPA. Since it is new, and attempts to represent the major varieties of cultivated speech, it has been more favorably received by scholars than by journalists.]

[2] [See The Linguistic Atlas of New England, *Orbis*, Vol. I, June 1952, pp. 167–75; Regional Linguistic Atlases in the United States, *Orbis*, Vol. V, Dec. 1956, pp. 349–86; The Dialects of American English, Ch. 9 of The Structure of American English, by W. Nelson Francis (New York, 1958), pp. 480–544; and the annual reports of the Committee on Linguistic Geography and Regional Speech of the American Dialect Society.]

major linguistic centers, is any understanding of the national idiom expected of the Ph.D. in English, and in most others such a requirement is accepted grudgingly.]

As we have seen, the early American philologists—Witherspoon, Pickering and their like—preached conformity to English precept. True enough, George Perkins Marsh, in his "Lectures on the English Language,"[3] argued that "in point of naked syntactical accuracy, the English of America is not at all inferior to that of England." But even Marsh expressed the hope that Americans would not, "with malice prepense, go about to republicanize our orthography and our syntax, our grammars and our dictionaries, our nursery hymns [*sic*] and our Bibles" to the point of actual separation. Moreover, the regularly ordained brethren were all against him. The fear of William C. Fowler, of Amherst, that Americans might "break loose from the laws of the English language"[4] altogether, was echoed by the whole fraternity.

Two sages of a later day actually preached that the independent growth of American was not only immoral but a sheer illusion. They were Richard Grant White, for long the most widely read American writer upon language questions, and Thomas R. Lounsbury, for thirty-five years professor of the English language and literature in the Sheffield Scientific School at Yale. White's "Words and Their Uses" (1872) and his "Everyday English" (1880) were mines of erudition. Lounsbury effectively attacked the follies of the grammarians; his two books "The Standard of Usage in English" and "The Standard of Pronunciation in English," not to mention his excellent "History of the English Language" and his numerous magazine articles, showed a sound knowledge of the early history of the language, and an admirable spirit of free inquiry. But when these laborious scholars turned from English proper to American English, they tried to deny its existence altogether, and to support that denial brought a critical method that was anything but scientific. After eight long articles in the *Atlantic Monthly*[5] on the fourth edition of Bartlett's "American Glossary" (1877), White had disposed of nine-tenths of Bartlett's specimens and questioned the authenticity of at least half the remainder. He erected tests so difficult and so arbitrary that only the exceptional word or phrase could pass them, and then only by chance. "To stamp a word or a phrase as an Americanism," he said, "it is necessary to show that (1) it is of so-called 'American'

---

[3] They were delivered at Columbia College during the winter of 1858–9, and were published in New York in 1859. They had reached a fourth edition by 1861. Marsh also published The Origin and History of the English Language; New York, 1862.

[4] The English Language; New York, 1850; rev. ed., 1855. This was the first American textbook of English for use in colleges.

[5] Americanisms, parts i–viii, Apr., May, July, Sept., Nov. 1878; Jan., Mar., May 1879.

origin—that is, that it first came into use in the United States of North America, or that (2) it has been adopted in those States from some language other than English, or has been kept in use there while it has *wholly* passed out of use in England." He further argued that unless "the simple words in compound names" were used in America "in a sense different from that in which they are used in England" the compound itself could not be regarded as an Americanism. One of these absurd rules would bar out such obvious Americanisms as *sick* in place of *ill*, *molasses* for *treacle* and *fall* for *autumn*, for all these words, while archaic in England, are by no means wholly extinct; the other would reject such unmistakably characteristic Americanisms as *joyride, showdown, rubberneck, chair warmer* and *backtalk*. Lounsbury went even further to lay down the dogma that "cultivated speech . . . affords the only legitimate basis of comparison between the language as used in England and America." He went on:

> In the only really proper sense of the term, an Americanism is a word or phrase naturally used by an educated American which under similar conditions would not be used by an educated Englishman. The emphasis, it will be seen, lies in the word "educated."

Finally he announced that his discussion was "restricted to the *written* speech of educated men." The result was a wholesale slaughter of Americanisms. A word not rejected on the ground that some stray English poet had once used it, could thus be rejected on the ground that it was not used by a college professor when he sat down to compose formal book-English. What remained was a small company, indeed—and almost the whole field of American idiom and American grammar, so full of interest for the less austere explorer, was closed without even a peek into it.

Despite its absurdity, this position was taken by most of the American *Gelehrte* of the day. The dull and humorless spokesmen of the American Academy of Arts and Letters have long tried to convert themselves into an American counterpart of the Académie Française, with the power of life and death over new locutions.[6] In 1916 they published a subsidized volume

---

[6] The Académie itself pretends to no such omniscience. In the preface to the first edition of its dictionary (1694), it disclaimed any purpose "to make new words and to reject others at its pleasure." In the preface to the second edition (1718) it confessed that "ignorance and corruption often introduce manners of writing" and that "convenience establishes them." In the preface to the third edition (1740) it admitted that it was "forced to admit changes which the public has made," and so on. Says D. M. Robertson, in A History of the French Academy (London, 1910): "The Academy repudiates any assumption of authority over the language with which the public in its own practise has not first clothed it. So much, indeed, does it confine itself to an interpretation merely of the laws of language that its decisions are sometimes contrary to its own judgment of what is either desirable or expedient." But despite this, its natural leaning is toward tradition, and that leaning has greatly diminished its authority. Even some of its own members repudiate its judgments.

of nine essays,[7] beginning by approving English models and ending by attacking Edgar Lee Masters, Amy Lowell and Carl Sandburg—with a bow to Don Marquis! The brethren seemed to believe that the only sound models of English are to be found in the thunderous artificialities of Eighteenth Century England, and that the only remedy for "entire abandonment to the loose-lipped lingo of the street" is "a little study of Latin and translation of Cicero and Virgil." Even though some of the contributors dissent, the book presents a depressing proof of the stupidity of the learned.

In 1923 a Conference of British and American Professors of English at Columbia University became an assault upon Americanisms in the national speech. If any speaker at the conference defended American speechways, the fact did not appear in the published reports. [On the lower levels of pedagogy the same general attitude was encouraged for a long time by the National Council of Teachers of English. But for the NCTE, those days are gone forever.

[One of the first to suggest that it was not unfitting to teach the actual usage of cultivated Americans was Sterling A. Leonard, in his "Current English Usage." [8] Other investigators, skeptical of his iconoclastic findings, discovered that the facts of usage were even more startling than he had indicated—that many expressions even Leonard was dubious about were in good standing on both sides of the Atlantic. But the savant who did most to irritate the American gogues into accepting the national idiom on its own merits was C. C. Fries, who took the lead in making the University of Michigan not only the pre-eminent center in the United States for the study of the English language but also the only center where the study of linguistics had a solid base in the English Department. He began by calling for an appraisal of how the language works, in the first edition of his often reissued book "The Teaching of the English Language" (1927). He brought to Ann Arbor the files of the Middle English Dictionary and the proposed Dictionary of Early Modern English. He induced the Linguistic Society of America to conduct at Ann Arbor in 1936 the first summer Linguistic Institute west of tidewater, renewed it for four consecutive summers and re-established it in 1945 as a regular feature of the summer program. Because of his interest, Albert H. Marckwardt began the study of Midwestern dialects and Kurath was called from Brown to edit the Middle English Dictionary. His book "The Structure of English" [9] ap-

---

[7] Academy Papers: Addresses on Language Problems by Members of the American Academy of Arts and Letters; New York, 1925. The contributors were Paul Elmer More, William M. Sloane, William C. Brownell, Brander Matthews, Bliss Perry, Paul Shorey, Henry Van Dyke and Robert Underwood Johnson.
[8] [Chicago, 1932.]
[9] [New York, 1952. It was hailed by Louella B. Cook as marking the coming of age of a truly functional grammar; The End of the Trail, *EJ*, Vol. XLI, Dec. 1952, pp. 540-3. A typical uncom-

praises the parts of English sentences, not by the way they might fit the norms of a Second Century Latin grammar, but by the way they are actually used in conversation by educated Midwestern Americans. Yet none of these did as much for the student of American *Sprachpraktik* as Fries's "American English Grammar."[1] Sponsored by the NCTE and based on thousands of holograph letters written to federal bureaus, this study showed a wide discrepancy between what was currently taught as good usage and what was the actual practice of educated people. For example, *those kind of things,* far from being a mark of illiteracy, is unknown to the unwashed and used only by those of superior education.[2]

[Moreover, Fries was a shrewd lobbyist and an effective public speaker, who could fight the traditionalists with their own weapons but with better ammunition. Realizing that the teachers colleges shape the attitude of pedagogues and therefore of the next generation, he cannily placed his best students in strategic teacher-training institutions, even in the Lhasa of pedagogy, Teachers College, Columbia.[3] At the beginning of World War II he set up the first successful center for using modern linguistic principles to teach American English to native speakers of other languages. His example and many of his methods were emulated by other universities, by army courses for teaching English to Italian and German prisoners of war and to our allies of various linguistic origins, and more recently by government-sponsored American Language centers spread from Pakistan to Peru.

[At the same time, Fries—first alone and then with his students—kept reminding the NCTE that no program for teaching English could be successful unless it was based on the actual practice of educated Americans. The NCTE finally capitulated, perhaps because, with the decline in the study of Latin, relatively few high-school and college students knew even the terminology of the older grammar, much less how to apply it to the very un-Latin behavior of English. A sympathy with American practice was found increasingly in *College English, The English Journal* and especially in the bulletins of the College Conference on Composition and Communication, a new group within the NCTE devoted to the practical

---

prehending attack is What Sort of Double Talk Is This? by Arnold Starbuck, *EJ,* Vol. XLV, Mar. 1956, p. 163; he is disturbed because Fries recognizes that *Let's us* occurs in standard colloquial American English.]

[1] [New York, 1940.]

[2] [p. 58.]

[3] [Some of the other significant works by Fries are the books Linguistics and Reading (New York, 1963) and English Word Lists (with Aileen Traver; American Council on Education, Washington, D.C., 1940); and the articles Implications of Modern Linguistic Science (*CE,* Vol. VII, Mar. 1947, pp. 314–20) and American Linguistics and the Teaching of English (*Language Learning,* Vol. VI, 1955, pp. 1–22). See The Man Behind the New Grammar, by Ethel Strainchamps, *Saturday Review,* Mar. 18, 1961, pp. 34–5, 61.]

problems of teaching students how to write. As at the MLA, the sessions of the NCTE devoted to problems of American English grammar have become the most popular with the rank and file.[4] The new attitude was dramatically symbolized in 1961 by two events. A Commission on English, established by the College Entrance Examination Board, recommended to the NCTE that every prospective teacher of English be trained in the actual structure of the language. And simultaneously, the die-hards among the schoolma'ams began to denounce the NCTE for succumbing to the "doctrine of permissiveness," and thus corrupting the standards of English.

[And it is the NCTE that sponsored "Current American Usage," a dictionary based on the actual practice of mid-century Americans.[5]

[The successful wooing of the NCTE has had its disadvantages. That many teachers of composition favor linguistic realism makes it suspect to the literary lamas who dominate university departments;[6] that many teachers colleges favor it is enough to damn it in the eyes of caste-conscious humanists.[7] Nor are these suspicions groundless: just as do-gooder social

---

[4] [The linguists' concern with teaching and the reception of linguistics by active teachers are presented in James B. McMillan, The Descriptive Grammarian's Point of View, *EJ*, Vol. XXXIV, Sept. 1945, pp. 395–6, and A Philosophy of Language, *CE*, Vol. IX, Apr. 1948, pp. 385–90; Archibald A. Hill, A Survey of Accomplishments and Trends in Research in Present-Day English, *AS*, Vol. XXIV, Apr. 1949, pp. 81–9, and Prescriptivism and Linguistics in English Teaching, *CE*, Vol. XV, Apr. 1954, pp. 395–9; Thomas Pyles, Linguistics and Pedagogy: The Need for Conciliation, *CE*, Vol. X, Apr. 1949, pp. 389–95; L. M. Myers, Linguistics and the Teaching of Rhetoric, *College Composition and Communication*, Vol. V, Dec. 1954, pp. 166–71; R. C. Simonini, Jr., Linguistics in the English Curriculum, *CE*, Vol. XIX, Jan. 1958, pp. 163–5; Henry Lee Smith, Jr., The Teacher and the World of Language, *CE*, Vol. XX, Jan. 1959, pp. 172–8; Paul Roberts, The Relation of Linguistics to the Teaching of English, *CE*, Vol. XXII, Oct. 1960, pp. 1–9. A useful collection of essays is Readings in Applied English Linguistics, ed. by Harold B. Allen; New York, 1958.]

[5] [Edited by Margaret M. Bryant; New York, 1962. This should not be confused with A Dictionary of Contemporary American Usage, by Bergen Evans, of Northwestern University, and his sister Cornelia (New York, 1957). Actually, the Evanses' book, like H. W. Fowler's popular Modern English Usage (Oxford, 1926), is a dictionary of opinions about usage—perceptive, learned, urbane and often witty opinions, but opinions nonetheless.]

[6] [*E.g.*, Harry R. Warfel, Who Killed Grammar? (Gainesville, Fla., 1952); Robert Withington, A Plea for Normative Grammar, *AS*, Vol. XXIX, May 1954, pp. 139–41; John C. Sherwood, Dr. Kinsey and Professor Fries, *CE*, Vol. XXI, Feb. 1960, pp. 275–80; Alain Renoir, Traditional Grammar or Structural Linguistics: a Buyer's Point of View, *CE*, Vol. XXII, Apr. 1961, pp. 484–8. These viewers-with-alarm often exhibit their ignorance of the discipline they deplore; Renoir, for instance, makes the incredible charge against the linguists that "their methods are no longer readily interchangeable from one language to another."]

[7] [The fear that an alliance between linguists and colleges of education may produce a power *coup* to dominate the teaching of English has been expressed in The Way They Say It, by William R. Bowden, *CE*, Vol. XXII, Apr. 1961, pp. 478–84. The cultural lag in the adoption of linguistics is surveyed objectively by John McGalliard, Resistance to Change

workers may abuse psychology to keep adolescent thugs out of the pokey, do-gooder English teachers may abuse descriptive linguistics to keep adolescent morons in the classroom—and graduate them. Furthermore, some once-vocal opponents of modern linguistics show an almost obscene haste in announcing their conversion and setting out to preach the faith without waiting to understand it.

[A greater hindrance to the spread of the new attitudes has been the lack of teaching materials. Discoveries in linguistics, as in other disciplines, are made by a relatively small group, accustomed to writing in a tightly technical style for one another. Lacking direct contact with this group, an outsider can hardly set his sail to one linguistic wind, let alone steer through the gusts and squalls of conflicting dogmas. The attempts of new converts to present linguistics for popular consumption fail to convince the old-fashioned grammarian and only disgust the serious linguist. Not until 1958 was a unified presentation [8] available to undergraduates curious about the nature of American English. The adaptations for elementary courses are still to come.[9] But the national language has generally won its place both as an object of serious study and as the model to be taught.]

6: THE VIEWS OF WRITING MEN

"American authors," said Alexis de Tocqueville in 1835,[1] "may truly be said to live more in England than in their own country, since they constantly study the English writers and take them every day for their own models. But such is not the case with the bulk of the population, which is more immediately subjected to the peculiar causes acting upon the United States. It is not then to the written, but to the spoken language that attention must be paid if we would detect the modifications which the idiom of an aristocratic people may undergo when it becomes the language of a

---

in Language Teaching, *CE*, Vol. XX, Apr. 1959, pp. 347–50; somewhat sardonically by James H. Sledd, Grammar or Grammarye? *EJ*, Vol. XLIX, May 1960, pp. 293–303. In Thorstein Veblen and Linguistic Theory (*AS*, Vol. XXXV, May 1960, pp. 124–30), Robert A. Hall, Jr., suggests that traditional grammar, like most marks of class distinction, is valued precisely because it is painful to acquire and useless when acquired.]

[8] [W. Nelson Francis, The Structure of American English, New York, 1958; James H. Sledd, A Short Introduction to English Grammar, Chicago, 1959. Of transitional books, the most successful are Paul M. Roberts, Understanding Grammar, New York, 1954, and Understanding English, New York, 1958; L. M.

Myers, American English, Englewood Cliffs, N.J., 1952; revised as Guide to American English, 1959.]

[9] [The most successful are Paul Roberts, Patterns of English, New York, 1956; and English Sentences, New York, 1962. Others are Donald J. Lloyd and Harry R. Warfel, American English in Its Cultural Setting, New York, 1956; and Harold Whitehall, Structural Essentials of English, New York, 1956.]

[1] De la démocratie en Amérique; Paris, 1835, Vol. II, Book I, Ch. XVI. Translated as The Republic of the United States of America and Its Political Institutions, Reviewed and Examined by Henry Reeves, with notes and a preface by John C. Spencer; New York, 1858.]

democracy." [2] Tocqueville visited the United States in 1831, when the two American writers principally admired and influential, Washington Irving and James Fenimore Cooper, were properly regarded by their contemporaries as Anglomaniacs. The revolt against English precept and example, as against English libel and invective, was left to lesser men. The most effective of these, James K. Paulding, whom we have mentioned before, greeted the War of 1812 with a "Diverting History of John Bull and Brother Jonathan," which must have had a powerful effect, for it remained in print until 1835 and was brought out again in 1867. This last edition had a preface by William I. Paulding, a son of the author, who was apparently upset by the bitterness of his pa's satire, and sought to apologize for it:

> He wrote in an atmosphere of acerbity, about matters then really of almost national [*sic!*] concern, though at the present day they can scarcely be made to appear in that light. He looked upon the whole detracting tribe [of English travelers] as mercenary calumniators of an entire people, with no claim to either courtesy or grace; and pitched upon the individual subjects of attack rather as types of the different styles of the British objector than from any personal feeling or knowledge of the parties.

This was poppycock. Paulding's savage thrusts were aimed at easily recognized offenders, and he must have known some of them well enough. In 1825 he returned to the attack with a still more devastating buffoonery under the title "John Bull in America, or, The New Munchausen." Here he singled out individual travelers so plainly that even his dunderhead son, writing forty-two years later, could not help identifying them. The book still makes excellent reading, as a burlesque with no squeamish pulling of punches. In his preface Paulding suggests waggishly that the author was probably William Gifford, editor of the *Quarterly Review* and grand master of English America-haters. Throughout he very adroitly parodies Gifford's condescending style, and the book is full of other devices that make the thing a capital example of a kind of writing that has been curiously little practiced in the United States. Paulding got some help in his counterattack—from Edward Everett, from Timothy Dwight and even from the timorous Cooper—but for twenty years he bore most of the

[2] The superior importance of the spoken language, often overlooked by writers on the subject, was stressed again nearly a century later by another French observer, A. G. Feuillerat, professor of French at Yale, in A Dictionary of the American Language, *Yale Review*, June 1929, p. 830. "It is," he said, "the most vital part of the language, the one that will in the end impose its laws when American civilization, having severed all links from English civilization, may eventually desire to assert itself in the adoption of a truly national mode of expression."

burden and heat of the day. Everett (1794–1865) was a convert to the cause of American independence in speech and had no truck with it until he visited England in 1815, and then proceeded to Göttingen to take his doctorate. He had several encounters with Gifford in London and stood up to him boldly, even criticizing the English of the *Quarterly*. He was unfavorably impressed, not only by the multiplicity of English provincial dialects, but also by the accepted speech of the higher circles of London. When, on returning home, he became editor of the *North American Review*, he denounced one of the slanderous English travelers of the time as a "miscreant" and another as a "swindler." In July 1821, in a review of an anti-American article in the *New London Monthly Magazine* for February of the same year, Everett argued that "on the whole, the English language is spoken better here than in England," and that "there is no part of America in which the corruption of the language has gone so far as in the heart of the English counties." He insisted that where differences were noticeable, the American practice was better than the English. "We presume," he concluded loftily, "that the press set up by the American missionaries in the Sandwich Islands will furnish a good deal better English than Mr. Bentham's Church-of-Englandism." Even when, in 1841, he was made American minister to England, he resisted stoutly the notorious tendency of that exalted post to make its incumbents limber-kneed, and came back in 1845 still convinced that American English was better than British English. He was the first, in fact, to suggest a dictionary of Briticisms. In one of his last publications, the "Mount Vernon Papers" of 1860, he quoted David Hume's prophecy to Edward Gibbon in 1767: "Our solid and increasing establishments in America . . . promise a superior stability and duration to the English language," and added: "What a contrast between these sensible remarks . . . and the sneers of English tourists and critics on the state of the English language as written and spoken in America." [3]

Cooper blew both hot and cold—and not so briskly hot as cold. According to Robert E. Spiller, the purpose of "Notions of the Americans," which was published in London and Philadelphia in 1828, was twofold: "the misinformed and prejudiced criticism of the English must be silenced, and the slavish mental dependence of the American mind upon British opinion must be brought to an end." [4] But Cooper faintheartedly withheld his name from the book and ascribed it instead to an anonymous "travelling bachelor," seeking to make it appear that this bachelor was an Englishman. In

---

[3] Allen Walker Read, Edward Everett's Attitude Towards American English, *New England Quarterly*, Vol. XII, Mar. 1939, pp. 112–29.

[4] Fenimore Cooper, Critic of His Times; New York, 1931, Ch. X.

"The American Democrat," ten years later, he forgot altogether the denunciations of American speechways by the English, and devoted himself mainly to drawing up an indictment on his own account. In part he said:

> The common faults of American language are an ambition of effect, a want of simplicity, and a turgid abuse of terms. To these may be added ambiguity of expression. Many perversions of significances also exist . . .
>
> *Creek*, a word that signifies an *inlet* of the sea, or of a lake, is misapplied to running streams, and frequently to the *outlets* of lakes.[5] A *square* is called a *park;*[6] *lakes* are often called *ponds;*[7] and arms of the sea are sometimes termed *rivers*.[8]

He denounced the pronunciation of *new* as *noo*,[9] and plumped for *clark, cowcumber, goold, levtenant* and *eye-ther*,[1] rather than the usual American pronunciations of *clerk, cucumber, gold, lieutenant* and *either*. He also criticized the democratic substitution of *boss* for *master* and of *help* for *servant*, and preached a smug sermon upon the true meaning of *lady* and *gentleman*. "To call a laborer, one who has neither education, manners, accomplishments, tastes, associations, nor any one of the ordinary requisites, a *gentleman*," he said, "is just as absurd as to call one who is thus qualified a *fellow*. . . . [A true gentleman] never calls his wife his *lady*, but his *wife*, and he is not afraid of lessening the dignity of the human race by styling the most elevated and refined of his fellow creatures *men* and *women*."

Cooper's pleas for "simplicity of speech, . . . totally without strut . . . or any other bloated feeling," had little effect upon his contemporaries.

---

[5] The American use of *creek* to designate any small stream had been remarked by various earlier commentators on American English, including Pickering and Dunglison; the DA's first example is dated 1622.

[6] *Square,* in the sense of a small city park, is not an Americanism. But *public square* is; the DA traces it to 1786. *Square,* in the sense of a city block or of the distance between one street and the next, apparently originated in Philadelphia, where William Penn laid out the city in rectangles—the first time this was done in America, and possibly in the world. All the other early American cities, at least in their older parts, have many crooked streets. But the DA's first example (1770) is from a description of New Orleans.

[7] *Pond* began to be applied to natural lakes in America so early as 1622, and in the name of Walden *Pond* it is familiar in that meaning to all readers of Thoreau.

[8] The misapplication of *river* to arms of the sea is as common in England as in America; the lower Thames, for example, is actually an inlet of the North Sea, and is often called, more properly, an *estuary*.

[9] [For the distribution of the two pronunciations today, see Hans Kurath and Raven I. McDavid, Jr., The Pronunciation of English in the Atlantic States (University of Michigan Publications in American English: III, Ann Arbor, 1961), pp. 113, 174, and Maps 33, 163–5.]

[1] [See The Pronunciation of English in the Atlantic States, p. 149 and Map 98.]

All were under the influence of the Johnsonian style of the Eighteenth Century, and not many attempted to make any use of the new and vivid native vocabulary flourishing about them. Bryant, born in 1794 and surviving until 1878, was essentially a conformist, and after he became editor of the New York *Evening Post*, he drew up an *Index Expurgatorius* which included some of the Americanisms denounced by the English reviewers, *e.g., reliable, standpoint, to jeopardize* and *to progress*—all now perfectly sound American and even sound English. This index is still imitated in American newspaper offices.[2] Mamie Meredith has observed that Emerson, in the seclusion of his diaries, was not afraid to experiment with words,[3] but in his published work he wrote like a university-trained Englishman. Poe and Melville delighted in strange words, but very few of them came out of the rising American vocabulary of their time. In James Mark Purcell's list of 180 terms found in Melville before the earliest dates of their recording from other sources, only a small number are properly describable as Americanisms: the overwhelming majority are either borrowings from or adaptations of the argot of English sailors, or nonce words of no significance.[4] As for Poe, a similar study shows even rarer inventions of any substance, and none that reveal genuinely American influence or have got into the common store.[5] Poe was fond of such monsters as *circumgyratory, concentralization* and *paragraphism,* but his actual vocabulary was small; Robert L. Ramsay estimates that in his poetry it was limited to about 3,200 words.[6] He used the phrase *American language* in "The

---

[2] I should add in fairness that some of the other words that Bryant banned belonged to the worst newspaper jargon of the time, and probably deserved to be frowned upon, *e.g., casket* for *coffin, devouring element* for *fire, to inaugurate* for *to begin, juvenile* for *boy, posted* for *informed,* and *on the tapis.* The index is reprinted in Helpful Hints in Writing and Reading, comp. by Grenville Kleiser; New York, 1911, pp. 15–17.

[3] Emersonian Unconventionalities, *AS,* Vol. XI, Oct. 1936, p. 172. [See also Some Notes on Emerson's Prose Diction, by Morton Cronin, *AS,* Vol. XXIX, May 1954, pp. 105–13. Thoreau's Journals are full of Americanisms, some of them antedating the DA citations by fifty years; a preliminary report has been completed by Lee Pederson.]

[4] Melville's Contributions to English, *PMLA,* Vol. LVI, Sept. 1941, pp. 797–808. Under the same title Purcell corrected a few errors, in *AS,* Vol. XVIII, Oct. 1943, p. 111. [Recently Melville has

been studied intensively by C. Merton Babcock, who finds few coinages but many adaptations: The Language of Melville's "Isolatoes," *Western Folklore,* Vol. X, Oct. 1951, pp. 285–9; The Vocabulary of "Moby Dick," *AS,* Vol. XXVII, May 1952, pp. 91–101; Herman Melville's Whaling Vocabulary, *AS,* Vol. XXIX, Oct. 1954, pp. 161–74; Some Expressions from Herman Melville, *PADS,* No. 31, Apr. 1959, pp. 3–13.]

[5] J. H. Neumann, Poe's Contributions to English, *AS,* Vol. XVIII, Feb. 1943, pp. 73–4.

[6] Review of A Concordance of the Poetical Works of Edgar Allan Poe, by Brandford A. Booth and Claude E. Jones (Baltimore, 1941), in *AS,* Vol. XVII, Apr. 1942, p. 112. Ramsay handles this concordance roughly; it is of very small value. It should be remembered that Poe's poetic output was not very large, and that this fact reduces his apparent vocabulary.

Rationale of Verse," and denounced Noah Webster, in "Fifty Suggestions," as "more English than the English—*plus Arabe qu'en Arabie*," but his other discussions of language, in "Marginalia" and elsewhere, showed that he was a rigid purist who could imagine no standards for American English save those in favor in England. Nor could Hawthorne, or Longfellow, or Holmes.

The first full-length defense of American by an American appeared in a volume of "Cambridge Essays, Contributed by Members of the University," published in London in 1855. Its author was Charles Astor Bristed, a grandson of John Jacob Astor.[7] Entitled "The English Language in America," it remains to this day the most intelligent brief discussion of the subject ever printed. He denounced the ever-prevalent notion that the study of American was undignified, and argued that it was worth any scholar's while "to investigate the course of a great living language, transplanted from its primitive seat, brought into contact and rivalry with other civilized tongues, and exposed to various influences, all having a *prima facie* tendency to modify it." He then disposed of the familiar arguments against the existence of an American form of English: (1) that most Americanisms "can be traced to an English source," (2) that "the number of actually new words invented in America is very small," (3) that "the deviations from standard English which occur in America are fewer and less gross than those which may be found in England herself," and so on. Here is a specimen passage from his caveat to the first two propositions, which he grouped together as embodying a single argument:

> We admit this argument to be true, *so far as it goes;* but it does not go so far, by any means, as its supporters imagine. They seem to forget that there is such a thing as applying a new *meaning* to existing words, and of this novelty the examples in America are sufficiently numerous. Thus *creek* is a perfectly legitimate English word, but its legitimate English meaning is "a small arm of the sea," whereas in America it is invariably used to designate a small river, except when it happens to be used to designate a large one. *Draw* is an old-established English verb, but the Americans have further employed it as a noun, and made it do duty for *draw-bridge*.

The third proposition Bristed answered thus:

> Such reasoning is on a par with that of one who should consider himself to have demonstrated that the upper classes of America were richer than those of England by showing that the lower classes of

---

[7] He was graduated from Yale in 1839 and then went to Cambridge to take a degree in 1845. During the next thirty years he lived chiefly at Washington. In 1852 he published Five Years in an English University, and three years later he was asked to contribute to Cambridge Essays.

England were poorer than those of America, or that the average wealth of the American population per head was greater than that of the English. There is no inconsistency in admitting that the worst English *patois* may be less intelligible than the worst American, and yet maintaining that the best currently spoken American contains appreciable deviations from the true English standard. The English provincialisms *keep their place;* they are confined to their own particular localities, and do not encroach on the metropolitan model. The American provincialisms are most equally distributed through all classes and localities, and though some of them may not rise above a certain level of society, others are heard everywhere. The senate or the boudoir is no more sacred from their intrusions than the farmhouse or the tavern.

Bristed argued boldly that in many ways American usage was already superior to English. He defended the American use of *sick,* and the practice, derived from the northern British dialects, of sounding the *h* in such words as *which* and *wheel.* In any case, he said, the Americans were perfectly free to modify their language as they pleased, and no conceivable pressure could dissuade them. Many American inventions had already "settled down into and become established in the language. *Talented* is a familiar example. It is of little use to inveigh against such words—there they are in full possession and cannot be turned out."

Whitman was very language-conscious, for it fitted into his romantic confidence in democracy to praise the iconoclastic and often uncouth American speechways of his time. Two formal treatises on the subject survive, in addition to a number of notes and reports of conversations. In November 1885, he contributed a paper to the *North American Review* under the title "Slang in America," and three years later he included it in "November Boughs." [8] Thirty years before, in the period of "Leaves of Grass," he prepared a lecture entitled "An American Primer," but it did not get into print until 1904, twelve years after his death.[9] Both the paper and the lecture, like all of Whitman's prose writings, are vague and flowery, but their central purpose remains plain enough, to make war upon the old American subservience to Eighteenth Century English pedantry, and open the way for the development of a healthy and vigorous autochthonous language in the United States.

At a time, says Louis Untermeyer, "when the rest of literary America was still indulging in the polite language of pulpits and the lifeless rhetoric of its libraries, Whitman not only sensed the richness and vigor of the

---

[8] Philadelphia, 1888.
[9] It was published in the *Atlantic* *Monthly* (Apr., pp. 460 *ff.*) by his faithful retainer, Horace Traubel.

casual word, the colloquial phrase—he championed the vitality of slang, and freshness of our quickly assimilated jargons, the indigenous beauty of vulgarisms. He even predicted that no future native literature could exist that neglected this racy speech, that the vernacular of people as opposed to the language of literati would form the living accents of the best poets to come. One has only to observe the contemporary works of Carl Sandburg, Robert Frost, Edgar Lee Masters, Vachel Lindsay and a dozen others to see how his prophecy has been fulfilled. Words, especially the neglected words regarded as too crude and literal for literature, fascinated Whitman. The idea of an enriched language was scarcely ever out of his mind. . . . it became almost an obsession." [1]

But this interest found little realization in Whitman's actual practice. His early prose was the dingy, cliché-laden journalese of the era, and after his discovery of Carlyle he indulged himself in a heavy imitation of the Scotsman's gnarled and tortured style. Not many specimens of the popular speech ever got into his writings, either in prose or in verse. He is remembered for few besides *yawp* and *gawk*.[2] His own inventions were mainly cacophonous miscegenations of roots and suffixes, *e.g.*, *scientism, presidentiad, venerealee, to memorandize, diminute* (adjective) and *infidelistic*, and not one of them has ever gained any currency. Moreover, more than half his innovations were simply borrowings from finishing-school French,[3] with a few examples of Spanish and Italian added for good measure. His French loans were pearls from the vocabulary of the primeval society editors of his time, *e.g.*, *coiffeur, restaurateur, mélange, faubourg, ennui, aplomb* and *éclat*.[4] A number of these have been naturalized, but Whitman had little to do with the process. Nor did he succeed any better with his Spanish and Italian favorites, *e.g.*, *camerado, libertad* and *cantabile*. Like Poe, he would air foreign words that struck him as tony. but like Poe again, he wrote a stiff and artificial English, and seldom showed any command of the vernacular riches that he professed to admire.[5]

Of the lesser American writers in the era from the publication of

---

[1] Whitman and the American Language New York *Evening Post*, May 31, 1919.

[2] The DAE traces *yawp* to 1835, when it was used by J. H. Ingraham in The South-West; it is found in many British dialects. *Gawk* has been in use in England since the early Eighteenth Century.

[3] Walt Whitman and the French Language, *AS*, Vol. I, May 1926, p. 425.

[4] Poe had a weakness for terms of the same sort, *e.g.*, *recherché, outré, dégagé* and *littérateur*. See The French of Edgar Allan Poe, by Edith Philips, *AS*, Vol. II, Mar. 1927, pp. 270–4.

[5] His unhappy efforts to devise new words of English material are described in Walt Whitman's Neologisms, by Louise Pound, *American Mercury*, Feb. 1925, pp. 199–201. His writings on language are well summarized in Walt Whitman and the American Language, by Leon Howard, *AS*, Vol. V, Aug. 1930, pp. 441–51. In A Study of Whitman's Diction, *University of Texas Studies in English*, No. 16, 1936, pp. 115–24, Rebecca Coy shows that the Americanisms in Leaves of Grass are not numerous.

"Thanatopsis" in 1817 to that of "Leaves of Grass" in 1855, N. P. Willis, like Paulding, resented the gross libels of all things American in the current English reviews and travel books, and sought revenge in 1835, in his "Pencillings by the Way." This work is an impudent and often satirical picture of the English life of the time, especially on the more pretentious intellectual levels, and in it there are some effective hits, as when, for example, Willis compliments the second Lord Grenville, who had visited America, on speaking "American English . . . with all the careless correctness and fluency of a vernacular tongue, [and without] a particle of the cockney drawl, half Irish and half Scotch, with which many Englishmen speak." [6] Willis unfortunately wrote in what he regarded as the best English fashion of the period, and disdained the neologisms that were beginning to show themselves in the work of the popular humorists. His own contributions to the vocabulary were such banalities as *haughty culture* (for *high culture*), *superfinery*, *whirlsated* (confused), *Caesar-or-nobody-dom* and *to brickify*. No one, as yet, has searched the American reviews of the pre-Civil War era, as the English reviews have been searched by Cairns and Read, but some light upon their position with regard to American English may be gathered from their treatment of the early American dictionaries.[7] Noah Webster's first dictionary in 1806 was generally denounced for its inclusion of Americanisms, and the same treatment was given the works of John Elliott, Caleb Alexander, William Woodbridge and the American Samuel Johnson, Jr., for somewhat less conspicuous offendings. Both the *American Review* and the *Monthly Anthology* protested bitterly against the listing of *composuist*, a substitute for *composer*, then "much used" according to Pickering, "at some of our colleges," but now happily obsolete. The *Monthly Magazine* laid down the doctrine that, save for a few "technical and scientific terms . . . any other species of American words are manifest corruptions, and to embalm these by the lexicographic process would only be a waste of time and abuse of talents." Two eminent pedagogues of the time took the other line. Jeremiah Atwater, president of Middlebury College in Vermont, declared that "local words are always with propriety inserted in dictionaries, especially when marked as being local." Timothy Dwight, president of Yale, already mentioned as giving aid and comfort to Paulding, drew up, in 1807, and not only signed himself but had nine members of his faculty sign, a letter to Webster saying:

---

[6] Pencillings by the Way made a considerable uproar in England and was attacked violently by the *Quarterly Review*, but it seems to have been read, and there was an English reprint so recently as 1943.

[7] Discussed incidentally by Read in The Development of Faith in the Dictionary in America, read before the Present-Day English section of the Modern Language Association at Philadelphia, Dec. 29, 1934.

The insertion of local terms in your small dictionary we approve. No good reason can be given why a person who meets with words of this kind should not be able to find their meaning in a dictionary—the only place where they can usually be found at all.

It was not, however, such scholastic bigwigs as Webster and Dwight who forced the seasoning of American writing with the pungent herbs of the vernacular, nor was it such literary rebels as Paulding and Whitman; it was the lowly humorists whose buffooneries began to appear in the newspapers soon after the War of 1812, and whose long line culminated in James Russell Lowell and Samuel L. Clemens. The first of them whose work got between covers was Seba Smith, who published his "Letters of Major Jack Downing" in 1830. According to Will D. Howe:

> These illustrated fairly well the peculiarities of New England speech and manners, and doubtless had a great influence in encouraging similar sketches in other parts of the country. Smith . . . was the first in America . . . to create a homely character and through him to make shrewd comments on politics and life.[8]

Smith was imitated at once by Charles A. Davis, who borrowed not only his method and manner but also his Jack Downing, and in a little while he had a long stream of followers—Augustus Baldwin Longstreet, Charles Henry Smith (Bill Arp), George W. Harris (Sut Lovengood), Samuel G. Goodrich (Peter Parley), Benjamin P. Shillaber (Mrs. Partington), Thomas G. Haliburton (Sam Slick),[9] Charles G. Leland (Hans Breitmann), Henry W. Shaw (Josh Billings), David R. Locke (Petroleum V. Nasby) and Charles Farrar Browne (Artemus Ward). Most of these created characters which, like Smith's Major Downing, were their spokesmen, and as humorists multiplied, their characters began to represent many national types—the Southern cracker, the Western frontiersman, the Negro, the Irishman, the German, as well as the New Englander. The result was a steady infiltration of the new American words and ways of speech, and the laying of foundations for a genuinely colloquial and national style of writing. The first masterpiece of this national school was Lowell's "The Biglow Papers," Series I of which appeared in 1848. Lowell not only attempted to

---

[8] The Cambridge History of American Literature; New York, 1918, Vol. II, p. 151. See also American Idiom in the Major Downing Letters, by Ernest E. Leisy, *AS*, Vol. VIII, Apr. 1933, pp. 78–9.

[9] Haliburton was not an American, but a Nova Scotian, and his Sam Slick, the Yankee clock peddler, was depicted with British bias. He served as a judge from 1828 to 1856, and contributed his first Sam Slick sketches to the *Nova Scotian* of Halifax in 1835. Collections of them were brought out in 1837, 1838 and 1840. Despite their prejudiced tone they were widely reprinted in American newspapers. [In recent years the Clockmaker sketches have been studied intensively by W. S. Avis. See Further Lexicographical Evidence from the "Clockmaker," *AS*, Vol. XXVII, Feb. 1952, pp. 16–19.]

depict with some care the peculiar temperament and point of view of the rustic New Englander; he also made an extremely successful effort to report Yankee speech.[1] His brief prefatory treatise on its peculiarities of pronunciation was the first to deal with the subject with any comprehensiveness, and in his introduction to Series II (1867) he expanded this preliminary note to a long and interesting essay, with a glossary of nearly 200 terms. In that essay he said:

> In choosing the Yankee dialect I did not act without forethought. It had long seemed to me that the great vice of American writing and speaking was a studied want of simplicity, that we were in danger of coming to look on our mother-tongue as a dead language, to be sought in the grammar and dictionary rather than in the heart. . . . Very few American writers or speakers wield their native language with the directness, precision and force that are common as the day in the mother country. We use it like Scotsmen, not as if it belonged to us, but as if we wished to prove that we belonged to it, by showing our intimacy with its written rather than with its spoken dialect. And yet all the while our popular idiom is racy with life and vigor and originality.[2]

Unhappily, Lowell assumed that he had sufficiently excused any given Americanism when he had proved that it was old English, and so a large part of his essay was given over to that popular but vain exercise. But despite this he did a great service to the common tongue of the country, and must be numbered among its true friends.[3] His own writing, however, did not differ materially from that of his New England contemporaries. The business of introducing the American language to good literary society was reserved for Clemens—and Clemens had a long wait before any of the accepted authorities of his generation recognized that he was not a mere zany like Browne and Locke, but a first-rate artist. The first academic dignitary to admit that he belonged at the head of the table was William Lyon Phelps in "Essays on Modern Novelists" in 1910, just as old Mark departed this earth for bliss eternal.[4] Since then his importance has

---

[1] [The best study is The Dialect of the Biglow Papers, by James W. Downer; diss. (microfilm), U. of Michigan, 1958.]

[2] In The Policies of the Dictionary of American English, *DN*, Vol. VI, July–Dec. 1938, p. 639, Allen Walker Read called this essay "probably the most important discussion of American English in the Nineteenth Century."

[3] Speech was not the main theme of his On a Certain Condescension in Foreigners, 1869, but that famous essay did not

altogether overlook it. [See James Russell Lowell: Linguistic Patriot, by Jayne Crane Harder, *AS*, Vol. XXIX, Oct. 1954, pp. 181–6.]

[4] I hailed the marvel in The Greatest of American Writers, *Smart Set*, June 1910, pp. 153–4. It was an astonishing event indeed, and without a parallel until May 1944, when the empurpled illuminati of the American Academy of Arts and Letters discovered at last that Theodore Dreiser was an important novelist,

come to be generally recognized, though a number of the heirs and converts to the standards of the Haircloth Age have continued to hack away at him. In 1938 the members of the English Department of the University of Missouri, led by Robert L. Ramsay and Frances Guthrie Emberson, completed an exhaustive study of his vocabulary, bearing the title of "A Mark Twain Lexicon." [5] It shows that Mark not only made free use of the swarming Americanisms (especially the Westernisms) of his time, but also contributed a number of excellent inventions. He was the first American author of world rank to write a genuinely colloquial and native American. Once he had thrown off the journalese of his first years, he achieved his effects without any resort to the conventional devices. Ramsay and Emberson, in an elaborate preface, show that of the 7,802 words they list as characteristic no less than 2,329 appear to be Americanisms, with 2,743 others possibly deserving that classification. Of all the authors listed in the DAE's bibliography Mark Twain occupies by far the largest space. Only "Personal Recollections of Joan of Arc" failed to yield something to the DAE's searchers. "The flavor of his style," say Ramsay and Emberson, "is always racy of the American soil, and it owes this quality largely to the prodigious store of native phrases and idioms which he employs." Nor did he employ them without deliberate purpose. He was always very language-conscious, and wrote upon the subject not infrequently. So early as 1872, in "Roughing It," he testified to his delight in "the vigorous new vernacular of the occidental plains and mountains," and in a prefatory note to "Huckleberry Finn," in 1884, he showed a pardonable pride in his grasp of it by warning his readers that what followed attempted to differentiate between "the Missouri negro dialect, the extremest form of the backwoods Southwestern dialect, the ordinary Pike County dialect, and four modified varieties of this last." [6] There was a chapter, "Concerning the American Language," crowded out of "A Tramp Abroad" in 1880, which antedated all the enormous accumulation of latter-day writing on the subject. In it he said:

> Our changed conditions and the spread of our people far to the
> South and far to the West have made many alterations in our
> pronunciation, and have introduced new words among us and changed
> the meaning of many old ones. . . . A nation's language is . . . not

---

and paid him $1,000 in cash, apparently as an indemnity for 44 years' lofty neglect of him.

[5] *University of Missouri Studies*, Jan. 1, 1938. Dr. Emberson's Mark Twain's Vocabulary: A General Survey was published in the same series. [Some qualifications of Ramsay and Emberson's con-

clusions are discussed in Backgrounds of Mark Twain's Vocabulary, by Charles J. Lovell, *AS*, Vol. XXII, Apr. 1947, pp. 88–98.]

[6] An attempt to sort out some of these dialects is made in Mark Twain and American Dialects, by Katherine Buxbaum, *AS*, Vol. II, Feb. 1927, pp. 233–6.

simply a manner of speech obtaining among the educated handful; the manner obtaining among the vast uneducated multitude must be considered also. . . . English and American are separate languages. . . . When I speak my native tongue in its utmost purity an Englishman can't understand me at all.[7]

Mark's influence upon the development of American prose was large, but most of his immediate contemporaries fought against it. William Dean Howells, however, came out in the Editor's Study of *Harper's Magazine*, in January 1886, for American autonomy in speech. "Languages, while they live," he said, "are perpetually changing. God apparently meant them for the common people . . . and the common people will use them freely, as they use other gifts of God. On their lips our continental English will differ more from the insular English, and we believe that this is not deplorable, but desirable." In the same article Howells advised the young American novelists of the day to give their ears to the regional speechways, and quoted what Alphonse Daudet once said of Turgenev: "What a luxury it must be to have a big untrodden barbarian language to wade into!" "We hope," he concluded, "that our inherited English may be constantly freshened and revived from the native sources which literary decentralization will help to keep open."

The spirit of the time, however, was against yielding to the national speech habits, and most of its other salient writers were not only careful conformists to English precept and example in their writing but abject colonials otherwise. A typical, if minor, example was Henry Van Dyke, now chiefly remembered, if at all, for his lachrymose sermon in fiction, "The Other Wise Man," but in the period 1890–1910 an arbiter of literary elegance as well as a prolific author of miscellaneous inanities. At the 1923 Conference of British and American Professors of English at Columbia University, he declared that "the proposal to make a new American language to fit our vast country may be regarded either as a specimen of American humor or as a serious enormity."[8] He was echoed by Fred Newton Scott, of the University of Michigan, who denounced my burlesque translation of the Declaration of Independence into the American vulgate,[9] quite seriously, as a crime against humanity, fit "for the hair shirt and the lash, or tears of shame and self-abasement." A year or two later Van Dyke and seven of his colleagues published "Academy Pa-

---

[7] Concerning the American Language was included in The Stolen White Elephant; Boston, 1882. [See also John J. Hoben, Mark Twain: On the Writer's Use of Language, *AS*, Vol. XXXI, Oct. 1956, pp. 163–71; and Robert J. Lowenherz, Mark Twain on Usage, *AS*, Vol. XXXIII, Feb. 1958, pp. 70–2.]

[8] Van Dyke Scoffs at Ideas of New Language in U.S., New York *Tribune*, June 4.

[9] AL3, pp. 398–401.

pers: Addresses on Language Problems," a series of earnest pleas for a rigid yielding to English standards, with bitter flings at all the current American authors guilty of stooping to the use of Americanisms. The most idiotic chapter in this preposterous volume was by Van Dyke himself: in it he denounced Carl Sandburg with Calvinistic rancor, and said of "The Spoon River Anthology" (including "Ann Rutledge"!) that "to call it poetry is to manhandle a sacred word."

In recent years the American idiom has been discussed by authors as diverse as Vachel Lindsay and Rupert Hughes, Ernest Boyd and Richard Burton,[1] who, with a long career as a teacher of English behind him, declared: "The pundit, the pedant, and the professor who are fain to stem the turbid tide of the popular vernacular may suffer pain; but they can have little influence on the situation. Even college-bred folk revert to type and use people's speech—when they are from under the restraining, corrective monitions of academic haunts—in a way to shock, amuse, or encourage, according to the point of view." [2] Hughes has often written on the subject with great vigor. "Could anyone imagine an English author hesitating to use a word because of his concern as to the ability of American readers to understand it and approve it? . . . Why should we permit the survival of the curious notion that our language is a mere loan from England, like a copper kettle that we must keep scoured and return without a dent?"

Lindsay, who gave the subtitle "Rhymes in the American Language" to "The Golden Whales of California," published in 1920, had his say on "The Real American Language" in the *American Mercury* for March 1928. He began by recounting "a few delusions in regard to the United States language." One of them, he said, "is that it came in with the ultra-flappers and the most saxophonish of the jazz, after Armistice Day." Another is that "the United States language is a New York novelty."

> It is really a new vocabulary arranged on an old British framework. It is true that the new vocabulary pours every day into our growing dictionaries, but this vocabulary is apt to mislead one. A smart phrase or new word is not the United States language. The very framework is as old as the writings of Captain John Smith of Virginia.

To which may be added a few reflections by Ernest Boyd:

> The time has passed when the English language could be claimed as the exclusive idiom of Britain, much less of any restricted area

---

[1] [See also J. H. Neumann, American Newspaper Interest in English Language Problems, *AS*, Vol. XX, May 1945, pp. 99–105.]

[2] English As She Is Spoken, *Bookman*, July 1920.

of England. Today it is the tongue of millions who have no other language, but have also no other tie with the mother country from which English came. There is no authority which can enforce the recognition of a Standard English that does not exist, save in the imagination of a few people in London. When these people write or speak they betray their place of origin as definitely as a native of New York or Edinburgh. Their assumption that, while the latter are strange and provincial, they are standard and authoritative, is merely an illustration of self-complacent provincialism. It is an assumption which the great English-speaking world does not and cannot admit.[3]

World War II brought on another upsurge of literary colonialism, but this time its leaders were mainly writers of palpable trash. Nevertheless, it will probably keep on showing itself. England is still the fount of honor for America, and almost the only native literati who disdain English approval are those to whom it is plainly sour grapes. But independence and self-respect have grown since the days when Lowell could write:

> *You steal Englishmen's books and think Englishmen's thought;*
> *With their salt on her tail your wild eagle is caught;*
> *Your literature suits its each whisper and motion*
> *To what will be thought of it over the ocean.*[4]

The whole swing of American style, for a half-century past, has been toward greater freedom in the use of essentially national idioms. The tart admonitions of English purists are no longer directed solely or even mainly to writers who need apology at home; the offenders now include many of our best. And they begin to get the understanding and approval of a larger and larger fraction of intelligent Englishmen.[5]

7: THE POLITICAL FRONT

Occasionally politicians looking for popularity propose to establish linguistic independence by the characteristic American device of passing a law, but such plans usually expire in tall talk. They go back to the earliest days of the Republic. William Gifford, the anti-American editor of the *Quarterly Review*, is authority for the story that at the close of the Revolution certain members of Congress proposed that English be formally pro-

---

[3] Translations, *Saturday Review of Literature*, Dec. 26, 1925.

[4] A Fable for Critics, 1848.

[5] [Studies of the usage of representative authors after World War II include Hensley C. Woodbridge, Slang in Farrell's "Young Lonigan," *AS*, Vol. XXXVI, Oct. 1961, pp. 225–9; C. Merton Babcock, Americanisms in the Novels of Sinclair Lewis, *AS*, Vol. XXXV, May 1960, pp. 110–16; Donald P. Costello, The Language of "The Catcher in the Rye," *AS*, Vol. XXXIV, Oct. 1959, pp. 172–81.]

hibited in the United States, and Hebrew substituted for it.[6] The substitution of Greek for Hebrew in this legend was apparently made by Charles Astor Bristed in his essay "The English Language in America" (1855).[7] But Bristed probably intended to be jocular, for he reported that Congress had rejected the proposal on the ground that "it would be more convenient for us to keep the language as it is, and make the English speak Greek." Eight years earlier a German named Franz Loher had alleged that, in Pennsylvania, an effort had been made to displace English with German.[8] The story, afloat a long while, was finally discovered to be a fable based upon a misunderstanding. The proposal before Congress in 1794 was simply to provide for the publication of some of the laws in a German translation, for the accommodation of immigrants—in Virginia, not Pennsylvania—who had not yet learned English. A petition from the Virginia Germans was favorably reported, on two occasions, but both times was voted down on the floor of the House.[9] Such translations of state laws, however, had already appeared in two of the states—in Pennsylvania in 1776, 1778, 1785, 1786 and 1787, and in Maryland in 1787. The Germans of Pennsylvania were extraordinarily tenacious of their mother tongue, and even to this day thousands of their descendants speak it.[1]

[Louisiana still has half a million speakers of French; in the bayou country of southwestern Louisiana, where the Acadians from Nova Scotia were dumped in the Eighteenth Century, it is possible to pass through high school without acquiring a nodding acquaintance with any variety of English.] French is still permitted in the courts of the state, and the constitution of 1819 permitted the legislature to publish the laws in French for the convenience of the French-speaking parishes (counties). Under that discretion they were so published until 1915 or 1916. In California and Texas, in the early days, the laws were printed in both English and

[6] This charge appeared in the *Quarterly* in Jan. 1814, in the course of a review of Inchiquin, the Jesuit's Letters, . . . Containing a Favorable View of the Manners, Literature and State of Society of the United States, brought out by Charles Jared Ingersoll in 1810. Gifford apparently lifted this tale from the Marquis de Chastellux, who served as a major general under Rochambeau during the Revolution and printed Voyages dans l'Amérique septentrionale in 1786 (English translation in 2 vols.; London, 1787, New York, 1828). See Allen Walker Read, The Philological Society of New York, *AS*, Vol. IX, Apr. 1934, p. 131.

[7] [The story is repeated in Randolph Quirk, The Use of English; London, 1962, pp. 2–3.]

[8] Franz Loher, Geschichte und Zustande der Deutschen in Amerika; Cincinnati, 1847, pp. 194–8.

[9] Theodore G. Tappert, Language and Legislation, the *Lutheran* (Philadelphia), Nov. 15, 1939, pp. 11–19. The paper is summarized in German the National Language, by W. L. Werner, *American Notes and Queries*, Vol. II, July 1942, p. 64, and in The Official German Language Legend, by the same, *AS*, Vol. XVII, Dec. 1942, p. 246.

[1] [It has been studied seriously by several competent linguists, notably J. William Frey, of Franklin and Marshall College; Carroll E. Reed, of the University of Washington; Paul Schach, of the University of Nebraska; and Lester Seifert, of the University of Wisconsin.]

Spanish. In 1842, after the beginning of the German immigration into Texas, the state legislature ordained that the laws be printed in German also, and in 1858 it added Norwegian.[2] In New Mexico, until 1941, the legislature was bilingual, and the laws were printed in both English and Spanish. Spanish is still permitted in the justices' courts, the probate court and the district courts of the state. There are many New Mexicans who cannot speak English, and when they face a jury which includes members who know little or no Spanish it is necessary to employ interpreters. [Naturally, both political parties are careful to cultivate the Spanish-American vote.] [3]

The English tried to wipe out Dutch in New York after the conquest of the colony in 1664, but it carried on an underground existence for many years. [A few native speakers survived in the remoter parts of the Hudson Valley as late as 1941.[4]] In Baltimore, down to World War I, there were actually public schools, the so-called German-English schools, in which German was used in the teaching of the elements [and many fairly young natives of Cincinnati and Milwaukee are more at home in German than in English].

A committee of the Continental Congress, in 1778, recommended that "the language of the United States" be used in all "replies or answers" to the French ambassador. [Five years later the term "American language" was used in the Continental Congress.[5]] In 1854 William L. Marcy, author of the political maxim "to the victor belong the spoils," then Secretary of State under Pierce, issued instructions to all American diplomatic and consular officers to employ only "the American language" in communicating with him. After another septuagenarian interval, on May 9, 1927, Andrew W. Mellon, as Secretary of the Treasury, ordered that the redemption call for the Second Liberty Loan be advertised "in every daily paper printed in the American language throughout the United States."

In the *North American Review* for April 1820, Edward Everett printed "a *jeu d'esprit* which has fallen in our way, under the name of 'Report of Resolutions to be proposed in the House of Representatives' . . . to return the compliment paid to us by the Marquis of Lansdowne, in the session [of Parliament] of 1819, in moving for an inquiry into the conduct

---

[2] State Laws in Other Languages, by Richard F. Burges, *American Notes and Queries*, Vol. III, Dec. 1943, p. 144.

[3] On Oct. 25, 1943, the Associated Press reported from Yuma, Ariz., that a magistrate there, J. T. Hodges, had that day tried and sentenced three successive prisoners in an Indian language, in English and in Spanish.

[4] [One of them, in Bergen County,

N.J., was interviewed for the Linguistic Atlas early in 1941 by Guy S. Lowman, Jr. See William Z. Shetter, A Final Word on Jersey Dutch, *AS*, Vol. XXXIII, Dec. 1958, pp. 243–51.]

[5] [See Early Examples of the Expression "American Language" and "langue américaine," by Joseph M. Carrière, *MLN*, Vol. LXXXV, June 1960, pp. 485–8.]

of General Jackson." The resolutions, probably concocted by Everett himself or by one of his collaborators on the *North American*, began with long satirical whereases directed at the English reviewers, and proceeded to deplore the corruption of the language in the Motherland, "to the degree that the various dialects which prevail, such as those in Yorkshire, Somersetshire, and Cumberland, at the same time that they are in themselves utterly uncouth and hideous, are unintelligible to anyone but a person born and educated in these counties respectively." Then came this:

> The House further regards, as still more pernicious, . . . that barbarity which from various causes is fast creeping into the language of the highest and best educated classes of society in England . . . an affectation, at one time, of forgotten old words, and at another of pedantic new ones, each equally unauthorized in a pure and chaste style of writing and of speaking.

Finally, after a sonorous declaration that in the United States the language has been "preserved in a state of admirable purity" and was, "by the blessing of God, quite untainted with most of the above mentioned vulgarities prevalent in the highest English circles," the resolutions concluded:

> *Resolved*, in consideration of these premises, that the nobility and gentry of England be courteously invited to send their elder sons, and such others as may be destined to appear as public speakers in church or state, to America, for their education, that the President of the United States be requested to concert measures with the presidents and heads of our colleges and schools for the prompt reception and gratuitous instruction of such young persons, and to furnish them, after the expiration of a term of —— years, certificates of their proficiency in the English tongue.

The Midwest has always been the chief center of linguistic chauvinism, and so early as 1838, the legislature of Indiana, in establishing the state university, provided that it should instruct the youth of the new Commonwealth "in the American, learned and foreign languages and literature." Nearly a century later, in 1923, there was a violent upsurging of the same patriotic spirit. The Hon. Washington Jay McCormick, then a Republican member of the House of Representatives from Montana, offered a bill in Congress making the American language official. It was dealt with jocosely by most of the newspapers that noticed it at all, but a few discussed it more seriously—for example, the Portland *Oregonian*, which said:

> Notwithstanding the obvious chauvinism of the movement, more might be said in its behalf if it were practicable to designate spe-

cifically, as the Montana congressman would do, which are the "words and phrases generally accepted as being in good use by the people of the United States." Right here the difficulty lies. Neither in the United States nor in England is there an equivalent of the French academy as a recognized arbiter of propriety in diction. With certain not very well-defined exceptions, language is with us largely a matter of individual preference.[6]

The McCormick bill died in the House Judiciary Committee, but others substantially like it were offered in the legislatures of various states. One of them was signed by Governor Len Small, of Illinois, on June 19, 1923, and is still on the books of the state as Chapter 127, Section 178, of the Acts of the Legislature of that year. Its father was a Chicago legislator bearing the ancient Irish name of Frank Ryan, and the Chicago papers, then in the midst of their gory battle with Mayor Big Bill Thompson, professed to see the same Anglophobia in it that prompted His Honor's historic warning to King George V to keep out of Chicago. The *News* headed a sneering article on the new law "Illinois State Assembly Adopts Menckenese as Official Language," and then proceeded to the astonishing disclosure that "the term *American Language* was first substituted for *English* by the Germans during the war, because of their hatred of all things English."[7] The New York *Sun*, rather less upset by Big Bill, had thus commented on the act while it was still before the legislature:

> There was a time in American life when it was possible to be both well-fed and 100% American by ordering *liberty cabbage;* in these saner times *sauerkraut* is to be found on the bill-of-fare. Giving a new tag to our language would be just such an adventure in hair splitting.[8]

As finally enacted, the Ryan Law read:

> *Whereas,* Since the creation of the American Republic there have been certain Tory elements in our country who have never become reconciled to our republican institutions and have ever clung to the tradition of King and Empire; and
>
> *Whereas,* America has been a haven of liberty and place of opportunity for the common people of all nations; and
>
> *Whereas,* These strangers within our gates who seek economic betterment, political freedom, larger opportunities for their children and citizenship for themselves, come to think of our institutions as American and our language as the American language; and
>
> *Whereas,* The name of the language of a country has a powerful

---

[6] The "American" Language (editorial), Mar. 1, 1923.

[7] July 25, 1923.

[8] We Still Understand English (editorial), Apr. 9, 1923.

psychological influence in stimulating and preserving the national ideal; and

Whereas, The languages of other countries bear the names of the countries to which they belong, . . . now therefore

Sec. 1. Be it enacted by the People of the State of Illinois, represented in the General Assembly: The official language of the State of Illinois shall be known hereafter as the "American" language and not as the "English" language.

But all the similar bills introduced in other legislatures seem to have failed of passage.

In February 1934, the Hon. Fred A. Britten, of Chicago, moved in the national House of Representatives that the members of the American *corps diplomatique* be instructed to carry on their legerdemain in American. "When an American envoy begins to *lawf* and *cawf* and ape the British, he ought to be brought home and kept here until he speaks the language as we speak it in the United States." [9] Early in 1937 a state senator of North Dakota named William A. Thatcher introduced a resolution declaring that American, not English, should be the language of that state; it was passed by the Senate, but killed in the House of Representatives. On June 3, 1940, Senator Claude D. Pepper, of Florida, in the course of a speech advocating all-out aid for the English and their allies, nevertheless gave formal notice that a resolution he had introduced to that effect was "set down in the American language, in black and white." [In 1952 a bill similar to the Illinois one was introduced in the Massachusetts legislature, but it got nowhere.[1]]

Meanwhile, the plain people of England and the United States, whenever they come into contact, find it difficult to effect a fluent exchange of ideas. This was made distressingly apparent during both world wars. Fraternizing between American troops and the British was impeded not so much by hereditary animosities as by the wide divergence in vocabulary and pronunciation. There was very little movement of slang from one camp to the other, and that mainly from the American side to the British. The YMCA, always pathetically eager for popularity, made a characteristic effort to turn to account the feeling of strangeness among the Americans. In the Chicago *Tribune*'s Paris edition of July 7, 1917, is a large advertisement inviting them to make use of the YMCA clubhouse in the Avenue Montaigne, "where *American* is spoken." At about the same time an enterprising London tobacconist, Peters by name, affixed a sign bearing the legend "*American* spoken here" to the front of his shop, and soon he

---

[9] Diplomats Should Be Understood (editorial), San Antonio *News*, Feb. 15, 1934.

[1] [The full text is printed in *The New Yorker*, Aug. 23, 1952, p. 41.]

was imitated by hundreds of other London, Liverpool and Paris shop-keepers. Such signs are familiar all over Europe, and they have begun to appear in Asia.

8: FOREIGN OBSERVERS

The Continental awareness of the differences between English and American is demonstrated by the fact that some of the popular German *Sprach-führer* now appear in separate editions, *Amerikanisch* and *Englisch*. There are many special guides to the American language in German—*e.g.*, "Uncle Sam and His English," by W. K. Pfeiler and Elisabeth Wittman (Berlin, 1932); and "Spoken American," by S. A. Nock and H. Mutschmann (Leipzig, 1930). It is also dealt with at length in various more general guides—*e.g.*, "Hauptfragen der Amerikakunde," by Walther Fischer (Bielefeld, 1928); "The American Wonderland," by S. A. Nock and G. Kamisch (Leipzig, 1930); and "America of Today," by Frau Voight-Goldsmith and D. Borschard (Berlin, 1929). Nor is it overlooked by pedagogues. In 1936 the Lessing Hochschule in Berlin offered courses in both Amerikanisch and Englisch—two for *Anfänger,* one for *Vorge-bildete* and one for *Fortgeschrittene.* The standard guidebooks for tourists always call attention to the differences between the English and American vocabularies. Baedeker's "United States" has a glossary for Englishmen likely to be daunted by such terms as *el, European plan* and *sundae,* and in Muirhead's "London and Its Environs" there is a corresponding one for Americans, warning them that *bug* means only *bedbug* in England, that a *clerk* there is never a shopman, that *homely* means domestic, unpretending, homelike, never plain-looking, and giving the meaning of *trunk call, hoarding, goods train, spanner* and *minerals.*

From the earliest days the peculiarities of American have attracted the attention of Continental philologians, and especially of the Germans. The first edition of Bartlett's Glossary (1848) brought forth a long review by Dr. Felix Flügel in the *Archiv für das Studium der neueren Sprachen und Literaturen* (Braunschweig), and four years later "Die englische Philologie in Nordamerika" in *Gersdorf's Reportorium.* In 1854 appeared the Dutch "Woordenboek van Americanismen," by M. Keijzer (Gorinchem, Holland), based on the first edition of Bartlett, and in 1866 the German "Wörterbuch der Americanismen" by Friedrich Köhler (Leipzig), based on Bartlett's third edition. The third edition of the present work was translated into German with a commentary by Heinrich Spies of Berlin.[2] In the German philological journals there have been frequent discus-

---

[2] Die Amerikanische Sprache (Das Englisch der Vereinigten Staaten) von   H. L. Mencken; Deutsche Bearbeitung von Heinrich Spies; Leipzig, 1927.

sions by Johannes Hoops, Walther Fischer and others. [During World War II many German *Gelehrte* came in intimate contact with American speechways, both informally in the hospitals and prisoner-of-war camps of both nations, and formally as a part of the American denazification program when hostilities ceased.[3] Under the Fulbright program—the post-war academic fraternization sponsored and partially subsidized by the State Department—many American linguists have lectured on the national idiom at German institutions, including C. C. Fries and A. H. Marckwardt, of Michigan, David W. Maurer, of Louisville, and Thomas Pyles, of Florida. In turn, several new treatments of American English from the German point of view have been published, particularly by Hans Galinsky, of the Johannes Gutenberg Universität at Mainz.[4]]

In 1934 R. W. Zandvoort reported that Americanisms were being picked up in large number by students in the Netherlands and that a demand for their consideration in university courses was in the making. Unhappily, the practical difficulty of giving instruction in two forms of the same language was a serious one, especially since Dutch *Gymnasium* students, by the time they came to English, were already more or less worn out by hard drilling in French, German, Latin and Greek. But Zandvoort and his fellow advocates of American refused to be daunted. "We look upon American English not as a mere lapse from 'good' English, but as a legitimate development, autonomous within its own domain, and from the European point of view subordinate to British English for historical and practical reasons only." [5]

Nor have the differences between Standard English and American been

---

[3] [This program was conducted by Henry Lee Smith, Jr. (now of the University of Buffalo), William G. Moulton (now of Princeton) and Edward Kennard (now of the University of Pittsburgh), with the assistance of a platoon of other linguists and a battalion of teaching assistants.]

[4] [Die Sprache des Amerikaners (Band I, Heidelberg, 1951; Band II, 1952); Amerikanisches und Britisches Englisch, Mainz, 1957. Other important contributions are Gustav H. Blanke, Die Amerikaner: eine sozio-linguistische Studie, Meisenheim am Glan, 1957; Georg Friederici, Amerikanistisches Wörterbuch, 1947; Günter Panten, Die Amerikanismen im "Manchester Guardian Weekly" (1948–54), Munich, 1959; Kurt Wittig, Phonetik des Amerikanisches Englisch, Heidelberg, 1956. For a summary see Die Amerikastudien an den deutschen Universitäten, *Mitteilungsblatt*

der Deutschen Gesellschaft für Amerikastudien, Heft. 5, Munich, 1959.]

[5] [Zandvoort's A Handbook of English Grammar has gone through several editions, and is better than most of its American counterparts. In 1957 he and his assistants published Wartime English: Materials for a Linguistic History of World War II (*Groningen Studies in English*, VI); this omits "exclusively American usages." John Vandenbergh has produced two popular works: Lexicon van het moderne Amerikaans, 's Graveland, 1950; and Zo spreekt Amerika, Hoorn, 1947. Interest in American in France is typified by Étienne Deak, Dictionnaire d'Américanismes; Paris, 1956, 2nd ed., 1957. Norman Eliason has summed up the status of American English in contemporary Europe in American English in Europe, *AS*, Vol. XXXII, Oct. 1957, pp. 163–9.]

noted only in western Europe. In 1858 Czar Nicholas I ordered that "the American language" be included in the curriculum of the Russian military academies. Under the Communists, an interest in American English has continued, largely because of the Russian desire to emulate American industrial technology. [In the great debate on the relative merits of American and Russian education, following Russian success with their sputniks, no one has revealed how many of the millions of Russians studying English are actually becoming familiar with the American variety,[6] but works on American usage are in great demand in both the Soviet Union and the satellite countries, and academic visitors from behind the Iron Curtain show a lively interest in the current slang as well as in the more decorous varieties of American.] Even the now sovietized Baltic Republics produced their Americanists. At Tartu-Dorpat in Estonia, Heinrich Mutschmann, professor of English in the university there, printed a "Glossary of Americanisms" (1931) which is much better than any that has come out in America since Thornton's.

In 1861 a memorial petitioned the Chinese Emperor Hsien-fung to establish a Foreign Office on Western lines, and asked that men be appointed who were familiar with English, French and American. [Missionaries and exchange students kept up the Chinese interest in American until the Communists took over the Celestial Empire; and the presence of American troops on Formosa assures American idioms an inlet into Chinese. Before World War II, several eminent Chinese philologians came to the United States as visiting professors, and some have remained, notably Fang-Kwei Li, of the University of Washington, and Y. R. Chao, of the University of California. Chao, one of the best living phoneticians, has written perceptively on both British and American varieties of English.]

But it is the Japanese who have taken the liveliest interest in American peculiarities of speech and have shown the keenest understanding of their significance. In this work they have been given active aid by Western teachers of English resident in Japan, including several Englishmen. Among the latter was H. E. Palmer, linguistic adviser to the Japanese Ministry of Education, who, when he brought out "A Dictionary of English Pronunciation" in 1926, included "With American Variants" in its title, and listed hundreds of them.[7] The literature on Americanisms in Japanese is already of some weight. It includes an excellent formal treatise, "English and American of Today," by G. Tomita (1930), which not only discusses the differences between the English and American

---

[6] [See The Teaching of English in the Soviet Middle School, *EJ*, Vol. XLVIII, Oct. 1959, pp. 393–7. Some indications of recent Russian and Polish interest in American and British English are found in Margaret Schlauch, The English Language in Modern Times; Warsaw, 1959.]

[7] This useful work was written in collaboration with J. Victor Martin, also resident in Japan, and F. G. Blandford. It was published in Cambridge, England, but Palmer's preface was dated Tokyo.

vocabularies but also gives an account of the grammar of vulgar American. Satoshi Ichiya, a well-known journalist, has set English and American in direct opposition in "King's English or President's English?" [8] and decided that the Japanese had better learn American. [Under the American occupation following World War II, the opportunities for the Japanese to learn American naturally increased, and several distinguished American linguists have helped organize a nation-wide program for teaching English in the Japanese public schools.] As in Germany, there is a considerable scholarly and popular literature on the English language, with notes on American variants.[9] In the days before World War II all the stewards and waiters on the Japanese Pacific liners were provided with handbooks instructing them in the mysteries of English idiom, with special attention to the idioms of Americans.

The feeling of many American philologians that the serious study of the common speech of their country is beneath their dignity is not shared by their European colleagues. In England the local dialects have been investigated for many years, and there is a formidable literature on slang, stretching back to the Sixteenth Century and including a glossary in seven large volumes. The Société des Parlers de France makes diligent inquiries into changing forms; moreover, the Académie itself is endlessly concerned with the subject. In Germany there are admirable grammars of the principal dialects. In Sweden there are several journals devoted to the study of the vulgate, and the government grants a generous annual subvention to an organization of scholars formed to investigate it systematically. In Norway there is a widespread movement to overthrow the official Dano-Norwegian and substitute a national language based on the speech of the peasants.[1] In Spain the Academia Española de la Lengua is constantly at work upon its great Diccionario, Ortografía and Grammática, taking in new words and new forms of old ones. And in Latin America, the native philologists have produced a large literature on the matter closest at hand: the Portuguese of Brazil and the variations of Spanish in Mexico, the Argentine, Chile, Peru, Ecuador, Uruguay and even Honduras and Costa Rica.

---

[8] Kobe, n.d.

[9] [Typical are Studies in English Grammar and Linguistics: A Miscellany in honour of Takanoba Otsuka, ed. by Kazuo Araki, Taiichiro Egawa, Toshiko Oyama and Minoru Yasui, Tokyo, 1958; and four studies by Jiro Takenaka: Studies in American Pronunciation, Tokyo, 1938; The Background of the American Language, Tokyo, 1948; An Anglo-American Dictionary, Tokyo, 1949; and The Outline of the American Language, Tokyo, 1949. Some of the more recent works of Fries and other American linguists first reached print in Japan.]

[1] This movement owes its start to Ivar Aasen (1813–96), who published a grammar of the *landsmaal*, or peasant speech, in 1848, and a dictionary in 1850. It won official recognition in 1885. [It is now favored by the Norwegian government, and called *Nynorsk* (New Norse).] See The Linguistic Development of Ivar Aasen's New Norse, by Einar Haugen, *PMLA*, Vol. XLVIII, Pt. 1, 1933.

I I

The Materials of
Inquiry

1: THE HALLMARKS OF AMERICAN

The characters chiefly noted in American English are, first, its general uniformity throughout the country; second, its impatient disregard for grammatical, syntactical and phonological rule and precedent; and third, its large capacity (distinctly greater than that of the English of present-day England) for taking in new words and phrases from outside sources, and for manufacturing them of its own materials.

The first of these characters has struck every observer, native and foreign. In place of the discordant local dialects of nearly all the other major countries, including England, we have a general *Volkssprache* for the whole nation, conditioned only by minor differences in pronunciation and vocabulary and by the linguistic struggles of various groups of newcomers. No other country can show such linguistic solidarity, not even Canada, for there a large minority of the population resists speaking English altogether. The Little Russian of the Ukraine is unintelligible to the citizen of Moscow; the northern Italian can scarcely follow a conversation in Sicilian; the Low German from Hamburg is a foreigner in Munich; the Breton flounders in Gascony. Even in the United Kingdom there are wide divergences. There are some regional peculiarities in American English, and they will be examined in Chapter VII, but all Americans use pretty much the same words in the same way.

Of the intrinsic differences that separate American from English the chief have their roots in the disparity between the environment and traditions of the two peoples since the Seventeenth Century. The English have lived under a relatively stable social order, and it has impressed upon their souls their characteristic respect for what is customary and of good report. Their whole lives are regulated by a regard for precedent. [Until the 1950s] the Americans felt no such restraint and acquired no such habit of conformity. They plunged to the other extreme, for life in their country put a high value upon the qualities of curiosity and daring, and so they acquired that character of restlessness, that disdain for the dead hand, which still broadly marks them. The American is not, of course, lacking in a capacity for discipline; he submits to leadership readily, and even to tyranny. But, curiously, it is not the leadership that is old and decorous that commonly fetches him, but the leadership that is new and extravagant [—even when, as in the demagogue-infested South, it purports to defend tradition]. He will resist dictation out of the past, but he will follow a new messiah with almost Russian willingness, and into the wildest vagaries of economics, religion, morals and speech. A new fallacy in politics spreads faster in the United States than anywhere else on earth, and so does a new revelation of God, or a new shibboleth, or metaphor, or piece of slang. The American likes to make his language as he goes along. A novelty loses nothing by the fact that it is a novelty, particularly if it meets the national fancy for the terse, the vivid and, above all, the bold and imaginative. The characteristic American habit of reducing complex concepts to the starkest abbreviations was already noticeable in colonial times, and such typical Americanisms as *O.K.*, *N.G.* and *P.D.Q.* have been traced back to the early days of the Republic. In so modest an operation as that which has evolved *bunk* from *buncombe* there is evidence of a phenomenon which the philologian recognizes as belonging to the most lusty stages of speech.

But more important than the sheer inventions, if only because more numerous, are the extensions of the vocabulary by the devices of rhetoric. The American, from the beginning, has been the most ardent of recorded rhetoricians. His politics bristles with pungent epithets; his whole history has been bedizened with tall talk; his fundamental institutions rest far more upon brilliant phrases than upon logical ideas. He exercises continually an incomparable capacity for projecting hidden and often fantastic relationships into his speech. Such a term as *rubberneck* is almost a complete treatise on American psychology; it has precisely the boldness and contempt for ordered forms that are so characteristically American. The same qualities are in *roughhouse, has-been, lame duck* and a thousand other such racy substantives, and in all the great stock of native verbs and adjectives. There is, indeed, but a shadowy boundary in these new coinages between the various parts of speech. *Corral,* borrowed from the Spanish, immediately becomes a verb and the father of an adjective. *Bust,* carved out of *burst,* erects itself into a noun. *Bum,* coming by way of an earlier *bummer* from the German, becomes noun, adjective, verb and adverb. Verbs are fashioned out of substantives: *to engineer, to stump, to hog, to style.* Others are made by torturing nouns with harsh affixes, as *to burglarize* and *to itemize,* or by groping for the root, as *to resurrect* and *to jell.* Yet others are changed from intransitive to transitive: a sleeping car *sleeps* thirty passengers.

All these processes are to be observed in the history of the English of England; at the time of its sturdiest growth they flourished. More than one observer has noted the likeness between the situation of American English today and that of British English at the end of the Sixteenth Century. The Englishmen of that time had not yet come under the yoke of grammarians and lexicographers, and were free to mold their language to the throng of new ideas that marked an era of adventure and expansion. Their situation closely resembled that of the American pioneers who swarmed into the West following the War of 1812, and they met linguistic needs with the same boldness. By a happy accident they had a group of men who could bring to the business of word-making a degree of ingenuity and taste far beyond the common; above all, they had the aid of a really first-rate genius, Shakespeare. The result was a renovation of old ways of speech and a proliferation of new and useful terms that has had no parallel, to date, save on this side of the Atlantic [and, to a lesser degree, in Australia]. Standard English, in the Eighteenth Century, succumbed to pedants whose ignorance of language processes was only equaled by their impudent assumption of authority: Swift, Horace Walpole, Thomas Gray of the oft-misquoted "Elegy" and, above all, Samuel Johnson. No eminent lexicographer was ever more ignorant of speechways than he was. In his Dictionary of 1755 he thundered idiotically against many words that are now universally recognized as sound English, *e.g., to wabble, to bamboozle* and *touchy. To wabble* he described as "low, barbarous," and *to bamboozle* and *touchy* as "low," and at other times he denounced *to swap, to coax, to budge, fib, banter, fop, fun, stingy, swimmingly, row* (in the sense of a disturbance), *chaperon* and *to derange.* Under the influence of Johnson and his Nineteenth Century apes, the Standard Southern dialect of English has been arrested in its growth and burdened with irrational affectations. Its tendency is to combat all that expansive gusto which made for its pliancy and resilience in the days of Shakespeare. In place of the old loose-footedness there is a preciosity which, in one direction, takes the form of clumsy artificialities in the spoken language, and in another shows itself in the even clumsier Johnsonese of so much current English writing—the jargon denounced by Sir Arthur Quiller-Couch in his Cambridge lectures [and more recently by Sir Ernest Gowers, of Her Majesty's Stationery Office [1].

American has so far escaped such suffocating formalism. Of course, we have our occasional practitioners of the authentic English jargon [and have seen some weird mutations develop under the green thumbs of federal bureaucrats, educationists, literary critics and the gray-flanneled admen of Madison Avenue]. "Once upon a time," says Jacques Barzun, of Columbia University, "American speech was really known for its racy, colloquial creations—*barnstorm, boom, boost, bulldoze, pan out, splurge* and so on. Now it is the flaccid polysyllable that expresses the country's mind. Pioneer has yielded to pedant, and one begins to wonder whether the German word-order had better not be adopted to complete the system." [2] What fevers Barzun, of course, is the artificial pseudo-English that school-ma'ams, whether in panties or in pantaloons, try to foist upon their victims, and the even worse jargon that Dogberrys in and out of office use for their revelations to the multitude. But in the main our faults lie in precisely the opposite direction. That is to say, we incline toward a directness of state-ment which, at its greatest, lacks restraint and urbanity altogether, and toward a hospitality which often admits novelties for the mere sake of their novelty, and is quite uncritical of the difference between a genuine improvement in succinctness and clarity, and mere extravagant raciness.

This revolt against conventional bounds and restraints is most noticeable, of course, on the lower levels of American speech. But even in the upper regions there are rebels aplenty, some of such authority that it is impossible to dismiss them. A glance through the speeches of Woodrow Wilson, a conscientious purist and Anglomaniac, reveals in a few moments half a dozen locutions that an Englishman in like position would certainly hesitate to use, among them *we must get a move on*,[3] *to gumshoe*,[4] and *that is going some*.[5] John Dewey, the country's most respectable metaphysician, unhesitatingly used *dope* for *opium*.[6] In recent years certain English magnificoes have shown signs of going the same route, but whenever they yield they are accused, and rightly, of succumbing to American influence.

Let American confront a novel problem alongside English, and immedi-ately its superior imaginativeness and resourcefulness become obvious. *Movie* is better than *cinema* [—though the English *telly* excels *video* or

[1] [Plain Words, London, 1948; The ABC of Plain Words, London, 1951; The Complete Plain Words, London, 1954.]

[2] How to Suffocate the English Lan-guage, *Saturday Review of Literature*, Feb. 13, 1943, p. 3.

[3] Speech before the Chamber of Com-merce Convention, Washington, Feb. 19, 1916.

[4] Wit and Wisdom of Woodrow Wil-son, comp. by Richard Linthicum; New York, 1916, p. 54.

[5] *Ibid.*, p. 56.

[6] *New Republic*, Dec. 24, 1919, p. 116.

even *TV*]. *Billboard* is better than *hoarding*. *Officeholder* is more honest, more picturesque, more thoroughly Anglo-Saxon than *public servant*. Turn to the terminology of *railroading* (itself, by the way, an Americanism): its creation fell upon the two peoples equally, but they tackled the job independently. The English, seeking a figure to describe the wedge-shaped fender in front of a locomotive, called it a *plough;* the American gave it the pungent name of *cowcatcher*. So with the casting which guides the wheels from one rail to another. The English called it a *crossing-plate;* the Americans, more responsive to the suggestion in its shape, called it a *frog*. One pictures the common materials of English dumped into a pot, exotic flavorings added, and the bubblings assiduously and expectantly skimmed. "When we Americans are through with the English language," says Mr. Dooley, "it will look as if it had been run over by a musical comedy."

All this boldness of conceit, of course, makes for vulgarity. It flowers in such barbaric inventions as *tasty, goof* and *semi-occasional*. But vulgarity, after all, means no more than yielding to natural impulses in the face of conventional inhibitions—the heart of all healthy language-making. The history of English, like the history of American and of every other living tongue, is a history of vulgarisms that, by their accurate meeting of real needs, have forced their way into sound usage, and even into the lifeless catalogues of the grammarians. In our own case the greater conservatism of the English restrains our native tendency to go too far, but the process itself is as inexorable in its workings as the precession of the equinoxes, and if we yield to it more eagerly than the English, it is only a proof, perhaps, that the future of what was once the Anglo-Saxon tongue lies on this side of the water.

Attempts to force the language into a strait jacket all come to grief in America, though the schoolma'am to this day clings to the doctrine that there is such a thing as "correct English," that its principles have been laid down for all time by the English purists and that she is under a moral obligation to inculcate it. But not many American grammarians above the level of writers of school texts subscribe to any such idea. They have learned by their studies that every healthy language has ways of its own, and that those of vernacular American are very far from those of Johnsonese English. Said Robert G. Pooley in his presidential address to the National Council of Teachers of English in 1941:

American English may be derided by conservative critics for the readiness with which neologisms become accepted and flash overnight to all parts of our land, but the fact itself is a sign of health. The purpose of a language is to communicate; if a new word or a new phrase carries with it a freshness of meaning, a short cut to communication, it is a desirable addition to our tongue, no matter how low its source, or how questionable its etymology. We need not fear word creation as harmful; what we must fear is crystallization, the preservation of a conventional vocabulary by a limited minority who resent the normal steady changes which inevitably must take place within a language. . . . We need not fear exuberance. What we must fear and guard against is senility, the complacency of old age, which is content with things as they are and mockingly derisive of change.[7]

2: WHAT IS AN AMERICANISM?

As we have seen, Americanisms were first defined by the Rev. John Witherspoon in 1781 as "ways of speaking peculiar to this country." Pickering in turn divided them into three categories:

1. "We have formed some new words."

2. "To some old ones, that are still in use in England, we have affixed new significations."

3. "Others, which have been long obsolete in England, are still retained in common use among us."

The other early writers on the subject did not attempt to define categories of Americanisms.[8] Noah Webster omitted all discussion of them from his "Dissertations on the English Language" (1789), and not before the preface of his American Dictionary of 1828 did he undertake any formal consideration of them:

Language is the expression of ideas; and if the people of one country cannot preserve an identity of ideas they cannot retain an identity of language. Now, an identity of ideas depends materially upon the sameness of things or objects with which the people of the two countries are conversant. But in no two portions of the earth, remote from each other, can such identity be found. Even physical objects must be different. But the principal differences between the people of this country and of all others arise from different forms of government, different laws, institutions and customs.

---

[7] One People, One Language, *EJ*, Vol. XXXI, Feb. 1942, pp. 110–20.

[8] One of them, the Rev. Jonathan Boucher, alleged in the preface to his Glossary of Archaic and Provincial Words (2nd. ed., London, 1832, p. xlix) that the only additions the Americans had made to the English vocabulary were "such as they have adapted either from naval or mercantile men, with whom, on their first settlement, they were principally connected, or else from the aboriginal inhabitants," but the evidence offered by a poem from his hand, printed in the same volume, was strongly against him.

The other lexicographers of the Webster era attempted no categories of Americanisms: David Humphreys, whose glossary of 1815 has been noticed; and Theodoric Romeyn Beck, whose "Notes on Mr. Pickering's Vocabulary" was published in 1830. Robley Dunglison, in the articles headed "Americanisms" in the *Virginia Museum* for 1829–30, contented himself with setting up two classes—"old words used in a new sense," and "new words of indigenous origin." He excluded old words preserved or revived in America in their original sense. Also, he frowned upon native inventions that were not absolutely essential. The English travelers who denounced Americanisms were negligent about defining them. William C. Fowler, in his brief chapter on "American Dialects" in "The English Language" (1850), offered the following formidable classification, the first after Pickering:

1. Words borrowed from other languages.
   a. Indian, as *Kennebec, Ohio, sagamore, succotash*.
   b. Dutch, as *boss, stoop*.
   c. German, as *spuke* [?], *sauerkraut*.
   d. French, as *bayou, cache, levee*.
   e. Spanish, as *calaboose, hacienda, rancho*.
   f. Negro, as *buckra*.
2. Words "introduced from the necessity of our situation, in order to express new ideas."
   a. Words "connected with and flowing from our political institutions," as *selectman, presidential, mass meeting, lynch law, help* (for *servants*).
   b. Words "connected with our ecclesiastical institutions," as *associational, to fellowship*.
   c. Words "connected with a new country," as *lot, squatter*.
3. Miscellaneous Americanisms.
   a. Words and phrases become obsolete in England, as *talented, offset* (for *set-off*), *back and forth* (for *backward and forward*).
   b. Old words and phrases "which are now merely provincial in England," as *hub, to wilt*.
   c. Nouns formed from verbs by adding the French suffix -*ment*, as *publishment, requirement*.
   d. Forms of words "which fill the gap or vacancy between two words which are approved," as *obligate* (between *oblige* and *obligation*) and *variate* (between *vary* and *variation*).
   e. "Certain compound terms for which the English have different compounds," as *bookstore* (*bookseller's shop*), *bottom land* (*interval-land*), *clapboard* (*pale*), *seaboard* (*seashore*).

f. "Certain colloquial phrases, apparently idiomatic, and very expressive," as *to cave in, to fork over, to hold on, to stave off.*

g. Intensives, "often a matter of mere temporary fashion," as *dreadful, powerful.*

h. "Certain verbs expressing one's state of mind, but partially or timidly," as *to calculate, to expect* (*to think* or *believe*), *to guess, to reckon.*

i. "Certain adjectives, expressing not only quality, but one's subjective feelings in regard to it," as *clever, grand, smart, ugly.*

j. Abridgments, as *stage* (for *stagecoach*), *spry* (for *sprightly*).

k. "Quaint or burlesque terms," as *to tote, humbug, loafer, plunder* (for *baggage*), *rock* (for *stone*).

l. "Low expressions, mostly political," as *locofoco, hunker, to get the hang of.*

m. "Ungrammatical expressions, disapproved by all," as *do don't, used to could, there's no two ways about it.*

John Russell Bartlett, in the second edition of his "Glossary of Words and Phrases Usually Regarded as Peculiar to the United States" (1859), offered nine classes:

1. Archaisms, *i.e.*, old English words, obsolete, or nearly so, in England, but retained in use in this country.

2. English words used in a different sense from what they are in England. "These include many names of natural objects differently applied."

3. Words which have retained their original meaning in the United States, though not in England.

4. English provincialisms adopted into general use in America.

5. New-coined words, which owe their origin to the productions or to the circumstances of the country.

6. Words borrowed from European languages, especially the French, Spanish, Dutch and German.

7. Indian words.

8. Negroisms.

9. Peculiarities of pronunciation.

Alfred L. Elwyn confined his "Glossary of Supposed Americanisms" (1859) to archaic English words surviving in America, and sought only to prove that they had come down "from our remotest ancestry" and were thus undeserving of English scorn. Schele de Vere's "Americanisms" (1872) followed Bartlett, concentrating on borrowings from the Indian languages and from the French, Spanish and Dutch. But John S. Farmer, in his "Americanisms Old and New" (1889), ventured upon a new classification, prefacing it with the following definition:

> An Americanism may be defined as a word or phrase, old or new, employed by general or respectable usage in America in a way not sanctioned by the best standards of the English language. . . . However, the term has come to possess a wider meaning, and it is now applied not only to words and phrases which can be so described, but also to the new and legitimately born words adapted to the general needs and usages, to the survivals of an older type of English than that now current in the mother country, and to the racy, pungent vernacular of Western life.

He then proceeded to this classification:

1. Words and phrases of purely American derivation, embracing words originating in:
   a. Indian and aboriginal life.
   b. Pioneer and frontier life.
   c. The church.
   d. Politics.
   e. Trades of all kinds.
   f. Travel, afloat and ashore.
2. Words brought by colonists, including:
   a. The German element.
   b. The French.
   c. The Spanish.
   d. The Dutch.
   e. The Negro.
   f. The Chinese.
3. Names of American things, embracing:
   a. Natural products.
   b. Manufactured articles.
4. Perverted English words.
5. Obsolete English words still in good use in America.
6. English words, American by inflection and modification.
7. Odd and ignorant popular phrases, proverbs, vulgarisms and colloquialisms, cant and slang.
8. Individualisms.
9. Doubtful and miscellaneous.

Sylva Clapin's "New Dictionary of Americanisms" (1902) reduced these categories to four:

1. Genuine English words, obsolete or provincial in England, and universally used in the United States.

2. English words conveying, in the United States, a different meaning from that attached to them in England.

3. Words introduced from other languages than the English: French, Dutch, Spanish, German, Indian, etc.

4. Americanisms proper, *i.e.*, words coined in the country, either representing some new idea or peculiar product.

Richard H. Thornton's "American Glossary" (1912) substituted the following:

1. Forms of speech now obsolete or provincial in England, which survive in the United States, such as *allow, bureau, fall, gotten, guess.*

2. Words and phrases of distinctly American origin, such as *belittle, lengthy, lightning rod, to darken one's door, to bark up the wrong tree, blind tiger, cold snap.*

3. Nouns which indicate quadrupeds, birds, trees, articles of food, etc., that are distinctively American, such as *ground hog, hangbird, hominy, live oak, locust, opossum.*

4. Names of persons and classes of persons, and of places, such as *Buckeye, Hoosier, Old Hickory, Dixie, Gotham,* the *Bay State,* the *Monumental City.*

5. Words which have assumed a new meaning, such as *card, clever, fork, help, penny, plunder.*

In addition, Thornton added a provisional class of "words and phrases of which I have found earlier examples in American than in English writers; . . . with the *caveat* that further research may reverse the claim" —a class offering specimens in *alarmist, capitalize, horse of another colour* [*sic!*], *the jig's up, omnibus bill* and *whitewash.*

Gilbert M. Tucker's "American English" (1921) attempted to reduce all Americanisms to two grand divisions:

1. Words and phrases that originated in America and express something that the British have always expressed differently if they have mentioned it at all.

2. Words and phrases that would convey to a British ear a different meaning from that which they bear in this country.

To this he added seven categories of locution *not* to be regarded as Americanisms:

1. Words and phrases stated by the previous compiler himself to be of foreign (*i.e.*, chiefly of English) origin, like Farmer's *hand-me-down.*

2. Names of things exclusively American, but known abroad under the same name, such as *moccasin.*

3. Names of things invented in the United States, like *drawing-room car*.

4. Words used in this country in a sense hardly distinguishable from that they bear in England, like *force* for a gang of laborers.

5. Nonce words like Mark Twain's *cavalieress*.

6. Perfectly regular and self-explanatory compounds, like *office-holder, planing machine, ink slinger* and *flytime*.

7. Purely technical terms, such as those employed in baseball.

A glance at these discordant classifications shows that they hamper inquiry by limiting its scope. They leave out of account some of the most salient characters of a living language. Only Bartlett and Farmer establish a separate category of Americanisms produced by phonological changes, though even Thornton is obliged to take notice of such forms as *bust* and *bile*, and even Tucker lists *buster*. Obviously many words and phrases excluded by Tucker's *Index Expurgatorius* are genuine Americanisms. Why bar *moccasin* because it is also known in England? So is *caucus*, which he includes. He is also too hostile to characteristic American compounds like *officeholder* and *flytime*. True enough, their materials are good English, with no change in the meaning of their component parts, but they were put together in the United States, and an Englishman always sees a certain strangeness in them. *Pay dirt, passageway, night rider, know-nothing* and *hog wallow* are equally compounded of pure English metal, and yet he lists them all. Again, he is too ready to bar archaisms. It is idle to prove that Chaucer used *to guess*. The important thing is that the English abandoned it centuries ago, and that when they happen to use it today they are conscious that it is an Americanism. *Baggage* is in Shakespeare, but not often in the London *Times*. Here Mr. Tucker's historical principles run away with his judgment. His book, the labor of nearly forty years, is full of shrewd observations and persuasive contentions, but is sometimes excessively dogmatic.

James Maitland did not categorize Americanisms in "The American Slang Dictionary," [9] nor did Brander Matthews in his "Americanisms and Briticisms,"[1] nor did George Philip Krapp in "The English Language in America."[2] The editors of "A Dictionary of American English," when they brought out their first volume in 1938, contented themselves with saying in their preface that "the different types of words and phrases"

---

[9] Chicago, 1891.
[1] First published in *Harper's Magazine*, 1891, pp. 214–22; republished in Americanisms and Briticisms, With Other Essays on Other Issues; New York, 1892, pp. 1 *ff*.

[2] Two vols.; New York, 1925. In the chapter on Vocabulary in Vol. I, Krapp discussed Americanisms at great length, but did not undertake a formal classification of them. He was greatly inclined to pooh-pooh them.

listed in it could "be more readily ascertained by inspection than by any attempt at classification," but their chief, Sir William Craigie, went into rather more detail in a paper published in 1940.[3] After excluding loan words, the topographical terms derived from them, and "composite names of plants and trees, animals, birds and fishes, of the type *black alder, black bear, black bass,* etc.," he listed the following categories:

1. Words showing "the addition of new senses to existing words and phrases."
2. "New derivative forms and attributive collocations or other compounds."
3. "Words not previously in use, and not adapted from other languages of the American continent."

[Finally, in the Preface to the "Dictionary of Americanisms," M. M. Mathews defines an Americanism as a word or expression or meaning that originated in what is now the United States. He is less concerned than the DAE with American survivals of words or meanings that have disappeared in England. And like his predecessors he avoids the complicated problem of the difference in status of the same word or meaning.]

The most scientific and laborious collection of Americanisms, before the DAE, was Thornton's. It presents an enormous mass of quotations, carefully dated; but its very dependence upon quotations limits it chiefly to the written language, and so the enormously richer materials of the spoken language are passed over, particularly the materials evolved during the past generation. In vain one searches for *buttinski, sure* as an adverb, and *well* as a sort of general equivalent of the German *also.* These grammatical and syntactical tendencies lay beyond the scope of Thornton, and some of them lie outside the field of the DAE and DA, but they are prime concerns of any student who essays to get at the inner spirit of the American language. Its difference from Standard English is not merely a difference in vocabulary, to be disposed of in an alphabetical list; it is also a difference in pronunciation, in intonation, in conjugation and declension, in metaphor and idiom, in the whole fashion of using words. The vocabulary, of course, must be given first attention, for in it the earliest American divergences are embalmed, and it tends to grow richer and freer year after year, but attention must be paid to materials and ways of speech that are less obvious, particularly to tendencies in vulgar American, the great reservoir of the language, and perhaps the forerunner of what it will be on higher levels in the years to come.

---

[3] The Growth of American English, I, *SPE Tract,* No. LVI; Oxford, 1940, p. 204.

III

The Beginnings of American

1: THE FIRST LOAN WORDS

The earliest Americanisms were probably words borrowed bodily from the Indian languages—words, in the main, indicating natural objects that had no counterparts in England. Thus Captain John Smith's "True Relation" (1608) mentions a strange beast described variously as a *rahaugcum* and a *raugroughcum*. Four years later, in William Strachey's "Historie of Trevaile into Virginia Britannia," it became an *aracoune*, "much like a badger," and by 1624 Smith had made it a *rarowcun* in his "Virginia." It was not until 1672 that it emerged as the *raccoon* we know today. *Opossum* has had much the same history. It first appeared in 1610 as *apossoun*, and two years later Smith made it *opassom* in his "Map of Virginia," at the same time describing the animal as having "an head like a swine, a taile like a rat, and is of the bigness of a cat." The word became *opossum* by 1763. In the common speech *raccoon* is almost always reduced to *coon*, and *opossum* to *possum*. The DA traces the former to 1742 and the latter to 1613. *Moose* is another American primitive, derived from a Passamaquoddy Indian word which refers to the animal's habit of stripping the lower branches and bark from trees when feeding. It had become *mus* by 1613, *mose* by 1637 and *moose* by 1672.

Most of these early loans came from the Indian languages of the Algonquian group. This group was only one of nearly sixty north of the Rio Grande, but the Indians who spoke it covered most of the region invaded by the first settlers, and out of it came the native personages who most dramatically appealed to the colonial imagination, *e.g.*, King Philip, Pontiac, Tecumseh and Pocahontas. In 1902 the late Alexander F. Chamberlain, professor of anthropology at Clark University, compiled a list of

132 words borrowed from Algonquian dialects, of which 34 survive to-day; [1] appended is the date of the first example given by the DA:

caribou, 1610

chinquapin, 1645

chipmunk, 1832

hickory, 1618

hominy, 1629

mackinaw, 1812

menhaden, 1643

moccasin, 1612

moose, 1613

mugwump (1663), 1832

muskellunge or *maskinonge,* 1789

opossum, 1610

papoose, 1634

pecan, 1773

pemmican, 1791

persimmon, 1612

podunk, 1666

poke (plant), 1634

pone, 1612

powwow, 1624

raccoon, 1608

sachem, 1622

scuppernong, 1811

skunk, 1588

squash, 1634

squaw, 1634

succotash, 1751

Tammany, 1771

terrapin, 1672

toboggan, 1829

tomahawk, 1612

totem, 1609

wigwam, 1628

woodchuck, 1674

Some of these—e.g., *chipmunk*—are probably materially older than the DA's first examples. The other words on Chamberlain's list survive, if at all, in more restricted use. Some specimens follow, with the dates of the DA's first examples:

carcajou (a wolverine), 1744

cashaw or *cushaw* (a squash), 1588

cisco (a Great Lakes fish resembling the herring), 1848

hackmatack (an evergreen tree), 1792

kinnikinnick (a mixture of tobacco with other dried leaves), 1817

manito or *manitou* (a deity), 1588

pocosin (a swamp), 1631

quahog or *quahaug* (a hard clam), 1753

sagamore (a chief), 1613

samp (corn porridge), 1643

scuppaug or *scup* (a marine fish), 1807

supawn (corn-meal mush), 1617 ?

tamarack (the red larch), 1805

wampum (shell money), 1638

wangan (a boat), 1848

whiskey-jack or *whiskey-john* (in Canada and parts of the Northwest, a blue jay; the word is a corruption of the Cree *wisket-jan*), 1839

Here, too, some dates probably fall considerably short of the earliest use of the words. "The Indian element in American English," said Chamber-

---

[1] *JAF*, Vol. XV, 1902, pp. 240–67. [*Caucus* and *porgy*, which Chamberlain included, are no longer generally believed to be of Algonquian origin.]

lain, "is much larger than is commonly believed to be the case. . . . In the local speech of New England, especially among the fishermen of its coasts and islands, many words of Algonquian origin, not familiar to the general public, are still preserved, and many more were once current, but have died out within the last 100 years."

If we examine the aboriginal sources of these words, we can see that most of them have been shortened or otherwise modified on being taken into colonial English. Thus *chinquapin* was originally *checkinquain* or *chincomen*, and *squash* appears in early documents as *askutasquash*, *isquontersquash* and *squantersquash*, the original significance apparently being "that which is eaten raw." These variations show a familiar effort to bring a new and strange word into harmony with the language. By it the French *route de roi* has become *Rotten Row* in English, *écrevisse* has become *crayfish* and the English *bowsprit* has become *beau pré* (beautiful meadow) in French. *Woodchuck* originated in this way. Its origin is to be sought, not in *wood* and *chuck*, but in *wejack*, the Indian name for the animal.

All of these words reflect the need of the colonists to describe the unfamiliar: strange flora and fauna, Indian foods, tools and artifacts, social institutions and relationships. These are in addition to a vast number of Indian names for rivers, mountains, islands, bays and—less often—inhabited places.

The etymologies of the early Indian loan words are sometimes obscure.[2] The early settlers had something less than a scientific interest in the exact names of the tribes and languages of their red-skinned neighbors, much less in their relationships with one another. Since many of these languages have died out, we may never know the exact one from which a particular word was borrowed. Even when the colonial records tell us the exact language source, we often do not know the aboriginal form. [When we relate it to something from the surviving Algonquian languages, we have to remember that some of these languages, *e.g.*, Cree and Ojibwa, were never spoken within hundreds of miles of the first settlements.]

Some of these words, *e.g.*, *caribou, mackinaw* and *toboggan*, came into colonial English by way of Canadian French. *Caribou* may be derived from Micmac *khalibu*, signifying pawer or scratcher, according to Weekley, because "the deer shovels away the snow with its hoofs to get at the moss on which it feeds. The French associations of *caribou* are reflected in the 1744 spelling of the plural as *cariboux*."

---

[2] [The best easily accessible authorities are the DA and Webster 1961. For a general discussion of the processes of linguistic loans, see Einar Haugen, The Analysis of Linguistic Borrowing, *Lg.*, Vol. XXVI, Apr.–June 1950, pp. 210–31; and Henry M. Hoenigswald, The Phonology of Dialect Borrowing, *SIL*, Vol. X, Mar. 1952, pp. 1–5.]

Chipmunk is related to the Ojibwa *atchitamon*, meaning a squirrel, and referring to the animal's habit of coming down a tree head first. *Hickory* comes from *pawcohiccora*, a word used by the Indians of Virginia to designate a dish made of the pounded nuts. It has produced many derivatives, *e.g., hickory nut, -stick, -shirt* and *-pole*.

Hominy is derived from a Virginia Algonquian word, *rockahominy*. In the DAE's first quotation, from John Smith, *milke homini* is described as "bruized Indian corne pounded, and boiled thicke, and milke for the sauce." Smith added: "but boiled with milke the best of all." The later settlers used lye water to soften the hulls of the grain, and by 1821 *lye hominy* was recorded. Many other obvious derivatives have been in use at different times, *e.g., hominy sifter, -pot* and *-grits*.

Mackinaw is derived from the Ojibwa *mitchimakinak*, meaning a large turtle. The same word provided the names of the Strait of Mackinac and the Michigan island, county, fort and town. *Mackinaw* was applied in the 1820s to the gaudy blankets which the government provided for the Indians of the vicinity, and soon afterward was used to designate a gun and a boat. The *mackinaw jacket*, [now usually shortened to *mackinaw*], originally made of blanket material in loud designs, apparently did not appear until toward the end of the Nineteenth Century. *Menhaden* was borrowed from the Indians of the lower New England coast; in the Massachusetts dialect it appeared as *munnoquohteau*, meaning "that which enriches the soil." The Indians buried one of the fish in each hill of corn, a custom borrowed by the settlers. It has many other names, *e.g., bunker, skippaug, Long Island herring* and *American sardine*. It is still taken for fertilizer, and also yields an oil and a cattle food. Its young are often canned under the guise of sardines.

Moccasin comes from a New England Indian word variously rendered by the early chronicles. The object designated, a soft-soled shoe, seems to have been borrowed by the settlers along with the word, since it was better suited for wilderness travel than their leather boots. The name was eventually transferred to a flower and a snake. *Mugwump*, now obsolescent, signified a chief. When the Rev. John Eliot translated the Old Testament into the Massachusetts language in 1663, he used it to translate the Authorized Version *duke* as a title for the lesser potentates of Edom (Genesis xxxvi). *Muskellunge*, the name of a pike much sought by sportsmen in the Great Lakes region, probably comes from the Ojibwa. *Possum* we have discussed; *to play possum* is traced by the DAE to 1822 and *to possum* to 1846. *Papoose* comes from an Algonquian word signifying a suckling baby. *Pecan* comes from one meaning any hard-shelled nut, and may have reached American English by way of Spanish. *Pemmican*, from the Cree word *pimmikan*, meaning fat, was brought in by the movement into the

West, and is not recorded before the time of the Lewis and Clark expedition. *Poke*, from the Indian word *uppowoc*, was first applied to the tobacco plant, but has since been transferred to the skunk cabbage, to a plant whose berries are used in dyeing, to a species of hellebore and to various common weeds. The DAE traces *pokeberry* to 1774, *pokeroot* to 1687 and *pokeweed* to 1751.

Pone, most often encountered in *corn pone*, is derived from an Algonquian word signifying anything baked. John Smith, in 1612, wrote *ponap*, but it had acquired its present spelling before the end of the Seventeenth Century. The DA's first example of *corn pone* comes from Bartlett, 1859, but it must be much older. *Pone*, in the regions where it is still in common use, signifies especially a bread made in small oval loaves, flat on the bottom and rounded on the top. *Powwow* comes from the Indians of the New England coast; it was applied at first to an Indian medicine man, and then transferred to an Indian ceremonial rite and finally to any Indian meeting. It came to designate a meeting of whites early in the Nineteenth Century, and usually today signifies a political palaver. The earliest meaning is still preserved in the Pennsylvania German region, where a *powwow man* or *woman* designates a witch doctor. *Sachem*, like *powwow* and *wigwam*, has been preserved in the argot of politics, and especially in that of Tammany Hall. A cognate, *sagamore*, of the same meaning (*i.e.*, chief), has almost vanished from American speech, though surviving in proper names. *Scuppernong*, the name of one of the principal varieties of American grapes, comes from an Indian word, *askuponong*, signifying the place of the magnolias. It first appeared in American use as a proper name for a river and lake in North Carolina,[3] and was later applied to the grapes growing in the vicinity. *Skunk* is applied to several species of the genus *Mephitis*, all of them characterized by the ejection of a foul-smelling secretion when disturbed. The word has been transferred to various animals and plants, *e.g.*, *skunk cabbage* (or *-weed*), *skunk bear* and *skunk spruce*. Its application as a pejorative to human beings is traced by the DAE to 1840. It also appears as a verb, signifying to defeat an opponent overwhelmingly, to slink away from danger and to evade a debt.

Squaw, in its various Indian forms, signified any woman, but the early settlers seem to have given it the special significance of a wife. Its derivatives include *squaw man* (the white consort of an Indian woman), *squaw winter*, and *squaw ax*, *-fish*, *-flower* and *-weed*. *Succotash*, derived from the Narragansett *misickquatash*, signifying an ear of corn, designates an American dish invented by the Indians and borrowed by the white set-

---

[3] [Norman E. Eliason, Tarheel Talk: An Historical Study of the English Language in North Carolina to 1860; Chapel Hill, 1956, p. 123.]

tlers of New England. *Terrapin*, in its original form, meant little turtle, and the DAE indicates that it was first borrowed by the whites in Virginia. The *diamond-backed terrapin*, so called because of the markings on its carapace, is not recorded before Bartlett's fourth edition of 1877, but it must be much older. There is a Maryland legend that *terrapin* were once so plentiful on the Eastern Shore that a law had to be passed forbidding the planters to feed them to their slaves more than twice a week. *Toboggan* came into American English through the Canadian French *tobagan*, a borrowing from the Micmac Indian *tobakun*, signifying a sled made of skins. The sport of *tobogganing* is first recorded by the DAE in 1856. *Totem*, now in universal use by anthropologists to signify an animal or plant associated with a given group and supposed to exercise some sort of influence over them, is said by F. W. Hodge[4] to be derived "from the term *ototeman* of the Chippewa and other cognate Algonquian dialects." It goes back to 1609, and *totemism* followed in 1791, but *totem pole* is a relatively late addition to the American vocabulary. *Wigwam* is derived from an eastern Algonquian cognate of Ojibwa *wigiwam*, signifying a dwelling place. [*Wigwam*, of course, was used only by the Algonquian groups, but the whites have often applied it indiscriminately to any kind of Indian habitation. The Plains Indians, mostly Siouan tribes, actually used *tipi* (more familiar in the spelling *tepee*); the Navaho still use *hogan*.]

The Indian loans in American English are by no means confined to terms borrowed from the languages of Indians inhabiting the present territory of the United States. Through the Spanish a great many Nahuatl words from Mexico have come in, and not a few of them have gone over into British English. George Watson, of the University of Chicago, listed a large number,[5] *e.g.*, *chocolate*, in English use, traced to 1604; *tomato*, to the same year; *coyote*, traced by the DAE to 1834; *chicle*, the basis of chewing gum; *avocado* (pear), mentioned in George Washington's diary, 1751; and *Mexico*. From the West Indian dialects, also through the Spanish, have come a number of words. *Barbecue* is derived from the Spanish *barbacoa*, itself a loan from a Haitian dialect. Since this Spanish *barbacoa* originally indicated a sleeping bench elevated on stilts, not a device for roasting meat, there has been some difficulty about accounting for the change in meaning. [However, early Spanish colonial records show that within a few years of its first recorded occurrence, *barbacoa* was being used throughout the Caribbean area to designate not only a variety of latticelike structures but things roasted or dried on them; it also designated

---

[4] Handbook of American Indians North of Mexico; Washington, 1907–10.

[5] Nahuatl Words in American English, *AS*, Vol. XIII, Apr. 1938, pp. 108–21.

a kind of fish trap.[6] In any event] the DAE shows that *barbecue* was in American use in the sense of a roasted animal by 1709, and in the sense of a social gathering by 1733.

Canoe was picked up from the Indians of the West Indies by Columbus's sailors as a Haitian word, *canoa*. It was taken without change into Spanish, where it remains *canoa* to this day.[7] Like *maize*, it appears in English for the first time in Eden's "Decades" (1555), where its form is still *canoa*. At the start it referred only to a craft made of a hollowed tree trunk, but after a while it came to mean any sort of native vessel operated by paddles. In the course of time the more limited American sense of a small craft sharp at both ends, made of bark, canvas or some other light material, and operated by paddles, supplanted the various English senses, and at present the English use the word exactly as Americans do. The familiar American phrase *to paddle one's own canoe* is traced by the DAE to 1828. *Canoeing* as a sport did not arise until after the Civil War. The DAE's first reference to a *canoe club* in the United States is dated 1872. By that time *canoeists* were already numerous on the rivers and lakes of the East.[8] *Canoe* hatched the usual derivatives before 1800. The DA traces *canoe tree* (a tree suitable for making a canoe) to 1638, *canoe load* to 1691, *canoeing* to 1752, and *canoe wood* to 1649. Its first example of *to canoe* is dated 1732, but the verb undoubtedly arose much earlier.

A curious phenomenon is presented by *maize*, which came into the colonial speech from the West Indies by way of the Spanish, went over into orthodox English, and from English into French, German and other Continental languages, and was then abandoned by the Americans, who substituted *corn*, which commonly means wheat in England. [But *maize* survives in American to designate a shade of yellow; *e.g.*, the colors of the University of Michigan are officially *maize* and blue.]

Finally, new words were made by translating Indian terms, whether real or imaginary, *e.g.*, *warpath*, *war paint*, *paleface*, *big chief*, *medicine man*, *pipe of peace*, *firewater* and *to bury the hatchet*; and by using the word *Indian* as a prefix. Many of the former class had to do with war, for it was as an enemy in the field that most colonial Americans were conscious of Indians. The DAE traces *war dance* to 1711, *war whoop* to 1725, *warpath* to 1755, *war club* to 1776, *war party* to 1755, *war paint* and *to go upon the warpath* to 1826 and *war trail* to 1840. The first examples of the last three come from Cooper, who also was the first, apparently, to use *paleface* (1821). The DAE traces *big medicine* to 1846,

---

[6] [Lawrence B. Kiddle, *Barbecue*, an unpublished paper read at the summer meeting of the Linguistic Society of America, Ann Arbor, Mich., July 1958.]

[7] [See Douglas Taylor, Spanish *Canoa* and Its Congeners, *IJAL*, Vol. XXIII, 1957, pp. 242–4.]

[8] The Cruising *Canoe* and Its Outfit, by C. E. Chase, *Harper's Magazine*, Sept. 1880, pp. 395 *ff*.

and records various other words and phrases embodying *medicine* to the 1790–1860 era, *e.g.*, *bad medicine* to 1815, *medicine man* to 1806, *medicine dance* to 1808 and *to make medicine* to 1805. *Pipe of peace* is traced to 1705, *Great Spirit* to 1790, *firewater* to 1817 and *to bury the hatchet* to 1754. The last-named seems to have been preceded by *to bury the ax* (1680) and *to lay down the hatchet* (1724). Many such terms, once much more familiar than they are today, were introduced by the reports of the Lewis and Clark expedition of 1804–6, especially those involving *medicine*.[9]

Of compounds embodying *Indian*, the candidly incomplete DA lists more than 200, of which the earliest seems to be *Indian cake*, 1607. Others recorded before 1625 are *Indian town*, 1608; *-meal*, *-wheat*, 1609; *-corn*, 1617; *-hemp*, 1619; *-king*, 1621; *-bean*, *-fig*, *-house*, *-nation*, 1622. It used to be assumed that *Indian summer* was one of the earliest of these compounds, but in 1902 Albert Matthews produced evidence that it was actually relatively recent.[1] The DAE traced it to Hector St. John de Crèvecoeur (1731–1813), in 1778, in a paper describing the season as "a short interval of smoke and mildness."[2] In its figurative sense, designating the closing days of life, the term was used by De Quincey in 1830, but it is still regarded as an Americanism in England, for the English climate offers nothing comparable to the balmy, smoky weather that usually prevails along the Atlantic coast of the United States from the end of October until the onset of winter. It was not listed by John Pickering in his Vocabulary of 1816, and Noah Webster did not admit it to his American Dictionary of 1828. There is, in fact, no mention of it in any of the early writers on Americanisms brought together by M. M. Mathews in "The Beginnings of American English."[3] Harry Morgan Ayres, in 1942, offered the theory that it got its name because the early settlers associated the word *Indian* with a concept of bogusness:

> In Europe, where the phenomenon is less striking than with us, it had long been known as *St. Martin's Summer*. . . . To Englishmen, unlike other Europeans, the name *St. Martin* suggested something false, a sham or imitation, for the dealers in cheap jewelry were gathered in the parish of St. Martin-le-grand in London. . . . For English-speaking folk, though clearly this was not the reason the

---

[9] An account of the neologisms thus launched is in Lewis and Clark: Linguistic Pioneers, by Elijah Criswell, *University of Missouri Studies*, Apr. 1, 1940.

[1] The Term *Indian Summer*, *Monthly Weather Review*, Jan. and Feb. 1902.

[2] [Most observers would now add "after the first frost."]

[3] Regarding the origin of the term there is a considerable difference of opinion. The DAE contents itself with recording some of the guesses. [The DA declares all these theories unconvincing, and directs the reader to the article by Albert Matthews.]

name was given to it,[4] the gentle hazy weather of late Autumn was indeed a *St. Martin's Summer*, an imitation and a sham.

The first of our American forefathers, then, whoever he or quite possibly she was, that may have said, " 'Tis but an *Indian* kind of Summer after all, as false and fickle as they," was only following the early habit among them of characterizing by the term *Indian* whatever in the New World looked something like the real thing but was not. *Indian-corn* is not wheat. An *Indian-barn* is a hole in the ground.[5] There were *Indian-beans*, *Indian-cucumbers*, . . . *Indian* this and *Indian* that, and so most appropriately, by a happy and enduring stroke of creative language, *Indian summer*.

On the exact duration and nature of *Indian summer* there seems to be no agreement among meteorologists. John R. Weeks, then the weather man at Baltimore, proposed in 1938 that it be defined as "a mild period of five or more days with no daily mean temperature below 40 degrees and with no rain on any day," [6] but it would be quite as rational to define it as a period of ten or fifteen or thirty or even more days during which the *average* daily temperature is above 40. In the Baltimore-Washington area *Indian summer* often runs on until beyond Christmas; indeed, it included Christmas nine times during the 66 years from 1872 to 1938. "Warm periods in January," said Weeks, "when snow and ice melt . . . were in the early days called by many *Indian Summer*, but now they are universally called the *January thaw*."

The use of real or supposed Indian terms by Tammany and by various fraternal organizations, sometimes as translations, is familiar to most Americans. The DAE's first example of *sachem* in the Tammany sense is dated 1786. In the Improved Order of Red Men,[7] the chief national dignitary is the *great incohonee*, and is supported by two *great sagamores*, a *great keeper of wampum* (treasurer), a *great tocakon* and a *great minewa* (guards). The head of a state-wide jurisdiction is a *great sachem*, and in his suite are two *great sagamores*, a *great sannap* and a *great mishinewa*. Of these terms, only *sachem, sagamore, wampum* and *sannap* (or *sannup*)

---

[4] The OED traces *St. Martin's Summer* to 1591 (Martinmas is Nov. 11). The English sometimes say *St. Luke's Summer* (St. Luke's Day is Oct. 18) or *All Hallows' Summer* (All Saints' Day is Nov. 1). See *Indian Summer*, by J. E. T. Horne, London *Daily Telegraph*, Oct. 10, 1936.

[5] Traced to 1634; defined by a writer of a century later as a hole in the ground "lined and covered with bark, and then with dirt."

[6] *Indian Summer* in Maryland, Baltimore *Evening Sun* (editorial page), Dec. 20, 1938.

[7] It claims to be an offshoot of the colonial Sons of Liberty from which Tammany is also alleged to be sprung. This claim, like that of the Freemasons to descent from the trade unions of King Solomon's time, has been disputed by cynics. The present order seems to have been organized in Baltimore during the winter of 1833–4.

are listed by the DAE. A lodge is a *tribe* and its head is a *sachem*. Tribal jurisdictions are *hunting grounds*, a meeting place is a *wigwam* or *tepee*, a member is a *warrior*, and a non-member is a *paleface*.[8]

The names of two American Indian groups, the Mohawks and the Apaches, have acquired special meanings in British English and French, respectively. *Mohawk* (or *Mohock*) is traced by the OED to 1711 as "one of a class of aristocratic ruffians who infested the streets of London at night in the early years of the Eighteenth Century." The *Gentleman's Magazine*, in 1768, said that they had been so called because they mauled passers-by "in the same cruel manner which the *Mohawks*, one of the Six Nations of Indians, might be supposed to do." *Apache* was introduced into French about 1901 by Émile Darsy, then a reporter on *Le Figaro*. M. Darsy, an ardent reader of the Western fiction of the time, tried the experiment of giving the Paris gangs names of Indian groups, and after failing to make *Sioux, Pawnee, Comanche* and various others stick, scored a ten-strike with *Apache*, which was adopted at once by M. Lepine, then prefect of police, and soon became a generic name for all gangs. In 1924 it was formally admitted to the language by the French Academy.[9] The *Apache dancers* of the 1920s always came in pairs, a man and a woman, and were dressed in costumes supposed to be those of the Paris *Apaches* and their doxies. In the dance they performed, the man always handled the woman violently, sometimes swinging her about him by the hair.

The language of the settlers also received accretions from the languages of the other colonizing nations. The contributions of the New Amsterdam Dutch during the half-century of their conflicts with the English included *cruller, cole slaw, cookie, stoop, sleigh, span* (of horses), *spook, hay barrack* (a haystack with a sliding roof on poles), *pot cheese, pit* (as in *peach pit*), *waffle, scow, boss* and *Santa Claus*, which comes from a dialect form of *Sint Klaas*, meaning St. Nicholas, the patron saint of children. Both the name and the gift-bearing old fellow it designates were introduced to America by the Dutch of the New York region. The Puritans knew nothing of either, and neither did the more genial English settlers of the Southern colonies. The DA's first example of *Santa Claus* comes from the New York *Gazette*, 1773. The Dutch did not bring in the *Christmas tree*, which had to wait for the Germans. [The first one we can be sure of was set up in 1832 by Charles Follen, a Hessian, the first professor of German at Harvard. During the next few years trees appeared at Belleville, Ill. (1833), Philadelphia (1834, 1842), Cincinnati (1835), Fort Motte, S.C. (1839), Rochester, N.Y. (1840, 1841), New York City (1843), Williamsburg, Va. (1845), Richmond, Va. (1846). All were set up by people of

---

[8] Revised Red Men Illustrated; Chicago, 1928.

[9] *Apaches* in the Dictionary, *The New York Times* (editorial), Aug. 17, 1924.

German descent, or in communities with a strong German background, before August Imgard, a tailor from Wetzler, Hesse, supposedly introduced the Christmas tree in Wooster, Ohio.[1]] The Germans, of course, know nothing of *Santa Claus;* their name for the saint who brings presents at Christmas is *Belsnickel*, and that name is retained by the Pennsylvania Germans.[2] The American *Krisskring'l* or *Kriss-Kingle*, now rare, arose from a misunderstanding of the German *Christkindlein* or *Christkind'l*, which means, not St. Nicholas, but the Child in the Manger.[3] *Kriss Kringle* is traced to 1830, and marked an Americanism.[4]

Boss had come into American English from the Dutch of New York by 1650. The verb *to boss* is not traced beyond 1856, but it must be older. The original Dutch form, *baas*,[5] is used in South African English precisely as we use *boss*. *Bedpan* dates from 1678. *Cole slaw* comes from the Dutch *koolsla*, which is made up of *kool*, meaning cabbage, and *sla*, a shortened form of *salade*, meaning salad. It is traced by the DAE to 1792. Folk etymology frequently converts it into *cold slaw;* [*hot slaw*, which the DA traces back to 1870, is an anemic substitute for sauerkraut]. *Cookie* comes from the Dutch *koekje*, a small cake, and seems to have been borrowed independently in the Scotch Lowlands. The DA's first example is dated 1703. *Cruller* is related to the Dutch verb *krullen*, to curl or crisp. The DAE traces it to 1805, but it is probably older.

Pit, the hard seed of a fruit, as in *peach pit* and *cherry pit*, is not recorded before Bartlett listed it in 1848, but it is no doubt older. If from the Dutch, it was probably helped into American by its resemblance to *pip*, traced by the OED to the late Eighteenth Century. [*Rolliches*, pickled rolls of meat, are still occasionally made in the Hudson Valley, and sometimes anglicized to *relishes*.] *Scow* was borrowed from the Dutch so early as 1669. *Sleigh*, from the Dutch *slee*, is traced to 1696. *Span*, in the sense of a harnessed pair of horses, came from an identical Dutch word, with

---

[1] [Personal communication from William I. Schreiber, The College of Wooster, Ohio.]

[2] A Dictionary of the Non-English Words of the Pennsylvania-German Dialect, by M. B. Lambert; Lancaster, Pa., 1924, p. 26.

[3] An anonymous article, The American Language, in *Putnam's Magazine*, Nov. 1870, p. 523, says that at that time, among American children in general, *Kriss-Kingle* was "only subordinate to *Santa Claus* as a designation for that obese personage who, in their philosophy, stands far beyond king or kaiser." *Kriss-Kingle* was still in wide use in the Baltimore of 1885–90.

[4] St. Nicholas is the patron saint, not only of children, but also of scholars, travelers, sailors, pawnbrokers and the Russian Orthodox Church. He flourished somewhere in the eastern Mediterranean in the Fourth Century and is said to have taken part in the Council of Nicaea. His feast day, Dec. 6, was assimilated to Christmas during the Middle Ages.

[5] Defined in Kramer's Nieuw Engelsch Woordenboek, ed. by F. P. H. Prick van Wely (Gouda, 1921), as meaning master, foreman. It is used in Dutch in many figurative senses, *e.g.,* to designate a jolly fellow, a big baby, a shrewish wife.

cognates in other Germanic languages, which apparently meant, originally, a yoke of oxen. The DAE traces it to 1769. Webster 1828 recorded a verb *to span*, meaning to agree in color and size, but it seems to have dropped out. Neither noun nor verb was ever taken into British English. *Spook*, in the sense of a specter, is from an identical Dutch and German word of the same meaning.[6] The OED runs it back to 1810 in American use, but it is probably older. By the middle of the century it had been adopted by the English; it produced a number of derivatives, of which only *spooky* and *spook dancing* are listed by the DA.

Stoop, from the Dutch *stoep*, is traced to 1735 in American use. In cities it usually means the front steps of the house, but in rural areas it sometimes designates a porch, especially a small one at the back of the house. *Waffle*, from the Dutch *wafel*, is not recorded before 1817, but it is obviously much older, for *waffle party* is recorded for 1808, *waffle iron* for 1794 and *waffle frolic* for 1744. *Waffle iron* is a direct translation of the Dutch *wafelijzer*. Schele de Vere, in his "Americanisms," first directed attention to a number of Dutch geographical terms that survive in the vicinity of New York, sometimes anglicized out of recognition, e.g., *kil*, a channel, as in *Kill van Kull, Catskill, Schuylkill* and *Fishkill; clove*, a ravine; *dorp*, a village; *hoek*, a bend or corner, as in *Kinderhook* and *Sandy Hook;* and *gat*, a pass in a channel, as in *Barnegat* and *Hell Gate* (*Helle-gat*);[7] to which may be added *fly*, a swamp, traced by the DA to 1645, [and *pol*, a tidal marsh, as in *Canarsie Pol*]. Schele de Vere also lists many Dutch terms still surviving in his time (1871) in the New York area only, e.g., *overslaugh*, a sand bar; *noodleje*, a noodle; *fetticus*, a salad; and *hoople*, a child's rolling hoop. The American use of *dominie* to indicate a clergyman (it exists in Scots, but only in the sense of a schoolmaster) and of *bush* to indicate wild land was probably influenced by the Dutch *dominee* and *bosch*. How *filibuster*, a Dutch loan, has been changed in meaning in the United States is discussed in Chapter IV, Section 2. *Hunky-dory* is probably derived from the Dutch *honk*, signifying the base or goal in children's tag games. The elegant euphemism *cuspidor*, ultimately from the Portuguese *cuspidiera*, comes immediately from the Dutch *kwispedoor* or *kwispeldoor*. In 1875 Mark Twain told of "a *cuspidor* with the motto 'In God We Trust,' " and in 1892, in "The Quality of Mercy," William Dean Howells spoke with quite natural pride of "a nickel-plated *cuspidor*."

---

[6] [The LA materials show it concentrated both in the Hudson Valley and in eastern Pennsylvania, as well as in German settlements to the south.]

[7] Washington Irving, in A History of New York . . . by Diedrich Knicker-bocker; New York, 1809, Ch. IV: "Certain mealy-mouthed men of squeamish consciences, who are loath to give the Devil his due, have softened [this] into *Hurlgate*, forsooth!"

Perhaps the most notable of all the contributions of Knickerbocker Dutch to American is the word *Yankee*. [The most probable etymology derives it from *Jan Kees* (a diminutive of *Cornelius*, a common Dutch name), as a sort of Dutch equivalent of *Joe Doakes* or *John Doe*.[8]] In the form *Jan Kaas* it has been a nickname for a Hollander, in Flanders and Germany, for a great many years. In the days of the buccaneers the English sailors began to use it to designate a Dutch freebooter, and in this sense it became familiar in New York. Possibly the New York Dutch applied it derogatorily to the English settlers of Connecticut, as persons whose commercial enterprise outran their moral scruples. Later it came into general use in the colonies to designate a disliked neighbor to the northward, and there was a time when the Virginians applied it to the Marylanders. In the end the New Englanders saw in it a flattering tribute to their cunning, and not only adopted it themselves, but converted it into an adjective signifying excellence. The DAE's first example of *Yankee*, then spelled *Yankey*, is dated 1683, as the proper name of one of the Dutch pirate commanders in the West Indies. By 1758 General James Wolfe was using it to belittle the New England militia in the Quebec campaign, and by the Revolution the English were using it to designate any American. During the Civil War, as everyone knows, the Southerners used it, usually contemptuously, of all Northerners,[9] and in consequence its widened meaning became restricted again. [In the two world wars it was applied by the British to all Americans; a number of unrecorded skirmishes in pubs demonstrated that to many Southerners it was still a dirty word, but—so long as they are overseas—few of them object any more.] The shortened form *Yank*, popularized in George M. Cohan's "Over There" (1917), is traced to 1778.

Many derivatives are listed by the DAE and DA, *e.g.*, *Yankee trick*, traced to 1776; *-land*, to 1788; *-ism*, to 1792; *-phrase*, to 1803; *-peddler*, to 1820; *to catch a Yankee* (to catch a Tartar), to 1811; and *to play Yankee* (to reply to a question by asking one), to 1841. *Yankee Doodle* as the name of a song is traced to 1767. Its history was detailed at length in a report by O. G. T. Sonneck, chief of the music division in the Library of Congress, in 1909.[1] In the same document he discussed at length the various etymologies proposed for *Yankee*:

---

[8] [Personal communication from J. J. Lamberts, of Arizona State University.]

[9] The Field, the Dungeon and the Escape, by Albert Richardson; Hartford, Conn., 1865, p. 90: "The Southern politicians and newspapers have persuaded the masses that the *Yankees* (a phrase which they no longer apply distinctly to New Englanders, but to every person born in the North) mean to subjugate them, but are arrant cowards, who may easily be frightened away." After the war the pejorative usually appeared as *damyankee*, and that form still survives in the South.

[1] Report on The Star-Spangled Banner, Hail Columbia, America, and *Yankee Doodle;* Washington, 1909.

The word gradually came to fascinate the historian of words until about 1850 fascination reached its climax. Since then the craze has subsided, yet any number of explanations are still current and proposed as facts, usually on the presumption that embellished reiteration of statements correctly or incorrectly quoted produces facts.

The most fantastic of these etymologies, that *Yankee* comes from the Persian word *janghe* or *jenghe,* meaning a warlike man or a horse, was actually proposed as a hoax, in the *Monthly Anthology and Boston Review* for 1810,[2] in a letter allegedly copied from "the *Connecticut Herald,* a paper printed in New Haven," and signed *W.* It was intended to be a burlesque upon the philological writings of Noah Webster, and the *Monthly Anthology* pretended to be "credibly informed" that it was "from the pen of N—— W——, jun., Esq.," himself. It was as follows:

> *Yankee* appears to have been used formerly by some of our common farmers. . . . Now in the Persian language, *janghe* or *jenghe*— that is, *Yankee*—signifies "a warlike man, a swift horse; also, one who is prompt and ready in action, one who is magnanimous." The word is formed from *jank, jenk,* battle, contest, war; and this from a like word signifying the fist, the instrument of fighting; like *pugna,* from *pugnus,* the fist. In Persian *jankidan* (*yankidan*) is to commence or carry on war.
>
> We hence see the propriety of the use of *Yankee* as applied to a high-spirited, warlike horse.
>
> The word *Yankee* thus claims a very honorable parentage; for it is the precise title assumed by the celebrated Mongolian khan, *Jenghis;* and in our dialect his title, literally translated, would be *Yankee King,* that is, *Warlike Chief.* . . .
>
> New Haven, March 2, 1810.

Jan Kaas, or *Jan Kees,* to English ears, must have seemed like a plural. "The loss of the *s* would be on a par with that in *Chinee, pea* and *cherry,* from *Chinese, pease* and *cherries.*"[3]

Many of the early loans from the French, *e.g., caribou* and *toboggan,* had been borrowed, in turn, from Indian languages. To these *bayou* may be added, influenced by the Choctaw *bayuk,* a small stream. But there were also direct borrowings, *e.g., chowder* (from *chaudière,* a kettle or pot),

---

[2] Vol. VIII, pp. 244-5.

[3] Henri Logeman, The Etymology of *Yankee,* in Studies in English Philology . . . in Honor of Frederick Klaeber; Minneapolis, 1929, pp. 403-13. This paper was summarized, with the addition of other matter, in On the Origin of *Yankee Doodle,* by Harold Davis, *AS,* Vol. XIII, Apr. 1938, pp. 92-6.

traced by the DAE to 1751; [4] *batteau,* traced to 1711; *calumet* (a tobacco pipe), to 1705; *carryall* (from *cariole,* by folk etymology), to 1714; *gopher* (meaning a burrowing rodent, probably from French *gauffre,* a honeycomb, etymologically related to *waffle;* in the sense of a land turtle, possibly from a Muskhogean Indian word), to 1791; *levee,* to 1719; *portage,* to 1698; and *prairie,* to 1773. Most of these came in along the Canadian border, but others were picked up in the West or South, *e.g., voyageur, bagasse* and *crevasse.* Those of the latter class are mainly unrecorded before the Nineteenth Century, though they were probably in local use before. A number of French terms found in proper names, *e.g., sault,* meaning rapids in a river, were taken over in the West, and the colonists freely used, in town names, the French suffix *-ville,* which had been used very rarely in England. *Buccaneer,* from the French *boucanier,* is chiefly associated with American history, and in consequence it is sometimes reckoned an Americanism, but it was previously in use in England. Several familiar terms came into American from the Spanish by way of Louisiana French, *e.g., calaboose,* traced to 1792, and *quadroon,* which is discussed in Chapter VI, Section 9.

Direct loans from the Spanish were very rare before 1800, though some words may have been borrowed independently here and in England. A good many Spanish words, or Spanish adaptations of native words, went into English during the Sixteenth Century without any preliminary apprenticeship as Americanisms, *e.g., mosquito, chocolate, banana* and *cannibal.* But *cockroach* (from the Spanish *cucaracha,* assimilated by folk etymology to *cock* and *roach*) is first heard of in Captain John Smith's "General Historie of Virginia" (1624). [5]

Such familiar Spanish loans as *lasso, corral* and *ranch,* now almost as thoroughly American as *ambulance chaser* and *hitchhike,* did not come in until after the beginning of the movement into the West. The early Americans, in fact, had very little contact with the Spaniards; they knew the Dutch and French much better. Of the early Germans they knew still less, for the Germans had a numerous colony only in Pennsylvania, and there they kept to themselves. *Sauerkraut* and *noodle* are apparently first recorded in England, but may have been independently borrowed in America. *Smearcase* may have been borrowed from both the Germans and

---

[4] Steven T. Byington suggests that it was borrowed from the Acadians in the early Eighteenth Century, after Nova Scotia (then including New Brunswick) was ceded to England by the Treaty of Utrecht in 1713. The English-speaking settlers who moved into Nova Scotia were largely from New England, so it is not surprising that a recipe for *chowder* appears in Boston by 1751. *AS,* Vol. XIX, Apr. 1944, p. 122.

[5] [See The Spanish Language as a Medium of Cultural Diffusion in the Age of Discovery, by Lawrence B. Kiddle, *AS,* Vol. XXVII, Dec. 1952, pp. 241–56.]

the Dutch. *Dumb,* in the sense of stupid, like *spook,* probably owes something to both Dutch and German. Most German words in the American vocabulary seem to have come in after the War of 1812.[6]

Very few words were borrowed from the languages of the Negro slaves, even in the South. *Buckra,* meaning a white man, is traced to 1736 in white American use. It was never widespread, and now it is unknown to most Americans. *Cooter,* a name applied to a turtle in the Carolinas and Georgia, is derived from an African word, *kuta* or *nkuda,* but is not traced before 1832. *Goober,* a Southern name for the peanut, is derived from the African *nguba,* but the DA's first example of its printed use is dated so late as 1834. *Pinder,* the South Carolina name for the peanut, is first found in American print in 1848, though it had been used in Jamaica as early as 1707. It is also of African origin. *Gumbo,* the common Southern name for a soup with an okra base, less common as a synonym for okra, is from the Angolan *kingombo,* and traced to 1805. In the sense of a Negro patois of French it may be derived from a quite different word, *nkombo,* a runaway slave, used by the tribes of the Congo region. *Gumbo* has produced a number of derivatives, *e.g., gumbo ball,* a kind of harlequinade, traced by the DA to 1819; *gumbo box,* a drum, derived from *nkumbi,* of the same meaning, and traced to 1861; and *gumbo soup,* traced to 1813. *Voodoo* seems to be derived from the African *vodu,* but it got into American English from the French of Haiti or New Orleans. *Hoodoo* is later. *Juba,* a dance, possibly of African origin, apparently did not get into the general American vocabulary until the rise of the minstrel show, *c.* 1830.

But the African languages undoubtedly had a considerable influence upon the dialect of the Southern Negroes, especially in such remote backwaters as the Sea Islands of South Carolina and Georgia, where the local Negro dialect, called Gullah, is almost unintelligible to white Southerners. Lorenzo D. Turner, of Roosevelt University, has found over 6,000 Africanisms among the Gullah-speaking Negroes.[7] Most of them are personal names, and all save a few of the remainder are used only in speaking to other Gullahs; in their dealings with the local whites, the Negroes make a larger use of what they take to be English. But even this polite dialect contains many African words that white observers have mistaken for debased forms of English words. A more detailed account appears in Chapter VII.

---

[6] [But, to the surprise of most Americans, the DA suggests that *The Father of His Country,* as a designation for the sacred Washington, is apparently an early loan translation from the German *Des Landes Vater,* which appeared in a Nord Amerikanische Kalender for 1779, issued at Lancaster, Pa., by Francis Baily. Paul Schach adds that "the common German designation for a sovereign during this period was Der Landesvater." Pennsylvania-German Words in the DA, *AS,* Vol. XXIX, Feb. 1954, pp. 45–54.]

[7] [Africanisms in the Gullah Dialect; Chicago, 1949.]

2: NEW WORDS OF ENGLISH MATERIAL

Of far more importance than such small borrowings was the great stock of new words that the early colonists coined in English metal—sometimes by giving an English word a new meaning but oftener by arranging English elements in new combinations. Such words were primarily demanded by the "new circumstances under which they were placed," but also frequently suggested a delight in the business for its own sake. The American of the Seventeenth Century already showed the characteristics that were to set him off from the Englishman later on—his bold and somewhat grotesque imagination, his contempt for dignified authority, his lack of aesthetic sensitivity, his extravagant humor. The few men of education, culture and gentle birth among the early settlers were soon swamped by hordes of the ignorant and illiterate, and the latter soon laid their hands upon the language. In Boston, so early as 1628, there was a definite class of blackguard roisterers, chiefly made up of sailors and artisans; in Virginia, nearly a decade earlier, John Pory, secretary to Sir George Yeardley, Deputy Governor, bemoaned the ignorance of the newcomers. The generation born in the New World was uncouth and iconoclastic;[8] the only world it knew was a rough world, demanding not niceness, but enterprise and resourcefulness.

Upon men of this sort fell the task of bringing the wilderness to the ax and plow, and the task of inventing a vocabulary for the great adventure. Out of their loutish ingenuity came a great number of picturesque names for natural objects, chiefly boldly descriptive compounds: *bullfrog, catbird, muskrat, garter snake* and so on. Out of an inventiveness somewhat more urbane came *live oak, turkey gobbler, canvasback, pokeweed, copperhead, eelgrass, eggplant, katydid, lightning bug* and *butternut. Live oak* appears in a document of 1610; *bullfrog* was familiar in 1705. These early Americans were often ignorant of the names of the plants that they encountered, even when those plants already had English names, and so they exercised their fancy upon new ones. So arose *Johnny-jump-up* for the *Viola tricolor,* and *basswood* for the common European *linden* or *lime tree (tilia),* and *locust* for the *Robinia pseudacia* and its allies. The grosser features of the landscape got a lavish renaming, partly to distinguish new forms and partly out of an obvious desire for literal descriptiveness. In addition to *key* and *hook,* borrowed from Spanish and Dutch, came *branch, fork, run* (stream), *bald, bluff, cliff, neck, barrens, bottoms, salt meadows, watershed, foothill, hollow, water gap, underbrush, bottom land, clearing, notch, divide, knob, riffle, rolling country* and *rapids,* and the extension of

---

[8] See The Cambridge History of American Literature, Vol. I, pp. 14 and 22.

pond from artificial pools to small natural lakes, and of *creek* from small arms of the sea to shallow feeders of rivers. Such common English topographical terms as *down, fen, bog, chase, dell* and *common* disappeared, save as fossilized in a few localisms and proper names.[9]

With the new landscape came an entirely new mode of life—new foods, new forms of habitation, new methods of agriculture, new kinds of hunting. A great swarm of neologisms thus arose, and, as in the previous case, they were chiefly compounds. *Backwoods, back land* and *back country* were all in common use before the Revolution; *back street* has been traced to 1638.[1] *Log house* appears in 1662, *log cabin* in 1770. *Hoecake* and *roasting ear* belong to the colonial period. So do *pine knot, snowshoe, cold snap, apple butter, salt lick* and *canebrake*. *Shingle*, in the American sense, was a novelty in 1705, but one S. Symonds wrote to John Winthrop, of Ipswich, about a *clapboarded* house in 1637; *clapboarding* appears the same year, and *frame house* in 1735. *Selectman* is first heard of in 1635, displacing the English *alderman*. *Mush* had displaced *porridge* by 1671. *Hired man* is in the Plymouth town records of 1737. *Camp meeting* did not appear until 1799. But *land office* was recorded in 1681, and *sidewalk* and *stamping ground* were in daily use before the Revolution.

Under *B* the DAE cites the following additional compounds made of English material during the Eighteenth Century:

back settlement, 1759	*beef packer,* 1796
back taxes, 1788	*bee tree,* 1782
bake oven, 1777	*bell horse,* 1775
bale cloth, 1797	*blue laws,* 1781
ball ground, 1772	*breadstuffs,* 1793
barn swallow, 1790	*breech clout,* 1757
bay vessel, 1789	*broom corn,* 1781
bear hunter, 1765	*broom straw,* 1785
beef cattle, 1776	*buckshot,* 1775

Under the letter *S* we find:

sheet iron, 1776	*shotgun,* 1776
shingle roof, 1749	*shower bath,* 1785
ship canal, 1798	*sinkhole,* 1749
ship channel, 1775	*smokehouse,* 1759
shooting iron, 1787	*smoking tobacco,* 1796

---

[9] For example, Chevy *Chase*, Boston *Common*, the Back Bay *Fens* and *cranberry bog*.

[1] A long list of compounds based on *back*, from the collections of the DAE, is to be found in *AS*, Vol. VI, Oct. 1930. It runs to no less than 120 terms, all of them of American origin. In addition there is a list of eleven peculiarly American uses of *back* as a verb, and five of its uses as an adjective.

snow plow, 1792   *spring house,* 1755
spoon victuals, 1777

Among the new names for natural objects are many more, most of them descriptive. Under *G,* for example, are:

gallberry, 1709   *grizzly bear,* 1791
German corn (rye), 1741   *ground pea,* 1769
glass snake, 1736   *ground squirrel,* 1709
gray eagle, 1778   *gum swamp,* 1799
green snake, 1709

And under *S:*

shagbark, 1751   *sourwood,* 1709
shortleaf pine, 1796   *spicewood,* 1756
slippery elm, 1748   *sugar maple,* 1731
snap bean, 1775

And these at random:

blue grass, 1751   *pond lily,* 1748
blue jay, 1709   *tree frog,* 1738
clingstone (peach), 1705

Under *blue* the DAE lists scores of such coinages, and under *black* and *white* almost as many. Some of the strange natural objects encountered by the first settlers, *e.g.,* the *bear,* the *beaver,* and the *eagle,* stimulated their word-making proclivities, and thus enriched their vocabulary. Allen Walker Read lists a large number of Americanisms using *bear* dating from the Eighteenth Century, *e.g., bear's oil,* 1674; *bear's fat,* 1709; *bear ham,* 1766; *bear bacon* and *bear's meat,* 1772; *bear steak,* 1788; and *bear ground,* 1797.[2] The term was also used in a figurative sense, as in *bear grass,* 1750. The new political and social conditions under which the settlers lived also suggested a large number of new compounds, some of which survive to this day. *Fence rails* were defined for British readers by Lt. Thomas Anburey, of the British Army, who surrendered with Burgoyne at Saratoga on October 17, 1777, and spent several years as a prisoner in America.[3] The DAE does not claim the compound as an Americanism, but its first example goes back to 1733, and the OED does not list it at all. *Fencing stuff,* material for making fences, has been traced to 1644; *fence viewer,* an offi-

---

[2] Allen Walker Read, The Bear in American Speech, *AS,* Vol. X, Oct. 1935, pp. 195–202.
[3] Travels Through the Interior Parts of America; London, 1789, Vol. II, p. 323.

I am indebted here to The Comment of British Travelers on Early American Terms Relating to Agriculture, *Agricultural History,* July 1933, pp. 99 *ff.*

cial appointed to inspect fences, to 1661; *fencing rail* to 1780; and *under fence* to 1796; but *fence law, fence rider, fence row, fence war* and *fencing wire* belong to the Nineteenth Century. All are Americanisms, and so is *fence corner*. The DAE traces *worm fence* to 1652, *rail fence* to 1649 and *snake fence* to 1805. *Back log*, traced to 1684, is still a stranger to the English; [*back stick*, its Appalachian synonym, is omitted by the DAE and the DA, but is obviously old].

The new money of the Confederation brought in a number of new words. In 1782 Gouverneur Morris proposed to the Continental Congress that the coins of the Republic be called, in ascending order, *unit, penny-bill, dollar* and *crown*. Later Morris substituted *cent* for the English *penny*. In 1785 Jefferson proposed *mill, cent, disme, dollar* and *eagle*, and this nomenclature was made official by the Act Establishing a Mint, approved April 2, 1792. Jefferson apparently derived *disme* from the French word *dixième*, meaning a tenth; the original pronunciation seems to have been *deem*. But it soon became *dime*.

Various nautical terms peculiar to America, or taken into English from American sources, came in during the Eighteenth Century, among them, *schooner, mud scow* and *pungy*. According to a historian of the American merchant marine,[4] the first *schooner* was launched at Gloucester, Mass., in 1713. *To scoon* was a verb borrowed by New Englanders from some Scots dialect, and meant to skim or skip across the water like a flat stone. Perhaps *pungy* is related to *pung*, a one-horse sled. *Pung* was once widely used in the United States, but later sank to the estate of a Northern provincialism. Longfellow used it, and in 1857 a writer in the *Knickerbocker Magazine* reported that *pungs* filled Broadway, in New York, after a snowstorm. [They were common in rural Michigan and Wisconsin until the automobile supplanted horse-drawn vehicles.]

Statehouse used to be credited by etymologists to the Dutch *stadhuis*, but it was in use in Virginia in 1638,[5] and had reached Maryland by 1662, and did not appear in New York until 1671. The DAE traces *best room* to 1719, *leaf tobacco* to 1637, *hoecake* to 1774, *state's attorney* to 1779, *hay scales* to 1773, *dry goods* to 1701, *bottom land* to 1728, and *double house* to 1707. The second element of *spinning bee* may have been invented by some ingenious Americano, for etymologists have been unable to find any trace of it in the vocabulary of England. The first *spinning bee* seems to have been recorded in 1769, but the term did not come into general use until after the Revolution.

Many of the early American terms had to do with food, *e.g., buckwheat*

---

[4] William Brown Meloney, The Heritage of Tyre; New York, 1916, p. 15.
[5] Albert Matthews, The Term State-House, DN, Vol. II, Pt. VI, 1902, pp. 199–224.

cake, first recorded in John Adams's diary, September 21, 1774; *corn bread*, 1796; *johnny cake*, 1739; *breadstuffs*, first recorded in a report by Thomas Jefferson, December 16, 1793; and *hog and hominy*, 1792. The inventor of the *buckwheat cake*, though immortal, remains unknown. Buckwheat was being grown for human food in Pennsylvania so early as 1698, and was then sometimes called *French wheat*. *Johnny cake*, which appears in both Yankeeland and Appalachia, albeit in different shapes, had acquired the variant form of *journey cake* by 1754,[6] and in consequence Noah Webster surmised that this was the original term, and that it signified a hard loaf baked for use on a journey. Both *johnny cake* and *journey cake* may have been related to *jonokin*, traced to 1675 and still surviving on Delmarva and in eastern North Carolina.[7] *Breadstuffs*, invented by Jefferson, was defined in his reports as "bread grains, meals and bread." Said Pickering in 1816: "It has probably been more readily allowed among us because we do not, like the English, use the word *corn* as a general name for all sorts of grain."

The rowdy personal habits of the early Americans are naturally reflected in their vocabulary. The DAE traces *tarring and feathering* to 1774, *gouging* ("the action of squeezing or pushing out a person's eye") to the same year, *Lynch's law* to 1782, and *rough and tumble* to 1792. Thomas Hutchinson's diary for 1774 indicates that *tarring and feathering* was already so well established a practice that regular committees were formed to carry it on, and that they objected to amateur competition. *Gouging* reached its highest development among the boatmen of the Western rivers after the beginning of the movement across the Alleghanies, but it was already practiced before the Revolution, along with biting, butting and scratching. Unhappily, etymologists differ regarding the identity of the man who served *Lynch's law* (and its progeny, *lynch law, lynching, lyncher, lynching bee* and *to lynch*) as eponym. James Elbert Cutler [8] came to the conclusion that its father was Colonel Charles Lynch (1736–96), a Quaker magistrate and militia officer of Bedford County, Va., but the DAE and DA say that the practice was "named after Captain William Lynch (1742–1820) of Pittsylvania County, Virginia, and later of Pendleton district, South Carolina." Local tradition at Lynchburg, Va., founded in 1786 by Charles Lynch's younger brother, John, supports the former theory, but

---

[6] In 1780 a Moravian bishop, Reichel by name, made a journey from the Moravian headquarters at Lititz, Pa., to the outpost at Salem, N.C. On June 8 he recorded in his diary that he had made his first acquaintance with a *journey cake*. The diary was in German, but he entered the words in English. Records of the Moravians in North Carolina, ed. by Adelaide Fries, Vol. IV, p. 1894.

[7] [Hans Kurath, A Word Geography of the Eastern United States; Ann Arbor, 1949, p. 68 and Fig. 117.]

[8] Lynch Law: An Investigation into the History of Lynching in the United States; New York, 1905.

an interview with Richard Venable, an aged and much respected citizen of Prince Edward County, published in *Harper's Magazine* in 1859,[9] brought personal recollection to the support of the latter, and the Eighteenth Century citations in the DA seem to be conclusive. Both traditions assert that the eponymous Lynch was a judge in one of the impromptu courts set up on the Virginia frontier during the troubles incident to the American Revolution. Crimes of violence had multiplied; it was inconvenient to transport apprehended offenders and witnesses to the Tidewater area, where the only duly constituted courts were held, and the frontiersmen were suspicious of the speed and efficacy of the justice meted out in those courts. Lynch joined with other substantial citizens in setting up a court with the power to try all classes of offenders. They were, of course, what later came to be called *vigilantes*, not lynchers in the current sense. They always gave prisoners fair and public trials. Since the two traditions, save for the identity of the eponymous Lynch, are virtually identical, it is highly probable that they are grounded upon historical facts; and that southwestern Virginia is thus entitled to public veneration, not only for the invention of lynching, but also for the launching of the name.

Half a dozen other terms are worth noticing, though some of them are not certainly of American origin: *bobolink, bootee, bundling, sophomore, Jimson weed* and *harmonica*. Although *bobolink* is first recorded in the writings of John Adams, it has a decidedly English sound and may have been borrowed from some English dialect. The term probably arose by onomatopoeia; the DAE calls it "an imitation of the metallic clinking note of the bird," *i.e.*, the reed- or ricebird. Adams used it in a figurative sense in speaking of a foppish young man, one of the South Carolina Rutledges. *Bootee* appeared in the Eighteenth Century, dropped out of use in the Nineteenth and was revived just before the Hoover Depression. The original *bootee,* defined as a "half boot or high shoe, covering the ankle but not the leg," goes back to 1799. *Bootees* were issued to the Federal troops during the Civil War, but soon afterward disappeared, though the word was still listed by the Century Dictionary in 1889. The revived *bootee* is defined as "a boot having a short leg; for men, usually made with elastic gore over ankle or with laced front; for infants, usually knitted and tiny or half-leg length." [1] A correspondent defines the modern *bootee* as "usually knitted or crocheted, and used for very small babies." [2] [*Bootees* are favorite presents to newborn babies, and mothers sometimes have a problem disposing of surplus pairs without offending friends and relatives.]

The art of *bundling* was not an American invention, nor was the word, but both flourished in this country more luxuriantly than in the British

[9] Lynch Law, May 1859, pp. 794-8.
[1] Mary Brooks Picken, The Language of Fashion; New York, 1939, p. 11.
[2] Miss Ruth Wilson, of New York.

Isles. The DAE's definition is "the practice of unmarried couples (partly undressed) occupying the same bed," and its first American example is dated 1781, from Samuel Peters's "General History of Connecticut,"[3] a work remembered today mainly because the author printed a list of ferocious Connecticut Blue Laws that have been denounced by other historians as imaginary, but are still generally accepted as authentic.[4] Peters says that bundling, in 1781, had prevailed in New England since "the first settlement in 1634," but that it went on "only in the cold seasons of the year." The OED's first example of *to bundle* comes from his book, but the practice seems to have previously existed in remoter parts of Britain, especially Wales. It attracted, however, but little attention from the primeval sociologists of the time, and Grose did not mention it until the third edition of his "Classical Dictionary of the Vulgar Tongue" (1796), after news of it reached England from America:

> A man and woman sleeping in the same bed, he with his small clothes and she with her petticoats on; an expedient practised in America on a scarcity of beds, where, on such an occasion, husbands and parents frequently permitted travelers to bundle with their wives and daughters.

Sophomore, a second-year student in a four-year college course, is probably an Americanism. The DAE's first example is from a Latin document of Harvard, dated 1654. By 1684 it was appearing in the Harvard records as an English word, but it is recorded in England only four years later, with every sign of being in familiar university use. [The DA omits it, but lists *soph* (1778), *sophomore class* (1765) and *sophomoreship* (1698).] It has bred *sophomoric* (1837) and *sophomorical* (1839), in each case in the United States. It seems to have been extended to second-year students in high schools during the 1890s, and has since been used to designate even post-freshmen in kindergartens. *Freshman* was current in England so early as 1596, and is still in use there. *Junior* and *senior,* however, are both American; the first is traced to *c.* 1764 and the second to 1741. *Campus* is traced to 1774, and was probably introduced at Princeton by John Witherspoon.[5] At all save a few colleges, *e.g.,* Harvard, it has displaced the earlier *yard.* [The local term at the University of Virginia is *lawn.*]

---

[3] The DAE overlooks an earlier example cited by Peters, from Travels Through the Middle Settlements of North America in the Years 1759 and 1760, by Andrew Burnaby; London, 1775. Burnaby was an English clergyman.

[4] See The True Blue Laws of Connecticut and New Haven and the False Blue Laws Invented by the Rev. Samuel Peters, by J. Hammond Trumbull; Hartford, 1876.

[5] Albert Matthews, The Use at American Colleges of the Word *Campus, Publications of the Colonial Society of Massachusetts,* Vol. III, 1900, pp. 3–9.

Jimson weed or *Jimpson weed* is a degenerate form of *Jamestown weed*, which the DAE traces to 1687. The plant (*Datura stramonium*) was discovered growing at Jamestown in Virginia by the English settlers who landed there in 1607, but they seem to have been unaware of the kick in it until 1676, when Nathaniel Bacon's rebellion reduced them to short commons, and they ate it.[6]

The *harmonica* was invented in 1762 by Benjamin Franklin, who first called it the *armonica* (from Italian *armonico*, harmonious), but had changed its name by 1765. It was no more than an improvement of the *musical glasses* mentioned in an oft-quoted passage in "The Vicar of Wakefield."[7] In their crude form they consisted simply of goblets filled with different amounts of water, and the musical notes produced by rubbing the rims of these goblets varied according to the height of the water in them. Franklin substituted a series of revolving glass basins operated by a treadle. Below them was a trough full of water, and as they revolved they picked it up. Musical notes were then produced by touching their wet rims. This contrivance was superior to the old *musical glasses* in two particulars: the glass basins were of fixed tonality, and more than one tone could be produced at the same time. The modern *harmonica* or *mouth organ*, also known in the Southern uplands as a *French harp*, invented in 1829 by a Viennese named Damien, is a reed instrument and bears no sort of relation to the *musical glasses*.[8]

The early colonists freely interchanged the parts of speech, turning verbs into nouns, nouns into verbs, and adjectives into either or both with an abandon that is still one of the hallmarks of American English. The New Englanders had made a verb of *scalp* before the end of the Seventeenth Century, and early in the next century they followed with *to tomahawk*. *To top*, in the sense of to remove the top of a growing tobacco plant, is traced by the DAE to 1688, and *to tote*, to 1677. The true origin of the latter remains mysterious. [In the sense of to carry on the person, it is almost universal in the Southern plantation country but rare in the mountains, where *pack* is the usual term. The word is unknown in Pennsylvania and the southern part of the Great Lakes area, but it shows up again in the lumbering country of Maine, the Adirondacks and Lake Superior, usually meaning to transport in a conveyance, as a canoe, sled or wagon, and giving rise to such combinations as *tote road, tote sled, tote team* and *tote wagon*. All of these last terms are related to the operation of bringing in supplies to lumber camps. Whether the two senses are related, or came independently from two different sources, is a matter on which philologists

[6] Robert Beverley, History and Present State of Virginia, 1705, Vol. II, p. 24.
[7] London, 1766, Ch. X.

[8] I am indebted here to D. F. Munro, of Lexington, Mo.

have not yet agreed, but Lorenzo Turner convincingly suggests that at least the Southern word is related to verbs of similar sound and meaning in several West African languages.[9]] *Tote* occurs in such other combinations as *to tote fair*, traced by the DAE to 1866; *tote bag, pistol toter* and *gun toter*. Some of these have been made more or less familiar to the English by American movies. *Tote* as a shortened form of *totalizer* or *totalization* is a Briticism, little used in the United States, where the *tote system* of betting on races is usually called *pari mutuel*.

Not all of these innovations were established peacefully. Pickering made a belated protest against the reduction of the English law-phrase *to convey by deed* to *to deed,* and argued that no self-respecting attorney would employ it, but American attorneys had been employing it for years and still are. So with *to table* for *to lay on the table*. Franklin deprecated *to advocate, to progress* and *to oppose*—a vain *caveat*, for all of them are now perfectly good.

Webster, though he agreed with Franklin in opposing *to advocate*, gave his *imprimatur* to *to appreciate* (to rise in value) and *to obligate*, and is credited with the invention of *to demoralize*.[1] He claimed to have "enriched the vocabulary with *absorbable, accompaniment, acidulous, achromatic, adhesiveness, adjutancy, admissibility, advisory, amendable, animalize, aneurismal, antithetical, appellor, appreciate, appreciation, arborescent, arborization, ascertainable, bailee, bailment, indorser, indorsee, prescriptive, imprescriptible, statement, insubordination, expenditure, subsidize* "and other elegant and scientific terms, now used by the best writers in Great Britain and America."[2] But most of these, though not found in Johnson's Dictionary (1755), were already in English before Webster began to write dictionaries, and some were very old.[3] *To antagonize* seems to have been given currency by John Quincy Adams, *to immigrate* by John Marshall, *to eventuate* by Gouverneur Morris and *to derange* by George Washington. Jefferson, as we saw earlier, used *to belittle*.

Many new verbs were made from common nouns, *e.g., to cord* (*i.e.,* wood), *to stump* and *to room*. Others arose as metaphors, *e.g., to whitewash* (figuratively) and *to squat* (on unoccupied land). Others were made by hitching suffixes to nouns, or by groping for roots, *e.g., to deputize, to locate* and *to legislate*. Yet others seem to have been produced by onomatopoeia, *e.g., to fizzle*. With them came an endless series of verb

---

[9] [Africanisms in the Gullah Dialect; Chicago, 1949.]

[1] Sir Charles Lyell, Travels in North America in the Years 1841–42; London, 1845; New York, 1852, p. 53.

[2] Letter to Thomas Dawes, Aug. 5, 1809. It is reprinted in Mathews, pp. 48 ff.

[3] The OED traces *amendable* to 1589, *antithetical* to 1583, *bailee* to 1528 and *appellor* to c. 1400.

phrases, *e.g.*, *to draw a bead* and *to fly off the handle*—obvious products of pioneer life. Fierce battles raged round some of these verbs, and they were all violently derided in England. Even *to locate*, now in quite respectable usage, was denounced in the third volume of the *North American Review*, and other purists of the times tried to put down *to legislate*.

The young and tender adjectives had quite as hard a row to hoe, particularly *lengthy*. The *British Critic* singled it out, and it also had enemies at home, but the authority of John Adams and Jefferson and Hamilton helped it survive. By 1816, indeed, Jeremy Bentham was using it in England. Years later James Russell Lowell boasted that American had given it to English.[4] *Dutiable* also met with opposition, and moreover it had a rival, *customable;* but Marshall wrote it into his historic decisions, and thus it took root. The same anonymous watchman of the *North American Review* who denounced *to locate* proscribed *presidential* and *congressional*, but the need for them kept them in the language. *Gubernatorial* had come in long before this, in the New Jersey Archives of 1734. *Influential* was denounced by the Rev. Jonathan Boucher and by George Canning, who argued that *influent* was better, but it was ardently defended by William Pinkney of Maryland. *Handy, kinky, law-abiding, chunky, solid* (in the sense of well-to-do), *complected* and *cute* were already secure in Revolutionary days. So with many nouns. *Balance*, in the sense of remainder, got into the debates of the First Congress. *Mileage* was used by Franklin in 1754, and is now sound English. *Draw*, for *drawbridge*, comes down from Revolutionary days. So does *slip*, in the sense of a berth for vessels. So does *addition*, in the sense of a suburb. So, finally, does *darky*.

The history of these Americanisms shows how vain is the effort of grammarians to combat the normal processes of language development. *To oppose, to legislate, to progress, bogus, reliable* and *standpoint* were constantly under academic fire. All are to be found in William Cullen Bryant's *Index Expurgatorius* (*c.* 1870),[5] and *reliable* was denounced by Bishop Coxe as late as 1886.[6] Edward S. Gould, another uncompromising purist, said of *standpoint* that it was "the bright particular star . . . of solemn philological blundering."[7] Gould also protested against *to jeopardize, leniency* and *to demean*, though the last was old in English in the different sense of to conduct oneself, and Richard Grant White joined him in an onslaught upon *to donate*. But all these words are in good usage in the United States today, and some of them have gone over into English.

---

[4] The Biglow Papers, Series II, 1866, pref.

[5] Reprinted in Helpful Hints in Writing and Reading, comp. by Grenville Kleiser; New York, 1911, pp. 15–17.

[6] A. Cleveland Coxe, Americanisms in England, *Forum*, Oct. 1886.

[7] Edward S. Gould, Good English, or Popular Errors in Language; New York, 1867, pp. 25–7.

3: CHANGED MEANINGS

The early Americans also made many new words by changing the meaning of old ones. *To squat*, in the sense of to crouch, had been sound English for centuries, but they gave it the meaning of to settle on land without the authority of the owner, and from it the noun *squatter* quickly emanated. Of *lot* Krapp says:

> The method of portioning out the common lands to the townsmen of the first New England communities has led to the general American use of *lot* to designate a limited section of land. . . . In the Norwalk Records (1671) the agreement is recorded that "all those men that now draw *lots* with their neighbors shall stand to their *lots* that they now draw." [8]

Other examples of the application of old words to new purposes are afforded by *freshet* and *barn*. A *freshet*, in Eighteenth Century English, meant any stream of fresh water; the colonists made it signify an inundation. A *barn* was a house or shed for storing crops; in America it became a place for keeping cattle also. The process is even more clearly shown in the history of such words as *corn* and *shoe*. *Corn*, in orthodox English, means grain for human consumption, and especially wheat, *e.g.*, the *Corn Laws*. Our corn is *maize;* as the staple grain of the New World, it soon became known as *Indian corn*, to distinguish it from *corn* in the English sense; but by the middle of the Eighteenth Century simple *corn* usually sufficed. Such derivatives as *corn field, -husk, -fed, -starch* and *-whiskey* all relate to *maize*,[9] and so does the familiar American phrase *to acknowledge the corn*. The DA traces *corn field* to 1608, *-stalk* to 1645, *-land* to 1654, *-crib* to 1687, *sweet-* to 1646, *-house* to 1699, *-hill* to 1616, *-row* to 1769, *-patch* to 1784, *-bread* to 1775, *-flour* to 1674, *pop-* to 1819, *-barn* to 1780. Most of these are probably older. The American colonists borrowed not only the Indian method of growing corn by planting a fish in every row, for fertilizer, but also some of the Indian ways of preparing it for the

---

[8] Krapp, Vol. I, pp. 85–6.

[9] Says Edgar J. Goodspeed in his preface to The Goodspeed Parallel New Testament: the American Translation and the King James Version (Chicago, 1943): "Differences of meaning have . . . grown up in different parts of the English-speaking world since Tyndale's day. What he called a *corn-field* we call a *wheat-field*, and his account of the disciples plucking the ears of *corn* conjures up a wholly false picture before the American mind; they were picking ears of wheat. King James's *corn of wheat*, of course, means a grain of wheat. Neither of them ever saw what we understand by a *corn-field*." *Corn*, as a general term, would of course include not only wheat and maize but oats, barley, rye and rice.

table, *e.g.*, by making hominy. But the English at home did not like it; [1] nor do they like it yet.

Shoe, in England, meant (and still means) a topless article of footwear, but the colonists extended it to varieties covering the ankle, thus displacing the English *boot*, which they reserved for foot coverings reaching at least to the knee. This distinction between English and American usage still prevails; such Americanisms as *bootblack* (1817) and *to bootlick* (1845) originally referred to the American *boot*, not the English. *Bureau*, to an Englishman, means an article of furniture including a writing desk—what we ordinarily call a *secretary;* in the United States it means a chest of drawers for holding linens, usually with a mirror attached. The English use it occasionally in our sense of a government or other office, but they prefer *office*. But they use *bureaucrat* and *bureaucracy* just as we do.

In colonial America, *shop* originally designated a small retail establishment, as it still does in England. But *store* had come in by 1721; by 1741 it had yielded *storekeeper*. In England, even yet, *store* means primarily a large establishment, like what we call a *warehouse*,[2] but the word in the American sense has been used for a co-operative retail store since about 1850, and recently there has been some currency for *department store*. Contrariwise, the English *shop* has been reintroduced in the United States, often in the elegant form *shoppe*. The DA traces *bookstore* to 1763, *grocery store* to 1774, *to keep store* to 1752 and *store book* to 1740, but most of the other familiar derivatives of *store* came later.

Rock, to an Englishman, commonly signifies a stone of large size, and the Pilgrims so used it when they named *Plymouth Rock* in 1620. But the colonists applied it to small stones during the Eighteenth Century, and in 1816 Pickering remarked that "in New England we often hear the expression of *heaving rocks* for throwing stones." Webster omitted the American sense from his dictionaries and Sherwood denounced it in his "Gazetteer of the State of Georgia." [The English preference for *stone*, as something to throw, is maintained in New England and its western dependencies; but from Pennsylvania south, *rock* is preferred.]

---

[1] In John Gerard's Herball, or Generall Historie of Plants, enlarged and amended by Thomas Johnson (London, 1638), it was denounced as unfit for human food: "The bread which is made thereof is meanly white, without bran; it is hard and dry as bisket is, and hath in it no clamminess at all; for which cause it is of hard digestion, and yieldeth to the body little or no nourishment; it slowly descendeth and bindeth the belly, as that doth which is made of millet or panick [an Italian variety of millet]."

[2] "In England," says H. W. Horwill (Dictionary of Modern American Usage), "*store* has normally much the same meaning as storehouse." He quotes the following from Some Impressions of the United States, by E. A. Freeman; London, 1883, p. 63: "In the early settlements a shop was really a *store* in a sense in which it hardly is now on either side of the ocean."

Cracker for what the English commonly call a *biscuit* is traced by the DAE to 1739. In recent years *biscuit,* in the English sense, has been borrowed in America, as in *National Biscuit Company,* and the English have made increasing use of *cracker,* which first appeared in England in 1810. The word seems to come from the verb *to crack,* and probably was suggested by the cracker's crispness. *Block,* in the Northern United States sense of a group of houses, is sometimes used in England, as in *block of shops,* but perhaps only as a conscious Americanism.[3] The first American example is dated 1796, but the OED does not report the form in English use until fifty-five years later. In the sense of the whole territory or mass of buildings between four streets it goes back to 1815 in the United States, and is still exclusively American, as also in the sense of the distance from one street to the next, as in "a *block* further on," and "He walked ten *blocks.*"

Creek, in England, means a tidal inlet of the ocean or of some large river, but in American it began to designate any small stream so long ago as 1622. It is still used along the Atlantic coast in the English sense, as in *Curtis Creek* (Maryland) and *Deep Creek* (Virginia), but the English never use it in the more usual American sense. The use of *spell* in various familiar phrases, *e.g., spell of sickness,* is apparently indigenous to America. *Spell of work* is old in English, but the first known examples of *spell of weather, cold spell, rainy spell* and *hot spell* are American, and so is the first recorded use of *spell* standing alone, as an indicator of "a time or while." *Lumber,* in England, means articles left lying about and taking up needed room, and in this sense it survives in America in a few compounds, *e.g., lumber room;* in the sense of timber it is an Americanism, traced by the DAE to the Seventeenth Century. Its familiar derivatives, *e.g., lumberyard, lumberman, lumberjack,* greatly reinforce this usage. *Dry goods,* in England, means "non-liquid goods, as corn" (*i.e.,* wheat); in the United States the term means "textile fabrics, cottons, woolens, linens, silks, laces, etc." The difference had appeared by 1725.

In England *college* ordinarily means one of the constituent corporations of a university, though sometimes it is also applied to a preparatory school, *e.g., Eton College;* in the United States, since the Seventeenth Century, it has been applied to any degree-giving institution short of university rank,[4] [to say nothing of such citadels of *Kultur* as *barber colleges, beauty colleges* and *colleges of mortuary science*]. In England *city* is restricted, says

---

[3] The more usual term seems to be *parade of shops. Business block* is unknown to the English.
[4] There is an interesting discussion of its early uses in America in On the Use of the Words *College* and *Hall* in the United States, by Albert Matthews, *DN,* Vol. II. Pt. II, 1900, pp. 91–114.

Horwill, to "a large and important town, or one that contains a cathedral"; in America it has long been applied to much smaller places.[5]

Many English zoological and botanical terms were applied by the colonists to species generally resembling what they had known in England, but actually different. In America since colonial times *partridge* has been used to designate not only the true partridge but also the ruffed grouse, the common quail and various other tetraonid birds. So with *rabbit*. Zoologically speaking, there are no native rabbits in the United States; they are all hares. But *hare* to an American normally means the so-called Belgian hare, which is not a hare at all, but a true rabbit. The American *robin* is really a thrush, second cousin to the mockingbird. In England *bay* is used to designate the bay tree (*Laurus nobilis*); in America it designates a shrub, the wax myrtle (*Myrica cerifera*), whose berries are used to make the well-known *bayberry* candles. Other botanical and zoological terms to which the colonists gave new significances are *blackbird, beech, hemlock, lark, laurel, oriole, swallow* and *walnut*.

The impact of a new landscape caused the early colonists to abandon several English topographical terms, e.g., *moor*, and use others that were rare or dialectal in England, e.g., *run* and *branch*. They also invented new ones, usually by giving familiar English words new meanings, e.g., *divide* and *bluff*. *Bluff*, the first Americanism to be denounced in England, was apparently borrowed from the Dutch in the Seventeenth Century, as an adjective describing blunt and nearly vertical ships' bows. [In the Savannah Valley it was made a noun, and by the Nineteenth Century it had spread west. It has been legitimized in England by Lord Tennyson (1830) and by the geologist Sir Charles Lyell (1842). The other American *bluff*, in the sense of bluster or pretense, probably owes something to both adjective and noun. Records do not tell us whether it originated as a poker term, but it has been in general use for more than a century.]

4: ARCHAIC ENGLISH WORDS

The notion that American English is fundamentally an archaic form of British English has been propagated both by Americans who seek to legitimize our English by identifying it with Shakespeare's, and by Englishmen who deny Americans any originality whatsoever in speech by showing that every new Americanism was used centuries ago. The latter enterprise has been carried to such extravagant lengths that one might find a correspondent of the London *Times* reporting that he had found *duck soup*

---

[5] Not infrequently it is embodied in their names, [as in *Ellicott City*, Md., with 2,109 inhabitants in 1950, *Dow City*, Iowa, with 524 and *Filer City*, Mich., with 320].

and *hitchhike* in a state paper of Henry VII. But despite all this absurdity there is a certainly recognizable substratum of archaic English in the American vocabulary, including many terms that Englishmen have denounced as American barbarisms. Ready examples are *to guess, to advocate, to notify, to loan* and *mad* for *angry*.

To guess has already been discussed. The American use of *to notify*, as in "The police were *notified*," has been in English use since 1440, though it has been rare since about 1700. *To loan*, in American use since 1729, strikes Englishmen as a typical Americanism, but the OED traces it to *c.* 1200, and it appears in one of the acts of Henry VIII. Since 1750, however, the English have preferred *to lend.* So with *sick* for *ill,* which the OED traces to the King Alfred translation of Boethius's "De Consolatione Philosophiae," *c.* 888. It began to be displaced by *ill* in the Fifteenth Century, and the English now regard the latter as more chaste and elegant, and have given *sick* the special sense of nauseated. In many compounds the original (and now American) sense survives, *e.g., sickness, sick bed, sick bay, sick leave* and *sick* (noun).

The list of such old English terms still alive in American would include many other words and phrases that have been denounced by English purists as abominable Americanisms, *e.g., patch* (of land), *druggist, gotten, gap* (a break in a range of hills), *to wilt, deck* (of cards), *shoat* and *fall* (for autumn). But, as Krapp argued, it is easy to overestimate the size and importance of this archaic element in American speech. It is largest in the dialect of certain remote communities, notably the Maine coast, Delmarva (*i.e.,* the eastern shore of Chesapeake Bay), eastern North Carolina and the southern Appalachians, but even in such communities it is smaller than is commonly assumed. The theory that the English brought by the early colonists underwent a sort of freezing here was first propagated, according to Krapp, by A. J. Ellis,[6] analogizing from the fact that the Old Norse of *c.* 1000 has survived with relatively little change in Iceland. But Ellis was densely ignorant of the history of the English settlements in America, and ascribed to them a cultural isolation that never existed. Krapp goes on:

> The American community has not been segregated, unadulterated, merely self-perpetuating. Relations with the parent country have never been discontinued. . . . The absurdity of describing American Eng-

---

[6] In his Early English Pronunciation, brought out at intervals from 1869 to 1889. [A century of scientific dialectology has demonstrated that the problem is far more complicated, anyhow, than Ellis realized: the focal areas in a speech community may preserve relics, while isolated areas may undergo radical changes. See William M. Austin, The Scientific Method and Historical Linguistics, *Journal of the American Oriental Society*, Vol. LXV, Jan.–Mar. 1945, pp. 63–4.]

lish as the archaic speech of an isolated community may be realized by considering what might have happened if the conditions favoring isolation had been present. If migration to New England had ceased in the year 1700, if New England had remained after that time a separate state, severed not only from Europe but from the rest of America, it is not improbable that something approximating the language of Dryden might still be heard in New England. But Dryden's speech is forever lost in the medley of later voices that sound more loudly in our ears.[7]

The argument for the archaic quality of American English did rest upon certain observable facts. In most of the colonies, *e.g.*, New England after 1640,[8] Virginia after 1660, Pennsylvania after 1700, the population growth was mainly from natural increase and from non-English immigration: Ulster Scots, Germans, Welshmen, Highlanders, Huguenots, Moravians and Sephardic Jews. Moreover, few of the colonists visited the mother country, for a sea voyage was long and dangerous and expensive. Furthermore, the centers of colonial literacy were not centers of interest in belles-lettres; neither the New England Puritan nor the Philadelphia Quaker patronized the theater, nor, when one of them did venture to England, did he find himself at home in the amiable profligacy of Eighteenth Century London society. Benjamin Franklin admitted modeling his prose style on that of Addison and Steele, but Franklin was exceptional, and even he seems not to have quoted or mentioned Shakespeare despite having access to his works.[9] Few of the traditional masterpieces of English literature were to be found in institutional, much less private, libraries; the works most often read were those that catered to the practical needs of the colonists: manuals of religious instruction, law books, arithmetics, treatises on surveying, and—as the agitation grew that led to the Revolution—works of political theory, especially those of the French encyclopedists.[1] And, finally, the expanse of the Atlantic and the practical business at hand kept the colonists from falling prey to the Eighteenth Century movement in England to petrify the language as insurance against the corruption of time. Johnson thundered against such novelties as *fun*, and read the death warrants of many archaisms that were not really archaisms at all, *e.g.*, *glee, jeopardy* and *to smoulder*. The Americans, largely cut off from this double policing, went on making new words and cherishing old ones.

[7] Is American English Archaic? *Southwest Review*, Summer 1927, pp. 292-303.

[8] Prescott F. Hall, Immigration; 2nd ed.; New York, 1913, p. 4. See also The Founding of New England, by James Truslow Adams; Boston, 1921, pp. 221 ff.

[9] "No allusion to Shakespeare has been discovered in the colonial literature of the Seventeenth Century, and scarcely an allusion to the Puritan poet Milton." Bliss Perry, The American Spirit in Literature; New Haven, 1918, p. 61.

[1] See The Cambridge History of American Literature, Vol. I, p. 119.

But it would be a mistake to assume that the colonists were simple children of nature. The wilderness was close at hand, to be sure, but in the wilderness the colonists had built an urban society that compared favorably with anything in Europe outside the major centers. In 1775 Philadelphia and Boston were the second and third most important cities under the British flag, and the sons of Southern planters often attended the English universities and the Inns of Court; even earlier, the library of William Byrd, of Westover, excelled that of most English gentlemen. The distinctiveness of American English developed with American political independence, and with the new cultural independence, not only of the frontier but of the cities that had been established in colonial times.[2]

---

[2] [See Carl Bridenbaugh, Cities in the Wilderness: The First Century of Urban Life in America, 1625-1743; New York, 1938; and Cities in Revolt: Urban Life in America, 1743-1776; New York, 1955.]

I V

The Period of Growth

Though the American language had begun its dizzy onward march before the Revolution, it did not begin to show its vigor and daring until the Nineteenth Century. Until then its free proliferation was impeded by the lack of a consequential national literature and by an internal political disharmony. Conflicting interests, suppressed during the Revolution by common aims and common dangers, reappeared with peace and yielded suspicions and hatreds which often came near wrecking the new Confederation. Few Americans of the period were able to detach themselves from the struggle for domination then going on in Europe. Not only the surviving Loyalists—perhaps a third of the population in 1776—but also many propertied patriots were ardently in favor of England, and such patriots as Jefferson were as ardently in favor of France. This engrossment in the rivalries of foreign nations made it difficult for the people of the new nation to think of themselves, politically and culturally, as Americans.[1] Soon after the Treaty of Paris was signed, someone referred to the late struggle, in Franklin's hearing, as the War for Independence. "Say, rather, the War of the Revolution," said Franklin. "The War for Independence is yet to be fought."

"That struggle," adds B. J. Lossing in "Our Country" (1873), "occurred, and that independence was won, by the Americans in the War of 1812."[2]

---

[1] According to R. E. Spiller (The American in England during the First Half Century of Independence; New York, 1926), Benjamin Silliman's Journal of Travels in England, Holland, and Scotland, and of Two Passages Over the Atlantic, in the Years 1805 and 1806 (New York, 1810), was "the first book of travels by an American which attempted to describe and discuss England as though she were actually a foreign land."

[2] [An article on the War of 1812 by Henry Steele Commager, The New York Times Magazine, June 17, 1962, pp. 15–20, is entitled The Second War of Independence.]

In the interval the new Republic had passed through a period of *Sturm und Drang* whose gigantic perils and passions we have begun to forget. The poor debtor class was fired by the French Revolution to demands which threatened the country with bankruptcy and anarchy,[3] and the class of property owners, in reaction, went far to the other extreme. On all sides flourished a strong British party, particularly in New England, where the codfish aristocracy exhibited an undisguised Anglomania, and looked forward to a *rapprochement* with the mother country.[4] This Anglomania showed itself, not only in ceaseless political agitation, but also in an elaborate imitation of English manners.

The first sign of the dawn of a new national order came with the election of Thomas Jefferson to the Presidency in 1800; he was the man who introduced the bugaboo of English plots into American politics. His first acts after his inauguration were to abolish all ceremonial at the court of the Republic, and to abandon spoken discourses to Congress for written messages.[5] Both reforms met with wide approval; the exactions of the English, particularly on the high seas, were beginning to break up the British party. But confidence in the solidarity and security of the new nation was still anything but universal. Democracy was still experimental, doubtful, full of gunpowder. Jefferson, its protagonist, was the hero of the populace, but he was not a part of the populace himself, nor did he ever quite trust it.

It was reserved for Andrew Jackson to lead the rise of the lower orders with dramatic effectiveness. Jackson was the archetype of the new American who appeared after 1814—ignorant, pushful, impatient of restraint and precedent, an iconoclast, a Philistine, an Anglophobe in every fiber. He came from the extreme backwoods, and his youth was passed, like that of Abraham Lincoln after him, amid surroundings but little removed from savagery. Thousands of other young Americans of the same sort were growing up at the same time. They swarmed across the mountains and down the great rivers,[6] wrestling with the naked wilderness and setting up

---

[3] The best brief account of this uprising that I have encountered is not in any history book, but in Mr. Justice Sutherland's dissenting opinion in *Home Building & Loan Ass'n* v. *Blaisdell et al.*, 54 *Supreme Court Reporter*, pp. 224 ff.

[4] In 1812 an actual conspiracy was unearthed to separate New England from the Republic and make it an English colony. The chief conspirator was one John Henry, who acted under the instructions of Sir John Craig, Governor-General of Canada.

[5] That ceremonial was in imitation, he believed, of the formality of the abhorrent Court of St. James's; the speeches to Congress were modeled upon the speeches from the throne.

[6] Indiana and Illinois were erected into territories during Jefferson's first term, and Michigan during his second. Kentucky was admitted to the Union in 1792, Tennessee in 1796, Ohio in 1803. Lewis and Clark set out for the Pacific in 1804. The Louisiana Purchase was ratified in 1803, and Louisiana became a state in 1812.

a casual, impromptu sort of civilization where the Indian still menaced. Schools were few and rudimentary; any effort to mimic the amenities of the East, or of the mother country, in manner or even in speech, met with instant derision. In these surroundings at this time the thoroughgoing American of tradition was born. America began to stand for something new in the world—in government, in law, in public and private morals, in customs and habits of mind. And simultaneously the voice of America began to take on its characteristic tone colors, and the speech of America began to differentiate itself unmistakably from that of England. The Philadelphian or Bostonian of 1790 had no difficulty in making himself understood by a visiting Englishman. But the Ohio boatman of 1810 or plainsman of 1815 was already speaking a dialect that the Englishman would have shrunk from as barbarous and unintelligible, and before long it began to leave its marks upon a distinctively national literature. The same year, 1828, which saw Jackson elected for his first term also saw the publication of Noah Webster's "American Dictionary of the English Language," and a year later followed Samuel Lorenzo Knapp's "Lectures on American Literature," the first formal treatise on the national letters. Knapp, by that time, had enough material at hand to make a very creditable showing—Bryant's "Thanatopsis" (1817); Irving's "Knickerbocker" (1809), "Sketch Book" (1819) and "Columbus" (1828); Cooper's "The Spy" (1821), "The Pilot" (1823) and "The Prairie" (1826); Hawthorne's "Fanshaw" (1828); and Poe's "Tamerlane and Other Poems" (1827); not to mention Schoolcraft's "Through the Northwest" (1821) and "Travels in the Mississippi Valley" (1825), Kent's "Commentaries" (1826), Marshall's "Washington" (1804) and Audubon's "Birds of America" (1827).

The national feeling, long delayed in appearing, leaped into being at last in truly amazing vigor. "One can get an idea of the strength of that feeling," says R. O. Williams,

> by glancing at almost any book taken at random from the American publications of the period. Belief in the grand future of the United States is the keynote of everything said and done. All things American are to be grand—our territory, population, products, wealth, science, art—but especially our political institutions and literature. Unbounded confidence in the material development of the country . . . prevailed throughout the . . . Union during the first thirty years of the century, and over and above a belief in, and concern for, materialistic progress, there were enthusiastic anticipations of achievements in all the moral and intellectual fields of national greatness.[7]

[7] Our Dictionaries and Other English Language Topics; New York, 1890, pp. 30-1. See also, for an excellent account of the spirit of the time, Localism in American Criticism, by Carey McWilliams, *Southwest Review*, July 1934.

Nor was that vast optimism wholly without warrant. With the memory of old wrongs shutting them off from England, the new American writers turned to the Continent for inspiration and encouragement. Irving had already drunk at Spanish springs; Emerson and Bayard Taylor were to receive powerful impulses from Germany, following Ticknor, Bancroft and Everett before them; Bryant was destined to go back to the classics. Moreover, Irving, Cooper, John P. Kennedy and many another had shown the way to native sources of literary material, and Longfellow was making ready to follow them; the ground was preparing for "Uncle Tom's Cabin." Finally, Webster himself worked better than he knew. His American Dictionary was not only thoroughly American; it was superior to any of the current dictionaries of the English.

Thus all hesitations disappeared, and there arose a national consciousness so soaring and so blatant that it began to dismiss every British usage and opinion as puerile and idiotic. The debate upon the Oregon question gave a gaudy chance to the new breed of super-patriots who raged unchecked until the Civil War. Thornton quotes a typical speech in Congress:

> The proudest bird upon the mountain is upon the American ensign, and not one feather shall fall from her plumage there. She is American in design, and an emblem of wildness and freedom. I say again, she has not perched herself upon American standards to die there. Our great Western valleys were never scooped out for her burial place. Nor were the everlasting, untrodden mountains piled for her monument. Niagara shall not pour her endless waters for her requiem; nor shall our ten thousand rivers weep to the ocean in eternal tears. No, sir, no! Unnumbered voices shall come up from the river, plain, and mountain, echoing the songs of our triumphant deliverance, wild lights from a thousand hill-tops will betoken the rising of the sun of freedom.[8]

This tall talk was not reserved for occasions of state; it decorated everyday speech, especially in the Jackson country to the southward and beyond the mountains. It ran to grotesque metaphors and farfetched exaggerations, and out of it came a great many Americanisms that still flourish. A noble example comes from Mark Twain's "Life on the Mississippi," the time being *c.* 1852:

> Whoo-oop! I'm the old original iron-jawed, brass-mounted, copper-bellied corpse-maker from the wilds of Arkansaw! Look at me! I'm the man they call Sudden Death and General Desolation! Sired by a hurricane, dam'd by an earthquake, half-brother to the cholera, nearly related to the smallpox on the mother's side! . . . Blood's my natural

---

[8] The orator was the Hon. Samuel C. Pomeroy, of Kansas.

drink, and the wails of the dying is music to my ear! Cast your eye on me, gentlemen, and lay low and hold your breath, for I'm 'bout to turn myself loose!

This extravagance of metaphor, with its naïve bombast, was borrowed eagerly by the humorous writers and was to leave its marks upon Whitman and Mark Twain, but the generality of American authors eschewed it. "Whatever differences there may be," says Sir William Craigie,[9] "between the language of Longfellow and Tennyson, of Emerson and Ruskin, they are differences due to style and subject, to a personal choice or command of words, and not to any real divergence in the means of expression." But meanwhile, says Sir William, there was going on

> a rise and rapid growth within the United States of new types of literature which would either give fuller scope to the native element by mingling it with the conventional, or would boldly adopt it as a standard in itself.

On the levels below the Olympians a wild and lawless development of the language went on, and many of the uncouth words and phrases that it brought to birth gradually forced themselves into more or less good usage. The old hegemony of the Tidewater gentry, North and South, had been shaken by the revolt of the frontier under Jackson, and what remained of an urbane habit of mind and utterance began to be confined to the narrowing feudal areas of the South and the still narrower refuge of the Boston Brahmins. The typical American, in Paulding's satirical phrase, became "a bundling, gouging, impious" fellow, without either "morals, literature, religion or refinement." Next to the savage struggle for land and dollars, party politics was the chief concern, and with the entrance of pushing upstarts from the backwoods, political controversy sank to an incredibly low level. First the enfranchised mob, whether in the city wards or along the Western rivers, invented fantastic slang words and turns of phrase; then they were "seized upon by stump-speakers at political meetings"; then they were heard in Congress; then they got into the newspapers; and finally they came into more or less good repute.[1] W. C. Fowler, in listing "low expressions" in 1850, described them as "chiefly political." "The vernacular tongue of the country," said Daniel Webster, "has become greatly vitiated, depraved and corrupted by the style of the congressional debates." This flood of racy and unprecedented words and phrases beat upon and finally penetrated the austere retreat of the literati, but the dignity of speech cultivated there had little compensatory influence upon the vulgate. The newspaper was enthroned, and belles-lettres

---

[9] The Study of American English, *SPE Tract*, No. XXVII, 1927, p. 203.

[1] Bartlett, 2nd ed., intro.

were cultivated almost in private, and as a mystery. "Uncle Tom's Cabin" and "Ten Nights in a Bar-room," both published in the early 1850s, were probably the first contemporary native books, after Cooper's day, that the American people, as a people, ever really read. Nor did the pulpit lift a corrective voice; it joined the crowd, and contributed to the vernacular such treasures as *to doxologize* and *to funeralize.*

This pressure from below eventually broke down the defenses of the purists, and forced the new national idiom upon them. "When it comes to *talking,*" wrote Charles Astor Bristed for Englishmen in 1855, "the most refined and best educated American, who has habitually resided in his own country, the very man who would write, on some serious topic, volumes in which no peculiarity could be detected, will in half a dozen sentences, use at least as many words that cannot fail to strike the inexperienced Englishman who hears them for the first time."

American slang, says Krapp,[2] was "the child of the new nationalism, the spirit of joyous adventure that entered American life after the close of the War of 1812." He goes on:

> One will search earlier colonial literature in vain for any flowering of those verbal ingenuities which ornament the colloquial style of Americans so abundantly in the first great period of Western expansion, and which have ever since found their most favorable conditions along the shifting line of the frontier.

The old American frontier vanished by the end of the Nineteenth Century, but to the immigrants who poured in after 1850, even the slums of the great Eastern cities presented essentially frontier conditions, and there are still cultural, if not geographic, frontiers at Las Vegas and Miami, not to mention Alaska and Mississippi. From 1814 to 1861 the influence of the great open spaces was immediate and enormous, and during those gay and hopeful and melodramatic days all the traditional characteristics of American English were developed—its disdain of all scholastic rules and precedents, its tendency toward bold and often bizarre tropes, its rough humors, its not infrequent flights of what might almost be called poetic fancy, its love of neologisms for their own sake. Recently most neologisms have come from the East, not a few of them painfully artful, but before the Civil War the great reservoir was the West, which then still included a large part of the South, and they showed a gaudy innocence.

"American humor," says Thomas Low Nichols, "consists largely of exaggeration, and of strange and quaint expressions. . . . Much that seems droll to English readers in the extravagances of Western American is very

[2] Is American English Archaic? *Southwest Review,* Summer 1927, pp. 292–303.

seriously intended. The man who described himself as 'squandering about permiscuous' had no idea that his expression was funny. When he boasted of his sister that 'she slings the nastiest ankle in old Kentuck' he only intended to say that she was a good dancer." [3] Yet, however much this may have been true in the earliest days, among the loutish fur trappers and mountain men who constituted the first wave of pioneers, it had ceased to be so by the time the new West began to develop recorders of its speech. The identity of its first recorders has been forgotten, but some of them were professional humorists, for by the end of the 1840s the stars of the craft were beginning to turn from the New England Yankee to the trans-Alleghany American, often a Southerner and usually only theoretically literate. The discovery of gold in California attracted not only fortune seekers but also journalists, and out of their ranks came a large number of satirical historians of the rise of Western civilization, with Mark Twain, in the end, overshadowing all the rest. These wags really made "tall talk" the fearful and wonderful thing that it became during the two pre-war decades, though no doubt its elements were derived from authentic folk speech. It was, said William F. Thompson,[4]

> a form of utterance ranging in composition from striking concoctions of ingeniously contrived epithets, expressing disparagement or encomium, to wild hyperbole, fantastic simile and metaphor, and a highly bombastic display of oratory, employed to impress the listener with the physical prowess or general superiority of the speaker or of his friends.

It survives more or less in Western fiction, and there are even traces of it remaining in real life,[5] but the best of it belongs to the Jackson era, when it first burgeoned: *to absquatulate, bodaciously, to obflisticate, to ramsquaddle, ringtailed roarer* and *screamer.*[6] *To absquatulate,* meaning to depart stealthily, is traced by the DA to 1830, and *bodaciously,* meaning completely, to 1837; in the form *body-aciously* it was used by James Hall in his "Legends of the West" (second edition, 1832). *To obflisticate,* meaning to eclipse or obliterate, is traced to 1832, with *to obflusticate* and *to obfusticate* as variants. *To ramsquaddle,* which dates from 1830, seems to have been a synonym for its contemporary *to exflunct, i.e.,* to beat, which soon developed a host of variants and derivatives. *Ringtailed roarer,* a big and hearty fellow, is traced to 1830, and *screamer,* a strong man,

---

[3] Forty Years of American Life, 1821–1861; London, 1864; reprinted, London, 1874; New York, 1937.

[4] Frontier Tall Talk, *AS*, Vol. IX, Oct. 1934, p. 187.

[5] Tall Talk of the Texas Trans-Pecos, by Haldeen Braddy, *AS*, Vol. XV, Apr. 1940, pp. 220–2.

[6] B. A. Botkin, Treasury of American Folklore; New York, 1944, p. 273.

to 1831. Many other similar coinages date from the period. *Rip-roaring,*
now almost standard American, is traced to 1834, and *rip-snorter* to 1840.
The DAE's first example of *teetotal* is dated 1837, three years later than
the date of the first English example, but *teetotaciously* had appeared in
1833, and *tetotally* (soon *teetotally*) in the letters of the celebrated Parson
Weems (1807). *Conbobberation,* a disturbance, is traced to 1835; *to hornswoggle,* to cheat, to 1829; *rambunctious,* uncontrollable, to 1830; and
peedoodles, a nervous disorder, to 1835.

Some of the Western terms of the 1812–61 era remain mysterious, *e.g.,*
bogus and *burgoo.* The noun *bogus* first signified an apparatus for making
counterfeit money. By 1839 it was being applied to counterfeit money, and
had become an adjective with the general sense of not genuine. *Burgoo*
was borrowed originally from the argot of British sailors, to whom it
meant a thick oatmeal porridge. It came to designate a meat-and-vegetable
stew in the West in the early 1830s, and since then it has been generally
associated with Kentucky, especially with the Derby. Arthur H. Deute, a
culinary authority,[7] says that it is composed of a mixture of rabbit or
squirrel meat, chicken, beef, salt pork, potatoes, string beans, onions, lima
beans, corn, okra, carrots and tomatoes, and is made in two pots, the
meats in a small one and the vegetables in a large. The two are well stirred
together, and the *burgoo* is ready. [*Charivari* seems to have been adopted
from the French in the Mississippi Valley, to replace a variety of Eastern
terms.[8]] It signifies, primarily, a rowdy serenade of a newly married couple,
but it is also used to designate any noisy demonstration. In various spellings,
it dates from the early Nineteenth Century. The *shivaree* (the simplest
phonetic spelling) still survives in many rural areas, East and West, under
such other names as *belling, warmer, serenade, horning, rouser, wake-up,*
jamboree, tin-pan shower, skimmelton and *callithumpian. Callithumpian*
was once used "in New York as well as other parts of the country," to
designate a noisy parade on New Year's Eve, but such parades have gone
out of fashion; [in the Midwest a *callithumpian band* or *parade,* of
children in false faces, was often a part of Independence Day festivities
down to World War I].

Stogy, in the sense of a crude cigar, made with a simple twist at the
mouthward end instead of a fashioned head, is not traced beyond 1893, but
it must be very much older. It is a shortened form of *Conestoga,* the name
for a heavy covered wagon with broad wheels, much in use in the early

---

[7] Pages from the Notebook of a Gour-
met, Chicago *Daily News,* May 4, 1944,
p. 21.

[8] [See *Shivaree:* an Example of Cultural Diffusion, by Alva L. Davis and
Raven I. McDavid, Jr., *AS,* Vol. XXIV,
Dec. 1949, pp. 249–55. It reappraises previous studies in the light of the LA
evidence.]

days for transport over the Alleghanies. This name came from that of the Conestoga Valley in Lancaster County, Pa., which came in turn from that of a long-extinct band of Iroquois Indians. The term *Conestoga wagon* was used in Pennsylvania before 1750, but it was apparently but little known to the country at large until the westward migrations after 1800. Many of the Conestoga wagoners were Pennsylvanians, and they prepared the tobacco of Lancaster County for smoking on their long trips by rolling it into what soon became known as *Conestogies* and then *stogies*. The commercial manufacture of these pseudo-cigars is now centered, not in Pennsylvania, but at Wheeling, W. Va. The *Conestoga wagon* survived until the Twentieth Century, not only in the Pennsylvania German country, but in the southern Appalachians. The covered wagon of the Western pioneer was often a *Conestoga*.

2: THE EXPANDING VOCABULARY

The pioneers who trekked westward between the War of 1812 and the Civil War stood a great deal closer to the 1937 Okies than to the heroic figures in historical fiction. They were not, perhaps, as vicious as the Puritans of early New England, but they lacked the cultural aptitudes that, in the Puritans, even Calvinism could not kill. Most were bankrupt small farmers or down-at-the-heel city proletarians, and the rest were mainly chronic nomads of the sort who, a century later, roved the country in caricatures of automobiles. If they started for Kentucky or Ohio, they were presently moving on to Indiana or Illinois, and after that, doggedly and irrationally, to even wilder and less hospitable regions.[9] When they halted, it was simply because they had become exhausted. There ensued, commonly, a desperate struggle with the climate, the Indians, the local Mammalia and Insectivora and assorted plagues and pestilences, and if, by some chance mercy of their sanguinary God, they survived and an organized community arose, it was quickly afflicted by a fresh scourge of moneylenders, theologians, patent-medicine quacks and politicians. The loutish humor of these poor folks was their Freudian reply to the intolerable hardships of their existence. They had to laugh to escape going crazy—and not infrequently the remedy did not work. It was not in relatively civilized centers like Cincinnati and St. Louis that the "tall talk" of the West developed or that the racier new words and phrases of the era were coined; it was along the rivers, in the mountains and among the lonely and malarious settlements of the prairies.

---

[9] How the last wave of them was finally brought up by the Pacific on the coast of Oregon was described in Honey in the Horn, by H. L. Davis; New York, 1935. The Oklahoma backwash was dealt with sentimentally in Grapes of Wrath, by John Steinbeck; New York, 1939; and more realistically in Prairie City, by Angie Debo; New York, 1944.

These words lacked subtlety, but were pungent and picturesque; and like every other trait of the crude, autochthonous trans-Alleghany culture, they had repercussions in the East.

Along the seaboard, not only Boston but also New Haven, New York, Philadelphia, Baltimore and Charleston had their caste of austere and hopeful Brahmins who knew precisely what was right and what was wrong in the most minute details of private conduct. Reformers of a thousand varieties swarmed the land, whooping up their new arcana and passing the hat. Their common aim was to polish and refine the country; they frowned, like William Jennings Bryan in 1925, upon the suggestion that *Homo americanus* was a mammal. But the West was fast devouring the East, and a true Century of the Common Man was beginning. The tide turned with Jackson's election in 1828. By the time the fumes of the Civil War cleared away, the whole American empire was closer to a mining camp in its life and thought than to the grove of Academe. Emerson had shrunk to a wraith almost as impalpable as his own Transcendentalism, and the reigning demigod was a river boatman and rail splitter of the West. Of all the evangelists of Better Things only Noah Webster left any mark. He taught the American people how to spell, but he taught them nothing else.[1]

During the period from 1815 to 1865 thousands of characteristic Americanisms were hatched by ingenious men—to the probable horror of all the visionaries sneered at by Emerson,[2] and to the equal horror of Emerson himself, but to the delight of the populace that these visionaries were bent on serving. There were plenty of antinomians well fitted for the job—the journalists of the new penny press, the humorists who came from their ranks, the itinerant traders and schemers, the politicians who roared from 10,000 stumps.

Examining the letter *S* in the DAE or the DA, we can find an unschooled and uninhibited boldness of trope in such coinages as *to keep one's shirt on, to slop over, stag party, swell head* and *spread-eagle;* the frequent brutal literalness, *e.g., shakes, smash up, spitball* and *sure thing;* and also a great fondness for harsh debasements of more seemly words, *e.g., to scoot, slick* and *to smooch.* The origins of many of these are still unknown or violently disputed.

To scoot, says the OED, may be derived from a sailor's verb, *to scout,*

---

[1] The influence of Webster is presented by Warfel, especially pp. 76 ff. There is more in The Development of Faith in the Dictionary in America, by Allen Walker Read, a paper read before the Present-Day English section of the Modern Language Association at Philadelphia, Dec. 29, 1934; [and in Words and Ways of American English, by Thomas Pyles; New York, 1952, especially pp. 93–124].

[2] In speaking of a congress of reformers of all wings, held in Boston in 1840.

meaning to go away hurriedly, but in its current meaning it was "apparently imported into general British use from the United States," where it is traced to 1841. *Slick*, a variant of *sleek*, is old in England, but it seems to have dropped out there to be revived in the United States. Most of the phrases in which it occurs, *e.g.*, *slick as a whistle* and *to slick up*, are unquestionable Americanisms. *To smooch*, meaning to dirty, is old in English, but has been almost exclusively in American use since the early Nineteenth Century. It apparently comes from *to smutch* or *to smudge*. *To smouch*, meaning to pilfer, is also an English archaism revived in the United States. Mark Twain used it so often that Ramsay and Emberson call it one of his favorite words.

The period under review was rich in uncouth neologisms of the class of *shebang, shindig, to skedaddle, skeezicks, slangwhanger, slumgullion, sockdolager, splendiferous* and *spondulicks*, many of which survive. *Shebang*, possibly related to the Irish *shebeen*, an unlicensed drinking place, came into great popularity during the Civil War. *Shindig* was used in the South, before the Civil War, in the literal sense of a blow on the shins, but it soon took on the meaning of a rowdy party [and is now often used for any informal social event]. *To skedaddle*, which came into use during the Civil War, has long intrigued etymologists. [Most probably it is related to a Scottish and Northern English dialect word meaning to spill potatoes or lumps of coal. But it remained for some mute inglorious American Milton to extend the metaphor to the precipitate departure of Confederates from the battlefield.[3]]

Skeezicks, originally meaning a good-for-nothing but later used mainly in playful and affectionate senses, is traced by the DAE to 1850. *Slangwhanger* was used in 1807 by Irving for a bitterly partisan political journalist, but by the time of Pickering's Vocabulary (1816) it had come to mean also a demogogic orator.

Slumgullion came into use during the California gold rush to signify a muddy residue left after sluicing gravel, but it had already been used to designate anything disgusting, especially food or drink. American tramps now use it as a synonym for *mulligan*, a stew made of any comestibles they can beg or steal. Not infrequently it is shortened to *slum*, like *slum-*

---

[3] [See Three Keys to Language, by Robert M. Estrich and Hans Sperber; New York, 1952, pp. 290–2. In New Brunswick those New Englanders who crossed the border to improve their health during the Civil War were known as *Skedaddlers*, and one of their settlements is still called *Skedaddlers Ridge*. The Province, traditionally depressed economically, benefited in 1861–5 not only from these immigrants but from bonuses paid the New Brunswickers who served as substitutes for Yankee draftees. I am here indebted to William Acheson, of Fredericton, N.B.]

gullion an Americanism. *Sockdolager,* first recorded in 1830, originally meant a knock-down blow, but now signifies anything large or overwhelming. It is still used by prize fighters in its original sense, along with a variant, *sockeroo. Splendiferous,* first encountered in R. M. Bird's "Nick of the Woods" (1837), is now reduced to consciously whimsical usage, along with its congeners, *splendacious, grandiferous* and *scrumptious.*[4] *Spondulicks,* money, often spelled *spondulix,* is traced to 1856.

Not a few of the characteristic coinages of the era have become obsolete: *slantidicular, squirtish* and *to squizzle. Sposhy,* meaning soft or wet, flourished in the 1840s, but is now no more; it had a noun, *sposh,* meaning mud or slush, that has also gone to word heaven. A *snollygoster,* apparently confined to the South, was a political jobseeker, defined by "a Georgia paper," quoted by the DAE, as "a fellow who wants office, regardless of party, platform or principles, and who, whenever he wins, gets there by the sheer force of monumental talknophical assumacy." [It had dropped out of public existence until it was revived by Harry Truman in 1952 to characterize politicians who pray in public to get votes.[5] *Spizzerinctum* has also been revived. It originally meant money, but has recently been used by the austere *New York Times* to epitomize the indefinable qualities of leadership associated with Ralph Houk, manager of the New York Yankees.[6]] *Savagerous,* probably a fanciful association with *savage* and *dangerous,* dates from 1832, and seems to have been in general use till *c.* 1870. [A variant *se(r)vigrous* still occurs in the South in the shortened form *vigrous,* with the vowel of *tiger.*]

So far, the letter *S* only. It is astonishing how many of the common coins of American speech date from this period, *e.g.,* the terms in *dead-, horse-* and *ice-. Dead broke* is traced to 1851, *deadhead* to 1841 and *deadbeat* to 1863. *Dead right* and *dead wrong* may have originated in England, but most Englishmen now think of them as Americanisms. The figurative use of *deadline* (as in newspapermen's argot) is clearly American, and so are *dead to rights* and *on the dead run.* Of the common Americanisms in *horse-, horse sense* is traced to 1832,[7] *horse swapping* to 1800, *horse trading* to 1826 and *horse thief* to 1768. *Man on horseback* is an Americanism, and was apparently first applied to General Grant in 1879. So is the phrase

---

[4] A long list of such terms is in Terms of Approbation and Eulogy in American Dialect Speech, by Elsie L. Warnock, *DN,* Vol. IV, Pt. I, 1913, pp. 18–20. [See also The Social Significance of the Language of the American Frontier, by C. Merton Babcock, *AS,* Vol. XXIV, Dec. 1949, pp. 256–63.]
[5] [Leo Spitzer, *AS,* Vol. XXIX, Feb. 1954, p. 85.]

[6] [*The New York Times,* Nov. 18, 1960.]
[7] It does not refer, of course, to the intelligence of the horse, which is one of the stupidest animals on earth. The term originated, I fancy, among horse traders, and had reference to smartness at their science.

hold your horses, which the DA traces to 1844. *Horse show* is traced to
1856. *Harper's Magazine* praised it in 1860 as "good because it is descriptive," though noting that *show* had become somewhat vulgarized by *minstrel show.*[8] The English were aware of *iced cream* (borrowed from Italy)
by 1688, but the first appearance of *ice cream,* in 1744, was in America.
The DA traces *icebreaker* to 1816, *icebox* to 1846, *ice-cream freezer* to
1854, *ice-cream saloon* to 1847, *iceman* to 1844, and *ice wagon* to 1853.
Ice pick is not recorded until 1879, *iced tea* not until 1880, and *ice-cream
soda* not until 1886.

The stately word *anesthesia* appeared in Nathan Bailey's "Dictionarium
Britannicum" in 1721, defined as "a defect of sensation, as in paralytic or
blasted persons," but Oliver Wendell Holmes the elder launched it in the
meaning of an insensitiveness produced by a drug, as well as *anesthetic* as
a designation for the drug itself. Both words have gone into the vocabularies of all civilized languages, [as have *appendicitis* (1886), *appendec-
tomy* (1903) and *geriatrics* (1909)].[9] The Morse *telegraph,* first used in
1844, did not introduce the word, which had been used in England to
designate various other contrivances for transmitting messages. But *telegram* (1852) is an Americanism, as is *cablegram* (1868). *Telephone* was
introduced by Alexander Graham Bell in 1876.[1] The verb *to telephone* is
traced to 1880; *to phone* probably came in soon afterward. The introduction of photography in the early 1840s brought on a combat between
photographer and *photographist. Photographist* appeared in *Sartain's Magazine* (Philadelphia) so early as 1852 [2] and survived until the 70s, but was
then completely supplanted by *photographer.*

A few miscellaneous examples of words and phrases first recorded during the period under review: *blood and thunder* is traced to 1852, *to back
down* to 1848, *bulletin board* to 1831, *chewing gum* to 1850, *close shave*
to 1834, *caboose* (of a train) to 1861, *to raise Cain* to 1840, *to face the
music* to 1850, *to flunk* to 1823, *ornery* to 1830, *walking papers* to 1825,
wholehearted to 1840, *surprise party* to 1859, *buddy* to 1850,[3] *in cahoots*
to 1829, *grab bag* to 1855, *bridal tour* to before 1855, *one-horse* (in the
general sense of petty) to 1853, *to be mustered out* to 1834, *packing house*
(for meats) to 1835, *pilot house* to 1846, *extra* (of a newspaper) to 1842,

[8] Aug. 1860, p. 411.

[9] Holmes used the words in a letter,
dated Nov. 20, 1846, to W. T. G. Morton,
the discoverer of ether anesthesia. On
Oct. 16, 1846, Morton, a dentist, administered ether to a patient undergoing,
at the Massachusetts General Hospital,
an operation for removal of a tumor on
the jaw. Holmes spelled the words *anaesthetic* and *anaesthesia,* the form still preferred in England. [*Geriatrics* was
coined by I. L. Nascher in a paper which
appeared in the *N.Y. Medical Journal.*]

[1] His first patent was issued on Mar. 7
of that year.

[2] Jan., p. 94.

[3] *Buddy* is discussed in The Southwestern Word Box, by T. M. P[earce],
New Mexico Quarterly, Vol. II, Nov.
1932, p. 340.

firecracker to 1829, *wharf rat* to 1823 and *quick on the trigger* to 1808.

Some of the characteristic coinages of the time make one sympathize with the pious horror of Dean Alford. Bartlett quotes *to doxologize* from the *Christian Disciple*, a quite reputable religious paper of the 40s. *To funeralize* [4] and *to pastor*, along with *to missionate* and *consociational*, were other contributions of the evangelical pulpit; it also produced *hellroaring* and *hellion*, the latter a favorite of the Mormons and even used by Henry Ward Beecher. *To deacon*, a verb which in colonial days signified to read a hymn line by line, began to mean to swindle or adulterate, *e.g.*, to extend one's fences *sub rosa* or to mix sand with sugar. A great rage for extending the vocabulary by the use of suffixes seized upon the corn-fed etymologists, and they produced a formidable new vocabulary, in *-ize*, *-ate*, *-ify*, *-acy*, *-ous* and *-ment*. Such inventions as *to concertize*, *retiracy* and *citified* appeared in the popular vocabulary and even in more or less respectable usage. Fowler, in 1850, cited *publishment* and *releasement* with no apparent thought that they were uncouth. And many verbs were made by the simple process of back formation, as *to enthuse*.

Some of these inventions were retired during the period of plush elegance following the Civil War, but a large number have survived. No purist would object to *affiliate, to collide, to predicate, to resurrect* or *to Americanize* today, though all gave grief to the judicious when introduced in the debates of Congress by statesmen from the backwoods. Nor to such simpler verbs as *to corner* (*i.e.*, the market). Nor perhaps to *to boom, to splurge, to bulldoze, to aggravate* (in the sense of to anger) and *to crawfish*. These verbs have entered into the very fiber of the American language, and so have many nouns derived from them, *e.g.*, *boomer, boom town* and *splurge*. A few of them, *e.g.*, *to collide*, were archaic English terms brought to new birth; a few others, *e.g.*, *to muss*, were obviously mere corruptions. But a good many others, *e.g.*, *to bulldoze* and *to hornswoggle*, were genuine inventions, and redolent of the soil.

Along with these new verbs came a great swarm of verb phrases showing the national talent for condensing a complex thought, and often a whole series of thoughts, into a vivid and arresting image. Typical are *to fill the bill* and *to back water*. Somewhat more elaborate are such common coins of speech as *to make the fur fly, to handle without gloves, to freeze on to, to know the ropes, to paint the town red* and *to take a back seat*. We use these idioms without thought; they seem as authentic English as *to be left at the post*. And yet, all appear to be of American nativity, and for some the circumstances surrounding their origin have been accurately deter-

---

[4] The OED quotes an example of its use in the sense of to render sad or melancholy from Sir Thomas Browne's Urn Burial (1658). But in the sense of to conduct a funeral the verb seems to be American.

mined. Many others are as certainly products of the great westward movement: *to pan out, to pull up stakes, to rope in, to get the deadwood on* and *to do a land-office business.* In many others the authentic American flavor is no less plain, *e.g.,* in *to see the elephant, to do up brown* and *to bark up the wrong tree.*

Of adjectives the list is scarcely less long. Among the coinages of the first half of the century that are still in use today are *non-committal, highfalutin, played-out, under the weather* and *flat-footed.* The first appears in 1829;[5] *highfalutin* is in a political speech of 1848. Both are useful words; it is impossible, not employing them, to convey the ideas behind them without circumlocution. The use of *slim* in the sense of meager, as in *slim chance,* goes back still further.

Other and less respectable contributions of the time are *peart, beatingest, codfish* (to indicate opprobrium) and *go-to-meeting.* The use of *plumb* as an adverb, as in *plumb crazy,* is an English archaism that was revived in the United States in the early years of the century. Although the characteristic American use of *mad* for *angry*—an archaism dating from 1300 in England—had been denounced in 1781 by Witherspoon and in 1816 by Pickering, it got into much better odor soon afterward, and by 1840 it was passing unchallenged. In the familiar simile, *as mad as a hornet,* it is used in the American sense, but *as mad as a March hare* is English, connoting insanity, not anger. The English meaning is preserved in *madhouse* and *mad dog,* but American rustics often derive the latter from a vague notion, not that the dog is demented, but that it is in a simple fury.

It was not, however, among the verbs and adjectives that the word coiners achieved their gaudiest innovations, but among the substantives. Here they had temptation and excuse in innumerable new objects and relations, and they exercised their fancy without restraint. As earlier, three main varieties of new nouns were produced: English words rescued from obsolescence or changed in meaning; compounds manufactured of the common materials of the mother tongue; and entirely new inventions. Of the first class, good specimens are *gulch, gully* and *billion,* the first two restored to usage in American and the last changed in meaning. Of the second class, examples are offered by *mortgage shark, cutoff, dugout, buzz saw* and *chain gang.* Of the third there are instances in *buncombe, bloomer, maverick, bugaboo* and *blizzard.*

Of these coinages perhaps those of the second class are most numerous and characteristic. In them American exhibits its habit of achieving short

---

[5] It quickly bred two nouns, *non-committal* and *non-committalism,* and the latter had the political significance of *straddling* in the 50s, but both seem to have gone out. An adverb, *non-committally,* has survived, and the Oxford Dictionary quotes it from Howells's The Rise of Silas Lapham (1885).

cuts by bold combinations. Why describe a gigantic rainstorm with the lame adjectives of every day? Call it a *cloudburst* and immediately a vivid picture is conjured up. *Roughneck* is more apposite and savory than any English equivalent, and unmistakably American. The same instinct for the terse, the vivid and the picturesque appears in *boiled shirt, claim jumper, home stretch, comedown, bottom dollar, cold snap, crazy quilt, ticket scalper, prairie schooner* and *flatboat*. Such compounds give the American vulgate its characteristic tang and color. *Bellhop, square meal* and *chair warmer*, to name three charming specimens, are as distinctively American as jazz or the quick lunch.

The spirit of the language also appears clearly in coinages of the other classes. English words have been extended or restricted in meaning, *e.g.*, *docket* (for court calendar), *collateral* (for security), *crank* (for fanatic), *backbone* (for moral courage), *scrape* (for fight or difficulty), *flurry* (of snow, or in the market), *suspenders* and *range*. Again, English materials have been rearranged, *e.g.*, *rowdy, teetotaler* and *cussedness*. Yet again, there are purely artificial words, *e.g.*, *guyascutus* and *scrumptious*. Of course, fashions change. In the 1840s *to absquatulate* was in good usage, but it has since disappeared. Most inventions of the time, however, have survived, and most Americans still know the meaning of *scalawag, rambunctious* and *to skedaddle*, and occasionally use them.

The *bee* proliferated in the early Nineteenth Century. Whenever a pioneer had a job that was too much for him and his family, the neighbors pitched in to help, and there was usually a jollification when the work was over. The DAE traces *husking bee* to 1816, *quilting bee* to 1832, *sewing bee* to 1856 and *spelling bee* to 1875. All of them are probably older, especially *spelling bee*. The simple word *bee* was also used to signify a donation party for a pastor, and sometimes that party included repairs to his house. This sense goes back to 1823. *Beeline* is also an Americanism, traced to *c.* 1845.

Already by the 1830s the two languages were so differentiated that they produced wholly distinct railroad nomenclatures. Such commonplace American terms as *cowcatcher*,[6] *boxcar* and *airline* are still strangers to England. So are *flagman, switch, switch engine, track walker, baggage master, express car, flatcar, gondola, waybill, expressman, fast freight, depot, hotbox, stopover, tie, fishplate, run, chair car, club car, bumpers, mail clerk, truck* and *right of way*, and the verbs *to flag, to side-swipe, to fire*

---

[6] [*Cowcatcher*, points out Southworth Lancaster of Boston University, "has always been slang; the correct term is *pilot*. *Front end* displaced *cowcatcher* among railroad men a good many years ago, while I have traced *pilot* back to the early days, although I cannot put a date to it." Personal communication, Apr. 7, 1957.]

(*i.e.*, a locomotive), *to switch, to side-track, to commute* and *to clear the track*. These terms are in constant use in America; their meaning is familiar to all Americans; many of them have given the language everyday figures of speech. But the majority of them would puzzle an Englishman, just as the English *plough, crossing-plate, permanent way, shunt, metals* and *bogie* would puzzle the average untraveled American.

Blizzard, set afloat by the first wave of Western pioneers, did not acquire its present significance until after the Civil War.[7] As recorded by Dunglison in 1829, *blizzard* was defined as "a violent blow, perhaps from *Blitz* (German: *lightning*)" and ascribed to Kentucky. It next turned up in David Crockett's autobiography (1834), in the sense of a rifle shot, and a year later in the sense of a crushing retort, in Crockett's "Tour to the North and Down East." By 1846, it was used to signify a cannon shot and during the Civil War it came to mean a volley of musketry. The possibility of onomatopoetic origin is suggested by various English dialect words in *bliz-*, all of them signifying some sort of violent action, and by the German *Blitz*. It was first applied to a severe snowstorm, with high wind, in the village of Estherville, Iowa, probably in the pioneer village newspaper, the *Northern Vindicator*, sometime during the early spring of 1870.[8] In a little while the term was in wide use all over the upper Midwest. During the winter of 1880–1, which saw a long succession of severe storms, it reached the rest of the country and even England. Soon afterward the discussion of its etymology began, and there has been wrangling over it ever since.

One of the characteristic inventions of pre-Civil War days was the *guyascutus*, an imaginary animal that still survives in American folklore.[9] Its original name was *guyanousa*:[1] "a monster of gigantic proportions," inhabiting "the tallest branches of the poplar" in "the disputed territory of

---

[7] Allen Walker Read, The Word *Blizzard, AS*, Vol. III, Feb. 1928, pp. 191–217. Frank H. Vizetelly printed a far from effective criticism of this paper in *AS*, Vol. III, Aug. 1928, pp. 489–90, and Read replied in *Blizzard Again, AS*, Vol. V, Feb. 1930, pp. 232–5.

[8] Estherville, now a town of [7,000] people, is in the northwestern part of the state, near the Minnesota line. The *Vindicator*, now the *Vindicator and Republican*, a semi-weekly, is still its principal newspaper. O. C. Bates, its editor in 1870, was fond of contemporary neologisms and seems to have devised a number of his own, *e.g.*, *baseballism* and *weatherist*. He may have first applied *blizzard* to a storm, or he may have picked it up from a town

character known as Lightning Ellis, but he gave it a heavy play after Estherville was snowed in on Mar. 14, 1870, and ever thereafter that storm was spoken of locally as the *March blizzard* or the *great blizzard*.

[9] Such monsters, of course, go back to the infancy of humanity. The *basilisk*, the *phoenix*, the *dragon* and the *sea serpent* will be recalled.

[1] Adventures of a Yankee Doodle; Ch. VI: The *Guyanousa, Knickerbocker Magazine*, July 1846, pp. 36–8. Randall V. Mills suggests in Frontier Humor in Oregon and Its Characteristics, *Oregon Historical Quarterly*, Dec. 1942, p. 355, that the author may have been George P. Burnham, a forgotten humorist of the period.

Penobscot" in Maine.[2] Men of vision were going about the country offering to show an alleged specimen in a tent; as soon as a paying crowd of yokels was assembled, they would dash out of the tent yelling, "The *guyanousa* am loose!" and the customers would decamp. Within a few months the tale reached Oregon, the scene of the swindle was transferred to the South and the beast renamed *guyascutus*.[3] The habits of the bearer were described differently by different authorities. A San Francisco journalist, George H. Derby, differentiated between the *guyascutus* and a similar beast, the *prock,* as known in Oregon;[4] but in the East the two apparently remained identical, and the chief mark of the combined creature was that its legs were longer on one side than on the other, and it could thus graze on steep hillsides. The alternate name *sidewinder* and various forms in *sidehill* plainly refer to this.

The *guyascutus* quickly entered into the florid mythology of the North-west, and "The *guyascutus* am loose" became a popular catch phrase, signifying that skulduggery was abroad. *Guyastacutas* was also used in the 1850s to designate a drum used by the callithumpian bands of the period. This drum was made of "a nail keg with a raw hide strained over it. . . . Inside of the keg, attached to the center of this drumhead, a string hung, with which the instrument was worked by pulling in the string and letting fly." [5]

There were many other mythical beasts in those days, and the record of such marvels is not complete even now. In 1939 the United Press reported from Glastonbury, Conn., that a mysterious beast said to resemble a lion, a cougar, a panther and a boar was terrifying the people there, and that some learned man among them had given it the name *glawackus*.[6] In November 1944, a similar creature roved the vicinity of Frizzleburg, Md., and was reported to have fought and routed a bull.

A majority of the terms still used by American boozers—and taken by them from Stockholm to Sydney—date from the gaudy era before the Civil War. Here the DAE and DA offer less help than they should, for the

---

[2] The territory east of the Penobscot River had been occupied by the British since the beginning of the War of 1812. In 1842 it was restored to the United States by the Ashburton Treaty, but ratification did not follow until some time afterward.

[3] The *Guiaskuitas,* by an Ox Driver, *Oregon Spectator,* Oct. 16, 1846.

[4] According to Derby, the *prock* or *sidehill sauger* could shorten the legs on one side by dislocating its shoulder joints at will; the *guyascutus,* a large harmless rodent, was heavily armored like a small Stegosaurus. [See also Cecily D. Raysor, The British brock and badger: the American prock or side-hill gouger, *AS,* Vol. XXXIV, May 1959, pp. 152–3.]

[5] H. H. Riley, Puddleford and Its People; New York, 1854, p. 94.

[6] *AS,* Vol. XIV, Oct. 1939, p. 238. [The sacred *Whiffenpoof* of Yale might also be added; see B. A. Botkin, A Treasury of American Folklore; New York, 1944, p. 639. Botkin has reprinted the natural history of several of these monsters.]

editors seem to have fought shy of the inspiring vocabulary of bibbing.[7] The DAE defines *cooler* lamely as "a cooling spirituous drink," and in its first quotation, from the New Orleans *Picayune*, there is an effort to connect it with the *julep*. This is absurd, for a *cooler*, save when concocted obscenely of Scotch whiskey, must contain lemon juice, which would be as out of place in a *julep* as catsup or gasoline. The true father of the *mint julep* is the *smash*, traced in the form of *brandy smash* to 1850. The DAE's first example of *mint julep* is dated 1809, in the writings of Washington Irving. *Julep* is not an Americanism, for it came into English *c.* 1400, from the Spanish and Portuguese *julepe* by the way of the French. But the English *julep* of those early days was only a sweet and harmless chaser for unpleasant medicines, whereas the *julep* of today is something quite else again, and the honest OED marks it "U.S." [8]

[The earliest DA citation for *rickey*, in the form *gin rickey*, is dated 1895. Authorities agree that the drink was named after a distinguished Washington guzzler of the period, but his identity is disputed, as is the original formula of the *rickey*.[9]] The standard *rickey* of today is made of any ardent spirits (including applejack), lime juice, and soda water. Quack *rickeys*, containing syrups or decorated with slices of orange or pineapple, are not served in bars of any tone. The addition of sugar converts a *rickey* into a *Tom Collins*, supposedly named after its inventor, a distinguished bartender, and the substitution of Holland gin for dry gin makes a *Tom Collins* a *John Collins*.[1] The use of Scotch whiskey and the substitution of ginger ale for soda water produces a *Mamie Taylor*, which has been described as "a popular summer drink," but is actually almost undrinkable. But the use of genuine ginger *beer* instead of ginger *ale* [2] produces some-

---

[7] [For example, New Orleans, one of the citadels of Christian drinking during the dry era, has benefited mankind by developing the *Sazerac cocktail* and the *gin fizz;* both of these blessings are ignored. However, the *silver top*, defined tentatively by the DA as a glass of beer, is possibly a nickname for a *gin fizz*, since the quotation is from the New Orleans *Picayune*. For a longer discussion of some of these terms, see Mencken's Postscripts to the American Language: the Vocabulary of the Drinking Chamber, *The New Yorker*, Nov. 6, 1948, pp. 62–7.]

[8] The old and extremely bitter controversy over the spirituous content of the *julep* need not be gone into here. In Kentucky and its spiritual dependencies Bourbon is always used, but in the Maryland Free State it would be an indeco-

rum verging upon indecency to use anything save rye whiskey. There is every reason to believe that in the first *juleps* the motive power was supplied by brandy.

[9] For some of the theories see The Life and Letters of Henry William Thomas, Mixologist, by Charles V. Wheeler; 2nd ed.; Washington, 1939, p. 7; In Memoriam, by Albert Stevens Crockett, *American Mercury*, Feb. 1930, pp. 229–34; and One Evening on Newspaper Row, a one-act dramatic sketch published by the Gridiron Club, Washington, 1930.

[1] The Official Mixer's Manual, by Patrick Gavin Duffy; New York, 1934, p. 233.

[2] Ginger *beer* is fermented like any other beer; ginger *ale* is mixed in a vat.

thing that is magnificent, whether based upon gin, rum, rye whiskey or Bourbon.

The *sour* is simply a mixture of a hard liquor, sugar, lemon and/or lime juice, and chopped ice, and is usually served strained. [The *brandy sour* is traced by the DA to 1861, as favored by a distinguished South Carolinian; the *whiskey sour* is not recorded till 1891.] Fancy forms contain liqueurs and even eggs, but are not favored by connoisseurs. The *sour* was once in great request among bibuli as a morning pickup to allay gastritis. The *fix* is substantially an unstrained *sour*, the *fizz* is the same with soda water, and the *daisy* is a *fizz* with the addition of a dash of grenadine, maraschino or something of the sort. The DAE traces the *sherry cobbler* to 1841 and calls it an American invention. The OED says that the origin of *cobbler* "appears to be lost." "Various conjectures," it adds, "are current, *e.g.*, that it is short for *cobbler's punch*, that it 'patches up' the drinkers." The *cobbler's punch*, which is defined as "a warm drink of beer or ale with the addition of spirit, sugar and spice," is traced only to 1865, and may have been borrowed from the American *cobbler*. The modern *sherry cobbler* consists of sherry, sugar and cracked ice, with no addition of malt liquor or spice.

The *cocktail*, to multitudes of foreigners, seems to be the greatest symbol of the American way of life, but the etymology of its name is unknown, and the thing itself may not be of American origin. Of the numerous etymologies the only ones showing any plausibility are the following:

1. That the word comes from the French *coquetier*, an eggcup, and was first used in New Orleans soon after 1800.[3]

2. That it is derived from *coquetel*, the name of a mixed drink known in the vicinity of Bordeaux and introduced to America by French officers during the Revolution.

3. That it descends from *cock ale*, a mixture of ale and the essence of a boiled fowl, traced by the OED to *c.* 1648 in England.[4]

4. That its parent was a later *cock ale*, meaning a mixture of spirits and bitters fed to fighting cocks in training.

5. That it comes from *cock-tailed*, "having the tail docked so that the short stump sticks up like a cock's tail."

6. That it is a shortened form of *cock tailings*, the name of a mixture

---

[3] The *Cocktail*, America's Drink, Was Originated in New Orleans, *Roosevelt Review* (house organ of the Roosevelt Hotel, New Orleans), Apr. 1943, pp. 30–1. This unsigned article attributes the *cocktail* to Antoine Amédée Peychaud, inventor of *Peychaud bitters*. Since he used brandy made by Sazerac du Forge et Fils, of Limoges, his cocktails were called *Sazeracs*. Rye whiskey later replaced the brandy.

[4] Peter Tamony, Origin of Words: *Cocktail*, San Francisco *News Letter and Wasp*, Aug. 4, 1939, p. 4. The word has got into practically all modern languages, including Japanese, and C. K. Ogden includes it among the fifty "international words" taken into Basic English.

of tailings from various liquors, thrown together in a common receptacle and sold at a low price.

7. That "in the days of cock-fighting, the spectators used to toast the cock with the most feathers left in its tail after the contest," and "the number of ingredients in the drink corresponded with the number of feathers left."

[All are somewhat fishy.]

A cocktail today consists essentially of any hard liquor, any milder diluent and a dash of any pungent flavoring. The DAE's first example of the use of the word, dated 1806, shows that it was then compounded of "spirits of any kind, sugar, water, and bitters." [5] A later quotation, 1833, defines it as "composed of water, with the addition of rum, gin, or brandy, as one chooses—a third of the spirits to two-thirds of the water; add bitters, and enrich with sugar and nutmeg." Bartlett's second edition (1859) gave only the bare word *cocktail* as consisting of "brandy or gin mixed with sugar and a very little water," but his fourth edition (1877) listed no less than seven varieties—the *brandy*, the *champagne*, the *gin*, the *Japanese*, the *Jersey*, the *soda* and the *whiskey*. He did not, however, give their formulae.

The DAE lists only the *Manhattan*, and traces it only to 1894. [The DA finds *Manhattan* in 1890, *Martini* in 1899,[6] *Bronx* in 1919, but *old-fashioned* no earlier than 1943; like its predecessor, it ignores the *sidecar*, the *Daiquiri*, the *orange blossom*, the *Alexander*, the *Dubonnet* and other popular decoctions.]

American initiative and imagination continue to display themselves in the making and naming of drinks. A common bartender's manual lists well over a thousand, a civilized cookbook over a hundred; the potential permutations of the *materia bibulica* in a first-rate bar reach figures commonly associated only with interstellar mileage or Congressional spending.[7]

---

[5] [This is the basic formula for the *old-fashioned;* hence, perhaps, its name.]

[6] [Despite its sometimes lethal effect, the *Martini*, of gin and vermouth, has no direct connection with the Martini and Henry carbine used by the British Army in the 1890s; it is apparently derived from the firm of Martini and Rossi, makers of a popular brand of vermouth. Early formulae for the *Martini* permitted either sweet or dry vermouth, with bitters optional; since World War II bitters and sweet vermouth have been taboo, and the proportion of gin to vermouth has grown from 2/1 to 4/1 and even higher.

Whether an olive should be immersed in a *Martini* has produced endless debates; a sizable faction prefers a small sour onion, but another faction insists that an onion converts a *Martini* into a *Gibson*. Still other topers eschew olive and onion alike. The *Martini sandwich*, devised by John Kepke, of Brooklyn, is favored by many American linguists; consisting of a dry *Martini* between two glasses of draft beer, it is not recommended for beginners in either linguistics or drinking. The *vodka Martini*, substituting vodka for gin, is disappointing, like all imitations.]

[7] [The *entente cordiale* produced a

In the Gothic Age of American drinking and word making, between the Revolution and the Civil War, many fantastic drinks were invented, and given equally fantastic names: *stone fence, blue blazer* and *stinkibus*. The DA passes over all save the *stone fence*, a mixture of whiskey and cider, traced to 1843. As a gesture of appeasement, it adds the *switchel*, a banal drink of molasses and water, often flavored with ginger and vinegar,[8] but sometimes with rum, which it traces to 1790; the *anti-fogmatic*, "an alcoholic drink, jocosely reputed to be valuable for counteracting the bad effects of fog," which it traces to 1789; [9] the *timber-doodle*, first recorded (by Charles Dickens in his "American Notes") in 1842; the *blackjack*, 1863; and the *eggnog*, c. 1775. The touring Englishmen of those days always spread the news of such grotesque drink names, and some of these Columbuses embellished the list with outlandish inventions of their own; in 1868 an American protested the practice: [1] "Genuine American drinks have names strange enough; but the fact that certain decoctions are called *brandy smashes, mint juleps* and *sherry cobblers* scarcely justifies the invention of the Haymarket *corpse-reviver*." Such names began to pass out after the Civil War, and the new drinks of the 1865–1900 era, the Golden Age of American drinking, were largely eponymous and hence relatively decorous, e.g., *rickey* and *Tom Collins*. The *highball*, traced to 1898, was simply the English *whiskey and soda*, which had been familiar to American visitors to England for many years.[2] Some authorities say that *highball* was borrowed from railroad men, for whom the term is a signal to go ahead. Others say that *ball*, in the 90s, was bartender's slang for a glass, and the glass used for a *highball* was naturally taller than that used for an old-time straight whiskey. The *highball* came in on the heels of *Scotch whiskey*, which was but seldom drunk in America before 1895. It has been enor-

spate of vodka drinks, and some have continued to be popular, e.g., the *Moscow mule*, of vodka and ginger beer. Enterprising bartenders have produced others, e.g., the *Rob Roy*, of Scotch and dry vermouth. After the election of 1960 there were several putative formulae for the *Kennedy cocktail*, e.g., "two parts of Irish whiskey, one part of Southern Comfort, and a twist of Norman Vincent Peale"—an allusion to the fact that the reverend gentleman's anti-Catholic pronouncements were as beneficial to Kennedy as the Rev. S. D. Burchard's "rum, Romanism and rebellion" had been to Cleveland in 1884. If orange peel is used, it is actually very potable.]

[8] It survives in the more backward sections of New Jersey as the *belly whistle*. See Jerseyisms, by F. B. Lee, DN, Vol. I, Pt. VII, 1894, p. 328.

[9] It also lists the *fog cutter*, which it traces to 1833.

[1] English Hotels, by an American, *Tinsleys Magazine* (London); reprinted in *Every Saturday* (Boston), May 30, 1868, p. 691. [Allen Walker Read points out: "The English curiosity over American drink names goes back to the Seventeenth Century, when the West Indian name *Kill-Devil*, for rum, was first recorded in 1639." The Adjective *American* in England, *AS*, Vol. XXV, Dec. 1950, p. 285.]

[2] *Soda water* seems to have been invented in the Eighteenth Century. But the *whiskey and soda* was called *whiskey and water* down to the middle of the Nineteenth Century.

mously popular ever since. Prohibition brought the degenerate custom of substituting ginger ale for soda water, especially in rye *highballs,* but high-toned bartenders and enlightened boozers rejected it.

Many amusing generic names for alcoholic stimulants have been current in the United States, *e.g., nose paint* (1881), *tanglefoot* (1859), *sheep dip, snake medicine* (1865), *rotgut* (1819) and *coffin varnish* (1845).[3] There are also generic names for various kinds and classes of drinks, *e.g., joy water* and *fire water* (1817) for whiskey; *foolish water* and *bubble water* for champagne; *Jersey lightning* (1852) for applejack; *prairie oyster* for a drink with an egg in it; *red ink* and *dago red* (1910) for red wine; and *hard liquor* (1890) for any distilled stuff. The DAE traces *snake medicine* to 1865, in the chaste pages of *Harper's Magazine. Nose paint,* first recorded in 1881, is probably much older. *Smile,* as a euphemism for a drink, goes back to 1839; *phlegm cutter,* another, to 1806; *to set 'em up* to 1851; *pony* to 1849; *finger* to 1856; *snifter* to 1848; *shot in the neck,* the predecessor of *shot in the arm,* to 1851; and *long drink* to 1828.[4] *Jim-jams,* an Americanism, is traced to 1852. *Straight* is also an Americanism, first recorded in 1855; the English use *neat.*

The earliest recorded example of *schooner* is from Bartlett's fourth edition (1877), but it must be considerably older. *To rush the growler,* traced to 1888, is also older. *To rush the can* is not listed by the DAE or DA, nor are *bucket of suds, hooker, nip, pick-me-up, on a binge, slug* (though *to slug up* is traced to 1856), *water wagon, bung starter,*[5] *bar rail* or *booze hoister.* Some of these may be omitted on the ground that they are also used in England, but probably not many. The DAE traces *eye opener* to 1818, *on a bender* to 1846, *on a bat* to 1848, *to liquor up* to 1850, *barrel house* to 1883 and *redeye* to 1819. [In addition the DA traces *to brace up* to 1802, *chaser* to 1897, *bartender* to 1836, *saloonkeeper* to 1860, *kick* to 1903, *katzenjammer* to 1849, *bust* to 1843, *to spike* (a drink) to 1889, *hangover* to 1912, *booze fighter* to 1903 and *Keeley cure* to 1892; un-accountably, it traces *booze hound* only to 1928 and *jitters,* glossed as "nervousness," to 1931.]

Prohibition multiplied the number of American boozers and made the whole nation booze-conscious. Everyday speech was soon peppered with such terms as *law enforcement, home brew, bathtub gin, rum runner,*

---

[3] Some of these were Southern. Says Bell Irvin Wiley in The Plain People of the Confederacy; Baton Rouge, La., 1944, pp. 26–7: "The potency of Confederate liquor, as well as the esteem in which it was held, were reflected by nicknames applied to it by the campaign-hardened butternuts; among the appella-tions were: *How Come You, Tanglefoot, Rifle Knock-Knee, Bust Skull, Old Red Eye,* and *Rock Me to Sleep, Mother.*"

[4] A *Long Drink* and the American Chesterfield, by Kenneth Forward, *AS,* Vol. XIV, Dec. 1939, p. 316.

[5] The English call a *bung starter* a *beer mallet.*

rum row, highjacker (or *hijacker*), *bone-dry, needle beer* and *Jake* (Jamaica ginger). [*Bootlegger* is older, traced to 1889 in Oklahoma, the latest state to legalize the sale of liquor. In Mississippi, still officially dry, the enterprising legislature has imposed a lucrative tax on bootlegging.] A number of early terms for crude varieties of whiskey were revived, *e.g.*, *bald face, bust head, forty-rod* (traced to 1858 and defined as "warranted to kill at forty rods"), *pine top, tarantula juice* (traced to 1861), *white mule, white lightning, squirrel whiskey* and *panther sweat*; and such novelties as *depth bomb* [6] and *third rail* were added. Denatured alcohol from which a token effort had been made to remove the usually poisonous denaturant acquired the special name of *smoke*, also applied, along with *canned heat*, to alcohol and paraffin preparations sold for heating purposes; the user of such exhilarants was called a *smoke eater*. [The DA traces *smoke*, as a term for cheap whiskey, to 1904. The troglodytes of western South Carolina coined *jump stiddy* for a mixture of Coca-Cola and denatured alcohol (usually drawn from automobile radiators); connoisseurs reputedly preferred the taste of what had been aged in Model-T Fords.]

The Prohibitionists, throughout the Thirteen Years, kept on using *rum* to designate all alcoholic drinks, including even beer. Its employment went back to colonial days, when rum was actually the chief tipple of American dipsomaniacs, particularly in New England.[7] Some of its derivatives date from the Eighteenth Century: *rum seller* from 1781, *rum guzzler* from 1775, *rum house* from 1739 and *rum shop* from 1738. *Rum blossom* is ignored, except by the slang thesaurus of Berrey and Van den Bark, which gives no dates, but *rum bud*, possibly earlier, is credited by Bartlett to Dr. Benjamin Rush, who died in 1813. The DA traces *speakeasy* to 1889, *wet* and *dry* to 1870; *to go dry* has been found in 1888, and *to vote dry* in 1904 (both are probably older). *Wet goods* goes back to 1779. *Local option* is first recorded in 1884. During the thirteen theoretically dry years the *wets* invented *dry dry* to designate the atypical legislator who voted with the Anti-Saloon League yet was dry personally.

Prohibition gave hard service to the splendid repertoire of American synonyms for *drunk*, and brought in a number of new ones.[8] In the main, however, old ones were preferred, *e.g.*, *cockeyed, pifflicated, boozed-up, paralyzed, soused, corned* and *stewed*. Although the English have gener-

---

[6] [Its formula, according to Capt. Milledge B. Seigler, USNR, requires one cube of ice, one dash of Angostura bitters, one jigger of Scotch, one jigger of rum, one jigger of cognac. It is deceptively smooth.]

[7] [It still is in Newfoundland, where *screech* or *Newfie screech* designates the cheapest grade.]

[8] [A glossary of 108 terms denoting drunkenness is included in Edmund Wilson, The American Earthquake; New York, 1958.]

ously contributed many of their better terms, *e.g., half seas over*,[9] Americans have long been rolling their own. Benjamin Franklin was apparently the first to attempt to list them. His first list included only 19 terms, but fifteen years later he expanded it to 228. He published it, he declared, as a warning against drunkenness, then as prevalent in the colonies as in England. At the end of his list he said: "The phrases in this dictionary are not (like most of our terms of art) borrowed from foreign languages, neither are they collected from the writings of the learned in our own, but gathered wholly from the modern tavern conversation of tipplers." Of his 228 terms, 90 are not to be found in either the OED or the EDD.[1] Some of the latter are pungent and picturesque, *e.g., been to Barbados, got a brass eye, flushed, has his flag out, gold-headed, has bet his kettle, nimptopsical, pigeon-eyed* and *as stiff as a ring bolt*. At least two are still in use—*oiled* and *stewed*. There are also some good ones among those apparently borrowed from England,[2] *e.g., in his airs, bungey, cherubimical, cherry-merry, dipped his bill, seen the devil, fuzzled, glaized, top-heavy, loose in the hilt, lordly, lappy, limber, moon-eyed, overset, raddled, seafaring in the suds* and *out of the way*. Some have survived till now, *e.g., boozy, cockeyed, jagged* and *soaked*.[3]

Of American terms for drinking places, *café* is traced to 1893, *buffet* to 1890, *sample room* to 1865 and *exchange* to 1835—all euphemisms for *barroom*, which goes back to 1797, or *saloon*, which is traced to 1841. During the last gory battle against Prohibition, most of the wet leaders promised waverers that, in case of repeal, the old-time saloon would not be revived. When victory followed in 1933, and it appeared that the triumphant antinomians of the country demanded its restoration exactly as it was, with the brass rail, the mirror behind the bar and even something resembling a free lunch, there arose a need for new and mellifluous names. There is probably not a single undisguised *saloon* in the United States today. They are all *taverns, cocktail lounges, taprooms, grills* or the like. Some are called *bars, lounge bars* or *cocktail bars*, but *saloon* is definitely out.[4] The snobbish English *saloon bar* never got a lodgment in this country, nor did *bar parlour* or *snug*. [A few saloons call themselves *pubs*.[5]] Nor are our wets fa-

---

[9] For a list of them see Farmer and Henley, Vol. II, p. 327.

[1] Edward D. Seeber, Franklin's Drinkers Dictionary Again, *AS*, Vol. XV, Feb. 1940, pp. 103–5. The full text is to be found in The Drinkers Dictionary, by Cedric Larson, *AS*, Vol. XII, Apr. 1937, pp. 87–92. It was Seeber who unearthed the earlier dictionary of 1722.

[2] He was a diligent borrower, and at least a third of the maxims in Poor Richard's Almanac were lifted from various English authors, especially Pope.

[3] For modern terms see especially Berrey and Van den Bark, pp. 122 ff.

[4] That is, save in the more elegant form of *salon*.

[5] [There are a few soi-disant *pubs* in Chicago, but not a single confessed *saloon*.]

miliar with such English names for drinks as *pint of bitter, gin and French* and *audit ale. Bitter,* an abbreviation of *bitter beer,* signifies in general a beer containing a reasonable sufficiency of hops. *Gin and French* (sometimes *gin and it*) is a mixture of dry gin and French vermouth, differing from a *Martini* in containing more vermouth and no ice. *Audit ale* is a strong ale that used to be brewed in the English universities for drinking on audit day, when the students had to settle their college accounts. Two other English drinks are occasionally drunk in this country. They are *half and half* and *shandygaff.* The former is defined by the OED as "a mixture of two malt liquors, especially ale and porter," and traced to 1756. The latter is defined as "a mixture of beer and ginger beer" and traced to 1853. *Half and half* (often pronounced *ahf 'n' ahf* in deference to the English) is also used for compounds of beer and porter or beer and brown stout, less frequently of beer and ale. *Black velvet* is a mixture of beer and champagne. [Canadian topers have an array of combinations, some quite potable, as *gin and ginger* (gin and ginger ale), some obscene, as *rye and orange* (Canadian whiskey and orange pop), but few have crossed the Undefended Frontier.]

So much for the vocabulary of bacchanalia. The American contributions to that of politics have been almost as lush. Some of the characteristic terms, like *caucus* and *mileage,* originated in colonial times, but the majority were coined during the expansions of the democratic process in the Nineteenth Century.[6] Characteristic specimens include the simple compounds: *omnibus bill, gag rule, executive session, mass meeting, steering committee* and *office seeker;* the humorous metaphors: *pork barrel, pie counter* and *lame duck;* the old words put to new uses: *wheel horse, precinct* and *regular;* the new coinages: *mugwump* and *bulldozing;* the new derivatives: *abolitionist, candidacy* and *per diem;* and the almost innumerable verbs and verb phrases: *to knife, to straddle, to crawfish, to split a*

---

[6] [No completely satisfactory dictionary of political terms exists. The deficiencies of three of the best (Wilbur W. White, White's Political Dictionary, Cleveland and New York, 1947; Harold D. Lasswell, Nathan Leites and associates, The Language of Politics, New York, 1949; and Uno Philpson, Political Slang, 1750–1850, *Lund Studies in English,* No. IX, Lund, 1949) are indicated in Francis Lee Utley, Language and Politics, *AS,* Vol. XXV, Feb. 1950, pp. 41–51. American Political Terms: An Historical Dictionary, by Hans Sperber and Travis Trittschuh, Detroit, 1962, is a sounder and livelier work. For particular aspects of the political vocabulary, see Military Phraseology in Presidential Campaigns, by Kathryn Anderson McEwen, *AS,* Vol. XXX, Feb. 1955, pp. 38–43; Words and Phrases in American Politics: Hunting Terms, by Hans Sperber and Travis Trittschuh, *AS,* Vol. XXVII, Oct. 1952, pp. 165–8; Political Words and Phrases: Card-Playing Terms, by James N. Tidwell, *AS,* Vol. XXXIII, Feb. 1958, pp. 21–8; Corruption Words in American Politics, *Inside the ACD,* Oct. 1952, p. 1. Of older works, perhaps the best is Political Americanisms, by Charles Ledyard Norton; New York, 1890.]

ticket, to lobby and *to boodle. To run* was already used in America in 1789; it was universal by 1820. *Anxious bench* (or *anxious seat*) at first designated only the place occupied by the penitent at revivals, but was used in its political sense in Congress so early as 1842. *Favorite son* appears in an ode addressed to Washington on his visit to Portsmouth, N.H., in 1789, but it did not acquire its present ironical sense until 1825. *Split ticket* goes back to 1842, *bolter* to 1812. In 1832 *lobbying* had already extended to Washington. *Regularity* was an issue in Tammany Hall in 1822. All of these terms are now as firmly imbedded in the American vocabulary as *election* or *congressman*.[7]

The most successful of these innovations—indeed, the most successful of all Americanisms—is *O.K.* Its long-disputed etymology has been practically settled by Allen Walker Read.[8] [It arose from a vogue for acronyms which developed in Boston in the summer of 1838. In the Boston *Morning Post* for June 12 appeared the following announcement:

> *Melancholy.*—We understand that J. Eliot Brown, Esq., Secretary of the Boston Young Men's Society for Meliorating the Condition of the Indians, F.A.H. (fell at Hoboken, N.J.) on Saturday last at 4 o'clock, p.m. in a duel W.O.O.O.F.C. (with one of our first citizens). What measures will be taken by the Society R.T.B.S. (remains to be seen).

[The most popular of the acronyms, according to Read, was *O.F.M.*, for "Our First Men," a semi-satirical phrase. In the *Morning Post* for June 20 appeared the query: "Does he [a turtle] *rare up* when you suggest to him that soup is called for by O.F.M. (our first men), and he is 'wanted'?" A clear forerunner of *O.K.* is the frequent and still surviving *n.g.* for *no go* (or *no good*), as in the comment on a lawsuit in the *Morning Post* for June 25: "They then went to the plaintiff's to try to settle, but it was *n.g.*" Drink names were often abbreviated, such as *G.C.* for *gin cocktail* and *m.j.* for *mint julep*. The use of abbreviations was so prevalent that it was denounced on June 19:

> Mr. Greene.—The present age is one pregnant with experiments. . . . There is yet one other sect, whose efforts carry them back to still remoter ages—disciples, it may be, of the illustrious Noah [Webster]—who, in their fondness for a brevity in writing, would discard every letter in a word, but that with which it commences.

---

[7] See American Political Cant, by Lowry Charles Wimberly, *AS*, Vol. II, Dec. 1926.

[8] [The First Stage in the History of *O.K.*, *AS*, Vol. XXXVIII, Feb. 1963, pp. 5–27; The Second Stage in the History of *O.K.*, *ibid.*, May 1963; The Evidence on *O.K.*, *Saturday Review of Literature*, July 19, 1941, pp. 3–11. See also Postscripts to The American Language: The Life and Times of *O.K.*, by H. L. Mencken, *The New Yorker*, Oct. 1, 1949, pp. 56–61.]

They extend this principle to speech too—they glory in hyro-glyphics—they rejoice in *stenographics*—but it is to this very class that I would send forth my denunciations—let it be understood that they are a dangerous sect—men whom Caesar would have regarded with a suspicious eye—for they do not "sleep o' nights"—they may be men of high standing in the community—for they speak of our "leading citizens" with a familiar air, and seem conversant with "our first people," and they claim to be literary, and aver that the efforts of their Society will be truly beneficial to the cause of *Letters*. But sir, I mistrust them—let them come out freely and openly, and show us that their cabalistic signs are not omens of evil. . . . Above all, let them give us the lengthy English signification of their W.B.'s—G.C.'s—B.C.'s and last, though not least, their P.W.S. Garee's that we may rest in the assurance that they are not incantations unholy, to call up spirits withal!

Yours,

I. C.

["The background for *O.K.*," Read goes on to say, "was so thoroughly set by the summer of 1838 that it is surprising that it was not yet found. Probably it was delayed by a close forerunner, *O.W.*, standing for 'All Right,' as if spelled *Oll Wright*. See the Boston *Morning Post*, June 18, 1838, in a reporter's account of taking a hack in Newport, R.I.: 'We jumped in, and were not disappointed either with the carriage, distance, or price. It was O.W.—(all right).' "

[Next Read presents "the very matrix out of which the first known instance of *O.K.* was parturiated":

An organization called the Anti-Bell-Ringing Society (usually referred to as the A.B.R.S.) was founded on October 26, 1838, to combat an ordinance of the Boston Common Council prohibiting the ringing of dinner bells. In December it instituted a suit in the police court to show the ridiculousness of the law; and throughout the next year they had high-spirited meetings. Concerning a visit of members of the A.B.R.S. to New York by way of Providence, the following appeared in the Boston *Morning Post*, March 23, 1839: "The 'Chairman of the Committee on Charity Lecture Bells' [Thomas B. Fearing] is one of the deputation, and perhaps if he should return to Boston, via Providence, he of the [Providence] Journal, and his *train*-band, would have the 'contribution box,' et ceteras, *o.k.*—all correct—and cause the corks to fly, like *sparks*, upward." Ah! This contains the first instance of *O.K.* so far known. Inasmuch as it appears in repartee between editors, it can be pinpointed to the writing of Charles Gordon Greene, nationally famous for his wit.

[Later in 1839, Read shows, the interest in initials was transferred to New York. "On July 8th two of the leading literary figures, Park Benjamin and Rufus W. Griswold, founded the New York *Evening Tatler*, and they were so waggish as to use *K.G.*, standing for 'No Go,' as if spelled *Know Go*, and *K.Y.*, standing for 'No Use,' as if spelled *Know Yuse*." Both appeared in the first month of the *Evening Tatler*'s existence. On September 2 *O.K.* appeared, glossed as "all correct," in commenting on a proposed lecture tour by Thomas Carlyle. The vogue of acronyms in New York was attested in the New York *Evening Signal* for November 14:

Wall Street Phraseology.—The editor of the Philadelphia Gazette, who appears to have flitted through our city a day or two since, writes as follows to his "round table":

They have a curious, short-handed phraseology in Wall-street which it is amusing to hear. A man offers another a note with the endorsement of a third—and saying of it—"You see it's A 1, the man is decidedly O.F.M."

"Yes—that's good—O.K.—I.S.B.D."

"Will you make that contract we spoke of yesterday?" says a fourth person to a fifth. "I have brought my friend as witness."

"Yes; we'll close it to-morrow."

"A.R., N.S.M.J.," is the reply; and the parties bow and separate. O.K., all correct; I.S.B.D., it shall be done; A.R., N.S.M.J., all right, 'nough said 'mong gentlemen—and so forth. This tongue-relieving process is quite in vogue here—it saves the common enemy, and is considered extremely useful.[9]

[However, *O.K.* owes its vogue to the political campaigns of 1840, when it took a second, independent start as a symbol of the Democrats to counteract the "log cabin" and "hard cider" of the Whigs.] In this new sense it made its first appearance in print in the New York *New Era* on March 23,

---

[9] [The original of this, in the Philadelphia *Gazette*, Nov. 12, 1839, was discovered by Woodford A. Heflin, and was presented by him in *O.K.* and Its Incorrect Etymology, *AS*, Vol. XXXVII, Dec. 1962, pp. 243–8. It was reprinted not only in the New York *Evening Signal* but also in the Baltimore *Patriot and Commercial Gazette* (country ed., tri-weekly), Nov. 13, 1839. The knowledge of *O.K.* lingered on in Baltimore, as we find in the Baltimore *Sun*, Feb. 24, 1840, concerning the gift of a mint julep: "We hope this will satisfy him, and that he will give us an acknowledgment that it is *o.k.* (all correct)." This was found by Robert G. Gunderson and referred to in his book The Log-Cabin Campaign (Lexington, Ky., 1957), p. 235, *n.* 7, and the significance of it admirably presented by Ralph T. Eubanks, The Basic Derivation of *O.K.*, *AS*, Vol. XXXV, Oct. 1960, pp. 188–92.]

1840, as part of the name of the Democratic *O.K. Club*, an organization of supporters of Martin Van Buren for a second presidential term, and was an abbreviation of *Old Kinderhook*, the Hudson Valley village in which he had been born in 1782. Van Buren had been known to his political enemies since the early days of the Albany Regency as the *Kinderhook Fox*, and to his followers as the *Sage*, *Magician* or *Wizard of Kinderhook*, and it was natural for the name to extend to one of the rowdy clubs which supported him. Reducing the name to *O.K.* was in accord with the liking for mystification that then marked politics. The Democratic *O.K. Club* held its first recorded meeting in the house of Jacob Colvin, at 245 Grand Street, on March 24, 1840, and the new name caught on at once. It was brief, it had a bellicose ring, and it was mysterious enough to suggest the sinister. By the next day *O.K.* had become a slogan among the other Locofocos of the city, the lower orders of whom had been masquerading under similar dark and puzzling names, *e.g.*, *Butt Enders*, *Huge Paws* and *Ball Rollers*. On March 27, when the New York Whigs held a meeting in Masonic Hall, a gang of Locofocos, using *O.K.* as their war cry, tried to break it up. "About 500 stout, strapping men," said the New York *Herald* the next morning, "marched three and three, noiselessly and orderly. The word *O.K.* was passed from mouth to mouth, a cheer was given, and they rushed into the hall upstairs like a torrent." Naturally *O.K.* provoked speculation, and at once the anti-Locofoco newspapers began to print derisory interpretations. A categorical statement of the *New Era*, that the term was "significant of the birthplace of Martin Van Buren, *Old Kinderhook*," did not shut off the rising flood of rival etymologies. One of these, appearing in the *Herald* on March 30, was accepted gravely, in one form or another, for a full century:

> A few years ago some person accused Amos Kendall to General Jackson of being no better than he should be. "Let me examine the papers," said the old hero. "I'll soon tell you whether Mr. Kendall is right or wrong." The general did so and found everything right. "Tie up them papers," said the general. They were tied up. "Mark on them *O.K.*," continued the general. *O.K.* was marked on them. "By the eternal," said the good old general, taking his pipe from his mouth, "Amos is *Oll Kurrect* and no mistake." [1]

Various other jocose etymologies for *O.K.* were suggested during the years following its appearance in the New York *New Era*, for the term seized the fancy of the country, and was soon in wide use. So early as

[1] Kendall (1789–1869) was perhaps the most influential of Jackson's Kitchen Cabinet. He was made Postmaster General in 1835, and founded the tradition that the holder of that office should be a practical politician.

December 18, 1840, a Philadelphia music publisher named George Willig was copyrighting "The *O.K.* Quick Step," "composed and arranged for the piano-forte and especially dedicated to the citizens of Richmond, Va., by Jos. K. Opl." Willig's son, George, Jr., operated a music publishing business in Baltimore, and before the end of 1840 he brought out an "*O.K.* Gallopade," "dedicated to the Whig ladies of the United States by John H. Hewitt." [2] Thus by the end of 1840 *O.K.* had already lost its exclusively Democratic significance. On April 2 the New York *Daily Express*, referring to the fact that the *O.K.* raid on the Whigs was repulsed, said that it was an Arabic word which, read backward, came to *kicked out*. After the Whigs had carried Connecticut over the Democrats, the *Express* reported that *O.K.* meant *Old Konnecticut*. Says Read:

> Another Whig version, soon current, was *Out of Kash, Out of Kredit, Out of Karacter* and *Out of Klothes*. Some months later a congressman from Illinois, on the floor of the House of Representatives, offered the interpretation *Orful Kalamity*.

Read's reports, of course, have not abated the efforts of amateur etymologists to account for *O.K.*, and new guesses are being added all the time. A few of the more picturesque or preposterous:

1. That *O.K.* comes from *aux quais*, used "in the American War of Independence by French sailors who made appointments with American girls." [3]

2. That it may be derived from *oikea*, a Finnish word signifying correct.[4]

3. That it arose during the Civil War, when "the War Department bought large quantities of crackers from the Orrins-Kendall Company. This company always put their initials on their boxes and as the crackers were of a high quality the initials gradually came to be used as a synonym for *all right*." [5]

4. "Certain bills in the House of Lords must be read and approved by the Lord Chairman of Committees, Lord Onslow, and by his counsel, Lord Kilbracken, and then initialed by them. They are then *O.K.*" [6]

5. "*O.K.* had its origin several hundred years ago in an expression common among Norwegian and Danish sailors: *H.G.* (pronounced

[2] See *O.K.*, 1840, by H. L. Mencken, *AS*, Vol. XVII, Apr. 1942, p. 126.

[3] *Aux Quais*, by Beachcomber, London *Daily Express*, June 28, 1940.

[4] *Main Library News Notes*, Cleveland Public Library, July 1940.

[5] *O.K.*, by Robert Greenburger, *Linguist* (Horace Mann School for Boys, New York), Vol. IV, 1939, p. 15.

[6] *O.K.*, by John Godley, London *Times*, Nov. 2, 1939.

hah gay), meaning shipshape, ready for action. *H.G.* was short for the Anglo-Saxon *hofgor*, meaning ready for the sea." [7]

6. "Liddell and Scott have an entry, ὤχ, ὤχ, a magical incantation against fleas. The authority is a work called 'Geoponica,' the date of which is given with a query, as 920 A.D." [8]

7. "The Prussian general Schliessen, who fought for the American colonies in the War of Independence, endorsed his letters and orders *O.K.* (*Oberst Kommandant*). Consequently the letters *O.K.* came to be applied to anything having the meaning of official assent." [9]

8. That *O.K.* may have some sort of connection with the Scotch *och aye*.[1]

9. "*O.K.* is an abbreviation of *orl korrec*, all correct. It is English, I think Cockney—not an Americanism. I was born in the 60s and remember it when I was a boy." [2]

10. That *O.K.* may come from *O qu-oui*, an emphatic French form of *yes*, to be found in Sterne's "A Sentimental Journey" (1768).[3]

Of all Americanisms *O.K.* has been the greatest success. It was in use by English telegraphers, as a signal that a message had been clearly received, so early as 1873, and first appeared in an English slang dictionary a year earlier.[4] Before 1888 it was already familiar enough to the patrons of London music halls to enter into the refrain of a popular song.[5] But it remained for the American movies to make *O.K.* familiar to all Englishmen, low or high. When it began to displace the English *righto*, there were the usual vain protests from patriots and pedants. An especially violent war upon it in 1935 was supported by the Anglomaniac Mrs. Nicholas Murray Butler, who was then in London, but before the end of the year the London *Times* heaved a bomb into the patriot ranks by giving its awful *O.K.* to *O.K.* H. W. Horwill did not think it necessary to explain *O.K.* or even to

---

[7] Reported but by no means certified by Frank Colby in his newspaper column Take My Word for It, Mar. 21, 1943.

[8] *O.K.*, by W. Snow, London *Times*, Oct. 26, 1935. The first edition of the Greek Lexicon of Henry G. Liddell and Robert Scott was published in 1843.

[9] *O.K.*, by Sir Anthony Palmer, London *Times*, Oct. 28, 1939. *Oberst Kommandant* is German for colonel in command. In *AS* for Oct. 1938 Gretchen Hochdoerfer Rogers published a translation of an article in the Omaha (Neb.) *Tribune*, a German daily, of Jan. 23, 1938, in which the German officer was changed to Baron F. W. von Steuben, inspector general of the Continental Army, and *Oberst Kommandant* to *Ober-Kommando*, meaning high command.

[1] The Cry of the English: Words That Bless and Burn, Nottingham *Journal*, Apr. 30, 1943.

[2] *O.K.*, by Charles A. Christie, London *Times*, Oct. 24, 1939.

[3] I am indebted here to William McDevitt, of San Francisco.

[4] Sir William Power, *O.K.*, London *Times*, Oct. 21, 1939.

[5] *O.K.*—The Victorians Used It, by J. W. Lee, *John o' London's Weekly*, Aug. 29, 1936. See also *O.K.* in History, by M. E. Durham, London *Spectator*, Jan. 14, 1938, p. 57.

list it in his "Dictionary of Modern American Usage." [6] During this same *annus mirabilis* the Judicial Committee of the Privy Council decided formally that inscribing *O.K.* upon a legal document "meant that the details contained . . . were correctly given." [7]

In 1937 the Edinburgh *Evening News* described *O.K.* as "now universal" in Great Britain,[8] and in 1940 a provincial journalist was reporting that "almost everybody says *O.K.* now instead of *all right*." [9] Finally Lord Beaverbrook made *O.K.* impeccable by using it at the Moscow Conference in a formal pledge as official representative of the British Commonwealth of Nations.[1]

O.K. is sometimes spelled *okeh*, *okay* or *okey*, and about 1930 an abbreviation *oke* appeared, quickly followed by *oke-doke* (more often *oky-doke*), *oky-doky* and *oky-dory*. The forms terminating in -*y* were perhaps suggested by the current *all-righty*, and maybe *oky-dory* was also influenced by *hunky-dory*. Woodrow Wilson used *okeh* in *O.K.-ing* documents, and seems to have subscribed to the theory that the term came from a Choctaw word, *oke, hoke*, signifying "yes, it is."

During their far-flung operations in World War II, American troops rarely encountered a people to whom *O.K.* was unknown. Lieutenant Colonel W. E. Dyess recorded that it was known to and used by every Japanese guard in Davao prison camp.[2] It was equally familiar to the Moslem allies of the Allies in North Africa,[3] and even earlier the American volunteers in the Spanish Civil War found that it had displaced *salud* as a greeting among the village children of Spain.[4] In several places *O.K.* encountered congeners which coalesced with it, *e.g.*, *ola kala* in Greece, *o-ke* in the Djabo dialect of Liberia and *hoak-keh* (literally "is so") in Burmese.

The familiar American use of *administration* as an adjective began soon after the opening of the Nineteenth Century: *administration paper* (*i.e.*, newspaper) in 1808, *administration man* in 1810, *administration candidate* in 1827, *administration party* in 1837 and *anti-administration* in 1850. *Administration*, signifying the President and his Cabinet, appeared in 1803. In the sense of the term or terms during which a President holds office, as in *first administration*, etc., the first recorded example is from Washington's Farewell Address (1796). The English have borrowed these terms in *ad-*

[6] Oxford, 1935.
[7] *Chemical Trade Journal* (London), quoted in *The New Yorker*, Oct. 19, 1935, p. 70.
[8] The Mystery of *O.K.*, June 4.
[9] How the Tank Got Its Name, by Sam Bate, *Northern Daily Telegraph* (Blackburn), Aug. 19, 1940.
[1] The Moscow Conference, by Lord Beaverbrook, *Listener* (London), Oct. 16, 1941, p. 320.
[2] Installment published in the newspapers of Feb. 18, 1944.
[3] Amen, *The New Yorker*, Aug. 28, 1943.
[4] Associated Press dispatch from Madrid, June 24, 1937.

ministration, as they have also borrowed *campaign* in the political sense. Their own word for pre-election political activity is *canvass*, but they know what *campaign* means, and often use it. The DAE traces it in this country to 1809. At the start it was commonly preceded by *electioneering*, but was soon used without explanation. Most of its derivatives, curiously, did not come in until years later: *campaign paper*, 1844; *campaign document*, 1871; *campaign speech*, 1880; *campaign manager*, 1882; *campaign orator* and *to campaign*, 1896; *campaign button*, 1900; and *campaign fund*, 1905. All of them are undoubtedly older than these dates indicate, but only the first seems to have been in use before the Civil War.

To back and fill, a phrase taken from the terminology of sailors, began to be used of elusive candidates for office in the 1850s. *Ballot-box stuffer* is traced to 1856, *to bolt* to 1833, *dyed-in-the-wool* to 1830, *to electioneer* to 1806 (*electioneering* goes back to 1787), *exposé* to 1830, *floater* to 1847, *landslide* to 1895, *lobby* to 1808, *logrolling* to 1812, *office hunter* to 1806 and *officeholder* to 1818, *party line* to 1834, *party machinery* to 1829 and *party hack* to 1848, *platform* (in the sense of a formal document) to 1844, *plank* to 1848, *on the fence* to 1828, *to mend fences* to 1879,[5] *peanut politics* to 1887, *picayune* (in the political sense) to 1837, *plum* to 1887,[6] *love feast* to 1876, *pull* to 1887,[7] *reformer* (nearly always in a derogatory sense) to 1848, *ring* to 1862, *safe* (meaning not radical) to 1862, *scattering* (of votes) to 1766, *to scratch a ticket* to 1841, *to see* (to bribe) to 1869, *solid South* to 1876,[8] *slate* to 1854, *to be snowed under* to 1880, *spellbinder* to 1888, *split ticket* to 1836, *straight ticket* to 1856, *straw vote* to 1887, *tidal wave* to 1868,[9] *timber* (e.g., presidential, gubernatorial) to 1831, *propaganda* (in the evil sense) to 1880 and *propagandist* to 1824, *rabble rouser* (perhaps borrowed from England) to 1843, *repeater* to 1861, *spoils* to 1812, *spoils system* to 1838 and *spoilsman* to 1842, *stump* to 1816, *stump orator* to 1813, *to whitewash* to 1800 and *wirepuller* to 1832. *Fat cat*, a

---

[5] In that year Senator John Sherman, of Ohio, made a visit home, ostensibly to look after his farm but actually to see to his political interests. When tackled by reporters he alleged that he had made the trip "only to repair my fences."

[6] *Plum* seems to have been launched by Matthew S. Quay, who, on being elected senator from Pennsylvania in 1887, promised his followers that he would "shake the plum tree." [This word may also be related to the legend, partly historical, of Little Jack Horner.]

[7] [The local term in Chicago is *clout*. This was first called to my attention by Lee A. Pederson. A dispenser of influence is a *Chinaman*.]

[8] Edward Clark in The *Solid South*, *Century Magazine*, Apr. 1885, p. 955: "The *Solid South* . . . came into vogue during the Hayes-Tilden canvass [*sic*] of 1876." At the time the Democrats were gaining strength in both the border states and those which had seceded, including even the ones where Republican governments were maintained by the occupation troops.

[9] [A Republican victory in Maine coincided with a disaster on the Pacific coast of South America. Hans Sperber and Travis Trittschuh, Words and Phrases in American Politics: *Tidal Wave*, *AS*, Vol. XXV, Dec. 1950, pp. 259–63.]

wealthy contributor to campaign funds, was coined by Frank R. Kent, of the Baltimore *Sun*, and was first used in his book "Political Behavior" (1928). [*Egghead* dates from 1952.]

Most of these terms are opprobrious. The American people have always viewed politicians with suspicion, and the word has a derogatory significance in the United States which it lacks in England. An *honest politician* is regarded as a sort of marvel, like a calf with five legs, and the news that one has appeared is commonly received with derision. It is casually assumed that a professional politician will do anything for votes, and that assumption is seldom controverted by plausible evidence. From the earliest days of the Republic, American politics have consisted mainly of a continuing auction sale, with pressure groups of voters offering their votes and gangs of politicians bidding for them with public money. The typical American campaign slogans from the pledges to the veterans of the Revolution down to [the "total victory" of the John Birch Society] have voiced engagements to loot A for the use and benefit of B.[1] In the popular political proverbs there is a matter-of-course acceptance of the theory that politicians are wholly vicious, *e.g.*, "In politics a man must learn to rise *above* principle," "Root, hog, or die," "To the victor belongs the spoils," "Few die and none resign" and "When the water reaches the upper deck, follow the rats." [2]

Some of the older political Americanisms have long engaged etymologists, *e.g.*, *caucus, buncombe, mugwump, gerrymander, roorback, scalawag* and *filibuster. Caucus* was first explained by Pickering as due to a mispronunciation of *caulkers*, since the meetings were held in the shipping district of Boston. This etymology was cited by Dunglison in 1829, and Bartlett apparently accepted it in his Glossary of 1848, but the Webster American Dictionary of 1847, edited by the lexicographer's son-in-law, Chauncey A. Goodrich, said that "the origin of the word is not ascertained." In 1872 Dr. J. Hammond Trumbull, an early authority on American Indian languages, suggested in the *Proceedings of the American Philological Association* that *caucus* may have been derived from an Algonquian

---

[1] The historian will recall *forty acres and a mule*, used to inflame the slaves toward the end of the Civil War; the more modest *three acres and a cow* launched by Jesse Collings in 1886; and the *two cars in every garage* of the unfortunate Hoover, *c.* 1928.

[2] These blistering sayings, like American proverbs in general, still lack scholarly investigation, though there are a few good local studies, such as Archer Taylor's Proverbial Comparisons and Similes from California, *University of California Folklore Studies*, No. 3; Berkeley and Los Angeles, 1954. There have been exhaustive studies of the proverbs of other nations, including England, but American proverbs continue to be neglected, though some of them are extraordinarily pungent, *e.g.*, "Don't monkey with the buzz saw," "I'd rather have them say 'There he goes' than 'Here he lies,' " "It will never get well if you pick it," "No tickee, no shirtee," "Cheer up; the worst is yet to come" and "Life is one damn thing after another."

word, *caucausu*, meaning one who advises. This surmise was adopted by the later Webster dictionaries, but the OED marked the word "origin obscure." The DAE says that the Indian etymology is "more plausible" than Pickering's, but calls attention to the possibility that the word may be derived from the name of a forgotten Boston neighborhood, and cites a notice that a "general meeting" of "lay brethren, to take into serious consideration the conduct of those reverend clergymen who have encouraged the itineration of Mr. George Whitefield" was to be held "at West-*Corcus* in Boston." Finally, the Standard Dictionary (1906) notes that there was a Latin word, *caucus*, signifying a drinking vessel, and observes darkly that "the *Caucus Club* perhaps had convivial features." [The DA accepts this happy marriage of alcohol and politics, but the debate still continues.]

In 1943, LeRoy C. Barret, of Trinity College, Hartford, announced that in one of Pickering's unpublished papers in the library of the American Oriental Society is an explanation of *caucus* as made of the initials of six men: *Cooper* (Wm.), *Adams, Urann* (Joyce, Jr.), *Coulson, Urann, Symmes*.[3] Unfortunately, all of Pickering's evidence is hearsay—"from B[enjamin] Russell, who had it from Samuel Adams and Paul Revere." There is, furthermore, an unhappy tendency among amateur etymologists to derive words from the initials of proper names. *Cabal* is often said to come from the names of the five ministers of Charles II who made an alliance with France for war against Holland in 1672, to wit, Clifford, Arlington, Buckingham, Ashley and Lauderdale, but the OED shows that the word was in use so early as 1646–7, and was actually borrowed from the French *cabale*, of precisely the same meaning. The Russell memorandum could not have reached Pickering before 1816, for he does not mention it in his Vocabulary of that year, when *caucus* was nearly a century old.

In the United States *caucus* has always meant a meeting of politicians to pick candidates, agree upon plans of action and so on. The *congressional caucuses* of the major parties dictated the nominations of presidential and vice-presidential candidates from 1804 to 1824, and were finally overthrown only by the adoption of the revolutionary national convention system in 1831.[4] *Caucuses* are still held by congressmen whenever a pending question calls for united party action, but they normally deal with measures rather than men. The early English commentators on American speechways denounced *caucus* as low and uncouth, but it was already respectable by 1762, and John Adams was using it soon afterward. The English finally adopted the word in the 1870s, and, as the OED shows, altered its meaning to what we call a *party organization* or *machine*. But lately they have begun to use it, somewhat gingerly, in the original Ameri-

---

[3] *Caucus, AS*, Vol. XVIII, Apr. 1943, p. 130.

[4] An *anti-caucus* movement is traced by the DAE to 1824.

can sense. Indeed, it had so appeared in "Alice in Wonderland" in 1865.

Popular tradition indicates that *buncombe* was introduced by Felix Walker, representative from the western district of North Carolina (1817–23), where Asheville, the county seat of Buncombe County, is the principal city. During a debate—possibly on the Missouri Compromise—he appealed to Speaker Lowndes for five minutes more time to get into the newspapers some remarks directed to Buncombe. [The papers of Governor D. L. Swain, of North Carolina, indicate that the incident took place before 1822, when Swain learned it from one of Walker's former colleagues.[5]] By 1827 "talking to *Buncombe*" was reported as an old and common saying in Washington.[6] [*Bunkum*, of course, is only a phonetic spelling by those unfamiliar with North Carolina geography.]

The English, who prefer *bunkum*, began to use the term about 1850, but they have stoutly resisted *bunk*, and *to debunk* arouses their indignation. The verb *to buncombe* appeared in 1855, but it seems to have been assimilated in the course of time to *to bunco*, an entirely different word. *To bunco* is traced by the DAE to 1875, and *bunco steerer* to the same year. The short form *to bunk* appeared in Bartlett's fourth edition (1877).

Gerrymander as noun and verb is traced to 1812, following a redistricting of Massachusetts to assure the Jeffersonian party, led by Governor Elbridge Gerry, continued control of the state senate.[7] The editor of a Federalist paper, possibly the same Russell who gave Pickering the story about *caucus*, hung over his desk, as a *memento irae*, a map of a serpentine-shaped new district in Essex County. Gilbert Stuart, best known for his portraits of Washington, affixed head, wings and claws and called it a salamander. "Gerrymander," said Russell, and the name stuck.

Pickering overlooked *gerrymander* in 1818, but three years earlier it was being used "throughout the United States as synonymous with *deception*." The Stuart map, headed "The Gerrymander," was printed in large numbers, and the copies propagated the term. The verb *to gerrymander* appeared almost simultaneously, and has been in use ever since. The English did not adopt it until the 80s, but they now employ it as we do. It is commonly given the *g* of *George*, though *Gerry* has that of *get*.

Mugwump, derived from an Algonquian word signifying a chief, was used in John Eliot's Indian Bible (1663) as an equivalent of the *duke* which appears forty-three times in the Authorized Version of Genesis xxxvi. It was seldom used before June 15, 1884, when the New York *Sun* applied it derisively to the Republicans who refused to support James G.

---

[5] [Norman Eliason, *Tarheel Talk*; Chapel Hill, N.C., 1956, p. 123.]
[6] *Niles' Register*, Sept. 27, p. 66.
[7] The origin of the term is recounted in A Memorial History of Boston, ed. by Justin Winsor; 4 vols.; Boston, 1880–1, Vol. III, p. 222.

Blaine for the Presidency—many of them men of means and consequence. Some of the independents, far from resenting the term, boldly adopted it as emblematic of their intellectual and moral superiority. Since 1884 *mugwump* has been in general use to indicate a political bolter, but it still suggests an assumption of undemocratic superiority. General Horace Porter defined it rather early as "a person educated beyond his intellect"; it is now popularly defined as a bird who sits on the political fence "with his *mug* on one side and his *wump* on the other."[8] The DAE traces *mugwumpery* and *mugwumpian* to 1885, *mugwumpism* to 1886, *mugwumpcy* to 1887 and *to mugwump* to 1889. The English adopted *mugwump* promptly, and by 1918 it had produced an adjective in England, *mugwumpish*. It is still, however, regarded as a somewhat uncouth term by the English.

Filibuster, derived originally from the Dutch *vrijbuiter*, a freebooter, has been in the language since *c.* 1587. In the 1850s it was used in this country to designate the adventurers who were promoting revolutions in Latin America. In 1853, a member of Congress termed the tactics of his opponents "*filibustering* against the United States," and by 1863 *to filibuster* had come to mean a delaying action on the floor, though it was not in wide use until the 80s.

Roorback, a political canard, [especially one that backfires,] arose in the campaign of 1844, when the Ithaca (N.Y.) *Chronicle* printed some alleged extracts from an imaginary book entitled "Roorback's Tour Through the Western and Southern States," containing grotesque charges against James K. Polk, then the Democratic candidate for the Presidency, and they were promptly copied by other Whig newspapers.[9] A typical story was to the effect that Roorback, in traveling through the South in 1836, had encountered an encampment of Negroes, every one of whom was branded with the letters J.K.P. *Roorback* was overlooked by Bartlett when he compiled his Glossary in 1848, and by Schele de Vere in 1872, but it is still occasionally encountered.[1] [Since the exposure of the fraud actually helped Polk, it is sometimes spelled *roarback*.]

Scalawag originated in western New York and at first meant "a mean fellow, a scapegrace." After the Civil War it was applied to the white

---

[8] Albert J. Engel, Speech in the House of Representatives, Apr. 23, 1936.

[9] The author of the book was supposedly a visiting German named Baron von *Roorback*. In part his adventures were suggested by those of Baron Munchausen, but there were also borrowings from An Excursion Through the Slave States (2 vols.; London, 1844), by an Englishman named George William Featherstonehaugh, who had spent many years in the United States but had never quite overcome his dislike of the country.

[1] See Abraham Lincoln: The Prairie Years, by Carl Sandburg; New York, 1926, Vol. I, pp. 343-4; and Something about Polk, *The New Yorker*, Aug. 8, 1936, p. 13.

Southerners who collaborated with the occupation, and since then it has been used to designate any lowdown politician.

[For more than a hundred years *to be rowed up Salt River* has meant *to lose an election*. The usual explanation has been that in the campaign of 1832, the Whig presidential candidate, Henry Clay, hired a boatman to row him up the Ohio to Louisville, where he was to deliver an important speech; the boatman, a Jackson man, instead rowed Clay up Salt River, a tributary of the Ohio, and caused him to miss the engagement, and consequently to lose Kentucky, and the election. Unfortunately, no evidence exists that Clay missed a Louisville engagement in either 1832 or in his previous campaign of 1824, and there is considerable evidence that *Salt River* had been earlier associated with the perils of the Wild West, and that *to row someone up Salt River* meant simply to give him a thrashing. It is in the political sense, however, that the phrase has stuck, though the river has sometimes become a creek, with something other than salt in solution.[2]]

Of the political terms not already discussed, *mileage*, signifying a legislator's allowance for traveling expenses, is probably the oldest, for it was used by Benjamin Franklin in 1754. *Machine*, in the political sense, is traced to 1865, *machine politician* and *machine politics* to 1876 and *machine ticket* to 1887. *Band wagon*, an Americanism first thrown to the world by P. T. Barnum in 1855, does not appear to have been taken into the political vocabulary until after 1906. *Banner state*, in the sense of the state which, in a presidential election, gives the winning (or losing) candidate the largest majority (or plurality, or vote), was first used by the Whigs in the Harrison campaign of 1840. *Barrel*, in the sense of a political fund (often *bar'l*), is traced to 1876, *barrel campaign* to the same year and *barrel candidate* to 1884. *Bee*, as in *presidential bee*, is not listed, but must be old. *Presidency* appeared about 1800, and has since elbowed out the earlier English *presidentship*. The DAE does not list *bell ringer*, in the sense of a bill introduced in a legislative body to extort money from those whose interest it threatens, or the analogous *holdup* and *shakedown* as political terms. *Strike*, meaning "a form of legislative blackmail," is traced to 1885, and Thornton, in his supplement,[3] traces the synonymous *fat frying* to 1890. The DA traces *ripper* to 1893, in the sense of a bill designed to legislate members of the opposition party out of office.

On a local level *heeler* is traced to *c.* 1877, *ward heeler* to 1888, *ward politics* to 1883 and *ward politician* to 1807. *Boss*, from the Dutch *baas*, has been in common use in the United States since colonial days, but it did not acquire its political significance until 1861. The DA traces *bossism* to

[2] [Hans Sperber and James N. Tidwell, Words and Phrases in American Politics: Fact and Fiction about *Salt River*, AS, Vol. XXVI, Dec. 1951, pp. 241–7.]

[3] *DN*, Vol. VI, Dec. 1932, p. 287.

1881 and *boss rule* to 1882. *Boodle,* from the Dutch *boedel,* meaning property or goods, came into use in the New York region so early as 1699, but it did not acquire the meaning of money (at first, counterfeit) until the 1850s, and was apparently not used to signify political bribes and loot until after 1880. The DA traces *to boodleize* to 1886, *boodler* and *boodlerism* to 1887 and *boodleism* to 1889. *Carpetbagger,* for a politico operating outside his home territory, came into general use in the era of Reconstruction, when the South was invaded by thousands of Northern entrepreneurs, but it was used to indicate a dubious stranger so early as 1846. The first political use of *dark horse,* borrowed from racing, was in 1865. *Dicker* and *divvy* are old words, but the former did not appear in the political vocabulary until 1888 and the latter not until *c.* 1900. *To engineer* became a political term in 1859. The *black-horse cavalry,* which *engineers* *bell ringers, strikes* and *shakedowns,* was first heard of in 1893. *Boom,* in the political sense, is traced to 1878,[4] and with it came *to boom* and *boomster. Boomlet* followed in 1887. *Brave* for a Tammany man, borrowed from the common name for an Indian warrior, does not appear to have come in until 1871. *Sachem* has been used by Tammany since 1786, *wigwam* since 1787. Another political term of Indian origin that deserves greater popularity than it enjoys is *wikinski* or *wiskinski,* signifying a functionary told off to collect campaign assessments from officeholders. [With the growth of public relations as a profession, more subtle techniques are used everywhere except in small towns, and the *wikinski* as such is seldom encountered. However, the functionary who peddles tickets to party shindigs—such as the $100-a-plate dinner—may be considered to be operating in the apostolic succession of *wikinskism.*]

Graft, in the political sense, is said to have been introduced by Joseph W. Folk, circuit attorney in St. Louis, *c.* 1900. Josiah Flynt's "Tramping with Tramps" (1899) had made Americans familiar with the significance of the term in the argot of criminals, and it was naturally transferred to the operations of political scoundrels. The DAE's first example in the new sense is 1903, but it was undoubtedly current before then. When *graft* began to denote the thieving of crooked politicians the more elegant of the regular or dirt crooks abandoned it for *grift.*[5] Various verb phrases based on *to go* have been long in use: *to go for,* 1830; *to go with the party,* 1829; and *to go Democratic,* 1877. *Freeze-out* and *to freeze out,* in the political sense, are traced by Thornton to 1882. *Has-been, immunity bath, mud slinger, public teat, public trough, rake-off* and *to view with alarm* are all omitted

---

[4] [Travis Trittschuh, Words and Phrases in American Politics: *Boom, AS,* Vol. XXXI, Oct. 1956, pp. 172–9.]

[5] According to a correspondent of the New York *Post,* June 2, 1923, signing himself H.P.S., the beautiful term *honest graft* was invented by "Ex-Senator Plunkett of New York." The date was not given.

by the DAE and DA. [The latter traces *keynote speech* only to 1911 and *keynoter* to 1932; both are older.] *Third party* goes back to 1801, and *third term* to 1833. *Steamroller* was invented by Oswald F. Schuette, Washington correspondent of the Chicago *Inter-Ocean*, to designate the rough devices used to force through the nomination of William H. Taft as the Republican presidential candidate in 1908. It has produced the inevitable verb, *to steamroller*, and the adjective, *steamrollered*. *Smoke-filled room* dates from 1920. *Bloc* is probably recent; the *farm bloc* officially appeared in 1921, though it had been in existence for a century. [*Dirt farmer* is traced to 1920, *grass roots* only to 1932; both are much older.] *To carry an election* is traced to 1848, *to crowd the mourners* to 1848 and *crowd*, in the sense of a political group, usually nefarious, to 1840. *To deliver the vote* is not recorded before 1893, but *to deliver the goods* was used in 1879. A number of terms embodying *election* are peculiarly American and relatively ancient. *Election district* was in use before 1800, *election day* by 1809 and *election time* by 1807. The DAE's first example of *election fraud* is dated 1883, and of *election bet*, 1925. Both are much older. In the early days the victors in an election celebrated with an *election ball*, but it survives into our own time only in the sporadic *inaugural ball* or *inauguration ball*, which the DAE traces to 1817. *Inaugural address* goes back to 1804, and *to inaugurate* to 1789.

The trade argot of Congress contains some relatively ancient Americanisms. *To get the floor* has been traced by the DAE to 1816, *to yield the floor* to 1835, *to take the floor* to 1846, *to have the floor* to 1848 and *floor leader* to 1899. *Gag rule* goes back to 1810, *junket* to 1886, *joker* (inserted in a bill) to 1904, *insurgent* to 1904,[6] *cloakroom gossip* (the congressional equivalent of soldiers' *latrine gossip*) to 1920 (it must be much older), *pork* to 1879, *salary grab* to 1873, *senatorial courtesy* (whereby a senator may veto a presidential nomination to office of anyone from his own state) to 1884, *slush fund* to 1864, *to stand pat* (from poker terminology) to 1896 and *standpatter, standpattism* and the adjectival *standpat* to 1904, *smelling committee* to 1877,[7] *steering committee* to 1887, *sectional* to 1806 and *sectionalism* to 1855 and *calamity howler* to 1892. The DAE and DA omit both *closure* and *cloture*. The latter was borrowed from the French by the English in 1871 or thereabout, but when the House of Commons adopted rules for the limitation of debate in 1882, *cloture*

---

[6] The first *insurgents* to attract general attention were the congressmen who revolted against the iron rule of Speaker Joseph G. Cannon in 1909. It was obviously suggested by memories of the Cuban *insurgents*.

[7] Bartlett, quoted by the DAE and DA, says that the term originated "in the examination of a convent in Massachusetts by legislative order."

was dropped for *closure*. Both have been used in this country, but *cloture* the more often.

The business of congressmen, like that of all other politicians, consists largely of the discovery, pursuit and laying of hobgoblins; this, indeed, is the chief phenomenon of the democratic process. The two houses have devoted immeasurable time and wind to pursuing *slavocrats, nullifiers, embalmed beef, isolationists, nigger lovers, pacifists, European pauper labor*, the *whiskey ring, pro-Germans, Japanese spies, land grabbers, land sharks, mossbacks*,[8] the *open shop*, the *closed shop*, and *labor* and other *racketeers*. Washington made a contribution to the menagerie with *foreign entanglements;* Jefferson produced two of the best bugaboos of all time in *war hawks* and *monocrats*. From 1875 onward until the late 80s *waving the bloody shirt* was the chief industry of Republican congressmen, and from the early 90s onward *the crime of '73* enraged the Democrats. *Bourbon*, borrowed from the name of the French royal family, the members of which were said to never learn anything and never forget anything, has been traced to 1859; after the Civil War, it was applied to unreconstructed Southern Democrats. *Tory* has been a term of opprobrium since the Revolution, when it was applied to one loyal to England; *Loyalist* was a synonym, but not quite so offensive. [The *United Empire Loyalists* of Canada match our *Daughters of the American Revolution* in patriotic zeal.] *Tory* served so well that it was revived in 1812 to designate New England opponents of the second war with England, in 1861 for Southerners who favored the Union, in 1896 for advocates of the gold standard, and in 1933 for persons who refused to accept the New Deal. *Gold bug*, always contemptuous, is traced to 1878. *Reactionary* was used so long ago as 1858,[9] but it did not begin to appear in the American political vocabulary until the Bryan era, and it was dying when the New Dealers revived it in 1933. *Plutocrats* were first heard of in the late 70s [1] and the *trusts* at about the same time.[2] Since 1880, at least forty different *trusts*, real and imaginary, have had the attention of Congress, *e.g.*, the *coal, whiskey, oil, gas*,[3] *lumber, railroad, fertilizer, gold, meat, telephone, elevator, money, shipping, steel, beer, flour* and even *baseball* and *civil service trusts*. *Imperialism* became so infamous under Democratic attack after the Spanish-American War that its Republican defenders sought to disguise it under the milder name

---

[8] *Mossback*, now applied to any conservative, was first used in 1885 for an Ohio Democrat of the conservative wing.

[9] In J. A. Froude's History of England.

[1] The word is not an American invention. The OED traces it in English use to 1850, and *plutocracy* to 1652.

[2] That is, in the sense of large industrial organizations, approaching or alleged to be approaching monopolistic proportions. In the common legal sense *trust* is traced to 1700, and in the titles of trust companies to 1834.

[3] It first appeared in 1888 as the *Coal-Oil Trust*.

of *expansion*. The *interests*, not listed by the DAE or DA, were discovered during the Bryan saturnalia of vituperation at the end of the Nineteenth Century, but *Wall Street* had been under fire since the Civil War, and *money sharks* were denounced so early as 1844. The Bryanists invented *hell hounds of plutocracy*, but *economic royalist, prince of pelf* and *rotten rich* had to wait for the New Deal. The DAE and DA omit *vice crusade*, *white-slave trade* and *vice trust*, which, in a vocabulary of Americanisms, is almost as sad an oversight as omitting *buffalo, home run* or *Rotary*.

Virtually all the more eminent politicos in American history have enlarged the roster of political terms and slogans. Lincoln is chiefly remembered for his more sonorous phrases, *e.g., government of the people, by the people and for the people,*[4] but he also invented or introduced many more homely things, *e.g., yellow dog* as a general indicator of inferiority. He probably invented *the great masses of the plain people*, later worked so hard by Bryan. The heroes between Lincoln and Cleveland were not phrase makers, but some of them were the beneficiaries or victims of phrases made by others, *e.g., plumed knight*, applied to Blaine by Robert Ingersoll in 1876,[5] and the *rum, Romanism and rebellion* of the Rev. S. D. Burchard in 1884.[6] With Cleveland came a revival of phrase making: he was responsible for *innocuous desuetude*[7] and was falsely credited with "Public office is a public trust." McKinley was likewise credited with *manifest destiny*, but it had been used in 1845. He seems to have actually coined *benevolent assimilation* in 1898, to describe the annexation of the Philippines. His followers revived and propagated *honest dollar* and *full dinner pail*, neither of them new. Bryan's masterpiece was *cross of gold and crown of thorns*, launched at the Democratic National Convention in Chicago, July 9, 1896, but he also made other phrases, including *deserving Democrat*.[8] Theodore Roosevelt made or revived scores, *e.g., big stick, malefactors of great wealth, Ananias Club, mollycoddle, weasel word, nature faker, to pussyfoot, strenuous life, one hundred per cent American, muckraker, square deal* and *lunatic fringe*. Woodrow Wilson was also fertile in neologisms: *little group of willful men, new freedom, peace without victory, too proud*

---

[4] This was in his Gettysburg Address, Nov. 19, 1863. It was by no means original with him. See my New Dictionary of Quotations; New York, 1942, p. 902.

[5] Speech at the Republican National Convention, June 5. "Like a *plumed knight*, James G. Blaine marched down the halls of the American Congress."

[6] Speech as chairman of a delegation calling upon Blaine, Oct. 29: "We are Republicans, and don't propose to leave our party and identify ourselves with the party whose antecedents have been *rum, Romanism* and *rebellion*." [This endorsement of Blaine is often considered the force which provided the Democrats with a narrow victory in New York, and hence in the country at large.]

[7] Message to Congress, Mar. 1, 1886.

[8] Letter to Walter W. Wick, receiver-general of the Dominican Republic, Aug. 20, 1913. Bryan was then Secretary of State in Wilson's Cabinet, but kept a watchful eye on the party fences.

to fight, watchful waiting, to make the world safe for democracy, open
covenants openly arrived at and pitiless publicity. Then came Harding
with normalcy,[9] followed by Coolidge with "Well, they hired the money,
didn't they?" and "I do not choose to run." Both of these were sound old
American terms. Al Smith later introduced baloney (dollar), alphabet soup
and off the record. Senator George H. Moses, of New Hampshire, contributed sons of the wild jackass to designate the insurgent Western Republicans. Hoover will be remembered chiefly for rugged individualism
and noble experiment, both of which helped to ruin him. So did Hoover-
ville [and Hoover cart [1]], which he certainly did not invent.

With the Depression [2] and the New Deal came the greatest flood of
novelties since Roosevelt I: forgotten man,[3] horse-and-buggy days, to
prime the pump, yardstick, rendezvous with destiny, coordinator, direc-
tive, ceiling price, underprivileged, boondoggling,[4] more abundant life,
court packing, client (for beneficiary), isolationist and good-neighbor
policy. New Deal, launched in Roosevelt's speech of acceptance, July 2,
1932, was apparently an amalgam of the Square Deal of Roosevelt I and
the New Freedom of Woodrow Wilson, and is said to have been devised
by Samuel I. Rosenman, the candidate's private counsel and intimate adviser and later a judge of the New York Supreme Court.[5] Brain Trust was
invented by James M. Kieran, a reporter for The New York Times, at
Hyde Park, N.Y., where Roosevelt was preparing campaign speeches with
the aid of three Columbia University professors, Raymond Moley, Rex-
ford G. Tugwell and Adolph A. Berle, Jr.[6] Some of Roosevelt's advisers
did not like the term, but Roosevelt himself favored it. Brain trust had

---

[9] A word much derided by American
intellectuals, but of respectable ancestry.
The OED quotes its use in a mathematical treatise of 1857. Abnormalcy has also
appeared.

[1] [The Hoover cart, which flourished
in the rural South, 1930–3, was a horse-
or mule-drawn vehicle made from the
rear axle and chassis of a worn-out automobile.]

[2] Language of the Depression, by
Charles Carpenter, AS, Vol. VIII, Dec.
1933, pp. 76–7.

[3] Borrowed from the title of a speech
by William Graham Sumner, delivered
in 1883, and reprinted in The Forgotten
Man and Other Essays; New Haven,
1919, and again as a pamphlet. The forgotten man of Sumner was the hard-
working, self-supporting fellow who
pays his own way in the world and
asks for no favors from anyone. Roosevelt converted him, by a curious perver-

sion, into a mendicant beneficiary of the
New Deal doles.

[4] Boondoggle, coined by Robert Link,
of Rochester, came into general use as a
name for the braided leather lanyard
worn by Boy Scouts (Word Study, Sept.
1935, p. 2). Under the New Deal the
term was transferred to the useless tasks
performed by the recipients of its doles.

[5] The Roosevelt Revolution, First
Phase, by Ernest K. Lindley; New York,
1933, pp. 26–7.

[6] When he learned that they were in
residence Kieran exclaimed: "The Brains
Trust!" and soon afterward he introduced it in his dispatches. "Some inspired
Times copyreader kept cutting it out
before it finally sneaked by and got into
actual print." (Letter to AS, Vol. XIV,
Dec. 1939, p. 247.) It was then adopted
by other reporters, and soon Brains was
reduced to the singular.

been "used by the line of the Army as a sort of sour grapes crack at the first American general staff established by Elihu Root in 1901."[7] The coiner of *That Man* is unknown.

The *reds* who emerged from hiding on the establishment of the *entente cordiale* with Russia in 1941 gave us *fellow traveler, cell, people's* (or *popular) front, people's democracies, to bore from within* and *transmission belt,* have revived and propagated *left, left wing, leftist,*[8] the corresponding forms of *right* and *center, to indoctrinate, underground, class struggle, reactionary, counter-revolutionary,*[9] *proletarian* and its derivatives, *Trojan horse* and *Trotskyite,* and have helped make *fascist* and *bourgeois* general terms of abuse.[1] [Americans captured in Korea by the Chinese Communists were subjected to a particular form of *indoctrination* called *brain washing,* a literal translation of the Chinese word, which has been extended to other contexts. *Premature liberal* and *premature anti-fascist* have been used for non-Communists who supported Russian policy against Germany before 1941; during the era of *McCarthyism* (1949–54) some of them had hard going.[2]]

Some of the eulogistic nicknames for American statesmen are familiar to every schoolboy, *e.g.,* the *Father of His Country* for Washington, *Honest Abe* for Lincoln, *Old Hickory* for Jackson, *the Little Giant* for Stephen A. Douglas, *the Great Commoner* for Clay and *the Commoner* for Bryan. But respectable schoolboys are not informed that Washington was often spoken of by his critics as *the Stepfather of His Country* and *the Old Fox,* or that the sainted Lincoln was derided by Confederates and Northern Democrats alike as *the Baboon,* a brilliant but indelicate reference to his aspect.[3] Grant, the soldier more than the politician, escaped with *the Butcher,* but his successors got it hot and heavy. Hayes was *the Fraud* and *Granny,* Arthur was *the Dude,* Cleveland was *the Stuffed Prophet* and

---

[7] General Hugh S. Johnson, letter to *AS,* Vol. XV, Feb. 1940, p. 79.

[8] See Right and Left Words, by George P. Wilson, *Words,* May 1937, pp. 102–5. *Left,* in the sense of a radical faction, was introduced by Carlyle in his French Revolution (1837). It comes from the French *côte gauche* (left side). In the French Assembly of 1789 the conservative nobles sat to the presiding officer's right, the radicals of the Third Estate to his left, and the moderates directly before him, in the center.

[9] Gouverneur Morris used *counter-revolutionary* in 1791 and *counter-revolution* in 1793 and may have invented them, for the OED offers no earlier examples.

[1] *Bourgeois* simply means citizen, but is commonly used in France to denote the middle class. With the rise of European socialism it became a term of reproach, and a symbol of dowdy unpleasantness. See the London *Observer,* Dec. 11, 1938.

[2] [The best satirizing of Communism has been done by an Englishman, George Orwell (Eric Blair) in a novel entitled 1984; Americans have generally been content to borrow his *Big Brother, Inner Party, Newspeak, Doublethink* and *duckspeaker* rather than invent their own terms.]

[3] He was also called *the Ape,* probably influenced by *Abe.* The White House secretariat called him *the Tycoon.*

the Hangman,[4] Roosevelt I was *the Bull Moose*, *the Man on Horseback* [5] and *Teddy the Meddler*, Wilson was *the Phrasemaker* and *the Schoolmaster*, Coolidge was *Silent Cal* (always with a sneer) [and Hoover (with an equal sneer) *the Great Engineer*. Eisenhower seemed safe with *Ike*, but antinomians soon launched *Lydia Pinkham*, in honor of the patent-medicine campaign which peddled him as a sovereign remedy for female complaints.[6]] Of willing but unwanted candidates, Calhoun was *the Great Nullifier*, Webster was *Black Dan*, Blaine was *the Tattoed Man*, Charles Sumner was *the Bull of the Woods*, Charles G. Dawes was *Hell and Maria*, W. R. Hearst was *the Yellow Kid*, Charles E. Hughes was *the Feather Duster*, John Nance Garner was *Cactus Jack*, *Poker Face* and *the Owl* [and Richard M. Nixon was *Tricky Dick*]. Even Mrs. Lincoln had a nickname, *the She-Wolf*. [Mrs. Hayes escaped with *Lemonade Lucy;* a passionate dry, she refused to serve alcoholic beverages in the White House.]

More than one figure in American politics is remembered for his prodigies of invective, *e.g.*, the two Roosevelts and Wilson. One of the most gifted and industrious was Roosevelt II's Secretary of the Interior, Harold L. Ickes,[7] who coined *Trilby* for Alfred M. Landon and *Svengali* for W. R. Hearst, *condottieri* for the newspaper columnists hostile to the New Deal, *jeer leader* for one of them and *intellectual Dillingers* [8] for other persons he disliked. General Hugh S. Johnson was both in and out of the New Deal corral, and did some loud howling on both sides of the barbed wire. As administrator of the NRA, he denounced his Republican critics as *intellectual prostitutes, academic mercenaries, kippered herring* and *hippopotami*, and after he became debamboozled he flayed his late colleagues as *breast beaters, wand-waving wizards, janissaries* and *Adullamites*.[9] He is

---

[4] As sheriff of Erie County, N.Y., he hanged a murderer.

[5] [The term goes back to 1860, when it was coined by Caleb Cushing, of Maine, under the inspiration of the romances of G. P. R. James. It was also applied to Grant. See Hans Sperber and James N. Tidwell, Words and Phrases in American Politics, *AS*, Vol. XXV, May 1950, pp. 93-5. Many other such nicknames are listed in Shankle.]

[6] [For the story of the original Lydia, see Lydia Pinkham Is Her Name, by Jean Burton; New York, 1949. As a political epithet *Lydia Pinkham* is old; Mr. Dooley (Peter Finley Dunne), as quoted by Edward F. Murphy, *The New York Times Magazine*, Sept. 9, 1962, p. 107: "An' did ye iver notice how much the candydates . . . looks like Lydia Pinkham." Mr. Eisenhower did not con-

tribute to the roster of political phrases; on the contrary, his own addiction to gobbledygook inspired antinomians to circulate a purported translation of the Gettysburg Address into Eisenhese. At the 1962 convention of the NCTE, Gordon Ray, director of the Guggenheim Foundation, labeled Webster 1961 "a Republican conspiracy to make us all talk like Eisenhower."]

[7] Some of his masterpieces are assembled by Fon W. Boardman, Jr., Political Name Calling, *AS*, Vol. XV, Dec. 1940, pp. 353-6.

[8] From *John Dillinger*, an eminent bandit of the early 30s, butchered by FBI agents on July 22, 1934. He was the first *Public Enemy No. 1*, a phrase apparently invented by Homer S. Cummings, then Attorney General.

[9] I Samuel XXII, 1-2.

also said to have invented *third termite*. The series of nicknames that began with *Tommy the Cork* for Thomas G. Corcoran is said to have been launched by Mr. Roosevelt himself. Other hands pitched in, and it presently included *Henry the Morgue* for Henry Morgenthau, Jr., *Leon the Hen* for Leon Henderson, *Benny the Cone* for Benjamin V. Cohen and *Harold the Ick* for Ickes.

It would be possible, too, to compile a formidable roster of theological and ecclesiastical Americanisms, *e.g., anxious bench* or *seat* (first noted in 1839), *mourners' bench, amen corner, hard shell* (1842), *camp meeting* (1801), *circuit rider* (1838), *desk* for pulpit (1770), *experience meeting, foot wash, donation party, pounding* and the verbs *to get* (or *experience*) *religion, to fellowship* and *to shout*. [Many of these, as we have seen, have also been taken into politics.]

3: LOAN WORDS AND NON-ENGLISH INFLUENCES

The Indians of the Far West added little to the American vocabulary. Most of the new loan words that were picked up west of the Mississippi came in either through the Spanish, *e.g., coyote,* or through the Chinook trade jargon of the Columbia River region,[1] *e.g., cayuse. Coyote,* ultimately from the Nahuatl language of Mexico, designates a prairie wolf, *Canis latrans,* never encountered in the East, but Western fiction and the movies have made its meaning familiar to all Americans. *Cayuse,* probably from the name of a tribe of Oregon Indians, is sometimes confused with a genuine Chinook word, *cultus,* meaning inferior. There is a strong tendency to ascribe all otherwise unidentified Indian loans to Chinook, but actual borrowings seem to have been few: *potlatch,* a gift, or, by extension, a party marked by lavish hospitality and gift giving, traced to *c.* 1861; *skookum,* large or powerful,[2] and *siwash* (1847), a generic term for Indian, borrowed by the Chinook from the French *sauvage.*[3] In Alaska and the Oregon country, a number of Chinook terms, unknown elsewhere save

---

[1] An amalgam of Chinook proper and various other Indian languages, *e.g.,* Nootka, Chehalis, Klickitat and Wasco, with contributions from French, English and probably also from Russian. A good account of it, with a vocabulary, is in Gill's Dictionary of the Chinook Jargon; 15th ed.; Portland, Ore., 1909. It was in use all over the Northwest from the Cascade Mountains to the coast. See also The Chinook Jargon, by Douglas Leechman, *AS*, Vol. I, July 1926, and The Chinook Jargon, by E. H. Thomas, *AS*, Vol. II, June 1927. [Other contact languages existed elsewhere on the continent. See American Indian Pidgin English, by Douglas Leechman and Robert A. Hall, Jr., *AS*, Vol. XXX, Oct. 1955, pp. 163–71.]

[2] *Skookum house*, in the West, is a name for the jail on an Indian reservation.

[3] [It has since become a designation for any fresh-water college; *to die for dear old Siwash* was a proverbial phrase for athletic posturing, before the industrialization of football following World War II.]

in fiction, are familiar locally, *e.g.*, *klootchman*, a woman; *muckamuck*, food; *cheechako*, a stranger; *keekwilly*, a house; and *kla-how-ya?*, "How are you?"

In the same way borrowings from the Indians of the Southwest are current in that region, though not in general use elsewhere, *e.g.*, *katchina*, a spirit; *kiva*, the central building of a pueblo; *mesquite*, a shrub; *peyote*, an intoxicant made of cactus; *tequila* or *mescal*, an intoxicant distilled from agave bulbs; and *wickiup*, a brush hut, now used to designate any mean habitation. *Wickiup* comes from a Mississippi Valley Algonquian language; the rest are from languages of the Southwest. The DA traces *mesquite* to 1805 and *mescal* to 1808. There were few additions to the translated Indian terms (or supposed Indian terms) previously listed. The forest Indians applied *Father* to a friendly white in the Eighteenth Century, but not until the reservation Indians of the West began trooping to Washington with their grievances was *Great White Father* heard of. *Snake dance*, traced to 1772, remained rare in American use until nearly a century later. *Happy hunting grounds* first appeared in Irving's "Bonneville" (1837), and in 1763 the Mississippi (literally "big river") begins to appear as the *Father of Rivers, of Floods* or *of Waters*.[4]

From the Canadian French *prairie, batteau, portage* and *rapids* had been borrowed during colonial days. After the Louisiana Purchase and the settlement of the Mississippi Valley and the Great Lakes region, there was a considerable accession of new French terms, not a few of them geographic. *Prairie* begat an enormous progeny during the great movement into the West. In 1828 Noah Webster omitted it altogether from his "American Dictionary of the English Language," but its use to designate the Western steppes was common before the Revolution, and *prairie hen* and *prairie dog* had come in by 1805. The Century Dictionary (1889–91) records thirty-four *prairie* combinations, the Oxford Dictionary (1909) sixty-three, Webster 1961 eighty-seven and the DA more than a hundred.

The DA traces *butte, cache* and *picayune* to 1805, *chute* to 1804, *coulee* to 1807, *crevasse* to 1813 and *depot* (railroad) to 1832. There have been bitter etymological battles over *shanty*. Over the claims of professional Hibernians (and earlier etymologists) that it is "probably from Irish *sean*, old, and *tigh*, house," [5] the DAE, DA and Webster 1961 derive it from the Canadian French *chantier*. *Lagniappe* came into American from the French, but is not actually a French word. "A trifling gift presented to a customer by a merchant," it is a French adaptation of the Spanish *ñapa*, which is taken in turn from the Kechuan (Peruvian Indian) *yapa*, a present made to

[4] Charles F. Hockett, Reactions to Indian Place-Names, *AS*, Vol. XXV, May 1950, pp. 118–21.

[5] P. W. Joyce, English as We Speak It in Ireland; 2nd ed.; Dublin, 1910, p. 319.

a customer.[6] It is one of a large number of French or pseudo-French loans that survive in the speech of the lower Mississippi region but are seldom heard elsewhere. Similar loans are to be encountered in the English of the French-speaking sections of Canada. *To sashay* (1836), from the French *chasser*, is defined by the DAE as "to glide or move around, to go about, to go."

Direct loans from Spanish, in Texas and farther west, first appeared in large number between 1800 and 1850, and many additions have been made since. Indeed American English has possibly borrowed more terms from the Spanish than from any other language. "In some instances," says Harold W. Bentley, they "have been adopted because there existed no adequate words in English. More often Spanish elements are taken over for local color effects, for their richness of connotation, including humor, for picturesqueness, or for descriptive contribution of some kind."[7] *Siesta* is an example of the first class, *savvy* and *juzgado* (corrupted to *hoosegow*) of the second. Of loans familiar to every American, *adobe* is traced to 1759, *alfalfa* to 1855, *bonanza* to 1844, *bronco* to 1850, *burro* to 1844, *calaboose* (by way of Louisiana French) to 1792, *canyon* to 1834, *chaparral* to 1845, *corral* to 1829, *fiesta* to 1844, *frijole* to 1759, *lariat* to 1832, *lasso* to 1831, *loco* to 1844, *mesa* to 1759, *mustang* to 1808, *padre* to 1792, *patio* to 1827, *peon* to 1826, *placer* to 1842, *plaza* to 1836, *pronto* to 1850, *ranch* to 1808, *rodeo* to 1844, *sabe* (or *savvy*) to 1850, *señorita* to 1823, *sierra* to 1759, *sombrero* to 1823, *tortilla* to 1831 and *vigilante* to 1867. The Mexican War brought in a large number of Spanish terms,[8] and the California gold rush brought in more. The Spanish-American War made all Americans familiar with *insurrecto*, *incommunicado*, *machete*, *junta* and *rurale*. Others filter in more or less steadily. So far there are no known examples of *mañana* before 1885, of *marijuana* before 1894, of *chili con carne* before 1895 or of *wrangler* (as in *horse wrangler*) before 1888. The first example of *rodeo* in the sense of a traveling show is dated 1914, and of *hoosegow*, 1920.

Some of the borrowings underwent phonetic change. The Spanish *cincho*, meaning a saddle girth, quickly became *cinch*, and soon took on a figurative significance. *Vamos*, Spanish for "Let's go," became *vamoose* in American and presently begat *to mosey*. The Spanish *chinche*, borrowed by the English in the Seventeenth Century but later abandoned, was reborrowed on the frontier, and became the still familiar *chinch*, a bedbug. *Estampida* was converted into *stampede*, *frijol* into *frijole* (pron. *free-*

---

[6] William A. Read, Louisiana French; Baton Rouge, 1931, p. 142.

[7] A Dictionary of Spanish Terms in English, with Special Reference to the American Southwest; New York, 1932. [See also Southwestern Plant Names from Spanish, by Ralph W. Sorvig, *AS*, Vol. XXVIII, May 1953, pp. 97–105.]

[8] One of them was *staked plains*, now obsolete. It came from the Spanish *llano estacado*. The first recorded example is from 1848.

holay), *tamal* into *tamale* and *vaquero* into *buckaroo*.[9] Americans soon outfitted many Spanish loan words with derivatives, *e.g.*, *rancher, ranch house,
to ranch, to lasso, to corral, to cinch, hot tamale, bronc, box canyon, peonage, burro load, -train* and *-trail, locoweed* (Sp. *loco*, crazy). Western fiction, the movies, TV serials, pseudo-Spanish bungalow architecture and
the constant invasion of southern California by transient visitors have kept
Spanish loan words alive in American speech. Thus *pinto* and *hombre* are
not often used save in the Southwest; nevertheless they are understood
almost everywhere.

This period saw the beginning of the great immigrations, particularly
Germans, Irish Catholics from the South of Ireland (the Irish of colonial
days "were descendants of Cromwell's army, and came from the north of
Ireland" [1]) and, on the Pacific coast, Chinese. So early as the 1820s the immigration to the United States reached 25,000 in a year; in 1824 the legislature of New York, in alarm, passed a restrictive act. The immigration of
1845 passed the 100,000 mark, and that of 1854 came within sight of 500,-
000. These new Americans did not all remain in the East; many spread
through the West and Southwest with the other pioneers.

Next to Spanish, German has probably made the heaviest contributions
to the American vocabulary. They range from such familiar words as
gesundheit, delicatessen, kindergarten and *ouch* to such phrases as *so long,
wie geht's* and *raus mit 'im*. Unhappily, there have been few scientific
treatments of their history, and only too often, especially since 1916, their
discussion has been incommoded by partisan heat. The OED's first example of *sauerkraut* is from the "Itinerary" of Fynes Moryson (1617), but as
the foreign name of a foreign comestible, and both name and comestible
retain a foreign smack in England. The thing itself seems to have been introduced to Americans by the Pennsylvania Germans; the first occurrence
recorded by the DA is in John Leacock's play "The Fall of British Tyranny" (1776). There has been a considerable controversy over *shyster*,
traced to 1846. [It is probably based on German *Scheisse*, excrement.]
The American *bum*, from an earlier *bummer*, is commonly believed to
have been suggested by the German verb *bummeln*, meaning to waste time.
The DA's first example of *bummer* is dated 1856. During the Civil War
bummer was used to designate a soldier who went foraging on his own
and later to Sherman's foragers. *Bumming*, in the sense of going on a
carouse, is traced to 1857, but the DA's first example of *bum* to designate

---

[9] *Vaquero* means cowboy, and is used
in that sense in Argentina. In the American West it quickly acquired the sense of
a *Mexican* cowboy. *Buckaroo* seems to
have dropped out. [Julian Mason would
derive it from Gullah *buckra*, "white
man," through the tradition of the
Negro cowboy. The Etymology of
buckaroo, AS, Vol. XXXV, Feb. 1960,
pp. 51-5.]
[1] Prescott F. Hall, Immigration; New
York, 1913, p. 5.

such a carouse is from 1871. *To bum* in the sense of to loaf or wander about is traced to 1863. *On the bum* and *to bum a ride* did not come in until the last decades of the century. To the English, *bum* means the backside, and is hence inelegant, but they use it without blushes in *bum-bailiff* and *bum-boat*. There is no evidence that the American permutations of *bum* owe anything to the English *bum*.

Loafer is apparently derived from the German *Landläufer*, meaning a vagabond, and on its first appearance in print, in the 1830s, was sometimes *landloafer* and sometimes simply *loafer*. The DA traces the verb *to loaf* to 1835. R. H. Dana, in "Two Years Before the Mast" (1840, expanded from notes made in 1834–6), spoke of *loafer* as "the newly invented Yankee word." In 1855, in "Leaves of Grass," Whitman used a phrase that seems destined to live: "I *loafe* [note the original spelling] and invite my soul." Both *loafer* and *bummer* have provided numerous derivatives: *loaf* (noun), *loafing place, corner loafer, bum* as an adjective (as in *bum steer* and *bum food*) and *bum's rush*. *Loafer* has migrated to England, but *bum* is still unknown there in the American sense.

The DAE is anything but strong in the department of German loans; [the DA is better but still omits *sauerbraten, stein, wanderlust, hausfrau, Schweizer cheese* and even *ouch* (which the DAE runs back to 1837). It traces *zwieback* to 1894, *spieler* to 1891, *pumpernickel* (in Longfellow's "Hyperion") to 1839, *katzenjammer* to 1846 and *smearcase* to 1829. It finds *dumb*, in the American sense of stupid, a borrowing from German *dumm* or Dutch *dum*, in 1823, but *dumbhead* (from *Dummkopf*) doesn't appear till 1887; Irving's *dum kop* (1825) is probably from Dutch. It lifts *fresh* (from *frech*), in the sense of impertinent, from Bartlett, 1848, and runs *bower* (in cards, from *Bauer*) to 1830, *lager* to 1854 and *turnverein* to 1852. Its first example of *pretzel* is dated *c.* 1824, of *bock beer*, 1856, and of *rathskeller*, 1900.] *Check*, in the sense of a restaurant bill, is traced to 1868, but there is no mention of the German *Zeche*. *To dunk*, from the Pennsylvania-German *dunke*, is traced to 1867. *Nix, nixie* and *nixy* are recorded, and their relation to the German *nichts*, [as well as the *nixie division* of the postal service, and its *nixie clerks* who handle misdirected mail, but there is no mention of *aber nit* or *nitwit*].

The American *bub*, "a playful form of address to boys," is probably related to the German *Bub(e)*, and its history is traced to 1839. *Bushelman*, a repairer of men's clothes, is probably related to the German *böscheln*. Scattered in the etymological literature, professional and lay, are discussions of various other possible American loans from the German. For example, *and how* may be a translation of the German *und wie*,[2] *standpoint*

---

[2] *And how* and *und wie*, by E. E. Ericson, *Beiblatt zur Anglia*, June 1937, p.   186; *And how*, by J. R. Schultz, *AS*, Vol. VIII, Dec. 1933, p. 80.

from *Standpunkt*. *Cant hook*, first recorded in 1848, may be from the German *Kanthaken;* the substitution of the American *shoe* for the English *boot* may have been helped by the German *Schuh;* [3] *bake oven* (1787) may come from the German *Backofen; slim* (1815) as in *slim chance* may be from the German *schlimm*. Such shortened and characteristically American forms as *cookbook* (1809) and *barbershop* (1852) [4] (for the preferred English *cookery-book* and *barber's shop*) may have been promoted by German example, and the numerous American terms in *ker-*, *e.g.*, *ker-flop*, *ker-smash* and *ker-thump*, may owe something to the German *ge-*. [5]

However cautiously one must handle these suggestions, they at least reveal the lack of scientific investigation. Many German words and phrases have been completely assimilated into American, and a formidable number of others are generally understood, though not altogether assimilated, *e.g.*, *eins, zwei, drei, Hofbräu, Knackwurst, hoch, wie geht's, ganz* (or *sehr*) *gut, prosit, auf Wiedersehen* and *Gemütlichkeit*. The latter class is greatest in the big cities of the Middle Atlantic and Midwestern States, and smallest in the South. In regions heavily settled by Germans, *e.g.*, Pennsylvania and Wisconsin, many German phrases are understood, and a great many Germanisms are in circulation. [6] *That* equals *so that*, as in "We like our mince

---

[3] German Influences upon English, by Ruth M. Stone, *AS*, Vol. VIII, Apr. 1933, p. 77.

[4] The OED has one example from 1579; the phrase has been formed anew in the United States.

[5] See German Influences on the American Language, by Andreas Dorpalen, *American-German Review*, Aug. 1941, p. 14. See also American Variations, by H. W. Horwill, *SPE Tract*, No. XLV, 1936, p. 176.

[6] See R. Whitney Tucker, Linguistic Substrata in Pennsylvania and Elsewhere, *Lg.*, Vol. X, Mar. 1934, pp. 1–5; George W. Struble, The English of the Pennsylvania Germans, *AS*, Vol. X, Oct. 1935, pp. 163–72; [Fred Eikel, Jr., The Use of Cases in New Braunfels (Texas) German, *AS*, Vol. XXIV, Dec. 1949, pp. 278–81;] J. W. Frey, A Simple Grammar of Pennsylvania Dutch, Clinton, S.C., 1942; The English of the Pennsylvania Germans in York Co., Pa., *'S Pennsylfawnisch Deitsch Eck* (Allentown, Pa.), May 18, 1940; [Jesse W. Harris, German Language Influences in St. Clair County, Illinois, *AS*, Vol. XXIII, Apr. 1948, pp. 106–110; Henry Kratz and Humphrey Milnes, Kitchener German: a Pennsylvania German Dialect, *Modern Language Quarterly*, Vol. XIV, 1953, pp. 184–98, 274–83; Hans Kurath, German Relics in Pennsylvania English, *Monatshefte für deutsche Unterricht*, Vol. XXVII, 1945, pp. 96–102; Carroll E. Reed, The Pennsylvania German Dialect Spoken in the Counties of Lehigh and Berks, Seattle, 1949; A Survey of Pennsylvania German Phonology, *Modern Language Quarterly*, Vol. VIII, Sept. 1947, pp. 267–89; A Survey of Pennsylvania German Morphology, *ibid.*, Vol. IX, Sept. 1948, pp. 322–42; The Adaptation of English to Pennsylvania German Morphology, *AS*, Vol. XXIII, Oct.–Dec. 1948, pp. 239–50; Double Dialect Geography, *Orbis*, Vol. X, June 1961, pp. 308–19; Carroll E. Reed and Lester W. Seifert, A Study of the Pennsylvania German Spoken in the Counties of Lehigh and Berks, *Modern Language Quarterly*, Vol. IX, Dec. 1948, pp. 448–66; A Linguistic Atlas of Pennsylvania German, Marburg an der Lahn, 1954; Carroll E. Reed and Herbert F. Wiese, Amana German, *AS*, Vol. XXXII, Dec. 1957, pp. 243–56; Paul Schach, Hybrid Compounds in Pennsylvania German, *AS*, Vol. XXIII, Apr. 1948, pp. 121–34; Semantic Borrowing in Pennsylvania German, *AS*, Vol. XXVI, Dec. 1951, pp. 257–67; Arthur Herman Wilson, The

pie piping-hot that it steams inside." A *tut* or a *paper tut* is a paper bag. *Verdrubt* means sad. The *freinschaft* is the relationship. *Schnitz* means dried apples. *All* is *all gone*, as in "The butter is *all.*" *Look* means *be fitting*, as in "It doesn't *look* for two girls to go there alone." Many other localisms have been found, among them *glick*, to come out right (Ger. *glück*); *siffer*, a heavy drinker (Ger. *Saufer*); and *ritschi*, a frozen pond used for sliding (Ger. *rutschen*, to slide). Santa Claus, in such areas, is usually *Belsnickel*, as indeed he was once among the Germans of Baltimore. Mixed forms are often found in the Midwest, *e.g.*, *brickstein* for *brick* (Ger. *Backstein*), *heurack* for *hayrack* (Ger. *Heu*, hay) and *büchershelf* for *bookshelf* (Ger. *Bücher*, books).[7] A peculiar intonation is remarked by visitors to the Pennsylvania-German towns. "The voice is raised at the beginning of a question and lowered at the end." This intonation is also noticeable when the native speaker is using what passes locally for German. Furthermore, questions frequently contain an *ain't*: "You'll do that, *ain't* you will?" "You won't do that, *ain't* you won't?"[8]

A number of German loans, once flourishing in American, have passed out. *Shenk beer* is completely unknown today. *Cylinder* for plug hat, probably from the German *Zylinder*,[9] disappeared before the object became a rarity. *Kindergraph*, a photograph of a child, went the way of most nonce words.[1]

The influence of Irish English upon American awaits serious investigation. Bristed, in 1855, declared that the only Irish mark upon the speech of New York at that time was the general abandonment of *shall* for *will*, but this was a palpable underestimate. The Irish gave American very few new words; *shillelagh*, *smithereens* and possibly *speakeasy* almost exhaust the list. *Lallapalooza* may also be an Irish loan word, apparently from *allay-foozee*, a Mayo provincialism, signifying a sturdy fellow. *Allay-foozee*, in turn, comes from the French *allez-fusil*, meaning "Forward the musket!" —a memory, according to P. W. Joyce, of the French landing at Killala in

English Spoken by Pennsylvania Germans in Snyder County, Pennsylvania, *AS*, Vol. XXIII, Oct.-Dec. 1948, pp. 236-8.]

[7] A. W. Meyer, Some German-Americanisms in the Middle West, *AS*, Vol. II, Dec. 1926.

[8] W. H. Allen, *DN*, Vol. IV, Pt. II, 1914, pp. 157 *ff.*

[9] *Harper's Magazine*, The Man in the Rocking Chair, Aug. 1861, p. 429.

[1] It appeared in an advertisement of Weller-Lewis *Kindergraphs* in the rotogravure section of the Baltimore *Sun*, May 31, 1925.

Poker (1834), according to the OED, comes from *Pochspiel*, "a similar bluffing card-game of considerable age, from *pochen*, to boast, brag, literally to knock, rap." However, Schele de Vere in his *Americanisms* (1872) derived it from the French *poche*, a pocket, [and the DA accepts this etymology]. Of more decorous terms, *academic freedom* is probably a loan translation, as is *Doctor of Philosophy*; *festschrift*, *semester* and *seminar* are straight loans. Leo L. Rockwell, Older German Loan-Words in American English, *AS*, Vol. XX, Dec. 1945, pp. 246-57.

1798.[2] But of far more importance may be certain Irish habits of pronunciation, syntax and grammar—in part the fruit of efforts to translate the idioms of Gaelic into English, and in part survivals from the English of the age of James I. The latter may well have reinforced American archaisms. The Yankees have lived down *tay* for *tea* and *desave* for *deceive*, and these forms, on Irish lips, strike them as uncouth and absurd, but they still cling, in their common speech, to such forms as *h'ist* for *hoist*, *bile* for *boil*, *chaw* for *chew*, *jine* for *join*, *sass* for *sauce*, *heighth* for *height* and *rench* for *rinse*, and the thousands of Irish immigrants who spread throughout the country undoubtedly gave them support. To this day some of the old forms survive on the lower levels of the national speech.

Certain uses of Gaelic, carried over into the English of Ireland, fell upon fertile soil in America. One was the employment of the definite article before nouns, as in French and German. An Irishman does not say "I am good at Latin," but "I am good at *the* Latin." In the same way an American does not say "I had measles," but "I had *the* measles." A use of intensifying prefixes and suffixes, often set down as characteristically American, may have been borrowed from the Irish. Examples of such stretch forms are *yes indeedy* and *teetotal*. The Irishman is almost incapable of saying plain *yes* or *no;* he must always add some extra and gratuitous asseveration. The American liking for intensives, especially marked during the pre-Civil War period, undoubtedly got a lift from the Irish newcomers. The DA traces *no sir-ee* to 1845 and *yes sir-ee* to 1846.

The Dutch, after the opening of the Nineteenth Century, contributed few additions to the American vocabulary. The DA traces *bedspread* (perhaps from the Dutch *beddesprei*) to *c.* 1845. *Dope*, derived from a Dutch word meaning a sauce, first recorded in that sense in 1807, acquired the meaning of a mysterious mixture by 1872, that of a thick lubricant or other substance by 1876, that of opium or other narcotics by 1895 and that of inside knowledge by 1901. The word has picked up various other significances, *e.g.*, a fool. Its derivatives, *dope fiend*, *dope peddler*, *dope sheet*, *dopester*, *to dope* and *to dope out*, are also in frequent use.[3]

To snoop, from the Dutch verb *snoepen*, meaning to eat sweets on the sly, is traced, in its American sense, to pry or spy, to 1832. Bartlett, so late as his 1877 edition, records the earlier sense. It now means any sort of surreptitious prowling. Thus Mark Twain, in "A Connecticut Yankee at King Arthur's Court" (1889): "They always put in the long absence *snooping* around . . . though none of them had any idea where the Holy Grail really was."

---

[2] English as We Speak It in Ireland; 2nd ed.; London, 1910, pp. 179–80.
[3] [*Dope* was the popular Southern designation for Coca-Cola down to the 1930s, but is rarely heard nowadays.]

From other languages the borrowings during the period of growth were naturally less. Down to the last decades of the Nineteenth Century, the overwhelming majority of immigrants were either Germans or Irish; the Jews, Italians, Scandinavians and Slavs were largely yet to come. But the first Chinese appeared in 1848, and soon their speech began to contribute loan words, such as the verbs *to yen* (meaning to desire strongly, as a Chinaman is supposed to desire opium) and *to kowtow*. *Chow* is traced by the DA to 1856, in a Sacramento paper. It is Pidgin English and was probably brought to the United States at the time of the gold rush, for *chow-chow* (the condiment) is recorded for 1850. *Chow* has never got above the level of slang, but *chow-chow* is in perfectly respectable usage. It reached England by 1857. *Fan-tan* is not listed by the DAE or the DA, but the first English example given by the OED Supplement is dated 1878, and the game was well known in California at least twenty years before. But *hop* is not Chinese. It is simply the common name of the *Humulus lupulus*, which, in English folklore, has long been held to have a soporific effect. *Hop pillows* were brought to America by the first English colonists. Neither is *highbinder* a translation from a Chinese term. In 1840 Edgar Allan Poe wrote in his Marginalia:

> As to *high-binder* which is so confidently quoted as modern ("not in use, *certainly*, before 1819") I can refute all that is said by referring to a journal in my own possession—the *Weekly Inspector*, for Dec. 27, 1806—published in New York. "On Christmas Eve, a party of banditti, amounting, it is stated, to forty or fifty members of an association, calling themselves *high-binders*, assembled in front of St. Peter's Church, in Barclay-street, expecting that the Catholic ritual would be performed with a degree of pomp and splendor which has usually been omitted in this city. These ceremonies, however, not taking place, the *high-binders* manifested great displeasure." In a subsequent number, the association are called *hide-binders*. They were Irish.

V

The Language Today

1: AFTER THE CIVIL WAR

American English has maintained its general characteristics since Jackson's day, though there was a formidable movement to bring it into greater accord with English precept and example during the years following the Civil War. This movement, led by such purists as Edward S. Gould and Richard Grant White, seems to have got its chief support from school-ma'ams, male and female, on the one hand, and from Anglomaniacs on the other.[1] Gould's "Good English" (1867),[2] the first of a long series of hortatory deskbooks, accepted, in principle, "the fabrication of new words, and the new use of old words," but such changes should be undertaken only by "educated men," capable of assuming the burden of proof in support of innovation. For the inventions of the ignorant he had only contempt, especially "the men generally who write for the newspapers." He then proceeded to denounce familiar bugaboos, including *to jeopardize* (he agreed with Noah Webster that *to jeopard* was better), *controversialist* (previously used by Macaulay), *leniency* (used by Coleridge and even by the *Edinburgh Review*), *standpoint, over his signature* and *to open up.*

---

[1] Henry Cabot Lodge says in his essay Colonialism in the United States, printed in his Studies in History (1884), that "the luxurious fancies which were born of increased wealth, and the intellectual tastes which were developed by the advances of the higher education . . . revived the dying spirit of colonialism." This spirit was confined largely to "young men who despised everything American and admired everything English." Such persons, says Lodge, "flatter themselves with being cosmopolitans, when in truth they are genuine colonists, petty and provincial to the last degree."

[2] Gould was born at Litchfield, Conn., in 1805, and died in New York in 1885. In 1836 he published his Lectures Delivered Before the Mercantile Library Association, apparently as a counterblast to Samuel Lorenzo Knapp's Lectures on American Literature (1829); he deplored the whooping up of American authors and argued for the superiority of the British.

White pretended to a broad tolerance, to the length of admitting that "language is rarely corrupted, and is often enriched, by the simple, unpretending, ignorant man, who takes no thought of his parts of speech." More, he argued [3] that the English spoken and written in the United States was at least as good as that spoken and written in England. But he assumed that the Boston dialect was Standard American: "the full, free, unconscious utterance of the broad *ah* sound of *a* is the surest indication in speech of social culture which began at the cradle." He then denounced most of the Americanisms in Gould's *Index Expurgatorius*, adding *gubernatorial, presidential, reliable, balance* (remainder), *editorial, real estate, railroad* (he preferred the English *railway*), *telegrapher* (he preferred *-ist*), *dirt* (as in *dirt road;* he believed it should be restricted to its English sense of *filth*), *ice water* (he preferred *iced*) and the verbs *to locate* ("a common Americanism, insufferable to ears at all sensitive"), *to enthuse, to aggravate* and *to resurrect.*

Gould's pedantries were attacked by G. Washington Moon, the antagonist of Dean Alford, with the same weapon that had proved so effective against the dean—that is, by showing that Gould himself wrote very shaky English, judged by his own standards. White was belabored by Fitzedward Hall in "Recent Exemplifications of False Philology" (1872) and again in "Modern English" (1873). As one of the collaborators in the Oxford Dictionary, Hall had access to its enormous store of historical material,[4] then still unpublished, and that material he flung at White with great precision and effect, in particular, at White's reverence for the broad *a* of Boston, and at the doctrine that "the authority of general usage, or even of the usage of great writers, is not absolute in language"—that "there is a misuse of words which can be justified by no authority, however great, by no usage, however general." He said:

> The critic neglects to furnish us with any criterion, or set of criteria, his own mandates and ordinances excepted, by which to decide when

[3] In the third chapter of his *Words and Their Uses* (1870), a book made up of articles contributed to the *New York Galaxy* in 1867, 1868 and 1869. His attempt to limit the field of Americanisms has been described in Chapter I, Section 5. Perhaps White's chief claim to fame is the fact that he was the father of Stanford White, the celebrated architect, put to death by Harry K. Thaw on June 25, 1906.

[4] He was born at Troy, N.Y., in 1825, and educated at Harvard. He then went to India in search of a runaway brother. Settling there, he undertook the study of Sanskrit, and soon mastered it sufficiently to be made professor of it at Benares. In 1862 he became professor of Sanskrit, Hindustani and Indian jurisprudence at King's College, London. In 1864 he became examiner in Hindustani for the British Civil Service Commission, and in 1880 he succeeded Max Müller as examiner in Sanskrit. He had a hand not only in the OED but also in Joseph Wright's *English Dialect Dictionary* (1896–1905). He died in 1901, much honored in England but barely known in his own country.

the misuse of a word becomes impossible of justification. His animadversions, where original, are, I believe, in almost every case, founded either on caprice, or defective information, or both. . . . We shall search in vain—for all the world, as if he had been bred at Oxford—to find him conceding, as within the compass of the credible, the fallibility of his private judgments, or the inexhaustiveness of his meagre deductions.

Hall's evidence should have been sufficient to destroy White, whose learning was mainly pretension. But his scholarly approach and forbidding accumulation of facts failed to prevail against his "amateurish rivals and opponents," though "the soundness of his methods has been generally recognized by the expert." [5] Gould and White thus had it all their own way. White's "Words and Their Uses" was in print till the 1930s, and there are many latter-day imitations of it, most of them as cocksure as it was, and as dubious.

The new purism was at its height in the 70s and 80s, and has been ebbing steadily since 1900, but there is still energy in its backwash.[6] There is little reason, however, to believe that what is left of this old innocent belief in authority is having any serious effect upon the national speech. The schoolma'am's victims forget her hortations the moment they escape her classroom, and she is herself increasingly frustrated and demoralized by the treason of the grammarians, most of whom, being only pedagogues of a larger growth themselves, are highly susceptible to the winds of doctrine, and thus accept without much resistance the current allegation (not actually taught by serious linguists) that one man's "grammar" is as good as another's, and maybe a damned sight better. Even Anglomania cuts much less a figure than it used to in the field of language. Only an inch or so below the level of Harvard and Groton, English speechways are regarded as preposterous, and even as a shade indecent. When Charles Dudley Warner complained in 1882 that Standard English had "more and more diverged from the language as it was at the time of the separation," and concluded that "we must expect a continual divergence in our literature," [7] there was a vast lifting of eyebrows, but today such notions pass unnoticed.

Warner probably realized how powerful an influence Mark Twain was to exert on American writing, for the two had done a book in collaboration only nine years before.[8] By the turn of the century, only eighteen

[5] George H. McKnight, Modern English in the Making; New York, 1928.

[6] [*E.g.*, Harry R. Warfel, Who Killed Grammar?; Gainesville, Fla., 1952. Most of the journalistic resentment against Webster 1961 stems from the school of White. See also The Ordeal of American English, ed. by C. Merton Babcock; Boston, 1960.]

[7] England, *Century Magazine*, Nov. 1882, p. 141.

[8] The Gilded Age; Hartford, 1873.

years ahead, that influence was to produce a wholly new style of writing— a new and freer choice of words, a new way of putting them together—as clearly American as the style of Hawthorne, dead eighteen years before, had been clearly English. Even the prissy Howells was to yield to it, though he could never get over the uneasy feeling that Mark went too far. On the lower levels the revolution was even more complete. The American journalist of today has forgotten the banal clichés of the Horace Greeley era, and devotes himself joyously to embellishing and glorifying the national vulgate. Charles A. Dana's bright young men of the old New York *Sun* showed the way, but the thing has gone a great deal further, and the journalese of tomorrow may be indistinguishable from the barbaric (but thoroughly American) jargon of *Variety* and *Time*. Even the politicos no longer try to write like Junius and Samuel Johnson of the *Rambler*. They still write badly, but they at least try to write in the actual language of the people they address. It was Abraham Lincoln, fresh from the Western wilds, who first made a deliberate effort to speak and write in the simple terms of everyday American.[9] He did not succeed as thoroughly as Mark Twain did, but his effort had a long-reaching influence. "The new words of the American language," says Carl Sandburg, "streamed across the Lincoln addresses, letters, daily speech. The Boston *Transcript* noted old Abe's use of 'the plain homespun language' of a man of the people who was accustomed to talk with the 'folks' and 'the language of a man of vital common sense, whose words exactly fitted his facts and thoughts.' That ex-President John Tyler should protest his grammar was natural. W. O. Stoddard wrote that the President knew how some of his plainer phrasing would sound in the ears of millions over the country and did not 'care a cornhusk for the literary critics.' "[1]

That Lincoln and Mark Twain, rather than Gould and White, spoke for their age is shown by the way the language ignored its self-appointed guardians and went on developing in innocent accord with its native genius. In the very heyday of White appeared such new Americanisms of characteristic vigor and vulgarity as *to strike oil* (1860), *boom* (1878) and *to boom* (1871). A glance through the records turns up *mule skinner* (1870), *jack rabbit* (1863), *cuss word* (Mark Twain, 1872), *hoodlum*

[9] The Gettysburg Address, so much esteemed, was not a specimen of his new style, but an evidence of literary stage fright on a great occasion. Many of its phrases—*fourscore and seven years ago, final resting-place, honored dead*, etc.— belonged to the age of Daniel Webster. But, as the anthologists are beginning to see, the address was poetry, not prose, and so criticism must stand silent before its astounding declaration that the Union soldiers killed at Gettysburg were fighting for self-determination. That, in fact, is precisely what they were fighting against. Poetry is not to be judged by the laws of evidence. It is always, at bottom, a sonorous statement of the obviously *not* true.

[1] Abraham Lincoln: The War Years, II; New York, 1939, p. 305.

(1871), *grubstake* (1863), *holdup* (1878), *freeze-out* (1861), *crook* (1879), *joint* (a low den, 1883), and *spellbinder* (1888). To them may be added the adverbs *to a frazzle* (General John B. Gordon to General Robert E. Lee, 1865) and *concededly* (1882), and the verbs *to go through* (to plunder, 1861), *to go back on* (1868), *to light out* (1870) and *to side-track* (1880). Some lasted for no more than a few brief months, or even weeks; others got no higher in the vocabulary than the level of slang or argot, and linger there yet; still others gradually made their way into standard usage. It is, indeed, very difficult to rate neologisms. The most seemly, etymologically speaking, are often rejected in the long run, and the most grotesque are accepted. Many more go on dwelling in a twilight region, including large numbers of the words that everyone who investigates the American language must discuss.

Today it is no longer necessary for an American writer to apologize for writing American. Indeed, he seems a bit stiff and academic if he doesn't make some attempt to add to the stock of neologisms himself. In 1926 a lexicographer of experience reported that "the accepted language grows at the rate of 3,000 words a year—of sufficient currency to be inserted in the dictionary." "In days of stress, in times of war, in an era of discovery and invention," he continued, "5,000 or more words will win the favor of the public so that their inclusion in the dictionary is demanded by scholar and layman." [2] So many novelties swarm in that it is quite impossible for the dictionaries to keep up with them; indeed, a large number come and go without the lexicographers so much as hearing of them. We Americans live in an age and society given over to enormous word-making—the most riotous seen in the world since the break-up of Latin. It is an extremely wasteful process, for with so many newcomers to choose from, large numbers of pungent and useful words and phrases must be discarded and in the end forgotten by all save linguistic paleontologists.[3] But all the great processes of nature are wasteful, and it is by no means assured that the fittest always survive.

2: THE MAKING OF NEW NOUNS

All of the recognized processes for the formation of new words have been in active operation in the United States since Jackson's time, and after the

---

[2] Let's Look It Up in the Dictionary, by Spencer Armstrong, *The Saturday Evening Post*, Mar. 6, 1926, p. 16.

[3] For example, *upper ten, over the left* and *shad-bellied*. The chief cause of the obsolescence of nouns, of course, is the disappearance of the things they designate, *e.g., antimacassar, lambrequin, ear-* *pick*. An interesting discussion of the subject is in Obsolete Words, by Edwin Berck Dike, *Philological Quarterly*, Vol. XII, Apr. 1933, pp. 207–19. [See also New Words for Our Language, by Mildred Landau, Baltimore *Sun*, Oct. 14, 1962.]

Civil War their workings took on a new impetus. Clipping, or back formation—a sort of instinctive search for short roots in long words—in Restoration days precipitated a quasi-English word, *mobile,* from the Latin *mobile vulgus,* which, in turn, was soon distilled into *mob. Mob* is now sound English, but in the Eighteenth Century it was violently attacked by purists,[4] and though it survived their onslaught, they undoubtedly greatly impeded the formation and adoption of other words of the same category. There are, however, many more in Standard English, *e.g., patter* from *paternoster, van* from *caravan, cab* from *cabriolet* and *curio* from *curiosity.* In Eighteenth Century America they went largely unchallenged, and multiplied. *Rattler* for *rattlesnake, coon* for *raccoon, squash* for *askutasquash* are already antique; *Sabbaday* for *Sabbath day* has reached the dignity of an archaism, as has the far later *chromo* for *chromolithograph.* Today, scarcely a new substantive of more than two syllables comes in without bringing one or more in its wake: *gas* from *gasoline* (1905), *photo* from *photograph* (1863), *auto* from *automobile* (1899), *phone* from *telephone* (1886) and *Coke* from *Coca-Cola* (1909). Some newcomers linger below the salt, *e.g., pen* for *penitentiary, beaut* for *beauty, copter* for *helicopter, combo* for *combination* (a small group of musicians), *champ* for *champion, sap* for *saphead, lube* for *lubricating oil* and *semi* for *semi-trailer,* but many others, once viewed askance, are now in more or less decorous usage, *e.g., Yank* for *Yankee, sleeper* for *sleeping car, flu* for *influenza, drapes* for *draperies, memo* for *memorandum, mum* for *chrysanthemum* and *quotes* for *quotation marks.* Back formations often originate in college slang, *e.g, prof* for *professor, grad* for *graduate* (noun), *co-ed* from the adjective *co-educational* (1889), *medic* for *medical student, dorm* for *dormitory, plebe* for *plebeian,* or in other varieties of slang, argot or dialect, *e.g., con* for *convict, doc* for *doctor, pard* for *partner, sarge* for *sergeant, typo* for *typographer* or *typographical error* and *prelim* for *preliminary. Ad* for *advertisement* and some of its compounds, *e.g., ad writer, want ad* and *adman,* are standard English. American advertising men, in the glorious days when the more forward-looking of them hoped to lift their art and mystery to the level of dogmatic theology, astronomy, ophthalmology and military science, denounced *ad* as "the language of bootblacks, and beneath the dignity of men of the advertising profession."[5] But to most Americans *want advertisement* would sound quite as affected as *taximeter-cabriolet;* the term is *want ad. Boob* for *booby* is almost sound American; its synonyms are no more respectable than it is. At its heels are *bo* for *hobo* and *bunk* for *buncombe,* two fit successors to *bum* for *bummer.*

---

[4] Among them, Jonathan Swift. In the *Tatler,* Sept. 28, 1710, he contended that "monosyllables are the disgrace of our land."

[5] See *Associated Advertising,* Jan. 1925.

Bike, for *bicycle,* is traced to 1882. *Pep* is traced by the DA to 1912, and called "an abbreviation of *pepper.*" The same etymology is given by Webster 1961, the OED Supplement and Partridge. Others, however, suggest that *pep* is really a shortened form of *pepsin.*[6] In Baltimore it appeared in 1890, or thereabouts, at which time there was a rash of confidence in the prophylactic virtues of pepsin, comparable to the later faith in vitamins. One of the most widely selling chewing gums of the time contained it, and millions believed that it would improve the digestion and stimulate the energies. There has never been any similar belief, in the United States, about pepper: it is thought of as a flavor, not as a metabolic booster.

Not only nouns are clipped by apocope. From adjectives, for example, come *fed* (usually a noun) for *federal, gat* for *Gatling gun, Met* for *Metropolitan* and *legit* for *legitimate,* not to mention such borrowings from England as *zoo.*[7] Many short forms of verbs are cognate with nouns, *e.g., to phone, to auto* and *to con.* Finally, there is an apparently growing tendency to shorten a phrase made up of an adjective and a noun to the adjective alone, and then to convert it into a noun, *e.g., flat* for *flat tire* and *permanent* for *permanent wave.* [The English and Canadians reduce *permanent* to *perm,* as they do *refrigerator* to *fridge.*]

Blends are also plentiful among the new American nouns. A number are in standard English, *e.g.,* Lewis Carroll's *chortle* (from *chuckle* and *snort*), *dumfound* (from *dumb* and *confound*) and *luncheon* (from *lunch* and *nuncheon,* the first going back to the Sixteenth Century and the second to the Fifteenth), but American soon made contributions, *e.g., gerrymander* (from *Gerry* and *salamander,* 1812), and it has been supplying others ever since, *e.g., cablegram* (from *cable* and *telegram,* 1868), *radiogram* (*radio* and *telegram*), *telecast* (*television* and *broadcast*), *Aframerican* (*African* and *American*), *Dixiecrat* (*Dixie* and *Democrat,* 1948), *Hoovercrat* (*Hoover* and *Democrat,* 1928), *insinuendo* (*insinuation* and *innuendo,* 1885), *pulmotor* (*pulmonary* and *motor*), *travelogue* (*travel* and *monologue*) and *squadrol,* a Chicago police vehicle combining the virtues of *squad* car and *patrol* wagon. Many words of this class are trade names, made of initials or other parts of proper names: *Socony* from *Standard Oil Company of New York, Dokkie* from *Dramatic Order of Knights of Khorassan* and *Bancamerica* from *Bank of America.*[8]

---

[6] For example, E. H. Peabody, president of the Peabody Engineering Corporation, New York (private communication, June 8, 1936).

[7] *Zoo,* from *zoological* (garden), is traced by the OED to *c.* 1847.

[8] Louise Pound, Blends: Their Relation to English Word Formation, *Anglistische Forschungen,* Vol. XLII, Heidelberg, 1914; Harold Wentworth, Blend Words in English, diss. (MS), Cornell, 1933; Lester V. Berrey, Newly-Wedded Words, *AS,* Vol. XIV, Feb. 1939, pp. 3–10; Robert Withington, Some New Portmanteau Words, *Philological Quarterly,* Vol. IX, Apr. 1930; More Portman-

Some authorities would include *boost* as a blend of *boom* and *hoist*, but *boom* in the sense of sudden activity did not come in till the 1870s, whereas *boost* as a verb was included in David Humphreys's Glossary of 1815. But the great vogue of the word was delayed until the last years of the Nineteenth Century, when *boosters* began to infest the land, and the American proverb "Every knock is a *boost*" was invented by some forgotten Solomon.

Novelties are produced in great number by *Time* and the newspaper columnists, but many of them involve puns, most are banal and only a few have got into general circulation. Wentworth's doctoral thesis lists 3,500, and includes examples long standard in English, *e.g., tragicomedy, squire-archy, luncheon* and *aniseed;* others slowly making their way into good usage, *e.g., anecdotage;* and a large number of American inventions, *e.g., pulmotor.* The English devote themselves diligently to such forms, and some of their less painful inventions have crossed the ocean, *e.g.,* Lewis Carroll's *chortle* and the later *brunch* (*breakfast* and *lunch*) and *smog* (*smoke* and *fog*). *Smog* was invented by an English medical man named Des Voeux in 1905, but not used by the United States Weather Bureau until 1926.

[The blending process keeps up with the changing culture. Aviation soon yielded *aeronautical* (*aero-* and *nautical*), which gave the science of *aeronautics,* and by back formation, *aeronaut. Avigation* (*aviation* and *navigation*) and *avigator* were short-lived, but a world on the threshold of space travel is already discussing *cosmonauts, astronauts* and *astronautics.*[9]]

Elsewhere, the old American faculty for making picturesque compounds shows no sign of abating. Many of them originate as slang, *e.g., roadhouse, glad hand, hot spot* and *hangout,* and never attain to polite usage, but others gradually make their way up, *e.g., sob sister, bellhop* and *rabble rouser,* and yet others are taken into the language almost as soon as they appear, *e.g., college widow* (1871), *loan shark* (1913), *highbrow* and *low-*

teau Coinages, *AS,* Vol. VII, Feb. 1932; Dickensian and Other Blends, *AS,* Vol. IX, Oct. 1933; Verbal Pungencies, *AS,* Vol. XIV, Dec. 1939; Coinage, *AS,* Vol. XV, Apr. 1940. [Among recent blended gems are *broasted* (*broiled* and *roasted*), widely advertised in the restaurant trade, and *cremains* (*cremated* and *remains*) from the private argot of morticians.]

[9] [*Cosmonaut* seems to have been borrowed from the Russian, in 1959. The science of *bioastronautics* was discussed in *The New York Times Magazine,* Oct. 20, 1957. More recently a news story has spoken of *astrowives* and *cosmospouses.*

For the terminology of the new field, see Woodford A. Heflin, ed., Aerospace Glossary; Maxwell (Ala.) Air Force Base, 1959. Mr. Heflin also edited the Air Force Dictionary, 1956. Bergen Evans discusses the Aerospace Glossary in New World, New Words, *The New York Times Magazine,* Apr. 9, 1961, pp. 62 *ff.* A brief glossary of Space Age Slang is found in *Time,* Aug. 10, 1962, p. 56. For space-age onomastics see The Names of Objects in Aerospace, by T. M. Pearce, *Names,* Vol. X, Mar. 1962, pp. 1–10.]

brow (1905), *hot dog* (*c.* 1900), *joyride* (1909), *lovenest* and *jaywalker* (1917) and *brain trust* (1932). Many popular American compounds are terms of disparagement: *four-flusher, roughneck* (which goes back to Davy Crockett's time, but did not become popular until the present century; [in the sense of a member of an oil-drilling crew, it has achieved respectability]), *gospel shark, back number, cheapskate, cow college* and *kill-joy.* Most of these linger below the salt, but now and then one edges its way into decorous usage.[1] Other compounds have been more or less fully accepted: *barb wire* (1880), *sharecropper, trouble shooter* (1931), *section hand* (1873), *bargain counter* (1888), *shanty town* (1888), *shore dinner* (1895), *Four Hundred* (1888),[2] *storm door* (1878), *summer kitchen* (1874), *sweatshop* (1867), *chewing gum* (1850), *monkey business* (1883) and *fox trot* (1905). Many of these compounds are metaphorical in origin: *rubberneck* (1900), *barfly* (1910), *doghouse* (place of imaginary incarceration for persons out of favor), *tightwad* (1900), *stuffed shirt* (1913), *bulldozer,*[3] *hayseed* (1889), *shuttle train* (1891), *skin game* (1868), *skyscraper* (1883), *square deal* (1883), *hot dog,*[4] *cowpuncher* (1878), *screwball, dust bowl* (1936)[5] and *road hog* (1893).

[Since the medieval atrophy of distinctive inflectional endings for the parts of speech, English has freely made nouns out of verbs, adjectives and other parts of speech. American has expanded the tradition. Except in the judicial sense, *trial* has almost completely given way to *try.* American technical competence is epitomized by *know-how,* which goes back to 1857.] Other familiar nouns made by the process are *hideaway, eats* (1910), *showdown* (1884), *strikeout* (1887), *shake-up* (1887), *shoot-the-chutes* (1895), *handout* (1882), *hangover* (1894), *standoff* (1843), *get-up-and-get* (1888), *shutdown* (1884), *shut-in* (1904) and *drive-in.*[6] From other parts of speech

---

[1] See Terms of Disparagement, by Marie Gladys Hayden, *DN,* Vol. IV, Pt. III, 1906.

[2] Coined by Ward McAllister. He said to Cecil Jerome Allen, a society reporter, "There are only 400 people in New York that one really knows," and Allen gave the term currency. See Cecil Allen, N. Y. *Sun* Society Editor Dies, *Editor and Publisher,* Dec. 18, 1937. McAllister died in 1895.

[3] First applied, *c.* 1876, to Louisiana *vigilantes* who specialized in flogging Negroes seeking to vote; later, 1881, to a revolver; still later to any persons applying duress to another; finally to a machine for pushing earth.

[4] Said to have been named by T. A. Dorgan, *c.* 1900.

[5] [Coined by Edward Stanley, Kansas City news editor of the Associated Press, in rewriting a news story by Robert Geiger of the Denver office. (Personal letter from Mr. Stanley, now of the National Broadcasting Company, May 15, 1957.)]

[6] [Originally (*c.* 1930) for *drive-in restaurant,* where customers may be served in their cars; since World War II, commonly for *drive-in theater.* Since the situation lends itself to uninhibited amorous activity, such a theater is often called a *passion pit,* to say nothing of less printable congeners. See also Verb + Adverb = Noun, by Edwin R. Hunter, *AS,* Vol. XXII, Apr. 1947, pp. 115–19.]

Americans have manufactured such nouns as *pink* (parlor socialist), *who-dunit, trusty* (1855), *sissy* (1846), *once-over* (1916), *hello girl* (1889), *high* and *low* (meteorological and financial senses, 1878).

The formation of artificial words of the *lallapalooza* and *rambunctious* class goes on constantly. Some are blends: *grandificent* (*grand* and *magnificent*) and *sodalicious* (*soda* and *delicious*); others are made up of common roots and grotesque affixes: *whangdoodle* and *peacherino;* yet others are stretch-forms or mere extravagant inventions: *scallywampus, dingus* (1876), *dingbat* (1861), *doodad* (1908), *floozy* and *goof* (1920). Many of these belong properly to slang, but there is a steady movement of selected specimens into the common vocabulary. [Advertising would be impossible without *blurb,* and mathematicians trying to cope with interstellar mileage or the national debt are thankful for *googol* (1 followed by 100 zeros) and *googolplex* (a googol of googols).] And few laymen boggle at such arbitrary coinages as *appendicitis, moron* and *sundae.*

Sundae is usually related to *Sunday.* The DAE's first example, taken from the New York *Evening Post* of May 21, 1904, spells the word *sundi,* and in an abridged dictionary issued by the Consolidated Book Publishers of Chicago in 1925 it is spelled *sondhi,* with *sundae* and *sunday* as variants. Perhaps the most plausible theory ascribes the introduction of the *sundae* itself to George Hallauer, of Marshall, Ill., and the invention of the name to George Giffy, of Manitowoc, Wis., in the early 90s. One night, so the story goes, Hallauer—then living in Two Rivers, Wis.—called at an ice-cream parlor kept by E. C. Berners and ordered a dish of ice cream. Being in an experimental mood, he asked for chocolate syrup on his ice cream, and the *sundae* was born. News of the novelty spread to nearby Manitowoc, where the thrifty George Giffy sold it on Sundays only, but the public—epitomized in the traditional little girl—demanded it every day, so that it acquired the name. How and when the spelling shifted from *Sunday* to *sundae* is still a mystery. It is rather astonishing that the *-ae* ending has produced so little progeny. The only known child of the *sundae* is the *mondae,* a mixture of *sundae* and soda water.[7]

Moron was proposed by Dr. Henry H. Goddard in 1910 to designate a feeble-minded person of a mental age of from eight to twelve years; it was promptly adopted by the American Association for the Study of the Feeble-Minded, and immediately came into wide use.[8] Soon popular usage

---

[7] The *ice-cream soda,* the forerunner of the *sundae,* made its first appearance in Philadelphia in 1874. See The Story of the Franklin Institute, by Sydney L. Wright; Philadelphia, 1938, p. 49. [Some of the new names devised for ice-cream sundaes recall the florid names bestowed upon alcoholic decoctions of the Gothic Age of American drinking, *e.g., undertaker's delight* and *crematory special,* both offered in Amsterdam, N.Y., in 1948.]

[8] The report of the committee on classification of the feeble-minded was printed

expanded its meaning to cover all kinds of mental dullness. In the Chicago area, since the Leopold-Loeb trial of 1924, a *moron* has come to mean a sexual pervert, and its use in the correct sense has overtones of libel.[9] *Moron* is the name of a character in Molière's play "La Princesse d'Elide," and this *Moron*, by a happy coincidence, is a fool, but his name was not in Dr. Goddard's mind when *moron* was coined. Nor was he likely aware that *Moroni* figures in the Book of Mormon as the son of Mormon and the author of about half of the text thereof, and that his name was not infrequently bestowed upon Mormon boys. *Moron* has been taken into English and other languages. The English *ament*, used to designate all three classes of the feeble-minded, is seldom used in America.[1] [Among American do-gooders, following the change in meaning of *moron*, so that it became offensive, new euphemisms became necessary: the current one for the young feeble-minded is *exceptional children;* the unfortunately bright child is branded an *over-achiever.*]

During the quarter-century following the Civil War, as during the same period preceding it, the West was the chief source of neologisms. But as the pioneer movement lost momentum, the industrialization of the country proceeded, and immigration reached a high tide, the center of language making moved back to eastward of the Great Plains, and there it has remained ever since, with outposts at Chicago and Hollywood. It is new objects and new procedures that make the largest share of new words, and both are now much more numerous in the big cities than they are on the land. *Tenderfoot* (1875) was redolent of the old West, and *trust buster* (1903) still suggested the great open spaces, but *go-getter* and *kibitzer* are unmistakably urban, if very far from urbane.[2]

New words are no more produced by the folk than are new ballads, but by concrete individuals, some of whom can be identified. As we have seen, the elder Roosevelt either coined or propagated many compounds that promise to survive, *e.g., pussyfooter* and *embalmed beef. Scofflaw* was coined simultaneously in 1924 by Henry Irving Shaw, of Shawsheen Village, Mass., and Miss Kate L. Butler, of Dorchester in the same state.[3] *De-*

---

in the *Journal of Psycho-Asthenics*, 1910, p. 61.

[9] See *Moron—A* Misconception, by E. E. Ericson, *AS*, Vol. XII, Dec. 1937, p. 323; and The Natural History of a Delinquent Career, by Clifford R. Shaw; Chicago, 1931, p. 4.

[1] Brightness and Dullness in Children, by Herbert Woodrow; 2nd ed.; Philadelphia, 1923, p. 45.

[2] [See Twentieth Century Humorists,

by Walter Blair, in his Native American Humor; San Francisco, 1960, pp. 162–80. See also The Effect of Urbanization on Regional Vocabulary, by James A. Drake, *AS*, Vol. XXXVI, Feb. 1961, pp. 17–33.]

[3] Late in 1923, Delcevare King, a rich Prohibitionist of Quincy, offered a prize of $200 for the best word to apply to "the lawless drinker to stab awake his conscience." Of more than 25,000 sug-

bunking, and its verb, *to debunk,* were launched by William E. Woodward in his book "Bunk" in 1923.

Two classes of professional word-makers have appeared in the national Gomorrahs since the turn of the century, and between them they produce a majority of all the new words. The first is composed of sub-saline literati, *e.g.,* gossip-column journalists, script writers, song writers, comic-strip artists and press agents. The second is composed of the persons who invent names for the new products and services, and the advertising agents who whoop them up. The mortality among the inventions of these innovators is almost as great as that among the fry of the oyster, but they keep the fires of transient slang burning. Walter Winchell runs largely to verbs and verb phrases, *e.g., to be Reno-vated, to infanticipate* and *to middle-aisle,* but he is also fertile in new nouns, many of them blends, *e.g., revusical* (a musical revue), *profanuage (profane language), Chicagorilla (Chicago* and *gorilla)* and *terpischorine* (a chorus girl). He is not averse to puns, *e.g., merry Magdalen* and *messer of ceremonies,* and does not hesitate to stoop to phonetic spellings in the manner of the newspaper humorists of the Civil War era, *e.g., Joosh* (Jewish), *phlicker* and *moom pitcher* (a movie) and *phewd* (feud). Inasmuch as he is chiefly concerned with the life of Broadway and its circumambient night clubs, his inventions have largely to do with the technics and hazards of its ethnology, *e.g., on the merge* (engaged), *on fire, that way* and *uh-huh* (in love), *welded* and *sealed* (married), *phfft, soured* and *curdled* (separated), *baby-bound* and *storked* (pregnant) and *melted* (divorced). Some of his phrases are old ones to which he has imparted an ironical significance, *e.g., bundle from heaven* (a child) and *blessed event* (the birth thereof), and he has made a number of ingenious contributions to the roster of Broadway place names, *e.g., Two-Time Square* and *Hard-Times Square* (Times Square), and *Hardened Artery, Bulb Belt* and *Baloney Boulevard* (Broadway). Many of his contributions are apparently not original, but he may be credited with giving them vogue, *e.g., pash* (passion), *phooey,*[4] *squaw* (wife), *giggle water* and *whoopee.*[5] He is not only an assiduous inventor and popularizer of new

---

gestions, *scofflaw,* twice suggested, was announced the winner on Jan. 15, 1924. The word was current till the collapse of Prohibition. [In 1961 it was revived in several cities to designate a wanton ignorer of traffic summonses. In April 1963 it was applied by *The New York Times* to citizens unwilling to return library books.]

[4] A borrowing from the Yiddish and German *pfui.*

[5] Winchell did not invent *whoopee,* but the verb phrase *to make whoopee* seems to be his. See Walter Winchell on Broadway, New York *Mirror,* Jan. 17, 1935. *Whoopee,* as an interjection, is traced by the DA to 1845; it was used as a noun by Mark Twain in *A Tramp Abroad;* 1880, p. 80.

words and phrases, but also no mean student of them, and has printed some interesting discussions.[6]

Winchell's closest rival was Arthur (Bugs) Baer, a master of buffoonery who never yielded to Winchell's weakness for throwing off the jester's motley and putting on the evangelist's shroud. Both had a forerunner in Jack Conway, a baseball player who took to vaudeville and ended his career on *Variety*.[7] He is credited with having launched *baloney*, possibly borrowed from the argot of the Chicago stockyards, where an old and tough bull, fit only for making sausage, has long had the name *bologna*. During the 1920s *baloney* was also used to designate a clumsy prize fighter, but it has given way to *palooka*, which Conway introduced in 1925. Conway's other contributions included *S.A.* (sex appeal), *Arab* (a Jew), *to click* (to succeed), *high hat* (1924), *pushover* (1906), *payoff*, *headache* (a wife), *belly laugh* and *to scram*. The sports writers are diligent coiners of neologisms, but on the whole they contribute only nonce words.[8] They are surpassed in ingenuity and success by some of the comic-strip artists, of whom Thomas A. (Tad) Dorgan, Elzie Crisler Segar and Billy De Beck are examples. Dorgan is said to have invented or introduced *skiddoo* (1909), *drugstore cowboy*, *nobody home* and the series of superlatives beginning with *cat's pajamas*, and to have launched such once popular phrases as "You tell him," "Yes, we have no bananas" and "You said it." Segar is credited with *goon*, *jeep* and various other terms that, at the hands of others, took on wide extensions of meaning, and with aiding the vogue for the words in *-burger*.[9] To De Beck are ascribed *heebie-jeebies*, *hot mama*, *hotsy-totsy* and *horse feathers*.[1] Damon Runyon's name is always included when lists of word coiners are published, but he insisted that he was only a popularizer of the inventions of others.[2] George Ade is likewise often mentioned as an introducer of novelties, but his long series of "Fables in Slang," begun *c.* 1900, borrowed from the slang of the day much oftener than they contributed to it.

The strange vocabulary of the American newspaper headline bewilders the stranger who knows only Standard English. It runs much more to short words than to long ones, and thus propagates back formations more often than compounds. When the custom arose of setting headlines in more or

---

[6] For example, in A Primer of Broadway Slang, *Vanity Fair*, Nov. 1927, pp. 67–134, and in his column in the New York *Mirror*, June 20, 1936.

[7] Winchell hailed him as "my tutor of the slanguage he helped me perfect" in an obituary notice in the New York *Graphic*, Oct. 4, 1928.

[8] Some examples of their hard effort are given in Varying the Football Jargon, by Willis Stork, *AS*, Vol. IX, Oct. 1934, pp. 237–9.

[9] A Word-Creator, by Jeffrey Fleece, *AS*, Vol. XVIII, Feb. 1943, pp. 68–9.

[1] Billy De Beck Dies, *Editor and Publisher*, Nov. 14, 1942.

[2] The Brighter Side, New York *Mirror*, Dec. 30, 1937, p. 10.

less uniform type, according to a relatively few fixed patterns, and with each section (or bank) self-contained, the copyreader took over the job of making them fit, and he soon found that he was greatly incommoded by long words, for if one of them filled a whole line it looked awkward, and if it was too long for a line it could not be used at all. Thus the search for shorter synonyms began, and whenever an effective one was unearthed, it was quickly endowed with extended and sometimes very strained meanings. Today *probe* is used to signify any sort of quest or inquiry, and *hint* is a synonym-of-all-work that may mean anything from rumor to accusation. Any sort of contest or combat is a *clash* or *bout*, any reduction in receipts or expenditures is a *cut* and all negotiations are *parleys* or *deals*. *Fiends* are so common in American criminology simply because the word is so short. Other favorite nouns of the headline writers are *ace, balm, blast, blow, chief, drive, fete, grip, hop, try, net, plea, slate, span* and *toll*. Many of these are converted freely into verbs, and in addition there is a large repertoire of midget verbs proper, *e.g., to back, flay* and *void*. Clipped forms are naturally much used, *e.g., ad, auto, gas, mart, photo* and *quake*. Even the compounds in use are commonly made up of very short words, *e.g., clean-up, comeback* and *pre-Yule*.[3] A constant search goes on for short forms of proper names frequently in the news, *e.g., J.F.K.* for Kennedy, *F.D.R.* for Roosevelt II, *Ike* for Eisenhower and *Khrushch* or *Nik* for Nikita Khrushchev. It was probably not moral indignation so much as the effort to conserve space that made the Germans *Boches* and *Huns* in World War I; in World War II they escaped with the happily short appellation of *Nazis. Norse, Japs, Reds* and the like are godsends to copyreaders. Onomatopoeia, of course, frequently enters in, and the copyreader, whenever possible, has adopted words "which not only express the meaning which he wishes to convey but also connote the quality of sound. He believes that *crash* or *smash* will signify more to the reader than *accident*."[4] This explosive headline terminology dates only from the era of the Spanish-American War and the memorable fight for circulation between Joseph Pulitzer and William Randolph Hearst. Previously the headline writer had aimed to keep all its parts within the bounds of a single sentence, and inasmuch as it sometimes ran halfway down the column he resorted to long words and a flowery style. Dean Alford's denunciation of the Newspaper English of 1870[5] described Newspaper American also. "You never read," he said, "of a *man*, or a *woman*, or a *child*. A man is an *individual*, or a *person*, or a *party*; a woman is a *female*, or if unmarried,

---

[3] I take most of these examples from Scribes Seek Snappy Synonyms, by Maurice Hicklin, *AS*, Vol. VI, Dec. 1930, pp. 110–22.

[4] Headline Words, by Harold E. Rockwell, *AS*, Vol. II, Dec. 1926, pp. 140–1.
[5] The Queen's English; 3rd ed.; 1870.

a *young person;* a child is a *juvenile,* and children *en masse* are expressed by that most odious term, *the rising generation.*" It was against such gaudy flowers of speech that William Cullen Bryant's famous *Index Expurgatorius* was mainly directed. We owe their disappearance, in part, to Charles A. Dana, of the New York *Sun,* who produced the first newspaper on earth that was decently written, but also in part to Pulitzer and Hearst, who brought in not only the fire-alarm headline writer, but also the comic-strip artist. The latter has been a very diligent maker of terse and dramatic words. In his grim comments upon the horrible calamities befalling his characters he not only employs many ancients of English speech, *e.g., slam* and *quack,* but also invents novelties of his own, *e.g., zowie, socko, plop, oof* and *grr.* Similar onomatopoeic forms of an older date are listed in the Supplement to the Oxford Dictionary as Americanisms, *e.g., blah, wow, bust* and *flipflop.*[6] All these and more are familiar to every American schoolboy. Their influence, and that of the headline vocabulary, upon the general American vocabulary must be very potent.

Nor is it only in vocabulary that liberties are taken with the language. There is a tendency to juggle parts of speech and to indulge in syntactical devices that dismay orthodox grammarians. A few examples: Gob Crabs Gal's *F.D.R.* Love Plea; Woman *Critical* after Nightgown Is Set Afire; *Smock Day* All Over, Girls Say. In this revolution there is some ingenuity and also some daring, but another of its principal constituents is simply philistinism. "This," says G. K. Chesterton, "is one of the evils produced by that passion for compression and compact information which possesses so many ingenious minds in America. Everybody can see how an entirely new system of grammar, syntax, and even language has been invented to fit the brevity of headlines. Such brevity, so far from being the soul of wit, is even the death of meaning; and certainly the death of logic." [7]

But the writing of American newspapers at its most advanced is as the writing of Walter Pater beside that of the two weeklies *Variety* and *Time.* Each has developed a dialect all its own, and both are heavily imitated. Their vocabulary and syntax are so bizarre that they have attracted much attention from students of the national language, and the literature of the subject is already formidable.[8] *Variety* bangs away

[6] See Exclamations in American Speech, by E. C. Hills, *DN*, Vol. V, Pt. VII, 1924.

[7] *G.K.'s Weekly* (London), May 2, 1931.

[8] For *Variety* see, for example, *Variety*, by Hugh Kent, *American Mercury,* Dec. 1926, pp. 462–6; Lord Broadway, by Dayton Stoddart, New York, 1941, pp. 268 *ff.*; The Story of *Variety,* by Bennett Cerf, *Saturday Review of Literature,* Apr. 17, 1943, pp. 32–4. [*Variety muggs* (the name used by the staff to designate its members) have often contributed to the discussion, *e.g.,* Abel Green, *The Variety Mugg, Esquire,* Sept. 1960; and The "Variety" of Language, *Variety,* Jan. 6, 1960, p. 12. See also *Variety*'s Lexicographical Variety Has Influenced American Language, by Robert Pollak, *Hyde Park Herald* (Chicago), Feb. 3, 1960.]

at the language in an innocent, hearty and insatiable manner. It invents and uses a great variety of back formations, *e.g.*, *pix* for *moving pictures*, *preem* for *première* and *sked* for *schedule;* and it launches many new and tortured blends, *e.g.*, *filmusical* (a movie with music), and bold compounds, *e.g.*, *chinfest* (a conference), *pic parlor*, *cowshed* (a summer theater), *cliffhanger* (a serial melodrama) and *oats opera* (a Western film). It puts old and new suffixes to use in a free and spacious manner, *e.g.*, *hoofologist* (a dancer), *flopperoo* (a failure), *socko* and *clicko* (a success), *nitery* (a night club), *peelery* (a burlesque show), *payola* (bribery),[9] *ghostitis, oldie, cinemaestro, microphonist, blurbist* and *lackage;* it makes verbs of nouns, *e.g.*, *to author*, and it converts all the other parts of speech into nouns, *e.g.*, *rave* (an enthusiastic review), *de luxer, personaling* (making personal appearances), *tie-in, pink* (a sexy picture), *clicky* (a picture making money), *brush-off* and *vocal* (a song). It also borrows freely from the argots of sports, of the circus, of hobos and of criminals, *e.g.*, *to beef* (to complain), *eight ball* (a failure), *G* ($1,000), *to gander* (to go sightseeing), *handle* (a title), *spieler* (an announcer) and *on the lam. Variety's* headlines are done in such a jargon that only the initiated can fathom them. One of the most famous, *Hicks Nix Sticks Pix*, attracted attention in faraway Egypt.[1] Its meaning, it turned out, was that bucolic movie audiences did not like pictures with rustic settings.

The jargon of *Time* is measurably less interesting than that of *Variety*, mainly because most of its neologisms are more or less obvious blends, *e.g.*, *shamateur, cinemactress, franchisler, bookritic* and *powerphobe*, but also because its assaults upon orthodox syntax are carried on under cover of a pretension to information and even learning. Among its gifts to American English are the heavy use of attributive nouns, sometimes in the possessive case, *e.g.*, *Hearsteditor* Jones, *Harvardman* Brown and *Columbia's* Nicholas Murray Butler, and the suppression of the definite article, *e.g.*, "*Report* was circulated today," etc. It also likes to begin sentences with adjectives, and it deals heavily in compounds of the Homeric variety, *e.g.*, *hot-eyed, moon-placid, legacy-stalking* and *Yankee-shrewd*.[2] Some of these

---

[9] [*Payola* became a national word after the disclosure of monkey business in popular TV quiz programs. See On the Air, *The New York Times*, Nov. 22, 1959, Sec. 4, p. 1; also Foreign Usage of *Payola*, by William Randle, *AS*, Vol. XXXVI, Dec. 1961, pp. 275-7. *Plugola*, a subspecies—payments to disk jockeys in return for frequently playing a record company's new recordings—was also disclosed during these scandals. *Nayola*, administrative do-nothingism, was reported in the Youngstown (Ohio) *Vindicator*, Feb. 13, 1960, p. 8. *Laundrola* has also been reported, as a name for the common practice among laundries of paying tribute to racketeers.]

[1] Headlines, *Egyptian Gazette* (Alexandria), May 12, 1937.

[2] I take these from *Time* Makes a Word for It, *Reader's Digest*, Mar. 1936, and The Vocabulary of *Time* Magazine, by Joseph J. Firebaugh, *AS*, Vol. XV, Oct. 1940, pp. 232-42. There are other discussions of the *Time* vocabulary and syntax in A Guide to the Pronunciation

idiosyncrasies have had a powerful influence upon current newspaper writing, both in the United States and in England. Conservative journalists in both countries have denounced them bitterly, but they are still widely imitated.

The American advertiser is also a very diligent manufacturer of wholly new terms, and many of his coinages, *e.g.*, *Coca-Cola* and *Kotex*, are as familiar as *tractor* and *sidewalk*. Many others are so well known at home that it surprises most persons to hear that they are, or ever were, registered or claimed as private trademarks, *e.g.*, *Tabasco sauce*, *Celluloid*, *Caterpillar tractor*, *Carborundum* and *Dictaphone*.[3] By law a trade name must be a word that does not really name or describe the article to which it is affixed, and must be sufficiently unlike the trade names of other articles of the same general type to prevent the buyer from mistaking one for the other. If it is applied to an entirely new article, having no other name, it may become that article's common name, and so lose its validity in law by becoming descriptive. The inventor of a new article, to be sure, may patent it, and so acquire a monopoly of its manufacture and sale under whatever name, but a patent is good for but seventeen years, whereas a trademark may go on so long as the article is offered for general sale. The Swiss inventor of *Cellophane*, Brandenberger, or rather his American assignee, Du Pont, lost the exclusive right to the name when the courts decided, on the expiration of the patent, that the article had no other general name, and that *Cellophane* was thus descriptive. Much the same thing happened in the cases of *Aspirin*, *Linoleum* and *Kerosene*. In the case of *Dry Ice* the name was clearly descriptive from the start.[4] Usually trade names are not common designations for a new article, but special designations for some special brand of a new or old article, and in con-

---

of Words in *Time*, by E. B. White, *The New Yorker*, Mar. 14, 1936 (reprinted in his Quo Vadimus?, New York, 1939), and Profiles: *Time, Fortune, Life*, Luce, by Wolcott Gibbs, *The New Yorker*, Nov. 28, 1936, pp. 20–5. The last is a merciless parody of the *Time* style.
[3] Louise Pound discussed them in Word Coinage and Modern Trade-Names, *DN*, Vol. IV, Pt. I, 1913, pp. 29–41. A number are listed in Pillaging the Dictionary, by Frank H. Vizetelly, *Atlantic Monthly*, Aug. 1932, pp. 228–34. [See also Trade-Name Irradiations, by Louise Pound, *AS*, Vol. XXVI, Oct. 1951, pp. 166–9; and Brand-New Brand Names, by Edith Efron, *The New York Times Magazine*, July 7, 1957, pp. 14, 30–1.]

[4] [*Thermos* is now in the public domain; see *Time*, July 6, 1962, p. 45. There is an excellent exposition of the intricate legal problems in Lost Monopolies of Names and Things, by E. W. Leavenworth, *Industrial and Engineering Chemistry*, Sept. 1937, pp. 1006–8. See also Trademarks: A Capital Tug of War, by S. V. Baum, *South Atlantic Quarterly*, Vol. LVIII, Winter 1959, pp. 55–63; Trade-Mark Feuding Revealed, by Robert Alden, *The New York Times*, Jan. 10, 1960, p. F–13; Marks of Pride, *Aramco World*, Aug. 1957, pp. 18–20; Predicting Trademark Effectiveness, by Harry A. Burdick, Edward J. Green and Joseph Lovelace, *Journal of Applied Psychology*, Vol. XLIII, Oct. 1959, pp. 285–6.]

sequence they are protected by law. In the early days of a new article the manufacturers are usually eager to get its name entered in the dictionaries, but when they discover that so entering it tends to give it the significance of a common word, and thus imperils their trademark, they are just as eager to have it expunged. The wise inventor of something really new first patents it and then devises two names for it—a common and more or less descriptive name and a name so wholly undescriptive that it qualifies as a trademark. If he is lucky the trademark will have become so firmly established by the time his patent runs out that other persons essaying to market the article will have hard going.

The history of some of the more familiar American trade names deserves the professional attention of etymologists. *Kodak*, coined by George Eastman in 1888, was suggested by the fact that *k* was the first letter of his mother's family name. *Vaseline* was coined by its first manufacturer, Robert A. Chesebrough, in 1870 or thereabout; it was made of the German *Wasser*, meaning water, and the Greek *elaion*, meaning oil. Both *Kodak* and *Vaseline* meet all requirements of the law and are still protected. *Nylon* has no etymological significance; it is applied to dozens of different substances, in different forms, and is protected, not as a trademark, but by the Du Pont patents on the manufacturing processes. [However, *Antron*, a subspecies of *nylon*, is protected by Du Pont as a trade name, as are *Orlon* and *Dacron*.] *Nabisco*, the name of a sugar wafer made by the National Biscuit Company, is composed of the first syllables of the company's name, and was registered in 1901. It is not descriptive, and under the terms of its registration may be used on "biscuits, crackers, bread, wafers, sugar wafers, cakes, snaps, jumbles, hard and soft boiled confectionary, including grainwork, creamwork, panwork, chocolatework, lozenges, and medicated candies." *Uneeda*, owned by the same company, was registered in 1898. It covers the same products as *Nabisco*, but may be used by others, apparently, on anything so unlike them as to preclude fraud or confusion. The name *Kelvinator* was coined by Major Nathaniel B. Wales, who joined in the incorporation of the first company to make the *Kelvinator* in 1914. The name was derived from that of Lord *Kelvin* (1824–1907), the English physicist whose theoretical studies paved the way for the development of the appliance. *Mazda*, as a name distinguishing electric lamps, was suggested to the General Electric Company by the late Frederick P. Fish, a Boston lawyer and one-time president of the American Telephone and Telegraph Company:

> In this case it seemed to me that a suggestion of the light-giving property of the lamp might well be indirectly involved. I naturally thought of *Apollo*, *Jupiter*, and *Jove*, but these names were relatively common-

place. . . . But I knew, of course, of the Zoroastrian god of the ancient Persians, who stood for the firmament with its light-giving characteristics and whose name was *Ahura Mazda*. It seemed to me that *Mazda*, with . . . its suggestion of the light-giving firmament, might prove an attractive trade-name for the tungsten incandescent lamp.[5]

Kewpie, the name of a once very popular doll, was invented by Rose Cecil O'Neill Wilson in 1912, and was first used in the decoration accompanying some verses that she contributed to the *Ladies' Home Journal*.[6] *Zipper*, as the name of a type of slide fastener, was coined by the B. F. Goodrich Company as a trademark for overshoes provided with such fasteners and was registered as a trademark for its overshoes in 1925. Although slide fasteners had been invented some thirty years earlier (Judson patent 504,038, Aug. 29, 1893), extensive use awaited the invention of automatic machinery. The name was chosen because of the observation that operation of the fastener produced an audible "zip" sound and the extensive use on overshoes was followed by use on many other common articles and by widespread use of *zipper* to designate the fastener itself. By 1928, as the OED Supplement shows, *zipper* was taking on the aspect of a common noun. The Goodrich Company thereupon appealed to the courts, and its rights were sustained.[7] However, its claim is now directed especially to footwear;[8] *zipper* as a generic name for a slide fastener is in general use. *Ivory*, as the name of a soap, was launched in October 1879. The soap itself, popular because it floats, was invented by accident when a workman in the plant of Procter & Gamble at Cincinnati let a machine introduce minute bubbles of air into a batch of soap. No one suspected that a great revolution had been effected until the soap reached the firm's customers and they began writing in demanding more of the same.[9] It lacked a name until Harley Procter, the senior partner in the company, heard a sermon on Psalms xlv, 8: "All thy garments smell of myrrh and

---

[5] Quoted in Scientific Terms in American Speech, by P. B. McDonald, *AS*, Vol. II, Nov. 1926, p. 70.

[6] *American Notes and Queries*, Vol. IV, Apr. 1944, p. 9.

[7] *Goodrich v. Hockmeyer*, 40 Fed. 2nd 99.

[8] The statement sent to me by the company on Apr. 27, 1944, said: "The trade-mark 'Zipper' . . . remains today the exclusive trade-mark of B. F. Goodrich for footwear, just as it was when adopted by B. F. Goodrich in 1923. No other has the right to use the trade-mark for footwear or in connection with a

business in footwear, nor has any other, to the knowledge of B. F. Goodrich, so used it." [On Mar. 8, 1963, Harold S. Meyer, Patent Counsel for the company, supplied an interesting short history of the word and its significance, concluding: "We would expect a phrase such as 'Zipper boot' or 'Zipper galosh' to be used only to refer to our footwear, but use of the word *zipper* without capitalization to refer only to the fastener is of no concern to us."]

[9] Into a Second Century with Procter & Gamble; Cincinnati, 1944.

aloes and cassia, out of the ivory palaces whereby they have made thee glad." The new floating soap was a dead white, so *Ivory* it became.

Rayon, chosen by the National Retail Drygoods Association in 1924, is not a trademark, but a generic name: the manufacturers of the different brands distinguish them by special names, usually embodying their own names. *Bakelite*, on the contrary, is a trademark suggested by the name of the inventor, Leo Hendrik *Baekeland*. Many trade names have fanciful and even romantic origins. An example is afforded by *Veronal*, invented by Emil Fischer and Freiherr von Mering, two distinguished German chemists. After long work upon the project, Mering took a holiday and went to Italy. One day, at *Verona*, he received a telegram from Fischer saying that the synthesis of the substance had been effected, and the name *Veronal* immediately suggested itself.[1] *Aspirin*, another German invention, is simply a blend of *acetyl* and *spiraeic acid*, the latter an old name for *salicylic* acid. *Coca-Cola*, a compound based on the names of two of the drink's constituents, was first used by J. S. Pemberton, an Atlanta druggist, in 1888, and was registered as a trademark on January 31, 1893. The Coca-Cola Company has been much plagued by imitations borrowing the word *Cola* or playing on *Coke*. The courts have been loath to prohibit others from using *Cola*, for it is descriptive, but in 1930 the Supreme Court of the United States decided that *Coke* is the exclusive property of the company. It once discouraged the use of *Coke*, for the term was also a name for cocaine, then present in *Coca-Cola* in microscopic amounts, and uplifters had convinced the country that cocaine was an extremely dangerous drug. But after cocaine was eliminated altogether from the formula, the company found the abbreviation *Coke* a good advertisement. *Coke*, of course, is a common word in other significances, and is traced by the OED to 1669 in the sense of the product remaining after coal is distilled, but in the sense of a non-alcoholic drink made of vegetable extractives it is now the property of the Coca-Cola Company.[2]

Louise Pound classified trade names by methods of coinage:

> Derivatives of proper names: *Listerine* from that of Sir Joseph Lister, *Postum* from that of C. F. Post.
>
> Shortenings or extensions of descriptive words: *Jello, Shinola, Wheatena.*

---

[1] Genesis of the Word *Veronal*, by Kurt F. Behne, *Jour. AMA*, July 18, 1931, p. 198.

[2] *The Coca-Cola Company* v. *The Koke Company of America, et al.*, 254 U.S. 143; 65 L. Ed. 189. This decision is printed in full, along with many decisions of lower courts, in Opinions and Decrees Involving *Coke*, the Abbreviation of the Trade-Mark *Coca-Cola;* Atlanta, 1943. [See also Safeguarding Our Trademarks, by Pope Brock, *The Red Barrel* (Coca-Cola Co.), Mar. 1949, pp. 20–5.]

Diminutives: *Chiclet.*

Compounds: *Palmolive.*

Disguised spellings: *Prest-O-Lite, Uneeda, Holsum.*

Blends: *Triscuit, Vaporub, Eversharp, Philco.*

Terms made from initials or other parts of proper names: *Pebeco* from P. Beirsdorf & Company, *Reo* from R. E. Olds.

Arbitrary coinages: *Kotex, Zu-Zu.*

A lucky hit in coining trade names establishes a fashion and brings in a host of imitators. *Kodak* was followed by a great many other terms beginning or ending or both beginning and ending with *k*, and *Uneeda* had a long progeny, *e.g., Uwanta, Ibuya.* In the 1920s there was a craze for the *-ex* ending in arbitrary coinages, and it produced scores of examples, *e.g., Lux, Celotex, Pyrex, Kleenex, Cutex,* etc.[3] Ten years later *master* came into fashion as both suffix and prefix, *e.g., Toastmaster, Mixmaster, Masterlite.*

Some of the current coinages show a considerable ingenuity, *e.g., Klim,* the name of a powdered milk, which is simply *milk* backward; *Flit,* a spray for obnoxious insects, suggesting very forcibly their precipitate departure; *Rem,* a cough cure, obviously based on *remedy;*[4] *Jonteel,* a perfume, from the French *gentile;* and *Gunk,* a "self-emulsifying colloidal detergent solvent."[5] Many trade names embody efforts to state claims for the product without colliding with the legal prohibition of descriptive terms, *e.g., Holeproof, Eversharp* and *Interwoven.*[6] The number of new ones registered in the United States in a normal year is about 10,000.[7]

The copious imitation of new suffixes among trade names is matched in

---

[3] Trade-Name Suffixes, by Walter E. Myers, *AS*, Vol. II, July 1927, p. 448; X-ploiting the La-z-y Letters, by Mabel E. Strong, *Words*, Dec. 1938, pp. 136–7; [Some Popular Components of Trade Names, Papers by Arthur Minton, Supplement to *AS*, Vol. XXXIII, May 1958, pp. 17–29].

[4] *Rem* was invented by Joseph Katz, a Baltimore advertising man.

[5] Launched by the Curran Corporation, Malden, Mass., in 1932.

[6] For the qualities required in such names, see 33 Check Points for Finding a Name for That New Product, by P. H. Erbes, Jr., *Printers' Ink*, Oct. 1, 1943, pp. 28–97. An account of the method of finding a new name by means of a prize competition is in $1,000 a Word, by Homer A. Parsons, *Writer's Digest*, Feb. 1927, pp. 102–3. [The latest method is to use a computer-printer to arrange the permutation of word-forming elements associated with the products of the company. In this way Chas. Pfizer and Co. have produced a 42,000-word lexicon (of some 350,000 names so produced) of trademarks for new drugs. See Trademarks "Authored" by Electronic Brain, by T. J. Connors and A. J. Schmitz, *Trademark Reporter*, Vol. XLVI, Aug. 1956, pp. 919–21. I am indebted to Andrew J. Schmitz, Jr., of the Pfizer office of research and development.]

[7] [The name *Mark Twain* is also registered, and may not be used upon the jacket, cover or title page of a book without the permission of the Mark Twain Co., through its agents, Harper & Brothers, now Harper and Row. For this information I am indebted to my colleague Walter Blair.]

the general speech of the Republic. These suffixes have various origins. The words in *-doodle*, e.g., *whangdoodle* and *monkeydoodle* (as well as the *Stammvater Yankee Doodle*), hint at German or Dutch influence, and those in *-ino* may owe something to Italian or Spanish. Such suffixes are often worked heavily. The first to come into fashion in the United States was apparently *-ery*. *Printery*, traced by the DAE to 1638 in America and not found in England until 1657, seems to have stood alone for a century and a half, but after *grocery* came in in 1791 it was quickly followed by other forms in *-ery*, and their coinage continues briskly to this day. *Bindery* is traced to 1810, *groggery* to 1822, *bakery* to 1827, *creamery* to 1858 and *cannery* to 1870. Dutch forms in *-ij*, e.g., *bakkerij* and *binderij*, may have helped produce the earlier examples, and the later ones may owe something to German forms in *-ei*, e.g., *Bäckerei* and *Konditorei*, but *-ery* and its attendant *-ory* are really old in English, and *buttery*, never in general use in the United States, goes back to the Fourteenth Century.[8] It is, however, on this side of the water that they have been hardest worked. In the United States, reported one English traveler in 1833, "shops are termed *stores*, and these again figure under the respective designation of John Tomkins's *grocery*, *bakery*, *bindery*, or even *wiggery*, as the case may be."[9] Bartlett, in the first edition of his Glossary (1848), listed *stemmery* as the designation of "a building in which tobacco is stemmed," and also all the terms just noted save *wiggery*, which is likewise omitted by the DAE and DA. *Dry-goodsery* was used by *Putnam's Monthly* in 1853 to describe the new A. T. Stewart store on Broadway.[1] Many others have been reported by lexicographical explorers, e.g., *cobblery*, *beefery* (a packing plant for beef), *shoe-fixery*, *juicery* (apparently a stand for the sale of fruit juices, but earlier a synonym for *groggery*),[2] *cyclery* (1892), *condensery* (a milk condensing plant, 1921), *chickery* (1859), *beanery* (1894), *eggery*,[3] (*fish*) *hatchery*, *car-washery*, *lunchery*, *mendery*, *drinkery* (1840), *drillery* (a civil-service cramming school),[4] *snackery* and *skunkery* (a place where skunks are bred for their fur, 1890). Some of these, of course, show an effort to be waggish, and there is more of that conscious humor in *ham-and-eggery*, *hashery*

---

[8] It survives in New England and its western dependencies as a synonym for *pantry*, the sense in which it is used at Oxford and Cambridge. At Harvard and Yale, in colonial times, it designated a room in which food and drink for sale to the students was stored.

[9] Notes of a Tour of the United States, by A. Fergusson.

[1] New York Daguerreotyped, Apr. 1853, p. 358, col. 1.

[2] *AS*, Vol. XVI, Apr. 1941, p. 120.

[3] The Living Language, by Dwight L. Bolinger, *Words*, May 1948, p. 69.

[4] Vogue Affixes in Present-Day Word-Coinage, by Louise Pound, *DN*, Vol. V, Pt. I, 1918, p. 10. [In *AS*, Vol. XXIV, Feb. 1949, p. 78, Miss Pound reported *papoosery* as the name of the nursery school at the University of Omaha, where the students are called *Indians*. *Riflery* (the art of rifle marksmanship) appears in the *Transylvania Times* (Brevard, N.C.), Aug. 9, 1962.]

(1870), *boozery, nitery* (a night club), *praisery* (a press agent's den), *sickery* (for hospital), *learnery* (for a girls' boarding school) and *stompery* (a dancing school).[5]

Perhaps the most fertile of the latter-day American suffixes is *-teria*, borrowed from *cafeteria*, whose oldest attestation in Spanish is in an 1862 dictionary of Cuban Spanish, meaning a shop where coffee is sold at retail.[6] In a later dictionary it is credited, not only to Cuba and Puerto Rico, but also to Mexico, and defined as an *establecimento donde se sirva esta bebida*. This ascription shows some gain in plausibility, for until recently there was little infiltration of Cuban Spanish into the United States, and all the available evidence indicates that *cafeteria* came into American English west of the Alleghanies, where the only Spanish prevailing is of the Mexican variety. Probably it made its appearance in Chicago at the time of the World's Fair of 1893. It has been reported in use in California *c.* 1853, but as "a place for drinking rather than for eating," as in the Mexican example just cited. The DAE's first example in the American sense is from the Chicago Directory for 1894, which listed a *Cafetiria* Catering Company (note the spelling) at 45 Lake Street. The names and addresses for this directory, in all probability, were gathered in 1893. By 1895 it was listing four *cafetirias*, and by 1896 one of them (now *caféteria*) had become so prosperous that gunmen were inspired to crack its safe.[7] Meanwhile the *cafeteria* had begun to spread, and before the end of 1893 there was at least one in St. Louis.[8]

Cafetera, in standard Spanish, means a coffeepot, not a coffeehouse. The Italian *caffetiere* is of precisely the same meaning, and it is not at all impossible that it, and not the Spanish word, suggested *cafeteria*. Meanwhile, California continues to claim its origin, and that great state, if not actually responsible for the word itself, is at least partly responsible for the proliferation of the *cafeteria*'s progeny. In the early days *-teria* was always used as an indicator of self-service, but its scope began to widen by 1930, and it is now used in many terms signifying establishments in which the customer is waited on by others. J. M. Steadman, Jr.,[9] distinguishes three meanings: (1) a place where articles are sold on the self-service plan, *e.g.*, *caketeria, groceteria;* (2) a place where certain articles are sold without the self-service plan, *e.g.*, *chocolateria, radioteria;* (3) a place where certain

---

[5] The last three are credited to Barney Oldfield, of the Lincoln (Neb.) *Journal and Star*, by *AS*, Vol. XVI, Oct. 1941, p. 207.

[6] Phillips Barry, *Cafeteria*, *AS*, Vol. II, Oct. 1927, p. 37.

[7] Chicago *Tribune*, June 28, 1898.

[8] Private communication from G. F. Longdorf, of Oakland, Cal., Oct. 18, 1939.

[9] *Basketeria* and the Meaning of the Suffix *-teria*, *AS*, Vol. V, June 1930, pp. 417–18. [Some of these derivatives, *e.g.*, *grocerteria*, have migrated to England. See *Grocerterias* in England Promote Foods of U.S., *The New York Times*, Aug. 25, 1962.]

services are rendered by others, not by the customer himself, *e.g.*, *bobateria* (where hair is bobbed), *beauteria*, *valeteria*. The majority of such terms, of course, are hardly more than nonce words, but some of them show signs of sticking as *cafeteria* itself has stuck.

The literature of *-teria* is extensive. The pioneer investigator of the suffix was E. C. Hills (1867–1932), professor of Romance philology at the University of California.[1] *Cafeterian* has come into use (apparently at the University of Nebraska) to signify "a student who visits classes for a week or two before registering in some of them,"[2] but it does not seem to have spread elsewhere. [Chicago has what is popularly called a *cafeteria court*, a tribunal where citizens accused of minor traffic violations may pay the assessed fine without the delay and expense of standing trial. It introduced a similar *cafeteria court* for minor building code violators in the spring of 1963.]

Among the other American suffixes that have produced notable progeny are *-orium* and *-cade*. The former has given *lubritorium* (the lubricating rack in a filling station), *printorium*, *corsetorium*, *hot-dogatorium*,[3] *parentorium* (a parent guidance center),[4] *puritorium* (a Jewish ritual bath)[5] and *eatatorium*. The analagous *-arium* has meanwhile produced *vocarium* (a collection of phonograph records of the human voice),[6] *oceanarium* (an underwater zoo),[7] *ritualarium* (a Jewish ritual bath, identical with a *puritorium*) and *terrarium* ("a covered glass globe or fish-tank containing flowers and plants to be grown indoors during the winter").[8] *Odditorium* was used by Robert L. Ripley to designate an exhibition of oddities at the Chicago World's Fair of 1933–4, but there was an *odditorium* in Kingston-on-Thames, a village near London, before World War I.[9] *Planetarium*, to designate a machine for exhibiting the motion of the heavenly bodies, may be an Americanism, though the DA does not claim it. The first example of its use offered by both the DAE and the OED comes from John Adams's diary (1774).

All the words in *-cade* seem to have been suggested by *cavalcade*, a loan

---

[1] New Words in California, *MLN*, Vol. XXXVIII, Mar. 1923; Irradiation of Certain Suffixes, *AS*, Vol. I, Oct. 1925; The Pronunciation of *Cafeteria*, *AS*, Vol. II, Nov. 1926, p. 114.

[2] M. C. McPhee, *AS*, Vol. XV, Oct. 1940, p. 335.

[3] Title of an article by Robert Littell, *Today*, June 6, 1936.

[4] *Survey Midmonthly*, Oct. 1940.

[5] More Notes on Neo-Suffixes, by Manuel Prenner, *AS*, Vol. XVIII, Feb. 1943, p. 71. [Lillian H. Hornstein reports a downtown *hairorium* advertised in the Washington *Times-Herald*, *AS*, Vol. XXVII, Feb. 1952, p. 72. The *cafetorium* and the *gymtorium*, dual-purpose rooms, were introduced in school buildings in the 1950s. Grace Partridge Smith reports a *libratory* at the State University of Iowa, *AS*, Vol. XX, Dec. 1945, pp. 307–8.]

[6] Profile of George Robert Vincent, *The New Yorker*, May 17, 1941.

[7] *E.g.*, the Marine Studios *Oceanarium*, Marineland, Fla.

[8] *AS*, Vol. XVII, Dec. 1942, p. 284.

[9] *Odditorium*—Believe It or Not, *AS*, Vol. XV, Dec. 1940, p. 442.

from the French traced by the OED in English use to 1591. The true suffix is not -*cade* but -*ade*. The latter got into French in loan words from the southwestern Romance languages, and many of the words embodying it subsequently passed into English, *e.g.*, *accolade*, *brigade*, *marmalade*, *parade* and *serenade*. But *lemonade*, which the OED traces to 1663, was apparently taken into English direct from the Spanish *limonada*. The invention of *motorcade*, first reported in *Notes and Queries* in 1924, has been ascribed to Lyle Abbott, automobile editor of the Arizona *Republican* of Phoenix, who used it for the first time "in 1912 or 1913 to describe the procession of motor-cars which took part in a Sociability Run from Phoenix to Prescott." [1] By 1930 it had been used to describe the conveyances of extension teachers from the University of North Carolina, of North Dakota politicians en route to the Republican National Convention [2] and of masked Georgia citizens who took a colored brother named John Will Clark from the Cartersville calaboose "and hanged him to the crossbeam of a telephone pole on the fair grounds a mile away." [3]

Despite its success, *motorcade* has produced only a meager progeny: *autocade*, *aquacade*, *communicade*,[4] *camelcade*, *aerocade* and *musicade*.[5] [*Icecapade*, often associated with the -*cade* family, is a blend of *ice* and *escapade*.] The more correctly formed *lemonade* has begotten *orangeade*, *fruitade*, *limeade* and a number of others.[6] "*Lemonade* is never written as two words, *lemon ade*, but its suffix sometimes detaches itself in the names of other fruit drinks. Signs advertising *orange ade*, *grapefruit ade*, *wild cherry ade* are not unusual. Drugstores and groceries sometimes announce lines of *ades*." [7] [Welch's grape juice has appeared in modified versions as *Welchade*, and the General Foods Corporation manufactures many kinds of *Kool-Aid*, a soluble powder for making flavored beverages at home.]

A number of the suffixes in continued use in both England and the United States show considerably more life in this country, *e.g.*, -*dom*, -*ster*, -*eer* and -*ette*. In 1912 Logan Pearsall Smith complained that -*dom* was being displaced in England by -*ness*, and that the effort of Thomas Carlyle and others to revive it during the Nineteenth Century had produced only one generally accepted word, *boredom*, which the OED traces to 1864.[8] But

---

[1] Garth Cate, in F. P. Adams's column, the New York *Herald Tribune*, June 29, 1931. See also The Earliest *Motorcade*, by W. L. Werner, *AS*, Vol. VII, June 1932, p. 388.

[2] *AS*, Vol. V, Aug. 1930, pp. 495–6; *AS*, Vol. VI, Dec. 1930, p. 155.

[3] Charlottesville (Va.) *Progress*, Oct. 1, 1930.

[4] *Gardens, Houses* and *People* (Baltimore), Jan. 1944, p. 8. Apparently a display of war equipment.

[5] [A Christmas *musicade*, presented over the Columbia Broadcasting System in 1945, was reported in *AS*, Vol. XXI, May 1946, p. 156.]

[6] *Apple-ade* appeared in an advertisement of the British Ministry of Food, London *Daily Express*, Dec. 3, 1940.

[7] *AS*, Vol. VIII, Oct. 1933, p. 76.

[8] The English Language; New York, 1912, p. 93.

this statement was too sweeping, for though some of Carlyle's inventions had but short lives, *e.g.*, *duncedom* (1829), *rascaldom* and *scoundreldom* (1837) and *dupedom* (1843), various other novelties of his era have survived, *e.g.*, *officialdom* (1863), *serfdom* (1850) and *stardom* (1865). In the United States the old suffix, which goes back to Anglo-Saxon days, is still very much alive, with such progeny as *fandom*, *moviedom* and *screendom*.[9] By 1927 *-dom* apparently had acquired four distinguishable significances: (1) realm or jurisdiction, *e.g.*, *filmdom*, *newspaperdom*; (2) state or condition, *e.g.*, *pauperdom*, *stardom*; (3) type or character, *e.g.*, *crookdom*, *loaferdom*, *thugdom*, *flapperdom*; and (4) common interest, *e.g.*, *cattledom*, *dogdom*, *puzzledom*, *turfdom*. In 1941 Harold Wentworth rounded up more than 200 dated examples of *-dom* words introduced since 1800, both in this country and in England, and so provided a refutation of the theory that the suffix is obsolescent.[1] Many of the earlier examples were English, but for the later years the American inventions were numerous, *e.g.*, *authordom* (1925), *bookdom* (1918), *crackerdom* (1934), *dictatordom* (1939), *folkdom* (1939), *freckledom* (1940), *gangsterdom* (1934), *Nazidom* (1933), *newsdom* (1931), *ringdom* (1940), *Sovietdom* (1931). New words in *-dom* are being coined all the time, *e.g.*, *retaildom*.[2]

The suffix *-ster*, as Old English *-estre*, was mainly used in the formation of feminine agent nouns, but by 1300 it had lost its suggestion of gender. In the Eighteenth Century it took on a disparaging significance, apparently because of its frequent appearance in the designations of the humbler sort of workmen. The OED traces *rhymester* to 1719, *trickster* to 1711 and *punster* to 1700. O. F. Emerson, in his "Outline History of the English Language" (1906), expressed the opinion that it was going out of use, but since then it has enjoyed a considerable revival, especially in the United States. In 1916 Miss Pound listed *clubster*, *funster*, *hopster*, *mobster* and *speedster* as recent American inventions, and *hymnster* and *wordster* as novelties in England, and in 1927 Josephine M. Burnham added *gangster*, *gridster*, *dopester*, *roadster*, *prankster*, *playster* and *workster*.[3] Since then various contributors to *American Speech* have reported *netster* (a tennis player), *thugster*, *pinster* (a bowler), *pollster* (a taker of polls) and *puckster* (a hockey player). Some of these deserve to be dismissed as nonce

---

[9] In Vogue-Affixes in Present-Day Word Coinage, *DN*, Vol. V, Pt. I, 1918, pp. 6–7, Louise Pound suggests that the influence of German *-tum* had something to do with the current popularity of *-dom*, but it had been in constant use for two generations. [See Robert M. Estrich and Hans Sperber, Three Keys to Language; New York, 1952, pp. 106–25.]

[1] The Allegedly Dead Suffix *-dom* in English, *PMLA*, Vol. LVI, Mar. 1941, pp. 280–306.

[2] *Women's Wear* (New York), quoted in the Baltimore *Evening Sun* (editorial page), Oct. 6, 1938.

[3] Three Hard-Worked Suffixes, *AS*, Vol. II, Feb. 1927. [*Pollster*, meaning an operative for a public-opinion poll, was used without derogatory significance in the *Hyde Park Herald* (Chicago), Sept. 12, 1962.]

words, but *gangster, ringster, speedster* and *mobster* have become firmly imbedded in American speech.

Another suffix that carries a disparaging significance is *-eer*, an anglicized form of the French *-ier*, as in *sonneteer*, which the OED traces to c. 1665, in *pulpiteer*, which goes back to 1642 and in *racketeer*. *American Speech* has recorded a large number of new words based on it in recent years, *e.g., conventioneer, fountaineer* (a soda jerker, said to be with "no suggestion of a derogatory flavor"), *vacationeer, budgeteer,*[4] *chariteer* (a professional charity monger), *unioneer, balladeer, gadgeteer, basketeer* (a basketball player), *black-marketeer, upper-bracketeer* and *sloganeer.*[5] *Profiteer*, traced by the OED Supplement to 1913, had existed in the verbal form of *profiteering* since 1814. The latter was popularized by a speech made by David Lloyd George in July 1917. "I believe," he said, "that the word is rather a good one. It is *profit-eer-ing* as distinguished from *profiting. Profiting* is fair recompense for services rendered; *profit-eer-ing* is an extravagant recompense, unfair in peace, and during war-time an outrage." *Patrioteer* is also English. It was reintroduced to the United States in 1939 by *Time*, which defined it as "the professional patriot, the kind of refuge-seeking scoundrel who waves a red-white-and-blue handkerchief when he should be wiping his own nose (not, it may be hoped, with that handkerchief)."[6]

Cellarette has been in English for more than a century, but *kitchenette* is American, and so are *farmerette, conductorette* and a number of analogous words. The English make the first of these words *cellaret*, not *cellarette*, though they are slow to follow American example in such words as *cigaret* and *etiquet*. The OED's first example of *cellaret*, which it defines as "a case of cabinet-work made to hold wine-bottles, etc.," or "a side-board with compartments for the same purpose," is dated 1806–7, and comes, with excessive inappropriateness, from a book called "The Miseries of Human Life." There are later quotations from Thackeray and Benjamin Disraeli. *Suffragette* also originated in England and is said to have been invented by Charles Eustace Hand, a reporter for the London *Daily Mail.*[7] The OED's example is from the *Daily Mail* of January 10, 1906. The *kitchenette* was invented by Andrew J. Kerwin, a New York real-estate operator, in 1901,

---

[4] Cf. Better Houses for *Budgeteers*, by Royal Barry Wills; New York, 1941. [Also The Mild *Budgeteer* (a story about James Felt, chairman of the New York City Planning Commission), *The New York Times*, Aug. 20, 1962.]

[5] *Sloganeer* was used by Franklin D. Roosevelt in a speech at Columbus, Ohio, Aug. 20, 1932. It had been used by Richard Connell, its apparent inventor, in the titles of three short stories contributed to *The Saturday Evening Post*, 1921–2. See The Invention of *Sloganeer*, *Word Study*, Jan. 1933, p. 6.

[6] Feb. 27, 1939.

[7] See the obituary of Hand, who died on Nov. 2, 1937, in *Editor and Publisher*, Nov. 6.

and named a little later. The story goes that Kerwin visited a young couple living in an apartment-hotel, and, struck by the inconvenience in their attempt to prepare a midnight supper over a gas ring, decided to include plans for a small kitchen in a hotel he was then building.[8] The *kitchenette* was quickly imitated by other builders of apartment houses, and after a while it acquired a brother (or sister) in the *dinette*. Presently someone called a small lunchroom a *luncheonette*, later reduced to *lunchette*, and a numerous progeny followed. But World War I really gave the *-ette* ending a start in the United States. It was first applied, apparently, to the *Yeomanettes*, who did clerical work for the Navy and were the *Stammütter* of the multitudinous *WACS*, *WAVES* and so on of World War II. The function of *-ette* as a diminutive began to recede, and in nearly all the new words ending with it, it served to indicate the feminine gender. The scouts of *American Speech*, especially Dwight L. Bolinger, have unearthed and recorded a great many, including *usherette*, *coppette* (a policewoman), *bachelorette*, *cabette*, *Latin Quarterette*, *dudette* (a female patron of a dude ranch), *drum majorette*, *chauffeurette*, *parkette* (a female police auxiliary who inspects parking meters and collects the money deposited therein), *tanksterette* (a woman swimmer) and *realtyette* (a female realtor).[9] In Hollywood, for some reason unknown, a larval movie queen is not a *starlette* but a *starlet*, and one full of malicious animal magnetism is an *oomph-let*. Despite this effeminization of the suffix it is still sometimes used as a diminutive, as in *blousette*, *roomette* (a sleeping compartment for one person on trains), *bathinette* (a portable bath for babies) [and the Canadian *champagnette*, a carbonated grape juice with slight traces of alcohol]. The English contributions include *sermonette*, *flannelette*, *wagonette* and *leather-ette*. In the San Francisco region before World War II the Italianate suffix *-etta* made some progress, *e.g.*, *cafetta* (a small café) and *tavetta* (a small tavern).[1]

Many other suffixes, new and old, have produced a plentiful offspring in the Republic. The hideous *-ite* is most frequently used to indicate residence or citizenship, *e.g.*, *Camdenite* and *Yonkersite*; in that field, indeed, it shows a tendency to drive out all other suffixes. But it has also been heavily employed to indicate other sorts of membership or allegiance, as in *Hicksite*,[2] *socialite*, *suburbanite*, *laborite*, *trailerite*, *third-termite*. The analogous *-ist*

---

[8] *The New Yorker*, Aug. 21, 1937, p. 11.

[9] *Realtyettes* to Instal, Portland *Oregonian*, Apr. 16, 1944.

[1] Harry Leon Wilson, Jr., private communication, Dec. 2, 1939. [Ronald K. Jones, North Hollywood, Cal., reports *haulette* as a designation for a small trailer. In *AS*, Vol. XXIV, Dec. 1949, p. 311, Mamie Meredith reported finding *terracettes* on pp. 295–6 of H. H. Bennett, Soil Conservation; New York, 1939.]

[2] A member of a sect of Quakers, traced to 1832, and still in use.

is rather more euphonious, and many of the terms embalming it are relatively respectable, *e.g., manicurist, behaviorist,*[3] *feminist, monopolist* and *alarmist. Receptionist,* not listed by the DAE or DA, is also well established, for no other word as clearly and conveniently designates the person referred to.[4] But there are also such uncouth examples as *swimmist, cigarist* and *misterogynist* (a man hater).[5] Among public performers of various sorts there has been a tendency for years to use the French *-iste* as an indicator of femininity, as in *artiste, violiniste* and so on, to which *cosmetiste* may be added. The new words in *-itis* no doubt stem from the multitudinous medical terms showing the same suffix, and not a few of them show a suggestion of pathology, *e.g., radioitis, headlineitis* and *golfitis.* As a suffix, it is pointed out, "*-itis* is always disparaging."[6] Some examples are highly grotesque: *crosswordpuzzleitis, let-George-do-it-itis* and *Phi-Beta-Kappaitis.* The suffix *-ism,* of course, is old in English, and has produced a huge list of words. New ones are coming in all the time, and not infrequently an old one enjoys a vigorous revival, as when *absenteeism* in the war plants began to attract notice in 1942. The miracle-working Henry J. Kaiser tried to get rid of it, along with its embarrassing connotations, by introducing *presenteeism.*[7] American political history and social life would be dull indeed without *greenbackism, Populism, Know-Nothing-ism, bossism, hoodlumism, rowdyism, Trumanism* and *McCarthyism.*[8]

Among words ending in *-ee* are the familiar *draftee* of World War I (supplanted in World War II by *selectee* and *trainee,* the latter subsequently adopted in business) and *honoree,* used widely in the South and Midwest to indicate the person for whom a party is given. Some fantastic forms have been recorded, *e.g., holdupee* (the victim of a holdup), *tryoutee* (one who tries for a position on a competitive basis), *rushee, quizee* and *parolee.*[9] *Jamboree* may owe something to *-ee* or to *spree;* it is traced by the DA to 1864 and was borrowed by General Sir Robert Baden-Powell in 1908 to designate a festivity for the newly organized Boy Scouts in Eng-

[3] Coined by John Broadus Watson in 1913.

[4] What's a *Receptionist?, The New York Times,* Oct. 5, 1924, indicated that the term was then a novelty. [*Chartist,* designating a habitual watcher of business and stock-market charts, appeared in *The New York Times,* Aug. 18, 1962.]

[5] Girls with Ideals Have Hard Sledding When Elders Are Lax, by Doris Blake, Chicago *Tribune,* Feb. 28, 1926, p. 28.

[6] Josephine M. Burnham, Three Hard-Worked Suffixes, *AS,* Vol. II, Feb. 1927, p. 245.

[7] *National Liquor Review,* July 1943, p. 4. I am indebted here to Fred Hansen.

[8] [*McCarthyism* was introduced by Max Lerner, Apr. 5, 1950. Current afflictions include *Birchism* (1961), *Parkinsonism* (1957), *Castroism, Fidelism* (1961), *Kennedyism* and *segregationism.* An imposing list is found in Among the New Words, by I. Willis Russell and Woodrow W. Boyette, *AS,* Vol. XXXII, Dec. 1957, pp. 292–6.]

[9] [See The Extraordinary Efflorescence of *-ee,* by Leo L. Rockwell, *Benedictine Review,* Vol. VI, 1956, pp. 24–30.]

land; when the Scout movement was taken up in the United States in 1910, *jamboree* returned to the land of its birth. It has produced a number of derivatives, *e.g.*, *yamboree* (a festival honoring the *yam*, or sweet potato)[1] and *camporee* (from *camp*). It has also revived *corroboree*, an unrelated rhyming word, which came into English from aboriginal Australian during the Nineteenth Century, but had practically died out by 1900. Other curious words in *-ee* are *beateree* (person or thing that "beats all"),[2] *tutoree* (or *tutee*) and *biographee*.

From *-ician* we have the lovely *mortician* and its sisters *beautician* and *cosmetician* (and *bootician*, to say nothing of *whooptician*, a college cheerleader).[3] Hollywood has spawned *dialogicians*. From *-(ol)ogist* and *-or* come *boyologist* (a specialist in the training and entertainment of boys), *truckologist*, *mixologist* (a bartender), *clockologist* and *hygiologist*, and *realtor*, *furnitor*, *chiropractor* and *merchantor* (a member of the Merchants' Bureau of a Chamber of Commerce).[4] The old suffix *-er* is also put to frequent use in American word coinage, as in *soap-boxer*, [traced to the Spokane *Industrial Worker* (1913)]. Among the more recent coinages are *first-termer*, *party-liner*, *inner-circler*, *low-incomer*, *rank-and-filer*, *WPAer*, *teen-ager*, *bobby-soxer*, *first-nighter*, *name dropper*, *draft dodger*, *Dust-Bowler* and *midnighter*. [*Moonlighter* designates a teacher or other public servant who also holds an evening job in an effort to remain solvent. Among union members it is applied to one who works after hours for less than the union scale.][5] Other old suffixes in continued request are *-age*, as in *teacherage* (a teachers' residence, obviously suggested by *parsonage*),[6] *outage*,[7] *readerage*[8] and *overage* (a bank term, the opposite of a *shortage*);

[1] *Jamboree Has Two Children*, by Atcheson L. Hench, *AS*, Vol. XII, Apr. 1937, p. 99. A *yamboree* was held at Gilmer, Tex., in Oct. 1935.

[2] *Beateree*, *AS*, Vol. XVII, Oct. 1942, p. 181. The term, traced by the DAE to 1861, apparently dropped out of use in the early 1880s. The history of *-ee* is *recounted* in The Fate of French *-é* in English, by C. T. Onions, *SPE Tract*, No. LXI, 1943.

[3] [According to Fred W. Householder and Thomas A. Sebeok, *AS*, Vol. XXVI, Oct. 1951, pp. 221–2, *linguistician*, to describe a student of language rather than a polyglot, was coined in 1895 by E. W. Fay, on the analogy of *statistician*, *logician*, etc. It was used in London and Tokyo in the 1930s, and there was some feeling for it in the United States following World War II; the American brethren, however, have not adopted it,

perhaps because of the pattern of *mortician* and *beautician*.]

[4] [Lena P. Smith, of S. Cottage Grove Ave., Chicago, proclaims herself a *healor*. A Chicago shoeshiner is described by his brethren among the Black Muslims as a *leatherologist*; Black Nationalism, by E. U. Essien-Udom; Chicago, 1962, p. 188.]

[5] [I. Willis Russell and Woodrow W. Boyette have published two long lists of new formations with *-er* in AS, Vol. XXXIII, Dec. 1958, pp. 280–3, and Vol. XXXIV, May 1959, pp. 131–3.]

[6] *Teacherage*, by Hugh Sebastien, *AS*, Vol. XI, Oct. 1936, p. 271.

[7] Used among public utility companies to describe the interruption of electrical service. [Morticians amiably discuss the annual *corpsage* in their community.]

[8] Office advertisement in the Oklahoma City *Times*, Oct. 27, 1924.

-arian, as in *Rotarian* and *charitarian; -ability*, as in *grindability*, *cleanability* and *clubability; -ography*, as in *Leicography* (from the name of the German *Leica* camera);[9] and *-ization*, as in *filmization* [and *tragerization*, from George L. Trager, deviser of a popular scheme for analyzing the sounds of English].

But of more interest, though many of them are strained and silly, are the words showing recent vogue affixes, e.g., *-(a)thon*, as in *talkathon* and *telethon; -eroo*, as in *flopperoo; -legger*, as in *bootlegger; -caster*, as in *newscaster* and *sportscaster; -(o)crat*, as in *Willkiecrat;*[1] and *-hog*, as in *road hog* and *gas hog*. All the *-thon* words derive from *marathon*, which came into general cognizance in 1896, when the first of the series of revived Olympic games was held at Athens, and rules were laid down for the famous *marathon race*. Twenty-one years later, when enterprising entrepreneurs began staging dance endurance contests in the United States, they borrowed the term. The first dance contests were actually continuous, but in 1930 a manager at Des Moines, Iowa, introduced rest periods, during which the contestants walked about the floor. This new form of a *marathon* was called a *walkathon*, and in a little while other derivatives followed.[2] *Readathon* most often appears as *Bible readathon;* it designates a relay reading of the Bible by a series of pious persons, usually led by their pastor. The popular *-eroo*[3] was likely borrowed from *buckaroo*, a corruption of the Spanish *vaquero*, a cowboy, traced through various forms, e.g., *buckeroo*, *bucchro* and *buckhara*, to 1827. *Jiggeroo*, used by tramps as a warning of the approach of police, was reported in 1919,[4] and *gazaroo*, meaning a boy, and *gozaroo*, meaning a fellow, were reported from Newfoundland in 1925,[5] but it was not until 1939 that *-eroo* and its congeners, *-aroo*, *-roo*, *-oo* and *-araroo*, began to flourish in a large way. Wentworth has presented nearly fifty examples, all dated: they include *antseroo* (ants in his pants), *bounceroo* (the grand bounce), *smackeroo* (a dollar), *sockeroo* (a success), *stinkaroo* (a bad play, movie or other

---

[9] *Canadian Stage*, 1936, p. 1.

[1] According to *Editor and Publisher*, Aug. 7, 1940, *Willkiecrat* was coined by James L. Verhoeff, assistant city editor of the *Arkansas Democrat*, of Little Rock.

[2] See *Billboard*, Aug. 18, 1934. [*Rockerthon*, *poolathon* and *pianothon* appeared in Canada in 1955. See also The *-thon* Suffix, by Eugene Nolte, *AS*, Vol. XXIX, Oct. 1954, p. 229.]

[3] Harold Wentworth, The Neo-Pseudo-Suffix *-eroo*, *AS*, Vol. XVII, Feb. 1942, pp. 10–15.

[4] F. H. Sidney, *DN*, Vol. V, Pt. II, 1919, p. 41.

[5] Newfoundland Dialect Items, by George Allen England, *DN*, Vol. V, Pt. VIII, 1925, pp. 332–3. [In Australia *jackeroo* (possibly itself from *vaquero*) has been used since c. 1880 to designate a "new chum," or greenhorn; the feminine analogue *jilleroo* is recent. See W. S. Ramson, Historical Study of the Australian Vocabulary, diss. (MS), U. of Sydney, 1962. Long but by no means exhaustive lists of compounds in these vogue suffixes are to be found in the appendix to Wentworth and Flexner, Dictionary of American Slang; New York, 1961.]

show) and *ziparoo* (energy). To them in 1942 and 1943 Bolinger[6] and Manuel Prenner[7] added *jugaroo* (a jail), *congaroo* (a dancer of the conga), *pepperoo* (a peppy story), *switcheroo, whackeroo* and *payeroo* (the pay-off). The *-ador* suffix was probably suggested by *humidor*, which the OED Supplement traces to 1903, and most of the words embodying it show analogous meanings, *e.g., beerador*.[8] The various words in *-legger* are all children of *bootlegger*. During the middle 1920s, when there was a great upsurge of comstockery and simultaneously a large flood of obscene books, *booklegger* came in to designate a person who either sold them or let them out for reading. Most of the *bookleggers* flourished in the college towns. *Votelegger* appeared in 1940, and in 1941 *Time* used *foodlegger* to designate the illicit foodsellers of rationed England. When rationing was set up in the United States *meatlegger* and *tirelegger* followed.[9] *Gas-leggers, coalleggers* and *carleggers* have also been reported.[1] *Broadcaster* apparently arose in England, but it is in the United States that it has pro-duced its chief derivatives, *e.g., gridcaster* (an announcer of football games), *dogcaster, smearcaster*[2] and *gamecaster*, and the verbs *to telecast, to radiocast, to colorcast, to sportcast* and *to newscast*.

The use of *-(o)crat* and *-(o)cracy* is by no means new. The OED traces *mobocrat* in English use to 1798 and *mobocracy* to 1754. *Monocrat* (a partisan of monarchy) was launched by Thomas Jefferson in 1792. *Shamo-crat* (from *sham* and *Democrat*) appeared in the political controversy of the 1850s, to designate the pro-slavery wing of the Democratic party; it soon died. *Technocracy*, which had a great vogue in the closing years of the Hoover era, is also now obsolete,[3] along with such derivatives as *sex-nocracy, pianocracy* and *healthocracy*. [Australia has boasted a *squattoc-racy*.] *Plutocrat* was borrowed from England, but *popocrat* made its first appearance in the Bryan campaign of 1896. [*Proctocrat* appeared in 1963 to designate a kind of bureaucrat common in small colleges.] The English are partial to *-crat* and have produced some forms so fantastic as to suggest American provenance, *e.g., shopocrat, poshocrat* and *demoplutocrat*. The words in *-buster* seem to be the children of *trust buster*.[4] *Gangbuster*

[6] Among the New Words, *AS*, Vol. XVII, Dec. 1942, p. 269.

[7] More Notes on Neo-Suffixes, *AS*, Vol. XVIII, Feb. 1943, p. 71.

[8] Melvin M. Desser advertised for sale, in the Baltimore *Sun*, May 29, 1941, a *beerador* of "23-case capacity."

[9] Among the New Words, by Dwight L. Bolinger, *AS*, Vol. XVIII, Feb. 1943, p. 63, and Dec. 1943, p. 303.

[1] Yes! We All Talk, by Marcus H. Boulware, Pittsburgh *Courier*, July 11, 1942.

[2] *Guild Reporter*, Aug. 15, 1944, p. 16.

[3] The term was coined in 1919 by Wil-liam H. Smyth, an inventor of Berkeley, Cal., but was given popularity by How-ard Scott, of New York. *Technology*, still respectable, is also older, dating from Jacob Bigelow, Elements of Technology, 1829.

[4] [A list of compounds in *-buster* is found in *AS*, Vol. XXIII, Oct.–Dec. 1948, pp. 290–5.]

appeared during the days of Thomas E. Dewey as a prosecutor of racketeers in New York, *c.* 1935. *Union buster* seems to be the invention of *The Nation*.[5] The first of the words in *-fiend* was probably *opium fiend*, which goes back to the early 80s, and maybe to the 70s. It was followed, *c.* 1890, by *cigarette fiend*, and a little later by *absinthe fiend*, *dope fiend* [6] and *cocaine fiend*. Then came *baseball fiend*, *dance fiend*, *jazz fiend* and the like. *Globaloney* (*global* and *baloney*) was launched by the Hon. Clare Boothe Luce in her maiden speech in Congress, February 1943. The following month *The New Yorker* contributed *verbaloney*. There was a time, *c.* 1925, when aviators of supposedly unusual daring (including Charles A. Lindbergh) were called *flying fools*, and from the term flowed *riding fool*, *writing fool* and so on, but they have apparently gone out. Many other words have produced from time to time, a small and transient progeny, but these derivatives are of hardly more than curious interest, *e.g.*, *bookmobile* and *clubmobile* from *automobile;*[7] *booboisie* and *joboisie* from *bourgeoisie; elegantsia* from *intelligentsia;*[8] *janissariat* from *proletariat; aquatennial* from *centennial;*[9] *carnapper* and *dognapper* from *kidnapper;*[1] *strippeuse* and *stripteuse* from *danseuse; typistry* from *artistry; motel* and *airtel* from *hotel; trainasium* from *gymnasium;*[2] and numerous forms in *-ology*, *e.g.*, *oilology, bagology*.[3]

The suffix *-ie* was far from new when it appeared in the back formation *movie*, soon followed by *quickie, Okie* and a host of other forms. The first verified example of *movie* is dated 1913, but the word was then already six or seven years old. Who invented it, no one knows. The magnates of the movie industry have always disliked the word, and vainly sought a more dignified substitute. When the talking pictures came in, in 1927, they were first called *speakies*, but *talkies* (actually dating from

[5] June 22, 1940, p. 746.

[6] In The Argot of the Underworld Narcotic Addict, Pt. II, *AS*, Vol. XIII, Oct. 1938, David W. Maurer says that *dope fiend* "is practically taboo among underworld addicts." *Pipe fiend* and *needle fiend* are also out of fashion.

[7] [*Bloodmobile*, for collecting blood donations, is common; *freezemobile*, a grocery store on wheels with frozen foods a specialty, was reported from Pawley's Island, S.C., by R. M. Lumiansky, *AS*, Vol. XXIII, Apr. 1948, p. 158. According to *The New York Times*, Sept. 30, 1962, two *artmobiles*, traveling art galleries on special truck-trailer bodies, operate in Virginia. The Somers (N.Y.) Circus Museum operates a *circusmobile*, a scale model of a big top in a large van; see What the Elephant Said, by Jean Cowles, *New York Folklore Quarterly*, Vol. XVIII, Spring 1962, p. 69. During the summer months the recreation service of the city of Chicago operates *craftmobiles* to teach handicrafts to children.]

[8] *AS*, Vol. XIV, Oct. 1939, p. 237.

[9] *AS*, Vol. XV, Dec. 1940, p. 371.

[1] *AS*, Vol. XVI, Oct. 1941, p. 239; *Words*, May 1940, p. 73.

[2] Used at the Army Parachute School in World War II. See Typical Parachute Injuries, by C. Donald Lord and James W. Coutts, *Jour. AMA*, Aug. 26, 1944, p. 1182.

[3] *Bagology* is the name of the house organ of the Chase Bag Company of Chicago.

1913) displaced it, [probably because *speakie* had been pre-empted by the speakeasy. As sound became universal, *talkie* faded into oblivion, and today the unqualified *movie* always implies sound.]

Jitterbug did not introduce *-bug*, for the DAE traces *tariff bug* to 1841 and *gold bug* to 1878, but *shutter bug*, *litter bug* and various like things seem to have flowed from it.[4] The suffix *-ine* came in during the middle 80s, first hitched to *dude*, itself an American invention of 1883. But both *dude* and *dudine* are now obsolete save in the Far West, where they survive to designate the Easterners who come out to cavort on *dude ranches* under the guidance of *dude wranglers*. About 1920 *-ine* had a brief revival, producing *doctorine*, *actorine*, *chorine*, etc., but only the last is ever heard today.[5]

"English," says Edwin Bercke Dike, "has picked up her affixes everywhere, and people have used them freely, and given them strange vogues"[6]—especially American people. But prefixes are used much more sparingly than suffixes. Indeed, the most productive over the years has been *anti-*, especially in the field of politics. "If it were possible to collect this material completely," says Allen Walker Read, "a 'History of Opposition Movements in America' could be written,"[7] beginning with *anti-episcopalian* (1769) and *anti-Federalist* (1788) and running down to the present *anti-desegregationist*. *Pro-*, which goes back to 1645 in English, usually carries a hostile significance, as in *pro-slavery* (1839), *pro-rebel* (1868) and *pro-German* (1914). Numerous words in *near-* began to appear about 1900, e.g., *near-silk*, *near-silver* and *near-porcelain*. A logical extension quickly produced *near-smile*, *near-accident*, *near-engagement* and others after their kind, and in 1920 came *near-beer* (known from 1909), to flourish obscenely for thirteen long years and then sink into happy obsolescence. *Super-* has been very popular since 1920 or thereabout, when the movie press agents began writing about *super-productions* and *super-films*, and various analogues have followed, e.g., *super-highway*, *supermarket*, *super-criminal* and *super-love*. The last signifies a kind of amour perfected by the virtuosi of

---

[4] [See *-wise*, *-ize*, *bar* and *bug*, CEA Critic, Jan. 1958, p. 1.]

[5] See *Chorine*, by Louise Pound, *AS*, Vol. III, June 1928, p. 368, and *Dudine*, by M. H. Dresen, *AS*, Aug. 1928. [The analogous *welderina* appeared in *Life*, Aug. 9, 1951, p. 8. Of miscellaneous new suffixes we may note *-cillin*, from *penicillin*, found in drug names; *-on* and *-lon* in trade names of fabrics, influenced by *rayon* and *nylon; clinic*, as in *car clinic; -rama*, from *panorama*, in such symbols of the entertainment world as *Cyclorama* and *Cinerama;* and the vogue slang *-sville*, as in "He's from *squaresville*," considered somewhat more *hip* than simply calling some out-of-date person a *square*. For a summary, see English Suffixation: a Descriptive Approach, by S. S. Newman, *Word*, Vol. IV, Apr. 1948, pp. 24–30.]

[6] Obsolete Words, *Philological Quarterly*, Vol. XII, Apr. 1933, p. 214.

[7] The Scope of the American Dictionary, *AS*, Vol. IX, Oct. 1933, p. 14. [*Anti-anti-Communist*, as less libelous than *pro-Communist*, dates from 1953.]

Hollywood: it partakes of the characters of riot, delirium tremens and mayhem. Sometimes *super-* is employed to strengthen adjectives, as in *super-colossal*. H. W. Horwill says that *semi-* "is in much more frequent use in America than in England," as in *semi-centennial* (English *jubilee*) and *semi-panic*. [*Semi-trailer* is normally abbreviated to *semi* by truck drivers.] There has been, of late, a use of *air-*, as in the adjectives *air-cooled*, *air-conditioned* and *air-minded*, and the nouns *airliner* and *air hostess*.[8] During the thirteen years of Prohibition *pre-Volstead* and *pre-war* threatened to bring in a flock of novelties in *pre-*, but the prefix seems to have died out of popularity. [*Mega-*, used by physicists in the sense of million, seems to be flourishing, as in *megacycles*, the number of million vibrations per second in the waves of short-wave radio. Nuclear physicists talk cheerfully of electric currents in *megavolts*, bomb effects in *megatons* (of TNT), the cost of apparatus in *megabucks* and the anticipated carnage in *megacorpses* or *megadeaths*.]

Many new words, launched with impressive ceremony, fail altogether. Edgar Allan Poe proposed that *suspectful* be used to differentiate between the two meanings of *suspicious*, one who suspects and one to be suspected,[9] but no one uses it. Most of Walt Whitman's inventions went the same way. The Pennsylvania Society for the Prevention of Cruelty to Animals awarded a prize to Mrs. M. McIlvaine Bready, of Mickleton, N.J., for *pitilacker*, in the sense of one cruel to animals, but it failed to make the success of *scofflaw*. The late Franklin H. Giddings proposed *taboobery* and *tomtomery*, but neither seized the public fancy. During the heyday of the IWW (1912–20) one of its chief propagandists, a writer calling himself T-bone Slim, invented many neologisms, and some of them were popular for a time, but only *Brisbanality*, signifying a platitudinous utterance by Arthur Brisbane of the Hearst papers, survived, and that but briefly. *Americanity* was coined by F. M. Kercheville, of the University of New Mexico, to designate "the broad but none the less profound concept of the genuine spirit—the fundamental elements and characteristics—common to all the Americas." [1] But it never caught on. Gelett Burgess, who launched *bromide* and *blurb*, proposed many others in "Burgess Unabridged" (1914), but they failed to make their way into the language. *Gwibit*, dedicated to the

---

[8] [The development of jet propulsion has brought *jetliner* and *jetport;* the helicopter has added *heliport and helibus*. *Neo-*, also used with adjectives, has produced, *inter alia*, *neo-Fascism* and *neo-Fascist; crypto-* has given *crypto-Communist*, on the analogy of the older *crypto-Catholic*. In Papers by Arthur Minton, Supplement to *AS*, Vol. XXXIII, May 1958, it is pointed out that *co-*, as in *co-pilot* and *co-chairman*, now indicates subordination.]

[9] In Fifty Suggestions, *c*. 1845.

[1] *Americanity*, by F. M. Kercheville, *AS*, Vol. XIV, Feb. 1939, pp. 71–3, reprinted in the *Congressional Record*, Mar. 31, 1939, pp. 5091–2.

nation by Congressman (later Senator) Karl E. Mundt, of South Dakota, in 1943, to designate "the guild of Washington incompetent bureaucratic idea throat-cutters," seemed to meet a need, but it nevertheless died the death.[2] When Charles H. Grandgent offered *osteocephic* as an elegant substitute for *bonehead* he seemed to be performing a public service, but it went unrequited by acceptance,[3] and the same fate befell *osseocaput*, launched in 1913, along with *lithocaput, ferrocaput* and various other analogues, [and *schizoceramic*, coined by Finley Foster, of Western Reserve University, as an elegant synonym for *crackpot. Coolant* was established by the need for high-performance liquid-cooled airplane engines in World War II.] But oblivion befell *homancing*, meaning house hunting, and *homancier*, meaning "one skilled in home financing."[4] At intervals some newspaper or magazine editor, struck with the thought that the vocabulary of the American language, despite its unparalleled richness, still has gaps in it, calls upon his readers to apply themselves to the invention of new words, but though many of the responses are ingenious and amusing they all fail to survive. Deliberate efforts to resuscitate obsolete words are also made from time to time, [but *sibling* (a brother or a sister) is an exceptional success].[5]

There was a transient craze in the second lustrum of the 1930s for nouns on the order of *maker-upper*, compounded of a verb and an adverb, with *-er* added to each. A somewhat similar fashion, before the Civil War, had produced such forms as *come-outer*, traced to 1840, and *comeuppance*, traced to 1859, but this new one was wilder and woolier, and some of the examples reported by Louise Pound and others were curious indeed, *e.g., fighter-backer; caller-, jotter-* and *tearer-downer; dropper-* and *taker-inner; putter-* and *topper-offer;* and *bracer-, setter, stayer-, waker-* and *warmer-upper.* Some genuine monstrosities have been recorded, *e.g., dance-mixer-upper, home-breaker-upper, haircut-putter-offer,* and *builder-upper-tearer-downer.*[6] The contagion spread to the adjectives, and some bizarre superlatives were concocted, *e.g., getting-aroundest, datingest* and *most-*

***

[2] *Congressional Record,* Dec. 15, 1943, p. 10835, and Dec. 18, 1943, p. A5999.

[3] Some Neologisms from Recent Magazines, by Robert Withington, *AS,* Vol. VI, Apr. 1931, p. 284.

[4] Both launched by the First Federal Savings and Loan Association of Lima, Ohio, in 1938, along with an explanatory poem by C. L. Mumaugh.

[5] In the New York *World,* Oct. 6, 1930, Richard Connell proposed the revival of *gomeral* (a fool), *nugacity* (frivolity), *appetent* (eagerly desirous), *docity* (quick comprehension) and *ges-* *tion* (management), but there were no seconds. [One of the latest complaints about gaps in the vocabulary is English at a Loss for Words, by Albert H. Morehead, *The New York Times Magazine,* Sept. 11, 1955, p. 27. *Booksneaf* (book + sneak thief) was coined about 1920 by Paul W. Stoddard, Hartford, Conn., and was awarded a prize by the Book Publishers Institute. See *AS,* Vol. X, Feb. 1935, p. 79.]

[6] On adding the Suffix of Agency, *-er,* to Adverbs, by Harold Wentworth, *AS,* Vol. XI, Dec. 1936, pp. 369-70.

workingest. But like the parent fashion, this one soon died away. *Hair-do* came in during the heyday of these locutions, and was followed by *up-do.* A series of terms in *walk-* is older: *walk-around* is traced by the DAE to 1869 and *walk-out* to 1888, and *walk-up,* an apartment without elevator service, to 1919.[7]

The etymology and history of many common American nouns remain undetermined: *phony, ballyhoo, hobo, hokum, jazz, jitney, maverick* and *Wobbly.* The earlier editions of Webster sought to relate *phony* to *funny,* but Webster 1961 lists it simply as "origin unknown." Its sources have been sought in *telephone* and in *Forney,* a manufacturer of cheap jewelry,[8] who made a specialty of supplying brass rings, in barrel lots, to street peddlers. [The DA derives it from Irish *fauney,* a ring, used in a ring-switching gyp popular among grifters.] Today anything not genuine is *phony* in the common American speech; a person suspected of false pretenses is a *phony.* Etymologists have unsuccessfully tried to connect *ballyhoo* with *Bally-holly,* a village in County Cork, Ireland; with a blend of *ballet* and *whoop;* with the Chicago World's Fair of 1893, as an imitation of the cry of the dervishes in the Oriental Village, to wit, *b'Allah hoo,* meaning "through God it is," [and with Spanish *balahú,* schooner, which may go back to Carib *balahua,* the sea].

So far, all reputable etymologists concede that the origin of *hobo* is unknown. The DA's first example is from the Ellensburgh (Wash.) *Capital* in 1891. A verb, *to hobo,* followed in 1906. It has been suggested that it might be from an identical Japanese word, the plural of *ho* (side), and meaning, in the plural, all sides or everywhere, or from *ho, bo!* (*boy!*), a cry. *Hokum* (1917) is usually related to *hocus;* Webster 1961 and the OED Supplement suggest a blend of *hocus-pocus* and *bunkum.* All the dictionaries report correctly that *maverick* comes from the name of Samuel A. Maverick (1803–70), a Texan who neglected to brand his calves, and so invited their bootleg branding by his neighbors. But when the word is discussed in the newspapers, which is not infrequently, it is sometimes stated that the thing ran the other way, and that Maverick himself did the stealthy branding.[9]

Jitney may "possibly" come from the French *jeton* (a counter or metal disk), from the verb *jeter* (to throw). The Oxford Supplement (1933) says that its origin is unknown, but quotes a statement in *The Nation* for February 4, 1915, that the word is "the Jewish slang term for a nickel."

---

[7] The earliest citation, in both DAE and DA, is from the first edition of this work, but the word probably dates from the turn of the century.

[8] All three were reported in *AS*, Vol. XII, Oct. 1937, p. 242.

[9] In Nov. 1889, one of his descendants, George M. Maverick, set the matter right in a letter to the St. Louis *Republic,* which was later reprinted as a pamphlet. But old libels die hard.

But nothing resembling *jitney* is to be found in any Yiddish wordbook, and it was used to designate a five-cent piece long before there was any considerable immigration of Eastern Jews. It began to be used to designate a cheap automobile bus in 1914, and is now nearly obsolete.

Webster 1961 says that *jazz* is of unknown origin. The Oxford agrees, but adds that it is "generally said to be Negro." Amateurs have made almost countless efforts to run it down, or, more accurately, to guess at its history. It has been derived from *Jasper*, the name of a dancing slave on a plantation near New Orleans, *c.* 1825; from *Chaz*, the stable name of Charles Washington, an eminent ragtime drummer of Vicksburg, Miss., *c.* 1895; and from the *chasse*, a dancing step.[1] The effort to trace the word to Africa has failed, though it was used by the Negroes in the Mississippi river towns long before it came into general use. But the meaning they—and most white Southerners, too—attached to it was that of sexual intercourse. Its extension to the kind of music it now designates would not be unnatural. Perhaps *jazz*, as we know it, is the resultant of several etyma. The origin of *Wobbly* is thus given by Mortimer Downing, a member of the IWW in its heyday:

> In Vancouver, in 1911, we had a number of Chinese members and one restaurant keeper would trust any member for meals. He could not pronounce the letter *w*, but called it *wobble*, and would ask "You I. Wobble Wobble?" And when the card was shown, credit was unlimited. Thereafter the laughing term among us was *I. Wobbly Wobbly.*[2]

Respectable lexicographers still cite this etymology for want of a better, but none really accepts it. The truth about the origins of *Wobbly*—as about the origins of *ballyhoo, hobo, hokum, jazz* and *jitney*—eluded the DAE and the DA. Perhaps future lexicographers will solve these and other vexing problems.

3: VERBS

American verbs made of simple nouns are as the leaves of Vallombrosa, but they are by no means new to the language.[3] Since early Middle English they have constituted one of the chief evidences of that almost complete abandonment of inflections which separates English from the other

---

[1] [See Jazz: The Word, and Its Extension to Music, by Peter Tamony, *Jazz*, Vol. I, Oct. 1958, pp. 42–3.]

[2] Quoted in How *Wobbly* Originated, by Richard W. Hogue, *The Nation*, Sept. 5, 1923, p. 242.

[3] [See Donald W. Lee, Functional Change in Early English, Menasha, Wis., 1948, and the shorter discussion of the same topic by Stefan Einarsson, *MLN*, Vol. LXIV, Dec. 1949, pp. 498–500.]

principal languages of the Indo-European family. Its nouns, save for the addition of *s* in the plural and of *'s* in the genitive, are the same in all situations, and many of them may be turned into verbs without any modification whatever, *e.g.*, *place* and *to place*. To be sure, a number of suffixes are still in use to notify the change, *e.g.*, *-ize* and *-ify*, as in *carbon, to carbonize; beauty, to beautify*, but often they are not necessary, and when they are used to make new verbs it is only because they seem to promote euphony. Many of the most common English verbs are borrowed nouns, and go back to a very early time, *e.g.*, *to ground, to house, to shackle* (*c.* 1460) and *to waltz*. The thing also runs the other way, and such verbs are matched by large numbers of common nouns that began as verbs, *e.g.*, *sleep* and *walk*. The process is going on constantly, and in both directions, but it is naturally most active at times when the language is in a stage of vigorous growth and radical change. The age of Shakespeare was a time of bold and often barbaric experiment in language, and some of its novelties were so extravagant that even the American of today finds them somewhat ultra. Shakespeare did not hesitate to use *to happy, to climate, to disaster, to furnace, to malice, to property* and *to verse*.[4] Some of his innovations, *e.g.*, *to fever* and *to foul*, made their way into respectability, but others died quickly. There is always a large turnover in such novelties, and no one can predict the ultimate fate of a given example.

A large number of new verbs are succinct substitutes for verb phrases, and so give evidence of the American liking for short cuts in speech, *e.g.*, *to service* for *to give service*,[5] *to intern* for *to serve as intern, to style* for *to cut in accord with the style, to model* for *to act as a model, to ready* for *to make ready, to vacation, to holiday* or *to weekend* for *to take a vacation* or *holiday* or *to go on a weekend trip* and *to yes* for *to say yes to*. Another class of verbs may be called "regular" substitutes for the forms that differ from the corresponding nouns and adjectives, *e.g.*, *to loan* for *to lend*,[6] *to host* for *to entertain* and *to signature* for *to sign*.

One of these newcomers destined to stick is *to contact*. It followed the addition of a new sense to the old noun *contact*, given by Partridge as "an acquaintance(ship), a connection, both with a view to business or self-interest." The earliest citation of the verb in the DA is from 1929, but on

---

[4] E. A. Abbott, Shakespearean Grammar; new ed.; London, 1879. Wilhelm Franz, Die Sprache Shakespeares in Vers und Prosa, unter Berüsichtigung des amerikanischen Entwicklungsgeschichtlich dargestellt; Halle, 1939.

[5] *To service* was used by R. L. Stevenson in Catriona (1893), but it remained a nonce word until American garages

began *servicing* cars *c.* 1910. It is now in almost universal use among the persons who keep machinery and fixtures in repair.

[6] *To loan* was once good English, and the OED gives examples going back to *c.* 1200, but it has been supplanted in England by *to lend* and the Oxford calls it "now chiefly U.S."

September 8, 1928, *Editor and Publisher* had noted its employment by an advertising executive. It apparently made relatively slow progress at the start, but after a couple of years it was in almost general use,[7] and soon afterward got to England. There it met with a hostile reception from purists, and by 1940 Ivor Brown, writing in the Manchester *Guardian*,[8] was throwing up his hands. "The war," he said,

> through the power it gives to bureaucracy and to the industrialist turned administrator, will certainly add to our language—or rather inflate it. The tendency of such people is always to prefer a new and heavy word to an old and short one. Instead of bidding us *meet* their Mr. Smith in Birmingham, they would have us *contact* him.

Brown's contention that in all the situations where *to contact* was being used the ancient *to meet* would suffice was not shared by other English observers. In 1941, an anonymous writer in the *Cheshire Observer*,[9] in noting its adoption by British Army headquarters in Greece, lamented that there was "no precise one-word substitute for it." It was attacked, in the 1930s, in the United States as well as in England, and in 1931, one of the high officials of Western Union denounced it as a "hideous vulgarism" and forbade its use by employees of the company.[1] But they are still using it, and so are multitudes of other Americans.

Many of the more recent verbs-from-nouns meet genuine needs, and deserve to be treated seriously, *e.g.*, *to thumb* (a ride), *to audition*, *to co-star*, *to curb* (take [a dog] to the curb, or force [a car] to the curb), *to cystoscope* (and its numerous medical analogues), *to deadhead*, *to highlight*, *to alert*,[2] *to package*, *to research*, *to pressure*, *to accession*,[3] *to sabotage*, *to franchise*, *to remainder* (unsalable books), *to panic*,[4] *to recess*, *to referee*, *to alibi*, *to gavel*,[5] *to steamroller*, *to pan*, *to option*, *to decision*

---

[7] Now It Is *Contacting*, Reno (Nev.) *Gazette* (editorial page), July 7, 1931. This was apparently a syndicated editorial.

[8] Verbs and Verbiage, July 20, 1940.

[9] *Contact* as Noun or Verb?, Apr. 19, 1941.

[1] See *The Commonweal*, Dec. 9, 1931, p. 145.

[2] *To alert* is to be found in Section IX of the report of the committee appointed to investigate the Pearl Harbor incident, submitted to the President on Jan. 24, 1942. The noun *alert* may have been borrowed from England. It was apparently new there on Oct. 12, 1940, when the London *Times Literary Supplement* an-

nounced magisterially that "it will pass muster."

[3] A librarian's term. We Do Odd Things to Words, by J.W.B., *The New York Times*, Mar. 27, 1932.

[4] Used by Thomas Hood in 1827, but apparently by no one else in England afterward. Reinvented in the United States, *c.* 1910, and since adopted in England. Denounced by the Manchester *Guardian* Nov. 24, 1939, as one of "our nastier newcomers."

[5] Associated Press dispatch from Washington, Feb. 26, 1926: "The Vice President *gaveled* through a motion." The noun *gavel*, to designate a mallet or hammer used by a presiding officer, is an

(defeat in a prize fight by decision rather than by a knockout), *to submarine, to solo, to bellyache, to pussyfoot, to railroad, to night-club, to mastermind, to blueprint, to needle* [6] and *to cold-deck.*

This list might be extended almost indefinitely, especially if one includes citations from the iconoclastic vocabulary of *Variety, e.g., to ash-can, to angel, to showcase, to emcee* or *m.c.* (serve as master of ceremonies),[7] *to background, to music, to guest, to biography, to bankroll, to première* (often shortened to *to preem*) and *to barnum. Variety* frequently reduces verb phrases to simple verbs, *e.g., to siesta* for *to take a siesta, to train* for *to go by train* and *to outlet* for *to serve as an outlet.* Rather curiously, it also affects a number of new and clumsy verbs, made from nouns, that are not nearly so vivid as the old verbs they displace, *e.g., to author* for *to write, to guest* for *to entertain* [8] and *to destruct* for *to destroy.*[9] Such forms are by no means confined to *Variety.* Walter Winchell and his disciples produce them in large number, and they are also plentiful in presumably more decorous circles; *to teacher* appeared in a learned journal of Florida.[1] Indeed, the manufacture of such new verbs goes on on all levels. *To letter*, probably suggested by *to major*, is used to indicate prowess in sports, *e.g.,* "He *lettered* in wrestling." One may add at random *to air* (to disseminate by radio), *to wax* (to record for the phonograph), *to canary* (to sing), *to true-bill* (to indict), *to statistic* (and *to outstatistic*), *to landslide, to lobby-display,*[2] *to front-page, to battle-test, to byline, to lyric* (to write the lyrics for a musical piece), *to waste-basket,*[3] *to press-agent, to brain-trust* and *to third-degree.* Nor are the English out of the running, for *to stonewall* has graced the London *Morning Post,*[4] *to partner* the *Western Morning News,*[5] *to town-plan* the austere Edinburgh *Scotsman,*[6] and a revival of the archaic *to servant* the *Countryman.*[7] *To park* was borrowed from the French early in the Nineteenth Century to indicate the storing of artillery, and was taken into the vocabulary of automobilists

---

Americanism, traced to 1860; it comes from the name of a hammer used by stonemasons, also an Americanism and traced to 1805.

[6] Used in various metaphorical senses, all suggesting penetration.

[7] [As a noun, *emcee* is old in *Variety*. A female counterpart, *femcee,* appeared June 1, 1955.]

[8] I find *to luncheon-guest* in the *Goldfish Bowl*, house organ of the National Press Club, Washington, Mar. 1937, p. 2. Along with it is *to luncheon-hear, i.e.,* to listen to a speaker invited to disburden himself at lunch.

[9] [*Destruct* as a Verb, by Elizabeth G. Christensen, *AS*, Vol. XXXVI, Oct. 1961, p. 234.]

[1] *Florida Review,* Spring 1938, p. 2.

[2] Used in the theater in the sense of to display photographs or lithographs in a theater lobby.

[3] And Here's Another, by H. H. Williams, Philadelphia *Record*, Nov. 7, 1930. [A story in the Chicago *Sun-Times*, July 24, 1962, described a firm as "*headquartered* at 111 W. Jackson."]

[4] Now absorbed by the *Daily Telegraph*. Mr. Eden as *Stonewaller*, Dec. 17, 1935: "Mr. Anthony Eden *stonewalled* persistent attacks."

[5] Nov. 27, 1937.

[6] Mar. 1, 1937.

[7] July–Sept. 1938.

c. 1910. Since then it has been extended in meaning to indicate any deposit of an article that must be kept safely, and Americans *park* not only their automobiles but also their dogs, their children and their consciences. The OED Supplement traces *to streamline* in English use to 1913; [it may have been in use in the United States earlier, but the DAE and DA do not list it]. It came into popularity *c.* 1937, and was greatly extended in meaning, so that it now designates any attempt at simplification. When *to broadcast* began to be used widely, in 1925, there was a debate among American grammarians over its preterite. The majority appear to have preferred *broadcasted,* as more regular, and they were supported by the English grammarian H. W. Fowler, but *broadcast* seems to have prevailed. It has bred the inevitable noun. [With the advent of television, *telecast* and *colorcast* have followed suit.]

One of the most mysterious American verbs is *to goose.* Its meaning is known to every schoolboy, but no lexicographer has ever worked out its etymology. The corresponding adjective, *goosey,* was noted in *American Speech* in 1933 as meaning "nervous, touchy," [8] and the diligent Bolinger has recorded that *to goose* itself has been taken over by truck drivers and aviators to signify feeding gasoline to an engine in irregular spurts,[9] but beyond this the philological literature is a blank. The preponderance of medical opinion inclines to the theory that the verb was suggested by the fact that geese, which are pugnacious birds, sometimes attack human beings, and especially children, by biting their fundaments.[1] There is also the possibility that the term may be derived from the old custom of examining a goose before turning it out to feed in the fields by feeling of its rear parts; if an egg could be felt it was kept in its pen for the day.[2] This method of exploration is still used by some housewives in order to

---

[8] Ranch Diction of the Texas Panhandle, by Mary Dale Buckner, Vol. VIII, Feb. 1933, p. 31.

[9] Among the New Words, *AS,* Vol. XVIII, Feb. 1943, p. 64.

[1] I am indebted here to the late Admiral Charles S. Butler, M.C., U.S.N. (1875–1944), to Dr. Logan Glendenning, and to Dr. Morris Fishbein, sometime editor of the *Journal of the American Medical Association.* In some of the countries of Europe, where geese are plentiful, they are also said to attack women by striking at the pudenda. An illustration of both methods of attack is in Illustrierte Sittengeschichte, by Eduard Fuchs; Munich, 1912, p. 86. [In Oklahoma, *c.* 1944, Thomas Pyles was shocked to hear *to goose* used by persons of refinement in the sense "to encourage, to incite, to accelerate," a sense that is apparently fairly common, though not recorded in Webster 1961. As with *to jazz up, to bollix up, nuts!* and much of the beatnikoid argot, the user is often ignorant of its indecorous origins. James H. Sledd has suggested that, since *Roger* was a conventional English folk name for the goose, like *Dobbin* for the horse, *to goose* may be a euphemism for *to roger,* a verb unaccountably omitted by the OED and cited only from 1750 by Farmer and Henley and by Partridge, but very popular among Eighteenth Century gentlemen, as in the secret diaries of William Byrd, of Westover. As a nickname for the goose, *Roger* is cited by the OED from 1570.]

[2] I am indebted here to Dr. Carey P. McCord, medical director of the Industrial Health Conservancy Laboratories, Detroit.

estimate the fatness of a dressed goose. The term appears to be unknown in England, and there are no analogues in the other European languages.

Verbs are made not only of nouns but also of other parts of speech. *To up* has had a twilight sort of life in English for many years, but it did not flower in American until *Variety* began to use it. Nothing whatever can be said against it, for its brother, *to down*, has been accepted since Shakespeare's time. *To up* is now in very respectable usage, especially around the poker table. *Variety* has also used *to in* and *to out*, but only with apparent timidity, and not often. To the same general category belong *to ad-lib* and *to yes* and the verbs made of interjections, *e.g.*, *to shush* and *to wow*, all of which have a reputable forerunner in *to hem and haw*, which goes back, in various forms, to the Fifteenth Century. Also, the pathologist of speech must not overlook the verbs made of adjectives, *e.g.*, *to obsolete* [3] and *to à-la-mode*, *i.e.*, to spread ice cream on a slice of fruit pie, thus converting it into *pie à la mode*.[4]

New verbs are frequently formed by adding prefixes or suffixes to old ones, or to nouns or adjectives. Of the prefixes, *de-* seems to be the most popular, with *un-* as its only serious competitor. *To debunk* (1923), popularized by William E. Woodward, was denounced not only on the ground that it was an uncouth word, but also on the ground that the activity it described was immoral and against God, but it has survived. It may have been suggested by *to delouse*, which appeared during World War I, probably in imitation of the German *entlausen*.[5] Before it came in, the English used *to disinfest*. The DA records but five American verbs in *de-* before 1900: *to defoliage* (1879), *to dehorn* (1888), *to demoralize* (1806), *to demote* (*c.* 1891) and *to detassel* (1892). Even *to derail* seems to have been borrowed from England,[6] which also produced *to detrain*.[7] But the crop has been larger in recent years, *e.g.*, *to dewax*, *to dejell*, *to dejelly*, *to degerm*,[8] *to dewater*, *to debulk*, *to detooth*, *to depledge* (to retract one's

---

[3] *AS*, Vol. XIV, Dec. 1939, p. 186.

[4] New Verbs, by Mabel E. Strong, *AS*, Vol. I, Feb. 1926, p. 292.

[5] *Debunk*, *AS*, Vol. II, May 1927, p. 374.

[6] [Ultimately from French, it was first used by the Anglo-Irish economist Dionysius Lardner, Railway Economy; American ed.; New York, 1850, p. 279: "I have adopted this word [*derailment*] from the French: it expresses an effect . . . for which we have not yet had any term in our railway nomenclature. . . . The verb *to derail* . . . may be used in a corresponding sense." Letter from Southworth Lancaster, July 7, 1957.]

[7] *To detrain*, originally a military term, is traced by the OED in army usage to 1881. It came into general use soon afterward and was borrowed in this country. In recent years the English have toyed with new words in *em-* and *en-*, imitated from *to embark*, e.g., *to embus*, *to emplane*.

[8] Defined as follows in the *Journal of Infectious Diseases*, Nov.–Dec. 1938, p. 301: "*To degerm* an object is to reduce, by any means, the number of microbes, pathogenic or nonpathogenic, in or on it."

promise to join a college fraternity), *to deflea, to derat, to debamboozle, to denazify* and *to desegregate*. [*To declassify* is Federalese for to release information previously hidden under a censor's stamp, *to debrief* for to elicit information from one who has performed a mission.[9]] The new verbs in *un-* are not numerous. The Nineteenth Century yielded only *unbank* (to deprive a bank of its functions; *cf. to unman, to unsex*) (1834) and *to unbank a fire* (1890). *To unquote*, meaning to finish a quotation, has been borrowed from the cablese of newspaper correspondents, who must indicate when a quoted passage ends and are forced by high cable tolls to avoid two-word phrases when they can find or invent a single word. *To unstink*, as in "The American Reds have attempted to unstink themselves," seems to have been coined by Westbrook Pegler. Walter Winchell and *Variety* have launched a number of analogues, but they have not come into general use. [The negative *in-* is apparently yielding *to incomplete*, in the jargon of football; sportcasters now report unsuccessful passes as *incompleted* rather than *incomplete*.[1]]

Suffixes are used far more freely; the old suffix *-en* is used to produce new verbs from nouns, adjectives and even other verbs, *e.g., to mistaken, to thinnen, to safen, to hotten, to outen, to quieten* and *to loaden*. Most of these belong mainly to the vulgar speech, as do most of the new formations in *-ify, e.g., speechify*.[2] A more productive suffix, however, *-ize*, has permeated every stratum of American society. Like most other word-forming elements, it is not new, but has been used to make verbs in English for many centuries.[3] It was reinforced in the Seventeenth Century by the French *-iser*, and English fashion still prefers spelling such words in *-ise*. *To apologize* and *to latinize* came in before 1600, and *to barbarize, to criticize* and *to sermonize* in the age of Shakespeare. *Burglarize*, an indubitable Americanism, is traced to 1871. When August Kemmler, the first murderer to be put to death by electricity, was waiting to be executed at

---

[9] [Denounced in We Don't Dig *Debrief* (editorial), Indianapolis *Sunday Times*, Feb. 25, 1962. It dates from World War II. I am here indebted to Mrs. Ruth W. Lieber.]

[1] [Because the *in-* is so often a negative prefix, combustible liquids are now normally labeled *flammable* rather than *inflammable*. In The Rise and Decline of Negative Doublets in English, *AS*, Vol. XXXV, Oct. 1960, pp. 206–9, Lea L. Seale points out that only 70 *un-* and *in-* pairs survive today, against 130 pairs current in the Eighteenth Century and 350 pairs in the Seventeenth. Of 50-odd pairs in use in 1500, only five have survived.]

[2] [Note, however, Military *Minifies* Big Bomb's Value, headline in *The New York Times*, Sept. 1, 1961, p. 2.]

[3] A large number of examples are listed in Lexicological Evolution and Conceptual Progress, by John Taggart Clark, *University of California Publications in Modern Philology*, Sept. 21, 1918, pp. 175–200. [A list of recent formations is found in Among the New Words, by I. Willis Russell, *AS*, Vol. XXXV, Dec. 1960, p. 286. The overworking of the suffix is attacked in The *IZE* Have It, by William Lee Miller, *The Reporter*, Dec. 29, 1955, p. 19.]

Sing Sing, many of the newspapers reported that he was to be *electrized*,[4] and it was some time before they abandoned *to electrize* for *to electrocute*. A few days after the first regulations of the Food Administration were issued, in 1917, *to Hooverize* appeared spontaneously in scores of newspapers, and it retains sufficient repute to be in Webster 1961. *To Bryanize, to Fletcherize* [5] and *to Oslerize* [6] came in just as promptly, the first in 1896, the second in 1904 or thereabout and the third in 1905. *Pasteurize* is older and comes directly from the French. But it is in recent years that the coinage of such verbs has been most active, and putting together anything approaching a comprehensive list would be impossible.

The most obvious are those derived from proper names, including trade names: *to Peglerize, to Texanize*,[7] *to Sanforize, to Sovietize, to Simonize*. Many are made of common nouns: *to pressurize* (as the cabins of high-flying aircraft), *to routinize, to glamo(u)rize* (to make more appealing, at least superficially),[8] *to flavorize, to sloganize, to picturize, to machinize, to moisturize, to powerize, to customize* (to give something the appearance of custom-made merchandise), *to winterize, to satinize*. From adjectives and adverbs are formed such lovely creatures as *to socialize* (in the sense of to go into society), *to tenderize* (to make tender, as meat, by artificial means), *to permanentize*. And from other verbs come *to prosperize* and *to renovize*.

In most of these verbs the *-ize* suggests nature-faking or other kinds of monkey business, and not infrequently such verbs are used with humorous intent. Thus when the Hon. Tom Connally, of Texas, used to *intelligencize* during a Senate debate on May 9, 1944, the reporters for the *Congressional Record* dutifully inserted "[laughter]" after it. [*Customize* and *finalize* are endemic in the advertising business; the latter has been used by Presidents Kennedy and Eisenhower, to the horror of purists.] *To expertize*, apparently suggested by the French noun *expertise*, meaning a survey or valuation by experts, is in universal use among American art and

---

[4] He went to the chair Aug. 3, 1890. The earliest recorded example of *to electrocute* is Aug. 1, 1889. Neither the DAE nor the DA lists *electrize*.

[5] From Horace *Fletcher* (1849–1919), a fanatic who advocated chewing food until all its taste was lost. His cure-all, once popular, is now happily forgotten.

[6] Contrary to Dr. Osler's actual scheme, which would have provided for retirement at sixty on a generous pension, *to Oslerize* came to mean to put a man to death as useless, and the age recommended was commonly understood to be forty.

[7] Motto of the Texas centennial celebration at Corsicana, 1936: Let's *Texanize* Texas.

[8] A Hollywood coinage, borrowed by the *News of the World* (London), June 12, 1938. [*Inventorize* seems to be favored by certain of the linguistic brethren, *e.g.*, "We can do more than *inventorize*—we can approximate an exhaustive list," and "So also, we can *inventorize* all affixes." Both of these appear in C. F. Voegelin, Criteria for Alternatives, *SIL*, Vol. XVI, 1962, p. 46.]

antique dealers, but it does not appear to prevail in England (though the French noun does), and the OED's only example is taken from *Harper's Magazine* for February 1889. *To backwardize* comes from the *Farm Journal*, a very sedate periodical, for March 1926; it is also common in *Variety*. *To slenderize* is used by nearly all the vendors of reducing salts and other such quackeries. *To sanitize* was described by the Associated Press, on July 6, 1934, as the invention of Leon Henderson, one of the economic advisers to the NRA [and later more widely, if hardly better, known as the first director of rationing in World War II], and its meaning was given as "to put sanity and sanitation in[to] business." [9]

The common American tendency to overwork a favorite verb has often been noted by English observers. *To fix* is no less common today than when it first shocked travelers of delicate sensibilities.[1] *To get*, however, does the heaviest service. As Ernest Weekley comments:

> It has become a verb of motion, commonly used in the imperative, and a euphemism for *kill*, as when the gunman *gets* the sleuth or the sleuth *gets* the gunman. The successful yeggman makes his *getaway*, and the successful artist *gets away with it*, while comprehension of a speaker's meaning can be conveyed by the formula, "I *get* you, Steve." [2]

One might add *to get going, to get religion, to get ahead, to get by, to get sore, to get on to* and scores of other phrases, many going back to the Revolutionary era and all of them in everyday American use. Of phrases with other verbs, we would be hard put to do without *to stay put* (traced to 1848), *to slip up* (1854), *to sit in* (1868), *to keep one's shirt on* (1854), *to shell out* (1825), *to go in for* (1835), *to go it alone* (1855), *to fork over* (1839), *to sell short* (1852), *to scare up* (1841), *to stand off* (1878), *to stop off* (1855), *to win out* (1896) and *to play up* (or *down*).

Most of them, it will be noted, are made by the simple device of adding a preposition or adverb to the verb. English commentators often mark the American fondness for the practice, and note sadly its spread to England.

---

[9] I had hardly got this paragraph on paper when someone sent me a copy of the *Literary Supplement* of the London *Times* for June 7, 1934, with the ghastly verb *to obituarize* marked with a red circle. Worse, I discovered on investigation that it was in the OED, credited to the London *Saturday Review* for Oct. 17, 1891. If I may intrude my private feelings into a learned work I venture to add that seeing a monster so suggestive of American barbarism in the *Times* affected me like seeing an archbishop wink at a loose woman.

[1] [See *Fix* (notes by Robert Withington and Atcheson L. Hench), *AS*, Vol. XXX, Dec. 1955, pp. 308–10.]

[2] Adjectives—and Other Words; London, 1930.

The differences in meaning between such compounds and the verbs they come from are often great. Compare, for example, *to give* and *to give out*, *to go back* and *to go back on*, *to butt* and *to butt in*, *to show* and *to show up*, *to pass* and *to pass out*, *to call* and *to call down*, *to try* and *to try out*. *To check* has bred a whole series, *e.g.*, *to check up*, *to check in*, *to check with* and *to check over*. Sometimes the addition seems only rhetorical and even irrational, as between *to lose* and *to lose out* (1869), and many of the resultant forms strike an Englishman as redundant. *Hurry up*, in the imperative, is common in England, but *to hurry up* in the indicative is used less than the simple *to hurry*. *Brush your hat off* would seem American there, and so would *to beat up*, *to try out*, *to start off* and *to stay put*. But such forms are almost innumerable in this country. Characteristic American verb phrases often embody bold and picturesque metaphors, *e.g.*, *to turn up missing*, *to shoot the chutes*, *to chew the rag*, *to kick in* and *to saw wood*. And some of the simple verbs show equally bold and picturesque transfers of meaning, *e.g.*, *to fire* (in the sense of to dismiss), *to can* (in the same sense), *to star* and *to neck*.

New verb phrases of a more elaborate sort are coming in all the time, *e.g.*, *to go Hollywood*,[3] *to bottom out*, *to pull a fast one*, *to pitch woo* (to make love) and *to eat a little higher on the hog*. *To go haywire*, familiar to every American, is not listed before 1929, but it is much older. Stewart H. Holbrook asserts that it originated in Maine logging camps, where old haywire was used for all kinds of crude repairs.[4] But no one who has ever opened a bale of hay with a hatchet, and had the leaping wire whirl about him and its sharp ends poniard him, will ever have any doubt as to how *to go haywire* originated. *To faze* also deserves attention from philologians. In the sense of to put to flight it is very old in English, but in the sense of to disconcert it seems to be American. It is spelled variously, *e.g.*, *faze*, *faeze*, *feaze*, *phase* and even *pheeze* and *pheese*. Thornton traces it, in its usual American sense, to 1843, and the DAE to 1830. In those early days it had a corresponding noun, signifying perturbation, traced by the DAE to 1647. It is now obsolete. But the verb *to faze*, though seldom used in England, is very familiar in the United States. *To interview* is unquestionably an Americanism. The first example listed is from *The Nation* (New York) of January 28, 1869, and the quotation is: "*Interviewing* is confined to American journalism." The first example of the noun is from the same issue. There is a newspaper tradition that the *interview* was invented by James Redpath, a Scotsman who followed Sherman's and Thomas's armies for the New York *Tribune* during the latter part of the Civil War.

---

[3] Neologisms, by Dwight L. Bolinger, *AS*, Vol. XVI, Feb. 1941, p. 66.

[4] Holy Old Mackinaw; New York, 1938, p. 49.

Verbs produced by back formation are usually challenged by high-octane purists, and sometimes denounced with great bitterness: as a result many linger in the Alsatia of slang. But others such as *to commute* have won their way into decorous American usage. The DAE traces *to commute* to 1865, the date, also, for its first example of *commuter*. *To enthuse* was first used in 1827 by a young Scot not long in this country. For years it was derided as fit only for bad newspaper reporters, worse politicians and other such *Simiidae*, but in recent years it has gathered respectability.[5] At the start it was a transitive verb only, but it began to be used as an intransitive in the 70s. By 1929, J. Y. T. Greig was listing it as an Americanism that had forced its way into English,[6] and by 1944 John B. Opdycke was reporting that, though still "a low colloquialism," it was prevailing "in spite of all efforts made by grammarians and lexicographers to discourage its use." [7]

Various other American verbs of the same non-Euclidean sort are still on probation, *e.g., to razz* (from raspberry), *to perc* (to make coffee in a percolator), *to reune, to housekeep, to orate, to elocute, to bach* (*i.e.,* to live in bachelor quarters) and *to emote;* and yet others remain on the level of conscious humor, *e.g., to jan* (from *janitor*) and *to chauf* (from *chauffeur*). "There is a much greater percentage of humorous shortenings among verbs," says Elizabeth Wittman, "than among other parts of speech. Especially is this true of verbs shortened from nouns and adjectives by subtracting what looks like a derivative suffix, *e.g., -er, -or, -ing, -ent* from nouns, or *-y* from adjectives. Many clipped verbs have noun parallels, while some are simply clipped nouns used as verbs." [8] Of these are *to stenog,*[9] *to chiropract, to taxpay, to liase,*[1] *to ghost-write, to baby-sit, to brainwash, to bookkeep, to collab* and *to best-sell.*[2] Some verbs of this class are already of respectable antiquity. The first example of *to jell* yet found comes from Louisa M. Alcott's "Little Women" (1869), and the DA traces *to resolute* to 1860, *to ush* to 1890, *to bootleg* to 1906. The

---

[5] *PMLA,* Vol. LIX, Mar. 1944, p. 91. [When the label *colloq.* was removed from *enthuse* in Webster 1961, many of the aesthetic gentry shook; it was the target of special fulminations in The String Untuned, a long diatribe by Dwight MacDonald in *The New Yorker,* Mar. 10, 1962, pp. 130–60.]

[6] Breaking Priscian's Head; New York, 1929, p. 80.

[7] Say What You Mean; New York, 1944, p. 230. [In contrast to the pother over *to enthuse, to automate,* from *automation,* has won acceptance without the quiver of an eyelash.]

[8] Clipped Words, *DN,* Vol. IV, Pt. II, 1914, p. 137.

[9] O. Henry, Springtime à la Carte, in The Four Million; New York, 1906.

[1] This lovely verb may be English. *American Notes and Queries,* Vol. I, Dec. 1941, p. 141, reports its appearance in a Home Guard instruction sheet. But Paul W. Kesten, of the Columbia Broadcasting System, says that it is also used in the American Army.

[2] [See How We Noun-Incorporate in English, by Robert A. Hall, Jr., *AS,* Vol. XXXI, May 1956, pp. 83–8. In *AS,* Vol. XXX, Feb. 1955, pp. 72–3, Mamie Meredith reports a cluster of verbs in *-hop,* with derivative nouns in *-er* and *-ing, e.g., to plane-hop, to mail-hop, booth-hopper, castle-hopping, party-hopping.*]

noble verb *to combust* apparently originated in Bloomington, Ill., where the first oil-burning heating plants for private houses were made. It is universally used by the workmen engaged in the industry. "To properly *combust* the oil means to so shatter it into minute particles as to achieve complete burning." [3] Thus *to combust* may owe almost as much to *to bust* as to *combustion*.

The American fondness for shortened forms is shown by the prevalence of transferred verbs of the *to sleep* class, as in "A Pullman sleeper *sleeps* forty passengers." Such forms are by no means rare in Standard English, *e.g.*, "He *walked* his horse," traced by the OED to the Fifteenth Century; but in late years the chief reservoir of new ones has been the United States. They serve a real need, for without them the only recourse is to long and sometimes unclear circumlocutions. Bartlett, in his first edition of 1848, recorded of a landlady that "she could *eat* fifty people in her house, although she could not *sleep* half that number." *To meal* and *to room* have likewise been noted. [4] *To fly* (in the sense of to convey by aircraft) is standard American. *To subsist* is apparently official in the Navy. [5] *To go* has arisen by analogy with *to stop*, as in "We'll see traffic cops *stopping* and *going* the entrants." [6] The medical men seem to have not only adopted *to sleep*, [7] but also to have invented a verb *to belch;* and every parent *burps* his babies after bottles. So far, however, no saloon or night club has been recorded as *drinking* so many clients an evening. Analogous forms are in common use among American farmers, *e.g.*, *to barn*, in the sense of to drive cattle to a barn, *to grain*, in the sense of to feed them with grain, and *to bug*, in the sense of to spray potatoes with insecticides; and in *to dessert*, in the sense of to serve a dessert. [8]

Also there are the verbs *to sell*, meaning to snare a customer, and by extension, to propagate an idea; and *to shave* (to get a shave) as in "I *shave* at the Terminal barbershop." The movement toward simplicity is also responsible for the triumph of *to graduate* over *to be graduated* and of *to operate* over *to operate on*. The latter is denounced regularly by the *Journal of the American Medical Association* and other medical authorities, but it makes steady headway. [9]

Verbs like *to fire*, *to star* and *to neck* are heavily patronized by headline writers, partly because they are pungent but mainly because they are short.

---

[3] Private communication from R. P. Whitmer of the American Foundry and Furnace Co.

[4] *AS*, Vol. III, June 1928, p. 414; Oct. 1927, p. 25.

[5] Rear Admiral W. A. Moffett in Flying Boats and Seaplanes, *Liberty*, Aug. 18, 1926, p. 46.

[6] Baltimore *Post*, Sept. 1, 1925.

[7] *Jour. AMA*, May 8, 1943.

[8] Personal communication from Dayton Stoddart.

[9] See The Art and Practise of Medical Writing, by George H. Simmons and Morris Fishbein; Chicago, 1925, p. 43.

The newspaper copy desk favors verbs of three letters, *e.g., to cut, to bar, to aid, to nab, to map* and *to rap.* It has revived an archaism, *to ire,* and has produced *to null* from *to nullify* by clipping. *Gassed* is always used in place of *asphyxiated. To admit* is used as a substitute for *to confess, to acknowledge, to concede, to acquiesce* and *to recognize. To back* is to give any sort of support or recognition, *to ban* indicates any sort of prohibition and *to hit* connotes every variety of criticism. A few headline verbs are of five letters, *e.g., to claim, to blame, to quash, to stage* and *to score,* and some are even of six, *e.g., to attack, to debunk* and *to battle,* but that is only because the copy-desk Websters have not, as yet, discovered shorter synonyms. Their preference, after their three-letter favorites, runs to four-letter verbs, *e.g., to best, to cite, to curb, to loom, to lure, to oust, to push, to bare, to raze* and *to spur,* and among them, as among the nouns, their first choice is for those of onomatopoeic tang.

4: OTHER PARTS OF SPEECH

The difference between adjective and adverb in English has always been a tenuous one. Most of the adverbs in Old English were dative-case adjectives ending in *-e;* even our adverbs in *-ly* go back to an Old English *-lice,* originally a dative of an adjective-making suffix *-lic,* which has given us the *-ly* terminal in such familiar adjectives as *ugly, friendly* and *lovely.* As case endings and other inflections faded during the Middle English period, adverbs were left without a distinguishing mark, except that most words in *-ly* were adverbs. From Early Modern English on, *-ly* has been freely tacked on to adjectives to provide new adverbs. But many common adverbs without the *-ly* remain, sometimes alongside words with the suffix, as *quick* and *quickly, slow* and *slowly.* When the situation permits, American common sense votes for the shorter form, so that *drive slow,* for instance, has survived a million onslaughts from the schoolma'ams. In the common speech *in bad* begins to take on the dignity of a national idiom, and *sure* has become respectable. When, in World War I, the Tank Corps chose "Treat 'em *rough*" as its motto, no one thought to raise a grammatical objection, and the clipped adverb was displayed on posters in every town in the country, with the imprimatur of the national government.

Most of the processes that result in new nouns and verbs are also used to produce new adjectives. There are adjectives made of nouns unchanged, *e.g., bum* and *bogus,* or from verbs or verb phrases, *e.g., sit-down* (1936), *gimme* (as *gimme farmer*), *back-to-work* and *cash-and-carry* (1921; but *cash-on-the-nail-chaps* had appeared in 1892), or from pronouns, *e.g., she-gal* and *he-man* (1832; *he-man* itself was used adjectivally by 1925), or by telescoping, *e.g.*, *radiopaque* (*radiation* and *opaque*) and *sophomoronic*, or by the use of prefixes and suffixes, *e.g.*, *Pan-American*, *Pan-Hellenic*, *super-colossal*, *underbibled*, *non-skid*, *food-conscious*, *plushy* and *bosom-atic*.[1] Of these devices, the last is the most productive. The *super-* prefix, of course, is old in English (the OED traces it to the middle of the Fifteenth Century, and John Donne used *super-supreme* and *super-sovrain*), but the movie press agents have given it a new lease on life, and their inventions include not only *super-colossal* but also *super-modern*, *super-maximum*, *super-superlative*, *super-ultra* and even *super-super*,[2] [although the DA fails to recognize adjectives in *super-*]. Whatever uplifter launched the vogue for *-minded* and *-conscious* succeeded beyond most ravishers of the language. *Social-minded*, the first of the class to make its way, was early followed by *civic-minded* and has since produced a long progeny, *e.g.*, *hospital-minded*, *air-minded*, not to forget a child by the left hand, *presence-of-minded*.[3] The related *-conscious* has been even more fecund, *e.g.*, *America-conscious*, *constitution-conscious* and *cosmetic-conscious*; moreover, it has had offspring in England, *e.g.*, *herb-conscious*.[4] Sir Oswald Mosley, boss of the English Fascists, launched such forms as *bamboozle-conscious* and *hocus-pocus-minded*.[5] Whenever a new suffix appears in the United States, it is put to use. An example is *-genic*, apparently borrowed from the *pathogenic* of the medical men; it has yielded *photogenic*, *radiogenic*, *telegenic* and *cosmogenic*.[6] Another is *-phobia*, borrowed from the psychiatrists, and made to do heavy duty in a multitude of nouns designating violent aversions, *e.g.*, *radiophobia*, *Negrophobia*, *ergophobia* and *sexophobia*, all of them with attendant adjectives in *-phobic*. The DA lacks them all, but includes *Negrophilism* and *Negrophile*. A third is *-worthy*, old in English but recently revived in this great Republic, as in *newsworthy*, *earworthy* and *prizeworthy*. [The DA, however, fails to list *-worthy*, *-conscious* or *-minded* among the adjective-forming suffixes.] A fourth is *-matic* (from *automatic*), as in *traffomatic* and *adjustomatic*.[7]

---

[1] Used by Rudolph Justice Watson, in the *Capitol Daily* (Washington), to describe the dames of the DAR, and noted in New Words for Old, Baltimore *Evening Sun*, June 18, 1938.

[2] [The DA also ignores compounds in *ultra-*, a favorite before the Civil War (Mamie Meredith, *Super-power*, *AS*, Vol. XIV, Feb. 1939, p. 79). Today it is usually associated with scientific terminology, as in *ultra-violet* and *ultra-high-frequency* television reception (often abbreviated to UHF), but it may be applied to shades of opinion, as *ultra-New Deal* or *ultra-conservative*. In 1932, in a heresy hunt at Furman University, Baptist fundamentalists charged a professor of Greek with *ultra-modernism*—the greatest tribute to the classics in the Twentieth Century.]

[3] Sired by Westbrook Pegler, and recorded in New Words for Old, Baltimore *Evening Sun*, July 17, 1939.

[4] London *Morning Post*, Feb. 14, 1936.

[5] *Action*, Aug. 19, 1939.

[6] *AS*, Vol. XV, Dec. 1940, p. 360.

[7] [In the early days of automatic transmissions for automobiles, such trade designations as *Hydramatic*, *Traffomatic* and *Ford-o-matic* flourished, but their use among the laity waned as the novelty wore off. More recently, in the United

A fifth is *-ific* as in *flavorific*. All the traditional adjectival suffixes are used for new words, e.g., *-y*, as in *plushy*, *ritzy* (1924) and *corny* (1933), to which may be added *nifty* (1865) and *iffy*. But American word makers show little liking for the English *-ish*, as in *fairish*, *liverish* and *biggish*; *-oid*, certainly full of possibilities in a country swarming with imitations, is not in American use, and the excellent English *bungaloid* has not been borrowed.[8] A few miscellaneous marvels are *slap-happy*,[9] *alco-joyed*, *fishful* (favorable to fishing), *cosmeticulous*, *glitterous*, *sexotic*,[1] *snazzy* (elegant), *must* (as an adjective), *stumble-bum*, *teen-age*, *hard-boiled*,[2] *comedic*[3] and *untouristed*.

Adverbs, of course, are made with the same freedom, e.g., *ritzily*, *productionally* and *classically*. [To make adverbs directly from nouns, the advertising wordsmiths have revived the suffix *-wise*, which in earlier times had given such familiar forms as *crosswise* and *lengthwise*.[4] Beginning about 1950 such forms as *budgetwise*, *housewise*, *moneywise* and *savingswise*

States exhibit at the 1962 London Food Fair, a supermarket was set up in which the shoppers could pick from hundreds of items in a self-feeding dispensing device called a *Food-o-Matic*. The New York Times, Aug. 8, 1962. The suffix *-ic* is hard worked by linguists, as by other scientists, in such adjectives as *phonemic*, *graphemic*, *morphemic*, *tagmemic*, with the underlying concepts of the *phoneme* and the like, and such branches of study as *phonemics* and *morphemics*. From *phonemic* and *phonetic* Kenneth L. Pike has coined the two adjectives *emic* and *etic*, referring to significant and non-significant details of behavior. Some of the more waggish brethren apply these suffixes to concepts or theories of their colleagues: in the 1930s Bernard Bloch invented (or at least popularized) *Joneme* to indicate the theory of the phoneme held by Daniel Jones, of University College, London; about 1950 E. Bagby Atwood coined *Trageremics* to designate phonemics according to the specifications of George L. Trager; most recently has appeared *Chomskemics*, honoring the doctrines of Noam L. Chomsky, of the Massachusetts Institute of Technology.]

[8] The OED Supplement's first example is from Dean W. R. Inge, writing in the London *Daily Express*, Nov. 22, 1927.

[9] Defined as "a synonym of *punch-drunk*" by Dwight L. Bolinger in *AS*, Vol. XIX, Feb. 1944, p. 60. He lists *sap-happy*, *scrap-happy*, *snap-happy* and *tap-*

happy as congeners. [Other scouts have found *sand-happy* and *bomb-happy*; an inventory, by no means exhaustive, is found in Among the New Words, *AS*, Vol. XXII, Oct. 1947, pp. 226-31.]

[1] Program of the National Theatre, Detroit, for the week of Aug. 9, 1940, p. 1. [*Sexciting* and the noun *sexcellency* are reported by Lillian Hornstein in *AS*, Vol. XXVII, Feb. 1952, p. 71. In art publications *exotic* is often used as a euphemism for *erotic*.]

[2] *Hard-boiled* is first cited from one of Mark Twain's speeches, 1886, in the sense of pedantic, but it did not have much popularity until T. A. Dorgan began using it in the noun form *hard-boiled egg*, in 1915. The vogue of the adjective followed during World War I. See The Origin of *Hard-Boiled*, by Peter Tamony, *AS*, Vol. XII, Dec. 1937, pp. 258-61.

[3] ["The wedding, which took place at Caxton Hall, was *comedic*." From The Screen's Fastest Rising Star, Horst Buchholz, *Parade*, June 24, 1962, p. 10. In *AS*, Vol. XXVI, Dec. 1959, p. 310, C. Merton Babcock reported *yesterlayed* eggs from Michigan.]

[4] [Henry Burton, A Plea to an Appeale: Traversed *Dialogue Wise*, 1626; from John Milton's Areopagitica: "Sometimes five imprimaturs are seen together, *dialogue wise*, in the piazza of one title-page." *Seneca-wise* is reported as occurring in an English literary text of 1920, by Harry T. Antrim, *AS*, Vol. XXXVII, May 1962, p. 159.]

began to proliferate. Most of these first inventions, of course, were playing on the resemblance between the suffix and the adjective *wise*. But the practice quickly spread from the admen to the bureaucrats and the educationists and soon yielded *curriculumwise, educationwise, officerwise, personnelwise* and *weatherwise*. Even the parsons have succumbed, with *sermonwise*.[5]

[Parallel with the proliferation of *-wise* has come the establishment of *-type* as an adjective maker, from an earlier *type of*. Originally it seems to have been added chiefly to nouns, as *a Hitler-type referendum* or *a New Deal-type administration*, but it was soon affixed to extant adjectives, giving such beauties as *a nice-type girl, a hard-type nose cone* and *a conversational-type dinner*.[6]]

The schoolma'am continues the heroic task of trying to make her charges grasp the difference between *who* and *whom*, but the speechways of the American public are against her. Nor do they respond to her efforts to promote *it is I*. To cite a few more details, American, in its spoken form, tends to obliterate the distinction between nearly related adjectives, *e.g.*, *healthful* and *healthy*, so that the phrase *healthy respect* is quite respectable. And to substitute *as though* for *as if*. And to dally lavishly with a supererogatory *but*, as in "I have no doubt *but* that." And to intrude *of* between *question* and *whether*. The last, denounced by Edward S. Gould so long ago as 1867,[7] was used often by the highly correct Henry Cabot Lodge I,[8] and has been written into a decision of the Supreme Court of the United States by Charles Evans Hughes.[9] [Such forms as *downwards, forwards* and *somewheres* have long been labeled Americanisms. As adverbs, par-

---

[5] ["The two services will be identical *sermon-wise*," reads a bulletin of St. Paul's Episcopal Church, Cleveland Heights, Ohio, June 1957. The popularity of *-wise* is noted in *AS*, Vol. XXVIII, Feb. 1953, p. 65. Although *-wise* has been used sporadically as an adverb maker throughout modern English, it was not active enough as a suffix in American to be noted in either of Mencken's Supplements. By 1952, however, it was sufficiently epidemic for Thomas Pyles to comment on it in his Words and Ways in American English. The earliest example I have personally found of its postwar proliferation is on p. 56 of Noah's Ark, New England Yankees and the Endless Quest, by Robert Keith Leavitt (Springfield, Mass., 1947), marking the hundredth anniversary of the first Webster dictionary under the Merriam imprint: "And *saleswise*, the

Webster dictionary gained out of all proportion to its rival." However, as Philip Gove, editor in chief of Webster 1961, pointed out in a letter of Mar. 6, 1963, occasional new coinages in *-wise* had been observed over the preceding decade; the recent vogue came from its use in advertising.]

[6] [Citations of *-type* adjectives, beginning with 1945, are found in *AS*, Vol. XXIII, Apr. 1948, p. 150; see also Esther K. Sheldon, A Very *Nice-Type* Girl, *AS*, Oct.–Dec. 1948, pp. 251–6, and Donald A. Bird, *Type* Compounds, *CE*, Vol. XVII, Dec. 1955, p. 179.]

[7] Good English, p. 59.

[8] For example, see the *Congressional Record*, May 14, 1918, p. 6996.

[9] *Principality of Monaco* v. *State of Mississippi*, May 21, 1934 (54 S. Ct. R., 748 note).

ticularly at the end of a clause, the first two are as respectable as *downward* and *forward,* though the latter forms alone are used as adjectives. The preposition is either *toward* or *towards,* occurring in both one-syllable and two-syllable pronunciations. *Anywheres, somewheres* and the like still linger below the salt, but are heard on every street corner and in many classrooms.[1] *Towards,* which drew White's fire in the late 1860s, is the prevailing form even in England.] *Anyways,* found in the Book of Common Prayer (1560), has perhaps been preserved by analogy with *sideways.* Henry James attacked "such forms of impunity [*sic*] as *somewheres else* and *nowheres else, a good ways on* and *a good ways off*" as "vulgarisms with which a great deal of general credit for what we good-naturedly call 'refinement' appears so able to coexist," [2] but his shrill complaint seems to have fallen upon sound-proofed ears. Perhaps he would have been even more upset, on his unhappy American tour, if he had encountered *no place* and *some place,* which occur alongside *nowheres* and *somewheres* in the common speech, and occasionally supplant *nowhere* and *somewhere* at the high table.

5: FOREIGN INFLUENCES TODAY

The great flow of European immigration to the United States, perhaps the most significant event in human history since the close of the Middle Ages, began with the Irish potato famine of 1847 and the German political disturbances of the two years following. Between 1776 and 1846, a stretch of more than two generations, less than 1,600,000 immigrants from overseas had come into the country, though its population had increased nearly sevenfold, from 3,000,000 to 20,000,000. But after 1850 the movement began in earnest, and thereafter it continued for sixty-five years, with only two considerable interruptions, the first caused by the Civil War and the second by the Depression of 1893. In each of the years 1905, 1906, 1907, 1910, 1913 and 1914 more than a million immigrants were admitted, and by 1927 the total number arriving since 1820 reached 37,000,000. In 1930 there were 13,366,407 white persons in the United States who had been born in foreign countries, 16,999,221 whose parents were both foreign-born, and 8,361,965 of mixed parentage—a total of 38,727,593, or more than 35% of the whole white population. In addition, there were perhaps 200,000 Negroes, Chinese, Japanese, Filipinos, Hindus and Koreans who

---

[1] LA investigations show them occurring in cultivated speech in almost every area.

[2] The Question of Our Speech; Boston, 1905, p. 30. See also *DN,* Vol. IV, Pt. I, 1913, p. 48.

were either foreign-born or the children of foreign-born parents, and nearly 1,500,000 Mexicans.[3]

With the passage of the Immigration Act of 1921 the flow of immigrants was considerably reduced, and when the Immigration Act of 1924 followed, it was virtually halted. Both acts were qualitative as well as quantitative in purpose and effect.[4] It was generally felt that immigrants from Eastern and Southern Europe were harder to assimilate than those from the West and North, and that the country already had enough of them, and to spare. So the number of Italians admitted annually was reduced from 42,128 under the Act of 1921 to 3,845 under the Act of 1924, and the number of Poles from 30,977 to 5,977. A certain amount of anti-Semitism also got into the matter, for a large proportion of the immigrants from Eastern Europe were Jews. The two acts worked so well that by 1930 the year's immigration was reduced to 241,700 and by 1933 to 23,068. Indeed, since 1930 the number of immigrants coming in annually has been more than

---

[3] [According to the 1960 census, there were 9,738,143 foreign-born persons residing in the United States. Of those who specified their mother tongue, a little over 9 million, 1,852,992 spoke English. Other languages were listed in the following order:

Norwegian	140,774
Swedish	211,597
Danish	79,619
Dutch	123,613
French	330,220
German	1,278,772
Polish	581,936
Czech	91,711
Slovak	125,000
Hungarian	213,114
Serbo-Croatian	88,096
Slovenian	32,108
Russian	276,834
Ukrainian	106,974
Lithuanian	99,043
Finnish	53,168
Romanian	38,019
Yiddish	503,605
Greek	173,031
Italian	1,226,141
Spanish	766,961
Portuguese	87,109
Japanese	95,027
Chinese	89,609
Arabic	49,908

These figures are far from satisfactory. No matter how many languages a person speaks natively—and polyglottism is common in Switzerland, Finland and many of the states of Central and Southern Europe—he is recorded as speaking only one. Moreover, the figures ignore the native-born who are native speakers of something other than English, so that the figure for speakers of French in Louisiana is the incredibly low 1,642. Puerto Ricans also seem to qualify as native-born, so that only 87,776 speakers of Spanish are recorded for New York state.]

[4] The first limited the annual immigration from each country to 3% of "the number of foreign-born persons of such nationality resident in the United States" in 1910, and the second reduced the quota to 2% and changed the year to 1890. The aim of the latter amendment was to diminish the relative number of immigrants from Eastern and Southern Europe. Down to 1890 the overwhelming majority of entrants had come from Great Britain, Germany and the Scandinavian countries, but after that year those from Italy, Russia and the Austrian dominions had taken the lead. In 1914, for example, 383,-738 came in from Italy, 255,660 from Russia and 278,152 from Austria-Hungary, whereas the arrivals from Germany were but 35,734, from Scandinavia 29,391, and from the United Kingdom and Ireland 73,417.

once surpassed by the number of former immigrants returning home, and from 1930 to 1935 the total excess amounted to 229,363.[5]

[Toward the end of the 1930s a new wave of immigration began to strain at the quotas: religious or ethnic minorities made the scapegoats of the new messianic creeds of Russia, Italy and Germany, or individuals whose economic, cultural or political positions in the previous regimes made their existence somewhat less than tolerable in Utopia. Like other immigrants after 1900, most of these *displaced persons* (a do-gooder euphemism), or simply *DP's,* hail from Southern and Eastern Europe, with Hungarians, Lithuanians and Poles making up the majority. Since the present demand for American visas exceeds the legal quotas from these countries, sometimes for as much as the next thirty years, and since most of those seeking to migrate have relatives already in this country, Congress is understandably under constant pressure to enlarge the quotas. Some concessions have been made, but far less than philanthropy would urge. Other new Americans are the brides and children of American servicemen stationed abroad during World War II and afterwards. The official policy of the Army and the civilian authorities is to discourage such unions, but biological urges, as usual, are more powerful than bureaucratic restraint, and these marriages have turned out at least as well, on the whole, as those the servicemen might have made at home. To the consternation of the *Übermenschlein* of the KKK, some of the most successful have been those with Japanese girls. Immigration now averages a little over 250,000 a year.]

Of the 13,366,407 foreign-born whites in the country in 1930, 13,216,928 were ten years old or older, and of this number only 3,907,021 spoke English as their native language. Nevertheless, all save 869,865 of the remainder managed to convince the census enumerators that they had acquired a workable command of the language. The immigrants of the older immigrations had naturally made the most progress. The Scandinavians, about half of whom arrived before 1900, topped the list, with hardly more than 2% of them unable to speak English, and less than 1% of the males. Next came the Germans: 58.3% of them arrived before 1900, and all save 2.9% (1.8% of males) could speak English. The Poles, Russians, Italians, Greeks and Czechs, and the Baltic and Balkan peoples, most of whom came in between 1900 and 1914, fell much behind. Of the Poles, for example, 12.8% were still unable to speak English in 1930 (7.7% of males and 18.7% of females), and of Italians 15.7% (8.9% and 25.1%). Here something more than mere duration of residence in the country seems to have had

---

[5] *Congressional Record,* Feb. 19, 1935, p. 2290. [See also George W. Pearson, The M Factor in American History,

American Quarterly, Vol. XIV, Summer 1962, pp. 275–89.]

some influence, for though 12.7% of the Germans came in after 1925, only 2.9% were without English in 1930. These late-coming Germans were, on the whole, much better educated than the Eastern and Southern Europeans who arrived at the same time, and large numbers of them had probably received some instruction in English at home. Moreover, they dispersed themselves throughout the country, and did not collect in ghettoes, like a majority of the Italians, Slavs and Jews. Of the 1,808,289 Italians here in 1930, more than 1,500,000 were crowded into relatively few cities, and of the 1,222,658 Jews who reported Yiddish as their native language, all save 19,000 were living in cities.[6] [By and large, these latest immigrants have given far fewer words to the American vocabulary than their numbers might suggest, possibly because urban contacts between ethnic groups are less persistent than rural, possibly because these recent groups were largely peasants, with little literacy and less regard for their cultural traditions. At all events, in cities such as Cleveland and Chicago it is a rare second-generation American of Polish, Hungarian or Croatian stock who even pretends to know his parents' native language. In rural and small town settlements, of course, the foreign influence lasts longer.] How long may be observed in the so-called Pennsylvania-Dutch region of Pennsylvania, where a dialect of German is still a living speech after more than 250 years of settlement and the local dialect of English shows plain traces of it, both in vocabulary and in pronunciation. In the same way, the everyday speech of lower Louisiana is full of French terms not in use elsewhere, *e.g., brioche, lagniappe, jambalaya* and *bogue*. In Minnesota and adjacent states many Swedish and Dano-Norwegian terms are in common use. From Swedish come *lutfisk* (a fish delicacy), *lingnon* (a berry), *lefse* (a potato pancake) and *lag* (an association of Swedes from the same province); from Dano-Norwegian, *gubbefest* (a men's party) and *lefsi* (a pastry served with coffee). There is also a considerable borrowing of Scandinavian idioms, as in *to cook coffee* (*koka kaffe*), *forth and back* (*fram och tillbaka*) and *to hold with* (*håller med*) in place of *to agree with*.

In the same way Czech words have got into American, and Czech idioms have influenced usage in the regions in which Bohemian immigrants are numerous. One of the former, listed in Webster 1961, is *kolacky* or *kolach*, defined as "a bun made of rich sweet yeast-leavened dough filled with jam or fruit pulp." *Kolach* is the Czech *koláč*, with its accent lost in the melting pot. Other Czech loan words and phrases in local use are *rohlík* (a roll

---

[6] [In 1960, of the 503,605 reported foreign-born native speakers of Yiddish, 497,270 were urban residents.] These figures, of course, do not show the total number of foreign-born Jews, since (as the Census Bureau observed in connection with the 1930 figures) many report German, Russian or other languages as their mother tongue.

brushed with egg yolk, salted and sometimes sprinkled with caraway or poppy seeds), *povidla* (a prune marmalade), *buchta* (a coffeecake), *počkej* (wait, hold on), *sokòl* (literally, a falcon, but used to designate an athletic association), and *to soč* (from the verb *sočiti*, meaning to scold or grumble). *Pantáta* (literally, Mr. Father, and signifying a father-in-law) was apparently once in use in New York to designate a corrupt police captain, but it has gone out.[7] In Bristol County, Mass., where there are many Portuguese immigrants, a number of Portuguese loan words are encountered, e.g., *cabeca* (head), *lingreese* (Port. *linguica*, a sausage) and *jick* or *jickie* (Englishman). *Cuspidor* comes ultimately from the Portuguese verb *cuspir* (to spit). The OED's first example of its use (spelled *cuspadora*) is taken from Forrest's "Voyage to New Guinea," dated 1779, but after that there is no quotation until 1871, at which time an Englishman named Heath, resident in New York City, took out a patent for "an improvement in *cuspidores*." The word seems to have been in general use in the United States before 1870.

Since the Civil War the chief contribution of German has been the domestication of the suffix *-fest*. It came in with *sängerfest* and *turnfest* in the early 1850s, but the manufacture of American analogues did not begin until 1900 or thereabout. In 1916 Louise Pound rounded up twenty-three specimens from the current vocabulary: *Ananiasfest*, *batfest* (a baseball game), *blarneyfest*, *bloodfest* (war), *crabfest*,[8] *eatfest*, *gabfest*, *gabblefest*, *gadfest*, *grubfest*, *jawfest*, *olymphest*,[9] *singfest*, *slugfest* (a prize fight), *smilefest*, *smokefest*, *sobfest*, *songfest*, *spooffest*, *stuntfest*, *swatfest* (a baseball game marked by many hits), *talkfest* and *walkfest*.[1] Many others appeared during the years following, e.g., *hoochfest*, *lovefest*, *bullfest*, *boozefest*, *bookfest* and *applefest*,[2] and in 1918 Miss Pound herself added *chatfest*, *egofest*, *funfest* and *gossipfest*. Since then linguistic explorers have

[7] See Czech Influence upon the American Vocabulary, by Monsignor J. B. Dudek, *Czecho-Slovak Student Life* (Lisle, Ill.), June 1928; [also Selected Problems of Bilingualism Among Immigrant Slovaks, by Goldie Piroch Meyerstein, diss. (microfilm), U. of Michigan, 1959. For other groups see The Norwegian Language in America: a Study in Bilingual Behavior, by Einar Haugen, 2 vols., Philadelphia, 1953; Portuguese-American Speech, by Leo Pap, New York, 1949. General problems of bilingualism are surveyed in Languages in Contact: Findings and Problems, by Uriel Weinreich, *Publications of the Linguistic Circle of New York*, No. 1, New York, 1953, and in two publications by Haugen: Problems of Bilingualism, *Lingua*, Vol. II, Aug. 1950, pp. 271–90, and Bilingualism in the Americas: a Bibliography and Research Guide, *PADS*, No. 26, Nov. 1956.]

[8] But in Maryland *crabfeast* has never yielded to *crabfest*.

[9] Coined at Hays, Kan., to designate a series of contests at the normal school there, not only in athletics but also in spelling, cookery, drawing, music and handicrafts.

[1] Domestication of the suffix *-fest*, *DN*, Vol. IV, Pt. V, 1916, pp. 353-4.

[2] Vogue Affixes in Present-Day Word Coinage, *DN*, Vol. V, Pt. I, 1918, p. 11.

unearthed *beerfest, hymnfest, gagfest, hamfest,*[3] *suitfest, bundesfest, blab-fest, chawfest, chinfest, gasfest, hashfest, pipefest, joshfest, laughfest, nude-fest, stripfest, pepfest, folkfest* and *henfest.* On April 9, 1927, the Pittsburgh *Courier* announced that the Northside Community Club of that city, a colored organization, was about to hold a *sangerfest* (no umlaut). The Spanish *fiesta* seems to have reinforced *fest* in the West, and *funfesta, jubilesta* and *hallowesta* have been reported.[4] The DA traces *sängerfest* to 1865, and *schützenfest* (an entertainment, usually a picnic, at which rifle-shooting competitions were held), to 1870. Webster 1961 lists both, along with *sängerbund.* There was a fashion about 1900 for words in *-bund,* and *moneybund* and *plunderbund* were in wide use. The pejorative significance of the suffix was accentuated when the FBI began running down *bundists, i.e.,* members of the German-American *Bund,* a Nazi-oriented organization. The latest word in *-bund* seems to be *smearbund,* signifying a band of de-famers. Other German suffixes that have produced progeny in American are *-lust, -heimer* and *-burger.* The first was introduced by *wanderlust,* which was in wide use for some years, and produced the derivatives *wan-derluster* (Eng. *rambler*), *wanderlust club* (Eng. *rambling club*), *wander-lusting* and *wanderlustful.* In 1933 the Hon. Louis Ludlow, a member of Congress from Indiana, launched *squanderlust* in a book, "America Go Bust," but it did not catch on. The suffix *-heimer* begat *wiseheimer* and various other terms. It was probably helped into American English by Yid-dish influence. Along with it came *-sky* or *-ski,* as in *allrightsky, buttinski* and *damfoolski,* but of these only *buttinski* shows any sign of surviving. All the American words in *-burger* appear to be derived from *hamburger.* In its early days in the United States the chopped beef now known as a *hamburger* was called a *hamburg steak,* and was served like any other steak, not in the form of a sandwich. The DAE traces *hamburg steak* to 1884 and it is probably older. By 1889 it had become *hamburger steak,* and soon afterward it degenerated from the estate of a steak to that of a sandwich and became a simple *hamburger.* It began to produce numerous offspring. As Arnold Williams says, "*-burger* has come to mean almost any meat or meat-substitute ground or chopped and, fried or grilled, made into sand-wiches."[5]

Williams lists *chickenburger, cheeseburger, clamburger, lamburger* (made of ground "lamb," and tasting, he notes, like ram), *rabbit burger, nut-burger, porkburger* and *wimpyburger.* He says:

---

[3] Defined by William White, in Radio Jargon, *Words,* Dec. 1941, p. 99, as "a convention of amateur radio broad-casters."

[4] *AS,* Vol. XIII, Apr. 1938, p. 157;

Dwight L. Bolinger, *Words,* Mar. 1940, p. 41.

[5] *Hamburger* Progeny, *AS,* Vol. XIV, Apr. 1939, p. 154.

Wimpyburger suggests to the student of etymology a clue to the popularity of *-burger* as a suffix. Popeye, the popular comic strip of the late Segar, though it cannot be credited with the popularity of the *hamburger* sandwich, did, in the character of Wimpy, endow hamburger with *mythos*. Like all of Segar's characters, Wimpy is an inveterate coiner of new words. Several years ago he created *goonburger*. More recently *demonburger* has appeared.

Among other concoctions reported are *beefburger* (1940), *kirschburger, shrimpburger, glutenburger, huskiburger, sausage burger, pickleburger, Meet-the-People-burger* (named after a musical comedy called "Meet the People"),[6] *tomatoburger, liverwurst burger* (rechristened *liver-sausage burger* by the austere sausage engineers of the Institute of American Meat Packers), *horsemeat burger, Mexiburger, chuckburger, dogburger, seaburger, fishburger* and *whinnyburger* (a euphemism for *horsemeat burger*).[7] [The ultimate horror, *Trumanburger*, coined during the dying days of meat rationing in 1946, consisted of mashed baked beans.[8]]

The DAE's first examples of *frankfurter* and *wienerwurst* are both dated 1899, but the two sausages were well known in the United States long before. The former is the variety commonly used in the hot dog; the latter is smaller. But the terms are frequently interchanged, even by Germans. Two clipped forms of *wienerwurst, wiener* and *wienie*, are in wide use. *Liver pudding*, corresponding to the German *Leberwurst*, may be an Americanism, though the DAE and DA do not list it, for it is not recorded by the OED either. In Nineteenth Century Baltimore *leberwurst, liverwurst, liver pudding* and *liver sausage* were used interchangeably. In 1930 Swift & Company began calling the sausage *braunschweiger*—the adjective often prefixed to *leberwurst* by the Germans, for the variety most esteemed in their homeland comes from Braunschweig (Brunswick). Swift has also reduced *frankfurter* to *frankfurt*, and put on the market a preparation of liver called *liver cheese*. Sometimes these German borrowings are sadly misspelled: *brownswoger, weanerwust* and even *wienna shitzel* (for *Wiener Schnitzel*).[9]

On the repeal of Prohibition, American legislators began to search for euphemisms for *saloon;* one of the words they hit upon was the German

---

[6] Among the New Words, *AS*, Vol. XVIII, Apr. 1943, p. 148.
[7] *AS*, Vol. XVIII, Oct. 1943, p. 237. [See also More *Burgers*, by Joseph Prescott, *AS*, Vol. XXIII, Feb. 1948, pp. 73–4; More and More *Burgers*, *AS*, Vol. XXV, Dec. 1950, pp. 315–16.]
[8] [Thomas Pyles, Words and Ways of American English; New York, 1952, p.

207. It should be noted that for a sandwich to be called a *-burger* it should be served in a bun, rather than between slices of bread.]
[9] This last appeared on a restaurant bill of fare in Reading, Pa., and may have been due to Pennsylvania-German influence.

Stube, signifying, alone, simply a room, but often combined with *Bier* (beer) or *Wein* (wine) in *Bierstube* or *Weinstube.* According to Sir William Craigie, *beer garden,* which came in about 1870, is "clearly from the German," *i.e.,* from *Biergarten. Living room* may have been influenced by the German *Wohnzimmer.* The OED cites a single use of it in England in 1825, but in the sense of "the room usually occupied during the day" it is called an Americanism in the Oxford Supplement, and assigned to 1867. F. L. Olmstead, however, had noted it as a Southern term in 1860.[1] *So long,* the phrase of parting, has been credited similarly to the German *so lange* (and also to the Yiddish *sholom*), but it is actually of English origin and does not appear to be an Americanism. In all probability *it listens well* was introduced by the German comedians who flourished before World War I. Like their Irish and Yiddish colleagues, they enriched the current slang with many fantastic locutions. The influence of Charles Godfrey Leland's "Hans Breitmann's Ballads" and other books also helped to familiarize Americans with many German and pseudo-German words and phrases. *Phooey,* which plainly comes from the German (and Yiddish) *pfui,* seems to have been popularized by Walter Winchell, *c.* 1930. During World War I an effort was made by super-patriots to drive all German loans from the American vocabulary. *Sauerkraut* became *liberty cabbage, hamburger steak* became *Salisbury steak, hamburger* became *liberty sandwich,* and a few extremists even changed *German measles* to *liberty measles.*[2] A similar movement got under way during World War II, but at the end of 1942 the Army's model menu still included spareribs and *sauerkraut.*[3] But attacks were made from time to time on *hamburger, kindergarten* and even *crème vichysoisse.* I also heard a suggestion that the reminder of things German, and hence abhorrent, in *Bismarck herring* be got rid of by substituting *Eisenhower herring.* After Pearl Harbor it was proposed in Washington that the name of the *Japanese* cherry trees around the Tidal Basin be changed to something less obscene, but nothing more seemly could be thought of, and such gestures were conveniently forgotten in the post-war reconciliation.

World War II, of course, introduced Americans to a great many new German terms, and a few of them, such as *snorkel* and *blitz,* promise to linger on to naturalization and even to produce derivatives,[4] but most of

---

[1] A Journey in the Back Country; London, 1860.

[2] In 1917 a theater manager in Cleveland complained to the United Booking Office of the Keith Circuit against a vaudevillian who used the word *Gesundheit* in his act. See Reporting the Acts, *Variety,* Jan. 12, 1944.

[3] *Consumer Reports,* Oct. 1942, p. 273. [Several Japanese restaurants, in New York City and elsewhere, became *Chinese,* or indefinitely *Oriental,* or simply advertised *chop suey.*]

[4] [*Snorkel* is applied to an underwater breathing apparatus for divers; the Chicago Fire Department uses it to designate a piece with an elevated pumping platform, for fighting fires in tall buildings. It is also applied to a patented type of fountain pen.]

them were also borrowed by the English, and hence do not concern us as Americanisms.

Two undoubted Americanisms that have puzzled etymologists may also be loans from the German: *to scram* and *hoodlum*. John T. Krumpelmann suggested that *hoodlum*, first recorded in the San Francisco area *c.* 1870, may come from a Bavarian dialect term, *hodalump*, of precisely the same meaning.[5] In the San Francisco of those days, he said, "the Germans constituted the largest foreign-language" group, and many of them were Bavarians. The theory that *to scram* may be of German origin was set forth by Dr. G. Kirchner, of Jena, who argued that it probably comes from "the German word *schrammen*, of exactly the same meaning." [6] Partridge suggests that it may come from a South Cheshire dialect word, *to scramble*, meaning "to get away with, with a notion of fear or stealth," but he admits that the English were unaware of it until American movies introduced it, *c.* 1930. *Yes man* also may be of German origin. The equivalent German *Jaherr* is defined by Cassell's New German and English Dictionary as "a compliant person, one unable to say no," and the aforesaid Krumpelmann has shown that it was used in that sense by a German writer on America, Charles Sealsfield (Karl Postl), in "Die Vereinigten Staaten von Nordamerika" (1877).[7]

A number of German terms are still in common use among Americans of the learned faculties, *e.g.*, *Arbeit*, designating a scientific enterprise, and *Fach*, meaning a specialty. The influence of German is also shown in the vocabulary of American musicians, *e.g.*, in *concertmaster*, from *Konzertmeister*. The OED's first example, 1889, is from an American source. The English commonly use *leader*.[8] The use of *German* as an adjective has made Americanisms since the Eighteenth Century. *German corn* (rye) is traced to 1741, *German Lutheran* to 1799, *German Reformed* (church) to 1812, *German cotillion* to 1839, *German Methodist* to 1788, *German* (from *German cotillion*) to 1863, *German Jew* to 1865 and *German-American* to 1824.

German brought in a number of Yiddish terms even before Yiddish became one of the principal languages of New York, *e.g.*, *ganef* (a thief),

---

[5] *MLN*, Vol. LIII, Feb. 1938, pp. 93–5.

[6] *Scram*, *AS*, Vol. XIII, Apr. 1938, pp. 152–3. [Borrowings through the occupation troops in Germany are discussed in German and the G.I., by Philip Neubaur and Arthur M. Z. Norman, *AS*, Vol. XXXI, May 1956, pp. 142–3.]

[7] Charles Sealsfield's Americanisms, *AS*, Vol. XVI, Feb. 1941, p. 27.

[8] Besides the works already cited, the bibliography includes The German Influence on the English Vocabulary, by Charles T. Carr, *SPE Tract*, No. XLII, 1934; Germany's Contribution to the English Vocabulary, by Harold G. Carlson, *Words*, May 1937, pp. 114–16; German Influence on the English Vocabulary of the Nineteenth Century, by Edward Taube, *JEGP*, Vol. XXXIX, Oct. 1940, pp. 486–93; and Studien über den deutschen Eingluss auf das amerikanische Englisch, by R. M. Stone, a dissertation submitted for the doctorate at Marburg in 1934.

kosher, mashuggah (crazy), *mazuma* (from Chaldean, through Hebrew and Yiddish), *shekels* (from Hebrew) and *tochos* (backside). All were used by German schoolmasters in Baltimore in the 1880s. In the early days of Hitler, the Nazis made some effort to purge German of these words, but apparently it was a failure. Most of the Yiddishisms in the cant of criminals were not introduced by Jewish immigrants to the United States: they go back to the Europe of the Middle Ages, and Martin Luther called attention to them so long ago as 1528 in his introduction to a reprint of Gerold Edilbach's "Liber Vagatorum," the first dictionary of thieves' jargon ever compiled.[9] The first such compilation in English, published in 1698,[1] contained several, *e.g., gelt* (from German), and there were more in Grose's "Classical Dictionary of the Vulgar Tongue" (1785). Partridge says that variations of *ganef* have been current among English criminals since *c.* 1835.

There are many German loan words in Yiddish, and one of them, *kibitzer*, has come into American by the Yiddish route. In German *Kiebitz* signifies the peewit or lapwing, and has long been in figurative use to designate a looker-on at cards, and especially one who offers unsolicited advice.[2] The word apparently acquired the agent suffix *-er* on coming into American. Another contribution is *schul* (the German word for school), used to designate a synagogue. The influence of Yiddish upon American has been felt, at least in the past, mainly in the urban areas; Dr. A. A. Roback, of New York, points out that most New York Yiddishisms have come in on the lower levels of speech:

> The majority of such locutions are slang, and quite a few find a place in the underworld vocabularies. Numerous expressions derived from the Yiddish constitute the backbone of commercial lingo. There is an auction jewelry jargon as well as a furniture jargon and a shoe business cant. . . . [Yiddish] has not been able to influence literary English yet, simply because, as a rule, Yiddish people do not move in higher society, and if they do, they find no need to resort to foreign phrases or expressions.[3]

Many of these expressions, most of which are originally German, are familiar to non-Jews as well; among them are:

---

[9] The first edition was published at Augsburg in 1512 or thereabout. Luther's edition was published at Wittenberg. The material in the book was mainly derived from the records of a series of trials of rogues and vagabonds at Basel in 1475.

[1] The Dictionary of the Canting Crew. The author signed himself B.E., and his identity has not been established.

[2] [See *Kibitz*, by John T. Krumpelmann, *AS*, Vol. XXV, May 1950, p. 154.]

[3] *You Speak Yiddish, Too! Better English*, Feb. 1938, p. 50. [See also Yiddish and American English, by Lillian M. Feinsilver, *Chicago Jewish Forum*, Vol. XIV, Winter 1955-6, pp. 71-6, and TV Talks Yiddish, *ibid.*, Vol. XV, Summer 1957, pp. 228-9.]

bagel: a doughnut-shaped hard roll.

blintz: a rolled pancake with a filling.

borax: cheaply made, gaudy furniture.

dreck: excrement (*cf.* Herr *Teufelsdröckh,* of Carlyle's "Sartor Resartus").

gefilte fish: chopped, spiced fishmeat in patties.

goy: a non-Jew; fem. *goya.*

kishkes: the intestines, guts.

lokschen: noodles.

macher: a fixer, an operator in the slang sense; a clever fellow.

mashuggah: crazy.

mazel tof: congratulations, good luck; on serious or ceremonial occasions.

momzer (pl. *momzayrim*): bastard; a general term of opprobrium, and also of affection as when used of a mischievous or clever child.

nash: a bit of food between meals.

nasher: one who habitually eats between meals.

schikse: a Christian girl.

schlemiehl: a clumsy, inept fellow; a blunderer.[4]

schlepper: a poorly dressed person, who, both literally and figuratively, has a hard time getting along.

schmaltz: corn, in the slang sense; sentimentality (lit. chicken fat).

schmaltzig: sentimental.

schmeer: to flatter, bribe.

schmo: a stupid person (originally a shortening of *schmok,* the *membrum virile*).

schmus: idle talk.

schnook: a jerk in the slang sense; a man who is thoughtless and does petty and cheap things.

schnorrer: a beggar or chiseler (especially one who works a religious angle), or even one who dresses poorly or as if poor to gain an advantage.

schnozzle: a large nose.

shamus: a deacon or caretaker of a synagogue; by extension, a plainclothes policeman.

---

[4] [The *Schlemihl* Problem, by Arthur M. Z. Norman, *AS,* Vol. XXVII, May 1952, pp. 149–50; see also Don't Be a *Schlemeel;* Avoid *Flufniks* When Buying a Car, Omaha *World-Herald,* Sept. 15, 1953, p. 4. This last was a syndicated article, from the North American Newspaper Alliance. *Nash* (pronounced and often spelled *nosh*) has yielded *noshery* as a designation for a snack bar. Miami Beach and similar outposts of civilization are full of *nosheries.* According to William M. Austin, a *Chinese Noshery* was opened in the posh Georgetown section of the District of Columbia, *c.* 1955. This dietary marriage is matched by a *Chinese smorgasbord,* offered by Joyce Chen, Cambridge, Mass., and a *Chinese Rathskeller* in New York.]

tochos: backside.

tzorris: troubles.

zaftig: well developed, curvaceous, sexually attractive, as of girls or women.

One gem is *T.L.* from *tochos lekker* (backside kisser), for one who tries to ingratiate himself with his superiors.[5] Not a few of the words and phrases thus borrowed have, in the original, a scatological or obscene significance, *e.g., to futz around, A.K.* (from *alter kacker*), *pisher* and *schmo.*[6] *Canary,* heard in New York in such phrases as "He's giving me a *canary,*" is derived from a Yiddish word compounded of the German *kein* (no) and the Hebrew *ayin* (eye) and *harrah* (evil). The intent is to ward off evil, much as in knocking on wood. Even some terms more or less closely associated with Judaism are known by non-Jews:

bar mitzva: the Jewish confirmation ceremony for boys.

kosher: ritually clean; hence, anything acceptable, in accordance with prescribed form.

matzoth: unleavened bread.

menora: a candelabrum.

minyan: the synagogue quorum of ten men.

mohel: a functionary licensed to perform circumcision.

schochet: a ritual slaughterer.

shabbath: the Sabbath.

shadchen: a marriage broker.

shalom aleichem: peace be with you.

shofar: a ram's horn blown in the synagogue on solemn holidays.

tref: ritually unclean.

Some of these have become so far naturalized that they are often given the English *-s* plural instead of the Hebrew *-im, e.g., schochets* instead of *schochtim.*

[The most fruitful sources of Yiddish loans are the media of mass communication—journalism, radio and television. In addition to *schlemiehl, schmaltz* and *schnook,* commonly heard currently, there is the deprecatory rhyming slang with *schm-* substituted in the second element, as in *phoneme-*

---

[5] See Lingo of the Shoe Salesman, by David Geller, *AS,* Vol. IX, Dec. 1934, pp. 283–6. This paper includes a glossary compiled by J. S. Fox. [See also *T.L., AS,* Vol. XXIII, Oct.–Dec. 1948, pp. 300–2, and American-Jewish Alphabetical Expressions, by Donn O'Meara, *AS,* Vol.

XXIII, Oct.–Dec. 1948, pp. 315–16.]

[6] [See also *Schnook* and *Nudnik,* by M. J. Bruccoli, *AS,* Vol. XXXII, May 1957, pp. 154–5, and *Hutzpa/Chuzpa,* "gall, nerve," *AS,* Vol. XXXIII, Oct. 1958, p. 230.]

schmoneme,[7] often with an explanatory clause following, as in the joke, "*Oedipus-schmoedipus,* so long as he loves his mother." The final intensive *yet,* as in "Five programs a week, *yet,*" comes from a similar use of *noch.* Other partial or complete translations of Yiddish expressions, some familiar from at least the 1930s, are: "I should worry," "I should live so long," "If you'll excuse the expression," "Get lost," "He don't know from nothing," "I need it like a hole in the head" (or "a third leg," or something equally useless) and "Give a look."]

"We may take it as a fixed rule," said Engelbrecht Kaempfer in his "History of Japan,"[8] "that the settlement of foreigners in a country will bring a corresponding proportion of foreign words into the language; these will be naturalized by degrees, and become as familiar as the native words themselves." The truth of this is well demonstrated by the foregoing record. Every fresh wave of immigrants has brought in new loan words, and some of them have become so thoroughly imbedded in the language that they have lost their air of foreignness, and are used to make derivatives as freely as native words, *e.g., peonage* (from the Spanish *peón,* traced to 1849), *spaghetti joint* and *to stevedore* from the noun (Spanish *estivador,* a stower of cargo). Not infrequently naturalization brings in a change of meaning, as when the Spanish *silo,* signifying an underground chamber for the storage of grain, came to mean, in most states, an aboveground structure in which green crops are fermented,[9] and *rodeo,* originally a cattle round-up, was transferred to an exhibition of cowboy tricks.[1] *Alfalfa,* also from the Spanish, is not an Americanism, but only in the United States has it picked up such connotations as are to be seen in *Alfalfa Bill*[2] and *Farmer Alfalfa.* As previously noted, American has probably made more loans from the Spanish than from any other language. They are, indeed, coming in all the time. *Marijuana* dates from 1894. The Spanish-American War added *trocha, ladrone, incommunicado* and *ley fuga,* some of which are already obsolete; and the popularity of Western movies and fiction has brought in a few more, *e.g., wrangler* (from *caballerango,* a horse groom), and

[7] [See Confusion Schmooshun, by Leo Spitzer, *JEGP,* Vol. LI, Apr. 1952, pp. 226–33; *Shmo, Shmog* and *Shnook,* by Lillian M. Feinsilver, *AS,* Vol. XXXI, Oct. 1956, pp. 236–7, On Yiddish *shm-, AS,* Vol. XXXVI, Dec. 1961, pp. 302–3, and Yiddish Idioms in American English, *AS,* Vol. XXXVII, Oct. 1962, pp. 200–6. For a historical study, see Jewish Literary Dialect, by John J. Appel, *AS,* Vol. XXXII, Dec. 1957, pp. 313–14.]

[8] Kaempfer (1651–1716) was a German doctor who entered the Dutch service and traveled extensively in the Far East.

The MS of his History of Japan was translated into English by J. G. Scheuchzer and published in London in 1727. The original German was not published until 1777.

[9] [Something of the original meaning survives in the West in *pit silo* and *trench silo.*]

[1] [It has yielded *roadeo,* an exhibition of the skill of truck drivers, and *showdeo,* reported by Louise Ackerman in *AS,* Vol. XXX, Dec. 1955, pp. 311–12.]

[2] The nickname of William H. Murray, governor of Oklahoma, 1931–5.

greatly increased the use of others. *Chile con carne* did not enter into the general American dietary until after 1900. The suffix *-ista* came in during the troubles in Mexico, following the downfall of Porfirio Díaz in 1911. *Político* appeared in the 1920s; *pachuco* in the 1940s; [and the recent influx of Puerto Ricans has spread *bodega* (a grocery-*cum*-liquor store) and given New York City (especially East Harlem—now often called *Spanish Harlem*) the nickname of *El Barrio* (the community). Spanish may share with Italian the credit for the current vogue of *marina*, as a de luxe designation for a yacht basin. The term has spread as far north as New Brunswick, and a new luxury river-front apartment development in downtown Chicago is called *Marina City*.[3]]

There are other related loan words from immigrant languages, notably the Swedish *smörgåsbord*, which has been taken in since World War I, with the loss of its diacritical marks. From French there is a continual borrowing, e.g., *brassière* (commonly shortened to *bra*), which did not appear till c. 1910. The Italian *macaroni* had been in American use since 1802, and *spaghetti* since the 1880s, but *ravioli*, *pizza* and *espresso* are more recent. *Policy* (from Italian *polizza*), a type of poor man's gambling, is traced to 1830. It has largely been supplanted by *numbers*. *Policy ticket* is recorded in 1872, *policy dealer* in 1865, *policy backer* and *to play policy* in 1882 and *policy shop* in 1858.

The contributions of Chinese to the American vocabulary are few in number, and most of them are confined to the Pacific coast and its immediate hinterland. The DA traces *chow mein* to 1927 and *chop suey* to 1903, but they must be much older. *Chow mein* means, primarily, fried noodles, and is derived from the Chinese words *ch'ao*, to fry, and *mien*, flour. *Chop suey* represents the Cantonese cognate of the standard Chinese *tsa-sui*, meaning miscellaneous pieces. *Joss* and its derivations got into English in the Eighteenth Century, but they seem to have been taken into American independently. The DAE traces *joss* in American use to 1873, and *joss house* and *joss stick* to 1871. *Tong* came in in the early 1880s and was soon followed by *tong war*. *Highbinder*, as we have seen, was first used in 1806 to designate a variety of Irish gangster in New York; it was not applied to Chinese until the late 1870s. The Chinese loan *yuen*, a vegetable garden, is known only on the West Coast. *Brainwash*, a loan translation, came in during the Korean police action. The Chinese, it should not be forgotten,

---

[3] [There seems to be a slackening of borrowing into English, even in the Southwest, since the new Spanish-speaking immigrants tend to be unskilled laborers. See Janet B. Sawyer, Aloofness from Spanish Influence in Texas English, *Word*, Vol. XV, Aug. 1959, p. 270, and her A Dialect Study of San Antonio, Texas: a Bilingual Community, diss. (microfilm), U. of Texas, 1957. See also Spanish-Speaking Groups in the United States, by John H. Burma; Durham, N.C., 1954.]

also contributed one of the most pungent American proverbs: "No tickee, no shirtee."

It is the custom on the Pacific coast to ascribe to Japanese any strange word that cannot be ascribed to Chinook, but it is seldom that plausible evidence is forthcoming. The Japanese etymologies proposed, for example, for *hobo* and *hunky-dory* are far from persuasive. *Tycoon* was brought in by the Perry expedition of 1852–4, and seems to have come into use in the United States before the English became aware of it. It was used as an affectionate nickname for Abraham Lincoln by the members of his secretariat, and has been worked to death in fairly recent years by *Time*. *Hara-kiri*[4] first appeared in *Harper's Magazine* in 1856, and *jujitsu* seems to have been introduced by Lafcadio Hearn in 1891, but *geisha* (1887), *jinricksha* (1874), followed by *rickshaw* (1886), *kimono* (1867) and *soybean* (1902) came to the United States by way of England.[5] World War II brought in *banzai*, *kamikaze* and *zaibatsu*, and made all Americans familiar with the older *Nisei*.[6]

[Russian undoubtedly has helped introduce such nonce forms as *buttinski*, previously mentioned. Reference to the Russians as *Russkis*, popularized by American soldiers in World War II, comes from *Ya Russki* (I am a Russian). The Russian success, in 1957, in launching the *sputnik*, their first artificial earth satellite, not only gave that word to all varieties of English but created a new vogue for words in *-nik: muttnik* for the dog-carrying Sputnik II, and *pfuttnik* and *dudnik* (along with less printable congeners) for the unsuccessful early American attempts. The 1959 Russian satellites in solar and lunar orbit were both named *Lunik*. The suffix *-nik* had previously been used in *nogoodnik*, a maliciously destructive animal species, by the cartoonist Al Capp (1949); and *nudnik* (a bore, a sickening person) is widely used by Russian-Jewish immigrants and is pos-

---

[4] It is often turned into *hari-kari*. For its etymology and true spelling see A Distorted Japanese Word, by E. E. Ericson, *AS*, Vol. XI, Dec. 1936, pp. 371–2.
[5] A long list of Japanese words that are more or less understood in England and the United States is in The Influence of Japanese on English, by E. V. Gatenby, *Studies in English Literature* (Tokyo), Vol. XI, 1931, pp. 508–20, and in his Additions to Japanese Words in English, *ibid.*, Vol. XIV, 1934, pp. 595–609.
[6] [The American troops in Japan have developed a *lingua franca* called *Bamboo English*, which is discussed by A. M. Z.

Norman, *AS*, Vol. XXIX, Dec. 1954, pp. 301–2, and Vol. XXX, Feb. 1955, pp. 44–8; the most widely known word is *moose* (from Japanese *musume*, daughter or young girl), for an American's Japanese mistress. Korean *Bamboo English* is discussed by John T. Algeo, *AS*, Vol. XXXV, May 1960, pp. 117–23, and by Grant Webster, *AS*, Vol. XXXV, Dec. 1960, pp. 261–5. Borrowings in Egypt are discussed by Morroe Berger and Louis T. Milić, *AS*, Vol. XXII, Dec. 1947, pp. 265–70; those in India and Burma by Eugene B. Vest, *AS*, Vol. XXIII, Oct.–Dec. 1948, pp. 223–31. But few of these borrowings have been domesticated at home.]

sibly the prototype of Capp's coinage. But it is not the prototype of all, since *-nik* is a highly productive suffix in Russian.[7]]

From the Indian languages the only recent acquisitions seem to be *chautauqua* and *hooch*. The latter goes back to the American occupation of Alaska in 1867. The first soldiers sent there were forbidden to have any spirituous liquors, so they set up stills and manufactured a supply of their own, of sugar and flour. The product was called *hoocheno* or *hoochino*, after a local Indian tribe, and continued to bear that name until the Klondike gold rush in 1897. Then it was shortened to *hooch*. *Chautauqua* was borrowed from the name of the county and lake in southwestern New York. The first *chautauqua* was opened on the shore of the lake on August 4, 1874, but the word did not come into general use until the end of the century. It was borrowed in the first place from the language of the Senecas, in which it meant the place of easy death, the place where one was lost, the foggy place, a place high up, two moccasins tied in the middle, and a pack tied in the middle. The French spelled it *tchadakoin*, and in early maps and books it appeared also as *tjadakoin, chataconit, chadakoin, chautauque, chatacoin, judaxque* and *jadaque*. In 1859, by a resolution of the county board of supervisors, the present spelling was made official.[8] At the start *chautauqua* meant a summer school, permanently housed and of some pedagogical pretensions. But toward 1900 it began to signify a traveling show, often performing under canvas, and including vaudeville acts as well as lectures.

---

[7] [See discussions of *-nik* by William White, *AS*, Vol. XXXIII, May 1958, pp. 153–4, and by Louise M. Ackerman, *ibid.*, pp. 154–6; a more extensive study is Russianisms in the American Press, by Morton Benson, *AS*, Vol. XXXVII, Feb. 1962, pp. 41–7.]

[8] See *Chautauqua* Notes, by J. R. Schultz, *AS*, Vol. IX, Oct. 1934, p. 232.

V I

American and English

The English travelers and reviewers whose pious horror of Americanisms has been recorded in Chapters I and III were able, for a while, to shut off their flow into Standard English, but only for a while. The tide began to turn, according to Sir William Craigie,[1] in 1820, and soon thereafter a large number of Yankee neologisms came into common use in England, *e.g.*, *reliable, influential, talented* and *lengthy*. Charles Dickens was credited with responsibility for the final acceptance of all four words by putting them into his "American Notes" in 1842.[2] But they had all come in earlier. Coleridge used *reliable* in 1800 and *influential* in 1833, and though he denounced *talented* as "that vile and barbarous vocable" in 1832, it had been used by no less an Americophobe than Robert Southey in 1828. Southey, in turn, sneered at *lengthy* in 1812 and again in 1834, but it was used by Jeremy Bentham so early as 1816, by Scott in 1827 (though still as a conscious Americanism) and by Dickens himself in "Pickwick" in 1837, five years before the publication of "American Notes." *Talented, reliable, influential* and *lengthy* appeared in the Concise Oxford Dictionary of 1911, and only *lengthy* was noted as "originally an Americanism." [3] During the half-century following 1820 many other Americanisms, *e.g., prairie, caucus* and *bluff*, also made their way into English. Even *to belittle*, which had provoked an almost hysterical outburst when Thomas Jefferson used it in

---

[1] *SPE Tract*, No. XXVII, 1927, p. 208.
[2] Americanisms in England, by A. Cleveland Coxe, *Forum*, Oct. 1886.
[3] The Fowlers call *reliable* "an established word avoided by purists as of irregular formation." It has actually been in good usage in England since the 1860s.

In 1871, when the United States claimed a large sum from England as indemnity for the depredations of the Confederate cruiser *Alabama*, *Punch* suggested that the injury England had suffered through the introduction of the word was sufficient compensation.

1787, was so generally accepted by 1862 that Anthony Trollope admitted it to his chaste vocabulary.

Englishmen would sharply disagree on how many Americanisms have actually got into accepted English. But a large number have become so thoroughly naturalized that the English dictionaries no longer mark them aliens. Others with the sharp tang of novelty are avoided by all persons careful of their speech, and in between these extremes is a vast body of Americanisms that have more or less current popularity but whose status in English is still to be determined. The earlier exchanges in both directions were on the upper level of usage, and most Americanisms were introduced to England by the writings of such illuminati as Jefferson, John Adams, James Fenimore Cooper and Noah Webster, but since 1900 the chief English borrowings have been from American slang. English observers generally attribute the shift to the influence of American movies, but the American comic strips, American popular songs and American pulp magazines—not to mention the American soldier—have also had a powerful influence. In fact, the American popular humorists of the post-Civil War era had already broken down many of the barriers against Americanisms.[4] The influence of these men, according to Farmer, was still strong in the late 80s; they had popularized "American peculiarities of speech and diction to an extent which, a few years since, would have been deemed incredible."[5]

But before the great invasion of England by American movies, beginning in the first years of World War I, Americanisms had to linger in a sort of linguistic Alsatia a long while before they were accepted, and even then they were sometimes changed in meaning. The cases of *caucus* and *buncombe* are perhaps typical. The former was in general use in the American colonies by the Revolution, but not until 1878 did it come into general use in England, and then, in the words of the Oxford Dictionary, it was "grossly misapplied." In the United States it had the settled meaning of a meeting of some division, large or small, of a political or legislative body for the purpose of agreeing upon a united course of action in the main assembly, but in England it was applied to what we would call the *organization*. *Buncombe*, in use in the United States since the 1820s, did not come into general use in England until the late 1850s, and then its spelling was changed to *bunkum*.

But when the American clipped form *bunk* arose toward the end of

---

[4] Says H. W. Seaman (private communication, May 9, 1944): "Hard-boiled fiction from America has influenced English speech and writing. The boys' papers have heroes who speak as nearly American as the authors can manage to make them."

[5] Farmer, p. vii.

World War I, it appeared in England almost instantly by way of American movies, and ten years later the verb *to debunk* got into use quite as quickly. Hundreds of other saucy Americanisms have followed it, often in successful competition with English neologisms. Although this invasion is resisted valiantly by swarms of volunteer guardians of the national linguistic chastity in sporadic crusades,[6] many of the more colorful innovations now get into circulation very rapidly. Among the large number that have "become naturalized since the beginning of the present century" are the compounds *hot air, comeback, highbrow, jaywalker* and *round-up*, the simple nouns *boom, kick* (a powerful effect), *publicity* (advertising) and *conservatory* (musical), the verbs *to park* (automobiles), *to rattle* and *to boom*, and the verb phrases *to get away with, to make good, to get a move on* and *to turn down;* and an even larger number are "apparently becoming naturalized," *e.g.*, the compounds *bargain counter, bellboy, comedown, joyride, holdup, horse sense, soap box, frame-up, roughhouse, close-up, goldbrick* and *logrolling*, the simple nouns *rally, bromide, cut* (reduction), *fan* (enthusiast), *quitter, pull* (political), *pointer, mixer* and *cereal* (breakfast food), the simple verbs *to ditch, to feature, to fire* (dismiss), *to pass* (a dividend) and *to hustle*, the verb phrases *to bank on, to get busy, to try out, to hand-pick, to iron out, to soft-pedal, to sandbag, to sit up and take notice, to snow under, to stay put, to side-step, to side-track* and *to win out*, and the miscellaneous idioms *good and, on the side, up to* and *up against*.[7] Many of these, of course, belong to slang, but some of them are making their way into relatively decorous circles. Paul Shorey, professor of Greek at the University of Chicago, used to collect thumping Americanisms used by English authors of dignified standing. He found *to make good* and *cold feet* in John Galsworthy, *rubberneck* in Sir Arthur Quiller-Couch (King Edward VII professor of English literature at Cambridge!), *nothing doing* in Lowes Dickinson, *proposition* "as a word of all work" in Mrs. Humphrey Ward and *to cough up* in John Masefield.[8] Such literati seldom use the current slang of their own country, except in depicting low or careless char-

---

[6] In the spring of 1935, for example, Major Brooke Heckstall-Smith, yachting correspondent to the London *Daily Telegraph*, raised a holy war against *to debunk*, and was presently joined by other viewers-with-alarm. One of them, A. E. Sullivan (Mar. 2), ascribed its origin to "the inability of an ill-educated and unintelligent democracy to assimilate long words." But it was defended by Hubert Furst (Mar. 2), author of a book entitled *Art Debunked*, and by Pearl Freeman (Mar. 4), who called it "a full-blooded descriptive word." On Mar. 2 *radio* was put at the head of a list of "bastard American expressions" by John C. Mellis (with *O.K., sez you, nerts, cute* and *big fella* following), but on Mar. 6 it was defended by Jan Stewer as "a beautiful coinage," and its English equivalent, *wireless*, denounced as "an abomination."

[7] Horwill.

[8] Academy Papers; New York, 1925, p. 150.

acters. But they are fetched by the piquancy of Americanisms, and employ them for their pungent rhetorical effect. The same consideration influences English politicians too, and "a veteran Parliamentarian" once said:

> Even Mr. Baldwin, one of the few authorities on the King's English in the House, used in his speech yesterday the expressions *backslider*, *best-seller*, and *party dog-fight*. I have heard him use *to deliver the goods*. The House is undoubtedly Americanized in some of its phrases. I have heard *whoopee* and *debunked* in the debating chamber, and *oh, yeah* and *you're telling me* in the lobby. *To pass the buck* is a well-known House expression and it is often used.[9]

The argot of English politics has naturalized many Americanisms besides *caucus* and *buncombe*. *Graft*, wrote Harold Brighouse in 1929, is "acclimatized in England." [1] So are *platform, carpetbagger, wirepuller, logrolling, on the fence, campaign*,[2] *to stump* and *to electioneer*.[3] In other fields there has been the same infiltration. The meaning of *bucket shop* and *to water*, for example, is familiar to every London broker's clerk. English trains are now *telescoped* and carry *deadheads*, there is an Associated Society of Locomotive *Engineers* and *Firemen* and in 1913 a rival to the Amalgamated Order of Railway *Servants* was organized under the name of National Union of *Railway Men*. With the advent of the welfare state, servants have become only slightly less rare in Britain than in the United States. But even earlier a movement against the use of the ignominious *servant* was visible, and the American *help* threatened to be substituted; at all events, *Help Wanted* advertisements are occasionally printed in English newspapers. The American *to phone* is now in general use, and *Hello* has displaced *Are you there?* as the standard telephone greeting. English journalists are ceasing to call themselves *pressmen*, and have begun to use the American *newspapermen*. They begin to write *editorials* instead of *leaders*. The English theaters continue to have *dress circles* where ours have *balconies*, but there are *balconies* in the moviehouses. Since England began to grow sugar beets, the English *beetroot* has succumbed to the American (and earlier English) *beet*, and the American *can* seems to be ousting the English *tin*. *Skyscraper, straphanger* and *foolproof* were naturalized long ago;[4] *cafeteria, kitchen cabinet, filing cabinet, nut sundae, soda fountain, ice-cream soda* and *popcorn* have appeared on shop signs in London, and

[9] Sunderland *Echo*, Oct. 31, 1934.
[1] Manchester *Guardian*, Apr. 5, 1929.
[2] For example, Gladstone's *Midlothian Campaign* of 1880.
[3] The Study of American English, by

W. A. Craigie, *SPE Tract*, No. XXVII, p. 208.
[4] See British English and American English, by Thomas G. Tucker, *Scribner's*, Dec. 1921.

chain store in a headline in a 100% British provincial newspaper.[5] Sometimes an Americanism of long standing is suddenly taken up in England, and becomes popular almost overnight. Thus *shyster*, in use here since the 1840s, was introduced by Robert Louis Stevenson in "The Wrecker" in 1892;[6] *Indian summer*, which goes back to colonial days, was given a start by John Galsworthy's use of it in the title "The *Indian Summer* of a Forsyte" (1918); and the then Prince of Wales popularized the Theodore Rooseveltian *bully* by using it in a speech to a Leicestershire hunt in 1930.

When the silent movie began to be supplanted by talkies many hopeful Englishmen believed that the American accent would be unendurable to their countrymen, that English-made talkies would thus prevail over those from Hollywood and that the inundation of Americanisms would be stayed at last. But Hollywood was soon deluging the English plain people with even more Americanisms than had ever appeared in the legends on the silent films.[7] The battle between English and American talkies that ensued came to highly significant issues in both countries. In England the commonalty rejoiced in the new influx of American neologisms and soon adopted large numbers of them, but in America the movie fans refused to tolerate the pseudo-Oxford accent and frequent Briticisms of the English actors.[8] Simultaneously, the educated classes in England resented and resisted the American talkies, and the Anglomaniacs of the United States welcomed the English talkies with colonial enthusiasm. The educated Englishmen procured the enactment of laws limiting the importation of American films, but the English middle and lower classes found them perfectly satisfying, and soon the Americanisms they introduced were in wide use, and many began to penetrate to the higher levels of speech.[9] In the lin-

---

[5] *Eastern Evening News* (Norwich), Mar. 27, 1935.

[6] Harold Brighouse in the Manchester *Guardian*, Apr. 5, 1929.

[7] At the start they made some effort to placate English prejudices. On July 10, 1929, *Variety* reported that a movie called No! No! Napoleon was being done in both an "American version" and an "English translation." The sentence "A *nut factory*, eh?" was translated into "A *madhouse*, eh?" This spirit of concession was well received by the English cinema magnates, and one of them contributed an article to the London *Star* on Feb. 4, 1930, in which he expressed the opinion that the day of American slang in England was over. "English actors of both sexes," he reported, "are being employed in ever increasing number, and a superior type of American artist is being engaged who has the culture and ability to acquire English cadences and intonations." But Hollywood soon discovered that the English fans, at least in the lower orders, really enjoyed American slang, so *nut factory* and many congeners were restored to use, and the "superior type of American artist" was displaced by the traditional recruits from the ten-cent stores and barbecue stands.

[8] Hollywood *Reporter*, quoted in Language Trouble, by Stephen Watts, London *Sunday Express*, Nov. 20, 1938: "It's next to impossible for Americans to understand an English accent on the screen."

[9] "If half the members of a talkie audience," said a contributor to the Liverpool *Daily Courier*, signing himself H.W.S., on Sept. 4, 1929, "shudder every time a character on the screen says 'Get

guistic interchanges between England and the United States this curious dichotomy has been witnessed for a long while. Americanisms get into English use on the lower levels and then work their way upward, but nearly all the Briticisms that reach the United States first appear on the levels of cultural pretension, and most of them stay there, for the common people will have none of them.

The old English battle against the American invasion has now begun to abate. Nothing short of a war with the United States is likely to shut off the flow of Americanisms, at all events on the lower levels of the population, or to keep them from penetrating upward. Such familiar Americanisms as *back number, crook, filling station, up against* and *up to* have now become so familiar in England that it is no longer necessary to interpret them. So late as 1932 the New York correspondent of the London *Observer* was at pains to explain that *hot dogs* were "broiled sausages in split rolls," [1] but since then the austere London *Times* has given its countenance to *highbrow*, the *Daily Express* has quite nonchalantly characterized the chaplain to a bishop as a *fence sitter*,[2] and the eminent *News of the World* has adopted *gate crasher*.[3] The English newspapers frequently philosophize upon a recent novelty, and usually advise their readers to avoid it, but most of them seem to be convinced that stemming the influx has now become hopeless.

In 1931 C. T. Onions, one of the editors of the Oxford Dictionary, described it as a "grievance" that English was being "invaded—and degraded —by the current idiom from the United States," [4] and so late as 1936 he was trying to get rid of that grievance by arguing stoutly that the extent of the invasion was "much exaggerated." [5] But even Onions conceded that "a certain proportion of the American language of the film caption" would "*catch on* [6] and become permanent." He noted that *to put it across, to get it across* and *to put it over* [7] were already "firmly domiciled" in England and apparently "entered upon a large career of metaphorical use." He proclaimed that *to make good* "no longer gives the impression of being an alien idiom" in England, that "the American applications of the word *dope* have generally commended themselves and have obtained a wide

a *load* of this' or 'It's *in the bag*,' the other half make a mental note of the expression for future use."
[1] The Democratic "Vaudeville," July 3, 1932.
[2] The Wrath of the Church, July 14, 1936.
[3] Precautions Against *Gate-Crashers* at Ascot, June 12, 1938.
[4] Is English Becoming Too American?, London *Evening News*, Nov. 19, 1931.

[5] Oxford correspondence of the Hong Kong *Telegraph*, Oct. 6, 1936.
[6] "Is that," he asked in parenthesis, "an Americanism?"
[7] Dr. Onions described all these verb phrases as "idioms derived from the stage footlights." This is possible, but it seems more likely that they really got their vogue in the United States as baseball terms.

currency" and that *yep* and *nope* "have penetrated even into the speech of the educated of the younger generation." [8] Other Americanisms that he spoke of politely, if not enthusiastically, were *mass meeting, best girl* [9] and *to fizzle out.* Sir William Craigie made it plain in 1936 that he did not agree with Onions that the number of Americanisms taken into English was "much exaggerated." To the contrary, he told a correspondent of the London *Morning Post* [1] that "current English contains many more real Americanisms than most people imagine." Many other authorities, high and low, agreed with him, then and afterward. "England," wrote Alistair Cooke in 1935,[2] "has been absorbing American words at an unbelievable rate. . . . There are thousands of these borrowings—debts which I am afraid we are never going to pay back to America. . . . Every Englishman unconsciously uses thirty or forty Americanisms a day, however much he is opposed to American idiom on principle." In 1936 H. W. Horwill reported from London in *The New York Times* [3] that the sales of American books were increasing in England, and ascribed it to the ever wider English familiarity with and use of Americanisms. "However much the pedants may rail and the grammarians quake," wrote an observant Englishman in 1939,[4] "American is steadily entering more and more into the Englishman's written and spoken language. Nobody now would jibe at *governmental, holdup,* or *junk,* and the use in conversation of such a phrase as 'an idea *resurrected* [5] from the Nineteenth Century' breaks no one's heart except the ultra-purist's, while the *Times Educational Supplement* (of all papers), has used *to enthuse* in its book reviews."

The arrival of American troops in England and Northern Ireland in 1942 helped along the process that American movies and comic strips had started. A correspondent of the Belfast *News-Letter,* early in 1943,[6] reported that the erstwhile *sonsy wee lassies* of the Scotch-Irish North had become *swell dames,* and that "farmers' children deep in the heart of Ulster" had learned "Aw, *lay off.*" The Belfast *Telegraph* [7] reported that *truck* for *lorry* had come into universal use in Ulster, and that the American *guy,* meaning simply anybody, had begun to displace the English *guy,* meaning a grotesque and ridiculous person.

---

[8] London *Evening News,* Nov. 19, 1931, *op. cit.*

[9] First noted as an Americanism by Barrère and Leland, Dictionary of Slang, Jargon and Cant; London, 1889-90.

[1] Americanisms Now Used in English, Aug. 26, 1936.

[2] English on Both Sides of the Atlantic, *Listener* (London), Apr. 3, 1935, p. 572.

[3] News and Views of Literary London, Oct. 4, 1936.

[4] Arthur D. Jacobs, of Manchester; private communication, July 19, 1939.

[5] *To resurrect* has been found in English use in the Eighteenth Century, but it came to flower in pre-Civil War America, and to the English of today it seems an Americanism.

[6] Sticking Out, Apr. 6, 1943.

[7] Fair Exchange, May 20, 1943.

It is curious, reading the fulminations of American purists of the last generation, to note how many of the Americanisms they denounced have broken down all guards across the ocean. *To placate*, attacked vigorously by all native grammarians down to (but excepting) White, now has the authority of the *Spectator*. Other old bugaboos that have been embraced are *to donate, reliable, gubernatorial, presidential* and *standpoint. To engineer, to collide* [8] and *to obligate* are in Cassell with no hint of their American origin, and so are *homespun, outhouse, cross purposes, greenhorn, blizzard, tornado, cyclone, hurricane, excursionist, washstand* and *washbasin.* J. Y. T. Greig, in "Breaking Priscian's Head," [9] printed a long list of Americanisms firmly lodged in English, and said that "few of us who have not taken the trouble to go into the matter are aware how many of our common expressions derive from the United States."

Horwill, after discussing the influence of the movies in this Americanization of English, adds that two other factors have had an important effect: "the increasing attention . . . paid in England to American books and magazines," and "the fact that . . . many members of the staffs of English newspapers are either Americans or English journalists who have spent several years in the practice of their profession in the United States." [1] One of these, H. W. Seaman, returning to England after ten years in the United States, has recorded a large number of observations of American influence upon English: [2]

> *To stop*, meaning to stay, has not been adopted in England, but the railways issue *stopover* tickets.
>
> *Peanut* has completely ousted *monkey-nut*.
>
> *Cooler*, meaning a jail, is now fairly current in England, and even *calaboose* is understood, thanks to a popular song.
>
> No English dramatic critic would shrink from writing of a *flop*.
>
> Headline in *Daily Express*, May 16, 1944: Russia *Puts Heat* on Sweden. No quotes or explanation now necessary.
>
> *Tuxedo* was used without quotes in the head and body of a story on the sports page of the London *Sunday Chronicle*, May 14, 1944.

---

[8] *To collide* is barred by many English newspapers, which prefer *to come in collision*. But the aim here is simply to avoid any direct imputation of agency, and so head off possible libel suits.

[9] London, 1929, pp. 79 *ff*.

[1] In The American Impact on Great Britain, 1894–1914; Philadelphia, 1940, p. 310, Richard Heathcote Heindel says that *Punch* noted the influence of American on the English press so early as the 90s. He also says that many terms "in the category of business . . . came into English usage before 1914." "Such invasion of the language as has taken place," he concludes, "proves the power of the cinema, press and business, not the connivance of English literary masters."

[2] Private communications at different times in 1944.

Through, meaning finished, is now respectable English. This has come to pass within ten years or less.

Radio has driven *wireless* virtually out of use. Even the London *Times,* which clings to *aether,* has surrendered to *radio.*

What it takes is now used freely. Few Englishmen realize that the idiom in "Britain *can take it*" is American.

Double-cross and *four-flush* are now respectable English, though poker is not an English popular game.

Pin-up girl is in wide use.

To lay off, meaning to desist from, is used editorially in the London *Sunday Times,* June 11, 1944.

Racket, for a swindling conspiracy, is well known and much used, but so is its English equivalent, *ramp.*[3]

2: SURVIVING DIFFERENCES

Despite the heavy American influence upon English in recent years, the two languages still show many differences. The English often use different words for the same common objects, they make frequent use of words and phrases that are seldom or never heard in America, they have different repertoires of everyday intensives and cuss words, they pronounce many words differently and their talk is based upon different speech tunes. The same thing, of course, runs the other way, but Englishmen probably find American considerably less difficult than Americans find English, if only because they have become so familiar with large numbers of American terms and idioms. Each preceding edition of "The American Language" included lists of the surviving differences between the current vocabularies of American and English, and in every instance that list had become archaic in some details before it could reach print. The English reviewers had their sport demonstrating that a number of Americanisms were really in wide use in England, but all they usually proved was that the exotic had become familiar. The more chauvinistic not only boggled at details but suggested that the real motive of such cruel labors was to drive a wedge between the two great branches of the Anglo-Saxon peoples, and thus prosper the enemies of democracy and Christianity, and more than one American Anglomaniac has played with the same idea. There is in each country a highly articulate group which holds that any notice of linguistic disparities between them, however academic, is seditious, immoral and against God. But, fortunately, when World War II brought American and British troops into contact for the second time in a generation, the

---

[3] There are earlier examples in Seaman's article Ninety-nine Percent British, *American Mercury,* Sept. 1937, pp. 46–53.

General Staffs of both armies, recalling the unpleasant misunderstandings in World War I, proceeded to issue what amounted, in substance, to American-English dictionaries. That of the American Army, included in a pamphlet entitled "A Short Guide to Great Britain" and first published in 1942, presented 183 everyday American terms, unknown or unfamiliar in England, that are represented in English by equivalents similarly strange in the United States. There followed a dictionary for American supply men,[4] and at other times yet other vocabularies for other special purposes.[5] Meanwhile, the English brought out various pamphlets of the same general tenor. Early in 1942, when RAF cadets began coming to the United States for training, the Air Ministry prepared a little pamphlet, "Notes for Your Guidance," and soon afterward the Ministry of Information issued a word list for artists invited to exhibit at an Anglo-American show at the Metropolitan Museum of Art.

So far the English foes of the notion that American and English differ have not complained of these official lists, but they are sure to denounce any list less authoritatively supported; consequently the one that follows is based on the vocabulary in the War Department's "Short Guide to Great Britain," and on printed evidence, usually English, for most of the other differences. Often it is genuinely difficult to establish the facts, for a great many Americanisms have got into English use in recent years, and not a few terms that seem distinctively American today are actually English archaisms. It is easy for the English guardians of the language to produce evidence that these archaisms were used, say, by Chaucer or Shakespeare, and to argue thereby that they are not Americanisms at all. This attitude recalls that of Holy Church toward embarrassing scientific discoveries, as described by Andrew D. White, *viz.*, they first denounce it violently, then admit it quietly, and then end by denying that they were ever against it. This was the history in England of *reliable* and *caucus*, and no doubt many an Americanism that is still below the salt will follow the pattern. That there are still wide divergences between American and English usage on the level of everyday speech was demonstrated beyond cavil by Horwill in his "Dictionary of Modern American Usage" and again in his "Anglo-American Interpreter." Despite inevitable slips and misunderstandings in both

---

[4] The headline on this vocabulary in the *Stars & Stripes* was British Names Headache to Supply Men: *GI Can* is *Dust Bin, Hot Water Bottle* a *Stomach Warmer.*

[5] One showing differences in the American and English names for various maintenance items was prepared for the Staff Officers' School, and another on the same topic was published in the *Quartermaster Review,* Mar.–Apr. 1943, by Col. Wayne Allen, of the Quartermaster Corps. Dave Breger, the Army cartoonist, did one for the troops in general in the form of an illustrated alphabet, beginning with *absorbent cotton–cotton wool* and running down to *zee–zed.*

books, on the whole Horwill is well informed and painstaking. In the following list [6] all doublets taken from the Army's "Short Guide to Great Britain" are indicated by an asterisk (*).

American	English
*absorbent cotton	cotton wool
ad (advertisement)	advert [7]
admit to the bar (law)	call to the bar
advertising manager, or director	advertisement manager
*ale	beer, or bitter
alumnus (of a college)	graduate
*apartment	flat
apartment-hotel	service flats
baby carriage, or baby buggy	perambulator (pram), or baby coach [8]
*baggage car	luggage van [9]
bath (noun, as in *sea bath*)	bathe [1]
*bathrobe	dressing gown
*beer	lager
beet	beetroot
bellboy, or bellhop	page, or buttons
*bill (money)	banknote, or note
*billboard	hoarding
billfold	wallet
billion	milliard

[6] Some of the terms listed are discussed at greater length in other places. See the List of Words and Phrases. [I am particularly indebted to my colleague Kenneth Northcott for providing the latest information on British usage.]

[7] Advertisement in *News of the World* (London), Jan. 23, 1938: "Why are you publishing this *advert*?"

[8] Americans, of course, know the meaning of *perambulator*, and even of *pram*. [And *baby coach* is typical of the Philadelphia area. See Hans Kurath, A Word Geography of the Eastern United States, *University of Michigan Studies in American English*, No. 1, Ann Arbor, 1949, pp. 35, 36, 77; Figs. 20, 147. As for British practice, Andrew Levens observes that *perambulator* is now archaic, and Kenneth Northcott that *baby carriage* is common.]

[9] Mournful Numbers, by Colin Ellis; London, 1932:
I'm certain we shall miss the train!
   Is all the luggage in the van?
Oh, George, you've dropped that box *again*!
I'm certain we shall miss the train—
Well, don't swear, if you *are* in pain—
   Oh, how I wish I were a man!
I'm certain we shall miss the train!
   Is all the luggage in the van?
(Note the. use of *miss* for the former British term *lose*.)

[1] H. W. Seaman: "We go for a *bathe* in the sea or a river or a swimming pool. We take a *bath* in the bathtub. *Bathe*, verb or noun, always rhymes with *lathe*, and *bath* with *lath*." [According to Kenneth Northcott, a *bathrobe* in England is made of terry cloth, a *dressing gown* of wool or silk.]

American	English
bingo	house, or housey-housey, or tombola
*biscuit	scone, or teacake
blank (noun)	form [2]
boards	deals [3]
boulevard, or main road	arterial road, or trunk road
*bouncer	chucker-out
boxcar	goods van
briefcase	portfolio, or despatch case [4]
*broiled (meat)	grilled
bug	insect
bulletin board	notice board
business suit [5]	lounge suit
caboose (railroad)	brake van
cab stand	cab rank
callboy (railroad)	knocker-up
can (container)	tin [6]
*cane	stick [7]
*car (railway passenger)	coach
carnival	fun fair
catalogue (school or college) [8]	calendar
catnip	catmint
*chain store	multiple store(s) [9]
check (restaurant)	bill
*checkers (game)	draughts
checkroom	left-luggage office, or -room
cigar store	tobacconist's shop
city hall	town hall, or guildhall
clean-up campaign	cleansing campaign
clipping (newspaper)	cutting

[2] As She Is Spoke in the United States, by J.H.M., Glasgow *Evening Citizen*, Aug. 29, 1936: "During the voyage the purser will send out at least one *form* to be *filled in*, but to the Americans it will be a *blank* to be *filled out*."

[3] The OED says that *deals* now commonly means fir or pine cut in planks not more than three inches thick.

[4] [According to Mrs. Helen Starr, *despatch case* is now more common, as well as newer and more fashionable. Kenneth Northcott describes *briefcase* as now the usual English term.]

[5] *Sack suit*, seldom used today, is an Americanism traced to 1895; *business suit* is traced to 1870.

[6] In England, says Horwill, *can* means a vessel for holding liquids, but it seems to be ousting *tin* for other purposes.

[7] In England *cane* is used for a very slender stick.

[8] The Harvard *catalogue* of 1682 corresponds to the present-day student and alumni *directories*.

[9] Since c. 1930 *chain store* has been in increasing use in England. [*Multiple shop(s)* now sounds quaint.]

American	English
closed season (for hunting)	close season
clothespin	clothespeg
*coal oil, or kerosene	paraffin
*collar button	collar stud, or back stud
common stock	ordinary shares
commutation ticket	season ticket
commuter	season-ticket holder
*conductor (railroad)	guard
cone (ice cream)	cornet [1]
confidence game	confidence trick
copyreader (newspaper)	sub-editor
*corn	maize (cattle food); sweet corn, corn on the cob (for table use)
corner (street)	turning [2]
corporation	limited liability company
*cracker	biscuit
cruising (taxi)	crawling
crystal (watch)	watch glass [3]
*deck (cards)	pack
delegation	deputation
deliveryman (*e.g.*, of milk or bread)	roundsman [4]
detour (road)	road diversion, traffic diversion, or loopway
dining car, or diner	restaurant car
*dishpan	washing-up bowl, or washer
distributor (merchandise)	stockist
district (legislative)	division, or constituency
district attorney, or state's attorney	public prosecutor [5]

---

[1] Advertisement in the London *Morning Post*, July 24, 1936, under a picture showing a small girl eating a banana and a boy holding an *ice-cream cone*: "A banana for the lady, a *cornet* for the gent."

[2] *The New York Times Magazine*, quoted in *Writer's Monthly*, Oct. 1927, p. 335: "A street does not have *corners* in England, but *turnings*; neither does it have a *head* or *foot*. English thoroughfares possess *tops* and *bottoms*."

[3] In England, says Horwill, "*crystal* is used in this sense by watchmakers only."

[4] An assault upon a *baker's roundsman* was reported in the London *Morning Post*, Nov. 25, 1935.

[5] Though every criminal offense is prosecuted in England in the name of the Crown, the actual prosecution was left, until 1870, to persons aggrieved. Since then, something like the American system has been set up, but even today the director of public prosecutions and his staff do not invariably intervene.

American	English
domestic mails	inland mails [6]
*dry-goods store	draper's shop
dumb-waiter	service lift
editorial (noun)	leading article, or leader [7]
electric heater	radiator, or electric fire [8]
eraser	Indian rubber
excelsior	wood wool
express company	carrier
extension (university)	extramural studies
extension wire	flex
fall (season)	autumn
*fender (automobile)	wing, or mudguard
filling station	petrol pump
fire department	fire brigade [9]
flashlight	torch
*floorwalker	shopwalker
flophouse	doss house
fraternal order	friendly society
freight car	goods waggon, or goods van
French fries	chips [1]
full time (adverb)	full out [2]
game (*e.g.,* football)	match
garbage can	dust bin
garbageman	dustman
*garter (men's)	sock suspender [3]
general delivery (post office)	poste restante
*generator (automobile)	dynamo
gingersnap	gingernut [4]
given name, or first name	Christian name
grab bag	lucky dip

[6] In England the *domestic* postal rates are *inland* also.

[7] *Editorial*, traced to 1830, was denounced by Richard Grant White in Words and Their Uses, 1870, but has survived.

[8] [Again, I am indebted to Mrs. Starr.]

[9] *Fire brigade* was used in the official program of the Oriole Pageant in Baltimore, Oct. 10-12, 1881. It is never heard in the town today. [It was common in South Carolina in the 1920s.] *Fire department* is traced to 1825.

[1] As in *fish and chips.*

[2] London *Sunday Express,* Nov. 13, 1938: "Alvis are working *full out* to supply the demand." [According to Kenneth Northcott, *full out* means under full pressure.]

[3] Or simply *suspender. Garter,* of course, is an old word in English, and the *Knights of the Garter* go back to Apr. 23, 1349. The term was not used to indicate an article of men's wear until the 1880s.

[4] Advertisement in the London *Telegraph and Post,* Feb. 22, 1938, with a picture of *gingersnaps:* "Romary's *gingernuts* just melt!" [But *gingersnap* is common.]

American	English
grade (noun, as of a road)	gradient
grade (school)	form, standard, or class
grade crossing (railroad)	level crossing
grocery	grocer's shop, or grocer's
*ground wire (radio)	earth wire
hall, or hallway (in a private house)	passage [5]
hash	shepherd's pie [6]
*highball	whisky and soda
highway patrolman	mobile police
hike (verb)	tramp
hitchhike	lorry jump, or -hop
hogpen	pig sty [7]
hog raiser, or -grower	pig breeder
holdup man, or stickup man, or highjacker	raider
*hood (automobile)	bonnet
hook-and-ladder	fire escape
horn (automobile), or siren	hooter
hot-water bottle	stomach warmer
ice cream	ice [8]
identification tag	identity disk
information bureau	inquiry office
installment plan	hire-purchase system, hire system, or "never-never"
insurance (life)	assurance
internal revenue	inland revenue
*janitor	caretaker, or porter
junk	rubbish
landslide	landslip
lease (verb)	let
lifeguard	lifesaver
life preserver	life belt
limited (in the name of a train)	express
*line up (verb)	queue up

[5] *Hall* in England ordinarily means a large apartment, *e.g.*, *music hall* or the *hall* of a castle. It is also used in special senses at the universities. *Servants' hall* likewise shows a special British use. But *hall bedroom*, *hall room*, *hallboy* and *hallway* are all Americanisms.

[6] [Mrs. Starr reports that *mince* is also common.]

[7] *Hog*, says Horwill, "is rarely used in England nowadays except figuratively, *e.g.*, *road-hog*."

[8] [Or *cream ice*. But *ice cream* is very common.]

American	English
*low gear (automobile)	first gear, bottom gear
lumber	timber
mail car, or railway post office	postal van
master of ceremonies (of a show)	compère
*monkey wrench	adjustable spanner [9]
motorman	driver
*movies	cinema, films, flick(er)s, or pictures
moving (changing residence)	moving house [1]
*mucilage, glue	gum
*muffler (automobile)	silencer
*newsstand	kiosk
nightstick, or club (policeman's)	truncheon
oarlock	rowlock
*oatmeal (boiled)	porridge
office (doctor's or dentist's)	surgery
office (lawyer's)	chambers
*oil pan (automobile)	sump
one-way ticket	single ticket
operating cost	running expense, or working expense
*orchestra seat (theater)	stall
overcoat	greatcoat [2]
pantry	larder
parking lot	car park
parole (for a criminal)	ticket of leave [3]
patrolman (police)	constable
*pebbly beach	shingle
penitentiary	prison [4]
penpoint	nib

---

[9] London *Daily Mail*, June 17, 1936: "Life is complicated enough without any help from outside in the way of throwing *spanners* into the works."

[1] London *Morning Post*, Aug. 25, 1936: "Take, for instance, the question of *moving house*. Every woman in her heart rejoices in the event as in a festival."

[2] But *overcoat* is also used in England.

[According to Kenneth Northcott, *greatcoat* is restricted to the military garment.]

[3] Horwill says that in England *parole* "is used in relation to prisoners of war only."

[4] *Penitentiary* in England designates a reformatory. The DA traces it, in the sense of a prison, to 1812, and *penitentiary offense* to 1855.

American	English
period (punctuation)	full stop
personal (business)	private
*pie (fruit)	tart
porterhouse (steak)	sirloin
*poolroom	billiards saloon
*potato chip	crisp
pot pie	meat pie
preferred stock	preference shares
pry (to raise or separate)	prise
public comfort station	public convenience
publisher (newspaper)	proprietor
*race track	race course
*radio	wireless [5]
railroad	railway
*raise (in pay)	rise
rare (of meat)	underdone
recess (school)	break
room clerk (hotel)	reception clerk
*roomer	lodger
rotogravure	intaglio
roundhouse (railroad)	running shed [6]
*round trip	return trip
*run (in a stocking)	ladder [7]
rutabaga	Swede, or horse turnip [8]
saloonkeeper	publican
scab (labor), or fink [9]	blackleg
scholarship	studentship [1]
*scrambled eggs	buttered eggs
scratch pad	scribbling block
*sedan (automobile)	saloon car
sell out (verb)	sell up
*shoulder (of road)	verge

[5] [M. M. Mathews points out that it is derived from the name of the Marconi *Wireless* Telegraph Co., which for many years attempted to establish a monopoly in the North Atlantic. *AS*, Vol. XXXII, Feb. 1957, pp. 59–60.]

[6] [With the disappearance of steam locomotives in America, the *roundhouse* is obsolete and has been replaced by the *diesel shop*, an entirely different type of building.]

[7] But *run* is making headway.

[8] The *rutabaga* was introduced into England from Sweden *c.* 1800, and into the United States soon afterward.

[9] [*Fink* reputedly goes back to the Homestead strike of 1892; *scab* is traced indubitably to 1806, but there are suggestions of its present use in Cotton Mather. See *AS*, Vol. XXV, Feb. 1950, p. 18.]

[1] *Scholarship* is also used in England.

American	English
sidewalk	pavement [2]
sirloin	rump
slingshot	catapult [3]
*smoked herring	kipper
*soda biscuit, or cracker	cream cracker
soda fountain	soda bar
*spark plug	sparking plug
*spigot, or faucet	tap [4]
spool (of thread)	reel of cotton
sporting goods	sports requisites, or sports goods
*squash	vegetable marrow
stenographer	shorthand writer [5]
*store	shop
straight (of a drink)	neat
straw hat	boater
streamlined	swept-out [6]
*string bean [7]	French bean
*subway	underground [8]
surplus (corporation) [9]	reserve
*suspenders	braces
*sweater	pull-over [1]
*taffy	toffee
*taxi stand	cab rank
telephone booth	call box

[2] A correspondent of the Liverpool *Daily Post,* Nov. 9, 1939, called attention to the fact that the Liverpool Corporation uses *pavement* to indicate the roadway, not the *sidewalk.* The *Industrial News,* Sept. 22, 1936, indicates that it also uses *sidewalk* as Americans do. [On the other hand, in Philadelphia and its environs, *pavement* is used in the English sense. See Hans Kurath, Word Geography, pp. 33, 62, Fig. 20.]

[3] In Australia a *slingshot* is a *shanghai;* [in the South it is still sometimes called a *nigger-shooter*]. The slingshot is becoming obsolete in America, as American boys forget their old sports and games.

[4] [The LA has recorded all three, as well as *hydrant,* an Americanism traced to 1806 in the sense of a fireplug, and to 1846 in that of a simple *spigot* or *spicket.* *Tap* is the common Canadian term.]

[5] [According to Mrs. Starr, *shorthand-typist* is now the more common term.]

[6] *Streamlined* is also used in England.

[7] [With the development of stringless varieties, *string bean* is largely an unhappy memory, except in the metaphorical sense. Two regional terms, the Midland *green beans* and the Southern *snap beans,* are favored in commercial usage.]

[8] Or *tube.* In England, and some American cities, *subway* means an underground passage for persons on foot. [In the upper Midwest it is used for a highway underpass.]

[9] [Some American corporations, embarrassed by the term *surplus,* designate it as *reinvested in the business.*]

[1] Or *cardigan,* or *jumper. Sweater* designates the American *sweat shirt.*

American	English
*tenpins	ninepins
thriller	shocker [2]
*thumbtack, or pushpin	drawing pin
ticket agent (railroad)	booking clerk
*ticket office (railway)	booking office
tie (railroad)	sleeper [3]
tie-up (traffic)	hold-up
*top (automobile)	hood
touchdown (football)	try
*transom (door)	fanlight
transport (Army ship)	troopship, or trooper
*trolley, or streetcar	tram, or tramcar
*truck	lorry
truck farmer	market gardener
truck line	road haulier
trunk	box
tube (radio)	wireless valve
T.V.	telly
*undershirt	vest, or singlet
union station	joint station
*union suit	combinations
vacationist	holiday maker
*vaudeville	variety
*vaudeville theater	music hall
*vest	waistcoat
*vomit (verb)	to be sick
washday	washing day
*washrag	face flannel [4]
*water heater	geyser
weather bureau	meteorological office
white-collar (worker)	black-coat
witness stand	witness box

[2] Murder for Pleasure, by Howard Haycraft; New York, 1941: "In England [*thriller*] has come increasingly to mean the bona fide detective story. When the English wish to signify the sensational novel, they say *shocker*." I take this from *AS*, Vol. XVII, Feb. 1942, p. 70.

[3] [According to Southworth Lancaster (private communication Apr. 1, 1957): "The difference in terminology is attributable to differing construction practices. In England *sleepers* were laid at right angles to the rails. In the first

American railroads, *sleepers* were laid lengthwise, with the rails attached to them. Later the *sleepers* were further secured by *crossties* or *ties*. The first reference I have found is in the B. & O. annual report for 1831."]

[4] [Private communication from Mrs. Helen Starr: "When I was in Newport, Monmouthshire, in 1928, it was *face flannel* and made from worn-out flannel garments. Now they have *face cloths*, and we buy ours too and call them *wash cloths*."]

A similar list of words which occur in both American and English but in quite different senses would run to like length. *Overalls*, to an Englishman, means "tight trousers which fit over the boots," [5] *corn* means any kind of grain for human consumption, *lumber* means disused articles of furniture, a *longshoreman* may mean a man who takes oysters along the seashore, *partridge* never means grouse or quail, a *frontier* is always a boundary between two countries, an *orchestra* is always a band of music and never a section of seats in a theater, and so on. Horwill adds that *precinct*, to an Englishman, means an enclosed space, especially one including a church, and that the American sense of a political subdivision is unknown to him. So is *dues* used for what the English call a *subscription* to a club or other such organization. *Homestead* they know, but not in our special sense of a grant of free land. They distinguish between *hunting* foxes or stags and *shooting* birds. They never call a judge a *jurist*, but reserve the term for "one versed in the science of the law," *i.e.*, a legal writer or professor. They do not regard *politics* as an opprobrious word; they know nothing of *office politics* or *campus politics* or *church politics*, [though they have come to be afflicted by *university politics*]. What we call a *citizen* they commonly call a *subject*. They think of *tardy* as meaning slow-moving rather than behind time. We have many words in *blue* that they do not use, *e.g.*, *blue laws*, *blue-sky laws*, *bluegrass* and *bluenose*. They know nothing of the policeman's *nightstick*, nor of *night riders*, nor of *scratch pads*.

A *davenport*, which is a couch here, is a desk or escritoire there; and a *dumb-waiter*, which is an elevator here, is a revolving table there, like our *lazy susan*. *Haberdashery*, in the United States, means men's wear, excluding shoes and outer clothes; in England it designates what we call *notions*. Before Damon Runyon became popular, a *guy*, in England, was a ridiculous figure, and the word was opprobrious; in the United States the word is an amiable synonym for *fellow*. The English *guy* owes its origin to the effigies of *Guy Fawkes*, leader of the Gunpowder Plot of 1605, which used to be burnt in public on November 5. But the English sense of the word is preserved in the American verb *to guy*. That verb gave birth to the verb phrase *to guy the life out of* not later than 1880, and by 1890 *to guy* itself was being used by American actors in the sense of to trifle with a part. But the noun *guy*, with no derogatory significance, seems to have come in a bit later, and the DAE's first example is from George Ade's "Artie" (1896). Partridge says that it began to be heard in England *c.* 1910, and soon afterward it was made familiar by American movies, but it still strikes the more elegant sort of Englishman as rather strange.[6]

[5] Right Dress, London *Daily Express*, June 27, 1936.

[6] [See The Ambivalence of *Guy*, by Edward Hackett, *Western Humanities Review*, Vol. VIII, Summer 1954, pp. 273-4.]

Homely, in the United States, always means ill-favored, but in England its principal meaning is simple, friendly, home-loving, folksy. The American meaning was formerly familiar to the English, and in 1590 Shakespeare wrote:

> *Hath* homely *age th' alluring beauty took*
> *From my poor cheek?*[7]

The use of *homely* in this sense of "commonplace in appearance or features, not beautiful, plain, uncomely" has been rare in England since the Eighteenth Century, and the Englishman of today always understands the word to be complimentary rather than otherwise. The English meaning may be discerned in certain phrases that have survived in America, *e.g.*, *homely fare* and *homely charm*, but no American, without hostile intent, would apply *homely* to a woman.

Sick is in common use attributively in England, as in *sick leave*, *sickbed* and *sickroom*, but in the predicative situation it has acquired the special meaning of nauseated, and so *ill* is usually used in place of it. An Englishman seldom speaks of a *warm* day; he prefers to call it *hot*, [being thankful for such a day when he can get it[8]]. He seldom uses *to peek* in the sense of to peep, and the Oxford marks *peek-a-boo* as "now chiefly U.S." He likewise knows *to slew*, but prefers *to swerve*, and is unacquainted with *slew-foot*.

That an Englishman calls out "*I* say!" and not simply "Say!" when he desires to attract a friend's attention or register a protestation of incredulity —this perhaps is too familiar to need notice. The movies, however, have taught his children the American form. His *hear*, *hear!* and *oh*, *oh!* are also well known. He is much less prodigal with *good-by* than the American; he uses *good day* and *good afternoon* far more often. He has no equivalent for *over his signature*; an Englishman who issues a signed statement simply makes it *in writing*. In American *just* is almost equivalent to the English *quite*, as in *just lovely*. The word is also used in place of *exactly* in other ways, as in *just in time*, *just how many?* and *just what do you mean?*

Thornton shows that the use of *right* in *right away*, *right good* and *right now*—familiar to all readers of Chaucer—was widespread in the United States early in the last century; his first example is dated 1818. Dickens noted *right away* as an almost universal Americanism during his first American tour (1842), and poked fun at it in Chapter II of "American Notes." *Right* is also used as a synonym for *directly*, as in *right off*; for *moderately*, as in *right well* and *right often*; and in place of *precisely*

---

[7] The Comedy of Errors, II.
[8] [This happy comment was made in a private communication from Andrew Levens.]

or *certainly*, as in *right there* and "I'll get there *all right*." The American use of *some* as an adjective indicating the superlative, as in "She is *some* girl," is now common in England, but its employment as an adverb to indicate either moderation or intensification, as in "I play golf *some*" and "That's lying *some*," is still looked upon as an Americanism there. The former usage has respectable English precedents, but the latter seems to be American in origin. Thornton has traced it to 1785. It enjoyed a revival during World War I, and produced a number of counter phrases, *e.g.*, *going some*.

The American visitor to England is often brought up by Briticisms so seldom heard in the United States, even as quotations, that they have the effect on him of foreign words. When, on passing a butcher's shop, he sees a sign offering *offals*, he is unpleasantly affected until told that, to an Englishman, the word simply means liver, kidney, tongue, heart, etc. Nor can he grasp without aid the meaning of the *silversides*, *gigots* and *stewing steak* offered at the same place, nor of the *fireside suites* and *surrounds* advertised by the dealers in house furnishings, nor of the *judge's kettles*, *secateurs*, *coal cauldrons* and *spark guards* to be had of the same. He is puzzled by the rubric *Au Pair* in the want-ad columns of the newspapers—until he reads the ads and finds that it simply indicates an offer of services for board and lodging. *To tout*, he finds, may have the harmless meaning of to collect party funds, and making a *whip-round* is only passing the hat. But what is a *tomasha*, and what are *gold sticks*, *crocodiles*, *tied houses*, *hooroosh*? How can there be such a thing as a *proper* bungalow? What, precisely, is *good form*? [9]

Conversely, a number of very common words, entering into many compounds and idioms in the United States, are known in England only as exoticisms, *e.g.*, *swamp*. It may have been in use in some English dialect before it was adopted in this country, but the first example so far unearthed is from Captain John Smith's "General History of Virginia" (1624). The word is old in English as an adjective meaning lean, unthriving, and it is possible that the American noun was derived from this adjective, but Weekley prefers to connect it with the German noun *Sumpf*,

---

[9] A Thing Called Not Done, London *Morning Post*, Aug. 4, 1936: "*Good form*—that mysterious ideal of schools—was the subject of pointed comment by Mr. W. B. Curry, headmaster of Dartington Hall, Devon, yesterday. '*Good form*, so far as I understand it,' he told the New Education Fellowship at Cheltenham, 'is a way of making important things seem trivial and trivial things seem important. It is concerned with manners and behaviour and a thing called *not done*. In schools where *good form* is thought important, it is much more serious to violate the canons of *good form* than to violate the Ten Commandments. Serious worship of *good form* among the young seems inevitably to lead to inflexibility of temper, because the essence of *good form* is that you do not question it.'"

which means precisely what Americans call a *swamp*. *Swamp* has produced many derivatives in the United States, *e.g.*, *to be swamped* in the sense of to be overwhelmed, traced to 1646; *swamp angel*[1] and *swamper*, a dweller in a swamp, traced to 1857 and 1735, respectively; *swamp land*, 1663; *swamp lot*, 1637; *swamp oak*, 1681; *swamp pine*, 1731; *swamp pink*, an azalea, 1784; *swamp rabbit*, 1845; *swamp sparrow*, 1811; and *swamp wood*, 1666.

Many other familiar and characteristic Americanisms have not been adopted in England and are little known there, *e.g.*, *snarl* (tangle), *lye* (household), *to hospitalize*, *truck garden*, *to shuck* (oysters), *gum* for chewing gum (in England it always means mucilage), *in back of* (though the English use *in front of*), *dirt* (for *earth*, though *dirt track* is coming into use), *jigger*, *powder room* (though it is occasionally used), *waist* and *shirtwaist* (the English always use *blouse*, as many modern Americans do), *lima bean*, *pipe dream* and *goose pimple* (the English use *chicken flesh*). Some of these are old English terms that have become obsolete in England. In this country *luggage* is coming to have the special meaning of the bags in which *baggage* is packed; in England it means their contents, though *baggage* is still used by military men. A *lobbyist*, in England, is not a legislative wire-puller, but a journalist who frequents the lobby of the House of Commons, looking for news and gossip. A *veteran* always means a soldier of long service; not, as with us, any ex-soldier. The English use the same measures that we do, but in many cases their values differ.[2] Their *bushel*, *peck*, *gallon*, *quart*, *pint* and *gill* are all larger than ours. Their *hundredweight* is 112 pounds, whereas ours is 100 pounds. Of their *quarter* of wheat we know nothing, nor have we their *quartern-loaf* or their *quarter-days*. A *billion*, in England, is not 1,000,000,000, but 1,000,000,000,000; for the former the word is *milliard*. According to Alistair Cooke, it is these words of differing meaning in England and the United States that give a visiting Englishman the most trouble:

If an Englishman reads "The floorwalker says to go to the *notion* counter," he knows at least one word he does not understand. If he reads a speech of President Roosevelt declaring that "our industries have little doubt of *black-ink* operations in the last quarter of the year," he is at least aware of a foreign usage, and may be trusted to

---

[1] *Swamp angel* was the nickname of a big gun used at the siege of Charleston in the Civil War. [*The Morris Island Swamp Angel* was published by the Union troops serving this piece. See Southern Newspaper Names, by James P. Jones, *Names*, Vol. X, June 1962, p. 118.] The

word was later used to designate a member of one of the bands of ruffians allied with the Ku Klux Klan.

[2] [How Do We Measure Up?, Or, When Is a Cup Not a Cup?, by Jill Elizabeth Little, *Christian Science Monitor*, Jan. 4, 1962.]

go off and discover it. But if I write "The *clerk* gave a *biscuit* to the *solicitor*," he will imagine something precise, if a little odd. The trouble is that, however lively his imagination, what he imagines may be precise but is bound to be wrong. For he is confronted with three nouns which mean different things in the United States and in England.[3]

An Englishman, walking into his house, does not enter upon the *first floor* as we do, but upon the *ground floor*. When he speaks of the *first floor*, he means what we call the *second floor*, and so on up to the roof, which is covered, not with *tin* or *shingles*, but with *tiles* or *leads*. He does not ask for *mail* but for *letters*. There are *mail trains* in his country, but in general he reserves the word *mail* for letters going to or from foreign countries, and he knows nothing of the compounds so numerous in American, *e.g.*, *mail car, -man, -box* and *-carrier*. He uses *post* instead. The man who brings his *post* or *letters* is always a *postman*, never a *mailman*. His outgoing letters are *posted*, not *mailed*, at a *letterbox*, not at a *mailbox*. If they are urgent they are sent, not by *special delivery*, but by *express post*. Goods ordered by post on which the dealer pays the cost of transportation are said to arrive, not *postpaid* or *prepaid*, but *post-free* or *carriage-paid*. The English have begun to use *freight* in our sense, though they prefer to restrict it to water-borne traffic, and they have borrowed *Pullman*, *ballast* and *track*, but they still get *in* or *out* of a train, not *on* or *off* it. They say a train is *up to* time, not *on* time; they call a railway bill of lading a *consignment note*, the aisle of a Pullman its *corridor*, and they know nothing, according to Horwill, of *way stations*, *flag stops*, *grade crossings*, *flyers*, *long* and *short hauls*, *trunk lines* and *tie-ups*.

In England a realtor is an *estate agent*, what we call a belt (as in *Cotton Belt, Corn Belt, Bible Belt*) is a *zone*,[4] a traffic blockade is a *block*, hand-me-downs are *reach-me-downs*, a laborer on the roads or railroads is a *navvy* (rhymes with *savvy*), and instead of signs reading "Post No Bills" the English put up signs reading "*Stick* No Bills." By *chicken* the English can mean any fowl, however ancient; [recently, however, they have begun to classify them as *boiling fowls, roasting chickens, broiling chickens* and *spring chickens*]. *Broilers* and *friers* are never heard of over there. The classes which, in America, eat *breakfast*, *dinner* and *supper* have *breakfast*, *dinner* and *tea* in England;[5] *supper* means a light evening meal or a late meal after a show. An Englishwoman's personal maid (almost an extinct

---

[3] The American Language, *Spectator*, Sept. 6, 1935.

[4] [But according to Andrew Levens, *belt* is coming in.]

[5] [With working wives, longer school-days and greater distances to travel to work, most American urban families now have a midday *dinner* only on Sundays or holidays.]

species in the welfare state) is not *Ethel* or *Maggie* but *Robinson*, and the woman who looks after the children is not *Lizzie* but *Nurse*. A general servant, however, is addressed by her given name, or, as the English always say, by her *Christian* name. A hospital that takes pay for entertaining the sick is not a hospital at all, but a *nursing home*, and its *trained* or *registered nurses* (as we would say) are plain *nurses*, or *hospital nurses*, or maybe *nursing sisters*. An English law student does not *study law* in his Inn of Court, but *reads the law*, though if he goes to a university to seek a doctorate in law he may be said to *study* it.

If an English boy goes to a *public school*, he is not getting his education free; his father is paying a good round sum for it and is accepted as a gentleman. A *public school* over there corresponds to the more elegant sort of American *prep school;* it is a place maintained chiefly by endowments, wherein boys of the upper classes are prepared for the universities. They normally attend a *prep school* to prepare for their *public school*. What we know as a *public school* is called a *council school* in England, because it is in the hands of the education committee of the County Council; it used to be called a *board school*, because before the Education Act of 1902 it was run by a school board. The boys in a *public school* are divided, not into *classes* or *grades*, but into *forms*, which are numbered, the highest usually being the *sixth;* [this terminology has also infected the council schools]. The benches they sit on are also called *forms*. An English boy whose father is unable to pay for his education goes first into a *babies' class* or *reception class* in *primary* or *infants' school* (corresponding to our elementary or grammar school). He moves thence to *class four, class three, class two* and *class one*, and then into the *junior school*, where he enters the *first form*. Until now boys and girls have sat together in class, but they are soon separated, the boy going to a boys' school and the girl to a girls'. The boy goes up a form a year. He reaches the seventh form, if he is bright, at the age of twelve and then goes into what is known as the *ex-seventh*. If he stays at school after this he goes into the *ex-ex-seventh*. But some leave the *public elementary school* at the *ex-seventh* and go into [a *grammar school*, a *secondary modern school*, a *technical college* or—the newest wrinkle—a *comprehensive school*, which is much like an American high school, except that it provides better instruction. *Grade schools* are unknown.[6]]

The principal of an English *public* (*i.e.*, private) *school* or *elementary school* is a *headmaster* or *headmistress*, but in a *secondary school* he or she may be a *principal*. Only girls' schools have *headmistresses*. The lower pedagogues used to be *ushers*, but are now *masters* or *assistant masters* (or

---

[6] [Here again I am indebted to Andrew Levens.]

mistresses). The titular head of a university is a *chancellor;* he is commonly an ornamental bigwig, and a *vice-chancellor* does the work.[7] Most English universities now have *deans* of faculties and some have *deans of women* and even *advisers to women students*. They have minor dignitaries of kinds unknown in the United States, *e.g.*, *proctors, orators* and *high stewards*. [The *proctor*, combining the functions of an American *dean of men* and *dean of women*, is responsible for the discipline and decorum of the entire university.[8]] In Scotland the universities also have *rectors*, who are chosen by election, and, like the chancellors, are mainly ornamental. The head of a mere college may be a *president, principal, master, warden, rector, dean* or *provost*. In the solitary case of the London School of Economics, he is a *director*. The students are simply *first-year men, second-year men*, and so on, though a *first-year man* is sometimes a *freshman* or *fresher*. Students do not flock together according to seniority, and there is no regulation forbidding an upperclassman, or even a graduate, to be polite to a student just entered.

The American stratified academic hierarchy, from *instructor* to *full professor*, is unknown in the English universities; they have *readers, assistant lecturers* (*assistants* in Scotland), *lecturers, senior lecturers* and *professors*. If his chair has been endowed by royalty, a professor prefixes *regius* to his title. A student, though technically a *member* of the university, has few rights as such until he is graduated (or, in some cases, until he takes his M.A.). The professors, lecturers and readers of a college or university do not constitute a *faculty*, but a *staff*,[9] and they are called, collectively, its *dons*, though all teachers are not, necessarily, *dons* (*i.e.*, fellows). An English university student does not *study;* he *reads*—whether for a *pass degree*, which was once easy but is becoming harder, or for *honours*, which demands serious work. [It used to be remarked that all a student needed to do to receive a *pass degree* was to maintain residence, pay his bills with reasonable promptness and avoid serious trouble with the police.] He knows nothing of *frats, class days, rushes, credits, points, majors, semesters, senior proms* and other such things; save at Cambridge and Dublin he does not even speak of a *commencement*, but of *degree day* or *speech day* or *prize day*. On the other hand, his speech has such un-American esoterica as *wrangler, tripos, head, greats* and *mods*. If he is expelled he is *sent down*. There are no *college boys* in England; only *university men*.

---

[7] [From 1946 to 1961 the University of Chicago was headed by a *chancellor*, with provision for a *president* as his subordinate; contrariwise, the University of North Carolina has a *president* at the head and a *chancellor* at each of its branches.]

[8] [Once more I am indebted to Andrew Levens.]

[9] But *faculty* is used to designate the *staff* of a special school, *e.g.*, of theology, medicine or law.

The upkeep of council schools in England, save for some help from the Treasury, comes out of the *rates*, local taxes levied upon householders. Thus an English municipal taxpayer is called a *rate payer*. The functionaries who collect and spend the money are not *office holders* or *job holders*, but *civil servants*, if employed by the national government, or *local government officials*, if by the community. A policeman is a *cop* or *copper* familiarly and a *constable* officially; the older *bobby* is going out.[1] He is sometimes mentioned in the newspapers, not by his name, but as P.C. 643 A—*i.e.*, Police Constable No. 643 of the A Division. When he belongs to what we call the traffic division he is said to be *on point duty*. The one rank between *sergeant* and *superintendent* is *inspector*. The blotter at a police station is the *charge sheet*. A counterfeiter is a *coiner*, and a fire bug is a *fire raiser*. The warden of a prison is the *governor*, and his assistants are *warders*. There is no *third degree*, and no *strong-arm squad*. An English saloonkeeper is officially a *licensed victualler*. His saloon is a *public house*, or colloquially, a *pub*. He does not sell beer by the *shell*, *seidel* or *stein*, but by the *pint*, *half-pint* or *glass*. He and his brethren, taken together, are the *licensed trade*, or simply the *trade*. He may divide his establishment into a *public bar*, a *saloon bar* and a *private bar*, the last being the toniest, or he may call his back room a *parlour*, *snug* or *tap room*. If he has a few upholstered benches in his place he may call it a *lounge*. He employs no *bartenders*. *Barmaids* do the work, with maybe a *barman*, *potman* or *cellarman* to help. [*Beer* is the generic term; the cheapest is *bitter*. Normal brews are *light ale*, *brown ale*, *dark ale* and *stout*. Imported light ale is known as *lager*. When an Englishman speaks of *booze* he means only ale or beer: for our *hard liquor* (a term he never uses) he prefers *spirits*. But he may refer to a friend as "a bit of a *boozer*," and say "He went out on the *booze*," "He came home full of *booze*" or "He spent the evening *boozing* around."] What we call *hard* cider is *rough* cider to him, [though all English cider is alcoholic]. The American *bung starter* is a *beer mallet* in England, and, as in this country, is frequently used for assault and homicide.

In England *corporation* commonly designates a municipal or university corporation, or some other such public body, *e.g.*, the British Broadcasting *Corporation*. But in 1920 Parliament passed an act (10 & 11 Geo. V, Ch. 18) levying a *corporation profits* tax. An Englishman writes *Ltd.* after the name of a limited liability (what we would call *incorporated*) bank or trading company, as we write *Inc.* He calls its president its *chairman* if a part-timer, or its *managing director* if a full-timer. Its stockholders are its *shareholders*, and hold *shares* instead of *stock* in it. Its bonds are called *debentures*, and the word is not limited in meaning, as in the United States, to securities not protected by a mortgage. The Wall Street of London is called the *City*,

---

[1] [This information—and that about imbibing—also furnished by Andrew   Levens.]

with a capital *C.* Bankers, stockjobbers, promoters, directors and other such leaders of its business are called *City* men. The financial editor of a newspaper is its *City* editor. Government bonds are *consols,* or *stocks,* or *the funds. To have money in the stocks* is to own such bonds. An Englishman has a *banking account,* his deposit slip is a *paying-in slip* and the stubs of his *cheque* book are the *counterfoils.* He makes a rigid distinction between a *broker* and a *stockbroker.* A *broker* means not only a dealer in securities, as in our *Wall Street broker,* but also "a person licensed to sell or appraise distrained goods." *To have the brokers* (or *bailiffs*) *in* means to be bankrupt, with one's very household goods in the hands of one's creditors.[2] What we call a *grain broker* is a *corn factor.*

Tariff reform, in England, does not mean a movement toward free trade, but one toward protection. The word *Government,* meaning what we call *the administration,* is always capitalized and usually construed as plural, *e.g.,* "The Government *are* considering the advisability," etc. A member of Parliament does not *run* for office; he *stands.* An English candidate is not *nominated,* but *adopted.* If he *stands* successfully, he *sits* at Westminster, and is a *sitting* member. When it is said of a man that he is *nursing a constituency,* it means that he is attending fairs, subscribing to charities and otherwise flattering and bribing the voters, in the hope of inducing them to *return* him. Once *returned,* he does not represent a *district,* but a *division* or *constituency.* At a political meeting (they are often rough in England) the ushers and bouncers are called *stewards.* A roll call in Parliament is a *division,* and an appropriation is a *vote.* A member speaking is said to be *up* or *on his legs.* When the House adjourns it is said to *rise.* The word *politician* has no opprobrious significance in England; it is applied to themselves by statesmen of the first eminence. [A government department is a *ministry,* under a *minister;* the most important ministers make up the *Cabinet,* headed by the *Prime Minister. Ministry* also corresponds to the American *administration;* Churchill's *ministry* designates his period as Prime Minister.[3]] A *contested* election, in England, is simply one in which there is more than one candidate; the adjective does not imply fraud.

The English keep up most of the old distinctions between physicians and surgeons, barristers and solicitors. A *barrister* is greatly superior to a *solicitor.*[4] He alone can address the higher courts and the parliamentary committees; a solicitor must keep to office work and the inferior courts. A man with a grievance goes first to his solicitor, who then *instructs* or *briefs* a

---

[2] A Glossary of Colloquial Slang and Technical Terms in Use in the Stock Exchange and in the Money Market, by A. J. Wilson; London, 1895.
[3] [This addendum furnished me by Andrew Levens.]

[4] An eloquent account of the pains and costs of becoming a *barrister,* by Viscount Castlerosse, was published in the London *Sunday Express,* Mar. 20, 1938.

barrister for him. Only barristers may become judges. An English barrister, like his American brother, takes a *retainer* when he is engaged, but the rest of his fee does not wait upon the termination of the case; he expects and receives a *refresher* from time to time. A barrister is never *admitted* to the bar, but is always *called*. If he becomes a *Queen's Counsel*, or *Q.C.* (a mainly honorary appointment, though it carries some privileges and usually brings higher fees), he is said to have *taken silk*. In the United States a lawyer *tries* a case and the judge either *tries* it or *hears* it; in England it is the judge who *tries* it, and the barrister *pleads* it. In the United States the court *hands down* a decision; in England the court hands it *out*. The calendar of a court is the *cause list*, and the lawyer's briefcase is an *attaché case*. The *brief* in it is not a document to be filed in court, as with us, but a solicitor's instructions to a barrister. What we call a *brief* is called *pleadings*. A *corporation lawyer*, of course, is a *company lawyer*.

The common objects and phenomena of nature are often differently named in England and America. The Englishman, instead of saying that the temperature is 29 degrees (Fahrenheit) or that the thermometer or the mercury is at 29 degrees, sometimes says there are *three degrees of frost*. Many of our names for common fauna and flora are unknown to him save as strange Americanisms, *e.g., terrapin, ground hog, poison ivy, persimmon, gumbo, eggplant, catnip, sweet potato* and *yam*. He is familiar with many kinds of sea food that we seldom see, *e.g., turbot, brill, raker, monkfish, coalfish, periwinkles* (or just *winkles*), *ling, dories* and *witches*, and eats some that we reject, *e.g., skate*. He also knows the *hare*, which is seldom heard of in America. But he knows nothing of *deviled crab, club sandwiches, clam chowder* or *oyster stew*, and he never goes to *oyster suppers, sea-food* (or *shore*) *dinners, clambakes* or *barbecues*, or eats *boiled dinners*.

An Englishman never lives *on* a street, but always *in* it,[5] though he may live *on* an avenue or road. He never lives in a *block* of houses, but in a *row* of them, or in a *block of flats* (not an *apartment*).[6] He often calls an office building simply a house, *e.g., Lever House*. [American branches of British firms have lately introduced this practice, and Anglophiles have spread it.]

The Englishman knows the *East End* and the *West End*, but the names of his streets are never preceded by *north, east, south* or *west*, and he never speaks of the *northeast corner* of two of them. English streets have no *sidewalks;* they are called *pavements* or *footpaths* or simply *paths. Sidewalk,*

---

[5] [Older New Yorkers and professional Charlestonians also live *in* a street; thanks to the subtle machinations of British agents, this idiom is also common in the 500% American Chicago *Tribune,* and was for a long time ordained by its style book. For this information I am indebted to Mrs. Jane Rosenthal.]

[6] [According to Andrew Levens, "*apartment* in English is a rather highfalutin' word meaning a set of rooms. The Queen has her private *apartment* in the Palace."]

however, is used in Ireland. A *road*, in England, is always a road, and never a railway. A *car* means a tramcar or motorcar, never a *railway carriage*. A telegraph *blank* is a telegraph *form*. The Englishman may have his shoes (or boots) *blacked, polished* or *shined*. He calls a *pócketbòok* a *purse* or *wallet*, and gives the name *pôcketbóok* or *pôcket diáry* to what we call a *memorandum book*. By *cord* he means strong string, almost what we call *twine;* his *twine* is the coarse sort of string used in a garden. He uses *dessert*, not to indicate the whole last course at dinner, but to designate the fruit only; the rest is the *sweet* or *pudding*.[7] If he inhabits bachelor quarters he commonly says that he lives in *chambers*. *Apartment houses* are often *mansions*. Both terms are relics of the old upper class. The janitor or superintendent is a *caretaker* or *porter*.

The Englishman is naturally unfamiliar with the countless phrases and metaphors that baseball has supplied to American. But he uses more racing terms and metaphors than we do, and a good many phrases from other games, particularly cricket. The word *cricket* itself indicates, in general, good sportsmanship. To take unfair advantage of an opponent is not *cricket*. Boating, once so popular on the Thames, has given colloquial English some familiar terms, almost unknown in the United States, *e.g., punt* and *weir*. The English vocabulary of racing differs somewhat from ours. When the odds are 2 to 1 in favor of a horse, we say that its price is *1 to 2;* the Englishman says that it is *2 to 1 on*. We speak of backing a horse to *win, place* or *show,* or *across the board*. The Englishman uses *each way* instead, meaning *win* or *place,* for *place*, in England, means both *second* and *third*. But the English have developed nothing comparable to the sporting argot used by American sporting reporters. When, during World War I, American soldier nines played baseball in England, some of the English newspapers employed visiting American reporters to cover the games, and the resultant emission of technicalities interested English readers much more than the games themselves. One of the things that puzzled them was the word *inning,* as in *second inning;* in England it is always plural.

As a set-off to American sports-page jargon, the English have an ecclesiastical vocabulary with which we are almost unacquainted, and it is in daily use, for the Church bulks much larger in public affairs over there than it does here. Such common terms as *vicar, canon, verger, curate, locum tenens, suffragan, dean, lay reader, holy orders* and *churchman* are seldom used in the United States, at least in their English senses, save by members

---

[7] [Comment by Andrew Levens: "*Sweet* and *pudding* are interchangeable, and the leaders of the U and non-U controversy cannot agree which is current, which is better, or which is U. Personally, I dislike both of them and stick to *dessert* or *second course,* but I am in a minority. *Pudding* implies what we normally call *stodge. Sweet* is a very unpleasant word."]

of the Protestant Episcopal Church, the crown colony of the Church of England. Except for Roman Catholics and High Church Episcopalians, to the average American a *curate* must seem as puzzling a mammal as an *archimandrite*, and a *locum tenens* (also used of doctors in England) must suggest inevitably what, in the vulgate, is known as *jim-jams*. The English use of *holy orders* is also strange to us. They do not say that a young man is *studying* for the ministry, but that he is *reading for holy orders*, though he may do the former if he is headed for the dissenting pulpit. Indeed, save he be a Presbyterian or Methodist, he is seldom called a *minister* at all, though the term appears in the Book of Common Prayer, and—except a Lutheran—never a *pastor;* a clergyman of the Establishment is always either a *rector, vicar* or *curate*, or colloquially a *parson*. According to Horwill, the term *clergyman* is seldom applied to any other kind. In America *chapel* simply means a small church, usually the dependent of some larger one; in England it has acquired the special sense of a place of worship unconnected with the Establishment. A Methodist wailing place in England, however large it may be, or any other dissenting house of worship, is still legally a *chapel*. But the London *Times* displays notices of services in Presbyterian, Congregational, Baptist, Christian Science and even Catholic *Churches*. *Chapel*, of course, is also used to designate a small house of worship of the Establishment when it is neither a parish church nor a cathedral, *e.g.,* St. George's *Chapel*, Windsor, and King's College *Chapel*, Cambridge. What the English call simply a *churchman* is an *Episcopalian* in the United States, and what they call the *Church* (always capitalized) is the *Protestant Episcopal Church*. The American language, of course, knows nothing of *nonconformists* or *dissenters*. The OED traces *dissenter* to 1663, and says that "in early use" it included Roman Catholics, but "is now usually restricted to those legally styled *Protestant* dissenters." Jews, like Catholics, are excluded. *Nonconformist*, of the same meaning, is traced to 1672, but *nonconformist conscience* is not listed, though every civilized Englishman (and American) is its goat. In Scotland one who refuses to swallow the national Presbyterianism is likewise a *dissenter*. The term was in use in America in colonial days, but disappeared when the battered fragment of the Church of England among us became converted into the Protestant Episcopal Church, and was disestablished everywhere.[8] The English have a number of *dissenting* sects whose very names are unknown in the United States, such as the *Methodist New Connexion*, but the American crop is much larger and considerably more bizarre. The Census Bureau's official

---

[8] [A learned if somewhat partisan discussion is The Origin and Meaning of the Name *Protestant Episcopal*, by Robert W. Shoemaker; New York, 1959. See also his The Nineteenth Century: Watershed of American Religious Appellations, *AS*, Vol. XXXIV, Feb. 1959, pp. 5–10.]

list of American denominations includes the *General Six Principle Baptists*, the *Two-Seed-in-the-Spirit Predestinarian Baptists*, the *Progressive Dunkers*, the *United Zion's Children*, the *Hutterian Brethren, Christ's Sanctified Holy Church*, the *Church of the Full Gospel*, the *Pillar of Fire*, the *Italian Pentecostal Assembly of God*, the *African Methodist Episcopal Zion Church*, the *Evangelical Unity of Bohemian and Moravian Churches*, the *Pentecostal Assemblies of Jesus Christ* and the *United Holy Church of America*, not to mention more than a dozen cubicles and cell blocks of the *Church of God*. The English get on without such American alarmers of God, and they give a *mourners' bench* the austere name of *penitent seat* or *form*. The Salvation Army, which is of English origin, uses *penitent form* even in America.

In music the English cling to an archaic nomenclature long since abandoned over here. Thus, they call a double whole note a *breve*, a whole note a *semibreve*, a half note a *minim*, a quarter note a *crotchet*, an eighth note a *quaver*, a sixteenth note a *semiquaver*, a thirty-second note a *demisemiquaver* and so on. This clumsy terminology goes back to the days of plain chant, with its *longa, brevis, semi-brevis, minima* and *semiminima*. In the same way, the English hold fast (though with a slacking of the grip of late) to a clumsy method of designating the sizes of printer's types. In America the point system makes the business easy; a line of *14-point* type occupies exactly the vertical space of two lines of *7-point*. But some old-fashioned English printers still indicate differences in size by such arbitrary and confusing names as *brilliant, diamond, small pearl, pearl, ruby, ruby-nonpareil, emerald, minion, long primer, small pica, pica, great primer* and *double pica*. The English also cling to various archaic measures. Thus, an Englishman will commonly say that he weighs eleven *stone* instead of *154 pounds*. A *stone*, in speaking of a man, is fourteen pounds, but in speaking of beef on the hoof it is only eight pounds. Instead of saying that his *back yard* is fifty *feet* long, an Englishman will say that his *back garden* is nearly seventeen *yards*. He employs such designations of time as *fortnight* and *twelvemonth* a great deal more than we do. He rarely says *fifteen minutes to* or *ten-thirty*; nearly always he uses *quarter to* and *half past ten*.[9]

In Standard English usage *directly* is always used to signify *immediately*; "in the American language, generally speaking," as Mark Twain once ex-

<hr>

[9] [Americans may say *quarter to, quarter of* or *quarter till*, the last being characteristic of Pennsylvania and its dependencies, including the upland South. The LA evidence for the Atlantic States is summarized in A Word Geography of the Eastern United States, by Hans Kurath; *University of Michigan Publications in American English*, No. 1, Ann Arbor, 1949, pp. 30, 47, 50. Fig. 44; preliminary findings further west are given in A Word Atlas of the Great Lakes Region, by A. L. Davis, diss. (microfilm), U. of Michigan, 1949.]

plained, "the word signifies after a little." [1] An Englishman never adds the pronoun in such locutions as "It hurts *me*," but says simply "It hurts." He never "*catches up* with you" on the street; he "catches *you up*." He never *brushes off* his hat; he *brushes* it. He never says "Are you *through*?" but "Have you *finished*?" or "Are you *done*?" He never uses *gotten* as the perfect participle of *get*; he always uses plain *got*.

One of the most striking differences between even nearly related languages is their varying use of fundamentally identical prepositions: it is almost unheard of for both members of an apparent pair to be used similarly in all situations. The German *über* may serve for *above, over, across* or *about* (concerning) in English, and the English *to* may call for *zu, nach* or *um zu* in German.[2] A few examples will show how, in this field, English usage sometimes differs from American:

> Since the sale of the property it has been offered for resale *by* auction.[3]
>
> He knows everything it contains *off by* heart.[4]
>
> "What is the use of waving a red flag *to* a bull?" he asked.[5]

Where the English speak of *up* and *down* tracks for trains, the American uses *eastbound, northbound, westbound* and *southbound*. Except for the London underground, the latter terms are foreign to English practice. The DA traces *eastbound, westbound, southbound* and *northbound* in railroad use to the early 80s. There are some other peculiarities, in American, in the use of indicators of geographical direction. Our *downtown* and *uptown* are seldom, if ever, encountered in England; the DAE records both in American use in the early part of the last century.[6] *Down East*, as noun, adjective and adverb, dates from the same period, and so does *down-country*, but *up-country* seems to have been in English use, at all events in the colonies, for many years.[7] *Upstate* designating New York State north and west

---

[1] Concerning the American Language, in The Stolen White Elephant; Hartford, 1882.

[2] The Loom of Language, by Frederick Bodmer; New York, 1944, pp. 126–7.

[3] Houses and Estates, London *Daily Telegraph*, Sept. 25, 1935.

[4] *John o' London's Weekly*, June 20, 1936.

[5] Socialist Repartee, London *Daily Telegraph*, Oct. 5, 1935.

[6] Anne Laurence Dodge reports in *American Notes and Queries*, Vol. III, Mar. 1944, p. 188, that in Newburyport, Mass., *up-along* and *down-along* are used.

[In *AS*, Vol. XXXVII, May 1962, p. 156, G. Thomas Fairclough points out that in Troy, N.Y., *down city* is used instead of *downtown* and that *down street*, which in some New England communities means *downtown*, is only part way down.]

[7] *Low Country*, especially in the South, denotes the Coastal Plain of South Carolina and Georgia, as distinguished from the Piedmont or *Up Country*; in England the plural *Low Countries* designates the Netherlands, and sometimes Belgium as well.

of Albany is recorded from 1901, but is probably older. The DAE records *up-boat* in 1857, *upbound* in 1884 and *upriver* [8] in 1836. *Up-south* and *up-east* are also to be found, but only, apparently, in nonce words. *Down* is in common use in New England when the journey is to Boston or to Maine.[9]

The use of *at* before points of the compass, as in *at the North*, is an Americanism, and Bartlett, in his second edition of 1859, recorded that it then "offended an English ear." [1] The English *West End*, which the OED traces to 1807, is in common use in the United States, but *West Side* seems to be preferred, and *East End*, traced to 1883 in England, is almost unknown. *East Side* is traced by the DAE to 1894, but is probably much older, for *West Side* is traced to 1858. *North Side* and *South Side* are also in use, particularly in the Chicago area, though the DAE and DA list neither.

In 1939 Stuart Robertson, of Temple University, published a discussion [2] of other differences in American and British usage of the minor coins of speech—a subject not often studied, for most observers seem to be chiefly interested in disparities in vocabulary. For example, the English rule that *to* may be omitted when the object is a pronoun, *e.g.*, "Give it me" instead of the usual American "Give it *to* me." There are also some curious differences in the use of the definite article. The English commonly insert it before *High Street*, and sometimes use it in situations wherein Americans would use *a*, *e.g.*, "ten shillings *the* bushel." Contrariwise, they omit it altogether before *government* and in *out of window*.[3] This last struck Mark Twain as one of the salient differences between American and English usage. In late years there has been a war upon the article in American journalistic writing, chiefly under the influence of *Time*, and the English have begun to join it. They have also imitated the American present subjunctive, as in "It was moved that the meeting *stand* adjourned," where orthodox English usage would ordain "*should stand* adjourned." [4] The English plural verb follow-

---

[8] [In *AS*, Vol. XXXII, Feb. 1957, pp. 75-7, it was pointed out that in Europe Americans often speak of going *up* the Rhine when traveling north, and thus downstream, and that *Ausländer* make the same mistake in Virginia, in speaking of the Shenandoah. There is also confusion about the Genesee, in upstate New York.]

[9] See R. Howard Claudius, *Up* and *Down*, *AS*, Vol. II, Oct. 1926, p. 19.

[1] [The DAE traces *at the East* in American use to 1636. The form seems to be going out, though it has been recorded by the LA; it was discussed by

E. E. Ericson in *AS*, Vol. XXXV, May 1960, pp. 156-8.]

[2] British-American Differences in Syntax, *AS*, Vol. XIV, Dec. 1939, pp. 243-54.

[3] Concerning the American Language, in The Stolen White Elephant; New York, 1888, p. 269.

[4] "Our journalists," said Ernest Weekley, in Words, American and English, London *Observer*, Oct. 9, 1938, "are gradually ejecting the English *should* in favor of the revived American subjunctive." [But whatever the case in England, the American pattern is not a revival but a petrified relic.]

ing collective nouns seems to be holding out better, though even here there are some signs of yielding. Nearly all the English newspapers still use the plural after *government, committee, company, ministry* and *vestry,* and even after proper names designating groups or institutions.[5] Such headlines as "Jesus *Outplay* All Souls" are still common in the newspapers. "The real proof for the existence of an American language," said *The New York Times* in 1938, "is not that we say *suspender* and *elevator* and the British say *braces* and *lift.* These are mere dialectical differences. The rub comes when the British newspapers say that their government *have* been exploring all possible channels, whereas we say our government *has* been exploring. The British say that Kent *face* an emergency, by which they mean that the Kent county cricket team *faces* an emergency. Reporting one of our own boat races, the British papers would say that Harvard *have* a big advantage over Yale."[6] The English are also fond of using *are* after United States. This was the early American custom, but *is* was substituted before the War of 1812. In 1942 a magazine called *Philippines,* published by the Philippine resident commission at Washington, protested against the use of *are* after Philippines, though it was allowed after Philippine Islands.[7]

The House of Lords has a watchman to see that consistency in number is maintained in government bills. He does not object to the singular verb *per se,* but insists that when a bill starts off with a plural verb, which is usually, it must so continue to the end. In 1936 he kicked up such a pother about the National Health Insurance Bill that the newspapers took notice.[8] He also insists that *who* instead of *which* shall be used in referring to the government. Englishmen, in fact, seem to prefer *who* after all collective nouns; *e.g.,* "Many big concerns *who* are excellent employers"[9] and "The Bank of France, *who* today lowered the bank rate."[1] But, following the practice of 1611, they use *which* in reference to God in their official version of the Lord's Prayer, and in 1944 the London *Times* actually dismissed the use of *who* therein as "American idiom."[2]

---

[5] In 1939 a Tasmanian journalist specializing in cricket and football news wrote to the lexicographer of *John o' London's Weekly* asking for advice about the use of the plural after, say, *Eton* and *Harrow,* and was told that he should use the singular when referring to "the team as a whole" and the plural when speaking of "the individual players in that team." "As a matter of literary grace," said the *John o' London* expert, "it is going too far to attach a plural verb to the name of the team."

[6] Editorial page, Aug. 3.
[7] Aug. 1942, p. 23. See A Protest from the Philippines, by M.J.M., *AS,* Vol. XIX, Apr. 1944, pp. 147–8.
[8] London *Daily Telegraph,* Aug. 8, 1936.
[9] 8 More Hours—for 6s., London *Daily Mirror,* Sept. 20, 1935.
[1] London *Daily Express,* Oct. 3, 1936.
[2] American Idiom, London *Times Literary Supplement,* Feb. 26, 1944, p. 103.

3: ENGLISH DIFFICULTIES WITH AMERICAN

Very few English authors ever manage to write realistic American. Their earlier attempts were usually upon the so-called Yankee or Down East dialect. The anonymous author of "The Adventures of Jonathan Corncob"[3] had his Americans use *I snore* and *I snort* as expletives, and stretched their vowels out into such forms as *blaaze away like daavils, get aloong* and *let me alo-one*. By 1866, in "Mugsby Junction," Charles Dickens had developed this Yankee dialect into the following:[4]

> And if I hain't found the eighth wonder of monarchical Creation, as finding Yew, and Yewer young ladies, and Yewer fixin's solid and liquid, all as aforesaid, established in a country where the people air not absolute Loonatocks, I am Extra Double Darned with a Nip and Frizzle to the innermost grit! Wheerfur—Theer!—I la'af! I Dew, ma'arm, I la'af!

This was so bad that even some English critics denounced it. But there was often more than bad reporting in such stuff; there was also a bitter dislike of all things American. Since 1866 many English authors have outgrown such loathing of the United States and its people, but even the most friendly of them runs into difficulties when he tries to report American colloquial speech. The only latter-day English novelist, said an American correspondent of the Manchester *Guardian* in 1937, "who can speak American" is P. G. Wodehouse.[5] At the time the American movies were first terrorizing English purists, the late W. L. George undertook a tour of this country and wrote a paper dealing with his impressions.[6] George was a very competent reporter, who delighted in Americanisms. But whenever he tried to write them he lapsed into unintelligible Briticisms: *back garden* for *back yard, perambulator* for *baby carriage, post* for *mail, petrol* for *gasoline* and so on. And to top them there were English terms with no American equivalents, *e.g., kitchen fender*. C. J. Cutliffe Hyne made a former American naval officer speak of *saloon corner men (corner loafers?)*. E. W. Hornung, in one of his "Raffles" stories, had an American prize fighter regale the London populace with: "Blamed if our Bowery boys ain't cock-angels to scum like this. . . . By the holy tinker! . . . Blight and

---

[3] London, 1787.

[4] I preserve the capitals he used for emphasis.

[5] American Slang in England, by D. B. Whitman, of Winthrop, Mass. His letter was reprinted in various American newspapers, *e.g.*, the Milwaukee *Journal*, Oct.

9, 1937. [A similar tribute to Wodehouse is found in Editor at Work, by Julie Eidesheim; New York and Toronto, 1939, p. 46.]

[6] Reprinted as Litany of the Novelist, in his Literary Chapters; London, 1918.

blister him! . . . I guess I'll punch his face into a jam pudding. . . . Say, sonny, I like you a lot, but I sha'n't like you if you're not a good boy." The American use of *way* and *away* seems to have daunted many of these authors; [7] they agree on forms never heard in the United States. Thus H. B. Marriott Watson makes an American character say: "You ought to have done business with me *away* in Chicago," and Walter Frith makes another say: "I stroll a block or two *way* down the Strand," "I'll drive him *way* down home by easy stages" and "He can pack his grip and be *way* off home." The American use of *gotten* also seems to present difficulties to English authors. For example, Rose Macaulay makes American characters say: "The kid's the only one who's *gotten* sense," "You've *gotten* but one small grip apiece" and "That about uses up all the energy they've *gotten*." [8]

At other times Americanisms are used in senses and situations that must inevitably give every actual American a start. In 1942 Margaret Louise Allingham, in a book review in the English edition of *Time and Tide*, described two quite respectable American girl characters as *floosies*.[9] During the same year Elizabeth Bowen used Americanisms in an amazing (if usually correct) manner in a serious historical work, "Bowen's Court":

> The Stuarts gestured, flattered and *double-crossed* (p. 47).
> Lord Muskerry was *putting something across* (p. 55).
> On the claim of having discovered a papist plot (which they *faked*), etc. (p. 58).[1]

Rosamund Lehmann did measurably better, and one of her American reviewers was moved to exclaim at her correct (and frequent) use of *boy friend*, *bunk* and *kidding*. But to counterbalance this, a he-novelist, Bruce Graeme, brought out a crime shocker, reprinted in the United States, in which American gangsters were made to use *blimey* and *ruddy*.[2] John Galsworthy, who frequently visited the United States, never came within miles of writing sound American. His stock device for indicating American characters was to lard his dialogue with *I judge, gee, cats* (exclamation), *vurry* (for *very*), *dandy* and *cunning*. He almost invariably confused *have got* and *have gotten*. Rather curiously, he sometimes put good American phrases into the mouths of English characters, *e.g., good egg* and *to say a*

---

[7] Frank M. Bicknell, The Yankee in British Fiction, *Outlook*, Nov. 19, 1910.

[8] Staying with Relations; London, 1930. See A British Misconception, by Stuart Robertson, *AS*, Vol. VI, Apr. 1931, p. 314.

[9] Oct. 10, 1942. She was brought to book in *Time and Tide*, Oct. 17, by D. W. Brogan.

[1] The page numbers are those of the American edition; New York, 1942.

[2] Gangsters, British Type, Detroit *Times*, May 5, 1935. The book was called Public Enemy No. 1 in England and John Jenkin, Public Enemy, in the United States.

mouthful.[3] Arnold Bennett, like Galsworthy, would make American he-men use *lovely* in such sentences as "It was a *lovely* party." Miss Mildred Wasson has commented on the cavalier way in which English writers disregard the touchstones of American regional and social dialects:[4]

> Mannerisms of speech that to an American would identify the speakers as from the Middle West, South, Boston, or Philadelphia are mixed freely in the speech of American characters as interpreted by English writers. . . . It is still more difficult for [these writers] to grasp that we have social lines of demarcation as definite as those in England and France. To ignore them stamps a writer, to Americans at least, as being a bit off his ground. An American writing of an English lord and making him speak music-hall Cockney would go just as far astray.

When they venture to deal with Americanisms humorously the British literati do even worse. The contributors to *Punch* often try, and with melancholy results, such as:

> He heard *foot noises* of quite a bunch.
> I *reckon* to work through that programme twice a day, and I *garntee* them bears gets to know eighty *barrel* oil leaving Central daily under my *tabs*.
> They *greased* for the trolley.
> *Young split*, your lil jaunt soaks me twelve *dollar* seventy-five.[5]

When English statesmen and other austere characters misuse American, they are often reported in the American newspapers, *e.g.*, Neville Chamberlain's extension of *jitterbug* to indicate an alarmist.[6] The Opposition leader,

---

[3] American Speech According to Galsworthy, by Stuart Robertson, *AS*, Vol. VI, Apr. 1931, p. 314. [See also On Englishmen Who Write American, by Cyril Connolly, *The New York Times Book Review*, Dec. 18, 1949, p. 1; and You Think You Speak English? (Translating American into English), *Christian Science Monitor*, Sept. 10, 1949, p. 12.]

[4] Cockney American, *AS*, Vol. VII, Apr. 1932.

[5] If You Know What I Mean, by C.W.M., *Independent*, Mar. 17, 1928. See also Speak the Speech, *Nation*, May 15, 1935, p. 562. The writer of the latter calls attention to the innocent way in which the brethren of *Punch* mix old and new American slang. A New York gangster is made to use *I swan* in the same sentence with *gun moll* and *gat*.

[6] Chamberlain seems to have been misled by Sir Samuel Hoare, then Home Secretary, who in a speech in the House of Commons on Jan. 26, 1939, said: "I am told that in the United States of America there is a class of people who sit listening in hysterical excitement to what is called *hot music*, and waiting for the final crash. Americans, in their forceful language, call them the *jitterbugs*. There are many people in Europe today that seem to be behaving in much the same way . . . waiting helplessly for the crash that, according to them, will destroy us all." This was a correct enough definition of *jitterbug*, but Chamberlain's subsequent use of it in the extended sense suggested by Hoare puzzled Englishmen who were familiar only with the original American sense.

Clement Attlee, in turn, accused Chamberlain of trying *to put sob stuff over the House*, forgetting the *on*, that, by American rules, should have followed *over*.[7] Chamberlain replied by describing himself as a *go-getter for peace*. He liked Americanisms, and occasionally used them correctly. His predecessor, Stanley Baldwin, had a formidable repertoire, and made precise use of *to try out*, *to deliver the goods*, *rattled*, *more to it*, *best seller* and party *dogfight*. As a switch on an old theme, he was sometimes accused of mouthing Americanisms when he was actually using ancient English terms, as when he adorned a debate with *backslider*, which the OED traces to 1581. In his heyday Winston Churchill, who is half American [and the first foreigner for whom Congress has voted honorary American citizenship (1963)], clung to the Oxford accent but larded his discourses with many American terms, *e.g.*, *proposition* and *cold feet*. Nevertheless, he once rebuked a Conservative M.P., Arthur Hugh Elsdale Molson, for using *stooge* in a question asked in the House of Commons. "I am not prepared," he said primly, "to answer a question couched in such very unseemly terms." In 1936 no less a character than the Archbishop of Canterbury used *up against* in a public pronunciamento, and during the same year King Edward VIII used both *radio* and *to broadcast* in his first fireside chat to his lieges.[8] The present Queen's cousin, Admiral Lord Louis Mountbatten (*geb.* Battenberg), speaks American fluently, for between the two world wars he made intensive linguistic and other studies in Hollywood. Some of the earlier American political terms, *e.g.*, *caucus*, *gerrymander* and *carpetbagger*, have been taken over, as we have seen, by the English politicos, but the meaning of *caucus* has been perverted, and the English have done almost as badly with *gerrymander*, which they employ to indicate any "method whereby one political party obtains an unfair advantage over another." [9] The *News of the World* even used *sawn-down* for *sawed-off* in a description of firearms.[1]

Colloquial English is just as unfathomable to most Americans as colloquial American is to Englishmen. Galsworthy not only puzzled his American readers with his bogus Americanisms; he also puzzled them with his attempts at English slang. When "The Silver Spoon" was published in this country in 1926, Harry Hansen was moved to print the following caveat:

> When a character says, "I shall *break* for lunch now" we understand what he means, but how are we to know what is meant by *bees too bee busy*, and again, *bee weak-minded*, which apparently is not a

[7] British Americanisms, *Newsweek*, Mar. 13, 1939.

[8] London *Morning Post*, Mar. 2, 1936; King's English, Manchester *Guardian Weekly*, Mar. 6, 1936.

[9] Premier's *Gerrymandering* Rebuked, London *Morning Advertiser*, Nov. 21, 1941.

[1] Shot Man's Legacy to Woman Friend, Aug. 2, 1936.

typographical error. Mr. Galsworthy's characters *take a lunar*, and enjoy the prospect of getting *tonked*. They are hit on the *boko*. "It's not my business to *queer the pitch* of her money getting," says one, and of another the author writes: "What was his image of her but a *phlizz?*" [2]

The last word was a borrowing from "Sylvia and Bruno" (1889), by Lewis Carroll, and no doubt not a few Americans recognized it, but the other terms, save maybe *to queer the pitch*, were wholly foreign to the American vocabulary.[3] Nor would it be easy to find Americans able, without some pondering, to comprehend such news items as the following:

> Lewis had driven the horse and *trap* laden with *milk churns* to a *collecting stage* on the main road, and to do so he had to cross Wood Green *level crossing*. . . . He apparently failed to see a train approaching around a *bend*. . . . The *driver* of the train pulled up promptly.[4]

Even ordinary business correspondence between Englishmen and Americans is sometimes difficult. In 1932 the publisher of the Decatur (Ill.) *Review* asked the London *Times* what its practice was in the matter of stereotyping halftones. The reply contained so many strange words and phrases that the *Review* was moved to print an editorial about them.[5] In England, it appeared, stereotypers' blankets were called *packing*, mat rollers were *mangles*, mats (matrices) were *flongs* and *to underlay a cut* was *to bump a block*. *To underlay* has since been adopted in England, but *cut* is seldom used.

The English often have difficulty understanding American books, and protest against their strange locutions with great bitterness. When my series of "Prejudices" began to be reprinted in London in 1921, many of the notices they received roundly denounced the Americanisms. But the 1926 translation into Standard English was reviewed very amiably and sold well. Changes are frequently made in American short stories reprinted in English magazines, and American advertisements are commonly rewritten for English use. In 1930 the Department of Commerce issued a business handbook of the United Kingdom, with a list of trade terms differing in England and the United States. In the early days of the movie invasion, the titles in American films were commonly translated, but that effort had to be abandoned, and for decades the talkies have poured a constant stream of

[2] The First Reader, New York *World*, July 9, 1926.

[3] [The difficulty of communicating is recognized by many British writers, *e.g.*, by Pamela Hansford Johnson (Lady Snow), in It's Easy to Get Americans All Wrong, *The New York Times Book Review*, Jan. 1, 1961, pp. 1, 20.]

[4] *News of the World*, Sept. 10, 1932.

[5] We Translate a Letter from London, Apr. 17, 1932.

American neologisms into English. Not infrequently they have been puzzling at first blush, and to the end that they may be understood, glossaries have been printed in the English newspapers.[6] Similar glossaries have sometimes been attached to American books, or inserted in the programs of American plays. When Carl Sandburg's "Collected Poems" was reprinted in London, a word list was given in the introduction, with definitions of *con man, honky-tonk, cahoots, leatherneck* and *floozy*, and when Sinclair Lewis's "Babbitt" was published there in 1922, there was added a glossary including *bellhop, to bulldoze, dingus, frame house, hootch, kibosh, nut, roommate, tinhorn* and *yeggman*. Nearly all of these are now understood in England.[7] In 1927 the Oxford University Press brought out an American edition, revised by George Van Santvoord, a former Rhodes scholar, of the Pocket Oxford Dictionary of F. G. and H. W. Fowler. It gave American spellings and pronunciations, and listed a great many words not to be found in the original English edition, *e.g., jitney, goulash, chop suey* and *drugstore*. In 1934 there followed a new edition of the Concise Oxford Dictionary, revised by H. G. LeMesurier and H. W. Fowler, with an appendix largely devoted to American terms, *e.g., alfalfa, badlands, bohunk, boob, burg, campus, chiropractic, cole slaw, coon, third degree, to doll up, to fade out* and *to get away with*. "The cinema, now vocal," says Mr. LeMesurier, "has made [the Englishman] familiar with many Americanisms at the meaning of which he has often to guess." And sometimes he guesses wrong, as when the London edition of Marjorie Hillis's "Live Alone and Like It" (1936) translated *Junior Leaguers* as *Girl Guides*.[8]

4: BRITICISMS IN THE UNITED STATES

"While England was a uniquely powerful empire state, ruled by an aristocratic caste," said Wyndham Lewis in 1934,[9] "its influence upon the speech as upon the psychology of the American ex-colonies was overwhelming. But today that ascendancy has almost entirely vanished. The aristocratic caste is nothing but a shadow of itself, the cinema has brought the American scene and the American dialect nightly into the heart of England, and the

[6] For example, American Without Tears, by Hamilton Eames, London *Times*, May 6, 1931. Mr. Eames undertook to define 118 terms, ranging from *alky-cooking* to *yen*. [More recently have appeared Swan's Anglo-American Dictionary, by G. R. Scott, New York, 1952; American into English: a Handbook for Translators, London, 1953; and Anglo-American Usage, by Margaret Nicholson, Oxford, 1957.]

[7] The Lewis glossary was made by Montgomery Belgion, an Englishman who once lived in New York. Despite his American experience he made a number of errors. Thus he defined *to buck* as to cheat, *bum* as a rotter, *highbinder* as an extravagant person and *roustabout* as a revolutionary.

[8] *The New Yorker*, Dec. 19, 1936.

[9] The Dumb Ox, *Life and Letters*, Apr. 1934, p. 42.

Americanizing process is far advanced. . . . There has been no reciprocal movement of England into the United States; indeed, with the new American nationalism, England is kept out." This is certainly true in the field of language. English neologisms are rarely taken up in this country, and when they are, only by a small class, mostly conscious Anglomaniacs. By the common people everything English, whether an article of dress, a social custom or a word or phrase, was long regarded as affected, effeminate and ridiculous. The stage Englishman is rarely a hero, and in his role of comedian he is laughed at with brutal scorn. To the average red-blooded American reader of comic strips, his tea drinking is evidence of racial decay, and so are the cut of his clothes, his broad *a* and his occasional use of such highly un-American locutions as *jolly, awfully* and *ripping*. The American soldiers who went to France in 1917 and 1918 did not develop either admiration or liking for their English comrades; indeed, they were better pleased with the French, and reserved their greatest fondness for the Germans. Of English songs, they adopted only one, "Mademoiselle from Armenteers." [1] In the elaborate but unpublished vocabulary of American soldiers' slang of World War I, compiled by E. A. Hecker and Edmund Wilson, Jr.,[2] are very few words or phrases of English origin. *To carry on* retains in American its old American meaning of to raise a pother, despite its widespread use among the English in the sense of to be (in American) *on the job*. *To wangle*, perhaps the best of the new English verbs of World War I, was a long time getting accepted. As for *blighty, cheerio* and *righto*, they would strike most members of the American Legion as almost as unmanly as *tummy* or *pee-pee*. After the success of "What Price Glory" by Laurence Stallings and Maxwell Anderson, in 1924, *what price* had a certain vogue, but it quickly passed, as did *at long last* from the 1936 abdication speech of Edward VIII.

[Except among the conscious Anglophiles, everything English was in pretty low esteem during the war-debt controversies of the 1920s and the era when the Conservatives were appeasing Hitler and Mussolini in the 1930s. But when the collapse of France left England to face Germany and Italy singlehanded, the British cause profited from the traditional American sympathy for the underdog, and the successful stubborn resistance against odds soon turned sympathy into admiration. There is nothing like common misfortune to breed mutual understanding, and American disasters in the months following Pearl Harbor brought the two English-speaking nations

---

[1] Eric Partridge, in his introduction to Songs and Slang of the British Soldier, 1914-1918, London, 1930, p. 6, says that it appeared in 1915 and (p. 48) that its tune was borrowed from the French music halls.

[2] [Through the courtesy of Mr. Wilson, HLM had access to it at the time of writing the fourth edition (1936) of this work; regrettably this glossary has not yet been published.]

closer together than ever before. Moreover, during World War II and the succeeding Cold War, Americans in large numbers actually lived among the English people for long spells and got to know English life at first hand. Nor was the newly gained respect lessened by the English ability—along with the German and French—to compete in the American market for the sale of the most typical American artifact, the automobile. But the linguistic effect of this new attitude has been scant so far, except in occasional advertisements of *tyres* for sports cars.]

World War II made all Americans familiar with such Briticisms as *commando,* but they were not numerous, even on official levels. On March 3, 1942, the word *rating* was used to describe enlisted men in a Navy communiqué, but the offense was not repeated. Other English military and naval terms that appeared during the war were *alert, quisling* and *paratroops,* and the German loans *snorkel, flak, panzer* and *lebensraum. Blitz* and its derivatives were apparently in use in the United States before they got into general circulation in England; [the patented *Blitz Cloth,* for polishing brass, was standard equipment, in the 30s, in American military schools]. Some of the phrases launched by English politicians of the war era, such as Neville Chamberlain's *to miss the bus* and Winston Churchill's *blood, sweat and tears,* were heavily labored by the American newspapers, but the vulgar were hardly aware of them. *Blood, sweat and tears,* in fact, was not Churchill's invention, though he had employed it even before it appeared in his speech of May 13, 1940.

On higher and less earthy planes there has long been greater hospitality to English example. Lacking a court, or a native aristocracy of any settled position and authority, persons of social pretensions are thrown back upon English usage for guidance, and the vocabulary and pronunciation of the West End of London naturally flavor their speech. Before 1900 *shop,* in American, always meant a workshop, but about 1905 the small, expensive stores of the larger American cities began turning themselves into *shops.* Today the word designates a store dealing in a limited range of merchandise, as opposed to a department store; [3] indeed, *shop* and *specialty shop* are interchangeable. Every American town of any pretensions now has *gift shops* (or *shoppes* [4]), *book shops, hat shops, tea shops, luggage shops* and *candy shops.* [The tonier drugstores of Madison and Lexington avenues

---

[3] [There are often *shops*—e.g., *luggage shops*—in department stores. These offer more expensive merchandise, presumably to a more select clientele, than do the regular departments of the store.]

[4] It is sometimes pronounced *shoppy,* and is often preceded by the archaic *ye,* historically just an abbreviation for *the*

but in such cases pronounced as spelled. [See Ye Olde Englysshe *Ye,* by Thomas L. Crowell, Jr., *AS,* Vol. XXIV, Apr. 1949, pp. 115–19. My own Platonic ideal of such signs is *Ye Olde Clyppe Joynte,* for the pseudo-archaic spelling betokens an increase in prices.]

in New York are often *chemist shops*, and, unlike most American drug-stores, largely confine themselves to pharmaceutical supplies.] But the plain people continue to call a *shop* a *store*, though they use *shopping* and *shopper*. The effort to substitute *boot* for *shoe* was less successful; there are not many *boot shops* left, and even fewer *boot makers*, save in the strict American sense. *Bootery* and *toggery* did not last long. But *tradesmen's entrance* fared better, and so did *charwoman*, which has pretty well now supplanted *scrubwoman*, and, in the cities at least, caused Americans to forget their native modification of *char* to *chore*. *Hired girls* began to vanish from the cities in the second Cleveland administration; their less frequent successors are all *maids* or *housekeepers*. *Drawing room*, always used in the South, began to challenge *parlor* about 1895, but soon both encountered stiff competition from *living room*. *Smog*, a mixture of smoke and fog, had long been in use among the astronomers at Yerkes Observatory, possibly owing to British influence, and in 1926 the Weather Bureau formally adopted the term.[5] How and when the National *Biscuit* Company acquired its name is a mystery. What it manufactures are *biscuits* in England, but *crackers* in the United States. The British *penny* survives in American usage, despite the fact that we have no coin bearing that name officially, and the further fact that the *cent* to which it is applied was long worth only half an English penny. It occurs in many compounds, *e.g.*, *penny bank* and *penny-in-the-slot*, and has even produced Americanisms, *e.g.*, *penny ante* and *penny arcade*.

Many Americans of social aspiration still make diligent efforts to imitate English cultural patterns, including the linguistic.[6] That fact helped change the old American sequence of *breakfast*, *dinner* and *supper* to *breakfast*, *luncheon* (often shortened to *lunch*) and *dinner*, with *supper* left hanging in the air as a designation for a nonce meal in the late evening.

The substitution of *postman* for *letter carrier* (traced by the DAE to 1825) was apparently given a lift by the great success of James M. Cain's novel "The *Postman* Always Rings Twice" (1934), but *postman*, as the DAE shows, was actually in use in the United States long before *letter carrier*, and it has always been favored in large parts of the country. The American telephone salutation "Hello" has never been supplanted by the English "Are you there?" even among Anglomaniacs, and any American telephone operator who said "You are through" to a subscriber in the sense of "Here is your party" would get an unpleasant earful. So would a federal jobholder who ventured to describe himself as a *civil servant*, or an invest-

---

[5] Associated Press dispatch from Washington, Feb. 7, 1926.

[6] [In the Chicago *Daily News*, Feb. 11, 1958, p. 25, it was pointed out that some 82% of the names in the Chicago Social Register have a "distinctive British ring," although Chicagoans of British descent are far outnumbered by Poles, Italians, etc. The article was appropriately headed Jove! British Rule Chicago.]

ment banker who attempted to float an issue of *preference shares*,[7] or a *baggage man* (once a *baggage smasher*) who began to talk of *luggage vans*, or a farmer who called his hired man an *agricultural laborer*, or a public-school principal who assumed the title of *headmaster*,[8] or a filling-station attendant who spoke of *gas* as *petrol* or the hood of a car as the *bonnet*, or an elevator starter who (outside a few fashionable shops and hotels) called his goons *liftmen*, or a candidate for any office of public honor or trust who dared to turn *secretary* into *secret'ry* or *been* into *bean*. When the theater bulked large in American life it supplied untraveled Anglophiles with a steady supply of Briticisms, both in vocabulary and in pronunciation. Thus small-town social aspirants became familiar with current Standard English pronunciation and with the current English phrases. An American of fashionable pretensions, say in Altoona, Pa., or Athens, Ga., learned how to shake hands, eat soup, greet his friends, enter a drawing room and pronounce the words *path, secretary, melancholy* and *necessarily* in a manner that was an imitation of what was done in Mayfair—in brief, an imitation in the fourth degree. Since the decay of the theater this influence has vanished, [but unemployable actors often set themselves up as teachers of speech, and in the fresh-water colleges titillate farm girls and grocers' wives with their air of elegance. Innocents from Kansas and Alabama fortunate enough to attend Harvard or Yale sometimes pick up a pseudo-British pronunciation, as Canadian boys hot off the prairies do at Toronto, but such elegancies as a *hawt hahm sahndwich* have little prestige value in American business.] American movie actors rarely try to imitate English pronunciation, and the dialogue put into their mouths seldom contains recognizable Briticisms. [Even the affectations of radio and television announcers have little genuine English in them.]

The Protestant Episcopal Church, affiliated with the Church of England and generally fashionable, is a distributing station for Anglomania in the United States, but its influence upon the language seems to be very slight. Even in New England and the South, most of its clergy use sound American.[9] The fashionable preparatory schools for boys, many under Protestant Episcopal control, have introduced a number of Briticisms into the vocabu-

---

[7] Indeed, such an investment banker might run some risk of getting into Sing Sing or Atlanta prematurely, and even unjustly.

[8] In England there is a distinction between a *headmaster* and a *head master*. The former is reserved for the chief pedagogues of so-called *public schools;* the latter may be applied to the head of what we would call a *public school* in the United States. See *News of the World*, Dec. 26, 1937.

[9] [But many of their patients feel that the Almighty understands only British; a letter to *Advance* (house organ of the Diocese of Chicago), Mar. 1962, complained that some of the rev. clergy pronounced *new* and *due* as *noo* and *doo*, like most educated Midwesterners. Some seminaries, like Virginia Episcopal (Alexandria) apparently teach pseudo-British pronunciations to their inmates.]

lary of their art and mystery, *e.g.*, *head master, house master, monitor, honors, prefect* and *form.* Dr. Henry Augustus Coit, first *rector* of the fashionable St. Paul's School at Concord, N.H., diligently promoted this Anglicization.[1] He encouraged the playing of cricket instead of baseball, and "introduced English schoolroom nomenclature to the American boy." But his successors suffered a relapse into Americanism, and while "St. Paul's still has *forms,* the *removes, evensong,* and *matins,* and even the cricket of Dr. Coit's time are now forgotten."[2] At Groton, the most consciously British of all the American prep schools, the boys are divided into *forms,* and there are *prefects, masters* and a *headmaster,* but an examination of the catalogue shows few other imitations of English nomenclature. The *staff* is actually called the *faculty,* and the *headmaster,* a Protestant Episcopal clergyman, is listed as *Rev.* without the *the.* [Virtually all American prep schools of any pretension show some British influence. *Headmaster* is by far the favorite designation for the director of a prep school for boys; but on the distaff side the analogous *headmistress* is still uncommon.]

Occasionally some American patriot launches an attack upon the few Briticisms that seep in. Richard Grant White, in 1870, warned against the figurative use of *nasty* as a synonym for *disagreeable,* but *nasty* quickly got into American. Merely fashionable slang has a harder time. When certain advertisers in New York began using such Briticisms as *swagger* and *topping* for snob appeal, the town wits, led by the watchful Franklin P. Adams, quickly routed them. To the average American of the plain people, indeed, any word or phrase of an obviously British flavor has an offensive smack. To call him *old dear* would be almost as hazardous as to call him *Percy,* and *bah Jove* and *my word* (now archaic in England) somehow set his teeth on edge. But the consciously elegant circles have less aversion to such forms as *rotter, priceless, cheerio* and *no end.*

Fashionable mothers teach their children to call them *Mummy.* This Briticism was not imported into the United States until the Twentieth Century; indeed, the OED reported in 1908 that it had come into vogue in England itself only "in recent years." It has been traced to 1839, and its short form *Mum* to 1823, but the earlier examples of both are all from low life. In the 1880s American children called their mothers *Mamma,* and not until the turn of the century was there any vogue for the formal and adult *Mother,* which was presently challenged by *Mummy. Mamma,* ancient in

---

[1] It is curious to note that Dr. Coit, for all his Anglomania, was born at Harrisburg, Pa., began life as the manager of a tube works at Cleveland and retired to Munich on resigning the rectorate of St. Paul's.

[2] [American Private Schools, by Porter E. Sargent; Boston, 1962, p. 90. Not unexpectedly, such private schools often peddle a pseudo-British accent along with their other prestige values; see Vance Packard, The Status Seekers; New York, 1961, pp. 123-4.]

English and with congeners in many other languages, was reinforced early in the Seventeenth Century by the French *Maman*, and soon became so fashionable that even adults used it. But not until the Nineteenth Century did the English lower orders adopt it. By the end of the century it had become so unfashionable that the way was open for *Mummy*. In England *Mamma* usually had the accent on the last syllable, but in the United States it more often fell upon the first. The OED does not list *Mom* as in English use; the Supplement thereof (1933) records it as a "U.S. abbreviation of *Mamma*." During World War II it occurred so frequently in published letters from American soldiers, greeting the folks at home, and in official morale-building propaganda, that it provoked a savage attack in Philip Wylie's "Generation of Vipers." [3] *Ma* is recorded as a Suffolk dialect form in 1823 by the DAE, and as in general use soon afterward. [In America it may have the vowel of *cot*, of *caught* or—especially in the South—of *cat*.[4]]

Papa, like *Mamma*, is based upon sounds uttered by babies, and was reinforced in England by French example in the Seventeenth Century. Again, it became fashionable during the century following, and fell out of vogue in the Nineteenth. The accent, at the start, was sometimes on the first syllable and sometimes on the second, but the latter form finally prevailed in England and the former in America. In America, as the DAE shows, a shortened form, *Pop*, had developed by 1840. *Pa* is traced by the OED to 1811, but it was not much favored by the English, since it was a nursery euphemism for nasty, indecent. *Pa* was popular in America before its first reported appearance in England, for Parson Mason L. Weems, in the original telling of the cherry-tree story (1800), made Washington say to his father: "I can't tell a lie, *Pa*; you know I can't tell a lie. I did cut it with my hatchet." *Pa* has the same variant pronunciations as *Ma*; *Pappy* is traced by the OED in English use to 1763 but is marked "now rare." Like *Mammy*, it is still heard among the whites of Appalachia, and does not denote that a colored person is being addressed or spoken of.

Dad and *Daddy* have long been in use, but not universally. In some areas *Daddy* was applied only to elderly Negroes, and everywhere *Dad* was a euphemism for *God* in such denatured profanity as *dad-blamed, dad burn me* and *dad gum*.[5] But *daddy-longlegs* for a spiderlike creature with long,

---

[3] New York, 1944. *Mammy* for a colored woman, especially a child's nurse, seems to have appeared in the 1830s. It was preceded by *Momma, Mauma* or *Maum*, whose stressed syllable had the vowel of *comma* or *dawn* rather than that of *slam*.

[4] [See The Pronunciation of English in the Atlantic States, by Hans Kurath and Raven I. McDavid, Jr., *University of Michigan Studies in American English*, No. 3, Ann Arbor, 1961, pp. 164–5.]

[5] [In the hospitals of Phoenix, Ariz., *father* is apparently restricted to the rev. clergy. A mere male parent is officially a *daddy*. See *The New York Times*, Nov. 18, 1962.]

slender legs was in common and unquestioned use, though it had rivals in *granddaddy-longlegs* and *grandfather-longlegs*. *Grandpa* and *Grandma*, variously pronounced, were in almost universal use as vocatives, with *Grandfather* and *Grandmother* heard only rarely, except in the third person. *Grandpappy* and *Grandmammy* were confined to Appalachia and the South, but *Grandpop* was a tolerated variant. *Dad* is traced by the OED to *c.* 1500, as is *Daddy*. They became fashionable in England toward the end of the Nineteenth Century and were soon afterward adopted widely in the United States. Few American boys above the age of five call their fathers *Papa*, though two generations ago the term was used by grown men. The effort to substitute *Father* arose simultaneously with the effort to substitute *Mother* for *Mamma*, but was presently challenged by *Dad*. In England, *Mummy* and *Daddy* seem a shade more elegant than *Mum* and *Dad*.[6] *Mater* and *Pater*, nearly always used in the third person and with the definite article, have never made any headway in the United States. The OED marks them both "chiefly schoolboys' slang," and they must have arisen among boys more or less familiar with Latin. *Governor* as a designation for father is traced by the OED to 1847. It is not unknown in the United States, but has never been in wide use.

Some of the Briticisms that actually come into use in America have rather curious histories. In England *flapper* goes back at least to 1892, when a discussion of it in *Notes and Queries* was summed up by an anonymous writer in the London *Evening News* on August 20. In 1893 Farmer and Henley listed it in "Slang and Its Analogues" as meaning both "a very young prostitute" and "a little girl." It had been listed in Barrère and Leland's "A Dictionary of Slang, Jargon, and Cant" (1889) in the sense of "a very young girl trained to vice, generally for the amusement of elderly men." Thus *flapper* probably acquired respectable significance in England between 1889 and 1892. The anonymous writer in the *Evening News*, just mentioned, thought that it represented a figurative borrowing of an earlier *flapper* meaning "a young wild duck, unable to fly," which has been traced by the OED to 1773, but the OED Supplement suggests that the term may really come from a dialect word, *flap*, meaning any unsteady young woman. Partridge says that in the English society slang of the early Nineteenth Century *flapper* meant "a very immoral young girl in her early teens,"[7] and that World War I "firmly established the meaning (already

[6] Lost *Mum* and *Dad:* headline in *News of the World*, Apr. 19, 1936, referring to two working-class orphans. "I lost my *Mummy* and *Daddy*": caption in an appeal for funds by the Shaftesbury Homes and *Arethusa* Training Ship in the London *Times Literary Supplement*, Jan. 1, 1914, p. 10.

[7] A definition borrowed from J. Redding Ware, Passing English of the Victorian Era, 1900. [See also A Point of Bibliographical Method, by Daniel Cook, *AS*, Vol. XXXIV, Feb. 1959, pp. 20–5.]

pretty general by 1905) of *any* young girl with her hair not yet up (or, in the late 1920s and the 30s, not yet cut short)." This transformation probably occurred at least a decade before the time set by Partridge. *Flapper* began to be heard in the United States not later than 1910, and it had, from the start, a perfectly unopprobrious signification. It is one of a long series of jocular terms for a young and somewhat foolish girl, full of wild surmises and inclined to revolt against the precepts and admonitions of her elders. The *filly* of the Eighteenth Century, occasionally heard nowadays, was of that general type, and so was the oft-revived *chicken* of the pre-1900 era. *Flapper* soon yielded *flapperhood, flapperdom, flapperism, flapper age, flapperish* and *flapper vote*.[8] All save the last reached America, but they survived only until *flapper* itself succumbed to various home-brewed terms, *e.g., sub-deb,* which was never used in England and in America has followed *flapper* into oblivion.

Some Briticisms have been taken into American only after long delays, and others have been changed in meaning or otherwise modified. *Bungalow,* from *bangla,* a Hindustani word meaning belonging to Bengal, appeared in English use in the sense of a one-story house in 1676, but was not adopted in this country until *c.* 1900. [For an ordinary residence it is rarely heard now, being replaced by *ranch house,* a bungalow turned sideways, but it often appears in advertisements of small houses to be rented during the summer at the seashore.] *Tabloid* was invented by Sir Henry Wellcome in 1884, and was registered by his pharmaceutical firm, Burroughs, Wellcome & Company, as a trademark for what in this country are commonly called *tablets;* it began to be used to designate newspapers smaller than the usual size in 1901. At some undetermined time afterward it reached the United States in both this new sense and in the original one. Since then its meaning has been greatly extended to designate anything small, from a prize fighter to an automobile. The familiar *cop* is an American shortening of the English *copper,* and has been renaturalized in England. All the slang authorities derive *copper* from an old cant verb, *to cop,* meaning to capture or catch, traced by the OED to 1704. *Copper* was in use in England by the early 1850s, and soon afterward made its way to New York, where it was presently reduced to *cop.*

Many Briticisms have not only been long delayed in getting here, but have continued on levels of affectation after coming in. Examples are *swagger* and *swank,* [and more recently *posh* and *queue*]. *Swank* first appeared in English, as university slang, at the beginning of the Nineteenth Century,

---

[8] [The *flapper vote* was an important force in the British election of 1929, the first in which women between 21 and 30 had the franchise. In the original Woman's Suffrage Act, following World War I, the voting age for women had been fixed at 30.]

but it was not heard in the United States until near the century's end. In England *swank* is the noun and verb, and *swanky* is the adjective, but in the United States *swank* also became an adjective.[9] To the English it has a suggestion of ostentation, and hence it would hardly persuade them in an advertisement, but in the United States it soon became virtually synonymous with *fashionable* and *chic*, [and now has passed into the vocabulary of unsuccessful social strivers]. *Brunch*, a combination of breakfast and lunch, eaten about noon, appeared in England about 1900, but it was thirty years later before it began to make any headway on this side of the water,[1] [chiefly for a late Sunday morning meal after a rough Saturday night]. *Snack bar* began to be used by some of the swagger American drinking places after the repeal of the Eighteenth Amendment; it now means only a lunch counter. The Federal Reserve System has *governors* in imitation of the Bank of England, but all other American banks continue to be operated by *directors*.[2] In the National Bank Act stock is designated by the English *shares* and stockholder by *shareholder*, but the New York Banking Act sticks to *stock* and *stockholder*, and so do virtually all American corporations. The introduction of golf to the United States in 1888 naturally brought with it the vocabulary of the game, and most Americans are now familiar with many of its terms, *e.g.*, *to tee off*, *to putt*, *hole in one*, *long drive*, *hazard* and *bunker*, and even with *cleek*, *mashie* and *niblick*. [By 1930, American manufacturers and players, following the example of the printers, had introduced a numerical system of designating clubs; but traces of the old nomenclature still survive.] The Americans have also added such terms as *birdie*, *eagle* and *nineteenth hole*, nearly all of which have passed to the British Isles.

The advertisement writers, especially for firms catering to the rich, show a considerable liking for Briticisms, and to them we probably owe the appearance of *master bedroom*, *swim suit* and the various terms ending in *-shop*. *Swim suit*, actually, is seldom used in England, though a common enough term in advertisements in this country. *Bathing suit*, still the popular term, is traced by the DA to 1881; the earlier American term may have been *bathing dress*.[3] *Parcel post* was undoubtedly borrowed, for *parcel*, save in the legal sense, is a word seldom used in the United States: *package*

---

[9] [Most Americans, I believe, rhyme it with *bank*, but in the Minneapolis area many rhyme it with *honk*.]

[1] On Apr. 10, 1941, the Fifth Avenue Hotel in New York was advertising a "Sunday strollers' *brunch*, $1 per person, served from 11 A.M. to 3 P.M.," in the *Villager*, p. 8. [*Brunch coats* for women are often advertised.]

[2] *Governor* was used in colonial America to indicate the college dignitary now known as a *trustee*, at some military colleges as a *visitor* or, at Harvard, an *overseer*.

[3] Omitted by the DA, traced by the DAE to 1864, found in *Harper's Magazine*, Aug. 1855, p. 429.

mail would have sounded more American. The English *parcels post* was set up in 1859, and the plural form continued in use until 1884, when *parcel post* was adopted. In the United States *parcels post* was used during the congressional discussion of plans for such a service, but when the project was at last executed, in 1912, *parcel post* appeared in the statute, and it has been that ever since. A number of other familiar terms may be borrowings from England, *e.g.*, *gadget* and *exchange* (telephone). *Gadget* appears to have come into the argot of British sailors about the middle of the Nineteenth Century, perhaps suggested by the French *gachette*, meaning a piece of machinery. It seems thoroughly and even typically American today. So with *exchange*. The original American word was apparently *central*, though the DAE's first example is dated 1889, two years after its first example of *exchange*, which has been in use in England since 1879.

Plenty of Briticisms, especially on the level of slang, deserve American adoption better than any of the shaky borrowings from the English upper classes, *e.g.*, *pub crawl* (a tour of drinking spots). Many more are to be found in the pungent slang of Australia, *e.g.*, *donk* (a fool), *fork* (a jockey), *hunk* (a large man), *to mizzle* (to complain), *rest* (a year in jail), *smoodger* (a flatterer) and *wowser* ("a drab-souled Philistine haunted by the mockery of others' happiness").[4] Every Puritan is not necessarily a *wowser:* to be one he must devote himself zealously to reforming the morals of his neighbors, and, in particular, to throwing obstacles in the way of their enjoyment of what they choose to regard as pleasures. The Prohibitionist of the thirteen dark years was an archetypical example.[5] "If Australia," said the London *Daily Telegraph* in 1937, "had given nothing more to civilization than that magnificent label for one of its most melancholy products, it would not have been discovered in vain."

The English *opposite number*, signifying a person in corresponding office or position, *e.g.*, the American Secretary of State with respect to the English Foreign Secretary, has made some progress in the United States in recent years, but only on relatively lofty levels: the common people know nothing of it. It has come in in England since World War I, and probably

---

[4] S. J. Baker, A Popular Dictionary of Australian Slang; Sydney, 1941. [In his Historical Study of the Australian Vocabulary, diss. (MS), U. of Sydney, 1962, W. S. Ramson quotes from a glossary appended to C. J. Dennis's, Backblock Ballads and Other Verses: "*Wowser*, an ineffably pious person who mistakes this world for a penitentiary and himself for a warder." Note the Australian use of *penitentiary* in the American sense.]

[5] The word was popularized by John Norton, editor of a somewhat saucy and even ribald weekly paper called *John Norton's Truth*, published simultaneously in Sydney, Melbourne and Wellington, N.Z. He invented other spicy terms, including *stink chariot* for automobile, but none has survived. [Traditionally he is credited with the invention of *wowser*, but Ramson, *op. cit.*, pp. 341 *ff.*, suggests it may have been derived from a Northern English dialect word meaning to whine, grumble, complain; in any event, Norton deserves eternal bliss for its dissemination.]

had a military origin. The most hard-worked of all the English counter words of recent years, *amenities*, is now beginning to be encountered in the United States. *Amenity* is the French word *amenité*, borrowed in the Fifteenth Century. To an American it is similar in meaning, in the plural, to *civilities*, as in "the *amenities* of the occasion," but the English have widened it, since *c.* 1916, to mean almost anything agreeable, from a beautiful view to a sound system of drains, and from the chance to hear a band of music to law and order. The English realtors have seized upon the term, and an advertisement of a country estate for sale seldom appears in the London papers without a long catalogue of the *amenities* offered with it, *e.g.*, central heating, electric clocks, elevator service and refrigerators.[6] In 1937 Lord Horder, physician-in-ordinary to the King, went about the country explaining the meaning of the term as he understood it. His definition, once revised, stood:

> What do I mean by *amenities*? Clean air to breathe. Close contact with the earth and sky and sun. The sight of beautiful things. The hearing of beautiful sounds. Quiet and leisure to enjoy all these.[7]

It is a wonder that this noble word is so rarely used in America.[8] It has an elegant smack.

5: HONORIFICS

Although the English bestow titles of honor upon their men of mark almost as diligently as the Germans, they are careful to withhold such titles from men who do not legally bear them. In America every practitioner of the healing art [9] is a doctor *ipso facto*, but in England a good many

---

[6] I am indebted for most of these examples to the collection of the late F. H. Tyson.

[7] At Last We Know What the *Amenities* Really Are, London *Daily Express*, Dec. 5, 1937.

[8] [In the Chicago *Sun-Times*, July 19, 1962, John Duba, Chicago Commissioner of Urban Renewal, stated that proposed legislation making rental and sales prices a factor in selling land specified that the *"amenities"* must be "excellent." Duba said that this will mean that good design and all the utilities will be required. The fact that Chicago reporters pressed him for a definition of *amenities*, and that the *Sun-Times* felt it necessary to print the word in quotation marks, suggests that the word has not yet found firm lodg-

ment in the American Heartland.]

[9] On April 1, 1926, *The New York Times* printed a warning by Assistant District Attorney Michael A. Ford that practitioners of the following non-Euclidean healing schemes were calling themselves *Doctor* in New York: aero-therapy, astral healing, autothermy, bio-dynamo-chromatic-therapy, chromo-therapy, diet therapy, electro-homeopathy, electro-napro-therapy, geo-therapy, irido-therapy, mechano-therapy, neuro-therapy, naprapathy, photo-therapy, physic-therapy, quartz therapy, san-itratorism, spondylo-therapy, spectro-chrome-therapy, theomonism, telather-apy, vitopathy, zodiac therapy, zonet-therapy and Zoroastrianism.

surgeons lack the title, and even physicians may not have it. It is customary there, however, to address a physician as *Doctor*, though his card may show that he is only *medicinae baccalaureus*, a degree unknown in America. Thus an Englishman, when ill, always consults a *doctor*, as we do. But a surgeon is usually plain *Mr.*, though he may have *M.D.* on his card, along with *F.R.C.S.* (Fellow of the Royal College of Surgeons).[1] A physician (or surgeon) who cures the right patients is often knighted, thus becoming *Sir Basil* and ceasing to be either *Dr.* or *Mr.* If royalty patronizes him, he may even become *Lord Bolus*. The Englishman prefers *medical man* to *physician*. An English dentist or druggist or veterinarian is never *Dr.*, but in this country these are, as well as a great variety of other healers, including osteopaths, chiropractors, optometrists and chiropodists. Most of these have set up doctorates of their own; some, like that of dentists, really represent advanced professional training, but those of some of the others are often highly dubious. [All of the non-Hippocratic varieties of leechcraft have energetic lobbies seeking, with some success, full recognition as practitioners of healing, on a par with orthodox *M.D.'s*. But in general these and their hospitals are required to operate under distinctive labels. The *M.D.'s* look with scorn upon all other doctorates but their own, no matter how much intellect or *Sitzfleischarbeit* went into the acquisition. Bona fide resurrection men, furthermore, resent the abbreviation *Doc;* on the other hand, druggists and veterinarians welcome it. In some localities *Doc* is also used as an informal salutation to a stranger, especially one wearing glasses, who is thus distinguished from the unbespectacled stranger, usually addressed as *Mac*.]

The title *Dr.* is infrequent among English pedagogues too. [The *Ph.D.* is an uncommon and recent degree. Oxford and Cambridge took it up after World War I, partly in an attempt to compete for the American postgraduates who had been going to Berlin and Heidelberg.] Even now it is seldom or never given for that congeries of quackeries which is promulgated, in American universities, under the title of "Education." [Nor do English universities offer the subsaline *Ed.D.* (Doctor of Education) which American schools of pedagogics dispense to their inmates too inept for a *Ph.D.*, even in "Education."] The tendency to multiply degrees has been marked in the United States since the turn of the century. The degrees of bachelor, master and doctor are now often followed by designations of particularity, *e.g.*, *in Ed.* (education), *in Eng.* (engineering), *in Mus.* (mu-

---

[1] In the appendix to the Final Report of the Royal Commission on Venereal Diseases, London, 1916, p. iv, I find the following: "*Mr.* C. J. Symonds, F.R.C.S., M.D.; *Mr.* F. J. McCann, F.R.C.S., M.D.; *Mr.* A. F. Evans, F.R.C.S." *Mr.* Symonds was consulting surgeon to Guy's Hospital, London, *Mr.* McCann an eminent London gynecologist and *Mr.* Evans a general surgeon in large practice. All would be called *Doctor* in the United States.

sic), etc. These distinctions are needed, lest the sheer multitudinousness of new bachelors, masters and doctors reduce them to an undifferentiated horde. [During the academic year 1954–5, for example, the various branches and substations of the University of California conferred 9,118 degrees and certificates, Columbia University 5,976, the University of Minnesota 4,362, and all the other great rolling mills of learning followed suit. Degree-bearing Americans are to be numbered in the millions: to 1955 California had laid hands upon 221,318, Columbia on 216,127, Illinois on 132,412, Minnesota on 121,614, and others in proportion. But Columbia is still most prodigal with the *Ph.D.:* during 1957–8 it awarded 357, of which 18 were in "Education," plus 212 in various branches of the latter from its Teachers College. The total number of accredited earned doctorates turned out in the United States numbered 8,799 in 1957–8; of these 1,485 were in various branches of "Education," but nearly all the rest represented mastery of a respectable discipline and the accomplishment of honest, if pedestrian, research. Since the doctorate is an almost indispensable union card for college teaching—and enjoys high prestige in business, industry and government service—there are repeated howls from those who see it barring the academic pastures to well-meaning mediocrity and repeated demands for setting up a less arduous "teaching degree." But so far the universities have held firm.[2] A few institutions without accreditation (such as Bob Jones University of Greenville, S.C.) award *soi-disant Ph.D's,* but no traditional academician takes them seriously. Occasionally a *Ph.D.* is given *honoris causa:* the crooner Bing Crosby has one from his alma mater, Gonzaga University. Governor James K. Vardamann once promised a Delta rabbi a *Ph.D.* from the University of Mississippi in return for twelve campaign speeches, but the rabbi declined on the ground that he already had a doctorate from Heidelberg.

[But if the American *Ph.D.* normally represents solid academic achievement, something less than that can be said of the honorary degrees which colleges and universities lavishly bestow. The most widely distributed is still the *LL.D.,* especially in run-of-the-mill institutions; but in late years the tonier seminaries have devised more sophisticated honors, such as *Doc-*

[2] [In Is There a Doctor of Philosophy in the House?, *AS*, Vol. XXVII, Oct. 1952, pp. 179–82. Arthur Minton points out the spread of technical medical terminology to education, as *clinic* (yielding *reading clinic* and *speech clinic*) and *diagnostic test. Clinic* has spread to other fields; some garages are *car clinics,* and (electric) *shaver clinics* are found in posh department stores. Frustrated baseball magnates have introduced *hitting clinics* and *pitching clinics. Football clinics* are sponsored by college and high-school coaches; see for example the Chicago *Sun-Times,* Mar. 10, 1962. According to Clifton Brock, Matters of Degree, *The New York Times Magazine,* Nov. 4, 1962, pp. 80 ff., American universities awarded 9,829 *Ph.D.'s* in 1960, of which 1,540 were in Education, a mere 8 in Journalism.]

tor of Science and *Doctor of Humane Letters.*] The champion degree bearer of all time seems to be the Hon. Herbert Hoover, who got his *A.B. in Eng.* at Stanford in 1895 by the sweat of his brow, and has since accumulated 85 honorary degrees of various sorts, chiefly *LL.D.'s* [At the struggling denominational colleges even the *LL.D.* is less frequent than the *D.D.* (Doctor of Divinity); and the more faction-ridden or unwashed the denomination, the more often is the honorific dispensed to potentially influential pulpit pounders.] The *D.D.* is often awarded by Baptist congregations—and perhaps some others—as a consolation prize when a pastor has been dislodged from his post. There are few members of Congress without at least one *LL.D.*, and few other politicos of any puissance.[3] It is also conferred wholesale upon the presidents and other high officers of rich corporations, newspaper editors and columnists, eminent radio crooners, college presidents who may be trusted to reciprocate and a miscellaneous rabble of contributors or potential contributors to college funds.

Professor, like *Doctor*, is worked less hard in England than in the United States, and is thus better esteemed. It is the normal title for any Englishman who holds a professorship, but any secular title he may acquire takes precedence. Thomas Henry Huxley was always called *Professor* until he became a Privy Councillor, with the right to have *Right Honorable* put before his name. Thereafter it was customary to call him simply *Mr.* Huxley, with the *Right Honorable*, so to speak, simply floating in the air. The combination, to an Englishman, was more flattering than *Professor*, for Englishmen esteem political dignities more than academic ones. [When knighted, like Huxley's grandson, a savant may become *Professor Sir Julian* Huxley, or simply *Sir Julian.*]

The misuse of *Professor* began in America at an early date and still prevails. It has been applied to an appalling range of virtuosi, mostly frauds.[4] Until recently, in all save a few of our largest cities every male pedagogue was a *professor*, and so was every band leader and dancing master. The title has been extended, *inter alia*, to balloon ascensionists, bartenders, colored hostlers who bit off the tails of puppies, rubbers of baseball players, paint-

---

[3] [Several studies have appeared, notably An Inside Look at the Honorary System, by David Boroff, *The New York Times Magazine*, June 12, 1960, pp. 18 *ff.*]

[4] [See In Pursuit of the Word *Professor:* An Exploration of the Uses and Associations of the Title, by Robert L. Coard, *Journal of Higher Education*, Vol. XXX, May 1959, pp. 237–55.] The title is frequently discussed in *AS*, beginning with The Title *Professor*, by N.R.L., Vol. III, Oct. 1927, p. 27. In Vol.

IV, Feb. 1929, pp. 71–2, Mamie Meredith reprints the protest of a Nebraska editor of 1869 who had been called *Professor* by a colleague. In his own paper he permitted the term to be applied to a horse trainer, a barber, the manager of a roller-skating rink and a dancing master. [In the South, where dancing ranks with Greek among the humanities, dancing masters bore the title at least so late as 1930.]

ers of black eyes, and distinguished crab-soup and oyster-flitter cooks. [In the Nineteenth Century the piano players in bordellos and the higher-class saloons held the title, and many of them deserved it for their distinguished contributions to American jazz.] The excessive misuse of *Professor* has brought it into disrepute, and more often than not it is applied satirically. The real professors try hard to get rid of it. In 1925 those at the University of Virginia organized a society "for the encouragement of the use of *Mister* to all men, professional or otherwise," and during the years since then its crusade has made such progress that most genuine professors now prefer to be called *Mister,* and that term is in wide use in the better colleges. [At those of the second rank, where nearly everyone has the *Ph.D., Professor* is still tolerated as a mark of distinction; in the academic Siberias where an earned doctorate is a rarity, even among the senior members of the faculty, *Doctor* takes precedence over *Professor.*[5]] There was a time when every county superintendent of schools and high-school principal was a *professor* by unanimous local consent, but of late years so many of these birchmen have been made *Ph.D's* or *Doctors of Education* that they are now usually called *Doctor,* even when they are not.

So with military titles. To promote a war veteran from sergeant to colonel by acclamation, as is often done in the United States, is unknown in England. The English have nothing equivalent to the gaudy tin soldiers of our governors' staffs, nor to the bespangled colonels and generals of the Knights Templar and Patriarchs Militant, nor to the nondescript captains and majors of our country towns.[6]

This American fondness for hollow titles goes back to colonial days. An English traveler, Edward Kimber, wrote in the *London Magazine* in 1746:

> Wherever you travel in Maryland (as also in Virginia and Carolina) your ears are constantly astonished at the number of colonels, majors,

---

[5] [There is an amusing discussion in A. H. Marckwardt, American English; New York, 1958, pp. 115–16. *Deans,* of course, proliferate in American academe. *Dean,* in the sense of the senior member of a body or of a profession, is less frequently heard than it used to be. A few years ago, when I referred respectfully in print to John S. Kenyon as "the *dean* of American phoneticians," he begged me not to repeat the offense, pointing out that it had been many years since the appellation of *dean* was a compliment. See also "Deans" in School and Out, by Mamie Meredith, *AS,* Vol. XXXIII, May 1958, pp. 151–3.]

[6] [In the early Twentieth Century it was a commonplace in the South that every white male old enough to have served in the Civil War, including some notorious draft dodgers, became *Captain* before his decease. In 1949 Southern members of the Linguistic Society of America organized a society restricted to those whose ancestors never rose above the rank of private in the Confederate Army. It remains slightly more exclusive than the French Academy or the Order of the Garter.]

and captains that you hear mentioned: in short, the whole country seems at first to you a retreat of heroes.

Two years earlier the Scottish physician Alexander Hamilton, traveling along the Hudson, found an immense number of colonels. "It is a common saying here," he wrote, "that a man has no title to that dignity unless he has killed a rattlesnake." [7] After the Revolution there was a great increase in these titles, for any veteran of respectable position—say, an innkeeper—was commonly called *Captain*, and all actual officers continued to use their titles, usually with an informal promotion of a rank or two. During the great movement into the West, they were multiplied enormously. "Every man who comes from Georgia," said a writer in the *Southern Literary Messenger* in 1852, "is a *major!*" But *Major* was never as popular as *Captain* and *Colonel*.[8] *Captain* got a great lift when on the coming of the railways it began to be applied to conductors. [It is now the official designation, on many airlines, for the chief pilot of a passenger plane. And any reasonably washed and tailored white Southerner can expect to be brevetted *Captain* by an elderly Negro in search of a patron.]

Colonel came into prominence when the governors of the states began appointing large and glittering staffs composed of their political cronies and financial benefactors. Some of these dignitaries were made *generals* but most became *colonels*. Ruby Laffoon, during his glorious reign as governor of Kentucky (1931–5), bestowed the silver eagle on whole brigades, divisions and army corps of them, and so helped to give the term *Kentucky colonel* a reinforced validity.[9] [As a special honor and innovation, he also created *admirals*, at least one of whom is still reputedly on active duty as *Admiral of the Kentucky River*.] *Colonel* is also often bestowed on American newspaper editors by common consent, as a sort of occupational honorific, especially in the South. [Thus the rare journalist who declines a colonelcy on the governor's staff gets it thrust upon him willy-nilly. In the Midwest the title is similarly given to auctioneers.[1]]

---

[7] Hamilton's Itinerarium . . . from May to September, 1744, edited by Albert Bushnell Hart; St. Louis, 1907, p. 94. See also Rattlesnake *Colonel*, by Albert Matthews, *New England Quarterly*, June 1937, pp. 341–5.

[8] [In the South *Captain* has always been applied to a stevedore boss and to the chief warder of a chain gang (who is also known as *The Man*).]

[9] It should be explained for the benefit of English readers that Ruby (1869–1941), despite his given name, was male. All American governors have some appointive power, but few in such un-

limited quantities as in Kentucky. A number of enlightened governors, in order to put down the pestilence of *colonels*, have declined to appoint honorary military staffs; in this reform Albert Cabell Ritchie (1876–1936), governor of Maryland from 1920 to 1935, was the pioneer.

[1] [With *captains* and *colonels* circulating at a discount, there recently has been an increasing vogue for *Chief*, once applied to foremen and plant superintendents. It has now left the assembly line for the white-collar ranks, and is often used for one's superior among executives

Judge seems to have come into courtesy use relatively late, for the first recorded example is from 1800.[2] Before this the lawyers of the colonies and the new Republic were apparently content with *Esquire*. But when the great march to the West got under way, *judges* began to proliferate in a dizzy manner, and by 1869 John Ross Browne was reporting in his "Adventures in the Apache Country"[3] that "all popular lawyers are *judges* in Nevada, whether they practice at the bar or sit upon the bench." This is true in large parts of the South and Southwest to the present day.[4] In England there are no *judges* at the bar, for a lawyer who has once been upon the bench is not permitted to practice thereafter. But in the United States there is no such squeamishness, and even retired federal judges are free to plead and beat their breasts before their late colleagues. Justices of the peace and police magistrates are also called *judge,* [as are local politicos of influence, whether trained in the law or not. An especially distinguished-looking figure may even find himself consecrated *Bishop.*] *Squire* survives occasionally in rural areas, but is disappearing from the towns, and is now almost unheard of in the cities. The DAE traces it to 1743. Horwill says that "the *squire* in an English country district is usually both a landowner and a magistrate, but it is in the former rather than the latter capacity that he is given the name; in America the *squire* is primarily a justice of the peace, but the name is loosely given, most commonly as a title, to any prominent resident in a village."

But perhaps the greatest difference between British and American usage is presented by *the Honorable*. In the United States the title is applied loosely to all public officials of any apparent respectability, and with some show of official sanction to many of them, especially congressmen, but it is questionable whether this application has any actual legal standing. Even the President of the United States, by law, is not *the Honorable*, but simply *the President*. Congressmen themselves are not *Honorables*. Nevertheless, a country congressman would be offended if his partisans, in announcing his appearance on the stump, did not prefix *Hon.* to his name. So would a state senator. So would a mayor or governor. The Style Manual of the Department of State, the highest American authority upon epistolary etiquette, grants it to a long list of functionaries, including ambassadors, gov-

---

and junior executives. Kelsie Harder points out that *subordinate* has now become a pejorative, like *servant;* in industry and even Academe, subordinate rank is indicated by the prefix *co-*, as in *co-pilot* and *co-chairman* (*AS*, Vol. XXIX, Oct. 1954, pp. 235–6).]

[2] John Maud, A Visit to the Falls of Niagara in 1800; it appears in Allen Walker Read, Words Indicating Social Status in America in the Eighteenth Century, *AS*, Vol. IX, Oct. 1934, p. 208.

[3] New York, 1869, p. 394.

[4] Most lawyers of any skill actually become *judges* soon or late, for there is rotation in the petty judgeships, and once a *judge* always a *judge*. There are occasional vain protests, as in Question of Title, by Lee Casey, *Rocky Mountain News,* Dec. 5, 1941.

ernors, cabinet officers, senators, members of Congress, judges and the mayors of large cities. In addition, it grants *the Hon.*, if not by precept then at least by example, to various other persons, including the secretary of the Smithsonian Institution, the archivist of the United States, the secretary general of the Pan-American Union, all members of international commissions who apparently rank as diplomats, and the acting heads of boards, commissions and other such bodies whose actual heads are entitled to it. But it is denied, *inter alia,* to all diplomatic officers under the rank of minister, to consuls and to the librarian of Congress. Congress is much more liberal with the *Hon.* It is bestowed in the *Congressional Record* upon a vast and miscellaneous congeries of dignitaries. In the *Congressional Record* proper, which is devoted mainly to a stenographic report of the previous day's debates in the two houses, all members are designated *Mr.*, even senators, but excluding, of course, females, who are *Miss* or *Mrs.*, as the case may be.[5] Even members lawfully bearing other titles, *e.g., Dr., Col.,* or *Bishop,* are denied them.[6] But in the Appendix to the *Record,* wherein members embalm speeches that they have made elsewhere and reprint all sorts of memorabilia, they are called *Hon.* without a preceding *the,* and in writing about themselves in state papers they often use the term, even in the first person.[7] But there has lately been visible a certain wobbling in usage. Even such austere dignitaries as Josephus Daniels, Sidney Hillman, Fiorello La Guardia and Wendell Willkie have appeared in the *Record* as non-*Hons.* The Hon. James A. Farley has appeared as *the Hon.*, as *the Honorable* and as plain James A. Farley without even *Mr.;* and the Hon. James F. Byrnes—successively congressman, senator, Supreme Court Justice, Director of War Mobilization, Secretary of State and governor of South Carolina —has been both *the Hon.* and James F. Byrnes, unadorned. There even seems to be some uncertainty about the Vice-President, who appears in the actual proceedings of the Senate without the *Hon.*[8] State governors are sometimes *Hons.*, but more often mere *Govs.*, always abbreviated. Most American newspapers refrain from calling a politico *the Hon.*, even when writing about him formally and favorably: when the term appears in them

---

[5] Even the Vice-President of the United States, who is *ex officio* president of the Senate, appears in its actual proceedings without the *Hon.* See *Congressional Record*, Sept. 14, 1943, p. 7599, top of col. 1.

[6] The Hon. Reed Smoot (1862–1941), who was a senator from Utah from 1903 to 1933, had been a Mormon bishop before he got into politics, and was promoted to the awful rank of *Apostle* before his election to the Senate.

[7] See for example, the *Congressional Record* for May 6, 1938, p. 8467, where the Hon. Mrs. Norton, a congresswoman from New Jersey, describes herself in a motion to discharge a committee as "I, *Hon.* Mary T. Norton."

[8] In the Appendix to the *Record,* during 1944, he was listed as *the Honorable,* as *Mr.* and as *Vice-President of the United States,* without any mention of his name.

at all, it is usually used satirically. [As such, *His Honor*, referring to a mayor, is often telescoped to *Hizzoner.*]

During the colonial era in America *Hon.* seems to have been in rather restricted use. By the time of the Revolution, however, the honorific was being applied to the members of at least some of the colonial legislatures, and a number of English travelers of the first part of the Nineteenth Century noted its wide use. The real stamping ground of *the Hon.* was in the South and West. There were, indeed, few politicos beyond the Alleghanies or below the Potomac who did not wear it proudly, and it was there that the custom arose of bestowing it indiscriminately upon all notables lacking other titles, whether real or imaginary. On March 24 and August 22, 1862, for example, Abraham Lincoln, whose English, despite its mellifluousness, always showed frontier influences, sent letters to Horace Greeley which addressed him as *Hon.* Lincoln, in fact, was very fond of the prefix, and not infrequently used it without a name, as in *Hon. Secretary of the Treasury.* It was also applied, in that genteel era, to distinguished foreigners.

In England the thing is more carefully ordered, and bogus *Hons.* are unknown. The title belongs as of right, in the British Isles, only to the younger sons of earls, to all the sons and daughters of viscounts and barons, to wives of these sons, to justices of the High Court, if not ranked as peers, during their terms of office, and to the Scotch Lords of Session. If the son of a peer entitled to bear it achieves baronetcy in his own right, he becomes *the Honble. Sir John Smith, Bt.,* and his wife becomes *the Honble. Lady.* (The English prefer *the Honble.* to *the Hon.*) All peers from baron up to and including earl are *Right Honble.,* and so are all members of the Privy Council, the Lord Chief Justice and various other higher judges, Lord Mayors, and with them their wives.[9] A marquis is *Most Honble.* and so is his marchioness. A member of the Cabinet is not *Right Honble.* as such, but only because he is a member of the Privy Council. His wife does not share his title, but he keeps it himself for life. An ordinary member of Parliament is neither *Right Honble.* nor *Honble.,* but simply *Esq.,* with *M.P.* following the *Esq.*

On the floor of the House of Commons, however, every member is at least *the honorable member* (or *gentleman*), and may be much more. If he is a legal officer—say, Attorney General or Solicitor General—or a

---

[9] The OED traces *Right Hon.* in English use to the Paston letters, *c.* 1450. Its first example of *Hon.* preceding a given name is dated 1674; it was then applied to Robert Boyle, the chemist, who was a son of the Earl of Cork. *Hon.* has been accorded in England to corporations as well as individuals, *e.g., the Hon.* East India Company. [In the novels of Nancy Mitford, the young women of the extended noble family about which she writes refer to themselves collectively as *the Hons.*]

practicing lawyer, he is *the honorable and learned gentleman;* [1] if he holds a commission in the armed forces he is *the honorable and gallant gentleman,* and if he is a member of the Privy Council, he is *the right honorable gentleman.*

The Commonwealth follows the jealous usage of the mother country. Even in Canada the lawless American example is not imitated. A "Table of Titles to be Used in Canada," laid down by royal warrant, lists those who are *Hons.* and those who are not *Hons.* in the utmost detail. Only privy councilors of Canada are permitted to retain the prefix after going out of office, and former speakers of the Dominion Senate and House of Commons and various retired judges may do so on application to the Crown, countersigned by the Governor General.

But though an Englishman or, following him, a colonial is thus very careful to restrict *the Hon.* to its legal uses, he always insists, when he serves without pay as an officer of any organization, upon indicating his volunteer character by writing *hon.,* meaning honorary, before the name of his office. If he leaves it off, it is a sign that he is a hireling. Thus the agent of the New Zealand government in London, a paid officer, is simply *the agent,* but the agents at Brisbane and Adelaide, in Australia, who serve for the glory of it, are *hon. agents.* In writing to a Briton of condition, one had better be careful to put *Esq.* behind his name and not *Mr.* before it. The English have long made a distinction between the two forms. *Mr.,* on an envelope, indicates that the sender holds the receiver to be his inferior. Any man who is entitled to the *Esq.* is a gentleman, by which an Englishman means a man of sound connections and what is regarded as dignified occupation—in brief, of ponderable social position, including recipients of the M.A., whether otherwise "gentlemen" or not.

Mr., an abbreviation of *master,* is traced by the OED to *c.* 1524. It originally indicated a certain social status, but, as the OED says, "the inferior limit for its application has been continually lowered," and "at the present time [in England] any man, however low in station, would be styled *Mr.* on certain occasions." In colonial America it ranked in the hierarchy of honorifics below *Esq.* and *gent.* In parts of the South it is still customary for a married woman to address her husband as *Mr.,* often followed by his first name instead of his surname.

Such forms as *Mr. President, Mr. Justice, Mr. Mayor* and so on are traced

---

[1] But not if he is actually a learned man. A Ph.D. would be simply *the honorable gentleman.* Only lawyers, by House of Commons rules, can be *learned.* [Similarly, as is evident at meetings of the National Education Association, the International Reading Association and the like, no linguist, historian or mathematician, however distinguished, or anyone else in a *subject-matter field,* deserves the title of *educator.* That is reserved for those versed in the arcana of pedagogics.]

by the OED in English use to *c.* 1524. They were brought to the United
States by the early colonists, and the DAE traces *Mr. Sheriff* to 1703. The
Style Manual of the Department of State ordains that letters to the Presi-
dent of the United States shall bear the simple inscription *The President,
The White House,* on the envelope, and that he shall be addressed inside as
The President (very formal; official), *Mr. President* (formal) or *My Dear
Mr. President* (informal). The First Congress debated his style and appella-
tion at great length, and in all probability it was the influence of Washing-
ton himself that induced Congress to adopt the simple form.[2]

The English avoid titles as much as possible in conversation between
presumed equals. The simple surname is employed by friends of any in-
timacy, even in addressing peers, and the excessive mistering that goes on
on certain levels in the United States is unknown. Not much success has
attended the occasional effort here to establish the simple surname in the
gap between *Mr.* and the given names and nicknames of Rotary.[3]

The American custom of dropping the definite aricle before *Hon.* extends to *Rev.* and the like, and has the authority of very respectable usage
behind it. The opening sentence of the *Congressional Record* is always:
"The Chaplain, Rev. _____, D.D., offered the following prayer." When
chaplains for the Army or Navy are confirmed by the Senate, they always
appear in the *Record* as *Revs.,* never as *the Revs.* The Episcopalians in the
United States, at least those of the High Church variety, usually insert the
the, but the rest of the Protestants omit it, and so do the ordinary Catholics; the Jews get rid of it by calling their rabbis *Dr.* Now and then some
evangelical purist tries to induce the Methodists and Baptists to adopt the
the, but usually in vain.

When it came into use in England, in the Seventeenth Century, *Rev.* was
commonly written without the article, and immediately preceding the surname. Thus Bishop Joseph Hall (1574–1656) did not hesitate to write
Reverend Calvin. But at the beginning of the Eighteenth Century *the* and
the given name began to be added, and by the end of the century that form
was almost universal in England. Here, as in many other cases, American
usage is archaic.[4] The use of *Reverend* as a vocative (usually pronounced
revrun or *rev*), with no name or title following it, seems to be American.
The DAE does not list this form, but it goes back to 1877 at least, when

---

[2] From The Inauguration of Washington, by Clarence Winthrop Bowen,
Century Magazine, Apr. 1889, p. 823.

[3] The English often remark another
American habit that strikes them as
strange, to wit, the frequent use of *Sir.*
They seldom use it save in addressing
indubitable superiors, especially royalty,

but in this country, more particularly in
the South, it is heard very frequently in
the palaver of equals, [and with the
proper intonation can be the most insult-
ing word in a man's vocabulary].

[4] See The Use of the Abbreviation
Rev. in Modern English, by Edward C.
Ehrensperger, *AS,* Vol. VII, Oct. 1931.

Mark Twain used it. Some years ago one of the suffering brethren was thus moved to protest in verse:

> Call me Brother, *if you will;*
> Call me Parson—*better still.*
> Or if, *perchance, the Catholic frill*
> Doth your heart with longing fill—
> Though plain Mister *fills the bill,*
> Then even Father *brings no chill*
> Of hurt or rancor or ill-will.
> To no D.D. do I pretend,
> Though Doctor *doth some honor lend,*
> Preacher, Pastor, Rector, Friend,
> Titles almost without end
> Never grate and ne'er offend;
> A loving ear to all I bend.
> But how the man my heart doth rend,
> Who blithely calls me Reverend! [5]

Not a few clergymen, revolting against being addressed as *Reverend*, and lacking the dignity of *divinitatis doctor*, have tried to induce their patients to call them *Mr.*, but seldom with success, for many Americans have a feeling that *Mr.* is rather too worldly and familiar for use in addressing a man of God.[6] The Catholics get around the difficulty by using *Father*, and the High Church Episcopalians imitate them. In the South *Reverend* is used in addressing colored clergymen for the purpose of avoiding calling them *Mr.* The Style Manual of the Department of State bans it, and also insists that *the* precede *Rev.* Incidentally, it prefers *Reverend* to the abbreviation, just as it prefers *the Honorable* to *the Hon.*

In general, ecclesiastical titles are dealt with somewhat loosely in the United States. In England an archbishop of the Established Church is *the Most Rev.* and *His Grace*, and a bishop is *the Right Rev.* and *His Lordship*, but there are no archbishops in the American Protestant Episcopal Church, and the bishops are seldom called *His Lordship*. The Methodists often omit the *Right*, contenting themselves with the simple *Rev.* Among Catholics, by the prevailing interpretation of a decree of the Sacred Congregation of Rites,[7] an archbishop who is not a cardinal is now *the Most Rev.* and *His*

---

[5] Its author, the Rev. Douglas H. Atwill, rector of St. Clement's Memorial Church, St. Paul, Minn., later became *the Right Rev.* as missionary bishop of North Dakota. The verses made their first appearance in his parish paper, *St. Clement's Chimes*, on July 25, 1925, and have been widely reprinted, often without mention of the authorship.

[6] *Mr.* for *Rev.*, *Time*, Nov. 27, 1939, p. 50.

[7] Dec. 31, 1930. The text is in *Acta Apostolicae Sedis*, Jan. 15, 1931.

Excellency, and so is a bishop. Formerly an archbishop was *the Most Rev.* and *His Grace*, and a bishop was *the Right Rev.* and *His Lordship*. A cardinal, of course, is *His Eminence*. Monsignori are divided into two sections: those who are prothonotaries apostolic or domestic prelates are *the Right Rev.*, and those of inferior rank, *e.g.*, papal chamberlains, *the Very Rev.*[8]

In the Salvation Army honorifics follow a strange pattern. The ordinary member is a *soldier*, and his status in his *post* is identical with that of a communicant in a church. He is forbidden to belong to any other church. He supports himself at whatever trade he knows, and pays a tenth of his income into the post funds. If he aspires to become an officer, he is called a *candidate* and is sent to a training college, where he becomes a *cadet*. On his graduation he is made a *probationary lieutenant*. He must serve for a year in the field before he may hope for promotion to full rank. Above the lieutenancy the ranks are those of *captain, major, brigadier* (not *brigadier general*), *lieutenant colonel, colonel, lieutenant commissioner, commissioner* and *general*. All ranks are open to women. A married woman always takes her husband's rank, and is known as *Mrs. Major, Mrs. Colonel* and so on. If he dies, her own future promotions begin where his left off. No unmarried officer may marry anyone save another officer without resigning from the corps of officers.[9]

In the South the question whether members of the Negro race should or should not be accorded the ordinary American honorifics constantly agitates publicists. Among the devices used by journalists to avoid *Mr.*, *Mrs.* and *Miss* are *Madame, Mademoiselle, Reverend, Doctor, Nurse, Professor, Uncle* and *Aunt*.[1] *Aunt* (or *Auntie*) and *Uncle*, like the older *Daddy*, are greatly disliked by the now emancipated colored folk, who see in them a contemptuous sort of patronage. As the DAE shows, both were formerly used in addressing white persons as late as 1801, and in parts of the South are still applied by children to intimate friends of their parents. But by the 1830s *Aunt* and *Uncle* had begun to be confined to Negroes, and the latter got a great boost in 1851, when Harriet Beecher Stowe started the serial publication of "*Uncle* Tom's Cabin." But both terms now seem to be going out, and the more advanced Aframericans use *Uncle Tom* to signify a subservient and pusillanimous member of their race. Whenever a Southern newspaper or instrument of government designates the darker brethren as *Mr.*, *Mrs.* and *Miss*, there is rejoicing in Aframerica.[2]

---

[8] Abbots are also *Right Rev.*, but in the United States they are not monsignors. See *Right Reverend*, by Prelatus Domesticus, *The Commonweal*, Oct. 18, 1935.

[9] This information was provided by Major Vincent Cunningham, sometime editor of the *War Cry* (Southern edition), [and by Robert Bowe, of Salvation Army territorial headquarters, Chicago].

[1] See Journalistic Headache, by R. E. Wolseley, *Ken*, Mar. 9, 1939, pp. 62–3.

[2] For example, when in 1940 the colored teachers in the Durham, N.C., public schools received notices of reappointment bearing *Miss, Mrs.* or *Mr.* before their names. Pittsburgh *Courier*, Apr. 27, 1940.

Few Englishmen of title settled in America in the early days, though some of the transitory colonial governors and other high officials were knights, baronets and even peers. Thus the English scheme of honorifics soon passed out of common knowledge. S. E. Morison suggests that the disappearance of its sonorous handles for the names of notables may have had something to do with the proliferation of more or less dubious military titles. But despite Article I, Section 9, of the Constitution, which provides that "no title of nobility shall be granted by the United States," there is no statute forbidding an American to accept one from a foreign state, or even to assume one on his own motion. Not a few, in fact, are counts, marquises and so on by creation of the Pope, and no one objects to their bearing these titles, though when they register for voting purposes they have to give their dirt names.[3]

American newspapers, in dealing with foreign titles, often use them ignorantly, to the horror of visiting Englishmen. When Sir William Craigie landed at the University of Chicago in 1925 to take charge of the Dictionary of American English, the campus newspaper, the *Maroon*, noted his arrival under the heading "Chicago Welcomes Sir Craigie and Lady Sadie" —a triple error, for it should have been *Sir William and Lady Craigie*, and the lady's name was not Sadie but Jessie.[4] It is almost an everyday occurrence for some paper to speak of a knight or baronet as a peer, or of a duke as *Lord So-and-so*.

During the mid-Nineteenth Century it was usual for American wives to borrow the honorifics of their husbands—a custom long prevailing in Germany and the Scandinavian countries. *Mrs. Captain* Voorhees appeared in the diary of Isaac Van Bibber of Maryland (1844),[5] and Mark Twain, in his famous appendix on "The Awful German Language" in "A Tramp Abroad" (1879), recorded *Mrs. Assistant District Attorney Johnson*. General McClellan, in letters referring to Mrs. Lincoln, spoke of her as *Mrs. President*.[6] This transfer of husbands' titles to wives is now old-fashioned and becoming obsolete in the United States, but another barbarism that seems to have arisen in Civil War days, the habit of prefixing long and cumbersome titles to names, still flourishes. The style of *Life* and *Time* promotes the creation of such monstrosities, and they are imitated by the newspapers. I could fill pages with them, but content myself with two

---

[3] General John J. Pershing, who was made a G.C.B. (Knight Grand Cross of the Most Honourable Order of the Bath) in 1918, thereby became *Sir* John J. Pershing by English law and custom. But he never used the honorific, [nor have the Americans similarly honored during and following World War II].

[4] [These difficulties have been discussed in *AS*, Vol. XXVIII, 1953, by Thomas Pyles in British Titles of Nobility and Honor in American English, May, pp. 69–79, and in a letter by Sir St. Vincent Trowbridge, Oct., pp. 199–200.]

[5] Mar. 18. *Maryland Historical Magazine*, Sept. 1944, p. 252.

[6] Sandburg, Abraham Lincoln: The War Years; Vol. II, p. 260.

magnificent specimens. The first is from *Life: "Episcopal Bishop in Japan's brother,* J. C. Reifsnider." [7] The second is from an Associated Press dispatch: *"Vice-President in Charge of Sales of Evaporated, Condensed, and Malted Milk, Cheese, Mince-Meat and Caramels* Arthur W. Ramsdell, and *Vice-President in Charge of Casein, Adhesives, and Prescription Products* William Callan were elected to those offices today by the board of directors of the Borden Company." [8]

The use of *Madam(e)* as a special title of honor for old women of good position survived in the United States until the 70s. It distinguished the dowager Mrs. Smith from the wife of her eldest son. After the Civil War *madam* (without the *-e*) as a common noun became the designation of brothel keepers, and so the title fell into bad repute. When women began to go into politics, after the proclamation of the Nineteenth Amendment in 1920, the widows of male politicians frequently became candidates for their dead husbands' jobs. One of the first of these ambitious relicts, the Hon. Nellie Tayloe Ross, of Wyoming, made her campaign under the style of *Ma*, and the title was soon extended to others of her kind, such as Miriam Ferguson, twice elected governor of Texas after her husband had been removed by impeachment. The term began to drop out of use in the 30s. The Hon. Frances Perkins, who became Secretary of Labor in 1933, was often called *Ma* in her early days, but after a while it became a custom in Washington to speak of her, and even to address her, as *Madam*. [Respectable women from the hinterland, who knew only the common garden meaning of *madam*, resented the title.]

Mistress, like *madam*, goes back nearly to Chaucer's time, but at the start it was always fully pronounced, and not reduced to *missus* or *missez*. Until the beginning of the Seventeenth Century the common abbreviation was not *Mrs.*, but *Mis.*, or *Mris*. The editor of an 1828 edition of John Walker's "Critical Pronouncing Dictionary and Expositor of the English Language" (1791) noted that to pronounce *Mrs. mistress* would "appear quaint and pedantick," and Noah Webster, in his American Dictionary of the same year, gave its "colloquial" pronunciation as *mis-ses*. But Schele de Vere reported in 1872 that "in the South it was still very frequently heard

---

[7] New Words for Old, Baltimore *Evening Sun* (editorial page), June 3, 1938.

[8] How's That Again? Department, *The New Yorker*, Jan. 6, 1940. Not infrequently such thunderous titles are preceded by *ex-* or *former*. *Former*, in this situation, is an Americanism, traced to 1885, but *ex-* is not, appearing in English use in an OED citation from 1793. Both the Style Manual of the Department of State and the Style Manual of the U. S. Government Printing Office seem to prefer *ex-* (with a hyphen) to *former*. [The spread of divorce has made *ex-husband* and *ex-wife* familiar to millions of Americans, and among the middle classes it is a mark of broad-mindedness to refer to a detached spouse casually as "my *ex*."]

pronounced fully, without the usual contraction into *misses*." [9] This full pronunciation continues to be heard occasionally from the lips of old-fashioned Southerners,[1] [but the familiar connotations of the common noun, like those of *madam*, have elsewhere caused most people to cease using it].

6: JARGON AND COUNTER WORDS

The proliferation of titles in a supposedly democratic society has brought with it an encouragement of the use of vague polysyllables with anything but clear meaning. This turgidity, deplored by a wide range of observers from Jacques Barzun to Thomas Pyles, afflicts all parts of American culture, but the longest and most ponderous words are likely to be employed to the most stultifying effect by those in public office, and especially by those who handle government correspondence.

It is hard to decide whether British or American jobholders write worse. On the higher levels, the British university tradition, to which most of their most puissant politicos have been exposed, imparts a feeling for language and a delight in the sharply turned phrase that few of their American counterparts can equal. But on lower levels their public jobholders, like ours, are generally shabby and pretentious writers, greatly given to counter words and clichés. So long ago as 1916 the official English style was denounced bitterly by Sir Arthur Quiller-Couch, and in recent years it has been given constant but far from loving attention by A. P. Herbert, M.P. Quiller-Couch defined it as the jargon that "has become the medium through which boards of government, county councils, syndicates, committees, commercial firms, express the processes as well as the conclusions of their thoughts, and so voice the reason of their being." [2] This bombastic style of English official utterance antedates even the great upsurge of pedantry in the Eighteenth Century. Some of its masterpieces are famous— for example, the sign reading "These basins are for casual ablutions only," formerly hanging in the men's washroom of the British Museum. [Even more beautiful is the example which the guardians of public safety posted in the windows of all business establishments in New York City during the blackout days of World War II: "Illumination is required to be extin-

---

[9] Americanisms: The English of the New World, p. 507.

[1] [See The Pronunciation of *Mrs.*, by E. Bagby Atwood, *AS*, Vol. XXV, Feb. 1950, pp. 10–18.] All old speechways seem to linger longer in the South than elsewhere, just as old theological doctrines and political hallucinations linger. It used to be common there for colored servants to address their mistress as *Miss Mary* instead of *Mrs. Smith*. The *Miss* was always heard in this combination, never the *Mrs.*

[2] Interlude on Jargon in On the Art of Writing; New York, 1916.

guished before these premises are vacated."] This sort of sonorous rubbish was denounced by the late Lord Tweedsmuir, Governor General of Canada,[3] and in 1940 Winston Churchill had at it in an official memorandum to the members of his government and the heads of the civil service, begging them to order their subordinates to write more simply. In the United States its chief critic in office was Maury Maverick, chairman of the Smaller War Plants Corporation, who boiled over on March 30, 1944, with a formal prohibition of what he called *gobbledygook language* by the tax eaters under his command:

> Be short and say what you're talking about. Let's stop *pointing up* programs, *finalizing* contracts that *stem from* district, regional or Washington *levels*. No more *patterns, effectuating, dynamics*. Anyone using the words *activation* or *implementation* will be shot.

Complaints about the unintelligibility of OPA directives became so bitter during the spring of 1944 that an expert was employed to attempt their translation into English. Characteristically, the savant selected was an Austrian who arrived in the United States so recently as 1938.[4] Whether or not he managed to effect a reform is not recorded. [Earlier, however, practical bureaucrats had quietly coped with officialese by having their subordinates prepare unofficial translations; thus an eighty-page set of instructions to ginners, under the Bankhead Cotton Control Act, became a sensible summary of two thousand words.] Meanwhile, the Army and Navy also succumbed to the official style.[5] By the end of 1943 such a monstrosity as the following was appearing in official handbooks: "Proper application of prescribed preventative maintenance measures must be a prime consideration in order to minimize replacements."

Among the favorites of the New Deal wizards between 1933 and 1944

---

[3] Quoted in Ponderous English, Manchester *Guardian Weekly*, Aug. 30, 1940, p. 149.

[4] [A sample of reactions against the plague: Rudolf Flesch, The Art of Plain Talk, New York, 1946; Sir Ernest Gowers, Plain Words, London, 1948, Plain Words: Their ABC, London, 1951, and The Complete Plain Words, London, 1954; James R. Masterson and Wendell Brooks Phillips, Federal Prose: How to Write in and/or for Washington, Chapel Hill, N.C., 1948; Thomas Pyles, Subliminal Words Are Never Finalized, *The New York Times Magazine*, June 15, 1958, pp. 16 ff., James Reston, Uniquack's Guide to the New Gobbledygook, *The New York Times*, Nov. 10, 1957. Most recently officialese has been attacked by

J. W. Goodrich, Civil Service Chief of New South Wales, who hopes to eliminate it in his jurisdiction; his ambitions were reported in *The New York Times*, Sept. 23, 1962. A longish glossary of current Washingtonese appeared in *Time*, Apr. 19, 1963, p. 31, headed Now Everybody, Escalate!]

[5] [In Supplement I, Mencken praised the "plain and excellent American" taught at West Point before World War II. But Jack R. Brown demurs from this generalization and demonstrates the existence of gobbledygook among the officers of the Regular Army, in *AS*, Vol. XXI, Oct. 1946, pp. 285-8. A short glossary of Marine Corps officialese was reprinted in *The New Yorker*, Apr. 27, 1963, p. 81.]

were *coordinator, pool, roll-back, rationale, objective, clearance, to be severed, to process* and the sententious saying "Time is *of the essence.*" Few if any of these were their inventions, but they gave all of them wide currency, and one of them, *to process,* though ignored by the DA, now threatens to take its place in the language alongside *to contact.* It is old as a law term, but in the sense of to subject to a mechanical or chemical process it seems to be an Americanism, first recorded by the OED in the New York *Evening Post* of January 28, 1884, where it was described as "a new verb invented to fit a new thing," to wit, the process of making photo-engravings. [Its original New Deal appearance was in *processing tax,* an ingenious but unconstitutional device to raise prices by taxing the process of manufacture.] But the later New Dealers gave it a much wider range by using it for purely ideational operations, and widening it to include human beings among its objects, such as the inmates of Army *processing centers* in World War II. It has since been adopted by large groups, mostly of learned pretensions, outside the ranks of officialdom, both in its older sense of doing something to inanimate materials and in its new sense of mauling and manipulating God's creatures.

There was no need for most of these groups to borrow it,[6] for they all have plenty of counter words and clichés of their own. [Business and advertising generate such terms as *convenience foods* and most of the new formations in *-ize* and *-wise.*] The medical brethren are notorious for their muggy writing. In part its defects are produced by mere garrulity, but in other part they flow out of a fondness for irrational and misleading terms, *e.g.,* the shortenings: *to operate* (a patient) for *to operate on* and *temperature* for *elevation of temperature.* Not a few use *case* for *patient,*[7] and some even lean toward such bizarre forms as *to diagnosticate,*[8] *to do a urine, rectal* and *basal* (as nouns) and *to clinic.* The psychiatrists, especially those of the psychoanalytical faction, have concocted a vast vocabulary of new words,[9] and some of them have got into the common speech, *e.g., complex (inferiority, Oedipus,* etc.), *libido, inhibition, repression, introvert, extrovert, fixation, subconscious, psychopathic personality* and various derivatives of *schizophrenia.*[1] From the repertoire of the internists has come

---

[6] [Technical writing, however, is rather favorably appraised by Julie Eidesheim, Editor at Work; New York and Toronto, 1939, pp. 89–90.]

[7] This may have been borrowed from the undertakers, now *morticians,* who have in turn adopted *patient.*

[8] Unfortunately the OED traces *diagnosticate* to 1846 and the more seemly *diagnose* only to 1861, so the former has seniority if not beauty. [See also The Spoken Language of Medicine, by Peter

B. Hukill, *AS*, Vol. XXXVI, May 1961, pp. 145–8.]

[9] *Psychoanalysis,* in the German form *psychoanalyse,* was coined by Sigmund Freud, *c.* 1900. It first appeared in English in 1907, the year of the first International Congress of Psychoanalysis.

[1] In *AS*, Vol. II, Nov. 1926, p. 95, Edna Heidbreder printed a sheaf of sapphics made up entirely of psychoneurotic terms.

the adjective *allergic*, now in wide use as a general indicator of aversion, whether physical or psychic.[2] The orthodox psychologists have also made contributions, *e.g.*, *reaction, conditioned, to stultify* and *psychological moment*.[3] But of all the bands of learned men who devote themselves to inventing new terms, and then to hugging them until the last drop of juice is squeezed out of them, the most assiduous are the pedagogues.[4] A few of their favorites, *e.g.*, *outstanding*, have got into the common stock, but on the whole their jargon remains esoteric, *e.g.*, *stimulus-response bond, creativity, overview, core curriculum, emphases, orthogenic, control of the learning situation, to motivate, to vitalize* and *to socialize*. The so-called progressive gogues, in the days of their glory, had a large and bristling vocabulary of their own, much of it lifted from the lingo of the psychoanalysts, the various warring wings of psychologists, the Rotarians and the Boy Scouts. The progressives are now in the doghouse, and the generality of public-school gogues are going back to what they call *essentialism, i.e.*, the teaching of such once-scorned subjects as reading, writing and ciphering. Pedaguese, as a special argot, has naturally drawn on the jargon of the more advanced and liberal sociologists, especially from the faction of pseudo-sociologists known as social workers.[5]

[Among humanistic technicians, the jargon of the social scientist is a favorite straw man for verbal clobbering, but the literary critics—New, Aristotelian and Freudulent—are at least as good at obfuscation.[6] American linguists also have an elaborate trade jargon. Much of its complexity comes from their practice, like that of their prototype, Leonard Bloomfield, of

[2] See The Living Language, by Dwight L. Bolinger, *Words*, Oct. 1937, p. 154, and Jan. 1938, p. 11. The parent noun *allergy* is traced by the OED Supplement to 1913, and *allergic* to 1925.

[3] [In 1942 the psychologists of the Air Force sired *stanine* (from *standard nine-point scale*) to indicate a composite aptitude rating.]

[4] [*Auding tests* (*auding* is pedaguese for listening) were mentioned in *EJ*, Vol. XLV, Dec. 1956, p. 543. Sketches of the argot are More on Pseudo-Medical Educational Jargon, by Paul Fussell, Jr., *AS*, Vol. XXIX, Oct. 1954, pp. 234–5; It's Teacher Talking, by E. John Long, *The New York Times Magazine*, Sept. 13, 1959, p. 111; A Short Primer of Educationese, by Sheldon P. Ziener, *CE*, Vol. XVIII, Oct. 1956, pp. 23–5. Nor is pedaguese confined to teachers colleges and departments of education. A rich lexicon of so-called *buzz words* flourished in the late 1940s at the Harvard Graduate

School of Business Administration, according to a letter by F. M. Hallgren and H. Weiss, *AS*, Vol. XXI, Oct. 1946, p. 263. The College (undergraduate school) of the University of Chicago, sired by Robert M. Hutchins and tended lovingly by platoons of philosophers, has an elaborate argot of such words as *to place out, comprehensive* (n.) and *mitigation* that are unfathomable by those in other parts of the University.]

[5] [There is a glossary, Sociological Terms, by M. J. Tarves; Minneapolis, 1951. See also Family Specialists Cautioned on Talk, *The New York Times*, Sept. 9, 1950.]

[6] [See The Vocabulary of the New Criticism, by Charles Moorman, *American Quarterly*, Vol. VII, Summer 1957, pp. 180–4, and The Auto-Beatnik, The Auto-Critic and the Justification of Nonsense, *Antioch Review*, Vol. XXI, Winter 1961–2, pp. 405–19.]

insisting on rigorous scientific method and precise terminology; but some of it simply comes from bad writing and probably muddled thinking. A recent "Glossary of American Technical Linguistic Usage, 1925–1950" [7] includes, *inter alia, alternation morph, belch timbre, constructional meaning, determinative compound, epilegm, fluctuant, glosseme, initiating stricture, literics, macrotagmeme, nonnucleus, operational sandhi, presequential* (noun), *referential symbolism, suprasegmental, tonomechanics, vocoid* and *zero affix.* [8]]

Words that are often used, in a technical argot or otherwise, tend to lose all definite meaning and become what linguists call counter words. There is a constant accretion of new ones. So long ago as September 27, 1749, Lord Chesterfield was noting and denouncing, in a letter to his son, the vogue for *vastly* in England. *Jolly*, still in use in England, is traced by the OED in English use, sometimes followed by *well*, to 1548, but it has never had a run in the United States, though the verb *to jolly* was adopted years ago (1891). The DAE marks *awful* and *awfully* Americanisms. The first is traced to 1809, more than sixty years before it appeared in England. "In New England," said Pickering in his Vocabulary of 1816, "many people would call a disagreeable medicine *awful*, an ugly woman an *awful*-looking woman; a perverse, ill-natured child that disobeys his parents would be said to behave *awfully*, etc." Pickering seemed to believe that *awful* and *awfully* were on their way out, but they still survive. He also noted *grand*, in the general sense of superior or noteworthy. *Swell*, as a noun signifying a person of fashion, seems to have been borrowed from the cant of thieves in England, *c.* 1800. In 1804 a number of young English officers were dismissed from the Army for forming what they called the *Swell* Club, but soon afterward the term was in general use, and the adjective seems to have followed almost immediately. *Swell* had a revival in the United States *c.* 1910; [its antonym *lousy* dates from 1839, and *lousy with* from 1850]. Both *swell* and *lousy* are counter words of the first virulence. Many other counter words of recent years will occur to the reader,

---

[7] [By Eric P. Hamp; Utrecht, 1957. For a confession of the problems, see Zellig Harris, Methods in Structural Linguistics; Chicago, 1952, p. v: "This book is, regrettably, not easy to read."]

[8] [Complaints against the style of linguists have been voiced by two of the brethren, Lee S. Hultzén, Communication in Linguistics, *AS*, Vol. XXVIII, Feb. 1953, pp. 3–11, and Hans Sperber, Linguistics in a Strait-Jacket, *MLN*, Vol. LXXV, Mar. 1960, pp. 239–52. See also Some Observations on the Language of Linguists, by L. R. Palmer, in Studies

Presented to Joshua Whatmough on His Sixtieth Birthday; 's Gravenhage, 1957, pp. 187–92. The problems in other disciplines are presented in J. R. Baker, English Style in Scientific Papers, *Science*, Apr. 27, 1956, pp. 713–14; Robert Gordon, A Question of Style, *American Association of University Professors Bulletin*, Spring 1957, pp. 22–33; Robert Graves, Diseases of Scholarship, *New Republic*, May 20, 1957, pp. 17–19; Britain and the Common Market Talk Same Language—Jargon, *The New York Times*, July 4, 1962.]

e.g., constructive (beloved of Rotarians), *consistent* and *definitely*. Observers have long commented on the way Americans overwork the verbs *to fix* and *to get;* the noun *proposition* began to take on wide and often preposterous significance in American during the 1870s, and was soon in a lamentably swollen state. It meant a problem, proposal, person, parallel, premise, postulate, parley, phenomenon, point, policy, philosophy, prospect, process, petition, paradox or possibility, to mention only a few of its meanings under its own first letter.[9] It went into English with the movies, and was denounced by H. W. Fowler in "Modern English Usage."

In 1910 or thereabout the more incompetent newspaper reporters of the United States began to use *angle* in the sense of any aspect of a person or an event, and *alibi* as a synonym for any word signifying an explanation or an excuse. Among recent counter words are *flair, personality, conference, analysis, plus,* the verbs *to function, to intrigue* and *to claim* and the adjectives *lurid, streamlined, meticulous* and *conscious*. Some of them began in the argot of a relatively small class, and then extended to the common tongue, *e.g., service,* which seems to have been launched by the visionaries of Rotary, *c.* 1910. [It was soon adopted by college administrators in *service courses,* those required offerings like English composition which few want to take or teach.[1]] *Outstanding* began its career among the pedagogues, and they still overwork it cruelly, but it is now also used by politicians, the rev. clergy, newspaper editorial writers and other such virtuosi of bad writing. *Consistent* came in *c.* 1925 as an adjective designating every sort of harmony or continuity. *Exciting* apparently arose in the jargon of art criticism, but in 1933 it was borrowed by the writers of book reviews, and presently had a great run in publishers' advertising, especially on the slip covers of books. *Plus* seems to have been the child of advertisement writers; it was noticed in *American Speech* for December 1927 as in high favor among them. *Classic* followed a year or so later.[2] The OED Supplement records *dingus* in the English of South Africa in 1898, but the DA records it in Nevada in 1876, so that it must be a much earlier borrowing from New York Dutch. It has been in heavy use in the United States since the automobile and the radio brought in a host of novel contraptions, and with it have flourished a number of congeners, *e.g., jigger, gadget* and *doodad*. The use of *gesture* as a general indicator of any sort of action, movement, offer, threat or deed

---

[9] In a speech in the Senate by Senator George W. Norris, of Nebraska, it was used in five or six distinct senses. See *Congressional Record*, Feb. 21, 1921, pp. 374 ff.

[1] [Antinomians, however, see a relationship to *service horse,* a folk euphemism for stallion.]

[2] See *Classic*, by R. G. Lewis, *AS*, Vol. III, June 1928, p. 433. [The more recent vogue word *historic* is discussed by Ralph H. Lane in *AS*, Vol. XXIV, Oct. 1949, pp. 181–8.]

began about 1925, possibly helped by the French *beau geste*, the title of a popular movie of the period. *Strenuous* should not be forgotten,[3] nor the counter words that occupy the intelligentsia without ever descending to lower levels, e.g., *sophisticated, perspective, rhetoric,*[4] *chemurgic, podium* and *ongoing* for *continuing*. Some English counter words have made the Atlantic journey, e.g., *knowledgeable,*[5] which had a great run in the 1935–8 era, and *unilateral,*[6] and the fashionable intensives of the *foul* and *putrid* order. Whether or not the *and/or* combination originated in England has not been determined. Like *alibi*, it comes from the argot of the law. It has been denounced in both England and America, even by judges, but it continues to flourish.

7: EUPHEMISMS

The American seldom believes that the trade he follows is quite worthy of his virtues and talents; he thinks that he would have adorned something far gaudier. Since it is often impossible for him to escape, or to dream plausibly of escaping, he soothes himself by pretending that he belongs to a superior section of his craft, and even invents a sonorous name to set himself off from the herd. Here we glimpse the origin of characteristic American euphemisms, e.g., *mortician* for *undertaker*, *realtor* for *real-estate agent*, *beautician* for *hairdresser*, *exterminating engineer* for *rat catcher* and so on. *Realtor* was devised by a high-toned real-estate agent of Minneapolis, Charles N. Chadbourn by name, who sought a distinctive title by which he and his fellow members of the Minneapolis Real Estate Board could distinguish themselves from fly-by-night dealers

---

[3] Popularized by Theodore Roosevelt's speech at Chicago, Apr. 10, 1899, and in vogue for a quarter of a century.

[4] [See The Melioration of *Sophisticated* and *Sophistication*, by Donald E. Houghton, *AS*, Vol. XXXV, Feb. 1960, pp. 73–6. Very complicated rocket instruments are said to be *sophisticated*. Newly concocted rocket fuels and fuel-delivery systems are *exotic*. In many walks of life a summary, especially a historical summary, is a *perspective*, e.g., *Perspectives on Linguistics*, by John T. Waterman, Chicago, 1963. Among the neo-Aristotelian critics *rhetoric* is a current fashionable synonym for *technique* or the older *craft*, as implying the superior intellectual status and cleaner hands of the philosopher: The *Rhetoric* of Fiction,

by Wayne C. Booth, Chicago, 1962, surveys essentially the same problems treated a generation ago by Percy Lubbock in The *Craft* of Fiction.]

[5] [Discussed by Charles Aughtry in *AS*, Vol. XXXIV, Feb. 1959, pp. 71–2. In *The New York Times*, May 6, 1963, a Washington dispatch reports *ongoing* as a bureaucratic novelty for *continuing*. But it had been in circulation for at least five years. Elder Olson calls my attention to the current vogue of *hopefully*. *Powerful* and *successful* are typical counter words in Noam Chomsky, Syntactic Structures, *Janua Linguarum*, No. 4, 's Gravenhage, 1956.]

[6] Denounced by A. P. Herbert, with many horrible examples, in Word-Skirmish, *Punch*, Mar. 17, 1937, pp. 288–9.

in houses and lots.[7] The Minneapolis brethren were so pleased with their new name that he went to the convention of the National Association of Real Estate Boards at New Orleans, and made a formal offer of it, which was accepted gratefully. The general counsel of the National Association is heard from every time *realtor* is taken in vain, and when, in 1922, Sinclair Lewis applied it to George F. Babbitt, there was an uproar. But when Mr. Chadbourn was appealed to he decided that Babbitt was "fairly well described," for he was "a prominent member of the local board and of the State association," and one could scarcely look for anything better in "a book written in the ironic vein of the author of 'Main Street.' "[8]

The suggestion that *realtor* is derived from two Spanish words, *real*, meaning royal, and *toro*, bull, and that it thus connotes *royal bull*, is spurned by the bearers of the name. The official pronunciation is not re*a*ltor, but *reel*-tor.[9] The agent suffix *-or* has always conveyed a more dignified suggestion in English than the allied *-er*, perhaps because it often represents the Latin *-ator* or the French *-eur*. *Professor*, to most persons, is superior to *teacher* not only in meaning but also in aspect and atmosphere, and in the same way *author* stands above *writer*, [and (at least in his own eyes) an *advisor* to students is more dignified than a mere *adviser*]. In this great free Republic there is little hostility to human aspiration, and in consequence *realtor* has suggested *insuror*[1] (an insurance agent), *furnitor* (a furniture dealer),[2] *publicator* (a press agent)[3] and *weldor*.[4] The radio trade has a long list of terms in *-or*, but they are applied to mechanical contrivances, not to God's children, *e.g.*, *resistor*, *inductor*, *capacitator* and *arrestor*, the last an elegant substitute for the

---

[7] Private communication, Sept. 28, 1935. [Some of the details of this section are elaborated in Postscripts to the American Language: Scented Words, by H. L. Mencken, *The New Yorker*, Apr. 2, 1949, pp. 70–4.]

[8] Letter to W. A. Frisbie, editor of the Minneapolis *Daily News*, 1922. The letter was subscribed "Yours *realtorily*." A copy was sent to Mr. Lewis, who preserved it in his archives.

[9] *Realtor: Its Meaning and Use*; Chicago, 1925, p. 3 *n*.

[1] *Insurors*, by G. P. Krapp, *AS*, Vol. III, June 1928, p. 432.

[2] San Francisco *Examiner*, Nov. 2, 1930, Sec. 1, p. 11.

[3] *AS*, Vol. XVII, Oct. 1942, p. 212. [Since 1951 *publicitor* has been very common, especially where athletic events are concerned. In England, according to Gerard Fay, "these people . . . are in-creasingly getting away with *publicist*, which used to have a nobler meaning. Unhappily, they are supported by the OED, which gives it as second meaning." Private communication, Feb. 26, 1957.]

[4] *Weldor* was launched as the result of a labor squabble. In 1941 the *welders* in the shipyards and on building construction petitioned the American Federation of Labor for a charter. When it was refused, they left the Federation and formed the Brotherhood of *Weldors*, Cutters and Helpers of America. See *Weldors*, *AS*, Vol. XVII, Oct. 1942, p. 214. [*Healor* is one of the professional titles of one Lena P. Smith, The Woman of God, who operates a religious studio on S. Cottage Grove Avenue in Chicago. Institutional purchasing agents favor *purchasor*; *The Chicago Purchasor* is their local house organ.]

earlier *lightning arrester*, which is traced by the DAE to 1860 and is probably an Americanism.[5]

Mortician is in the public domain. It was suggested by *physician*, for undertakers naturally admire and like to pal with the resurrection men.[6] From the earliest days they have sought to bedizen their hocus-pocus with mellifluous euphemisms, and during the Civil War they undertook their first really radical reform of its terms, by substituting *casket* for the older *coffin*. Many purists did not like it, including Nathaniel Hawthorne, who thus denounced it in "Our Old Home" (1863):

> *Caskets!*—a vile modern phrase [*sic*] which compels a person of sense and good taste to shrink more disgustfully than ever before from the idea of being buried at all.

But *casket* quickly made its way, and since the early 80s *coffin* has seldom appeared in an American undertaker's advertisement or in a newspaper account of the funeral of anyone above the dignity of an executed murderer.[7] *Casket* remains in almost universal use, though there are poetic morticians who root for *slumber cot* or *burial couch*. The Civil War also brought the embalming of the dead into common practice, thanks to the job of bringing home dead soldiers from distant battlefields, often in warm weather. All the pioneer embalmers of the time called themselves *Dr*.

The DAE's earliest example of *mortician* comes from an advertisement in the Columbus (Ohio) *Dispatch* of August 14, 1895, only six months after the term was launched by the *Embalmer's Monthly*.[8] But it was not until September 17, 1917, that 200 of the most eminent American undertakers banded themselves into an organization called the National Selected *Morticians*,[9] and began to strike out for a general reform of

---

[5] More Words in *-or*, by C. P. Mason, *AS*, Vol. IV, Apr. 1929, p. 329. [*Computor* appeared in a headline in the University of Chicago *Maroon*, Aug. 4, 1962.]

[6] Various correspondents write in to say that I use this term inaccurately. A *resurrection man*, they point out, was one who robbed graves for the doctors in the days before the Anatomy Acts gave them a lawful supply of cadavers. Nevertheless, I continue to think of them as *resurrection men* themselves, for the frequent (if not always beneficial, socially speaking) effect of their labor is cheating the grave.

[7] Some nascent morticians, in the Civil War era, preferred *case*. The DA traces *burial case* to 1851 and defines it as "a form of coffin, often of metal."

[8] Feb. 1895. According to Elmer Davis (The Mortician, *American Mercury*, May 1927, p. 33), "it owes its origin chiefly to Frank Fairchild of Brooklyn and Harry Samson of Pittsburgh, distinguished members of the profession."

[9] For this date I am indebted to W. M. Krieger, of the National Selected Morticians, with headquarters in Chicago. [Membership in this elite is rarely advertised. However, in the Miami *Herald*, May 4, 1963, an enterprising practitioner unblushingly announces his membership in an ad which modestly acknowledges that his four studios provide "Everything in Mortuary and Crematory Services.]

necrophoric nomenclature.[1] Some of their inventions are now familiar: *patient* or *case* for *body; funeral car, casket coach* or *ambulance* for *hearse; negligee, slumber robe* or *slumber shirt* for *shroud; slumber room, reposing room, funeral home* or *funeral residence* for *funeral parlor* or *undertaking establishment; operating parlor, operating room, preparing room* or *preparation room* for the cellar in which the embalmer does his work; *service car* for *dead wagon; limousine* for *mourners' coach;*[2] and so on. In September 1935, a Washington mortician was advertising by cards in the local trolley cars that the *reposing rooms* in his *funeral home* were *"autumn-breezed* by the finest air-conditioning equipment."[3] Meanwhile, the owners and press agents of places of sepulcher have followed their associates into the flowery fields of euphemism. Graveyards, in all the more progressive parts of the United States, are graveyards no longer, nor even cemeteries, but *memorial parks, burial abbeys* or *-cloisters,* or *mortaria.*[4] In some areas graveyards are giving way to elaborate buildings. Some of these new mausoleums are structures of great pretentiousness, usually either Gothic or Byzantine in style and as gorgeous as a first-rate filling station. They flourish especially in southern California,[5] and those of Los Angeles are heavily patronized, for one of

---

[1] A *mortician,* said D. W. Brogan in Our Uncle's Tongue, *Oxford Magazine,* June 10, 1937, "was once defined by a wit as 'the man who buries a *realtor.*'"

[2] [In the early days of the automobile, *limousine* was in wide use; in the larger cities it is still used in this connection, especially for an ostentatiously large chauffeur-driven car, and the rental of *limousines* (often with livery) is an important business for those who cater to conspicuous wealth. For most Americans, however, it survives only in the vocabulary of morticians and for taxi service to and from airports, though the vehicle in question may be an ordinary bus. According to Gerard Fay, "*Limousine* almost passed out but has been resurrected by the airport operators in Europe, as in *limousine service to city terminal.*" Private communication, Feb. 20, 1957. According to the Chicago *Sun Times,* May 19, 1963, the makers of *limousines* now distinguish between *executive limousines* and *funeral cars.*]

[3] At least one *mortician* has promoted himself to the estate and dignity of a *mortuary consultant,* and another has become a *funeral counselor,* but none has come to light who calls himself a *mortuary, obituary* or *obsequial engineer.*

[The rise of the profession is chronicled in The History of American Funeral Directors, by Robert W. Habenstein and William M. Lamers; Milwaukee, 1955. Like literary critics, osteopaths and veterinarians, the morticians now demand advanced education for entrance to their guild, specifically attendance at one of 24 *mortuary colleges* now operating. See Vance Packard, The Status Seekers; New York, 1961, p. 84. A somewhat jaundiced view of the profession is offered by Jessica Mitford in The Undertakers' Racket, *The Atlantic Monthly,* June 1963, pp. 56–62.]

[4] In Houston, Tex., there is a cemetery called the *Garden of Memories.* See *Billboard,* Oct. 2, 1943, p. 31, and Forest Lawn, *Life,* Jan. 5, 1944, pp. 65–75. [California cemeteries are delicately described by Aldous Huxley in After Many a Summer Dies the Swan, and by Evelyn Waugh in The Loved One. The term *necropolis* has not, to my knowledge, appeared in the United States; but Kenneth Northcott points out that the *London Necropolis Company* manages an estate in suburban Brookwood.]

[5] "Before long," said Elmer Davis in 1927, "they will probably be calling them *memorial cathedrals.* Ground burial, we

the inducements they offer is the chance to store the beloved dead cheek by jowl with a Clark Gable or a Marilyn Monroe. To be laid away in one runs into money. [Even a run-of-the-mine funeral costs over $1,000, and in a year the morticians and their satellites extract three times as much money from American pockets as is spent on doctors, hospitals and prescription drugs. Some of these virtuosi are folk of literary genius, as the *Charon Equipment Company*, of Chicago, which rents funeral appurtenances, or the Cooney Mortuary, of the same city, which describes itself as "A Homey Place for Funerals."]

A correspondent reported a *mortician* in the town of Driffield in Yorkshire (pop. 6,000) in 1925, but the term has made very little progress among the hunkerous English, who prefer *undertaker*. *Funeral director*, an Americanism traced to 1886, is not listed in the OED, but an older term, *funeral undertaker*, is traced to 1707. *Undertaker* itself goes back to 1698.[6] *Morgue*, to designate a dead house, was borrowed from the French in 1850, and *mortuary* dates from 1865.[7] *Crematory* is traced by the DAE in American use to 1885; the OED traces it to 1876 in England. It is now pretty well supplanted in the United States by the more mellifluous *crematorium*, which borrows elegance from *pastorium*, *lubritorium* and their congeners.

The resounding success of *mortician* brought in many other words in *-ician*, e.g., *beautician*, *cosmetician*, *radiotrician*, *linguistician*. The DA's first citation of *beautician* is dated 1926, but the owner of a beauty salon by the name of Miss Kathryn Ann was advertising in the November 1924 issue of the Cleveland, Ohio, telephone directory that she had a staff of "very efficient *beauticians*." By 1926 Dr. Morris Fishbein, editor of the *Journal of the American Medical Association*, was reporting in the *Amer-*

learn, is out of date and barbarous; mausoleum entombment is modern, progressive and humanitarian—'as sanitary as cremation and as sentimental as a churchyard.'" The ceremony of depositing ashes in one of these basilicas is called *inurnment*. See *Inurnment*, by C. Douglas Chrétien, *AS*, Vol. IX, Dec. 1934, p. 317. [Arthur H. Cole comments on these structures in The Price System and the Rites of Passage, *American Quarterly*, Vol. XIV, Winter 1962, p. 543: "One [mausoleum] in the neighborhood of New York City was described as encompassing several levels or stories, being equipped with elevators, electric lights and air conditioning, and capable of containing 30,000 bodies plus several thousand funeral urns. One recently erected in Los Angeles was advertised to possess fifty thousand crypts and several added thousands of niches for funeral urns."]

[6] It once had a formidable rival in *upholder*, the original meaning of which was a dealer in and repairer of old furniture. In that sense *upholder* is traced by the OED to 1333, but it does not seem to have come into use to designate a funeral contractor until the beginning of the Eighteenth Century. It still survives in England. [The art of the mortician and the trade of the furniture dealer are still combined in many American small towns.]

[7] Three years later a writer in the London *Spectator* was sneering at it as the invention of newspaper reporters. His sneer was reprinted in *Every Saturday* (Boston), May 16, 1868, p. 636.

ican Mercury[8] that *beauticians, cosmeticians* and *cosmetologists* were in practice from end to end of the country, and that nine states had already passed acts providing for their examination, licensing and regulation.

Beautician had reached England by 1937, but it was apparently collared there by beauty-preparation manufacturers, who also tried to lay hands on *cosmetician*. In the United States both are yielding to *cosmetologist*, and the chief organization of the beauty-shop operators is called the National Hairdressers and *Cosmetologists* Association. In the Nineteenth Century the dens of lady hairdressers were called simply *hairdressing parlors*, but *beauty parlor* began to appear before World War I, and soon afterward it was displaced by *beauty shop, beauty shoppe* and *beauty salon*.

Radiotrician, perhaps suggested by *electrician* rather than by *mortician*, was adopted by the radio repairmen in the late 1920s, a little while after the regular electrical jobbers began to call themselves *electragists;* [both terms now have little currency among the laity. *Shoetrician* is likewise uncommon; however, the earlier euphemism *shoe rebuilder* flourishes, and some brethren of the craft are still content to be *cobblers*.] *Fizzician*, a second stage (the first being *fountaineer*) in the advance from *soda jerk*, was reported by *PM* in 1938. [*Linguistician* has been proposed to distinguish the scientific students of language from mere polyglots—which is what the term *linguist* usually signifies to the hoi polloi—but the resemblance to *mortician* has repelled the sensitive-eared members of the profession.] *American Speech* has recorded such marvels as *whooptician, fermentician, bootblackitician* and *scholastician*. *Ecstatician* ("one who studies, or is versed in, ecstasies") turned up in the *Atlantic Monthly* in 1936,[9] and *jazzician* briefly in England in 1938.[1] *Bootician*, my own invention, launched in the *American Mercury* in 1925, to designate a high-toned bootlegger,[2] was followed in 1930 by *super-bootician*.[3] It came too late to be included in the DAE or DA.

The tendency to engaud lowly vocations with names presumably dignified goes back to the Revolution, and has been frequently noted by English travelers, beginning with Thomas Anburey in 1779.[4] In 1784 John Ferdinand Dalziel Smyth observed that the smallest American shopkeepers were calling their establishments *stores*, which indicated a large

[8] The Cult of Beauty, Feb. 1926, pp. 161–8.

[9] *Words*, Feb. 1938, p. 30.

[1] *Jazzicians* Voluntarily Join Discharged Colleagues, *Cavalcade* (London), Aug. 13.

[2] Philological Notes, Apr., p. 450.

[3] Some Neologisms from Recent Magazines, by Robert Withington, *AS*, Vol. VI, Apr. 1931, p. 287.

[4] His Travels Through the Interior Parts of America was published in London in 1780. See Words Indicating Social Status in America in the Eighteenth Century, by Allen Walker Read, *AS*, Vol. IX, Oct. 1934, pp. 204–8.

place to an Englishman. "The different distinct branches of manufacturers," he said, "such as *hosiers, haberdashers, clothiers, linen drapers, grocers, stationers*, etc., are not known here; they are all comprehended in the single name and occupation of *merchant* or *storekeeper*." [5] By 1846 the American barbershop had begun to be a *shaving salon*, and by 1850 a photographer was a *daguerrian artist*. By 1875 barbers were *tonsorial artists* or *tonsorialists*,[6] and in the early 80s presentable saloonkeepers became *restauranters* or *restauranteurs*.[7] By 1901 the *Police Gazette* was carrying on a campaign for the abandonment of the lowly *bartender* and the adoption of either *bar clerk* or *mixologist*, which last had been proposed sportively by the *Knickerbocker Magazine* in 1856 and had come into more or less use in the West by 1870.[8] The early American photographers called their working places *studios*, and the term was later adopted by the operators of billiard rooms, barbershops and even various sorts of stores. A contributor to *American Speech*, in 1926, reported encountering *tonsorial studio, food studio* and *shoe studio*.[9] In 1940 the makers of Fanny Farmer candies called their kitchens *studios*, as did a Canadian competitor.

The list of such euphemisms might be lengthened almost endlessly. A bill collector has described himself as a *collection correspondent*,[1] a tapeworm specialist has operated a *Helminthological Institute*,[2] and in some stores *section manager* (formerly *aisle manager*) has replaced *floor walker*. *Tree surgeon* appears in Webster 1961 without comment; in 1934 the man who coined it, Martin L. Davey, was elected governor of Ohio. [*Corn doctors* have progressed via *chiropodists* to *podiatrists*.] The old-time newsboy is now a *newspaper boy*, which seems to be regarded as somehow more dignified; a dog catcher is a *canine control officer* in Peoria, Ill., and a *humane officer* in Tulsa, Okla.; an iceman, in Denver, is an *ice attendant*; a grocer is a *provisioner* or *victualer*. A janitor is a *superin-*

---

[5] A Tour in the United States of America; London 1788, Vol. I, pp. 98–9.

[6] In 1924, 3,000 of the more aspiring of them met in Chicago and resolved to become *chirotonsors*, but a loud chorus of newspaper ribaldry wrecked the term and it did not stick. See *The Commonweal*, Nov. 26, 1924, p. 58. The *tonsor* part was recorded as a name for a barber in Thomas Blount's *Glossographia* (1656).

[7] Always with the *n*; never in the French form, *restaurateur*. See my Newspaper Days; New York, 1941, pp. 215–16.

[8] The DAE records that an effort was made in Jersey City in 1910 to outlaw *bartender* and substitute *server*.

[9] John T. Krumpelmann suggests in a note to *AS*, Vol. II, Dec. 1926, p. 158, that this craze, at least in the Central West, may have been influenced by the German partiality for *atelier*. [*Atelier* was used by a photographer in Greenville, S.C., in the 1920s.]

[1] In the *Saturday Review of Literature*, Jan. 20, 1934, Christopher Morley reported one who called himself an *arrears negotiator*.

[2] *Institute* often designates a trade organization formed to resist legislative attacks upon large industries. See Among the New Words, by Dwight L. Bolinger, *AS*, Vol. XVII, Apr. 1942, p. 120.

tendent, custodian, engineer-custodian or *custodial engineer*. [At some universities, when the janitors were elevated to *custodians*, the custodians of special library collections were in turn upgraded to *directors* or *archivists*.[3]] In 1940 the International Brotherhood of *Red Caps* changed its name to the United *Transport Service Employees* of America. In 1939, when the surviving customers' men in the offices of the New York stockbrokers formed an Association of *Customers' Men* there was diffidence about their title, which had suffered grievously from the town wits; they soon adopted *customers' broker*.[4] Three years before this the hod carriers of Milwaukee had resolved to be *mason laborers*,[5] and only a few months later the Long Island Federation of Women's Clubs decreed that housewives should become *homemakers*. In 1942 some reformer in Kansas City launched a crusade to make it *household executive*.[6] In 1943 the more solvent spiritualists of the country, fretting under the discreditable connotations of their name, resolved to be *psychists* thenceforth.[7]

Gardeners posturing as *landscape architects* and laborers posturing as *gardeners* are too numerous to be remarked. So are lobbyists under the guise of *industrial consultants* or *field engineers*, press agents disguised as *publicity directors, public relations counsel* or *publicists*, detectives as *investigators* or *operatives*, encyclopedia salesmen as *educational advisors* and messenger boys as *communications carriers*.[8] *Public relations counsel* was launched by Edward L. Bernays, of New York, one of the most distinguished members of the fraternity.[9]

The lowly garbageman and ashman (English: *dustman*) have begun to disappear from the American fauna; they are now becoming *sanitary officers*, and the bureau under which the former works (at all events in

---

[3] [See A. H. Marckwardt, American English; New York, 1958, p. 117. An elaborate glossary of euphemisms employed by the Hartford *Courant* to "protect the status of the *newspaper delivery boy* as a '*Little Merchant*'" was reprinted in *The New Yorker*, Apr. 20, 1963, p. 162. The *Courant*, in turn, had taken it from the Dec. 1962 official bulletin of the International Circulation Managers Association.]

[4] *Customers' Men, Newsweek*, May 8, 1939; *Brokerettes, Newsweek*, June 19, 1939.

[5] Associated Press dispatch from Milwaukee, July 31, 1936.

[6] This happy event, like many others mentioned here, was recorded in two *New Yorker* articles by W. E. Farbstein: Workers, Arise! Sept. 16, 1939, and In Other Words, Aug. 8, 1942. [In England,

says Gerard Fay, "*housewife* was almost dead by 1939 and we tended to make fun of the German *Hausfrau*. But the word leaped back into the vocabulary during the war and has not subsided yet —it gave propagandists a chance to flatter women who could not be put into any other category." Personal communication, Feb. 26, 1957. In the United States *homemaker* flourishes, *e.g.*, U.S. Studies Jobs for *Homemakers*, headline in *The New York Times*, Aug. 25, 1962.]

[7] *Psychists* Incorporated, *Psychic Observer* (Lily Dale, N.Y.), Nov. 10, 1943.

[8] The Western Union advertised for them in *The New York Times*, Aug. 16, 1943, p. 29.

[9] It had been preceded by *councilor in* (or *on*) *public relations*, occasionally used by Ivy L. Lee (1878–1934), another eminent publicist.

heavenly Pasadena) has become the *table waste disposal department*.[1] [In refreshingly conservative contrast, Chicago still has *public scavengers*.] Street sweeps are also becoming *sanitary officers* or *sanitation men*. The United States Post Office now calls its male sweepers *charmen*, and may be trusted on some near tomorrow to give a lift to its *charwomen*. The junkmen, by their own resolve, are now *waste material dealers*. An ancient bill sticker attached to a Baltimore theater once boasted the sonorous title of *chief lithographer*.

Before the Revolution *help* and *hired man* seem to have been descriptive merely; Albert Matthews maintains with his accustomed great learning that before 1776 there was not "the slightest indication of [*hired man*] having been employed in a euphemistic sense."[2] But after 1776 it began to be employed to distinguish a freeman from a slave, and after 1863 it became a general substitute for *servant*, a "hated appellation." It was not noted as an Americanism by any of the early writers on the subject, but Webster listed it in his American Dictionary of 1828. *Hired girl* is traced to 1818, *hired hand* to the same year and *hired help* to 1815. *Help* originally appears to have designated a person giving occasional assistance only, as opposed to a regular servant. It probably became a euphemism after the Revolution, when the servant problem became acute. *Help* and *hired girl* are now both abandoned, and *maid* or *housekeeper* is the almost universal designation of a female servant.[3]

Since *engineer* became a title of prestige in America, it has been assumed by a wide spectrum of charlatans. For a number of years the *Engineering News-Record*, the organ of the legitimate engineers, used to devote a column every week to uninvited invaders of the craft, some so fantastic that it was constrained to reproduce their business cards photographically to convince its readers that it was not spoofing. A favorite exhibit was a bedding manufacturer who first became a *mattress engineer* and then promoted himself to the lofty dignity of *sleep engineer*. No doubt he would have called himself a *morphician* if he had thought of it. A tractor driver advertised for a job as a *caterpillar engineer*. A beautician burst out as an *appearance engineer*. Elsewhere appeared *display engineers* who had been lowly window dressers until some visionary among them made the great leap, *demolition engineers* who were once content to be house wreckers and *sanitary engineers* who had an earlier

---

[1] [See *Garbician, Garbigian, Garbagian*, by John B. Virtue, *AS*, Vol. XXXI, Dec. 1956, pp. 307–8. According to the journal of Andy Jordan, Sept. 24, 1849 (cited in W. E. Woodward, The Way Our People Lived; New York, 1944), the Irish washerwomen of San Francisco were

calling themselves *clothing refreshers*.]
[2] The terms *Hired-man* and *Help, Publications of the Colonial Society of Massachusetts*, Vol. V, 1900.
[3] [See The Status Seekers, by Vance Packard; New York, 1961, p. 19.]

incarnation as garbagemen. The *wedding engineer* is a technician employed by florists to dress churches for hymeneal orgies. The *commencement engineer* arranges college and high-school commencements; he has lists of clergymen who may be trusted to pray briefly, and some sort of fire-alarm connection with popular commencement orators. The *packing engineer* crates clocks, radios and chinaware for shipment. The *correspondence engineer* writes selling letters guaranteed to pull. The *income engineer* is an insurance solicitor in a new false face. The *dwelling engineer* replaces lost keys, repairs leaky roofs and plugs up rat holes in the cellar. The *vision engineer* supplies spectacles at cut rates. The *dehorning engineer* attends to bulls who grow too frisky. Perhaps the prize should go to the *dansant engineer* (an agent supplying dancers and musicians to night clubs), or to the *hot-dog engineer*.

The Dictionary of Occupational Titles prepared by the Job Analysis and Information Section of the Division of Standards and Research of the Department of Labor lists many curious varieties of engineers, including the *rigging-up engineer*, the *yarder engineer* and the *roader engineer*, but all of them appear to have to do with some form of actual engineering or engine operation, however lowly, and so their titles, while perhaps rather florid, do not qualify as euphemisms. In this list a *sanitary engineer* appears, not as a plumber but as "a civil engineer who designs and supervises the construction and operation of sewers, sewage disposal plants, garbage disposal plants, ventilation tunnels, and other sanitary facilities," and such savants as the *termite engineer*, the *social engineer* and the *human engineer* are *non est*. Neither do any of these latter-day wizards appear on the list of engineers employed by the Tennessee Valley Authority, though it has room for *cost engineers*, *erosion engineers* and *material engineers*.[4] The rat, cockroach and bedbug eradicators of the country have had for years an organization called the American Society of *Exterminating Engineers*. On November 8, 1923, the *News-Record* reported that one of its members followed the sideline of a mortician in Bristol, Pa., and suggested sportively: "That's service for you. Kill 'em and bury 'em for the same fee." But the title of *engineer* seems to be reserved with some plausibility for the head men of this profession: its lowlier representatives are apparently content to call themselves *exterminators*.

Next to *engineer*, *expert* seems to be the favorite talisman of Americans eager to augment their estate and dignity in this world. Very often it is hitched to an explanatory prefix, *e.g.*, *housing-*, *hog-*, *marketing-* or *sheep-dip-*, but sometimes the simple adjective *trained-* suffices. When the Brain Trust was in power in Washington, the town swarmed with

---

[4] *Congressional Record*, Mar. 15, 1938, p. 4556. [In *American Notes and Queries*, Vol. IV, June 1944, p. 48, Wayland Hand reports from Los Angeles the profession of *spiritual engineer* and a *School of Human Engineering*.]

such quacks. A humorous member of Congress found at least one whose expertness was acquired in a seminary for chiropractors. During the John Purroy Mitchel "reform" administration in New York City (1914–18) so many bogus *experts* were put on the payroll that special designations ran out, and a number were carried as *general experts*.

After the invention of *bootician* in 1925 I hatched no neologism of the same high tone for fifteen years. Then I was inspired by a letter from a lady subscribing herself Georgia Sothern and designating her profession as strip teasing, who requested "a new and more palatable word to describe this art." As a help to her (or her public relations counsel) I replied as follows:

> It might be a good idea to relate strip teasing in some way or other to the associated zoological phenomenon of molting. Thus the word *moltician* comes to mind, but it must be rejected because of its likeness to *mortician*.
>
> A resort to the scientific name for molting, which is *ecdysis*, produces both *ecdysist* and *ecdysiast*. Then there are suggestions in the names of some of the creatures which practice molting. The scientific name for the common crab is *Callinectes hastatus*, which produces *callinectian*. Again there is a family of lizards called the *Geckonidae*, and their name produces *gecko*.[5]

In a little while articles in the public prints indicated that she (or her press agent) had decided to adopt *ecdysiast*.[6] It appeared by these articles that two popularizers of semantics had been consulted—S. I. Hayakawa, of the Illinois Institute of Technology and author of "Language in Action," and Stuart Chase, S.B. *cum laude* (Harvard), author of "The Economy of Abundance," "Your Money's Worth," "The Tyranny of Words" and other scientific works. Hayakawa seemingly demurred on the incredible ground that he had never seen a strip teaser in action, and Chase, busy with the salvation of humanity on a dozen fronts, made no reply at all; so I won by a sort of forfeit. Soon the British United Press correspondent cabled news of *ecdysiast* to London, and it was discussed gravely in many of the great English organs of opinion, though strip teasing itself was prohibited in the British Isles.[7] A suggestion by La Sothern (or her press agent) to the

[5] I learn from How It Happened, Philadelphia *Record*, Mar. 27, 1944, that the counsel in the woodpile was one Maurice Zolotow. A portrait of this literatus is in *Esquire*, Dec. 1944, p. 58.

[6] Strip Teasing Alters Name; Same Exposure, by Robert M. Yoder, Chicago *Daily News*, Apr. 19, 1940.

[7] What's in a Name, Manchester *Evening News*, May 25, 1940; Do You Know What an Ecdysiast Is?, Birmingham *Evening Dispatch*, May 25, 1940. [A subvariety of the *ecdysiast*, the *exotic dancer*, is discussed in *AS*, Vol. XXX, Feb. 1955, pp. 79–80.]

official censor of stage performances that the adoption of *ecdysiast* might perchance open the way for lifting the ban regrettably got nowhere. [But the inevitable Association of *Ecdysiasts* soon appeared in the United States.] Rather curiously, the most eminent of all the ecdysiasts, Gypsy Rose Lee, refused to adopt the new name.

Englishmen are a good deal less ashamed of their trades than Americans, and in consequence show less exuberance of occupational euphemism. But as long ago as the Seventeenth Century some of the more advanced English dressers of female coiffures called themselves *woman surgeons*,[8] and before the end of that century some English men's tailors claimed to be *master fashioners*. Today many of the buyers and sellers of old clothes in London pass as *wardrobe dealers*, and from time to time there are proposals to outfit street sweeps with some more delicate name. In 1944 the charwomen working in the government offices in London were organized into the Government Minor and Manipulative Grades Association of *Office Cleaners*,[9] and the Glasgow *dustmen* (American: garbagemen) were renamed *cleansing personnel*.[1] Meanwhile, the rat-catching department of the Ministry of Food had become the *directorate of infestation control*, and the rat-catcher became a *rodent operative*. Many English butchers already call themselves *purveyors*, usually in the form of *purveyors of quality*,[2] and those of Birmingham use *meat traders*, and have set up a *Meat-Traders'* Diploma Society which issues diplomas to its members, and calls its meat cutters *meat salesmen*,[3] just as American milk-wagon drivers are called *milk salesmen* and bakers' deliverymen *bread salesmen*. The fishmongers still vacillate between *fish specialist* and *sea-food caterer*, the latter borrowed from America. The English used-car dealers and other such idealists are also showing signs of unrest, for P. E. Cleator encountered a *car clinic* at Wrexham, in North Wales, in 1937. Finally, *Punch* reports that a Cheshire cobbler, disdaining both *shoe rebuilder* and *shoetrician*, calls himself a *practipedist*.[4]

The English euphemism-of-all-work used to be *lady*. In the Seventeenth Century the court poet Edmund Waller spoke of actresses, then a novelty on the English stage, as *lady actors*, and even today the English newspapers

---

[8] This term appears in John Ford's The Lover's Melancholy (1628), Act II.
[9] London *Times*, June 7, 1944.
[1] London *Daily Express*, Apr. 29, 1944. [In 1962 a correspondent reported to *The Literary Repositor* (house organ of J. Stevens Cox, Antiquarian Bookseller, of Beaminster, Dorsetshire) that not only had rat-catchers become *Pest Officers* and ashmen *Public Health Auxiliaries* or *Refuse Officers*, but that cattle drovers had been upgraded to *Express Mobile Herdsmen's Service*.]

[2] Butchers or *Purveyors?*, by S. W. Corley, London *Times*, Aug. 23, 1936.
[3] Random Thoughts on Education, by Adelantemnos, *Knife and Steel* (the organ of the society), Dec. 1936, p. 6. [In *American Notes and Queries*, Vol. IV, Apr. 1944, p. 10, it was reported that the drivers for a municipal bus company in New Jersey had likewise been metamorphosed into *salesmen*.]
[4] Word-Skirmish, Apr. 7, 1937, p. 370.

frequently refer to *lady secretaries, lady doctors, lady inspectors* and *lady champions. Women's wear*, in most English shops, is *ladies' wear*. But this excessive use of *lady* seems to be going out, and *women's singles* and *women's ice hockey* are seen on the sports pages of the London *Daily Telegraph*.[5] In the United States *lady* is more definitely out of favor.[6] The *salesladies* of yesteryear are now *saleswomen* or *salesgirls*, and the female superintendent of a hospital is simply the *superintendent*. The DA traces *saleslady* to 1856 and *forelady* to 1889. Now and then a new congener appears, *e.g., flag lady*, which the Union Pacific Railroad introduced in 1944 to designate female watchers at grade crossings. But the women at work in the shipyards and other war plants were seldom if ever called *ladies*, and the Pennsylvania Railroad, when it put female trainmen to work in 1943, marked their caps simply *trainman*. When women were first elected to Congress, the leaders of the House of Representatives used "the *lady* from So-and-so," but soon "the *gentlewoman*" was substituted. Its invention is commonly ascribed to Nicholas Longworth, son-in-law of Theodore Roosevelt. He probably suggested it jocosely, for it is clumsy and often as inaccurate as *lady*. The English normally use just *the hon. member* for women M.P.'s, though sometimes *the hon. lady* occurs.[7] The English use *gentleman* much more carefully than we do, and much more carefully than they themselves use *lady*. *Gentleman author* or *gentleman clerk* would make them howl, but they commonly employ *gentleman rider* and *gentleman player* in place of our *amateur*, though *amateur* seems to be gaining favor. Here the man referred to is always actually a gentleman by their standards. What with World War II and the welfare state, the English use of *lady* has gone into a decline. But it survives as a form of address hooked to *Lord* and *Sir*, as well as in *lady mayoress*. On May 7, 1937, the New York *Herald Tribune* printed a London dispatch saying that "the retiring rooms specially erected at Westminster Abbey for Coronation Day will be severally marked as follows: *Peers, Gentlemen,*

---

[5] Mar. 29, 1935.

[6] A review of the decay of *lady* in the United States, entitled *Lady, Woman* and *Person*, was published by Robert Withington in *AS*, Vol. XII, Apr. 1937, pp. 117–21; he furnished further details in the Oct. issue (p. 235), under the heading *Woman—Lady*. [William Card, of Chicago Teachers College and formerly a labor organizer, informs me that *chairlady* is common in the garment industry. At the Ninth International Congress of Linguists (Cambridge, Mass., 1962) *ladies' events* were listed on the program and described in the presidential address of Einar Haugen.]

[7] I am indebted for the following to James Bone, of the Manchester *Guardian*: "When a Minister answers a question in the House he says *Yes, sir*, or *No, sir*, whether the question is asked by a man or woman M.P. The reason is that he is supposed to be addressing the Speaker. There was some laughter among young members when a Minister replied *Yes, sir*, to a question by Lady Astor, but elderly members wrote to the papers at once, rebuking them and explaining the procedure."

Men, and *Peeresses, Ladies, Women*," but this seems to have been a rather unusual reversion to ancient forms. On the signs in the public lavatories of London *ladies* and *women* appear to be varied without rule, and *ladies* and *men* may grace adjacent doors. The English still cling to the suffix *-ess*, and use it much oftener than Americans. Such of these common forms as *mayoress* or *manageress* would strike most Americans as very odd, and so would *conductress* (of a streetcar).[8] But the older forms in *-ess* are still alive in the United States, *e.g.*, *deaconess, patroness* and *poetess*. During the era of elegance straddling the Civil War the termination was considered rather swagger, and some grotesque examples came into use. Mamie Meredith has assembled *doctress, lecturess, nabobess, rebeless, traderess, astronomess, editress* and *mulatress;* the comic writers of the time contributed *championess, Mormoness* and *prestidigitateuress*.[9] The OED traces *sculptress*, in English use, to 1662, and the DAE traces *presidentess*, in English use, to 1782, and, in American use, to 1819. James Fenimore Cooper used *Americaness* in his "Home as Found" (1838). But it never caught on.

Euphemisms for things are almost as common in the United States as euphemisms for avocations. Dozens of forlorn little fresh-water colleges are called *universities*,[1] and almost all *pawnshops* are *loan offices. City*, in England, used to be confined to the seats of bishops, and even today it is applied only to considerable places, but in the United States it is commonly assumed by any town with paved streets, and in the statistical publications of the federal government it is applied to all places of 8,000 or more population. [In Louisiana, hamlets of 450 population proudly advertise *city limits;* in Alaska, a first-class city needs only 400 inhabitants, and a second-class city a scant 50.]

---

[8] [Since the war, however, according to Gerard Fay, bus conductresses are widely called *clippies,* especially in headlines. Private communication, Feb. 26, 1957.]

[9] *Doctresses, Authoresses* and Others, by Mamie Meredith, *AS*, Vol. V, Aug. 1930, pp. 476–81. See also The Suffix *-ess*, by Edwin B. Dike, *JEGP*, Vol. XXXVI, Jan. 1937, pp. 29–34; [When Women Were Women with *-ess*, by Robert L. Coard, *Georgia Review*, Winter 1960, pp. 285–8; and *Chiefess*—A Hawaiian Word, by C. M. Wise, *AS*, Vol. XXVI, May 1951, pp. 116–21.]

[1] [This upgrading has been noticeable in the rush to college since World War II, particularly for the one-time *normal schools*, many of which had become *teachers colleges* before 1940. At present *Chicago Teachers College* and *Ball State Teachers College* (Muncie, Ind.) are the only remaining seminaries under this label in the Midwest. The others have become *state colleges, state universities* or just *universities*, occasionally with *normal university* as a way station. There is no statute that prevents any American institution from assuming the label, regardless of its standards; thus we have *Van Norman University of Law and Engineering, West Coast University* (engineering and mathematics) and the *Empire University of Beauty Culture*, all reported from Los Angeles by Ronald K. Jones. In Canada, however, as in England, such labels are awarded only after a severe scrutiny by existing universities and by Act of Parliament.]

Meanwhile, such harsh terms as *secondhand* and *ready-made* disappear from the American vocabulary. For the former, automobile dealers, who are ardent euphemists, have substituted *reconditioned, rebuilt, repossessed* and *used;* and for the latter, department stores offer *ready-tailored, ready-to-wear* and *ready-to-put-on.* [Los Angeles reported *experienced tires* during the early days of World War II rationing.] In New York a second-hand store is now often called a *buy-and-sell shop;* in Chicago it may also be a *resale store* or a *resale shop.* There is also a continuous flow of euphemisms for *damaged* or *shop-worn, e.g., second, slightly second, slightly hurt,*[2] *store-used* and *substandard.* The last had got to England by 1938.[3] In 1942 the *ersatz* articles introduced with rationing and priorities brought a demand for a word less offensive to the refined mind than *substitute.* In the canning industry materials used as substitutes for tin were called *alternates.*[4] The appearance of horse meat for human consumption in 1943 started a search for euphemisms to designate it. One reader of *Life* submitted a list of names for dishes designated "to tempt the most ticklish palates," including *braised fetlocks* and *fillet of Pegasus.*[5] But sometimes, in revulsion against euphemism, a bold advertiser tells the truth. Thus, from a correspondent in California comes a clipping of an advertisement of a Carmel restaurant, announcing *pseudo mint juleps,* and a Baltimore department store has advertised *fake pearls.*

The uplifters are naturally heavy users of ameliorative and disarming words. One of the best of recent coinage is *door-key children,* a humane designation for the youngsters who are turned loose on the city streets to shift for themselves.[6] In the lunatic asylums (now *state hospitals* or *mental hospitals* or *psychiatric institutes*) a guard is an *attendant,* a violent patient is *assaultive* and one whose aberration is not all-out is *maladjusted.*[7] In the federal prisons a guard is a *custodial officer;* among social workers *case work* has become *personal service,* and every surviving orphan asylum has become an *infant home* or something equally mellifluous. In many American cities what used to be the office of the overseers of the poor is now the *community welfare department.* The English, in this field of gilding the unpleasant facts of life, yield nothing to Americans. Their reform schools for wayward boys, which had been *Borstal institutions*[8]

---

[2] Used by a bookstore on Fifth Avenue, New York.

[3] Advertisement of Selfridge's in the London *Daily Express,* Mar. 13, 1938. It was applied to women's hose.

[4] Substitutes for *Substitute,* by M.J.M., *AS,* Vol. XVIII, Oct. 1943, p. 207.

[5] Names for Horse-Meat, *Life,* Aug. 2, 1943.

[6] Reported by Max Lerner, *PM,* Apr. 2, 1943; cited in *American Notes and Queries,* Apr. 1943, p. 7. [According to Gerard Fay, the English term is *key children.*]

[7] Straight Talk About Sick Minds, by Edith M. Stern, *Hygeia,* Mar. 1944, p. 195.

[8] From the name of the first such institution, at Borstal, a village near Rochester in Kent. [See also the autobiographical *Borstal Boy,* by Brendan Behan; London, 1958; New York, 1959.]

since 1902, are now called *approved schools*, and there is talk of further change to *hostels*. [*Slum clearance* still appeals to the British politician; *a special area*, formerly *a depressed area*, designates an industrially or economically depressed part of the country with heavy unemployment.[9] In the United States *slum clearance* has largely given way to *urban renewal*.]

The early moviehouses were called *parlors*, but in a little while *theaters* was substituted, and today *theater* ordinarily suggests movies to an American. The first *movie cathedral* to bedazzle the fans was the Paramount Theatre in New York. Unhappily, the newspaper wits began to poke fun at it by writing about *movie mosques*, *movie synagogues* and *movie filling stations*, and so it did not prosper. But as late as 1941 a *news cathedral* was opened in Poughkeepsie, N.Y.,[1] and in Pittsburgh the huge skyscraper housing the town university is called the *Cathedral of Learning*. For many years there has been a quiet effort to find a substitute for *mother-in-law*, which has been cursed with unpleasant connotations by the cheaper humor of the press and stage, and also, perhaps, by personal experience. Gene Howe, editor of the Amarillo (Tex.) *News-Globe*, a son of the cynical E. W. Howe, but himself a man of heart, began a movement for rehabilitating the lady in 1930, or thereabout, but did not invent a softer name. In 1942, however, the Mother-in-Law Association that flowed from his campaign adopted *kin-mother*, which had been proposed by Mrs. E. M. Sullivan. Other suggestions were *our-ma*, *law-ma*, *assistant mother*, *ersatz mother* and *motherette*. But *kin-mother* won.[2]

---

[9] [Here I am again indebted to Gerard Fay. On Oct. 6, 1961, in an editorial entitled A Slum Is a Slum, *The New York Times* protested against the euphemistic language favored by the Human Relations Unit of the New York City school system. Among favorite euphemisms of the 1960s one must note *underprivileged* and *culturally deprived* for slum dwellers, and *senior citizens* for the old. In international affairs one may no longer speak of *backward nations;* they are *developing areas*.]

[1] Beautiful Home of Poughkeepsie Newspapers to Be *News-Cathedral*, *Editor and Publisher*, July 12, 1941. The newspapers were the Poughkeepsie *Evening Star-Enterprise* and *Morning Eagle-News* and the *Hudson Valley Sunday Courier*.

[2] In Other Words, by W. E. Farbstein, *The New Yorker*, Aug. 8, 1942. [The problem of naming one's in-laws has recently been the subject of considerable speculation and research among social scientists. In Mother-in-Law: A Problem in Terminology, *Etc.*, Vol. XIX, July 1962, pp. 161–71, John M. Shlien suggests that the mother-in-law problem may be intensified by the fact that since the disuse of Old English *sweger* there has been no simple form of address to make conversation easy. Later in 1962 Constance E. Cronin prepared a Master's Essay (MS) in anthropology at the University of Chicago on The American Dual Conjugal Family System, as part of a long-term study of the American kinship system, directed by David M. Schneider and Alice S. Rossi, paralleling a similar study of the British kinship system under the direction of Raymond Firth, of the University of London. About 50% of the women interviewed report that parents-in-law are customarily addressed as *Mother* and *Father*. However, the percentage varies from group to group: *Mother* and *Father* are preferred by 60% of the Jewish couples but by only

Substitutes for *death* and *to die*, both euphemistic and facetious, have been numerous in America since the earliest days. Many of the latter class are heritages from England, *e.g.*, *to croak, to kick the bucket* and *to peg out*, but others are of American origin, *e.g.*, *to pass in one's checks, to go under* (traced by the DAE to 1848) and the short form *to kick*. *To go West* may be American also, though the DAE does not list it and it was used by the British soldiers in World War I. The same may be said with more certainty of *to blow off, to bite the dust, to fold, to hop off, to lose the decision, to pass out, to poop out, to shuffle off* and *to shoot the works*. Similarly, for *death* there are *the one-way ticket, the fade-out, the last call* and *the payoff*, and for *dead, checked out, finished, gone under* and *washed up*. In the days of Prohibition the racketeers invented (or had invented for them by newspaper reporters) a number of picturesque terms for *to kill, e.g., to take for a ride, to put on the spot, to put the finger on* and *to rub out*, and at other times ordinary criminals have launched synonyms for *to be executed, e.g., to fry, to take a hot squat* and *to walk the last mile* (electrocution), *to go up* and *to be topped* (hanging) [3] and *to be gassed* (lethal gas). There are also many more decorous terms in the field of mortality; seldom encountered of late in city newspapers but still flourishing in the country weeklies are: *breathed his last, called home, laid to rest, long home, the Grim Reaper* and *the Pale Horseman*.[4]

8: FORBIDDEN WORDS

The American people, once the most prudish on earth, took to a certain defiant looseness of speech during World War I and Prohibition. Today, after a second world war and threats of a third, words and phrases are encountered everywhere—on the air, on the screen, in the theaters, in the comic papers, in the newspapers, on the floor of Congress and even at the domestic hearth—that were reserved for use in saloons and bagnios a generation ago.

Victoria was not crowned until 1838, but a Victorian antipathy to naughty words had flourished in this country since the Seventeenth Century. The rage for euphemism which arose during Puritan times was

---

30% of Roman Catholics, who prefer first names or other forms of address not connoting parenthood. With scholarly objectivity Miss Cronin comments that this question customarily generates a great deal of emotion on the part of respondents.]

[3] [According to Gerard Fay *topped* is common in England.]

[4] American Euphemisms for *Dying, Death* and *Burial*, by Louise Pound, *AS*, Vol. XI, Oct. 1936, pp. 195–202. [See also If You Don't Mind My Saying So . . . , by Joseph Wood Krutch, *American Scholar*, Vol. XXIV, Autumn 1955, pp. 460–1.]

quickly transferred to the American colonies. The Restoration brought some abatement at home, but no real return to the free utterance of the Elizabethan era, and during the Eighteenth Century prissiness enjoyed a considerable revival. The Puritans not only made war upon all the old expletives and all the immemorial names for physiological processes; they also strove to put down the abhorrent vocabulary of Holy Church, which they described elegantly as the Whore of Babylon. The word *saint* was actually deleted from the titles of the principal London churches,[5] and some of the more fanatical Puritans began substituting an ironical *sir* for *saint* in the designations of the saints themselves, *e.g., Sir Peter, Sir Paul* and even *Sir Mary*. Some tried to substitute *Christ-tide* for *Christmas* in order to get rid of the reminder of the outlawed mass in the latter. The nasty revival of prudery associated with the name of Victoria went to extreme lengths in the United States, and proceeded so far that it was frequently remarked and deplored by visiting Englishmen. In 1830 or thereabout, as Mrs. Frances Trollope tells us, "a young German gentleman of perfectly good manners . . . offended one of the principal families . . . by having pronounced the word *corset* before the ladies of it." [6] James Flint, in his "Letters from America," [7] reported that *rooster* had been substituted for *cock* (the latter having acquired an indelicate anatomical significance) by 1821; indeed, there is a quotation in Thornton's "American Glossary" which indicates that it may have come in by 1809. A bit later a young man in Judge T. C. Haliburton's "Sam Slick" was telling a maiden that her brother had become a *rooster-swain* in the Navy.

Mrs. Trollope recorded that, to the more delicate Americans of that day, Shakespeare was obscene and unendurable, and that the very mention of Pope's "The Rape of the Lock" made them shrink in horror. It is one of the ironies of literary history that Pope himself, in his edition of Shakespeare, brought out in 1725, heavily bowdlerized the Bard. In the masquerade scene of "Romeo and Juliet," for example, he changed the word *toes* in the lines:

> *Gentlemen, welcome! Ladies that have their* toes
> *Unplagued with corns will have a bout with you.*

to *feet*, though letting *corns* stand. A century later, in the United States, *feet* was also under the ban.

When Captain Frederick Marryat, the author of "Mr. Midshipman Easy," came to the United States in 1837, he got into trouble at Niagara Falls when a young woman acquaintance slipped and barked her shin. As

---

[5] See Zachary Grey's notes to Samuel Butler's Hudibras, 1744.
[6] Domestic Manners of the Americans; London, 1832, Vol. I, p. 132.
[7] Edinburgh, 1822.

she limped home, he asked, "Did you hurt your *leg* much?" [8] She turned from him "evidently much shocked or much offended," but presently recovered her composure and told him gently that *leg* was never mentioned before ladies; the proper word was *limb*. Even chickens ceased to have *legs*, and another British traveler, W. F. Goodmane, was "not a little confused on being requested by a lady, at a public dinner-table, to furnish her with the *first and second joint*." [9]

The palmy days of euphemism ran from the 1820s to the 80s. Bulls became *male cows*, *cow creatures* (more commonly *cow critters*), *seed oxen* and *Jonathans*, the breast became the *bosom*, both a chair and the backside became *seats*, harlots became *fallen women*, cockroaches became *roaches*,[1] trousers became *inexpressibles*, *unmentionables*, *unwhisperables* or *nether garments*,[2] *stockings* (female) became *hose*,[3] *antmire* was substituted for *pismire*, *shirt* was forbidden, *to go to bed* became *to retire*, servant girls ceased to be *seduced* and began to be *betrayed*, and *stomach*, then under the ban in England, was transformed into a euphemism for the whole region from the nipples to the pelvic arch. The biblical *ass*, homonymous with *arse*, was displaced by *jackass*, *jack* or *donkey*, and *to castrate* became *to change*, *to arrange* or *to alter*, even on the farm. The very word *woman* became a term of reproach, and the uncouth *female* took its place. As a noun *female* was old in English and had been used by Steele in the *Guardian* in 1713, but it seems to have carried a suggestion of scorn in early Nineteenth Century England. In the United States, however, it was used perfectly seriously. There were *female* seminaries, boarding schools, institutes, orphan asylums and missionary societies in the 1820–70 era. The term did not go unchallenged, but it took a long while to put it down, for there was a span of nearly thirty years between the time the legislature of Maryland expunged it from the title of a bill on the ground that it was "an Americanism" and the time Mrs. Sarah Josepha Hale, editor of *Godey's Lady's Book*, succeeded in persuading the trustees of Vassar to drop it from the name of that great institution.[4] In 1833 Noah Webster actually undertook to bowdlerize the Bible.[5] His version substituted *breast* for *teat*, in

---

[8] A Diary in America; Philadelphia, 1839. [In the new edition published by Alfred A. Knopf (New York, 1962), the passage appears on pp. 273–4.]

[9] Seven Years in America; London, 1845, p. 16.

[1] An Americanism, traced to 1837.

[2] These terms were discussed by Mamie Meredith in *AS*, Vol. V, Apr. 1930, pp. 285–7.

[3] Bartlett, 1859, listed *hose* as a Western term. "*Stockings*," he said, "is considered extremely indelicate, although long socks is pardonable." [*Socks* for women's *stockings* is used today in Minnesota.]

[4] The Lady of *Godey's*, by Ruth E Finley; Philadelphia, 1931, p. 205.

[5] Noah Webster as a Euphemist, by Allen Walker Read, *DN*, Vol. VI, Pt. VIII, 1934. [On Apr. 16, 1963, the Philadelphia Board of Education announced that it had replaced the standard text of Huckleberry Finn with an "adapted" version which "eliminates much of the text of the original, tones down the vi-

embryo for *in the belly*, *peculiar members* for *stones* (Leviticus XXI, 20), *smell* for *stink*, *to nurse* or *to nourish* for *to give suck*, *lewdness* for *fornication*, *lewd woman* or *prostitute* for *whore*, *to go astray* for *to go a-whoring* and *impurities, idolatries* and *carnal connection* for *whoredom*. He got rid of *womb* by various circumlocutions, and expunged many verses altogether, as beyond the reach of effective bowdlerization. This mania for the chaste afflicted even the terminology of the arts and sciences. For example, the name of the device in which the percussion cap of a muzzle-loading gun was fixed and exploded was changed from *nipple* to *cone* or *tube*.[6]

After the Civil War there was a recurrence of delicacy, and many euphemisms that still adorn the American newspapers came into use, *e.g.*, *interesting* (or *delicate*) *condition*, *disorderly house*, *felonious attack*, *serious charge* and *criminal assault*. *Syphilis* became transformed into *blood poison*, *specific blood poison* and *secret disease*, and it and gonorrhea into *social diseases*. Various French terms, *enceinte* and *accouchement* among them, were imported to conceal the fact that careless wives occasionally became pregnant and had lyings-in. The passage of the Comstock Postal Act, in 1873, greatly stimulated the search for euphemisms. Once that amazing law was upon the statute book and Comstock himself was given the inquisitorial powers of a post-office inspector, it became positively dangerous to print certain ancient and essentially decent English words. To this day the effects of that reign of terror are still visible. We yet use *toilet, retiring room, washroom* and *public comfort station* in place of franker terms.[7] The list of such euphemisms is long, especially for women's rooms. In the high days of euphemy in the United States they were not called anything at all, but simply marked *For Ladies Only*. Later this was reduced to *Ladies Only*, then to *Ladies*, and finally to *Women*. Simultaneously, *For Gents Only* went through the stages of *Gents Only*, *Gents*, *Gentlemen* and *Men*. During the days of Prohibition, some learned speakeasy proprietor hit upon the happy device of calling his retiring room for female boozers a *powder room*,[8] and meanwhile various other euphemists had borrowed or invented

---

olence, simplifies the Southern dialect and deletes all derogatory references to Negroes." My colleagues in American literature confidently await the appearance of similar dephlogisticated versions of the Oresteia, Oedipus Tyrannus and the Memoirs of Fanny Hill, "adapted" to the requirements of the Epworth League and the Mormon Beehive Girls.]

[6] *Tube*, in this context, is still almost universal among older speakers in the coastal South as well as in Appalachia.

[7] The French *pissoir* is still regarded as indecent in America, and is seldom used in England, but it has gone into most of the Continental languages, though the French themselves avoid it in print and use the inane *Vespasien*.

[8] [It is reported that in the 1930s, when an American architect drew plans for remodeling the embassy in Berlin, he included a *powder room* among the new features. The blueprints prepared by the German contractor translated this literally as *Pulverkammer*, to the consternation of government functionaries, who angrily demanded to know why the Americans wanted a powder magazine, which is what *Pulverkammer* signifies in German.]

rest room, dressing room, ladies' room, cloak room and *lavatory. Lavatory* and *toilet* are in use in England, but the OED, which traces the latter to 1819, marks it "in U.S. esp." [9] Various other designations, sometimes very fanciful, have been recorded from time to time, *e.g., boudoir*, which appeared on the ladies' room at the Casa Italiana, Columbia University, and *Egypt* [common in Southern boys' camps and military colleges but not unknown in the Midwest].[1] In the American women's colleges, in the 30s, there arose a fashion for calling the retiring place the *John* or *Johnnie*. The term may be related to the English *jakes*, which the OED traces to 1530 or thereabout. When in 1596, Sir John Harington, one of Queen Elizabeth I's courtiers, invented the modern indoor toilet, with its flushing arrangement, he announced it in a work with the punning title of "The Metamorphosis of Ajax." [2] As Harold B. Allen reported, "the use of *John* . . . goes back to the second half of the Seventeenth century, at least"; [the Linguistic Atlas has recorded *johnny house* and *jack house* as dialect terms in Virginia]. The usual term among male students is *can*, which is also a common American word for jail. The outdoor latrine that still survives in country districts is often called a *Chick Sale*, in compliment to an entertainer whose amusing account of the building of one was widely circulated, *c.* 1920.[3]

The inventor of *public comfort station* remains unknown. The DAE's first example of the term comes from the New York *Evening Post*, June 30, 1904, announcing that excavations had been begun for New York's first such station, in Chatham Square. *Water closet*, which is commonly abbreviated to *W.C.* in England, is traced by the OED to 1755. It was preceded by *closet of ease*, which is traced to 1662. The shortened form *closet* is not found before 1869. The English term *necessary house*, traced by the OED to 1611, survives in American dialects in the shortened form *necessary*.

Hollywood, always under heavy pressure from official and volunteer censors, has its own *Index*, augmented from time to time. This *Index* was first adumbrated in 1921, when the Motion Picture Producers and Distributors of America, Inc., was organized, and Elder Will H. Hays, an eminent Presbyterian quasi-ecclesiastic, who had been Postmaster General in the

---

[9] [According to Nancy Mitford, in *Noblesse Oblige. toilet* is now non-U; the current fad in England is *loo* or *lulu*. I am indebted to Gerard Fay for this bit of aesthetic criticism.]

[1] An American Euphuism, by Ted Robinson, *American Notes and Queries*, Vol. III, Aug. 1943, p. 78.

[2] *Ajax* was then pronounced *a-jakes*. The Metamorphosis of *Ajax* included working drawings. It was followed by An Anatomie of the Metamorphosed *Ajax*, and Ulysses upon *Ajax*. [*John* has even invaded the men's dormitories of the University of Chicago, to the somewhat ribald reaction of males in neighboring institutions. *Head house* is used on construction projects as a designation for a portable toilet.]

[3] [Reprinted in England as The Expert, it sells well among all classes, according to Gerard Fay.]

Cabinet of President Harding, was offered the post of president and moral dictator. The Elder laid about him vigorously, preventing the completion of a number of bawdy films already in progress, and in the course of the next eight years gradually evolved a so-called Production Code by which all save a few outlaw producers are still bound. Its *Index Expurgatorius* includes, as permanent fixtures, *broad* (for *woman*), *chippy, cocotte, courtesan, eunuch, fairy* (in the sense of homosexual), *floozy, harlot, hot mamma, hussy, madam* (in the sense of brothel keeper), *nance, pansy, slut, trollop, tart* and *wench* and, of course, *whore. Sex* is also forbidden, as is the adjective *sexual. Jew* may be used only in complimentary connotations, and *kike, yid, dago* and *nigger* are prohibited altogether. *God* must be used circumspectly, and *Gawd* is under the ban. So are *Lord* ("when used profanely"), *Christ, guts, hell, hellcat, Jesus, Geez, son of a . . ., S.O.B.,*[4] *louse* and *punk. Traveling salesman* may not be used "where reference is made to a farmer's daughter," and *liar* is reserved for scenes "in a light comedy vein."

The office has remained watchful under the Elder's successors, and not only profanity and indecency but also what it chooses to regard as vulgarity are prohibited. Late in 1942 it ordered a producer to delete the word *louse* from a film lambasting the Japanese, and suggested *stinkbug* as a substitute.[5] It even frowns on such relatively harmless words as *belch*. Even the word *virtuous* is taboo. Nor is this office the only bugaboo in the movie zoo. The producers must also submit to censorship by a committee of Catholics, frequently very drastic in its demands, and to the whims of assorted state and local boards. In the days when the Motion Picture Producers and Distributors of America was organized, the speaking stage, and especially the vaudeville stage, was heavily beset by censors,[6] but it has since thrown most of them off, and save in Boston, New York and a few other cities, is virtually free. It can indulge in a vocabulary almost approaching that of Ernest Hemingway, James Joyce, *et al.*, and exhibit the female form in nearly complete nudity, whereas the movies are cribbed, cabined and confined by regulations that would now seem oppressive in a Baptist female seminary. Radio and television, in the department of speech, are policed quite as rigorously; since the Federal Communications Commission has the power to deprive an offending station of its license, station directors are very skittish, and some of them go to extreme lengths to avoid trouble. In

---

[4] The prohibition of two euphemistic forms of *son of a bitch*, of course, includes the term itself.

[5] Quoted in *The New Republic*, Jan. 4, 1943.

[6] Under the heading Verbotens of 1929, compiled by Joe Laurie, Jr., *Variety* printed a list of the words and phrases forbidden to vaudevillians in that year. It included *to hell with, cockeyed, wop, Arab* (signifying a Jew), *pushover, dammit, belly, fanny* and *lousy*. It should be added that these prohibitions were imposed by the Keith booking office, not by official censorship.

1934 the radio syndics actually forbade the verb *to do* in songs, feeling that it was "a bit too suggestive." [In 1960 the television raconteur Jack Paar temporarily quit because the Pecksniffs of the National Broadcasting Company deleted his innocuous version of a hoary anecdote whose point depends on the fact that in much of Europe the initials *W.C.* may—depending on context—designate an outdoor toilet or a Wesleyan (or wayside) Chapel.[7]]

But not even radio and television are under such oppressive censorship as the magazines and newspapers, which may be barred from the mails, and hence subjected to ruinous loss, at the fiat of the Postmaster General. In the proceeding against *Esquire* in 1943–4, the Post Office Dogberrys actually objected to its use of such perfectly harmless words as *backside, behind* and *bawdy house*. No wonder that American newspapers, with few exceptions, continue to use the euphemisms inherited from the Victorian age, *e.g., criminal operation, house of ill repute, statutory offense, intimate relations* and *felonious assault*. Sometimes the result is extremely amusing. Not long ago, for example, a New York paper reported that a *fiend* had knocked a girl down, "dragged her down the cellar-steps, beat her with an iron pipe, and *then* assaulted her." [8]

In 1925 or thereabout the *Atlantic Monthly* gave a cruel blow to the moribund Puritan *Kultur* by printing the word *whore*, but when, in 1934, Sean O'Casey's "Within the Gates" was presented in New York, with one of its characters appearing simply as "The Young Whore," three of the local papers changed the designation, and another avoided it by omitting the cast. The *Sun* changed it to "The Young Prostitute," the *World-Telegram* to "The Young Harlot" and the *American* to "A Young Girl Who Has Gone Astray." It should be added that the *Times, Post* and *Telegraph* printed it boldly, and that the *Herald Tribune*, which omitted the cast, gave the word in the third paragraph of its review. Back in 1916 even *virgin* was a forbidden word, at least in Philadelphia. On February 26 of that year a one-act play of mine, "The Artist," was presented at the Little Theatre there, and the same day the *Public Ledger* presented specimens of the dialogue. One of the characters was called "A Virgin," but the *Ledger* preferred "A Young Girl." *Romance* is constantly used to designate an illicit love affair,[9] and *lovenest* has been widened in meaning to include the more elegant varieties of houses of prostitution.

Ever since the beginning of the Sex Hygiene movement, *c.* 1910, *syphilis*

---

[7] [The complete text of this gentle fable is found in the Chicago *Sun-Times*, Feb. 13, 1960. The excessive concern with propriety often provokes Freudian slips on the air, as pointed out by R. C. Simonini, Jr., in *AS*, Vol. XXXI, Dec. 1956, pp. 252–63.]

[8] I am indebted here to William McNulty, of Bedford Village, N.Y.

[9] *Romance*, by Mary Mielenz, *AS*, Vol. XII, Oct. 1937, p. 237.

and *gonorrhea* have been struggling for recognition, but they worked their way into the newspapers only slowly. In 1918 the Army Medical Corps complained that the newspapers emasculated its bulletins regarding venereal disease in the Army by using euphemisms. Nevertheless, editors overwhelmingly declared against the use of the two words. On April 26, 1919, the New York *Tribune* quoted with approbation a declaration by Major W. A. Wilson, of the Division of Venereal Control in the Merchant Marine, that "the only way to carry on the campaign [*i.e.*, against venereal disease] is to look the evil squarely in the face and fight it openly," and yet the word *venereal* was carefully avoided throughout the article, save in the place where Major Wilson's office was mentioned.

In 1933 the newspapers were full of articles about improvements in the use of malaria for treating tertiary syphilis, but few if any of them mentioned the name of the disease. Radio and TV still share this prudery. But in the last thirty years *syphilis* and *gonorrhea* have forced their way into general newspaper use, and promise to shoulder out such former euphemisms as *social disease* and *vice disease*. In 1934 the *New York Times* Index listed no reference whatever to either *syphilis* or *venereal disease*, but in the 1935 volume there were 6 references; in that for 1936, 18; in that for 1937, 72; and in that for 1938, 92; and since then the old ban has been definitely off. The Chicago *Tribune* claims credit for being the first American newspaper to print *syphilis* and *gonorrhea*, in 1913, and may be correct, though I printed both words during the same year in the Baltimore *Evening Sun*. Today all save a few of the prissier papers use *syphilis*, and large numbers also use *gonorrhea*, which mysteriously seems to be regarded as a shade more offensive.[1] During World War II the surgeons of the Army and Navy discussed both *syphilis* and *gonorrhea* with the utmost freedom, and the plain people became weathered to placards and circulars telling the soldiers and sailors how to avoid both. The only surviving opposition to such plain speaking seems to come from Catholics, who hold that any open discussion of prevention breaks down moral restraints and so inspires to sin.

In England, the opposition to free discourse on venereal disease seems to come, not from religious bodies, but from the newspapers. When, in 1938, the Ministry of Health prepared the first of a series of very frank advertisements for insertion in the newspapers, the copy committee of the Newspaper Proprietors' Association objected to some of the terms used, and the ministry was forced to modify them. *The Lancet*, the principal organ of the English medical men, protested against this bowdlerization with great vigor, but little effect.[2]

---

[1] Perhaps because what even medical men used to conceal under the euphemism of *Neisserian infection* is more frequently the subject of folk ribaldry.

Albert L. S. Neisser (1855–1916) discovered the gonococcus in 1879.

[2] Hush-hush over V.D., *News-Review* (London), Mar. 11, 1943, p. 19.

When the rejuvenation quackery came into vogue in the early 1920s, American newspapers invented a new set of euphemisms for the word *testicles*. A few ventured upon *gonads*, but the majority preferred *glands*, or *interstitial glands*, with *sex glands* as an occasional substitution.[3] Even among medical men there is a faction which hesitates to violate the national canons of delicacy. Dr. Fishbein, sometime editor of the *Journal of the American Medical Association*, reports that not a few of them, in communications to their colleagues, still state the fact that a patient has syphilis by saying that he has a *specific stomach* or a *specific ulcer*. In all matters relating to the human body, of course, euphemisms are common and some of them are very old.

Outside the fields of anatomy, physiology and pathology, in which concepts of the disgusting may reinforce concepts of the indecent, American prudery has been abating since World War I. Leaving out the obscene fancies of Post Office censors, to find the hyper-delicacy of the Grant era in full flower one must resort to the remoter and more backward parts of the country—for example, the Ozark region, where Vance Randolph reports that *bull, boar, buck, ram, jack* and *stallion* are still taboo, and that even such harmless compounds as *bullfrog* and *buckshot* are regarded askance. So are all words involving *cock, e.g., cockeyed, cocksure* and even the proper names *Cox* and *Hitchcock*. A cock, to the hill men, is either a *rooster* or a *crower*. A stallion is a *stable horse*, a bastard is a *woodscolt* and a bull is a *cow brute*. Certain everyday words are avoided whenever possible, *e.g., stone, maiden, piece, bed, decent, bag, stocking, tail;* for one reason or another they suggest lustful ideas.[4]

The movement, apparently originating in Hollywood, to reintroduce the old four-letter words to polite society by inserting a euphemistic *r* into them—*nerts* for *nuts* is a relatively decorous example—has made but little progress. On one level they have come back unchanged, and on another they are still under the ban. The first effort to treat them scientifically and without moral prepossession, made by Allen Walker Read in 1934,[5] has

---

[3] *Hygeia*, Feb. 1925, p. 107. *Interstitial glands*, of course, was used inaccurately.

[4] Verbal Modesty in the Ozarks, *DN*, Vol. VI, Pt. I, 1928. This paper is reprinted in Randolph's The Ozarks; New York, 1931, pp. 78 *ff.* [The euphemistic substitution of *woodchuck* for *woodpecker*, not uncommon in South Carolina, was reported from Middle Tennessee by Kelsie Harder in *AS*, Vol. XXVII, May 1952, p. 157.]

[5] An Obscenity Symbol, *AS*, Vol. IX, Dec., pp. 264–78. [The participle of this symbol was represented as *flicking* in a scene involving two sergeants, in the British movie Seven Days Till Noon (1950). In recent years the agentive noun of this verb, with *mother-* prefixed, has attracted much philological attention. Apparently it was first printed in full by Arthur M. Z. Norman, in Army Slang and the Future of American English, *AS*, Vol. XXXI, May 1956, p. 111. In Stateville Names (MS), Nathan and Joanne Kantrowitz report more than thirty subclasses of this epithet (not including the elegant euphemism *Mr. Franklin*), probably the most popular term of abuse among the unwilling guests of the state of Illinois. It is a

been followed up by Read himself,[6] by Partridge [7] and by others. Such words, says Read,

> are not cant or slang or dialect, but belong to the oldest and best element in the English vocabulary. They are not even substandard, for they form part of the linguistic equipment of speakers of standard English. Yet they bear such a stigma that they are not even listed in the leading dictionaries of the language. But although they are in such marked disrepute it does not follow that they should be ignored by the student of the language. A sociologist does not refuse to study certain criminals on the ground that they are too perverted or too dastardly; surely a student of the language is even less warranted in refusing to consider certain four-letter words because they are too "nasty" or too "dirty." For the scientific linguist the propriety or respectability of a word is merely one aspect of its history.

Some of these words are in Shakespeare,[8] and others are in the King James version of the Bible. All are old in English, and nearly all were at one time quite respectable. They have many euphemistic substitutes, ranging from terms scarcely more decorous than themselves to terms acceptable in any society which does not deny altogether that sexual and excremental functions exist in *Homo sapiens*. There are also euphemisms for a number of terms measurably less shocking to the delicate but still highly indecorous, *e.g.*, the familiar derivatives of *bull* and *horse* and the common names for flatulence and eructation. The first-named is usually reduced, in the United States, to either *bull* or *b.s.*; in Australia it is turned into *bullsh* or *boolsh*.

Down in the Bible Belt the old taboos seem to be breaking down.[9] In 1936–7 Edwin R. Hunter and Bernice E. Gaines inquired into the use of *bull* among 280 freshmen, 48 seniors and 48 members of the faculty of "a coeducational college in East Tennessee." [1] They found that about 20%

---

common byword among Negroes, but like many other features of Negro speech it is a survival of rural Southern white usage; I first encountered it in 1928, at a Citizens' Military Training Camp, Fort Oglethorpe, Ga., patronized chiefly by Southern uplanders.]

[6] Lexical Evidence from Folk Epigraphy in Western North America; Paris, 1935. [The preface to this monograph, slightly revised, was reprinted in *Neurotica*, No. 5, Autumn 1949, pp. 23–30, as The Nature of Obscenity.]

[7] A Dictionary of Slang and Unconventional English; New York, 1938.

[8] [Eric Partridge, Shakespeare's Bawdy; London, 1947. See also Falk Johnson, History of Some Dirty Words, *Ameri-*

can Mercury, Vol. LXXI, Nov. 1950, pp. 38–45; The Ups and Downs of "Dirty" Words, *ibid.*, Vol. LXX, Jan. 1950, pp. 85–92; Bernard De Voto, The Editor's Easy Chair, *Harper's Magazine*, Dec. 1948, pp. 98–101; J. J. Lamberts, Slang and Taboos, *Language Learning*, Vol. V, 1953–4, pp. 56–60. A more pretentious but often inaccurate study is Edward Sagarin, The Anatomy of Dirty Words; New York, 1962.]

[9] J. M. Stedman, Jr., A Study of Verbal Taboos, *AS*, Vol. X, Apr. 1935, and Language Taboos of American College Students, *English Studies*, June 1935.

[1] Verbal Taboo in a College Community, *AS*, Vol. XIII, Apr. 1938, pp. 96–107.

of the males avoided it and about 40% of the females. Other words under the ban of these teachers and students, usually to a much greater extent, were *ass, bastard, belch, belly, bitch, bugger, drawers, guts, pregnant, sex, stink* and *whore*. The progress of frankness since the Golden Age of euphemism in America was shown by the fact that 72.3% of the men and 54.6% of the women reported that they saw no impropriety in *garter*, that 88.6% of the men and 72.8% of the women used *sex*, that 95.2% and 92.4% respectively used *leg* and that 97% and 93.3% used *sick*. The word most abhorred by the men was *puke*, and by the women *bitch*. Only 47.4% reported that they used *vomit;* what terms the others resorted to to indicate emesis was not indicated.[2]

The number of euphemisms for forbidden words in use in the United States is still large, [but only a few groups of terms have been systematically investigated over wide areas, as for the Linguistic Atlas]. Various correspondents report that *single child* is used by colored people in Baltimore to indicate a bastard, that *bastrich* is used in the Duluth area as a happy compound of *bastard* and *son of a bitch*, that the older rustics of Virginia use *Durham* for bull, that to castrate is *to make a Baptist minister of him* in Georgia, that to be pregnant is *to walk uphill* in southern Illinois and that *she* is a derogatory prefix in many parts of the country and is felt to be more or less indecent.[3] Many disarming names for a house of prostitution are in common use, *e.g., sporting house, cat house,*[4] *fancy house, crib* and *call house.*[5] There are even more for prostitute. Euphemisms also exist on the highest levels, *e.g., intestinal fortitude* for guts, *to burp* for to belch, *derrière* for the female backside, *to make, to lay* and so on. *Derrière*, borrowed from the French, is one of many such loans in the argot of fashion writers, *e.g., brassière;*[6] other familiar euphemisms are thoroughly American, *e.g., step-in* and *undie*.[7] But the general tendency is toward plainer speech. I have encountered an impassioned defense of *bastard* in the Washington *Post*,[8] and seen *womb* in a two-column head in the

---

[2] [A study of taboo words in metropolitan Chicago is now being conducted by Lee Pederson.]

[3] In my boyhood in Baltimore a loose paving brick was called a *she-brick*. On wet days it discharged a stream of dirty water on anyone who stepped on it.

[4] In the Midwest, in the days when harlots were itinerants, the conveyances they used were called *cat wagons*.

[5] *Call house* especially indicates a house whose inmates go out to clients on call. [The *call girl*, the aristocrat of the profession, is an example of individual enterprise, operating from her own base.]

[6] When, in 1943, the WPB allotted some synthetic rubber to makers of *brassières* it designated them *breast forms* and *breast shields*. See an article in the New York *Post* by Earl Wilson, reprinted in Tonics and Sedatives, *Jour. AMA*, Jan. 1, 1944, p. 30. *Brassière* is usually reduced to *bra*.

[7] A list of euphemistic brand names invented by American manufacturers of such things is in Glamour Words, by Charles E. Bess, *AS*, Vol. XVI, Apr. 1941, pp. 96–9, among them, *undikins, roll-ons, campus briefs* and *cup forms*.

[8] Much Ado (editorial), Dec. 14, 1942.

Baltimore *Sun*.[9] Rupert Hughes [1] calls attention to the fact that a few such words as *womb* have been "sanctified when used metaphorically," but are still frowned upon in "literal usage." When such areas must be discussed willy-nilly, the common device of decorum is to resort to Latin or Greek names, usually polysyllabic, as Chaucer substituted *hernia* for *rupture*. "A long word," says Hughes, "is considered nice and a short word nasty." And as with terms for organs and functions, so with terms for voluntary acts. "You can refer to anything under the sun if you will call it *illicit relations, soliciting, perversion, contributing to juvenile delinquency*. But the police will be after you if you print the short words." Euphemisms, of course, "may in time become too closely associated with the meaning, and in turn become taboo. Our word *whore*, cognate with the Latin *carus* (dear), must have been at one time a polite substitute for some word now lost." [2]

An American visiting England discovers quickly that different words are under the ban on the two sides of the ocean. An Englishman restricts the use of *bug* to the *Cimex lectularius*, or common *bedbug*, and hence the word has highly impolite connotations. All other crawling things he calls *insects*. The English aversion to *bug* has been breaking down of late, however, probably under the influence of such naturalized Americanisms as *jitterbug*, but it yet lingers in ultra-squeamish circles, and a *ladybird* is never called a *ladybug*. Not so long ago *stomach* was on the English *Index*, and such euphemisms as *tummy* and *Little Mary* were used in its place, but of late it has recovered respectability. *Dirt*, to designate earth, and *closet*, in the sense of a cupboard, are seldom used by an Englishman. The former always suggests filth to him, and the latter has obtained the limited use of *water closet*. But the Englishman will innocently use many words and phrases that have indecent significances in the United States, quite lacking in England, *e.g.*, *to be knocked up* (to be tired),[3] *to stay with* (to be the guest of), *screw* (as a noun, meaning salary or pay),[4] *to keep one's pecker*

---

[9] One of Twins Delivered Here Was Never in Mother's *Womb*, Aug. 25, 1944.

[1] The Latin Quarter in Language, Dutch Treat Club banquet book, 1937.

[2] Leonard Bloomfield, Language; New York, 1933, p. 401. [The vernacular of menstruation has been discussed by Lalia Phipps Boone, *AS*, Vol. XXIX, Dec. 1954, pp. 297–8, and by Natalie Jaffe, *Word*, Vol. IV, 1948, pp. 181–6. Some of the byways of euphemism are explored by Thomas Pyles in Innocuous Linguistic Indecorum: a Semantic Byway, *MLN*, Vol. LXIV, Jan. 1948, pp. 1–8, and by Allen Walker Read in English Words with Constituent Elements

Having Independent Semantic Value, Philologica: the Malone Anniversary Studies; Baltimore, 1949, pp. 306–12.]

[3] [Anne Lohrli, *Knocked Up* in England and the United States, *AS*, Vol. XXXV, Feb. 1960, pp. 24–8. She includes, of course, the information that in England the active form *to knock up* means to rouse by knocking, and hence to call for. American servicemen stationed in England are naturally aware of this meaning, and the possibilities of *double-entendre*. The English use of *rubber* for eraser also gives them pause.]

[4] Alistair Cooke tells me that as a verb it is banned from refined discourse in England as in America.

up,[5] *douche* (shower bath) and *cock* (a male chicken). The English use *bitch* a great deal more freely than Americans. Now and then an American, reading an English newspaper, is brought up with a start by a word or phrase that would never be used in the same way in the United States. I offer two examples. The first is from an advertisement of a popular brand of smoking tobacco in the *News of the World:* "Want a good *shag?*"[6] The second is from the *Literary Supplement* of the London *Times:* "On the whole we may congratulate ourselves on having chosen not to be born in that excellent and indispensable century when an infant of six could be hanged . . . and school boys were encouraged to match *cocks*."[7]

9: TERMS OF ABUSE

The converse of euphemisms are terms of opprobrium, of which the American language boasts a large stock, chiefly directed at aliens.[8] The English have fewer strangers within their gates, and hence their native armamentarium is smaller, and not a few of the achthronyms [or ethnophaulisms][9] they use come from the United States. But there has also been traffic in the other direction. *Frog* for a Frenchman was borrowed by Americans in World War I, and subsequently got into wide circulation at home, but it had been known before. In its present sense in England, according to Partridge, it goes back only to *c.* 1870. In the Seventeenth Century it was used to designate a Dutchman and also a Jesuit. At some time before 1870 a Frenchman came to be called a *frog eater* in England[1]—the OED's first

---

[5] In the sense of to keep up one's courage or resolution the OED traces this verb phrase to 1853. In W. S. Gilbert's Trial by Jury, 1875, is: "Be firm, my moral *pecker.*" [Lynn G. Rumer reports the consternation among the Methodist clergy of Iowa when an Englishwoman, the wife of the District Superintendent, used the phrase in an attempt to console a bereaved parson.]

[6] June 19, 1938, p. 15.

[7] Children of a Harsh Age (a review of The English Child in the Eighteenth Century, by Rosamond Bayne-Powell; London, 1939), June 24, 1939, p. 303. [Linguists have yet to make a systematic investigation of regional differences in the anatomical significance of *cock* in the United States.]

[8] [Not that the designations which one group of natives uses toward another are always respectful, as witness such terms current in South Carolina as *lint head* for cotton-mill worker, *shrimp dipper* for Low Countrymen and such more widely circulating coins as *hillbilly* and *swamp rat*. Most of the nicknames for states and their inhabitants, discussed in Ch. X, Sec. 4, were originally derogatory even if no longer so; so was *Yankee*, discussed in Ch. III, Sec. 1.]

[9] [*Ethnophaulisms* is used by A. A. Roback in his Dictionary of International Slurs; Cambridge, Mass., 1944. For an attempt to measure prejudice objectively, see Ethnophaulisms and Ethnocentrism, by Erdman B. Palmore, *American Journal of Sociology,* Vol. LXII, Jan. 1962, pp. 442–5. The purging of ethnic terms is examined in Social Awareness and Semantic Change, by Rossell Hope Robbins, *AS,* Vol. XXIV, Apr. 1949, pp. 156–8.]

[1] It is possible that this was a loan from the German. *Froschesser* was used by Karl Postl (Charles Sealsfield) in Der Virey und die Aristokraten, oder Mexico in 1812, published in 1814; see Charles

example is dated 1863—and soon this was shortened to *frog*. Although various etymologists derive *frog* from the formerly quaggy state of the streets of Paris or from the toads on the coat of arms of the city, more likely the eating of frogs by the French, a custom regarded with loathing by the English, is at the bottom of it. A derivative, *froggy*, is used by lower-class Londoners to designate any man with a French-sounding name. *Froggy* is in common use in the British Army to designate a French soldier. *Frog* is not applied in Canada to a French Canadian, [who is a *Canuck* or simply *Joe*, and prefers to be called a *Habitant*].[2] In the California gold rush the few Frenchmen who turned up were called *parleyvoos* (*parlez vous*) or *keskydees* (*Qu'est-ce qu'il dit?*) by the 49ers.[3] Both terms were revived by the American and British troops during World War I. Neither is American. The OED traces *parleyvoo* in English use to 1815, and in the sense of the French language to 1754. *Frencher* was used by Cooper in "The Last of the Mohicans" (1826), but it seems to have passed out. The DA traces *Cajan* or *Cajun* (from *Acadian*), the common term in Louisiana for a rustic of French descent, to 1868, but it is undoubtedly older. The word carries a derogatory significance, and is never applied to the high-toned French of New Orleans, who are *creoles*. The common—and resented—American assumption that *creole* connotes Negro blood [is repeated, in turn, by many *Cajans*. The dialect of the *Cajans* is locally known as *Bougalie*.] The etymological history of *creole* was summed up in 1926 by Lyle Saxon:

> The *creole* is one who is born away from his country—whatever that country may be. The New Orleans *creole* is our finest product. The women are lovely. The men are brave. They have charming manners. They are exclusive. They are clannish. They have their own language, their own society, their own customs. They still speak a pure French. The reason why the word *creole* has been so often misunderstood is that their slaves spoke a *creole* dialect, bearing about the same relation to pure French as our Southern Negro talk does to English purely spoken. Then, of course, there was the Acadian French, or *cajan* French, as spoken in the outlying districts of Louisiana. And *gumbo* French—that simply means French incorrectly spoken.[4]

Sealsfield's Americanisms, II, by John T. Krumpelmann, *AS*, Vol. XVI, Apr. 1941, p. 110. [In a later note, James N. Tidwell suggests that *frog eater* probably goes back to the Eighteenth Century in England, and shows that it is attested in the United States by 1812. Frogs and Frog-Eaters, *AS*, Vol. XXIII, Oct.-Dec. 1948, pp. 214–16.]

2 [In the *Canadian Journal of Linguistics*, Vol. VIII, Fall 1962, p. 49, W. S.

Avis observes that *Canuck* has been extended in meaning to any Canadian of European descent.]

3 Three Years in California, by J. D. Borthwick, 1857; cited in California Gold-Rush English, by Marian Hamilton, *AS*, Vol. VII, Aug. 1932, p. 424.

4 New Orleans *Times-Picayune*, Feb. 11, 1926, quoted in *Creole and Cajan*, by William A. Read, *AS*, Vol. I, June 1926, p. 483.

[Other Lousianians employ the term to designate any white person whose family lived in Louisiana before Jefferson bought it from Napoleon in 1803, and point with pride to families of *German creoles* and *Irish creoles*, as well as those of French or Spanish stock.]

From the first appearance of syphilis in England it was labeled *French*—first the *French pox* (1503), then the *French marbles* (1592) [5] and then the *French disease* (1598), which remained in common English use for more than two centuries. The adjective *French-sick* survived from 1598 to the end of the Eighteenth Century.[6] When, in 1776 or thereabout, a device for the limitation of offspring was invented, the English gave it the name *French letter*, and the French retaliated by calling it a *capote anglaise*. This last was changed to *capote allemande* during World War I, as a gesture in furtherance of the Entente Cordiale, but the English did not reciprocate, and *capote anglaise* was restored. To the English, anything French is likely to be suspicious, and their language embalms the fact in such phrases as *French leave*. The simple word *French*, to them as to Americans, connotes sexual perversion. The Germans, Spanish and Italians also have forms of *French leave*. Rather curiously, the French and Germans have few opprobrious phrases for one another. In Prussia lice are called *Franzosen*, but in other parts of Germany they are commonly called *Schwaben* (Swabians)—and cockroaches are *Preussen* (Prussians). The French call a louse an *espagnol* (Spaniard) and a flea an *espagnole:* the difference in gender is unexplained.[7]

Squarehead is applied not only to Germans but also to Scandinavians. Other opprobrious names for a German include *boche, dutchie, heinie, hun, kraut* and *sausage*. In June 1861, *Harper's Magazine* printed a caricature depicting the German immigrant as wearing a beer barrel as a coat, smoking a porcelain pipe with a long stem and carrying a long sausage and a sheet of music under his arm. General Joseph Heister, when a candidate for governor of Pennsylvania, was called *Old Sauerkraut* by supporters and opponents alike. In those days Germans were called *cabbageheads* also, but that term was apparently likewise applied to the Dutch.[8]

The early German immigrants acquired the name of *Dutch* from their use of *Deutsch* (pronounced *Deitsch*) to designate themselves. The DA's first example of *Pennsylvania Dutch* is dated 1863, but the term must be

---

[5] A corruption of the archaic French *morbilles*, pox.

[6] The use of *French* was not confined, of course, to the English. Sebastian Brant, in De Scorra Pestilentia (1496) called syphilis *mala de Franzos*, and other writers of the time called it *morbus Gallicus*. [According to *Time*, Mar. 22, 1963, p. 24, the new freedom of sexual behavior in England (or at least of discussion of sexual behavior) has given homosexuality the name, on the Continent, of *la vice anglaise*.]

[7] See Calling Names in Any Language, by Joachim Joesten, *American Mercury*, Dec. 1935, pp. 483–7; also A. A. Roback, Dictionary of International Slurs; Cambridge, Mass., 1944.

[8] See *Harper's Magazine*, Jan. 1854, p. 269, col. 2.

very much older. The use of *Dutch* in the sense of Germans in general is traced to 1742; [it is used earlier in "Gulliver's Travels" to designate the language]. In the California gold-rush days it was applied indiscriminately to Germans, Hollanders and Scandinavians.[9] During the Civil War, all Northern sympathizers in Missouri were called *Dutch* because many of them were Germans. The familiar American phrases *that's all Dutch to me* and *in Dutch* may allude to the actual Dutch of New York, but more likely to the Germans. The first is traced to 1899, the second to 1919. *To talk like a Dutch uncle* (*i.e.*, with brutal frankness) is also probably American; *Dutch supper* certainly is. Both apparently allude to Germans, not Dutchmen. *Hessian* is often used in folk speech to designate "anyone who is rough, uncouth, boorish, or, more particularly, an individual whose moral character is of the lowest."[1] It apparently came into American English in Revolutionary times, but is also found on the Isle of Man and in Ireland. It was used by the Confederates during the Civil War as a term of opprobrium for Northerners, and by 1877, according to Bartlett, had gained some currency as a designation for "a hireling, a mercenary politician, a fighter for pay."

The Seventeenth Century naval rivalry between England and Holland brought in many compounds in which *Dutch* appeared as a derisory adjective. The OED shows that in 1608 a *Dutch widow* meant a prostitute, and that in 1678 a *Dutch bargain* meant one made in drink. Not a few of the more familiar terms in *Dutch* originated in America from the hostility between the English and Dutch in early New York, or between the Germans and the other stocks in Pennsylvania and elsewhere. *Dutch courage*, meaning a false courage produced by alcohol, is probably an Americanism: the earliest known American example of its use, dated 1812, preceded the earliest English example by fourteen years. *To beat the Dutch* is also American; the first example, dated 1775, is from an American song of the Revolution. *Dutch route*, meaning suicide, is probably American. So, probably, is *Dutch auction*, one beginning with a high bid and then working downward; though it is not recorded in America earlier than in England, *Dutch auctioneer* is. Other terms based on *Dutch*, either English or American, are *Dutch feast*, at which the host gets drunk before his guests; *Dutch drink*, one that empties the pot at a gulp; *Dutch treat* (1904), one requiring each drinker to pay for himself; *Dutch wife*, a bolster; and *Dutch comfort*, the kind that does not comfort.[2] There are so many such terms that Farmer and

---

[9] California Gold-Rush English, by Marian Hamilton, *AS*, Vol. VII, Aug. 1932, p. 424.
[1] A Note on the Epithet *Hessian*, by Paul G. Brewster, *AS*, Vol. XVIII, Feb.

1943, p. 72.
[2] Grose, in his third edition, 1785, illustrates this term with "Thank God it is no worse."

Henley define *Dutch* itself as "an epithet of inferiority." The Netherlands government in 1934 tried to pull the teeth of the English pejoratives by ordering all its officials to drop *Dutch* and use *Netherlands* instead, but apparently the device did not succeed.[3] In the 80s, as Theodore Roosevelt once observed,[4] "anything foreign and un-English" was called *Dutch*. "It was in this sense," he said, "that a West Virginian member of the last Congress used the term when, in speaking in favor of a tariff on works of art, he told of the reluctance with which he saw the productions of native artists exposed to competition 'with *Dutch* daubs from Italy.'"

Hunk and *hunkie* (or *hunky* or *hunkey*) are proper applicable to Hungarians only, but they have been extended to include all Europeans coming from the region east of the German lands and west of Russia, save only the Greeks. Berrey and Van den Bark report extensions, in the United States, signifying a country bumpkin, a numskull, a common laborer and a foreign-born miner of any nationality. *Bohunk* (sometimes abbreviated to *boho* or *bo*) is probably a blend of *Bohemian* and *Hungarian*, recalling the ancient united kingdom, and is applied to both groups. In regions where Czech immigrants are numerous, *cheskey* is frequently heard. It is "an attempted transliteration of the Bohemian adjective *český* (Czech)."[5] *Mick* (1856), *harp* (1926) and *Turk* are well-known achthronyms for an Irishman;[6] *flannel mouth* (1870), *shamrock, spud* and *terrier* once flourished, along with *biddy* for an Irishwoman, but are no longer in wide use. *Flannel mouth*, in England, designates any well-spoken person, and *spud* means not only a potato but also a baby's hand. *Turk*, which may go back to Gaelic *torc*, pig, is used among Roman Catholic priests in the United States to designate a colleague of Irish birth; it is assumed that every such immigrant has a special talent for ecclesiastical politics. *Irish* has been an element in many English compounds, chiefly of a derogatory or satirical significance. *Irish evidence*, perjury, *Irish apricots*, potatoes, and *Irish legs*, thick ones, were listed by Grose in the first edition of his "Classical Dictionary of the Vulgar Tongue" (1785), and *Irish beauty*, a woman with two black eyes, was added in his third edition of 1796. The OED traces *Irish diamond*, a rock crystal, to 1796; *Irish blunder*, defined by Swift as "to take the noise of brass for thunder," to 1725; and *Irish bull* to 1802. The DAE adds *Irish*

---

[3] The Dutch Government *Beats the Dutch*, by J. F. Bense, *English Studies* (Amsterdam), Dec. 1934, pp. 215–16.

[4] Phases of State Legislation, *Century Magazine*, Apr. 1885, p. 827. [In England, according to Kenneth Northcott, *Dutch medley* describes a radio and a piano playing different pieces of music at the same time, and *Dutch cap* designates the female counterpart of a *capote anglaise*.]

[5] Czech Influence upon the American Vocabulary, by J. B. Dudek, *Czecho-Slovak Student Life* (Lisle, Ill.), June 1926, p. 16.

[6] Some Current Substitutes for *Irish*, by W. A. McLaughlin, *DN*, Vol. IV, Pt. II, 1914, pp. 146–8. [According to Lee Pederson, in Chicago *turkey* denotes a native Irishman; the second generation, reputedly weaklings, are *narrowbacks*.]

dividend, an assessment on stock, 1881; *Irish spoon*, a spade, 1862; and *Irish pennant*, a loose end of rope, 1840. Berrey and Van den Bark add many others, *e.g., Irish apple*, a potato; *Irish clubhouse*, a police station; *Irish confetti*, bricks; *Irish bouquet*, a brickbat; *Irish promotion*, a demotion;[7] and *Irishman's dinner*, a fast. In the days of the great Irish immigration, the American designation of almost anything unpleasant was hung with the adjective and it was converted into a noun to signify quick temper. A wheelbarrow was an *Irish chariot* or *buggy*, and there was a stock witticism to the effect that it was the greatest of human inventions, since it had taught the Irish to walk on their hind legs. Also, *No Irish Need Apply* was a sign as common as *Juden sind nicht erwünscht* was to become in Nazi Germany.

Wop has likely come from *guappo*, a Neapolitan term signifying a showy, pretentious fellow.[8] The early immigrants from southern Italy, *c.* 1885, brought *guappo* with them, and used it frequently in referring to one another, usually in a sportive sense. It was picked up by the Americans among whom they labored in tunnel and ditch, and by 1895 or thereabout had come to signify any Italian. *Wop* has produced a number of derivatives in the United States, *e.g., wop house*, an Italian restaurant, and *wop special*, spaghetti. During the first years of World War II it appeared often in the English newspapers, in a derogatory significance, but after the surrender of Italy it was used less. Rather curiously, it was adopted by the Royal Air Force to signify a wireless operator, and also occasionally an air gunner.[9] *Wop* is sometimes used to signify any European of dark complexion, and like *hunky* may even be applied to any man of uncertain nationality. In railroad slang it is sometimes used for a section hand, and among criminals it means a sentence of less than a month. *Woppage* appeared in England as a designation for the retreating Italian Army in North Africa,[1] but it did not survive.

Dago, which preceded *wop* in American favor, is traced by the DAE to 1832. It comes from the Spanish *Diego*, James, and was first used to designate a Spaniard. It was probably transferred to Italians during the 80s. In 1900 E. H. Babbitt listed it in his "College Words and Phrases"[2] as signifying (*a*) the Italian language, (*b*) a professor of Italian, (*c*) a student studying Italian and (*d*) any uncouth person, and reported it as in use in one or more of these senses in twenty American colleges, including Harvard, Princeton and Smith. *Dago red*, a cheap red wine, is in wide use. *Guinea*

---

[7] [In England, says Gerard Fay, it is an *Irishman's rise*.]

[8] See Word Vagaries, by Camillo P. Merlino, *Words*, Sept. 1936, p. 7.

[9] It's a Piece of Cake: R.A.F. Slang Made Easy, by C. H. Ward-Jackson; London, n.d., p. 63.

[1] London *Daily Express*, Jan. 20, 1943.

[2] *DN*, Vol. II, Pt. I, 1900, p. 31.

is probably another term of changed meaning. In the sense of a Negro from Guinea the DA traces it to 1789; by 1910 it had come to mean an Italian. Berrey and Van den Bark also list *dino, duke, gin, macaroni* and various proper names, but most of the former are heard but rarely, and of the latter only *Tony* seems to be in general use. The DAE shows that in the middle 90s, at least in the Pennsylvania mining region, Italians were called *hikes.* Among the Eastern Jews in New York and Chicago, and perhaps elsewhere, they are called *lukschen,* from a Yiddish word meaning noodle [3] —presumably a reference to spaghetti. In Louisiana *gi-gi* has been recorded; it is also a contemptuous term there for a creole, "especially from the country." Baker reports that the Australians call Italians *eyetos* or *skies.* The terms *mafia* (or *maffia*), *black hand* (from the Spanish *mano negra*) and *camorra,* which had come into frequent use in the early days of the great Italian immigration, began to die out before the butchering of Prohibition got under way. All three designated Italian secret organizations which preyed, in the main, not on Americans but on Italian immigrants.

Skibby, used on the Pacific coast to designate Japanese, is extremely offensive to them, for it was applied originally to a loose woman. Webster 1961 derives it from the Japanese *sukebei,* lewdness. In the British Navy *skivvy* is an interjection of greeting, and is commonly believed to have come from the Japanese; perhaps it was encountered as a salutation of Japanese prostitutes. [*Skivvy* also means underwear consisting of shorts and a T shirt; *skivvy shirt,* meaning the latter, has come into civilian use via the Navy.] Since 1905 or thereabout, according to Partridge, *skivvy* has been used in English slang to designate an English maidservant of the rougher sort. [No connection has been proved between *skibby* and *skivvy,* or the two meanings of the latter.]

The designation *nisei* for Japanese Americans of American birth was seldom heard before Pearl Harbor, save on the Pacific coast, nor was *kibei,* the name for those American-born Japanese who were sent to Japan for their schooling and so presumably underwent Japanese indoctrination. *Nisei* is simply the Japanese term for second generation. Before 1941 American-born Japanese objected frequently and vigorously to the use of *Jap* to designate their people. Their crusade made little progress, for *Jap,* as a very short word, was irresistibly tempting to headline writers, and during the electric days preceding and following Pearl Harbor, it appeared on almost every first page in the United States almost every day.[4] The related *Nip,* from *Nipponese,* was used in an NBC broadcast on January

---

[3] I am indebted for this to Harry Green, of Chicago, and Michael Gross, of New York. *Lukschen* also means extremely elongated in Yiddish and is ap-plied to any tall man.

[4] The OED reports it in colloquial use in England, *c.* 1880.

12, 1942, and by *Time* on February 23 of that year; [5] [it is much older]. The English use *Chink* for a Chinese, as we do, but Partridge says that it did not come in until *c.* 1890, and hints that it was probably borrowed from Australia. The DAE's earliest example of *Chink* in American use is dated 1901, but it may go back to the days of the gold rush in California. The Chinese greatly dislike the terms *Chinaman* and *Chinee*, just as the Japanese dislike *Jap*. [6] [Since World War II, *Asiatic* has become a taboo word, both as noun and adjective, and *Asian* has been substituted; perhaps the older term was felt to smack too much of colonialism. Even the *Asiatic flu*, which first appeared in the late 1950s, has been rechristened *Asian flu*.] The DAE traces *Chinaman* to 1849, *Chinee* to 1870 and *Chinawoman* to 1872, when it was used by Mark Twain in "Roughing It." *Chinatown* is traced to 1857. [The DA cites *Chinaman's chance* from 1928, but it is far older.]

Bartlett defines *greaser* as "a term vulgarly applied to the Mexicans and other Spanish Americans" and says that "it first became common during the war with Mexico." The DA's earliest example is from a letter from Texas, in 1836. Twelve years later George F. Ruxton explained in his "Life in the Far West" (published in 1849) that the Mexicans were so called "by the Western people" on account of "their greasy appearance." The Mexicans in the Southwest resent this explanation, and have concocted a number of more seemly etymologies. One holds that the term was first applied to a Mexican who set up a studio for greasing the ox carts of early settlers at the top of the Raton Pass, and that his designation, the *Mexican greaser*, was gradually extended to all his countrymen. [7] Its application has been further extended to include any Latin American, but it is still used mainly to designate a Mexican. It has had, at different times, various rivals, *e.g.*, *pepper-belly* (sometimes shortened to *pepper*), which embodies an obvious allusion to the Mexican cuisine, as do *chili eater* and *frijole eater*. [Mexican migrant laborers who enter the United States illegally—as by wading or swimming the Rio Grande—are known as *wetbacks*.[8]] In the Colorado sugar-beet fields the Mexican laborers are spoken of by the euphemism *Spaniards;* they are also called *primos*. In New Mexico they are often called *natives*. In the same state Americans are *Anglos* and Indians are *pueblos*.[9] The use of *spiggoty* and *spick* for any Latin American, but especially for a native of Panama, is presumably derived from a native pronunciation of "no spik Inglis."

---

[5] Reported by Dwight L. Bolinger, *AS,* Vol. XVIII, Apr. 1943, p. 151.
[6] [But the citizens of Burma prefer *Burman* to *Burmese*.]
[7] This tale is quoted in The Southwestern Word Box, by T. M. P[earce], *New Mexico Quarterly* (Albuquerque), Aug. 1932, p. 267, but the author does not vouch for it.

[8] [According to William Randle, *AS,* Vol. XXXVI, Feb. 1961, pp. 78–80, the term has been extended to a Volkswagen obtained in the United States through other channels than authorized dealers.]
[9] *AS,* Vol. XII, Oct. 1937, p. 141.

Gu-gu, for a Filipino, like *greaser* for a Mexican, may derive from the apparently oily skin. *Gook* is also applied to a Filipino or Korean, and sometimes either is applied to any native of the Pacific Islands, but the more usual term for the latter is *kanaka*, a Hawaiian loan signifying simply man, or, in a general sense, the people.[1] During World War II, General Carlos P. Romulo used *Filamericans* to designate his people, but the term made no headway.[2]

Grease ball is most often applied in the United States to Greeks, but it is also used to designate any foreigner of dark complexion. In the argot of Sing Sing, and perhaps of other American prisons, it designates an Italian. In the general slang of the country it means any dirty person, and in occupational argots it has various special significances, all having to do with some notion of unkemptness. So far, the Greeks in the United States have never undertaken a crusade against it.

Herring choker is used by the New England fishermen to designate not only a Scandinavian but also a Newfoundlander, [more commonly a *Newfie*,] and sometimes also a Nova Scotian or a Canadian in general. The more common name for a Nova Scotian is *bluenose*, which the DAE defines as "a native of Nova Scotia or New Brunswick" and traces to 1837.[3] Before this it had apparently been used to designate a New Englander. During the days of Prohibition *bluenose* was widely used to designate a Prohibitionist, and earlier it had been applied (as it still is) to reformers in general, especially the sort called *wowsers* by Australians. *Polack*, for a Pole, is old in English, and the OED traces it to 1599. Horatio uses it in "Hamlet," Act II, Scene I. [In conversation it usually rhymes with *dock*.]

The paucity of aliens in England makes it unnecessary for the English to pay as much heed as we do to the sensitivities of organized and vocal foreign groups, [though recent heavy migration from the West Indies has provoked strong anti-Negro feelings]. The English are free to laugh at stage Irishmen without bringing down the dudgeon of the Knights of Columbus; they use the word *Jew* freely and even retain the verb *to jew* in their vocabulary. *To jew*, in the original sense, now obsolete, of to cheat, may be an Americanism, and in the sense of to bargain for a lower price (usually *to jew down*) it certainly is. The OED's first example of the former is dated *c.* 1845, and the latter is not listed at all. The DA's first example of the former is dated 1824 and of the latter 1870.[4] The Jews of the United

---

[1] The Hawaiian Language, by Henry P. Judd; Honolulu, 1940, p. 99. At the turn of the century, during the Philippine insurrection against American control, *Filipino* in the Boston area signified an opponent of a regularly nominated candidate for office. It was more pejorative than the older *mugwump*.

[2] A Protest from the Philippines, by M.J.M., *AS*, Vol. XIX, Apr. 1944, p. 148.

[3] [In Canada, according to W. S. Avis, in the *Canadian Journal of Linguistics*, Vol. VIII, Fall 1962, p. 49, Nova Scotians are *bluenoses* and New Brunswickers are *herring chokers*.]

[4] The earliest citation of *to jew down* comes from the proceedings of Congress.

States have waged so successful a campaign against the verb that it seldom appears in any save frankly anti-Semitic writings, though it is still heard. This campaign began so long ago as the 70s, when they petitioned the publishers of Webster's and Worcester's dictionaries to omit it. Worcester's complied, but it still appears in Webster 1961. Webster throws a sop to the protestants by appending to its definitions of *to jew* and *to jew down* "usually taken to be offensive." Neither appears in Webster's Seventh New Collegiate Dictionary, the 1963 abridgment of the New International. [*To jew* and *to jew down* are both included in the American College Dictionary and in the World Publishing Company's Webster's New World Dictionary, but are quarantined as "offensive"; *to jew* is labeled "usually in an unfriendly way" by Barnhart's World Book Encyclopedia Dictionary.] In 1936 a vigilant male Jew from Chicago undertook a jehad against the publishers of a new edition of Roget's Thesaurus because it listed *Jew* as a synonym for lender.[5] Certain American Jews carry on a continuous campaign against the use of *Jew*, and American newspapers, in order to get rid of their clamor, often use *Hebrew* instead. Thus one encounters such forms as *Hebrew comedian, Hebrew holidays* and even *Hebrew rabbi*.[6] This movement originated among the so-called Reformed Jews, most of whom were from Germany or Austria. [However, if Chicago is representative of American *Kultur*, Conservative, Traditional and even Orthodox Jews assemble oftener in *Hebrew* than in *Jewish* congregations.] Certainly the sort of Jew who devotes himself to visiting editors[7] seems to prefer *Hebrew*. Even in the advertisements of *kosher* hotels in the Jewish papers the old term *Jewish cooking* has been abandoned. But no one finds *Hebrew cooking* in its place, [though the short-lived Sabra restaurant in Chicago proclaimed "*Israeli* and American dishes"]. In *The New York Times* the resorts which cater to a Jewish clientele normally advertise *dietary laws observed, dietary laws* or simply *dietary*. But *Jewish funeral directors* and *Jewish cemeteries* flourish uninhibited.

The very word *Jew* appears to be offensive to American Jews, and they

---

[5] His circular letter was dated July 21, 1936. The English still say of a spendthrift borrower that he is *in the hands of the Jews*, but the American term is *loan sharks*. [The *jew's harp*, so known since the Sixteenth Century, has been rechristened *jaws harp*, in Roy Smeck's Complete Method for the *Jaws Harp* (compiled and edited by Harry Reser, New York, 1953), on the ground that this was the original name. To any performer the term *juice harp*, widely known in the South, makes more sense as a folk etymology. Another euphemism, *Bruce harp*, is also reported by Lee Pederson.]

[6] *Variety*, which is owned and mainly staffed by Jews, reduces *Hebrew* to *Hebe*, obviously with jocose intent. Other sportive Jews use *Arab* or *Mexican*.

[7] [A rare defense of the ethnic joke as a safety valve was printed in Critic At-Large, the column of Hoke Norris, under the heading Value of Wit, Chicago *Sun-Times*, July 20, 1962.]

commonly avoid it by using *Jewish* with a noun. In "Who's Who in America," the majority of Jews who mention their faith at all use *Jewish religion*, not *Jew*. In New York, *Jewish boy, girl, man, woman* or *people* is often used as a sort of euphemism. In 1927 a statistician at Yale examined the replies made by ninety-one Jewish candidates for admission as freshmen to the question "Church affiliation?" Nineteen answered by giving the name of their congregation; of the rest, forty-eight answered *Jewish*, fourteen answered *Hebrew*, two answered *Jewish Orthodox*, one each answered *Judaism, Reformed Judaism, Jewish temple* or *synagogue, Jewish faith* or the like; not one answered simply *Jew*. There is apparently no objection to *Jews* in the plural to designate the whole body of Israel, but in the singular it is avoided, and *Hebrew* is used instead.

The American Jews themselves are inconsistent in their use of *Jew* and *Hebrew*. They have Young Men's *Hebrew* Associations all over the country, but they also have a Council of *Jewish* Women and many *Jewish* Community Centers. They have both a *Hebrew* Union College and a *Jewish* Theological Center. Their principal weekly is called the *American Hebrew and Jewish Tribune*. The distinction between the religious significance of *Jew* and the national significance of *Hebrew* is by no means always clear. Abraham was a *Hebrew* (*'Ibri*), but in the course of time his descendants divided into two moieties, the *Israelites* and the *Judeans*, and it is from *Judeans* that we get our word *Jew*. When the Northern Kingdom was destroyed by Shalmaneser the name *Israel*, as a territorial designation, disappeared except from poetry and prayer, until it was recently revived by the Zionists [8] [as the name of their Palestinian state, whose citizens are *Israelis*].

The deliberately offensive names for a Jew—*sheeny, kike, mockie* and so on—are of mysterious etymology. Webster 1961 labels *kike* and *sheeny* "usu. taken to be offensive," and *mocky, mockie,* "usu. used disparagingly." The OED marks *sheeny* "of obscure origin," and traces it to 1824. Ernest Weekley, in his "Etymological Dictionary of Modern English," calls it "East End Slang," and hazards the guess that it may have arisen from a "Yiddish pronunciation of the German *schön*, beautiful." Partridge says: "Very tentatively, I suggest that it arose from the *sheeny*, i.e., glossy or brightly shiny, hair of the average 'English' Jew." Barrère and Leland mark it Yiddish and say: "It is probably taken from *scheina—scheina, jaudea lischkol*—a stupid fellow who does not know enough to ask or inquire." They add: "*Schien*, a policeman, and *schiener*, a house-thief, may have contributed to form this rather obscure word." Farmer and Henley also list it as an adjective meaning "base, Jewish, fraudulent." Thackeray used *Sheeney*

---

[8] Private communication from Dr. Solomon Solis Cohen, of Philadelphia.

in "The Book of Snobs" (1847) as a generic name for a Jew, along with *Moses.* Partridge says that the word was apparently inoffensive so late as the 70s, but by the 80s it had become very obnoxious to the Jews of both England and the United States.

[*Kike,* first cited by the DA from 1917, is most commonly derived from the *-ki, -ky* endings of the surnames of many Slavic Jews, who first came to the United States in large numbers toward the end of the Nineteenth Century.] In 1926 J. H. A. Lacher commented in *American Speech:*

> Soon after the Russian invasion, the credit men of that period were greatly prejudiced against firms whose names ended in *-ki* or *-ky.* . . . Hence it was not long before *-ki* and *-ky* disappeared as tails to their names, and *Gordensky* became *Gordon* and *Levinski* became *Levin.* I have even known them to drop their Slavic-Jewish patronymics and to assume German names so as to disarm the credit man and escape the odium of being *kikes.* There are still plenty of surnames to be found in the city directories terminating in *-ki* or *-ky,* but almost invariably they are owned by Christians. The word *kike* remains, however, to designate a low type of merchant.

Kike has acquired a somewhat extended meaning since World War I, and now designates, not only an Eastern Jew, but any Jew who happens to be in ill favor. This extension is shown by a familiar witticism: "A *kike* is a Jew who has left the room." In the heyday of the Ku Klux Klan, the term was used to designate a Jew who opposed the ideals of that great Methodist-Baptist organization.[9] "There are good Jews, and there are *kikes*" is still frequently heard, and not only in the Bible country. *Mockie* seems to be confined to the New York area. Its etymology may have some sort of relation to the word *mock.*

Several English names for Jew, all more or less opprobrious, have never flourished in the United States, *e.g., shonk* and *smous(e).* A. F. Hubbell suggests[1] that *shonk* may be a recent innovation: it does not appear in any of the standard vocabularies of English slang. *Smous(e)* was listed by Grose in 1785, and defined as meaning a German Jew. It is traced to 1705 by the OED, which suggests that it is probably derived from the Yiddish *schmus,* which in turn is derived from the Hebrew *sh'muoth,* meaning tales or news. *Shmog* is reported as sometimes used as an obscene term to designate a Jew in England. [In Yiddish it signifies the *membrum virile*] but it is not listed in any dictionary of English slang. The British Fascist party used *yid,* which is relatively innocuous in the United States; American Jews use it them-

---

[9] In the South many prudent Jews joined it. This course offered them their only means of escape from its afflictions.

[1] A List of Briticisms, *AS,* Vol. XVII, Feb. 1942, p. 8.

selves jocularly, often in the form *yiddisher,* and sometimes as a plural, *yidden. Christ killer* was once familiar but passed out with the decay of Bible searching.

American Jews have generally succeeded in putting down the newspaper designation of Jewish criminals as *Jewish,* and the use of anti-Semitic phrases in advertising, especially of hotels. There was a time when hotels and apartment houses refusing Jewish patronage advertised that refusal in terms almost as frank as the Nazi *Juden sind nicht erwünscht,* but the protests of Jews gradually reduced them to such equivocal (but well understood) phrases as *restricted* (or *selected*) *clientele,* and eventually to the single word *restricted.* In 1942 the newspaper *PM* undertook to put down even *restricted,* and a year or so later all the dailies of New York banned it from their classified advertising.[2]

Bronx cheer may not embody an allusion to the local Jewry, but *Bronx vanilla* (garlic) obviously does.[3] *Jewish engineering* is sometimes used in colleges for the curriculum in business administration, and *Jewish cavalry* is an old Army term for the Quartermaster Corps.

The Jews are not the only indignant visitors to American editorial offices. In Chicago, during Prohibition, the local Italians objected so vociferously to the use of *Italian* in identifying gunmen that the newspapers began to use *Sicilian* instead. Why the thousands of law-abiding Sicilians and Neapolitans in the Chicago region did not protest in their turn is not known. The Negroes everywhere carry on a double campaign—first against the use of *nigger,* and secondly, for the capitalization of *Negro.* On March 7, 1930, when *The New York Times* announced that it would capitalize *Negro* thereafter, there was jubilation in the Negro press. In March 1933, the Style Manual of the Government Printing Office was revised to make *Negro* and *Negress* begin with capitals in all official publications of the United States, including the *Congressional Record.* The Pittsburgh *Courier,* the most widely circulated of Negro newspapers, hailed the conversion of the *Times* with an exultant editorial on March 15, 1930, but its star columnist, the sardonic George Schuyler,[4] refused to agree that the colored folk "universally wished" to become *Negroes.* Schuyler returned to the subject many times afterward. Thus on July 17, 1937:

> *Negro* clearly belongs with *blonde, brunette, ruddy, mulatto, octoroon* and such descriptive terms, and has no stronger claim on capitalization. . . . Capitalized, it tends to bolster the *status quo,* and

[2] Resort Ads Reformed, *Editor and Publisher,* Aug. 7, 1943.
[3] *AS,* Vol. XI, Dec. 1936, p. 374.
[4] Mr. Schuyler is the most competent journalist that his race has produced in America. There are few white columnists who can match him for information, intelligence, independence and courage.

thus is at best conservative and at worst reactionary, for it discourages differentiation and strengthens the superstition that "all coons are alike."

And again on March 29, 1943:

Negro is either an adjective meaning black or it is a caste name like *Sudra*.[5] When we eagerly accept it as a group designation, regardless of our skin tint, we are accepting all the "racial" nonsense of Hitler, Bilbo, and the myriads who believe as they do—at least in the day time.

Schuyler's ideas, of course, got but little support from the general run of American colored folk, or from their accepted fuglemen and haruspices. Even so intelligent and independent a leader of the race as Dr. Kelly Miller [6] was moved to dissent. In 1937 Dr. Miller contributed a thoughtful article, under the title "*Negroes* or Colored People?" to *Opportunity*, the organ of the National Urban League,[7] and in it said:

A printed list consisting of Englishmen, Germans, Italians, Jews and *negroes* would evidently be a case of unexplained typographical discrimination. If it be said that *Negro* is not derived from a country or geographical division, as other racial divisions are, an adequate rejoinder would be that neither is *Jew*.[8]

In this article Dr. Miller presented the history of the common American designations of persons of his race. In the first days of slavery, they were called *blacks*,[9] and even after interbreeding lightened their color the term continued in use. Then came *African*, which was accepted by the race "in the early years, after it first came to self-consciousness," and still survives in the titles of some of its religious organizations, *e.g.*, the *African* Methodist Episcopal Zion Church. (This, according to the DAE, was during the first half of the Eighteenth Century.) A bit later *darky* or *darkey* began to be used, and "at first it carried no invidious implication." (The DAE's first example is dated 1775.) Then came *Africo-American* (1835 or thereabout), but it was too clumsy to be adopted.[1] After the Civil War the war-

---

[5] A member of the lowest of the four Hindu castes.

[6] Dr. Miller was dean of the College of Arts and Sciences, Howard University, Washington, and a recognized Negro publicist.

[7] May 1937, pp. 142–6.

[8] Here Dr. Miller slipped. See the discussion earlier in this section.

[9] [*Black men* is favored by the Muslims, an urban organization with Black Supremacist overtones; they speak contemptuously of the "so-called Negroes." See Black Nationalism: A Search for an Identity in America, by E. U. Essien-Udom; Chicago, 1962.]

[1] It survives, however, in the *Africo-American Presbyterian*, a weekly published since 1879 by the Negro Presbyterian Church at Charlotte, N.C.

time coinage *freedman* was in wide use, but it began to die out before the end of the 70s.[2] In 1880, according to Dr. Miller, *Afro-American* was invented by T. Thomas Fortune, editor of the New York *Age* [though it had appeared in 1853, in the Windsor (Ont.) *Voice of the Fugitive*], and it still survives, but only in rather formal usage.[3] At some undetermined time after 1900, Sir Harry Johnston, the English African explorer and colonial administrator, shortened *Afro-American* to *Aframerican*, but the latter has had little vogue.[4] After rehearsing the history of all these appellations, Dr. Miller turned to *Negro* and *colored*, and proceeded to discuss their respective claims to general adoption. The latter, he concluded, could not qualify, for it was properly applicable to any person not white, including Chinese, Japanese, Indians and Mexicans, and had been so applied in various state laws, and even, at least by inference, in federal population statistics.[5]

Dr. Miller, going further than most other advocates of *Negro*, was also willing to accept *Negress*, which is intolerably offensive to most high-toned colored folk. Here the iconoclastic Schuyler agreed with him, saying,

> If we accept the term *Negro* there is no sound reason for spurning *Negress*, and yet its use is discouraged and condemned, without, of course, any sensible argument being advanced for this position. I understand Jews are similarly unreasonable about the term *Jewess*.[6]

Other Negro publicists have proposed various substitutes for any designation pointing directly to color, among them *race* and *group*. According to Dr. Miller, *racemen* was suggested in 1936 or thereabout by Robert S. Abbott, editor of the Chicago *Defender*. It has survived, more or less, and *group* is really flourishing. Many of the Negro newspapers use *our group, group man, group leader*, etc. At present the objection to *Negro*, now capitalized by nearly all American publications, takes two forms. First, there is a campaign against using it whenever a person of color comes into the

[2] *Contraband* came into use in 1861, when General Benjamin F. Butler issued a proclamation declaring slaves owned by Confederates contraband of war, but it was obsolete by 1870.

[3] It is the name of a Negro newspaper of wide circulation and influence, published in Baltimore with local editions in other places.

[4] It was preceded, and probably suggested, by *Amerindian*, a name for the American Indian coined by Major J. W. Powell, of the Bureau of American Ethnology, in 1899. *Amerindian* was quickly displaced by *Amerind*, which is still in use. In Liberia the descendants of returned American slaves who constitute the ruling caste of the country used to call themselves *Americo-Liberians* to distinguish themselves from the general mass of blacks. But now, according to Ben Hamilton, Jr., of the Liberian consulate in Los Angeles, "they prefer to be called *civilized* or *Monrovian Liberians* to distinguish themselves from the natives of the hinterland, who are generally called by their tribal names." Monrovia is the capital of Liberia, and the home of virtually all its *noblesse*.

[5] Mexicans were not formally classified as white until the 1940 census.

[6] Views and Reviews, Pittsburgh *Courier*, July 17, 1937.

news, on the ground that calling attention to his race is gratuitous, and usually damaging to the other members of it. Thus an anonymous Negro quoted by R. E. Wolseley:

> Why is it necessary to differentiate us so clearly? We don't see newspaper reporters identifying a man in a newspaper story as a *Catholic* or a *Methodist* or a *Brazilian* or a *Frenchman*. Why go to so much pains to explain that his color is black? [7]

In this objection, of course, there is a certain falsetto, for the question whether a certain person in the news is white or black is often of interest and even of importance. Very few Negroes object when a newspaper describes Leontyne Price as an eminent *Negro* singer and Ralph Bunche as a distinguished *Negro* diplomat (or reminds its readers that Joe Louis was a *Negro* pugilist who slaughtered a long line of whites): they are heard from principally when it is recorded that *Negro* pickpockets have been at work or that *Negro* students have staged a riot. Only Schuyler, apparently, has ever argued for "the doing away entirely of the word." "There is no more reason why we should say *Negro educator* or *Negro criminal*," he once wrote, "than we should say *white educator* or *white criminal*." [8] But this remains a feeble argument so long as Negro educators are differentiated in function from their white colleagues, and Negro criminals, at least in some areas, constitute a specialized faculty. In more logical moments Schuyler argues plausibly that all such verbal reforms and ameliorations are in vain—that the race conflict in the United States will never be abated until the overwhelming majority of whites are induced to look at Negroes with more tolerance, and with less than their present uneasiness.

The other objection to *Negro* has to do with the fact that the word is frequently pronounced as the hated *nigger*. In the South it is commonly heard as *nigrah* [or *nig-ro*], and not only from white lips; [in fact, before the current pother *nigrah* was the usual polite pronunciation from the Potomac south, and *nig-ro* in the Chesapeake Bay area. The racially favored *Negro*—with *ee* in the stressed syllable and a full final *o*—is rare in the South. It probably originated as a spelling pronunciation in New England, where Negroes were rare before Emancipation, and was adopted by the designees in recognition of New England's part in the abolition movement.[9]] *Nigrah*, in fact, is also used by Northern Negroes [and Chicago radio stations still favor *nig-ro*]. Worse, even the abhorred *nigger* is in wide use among the colored people themselves, at least upon the lower levels.

---

[7] Journalistic Headache, *Ken*, Mar. 9, 1939.

[8] Views and Reviews, Pittsburgh *Courier*, Nov. 7, 1936.

[9] [See Kurath and McDavid, The Pronunciation of English in the Atlantic States, pp. 149–50, Maps 99–100.]

Nigger is so bitterly resented by the more elegant blackamoors that they object to it even in quotations, and not a few of their papers spell it *n——r* when necessity forces them to use it.[1] On March 4, 1936, Garnet C. Wilkinson, first assistant superintendent of schools in Washington, in charge of the Negro public schools of the District of Columbia, actually recommended to Superintendent F. W. Ballou that *Opportunity*, organ of the National Urban League and for years a recognized leader among Negro magazines, be barred from the schools of the District on the ground that it used "the opprobrious term *N——* in its publications on Negro life." In 1943 there was an uproar over the belated discovery that the American Tobacco Company was making a brand of tobacco called *Nigger Head*. In this case the crusade for redress was carried on by the *Amsterdam Star-News*, of New York, and in a little while the company announced that the brand was being withdrawn.[2] *Nigger in the woodpile* is traced by the DA to 1852, and is defined as "a concealed or inconspicuous but highly important fact, factor or 'catch' in an account, proposal, etc." *Niggerhead*, in the more refined form of *negrohead*, is traced to 1809, and defined as a "low grade of strong, dark-colored tobacco." It was used by Huckleberry Finn in contradistinction to *store tobacco*. *Niggerhead*, in the sense of a piece of extraordinarily hard rock, goes back to 1847, and has been used in a report of the Smithsonian Institution; it also appears in "Chicago Poems" by Carl Sandburg (1916). After the Civil War it was used to designate a person who favored full political equality for Negroes. The use of *niggerhead* to signify a hard stone was no doubt suggested by the old American belief that the skull of the Negro is extraordinarily thick, and hence able to stand hard blows without cracking. That superstition is accompanied by one to the effect that the shins of the colored folk are extremely tender. The notion that they have an inordinate fondness for watermelon belongs in the same category. This last is so far resented by high-toned Negroes that they commonly avoid *Citrullus vulgaris* in their diet as diligently as the more elegant sort of German Americans used to avoid Limburger cheese.

Negro is not, of course, an Americanism. It was simply the Spanish and Portuguese word for black, and was borrowed by the English during the Sixteenth Century. By 1587 a Northern English form, *neger*, had appeared, and it was from this that both the Irish *naygur* and the English-American *nigger* was derived. The OED's first example of *nigger* comes from a poem

---

[1] See, for example, the Pittsburgh *Courier*, Nov. 1, 1941. [Some of the Pecksniffian pother about Huckleberry Finn is possibly due to the fact that its hero—the first Negro in American literature to be treated as a human being rather than as a prop or a caricature—is named *Nigger Jim*. But the dramatic effect of the characterization depends on the contrast between Jim's label in a slaveholding society and his dignity as an individual.]

[2] *The Nation*, Mar. 20, 1943.

of Robert Burns, published in 1786. In the United States, in the spelling *niger*, the DAE traces it to Samuel Sewall's diary (1700). But after that the DAE offers no example until the Nineteenth Century. *Nigger boy* is traced to 1825, *nigger wench* to 1837,[3] *nigger talk* to 1866 (*nigger* alone, meaning the manner of speech of Negroes, goes back to 1825), *niggerish* to 1825, *nigger killer* to 1855, *nigger luck* (meaning good luck) to 1851 and *nigger heaven* (the top gallery in a theater) to 1878. A *nigger* is 2 device used in sawmills to turn a heavy log, a capstan on a towboat and also a defect in an electrical conductor, causing a short circuit. *Niggertoe* is a widespread name for the Brazil nut, and was once used to designate a variety of potato. *To nigger lip* is "to moisten the tip of one's cigarette," [4] and *nigger tone* is "a buzzing tone produced in the lower register of a wind instrument by constricting the throat muscles." [5] *To work like a nigger* is traced by the DAE to 1836.

Before 1890, according to Dr. Miller, the Census Bureau "sought to subdivide the Negro group into *blacks, mulattos, quadroons* and *octoroons*," but found it "impossible to make such sharp distinctions, since these divisions ran imperceptibly into one another." Upon the advice of Booker T. Washington it began calling all colored persons of African blood *Negroes. Mulatto, quadroon* and *octoroon* have now almost disappeared from American speech. Of them, only *octoroon* seems to be an Americanism. *Mulatto*, which comes from the Spanish and Portuguese *mulato*, signifying a young mule, and hence a half-breed, is traced by the OED in English use to 1595, but the DAE's first American example is dated 1658. Originally, the word meant the immediate offspring of a Negro and a white person, but by the Eighteenth Century it was applied to anyone of mixed white and Negro blood. *Quadroon* is a loan from the *quateron* of the Louisiana French, who borrowed it in turn from the Spanish *cuarterón*. The OED's first example of *quarteron* is dated 1707; Thomas Jefferson used it in that form in 1793. In the form of *quadroon* it goes back to 1796 in English usage and to 1832 in American. *Octoroon* is traced only to 1860, in a sketch by Artemus Ward. *Griffe*, another loan from the French of Louisiana, is now obsolete. It signified, according to Miss Grace E. King, quoted in the DAE, a mixed breed one degree lighter than an octoroon, the series being *mulatto, quad-*

---

[3] *Negro wench* is cited by the DAE (in Boston!) from 1715. In 1807 Charles William Janson reported in The Stranger in America, London, p. 309 (quoted in Words Indicating Social Status in America in the Eighteenth Century, by Allen Walker Read, *AS*, Vol. IX, Oct. 1934, p. 208), that female slaves were "uniformly called wenches." The term remained in general use until the Civil War and is still used in the South. A male slave was called a *buck*, still occasionally heard.

[4] Smokers' Slang, by Robert H. Weber, *AS*, Vol. XV, Oct. 1940, p. 335. [More often the term is used to describe the habit of holding the cigarette continuously between the lips while smoking, so that the tip becomes moistened.]

[5] A Musician's Word List, by Russel B. Nye, *AS*, Vol. XII, Feb. 1937, p. 47.

roon, octoroon, griffe; [other authorities, however, associate the term with a darker hue, that of the offspring of a *Negro* and a *mulatto.* Misses Elaine Douglass and Juanita Williamson report the following gradations of pigment among the Negroes of Memphis:

1. *Black:* "Most do not like it now, but friends will use it in talking to each other."
2. *Dark brown.*
3. *Light brown.*
4. *Olive.*
5. *Meriny,* rhyming with *tiny* (from the curly wool of the *Merino* sheep?): "One younger informant says that it is not a term heard too often now."
6. *Fair.*

Various complex systems of pigment terminology have been reported from Latin America, but they are unknown in the United States.[6]]

The irreverent Schuyler, who does not hesitate to refer to his race as *dark brethren, Senegambians, tarbrushed folk* and so on, frequently discusses such opprobrious names as *darky, coon, shine, smoke, dinge* and *boogie.* In 1936, when the Baltimore *Afro-American* started a crusade against "My Old Kentucky Home" because *darky* occurs in it, he said:

> Will someone who has the gift of logic and intelligence tell me what is the difference between *darkey* and *Negro?* . . . There can be no more real objection to *darkey* than there can be to *blondie.* It is a far more acceptable term than *wop* or *kike.*[7]

---

[6] [See also Trends in the Naming of Tri-Racial Mixed-Blood Groups in the United States, by A. R. Dunlap and C. A. Weslager, *AS,* Vol. XXII, Apr. 1947, pp. 81-7. Charles Parrish and David W. Maurer, of the University of Louisville, have discovered more than 200 color designations in use among Southern Negroes. On Sept. 16, 1962, *The New York Times* reported the term *Hi-Lo* in use in Buras, Plaquemines Parish, southern Louisiana, as a designation for the mulatto group, who there have their own school, segregated from both white and Negro.]

[7] [An amusing note on racial nomenclature is found in What Is a *White* Man?, by Charles T. Dougherty, *AS,* Vol. XXII, Apr. 1947, p. 156: "The Hon C. S. Amsden, then of Milbank, S. Dakota, delivered an address before the fourth bicentennial meeting of the

State Historical Society of South Dakota on 'The Big Winter, 1880,' which has been preserved in *South Dakota Historical Collections,* Vol. V, pp. 92-94 (Pierre, 1910). In the course of his speech he said:

> When I came to Grant county practically the only white settlers in the county were a Frenchman named J. G. Lamreaux and a negro by the name of Williams; at least the negro always said: 'Lameraux [*sic*] and I were the two first white settlers in the county.' However, there were about a half dozen white families at the foot of Big Stone lake on the Dakota side in our county. . . .

By *white* Mr. Amsden simply meant non-Indian. The Negro was specifically included, and included himself in the term *white* man."]

Coon, though now one of the most familiar designations for a Negro, did not come into general use in that sense until the Civil War: the DA's first example is dated 1862. Earlier it had been used in the sense of a loutish white man, and in Henry Clay's time it had designated a member of the Whig party. It is generally assumed to have come from the name of the animal. The use of *coon* to designate a Negro apparently got its great vogue from the success of Ernest Hogan's song "All *Coons* Look Alike to Me" in 1896. Hogan, himself a colored man, used the term without opprobrious intent, and was amazed and crushed by the resentment it aroused among his people.[8]

"All *Coons* Look Alike to Me" was followed in 1899 by "Every Race Has a Flag but the *Coon,*" by Heeland and Helf, two white men, and in 1900 by "*Coon, Coon, Coon,*" by two others, Jefferson and Friedman, and from that time forward *coon* was firmly established in the American vocabulary.[9] The history of the other more or less opprobrious synonyms for *Negro* is mainly obscure. The DAE does not list *boogie* and its congeners, but reports that *booger* is an Americanism, traced to 1866, for a bogy. In 1891 a writer in *Harper's Magazine,*[1] quoted by the DAE, defined *boogah hole* as "the hiding place of cats and of children fleeing from justice," and of *boogars* or *boogahs,* whatever these mysterious beings may be. It is possible that the suggestion of darkness developed *boogie* from *booger* or *boogah.* The latter form hints at a Southern variant of *bogy* or *bogey,* which has been traced in England by the OED, in the sense of the Devil, to 1836, in the sense of a goblin to 1857 and in that of a bugbear to 1865. In the South *boogie man* is still one of the names of the Devil. From the early Eighteenth Century down to the 1880s *Cuffy* was a generic name for a Negro, comparable to *Pat* for an Irishman. It is derived from a common West African name, by custom applied to anyone born on Friday, and is traced to 1713.[2] It had a rival in *Sambo,* which apparently arose in England. [*Cuffy* and the abbreviated *Cuff* are still used as salutations among the Charleston Negroes and are not unknown in Chicago] but by 1880 they had disappeared in Baltimore, and *Sambo* was being supplanted by *Rastus.* During the same era *Liza* or *Lize* was the common name for a colored girl, apparently a reminiscence of "Uncle Tom's Cabin"; [later *Mandy* replaced *Liza,* but became obsolete in turn].

The DA cites *dinge* and *dingy* from 1909, in a story by O. Henry,

---

[8] See Edward B. Marks, They All Sang; New York, 1935, p. 91.

[9] In South Africa *coon* is sometimes used by the newspapers to designate a black native, apparently without derogatory intent.

[1] Oct., p. 825.

[2] [See Lorenzo Turner, Africanisms in the Gullah Dialect; Chicago, 1949.]

but omits *dinkey*, which in late Nineteenth Century Baltimore meant a colored child. Webster 1961 lists *dinge*, but omits *dinkey* in this sense. *Kink* shows an obvious allusion to the Negro's hair; the DA traces *kinky*, in this sense, to 1844. *Pickaninny*, in the sense of a Negro child, is not an Americanism: it was in use in the British West Indies by 1653, whereas the DAE's first American example is dated 1800. It is derived from the Spanish *piqueño nino*, meaning a small child. It is used in South Africa precisely as we use it, but it is commonly spelled *piccanin*. In Australia it designated a child of the aborigines, and has there produced a derivative, *piccaninny daylight*, signifying dawn.[3] In the South of quieter days, *pickaninny* was not used invidiously, but rather affectionately. So, indeed, was *tar pot*, also signifying a Negro child.

The DAE does not list such vulgar synonyms for *Negro* as *eight ball*, *jazzbo*, *jigabo* (with the variants *jigaboo*, *jig*, *zigabo*, *zigaboo*, *zig*),[4] *shine*, *smoke*, *snowball*, *spade* and *Zulu*. [The DA lists only *shine*.] *Crow* is traced to 1823, in "The Pioneers," the first of James Fenimore Cooper's Leatherstocking Tales. Whether it suggested *Jim Crow* or was suggested by *Jim Crow* is not known. The DA's first example of *Jim Crow* is dated 1835, but that example includes the statement that "'*Zip Coon*' and '*Jim Crow*' are hymns of great antiquity." The DA adds that Thomas D. Rice's song and dance "*Jim Crow*" was copyrighted in 1828. The verb phrase *to jump Jim Crow* appeared in 1833. By 1838 *Jim Crow* had become an adjective and was so used by Harriet Beecher Stowe in "Uncle Tom's Cabin" (1852); by 1923 it had also become a verb. The DA's first example of *Jim Crow car* is dated 1842; of *Jim Crow school*, 1903; of *Jim Crow bill*, 1904; of *Jim Crow law*, 1904; and of *Jim Crow regulations*, 1910.

Eight ball is probably derived from the game of pool, which is played with fifteen numbered and varicolored balls, No. 8 being black. *Blueskin*, as a synonym for *Negro*, occurs in Cooper's "The Spy" (1821), but had become obsolete before the Civil War. In Baltimore, in the 80s of the last century, the German-speaking householders, when they had occasion to speak of Negro servants in their presence, called them *die Blaue* (blues). In the 70s *die Schwarze* (blacks) had been used, but it was believed that

---

[3] A Popular Dictionary of Australian Slang, by Sidney J. Baker; 2nd ed.; Melbourne, 1943, p. 58. [See also An Historical Study of the Australian Vocabulary, by W. S. Ramson, diss. (MS), U. of Sydney, 1962, pp. 462, 514.]

[4] James Hargan, in The Psychology of Prison Language, *Journal of Abnormal and Social Psychology*, Oct.–Dec. 1935,

p. 36, says that the inmates of Sing Sing call a Negro a *jig* or *buggy*. Dorothy Bentz says in American English as Spoken by the Barbadians, *AS*, Vol. XIII, Dec. 1938, p. 310, that in the Canal Zone all West Indians are called *jigs*. [*Jazzbo* is the *nom de guerre* of one Al Collins, a popular disk jockey.]

the Negroes had fathomed it. *Ofay*, which Negro sophisticates have used to designate a white person, is often derived from the French *au fait*, but without convincing evidence; it is probably a pig Latin form of *foe*.[5] The Negroes use various other sportive terms for whites, *e.g.*, *paleface*, *chalk*, *gray* and *milk*. The militantly race-conscious sometimes call Africa *the mother country*.[6] Unhappily, the ideas and cultural criteria of the American blacks are so thoroughly American that such gestures always smack of affectation. Even their norms of personal beauty are white. "As Negroes," said a colored lady journalist in 1944,[7] "we usually say that a person is beautiful if they closely approach white standards, for we think of beauty as we have been taught since we have lived in this country. Straight noses, thin lips and skin that is not black come in for our share of admiration. Whether we like to admit it or not, this is true." [Confirming her judgment, beauty-preparation ads in Chicago's Black Belt advertise "Lighter Skin for Romance."] A curious euphemism for *Negro*, apparently originating in the South, is *nonpromotable*, signifying a locomotive fireman who is ineligible for advancement to engineer because of his color.[8] It has come to signify any Negro in a like unfortunate position.

The English have many derisive terms embodying references to Scotland and the Scots, *e.g.*, *Scotch fiddle*, the itch, and *Scotch warming pan*, a loose girl; but they are not in use in the United States. Nor are such derisive English names for Scotland as *Itchland*, *Scratchland* and *Louseland*. The inhabitants of the Northern kingdom greatly prefer *Scot* or *Scotsman* to *Scotchman*. *Scot* is traced by the OED to 1338, *Scotsman* to *c.* 1375 and *Scotchman* to 1570. The OED notes that, from the Seventeenth Century onward to recent times, *Scot* was "chiefly historical except in jocular or rhetorical use," but now it is dominant. Says an English correspondent: "To call a Scot a *Scotchman* is like calling a Negro a *coon*." Nearly all the English words and phrases based on *Scotch* embody references to the traditional penuriousness of the Scots, *e.g.*, *Scotch coffee*, hot water flavored with burnt biscuit; *to play the Scotch organ*, to put money in a cash register; *Scotch pint*, a two-quart bottle; *Scotch sixpence*,

---

[5] [*Ofay*, an urban word, is less frequently used than it used to be. For recent studies of urban Negro speech see If You're Woke You Dig It, by William Melvin Kelley, *The New York Times Magazine*, May 20, 1962, pp. 45 ff.; and *Man* and *Evil* in American Negro Speech, by Richard A. Long, *AS*, Vol. XXXIV, Dec. 1959, pp. 305–6. George Rowell is currently investigating in-group terms among Chicago Negroes.]

[6] America's Mother Country, by Rex Forrest, *AS*, Vol. XVI, Feb. 1941, p. 74. [The Muslims tend to reject Africa and think of themselves as *black Asiatics*. See E. U. Essien-Udom, Black Nationalism; Chicago, 1962.]

[7] New Yorker's Album, by Constance Curtis, *Amsterdam News*, Mar. 4.

[8] *Congressional Record*, Dec. 17, 1943, p. A5942, col. 3.

a threepence; and the *Scotchman's cinema*, Piccadilly Circus, because it offers many free attractions.[9]

In the interchange of international objurgations the United States gets off very lightly. The best-known have arisen in Spanish-speaking nations: *Yanqui-blofero* (in Cuba, *blofista*) and *gringo*. The latter is traced by the DA to 1849, in Audubon's "Western Journal," but it is probably older. In 1929 Frank H. Vizetelly printed its history in *The New York Times*, as going back to a slang term for foreigners who spoke bad Spanish.[1] Various other etymologies have been proposed, but they are all fanciful. The best insults the Nazis or Communists have yet been able to invent are tedious variations on the theme of *capitalist, plutocrat* and *warmonger*; perhaps as the quality of Marxist literature improves, superior epithets will arise. Meanwhile, Roback's "Dictionary of International Slurs" (1944) lists such unfavorable reflections on American traits as the Hungarian *amerikazni*, to loaf on the job; the Italian *americanata*, an advertising stunt; and the French *oeillade américaine*, goo-goo eyes.

Rather curiously, no pejorative for *Indian* has ever appeared in American speech. *Lo*, borrowed from Alexander Pope's line "Lo, the poor Indian," is merely sportive. It was a long time coming in, for the DAE's first example is dated 1871. *Buck* has been applied to a male Indian since the middle of the last century, but it was used to designate a male Negro somewhat earlier. The English use *wog* for a native of India, and it has been extended to indicate any native of the Red Sea and Indian Ocean country. It was borrowed by the American troops serving in Egypt during World War II, from the argot of the British troops. It is supposed to be an abbreviation of *wily oriental gentleman*.

10: EXPLETIVES

Perhaps the most curious disparity between the vocabulary of the two tongues is presented by *bloody*. This word is entirely without improper significance in America, but in England it is regarded as indecent, with overtones of the blasphemous. The sensation produced in London when George Bernard Shaw put it into the mouth of the elegant Mrs. Patrick Campbell in his play "Pygmalion" will be remembered. "The interest in the first English performance," said *The New York Times*,[2] "centered in

---

[9] A Dictionary of International Slurs, by A. A. Roback; Cambridge, Mass., 1944, pp. 61–3. [John Lyman suggests that *limejuicer* for an Englishman, like the later derivative *limey*, may be an Americanism. *AS*, Vol. XXX, Oct. 1955, pp. 172–5.]

[1] The Origin of *Gringo* (editorial page), Sept. 29.
[2] Apr. 14, 1914. In 1920 the English Licenser of Stage Plays ordered *bloody* expunged from a play dealing with labor. See *English*, Oct. 1920, p. 403.

the heroine's utterance of this banned word. It was waited for with trembling, heard shudderingly, and presumably, when the shock subsided, interest dwindled." But in New York, of course, it failed to cause any stir. Just why it is viewed so shudderingly by the English is one of the mysteries of the language. Various amateur etymologists have sought to account for its present evil fame by giving it loathsome derivations, sometimes theological and sometimes catamenial, but the professional etymologists all agree that these derivations are invalid, though when it comes to providing a better one they unhappily disagree. Some hold that *bloody* was born of the rich young *bloods* who beat up watchmen in the reign of Anne. Others argue that it is a brother to the German *Blut*, often used in such combinations as *blutarm*, meaning bloody poor. And yet others think it is a degenerate form of either *'s blood* or *by 'r Lady*, both of them favorite if harmless oaths in Shakespeare's day. But none of these justifies the present infamy of the word. In the Motherland, the more it is denounced by the delicate, the more it is cherished by the vulgar. It is in constant use as a counter word—in Dean W. R. Inge's phrase, simply a sort of notice that a noun may be expected to follow.[3]

The English have produced a number of euphemisms for *bloody*, e.g., *bleeding*, *ruddy* and *sanguinary*. Of these, says an English correspondent,[4] *bleeding* and *ruddy* have become "swear-words in their own right, as strong as *bloody* itself," and *sanguinary* is used "only facetiously." When, on January 22, 1887, a new operetta, *"Ruddygore,"* by Gilbert and Sullivan, was presented at the Savoy Theatre, London, the title caused a considerable raising of eyebrows. It was exactly descriptive, for the piece was a burlesque on the gory melodramas of the time, but the more queasy Savoyards raised such a pother against it that it was changed to *"Ruddigore"* after the fourth performance. Even then there were murmurs, and letters of protest flowed in on the authors.

The Australians, who are much more spacious in their speech than the English, use *bloody* with great freedom. They call it, somewhat proudly, *the great Australian adjective*,[5] and have embodied it in some of their folk

---

[3] See A Note on *Bloody*, by Robert Withington, *AS*, Vol. VI, Oct. 1930, and his Children of Linguistic Fashion, *AS*, Vol. IX, Dec. 1934.

[4] Arthur Jacobs, of Manchester.

[5] A contibutor signing himself R.G.H. reports in the Sydney (N.S.W.) *Morning Herald* (A Word of Fear, Feb. 11, 1939) that this phrase originated at the University of Melbourne, at the time the university conferred a doctorate of letters on Edward E. Morris, the first

serious lexicographer of Australian. Morris had omitted *bloody* from his Austral English (London, 1898), and the students, apparently resenting the prudery, staged a burlesque of the ceremony, in which a solemnly gowned candidate carried under his arm a huge tome inscribed The Great Australian Adjective. [The adjective is likewise omitted in W. S. Ramson, An Historical Study of the Australian Vocabulary, diss. (MS), U. of Sydney, 1962.]

poetry—for example, the following refrain of a song sung by Australian troops stationed in Newfoundland in 1942:

> *No* bloody *sports, no* bloody *games;*
> *No* bloody *fun with* bloody *dames;*
> *Won't even tell their* bloody *names;*
> *Oh,* bloody, bloody, bloody! [6]

Profanity has never had a scientific historian, though the literature on the subject is not inconsiderable.[7] The admonitions and threats of the Old Testament seem to be directed principally to perjury, which was regarded by the early sages as a kind of blasphemy. The more orthodox Quakers, in our own time, forbade all oaths, even on the witness stand, as savoring of blasphemy.[8] Profanity, like any other art, has had its ups and downs—its golden ages of proliferation and efflorescence and its dark ages of decay and desuetude. Medieval England appears to have had a large repertoire of foul language. The first serious war upon this vocabulary was opened by the Puritans in the first quarter of the Seventeenth Century, and it achieved considerable success. Two years after the death of the hard-swearing Elizabeth I, Parliament passed an act providing a fine of £10 for anyone who should "in any stage play, interlude, show, etc., jestingly or profanely speak or use the holy name of God, or of Jesus Christ, or of the Holy Ghost, or of the Trinity." This law greatly cramped the style of the playwrights of the Bankside, including Shakespeare. The quartos of his plays had been full of oaths and objurgations, but when his friends Heming and Condell assembled the First Folio in 1623 they undertook a prudent bowdlerization, and the editors of the bard in later years had the exhilarating job of restoring the denatured expletives.

At the Restoration the natural revival of profanity was apparently confined within rather cautious metes and bounds. The forthright *God's wounds* of 1535 became the euphemistic *zounds* by the beginning of the

---

[6] Robert Graves says in his Lars Porsena, or, The Future of Swearing, New York, 1927, p. 34, that this song originated during World War I and is called simply The Australian Poem. New stanzas are added from time to time. [On the current status of *bloody* see comments by W. Sprague Holden, *AS*, Vol. XXXV, Oct. 1960, pp. 236-7.]

[7] There is a brief bibliography in The Literature of Slang, by W. J. Burke; New York, 1939, pp. 152-3. To it may be added [The Lost Art of Profanity, by Burges Johnson, Indianapolis, 1948; Master List and Classification of Interjec-

tions, by Clyde Crobaugh, Knoxville, Tenn., 1954; Postscripts to the American Language: Hell and Its Outskirts, by H. L. Mencken, *The New Yorker*, Oct. 23, 1948, pp. 52-7;] The Psychology of Profanity, by G. T. W. Patrick, *Psychological Review*, 1901, pp. 113-27; Profanity, by Henry Woodward Hulbert, *Biblical World* (Chicago), 1920, pp. 69-75. The article on Profanity in Hastings' Encyclopedia of Religion and Ethics, New York, 1928, Vol. X, pp. 378 ff., is worth consulting.

[8] Based on Matthew v, 34-6.

next century and then vanished altogether, and the numerous old oaths naming the Virgin Mary were diluted down to the innocuous *marry*. The fashionable oaths of the 1650–1700 period ran to such banal forms as *strike me dumb, split my windpipe, gadzooks* and *dag take me. Lord* was reduced to *lard, devil* to *Harry, Jesus* to *Jeminy* and various resounding appeals to God to *dear me.*[9] By 1823, apparently the only oath surviving in English circles having "any pretension to fashion" was *by Jove.*[1] But on lower levels *bloody* was already making its way.

In the United States, probably because of the decay of the legal concept of blasphemy, there has been little organized opposition to profanity. Even in the heart of Puritan New England there was a large population of non-Puritans, some of them sailors come ashore and others wastrels and fugitives of a dozen varieties, and it was hard for the magistrates and clergy to dissuade them from sulphurous utterance. The frequency of prosecutions for profane cursing and swearing, as reported in the town records, shows that the offense must have been a common one.[2] The Revolution, like any other general war, greatly prospered both obscenity and profanity. The admonitions of George Washington and John Adams against profanity and blasphemy in the Army and Navy had no effect, and at the end of the century an English visitor named Richard Parkinson was recording that "the word *damned*" was "a very familiar phrase" in the new Republic, and that even the clergy used language that was "extremely vulgar and profane." Washington himself, despite his order to his men, used both *damn* and *hell* with considerable freedom, as have several other American officers since.

In 1931, writing in *American Speech*, L. W. Merryweather observed that "*hell* fills so large a part in the American vulgate that it will probably be worn out in a few years."[3] Merryweather regarded this deterioration as so likely that he proposed that "clerical circles should take it upon themselves, as a public duty, to invest some other theological term with a shuddering fearsomeness that will qualify it as the successor to *hell*, when the lamentable decease of the latter actually takes place." Fortunately, his fears have not been borne out by the event. *Hell* still flourishes in the

---

[9] A History of Modern Colloquial English, by H. C. Wyld; London, 1920, pp. 389–90.
[1] Modern English in the Making, by George H. McKnight; New York, 1928, p. 506.
[2] British Recognition of American Speech in the Eighteenth Century, by Allen Walker Read, *DN,* Vol. VI, Pt.

VI, July 1933, p. 328.
[3] *Hell* in American Speech, *AS,* Vol. VI, Aug. 1931, pp. 433–5. [The associations of *hell* have caused genteel Americans to alter the pronunciation of such words as *Helena;* see my Hidden *Hell* in *Helena, AS,* Vol. XXVI, Dec. 1951, pp. 305–6.]

Republic, insofar as profanity flourishes at all, and every one of the combinations and permutations of it that he listed remains in use:

1. *Hell* as "the equivalent of negative adverbs" or as an intensifier thereof, as in *the hell you say* and *like hell I will.*
2. As a super-superlative, as in *colder than hell.*
3. As an adverb of all work, as in *run like hell* and *hate like hell.*
4. As an intensifier of questions, as in *what the hell?, who the hell?, where in hell?,*[4] etc.
5. As an intensifier of asseverations, as in *hell, yes!*
6. As an intensifier of qualities, as in *to be hell on* and *hell of a price.*
7. As an indicator of intensified experience, as in *hell of a time, get the hell* and *to play hell with.*
8. In a more or less literal sense, as in *wouldn't it be hell?, go to hell, the hell with, hell on wheels, hell to pay, like a snowball in hell, till hell freezes over* and *to beat hell.*
9. As a synonym for uproar or turmoil, as in *to raise hell, to give him hell* and *hell is loose.*
10. As a verb, as in *to hell around.*
11. As an adjective, as *in a hellish hurry* and *hell-bent.*
12. In combination with other nouns, as in *hell's bells, hell and red niggers, hell and high water, hell and Maria, hell raiser, hell diver, hell bender* and *hell to breakfast.*
13. In derivatives, as in *hellion, hellcat* and *heller.*
14. As a simple expletive, as in *oh hell.*

Most of these are of American origin; the English have a much less inspiring repertoire of terms in *hell.* The DAE traces *to give him hell* to 1851, *to be hell on* to 1850, *hellion* to 1845, *hell diver* (a bird) to 1839, *hell-bent* to 1835 and *hell of a* to 1776, and marks them all Americanisms. It records a number of forms that have since become obsolete, *e.g., hell face* and *hell to split* (1871), *to smell hell* and *hellabaloo* (1840), *hell sweat* (1832) and *hell kicking* (1796). *Hellion* seems to have been invented by the Mormons, along with *by hell* and *son of hell,* apparently on the theory that "if it is evil to use celestial names profanely, it must be good to take infernal names in vain. *Hellion* and *son of hell* are obvious substitutes for a pair of obscene epithets, and *by hell* takes the place of *by God.*" New combinations embracing *hell* are being launched all the time, and

---

[4] The choice between *the* and *in* or both is determined by euphony and the taste of the speaker.

old and forgotten ones are frequently revived. In 1944, for example, a United States senator got a flattering editorial notice in *The New York Times* for "The hardtack was *as hard as the hubs of hell*." A few days later a correspondent wrote in to say that the simile was used by the soldiers during the Spanish-American War, and that *hubs* should have been *hobs*.[5]

Dwight L. Bolinger has called attention to the fact that *hell* and its derivatives make much milder oaths in English than in other languages. They are not as innocuous as the terms in *heaven*, but nevertheless they fall below those in *God, e.g., goddam*.[6] But that they have not lost altogether the character of profanity is proved by the continued use of euphemisms, *e.g., heck, blazes* and *thunder*. *By heck* is not listed in the DA, but the OED Supplement calls it "dial. and U.S." and traces it in American use to 1865, more than twenty years before the date of the first English dialect example. The provenance of *blazes* is uncertain. Among the phrases embodying it are *by blazes, as blue as blazes, as black as blazes, as hot as blazes, like blazes, oh blazes, where in blazes?* and *what in blazes? Thunder* is undoubtedly an Americanism, and the DAE traces it to 1841. It seems to have been preceded by *thunderation*, which was obviously a euphemism for *damnation*, but it had taken on the definite sense of *hell* by 1843, in *by thunder, go to thunder, why (how or what) in thunder?* and *to give him thunder*. *Go to Halifax* and *go to Guinea* are not Americanisms; they belong to an English series of which *go to Jericho* is perhaps the most familiar example. *Jesse*, as in *give him Jesse*, is also a euphemism for *hell*. *All-fired*, a softened form of *hell-fired*, is traced by the DAE to 1835 and marked an Americanism.

The only comprehensive collection of American swear words is in "A Dictionary of Profanity and Its Substitutes," by M. R. Walter, of Dalton, Pa. It has not been published, but a typescript is in the Princeton University Library and may be consulted there by learned men of reasonable respectability.[7] Walter's list is especially rich in euphemisms. Some of them follow, along with a few from other sources:[8]

> For *damn: drat, bang, blame, blast, bother, darn, cuss, dang, ding, bean.*
> For *damned: all-fired, blamed, blasted, blowed, confounded, darned, dashed, cursed, cussed, danged, deuced, dinged, switched, swiggered.*
> For *damnation: botheration, thunderation, perdition, tarnation.*
> For *goddam: goldarn, doggone, consarn, goldast, goshdarn* and

[5] It's Hard Enough, Anyway (editorial page), Mar. 10, 1944.
[6] Profanity and Social Sanction, *AS*, Vol. XIII, Apr. 1938, p. 153.
[7] I have had access to it by the grace of Dr. Julian P. Boyd, the librarian.
[8] Mainly, Exclamations in American English, by E. C. Hills, *DN*, Vol. V, Pt. VII, 1924, pp. 253–84.

various terms in *dad-*, e.g., *dad-blame, dad-blast, dad-burn, dad-shame, dad-sizzle, dad-rat, dad-seize, dad-swamp, dad-snatch, dad-rot, dad-fetch, dad-gum, dad-gast.*

For *hell: Sam Hill, blazes.*

For *Lord: land, law, lawks, lawdy, lawsy.*

For *God: gosh, golly, (great) guns, (great) Scott, (great) horn spoon, (great) snakes, (good) grief, gum, Godfrey.*

For *God Almighty: goshamighty, goramity.*

For *Jesus: gee,*[9] *jeez, jiminy* (or *jeminy*) or *gimini, Jemima, Jerusalem, Jehosaphat, jiminy-whizz, gee-whizz, gee-whillikin(s),*[1] *gee-whittaker.*

For *Christ: cripes, crickey, Christmas, cracky, Christopher.*

Many of these are Americanisms, but not all. *Blasted* in the sense of damnably goes back to 1854, *cracky* to 1830, *dinged* to 1843, *dad-blamed* to 1844, *dad-burn* to 1839, *switched* to 1838, *goldarn* to 1832, *goldast* to 1888, *land* (in *land's sake*) to 1834, *Jerusalem* to 1840 and *gosh* to 1832. Walter notes some Irish euphemisms, familiar to all Americans, but now obsolete, *e.g., bedad, faith, bejabers* and *begorrah.* He also notes some extensions of *Jesus* and *Jesus Christ, e.g., ke-rist, Jesus H. Christ, Jesus H. Particular Christ, Jesus Nelly* and *holy jumping Jesus.* He lists nearly 400 picturesque oaths in the *by* form, *e.g., by hell's peekhole, by the high heels of St. Patrick* and *by the ripping, roaring, jumping Jerusalem.* Finally, he notes that the Old Testament makes Jahveh Himself swear gently on occasion, as the pious will discover in Ezekiel xviii, 3.

Regarding the etymology of the euphemism *darn*, with its variants *dern* and *durn*, there is a difference of opinion among lexicographers. Noah Webster, in his "Dissertations on the English Language," sought to identify it with the Old English word *dern* or *derne*, meaning secret. This etymology was accepted by Krapp, and argued for with great learning in his excellent work "The English Language in America,"[2] and it is adopted by the DAE and mentioned favorably by the OED Supplement. Nevertheless, there is considerably more plausibility in Louise Pound's theory, launched in 1927,[3] that *darn* and its congeners, *dern* and *durn*, are

---

[9] *Hully gee* (for *Holy Jesus*) was introduced by Edward W. Townsend's Chimmie Fadden and Major Max (New York, 1895), but it disappeared with the decay of the Bowery boy as an American comic type.

[1] An Americanism traced to 1851.

[2] New York, 1924, Vol. I, pp. 118–26.

[3] The Etymology of an English Intensive, *Lg.*, Vol. III, June 1927, pp. 96–9.

See also her *Darn, Saturday Review of Literature*, Sept. 7, 1940, p. 19, and *Darn Again*, by Woodford A. Heflin, *AS*, Vol. XVII, Dec. 1942, pp. 276–7. [Miss Pound's thesis is further confirmed by W. S. Avis's research in Judge Haliburton's Sam Slick stories; see *Darn* in The Clockmaker, *AS*, Vol. XXVI, Dec. 1951, pp. 302–3.]

really derived from *tarnal*, an American contraction of *eternal* that arose during the Eighteenth Century and was in wide use as an intensive by the time of the Revolution. *Tarnal*, at the start, was a mere intensive, but it quickly gave rise to *tarnation* as a euphemism for *damnation*, and in a very short while *tarnation* was in use as an expletive. By 1798 it had assimilated the initial *d* of *damnation*, and in the course of time *tarnal* and its derivatives in *t* dropped out of use, and only *darn* remained.

Darn as a mere intensive, as in Webster's *darn sweet*, is traced by the DAE no further back than his mention of it in his "Dissertations on the English Language," but it must have been in use in America for some time before that. *Tarnal*, as an intensive, is traced to 1775. Both words took on the special sense of *damned* very soon afterward. The DAE's first example of *darnation* is dated 1825. *Tarnal* and all its derivatives, whether in *t* or in *d*, are Americanisms. Visiting Englishmen found them piquant, and took them home. Dickens reported *darn* as an expletive in his "American Notes" (1842), and made one of his Americans use it in "Martin Chuzzlewit" (1843). But it never really took hold in England. *Not by a darned sight* is traced to 1834. It was preceded by *not by a jugful*, 1833, and has been followed by various euphemisms of the second degree, *e.g.*, *not by a considerable sight*, used by Mark Twain in "Huckleberry Finn." *Darn* seems quite innocuous to most Americans today, but so recently as 1941 a federal judge sitting in New York was objecting to its use in his courtroom and threatening a lawyer who used it with punishment for contempt of court.[4]

Doggone is marked an Americanism by the DAE and traced to the middle of the last century. There is reasonable ground for deriving it from the Scotch *dagone*, of exactly the same significance and use, with changes in spelling and pronunciation through some vague association with going to the dogs. In the common speech, indeed, it is often *daggone*, with the first syllable rhyming with *drag*. As adjectives, both it and *darn* have produced superlatives by analogy with *damndest*, to wit, *doggondest* and *darndest* (*derndest*, *durndest*). They are by no means the only American euphemisms for *damn*. The Linguistic Atlas of New England [5] lists many others, *e.g.*, *dem*, *dum*, *dean*, *dang*, *drat*, *blame*, *blast*, *burn*, *confound*, *condemn*,

---

[4] *Darn* Upsets Court, *The New York Times*, July 15, 1941.

[5] Vol. II, Pt. I, Map 599; Providence, R.I., 1943. [The unpublished materials from Appalachia should yield similar riches. Mrs. Irene Mason, of Dunbar, W. Va., points out that contrary to the usual government practice of naming dams after the nearest community, *Summersville Dam* in Nicholas County was so named because people shuddered at the thought of naming it after the nearest community, *Gad*. In contrast—perhaps as a Freudian reaction to the headaches it causes them—the "flying officers" of the Chicago Police Department, in their helicopter-borne surveys of the traffic situation, usually convert the title of the *Dan Ryan Expressway* (a new and expensive focus of traffic jams) to *Dam Ryan*.]

consarn, condarn, curse, cuss, gast, hang, rat, torment, plague and *tarn.*
Dum is traced to 1787. *Dad*, usually combined, as in *dad-fetch* and *dad-gum*, is also apparently of American origin. *Shuck*, in the plural, is commonly used as an exclamation of disgust or regret without any reference to *damn*, and in that use the DAE traces it to 1847. *Tormented* is traced by the DAE to 1825.

Damn is a borrowing from the Old French *dampner*, which in turn was a borrowing from the Latin *damnare*. It goes back to the Ages of Faith. *Goddam* is first recorded in English use in 1633, and soon afterward the French were using it to designate an Englishman, apparently because it was often on the lips of English soldiers and travelers. Toward the middle of the Seventeenth Century the Puritans began calling the Cavaliers *goddammes*, but the term seems to have passed out at the Restoration. The expletive is now so rare among Englishmen that when it is heard the police take a serious view of it. An English friend reported that when, as a boy (*c.* 1905), he heard his father use it he was greatly shocked. It seemed as quaint to him as *egad* or *odsblood.*

Many euphemisms for *goddam* have flourished in America, as Walter indicates. *Gosh* itself was borrowed from England, but *goshdarn, goldarn, goshdad* and *goshdang* are Americanisms, and so are *goshamighty, goshwalader* and *goshawful.* The DA records the astonishing *goy blamed* as in use in 1832, long before the influx of European Jews had converted Christian Americans into *goyim. Golly* is not an Americanism, but *gravy*, as in *by gravy*, is, and the DA traces it to 1831. *I swan* (for I swear) and *I vum* (for I vow) are now obsolete save in a few remote country districts. The former is traced to 1754 and the latter to 1785. Both are apparently of American origin. The DA's first example of *by the great horn spoon*, also an Americanism, is from "The American National Song Book" (1842). Its original meaning remains a mystery.[6]

The American custom of inserting *goddam* into other words, to give them greater forensic force, is generally believed to have been launched by the late Joseph Pulitzer, of the New York *World*, a great master of profanity in three languages. In order to flabbergast the managing editor of the *World*, Foster Coates, Pulitzer is said to have roared, "The trouble with you, Coates, is that you are too inde*goddam*pendent."[7] This ingenious device has been borrowed by the Australians, who are great admirers of the American language, but they use *bloody* instead of *goddam*, no doubt as a concession to Commonwealth solidarity.

All recent writers upon the subject seem to be agreed that profanity is

---

[6] *The Great Horn Spoon*, by Mamie Meredith, *AS*, Vol. IV, Aug. 1929, pp. 499–500.

[7] See Reporters Become of Age, by Isabelle Keating, *Harper's Magazine*, Apr. 1935, p. 601.

now in one of its periods of waning. This is the melancholy thesis, for example, of "Lars Porsena, or, The Future of Swearing," by Robert Graves.[8] Graves believes that there has been a steady decline in England, marked by ameliorations in wartime, since the age of Elizabeth I.[9] The lower classes, he says, find *bloody* sufficient for all ordinary purposes, with *bastard* and three obscene auxiliaries to help out on great occasions. One of these auxiliaries, *bugger*, resembles *bloody* in that it is not generally considered obscene in the United States. When I was a boy my father used it often, as an affectionate term for any young male, and any flavor of impropriety today must be due to English influence.[1] All three auxiliaries are discussed at length in "Songs and Slang of the British Soldier, 1914–1918," by John Brophy and Eric Partridge.[2] They say of one of them, a word of sexual significance, [the only traditional four-letter word omitted by Webster 1961]:

> From being an intensive to express strong emotion it became a merely conventional excrescence. By adding *-ing* and *-ingwell* an adjective and an adverb were formed and thrown into every sentence. It became so common that an effective way for the soldier to express emotion was to omit this word. Thus, if a sergeant said, "Get your ——ing rifles!" it was understood as a matter of routine. But if he said, "Get your rifles!" there was an immediate implication of urgency and danger.

All American treatises on the subject likewise agree that there has been a marked decline in the Republic since the Civil War, with only faint revivals during the two world wars. In 1934, Burges Johnson declared that American profanity was fast losing its punch.[3] He noted that a number of intrinsically innocuous words, *e.g. plutocrat, capitalist, Bolshevik, Communist, Fascist, pacifist, radical, Rotarian* and *bourgeoisie*, were coming into use for purposes of invective, and predicted that they would gradually take on the dignity of general expletives. This prediction has been borne out by the event, and to them have been added many other terms, *e.g., isolationist* and *Nazi*, [*segregationist* and *appeaser*]. But this process, of course, is old in English and does not lead to the production of true profanity. The decline of American profanity has been helped by the extraordinary prudishness of the American newspapers, which always hesitate to report genuine profanity in full, or even any harmless discourse quoting its more

---

[8] London, 1927; rev. ed., 1936.

[9] A similar decline in Ireland is reported in Joyce, p. 66.

[1] It was defined by Dr. Johnson as "a term of affection common among sailors."

[2] London, 1930, pp. 15 *ff.*

[3] Modern Maledictions, Execrations and Cuss-Words, *North American Review*, Nov. 1934, pp. 467–71.

familiar terms. I had a curious personal experience of this in 1939, when, in the course of a lecture delivered at Cooper Union, New York, I ventured to observe: "American grammar is fast going to *hell*, which is where all grammars will land, I hope and pray, soon or late." In the New York *Journal-American*'s report of the lecture the next morning, *hell* was printed *h—l*.[4] Some American newspapers even hesitate to use such euphemistic forms as *damfino, damphool* and *helluva*. The movies, radio and television are still more prudish.

The Holy Name Society carries on a crusade against the use of the more forthright forms of profanity by American Catholics, apparently with some success among its actual members, who are all males. (It is apparently the theory of the spiritual directors that Catholic women do not swear.) But many Catholics do not belong to it, and numbers of those who are enrolled have apparently got wind of the fact that *hell* and *damn*, if unaccompanied by sacred names, are not, in the judgment of moral theologians, blasphemous, and hence do not involve mortal sin.

All expletives tend to be dephlogisticated by over-use. Of the non-profane pejoratives in common American use, *son of a bitch* is the hardest-worked, and by far. It rose to popularity in the United States during the decade before the Civil War,[5] and at the start was considered extremely offensive, but many other terms, including the simple *liar*, are now more apt to provoke actual blows. Not infrequently, indeed, it is used almost affectionately. It was so used in "The Virginian," a novel and movie by Owen Wister, wherein one character said to another, "You son-of-a——," and the other interrupted with "When you call me that, smile." [It was such a byword among the American Expeditionary Force of World War I that for a generation afterward Americans were collectively known in France as *les sommombiches*, analogous to the earlier *les goddammes* as a designation for Englishmen.[6]] But, as we have seen, it is now forbidden by the movie code of morals, along with its abbreviation, *s.o.b.*[7] The American newspapers avoid it diligently. [When Harry S. Truman used the abbreviated form in a letter from the White House, to a music critic who had spoken disparagingly of daughter Margaret's singing, the public reaction was only slightly less violent than if General Douglas MacArthur had been discovered to be a paid agent of the Kremlin.] But *son of a bitch* seems as pale and ineffectual to a Slav or Latin as *fudge* does to us. The dumbest police-

---

[4] The lecture was on Dec. 1, 1939. I should add that the Boston *Evening Globe*, in an editorial on it on Dec. 4, spelled out the word.

[5] Partridge traces it in English use to 1712. [The larval *bicchessone* is found in the Fourteenth Century poem Arthur and Merlin.]

[6] [For this I am indebted to William S. Price, of the University of Tulsa.]

[7] The cognate *s.o.a.b.* is embalmed in the name *Soab* Creek, on a map issued by the Canadian Geological Survey.

man in Palermo thinks up a dozen better ones between breakfast and the noon whistle. Worse, it is frequently transmogrified into the childish *son of a gun*. The latter is so lacking in punch that the Italians among us have borrowed it as a satirical name for an American: *la sanemagogna* is what they call him, and by it they indicate their contempt for his backwardness in the art that is one of their great glories. In Standard Italian there are no less than forty congeners of *son of a bitch,* and each and every one of them is more opprobrious, more brilliant, more effective. In the Neapolitan dialect there are thousands.

VII

The Pronunciation of
American

1: ITS GENERAL CHARACTERISTICS

The fact that there are differences between the way the average literate American speaks and the way the average literate Englishman speaks has long been noted. Many of these differences have to do with vocabulary, and some are so striking that they inevitably attract attention. But these differences are not as important as they used to be.

The differences in pronunciation, however, show a higher degree of resistance to change. They extend to many common words, *e.g.*, *can't*, *deficit* and *secretary*. The Englishman, using the first of these, gives it a broad *a* that is rare in the United States save in those areas—for example, the Boston region and the swankier suburbs of New York—where emulation of English usage is still potent in speechways. In words of the *deficit* class the difference is one of stress rather than of vowel quality, for the Englishman puts the accent on the second syllable, whereas the American commonly stresses the first. In *secretary* what the Englishman does is to get rid of a syllable altogether, so that the word becomes, to American ears, *secretry;* the American himself almost always gives it four syllables, and lays a slight but unmistakable second stress on the third, which he rhymes with *care*.

The last difference is typical of many others, for American speech, on the whole, follows the spelling more faithfully than English speech. Why this should be so is not known with any assurance, though a great many persons have put forth confident theories.

My own guess is that Americans speak more distinctly than Englishmen largely because their speechways were molded, for four generations, by

Noah Webster's famous Spelling-Book. From 1783, when it was first published, until the beginning of the Twentieth Century, it was the most widely circulated book in the country,[1] and the most influential. Indeed, it was the only work on language that the average American ever saw, or even heard of. It had no traffic with slurring, but insisted that all words be pronounced as Jahveh had spelled them out to Adam and Eve in the Garden of Eden, or to the sons of Noah after the Flood.[2] Webster gave *secretary* four syllables, and noted that there was what he called "a half accent" on the third; he insisted upon full *r*'s in such words as *fire* and *fore*, *heart* and *cargo;* he frowned upon pronouncing *bounteous* as *bountcheous*, and he even insisted upon spelling pronunciations in such proper names as *Norfolk*, *Thames* and *Greenwich*.[3]

But Webster was only giving voice and momentum to what was really a spontaneous natural tendency. The Americans were a highly matter-of-fact people, and could see nothing save folly in English pronunciations, especially the affected ones that became fashionable in England during the latter half of the Eighteenth Century. Those pronunciations arose in the court circles of London, were adopted by the more pretentious sort of actors and were propagated and given standing by the pronouncing dictionaries of Thomas Sheridan (1780) and John Walker (1791), both of whom had been actors and teachers of elocution before they put on the shroud of the lexicographer.[4] But in the United States such dubious authorities were combatted earnestly by the peppery Webster, and in consequence they were impeded in making converts for their stretched vowels and macerated consonants. Eighteenth Century Englishmen, accustomed to gross barbarisms the moment they got out of the ambits of the court, the theaters and the two universities at home, were astonished to discover that nearly all Americans talked alike, on the lower as well as the higher levels of society, and that their talk was generally clear and hence easily understood. There were, of course, some differences, and Webster himself often gave evidence that he was a New Englander and not a Southerner, but such differences were not numerous. Save for a few oddities in vocabulary, it was possible to understand any man encountered along the road, even in the Far South

---

[1] Down to 1814 it had sold more than 3,000,000 copies, and down to 1889, 62,000,000. Mrs. Emily E. F. Skeel, Webster's great-granddaughter, tells me that there were 304 editions before 1829. It is still in print.

[2] See Etymology, Anglo-Saxon, and Noah Webster, by Charlton Laird, *AS*, Vol. XXI, Feb. 1946, pp. 3-15.

[3] *Worcester*, to be sure, stumped him, and though he rejected *Wooster* he was willing to compromise on *Worster*. Also, he allowed that it was best to pronounce *Mishilimackanac* as if it were spelled *Mackinaw*. He spelled and pronounced *Chicago Chickaugo*.

[4] An elaborate and excellent study of the subject is in Standards of English Pronunciation According to the Grammarians of the 16th, 17th and 18th Centuries, by Esther K. Sheldon, diss. (MS), U. of Wisconsin, 1938. [See also E. J. Dobson, English Pronunciation, 1500-1700, 2 vols., Oxford 1957; and Hans Kurath's forthcoming study.]

or beyond the Alleghanies, and there was nothing anywhere that could be reasonably compared to the gnarled and difficult local dialects of Somerset, Lancashire and Yorkshire, to say nothing of Scotland and Wales, or of proletarian London.[5]

Such impressions of American pronunciation continued until near the end of the century, when the London reviews launched that ill-humored war upon American speechways which has gone on ever since. Even the unhappy success of the Revolution did not provoke the attack, for the English, during the decade following Yorktown, seem to have entertained some hope that the wayward colonies might return. Indeed, there were Englishmen who spoke favorably of American speech while the struggle was actually going on: the otherwise bitterly anti-American Jonathan Boucher wrote on December 23, 1777, that "in North America there prevails not only, I believe, the purest pronunciation of the English tongue that is anywhere to be met with, but a perfect uniformity." So late as 1791 the editor of an English reprint of Dr. David Ramsay's "History of the American Revolution" was moved to say in this preface:

> It is a curious fact that there is perhaps no one portion of the British empire in which two or three millions of persons are to be found who speak their mother tongue with greater purity or a truer pronunciation than the white inhabitants of the United States. This was attributed, by a penetrating observer, to the number of British subjects assembled in America from various quarters, who, in consequence of their intercourse and intermarriages, soon dropped the peculiarities of their several provincial idioms, retaining only what was fundamental and common to them all—a process which the frequency or rather the universality of school-learning in America must naturally have assisted.[6]

This Englishman's surmise as to the cause of the uniformity of speech visible in the United States is supported by the fact that immigration from one state to another has been active since the earliest days. Today it is a commonplace that the population of the big cities is made up largely of native Americans born elsewhere, and to a considerable extent in distant states. But the early leveling of dialects was more than a mere amalgamation, for the resultant general speech of the country was influenced much

---

[5] See Sir Charles Lyell, Travels in America in the Years 1841-42, New York, 1852; and two studies by Allen Walker Read, Amphi-Atlantic English, *English Studies*, Oct. 1935, pp. 161-78, and British Recognition of American Speech in the Eighteenth Century, *DN*, Vol. VI, Pt. VI, 1933, pp. 313-34.

[6] Ramsay, a native Pennsylvanian, made his career in South Carolina as a physician. From 1782 to 1786 he was a member of the Continental Congress, and during the last two years its president. Besides his History of the American Revolution, first published in 1789, he wrote a History of South Carolina, a History of the United States and a biography of Washington.

more by several of the British dialects than by all the rest. The preponderance of opinion seems to be that American English, at least in the North, got most of its characteristics from the speech of the southeastern counties of England. Said John Fiske in "The Beginnings of New England": "Perhaps it would not be far out of the way to say that two-thirds of the American people who can trace their ancestry to New England might follow it back to the East Anglian shires of the mother-country; one-sixth might follow it to those southwestern counties—Devonshire, Dorset and Somerset—which so long were foremost in maritime enterprise; one-sixth to other parts of England." [7] This is confirmed by Anders Orbeck, whose study of the Seventeenth Century town records of Massachusetts [8] leads him to conclude that if "Essex, Middlesex and London, as well as Norfolk, Suffolk, Cambridgeshire, Northamptonshire, Bedfordshire and Hertfordshire" are included in the East Anglian counties, slightly over 71% of the pioneers of Plymouth, Watertown and Dedham who can be traced came from that area. Further confirmation is provided by Read, who has shown that the Americans of the early Eighteenth Century were quick to notice peculiarities in the speech of recent immigrants from the British Isles, but saw nothing to remark in that of those who came from east of Wiltshire or south of the Wash.[9] The East Anglian theory is supported more or less by many familiar New England place names, *e.g.*, *Yarmouth*, *Ipswich*, *Haverhill* and the nearby (in England) *Cambridge* and *Boston*. In his "Americanisms: The English of the New World," Schele de Vere declared flatly that the early New England immigrants brought from Norfolk and Suffolk "not only their words, which the Yankee still uses, but also a sound of the voice and a mode of utterance which have been faithfully preserved, and are now spoken of as the 'New England drawl' and 'the high, metallic ring of the New England voice.' " [1] In another place, he said that Southern disregard for the letter *r* should be laid upon "the shoulders of the guilty forefathers, many of whom came from Suffolk and the districts belonging to the East Anglians." [2]

Hans Kurath, director of the Linguistic Atlas, agrees insofar as the coastal South is concerned. "Like the seaboard of New England," he says, "the Tidewater region of Virginia received most of its early population from Southeastern England." [3] Krapp [4] and others hold that in the South "the

---

[7] Boston and New York, 1889, p. 63.
[8] Early New England Pronunciation; Ann Arbor, Mich., 1927, p. 129.
[9] The Assimilation of the Speech of British Immigrants in Colonial America, *JEGP*, Vol. XXXVII, Jan. 1938, pp. 70–9.
[1] Schele de Vere, p. 427.
[2] *Ibid.*, p. 627. The old kingdom of East

Anglia comprised the present counties of Norfolk and Suffolk and part of Cambridgeshire.
[3] The Origin of Dialectal Differences in Spoken American English, *MP*, Vol. XXV, May 1928, p. 391.
[4] Krapp, Vol. I, pp. 248 *ff*., Vol. II, p. 226.

speech of the Negro and the white is essentially the same" and that what are commonly regarded as "specifically Negro forms" are often only "older English forms which the Negro must have originally taken from the white man, and which he has retained after the white man has begun to lose them." [5] Tidewater Southern differs in many ways from this bi-racial lingo, but it is confined to a relatively limited area, radiating from the lowlands to such inland islands as Richmond, Charlottesville and the northern Shenandoah Valley, but hardly extending beyond. Tidewater Southern, like the dialect of the narrow Boston area and that of the lower Hudson Valley, appears to have been considerably influenced by the fashionable London English of the Eighteenth Century. The reason is obvious. These regions, from the earliest days, maintained a closer contact with England than the other parts of the country, and their accumulation of wealth filled them with social aspiration and made them especially responsive to upper-class example. The Civil War shifted the money of the South from the Tidewater to the Piedmont, but the conservative lowland gentry continued faithful to the speechways acquired in their days of glory, and the plain people followed them. But all the more recent intrusions of English ways of speech have entered in the Boston and New York areas and on the level of conscious Anglomania.

There remains the speech of the overwhelming majority of Americans —according to some authorities, at least 120,000,000 of the 180,000,000 inhabitants of the continental United States. Once called General American, it is described by George L. Trager as "the pronunciation . . . of the whole country except the old South, New England, and the immediate vicinity of New York City." [6] More, it is constantly spreading, and two of its salient traits, the flat *a* and the clearly sounded *r*, are making heavy inroads in the territories once faithful to the broad *a* and the silent *r*. "Only in the immediate neighborhood of Boston and in the greater part of New Hampshire and Maine," says Bernard Bloch, "is the so-called Eastern pronunciation universal," and even in this region there are speech islands in which it is challenged.[7] New England west of the Connecticut River speaks pre-

---

[5] Cleanth Brooks, The Relation of the Alabama-Georgia Dialect to the Provincial Dialects of Great Britain, *Louisiana State University Studies*, No. 20, Baton Rouge, 1935, pp. 63–4.
[6] The Pronunciation of Short *a* in American Standard English, *AS*, Vol. V, June 1930, p. 396.
[7] Postvocalic *r* in New England Speech: A Study in American Dialect Geography, *Acts of the Fourth International Congress of Linguists*, Copenhagen, 1936, p. 198. [In the last thirty years research for the LA has disclosed that the so-called "General American" area is really made up of two major dialects: one, Inland Northern, based on the speech of western New England and upstate New York; the other, Midland, based on the speech of Pennsylvania and its derivatives. Both Inland Northern and Midland differ in much the same ways from Coastal Southern, Eastern New England and British Received Pronunciation, but the differences between the two are striking.]

dominantly like the northern Midwest, and so does all of New York State save the suburbs of New York.

What, then, was the origin of this widespread and now thoroughly typical form of speech, and why is it prevailing against all other forms? "The Piedmont of Virginia and the Carolinas, and the Great Valley," says Kurath, "were largely settled, during the half-century preceding the Revolution, by the Scotch-Irish, who spoke . . . the English of the Lowlands of Scotland and the north of England as modified by the Southern English Standard. They neither dropped their *r*'s nor did they pronounce their long mid-vowels diphthongal fashion. The large German element from Pennsylvania ultimately acquired this type of English." Moreover, it also found lodgment in western New England, which received a considerable admixture of Scotch-Irish during the same period, and the speechways of the region soon "became established in New York State and in the Western Reserve of Ohio," and thence moved into the whole of the opening West. Unquestionably, this influence of Scotch-Irish example was powerful all along the frontier, and even nearer the coast it must have had some effect, for many of the early schoolmasters were Scotsmen or Irishmen. Later tides of pedagogy considerably reinforced the movement away from the southeastern English speechways of the Atlantic seaboard and toward those of the Scottish lowlands and the English North. The original Scottish schoolmasters, to be sure, did not long outlast the Eighteenth Century, nor did the Irishmen who followed them. By the time the great movement into the West was well under way both were beginning to be displaced by native young men, and before the Civil War these men [8] were giving way in their turn to females. Not many of the latter, in their primeval form, had any education beyond that of the common schools they taught in; the great majority, indeed, were simply milkmaids armed with hickory sticks. They could thus muster up no authority of their own, but had to depend perforce upon that of the books in their hands—and the book that was there invariably, before and above all others, was the aforesaid Speller of Noah Webster. When it got any support at all, it was usually from his unfolding series of dictionaries.

Webster was not a Bostonian, and his central purpose was "to deliver . . . my countrymen from the errors that fashion and ignorance" were seeking to introduce from England.[9] He advocated clarity and consistency in utterance, and was against all the vowel changes, sacrifice of consonants and

---

[8] It was almost the rule, between 1800 and 1835, for poor young men to earn their way through college by teaching school, and large numbers continued until they were ripe for politics or one of the professions.

[9] Quoted by George H. McKnight in Modern English in the Making; New York, 1928, p. 484.

other perversions that were imitated from contemporary English usage. He was opposed to the artificial *Bühnenaussprache* that Sheridan had introduced and that Walker was soon to reinforce, for his opinion of actors was almost as low as his opinion of political and theological rhetoricians.[1] He thus gave powerful support to the northern British influences—always in favor of relatively precise utterance—that were operating upon American speech west of the Hudson, and he was supported in turn by the natural tendency of hard-driven pioneers to say what they had to say in very plain language.[2] The schoolma'am, without doubt, found it difficult to induce her pupils to speak with any elegance, just as her heirs find it difficult today, but she taught them to articulate clearly and her efforts were vastly facilitated by the popularity of the spelling class and the spelling bee, which broke up words into their component parts, and gave every part its full value.

The schoolmen were aided by what may be described as the influence of a class but lately risen in the social scale and hence a bit unsure of itself— a class intensely eager to avoid giving away its vulgar origin by its speech habits. The great historical changes in Standard English, says Wyld,[3] were synchronous with the appearance of new "classes of the population in positions of prominence and power in the state, and the consequent reduction in the influence of the older government classes." Some of the events that produced such shifts in the balance of power were: "the break-up of the feudal system, the extinction of most of the ancient baronial families in the War of the Roses, the disendowment of the monasteries, and the enriching of the King's tools and agents; the rise of the great merchants in the towns; the Parliamentary wars and the social upheaval of the Protectorate; the rise of banking during the Eighteenth and early Nineteenth Centuries." Precision in speech became the hallmark of those who had but recently arrived. Obviously, the number of those who have but recently arrived has always been greater in the United States than in England, not only among the aristocracy of wealth and fashion but also among the intelligentsia. The average American schoolma'am, our chief guardian of linguistic niceness, does not come from a tradition of culture, but from the class of small farmers and city clerks and workmen. This is true even of the average American college teacher. Such persons do not advocate and practice pre-

---

[1] Brander Matthews says in Essays on English, New York, 1921, p. 216, that the German *Bühnenaussprache* was revised in 1898 by a committee consisting of five professors of language and six actors and managers. American actors of the tonier sort still use some of the traditional pronunciations of the English stage.

[2] Said C. K. Thomas in *QJS Ed.*, Vol. XIII, Nov. 1927, p. 452: "The West, since it grew up with its attention on more urgent questions than niceties of speech, developed a more natural type, mainly free from the artificialities of polite speech."

[3] Wyld, pp. 18 *ff*.

cision in speech on logical grounds alone; they are also moved by the belief that it tends to conceal their own cultural insecurity. From them come most of the gratuitous rules and regulations that afflict schoolboys and harass the writers of the country. But it would be a mistake to think of their influence as wholly evil. They have thrown themselves valiantly against the rise of dialects, with such success that nothing so grossly unpleasant to the ear as the Cockney whine or so lunatic as the Cockney manhandling of the *h* is now prevalent anywhere in the United States. And they have policed the general speech to such effect that even on its most pretentious levels it is virtually free from the silly affectations of Standard English.

The beginnings of this prevailing speech of the country apparently date from the Revolution,[4] but until the closing years of the Eighteenth Century it seems to have attracted little notice. Even the alert and far from amiable John Witherspoon, writing from his rectoral stool at Princeton in 1781, had little to say about the pronunciation of Americans. And what little he said was mainly favorable, perhaps because he was a Scotsman. The true British aversion began to show itself soon after the War of 1812, when such travelers as Frances Trollope denounced the American accent as well as the American vocabulary:

> I very seldom during my whole stay in the country heard a sentence elegantly turned and correctly pronounced from the lips of an American. There is always something either in the expression or the accent that jars the feelings and shocks the taste.

The patriots of the time met these sneers with claims that the American accent was not only quite as good as the English but much better. Said James Fenimore Cooper in "Notions of the Americans": [5]

> The people of the United States, with the exception of a few of German or French descent, speak, as a body, incomparably better English than the people of the mother country. . . . In fine, we speak our language, as a nation, better than any other people speak their language.

But after this show of independence Cooper joined the group of native Americans who set up the doctrine that the only right way to speak English was the ever-changing way of the English upper classes. Benjamin Franklin seems to have inclined to this idea, perhaps because he had spent

---

[4] See Eilert Ekwall, American and British Pronunciation; Uppsala, 1946, pp. 29 and 32.

[5] London, 2 vols., 1828, as "By a Travelling Bachelor," but later acknowledged by Cooper. The quotations are from Vol. II, Letter VII.

so much time in England.[6] Irving, always eager for English notice and favor, ran the same way. Nor is there any evidence that any other American authors of the pre-Civil War era greatly resented the notion that spoken American, save for the differences in vocabulary, should conform to English standards. The first Americans to give the language of the country serious study were William C. Fowler and George P. Marsh; Fowler published "The English Language in Its Elements and Forms" in 1850, and Marsh followed with "Lectures on the English Language" in 1859. Fowler, a son-in-law of Noah Webster, was professor of rhetoric at Amherst and the first Northern pedagogue to undertake courses in Old English.[7] Marsh was a Vermonter who went in for politics and rose to high office, but he had many outside interests. Fowler distinguished between the language of New England, that of the South and that of the rising West, but predicted that "the system of school education, and the use of the same textbooks in the institutions of learning, and of the same periodicals and reading books in families—in short, the mighty power of the press" would eventually iron out these differences and make "the people of America one in language as one in government." [8] He was willing to be polite to English example on the higher levels of speech, but he argued that "the great mass of the people of the United States speak and write their vernacular tongue with more correctness than the common people of England." Marsh took much the same position, but he noted and deplored "a marked difference of accent" already separating the speech of the two countries.[9]

But it would be unjust to accuse Marsh of advocating an abject conformity to English standards. The first to do that in an all-out and undisguised manner was Richard Grant White, who apologized most humbly for occasional criticisms of English usage, saying that "no insinuation of a superiority in the use of their mother tongue by men of English race in 'America' is intended, no right to set up an independent standard is implied." [1]

White was challenged by a number of other writers on speech, but the most refined opinion of his time seems to have supported him, and his books remained authorities for many years. He received a heavy reinforcement in 1905, when Henry James, the novelist, broke his voluntary exile in England long enough to harangue the year's graduating class at Bryn Mawr

---

[6] On Sept. 27, 1760, he wrote from London to David Hume: "I hope . . . that we shall always in America make the best English of this island our standard, and I believe it will be so."

[7] This was in 1841. It had been taught at Randolph-Macon College since 1839 and at the University of Virginia since 1825.

[8] p. 94.

[9] Lectures on the English Language; 4th ed., revised and enlarged; New York, 1870, p. 676.

[1] Words and Their Uses; New York, 1870; a collection of essays first published in *Galaxy* in 1867, 1868 and 1869.

College on the evils of American speech.[2] James was no phonologist, and it was apparent that his notion of the speechways of his native land was picked up, not by direct observation, but by a study of the barbarisms credited to Americans in the English comic papers, *e.g.*, *popper, vanillar, vurry, Amurrica, tullegram* and even *Philadulphia.* He had, however, high prestige as a writer and imitated very effectively the lofty air of an Oxford don, so his ill-natured remarks made a considerable impression. So late as 1916, Fred Newton Scott was telling the National Council of Teachers of English that "almost everyone who touches upon American speech assumes that it is inferior to British speech." [3]

Scott was wrong here, as he was wrong in other matters, for philologians of more weight than he were already declaring for American autonomy in pronunciation. Louise Pound had noted the plain fact that English and American had already developed too many differences to "be treated as orally identical." She expressed the pious hope that these differences would not lead, at least in the near future, to a complete separation of the two tongues, but she saw clearly that they were bound to "increase, not lessen." Other experts on the national speechways soon joined her, and in recent years nearly all the better texts on pronunciation accept American English as it is, and avoid any vain attempt to bring it into harmony with current English standards. Krapp declared: [4] "It seems scarcely credible that one who knows the facts should think it possible to impose British standards upon American speech." To which may be added the verdict of a special committee appointed by the Modern Language Association to draw up a report on "The English Language in American Education":

> Contemporary linguistic science views . . . American English not as a corruption but as the accepted English of the United States. . . . The most practical pedagogical conclusion involved is that wherever the spelling, pronunciation, vocabulary and usage of the two great branches of the language differ, American students should be taught the American rather than the British form. . . . The English our American

---

[2] His address was delivered on June 8 and got a great deal of attention in the newspapers. It was printed in The Question of Our Speech; Boston and New York, 1905. [In Henry James and the American Language, *Transactions of the Wisconsin Academy of Sciences, Arts and Letters,* Vol. XLIX, Dec. 1960, pp. 237–47, Donald Emerson argues that James was really not unsympathetic to-

ward American speech patterns. This argument still leaves the overt effrontery to be explained.]

[3] Presidential address in New York, Dec. 1; it was printed in *EJ*, Vol. VI, Jan. 1917, and reprinted in The Standard of American Speech and Other Papers; Boston, 1926.

[4] The Pronunciation of Standard English in America; New York, 1919, p. x.

students should be helped to master is the standard English spoken and written in contemporary America.[5]

In 1927, C. K. Thomas. of Cornell, now of the University of Florida,[6] summarized professional opinion under five headings:

1. Is there a world standard of English pronunciation?
2. What claim has the speech of southern England to be considered a world standard?
3. What claim has the speech of southern England to be considered the standard for America?
4. Is there a distinct American national standard?
5. What are the criteria of a good standard?

Thomas found that the answer to the first question was no. He could find no trace of a generally acknowledged world standard. A few phonologists of small authority favored "the worldwide acceptance of the southern English standard," but all the rest seemed to favor national autonomy, and to regard it as inevitable. To the second question the answer was none. There were English authorities, to be sure, who defended Standard English as superior to any other form of the language, but there were other authorities, greater in number and fully equal in learning, who denounced it as one of the worst. The answer to the third question was likewise none. "The preponderance of authority," concluded Thomas, "is strongly against community of standard for British and American pronunciation." In answer he described the three major varieties of American then recognized—the Boston–New York, the Southern and the Western or General—and agreed with Kenyon and Krapp that the last-named was already dominant and showed plain indications of increasing its area and authority. The answer to the last question resolved itself into a plea for letting nature take its course. "A good standard," said Thomas, "is a natural growth, not a manufactured article, and attempts to improve on this standard are like attempts to graft wings on human shoulders." In other words, the voice of the people, in the last analysis, must decide and determine the voice of the people.

Unconscious of the monotony of their speech tunes and of the nasalization which offends Englishmen, Americans today clearly believe that their way of using English is better than the English way. In consequence, there is little imitation of the English usage, which the average American regards as effeminate and absurd. There was a time when all American actors of

[5] Published by the Association's Committee on Trends in Education; New York, 1945. The quotation is from pp. 5–6.

[6] Recent Discussions of Standardization in American Pronunciation *QJS Ed.*, Vol. XIII, Nov. 1927, pp. 442–57.

any pretensions employed a dialect that was a heavy imitation of the dialect of the West End actors of London. It was taught in all the American dramatic schools, and at the beginning of the present century it was so prevalent on the American stage that a flat *a* had a melodramatic effect almost equal to that of *damn*. But the rise of the movies broke down this convention. They attracted actors from all parts of the world, to many of whom English was a foreign language, and when the talkies followed it was found that most of these newcomers had picked up ordinary American. Moreover, the native-born recruits were mainly without formal professional training, so the majority of them also spoke the vulgate. From time to time Hollywood has made some effort to model its speech on that of its English-born luminaries, but never with much success.

The early radio announcers were not altogether to blame for their unhappy tendency to imitate English speech, for they were under pressure from various prophets of refinement, some of them of apparent authority. Part of this pressure came by way of the theater and the movies, which still followed, more or less, the traditional stage pronunciations. When the American Academy of Arts and Letters began offering medals to actors for chaste and genteel diction, it soon became apparent that those following English models were favored, for among the early winners were George Arliss and Julia Marlowe. Meanwhile, the showmen's weekly, *Billboard*, had employed a speech corrector named Windsor P. Daggett to police the pronunciation of public performers of all sorts, and he argued eloquently for the pseudo-English standard.[7] But public opinion turned out to be strongly against any movement to extend this artificial polish to the speech of the current announcers, commentators and crooners. On February 4, 1931, the Columbia Broadcasting System sought to allay the uproar by setting up a school for announcers and appointing Frank H. Vizetelly as its head. Vizetelly was born in London and lived there until he was well into his twenties, but he was no advocate of Oxford English and at once announced to his students that he was eager to "help in spreading the best traditions of American speech."

The effects of Vizetelly's pedagogy were soon visible, and in a little while the effort to talk like English actors was only a memory in the CBS studios. On his death he was succeeded by W. Cabell Greet, who listened to broadcasts at the heroic rate of 600 a month and kept his ears open for slipshod or affected pronunciations. In 1939, after two years of this service, he summed up his observations:

> Listeners are the arbiters of [the announcer's] success, and they have not hesitated to criticize. . . . Most listeners nowadays will sympathize

---

[7] The Spoken Word, *Billboard*, Apr. 4, 1928.

with an announcer who is in revolt against the pseudo-correctness and the insincere voice of the typical announcers of the 20s, who were encouraged in their fake culture by the Academy's medal for good diction.[8]

The National Broadcasting Company followed CBS by recruiting James F. Bender, director of the speech and hearing clinic at Queens College, Flushing, L.I., and speech clinician at the Vanderbilt Clinic, New York, and the New York Post-Graduate Medical School and Hospital. Bender turned out to be an advocate, like Greet, of American standards. He ordained the flat *a* in *dance, grass, aunt*, etc., a clear terminal *r*, the retention of every syllable in such words as *secretary* and the American pronunciations in *schedule, laboratory*, etc.[9] His labors, following those of Vizetelly and Greet, unquestionably influenced many American broadcasters, but others, especially among the more vapid news commentators, still affect something they take to be the English standard.

In the early days of the British Broadcasting Corporation (BBC), most of its announcers and commentators affected a somewhat extreme form of Oxford English. There were, in consequence, a great many protests from listeners in the North of England and in Scotland and Ireland, to whom this dialect was as strange, and indeed as offensive, as it would have been to Americans. In response to their protests the BBC appointed, in 1926, an Advisory Committee on Spoken English headed by the Poet Laureate, Robert Bridges, organizer in 1913 of the Society for Pure English and a diligent student of speechways. Among the Committee's members were George Bernard Shaw, H. C. K. Wyld, Dame Rose Macaulay, Lord David Cecil, Lady Cynthia Asquith, Lascelles Abercrombie and I. A. Richards. It also had the advice and comfort of professional phonologists. These last leaned, generally speaking, to the southern form of English, but some of the members, *e.g.*, Shaw and Bridges, were tart critics of it, and in consequence modifications were tolerated. [The Committee perished in World War II and subsequent decisions of the BBC have been purely *ad hoc*.]

So long ago as 1910, sixteen years before he was recruited, Bridges described Oxford English as "a degraded form."[1] What chiefly aroused his

---

[8] The Announcers Have a Word for It, *Broadcasting*, Oct. 15, 1939, pp. 24, 62. [In World War II, Greet prepared War Words, a manual showing the correct pronunciation of the multitudinous foreign place names in the news. Issued in 1943, it was reprinted the following year as World Words; a second edition appeared in 1948.]

[9] He is the author of the NBC Handbook of Pronunciation, [which had reached a second edition by 1951].

[1] His essay was first published in *Essays and Studies by Members of the English Association*, edited by A. C. Bradley. It was revised and republished as A Tract on the Present State of English Pronunciation; Oxford, 1913.

indignation was its slaughter of the final *r* in such words as *danger, pleasure, character* and *terror*. Shaw occasionally broke into the newspapers with general assaults upon Oxford English,[2] but it was seldom possible to make out just what he objected to. Various other Britons, including not a few 100% Englishmen, have criticized the Oxford dialect. But not many of these dissident Britons commend American pronunciation. Its monotonous speech tunes commonly seem unpleasantly drawling to their ears, and they are jarred by its frequent nasalization of vowels. As a Cockney once said after suffering an American movie: "It ain't so much their bleedin' leng-widge; it's their blawsted neysal tweng."

Nearly all the accepted speech experts of England stand up bravely for Oxford English, or for something closely resembling it. Daniel Jones, professor emeritus of phonetics at University College, London, describes it complacently as the Received Pronunciation (RP), and says that it is the form "usually heard in everyday speech in the families of Southern English people who have been educated at the public schools," among "those who do not come from the South of England but who have been educated in these schools" and, "to an extent which is considerable though difficult to specify, from natives of Southern England who have not been educated in these schools." [3] He disclaims any intent to depict it "as intrinsically better or more beautiful than any other form of pronunciation," but all the same he is for it. So, too, though with certain prudent reservations, was his colleague on the BBC board A. Lloyd James, professor of phonetics at the University of London.[4] So, to make an end, was Henry Cecil Wyld, professor of the English language and literature at Oxford and author of many books on the history of English speech. Wyld said that it might be called Good English, Well-Bred English or Upper-Class English, but he preferred to call it simply Received Standard English.[5] He described it as "easy, unstudied and natural," with "sonorous" vowels, each of them clearly differentiated from all the others, diphthongs of high "carry-power and dignity" and clearly articulated consonants.

Wyld, so far as I know, never ventured into the American wilderness, but Jones made the trip in 1925 and James in 1936. Jones gave a course in phonetics at Smith College, and seems to have made a hit with the ladies of the faculty, for one of them testified afterward that he was very polite

---

[2] For example, in the London *Times*, Jan. 25, 1934.

[3] [An English Pronouncing Dictionary; 11th ed., completely revised, enlarged, brought up to date and reset; London, 1960, p. xv.] He explains in a footnote that he means *"public school* in the English sense, not in the American sense." The difference is shown in Chapter VI of this work.

[4] The Broadcast Word; London, 1935, pp. 153–72.

[5] Wyld, p. 2; The Best English: A Claim for the Superiority of Received Standard English, *SPE Tract*, No. XXXIX, Oxford, 1934, p. 614.

about American English and "never antagonized the most tender-minded of us." [6]

Wyld described Received Standard as "the product of social conditions," showed how its origins went back to the Sixteenth Century, when, for the first time, "difference was recognized between upper-class English and the language of the humbler order of people." [7] It was, he said, by no means a regional dialect, despite the fact that it was often called Southern English. It was actually spoken by the upper social class, with inconsiderable local modifications, all over England. "Perhaps the main factor in this singular degree of uniformity," he went on, "is the custom of sending youths from certain social strata to the great public schools. If we were to say that Received English is Public School English we should not be far wrong." H. C. Macnamara, in 1938, described it as "the language necessary for all English boys who aspire to be archbishops, field-marshals, Lords of Appeal, butlers and radio announcers." [8] Macnamara's mention of butlers was a true hit, for the fashionable English pronunciation falls very short of being learned. Indeed, some of its characteristics suggest the paddock far more forcibly than they suggest the grove of Athene. Nor does every Englishman of high position affect it. Even Sir Winston Churchill, though he kept close enough to it in his heyday to enrapture American Anglomaniacs, ameliorated its rigors sufficiently to avoid alarming the plain people.

The nature of the differences between Wyld's Received Standard English and Midwestern American have been discussed at length by various authorities, particularly by Palmer, Martin and Blandford in their "Dictionary of English Pronunciation with American Variants." [9] They dis-

[6] Standards of English, by Elizabeth Avery, *AS*, Vol. I, Apr. 1926, p. 367.

[7] Wyld, pp. 2–3.

[8] Is There an American Language?; Hong Kong, 1938. [The Welfare State is perhaps more insistent on imposing Received Pronunciation than was the traditional English society of orders and degrees. A news story in *The New York Times*, Aug. 7, 1959, headed English Children to Be Taught to Speak Their Native Tongue, spoke of the use of mechanical aids in helping to erase undesirable traits, such as Cockneyisms and Americanisms. According to Vance Packard (The Status Seekers, New York, 1961, p. 12), the mastery of RP (as it is generally called) is necessary for a successful career as a naval officer. Problems of evaluating RP are discussed by John Spencer, *Lingua*, Vol. VII, Nov. 1957, pp. 7–29. The status symbols of upper-class British speech have been copiously discussed in the last decade, so that the terms *U* and *non-U* are widely known; the discussion was initiated by Alan Ross in Upper-Class English Usage, *Neuphilologische Mitteilungen* (Helsinki), Vol. LV, 1954, pp. 20–56, and amplified by Nancy Mitford in *Encounter*, Sept. 1955, and by Josef Vachek in On Social Differentiation of English Speech Habits, *Philologica Pragensis*, Ročnik III, Dec. 1960, pp. 222–7. The relative status of various styles of British pronunciation is urbanely discussed by David Abercrombie, in *English Language Teaching*, Vol. VII, Summer 1953, pp. 113–23; in Problems and Principles, Studies in the Teaching of English as a Second Language, London, 1956, he points out that outside England RP carries no privileges.]

[9] pp. xxxvii–xlvii.

tinguish twelve major variants and fourteen minor ones, and for the 20,000-odd terms (including inflections and derivatives) that they list in their vocabulary they note differences in more than 5,000. Their twelve major variants may be reduced to six classes, as follows:

1. The English *o* in such words as *hot, box* and *stop* becomes "a vowel more or less approximating" the broad English *a* of *ask* and *path*.
2. This English *a* is replaced by flat *a* in both of these words, and also in many others, *e.g., half, brass* and *last*.
3. The *r* following vowels, whether or not it is itself followed by consonants, is pronounced more clearly than in English.
4. There is a difference between the English *u* in such words as *hurry, worry* and *thorough* and the prevailing American *u*.[1]
5. The *-ary* at the end of a word has a clear *a* sound, whereas the English reduce it to the neutral vowel or omit it altogether.
6. So with *-ory*.

Palmer and his collaborators also note many minor variants, *e.g.,* the English pronunciation of *clerk* as *clark*, of *ate* as *et* (a vulgarism in the United States except among the proper Charlestonians), of *lieutenant* as *leftenant* and of *schedule* with its first syllable showing the *sh* of *she*. Finally, they show that it is sometimes difficult to find any logical pattern or general tendency in a major variation between English and American speech. Thus, if we take the phrase "Mr. Martin of Birmingham," and ask an Englishman and an American to speak it, the Englishman will reduce the *-ham* of *Birmingham* to a sort of *'m* but pronounce the second syllable of *Martin* distinctly, whereas the American will reduce *Martin* to *Mart'n* but give a clear pronunciation to the *-ham*. Here Englishman and American head both ways, and without apparent rhyme or reason. It would not be difficult, indeed, to make up a short list of words in which the typical American pronunciation is what one might expect to find in Standard English, and vice versa. This is true even in the matter of stress, where there are plenty of exceptions to the stronger American tendency to throw the accent forward. But in general the prevailing tendencies in the two forms of the language are pretty well maintained, both in the values given to letters and in the placing of stress. Thus when an American hears *laboratory* or *doctrinal* with the accent on the second syllable and *artisan* or *intestinal* with the accent on the third,[2] he gathers at once that he is not listening to a compatriot. In this field even the most colonial-minded Bostonian commonly speaks American.

[1] See Notes on the Pronunciation of *Hurry,* by C. K. Thomas, *AS,* Vol. XXI, Apr. 1946, pp. 112-15.

[2] I am indebted here to a list prepared in 1945 by Dr. James F. Bender.

The movement of stress toward the first syllable, of course, is by no means of American origin. It has been going on in English since Chaucer's day and there has been a considerable acceleration since the Eighteenth Century. Kökeritz has shown [3] that in 1723 *alcove, balcony, bombast, confiscate* and *expert* were all stressed on the second syllable, and that these pronunciations survived at least until 1791,[4] along with the accentuation of *advertise, complaisance, fornicator* and *paramount* on the third syllable. But his study offers proof of a number of forward shifts between 1723 and 1791, *e.g., arbitrator, expedite* and *reconcile*, in which the stress moved from the third syllable to the first, and *inbred, mischievous* and *theater*, in which it moved from the second to the first. Rather curiously, he also turns up a few words in which the stress was on the first syllable in 1723, but has since moved back, *e.g., accessory, construe, escheat* and *utensil*. But the prevailing movement is in the other direction, and is still in progress. It is in the United States, however, that the movement seems to have most momentum. I recall *mámma, pápa, ínquiry, céntenary, álly, récess, ídea, álloy* and *ádult;* I might add *défect, éxcess, áddress, súrvey, místache, résearch* and *rómance*. All these words have the accent on the second syllable in the Concise Oxford Dictionary.[5] But American retains a secondary accent in many words that have lost it in English. Most of these end in *-ary, -ery* or *-ory, e.g., necessary, monastery* and *preparatory*. In American the secondary accent in *necessary*, falling upon *ar*, is clearly marked;[6] in England only the primary accent on *nec* is heard, and so the word becomes *néces-s'ry*. In *laboratory*, which the English accent on the second syllable, the secondary accent on the fourth, always heard in American, is likewise omitted, and the word becomes something like *labórat'ry*, in contrast to the American *láboratòry*. The same difference in pronunciation is to be observed in certain words of the *-ative* and *-mony* classes, and in some of those of other classes. In American the secondary accent on *a* in *operative* is always heard, but seldom in English. So with the secondary accent on *mo* in *ceremony:* the third syllable is clearly enunciated in American, but in English everything after *cer* becomes a kind of glissando. So, finally, in *melancholy:* In English it sounds like *melanc'ly*. There is some exchange in fashions of pronunciation across the water. The English, after holding

---

[3] Mather Flint on Early Eighteenth Century English Pronunciation; Uppsala, 1944, pp. 159–60.

[4] His authorities are A Dictionary of All the Words Commonly Us'd in the English Tongue, by Thomas Dyche, London, 1723; and Walker's Dictionary.

[5] [An unfashionable initial stress often appears in individual words in the speech of prominent Americans; *e.g., ée-ficiency* was often said by President Eisenhower.]

[6] [Sometimes a non-Euclidean secondary stress appears, as on the final syllable of *president*, which in the vulgate often rhymes with *tent*, or on the second syllable of *obstacle*, which Mr. Eisenhower rhymed with *tickle*.]

out a while for *armístice*, seem to have yielded to *ármistice* but so far not many Americans have succumbed to the English *áristocrat*.[7] Running against the current, *barráge* and *garáge* survive in the United States against the British *bárrage* and *gárage*. But the American *réveille* balances the account by resisting the English *revéille*, pronounced *revélly*.[8]

"Language," said A. H. Sayce in 1879, "does not consist of letters, but of sounds, and until this fact has been brought home to us our study of it will be little better than an exercise in memory." [9] The theory, at that time, was somewhat strange to English and American grammarians and etymologists; their labors were largely wasted upon deductions from the written word. But since then, chiefly under the influence of Continental philologians, they have turned to the actual sounds of the tongue, and a number of the more recent grammar books are based upon the spoken language of the general body of cultivated folk.[1] Unluckily, this new method also has its disadvantages. The men of a given nation and time usually write a good deal alike, but in their speech there are wide variations. The result is that it is extremely difficult to determine the prevailing pronunciation at any time and place. The persons whose speech is studied pronounce it with minute shades of differences, and admit other differences according as they are conversing naturally or endeavoring to exhibit their pronunciation.

The bare sounds of spoken speech, of course, constitute only one of its characteristics, and that characteristic is a variable quality. Even syllable stress changes more or less with the position of a word in a sentence and with the mood and intent of the speaker. There are students of speech who hold that neither is as important, in distinguishing one dialect from another, as intonation or pitch pattern.[2] When an American hears a strange Englishman speaking it is not the unfamiliar pronunciation that chiefly warns him to be on his guard, nor even the occasional use of unintelligible words; it is the exotic speech tune. "What does an Englishman first notice on landing

---

[7] *AS*, Vol. IX, Apr. 1934, p. 155.

[8] The varying stress in the same word when used as noun or verb, *e.g.*, *prótest* and to *protést*, remains fairly uniform in the standard speech of both countries. See Stress in Recent English as a Distinguishing Mark between Disyllables Used as Noun or Verb, by A. A. Hill, *AS*, Vol. VI, Aug. 1931, pp. 443–8.

[9] Introduction to the Science of Language; 4th ed.; London, 1900, Vol. II, p. 339.

[1] The pioneer was A Grammar of Spoken English, by H. E. Palmer; Cambridge, 1922. [In the United States, of late, a spate of such textbooks has ap-

peared under various auspices, notably the series prepared by the English Language Institute of the University of Michigan, that of the War Department during World War II and that of the American Council of Learned Societies in the 1950s. Most of these are directed toward native speakers of other languages, particularly foreign students in American universities, but the method has possibilities in the slum areas of our cities.]

[2] For example, R. J. Menner, The Pronunciation of English in America, *Atlantic Monthly*, Mar. 1915, p. 366.

in America," asks Hilaire Belloc, "as the contrast between the two sides of the Atlantic so far as the *spoken* language is concerned?" The answer is: "The first thing which strikes him is the violent contrast in intonation." [3] "Though they use the same words," says John Erskine, "the Englishman and the American do not speak the same tune." [4]

Unhappily, there is a good deal of conflict of opinion regarding the precise nature of the difference in intonation between typically English and typically American speech. Some observers report that, to their ears, Englishmen cover a wider range of tone in speaking and carry it higher than Americans; others, while agreeing that Americans pitch their voices within a very narrow range, hold that their gamut lies further up the scale than that of the English. Some think that Englishmen speak the faster, and some believe that Americans do. In each case this may be only fresh evidence of the familiar fact that strange speech always sounds over-fast.

Finally, there is the question of timbre. To most Englishmen, American speech is unpleasantly harsh and unmusical, whereas to most Americans that of Englishmen is throaty and gurgling. These differences not only make it hard, on occasion, to take in the idea sought to be conveyed by a speaker from the wrong side of the Atlantic; they also produce emotional responses that are nearly always hostile, for each dialect has its characteristic speech tunes, and hearing a strange one substituted for a familiar one is always disconcerting and sometimes extremely irritating. There are Englishmen who, in their more reflective moments, admit that something is to be said for the superior clarity of American pronunciation, but they seldom hold to that line long. The general tune of American speech affects them as unpleasantly as the Cockney whine of the Australians.

The study of pronunciation, as hitherto noted, is of comparatively recent growth. The historical study of American pronunciation was put on a solid basis by the publication of the second volume of George Philip Krapp's "The English Language in America" in 1925.[5] Krapp was the first to under-

---

[3] A Note on Language, in The Contrast; New York, 1924, p. 219.

[4] Do Americans Speak English?, *The Nation* (New York), Apr. 15, 1925, p. 410.

[5] A bibliography of American and English pronunciations to the end of 1922 will be found in Arthur G. Kennedy's Bibliography of Writings on the English Language, Cambridge, Mass., 1927. New studies are reported in the bibliographies in each issue of *American Speech*. [A few of the more important descriptive works in recent years: Arthur J. Bronstein, The Pronunciation of American English, New York, 1960; J. S. Kenyon, American Pronunciation, 10th ed., Ann Arbor, Mich., 1952; Hans Kurath and Raven I. McDavid, Jr., The Pronunciation of English in the Atlantic States, Ann Arbor, 1961; Charles K. Thomas, The Phonetics of American English, New York, 1958; C. M. Wise, Applied Phonetics, Englewood Cliffs, N.J., 1957. Of historical studies the most imposing is E. J. Dobson, English Pronunciation, 1500–1700, 2 vols., Oxford, 1957. Alexander J. Ellis, On Early English Pronunciations, 5 vols., London, 1869–89, is still useful if somewhat dated. Other useful studies are

take an exhaustive examination of the available material—the early dictionaries, grammars and spelling books, the attempts at devising phonetic alphabets and the records of the Massachusetts, Connecticut and New York towns, many of them made by unlearned men and written phonetically. One of his conclusions was that most of the peculiarities of American pronunciation have historical precedents in England, and that many of them may be found to this day in the English dialects. Even the nasalization which Englishmen always mark in American speech "is by no means exclusively American." It was charged to the English Puritans by their critics, and is denounced in "Hudibras," Part I, Canto III. Krapp believed that "differences of practise among standard American speakers, that is, among members of good standing in the community, were formerly much more numerous than they are today," and that they "continue to show an increasing tendency to disappear in an all-embracing uniformity." Many forms now confined to isolated speech islands—for example, in rural New England or the remoter parts of the South—were once almost universal. [The current linguistic surveys of the British Isles [6] and the completed but largely unpublished records of the Atlantic seaboard states will eventually make it easier to trace historical connections.]

Even so late as 1926 Kemp Malone could say with perfect truth that "intonation, or pitch variation in speech," though "probably the most important constituent in the sum total of speech peculiarities that give one an accent," was "yet but little studied." [7] Since then, however, this study has flourished in a way that must delight him.[8] Its practitioners have got

---

The English Pronunciation at Shakespeare's Time, by R. E. Zachrisson, Uppsala, 1927; Pronunciation of English Vowels, 1400–1700, by the same, Göteborg, 1913; Shakespeare's Pronunciation, by Helge Kökeritz, New Haven, 1953; and English Pronunciation from the Fifteenth to the Eighteenth Century, by Constance Davies, London, 1934. Among theoretical works, one may cite a handful: Charles F. Hockett, A System of Descriptive Phonology, *Lg.*, Vol. XVIII, Jan.–Mar. 1942, pp. 3–21, and A Manual of Phonology, Memoir No. 11, *IJAL*, 1955; Roman Jakobson, Gunnar Fant and Morris Halle, Preliminaries to Speech Analysis, Cambridge, Mass., 1952; Kenneth L. Pike, Phonetics, Ann Arbor, 1944, and Phonemics, Ann Arbor, 1947; R. H. Stetson, Motor Phonetics, Amsterdam, 1951; Morris Swadesh, On the Analysis of English Syllabics, *Lg.*, Vol. XXIII, Apr.–June 1947, pp. 137–150;

George L. Trager and Henry Lee Smith, Jr., An Outline of English Structure, *SIL*, Occasional Paper No. 3, Norman, Okla., 1950; and W. Freeman Twaddell, On Defining the Phoneme, *Language Monograph* No. 16, 1935. The subject promises to remain exciting and controversial for a long time.]

[6] [The first volume of the English survey, directed by Eugen Dieth and Harold Orton, was issued by the University of Leeds in 1962; for Scotland, see Angus McIntosh, An Introduction to a Survey of Scottish Dialects; Edinburgh, 1953.]

[7] Pitch Patterns in English, *Studies in Philology*, Vol. XXIII, July 1926, p. 372.

[8] [The standard introduction is Martin Joos, Acoustic Phonetics, *Language Monograph* No. 23, 1948. Briefer but useful is Elements of Acoustic Phonetics, by Peter Ladefoged; Chicago, 1962. A more recent work is Ernst Pulgram, Introduction to the Spectrography of

together a really formidable armamentarium of instruments for detecting and recording precisely what goes on during the speaking of a sentence, and some of their discoveries, though rather beyond the comprehension of a layman, are of considerable importance.[9] Accent, for instance, has been found to be a far more complicated phenomenon than the old-time lexicographers ever suspected, and stress itself is by no means an isolated phenomenon, measurable wholly in terms of intensity.[1] Stress also drags out the duration of a syllable, raises its pitch and augments its tonal range. And as with syllables, so with words.

For many years past, philologians have been struggling with the difficulties of representing the gradations of speech in print. No alphabet of any actual language achieves the business. It is, in fact, full of downright impossibilities, as Robert Southey was saying more than a hundred years ago. "Sounds," he observed, "are to us infinite and variable, and we cannot transmit by one sense the ideas and objects of another." Nevertheless, during the last century, such eminent phoneticians as Prince Louis Lucien Bonaparte, a nephew of Napoleon, and the Englishmen Alexander J. Ellis and Henry Sweet devised various systematic ways of representing speech sounds, which were forerunners of the International Phonetic Alphabet (IPA) of the Association Phonétique Internationale, both alphabet and association being largely guided by the French phonetician Paul Passy.[2]

Speech; 's Gravenhage, 1959. Discussions of particular instruments and what they find appear in a variety of journals in the fields of linguistics, speech and physics, of which the *Journal of the Acoustical Society of America* deserves particular notice.]

[9] [Systematic study of intonation actually began in the Eighteenth Century, but was largely abandoned because the necessary instruments were lacking. See Joshua Steele and the Melody of Speech, by Paul K. Alkon, *Language and Speech*, Vol. II, July 1959, pp. 154–74. Important recent studies include Kenneth L. Pike, The Intonation of American English, Ann Arbor, Mich., 1945; Rulon S. Wells, The Pitch Phonemes of English, *Lg.*, Vol. XXI, Jan. 1945, pp. 27–39; Dwight L. Bolinger, Intonation: Levels versus Configurations, *Word*, Vol. VII, Dec. 1951, pp. 199–210; Wiktor Jassem, Intonation of Conversational English (Educated Southern British), Wroclaw, 1952; W. R. Lee, English Intonation: a New Approach, *Lingua*, Vol. V, Aug. 1956, pp. 345–71; William Whitney Gage, Grammatical Structures in American In-

tonation, diss. (microfilm), Cornell, 1958; Maria Schubiger, English Intonation: Its Form and Function, Tübingen, 1958.]

[1] A pioneer study was The Acoustical Nature of Accent in American Speech, by Wilbur L. Schramm, *AS*, Vol. XII, 1937, pp. 49–56. [Of recent studies, see Stanley S. Newman, On the Stress System of English, *Word*, Vol. II, Dec. 1946, pp. 171–87; W. A. Munson and M. B. Gardner, Loudness Patterns—a New Approach, *Journal of the Acoustical Society of America*, Vol. XXII, Sept. 1950, p. 678; Lee S. Hultzén, Stress and Intonation, *General Linguistics*, Vol. I, pp. 35–42; G. F. Arnold, Stress in English Words, *Lingua*, Vol. VI, Apr. and July 1957, pp. 221–67, 397–441; Dwight L. Bolinger, English Stress: The Interpenetration of Strata, in The Study of Sounds, Tokyo, 1957. All general texts on linguistics, and nearly all descriptions of English, now have sections on intonation and stress.]

[2] [See The International Phonetic Alphabet: Its Background and Development, by R. W. Albright; Bloomington, Ind., 1958.]

This alphabet, which included many new characters, has come into wide use, and there have been numerous modifications to cope with languages not known to the Founding Fathers. When, for example, the Practical Phonetics Group of the Modern Language Association adopted it in 1927, it was necessary to add a number of new symbols to indicate peculiarities of American speech.[3] Very few practical phonologists have ever attempted to use the IPA without modification. Krapp made some effort to use the IPA in both "The Pronunciation of Standard English in America"[4] and the second volume (on pronunciation) of "The English Language in America,"[5] but in the former volume he sounded a warning to the whole faculty (including himself) that no such artificial alphabet could ever solve the problem of representing all the shades of sound in print.[6]

In his "American Pronunciation," first published in 1924, John S. Kenyon used the IPA "in such ways as to adapt it to the peculiarities of American pronunciation." His larger "Pronouncing Dictionary of American English," in collaboration with Thomas A. Knott, retains the IPA; however, in addition to the symbols used to represent the most frequent sounds in American English, it lists about 25 other IPA symbols for "less common English sounds and the sounds of foreign languages." The explanation of this vitaminized IPA occupies nearly a dozen pages of fine print in the introduction to this dictionary. The common, or dirt, dictionaries of both England and the United States avoid the IPA with great diligence. Webster 1934, of which Knott was the general editor, offered an explanation of it in the prefatory "Guide to Pronunciation," written by Kenyon, but in the body of the work it was abandoned for an even more complicated system whose cumbersome and unsystematic nature is concealed behind the illusory familiarity of such indicators as ă, ă and ä. [More recent dictionaries, such as the American College Dictionary (1949) and Webster's New World Dictionary (1952; no kin to the New International),[7] while still eschewing IPA, have used simpler and more scientifically ordered diacritical systems, and Webster 1961 has completely revised its practice in representing pronunciation.]

Krapp's longing for a device to record speech sounds that would be "richer in possibilities than an alphabet" was already in process of realiza-

---

[3] The International Phonetic Alphabet, by John S. Kenyon, *AS*, Vol. IV, Apr. 1929, pp. 324-7.

[4] New York, 1919.

[5] [As pointed out elsewhere, the LA adopted an extensive modification of the IPA. Another derivative is in Bernard Bloch and George L. Trager, Outline of Linguistic Analysis; Baltimore, 1942.]

[6] p. vi.

[7] [Webster's New World Dictionary is published by the World Publishing Company, of Cleveland and New York; Webster's New International by the G. & C. Merriam Company, of Springfield, Mass.]

tion when he wrote in 1918. It was the phonograph, which the International Correspondence Schools had been using to teach foreign languages since 1901. But its use for embalming and studying spoken American had to wait until 1924, when Harry Morgan Ayres, of Columbia University, presented five records of the national speech at the annual meeting of the Modern Language Association. Three years later he and Greet began a diligent and systematic making of records at Columbia. In some cases radio speeches by eminent public characters, *e.g.*, Roosevelt II, Nicholas Murray Butler and Dorothy Thompson, were recorded, and in other cases volunteers from various parts of the country were recruited to provide specimens of their talk. The latter were found mainly on the campus of Columbia, where more than 10,000 students are gathered annually for the sessions of the Summer School. The same method has been employed by other phonologists, and it was used in accumulating materials for the Linguistic Atlas. [Since World War II, the development of lightweight high-fidelity tape recorders has given a new impetus to this trend. Every first-rate educational institution has a language laboratory with facilities for recording living speech; and in better institutions the number of specimens sampled runs into the thousands. Of late, such laboratory instruments of the 1930s as the cathode-ray oscillograph have been supplemented by new devices like the sound spectrograph and the speech stretcher, to provide accurate analyses of the complicated sound structure of connected discourse.]

Meanwhile the Linguaphone Institute in New York undertook, on a large scale, the teaching of both foreign languages and English pronunciation by phonograph,[8] and in 1943 it added an American English conversation course in which the teachers were Ayres, Greet and various other phonologists.[9] In 1941, cheered by these experiments, Bert Emsley, of Ohio State University, proposed boldly that the pronouncing dictionaries of the future be not printed, but recorded on phonograph plates.[1] So far this clarion call has not been answered. [But it is only a matter of time. Every recent text on spoken American English—and on other spoken languages as well—is designed to be accompanied by records or tapes, and the versatility of computers and retrieval systems is such that it would be simple to design apparatus which would make available to the public a continuously revised inventory of the entire English vocabulary—includ-

---

[8] [In 1942 the Army and Navy, in association with the Linguistic Society of America and the Intensive Language Program of the American Council of Learned Societies, began teaching foreign languages to soldiers and sailors by the same method. Several similar programs of courses on records and tapes have been issued by enterprising publishers.]

[9] Linguaphone for Languages; New York, 1945, p. 3.

[1] Talking Dictionaries, *QJS*, Vol. XXVII, Apr. 1941, pp. 274-81.

ing pronunciations, spellings, meanings and citations. The only problem is money.]

2: THE VOWELS

"Every vowel sound without exception," said Hilaire Belloc in "The Contrast," [2] "has taken on this side of the Atlantic [*i.e.*, the American side] some different value from what it has on ours [*i.e.*, the English side]. And in many cases the change is so great that the exact setting down of it in an accurate transliteration would involve a totally different spelling." Even the *a* of such words as *cab* and *hand* differs in the two countries. When Englishmen speak them rapidly they often sound, to American ears, like *keb* and *hend*. Or consider, for example, the much-debated broad *a* sound, a favorite gauge of the disparity between English speech and American. At one end of the scale is the solid *ah* that speakers of the Received Standard English put into *glass* and *dance*, and at the other end is the so-called flat *a*, as in *can* and *Daniel*, used by most Americans. Between the two stands the compromise of the Boston–Hudson Valley dialect. But most persons who attempt the compromise *a* vary it considerably in their own speech, so that it is sometimes difficult to make out whether they use it or not. The other vowels are all in a state of flux, and Arthur J. Bronstein hints that something analogous to the Great Vowel Shift of 1500, which separated Modern English from Middle English, may be in progress.[3]

The old-time grammar books were content to inform the young that there were five vowels in English, but this was true, of course, only of the letters used to represent them, not of the sounds. In 1791 John Walker was constrained to distinguish ten vowels and diphthongs,[4] and in 1837 Isaac Pitman, the pioneer of modern English shorthand, went on to six long vowels,[5] six short ones and four diphthongs. The number has been growing ever since. Daniel Jones, in the 1937 edition of his "English Pronouncing Dictionary," went to fifteen vowels and twelve diphthongs, and Leonard Bloomfield, in 1935, reported seventeen "syllabic phonemes" among "educated speakers in Chicago" alone.[6] [In 1941, George L. Trager and Bernard Bloch, following previous suggestions by Henry Sweet and Prince Nicholas

---

[2] New York, 1924, p. 224.

[3] Trends in American Pronunciation, *QJS*, Vol. XXXVIII, Dec. 1942, pp. 452–6.

[4] The Phonetic Concepts of John Walker and Daniel Jones, by Benjamin Newman, *QJS*, Vol. XXXVII, Oct. 1941, p. 365.

[5] To wit, *ah*, *eh*, *ee*, *aw*, *oh* and *oo*.

[6] The Stressed Vowels of American English, *Lg.*, Vol. XI, Apr.–June 1935, pp. 97–116. See also The Vowels of Chicago English, by Morris Swadesh, pp. 148–51 of the same issue.

Trubetzkoy, proposed an analysis of English vowels including six simple vowels and eighteen diphthongs—six ending in a *y* glide, six in a *w* glide and six in prolongation or a glide toward the neutral vowel. A year later the same authors discovered a seventh vowel and another trinity of diphthongs,[7] and in 1951 Trager and Henry Lee Smith, Jr., produced an analysis with nine vowels and twenty-seven diphthongs.[8] Known to American phonologists as "the over-all pattern," this analysis has been widely adopted in textbooks of linguistics and in manuals for teaching English to speakers of other languages. However, many scholars, notably James H. Sledd, have shown that even this system must be expanded by at least a tenth vowel and a fourth set of diphthongs (making forty in all).[9] In "The Pronunciation of English in the Atlantic States," [1] Kurath and McDavid use a basic system of six "checked vowels" which must be followed by a consonant, and twelve "free vowels" (long vowels and diphthongs) which may occur at the end of a word in a stressed syllable, but state that some dialects may require more.[2]]

The sounds of vowels are produced by columns of air going through the two resonator spaces above and below the tongue, with modifications affected by variations in the position of the tongue itself and the lips. Since no two human mouths are precisely alike, the mechanism of speech thus differs from individual to individual, and in the same individual from time to time. It is sometimes difficult to distinguish between *a* and *o* on the one hand and *a* and *e* on the other, or between *a* and the neutral vowel, but on most occasions they remain reasonably distinct, despite the wide range of sounds on both sides of the fence. The quantity, *i.e.*, the length, of any vowel is conditioned by its position with relation to other sounds. Thus the exclamation *ah*, in isolation, shows a longer *a* than the one in *father* or *palm*, and the quantity thereof is further affected by the surrounding consonants and the rapidity of speech.[3] "The pronunciation of a word in isolation," says R.-M. S. Heffner, "represents an unhampered shot at the goal of an ideal or normal pronunciation, while pronunciation in context represents a more or less disturbed or jostled shot at the same goal." [4] The most

---

[7] [The Syllabic Phonemes of English, *Lg.*, Vol. XVII, July 1941, pp. 223–46; and Outline of Linguistic Analysis; Baltimore, 1942.]

[8] [Outline of English Structure; Norman, Okla., 1950.]

[9] [See Sledd's Short Introduction to English Grammar; Chicago, 1959.]

[1] [Ann Arbor, Mich., 1961, pp. 1–9.]

[2] [The competing analyses are summarized in Arthur Bronstein, The Pronunciation of American English; New York, 1960.]

[3] See two studies by John W. Black, The Effect of the Consonant on the Vowel, *Journal of the Acoustical Society of America*, Vol. X, Jan. 1939, and The Stability of the Vowel, *ibid.*, Feb. 1939. [Of the host of detailed studies with newer instruments, The Phonetic Value of Vowels, by Gordon E. Peterson, *Lg.*, Vol. XXVII, Oct.–Dec. 1951, pp. 541–53, is representative.]

[4] Notes on the Length of Vowels, *AS*, Vol. XII, Apr. 1937, p. 128.

active factor, however, is stress, and Heffner concludes that "strong stress with falling intonation produces a slightly greater duration of the vowel than strong stress with rising intonation."[5] All such differences in quantity tend to become differences in quality, and in the long run they may produce entirely new vowels, or, at all events, variations so marked that they have to be represented by different symbols.[6]

Many words have short vowels in American instead of the long vowels or diphthongs usual in English. The English authorities ordain the long *e* in *evolution*, and the long *i* in words of the *fragile* class, but in the United States the short *e* and *i* seem to be dominant in these words. There is also a tendency to substitute the short *e* of *pen* for the long *e* of *scene* in *penalize;* the short *i* of *sin* for the long *i* of *line* in *sinecure;* and the short *u* of *sum* for the long *u* of *cube* in *quintuplet.*[7] In both English and American usage there is a strong movement, at least a thousand years old, toward substituting the so-called neutral vowel for clearer vowels in unstressed syllables, especially in colloquial speech. Thus the *a* of *about*, the *e* of *the*, the *i* of *habit*, the *o* of *hillock* and the *u* of *upon* are all reduced to a grunt.

One of the most noticeable differences between Standard English and Standard American lies in the varying pronunciation of *a* in about 150 words in everyday use. The English, in general, prefer the broad *a* of *dark* before *f*, *ft*, *nch*, *nd*, *nt*, *sk*, *sp*, *st*, *ss* and *th*, as in *laugh*, *draft*, *branch*, *command*, *chant*, *can't*, *ask*, *clasp*, *last*, *grass* and *path*, whereas most Americans use the flat *a* of *that*.

The broad *a* did not begin to flourish in England until the Eighteenth Century, though it was, of course, used before then, especially in dialects. C. Cooper, whose "Grammatica Linguae Anglicanae" was published in 1685 and who has been described by Wyld as "by far the most reliable phonetician among the Seventeenth Century writers," recorded the present-day American flat *a* not only in *bath*, *gasp* and *path* but also in *car*, *tar*, *quality*, *barge*, *carp*, *dart*, *larch* and *tart*. To this day, in fact, that *a* is retained by the English in a large number of words—perhaps in quite as many as show the broad *a* that Americans think of as so characteristic of England. Examples are *fancy*, *pants*, *vassal*, *pantry*, *lass*, *can*, *mandate*, *pamphlet*, *ant*, *ass* (the animal), *parasol*, *avoirdupois*, *bas-relief*, *candle*, *passenger*, *parrot*, *handsome* and *passive.*[8]

---

[5] *AS*, Vol. XVII, Feb. 1942, p. 48.

[6] Outline of English Phonetics, by Daniel Jones; New York, 1932, par. 879, quoted by Heffner.

[7] Henry A. Perkins, Our Changing Vowels, Hartford *Courant*, Apr. 27, 1938.

[8] [According to L. Foster, writing in *English Studies*, Vol. XXX, June 1949, pp. 86-91, in such words as *ass*, *bastard* and *Catholic* the symbolic association varies according to whether the flat *a* or the broad *a* is used. In the first word, the flat *a* is zoological, the broad *a* anatomical and therefore a term of contempt.]

As Wyld points out,[9] the change from the old (and still American) flat *a* to the broad *a* of the English *past, bath* and *after* was still hanging fire in the early Eighteenth Century, and it was "difficult for Englishmen at that time." During most of the Eighteenth Century, in fact, a broad *a* was regarded in both England and America as a rusticism, and careful speakers commonly avoided it. Thomas Sheridan's "General Dictionary of the English Language" (1790) actually omitted it from the list of vowels. It gave the pronunciation of *papa* as if both *a*'s were that of *pap* and the same *a* before *r*, as in *car* and *far*. Benjamin Franklin was in complete accord with Sheridan.[1] He favored the flat *a*, not only in all the words which now carry it in American, but also in *calm, far, hardly* and even *what*, which last was thus made to rhyme with *hat*. Franklin's pronunciations were presumably those of the best circles in the London of his time, and of Philadelphia, then the center of American culture. But the broad *a* continued in the folk speech of New England, as in that of Old England, and in 1780 or thereabout it suddenly became fashionable in Standard London English. How and why this fashion arose is not known. But educated New Englanders were using the broad *a* in many words at the time Noah Webster published his "Dissertations on the English Language" in Boston in 1789. In it he gave *quality, quantity* and *quash* the sound of *a* in *hat*, but he gave *advance, after, ask, balm, clasp* and *grant* the *a* of *arm*. In subsequent editions of "The American Spelling-Book" he favored the broad *a* before a final *r* or before *r* followed by a consonant, *e.g., bar, depart;* before *(l)m, e.g., embalm;* before a final *s* or *s* followed by a consonant, *e.g., pass, ask;* before *f, e.g., staff, half;* before *th, e.g., path;* before *lv, e.g., salve, calves;* before *n* followed by *ch, s* or *t, e.g., blanch, dance, ant;* in words spelled *au* before *n* followed by *ch, d* or *t, e.g., staunch, jaundice, aunt;* and in a number of other words, *e.g., chamber, slander, gape.*[2] Webster's immense authority was sufficient to implant the broad *a* firmly in the speech of the Boston area. Between 1830 and 1850, according to C. H. Grandgent,[3] it ran riot, and was used even in such words as *handsome, matter, apple, caterpillar, pantry, hammer, practical* and *Saturday*. Oliver Wendell Holmes protested against it in "The Autocrat of the Breakfast Table" in 1857, but it survived his onslaught.

Nevertheless, the imprimatur of the Yankee Johnson was not sufficient to establish the Boston *a* outside New England. His great antagonist, Joseph E. Worcester, whose "Comprehensive Pronouncing and Explanatory Dictionary of the English Language" appeared in 1830, set up a distinction

[9] Wyld, p. 204.
[1] A Scheme for a New Alphabet and a Reformed Mode of Spelling; Philadelphia, 1768.

[2] Krapp, Vol. II, p. 67.
[3] Fashion and the Broad *a* in Old and New; Cambridge, Mass., 1920, pp. 25–30.

between the true British broad *a* and the modified New England *a* and frowned upon the former. "His hesitation with respect to words like *ask, dance, chaff,* etc.," says Krapp, "was due not to the fear that the sound which he advocated might seem too near [the *a* of *hat*], but too near [the *a* of *bard*]. In other words, the vulgar extreme which was to be avoided was [the latter and not the former]." By 1850 the flat *a* was dominant everywhere west of the Berkshires and south of New Haven, save for what Grandgent calls "a little *ah*-spot in Virginia," and its sound had even got into such proper names as *Alabama* and *Lafayette*.[4] Outside New England the broad *a* has got into a few words, particularly those in which it is followed by *lm*. They were once pronounced to rhyme with *ram* and *jam,* but their pronunciation that way has begun to seem provincial and ignorant, except to older cultivated Charlestonians. Krapp says that the *a* has likewise broadened in *salmon* and *almond,*[5] but this is not yet generally true. The first syllable of *salmon,* true enough, does not quite rhyme with *ham,* but it is nevertheless still very far from *palm.* The broad *a,* by a fashionable affectation, has also appeared in *vase* and *drama.*

The broad *a* survives before *r,* as in *charm.* But in the early 1870s, William Dwight Whitney said that "until quite recently it was admitted in the United States in *calf, answer, chance, can't, alas, pass, bask, clasp, blaspheme, last, path, lath, laugh, staff, raft, after* and in many other words like them," but that, save in "local usage (I cannot say how extensive)," it was already being replaced by "the *a* of *fat* and *fan,*" or by some "intermediate" *a.*[6] According to Chad Walsh,[7] the broad Southern *a* is now losing ground even in Tidewater Virginia, but is holding out better among the women than among the men. "This," he says, "is probably because a man's friends are more likely to resent what they regard as a speech affectation. I have known several cases in which the mother used the broad *a* and the father

---

[4] Richard Meade Bache denounced it in *Lafayette,* in his Vulgarisms and Other Errors of Speech; 2nd ed.; Philadelphia, 1869, p. 65.

[5] The Pronunciation of Standard English in America, p. 60. [The difference between the vowels of *ham* and *salmon* is pointed out in Trager's studies with Bloch in 1941 and 1942 and with Smith in 1950.]

[6] Oriental and Linguistic Studies: Second Series; New York, 1874, pp. 206–7. [Further recession of the broad *a* in New England appears both in the LA and in a local survey conducted by Boston University. See *Newsweek,* Mar. 10, 1952, p. 92.]

[7] Broad *a* in Virginia, *AS,* Vol. XV, Feb. 1940, p. 38. [The assumed prestige value of a broad *a,* often in the wrong places, is discussed by Thomas Pyles in That Fine Italian *a* in American English, Philologica: The Malone Anniversary Studies; Baltimore, 1949. *Can't* is examined meticulously by Sumner Ives in *AS,* Vol. XXVIII, Oct. 1953, pp. 149–57, and the whole family summarized by Kurath and McDavid in The Pronunciation of English in the Atlantic States, pp. 135–43, Maps 67–80. The most striking feature of the Atlas evidence is the inconsistency with which the broad *a* is preserved or adopted; its occurrence in one "typical" word does not predict it in another.]

didn't, and the children imitated the mother's pronunciation. However, when the children grow up there is a tendency for the boys to adopt the short *a*."

One debate that frequently engrosses the newspaper phonologists has to do with *again*. Should it be pronounced to rhyme with *pain* or with *pen?* Palmer, Martin and Blandford say that the former is good English usage and Bender advises American crooners to use *agen*, but there is contrary advice and custom on both sides of the water. Down to the Nineteenth Century the English poets freely rhymed *again* with *pen*, but Shakespeare also rhymed it on occasion with *twain*, *plain* and *slain*. The OED, whose *A* volume was published in 1888, ventured the opinion that *again* was then displacing *agen* in England, and this seems to be confirmed by the later English authorities, including Daniel Jones, but most American authorities, *e.g.*, Webster 1934 and Kenyon and Knott, hold out for *agen*.[8] The English authorities sanction *et* for *ate*, but in the United States (except in Charleston) it is generally regarded as a vulgarism, as *eat* in the past tense is everywhere.

Amen with the broad *a* seems to be making progress. E. W. Howe tells a story of a little girl in Kansas whose mother, on acquiring social aspirations, entered the Protestant Episcopal Church from the Methodist Church. The father remaining behind, the little girl had to learn to say *amen* with the *a* of *rake* when she went to church with her father and *amen* with the *a* of *car* when she went to church with her mother. But the *a* of *rake* prevails in *amen corner* [and also in the *amen* of the Catholic proletariat].

Patent, in American, usually has the *a* of *cat*, but in English the *a* of *late* is often heard when the word is used in the sense of a license or monopoly. In England, *mater*, a common synonym for *mother*, has the same *a*, but in the American *alma mater*, which is seldom used in England, the third *a* is that of *bard*, though the first is commonly that of *pal*. In English the third *a* of *apparatus* is always that of *late*, but in the United States it is often that of *cat*. In *phalanx* it runs the other way, with the English preferring, for the first syllable, the *a* of *rack*, and Americans that of *mate*. In *radio* the usual American pronunciation shows the *a* of *mate*, but the plain people of New York City often have that of *rack*. The English use a broad *a* in the final syllable of *charade* and *promenade*, but most Americans prefer the *a* of *mate*. In the second syllable of *asphalt* the English always use the *a* of *rack*, but Americans prefer the *aw* of *bawl*. In England the *a* of *patriotism* is always the *a* of *rack*, but in the United States it is usually that of *late*. In *radish* the *a* is sometimes that of *cab* and sometimes the *e* of *red*. In such proper names as *Alabama*, *Alaska*, *Montana*, *Nevada* and *Colorado* the flat

---

[8] [See Kurath and McDavid, p. 131, Maps 60–1.]

a is normally heard, especially in the states themselves, but a broad *a* is not unknown. In the years before the Civil War the plain people converted the *a* of *care* into the *a* of *car* in *bear, dare, hair* and *where*, into a short *i* in the verb *can*, into a short *e* in *catch* and into a long *e* in *care, scarce* and *chair*, thus producing *bar, dar, har, whar, kin, ketch, keer, skeerce* and *cheer*. They reduced *sauce* to *sass, saucy* to *sassy* and *because* to *becuz* or *becaze*, and turned the *a* of *drain* into a long *e*, producing *dreen*. Some of these toyings with *a* survive, but not all. The rest have been exterminated by the schoolma'am or forced into exile among the remoter dialects.[9]

The pronunciation of *a* in this or that situation has changed often within the past two centuries. Boswell records how puzzled Samuel Johnson was when Lord Chesterfield advised him that "the word *great* should be pronounced so as to rhyme to *state*" and Sir William Younge insisted that "it should be pronounced so as to rhyme to *seat*, and that none but an Irishman would pronounce it *grait*." "Here," marveled the lexicographer, "were two men of the highest rank, the one the best speaker in the House of Lords, the other the best speaker in the House of Commons, differing entirely."[1] [Many cultivated Southerners, and a sprinkling in other regions, say *gret*.]

When it comes to *e* the chief battle in the Republic continues to be between the advocates of *ee-ther* and those who prefer *eye-ther*. *Eye-ther* and *nye-the*r have been common in New England for nearly two centuries. Noah Webster, in his "Dissertations,"[2] classed them as "errors," along with *desate* for *deceit, consate* for *conceit* and *resate* for *receipt*, but he conceded that the *eye* sound was in general use "by the Eastern people," though not common in the South and West. At that time (1789) *ee-ther* and *nee-ther* were favored in England. How the fashion for the *eye* pronunciation arose is not known, but it was raging on both sides of the ocean by the middle of the Nineteenth Century, and is still in force. James Fenimore Cooper, in "The American Democrat" (1838), came out strongly in favor of *eye-ther* and *nye-ther*, which he described as "polite."

Nearly all the American authorities of the Nineteenth Century were in favor of *ee-ther*,[3] and most of those of the present century have followed them. Whitney, in 1867, admitted that *eye-ther* and *nye-ther* were spreading in the United States, but denounced them as "the deliberate choice of

---

[9] [*Catch* is discussed in *CE*, Vol. XIV, Feb. 1953, pp. 290–1, and in Kurath and McDavid, pp. 139–40, Map 74; *apricot*, by Blanche Miller in *AS*, Vol. XXVI, May 1951, pp. 152–3; *radish, scarce, because* and *drain* in Kurath and McDavid.]

[1] Boswell's Life, Mar. 1772.

[2] p. 114.

[3] For example, James Russell Lowell, in On a Certain Condescension in Foreigners, wrote: "We said *eether* and not *eyther*, following therein the fashion of our ancestors, who unhappily could bring over no English better than Shakespeare's."

persons who fancy that there is something more *recherché*, more English" in them.[4] Seven years later he called the fashion for them "a relentless and senseless infection, which can only be condemned and ought to be stoutly opposed and put down," and said that those Americans who had succumbed to it "ought to realize with shame the folly of which they have been guilty, and reform." [5] Even Richard Grant White, who strongly favored the broad *a*, declared in 1870 that there was "no authority, either of analogy or of the best speakers, for *eye-ther* and *nye-ther*," and called their use "an affectation, and in this country, a copy of a second-rate British affectation." [6] The Oxford Dictionary, in 1897, gave the preference to *ee-ther* and *nee-ther*, but admitted that *eye-ther* and *nye-ther* were "somewhat more prevalent in educated English speech." H. W. Fowler, in "A Dictionary of Modern English Usage" (1926), predicted that they would "probably prevail," though adding that they were "not more correct" than *ee-ther* and *nee-ther*. Webster 1961 holds out for the latter, but gives *eye-ther* and *nye-ther* as variants. [The Linguistic Atlas archives show *ee* heavily predominant in all areas and all classes of speech. Along the Atlantic seaboard, *ither*, *nither*, and *uther*, *nuther*, are next most common, though largely confined to the vulgate. *Eye-ther* and *nye-ther* appear among the tony in Northern metropolitan areas, but not a single example is recorded in cultivated speech south of the Mason-Dixon Line, even among those who display the broad *a* in *aunt*, *dance* and *tomato*.] An older pronunciation, *ay-ther* and *nay-ther*, is still heard in Ireland, but it is rare in the United States.[7]

There are some other differences in the pronunciation of *e* in English and American, but not many. The English use the long *e* of *bee* in the first syllable of *evolution* and *epoch*, but Americans prefer it short. Contrariwise, the English use a short *e* in *lever* and *egoist*, whereas most Americans prefer a long one. The use of the long *e* in *deaf*, though historically very respectable and ardently advocated by Noah Webster,[8] has disappeared from cultivated American speech; it persists, however, in the vulgate. [Even rarer and more old-fashioned is the pronunciation *diff*.] In the same way the *i* sound, as in *sit*, has disappeared from *get*, *yet*, *general*, *steady*, *chest*, *kettle* and *instead*; Benjamin Franklin defended it, but now even the vulgate is losing it. This pronunciation was correct in the Seventeenth Century, and perhaps down to the middle of the next century; the colonists may have clung to such disappearing usages longer than the English. In Webster's

[4] Language and the Study of Language; New York, 1867, p. 43.
[5] The Elements of English Pronunciation, in Oriental and Linguistic Studies; New York, 1874, p. 221.
[6] Words and Their Uses, New York, 1870; the quotations are from the revised edition, 1876, pp. 263–4.
[7] [Kurath and McDavid, p. 149, Map 98.]
[8] See Dissertations on the English Language, 1789, p. 128; [Kurath and McDavid, pp. 131–2, Map 62].

time the *a* of *lame* was generally heard in *egg, peg, leg* and so on, but it too is receding.[9]

One of the Briticisms that Americans appear to be most conscious of is the change of *e* to a broad *a* in *clerk, Derby, Berkeley*, etc. Wyld[1] shows that this vowel shift began in the Thirteenth Century, and has left sediments in words that are now spelled with the *a* in both England and America, *e.g., to bark, dark, heart, parson* and *starve*. There was a time when what Webster called "the yeoman of America,"[2] like the contemporary English, used this broad *a* in many other words now pronounced *ur, e.g., servant, certain* and *search;* and it still survives in the dialect of Appalachia. In the general speech the only notable survivor seems to be *sergeant*. But let us not forget the proper names *Hartford, Barclay* and *Barney*, the last-named a diminutive for *Bernard*, as in *Barney* Baruch. Wyld says that the change from *er* (with our vowel of *get*) to *ar* (with our vowel of *father*) started in the dialects of southeastern England, and soon spread to East Anglia. It was rare in the London dialect before the Fifteenth Century, but became "increasingly fashionable until the last quarter of the Eighteenth," when it began to recede from all words save those which had come to be spelled with *a, e.g., dark*.

Crick for *creek* is commonly regarded as an Americanism, and it has been traced by the DAE to 1608, when Captain John Smith used it in his "Newes from Virginia," but the OED shows that, in the forms *crike, krike* and *cryke*, it was in English use before the discovery of America. William Allen Pusey (1865–1940), sometime president of the American Medical Association, was greatly interested in the distribution of *crick*. He found that it was almost unknown in the rural parts of his native state, Kentucky, and that it was rare in the South below North Carolina. He concluded that it was a Northernism, [a conclusion generally confirmed by the Linguistic Atlas materials].[3] Incidentally, *crick in the neck* is properly *crick* and not *creek. Sleek* has divided into two words, *slick* and *sleek*, the former signifying slippery, including the metaphorical sense of cunning and ingratiating, and the latter referring especially to appearance. Webster, in his "Dissertations," recommended *heerd* for *heard* as well as *deef* for *deaf*. For the

---

[9] [Kurath and McDavid, pp. 132–3, Maps 63–4. According to Lee Pederson, the vowel of *late* is still surprisingly common in *egg*, etc., among educated speakers in metropolitan Chicago. Throughout the country it is often heard in *measure, treasure* and other words of that type, and in some regions may be predominant.]

[1] Wyld, pp. 212–22.
[2] Dissertations, p. 105.
[3] Private communications, Aug. 23 and 27, Sept. 8 and Nov. 14, 1937. [See Kurath and McDavid, pp. 148–9, Map 97; and Linguistic Geography and Toponymic Research, *Names*, Vol. VI, June 1958, pp. 65–73.]

former he had the support of Samuel Johnson.[4] Webster said: "The Americans were strangers to [*hurd*] when they came from England, and the body of the people are so to this day. To most people in this country the English pronunciation appears like an affectation." Webster, in those days, was a fiery linguistic patriot, and refused absolutely to follow English example. "If it is erroneous," he said, "let it remain so: we have no concern with it." But by the time he came to his American Dictionary of 1828 he was admitting *hurd*, though insisting that *deaf* was more commonly *deef* than *def* in America. Of the so-called neutral vowel, Webster said in the introduction to his 1828 Dictionary:

> Let any man in genteel society or in public pronounce the distinct sound of *a* in the last syllable of *important*, or the distinct sound of *e* in the terminations *less* and *ness* in *hopeless, happiness*, and he would pass for a most inelegant speaker.

Difficulties with *i* in the United States occur mainly in relatively recent words of scientific provenance, *e.g.*, *appendicitis, iodine, quinine* and so on. Bender, in his counsel to radio message bringers,[5] follows what are probably the prevailing American pronunciations, which are far from consistent. Thus he gives the crucial *i* the diphthongal *ai* sound in *iodine*, but the *ee* sound in *chlorine* and *bromine* and the sound it has in *in* in *ephedrine*. In *appendicitis, bronchitis, tonsillitis, neuritis, gastritis* and the like he ordains the *ai* sound. Jones, in "An English Pronouncing Dictionary," gives precisely the same pronunciations for England, but notes that *iodine* is accorded the *ee* sound by English chemists. The *ai* sound, he says, "is an old-fashioned pronunciation used by people who are ignorant of chemistry, but are familiar with the substance as a household commodity." Kenyon and Knott note that the *ee* sound is likewise preferred by chemists in America, and give *iodin*, with the last syllable rhyming with *pin*, as an alternative to *iodeyn*. Bender recommends *kwi-nine*, with both *i*'s as in *nine*, for *quinine*, and so do Kenyon and Knott. Jones gives the *i* of *pin* to the first syllable and that of *nine* to the second. Vizetelly noted so long ago as 1917[6] that

---

[4] Boswell reported under date of Sept. 23, 1777: "[Johnson] said his reason was that if *heard* were pronounced *herd*, there would be a single exception from the English pronunciation of the syllable *ear*, and he thought it better not to have any exception." [For survivals of *heerd*, *heern*, see E. Bagby Atwood, A Survey of Verb Forms in the Eastern United States, Ann Arbor, Mich., 1953, p. 16, Fig. 12; and Virginia McDavid, Verb Forms in the North-Central States and Upper Midwest, diss. (microfilm), U. of Minnesota, 1956.]

[5] NBC Handbook of Pronunciation; New York, 1943, 3rd printing.

[6] A Desk-Book of 25,000 Words Frequently Mispronounced, p. 713.

kin-neen was already going out [but it still has some standing in Canada [7]]. *Dynasty*, in American, has a first syllable like *dine*, but in English it is *din*. *Been*, in American, is almost always *bin* or *ben; bean* never appears save as a conscious affectation. But in England *bean* is preferred, [though Shakespeare often wrote *bin*].

The differences between the English *o* in *rock* and the American *o* in the same word have long engaged phonologists. The former is a lightly rounded vowel, heard in eastern New England but rare in the Midwest, though it is close to the short form of the American *aw* heard in the opening syllables of *authentic* and *autocracy;* the latter is the shortened American *ah* sound usually heard in *not.* "Cultivated English speakers do not recognize this *ah* sound in the words commonly spelled in *o, e.g., not, rod, rock, fog, hop, rob, pomp, on, beyond, novel;* English phoneticians indeed condemn it as dialectal. . . . In American, on the other hand, both sounds are heard in all these words. . . . Both sounds are heard in American speech also in the *wa* words, *e.g., wander, want, wash, watch, swamp, swan, quarrel, squander, squalid.*"[8] [Native Chicagoans usually have the short rounded vowel in the name of their city. *Ausländer* have *ah.*]

Yet a third sound is sometimes heard in these *wa* words—a downright *aw.* One encounters it in *water, wash, swamp, swan* and *squalid,* which become, roughly, *wawter, wawsh, swawmp, swawn* and *squawlid.* It also appears in *God,* which may be variously *God, Gahd* or *Gawd.* The first of the three—the British and eastern New England variety—is regarded as the most formal. A speaker who says *Gawd* in his ordinary discourse will switch to *God* (or maybe *Gahd*) when he wants to show reverence. In the Eighteenth Century, as Krapp's researches show,[9] it was not unheard of for the *a* of *care* to be used in such words. Thus, the poets of the time rhymed *war* not only with *care* but also with *air, dare, glare, forbear, spare, share, blare, snare, despair, bear, bare* and *prepare.* But the rhymes of poets are not always to be trusted, and it is to be noted that those examined by Krapp also occasionally rhymed *war* with *car* and *tar.* In any case, it began to be rhymed with *more* after the beginning of the Nineteenth Century. In

---

[7] [Kurath and McDavid, pp. 165–6, Maps 139–41. The first syllable of the Du Pont synthetic *Dacron* is usually pronounced to rhyme with *bake,* but some tony haberdashers rhyme it with *back.* When the drug *thalidomide* was in the news in the summer of 1962, in one morning I heard radio announcers render it as *thuh-líd-o-myde, thuh-líd-o-mìd,* and *thàl-uh-dóh-myde.* The first vowel in *vinyl* is usually that of *vine,* but some educated speakers use the vowel of *tin.*]

[8] Pronunciation, a Practical Guide to American Standards, by Thorleif Larsen and Francis C. Walker; London, 1930, pp. 23 *ff.* [For a detailed examination of the variations along the Atlantic seaboard, see The Low-Central and Low-Back Vowels in the English of the Eastern United States, by Thomas H. Wetmore, *PADS,* No. XXXII, Nov. 1959.]

[9] Krapp, Vol. II, p. 83.

words containing *au* or *aw* the sound is usually *aw*, but in the vulgar speech a flat *a* like that of *land* gets into *haunt, jaundice* and sometimes *launch. Laundry* may be *lawndry, lahndry* or *londry*. *Aunt*, of course, is *ant* to the plain people and most others everywhere, save in the Boston area and parts of the South.[1]

As Louise Pound once indicated,[2] the short *o* of the British type is rare in American English [except in those areas—notably eastern New England, the Pittsburgh area and western Canada—where such pairs as *cot* and *caught, collar* and *caller*, are homonyms, both often having this short *o*]. Elsewhere Americans turn it "into a long open *o* or into *ah*. . . . There is a different usage for different parts of the United States, and there is no consistency observed even for words within the same group, *e.g.,* I say myself *dawg* but *fahg*." Since 1931, C. K. Thomas has investigated the pronunciation of *horrid, orange, Florida, forest, foreign, horrible* and a number of other such words. He finds that the territory they come from can be divided into an Eastern-Southern *ah* section and a Western short-*o* section, with the two divided by a line running southward from central Vermont, then westward across New York and Pennsylvania, then southward through Maryland and part of Virginia, then generally westward to southern Missouri and then southward again through Texas.[3] In some parts of the *ah* region the preference for it is overwhelming, *e.g.,* Massachusetts, lower New York, New Jersey, Virginia, Tennessee, Arkansas and Louisiana.

Harold Whitehall has studied the vicissitudes of the *u* sound in early American speech.[4] It became, on the one hand, *oo,* on the other hand a diphthong apparently identical with that of *how* and at other times various other sounds. These variations, in the main, have vanished, and one no longer encounters *bull* spelled *bool,* or *blood* rhymed with *load,* or *dew* with *bough*. But usage in the pronunciation of *u* still differs widely in the United States. Two sounds, that of *oo* in *goose* and that of *u* in *bush,* are used by different speakers in the same word. The *oo* sound prevails in *aloof, boot, food, groom, proof, rood, rooster, soon, spook, spoon* and *woof,* and the *u* sound in *butcher, foot, nook* and *rook*. Educated usage varies in *coop, Cooper, hoop, goobers, broom, room, hoof, roof* and

---

[1] [In the South it is often homonymous with *ain't;* see Kurath and McDavid, pp. 135–6, Map 67.]

[2] Pronunciation in the Schools, *AS,* Vol. VII, Oct. 1932, p. 476.

[3] The Dialectal Significance of the Non-Phonemic Low-Back Vowel Variants before *r,* in Studies in Speech and

Drama in Honor of Alexander M. Drummond; Ithaca, N.Y., pp. 244–54. A bibliography is appended.

[4] Middle English *ū* and Related Sounds: Their Development in Early American Speech, *Language Monograph* No. 19, 1939.

root. *Soot* usually rhymes with *foot,* but educated Southerners and the plain people in most of the country rhyme it with *cut,* and a few socially aspiring Northerners rhyme it with *toot.*[5] The English are far more careful than we are with the shadowy *y* preceding *u* in words of the *duty, tube, new* class. *Nooz* for *news* still remains the prevailing pronunciation outside the South, and *nyews, nyude, dyuke, Tyuesday, enthyusiasm, styupid* and *syuit* seem affectations, despite the English preference and the efforts of generations of schoolma'ams to import and propagate it. In *figure,* however, Americans retain the *y* sound, whereas the English drop it. Wyld[6] has produced evidence that it was in wide use in England in the early Seventeenth Century, and Walker argued for it in his "Critical Pronouncing Dictionary and Expositor of the English Language" (1791), but Webster in his "Dissertations"[7] dismissed it as a peculiarity of Virginia speech, and hence barbaric. In his Dictionary of 1828 he actually ordained *fig-ur, val-u, vol-um, moot* (for *mute*), *litera-tur,* etc., but he had to admit that it was already "the practise [in the North] to give *u* the sound of *yu* in such words as *nature, feature, rapture,* which are pronounced *nat-yur, feat-yur, rapt-yur,*" and after his death in 1843 his heirs and assigns quietly inserted the *y* in *figure, value* and *volume.* Kenyon and Knott give both *nyu* and *noo* for *new,* with the former first, but Bender prefers the latter. Most Americans use *doo* for *due, toob* for *tube, dooty* for *duty* and *nood* for *nude,* but I have never encountered a native who used *oo* after *p, b, m* or *f* to give *poor* (for *pure*), *booty* (for *beauty*), *moosic* or *foo* (for *few*).[8]

H. W. Fowler ventures the opinion[9] that, after *l, yu* is yielding to *oo* in English usage. "It was formerly *de rigueur,*" he says, "to put in the *y* sound; a *flute* had to be called a *flyoot,* or the speaker was damned in polite circles. . . . But for most of us [Southern English] anything but *bloo* [*blue*] and *gloo* [*glue*] is surely now impossible, however refined we like to be where the trials of articulation are less severe." Krapp shows that *lieutenant* was originally *leftenant* in this country,[1] as it is in England,

---

[5] [See Kurath and McDavid, pp. 151–7, Maps 107–19; a more detailed study for the South Atlantic States is found in *QJS,* Vol. XXXV, Dec. 1949, pp. 496–504. The variations in the San Francisco and Los Angeles areas are described by John P. Moncur, *QJS,* Vol. XLII, Feb. 1956, pp. 31–4. For earlier dictionary judgments, see the article by Arthur J. Bronstein and Esther K. Sheldon in *AS,* Vol. XXVI, May 1951, pp. 81–9.]

[6] Wyld, pp. 242–4.

[7] p. 159.

[8] [Kurath and McDavid, pp. 168, 172, Maps 147, 163–5. In Texas, according to Ernest S. Clifton, *oo* seems to be spreading, especially in the cities; see *AS,* Vol. XXXIV, Oct. 1959, pp. 190–3.]

[9] Modern English Usage; Oxford, 1926, pp. 335–6. [But Webster's New Collegiate Dictionary, 1949, seems to ordain *yu* in *lute, assume, revolution* and the like. See Pronunciation, by Charles N. Somers, *CE,* Vol. XXII, Apr. 1961, pp. 517–18.]

[1] Krapp, Vol. II, pp. 163–4.

but Webster, with his fondness for spelling-pronunciations, declared for *lootenant*, as had Walker, and *lootenant* it now is. An American police lieutenant is commonly *Loot* to his men, and the same abbreviation is not unknown in the Army and Navy.

Jones says in "An English Pronouncing Dictionary" that *route* is pronounced *rowt* by English soldiers but *root* by the rest of the population. Webster preferred *rowt*, but George R. Howells reported in 1883 [2] that "ninety Americans out of a hundred," at that time, used *root*. Bender gives *root* without mentioning *rowt*; Kenyon and Knott, and Webster 1961, give both.

The intrusion of the *y* before the broad *a*, as in *cyard* and *gyarden*, is still thought of by most Americans as a Southernism, but it actually goes back to Eighteenth Century England, when it was described by Walker (1791) as prevailing "in polite pronunciation." At the same time there was a fashion in London for inserting it before the diphthong of such words as *kind* and *cow*. Webster was against this intrusion, and denounced it in his "Dissertations" in 1789. In the case of *ow* he called it characteristic of the "barbarous dialect . . . of the Eastern country people." "It is presumed," he added prissily, "that the bare mention of such barbarisms will be sufficient to restrain their progress, both in New England and on [*sic*] the British theatre." After *k* and *g* the *y* sound is still frequently heard in the South.[3] Greet, himself a Southerner, says that there is much variety of usage among Southerners who affect the *y* sound, and that they are seldom consistent.[4] It is not fashionable, he says, in words showing the vowels of *gift*, *get* and *carry*, but it occurs before the *ur* sound, as in *gyirls* for *girls*. To insert the *y* sound before the *ow* of *cow*, he says, is "a real *faux-pas*." In this he agrees with Webster. But *cyow*, *cyounty* and their like, which were common in the New England of Webster's time, still survive there among the remoter country people.

In the dialect speech of the Republic the diphthongs have made heavy weather of it. Either they displace other sounds, as in the *thoid* of the Brooklyn [and New Orleans] dialect, or they are themselves displaced by other sounds, as in *pizen* for *poison* and *snoot* for *snout*. The use of the diphthong of *wine* in the words in *oi* was quite correct in England in the Seventeenth and Eighteenth Centuries. Samuel Butler's rhymes indicate that he heard it in *toil*, *purloin* and *enjoin*, Dryden's that it was then current in *toil* and *coin* and Pope's that it was admitted in *enjoy* and *join*. The colonists thus brought it with them, and at the same time it lodged in

---

[2] *Transactions of the Albany Institute*, Vol. X.

[3] Krapp, Vol. II, pp. 207 ff.; [Kurath and McDavid, p. 175, Map 167].

[4] Southern English, in Culture in the South, ed. by W. T. Couch; Chapel Hill, N.C., 1934, p. 610.

Ireland, where it still prevails. But in England, during the late Eighteenth Century, this *i* sound was displaced in many words by the original *oi* sound, not through historical research but by deduction on the part of pedagogues, from the spelling. William Kenrick's "New Dictionary of the English Language" (1773) indicated that *ai* was still normal in *boil* and *join*, but in *oil* and *toil* had become "a vicious custom" tolerated only "in common conversation." [5] The new pronunciation soon extended to the polite speech of America. In the common speech, however, the *ai* sound persisted, and down to the time of the Civil War it was constantly heard in such words as *join, spoil, joist* and *pennyroyal*, which thus became *jine, spile, jist* and *pennyr'yal*. Since then the schoolma'am has combatted the *ai* sound with such vigor that it has begun to disappear, and such forms as *pizen, bile* and *ile* are seldom heard. But in certain other words the *ai* sound still persists. Chief among them are *hoist* and *roil*. An unlearned American always says that he was *riled*. Desiring to examine the hoof of a horse, he never orders the animal to *hoist* but always to *hist*. In the coal mines of southern Illinois *hoist* is pronounced correctly in *hoisting engineer*, but he always *hists* the coal.[6] *Jine* as a verb has retired to certain dialects, but the noun *jiner*, signifying a man given to joining fraternal orders, is still in common use. Most of the other vowel changes in vulgar American are also to be encountered in the British dialects. A flat *a* displaces the long *e* of *beet* in *rear* (*e.g.*, as a horse) and the short *e* of *thresh* and *wrestle*, producing *rare, thrash* and *wrastle*. In the days before the Civil War a short *i* appeared in *cover*, producing *kiver. Jedge* for *judge* and *empire* for *umpire* survive more or less, as do *jest* and *jist* for *just* and *tech* for *touch. Shet* for *shut* is still common, [but *gal* for *girl* is now usually jocular, and deliberately so]. The substitution of *guardeen* and *champeen* for *guardian* and *champion* is very common, if hardly polite. So is *chaw* for *chew*. One *stamps* a letter but *stomps* with the foot.[7] This last differentiation seems to have a number of parallels in English: the case of *strap* and (razor) *strop* suggests itself at once. Similarly, a cow *tromps* her fodder, but a vagrant remains a *tramp*. All of these variants are gradually succumbing, though some of them— like *strop* and *stomp*—are still common in educated speech.

The English are rather more bold than we are in naturalizing foreign words, especially proper names, and the example of *Calais*, pronounced

---

[5] A Modern English Grammar, by Otto Jespersen; Heidelberg, Vol. I, 1922, pp. 329–30. Isaac Watts, in The Art of Reading and Writing English, 1721, listed *jice* as correct for *joist*, but Robert Nares, in Elements of Orthoepy, 1784, denounced *hist* for *hoist* as a "low vulgarism."

[6] Personal communication from Dr. H. K. Croessman, Du Quoin, Ill. [See Kurath and McDavid, pp. 167–8, Maps 143–6. Webster 1961 and Webster's Seventh New Collegiate (1963) accept *rile* in the sense of to irritate.]

[7] [*Judge, kettle, stamp* and *touch* are discussed in Kurath and McDavid.]

to rhyme with *palace* since Shakespeare's time, is in point. The consultants of the BBC do not hesitate to recommend essentially English pronunciations of such words as *carillon, conduit, cul-de-sac, liqueur* and *harem*, and they appear to have a hearty contempt for the French *u* and the German *ö* (they convert *Röntgen*, for example, into *Runtgen*), but in many other cases they are at pains to preserve something resembling foreign pronunciation, *e.g.*, in *compère*, (the English equivalent of the American *master of ceremonies* or *m.c.*), *enceinte, hors-d'oeuvre, entourage* and *ski*. The result is inevitably a series of sorry compromises. "The only French sound in the average English pronunciation of the word *restaurant*," observed Lloyd James sadly, "is the *s*, which is the same in English and French." [8] His colleagues on the BBC board have sometimes changed their decisions. On January 17, 1930, they ordained that *ski* should be *skee*, but by 1935 it had become the correct Dano-Norwegian *shee*.

Most American authorities seem to be willing to let nature take its course. They have learned by bitter experience that their admonitions, at best, never reach below the penthouse of the educational structure. Because of the presence of so many foreigners in the Republic, Americans on the lower levels have picked up many more loan words than Englishmen of the corresponding class, and not a few of those that have come in by word of mouth have retained more or less correct pronunciations, *e.g.*, the French *rouge*, the Spanish *cañon, mesa* and *tortilla*, and the German *sauerkraut, pumpernickel, hausfrau* and *delicatessen*. In other cases loan words have been preserved with changes in spelling, as *ouch* (*autsch*) and *bower* (*Bauer*). In yet other cases they have succumbed to folk etymology, *e.g.*, the Dutch *koolsla*, pronounced *cole slaw*, which has become *cold slaw*; or suffered changes in their vowels, *e.g.*, the Spanish *peón* (whose derivative, *peonage*, rhymes the first syllable with *see*), *loafer* (from the German *Laufer*) and *smearcase* (from *Schmierkäse*). Brander Matthews believed in the inevitability of such changes, and refused to denounce them. "The principle which ought to govern," he once said,

> can be stated simply. English should be at liberty to help itself freely to every foreign word which seems to fill a want in our own language. . . . Those which are retained ought to become completely English, in pronunciation, in spelling, and in the formation of their plurals. No doubt this is today a counsel of perfection; but it indicates the goal which should be strived for. It is what English was capable of accomplishing prior to the middle of the Seventeenth Century. [9]

---

[8] Broadcast English No. I, in which he had a hand, advises *réstarong*.

[9] The Englishing of French Words, *SPE Tract*, No. V; Oxford, 1921, p. 7.

When a foreign word in wide use presents difficulties, the plain people sometimes dispose of it by inventing a shortened form, as in *bra* (pronounced *brah*) for *brassière*. Not infrequently a loan which has had polite treatment on the higher levels is dealt with barbarously when it becomes known lower down. This happened, for example, to *coupé*. It was commonly pronounced in an approximation of the French manner so long as it designated a four-wheeled, one-horse carriage,[1] but when it was applied, *c.* 1920, to a car it quickly became *coop*.[2] In the same way *liqueur* became *lik-kewer, chassis* became *shassis* or *tshassis,* and *chic* came close to *chick. Hors-d'oeuvre* has always been a stumbling block to Anglo-Saxons. Many Americans, in despair, have turned to the Italian *antipasto,* which is much less painful to the national larynx.

Among other words first apprehended in print *brazeer* is common for *brassière, ratskiller* for *Rathskeller, huffbrow* for *Hofbräu, vawdvil* for *vaudeville, dash'und* for *Dachshund, shammy* for *chamois, fyancy* for *fiancée, massour* for *masseur, de-bút* for *début, nee* for *née, premeer* for *première, meenoo* for *menu* and *ródeo* for *rodéo.* In the *Hinterwald* the musical terms brought in by wandering performers undergo a radical transformation. *Prélude* becomes *prelood, étude* becomes *ee-tude, scherzo* becomes *shirt-so* and *Träumerei* becomes *trowmerai.* Some years ago the word *protégé* had a brief vogue in fistic circles and was often used by announcers at prize fights. They always pronounced it *proteege.* I once heard a burlesque show manager, in announcing a French dancing act, pronounce *M.* and *Mlle.* as *Em* and *Milly.*

In 1935, Emily Post, then the unchallenged arbiter of elegance in the United States, was appealed to for advice about pronouncing the French words currently in vogue. She replied that those which had "already been Americanized" should be turned into "plain English," *e.g., menyou* for *menu* and *valet* with a clear *t;* and that those having sounds nearly equivalent to English sounds should be given the latter, *e.g., mass-her* for *masseur* ("emphasis is the same on both syllables"), *brass-yair* for *brassière* and *show-fur,* not *showfer* or *showf'r* ("accent both syllables equally, or else slightly on the last"), for *chauffeur.* Such words as *garage, demitasse* and *fiancé* she described as "stumbling blocks," and advised her customers, in the last two cases, to substitute *black coffee* and either *betrothed* or *man I'm going to marry.*[3]

---

[1] The DAE says that it was first used in this country in the 1840s.

[2] Some Established Mispronunciations, by Annina Periam Danton, *Words,* Nov. 1937, p. 177.

[3] Mrs. Post added some advice about honorifics and proper names. Europeans, she said, always use their own titles in addressing Americans, so we should use *Mister, Misses* or *Miss* in addressing them, thus avoiding the snares of *Monsieur, Signora* and *Fräulein.* [See also On the Pronunciation of Recent French Loan-Words, by Knut Sørensen, *Eng-*

Charles James Fox, it is said, called the red wine of France *Bordox* to the end of his days. He had an American heart; his great speeches for the revolting colonies were more than mere oratory. John Bright, another kind friend in troubled days, had one too. He always said *Bordox* and *Calass.*

3: THE CONSONANTS

The generally more distinct utterance of Americans preserves a number of consonants that have begun to decay in Standard English. The English have not only made a general slaughter of *r*; they show a tendency to be careless about *l*, *d*, *g* and *t*, at least in certain situations, and even on the level of the best usage they drop a few *h*'s. An American always sounds the first *l* in *fulfill*; an Englishman commonly makes the first syllable *foo*. An American sounds the final *t* in *trait*; an Englishman makes it homologous with *tray*.

Next after the use of the broad *a*, the elision of *r* before consonants and in the terminal position is the thing that Americans are most conscious of in English speech. "In London and some parts of the South [of England]," said R. J. Lloyd in 1894, "the *r* following a vowel at the end of the word or syllable has disappeared, but there is no other part of the English-speaking world except Eastern New England where this is quite the case." [4] Lloyd might have excepted also the Tidewater South, but everywhere else in the United States, including even the Hudson Valley area, the *r* is usually sounded. Bernard Bloch, one of the collaborators on the Linguistic Atlas of New England, has since shown that in the western third of that area it prevails in more than 75% of the cases, and even within the Boston territory there are speech islands in which it is clearly sounded. [5]

The violent Anglophile Henry James, revisiting the United States after many years in England, was so distressed by this clear sounding of *r* that he denounced it as "a morose grinding of the back teeth," [6] and became so

---

lish Studies, Vol. XXXVII, Aug. 1956, pp. 162–8. Thomas Pyles has devoted two studies to the problem of Latin words: Tempest in Teapot: The Reform in Latin Pronunciation, *ELH*, Vol. VI, 1939, pp. 138–64, and The Pronunciation of Latin in English: A Lexicographical Dilemma, *AS*, Vol. XXII, Feb. 1947, pp. 3–17.]

[4] Standard English, *Die neuren Sprache*, 1894, p. 53. I take this from Sidelights on the Pronunciation of English, by Giles Wilkeson Gray, *QJS*, Vol. XVIII, Nov. 1932, p. 556.

[5] Postvocalic *r* in New England Speech, *Acts of the Fourth International Congress of Linguists;* Copenhagen, 1936, pp. 195–9. [Bloch's findings have been re-examined and the data from the rest of the Atlantic seaboard evaluated in The Loss of Postvocalic *r* in the Eastern United States, by William R. Van Riper, diss. (microfilm), U. of Michigan, 1958. See also Postvocalic /-r/ in South Carolina: a Social Analysis, by Raven I. McDavid, Jr., *AS*, Vol. XXIII, Oct.–Dec. 1948, pp. 194–203.]

[6] The Question of Our Speech; Boston, 1905, p. 29.

sensitive to it that he began to hear it where it was actually nonexistent, save as an occasional barbarism, *e.g.*, in *Cuba-r*, *vanilla-r* and *California-r*. He put the blame for it, and for various other departures from the strict canon of Oxford English, upon "the American school, the American newspaper, and the American Dutchman and Dago." James's observations, obviously, must have been made west of the Connecticut River and north of the Potomac.

H. C. Wyld offers evidence [7] that r was lost before consonants "at least as early as the Fifteenth Century," and especially before *s* and *sh*, as in *sca'cely* and *ma'sh*. Krapp gives many examples from the early American town records, and calls attention to the fact that there are survivals in vulgar American, as in *cuss*, *bust*, *passel* (for *parcel*) and *hoss*.[8] Toward the end of the Eighteenth Century it became fashionable in England to omit the *r*, and Samuel Johnson helped that fashion along by denouncing the "rough, snarling letter." Archibald A. Hill supports Wyld by showing that the loss of *r* after vowels and before consonants is frequent in the English dialects,[9] and has produced examples from as long ago as the Fifteenth and Sixteenth Centuries, *e.g.*, *assenycke* for *arsenic* (1530) and *cott* for *court* (1552). Today in England it is omitted when it stands at the end of a word, as in *car*, *fair* and *fur*. However, it is commonly restored when the word following begins with a vowel, as in "The *car* is at the door." [1] But this restoration is not invariable, and there are situations in which many speakers seem to find it difficult to decide whether they should sound the *r* or not. As a result, some of them insert it where it has no place, as in "The *idear* is" and "*vanillar* ice cream." This confusion is promoted by the fact that many quite dissimilar words, *e.g.*, *law* and *lore*, are pronounced precisely alike in Southern English. [In Boston and New York City, the prevailing practice is that of England. But in the South it is different. No proper Charlestonian or Tidewater Virginian says *over all*; he says *ovah all*.]

J. S. Kenyon observes, like Ring Lardner before him,[2] that the literary custom of representing the vulgar pronunciation of *fellow*, *window* and their like by *feller*, *winder*, etc., is misleading, for the final syllable usually does not show *r* at all, but is simply the neutral vowel.[3] Why has *r* survived in the American hinterland? Kenyon rejects the theory that the schoolma'am, egged on by Webster, preserved it by insisting on spelling-pronunciations, and points out very wisely that there were more of her

---

[7] Wyld, p. 298.

[8] Krapp, Vol. II, p. 220. [See also More Evidence of Early Loss of [r] in Eastern American Speech, by Gordon E. Bigelow, *AS*, Vol. XXX, May 1955, pp. 154-6.]

[9] Early Loss of *r* Before Dentals, *PMLA*, Vol. LVI, June 1940, pp. 308-59.

[1] See Broadcast English No. II, by A. Lloyd James; London, 1930, p. 14.

[2] Some Notes on American *r*, *AS*, Vol. I, Mar. 1926, pp. 329-39.

[3] [But see Kurath and McDavid, pp. 169-73, Maps 151-9.]

clan in eastern New England, where it vanished, than to the westward, where it persisted. He and Krapp [4] rather incline to believe that the character of the immigration to the West was mainly responsible. It was largely made up of Scotsmen, Irishmen and Englishmen coming from regions outside the influence of London speech, and "they brought their *r*'s with them." "There is much reason to think," Kenyon concludes, "that the Western treatment of *r* . . . is parallel to the Western pronunciation of words like *half*, which belongs to an 'older family' than Eastern *hahf*." Even more than the use of the flat *a*, the sounding of *r* is the chief hallmark of American speech; indeed, Leonard Bloomfield says that this "Central-Western type of American Standard English" may be defined as "the type which preserves old *r* in final position and before consonants." [5]

The dropping of the final *g* [more accurately, replacement of an *ng* sound by an *n*] in words ending in -*ing* seems to be more widespread in England than in America, and is tolerated, if not exactly recommended, by most of the English authorities. [In fact, it is often a touchstone for the speech of the best squirearchical families.] Kenyon says [6] that, in the United States, it "appears to be more common among the educated in the South than in the North and East." "The spelling-pronunciation," he goes on, "is now so general that it is in excellent usage, but it must not be hastily concluded that the pronunciation -*in* is necessarily a mark of ignorance or lack of cultivation. It is still commoner than most people suppose." [Even among the cultured, -*in* is used by about a fifth of the Atlas informants in New England and the Middle Atlantic States, and a good half of those in the South. In the North-Central States and the upper Midwest, despite the influence of the schools, -*in* is used by nearly half of the cultivated. Among the hoi polloi, of course, the proportion is much higher.[7]] Krapp shows [8] that -*in* is to be found plentifully in the early American records, and that it must have been general in the Seventeenth Century. He ascribes the prevalence of -*ing* to the rage for spelling-pronunciations, and notes that, among the innocent, "the analogy of words" has produced such forms as *kitching* and *garding*.

It is as grievous to an Englishman of tone to be accused of dropping his *h*'s as it is to a Southerner to be accused of using *you-all* in the singular. Nevertheless, both are guilty to some extent. Daniel Jones, in prescribing the usages of what he calls Received Pronunciation (RP), lists *hospital* with

[4] Krapp, Vol. II, p. 231.
[5] The Stressed Vowels of American English, *Lg.*, Vol. XI, Apr.–June 1935, pp. 97–116.
[6] American Pronunciation; Ann Arbor, Mich., 1945, p. 149.
[7] [E. Bagby Atwood, A Survey of Verb Forms in the Eastern United States, Ann Arbor, Mich., 1953, pp. 34–5; Virginia McDavid, Verb Forms in the North-Central States and Upper Midwest, diss. (microfilm), U. of Minnesota, 1956.]
[8] Krapp, Vol. II, pp. 13–17.

a clear *h* but allows both *hostler* and *ostler*, and when he comes to *hotel* says that "some use the form *otel* always; others use it occasionally, when the word is not initial."[9] All Americans believe that they sound the *h* invariably, but when they use *an* before *hotel*, which happens sometimes, they actually say *an otel*, for sounding the *h* after consonants is phonologically unhandy, as the cases of *on his* and *to kiss her* sufficiently show. They are saved from Cockneyism by the fact that, as a practical matter, they seldom use *an* before *hotel* and its allied words, despite the assumed influence on their speech of the King James Bible, which gives it before *haven*, *hedge*, *hidden*, *house*, *hypocrite*, etc. In late years the more popular American prints of Holy Writ have quietly substituted *a* for *an* before all these words, though in a few aberrant cases *an* is retained. In the only instances in which *hen*, *hind*, *hot* and *huge* appear in the text with an indefinite article the King James Version itself uses *a*, which is also used before *horrible*.

So far as I know, the only study of English and American practice with *an* and *a* has been one reported by Louis N. Feipel in 1929.[1] He investigated 300 contemporary books by authors of decent standing on both sides of the water and found that the English used *an* much oftener than the Americans. With *hallucination*, for example, the score ran three to one, with *horizon* four to one and with *hysterical* five to one. *An historical* was found in six English writers and four Americans, but *a* was likewise used by six Englishmen and four Americans, which left a sort of stalemate. *An heroic* was used by eight Englishmen and four Americans, but two Americans used *a heroic*, which all the English avoided. Mark Twain was noting these differences in 1879, when he said to an Englishman encountered on a German train:

> Your educated classes say *humble* now, and *heroic*, and *historic*, etc., but I judge that they used to drop those *h*'s because your writers still keep up the fashion of putting an *an* before those words, instead of *a*. This is what Mr. Darwin might call a rudimentary sign that *an* was justifiable once, and useful—when your educated classes used to say *umble*, and *eroic*, and *istorical*.[2]

When it appears in any save the initial position, *h* is frequently dropped, by British and Americans alike. No one, for example, sounds it in *exhaust*

---

[9] An English Pronouncing Dictionary, p. 211.

[1] *A* and *An* before *h* and Certain Vowels, *AS*, Vol. IV, Aug. 1929, pp. 442–54. [There is an unpublished study of *a/an apple* in the LA records, which shows that *a apple* is characteristic of the American South and South Midland, as it is of Scots.]

[2] Concerning the American Language, "part of a chapter crowded out of A Tramp Abroad" (1880), in The Stolen White Elephant; New York, 1882, pp. 265–9.

and *exhort*. The English long ago dropped it from *forehead,* which is *forrid* or *forred* in their speech. There was a time when they also dropped it in *blockhead, hothouse, hedgehog, greenhouse, abhor* and *adhere*. The compensatory insertion of *h* in situations where it does not belong is purely dialectal in English and does not occur in Standard Southern English. In American it is unknown, save in such vulgar forms as *overhalls*. But Americans sometimes retain the *h* where English usage does not sound it, especially in proper names, *e.g., Northampton.*

The English, at least in the London area, seem to have early abandoned all effort to sound the *h* in such words as *when* and *where*. [In the United States, however, words like *whip* and *wheelbarrow* generally have *hw*. But the *h* is usually lost in a triangular area of the Middle Atlantic States, from Albany to Baltimore and westward to the Pennsylvania Appalachians, and in two narrow coastal strips from Boston north and from Georgetown, S.C., south. *Wharf,* a coastal word, lacks *h* almost everywhere it is known. *Whoa* usually has *h* in the area of New England settlement, but lacks it elsewhere. Usage to the west is not yet known in detail, but the New Orleans area seems to lack *h* in all these words, as do a considerable proportion of speakers in metropolitan areas, particularly in groups whose ancestral language was something other than English.[3]]

The authority of Webster was sufficient to establish the American pronunciation of *schedule*. In England the *sch* is always given the soft sound, but Webster decided for the hard sound as in *scheme*. The name of the last letter of the alphabet, which is always *zed* in England and Canada, is *zee* in the United States. Thornton shows that this Americanism arose in the Eighteenth Century. Americans normally give *nephew* (following a spelling-pronunciation, historically incorrect) an *f* sound instead of the English *v* sound.[4] They tend to abandon the *f* sound in *diphtheria, diphthong* and *naphtha* for a plain *p* sound.[5] English usage prefers an *s* sound in such words as *issue* and *sensual,* but in America the sound is commonly that of *sh*. English usage prefers a *tu* sound in *actual, punctuate, virtue* and their like, but in America the *tu* tends to become *choo*.

The American plain people add a *t* to *across, close, wish, once* and *twice,* and displace *d* with *t* in *hold,* which becomes *holt*. In *told* and *old* they abandon the *d* altogether, preferring *tole* and *ole*. *Didn't* is pronounced *di'n't,* and *find* becomes indistinguishable from *fine*. The same sound is often dropped before consonants, as in *bran(d)-new, goo(d)-*

[3] [See *H* before Semivowels in the Eastern United States, by Raven I. McDavid, Jr., and Virginia McDavid, *Lg.,* Vol. XXVIII, Jan.–Mar. 1952, pp. 41–62.]

[4] [See Kurath and McDavid, p. 176, Map 169.]

[5] [See Kurath and McDavid, p. 179, Map 179.]

sized and *corne(d) beef.* The old *ax* for *ask* is now confined to a few dialects; in the current vulgate *ast* is substituted for it. The *t* is dropped in *bankrup, kep, slep, crep, quanity* and *les (let's).* The *l* is omitted from *a'ready* and *gent'man*, and the *g* from *reco'nize.* Medial *r* is also often dropped [even in *r*-sounding areas], as in *su'prise, qua'ter, co'ner, pe'form-ance, lib'ary, yeste'day, sa'sparilla, pu'sy* (for *pursy*, usually encountered in *pussy gut*), *pa'lor* and *Feb'uary.*[6] Some of these are to be found also in English usage. Other sounds that are likewise dropped on occasion are those of *k*, as in *e'cept;*[7] *th*, as in *scythe; v* as in *fi' cents.* The excrescent *b*, as in *chimbley*, and the addition of *th* for *t* in *height*, like that of *t* to *once*, seem to be heirlooms from the English of two centuries ago. There are many parallels for the English butchery of *extraordinary, e.g., bound'ry, int'res'* and *prob'ly. Ordinary* is commonly enunciated clearly, but it has bred a degenerate form, *onry* or *onery*, differentiated in meaning.[8] Some-times one consonant is substituted for another, as in *grampa* and *robm* (*robin*), or two for two, as in *sebm* (*seven*);[9] sometimes a cluster of con-sonants is omitted, as in *gra'ma;* and sometimes there is elision of a com-bination of consonant and vowel, as in *pro'bition* and *gov'ment.*

Hilaire Belloc, in 1924, alleged that *th*, in American speech, was be-coming *d*.[1] This change has never been acknowledged by any American phonologists, [except in such jungles as New York's East Side and New Orleans's Irish Channel], but many of them have studied the parallel change of *t* to a kind of *d*, as in *water, butter, battle, twenty*, etc. An Englishman commonly pronounces the *t* in *pity* much like that in *tippy*, but in col-loquial American speech the former often comes close to *piddy.* This change, acording to Kenyon,[2] "occurs most commonly between vowels, sometimes between a vowel and certain of the voiced consonants when it is at the end of an accented syllable before an unaccented one (*twenty*), or sometimes when it is at the beginning of an unaccented one where there is some doubt which syllable the *t* is pronounced with (*want to go*)." It also occurs between two unaccented syllables, as in *join us at eleven.* It does not occur at "the beginning of syllables initial in the phrase, whether ac-cented or unaccented (*table, today*), nor at the end of syllables final in the

---

[6] Loss of *r* in English Through Dissim-ilation, by George Hempl, *DN*, Vol. I, Pt. VI, 1893, pp. 279–81.

[7] Two Observations on Current Col-loquial Speech, by A. R. Dunlap, *AS*, Vol. XIV, Dec. 1939, p. 290.

[8] In the Baltimore of my youth *o'n'ry* was in general use; it was understood to signify, not ordinary, but vicious.

[9] Some Recurrent Assimilations, by Louise Pound, *AS*, Vol. VI, June 1931, pp. 347–8.

[1] The Contrast; New York, 1924, p. 225.

[2] American Pronunciation; 9th ed.; Ann Arbor, Mich., 1945, p. 232.

phrase, whether accented or unaccented (*repeat, rivet*), nor at the beginning of accented medial (*Miltonic*) or final syllables (*retain*)." [3]

The use of *s* for *sh* before *r*, noted in many English dialects, seems to be common in the South. It was denounced by a Baltimore orthoepist, so long ago as 1856, as "the affected pronunciation of over-refined school-girls who cannot bring themselves to utter the homely English sound of *sh* when combined with an *r* for fear apparently of distorting their faces," [4] but it survives widely below the Potomac, and is not unknown in other regions.

The displacement of consonants by metathesis, as in *prespiration, hunderd, modren, childern, calvary, neuraliga, govrenment, apurn* and *interduce*, is not pathognomonic of vulgar American but is ancient in English and has produced a number of everyday words, *e.g., third*, which started out as *thrid*. Equally widespread is the intercalation of redundant vowels, though many familiar examples are probably of American origin, *e.g., athaletic, reality (realty), fillum, Cubéan, golluf, cruality, mayorality* and *municipial*.[5] It was apparently commoner in the earlier days than it is today. The addition of *g* to the *n* of unstressed syllables has been traced by Wyld [6] to the Fifteenth Century. Some of his later examples are *chicking*, 1653; *lining (linen)*, 1657; *chapling*, 1662; *fashing*, 1664; *childering*, 1692; and *slouinglie (slovenly)*, 1549. In the American common speech such forms are still frequent, *e.g., capting*. Sometimes a *t* is added, as in *varmint (vermin)*, which is traced by Wyld to 1539 and is now reduced to dialect. Often the *t* follows an *s* sound, as in the familiar *wunst, twict, acrost* and *sinct*. Wentworth traces *grievious* and *bretheren* to 1837, *hunderd* (or *hundert*) and *childern* to 1840 and *modren* to 1905. The last is undoubtedly much older. [An analogue, *tavren*, is the normal pronunciation of Cleveland radio announcers. *Pronounciation* appears in the speech and even the writing of many educated Americans,[7] including some university presidents.] *Mountainious*, used quite seriously, is in *Harper's Magazine* for

---

[3] An attempt at a controlled experiment was conducted in Hazleton, Pa., by Victor A. Oswald, Jr. See Voiced *t*—a Misnomer, *AS*, Vol. XVIII, Feb. 1943, pp. 18–25. [Later observations on the phenomenon have been made in *AS* by W. P. Lehmann, Vol. XXVIII, Dec. 1953, pp. 271–5, and by Donald J. Sharf, Vol. XXXV, May 1960, pp. 105–9. It is my impression that for most younger speakers *latter* and *ladder* are now homonyms.]

[4] Punctuation and Improprieties of Speech; Baltimore, 1856, p. 68. I take this from Pronunciation of *Shrimp, Shrub*

and Other Words, by George H. Reese, *AS*, Vol. XVI, Dec. 1941, pp. 251–5. Reese says that *sr* became dominant in Standard English in the late Seventeenth or early Eighteenth Century, but was subsequently replaced by *shr*, "probably under the influence of the spelling."

[5] [On the assembly lines, *grieviance* seems to be the preferred pronunciation.]

[6] Wyld, p. 290.

[7] [For example, in a letter to *Advance* (house organ of the Episcopal diocese of Chicago), in Mar. 1962, complaining of the failure of the rev. clergy to follow British models.]

1860,[8] and *Patapsico* for *Patapsco* is common in Maryland. According to a writer in *American Speech*,[9] intrusive *n* remains a recurrent phenomenon in speech and writing, *e.g., menance, prowness* and *grimance*. Other familiar forms are *conflab, lozenger* (traced to 1850), *bronichal* and *portry*. Further changes have converted *licorice* to *likerish, recipe* into *receipt, picture* into *pitcher* and *larceny* into *larsensy*. A lovely example of double metamorphosis is offered by *savage corpse* for *salvage corps*.

4: DIALECTS [1]

All the early writers on the American language remarked its strange freedom from dialects. This freedom, of course, was only relative, for differences were noted even before the Revolution. But both local residents and the English travelers who toured the country between the Revolution and the War of 1812 were right in reporting that the linguistic differences

---

[8] Dec., p. 132.

[9] Vol. XV, Dec. 1940, p. 360.

[1] [The years since the publication of Supplement Two have seen a spectacular growth in our knowledge of American dialects—in the amount of over-all information, in the accuracy with which patterns can be described and in the understanding of the forces that created those patterns. To take the Linguistic Atlas alone, in 1947 all that was available was the New England part, plus a few interpretative articles based on preliminary investigations further south and in the Great Lakes region. Since then field work has been completed along the Atlantic seaboard, in the North-Central States (Wisconsin, Michigan, southwestern Ontario, Illinois, Indiana, Kentucky and Ohio), in the "Upper Midwest" (Minnesota, Iowa, Nebraska and the Dakotas), in Colorado and Utah in the Rockies and in California and Nevada on the Pacific slope, and is well under way in the Pacific Northwest (Washington, Oregon, Idaho and Montana). In Louisiana the students of C. M. Wise have made more than a hundred field records, and for the vocabulary there is a sizable body of evidence in the lower South. Investigators are now in the field in Missouri and Oklahoma. Out of the archives of these projects—and special studies of particular communities —have come dozens of articles and three major books: Kurath's Word Geography of the Eastern United States (1949), Atwood's Survey of Verb Forms in the Eastern United States (1953) and Kurath and McDavid's Pronunciation of English in the Atlantic States (1961). In addition to the Atlas projects, the collections of C. K. Thomas on pronunciation—particularly the *ah* and *aw* vowels—have continued to grow; Norman Eliason and his students have produced several studies of early North Carolina speech, based on historical records, including one first-rate book, Eliason's Tarheel Talk (1956); scholars have shown a growing interest in foreign-language communities and in bilingualism; and Frederic G. Cassidy has steered the American Dialect Society into systematic work toward a dialect dictionary, and has just completed Wisconsin Words with the help of Audrey Duckert. Elsewhere in this hemisphere, a linguistic atlas and a dialect dictionary are near completion in Jamaica, along with a Historical Dictionary of Jamaica English, comparable to the DAE; Cassidy's Jamaica Talk, a popular introduction, appeared in 1961. A linguistic atlas and a dialect dictionary are likewise under way in Newfoundland, and plans have been drafted for an imposing series of Canadian dictionaries as well as for completing Linguistic Atlas work in the Maritimes and ultimately throughout the Dominion.]

they found among Americans were vastly less than one could find in Britain.[2]

The first writer to deal with this fact at length, the Rev. John Witherspoon, explained it as due to the mobility of the American people.[3] Timothy Dwight and John Pickering took the same line, as did the Rev. Jonathan Boucher, whose glossary was published in 1832. "There is, properly speaking," said Boucher, "no dialect in America . . . unless some scanty remains of the croaking, guttural idioms of the Dutch, still observable in New York; the Scotch-Irish, as it used to be called, in some of the back settlers of the Middle States; and the whining, canting drawl brought by some republican, Oliverian and Puritan emigrants from the West of England, and still kept up by their unregenerated descendants of New England—may be called dialects." [4] James Fenimore Cooper said in 1828 that such meager dialects as were to be encountered in the United States were fast wearing down to uniformity. The differences between New England, New York and Pennsylvania speech, he said, "were far greater twenty years ago than they are now." [5] A generation later George P. Marsh reported that this ironing out had been arrested. "I think no Eastern man," he said, "can hear a native of the Mississippi Valley use the *o* vocative, or observe the Southern pronunciation of ejaculatory or other emphatic phrases, without perceiving a very marked though often indescribable difference between their and our utterance of the same things." But Marsh was still convinced that American was singularly uniform. He said:

> Not only is the *average* of English used here, both in speaking and writing, better than that of the great mass of the English people; but there are fewer local peculiarities of form and articulation in our vast extent of territory than on the comparatively narrow soil of Great Britain. In spite of disturbing and distracting causes, English is more emphatically one in America than in its native land.[6]

A great many other authorities might be quoted, all supporting the same doctrine. In 1919 Krapp declared:

> Relatively few Americans spend all their lives in one locality, and even if they do, they cannot possibly escape coming into contact

---

[2] See British Recognition of American Speech in the Eighteenth Century, by Allen Walker Read, *DN*, Vol. VI, Pt. VI, 1933, pp. 313–34, and Two Early Comments on American Dialects, by Robert J. Menner, *AS*, Vol. XIII, Feb. 1938, pp. 8–12.

[3] The Druid, No. V, May 9, 1781, reprinted in Mathews, p. 16.

[4] A Supplement to Johnson's Dictionary of the English Language; London, 1832–3.

[5] Notions of the Americans; London, 1828, Vol. II, pp. 164–5.

[6] Lectures on the English Language; New York, 1860; 4th ed., 1870; Lecture XXX, pp. 666–7, 674–5.

with Americans from other localities. . . . We can distinguish with some certainty Eastern and Western and Southern speech, but beyond this the author has little confidence in those confident experts who think they can tell infallibly, by the test of speech, a native of Hartford from a native of Providence, or a native of Philadelphia from a native of Atlanta, or even, if one insist on infallibility, a native of Chicago from a native of Boston.[7]

Krapp was discussing Standard American, but on the plane of the vulgate the leveling is almost as apparent. That vast uniformity which marks the people of the United States in general information, in reaction to new ideas, in deep-lying prejudices and enthusiasms, in the veriest details of domestic custom and dress, is nowhere more marked than in their speech habits. The differences in pronunciation between American dialects seldom impede free communication, for a man who converts *pass* into *pahs* or drops the final *r* in *father* is still usually able to palaver readily with one who gives *pass* the *a* of *Dan* and wrings the last gurgle out of his *r*'s. The differences in vocabulary are sometimes more puzzling, but they are not very numerous, and a stranger quickly picks them up. A newcomer to Maryland soon abandons *faucet*, or *tap*, or whatever it was that prevailed in his native wilds, and turns easily to the local *spigot*. In the same way an immigrant to the Deep South is rapidly fluent in the use of *you-all*, *yonder* and *to carry* in the sense of to convey. Even differences in intonation are much less marked between any two parts of the United States than they are between any two parts of England, or than between England and this country as a whole.[8] The railroad, the automobile, the mailorder catalogue, the movie and, above all, radio and television have promoted uniformity in even the most remote backwaters.

Nevertheless, there *are* dialectal differences in American English, and they have been observed and recorded by a multitude of investigators, professional and lay. Louise Pound has shown that the study of dialect, in both England and the United States, came in later than the study of folklore. The latter was "an offshoot of the Romantic Movement of the late Eighteenth and early Nineteenth Centuries," but the former had to wait for the organization of the English Dialect Society, which got under way in 1873, with W. W. Skeat (1835–1912) as its director and honorary secretary. The Society published a long series of excellent books, covering nearly all the English counties, and Joseph Wright, deputy professor

---

[7] The Pronunciation of Standard English in America; New York, 1919, p. viii.

[8] "The difference in speech between Boston and San Francisco," says the Encyclopaedia Britannica (14th ed., London, 1929, Vol. XIII, p. 698, col. 2), "is less than what may be observed between two villages in Great Britain that are only a few miles apart."

of comparative philology at Oxford, used the material thus amassed in his large "English Dialect Dictionary." [9] The American Dialect Society did not follow until 1889.[1] It probably owed its organization quite as much to the current discovery of and rage for dialect by American novelists as to the example of the English Society, but it had the advantage from the start of the interest of competent philologians. The Society has had its vicissitudes, including the mysterious loss of its collection of 26,000 examples of American dialect words and phrases. This collection has never been recovered, but enough of it had been printed in *Dialect Notes* to launch Harold Wentworth upon his "American Dialect Dictionary," published in 1944. Wentworth also mined *American Speech*, the newspapers and popular magazines and the writings of such lay observers as Edward Eggleston, James Russell Lowell, Roark Bradford, Joel Chandler Harris, Vance Randolph and the early humorists.[2] As a result, students of American speechways have a work which brings into one handy volume the accumulated observations of hundreds of men and women, extending over many years. Most of its materials come from printed sources, but Wentworth added firsthand examples whenever possible, some gathered in the field and the rest borrowed from other workers and the radio.

The book makes it clear that, in the United States as elsewhere, dialect is mainly a function of the lower orders of the population. Persons of the educated class, though they show the influence of the circumambient patois, nevertheless approach the standard speech of the region whenever any care in speaking is indicated. Individuals of this class, living in the country, says Wyld,[3] will "gain invariably a very fair knowledge of the local dialect in all its aspects." Yet they do not use this dialect in conversation among themselves, and seldom if ever in speaking to "their humbler friends," for if they did so "it would be felt as an insult." Wyld is discussing Englishmen, but the same thing is true of Americans [except for the more backward Southern politicians in rural areas]. The plain people, save on their very lowest levels, understand "good English" quite well, and many of them make not unsuccessful attempts, on occasion, to use it.

Wentworth's dictionary shows that any given dialect term may be considerably more widespread than is commonly assumed. *To tote* often seems to be a quite typical Southernism, but he finds examples of it from Maine, Pennsylvania, Illinois, Indiana and Oregon. *To carry*, in the sense of to transport or escort, is also associated in recent years with Southern

[9] Six vols., London, 1898–1905. It was reprinted in 1923 and 1962. An English Dialect Grammar is in Vol. VI.
[1] The story of its organization is told in The First Year of the American Dialect Society, *DN*, Vol. I, Pt. I, 1890, pp. 1–12.
[2] A list of his principal sources is in his dictionary, pp. 737–47.
[3] Wyld, pp. 15–16.

speech, but he cites its use in Maine.[4] Not infrequently the evidence makes it clear how a given locution got from one place to another. There is, for example, the Pennsylvania use of *all* in such a phrase as "The bread is *all.*" Its old home is in the German counties of its native state, and though it has got as far away as Nebraska and Kansas it is never encountered save in centers of German immigration. Many terms, sometimes thought of as regional, are really nearly universal, *e.g.*, *gallus*, suspenders; *h'ist*, hoist; *bub*, boy; and *sass*, sauce. Some specimens of this class belong to ignorant English everywhere, but others seem to be American inventions. Appreciable progress has been made in tracking down the history of the latter, chiefly in the colonial town records.[5] What is needed now is a co-operative dictionary on a comprehensive scale, following the method of the DAE. Since the resurrection of the American Dialect Society in 1942 there have been some efforts to interest a competent posse in such an enterprise. [Recently Frederic G. Cassidy, of Wisconsin, president of the ADS in 1958–9, devised a method for systematically investigating the most characteristic fields of the everyday vocabulary, along lines similar to those of the Linguistic Atlas, and has pushed to completion both a dialect dictionary of Wisconsin and one of his native Jamaica. Other scholars are emulating Cassidy—or at least urging their students to do so.[6]]

The Linguistic Atlas of the United States and Canada, launched in 1928, does not meet the need for the dialect dictionary, for it naturally confines itself to showing the distribution of a relatively small number of items. It offers the only feasible way to determine dialect boundaries with any precision, for the mere accumulation of terms is likely to lay too much stress upon those that are only aberrant and curious, and the collector has no means of checking their distribution.[7] [The work of Cassidy, himself a

---

[4] The OED traces it to 1513 in Scottish use, and shows that it was used by Pepys, Samuel Johnson and Benjamin Franklin.

[5] The pioneer in this investigation seems to have been Albert Matthews (1860–1946); his work was expanded by Krapp and by Miles L. Hanley. [Most recently the students of Norman Eliason, at the University of North Carolina, have begun to exploit the extensive materials in the local Southern Historical Collection. Eliason's Tarheel Talk (1956) is based upon those materials.]

[6] [See Cassidy, On Collecting American Dialect, *AS*, Vol. XXIII, Oct.–Dec. 1948, pp. 185–93; Cassidy and Audrey R. Duckert, A Method of Collecting Dialect, *PADS*, No. XX, 1953. Cassidy's techniques were utilized in A Dictionary

of the Folk Speech of the Eastern Alabama Negro, by Saunders Walker, diss. (MS), Western Reserve U., 1956.]

[7] [The development of systematic dialect study is sketched by Sever Pop in La Dialectologie: Aperçu historique et méthodes d'enquêtes linguistiques; Gembloux (Belgium), 1950. The most readily accessible summary of American research is that in Ch. IX of W. Nelson Francis, The Structure of American English; New York, 1958. The materials of inquiry are presented in A Compilation of the Worksheets of the Linguistic Atlas of the United States and Canada, by Raven I. McDavid, Jr., and Virginia McDavid, Ann Arbor, Mich., 1951; and A Compilation of Checklists Used in the Study of American Linguistic Geogra-

field worker for the Atlas in Ohio and Wisconsin, has done much to clarify the distinctions between a dialect dictionary and a linguistic atlas, and the once bitter debates between the proponents of general collecting and those of selective sampling seem destined to fade into history.]

The first part of the Linguistic Atlas, devoted to New England, was published between 1939 and 1943, along with an interpretative Handbook. Its six volumes are made up of 734 double-page tinted maps showing, in phonetic symbols, the vocabulary and pronunciation encountered in 223 communities in New England and six in New Brunswick. Successive maps show how typical people of the communities investigated pronounce common words, *e.g., class, theater* and *yesterday;* what names they use to designate common objects, *e.g., pail* or *bucket, garret* or *attic, purse* or *pocketbook;* how they conjugate common verbs, *e.g., swelled* or *swole, drove* or *driv, took* or *taken;* and what euphemisms they use for such words as *coffin, bull* and *ram.* The test words were adroitly chosen, and they produced a reasonably accurate and more or less representative report on New England speech.

One strange fact unearthed has been noted already—that the broad *a* of the Boston area seems to be gradually succumbing to the usual American flat *a,* even within cannon shot of the Harvard pump. Many other facts about American speech will reward the patience and stamina of any reader bold enough to struggle with the six hefty volumes and search the glosses accompanying the 734 maps. In 1933 the hideous *mummy,* for *mother,* borrowed from the English and now fashionable in all the big cities, was just beginning to invade New England. It was supported by a somewhat similar form, *mumma,* apparently indigenous, but the overwhelming majority of natives, whether urban or bucolic, appear to prefer the more ancient *ma, maw, mom, mahm, mum, mamma, mommy* or *mother.* So with names for the other parent. One example of *pater* is reported from the Boston area and one of *governor* from the Maine coast, but both seem to be innovations. Such innovations, says the Handbook, are "derived from the literary language" or "through contact with the upper classes of society." The maps show pretty clearly that the old Yankee dialect is fast losing many of what were once among its characteristic terms.

phy, by David W. Reed and David DeCamp, Berkeley, Cal., 1952. The possibilities of a streamlined "structural" examination of dialects, concerned chiefly with problems of pronunciation systems, have been explored by Uriel Weinreich in *Word,* Vol. X, Aug.–Dec. 1954, pp. 388–400, and by Robert P. Stockwell in *AS,* Vol. XXXIV, Dec. 1959, pp. 258–68, and again at the Ninth International Congress of Linguists, Cambridge, Mass., 1962. A balancing of the objectives will be found in *Orbis,* Vol. X, June 1961, pp. 35–46. LA investigators have repeatedly emphasized that methods are to be adapted to changing conditions and to new technological developments.]

Pantry is supplanting *buttery*, *clothes press* is yielding to *clothes closet*, *shopping* is driving out *trading* and *to home* is succumbing to *at home*.

The Linguistic Atlas was originally suggested by two linguistic scholars of eminence, Edward Sapir and E. H. Sturtevant, both of Yale and neither primarily a dialectologist. Hans Kurath, then of Ohio State University, later of Brown and now of Michigan, was in charge of it from the start, and his extraordinary learning and energy vitalized the whole enterprise. His principal collaborators included Miles L. Hanley, Bernard Bloch, Guy S. Lowman, Jr., and Marcus L. Hansen, and he was aided in organizing the field work by Jakob Jud, one of the editors of the Linguistic Atlas of Italy and Southern Switzerland,[8] and Paul Scheuermeier, a member of its staff. The gathering of materials in other parts of this country and Canada has been in progress for some years, [with Albert H. Marckwardt and Raven I. McDavid, Jr., in charge of the Great Lakes and Ohio Valley regions, Harold B. Allen in charge of the Upper Midwest, E. Bagby Atwood in charge of Texas, David W. Reed and Carroll E. Reed in charge of the Pacific Coast, and other competent linguists directing the work elsewhere. To this end funds have been provided by the American Council of Learned Societies and various universities and foundations, and Kurath, Bloch and others have undertaken the training of field workers. But none of the regional surveys to be brought out hereafter will be published on the heroic scale of the New England folios; Kurath and his colleagues are actually of the opinion that a less formidable format, without hand-lettered phonetic maps, will be more useful.

[How many major dialect areas exist in the United States is still a matter of dispute. As frequently happens, increasing knowledge has made generalization more difficult than it was a generation ago. Down to the publication of Kurath's "Word Geography of the Eastern United States"[9] it was customary to state that there were three of them: New England, Southern and so-called General American or Western. The most important was that which Kurath had earlier called] Western American, considered as the tongue which the overwhelming majority of Americans speak and the one that Englishmen always have in mind when they discuss American English. Its territory was defined to include all of New England west of the Connecticut River, the whole of the Middle Atlantic area save the lower Eastern Shore of Maryland and lower Delaware, and all the region west of the Cotton Belts of Texas and Arkansas and north of central Missouri and the Ohio River, with the mountain country of the South as an exclave. No other group of American dialects is so widespread, and

[8] Sprach- und Sachatlas Italiens und der Sudschweiz, ed. by Karl Jaberg and Jakob Jud; 16 vols.; Zofingen (Switz.), 1928–40.
[9] [Ann Arbor, Mich., 1949.]

none other is still spreading. [Because of its spread it was usually called General American. Its territory was so large that there was little surprise when subsequent research enabled Kurath and others to divide it into an Inland Northern area, derived from western New England by way of upstate New York, and a very different Midland area, derived from Pennsylvania.[1] Southern mountain speech is a subvariety of the South Midland area, which has spread southwestward from Pennsylvania, infiltrated the southern parts of Ohio, Indiana and Illinois and become the basis of the speech of Texas.]

Southern American marches with Kurath's Midland along the Potomac and the Blue Ridge, shows a few dips across the latter into the plantation country of the Kentucky bluegrass and the Tennessee Valley, and leaps the Mississippi into southern Missouri, Arkansas and eastern Texas. The people of the lower classes, whether white or black, still cling to their ancient speechways, and as a result "cultivated speech and dialects are more clearly separated than in the North." Greet distinguishes the coastal or Tidewater type from the general lowland speech. "The speech of the Virginia Tidewater," he says, "has been transplanted successfully to the northern Shenandoah region and to Charlottesville, but outside of Virginia it has made no headway against the General Southern of the lowlands."[2] This General Southern is spoken in "the plantation Up Country of Georgia and South Carolina, the cotton country of Alabama, Mississippi, Texas and Louisiana in so far as the speech is without French influence," and the Piedmont of Virginia. The speech of the hill people is quite different from both dialects of the Southern lowlands, [for it is basically derived from the Scotch-Irish of western Pennsylvania]. "There is no sharper speech boundary in the United States," says Kurath, "than that following the Blue Ridge from the Potomac to the James."[3] This mountain speech is also to be found in the Ozarks, which lie in the corner where Missouri, Arkansas

[1] [The first edition of C. K. Thomas's Introduction to the Phonetics of American English, New York, 1949, kept the term *General American,* though applying it to a much smaller territory than had been customary in the 1930s; the second edition, 1958, abandons it. However, it still appears in popular treatments, as that by Gilbert A. Schaye, *The New York Times Magazine,* July 30, 1961, p. 29. To describe the new type of speech arising in urban areas out of the contacts of various dialect types, Allen Walker Read proposes the term *Generalized American.* See The Labeling of National and Regional Variations in Popular Dictionaries, in Problems in Lexicography, ed. by Fred W. Householder and Sol Saporta, Publication No. 21, Indiana University Research Center in Anthropology, Folklore and Linguistics; Bloomington, Ind., 1962, p, 224.]

[2] Kurath, American Pronunciation, *SPE Tract,* No. XXX; Oxford, 1928, p. 292. [These observations have been borne out by the Atlas investigations; see Atwood, A Survey of Verb Forms in the Eastern United States, and Kurath and McDavid, The Pronunciation of English in the Atlantic States.]

[3] *Lg.,* Vol. XX, July–Sept. 1944, p. 151.

and Oklahoma meet. It was taken there by immigrants from Appalachia and has filtered into the adjacent lowlands.

The chief characteristics of the major dialects have been indicated in the preceding sections of this chapter. All show local variations, and in the midst of the areas of each of them there are islands of the others. Even the New England variety of American is anything but a homogeneous whole. In its coastal form, centering in Boston, it is very like the Standard English of southern England, but as one moves westward it gradually loses itself.

It was the dialect of New England that first attracted the attention of writers upon speechways in the United States, and as a result the literature upon it is very large. That literature began with Noah Webster's amateurish effort, in his "Dissertations on the English Language" (1789), to account for the Yankee drawl,[4] and it has culminated in our time in such competent and valuable studies as the Linguistic Atlas, Grandgent's "New England Pronunciation"[5] and Anders Orbeck's "Early New England Pronunciation."[6] Two years before Webster, in 1787, the Yankee made his first appearance as a stage type in "The Contrast," by Royal Tyler, and thereafter he gradually took on popularity, was borrowed by the writers of humorous fiction[7] and finally came to his apotheosis in "The Biglow Papers" of James Russell Lowell, the first series of which was published in the Boston *Courier* in 1846. When this series appeared in book form, two years later, Lowell added a preface on the Yankee dialect and a glossary thereof, and when a second series (begun in 1862) followed in 1867, he expanded these into a somewhat elaborate treatise. In the first series Lowell laid down seven rules for distinguishing the Yankee dialect, but Krapp has asserted that only the two of them relating to the pronunciation of *a* had any validity.[8] Krapp also showed that of forty words distinguished as dialect in six stanzas of Lowell's "The Courtin'," only six were really local to New England.[9] [Nevertheless, James W. Downer, of Michigan, has argued convincingly that, within the limits of his own dialectal system and the conventional English alphabet, Lowell has given

---

[4] p. 107. He believed that it was produced by the natural diffidence of a people unaccustomed to commanding slaves and servants and "not possessing that pride and consciousness of superiority which attend birth and fortune." This caused them "to give their opinions in an indecisive tone" and to drag out their words.

[5] A chapter in Old and New; Cambridge, Mass., 1920.

[6] Ann Arbor, Mich., 1927.

[7] The first of them was apparently Seba Smith, whose Letters of Major Jack Downing was published in 1830, but the most successful was Thomas C. Haliburton, whose Sam Slick sketches began to appear in 1835.

[8] Krapp, Vol. I, pp. 232–3.

[9] p. 235.

an effective literary presentation of rural New England speech of the early Nineteenth Century.¹]

Various authorities have sought to include New York City and Long Island in the New England speech area, but this is hardly justified by the facts. The broad *a* actually heard in the metropolitan region is confined to a very small class of persons, chiefly of social pretensions, and among them it is not the Boston *a* that is used but the English one. In the rest of the state the flat American *a* prevails, and the *r* is not elided.² The common people of New York City have a dialect of their own, first described scientifically by E. H. Babbitt, of Columbia, in 1896.³ Its most notable peculiarity lies in the pronunciation of *bird, nerve, girl,* etc., which become something that is usually represented as *boid, noive* and *goil.* Contrariwise, the *oi* sound of *oyster, noise* and *Boyd* also mutates, and in print these are often given as *erster, nerz* and *Byrd.* Normally the true sound is the same in both cases, and lies between *oi* and *er.* To a person unfamiliar with it, it sounds like *oi* in the *er* words and like *er* in the *oi* words.

At the time the New York vulgar dialect first appeared in literature, in the early 1890s, this confusion between *oi* and *er* was not stressed; instead, the salient mark of the dialect was thought to be substitution of *t* and *d* for the unvoiced and voiced forms of *th,* respectively, as in *wit* and *dat* for *with* and *that.* This substitution, said Babbitt, "does not take place in all words, nor in the speech of all persons, even of the lower classes; but the tendency exists beyond doubt." It has declined in late years, probably through the labors of the schoolma'am. But she has not been able to stamp out *foist* and *thoid,* if, indeed, she has been sufficiently conscious of them to make the attempt. It is frequent in the speech of educated New Yorkers, and it is very common in that of the high-school

---

¹ [The Dialect of The Biglow Papers, diss. (microfilm), U. of Michigan, 1958. A recent important study is C. K. Thomas, The Phonology of New England English, *Speech Monographs,* Nov. 1961, pp. 223–32.]

² [The distinction between Upstate New York and the Hudson Valley, with metropolitan New York City as a special dialect area within the Hudson Valley, is shown in Kurath, A Word Geography of the Eastern United States. Features of grammar and pronunciation are charted in Atwood, A Survey of Verb Forms in the Eastern United States, and in Kurath and McDavid, The Pronunciation of English in the Atlantic States.]

³ The English of the Lower Classes in New York City and Vicinity, *DN,* Vol. I, Pt. IX, 1896. [Recent discussions are C. K. Thomas, The Place of New York City in American Linguistic Geography, *QJS,* Vol. XXXIII, Oct. 1947, pp. 314–20; Yakira H. Frank, The Speech of New York City, diss. (microfilm), U. of Michigan, 1948; Allan Forbes Hubbell, The Pronunciation of English in New York City: Consonants and Vowels, New York, 1950; Arthur J. Bronstein, Let's Take Another Look at New York City Speech, *AS,* Vol. XXXVII, Feb. 1962, pp. 13–26. The folk vocabulary of New York State is discussed in the *New York Folklore Quarterly,* Vol. VII, Fall 1951, pp. 173–91.]

graduates who make up the corps of New York stenographers. It extends into New Jersey and up Long Island Sound into Connecticut; it has another strong focus in metropolitan New Orleans, and in an attenuated form occurs sporadically in the plantation South from South Carolina to Texas, without any of the derogatory associations it often has in New York. The origin of the New York dialect has not yet been accounted for with any plausibility; its *oi*, in particular, is found in no dialect of the British Isles.[4]

In the other Middle Atlantic States north of Baltimore, a Northern variety of Midland prevails, save only for a small part of New Jersey adjacent to New York City, where the New York vulgate has some footing. Most of the early observers of American speechways thought that the pronunciation of the Western Shore of Maryland was especially euphonious and correct. "When you get as far South as Maryland," said James Fenimore Cooper in 1828,[5] "the softest, and perhaps as pure an English is spoken as is anywhere heard." Two years earlier Mrs. Anne Royall said that "the dialect of Washington, exclusive of the foreigners, is the most correct and pure of any part of the United States I have ever yet been in." [6] Noah Webster also liked the pronunciation of this region, though he added that a *t* was added to *once* and *twice* by "a class of very well educated people, particularly in Philadelphia and Baltimore." [7] In parts of Pennsylvania the German influence not only has introduced a number of words that are not commonly heard elsewhere, but has also established some peculiar speech tunes. The Pennsylvania voice, indeed, is recognized instantly in the adjacent states. In the sentence "Are you going now?" for example, there is a sharp rise on *go* and a fall on *now*. For the rest, Pennsylvania speaks a Northern variety of Midland, with a flat *a* and a conspicuous *r*. The speech of New Jersey, save in the New York suburbs, is of the same basic type, but the vocabulary of the state is rich in local terms.

Next to New England speech, the American dialect that has been most studied is that of the Southern mountains, [a southwestward thrust of the Midland speech of Pennsylvania, with some infiltrations from Lowland Southern]. The people speaking it were isolated for many years, and thus preserved speech forms that have become archaic elsewhere. Until recently they were also, in the main, of low economic status, and it is

---

[4] [Based on an examination of both the materials of the English Dialect Survey and the records made in southern England by Guy S. Lowman, Jr. Here, as in many unspecified places, I am indebted to the generosity of Harold Orton and Hans Kurath.]

[5] Notions of the Americans, Vol. II, p. 175.

[6] Sketches of History, Life and Manners in the United States; New Haven, 1826, p. 58.

[7] Dissertations on the English Language; Boston, 1789, Vol. II.

among the poor that ancient forms are least affected by pedagogy and fashion. There are, of course, many local variations, due to the extreme isolation of the mountain communities. But these differences are yielding to good roads and the automobile, and in another generation the mountain folk, for the most part, will probably be speaking the general vulgate.[8] Southern mountain speech is encountered only sporadically in the mountains of Pennsylvania, but it begins to appear in the western tip of Maryland, and then sweeps southward through the mountain coves of West Virginia, southwestern Virginia and the Carolinas into Georgia and Alabama, with leaps into southern Illinois and the Ozarks. The persons who speak it undiluted are often called, by Southern publicists, "the purest Anglo-Saxons in the United States," but less romantic ethnologists describe them as predominantly Celtic in blood, though there has been a large infiltration of English and even German strains. The mountain type of speech has been taken to the Piedmont by hill folk going to work in the cotton mills, and Greet says that it is "well fixed on the Southwestern plains and in cities like Fort Worth and Dallas," and has echoes on the Delmarva Peninsula and on the islands of Chesapeake Bay. It is often slower than the speech of the lowlands, where rapid speech is more common than slow speech, and is often nasal and high-pitched.[9]

The speech of these poor folk, who have been called "our contemporary ancestors," was first described with any approach to scientific precision by Calvin S. Brown, Jr., in two papers published in 1889 and 1891,[1] but during the years thereafter various other linguists began to study it at length, notably Josiah H. Combs. Combs's first report, published in *Dialect Notes* in 1916,[2] was so good a conspectus of the subject that there has been little for later inquirers to do save run down the leads he furnished. On two points subsequent research has questioned his first conclusions: the Celtic element in the mountain population, including Welsh as well as Scotch-Irish fractions, is probably larger than he was disposed to grant, and there is doubt that the linguistic fossils he discovered in large number are really inherited directly from Elizabethan England. Many of them flourished along the Scotch-English border so late as the Eighteenth Century.[3] But the archaisms that appear in all American speech

---

[8] [It was noticeable that many characteristic mountain words were unfamiliar to the teachers from that area whom I encountered at West Virginia State College in the summer of 1962.]

[9] Southern Speech, in Culture in the South; Chapel Hill, N.C., 1934, p. 614.

[1] Dialectal Survivals in Tennessee, *MLN*, Vol. IV, 1889, pp. 409-16, and Other Dialectal Forms in Tennessee,

PMLA, Vol. VI, 1891, pp. 171-5.

[2] Old, Early and Elizabethan English in the Southern Mountains, Vol. IV, Pt. IV, pp. 283-97.

[3] And some survive to this day; Alexander Warrack's Scots Dialect Dictionary, London, 1911, cites such familiar forms as *afeared, steepy, tonguey* and *to argufy.*

are appreciably more numerous, whatever their immediate provenance, in the mountain dialect. The mountain phonology was dealt with both by Combs and, at greater length in 1942, by Joseph Sargent Hall,[4] who gathered his materials in two counties of western North Carolina and three of eastern Tennessee.

Vance Randolph says that the dialect of the Ozarks is "derived doubtless from the dialect of the Southern Appalachians,"[5] but that it has been reinforced in the remoter areas by words and phrases apparently of indigenous origin. It preserves many older pronunciations that have fallen out of use elsewhere, and reinforces and exaggerates most of those that remain. The flat *a* appears even in *balm* and *gargle*, but in *narrow* and *barrel* a broad *a* is substituted, so that they become *nahrr'* and *bahr'l*. In other situations the broad *a* is turned into a *u*, as in *fur* and *ruther* for *far* and *rather*. *Brush* is *bresh*, *such* is *sich* and *until* is *ontil*. The *au* sound is usually changed: *saucy*, as in the general vulgate, becomes *sassy*, and *jaundice* is *janders*, and *aunt* is often *aint*.[6] "Such nouns as *post* and *nest*," says Randolph, "drop the *t* in the singular, but in the plural the *t* is pronounced distinctly and an unaccented syllable added—*nestes* and *postes*. *T* replaces the final *d* in words like *salad*, *ballad*, *killed*, *scared* and *held*, so that they are best rendered *salat*, *ballat*, *kilt*, *skeert* and *helt*. Occasionally the final *t* is replaced by a *k* sound, as when *vomit* is turned into *vomick*." An excrescent *t* is added to many words besides the familiar *once*, *wish* and *close*; thus *sudden* becomes *suddint* and *cliff* is *clift*.[7] An intrusive *y* appears in *hear* and *ear*, which become *hyar* and *yar*. In many words the accent is thrown forward; thus, *catarrh*, *guitar*, *insane*, *police* and *hurrah* are accented on the first syllable. The Ozarker uses *hit* for *it*, but he uses it "only at the beginning of a clause, or when unusual emphasis is desired."[8] In the vocabulary Randolph notes some curious changes in meaning:

> A *stew* is not a dish of meat and vegetables in the Ozarks, but a drink made of ginger, hot water and corn-whiskey. . . . *Ashamed*, when used with reference to a child or a young girl, does not mean

---

[4] The Phonetics of Great Smoky Mountain Speech, *American Speech Reprints and Monographs*, No. 4.

[5] Is There an Ozark Dialect?, *AS*, Vol. IV, Feb. 1929, pp. 203–4. [See also Down in the Holler: a Gallery of Ozark Folk Speech, by Randolph and George P. Wilson, Norman, Okla., 1953; and An Ozarker's Reactions to Formal Language, by Ethel Reed Strainchamps, *AS*, Vol. XXIII, Oct.–Dec. 1948, pp. 262–5.]

[6] [The wide dissemination of many of these pronunciations in American folk speech is shown in Kurath and McDavid, The Pronunciation of English in the Atlantic States.]

[7] [*Clift* is also common in eastern Kentucky; the plural there is *clivs*.]

[8] On the Ozark Pronunciation of *It*, by Vernon C. Allison, *AS*, Vol. IV, Feb. 1929.

ashamed at all, but merely timid or bashful. *Gum* means a rabbit-trap
—when the hillman wants chewing-gum he calls for *wax.* . . . When
he says *several,* he doesn't mean two or three or four, but a large
number. . . . *Judge* or *jedge* is used to mean a fool or clown, and
there is even an adjective, *jedgy.* . . . *Enjoy* is used in the sense of
entertain. *Lavish* is used as a noun, meaning a large quantity. . . .
Portly, as applied to a man, means handsome. . . . *Out* is used as a
verb meaning to defraud. . . . *Fine-haired* means aristocratic.[9]

Randolph's account of the extreme prudishness of the Ozarkers has been
noticed earlier. Many common words, *e.g., bull, buck, bitch, virgin, bed,
leg, bag* and even *love,* are taboo among them,[1] but on the other hand they
are free in the use of terms, *e.g., to snot* and *to give tittie,* that are frowned
upon elsewhere.[2]

[Greet, Kurath and others have long noted that Southern speech is extremely varied, even leaving out the mountain dialect.] The most distinctive types are the Virginia Tidewater, the South Carolina Low
Country and the General Southern Lowland type.[3] The first prevails along
the coast from the Delmarva Peninsula to South Carolina. [The South
Carolina Low Country type extends from the Peedee River, in northeastern South Carolina, to northeastern Florida, with extensions along the
river valleys as far inland as Columbia, S.C., and Augusta and Macon, Ga.]
The Tidewater type embodies most of the peculiarities that Northerners
associate with sub-Potomac speech, *e.g.,* the intrusion of a *y* sound before
a after *k* or *g,* as in *cyar* and *gyarden.*[4]

General Southern is a variable quantity, and more than one observer has
noted the great range between the careful speech of an educated and
self-conscious inhabitant of, say, Atlanta, Richmond or New Orleans, and
the casual talk of a Georgia cracker or Mississippi Negro. The vowels of
the former include the flat *a* in *pass, dance, can't,* etc.[5] General Southern

[9] The Ozarks: an American Survival
of Primitive Society; New York, 1931,
pp. 70–1.
[1] [Besides terms generally regarded as
indecent, many are frowned on for other
reasons in the South. In Dialect Geography and Social Science Problems, *Social
Forces,* Vol. XXV, Dec. 1946, pp. 168–72,
it is pointed out that Henry Wallace's
century of the common man was regarded askance south of the Potomac because *common* is there "a term of contempt."]
[2] Verbal Modesty in the Ozarks, *DN,*
Vol. VI, Pt. I, 1928; reprinted in Randolph's The Ozarks, pp. 78–96.

[3] [See Kurath, A Word Geography of
the Eastern United States; Ann Arbor,
Mich., 1949, Fig. 2.]
[4] [See E. Bagby Atwood, Some Eastern
Virginia Pronunciation Features, English
Studies for James Southall Wilson, *University of Virginia Studies,* IV, 1951, pp.
111–24.]
[5] C. M. Wise, Southern American Dialect, *AS,* Vol. VIII, Apr. 1933, pp. 37–43.
[See also Kurath and McDavid, The Pronunciation of English in the Atlantic
States, Ann Arbor, Mich., 1961, pp. 19–
22.]

inserts a *y* glide before *u* after *t, n* and *d*, but not after *s, z* and *l, e.g.,* *tyune, nyew* and *dyew*, but not *presyume* or *absolyutely*. But this elegant Southern is a narrow class dialect, and is seldom encountered in its purest form. More commonly it is colored, even on the highest levels, by usages borrowed from below. These include the conversion of the flat *a* into long *a*, as in *kaint* for *can't;* the omission of the final *r* in *poor, floor* and *your,* and sometimes of the *r* following a consonant as in *throw* and *through;* the change of the diphthong in *cow* into a mixture of the flat *a* and *y;* the omission of the *l* from *twelve, self, help,* etc.; the voicing of the *s*, as in *greasy* and *blouse;* the use of *you-all;* and the omission of *t* from *next, best, soft,* etc., and of *d* from *land,* etc.

Southern observers generally agree that the intrusion into cultivated speech of elements borrowed from the folk speech is more frequent in the South than elsewhere. The Southerner uses habitually a dialect that marks him off instantly, and is not concealed by education. In the Tidewater region of Virginia and South Carolina, where the most elegant of all Southerners live and have their being, little effort seems to be made to conceal a way of speaking that sounds to many Northerners (as they say in their benighted fashion) somewhat niggerish. A Tidewater Virginian, escaped to the wilds of the damyankee, may throw off his native speechways more or less, but at home he clings to them.[6]

Southern American has been neglected by Northern philologians, but some of the Southern brethren have made and published excellent studies of it.[7] Southern speech has suffered cruelly on the stage and in the movies, where kittenish actresses from the North think they have imitated it sufficiently when they have thrown in a few *you-alls* and *honey-chiles* and converted every *I* into a long *ah*. The exact nature of the Southern long

[6] [During Linguistic Atlas interviews, "nearly every cultured informant . . . in South Carolina and Georgia used *ain't* at some time during the interview. In fact, one of the touchstones often used by Southerners to distinguish the genuine cultured speaker from the pretenders is that the latter are too socially insecure to know the proper occasions for using *ain't*, the double negative and other such folk forms, and hence avoid them altogether." Raven I. McDavid, Jr., and Virginia McDavid, The Relationship of the Speech of American Negroes to the Speech of Whites, *AS*, Vol. XXVI, Feb. 1951, p. 15.]

[7] James B. McMillan, Vowel Nasality as a Sandhi-Form of the Morphemes *-nt* and *-ing* in Southern American, *AS*, Vol.

XIV, Apr. 1939, pp. 120–3; N. M. Caffee, Southern *l* Plus a Consonant, *AS*, Vol. XV, Oct. 1940, pp. 259–61; [Raven I. McDavid, Jr., The Position of the Charleston Dialect, *PADS*, No. XXIII, Apr. 1955, pp. 35–49; Robert Ray Howren, The Speech of Louisville, Ky., diss. (microfilm), Indiana U., 1958; Christine Duncan Forrester, A Word Geography of Kentucky, M.A. thesis (MS), U. of Kentucky, 1952; Arthur M. Z. Norman, A Southeast Texas Dialect Study, *Orbis*, Vol. V, June 1956, pp. 61–79; Gordon R. Wood, An Atlas Survey of the Interior South (USA), *Orbis*, Vol. IX, June 1960, pp. 7–12, and Word Distribution in the Interior South, *PADS*, No. XXXV, Apr. 1961, pp. 1–10.]

i has been discussed by various sub-Potomac philologians. In standard English this phoneme, or phoneme sequence, is not a simple vowel, but a diphthong made up of the vowels *a* and *i* (*ah* and *ee*). In Southern speech, however, the latter half of the sound sequence is dropped off, leaving a remnant that sounds to many Northerners like *ah*. But it is not precisely *ah* to Southern ears; like the Boston broad *a*, it is pronounced nearer the front of the mouth than the true Southern *ah*. In educated Southern speech it appears only at the ends of syllables or before voiced consonants; the first person *I* sounds *ah* to a Northerner, and the same vowel occurs in *my, ride, time, fine* and *alive*. But in *night, hike, ice, life* and *type* the educated Southerner uses a diphthong comparable to that used in other regions. [The Southern unwashed, however, often use the undiphthongized vowel in all positions, so that phrases like *nice white rice* become effective social shibboleths.[8]]

Until recently the speech of the rest of the country was little studied, no doubt because the immense territory covered made it seem obvious and commonplace. [The speech of the United States from the Appalachians westward has many local varieties, as Inland Northern, South Midland and other influences combine in varying proportions.[9] Nevertheless, these

---

[8] [See Kurath and McDavid, The Pronunciation of English in the Atlantic States, pp. 109–10, Maps 26–7.]

[9] [Some recent studies in the Midwest are Harold B. Allen, The Linguistic Atlas of the Upper Midwest of the United States, *Orbis*, Vol. I, May 1952, pp. 89–94; Principal Dialect Areas of the Upper Midwest, Fries Festschrift, Ann Arbor, Mich., 1963; Minor Dialect Areas of the Upper Midwest, *PADS*, No. XXX, Nov. 1958, pp. 3–16; Alva L. Davis, A Word Atlas of the Great Lakes Region, diss. (microfilm), U. of Michigan, 1949; Virginia McDavid, Verb Forms of the North-Central States and Upper Midwest, diss. (microfilm), U. of Minnesota, 1956; A. H. Marckwardt, Folk Speech in Indiana and Adjacent States, *Indiana History Bulletin*, XVII, 1940, pp. 120–40; Principal and Subsidiary Dialect Areas in the North-Central States, *PADS*, No. XXVII, May 1957, pp. 3–15; Edward Earle Potter, The Dialect of Northwestern Ohio: the Study of a Transition Area, diss. (microfilm), U. of Michigan, 1953. For the Rocky Mountain area: Clyde T. Hankey, A Colorado Word Geography, *PADS*, No. XXXIV, Nov. 1960; Semantic Features and Eastern Relics in Colorado Dialect, *AS*, Vol. XXXVI, Dec. 1961, pp. 266–70; Marjorie M. Kimmerle, The Influence of Locale and Human Activity on Some Words in Colorado, *AS*, Vol. XXV, Oct. 1950, pp. 161–7; T. M. Pearce, Three Rocky Mountain Terms: *Park, Sugan* and *Plaza*, *AS*, Vol. XXXIII, May 1958, pp. 99–107; Marjorie M. Kimmerle, Virginia McDavid and Raven I. McDavid, Jr., Problems of Linguistic Geography in the Rocky Mountain Area, *Western Humanities Review*, Vol. V, Fall 1951, pp. 249–64. For the Pacific coast: Frederick H. Brengelman, The Native American English Spoken in the Puget Sound Area, diss. (microfilm), U. of Washington, 1957; David DeCamp, The Pronunciation of English in San Francisco, *Orbis*, Vol. VII, Dec. 1958, pp. 372–91, Vol. VIII, June 1959, pp. 54–77; Carroll E. Reed, The Pronunciation of English in the State of Washington, *AS*, Vol. XXVII, Oct. 1952, pp. 186–9; Washington Words, *PADS*, No. XXV, May 1956, pp. 3–11; David W. Reed, Eastern Dialect Words in California, *PADS*, No. XXI, Apr. 1954, pp. 3–15. The existence of clear dialect boundaries in the Midwest, along with the problems of finding them, is shown

varieties are not as distinctive as those along the Atlantic seaboard, and the fact that all of them share such non-British features as the flat *a* in *pass* and the conspicuous *r* was sufficient to persuade earlier savants to lump them all together as "General American."] In the early days the larval form of these inland dialects, then called Western speech, attracted the attention of the contemporary philologians as the source of nearly all the current neologisms, many of them of an extraordinary pungency. Webster and Pickering recorded only a few, for the great movement into the West, with its proliferation of words and phrases, did not begin in earnest until after the War of 1812, but by the time John Russell Bartlett put together his Glossary in 1848 many of them had come into notice in the East, and he listed a great number. The West was wild and woolly until the Civil War and for twenty years afterward, but in the middle 1880s it began to succumb to the schoolma'am and the evangelist, and today it shares with the South the custody of what remains of Puritanism and is quite decorous in its speech. Even in its palmy days the West introduced few novelties in pronunciation; its contributions were nearly all to the vocabulary. The two waves of pioneers, from the Inland North and the South Midland, met on its wide reaches; the misfits lingered in Appalachia or took refuge in the Ozarks, and there hung on to the archaic patois that we have been lately examining. The Pike County dialect of the Mississippi Valley was only a transient phenomenon: it long ago disappeared from all save a few remote backwaters.

The speech of the Western cattlemen, once romantic nomads but now mere drovers, is said to show a predominantly South Midland substratum.[1] But this speech remains a good deal less regional than occupational, and in any case most of its terms have been made so familiar by the movies and television and by pulp fiction that it hardly strikes the average American as peculiar. In 1913, when Bartle T. Harvey, of the United States Bureau of Ethnology, undertook the first vocabulary of it, he listed many words and phrases that are known to every schoolboy; *e.g., fall guy, to get in bad, to hit the hay, locoed, makings* (of a cigarette) and *to mooch*. All the later contributors to the subject offered only more and more evidence that the speech of the old Wild West was being rapidly assimilated.

---

in Roger W. Shuy, The Boundary Between the Northern and Midland Dialect Regions in Illinois, diss. (MS), Western Reserve U., 1962.]

[1] [E. Bagby Atwood, A Preliminary Report on Texas Word Geography, *Orbis*, Vol. II, June 1953, pp. 61–6, and The Regional Vocabulary of Texas, Austin, Tex., 1962; Mima Babington and E. Bagby Atwood, Lexical Usage in Southern Louisiana, *PADS*, No. XXXVI, Nov. 1961; William R. Van Riper, Oklahoma Words, *Round Table of the South Central College English Association*, No. 2, May 1961, p. 3; Katherine Wheatley and Oma Stanley, Three Generations of Texas Speech, *AS*, Vol. XXXIV, May 1959, pp. 83–94.]

The speech of the Southwest is, even today, more heavily laden with Spanish loans than other dialects, but a great many such loans have been generally disseminated, and meanwhile the Southwest seems to be gradually abandoning those that remain, so that New Mexican American promises, on some near tomorrow, to become indistinguishable from the American of the Midwest, as the American of New Orleans, once full of French loans, has become almost indistinguishable from that of the rest of the lowland South.[2] "Perhaps the Middle West language, whatever it is," said an intelligent newspaper commentator in 1937,[3] "will prevail because it is a composite. While it has its own sectionalisms, it has rejected to a large degree the radical departures of the older areas of the South and East."

The sectionalisms here mentioned, of course, are to be found all over the United States, for despite the general uniformity of speech in large areas there are still many local peculiarities. In Maryland, for example,[4] there are five quite distinct speech areas, and several sub-areas. In the two far western counties the prevailing speech is that of Appalachia. To the eastward, under the Mason and Dixon Line, the influence of the Pennsylvania-German area of Pennsylvania is plainly apparent. On the Eastern Shore, south of the Choptank River, the dialect shows the influence of Tidewater Virginia, with occasional suggestions of Appalachia. On the Western Shore, below Annapolis, it is predominantly General Southern. In Baltimore and vicinity, and around the periphery of Washington, it is North Midland, with a few touches of Southern. Moreover, there are innumerable gradations where these areas meet, so that it is often difficult to say of a strange Eastern Shoreman, for example, whether he comes from below the Choptank or above. The same differentiations are to be found in many other states, notably in such reputedly homogeneous areas as eastern New England and the Deep South. It is thus very misleading to sort out American speechways by states, as most local writers have hitherto done. [As the Linguistic Atlas project proceeds toward completion, with its emphasis on cultural rather than political boundaries, we may expect a clearer delineation of local areas and their roots elsewhere, as we have already had for the Atlantic seaboard.[5]]

---

[2] But see The English Language in the Southwest, by Thomas Matthews Pearce, *New Mexico Historical Review*, Vol. VII, July 1932, pp. 210–32.

[3] Editorial, Grand Rapids (Mich.) *Press*, Oct. 27. [Tentative observations on the speech of metropolitan areas suggest that as Americans are thrown together the sharp edges of all regional forms of speech tend to disappear. On the other hand, the new class segregation, particularly by residential suburbs, may speed the development of sharply distinctive social dialects.]

[4] It has but 12,210 square miles of area, and 2,319 of them are under water. Counting only dry land, Texas could hold 21.76413 + Marylands.

[5] [Kurath, A Word Geography of the Eastern United States, Ann Arbor, Mich., 1949.]

In Hawaii has arisen a dialect of American that is confined to the islands, and is full of interesting peculiarities. Its basis seems to be Beach-la-Mar, the common trade speech of the Western Pacific, in which, for many years past, there have been a number of terms of American origin, *e.g.*, *alligator, boss, schooner* and *tomahawk*, but since English began to be taught in the Hawaiian schools in 1853, this crude jargon has moved in the direction of Standard American. The original Beach-la-Mar still survives, but it is spoken only by "the immigrant generation of Orientals and Latins, and some elderly native Hawaiians." [6] The other non-American inhabitants, whether Japanese, Chinese, Koreans, Portuguese, Puerto Ricans, Filipinos or native Hawaiians, speak the dialect aforesaid, in varieties ranging from something rising but little above Beach-la-Mar to something hard to distinguish from the speech of native Americans. It is used, in one form or other, by probably two-thirds of the people of the islands. It resembles vulgar American in its disregard of grammatical niceties, but its vocabulary differs considerably from the speech of the mainland. Many common expressions have been changed in meaning, *e.g.*, *bogus* has come to mean boastful or a boaster, *meat* signifies only beef, and by a confusion between *laboratory* and *lavatory*, *lab* has come to mean the latter. There are, of course, many loan words from Hawaiian and the non-English immigrant languages, *e.g.*, *aloha* (farewell) and *haole* (a white of Germanic blood) from the Hawaiian; *jabon* (the shaddock) and *hekka* (a popular stew) from the Japanese; *stay* (from *está*, meaning is) from the Portuguese; *kaukau* (food) from the Chinese; and *bagoong* (a shrimpy sauce) from one of the Filipino languages. The articulation of those who speak this dialect is reasonably clear, but they have a habit of prolonging stressed vowels, and of clipping unstressed vowels and all consonants. "Sometimes it is difficult for an ear trained to Mainland American speech to catch words because of the comparative rapidity of utterance. There is little drawling, even where there is hesitation; the speed and pitch of utterance remind us more of the British norm than of the American." [7] But it is a form of American English, and in the course of time it will probably come closer and closer to everyday vulgar American.

[During the half-century of American domination of the Philippines, English made much more progress than Spanish had made in the nearly

---

[6] The English Dialect of Hawaii, by John E. Reinecke and Aiko Tokimasa, *AS*, Vol. IX, Feb. 1934, p. 50; [How to Talk in Hawaii, by A. Grove Day, *AS*, Vol. XXVI, Feb. 1951, pp. 18–26; The Fiftieth State: New Dimensions for Studies in Speech, by Elizabeth R. Carr, *The Speech Teacher*, Vol. X, 1961, pp. 283–90. The varieties of pidgin current in the Pacific and elsewhere have been most thoroughly studied by Robert A. Hall, Jr., of Cornell University.]

[7] Reinecke and Tokimasa, *AS*, Vol. IX, Apr. 1934, p. 130.

four centuries preceding.] At the end of 1945 it was estimated that no less than 5,000,000 of the 16,500,000 inhabitants spoke what is known locally as Bamboo English, as against but 500,000 speaking Spanish. Tagalog, the principal language spoken around Manila, was chosen to become the official language after independence, alongside English and Spanish.[8] [However, Tagalog is spoken by a minority of Filipinos, and it is evident that English will be in demand for a long time. At present, English is taught in the first two grades, and from the third grade on becomes the medium of instruction. There are two schools of thought on the variety of English to be offered in the schools. One group favors teaching a variety of Midwestern American; the other would promote Filipino English, which is a viable tongue, distressing as its phonology may seem to North Americans.[9]]

The language question likewise arose during the Puerto Rican movement for independence, and the discussion of it aroused bitter animosities. A minority of native Uncle Toms, derisively termed *pitiyanquis* (petite Yankees), declared they wished to use English even for the teaching of Spanish,[1] but the overwhelming majority of Puerto Ricans demanded that all elementary teaching be in Spanish, with English taught only as a second language and in the higher grades. [Under the Commonwealth status of Puerto Rico—a form of autonomy under which the United States grants tariff preferences and assumes the responsibility for defense—the debate on the role of English continues, but in more realistic terms. Perhaps the calmer view has been encouraged by the heavy recent Puerto Rican migration to New York and other metropolitan centers, where the lack of English has put the new arrivals at a severe disadvantage. The University of Puerto Rico has taken an active part in promoting the teaching of English, and has enlisted the co-operation of such institutions as Indiana University and the University of Michigan; in fact, some scholars have joint appointments in the University of Puerto Rico and one of the mainland universities.]

Peculiar dialects of English flourish at Key West and in the Virgin Islands. The Key West dialect is Southern American showing the influence

---

[8] *AS*, Vol. XVI, Dec. 1941, p. 303.

[9] [This point was repeatedly made at the Ann Arbor, Mich., conference on the teaching of English as a second language, July 1957. For specific details, see Some Structural Problems for Tagalog Students in English, by William Schwab, *Language Learning*, Vol. VI. 1955, pp. 68–72. Morris Finder, of Chicago, a former exchange professor in the Philippines, supplied other details in private correspondence.]

[1] [They were recently abetted by Adam Clayton Powell, Jr., of New York, chairman of the Committee on Education of the House of Representatives, who proposed that English be the official language of all schools in Puerto Rico. The effect of English on island Spanish has been shown in English Loan Words in Puerto Rico, by C. E. Schorer, *AS*, Vol. XXVIII, Feb. 1953, pp. 22–5.]

of Bahaman English and Cuban Spanish. The *i* is frequently given its Spanish sound, especially in proper names, so that *Olivia* becomes *Oleevia*. The *a* before *g* is transformed into a short *i*, so that *bag* becomes *big* and *rag* becomes *rig*. The *w* and *v* are confused, so that *west* becomes *vest* and *visit* becomes *wisit*. The *h* is treated in the Cockney manner, so that *horse* becomes *orse* and the letter *l* is called *hell*. *Ain't* is often used in place of *won't* or *haven't*. The *-ed* ending is omitted from the past tense forms of the verbs. Many Spanish idioms are translated literally, *e.g., Cuántos años tiene?* which becomes "How many years you got?" There are many loan words from the Spanish, and the inhabitants have invented the usual opprobrious terms for one another, *e.g., conch* (a West Indian) and *saw* (a native of Nassau).[2] The Virgin Islands dialect, of course, is not American, but English. The phonology shows Danish influence. Among the special characters are the omission of *s* before consonants, so that *stocking* becomes *tocking*, and the use of a collective pronoun *a-wee*, corresponding to the Southern American *us-all*. In addition to such West African loans as *buckra*, a white man, *shandrámadan*, a rascally act, and *caffoon*, a fall or other mishap, there are survivals of French, Dutch, Portuguese and Spanish loans, both directly and through Crucian (and St. Thomian) Creole, "a *lingua franca* invented [for the slaves] by early Moravian missionaries who combined the language of their European masters' families with their own African dialects."[3] The basis of the dialect is "late Seventeenth and early Eighteenth Century English—traditionally the language of trade and of the buccaneers throughout most of the West India islands." This dialect is not only "the language of the normally English-speaking islands, such as St. Kitts and Antigua, but also of Dutch Saba and Dutch and French St. Martin." It tends to throw the accent back whenever possible, so that *good morning* becomes *gu-marnín;* it changes *th* to *d*, and it includes many pronunciations recalling the American Negro, *e.g., sarmin, lebben, gwine, wuk* and *fotch*. A somewhat analogous dialect, but much less like Standard English, is spoken in Dutch Guiana (Surinam), on the South American mainland.

Palmer, Martin and Blandford, in their "Dictionary of English Pronunciation with American Variants,"[4] group American and Canadian speech

---

[2] See A Philologist's Paradise, by Thomas B. Reid, *Opportunity*, Jan. 1926.

[3] Henry S. Whitehead, Negro Dialect of the Virgin Islands, *AS*, Vol. VII, Feb. 1932, pp. 175–9. [Other representative studies of English in the Caribbean are: William Leonard Schwartz, American Speech and Haitian French, *AS*, Vol. XXIV, Dec. 1949, pp. 282–5; Robert A. Hall, Jr., Further English Borrowings in Haitian Creole, *AS*, Vol. XXV, May 1950, pp. 150–1; Frederic G. Cassidy, Iteration as a Word-Forming Device in Jamaican Folk Speech, *AS*, Vol. XXXII, Feb. 1957, pp. 49–53; English Language Studies in the Caribbean, *AS*, Vol. XXXIV, Oct. 1959, pp. 163–71; Robert B. LePage, General Outlines of Creole English Dialects in the British Caribbean, *Orbis*, Vol. VI, Dec. 1957, pp. 373–91, and Vol. VII, May 1958, pp. 54–64.]

[4] Cambridge (England), 1926, p. xxvii.

together as facets of the same gem. [Perhaps this assumption then satisfied speakers of British English resident in the Far East, or the students for whom their dictionary was originally designed, but it can no longer satisfy the serious student of North American English, whatever his nationality, and only a little knowledge of Canadian history is necessary to suggest that it was never an accurate statement of the facts. Like the English of the United States, Canadian English is far too complicated to be dismissed with a single categorical statement. True, Canadian English developed out of the familiar kind of colonial experience, borrowing new words and reshaping or recombining old ones to fit new experiences and new needs for communication. True again, there have always been currents of migration flowing in both directions across the border. Long before the Revolution, New Englanders were settling in Nova Scotia, and the displacement of the Acadians, so well publicized by Longfellow and by the tourist bureaus of southwestern Louisiana, was motivated not only by military considerations but also by traditional Yankee acquisitiveness; New Englanders wanted the Acadian farmlands and occupied them as soon as the Acadians had been removed. The migrations of the United Empire Loyalists into the Maritimes and Ontario was followed by a more peaceful intermingling of the two peoples in the settlement of the Great Lakes and prairie regions; [5] and even today the expanding petroleum industry in Alberta has drawn many Americans north. And American mass communications and supermarket culture are among the major forces shaping Canadian speech for better or for worse.

[But this is not all. At the same time there has been a continuous flow of immigration from the British Isles, some of it resulting in rather homogeneous settlements with strong British traditions in their speechways. The coast of Newfoundland is dotted with such settlements, some at least as old as Jamestown. The Ottawa Valley was settled by immigrants from the British Isles in the early Nineteenth Century, and similar origins characterize Vancouver Island and its satellites, settled later. Furthermore, membership in the Commonwealth and the common bond of the Crown foster a Canadian receptivity to changes in institutions and manners in England. It may well be for this reason that some British words and expressions find acceptance among Canadians but make no headway in the United States.

[And even this is not the whole story. One must reckon with Canadian nationalism, arising from autonomy attained not through a break with the Crown but by evolution within the Commonwealth and therefore less obvious than the nationalism derived from the autonomy which the United

---

[5] [Marcus Lee Hansen and John Bartlet Brebner, The Mingling of the Canadian and American Peoples; Toronto, 1941.]

States achieved through armed revolt. The Canadian is first of all a Canadian; his own nationality is more significant to him than the false dichotomy between things British and things of the United States, and he feels (much as his neighbors south of the border felt in the Jacksonian era) that it is high time his voice was heard in equal partnership with Britain and the United States in the destiny of the free world.[6]]

So long ago as 1857 Canadians were using *bug* in the general sense of insect; *to fix* as a verb of all work; *to guess, to locate* and *rooster*.[7] In 1890 A. F. Chamberlain noted that in the parts of Ontario settled by Loyalists from New York and Pennsylvania "much that characterized the English speech of those States" was "still traceable in their descendants," and that the speech of the Eastern Townships of Quebec did not differ "to a very marked extent" from that of the adjoining New England States.[8] In 1942 Martin Joos observed that "Ontario English differs from the neighboring General American speech (for instance, in rural New York or Wisconsin) in only two items of phonological consequence." These are (*a*) *pod* and *pawed* are homophones, and (*b*) the diphthongs *ai* and *ow* (as in *rite, ride, out, loud,* but not *oi* as in *boy*) each have two variants.[9]

A number of forces work against the spread of American patterns of speech in Canada, notably the survival of regional dialects in the Maritime Provinces and Newfoundland, the prevalence of French in Quebec and the

---

[6] [This statement is derived from Canadian English Merits a Dictionary, by W. S. Avis, *Culture*, Vol. XVIII, Sept. 1957, pp. 245–56, and from personal correspondence with the author. Avis, secretary of the Canadian Linguistic Association, is a former student of Kurath's and the scholar most intimately conversant with all aspects of Canadian English. His bibliography of writings on Canadian English, *Journal of the Canadian Linguistic Association*, Vol. I, Oct. 1955, pp. 19–20, is a bench mark for anyone concerned with the subject. Other important articles are Canadian English and Its Relation to Eighteenth Century American English, by Morton W. Bloomfield, *JEGP*, Vol. XLVII, 1948, pp. 59–67; and M. H. Scargill, Sources of Canadian English, *JEGP*, Vol. LVI, 1957, pp. 610–14. Under the sponsorship of the Canadian Linguistic Association work is under way on a Dictionary of Canadianisms, A Dictionary of Canadian English on Historical Principles and several dictionaries for the schools. Plans were summarized in the Edmonton *Journal*, June 13, 1958. The Avis bibliography was revised in 1963.]

[7] Canadian English, by the Rev. A. S. Geikie, *Canadian Journal*, Vol. II, 1857, pp. 344–5.

[8] Dialect Research in Canada, by A. F. Chamberlain, *DN*, Vol. I, Pt. II, pp. 43–56.

[9] [Both of these features occur elsewhere, but only in Ontario and western Canada do they occur together. *Pod* and *pawed* are homophones in much of eastern New England, the Pittsburgh area and parts of the Upper Midwest and Rocky Mountain areas; the diphthongs in *rite* and *ride*, and *out* and *loud*, have alternations similar to the Canadian ones in eastern Virginia and the South Carolina–Georgia tidewater. It is rather curious that these alternations should have developed in three separate parts of North America, since they have not yet been found in any dialect of the British Isles. See Kurath and McDavid, The Pronunciation of English in the Atlantic States, pp. 109–11, Maps 26–9.]

effects of social aspiration in the larger cities. The last-named has sufficed to keep English spelling in countenance, so that *cheque* and *centre* are still in use, though the American *tire, curb* and *jail* are preferred. A few fashionable private schools, as in the United States, still inculcate something vaguely approximating Oxford English, and many of their teachers are Englishmen. But among the plain people, even in Montreal, *baby carriage, streetcar* and the like are in everyday use, though *schedule* is pronounced with the *sch* soft and the letter *z* is *zed*, not *zee*.[1] Moreover, the movies, radio and television and the constant travel across the border bring in the newest American inventions as they appear. "The Great Lakes and the St. Lawrence River," said an observer in 1939,[2] "are highways of communication rather than barriers." This observer thinks, however, that pronunciation differences are sufficient "to enable Canadians and Americans usually to place one another very quickly by speech alone." He lists some of them, *e.g., cornet* is accented on the first syllable, not on the second, as in the United States; *economics* is *eek-*, not *ek-; lieutenant* "is always *leftenant*"; and "a few Canadians still say *clark* instead of *clerk*."

But such differences are obviously small, and set against them are many popular preferences for American as opposed to English usage, *e.g.,* the *r* is always sounded. Except in the Maritimes and in Victoria, B.C., the broad *a* is rarely heard, even in *aunt* and *rather*. "Most Canadians are inclined to regard American speech habits disparagingly, [but they] are no more fond of Southern British speech."[3]

The remoter parts of Canada, like the remoter parts of the United States, have developed local dialects that show some interesting oddities, but they are confined to small and thinly populated areas, and give no sign of spreading. [The speech of the Maritimes is largely derivative of New England. The dialects of Newfoundland—some of the longest established and most isolated in the New World—have long attracted amateur investigators, and are now being systematically examined by a group of scholars

[1] [See Languages Here and There, by John Lardner, *The New Yorker*, Sept. 26, 1959, pp. 171–4. For systematic investigation of the border as a linguistic boundary, see Harold B. Allen, Canadian-American Speech Differences along the Middle Border, *Journal of the Canadian Linguistic Association*, Vol. V, Spring 1959, pp. 17–24, and three articles by Avis in the same journal: Vocabulary, Vol. I, 1954, pp. 13–18; Grammar and Syntax, Vol. I, 1955, pp. 14–19; and Pronunciation, Vol. II, 1956, pp. 41–59. Typical Canadian words, according to Avis, are *riding* for parliamentary constituency (equivalent to our *congressional district*), *flying wing* (the fifth backfield man in Canadian football) and *homer*, a referee who favors the home team. American influence on Canadian French is discussed seriously by Douglas Leechman in *AS*, Vol. XXV, Dec. 1950, pp. 253–8, and more casually in L'Arbitre est un robber, *Time*, May 31, 1948, p. 30.]

[2] A Note on Canadian Speech, by Morley Ayearst, *AS*, Vol. XIV, Oct. 1939, pp. 231–3.

[3] Ontario Speech, by Evelyn Ahrend, *AS*, Vol. IX, Apr. 1934, pp. 136–9.

at the Memorial University of Newfoundland, with a dialect dictionary and
a linguistic atlas promised in the near future.[4]] The dialect of Lunenburg,
Nova Scotia, which was settled by Germans in the Eighteenth Century,
has been studied by competent phonologists, first by M. B. Emeneau, of
California, himself a native Lunenburger, [and more recently by H. R.
Wilson, of the Royal Military College of Canada, a student under Kurath
and Marckwardt].[5] German is no longer spoken there, but it is still understood by a few oldsters and its influence upon the local speech remains evident. Some of the examples cited by Emeneau are *to make* in the sense of
to prepare, as a meal; *to get awake* (Ger. *wach werden*); *with* used as an
adverb after *to go* and *to come* (Ger. *mitgehen*); *all* used in place of *all
gone; apple snits* (Ger. *Schnitte*); *lapish*, insipid (Ger. *läppisch*); *klotsy*,
heavy or soggy (Ger. *klotzig*); *shimmel*, a very blond person (Ger. *Schim-
mel*, a white mold); and *Fassnakday*, Shrove Tuesday (Ger. *Fastnacht*).
All these loans [typical of German-American communities] show signs of
dying out. The dialect has, in general, the characteristics of the general
speech of Canada, *e.g.*, to have sharply different varieties of *ai* and *ow* depending on what sound follows. But, unlike the rest of Canada, it does not
pronounce *r* after vowels.

In the late 1930s, Henry Alexander, of Queen's University, Kingston,
Ont., began an investigation of the speech of the Maritimes with a view to
the preparation of a part of the Linguistic Atlas of the United States and
Canada.[6] His researches were interrupted by World War II, and were
never resumed.[7]

Allen Walker Read has shown that the Americans of fifty years before
the Revolution were already acutely aware of the existence among them

---

[4] [Under the chairman of the English Department, E. R. Seary, and his New-foundland-born colleague George Story, Memorial has shown the most serious and systematic interest in folk speech and folk culture of all the colleges and universities in English-speaking North America. Typical Newfoundland words are *tickle*, a narrow strait, *bawn*, a beach, *dolly varden*, an earthenware cup, and *tilt*, a shanty. *Fish* to the Newfie always means cod; other varieties are specified.]

[5] M. B. Emeneau, The Dialect of Lunenburg, Nova Scotia, *Lg.*, Vol. XI, June 1935, pp. 140–7; [H. R. Wilson, The Dialect of Lunenburg County, Nova Scotia, diss. (microfilm), U. of Michigan, 1958. See also Eighteenth Century English in Nova Scotia, by M. H. Scargill,

Journal of the Canadian Linguistic Association, Vol. II, Mar. 1956, pp. 3 ff.]

[6] Alexander made a preliminary report at the Chicago meeting of the American Dialect Society, Dec. 1945.

[7] [Murray Wanamaker, of Acadia University, is currently investigating the Annapolis Valley in western Nova Scotia, and Wilson is conducting field investigations in other parts of the province. Elsewhere in Canada, R. J. Gregg has investigated the vowels employed in the Vancouver area, *Journal of the Canadian Linguistic Association*, Vol. III, Oct. 1957, pp. 78–83; and M. H. Scargill has contributed two preliminary studies on Alberta to the same journal, Vol. I, Oct. 1954, pp. 21–3, and Vol. I, Mar. 1955, pp. 26–30.]

of groups speaking English with telltale brogues and accents.[8] That awareness must have gone back to at least a century before, for it is hard to
imagine that the Indians who picked up the language of the colonists
learned to speak it correctly overnight, and before the middle of the
Seventeenth Century the English were in frequent contact with Frenchmen
and Dutchmen. Later came Swedes, Germans and Spaniards, and meanwhile the nascent Americans began to notice that the Scotch, Irish and
Welsh immigrants who came in, and even some of the English, spoke in
ways that were not their own. By 1775 the Southern Negro began to be
differentiated in speech, by 1797 the rustic Yankee, and after the War of
1812 the Westerner.[9] After the great Irish immigration of the late 40s and
the German immigration which followed it, the Irishman and the German
became standard types in American comedy, alongside the Negro minstrel
introduced by Thomas D. Rice (1808–60) in the 30s. They were followed,
in the 50s, by the Chinaman, and in later years by the Scandinavian, the
Italian and the Jew.[1] So early as 1823 James Fenimore Cooper had attempted German, French, Irish, English and Negro dialects in "The Pioneers," though he made his Indians speak conventional English.[2] But there
had been an attempt to render Indian English in a serious book published
in 1675, to wit:

> Umh, umh, me no stawmerre fight Engis mon. Engis mon got two
> hed, Engis mon got two hed. If me cut off un hed, he got noder, a put
> on beder as dis.[3]

German dialect apparently got its first literary recognition in 1856, when
Charles Godfrey Leland wrote the earliest of his long series of "Hans
Breitmann" ballads to fill an unexpected gap in *Graham's Magazine*. These
ballads were very popular during the Civil War, and Leland continued to

---

[8] Bilingualism in the Middle Colonies, 1725–1775, *AS*, Vol. XII, Apr. 1937, pp. 93–9.

[9] Literary Dialects, in Krapp, Vol. I, pp. 225–73. [See also A Theory of Liter-ary Dialect, by Sumner Ives, *Tulane Studies in English*, Vol. II, 1950, pp. 137–82, and the introductory chapters of The Dialect of the Biglow Papers, by James W. Downer, diss. (microfilm), U. of Michigan, 1958.]

[1] [See Jewish Literary Dialect, by John J. Appel, *AS*, Vol. XXXII, Dec. 1957, pp. 313–14. He feels that "Jewish" Eng-lish may have existed as a literary stereo-type since the Eighteenth Century. It is referred to in Landa's The Jew in Drama

and was employed in Brackenridge's Modern Chivalry and in Mrs. Rowson's play Slaves in Algiers; Philadelphia, 1794. Twentieth Century Jewish dialect is, of course, an attempt at realism (per-sonal communication, Apr. 5, 1957).]

[2] Cooper's Leatherstocking was given a dialect greatly resembling that of the contemporary Yankee. See The Dialect of Cooper's Leatherstocking, by Louise Pound, *AS*, Vol. II, Sept. 1927, pp. 479–88, [and the chapter on Cooper's use of dialect in the unpublished dissertation of Warren S. Walker, Cornell, 1951].

[3] The Present State of New England, by a Merchant of Boston; London, 1675, p. 12; quoted by Krapp.

bring out volumes of them until 1895.[4] In the 70s the so-called Dutch comedian became a popular figure on the American stage, and during the 80s and 90s that was a rare burlesque show or vaudeville which did not present at least one specimen of him. He perished in World War I, though perhaps not altogether in consequence of it, for the Irish, Scandinavian and Negro comic characters perished with him, and the Jew moved from the stage to books.

Since 1909, when Montague Glass's "Potash and Perlmutter" stories began to appear in *The Saturday Evening Post*, the speech of the immigrant Jews of New York, popular on the stage since the 90s, has been the dialect most cultivated by American comic writers, *e.g.*, Arthur Kober, Leo Rosten (Leonard Q. Ross) and Milt Gross. Robert Menner says that Gross's transcription is as accurate "as our poor alphabet will allow." One of the chief marks of the dialect is its change of the vowel of *bit* to that of *beet*, and vice versa. Says Menner:

> Mrs. Feitelbaum and her friends do not actually reverse these sounds. In both *slip* and *sleep* they use a sound which may loosely be described as midway between short *i* and long *e*. For in their native Yiddish, presumably, they have not the exact equivalent of either. Our popular designations disguise the close relationship between short *i* and long *e*. To the phonetician, as to the Continental, both are varieties of an *i* sound. In phonetic terms Mrs. Feitelbaum's *i* is probably a high-point tense *ee* shorter than the English *ee* in *sleep* and yet not slack like the *i* in *slip*. . . . But if Gross's symbols are not phonetically exact, they nevertheless reproduce exactly the effect on the ordinary hearer of the Yiddish attempt to pronounce our vowels.[5]

In the same way and for the same reason the speaker of this dialect confuses and interchanges the sound of *e* in *bed* and that of *a* in *bad*, so that *rang* becomes *reng* and *hat* becomes *het*. Again, the *o* of *don't* and the *u* of *run* are exchanged, so that *don't* becomes *dunt* and *punch* becomes *ponch*. Among the consonants *v* is changed to *f*, *w* to *v*, *v* to *w*, *d* and the *th* of *bath* to *t*, the *th* of *that* to *d*, and *g* to *k*. [Most of these orthographic devices, like the interchange of *oi* and *er* in representations of New York City speech, reflect the fact that the dialect does not have contrasts between sounds that contrast in Standard English.]

C. K. Thomas has studied the speech of educated Jews in New York

---

[4] He was an amateur philologist of some skill, and published books on Pidgin English and the language of Gypsies. In 1889–90 he and Albert Barrère brought out A Dictionary of Slang, Jargon and Cant in two volumes; rev ed. 1897.

[5] Popular Phonetics, *AS*, Vol. IV, June 1929, pp. 410–16.

City.[6] He points out that one of its chief characteristics is a slight change in tongue position in the pronunciation of *t, d, n, l, s* and *z*, producing the effect of a lisp. This lisp is even more noticeable in the speech of English Jews, and writers who attempt to transcribe that speech usually indicate it.[7]

But of all the ethnic dialects on exhibition in the United States the one that has got the most attention, both from the literati and from students of linguistics, is that of the Southern Negroes.[8] Tremaine McDowell says that it made its first appearance in American fiction in Part I of Hugh Henry Brackenridge's satirical novel "Modern Chivalry: Containing the Adventures of Captain Farrago and Teague O'Regan, His Servant," published in 1792,[9] but it had been attempted in plays so early as 1775 and there were traces of it in other writings even before. Then, as ever since, Negro speech has shown a simplified—or at least different—grammatical structure. The origins of that structure were described by Krapp[1] as the development of a dialect comparable to Pidgin English or Beach-la-Mar; and this dialect survives more or less in the Gullah of the sea islands of Georgia and South Carolina. But its vestiges are also to be found in the speech of the most ignorant Negroes of the inland regions, which still shows grammatical peculiarities seldom encountered in white Southern speech, however lowly, *e.g.*, the confusion of persons, as in "I *is*," "*Do* she?" "*Does* you?" "*Am* you de man?" and "He *am*"; the frequent use of present forms in the past, as in "He *been die*" and "He *done show* me"; and the tendency to omit all the forms of *to be*, as in "He *gone*" and "Where you *at?*"[2] The phonology

---

[6] Jewish Dialect and New York Dialect, *AS*, Vol. VII, June 1932, pp. 321–6.

[7] [This feature is also found in some Jews of Cleveland and Chicago.]

[8] [For a summary of the problem, see The Relationship of the Speech of American Negroes to the Speech of Whites, by Raven I. McDavid, Jr., and Virginia McDavid, *AS*, Vol. XXVI, Feb. 1951, pp. 3–17.]

[9] Notes on Negro Dialect in the American Novel to 1821, *AS*, Vol. V, Apr. 1930, pp. 291–6. [See also Negro Dialect in Eighteenth Century American Drama, by Richard Walser, *AS*, Vol. XXX, Dec. 1955, pp. 269–76, and The Speech of Negroes in Colonial America, by Allen Walker Read, *Journal of Negro History*, Vol. XXIV, 1939, pp. 247–58. Read points out that in the Eighteenth Century as today there were Negroes (as also representatives of other ethnic groups) in all stages of proficiency in the use of English.]

[1] The English of the Negro, *American Mercury*, June 1924, pp. 190–5. [The one serious investigation of urban Negro speech is A Phonological and Morphological study of the speech of the Negro of Memphis, Tennessee, by Juanita V. Williamson, diss. (microfilm), U. of Michigan, 1961.]

[2] [The simplification of the verb conjugation in Negro speech has been noted by E. Bagby Atwood, A Survey of Verb Forms in the Eastern United States; Ann Arbor, Mich., 1953, p. 44. These characteristics appear in the speech and writing of urban Negroes in the North, to their great disadvantage both in school and in their attempts to obtain better housing and better jobs. Unfortunately, the "professional Negro" often discourages any serious investigation of linguistic traits associated with his race and puts pressure on the schools not to mention the subject. The attitude is grimly reminiscent of the Nineteenth Century feeling about tuberculosis and the early Twentieth Century attitude toward venereal di-

of this mudsill Negro speech greatly resembles that of the lowest class of whites, so much so that many competent observers have declared that it is substantially identical, but in intonation, at least, it shows special characteristics. Even the educated Southern Negro seldom loses this intonation, though in vocabulary and pronunciation his speech is identical with that of the corresponding class of whites.[3] Indeed, he tends to speak a shade "better," in the schoolma'am's sense, than whites on his own level. The representation of Negro speech in literature has always been imperfect and often absurd. [An exception is the Uncle Remus cycle of Joel Chandler Harris. Sumner Ives, of Syracuse University, has shown that within the limits of the English alphabet, Harris has been remarkably accurate and effective in presenting the speech of a plantation Negro as heard by a cultivated white Southerner—though *Ausländer* often have difficulty in understanding the phonetic basis of Harris's orthography.[4]]

The Gullah or Geechee dialect of the Georgia and South Carolina coast is an anomaly among American Negro dialects, as it is indeed among American dialects in general, for it is the only one that is not easily intelligible in far parts of the country. Krapp was of the opinion that "very little of it, perhaps none, is derived from sources other than English," and not a few white linguists have supported him, notably John Bennett, an Ohio-born Charlestonian.[5] But this theory has now been considered weakened by the studies of Lorenzo D. Turner, of Roosevelt University, a Negro linguist who prepared himself for his task by acquiring a working knowledge of the principal West African languages. He began work between Georgetown, S.C., and the Georgia-Florida border in 1930, and by 1944 had assembled no less than 6,000 loans from twenty-eight languages and dialects. Of these about a thousand came from Kongo, spoken in Angola and the former Belgian Congo, and another thousand from Yoruba, spoken in Nigeria. About four-fifths of them appear today only as personal names, and others are used only in traditional African songs, mostly unintelligible to the singers, but the rest "are used daily in conversation."[6] Some of Turner's specimens from the surviving vocabulary follow, with the African terms from which they come:

Bong. A tooth. (Wolof *bong*.)
Bubu. Any insect, but usually one whose sting is poisonous. (Fula *mbubu*, a fly; Hausa *bubuwa*; Bambara *buba*; Kongo *mbu*.)

---

sease: that we can eliminate an evil from society if we just don't talk about it.]

[3] This approximation was noted by Nathaniel Beverly Tucker, a Virginian lawyer, so early as 1836. See McDowell, before cited, p. 295.

[4] [Dialect Differentiation in the Stories of Joel Chandler Harris, *American Lit-*

erature, Vol. XXVII, Mar. 1955, pp. 58–96; The Phonology of the Uncle Remus Stories, *PADS*, No. XXII, Nov. 1954.]

[5] Gullah: A Negro Patois, Part I, *South Atlantic Quarterly*, Oct. 1908, p. 33.

[6] [Africanisms in the Gullah Dialect; Chicago, 1949.]

Buckra. A white man. (Efik and Ibibio *mbakara*, white man, from *mba*, he who, and *kara*, to govern.)

Da *or* dada. Mother. (Ewe *da* or *dada*.)

Det. A hard rain. (Wolof *det.*)

Dindi. A small child. (Vai *din din.*)

Enufole. Pregnant. (Ewe *fo le enu*, she is with child.)

Fukfuk. The viscera of an animal. (Mende *fukfuk.*)

Guba. A peanut. (Kongo *nguba*, a kidney.)

Gumbo. Okra. (Tshiluba *tshinguhmbuh;* Umbundu *otshingumbo.*)

Hudu, *v.* To bring bad luck to. (Hausa *hudu*, a form of gambling; Ewe *hododo*, lending or borrowing; *hodada*, a dice game.)

Kuta. A tortoise. (Bambara and Malinke *kuta;* Dahomean *kulo;* Efik *ikut;* Buluba-Lulua *nkudu;* Djerma *ankura;* Hausa *kunkura.*)

Na. And. (Twi and Ibo *na.*)

Nanse. A spider. (Twi and Fante *ananse.*)

Nyamnyam *or* nyam, *v.* To eat. (Wolof *nyamnyam.*)

Pojo *or* ojo. A heron. (Mende *podzo.*)

Tot, *v.* To carry. (Umbundu *tuta*, to carry; Kikongo *tota*, to pick up; Mandingo *ta*, to carry on the head or in the hand.)

Ula. A louse or bedbug. (Umbundu *ola* or *ona*, a louse; *ula*, a bed; Yoruba *ola*, a moth.)

Vudu. Sorcery. (Dahomean *vodu*, a spirit or fetish; *vodudoho*, a curse; *voduna*, a cult or religion; Ewe *vodu da*, a snake that is worshipped; *vodusi*, a priest.)

Some of these have got into the general American vocabulary, especially in the South, *e.g., buckra, gumbo, vudu (voodoo), hudu (hoodoo), guba (goober)* and *kuta (cooter)*. In Gullah the conjugations of verbs are disregarded, so that "the simple form *run* does duty for *run, runs, is* or *are running, has* or *have run, ran*, etc., singular and plural of all tenses";[7] the possessive is indicated by juxtaposition, as in *Billy gun, we hat;*[8] adjectives and nouns are turned into verbs, and verbs into nouns; "there is no distinction of pronouns with regard to sex; the feminine form is practically unused";[9] and the singular of nouns commonly, though not invariably, also does duty for the plural.[1] [Turner presents evidence that these and other features of Gullah grammar reflect the underlying structure of most West African languages, where changes in syllable pitch do the work that in Indo-European languages is performed by inflectional endings. It is also

[7] Reed Smith, Gullah, *Bulletin of the University of South Carolina*, Nov. 1, 1926, p. 26.

[8] John Bennett, Gullah: A Negro Patois, Part II, *South Atlantic Quarterly*, Jan. 1909, p. 50.

[9] *Ibid.*, p. 49.

[1] Guy B. Johnson, Gullah, in Folk Culture on St. Helena Island, South Carolina; Chapel Hill, N.C., 1930, p. 35.

possible that the peculiar intonation of Gullah—and even of the white speech of the same region—owes something to the same source, but conclusive evidence is lacking.]

The popular belief ascribes some of the characteristics of Southern American—for example, the elision of the *r* before consonants and the intrusion of the *y* before certain vowels—to Negro influence. This belief is not of recent origin, for on April 15, 1842, Charles Dickens, who was then in the United States, wrote home to his wife: "All the women who have been bred in slave States speak more or less like Negroes, from having been constantly in their childhood with black nurses." But Greet argues convincingly that the thing has really run the other way.[2] "When the slaves were brought to America," he says, "they learned the accent of their masters. There is literally no pronunciation common among Negroes, with possible exceptions in Gullah, that does not occur generally in vulgar or old-fashioned American speech." Krapp argued that the common belief that the voice of the Negro differs from that of the white man is unsupported by the facts.[3] He was even indisposed to grant that the use of *I is* for *I am* among the lower orders of Negroes is a true Negroism: he tracked it down in Joseph Wright's English Dialect Dictionary, and found that it was common in England so long ago as the Thirteenth Century. Nevertheless, there is a conventionalized Negro dialect, perhaps launched by the minstrel shows of the past generation, that all Americans recognize, and it plays a large part in American literature.[4]

---

[2] Southern Speech, in Culture in the South; Chapel Hill, N.C., 1934, p. 614.

[3] The English of the Negro, *American Mercury*, June 1924.

[4] [Negroes are often aware of the dialect expected of them by the white man, especially by their patrons, and try to supply it; it is a flattering experience for an Atlas field worker to find a Negro informant who drops the dialectal veneer as soon as the white patron disappears around the corner. Even Negro investigators have difficulty achieving rapport with their informants. This was noticed by Turner, and more recently by Juanita Williamson in her study of the Negro speech of Memphis.]

VIII

American Spelling

1: THE INFLUENCE OF NOAH WEBSTER

At the time of the first English settlements in America the rules of English orthography were beautifully vague, and so we find the early documents full of spellings such as *aetaernall* for *eternal* and *jinerll* for *general*.[1] There had been attempts in England since the middle of the Sixteenth Century to put the spelling upon a more rational basis,[2] but it was not until about 1630, nearly a quarter of a century after the landing at Jamestown, that English printers began to differentiate clearly between *u* and *v*, *i* and *j*, two pairs still confused in the First Folio of Shakespeare (1623) [and not alphabetized separately till the Nineteenth Century[3]]. The redundant final *e* was much oftener encountered then than now, and almost any Seventeenth Century American public document shows *toune* for *town*, *halfe* for *half* and *yeare* for *year*.

As printing increased, a movement toward uniformity in spelling, if not toward rationality, began. By the beginning of the Eighteenth Century,

---

[1] See for example the collection of such forms made by the students of Miles L. Hanley in 1935.

[2] They are described in George H. McKnight's English Language in the Making, New York, 1928, especially pp. 119–20, 191–2, 229. [Several of the reforms associated with Webster had been proposed in James Howell, Familiar Letters (1630), and in Thomas Dyche, A Guide to the English Tongue (1719) and A Dictionary of All the Words Commonly Us'd in the English Tongue (1723). See The English Dictionary from Cawdrey to Johnson, by DeWitt Starnes and Ger-

trude Noyes; Chapel Hill, N.C., 1946, p. 127; and English Examined, by Susie I. Tucker; Cambridge, Eng., 1961, pp. 29–30, 62–4.]

[3] [The possibility that the separate alphabetizing of *i* and *j*, *u* and *v*, was a contribution of Webster has been considered by Joseph Friend, one of the editors of Webster's New World Dictionary of the English Language, and author of The Development of American Lexicography from Its Beginning through the Webster-Worcester Dictionary War, diss. (microfilm), Indiana U., 1962.]

English authors were spelling pretty much alike and substantially as we spell now, but it was not until Samuel Johnson's Dictionary (1755) that Englishmen had a universally accepted guide to orthography. In the presence of conflicting usage, Johnson always took the conservative side. He thus ordained that *critic, music,* and even *prosaic,* which he considered Old English words, should have a final *k,* though all were borrowed from Latin through French. He decided for the *-our* ending in words like *honor,* and it remains in use in England today. Naturally enough, he fell into contradictions, and Lindley Murray could point out such pairs as *deceit* and *receipt, exterior* and *interiour.* But on the whole his decisions ratified what had become customary usage oftener than they sought to change it. His influence was tremendous, both in England and in America.

Not until after the Revolution were his mandates challenged on this side of the water, and it was Noah Webster who divorced English precept and example and American practice. In his "Dissertations on the English Language" (1789), Webster proposed the omission of silent letters (*a* in *bread*), the elimination of certain consonant-and-vowel combinations for which there were more commonly used counterparts (*tuf* for *tough*) and the addition of diacritical marks to distinguish different ways of pronouncing the same letter. These changes, all in the direction of a consistent alphabet, would, said Webster, "render the orthography sufficiently correct and regular." His greatest argument, however, was the patriotic one; such reform would differentiate English and American orthography, it would encourage the printing of books in the United States and it would act as "a band of national union":

> However [Americans] may boast of Independence, and the freedom of their environment, yet their opinions are not sufficiently independent; and astonishing respect for the arts and literature of their parent country, and a blind imitation of its manners, are still prevalent among the Americans.

But, as Krapp points out, Webster was "above all a practical, not a theoretical reformer," [4] and in consequence he was slow to adopt the reforms he advocated. Not until his Dictionary of 1806 was there a wholesale assault upon the authority of Johnson.[5] He made an almost complete sweep of whole classes of silent letters: the *u* in *-our* words, the final *e* in *determine,* the silent *b* in *thumb,* the *s* in *island* and the redundant penultimate

---

[4] Krapp, Vol. I, pp. 332 *ff.* [See also Noah Webster's Conservatism, by Gerald A. Smith, *AS,* Vol. XXV, May 1950, pp. 101-4.]

[5] [In the preface he tried to dissociate himself from Franklin's scheme to reform the alphabet; in the dictionary itself he operated from Franklin's basic principles. See Benjamin Franklin on Spelling Reform, by Abraham Tauber, *Word Study,* Feb. 1956, pp. 4-6.]

consonant in *traveler* and *wagon* (English *traveller* and *waggon*). He lopped the final *k* from *frolick* and *physick*, and transposed the *r* and *e* in many of the words ending in *-re*, such as *theatre* and *centre*. He even antedated the simplified spellers by such phonetic spellings as *tung* for *tongue* and *wimmen* for *women*. Some of these spellings simply echoed an earlier English uncertainty, others were for analogy or uniformity, or for euphony or simplicity, or because it pleased him to stir up the academic animals. Webster, in fact, delighted in controversy, and was anything but free from the national yearning to make a sensation. Many of his innovations failed to take root, and in the course of time he abandoned some himself, such as the dropping of the silent letter in such words as *head*, *give*, *built* and *realm*. Successive editions of his dictionary show further concessions, but many, like *aker* for *acre* and *cag* for *keg*, did not begin to disappear until the edition of 1847, issued by other hands after his death. Three of his favorites, *chimist* for *chemist*, *neger* for *Negro* and *zeber* for *zebra*, are incidentally interesting as showing changes in American pronunciation. He abandoned *zeber* in 1828, but remained faithful to *chimist* and *neger* to the last.

But though he was thus forced to give occasional ground, Webster lived to see many of his reforms adopted. The influence of his Spelling-Book, first published in 1783, was tremendous. It took the place of Thomas Dilworth's "Aby-sel-pha," [6] which had been first printed in London in 1740, and later reprinted in Philadelphia in 1747 by Benjamin Franklin. Webster himself had been nourished upon it in youth, and was sufficiently convinced of its merits to imitate it, even to the extent of lifting whole passages. Dilworth's reading lessons, for example, began with a series of pious dithyrambs in monosyllables, reminiscent of the Old Testament, and Webster's began with a palpable paraphrase of them. Thus:

Dilworth	*Webster*
Pay to God his due.	The way of man is ill.
Go not in the way of bad men.	My son, do as you are told.
No man can see God.	But if you are bid, do no ill.
Our God is the God of all men.	See not my sin, and let me not go to the pit.

Dilworth shut down after six stanzas of this dismal doggerel, but Noah went to ten, and then followed with five more frankly printed as prose.

---

[6] A corruption of *abisselfa*, itself a corruption of *a-by-itself-a*. Allen Walker Read explains in The Spelling Bee: a Linguistic Institution, *PMLA*, Vol. LVI, June 1941, that at the old-time spelling bees a vowel which was also a syllable "was noted by a formula such as *a by itself a*, which was contracted into *abisselfa*." Read finds reference to the *a-by-itself-a* system of spelling in The Petit Schole, by F. Clement; London, 1587.

Webster's Spelling-Book, even in its heyday, was by no means without rivals, though it maintained its authority for nearly a century. There was no national copyright until 1790, and the states did not offer any protection to authors until 1782. In his preface to his revised edition of 1803 he complained bitterly that his imitators "all constructed their works on a similar plan," borrowing his lists of words (as he had borrowed some of Dilworth's).[7] But he had a stout heart and was a relentless salesman, and he could boast in the same preface that the sales to date had reached 3,000,000. How many copies were sold before it was at last displaced is unknown. It seems to have made its way in the South more slowly than in the North, but once it was established it became almost immovable. During the Civil War discreetly revised editions were brought out at Macon, Raleigh and Atlanta; it has never been out of print.

Even more influential than the old blue-back speller was Webster's series of dictionaries, and especially the "American Dictionary" of 1828. He began work on them in 1800, bringing out preliminary drafts in 1806 and 1807, and at the same time continued to amass materials for the larger dictionary that he had in mind. In 1824 he went to Europe to consult the philologians and libraries of England and France, and in January 1825 he finished his manuscript at Cambridge, England.[8] The first edition, two volumes quarto, was of 2,500 copies, selling at $20 a set. It went quickly enough, but there was no profit in it, and in 1829 Webster employed Joseph E. Worcester (1784–1865) to prepare a one-volume abridgment. This sold well, but Worcester followed it with a dictionary of his own, and for years thereafter this dictionary and Webster's fought for favor.

Worcester's had one advantage: it was free from the attempts at reform of spelling and pronunciation that Webster had undertaken. But Webster's, though its etymologies were often fanciful and most of its innovations in spelling had to be dropped after his death, gradually made its way with the plain people, and by 1840 it was accepted as the American authority par excellence. When he died in 1843, George and Charles Merriam, of Springfield, Mass., bought the rights to the dictionary from his quarreling heirs, and prepared a new edition which appeared in 1847, in one volume and selling for $6.[9] Warfel says that it "took immediate hold" and that "the presence of a Webster dictionary in almost every literate household dates from this year."

---

[7] Both he and Dilworth put *cag* among the *-ag* words.

[8] [Webster's considerable debt to Samuel Johnson is discussed by Joseph W. Reed, Jr., in *AS*, Vol. XXXVII, May 1962, pp. 95–105.]

[9] One of Webster's sons-in-law, Chauncey A. Goodrich, was the editor. [The Merriam tradition is presented by R. K. Leavitt in Noah's Ark, Two New England Yankees, and the Endless Quest: a Short History of the Original Webster Dictionaries; Springfield, Mass., 1947.]

During the century since then Webster has had to meet some very stiff competition—from the Century Dictionary after 1891, from the Standard after 1895, from the Concise Oxford after 1911, [from the American College Dictionary after 1949 and from Webster's New World Dictionary (published by another house, which asserted the right to the Webster name as something in the public domain) after 1952, and most recently from the Thorndike–Barnhart World Book Encyclopedia Dictionary of 1963,] but four Americans out of five, when they think of a dictionary, think of it.[1] The Merriams and their heirs have employed competent philologians to supervise the revisions, which have stretched from 1859 to 1961; [the 1961 work, in particular, represents a thorough overhauling [2]]. Even though the competition is keener today than ever, it still occupies a favored position. It is accepted as authority by all American courts, is widely used in colleges and schools, is the official spelling guide for the Government Printing Office and has the same standing in many newspaper, magazine and book publishing offices. How many copies of Noah Webster's dictionaries and its Merriam descendants have been printed and circulated cannot be determined, for as the copyrights on the successive editions expired, other publishers prepared photographic reproductions, added a few new words and entered into competition under new titles. That the total sales of all these have equaled the sales of the Webster Speller is certainly possible, if not exactly probable. Thus Webster lives in American history as the author of the two champion best-sellers of all time, the Bible only excepted.

2: THE ADVANCE OF AMERICAN SPELLING

American spelling is plainly better than English spelling, and in the long run it seems sure to prevail. The superiority of *jail* to *gaol* is manifest by the common mispronunciation of the latter by the Americans who find it in

---

[1] [Some of the new wrinkles in recent dictionaries are explained in Contributions of Dr. Thorndike to Lexicography, by Clarence L. Barnhart, *Teachers College Record*, Vol. LI, No. 1, Oct. 1949, pp. 35–42. The principles by which various popular dictionaries were edited are explored by James B. McMillan in *CE*, Vol. X, Jan. 1949, pp. 214–21, and by Karl W. Dykema in *AS*, Vol. XXIX, Feb. 1954, pp. 59–65.]

[2] [The hue and cry raised against the 1961 Webster in the public prints by the spokesmen for literary mandarinism and soft-headed gentility has so far prevented an objective evaluation by competent scholars, since the attack is also directed at the objective study of language. But oddly enough, the British reviews, including those in the London *Times* and Manchester *Guardian*, are generally favorable. See Dictionaries and *That* Dictionary: a Casebook on the Aims of Lexicographers and the Targets of Reviewers, by James H. Sledd and Wilma R. Ebbitt; Chicago, 1962. A generally favorable verdict was returned by a symposium of seven reviewers operating independently (Harold B. Allen, Margaret M. Bryant, Robert A. Hall, Jr., Raven I. McDavid, Jr., John B. Newman, Allen Walker Read and Robert Sonkin) in *QJS*, Vol. XLVIII, Dec. 1962, pp. 431–40.]

print, making it rhyme with *coal*. *Curb* has analogues in *curtain, curdle, curve* and *curt; kerb* has very few, and of them only *kerchief* and *kernel* are in general use. Nor would it be easy to argue logically against *gram, toilet, ax, draft* and *tire*. [Only a few English spellings are obviously superior, notably *whisky* for *whiskey*. Webster preferred *whisky*, but *whiskey* remains the common form in the United States. The Scotch variety is always labeled *whisky*, and the same practice is followed by Canadian distillers; in Ireland both spellings are in use, apparently without any guiding principle.[3]]

The Government Printing Office has followed Webster's dictionaries since 1864, when the Superintendent of Public Printing (he became the Public Printer in 1895) was authorized by law to determine "the forms and style in which the printing . . . ordered by any of the departments shall be executed." He issued his first Style Manual in 1887, and it has been revised a number of times since. A copy of this work is in the proofroom of nearly every American magazine and newspaper. It favors American spelling in all cases, and its rules are generally observed.

Even in England the uncompromising defenders of English spelling lead a forlorn hope. Not only is there a general movement toward American forms in newspapers, including the *Times* itself; there is also a general yielding by English "authorities." The Concise Oxford Dictionary of the brothers Fowler (1911) offers plenty of examples.[4] The authors say in their preface that they "stop short of recognizing forms that at present strike every reader as Americanisms," but they surely go far enough. In nearly all words ending in *-ise* and *-isation*, the English *s* is changed to the American *z*. They cling to *leveller* and *traveller*, but accept *-or*, conceding only that "in Britain many retain *-our*." They swap *y* for *i* in *tire* and *siphon*, concede that *jail* is as good as *gaol* and admit *program* and *wagon* without precisely endorsing them.

The monumental Oxford Dictionary upon which the Concise Oxford is grounded shows many silent concessions, and quite as many open yieldings

---

[3] [Bushmill's in Ulster and Jameson's in Dublin both use *whiskey;* so far as extensive research reveals, the only labels defaced with the Sassenach *whisky* bear the fiery Irish names *Paddy's* and *Murphy's. Whisky* has some currency in the United States; see for example *AS*, Vol. XXV, Dec. 1950, p. 257, and Vol. XXVIII, May 1953, p. 113. Not illogically, though perhaps surprisingly, the meaning of *proof* as an indicator of alcoholic voltage varies in the two countries. In the United States *proof* or *100 proof* means 50% alcohol by volume, in England 50% by weight (approximately *114 proof* U.S.). Canadians officially gauge their whisky *underproof: 30 underproof* Canadian = *70 proof* English, *80.4 proof* U.S. Russian spirits of the same potency would be labeled *40% alcohol by volume*. For this intelligence I am indebted to William M. Austin, of the Illinois Institute of Technology, and Robert P. Young, Director of Public Relations, Hiram Walker–Gooderham & Worts, Ltd.]

[4] 4th ed., rev. by E. McIntosh, 1951.

—for example, *ax*, which is admitted to be "better than *axe* on every ground." The Authors' and Printers' Dictionary,[5] the authority for printers and proofreaders in London, Edinburgh and Belfast, shows characteristic American spellings in the 1956 edition. For example it recommends the use of *jail* and *jailer* in place of the English *gaol* and *gaoler*, changes *burthen* to *burden* and prefers *fuse* to *fuze*.[6]

There is, however, much confusion among these authorities. The Concise Oxford and the Authors' and Printers' Dictionary prefer *bark* to *barque*, but the Oxford is for *czar* and the A. and P. for *tsar*. The Oxford admits *program;* the A. and P. sticks to *programme*. Both have abandoned *enquire* for *inquire* but remain faithful to *endorse* and *enclose*. The British Board of Trade detaches the final *-me* from *gramme* in *kilogram* and *milligram*, but insists upon *gramme* when the word stands alone.

The English tendency to follow American example is not extended to words ending with *-or*. Here orthographical logic has little to do with the matter; it is, rather, a matter of national pride. In American the *u* appears only in *glamour* and *Saviour*, and in the last only when the word is used in the Biblical sense. In England it is used in most words of that class, but omitted from agent nouns, *e.g.*, *ambassador*, *emperor*, and also from various other words, *e.g.*, *horror* and *torpor*. The derivatives of *honour* exhibit clearly the difficulties of the American who essays to write correct English. *Honorary*, *honorarium* and *honorific* drop the *u*, but *honourable* retains it. There is, indeed, no order in the business, for *laborious* stands beside *laboured*, *labourer*, *labouring* and *Labourite*, *odorous* beside *odourless*, *humorist* beside *humour*, etc.[7] In many cases the spelling has been changed, sometimes long ago and sometimes only recently. *Orator* was *oratour* to Chaucer but *orator* to Shakespeare. *Governor* was *governour* to Samuel Johnson in 1775, though Clarendon had written *governor* in 1647.[8] Coleridge was still spelling *honor* in 1809, though Wordsworth in the same year made it *honour*. H. W. Fowler seemed to be convinced that his fellow-Englishmen, soon or late, would adopt the *-or* endings, despite their present distaste for them. He said:

> What is likely to happen is that either, when some general reform of our spelling is consented to, reduction of *-our* to *-or* will be one of

---

[5] [Authors' and Printers' Dictionary . . . an attempt to codify the best typographical practices of the present day, by F. Howard Collins; 10th ed., revised; London, 1956.]

[6] [American Army usage, as represented by the official Dictionary of U.S. Army Terms, Washington, 1943, prefers *fuze* for a detonating device.]

[7] All these examples are from the Concise Oxford.

[8] [The novels of the South Carolinian William Gilmore Simms, which issued from Boston and New York publishers before the Civil War, leaned toward *governer* and the like. But this intelligent simplification had no following.]

the least disputed items, or failing general reform, we shall see word after word in *-our* go the way of *governour*. It is not worth while either to resist such a gradual change or to fly in the face of national sentiment by trying to hurry it; it would need a very open mind in an Englishman to accept *armor* and *succor* with equanimity.[9]

The rule in other classes of words is so complicated and full of exceptions that no lexicographer has been able to explain it. The use of *c* instead of *s* in *defense* and *offense* is etymologically incorrect, but the English cling to it tenaciously. The English use a *c* in *pretence*, but they have abandoned it for *s* in *expense* and *recompense*, so that there is some hope that they may come over to the American way in other words. In those beginning with *en-* or *in-*, *em-* or *im-*, they prefer the *e*, but there is inconsistency in their practice. Thus they use both *to ensure* and *insurance*, *to endorse* and *indorsation*.[1] They still use *ae* and *oe* in words in which, on this side of the ocean, simple *e* usually suffices, *e.g.*, *anaemia*, *anaesthetic*, *mediaeval* and *diarrhoea*, but there seems to be a movement toward the American *e*.[2] *Pediatrics*, *economy*, *pedagogy* and *penology* are now spelled by all English writers as in the United States.

Additional rocks upon which the Englishman founds his pride, patriotism and faith are *storey* (of a house), *waggon*, *for ever* (two words), *nought*, *grey*, *cheque*[3] and *pyjamas*. Some of these rocks, alas, begin to show signs of faulting. Amateur lexicographers often go to bat for *storey*, but the OED prefers *story*, as does the Rules for Compositors and Readers at the University Press, Oxford. One of the arguments commonly heard in defense of *storey* is that it serves to differentiate clearly the two meanings of the word, but how anyone could ever confuse a *story* in *The Saturday Evening Post* with one in the Empire State Building is more than I can make out. The Authors' and Printers' Dictionary has been recommending *wagon* with one *g* for years past, and the OED quotations show that making one word of the more usual *for ever* has been favored by eminent British authors of the past, including Carlyle. So with *naught;* the OED

---

[9] A Dictionary of Modern English Usage, p. 415.

[1] Even in the United States there is some wobbling, *e.g.*, in Philadelphia *Inquirer* and Cincinnati *Enquirer*.

[2] Urged on by Dr. George M. Gould (1848–1922), author of a standard medical dictionary (often revised by other hands) and part-author of the incomparable Anomalies and Curiosities of Medicine, the American Medical Editors' Association declared for the simple *e* at Milwaukee, June 1893.

[3] *Check* is always used in the United States for a *personal check* or a *certified check; Traveler's Cheques* are issued by the American Express Company and the Bank of America, *Traveler's Checks* by the First National City Bank of New York. [English authorities are apparently silent about *corney* vs. U.S. *corny*, but the former spelling appears in Coronet among the Weeds, by Charlotte Bingham; New York, 1963.]

prefers *nought* but the Authors' and Printers' Dictionary ordains the American *naught*.

There is not much movement of English spellings in our direction; the traffic, as with neologisms, runs heavily the other way. At Bar Harbor, in Maine, a few Anglophile summer residents are at pains to put *Harbour* instead of *Harbor* on their stationery, but the local postmaster stamps all mail *Bar Harbor*, the legal name of the place. In the same way American haberdashers of the more doggy sort sometimes advertise *pyjamas* instead of *pajamas*, just as they advertise *braces* for suspenders and *boots* for shoes, but this benign folly does not go very far. [Nor does the attempt of dealers in accessories for foreign sports cars to establish the spelling *tyres*.] However, *theatre* is favored in the stage world and *centre* occurs in the names of many buildings and some place names, such as Somerset *Centre*, Mass.

Thornton, in his "American Glossary," [4] says that the reduction of two *l*'s to one in such words as *traveller*, *jewellery*, etc., began in the United States "about the year 1835"; there seems to be every reason for believing that Webster was responsible for it, for in his "American Dictionary" of 1828 he not only gave the forms with one *l*, but defended them at length. The rule he set up was that when a final consonant appears in an accented syllable, it may be doubled in derivatives, but not when it appears in an unaccented syllable. Thus he arrived at *jeweler* and *traveler* but permitted *distiller* and *beginning*. His decision to keep Sir Humphry Davy's original *aluminum* in his dictionary of 1828 rather than the emendation to *aluminium* (on the analogy of *potassium, sodium*, etc.) [5] is responsible for its remaining *aluminum* in the United States today.[6]

The distinction between *practice* the noun and *to practise* the verb seems to be breaking down. Webster 1961 apparently prefers *practice* for both, as does the Government Printing Office. The spelling with *c* apparently arose in imitation of *justice, service*, etc. But all the English authorities continue to distinguish between noun and verb. Among minor differences between the two orthographies *specialty* and *alarm* offer examples. In England they are *speciality* and *alarum*, though *alarm* is also an alternative form. *Specialty*, in America, is always accented on the first syllable; *speciality* in England on the third. The American *aluminum* is similarly accented on the second syllable, the English *aluminium* on the third. Perhaps the *boric-boracic* pair also belongs here. In American *boric* is now almost

---

[4] Vol. II, p. 905.

[5] *Aluminum* was condemned by the *Quarterly Review*, Vol. I, 1812, p. 355, on the ground that this analogy was lacking, and *aluminium* was proposed as a more respectable choice.

[6] According to Percy A. Houseman, of Haddonfield, N.J., the decennial index of *Chemical Abstracts*, an official publication of the American Chemical Society, used *aluminium* before 1916, but has since used *aluminum*.

universal and is also making progress in England. How the difference between the English *behove* and the American *behoove* arose I do not know.

In Canada the two orthographies, English and American, flourish side by side. By an Order-in-Council of 1890, official correspondence must show the English spelling, and such quasi-official publications as highway maps seem to prefer *harbour*. Newspaper practice varies, and the new Canadian school dictionaries recognize that here, as elsewhere, Canadian English has mixed origins and considerable variety.[7] In Australia the English spelling is official, but various American forms appear in the newspapers and elsewhere.

3: THE SIMPLIFIED SPELLING MOVEMENT

Franklin's "Scheme for a New Alphabet and Reformed Mode of Spelling" (1768) was by no means the first attempt to revise English spelling. At the beginning of the Thirteenth Century a monk named Orm tried to reform the spelling of Middle English. He proposed to get rid of the chief difficulty—distinguishing between long vowels and short ones—by doubling the consonants after the short ones. Thus he spelled *fire, fir*, and *fir, firr*. His proposal got no support, but when the manuscript in which he made it was exhumed six centuries later, it turned out to be invaluable to philologians for the light it shed upon Middle English pronunciation.

Sir John Cheke (1514–57), professor of Greek at Cambridge and teacher of King Edward VI, proposed to amputate the now useless final *e*'s surviving from Middle English. He also wanted to differentiate between short and long vowels by doubling the latter, and to get rid of all silent consonants, thus making *doubt, dout*, and *fault, faut*, [as they had been when borrowed into English from French]. Cheke had influential support, including that of Roger Ascham, but English went on its wild way. Other attempts to bring it to rule were made by Sir Thomas Smith (1568), who produced a phonetic alphabet, and, a century later, by the Rt. Rev. John Wilkins, who came forward with another one, of 450 characters. Many later English authors of the classical line made attempts to regulate and improve the spelling of their time, notably John Milton, who used *sovran* for *sovereign*,

---

[7] [According to private communications from W. S. Avis, secretary of the Canadian Linguistic Association, the regular practice of newspapers and periodicals (and some publishers) is roughly this: *honor* and its analogues, *plow, program, jail, curb, omelet*, as in the American fashion; *cheque, storey, centre* and its analogues, *axe, kidnapped* and *skilful*, as in British practice; either *traveller* or *traveler, jeweller* or *jeweler, jewellery* or *jewelry, grey* or *gray*, with the first in each instance the more common. But *Shopping Centre* and *Shopping Center* may be advertised in the same newspaper, and the variants of common words may appear in the same news story or even in the same sentence.]

glimse for *glimpse* and *thir* for *their* [and attempted to distinguish the weak- and strong-stressed forms of *me, we, he, she,* by doubling the vowel letter to indicate unexpected strong stress, as *mee* [8]]. Swift seems to have been against simplified spelling, as Samuel Johnson was, and in 1712 denounced the "foolish opinion, advanced of late years, that we ought to spell exactly as we speak." [9] But neither these worthies nor their numerous successors had any hand in the determination of actual spelling practice. That was mainly the work of printers, and after 1650, their rules began to be accepted by English authors, and most of them remain in force to this day.[1] Since Franklin's time the literature of the subject has been large. In the last century the most noise was made by Sir Isaac Pitman, the inventor of a system of shorthand. In the early 1840s he and Alexander J. Ellis proposed a phonetic alphabet of forty letters, and during the years following he made vigorous propaganda for it.

But the real father of the simplified spelling movement was probably Noah Webster. The controversy over his new spelling aroused so much interest that the dons of the American Philological Association appointed a committee consisting of Professors Francis A. March, William Dwight Whitney, J. Hammond Trumbull, S. S. Haldeman and F. J. Child to look into it, and in 1876 this committee reported that a revision of spelling was urgent. The eleven new spellings they urged be adopted at once were *ar, catalog, definit, gard, giv, hav, infinit, liv, tho, thru* and *wisht.* Out of a convention in Philadelphia this same year grew the Spelling Reform Association, which endorsed the eleven new spellings. Three years later a similar body was organized in England, with such officers as A. H. Sayce, Charles Darwin, Alfred Tennyson, J. A. H. Murray, W. W. Skeat and Henry Sweet. In 1886 the American Philological Association made recommendations affecting about 3,500 words. Most of the new forms had been put forward earlier by Webster, and some were in unquestioned American usage at that time, *e.g.,* the deletion of the *u* from the *-our* words, the substitution of *-er* for *-re* and the reduction of *traveller* to *traveler.* The trouble with their other changes was that they were either too uncouth to be adopted without a long struggle (*e.g., tung* for *tongue, ruf* for *rough*) or likely to cause errors in pronunciation (*cach* for *catch, troble* for *trouble*). The movement suffered a setback, but twelve years later the National Education Association revived it with a proposal that a beginning be made with a very short list and nominated the following twelve changes:

---

[8] [This is shown by the English scholar Miss Helen Darbishire, and is the basis of her excellent edition of Milton's poems; Oxford, 1955.]

[9] A Proposal for Correcting, Improving and Ascertaining the English Tongue: a letter to the Earl of Oxford and Mortimer, London, Feb. 22, 1711/12.

[1] [The schemes of the early reformers are discussed in all standard histories of the English language, such as the one by A. C. Baugh; 2nd ed., New York, 1958.]

*tho, altho, thru, thruout, thoro, thoroly, thorofare, program, prolog, cata-
log, pedagog* and *decalog.*

Then, in 1906, came the organization of the Simplified Spelling Board,
with a subsidy from Andrew Carnegie, and such members as Henry
Bradley, F. J. Furnivall, C. H. Grandgent, W. W. Skeat and T. R. Lounsbury. The Board at once issued a list of 300 spellings, new and old, and
in 1906 President Theodore Roosevelt ordered their adoption by the Government Printing Office, which resisted, as did most departments. In the
end the use of the twelve new spellings was restricted to the White House.[2]
After Carnegie's death in 1919 there was a serious decline in the activities
of the Board.[3] A Handbook of Simplified Spelling (1919) summarizing its
successive recommendations was so long and unwieldy that a much shorter
list was distributed simultaneously. This too failed to win any considerable
public support, and its brash novelties (*det, tel, twelv, wil, yu*) gave the
whole movement a black eye. In the summer of 1921 the National Education Association, which had launched the campaign for reform in 1898,
withdrew its endorsement. Since Carnegie's death, spelling reform has been
promoted mainly by individuals, no two of whom agree.

On January 28, 1935, the Chicago *Tribune* announced out of a clear sky
that it had adopted twenty-four simplified spellings and was preparing to
add others from time to time.[4] Its first list, with *catalog, skilful, harken,* etc.,
was rather cautious, but the second list added *agast* for *aghast, aile* for
aisle, crum for *crumb,* and got into wider waters. In subsequent announcements it proceeded to *hefer* for *heifer, herse* for *hearse, lether* for *leather*
and *yern* for *yearn.* Some of its readers applauded, but others protested,
and in a little while it abandoned *iland,* [etymologically one of the soundest
on the list]. Its list did not include such favorites of the Simplified Spelling
Board as *tho, thru* and *filosofy.* After many vacillations, it abandoned the

[2] [See Spelling Simplified by Presidential Decree, by Clyde H. Dornbusch,
AS, Vol. XXXVI, Oct. 1961, pp. 236–8;
also Simplified Spelling in Government
Publications, by George R. Ranow, *AS,*
Vol. XXIX, Feb. 1954, pp. 36–44. Ranow
points out that without any spectacular
victory changes in the practices of printers and dictionaries have achieved the
adoption of simplified spellings "to a
much greater extent than was ever the
fondest hope of Theodore Roosevelt."]
[3] First and last, he is said to have spent
$283,000 on the movement.
[4] [Actually, the announcement should
have surprised no one familiar with the

history of the *Tribune.* Its great editor
Joseph Medill (1823–99) had been a
member of the council of the Spelling
Reform Association, and had spoken editorially in favor of spelling reform; moreover, several simplified spellings, of the
type associated with the *Tribune* in the
1930s, had been adopted by the *Tribune*
before 1880. See The Chicago *Tribune:*
Its First Hundred Years, by Philip Kins-
ley; 3 vols.; New York and Chicago,
1946. The *Tribune*'s spelling reforms
were evaluated skeptically by the Manchester *Guardian Weekly,* July 14, 1949,
p. 95.]

more extreme novelties, kept many of the original list and added such
favorites as *tho,.thru* and *altho.*[5]

Despite the fact that the activities of the Simplified Spelling Board have
much slowed down, it has probably had some influence upon the course
of American spelling. It brought *tho* almost to the point of acceptance, and
undoubtedly aided the acceptance of *catalog, program* and their congeners.
George Philip Krapp, who was certainly no Anglophobe, believed that
fonetic, fonograf and the like were "bound to be the spelling of the future"
in this country.[6] Louise Pound long ago suggested that the spelling reform
movement, if it had little effect upon standard spelling, may have fanned
the craze for whimsical spellings which still rages among advertisement
writers, who have produced *nabor, nite, foto, hi, lite, Holsum, thanx* and
kreem.[7] An early stage of the craze was visible in the name of the *Ku Klux
Klan,* organized in 1865, but the original Klan did not use all the strange
nomenclature that marked its successor of 1920, e.g., *klavern, kleagle,
klonvocation, kloran, klaliff* and *kludd.*[8] Miss Pound recalled that Walt
Whitman was curiously attracted to *k,* and cited his *Kanada* and *Kanadian.*
Meanwhile, *Variety* and its imitators continue to generate and disseminate
a large number of simplified spellings of their own, e.g., *laff, ayem* (A.M.),
whodunit, burlesk and *vodvil.* Hollywood seems to have been responsible
for the reduction of *and* to *'n,* as in *Sit 'n Eat, Park 'n Dine,* and perhaps for
hiway and *traler* (trailer).[9] The substitution of *x* for *cks* is apparently of
respectable age in the United States. *Sox* for *socks* has become universal,
as in *White Sox. Slax* has been found,[1] as have *trunx* and *chix.*[2] *Donut* is
so widely accepted that there is a *Donut* Institute and even a *National
Donut Week.*[3] Advertisement writers and authors combine in an attempt
to naturalize *alright,* a compound of *all* and *right,* made by analogy with

---

[5] [Many of the characteristic *Tribune*
spellings were dropped in the 1950s. The
1962 Style Book, p. 63, specifies the following: *aging, altho, ameba, analog,
apolog, burocracy, burocratic, *canceled,
cantaloup, catalog, cigaret, *controled,
controler, criscross, crystalize, decalog,
demagog, dialog, drouth, eclog, epilog,
etiquet, extoled, fulfilment, glamor, gly-
cerin, hiccup, instalment, intern, linage,
monolog, *patroled, pedagog, prolog,
*subpenas, synagog, tho, *thoro, thru,
thruout, tonsilitis, tranquility.* "*All
forms of these words use *Tribune* spelling, as when they end in *ed, ing,* and *er.*
Also words like *thoroly, thorobred,
thorogoing,* and *thruout.*" Only parts of
proper names are excepted.]

[6] Modern English; New York, 1910,
p. 181.

[7] The Kraze for *K, AS,* Vol. I, Oct.
1925; see also her papers in *DN,* Vol. V,
Pt. VI, 1923, and Vol. IV, Pt. I, 1913.

[8] [A glossary. of *Klan-guage,* taken
from a book copyrighted in 1953 by
Imperial Wizard Eldon Edwards, was
published in *The New York Times,*
Sept. 16, 1962.]

[9] Showing Hollywood, by Cecilia
Ager, *Variety,* July 23, 1930.

[1] *AS,* Vol. XI, Dec. 1936, p. 374.

[2] These by Louise Pound, in The
Value of English Linguistics to the
Teacher, *AS,* Vol. I, Nov. 1925, p. 100.

[3] *The Nation,* Aug. 15, 1942, p. 133.

already and *almost*. It has already migrated to England and has the imprimatur of a noble lord.[4]

The collapse of the Simplified Spelling Board put an end to organized and large-scale agitation for spelling reform in the Republic, but at the same stroke it revived and restimulated the same great moral movement in England. By the terms of a trust set up by Sir George Burton Hunter, and a subsequent legal decision, the Simplified Spelling Society, the British opposite number to the American Simplified Spelling Board, inherited, in 1939, £18,200,[5] and at once began bringing out a long series of books and pamphlets in promotion of the cause. These publications show that the Society hopes to reform English spelling without bringing in any new characters, without putting on accents and without departing from the more obvious phonetic values. What all this comes to is shown by the following:

> We instinktivly shrink from eny chaenj in whot iz familyar; and whot kan be mor familyar dhan dhe form ov wurdz dhat we hav seen and riten mor tiemz dhan we kan posibly estimaet? We taek up a book printed in Amerika, and *honor* and *center* jar upon us every tiem we kum akros dhem; nae, eeven to see *forever* in plaes ov *for ever* atrackts our atenshon in an unplezant wae. But dheez ar isolaeted kaesez; think of dhe meny wurdz dhat wood hav to be chaenjd if eny real impruuvment wer to rezult. At dhe furst glaans a pasej in eny reformd speling looks "kweer" and "ugly." Dhis objekshon iz aulwaez dhe furst to be maed; it iz purfektly natueral; it iz dhe hardest to remuuv. Indeed, its efekt iz not weekend until dhe nue speling iz noe longger nue, until it haz been seen ofen enuf to be familyar.[6]

Happily the shock to Britons on encountering the American *honor* is evaded by going the whole hog to *onor*. *Labor* is disguised as *laebor*, and *color* becomes *kulor*. At first glance, the new system simply looks like "bad" spelling, but it must be said for it that even its most radical innovations are usually readily fathomed.

---

[4] Viscount Harberton, in How to Lengthen Our Ears; London 1917, p. 28.

[5] London *Times*, Mar. 2, 1939.

[6] New Spelling, by Walter Ripman and William Archer; London, 1940, p. 90. In 1941 the Society published a Dictionary of New Spelling, compiled by Ripman and containing about 18,600 words. [It is now under formidable competition from the Augmented Roman Alphabet, described by I. J. Pitman in Learning to Read: An Experiment, *Journal of the Royal Society of Arts*, Feb. 1961, which is actually undergoing tests in British primary schools. An appraisal, though hardly impartial, was presented by John Downing, Director of the Reading Research Institute, University of London Institute of Education, at the 27th Educational Conference sponsored by the Educational Records Bureau in New York, Nov. 1-2, 1962. It was subsequently published as Experiments with an Augmented Alphabet for Beginning Readers in British Schools. Although the Augmented Alphabet has been subjected to searching criticism, several American school systems, notably that of Chicago, are planning to experiment with it.]

In England, as in the United States, there are many modern lone-wolf spelling reformers. George Bernard Shaw, in his heyday as a reformer, maintained a department of reformed spelling in his vast and bizarre Utopia.[7] But save for a few banal innovations, *e.g., havn't, program* and *Renascence,* most of which were not really innovations at all, he stuck closely to standard English spelling in his own writing, and even indulged himself in a few archaisms, *e.g., to shew.* In theory, however, he was always in favor of very radical changes, including the adoption of an entirely new alphabet, and provision for such a one was made in his will. [However serious the intent behind Shaw's bequest, no proposal met the stringent requirements laid down by the executors; and after a decent delay (and the ultimate amount of publicity) this bequest was divided among a group of museums which Shaw had named as alternative legatees in case no qualified alphabet should be forthcoming].[8]

In its early days, the spelling reform movement in both the United States and England had the support of many of the most eminent philologists then in practice in the two countries, and also of many distinguished literati, but it has never made any progress, and there is little evidence that it will do better. In this country it has been handicapped by the fact that, to Americans, phonetic spelling suggests the grotesqueries of the comic writers, stretching from Seba Smith to Milt Gross, and by the further fact that popular interest in and respect for spelling prowess, fostered by the institution of the spelling bee, still survive more or less. Furthermore, the endorsement by Roosevelt I in 1906 produced vastly more opposition than support, for Americans, in those days, had not yet got used to government by administrative fiat, and resented it violently whenever it touched what they regarded as their private affairs. Finally, the patronage of Andrew Carnegie likewise irritated a tender nerve. Memories of the bloody Homestead strike of 1892 were still playing about him, and it was not until later that he began to lose his diabolical character.

The advantages of spelling reform have always been greatly exaggerated

---

[7] [See The Case for Fonetik Spelling, reprinted in *The New York Times Magazine,* Aug. 20, 1961, from Shaw's preface to The Miraculous Birth of Language, by Richard Albert Wilson; London, 1948.]

[8] [The Public Trustee, under provisions of the will, did conduct a contest for a new alphabet, and announced on May 23, 1961, that a sizable prize was to be divided among four contestants: Mrs. Pauline M. Barratt, of Canada, and Mrs. J. F. Magrath, Dr. S. L. Pugmire and Mr. Kingsley Read, all of Great Britain. This information was obtained from Some Arguments for & against Reforming English Spelling, a Report Prepared for the Canadian Conference on Education by a Committee Representing the Canadian Linguistic Association and the Association of Canadian University Teachers of English; Kingston, Ontario, 1962. This report is perhaps the most intelligent summary of the problem now in print. In Sept. 1962 an edition of Androcles and the Lion was published in the new "Shaw alphabet," a compromise between the prize-winning suggestions. It greatly resembles shorthand.]

by its exponents, many of whom have been notably over-earnest and under-humorous men. Some of the favorite arguments of the reformers are so feeble as to be silly—for example, the argument that the new spelling would greatly reduce the labor of writing and the cost of paper and printing. In 1849 Alexander J. Ellis figured that his fearsome phonetic alphabet would result in a space saving of 17%. More modest estimates range from 1.6% to 4%, but these always overlook the fact that many of the gains would be wiped out by compensatory losses, for some changes, even those conservative ones of the Simplified Spelling Board, would only rearrange letters, and in a few cases even make words longer.

The argument that phonetic spelling would be easier to learn than the present spelling is not supported by the known facts. In some cases it no doubt would be, but in plenty of other cases it would certainly not. Moreover, the number of "hard" words in English is greatly overestimated.[9] It is not infrequently argued that the inconsistencies of English spelling are unknown in other languages, but this is moonshine. No civilized language is really spelled phonetically, not even German, Spanish or Italian; [and as accurately as the Finnish alphabet represents the vowel and consonant phonemes, it does no better than the rest in indicating stress and intonation]. German is actually full of sounds that are represented in its orthography by different characters, *e.g.*, *ch* and *g*, *f* and *ph*, *c* and *k*, and letters that have different sounds in different situations, *e.g.*, the *s* in *essen* and *Hase*. Spanish and Italian come much closer to phonetic spelling than German, but even in those languages there are difficulties in the orthography. Russian spelling, which had been static since it was fixed in the Eighteenth Century, was reformed by fiat of the Kremlin in 1924. But a proposal to abandon the Cyrillic alphabet for the Roman was rejected, [as have been most of the Roman alphabets which were devised to write the languages of hitherto illiterate minority groups]. In Turkey, a few years later, Kemal Atatürk had better luck, for the Army was under his thumb and at least nine out of ten Turks were illiterate. He was therefore successful in substituting the Roman alphabet of Europe for the clumsy and difficult Arabic alphabet, and in bringing in what almost amounted

---

[9] [The regular patterns of sound-letter association in English are sketched by W. Nelson Francis in Ch. VIII of The Structure of American English, New York, 1958, and more fully by Robert A. Hall, Jr., in Sound and Spelling in English, Philadelphia, 1960. More detailed treatments are by C. M. Wise, Some Contextual Guides to the Pronunciation of American English, in *The Study of Sounds*, 1957, pp. 251–72, and by Paul Friedrich Werner, English Pronunciation: the Relationship between Pronunciation and Orthography, trans. by R. A. Martin, London, 1958. Let's Read: a Linguistic Approach, by Leonard Bloomfield and Clarence Barnhart, Detroit, 1961, makes use of these regular associations, as do several new series of readers based on Bloomfield's experimental sketch, never published in his lifetime.]

to phonetic spelling. In France the learned men of the Academy began considering spelling reform in 1893; nothing came of it, and to this day French spelling is even less consistent than English.

All the American spelling reformers, beginning with Noah Webster, have made the capital mistake of trying to cover too much ground in one operation. An impressive number of Webster's innovations were accepted, but many, many more were rejected. When the Simplified Spelling Board began making its list longer and longer and wilder and wilder, the national midriff began to tickle and tremble, and soon the whole movement was reduced to comedy.

Sir William Craigie made the same point in a wise paper printed in 1944:

> There would be better prospect of some success if the aim were less ambitious. Gradual changes in certain words or types of words, such as have been made in the past, might well be introduced . . . which in time would become so familiar that the older forms would take their place with . . . *musick* and *physick, deposite* and *fossile, chymical* and *chymist.* Such changes, however, . . . would still leave the essentials of English spelling intact. . . . It is well to bear in mind that it has now stood the test of three centuries, and in spite of all its alleged defects has not prevented English from attaining the world-wide position it now holds.[1]

In another paper Craigie called attention to an impediment that nearly all spelling reformers have passed over too casually:

> The question of the possibility or advantage of change becomes more difficult when the normalized spelling would reduce to a common form those homophones which at present are differentiated and on that account are immediately recognizable.[2] If the postal *mail* were respelled as *male,* the meaning of *male carriers* might well be in doubt in certain contexts, and if *sew* became *sow* it would not only eliminate a useful distinction but would add a third homograph to the noun *sow.* This problem, of course, applies to all homophones with distinctive spellings, whether these have etymological justification or not.[3]

Craigie hints that English is one of the languages which resist the phonetizing process, and for two reasons. The first is that it is made up of words coming from widely different sources—"the native, Romanic,

---

[1] Problems of Spelling Reform, *SPE Tract,* No. LXIII; 1944, p. 75.
[2] *e.g., to, too* and *two.*

[3] Some Anomalies of Spelling, *SPE Tract,* No. LIX; 1942, p. 331.

classical and exotic"—and each element has brought in its own tradition in spelling. If, in a proposed spelling-reform scheme,

> the native standard is adopted, much of the Romanic and classical element becomes unrecognizable, *e.g.*, if *seed* is taken as the normal representation of the sounds *s, ee, d*, then *cede* and *recede* must become *seed* and *reseed*. . . . On the other hand if the Romanic and classical *fuse* or *muse* is taken as a model, then *news* will be *nuse*, and *huse* would represent both *hues* and the third person singular of the verb *hew*.[4]

The second obstacle lies in the fact that many of the commonest words in the language have traditional spellings that could not be changed without offending the eye and causing confusion. "No one will deny," says Craigie, "that . . . *ake, coff, enuff, enny, wimmen, tung, shure* and *berry* are better representations of the sounds of *ache, cough, enough, any, women, tongue, sure* and *bury* than the conventional spellings. The trouble is that to all who have a fair knowledge of orthography such forms, instead of being recognized as improvements, suggest only ignorance and illiteracy, since they are such as would occur to anyone whose schooling has been decidedly imperfect."

A third, and perhaps the most important difficulty, lies in the fact that many words are pronounced differently in England and the United States, and even in different parts of the same country. There is, for example, *schedule*, which would have to be *shedyul* or something of the sort in England and *skedyul* in America. Said George Sampson, a retired inspector of schools of the London County Council and formerly honorary secretary of the English Association:

> Radical reform in spelling means the exact phonetic representation of pronunciation. But whose pronunciation? There is Scottish English, Irish English, Welsh English, and American English of numerous kinds. There is even English English, of which I will offer some specimens:
>
> I was recently talking to some eminent persons about education. One spoke of "the *grät* (*ä* as in German) *vahyoo* of the *clahssics*," and mentioned "*Ahthuns*"; another spoke of "the *greet velyiew* of the *clessics*," and mentioned "*Ethins*"; a third thought it "a *gret shem* that the *univahsities* should *conten* so *mach infairior matairiel*." And the other day a lady told me she was "*afred bebby hed a pen* and *mäst hev gert* a *curled*." [5]

---

[4] Problems of Spelling Reform, p. 57.
[5] Reforms in Spelling, London *Times*, Feb. 26, 1936.

[The closest approach to a consistent scheme for reforming standard English spelling and simultaneously not doing violence to the association between sound and symbol in most of the major dialects of American English has been devised by Martin Joos, of the University of Wisconsin.[6] But there is no evidence that it has any effect in making the teaching of reading and writing an easier task in the public schools of Madison or in the University of Wisconsin, than it is in more distant precincts.]

Robert Bridges made a study of the homonyms in the OED, some 509 of them, embracing 1,075 words,[7] and showed that phonetic spelling would greatly increase their number. But he professed to be undaunted by that fact, for he argued that in the case of the average man, "as he learns new words, there will be a tendency, if not a necessity, for him to lose hold of a corresponding number of his old words, and the words that will first drop out will be those with which he had hitherto been uncomfortable, and among those words will be the words of ambiguous meaning." But all that this comes to is the doctrine that an increase in homographs would lead to a corresponding impoverishment of the vocabulary. [In all fairness, of course, we should recognize that no one has yet calculated the extent to which homography would be increased by a more nearly phonemic spelling. If the *bough* of a tree and the *bow* of a ship were to be spelled alike, there would arise at the same time an orthographic difference between the *bow* of a ship, rhyming with *cow*, and a *bow* of ribbon, rhyming with *dough*, that does not exist today. In the end, the distinction between homographic (and homophonic) forms would be resolved pretty much the way it is now, in terms of the context in which each is used.] [8]

Some years ago the London *Observer* sought to resolve the matter by advocating free trade in spelling. If a word is spelled so that it is instantly recognizable, what difference does it make, after all, *how* it is spelled? George Bernard Shaw was content to use the present alphabet in a free and easy manner in his ordinary writing, and the same system is followed by the overwhelming majority of average Americanos, and it works very well. Everyone can understand a policeman when he turns in the report of a *larsensy* or an applicant for a job when he alleges that he is a licensed *chuffer*, *shoffer* or even *shofar*. "Correct" spelling, indeed, is one of the arts that are far more esteemed by schoolma'ams than by practical men, neck-deep in the heat and agony of the world.

---

[6] [See his review of Regularized English, by Axel Wijk (Stockholm, 1959) in *Lg.*, Vol. XXXVI, June 1960, pp. 250–62.]

[7] On English Homophones, *SPE Tract*, No. II; 1919, p. 14.

[8] The most comprehensive study of homonyms is The Conflict of Homonyms in English, by Edna Rees Williams; New Haven, 1944. It is reviewed by Rudolph Willard in *AS*, Vol. XX, Feb. 1945, pp. 61–2.

4: THE TREATMENT OF LOAN WORDS

In the treatment of loan words, English spelling is much more conservative than American. This conservatism, in fact, is so marked that it is frequently denounced by English critics of national speech, and it stood first among the "tendencies of modern taste" attacked by the Society for Pure English in its original prospectus in 1913—prepared by Henry Bradley, Sir Walter Raleigh, Logan Pearsall Smith and others:

> Literary taste at the present time, with regard to foreign words recently borrowed from abroad, is on wrong lines, the notions which govern it being scientifically incorrect, tending to impair the national character of our standard speech, and to adapt it to the habits of classical scholars. On account of these alien associations our borrowed terms are now spelt and pronounced, not as English but as foreign words, instead of being assimilated, as they were in the past, and brought into conformity with the main structure of our speech.[9]

There has been some change in England,[1] but the more pretentious English papers continue to accent, and often italicize, words that have been completely naturalized in this country, *e.g.*, *café, naïveté, régime, rôle, divorcée* and *dénouement*. Even loan words long since naturalized are sometimes used in their foreign forms, *e.g.*, *répertoire* for *repertory*, *Muslim* for *Moslem* and *crêpe* for *crape*. The dictionaries seldom omit the accents from recent foreign words.

In the United States usage is much looser. *Dépôt* became *depot* immediately it entered the language, and the same rapid naturalization has overtaken *employée, matinée, débutante, negligée, exposé, résumé* and scores of others. *Café* is seldom seen with its accent, nor is *attaché* or *señor*. Even in the larger cities, the majority of American newspapers manage to get along without using foreign accents, even on foreign proper names, so that *Bülow* becomes *Bulow* and *Poincaré* becomes *Poincare*. This iconoclasm, while general, is by no means universal. *The New York Times*, at least in theory, uses the proper diacritical marks on all accented foreign words that have not been naturalized,[2] and the Baltimore *Sunpapers*[3] and the New York

[9] *SPE Tract*, No. I, Preliminary Announcement and List of Members; Oct. 1919, p. 7.

[1] Probably at least partly because of the Society, which in later tracts printed lists of proposed new spellings. In No. XIII (1923) it proposed *rencounter* for *recontre, tamber* for *timbre* and *intransigent* for *intransigeant*.

[2] [Style Book of *The New York Times*, ed. and rev. by Robert E. Garst; New York, 1956, p. 31. *The Times*, however, hedges on the German umlaut; "since it cannot be used in heads, preference should be given for the sake of uniformity to the use of the additional *e* instead of the mark." It therefore recommends *Fuehrer* and *Tannhaeuser*, rather than *Führer* and *Tannhäuser*.]

[3] [At one time the *Sunpapers* had the

Herald Tribune [4] go at least part way. Even the Chicago *Tribune* (despite its long-continued attempts to inflict simplified spelling on its readers) makes some provision for accents.[5] The Government Printing Office favors naturalizing loans as soon as possible, and thus ordains *blase, boutonniere, brassiere, cafe, debut, decollete, entree, facade, fete, role* and *roue,* but it still uses accents on *abbé, attaché, canapé, étude, métier, précis, résumé, risqué* and *vis-à-vis.*[6] The State Department, having a great deal of correspondence with foreigners, puts accents on all of these and also on *naïve.*[7]

With the shedding of accents Brander Matthews was in hearty sympathy. Writing in 1917, and dealing with *naïve* and *naïveté,* which he welcomed into the language because there were no English equivalents, he argued that they would "need to shed their accents and to adapt themselves somehow to the traditions of our orthography." He went on:

> After we have decided that the foreign word we find knocking at the doors of English [he really meant American, as the context shows] is likely to be useful, we must fit it for naturalization by insisting that it shall shed its accents, if it has any; that it shall change its spelling, if this is necessary; that it shall modify its pronunciation, if this is not easy for us to compass; and that it shall conform to all our speech-habits, especially in the form of the plural.[8]

same theoretical meticulosity about accents that *The Times* has today.] The necessary linotype matrices were laid in by the *Evening Sun* in 1914 or thereabout. I was at that time a member of the editorial staff of the paper, and had been carrying on an intra-office campaign for their purchase since 1910. It took about five years to induce the copy desk and proofroom to use them. The morning *Sun* followed ten or eleven years later. It was a long and bitter battle, and left me pretty well exhausted. [According to Miss Betty Adler, of the Enoch Pratt Free Library in Baltimore, "The *Sun* has done some backsliding since Mencken's day. Paul Banker, city-desk editor and co-author of the 1958 style book says they bought a new font that did not have accents or diacritical marks, so these have disappeared from news pages. However, as a redeemer, they continue to use accents, tildes and cedillas on the editorial page, especially as they must adorn so many foreign dignitaries. . . . Item 2 in the style book claims that the accents, etc., were so misused that they would be omitted except on the editorial page. From which one can infer that editorial writers and typesetters are more educated." Miss Adler is the editor of *Menckeniana,* a publication of the Enoch Pratt.]

[4] Style Book of the New York *Herald Tribune,* 1934, p. 2. [At that time the *Herald Tribune* used diacritics in "art, dramatic, literary and musical copy, and on the editorial and Sunday fashion page." However, current practices do not follow the precepts of this unrevised style book, but principles derived from the common knowledge of the staff. One of these principles is to ignore accents and other diacritics on foreign words. For this information I am deeply obligated to Allan F. Hubbell.]

[5] [Composing Room Style Book, 1962, The Chicago *Tribune* and Chicago's *American,* p. 4.]

[6] [United States Government Printing Office Style Manual; rev. ed.; Jan. 1959, p. 61.]

[7] Style Manual of the Department of State, by Margaret M. Hanna and Alice M. Ball; Washington, 1937, p. 113.

[8] Why Not Speak Our Own Language?, *Delineator,* Nov. 1917, p. 12. See also his French Words in the English Language, *SPE Tract,* No. V, 1921.

This counsel is heeded by many patriotic Americans. So far, *bozart* (for *beaux arts*) is not in any dictionary, but it has been used as the name of a magazine of verse, as the name of a lead pencil and in the title of business firms, including one with quarters in Radio City, New York. *Exposé*, shorn of its accent, is sometimes pronounced to rhyme with *propose*, and the *sauer* in *sauerkraut* and *sauerbraten* is often spelled *sour*. *Cole slaw*, by folk etymology, has become *cold slaw*, and one step further is found *hot slaw*. *Cañon* is *canyon* and *vaudeville* is sometimes *vodvil*. I have even seen *jonteel*, in a trade name, for *gentil*, and *parfay* for *parfait*. American newspapers seldom distinguish between the masculine and feminine forms of common loan words. *Blond* and *blonde* are used indiscriminately. The majority of papers, apparently mistaking *blond* for a simplified form of *blonde*, use it to designate both sexes. So with *employée, divorcée, fiancée,* etc. Here the feminine form is preferred; no doubt it has been helped into use by the analogy of *devotee*.[9]

In the formation of the plural, American adopts native forms much more quickly than English. Where English has *sanatoria, indices, formulae, libretti, media* and *monsignori*, American usage favors plurals of native design, and sometimes they take quite fantastic forms. One often meets *delicatessens, monsignors, virtuosos, rathskellers, nucleuses* and *appendixes*. *Banditti*, in place of *bandits*, would seem an affectation to an American, and so would *soprani* for *sopranos* and *soli* for *solos*.

Both English and American labor under the lack of native plurals for the two everyday titles *Mister* and *Missus*. In writing and in the more exact forms of speech, the French plurals, *Messieurs* and *Mesdames*, are used, but in the ordinary spoken speech, they are avoided by circumlocution. In place of *Mesdames* a more natural form, *Madames*, seems to be gaining ground in America. Thus *Dames du Sacré Coeur* has been translated as *Madames* of the Sacred Heart in a Catholic paper of wide circulation.[1]

Louise Pound[2] has noted that a number of Latin plurals tend to become singular nouns in colloquial American, notably *curricula, data, dicta, insignia* and *strata*, and with them a few Greek plurals, *criteria* and *phenomena*. The error leads to the creation of double plurals, *e.g.*, *curriculas, insignias, stratas, stimulis, bacillis, narcissis*. The Latin names of plants lead to frequent blunders. *Cosmos* and *gladiolus* are felt to be plurals, and from them, by folk etymology, come the false singulars *cosma* and *gladiola*. Such forms may be found plentifully even on higher levels. *Data* in the singular has reared its head, among other places, in the *Congressional*

---

[9] See Words from the French (*-é, -ée*), by Matthew Barnes, *SPE Tract*, No. XXX, June 1928.

[1] *Irish World*, June 26, 1918.

[2] The Pluralization of Latin Loan-Words in Present-day American Speech, *Classical Journal*, Dec. 1919.

Record [3] and in the *Saturday Review of Literature*,[4] and *media* to designate one newspaper in *Editor and Publisher*.[5] In *Etude*, the Bible of all small-town music teachers, *tympani* has been used for one drum.[6] *Data* is so wide-spread that even Webster 1961 recognizes it. In compensation for these barbarities there is an occasional resort to a pseudo-Latin plural, as in *prospecti* and *octopi*.[7]

The tendency to replace all non-English plurals with indigenous forms is not recent, but goes back many years. When *halo* came in during the Sixteenth Century, the Latin plural *halones* was used, but by 1603 it had become *haloes* and by 1646 *halos*. Many repectable authorities argue that most of the surviving Latin plurals had better be dropped. In 1925, for example, Robert Bridges declared for *nebulas* in place of *nebulae*, *vortexes* for *vortices* and *dilettantes* for *dilettanti*, though allowing that *automata* and *phenomena* had better be retained.[8]

Every now and then someone starts a crusade against loan words that seem to be unnecessary, *e.g.*, *questionnaire*,[9] *per* instead of *a* in *per year*, etc., but it seldom comes to anything. The changes undergone in the process of naturalization are often curious. The case of *smearcase* (Ger. *Schmierkäse*) is familiar, and in a travel article published in 1876 the Japanese *jinricksha* appears as *djinrichia*, *geisha* is *guecha* and *samurai* is *samourai*.[1]

The difficulties that 100% Americans have with the plural of loan words are matched by their difficulties with the plurals of certain native words. Is *buses* correct, or *busses?*[2] The problem has been debated with no con-clusion, and Webster 1961 gives both. And what of the plurals of *attorney general* and its cognates?[3] Again, is the plural of *roof*, *roofs* or *rooves? Proofs* pulls one way and *hooves* another, [though of late years, with the disappearance of the horse, *hoofs* has been supplanting *hooves*]. Yet again, is it *spoonsful* or *spoonfuls*, *brothers-in-law* or *brother-in-laws*, *Misses Smith* or *Miss Smiths?* Most authorities declare for the first of each of

---

[3] Extension of Remarks of Hon. Francis Case, of South Dakota, Nov. 23, 1945, p. A5440.

[4] Two examples are on p. 9, Aug. 7, 1937.

[5] Censor's Office Discusses Rules of Advertising, Mar. 7, 1942, p. 8.

[6] Drum Hunt, Jan. 1944, p. 10.

[7] I take the former from Dozen Periodicals Fold, *Variety*, June 23, 1937; the latter is ascribed to John Steinbeck in *Minimum? Minimis? Minima?* by Ernest Fuld, *Saturday Review of Literature*, Jan. 20, 1945, p. 23.

[8] *SPE Tract*, No. XXII, pp. 66-7.

[9] [Disliking *questionnaire*, Hans Kurath labeled the body of questions for the field interviewing of the Linguistic Atlas the *work sheets*, a happy choice since they are readily distinguishable from the *check lists*, employed in many areas for gathering Atlas material by mail. *Questionnaire* would be ambiguous.]

[1] The Japanese Stage, *Galaxy*, Jan. 1876, pp. 76, 78 and 79 respectively.

[2] See The Plural of *Bus*, by Mamie Meredith, *AS*, Vol. VI, Aug. 1930, pp. 487-90.

[3] *Attorney-Generals*, *State Government* (the official organ of the Council of State Governments), Jan. 1939.

these pairs, but the others are undoubtedly in wide use. *Sisteren* or *sistern*, now confined to the Christians, white and black, of the Get-Right-with-God country, was common in Middle English and is just as respectable, etymologically speaking, as *brethren*. And down to the Seventeenth Century *grieves* was the plural of *grief* and *strives* of *strife*.[4] Certain plurals of words ending in *-th* or *-se*, though their spelling is established, present problems in pronunciation, *e.g.*, *wreath* and *blouse*. Should the *th* of *wreaths* be that of *think* or that of *this?*[5] And should the *s* of *blouses* be the *s* of *sue* or the *z* of *zoo?* [In the ex-Confederate states, the latter pronunciation is common in the singular *blouse* as well, so that it rhymes with *cows* rather than with *mouse*.]

5: PUNCTUATION, CAPITALIZATION AND ABBREVIATION

In capitalization the English are much more conservative than we are. They invariably capitalize such terms as *Government*, *Prime Minister*, *Church* and *Society*, when used as proper nouns; they capitalize *Press*, *Pulpit*, *Bar*, etc., almost as often. In the Eighteenth Century there was a fashion for reducing all capitals to small letters, and Lord Chesterfield thus denounced it in a letter to his son, April 13, 1752:

> It offends my eyes to see *rome, france, caesar, henry the fourth*, etc., begin with small letters; and I do not conceive that there can be any reason for doing it half so strong as the reason of long usage to the contrary. This is an affectation below Voltaire.

But Thomas Jefferson thought otherwise, and in the first draft of the Declaration of Independence *nature* and *creator* and even *god* are in lower case. Sometimes, indeed, small letters appear at the beginning of sentences and even paragraphs.[6] But Franklin, a conservative in this field as in so many others, stuck to capitals for all nouns, whether proper or common, to the end of his days. During the early part of the succeeding century the movement against capitals went so far that the days of the week were often spelled with small initial letters, and even *Mr.* became *mr.* Curiously enough, the most striking exhibition of this tendency of late years is offered by an English work of the highest scholarship, the Cambridge History of English Literature. It uses the lower case for all titles, even *baron* and *colonel*, before proper names, and also avoids capitals in such words as *presbyterian*,

---

[4] The Irregularities of English, *SPE Tract*, No. XLVIII, 1937, p. 287.
[5] The Plural of Nouns Ending in *-th*, by C. T. Onions, *SPE Tract*, No. LXI, 1943, pp. 19–28.

[6] The Declaration of Independence: the Evolution of the Text, by Julian P. Boyd; Princeton, N.J., 1945, pp. 19–21.

catholic and *christian*. At present there is considerable variation in the practice of American newspapers. Very few capitalize the names of the seasons,
those of the points of the compass or the numerical designation of centuries.
All capitalize the name of *God* and His divine associates, and all pronouns
referring to them save those beginning with *w*, but these pronouns are not
capitalized in direct quotations from the King James Bible, where they are
all l.c. Nearly all American publications now capitalize *Negro*.

There are also differences between English and American practice in
punctuation. The English usually put a comma after the street number of a
house, making it, for example, *34, St. James's Street*. There was a time when
they inserted a comma instead of a period after the hour when giving the
time in figures, *e.g.*, *9,27*, and omitted the *o* when indicating less than 10
minutes, *e.g.*, *8,7*, instead of *8.07*, but now their practice is more like ours.[7]
In writing dates the usual order is day, month, year, *e.g.*, *5 September 1962*,[8]
but sometimes month, day, year, the normal American practice; [needless
to say, both usages are found in Canada]. During World War II the War
Department came out for day, month, year;[9] even before that the form
had been in more or less use in both the Army and the Navy, though not in
other departments in Washington.

In the use of the hyphen English and American practice seem to be substantially identical, though the English employ it in proper names rather
more than we do. They also cling to it in *to-day*, *to-night* and *to-morrow*,
which have long been supplanted by *today*, *tonight* and *tomorrow* in
America.[1] [The Webster dictionaries clung to the older form till the 1930s;
it is found in the fourth edition of Webster's Collegiate, but the modern
form has been offered since the second edition of the New International
(1934).] Of late there has been a tendency among American newspapers to
amalgamate *-man* with a long series of nouns that were formerly separated,
e.g., *garbageman* and *newspaperman*. Jacques Barzun has printed an eloquent protest[2] against excessive amalgamation of words that had better be
kept separate, listing some of the horrors that he has encountered, *e.g.*,
picturegallery, *fifteenyearold*, *hardshelled*, *ultraaustere* and *midsummer-
madness*.[3]

The English are more careful than we to retain the apostrophe in pos-

---

[7] [Authors' and Printers' Dictionary;
10th ed.; London, 1956, p. 403.]

[8] The Authors' and Printers' Dictionary so ordains (pp. 94–5) and indicates
that French and German practice is
similar. Note that no comma appears
after the name of the month. [See Com-
mas in Dates, by Howard Hoving, *CE*,
Vol. XII, Feb. 1951, pp. 286–7.]

[9] *The New Yorker*, Sept. 16, 1944, p.
11; *American Notes and Queries*, Vol.
VI, June 1946, p. 40.

[1] Reginald Skelton, in Modern English
Punctuation, London, 1933, p. 65, says
that *tomorrow* is also "in regular use" in
England.

[2] Unhyphenated American, *The Nation*, Sept. 5, 1942, pp. 194–5.

[3] I add *sweetpotato* from the *Congressional Record*, Apr. 2, 1946, p. 3050.

sessive forms of nouns used in combination, *e.g.*, *St. Mary's Church, ladies' room*. In the United States the apostrophe seems to be doomed, for the Board on Geographic Names has swept it out of such old forms as *Prince George's* and *Queen Anne's* (counties in Maryland), and it has been dropped from the title of *Teacher's* College, Columbia, the Lhasa of American pedagogy.[4] In other respects American and English punctuation show few differences. The English are rather more careful than we are, and commonly put a comma after the next-to-the-last member of a series, but otherwise they are not too precise to offend a red-blooded American. There are frequent proposals that the semicolon be abandoned, though its utility must be manifest,[5] and next to it, quotation marks seem to be the chief butt of reformatory ardor. The fact that quotes within quotes are often confusing, and unhinge the minds of thousands of poor copyreaders every year, has fanned these flames. Most American newspapers print the names of other newspapers, when they can't avoid mentioning them, in roman, enclosed in quotation marks, but the Government Printing Office prints them without the quotation marks.[6] The relatively few that use italics go on to caps and small caps when they mention themselves.[7]

The American liking for short cuts in speech, so plainly visible in the incessant multiplication of compounds and back formations, is also shown in the popularity of abbreviations. They are employed, in the United States, says John S. Farmer, "to an extent unknown in Europe. Life, they say, is short and the pace is quick; brevity, therefore, is not only the soul of wit, but the essence of business capacity as well. This trait of the American character is discernible in every department of the national life and thought —even slang being curtailed at times."[8] *C.O.D.*, *N.G.* and *P.D.Q.* are American masterpieces; *O.K.*, the most successful abbreviation ever coined, in the United States or elsewhere, has been borrowed by all the languages of Western Europe and some of those of Asia. In the days of the great immigrations the immigrants learned all four immediately after *hell* and *damn*.

The origins of *P.D.Q.*,[9] *S.O.L.* and *on the Q.T.* are still shrouded in mystery, but *N.G.* has been traced to 1839, *F.F.V.* (first families of Virginia) to 1847, *L* (elevated railway) to 1879, *C.O.D.* to 1859, *G.A.R.* (Grand

---

[4] It survives, however, in the names of many colleges named after saints, *e.g.*, *St. Mary's*, Winona, Minn.
[5] Modern English Punctuation, by Reginald Skelton; London, 1933, pp. 41–7. Topics of the Times, *The New York Times*, July 13, 1942.
[6] [Style Manual; rev. ed.; Jan. 1959, pp. 27, 173.]

[7] Many papers, and perhaps most, have no italic linotype matrices. Instead they use boldface.
[8] Farmer, p. 1.
[9] Said to have been coined by Dan Maguinnis, one of the comedians of the Boston Stock Company from 1867 to his death in 1889.

Army of the Republic—the organization of Union veterans of the Civil War, which established the right of all veterans to suckle perpetually at the public teat) to 1867, *G.B.* (grand bounce) to 1887, and *G.O.P.* (Grand Old Party, the official nickname of the Republicans) to 1887. In the days of the horsecars and the early automobiles, it was also popular as an abbreviation for *get out and push;* it was probably suggested by the English *G.O.M.* (1882) (Grand Old Man: W. E. Gladstone, 1809–98). *A No. 1,* as in *A No. 1* (or *A-1*) performance, is also an Americanism of English parentage: it is borrowed from *A 1,* used in Lloyd's Register to designate ships in first-class condition.[1] The English in turn have borrowed *C.O.D.,* but they always use it to mean *cash* on delivery, not *collect* on delivery. Other old-line Americanisms are *S.A.* (sex appeal), *D. and D.* (drunk and disorderly), *T.B.* (tuberculosis [and briefly, *c.* 1930, for tremendous buttocks]) and *B.V.D.,* the trade name for a brand of men's underwear, now applied ignorantly and unlawfully to the products of other manufacturers.[2] [*S.O.B.* stayed in limbo, known but not written, until it appeared in Harry S. Truman's essays on music criticism.[3]]

The number of such abbreviations has expanded tremendously since 1900. World War I brought in *A.E.F.* (American Expeditionary Force) and *A.W.O.L.* (absent without leave, often pronounced *ay-wall*). There was a similar abundance of new forms in England: of them *Anzac* (Australian and New Zealand Army Corps), *D.O.R.A.* (Defence of the Realm Act) and *Wren* (a member of the Women's Royal Naval Service) are examples. After the war the Russians contributed a large number, *e.g., Cheka* (*Chrezvychainaya Komissiya, i.e.,* Extraordinary Commission), *N.E.P.* (New Economic Plan) and *Ogpu* or *Gay-Pay-Oo* (*Obedinenneoe Gosudarstvennoe Politicheskoe Upravlenie, i.e.,* United Government Political Administration). To these was presently added *Nazi* (*Nationalsozialistische*) from Germany. The effect was to encourage the invention of similar forms in America, and when the New Deal dawned, in 1933, scores began to appear, *e.g., N.R.A.* or *Nira* (National Industrial Recovery Administration), *A.A.A.* (Agricultural Adjustment Administration), *T.V.A.* (Tennessee Valley Authority), *P.W.A.* (Public Works Authority), *C.C.C.* (Civilian Conservation Corps), *F.E.R.A.* (Federal Emergency Relief Administration) and

---

[1] [*No. 1, letter A* has been found in Thomas C. Haliburton's The Clockmaker, 1837, by Francis W. Palmer. See Gleanings for the DAE Supplement, *AS,* Vol. XXII, Oct. 1947, pp. 199–206.]

[2] [According to *Time,* Nov. 9, 1962, it is derived from *Bradley, Voorhees and Day,* who founded the company in 1876.]

[3] [Word That Came to Dinner, *Time,* Mar. 7, 1949, p. 24. Lea L. Seale proposes *eusystolism* to describe initials used in the interest of delicacy, as *S.O.B., V.D., D.T.,* etc. *AS,* Vol. XXX, Feb. 1955, pp. 69–70. Ruth Dunbar, educational editor of the Chicago *Sun-Times,* was known as Viola before she had to initial her news stories.]

its successor *W.P.A.* (Works Progress Administration), until Al Smith could describe the government as submerged in a bowl of alphabet soup. World War II brought in innumerable others, *e.g.*, *O.P.A.* (Office of Price Administration). [Most of these coinages were short-lived, for the organizations they designated succumbed to court decisions, lack of appropriations, public hostility or apathy and the exigencies of World War II; but a few tough customers survived and the oysterlike fertility of the bureaucratic mind provided others. The Chicago telephone directory for 1961 yields these specimens: *B.F.D.C.* (Bureau of Foreign and Domestic Commerce), *C.A.B.* (Civil Aeronautics Board), *C.C.C.* (Commodity Credit Corporation), *F.A.A.* (Federal Aviation Agency), *F.B.I.* (Federal Bureau of Investigation), *F.C.C.* (Federal Communications Commission), *F.C.I.C.* (Federal Crop Insurance Corporation), *F.D.I.C.* (Federal Deposit Insurance Corporation), *F.H.A.* (Federal Housing Authority), *F.H.L.B.B.* (Federal Home Loan Bank Board), *F.T.C.* (Federal Trade Commission), *F.W.A.* (Federal Works Agency), *G.P.O.* (Government Printing Office), *G.S.A.* (General Services Administration), *H.E.W.* (Health, Education and Welfare), *I.C.C.* (Interstate Commerce Commission), *N.L.R.B.* (National Labor Relations Board), *P.B.S.* (Public Buildings Service), *R.F.C.* (Reconstruction Finance Corporation), *S.E.C.* (Securities and Exchange Commission), *S.S.A.* (Social Security Administration), *U.S.E.S.* (United States Employment Service) and *V.A.* (Veterans' Administration). Other well-known current federal abbreviations include *A.E.C.* (Atomic Energy Commission), *C.I.A.* (Central Intelligence Agency), *F.N.M.A.* (Federal National Mortgage Authority, also affectionately known as *Fannie Mae*) and *F.S.I.* (Foreign Service Institute); a full listing of those current in Washington must run into the hundreds, for despite campaign hokum about cutting government payrolls, no administration ever abolishes more than a handful of agencies and soon replaces those with twice as many of its own creation. Contrary to legend, the alphabetical designation of agencies did not originate with the New Deal; the now moribund *R.F.C.* was a creation of Herbert Hoover, while the *I.C.C.* goes back to the trustbusting days of Roosevelt I and the *B.G.N.* (Board on Geographic Names) to Benjamin Harrison.]

Down to the advent of the New Deal the section on abbreviations in the average American style book filled only a few pages. But now the number of them, chiefly emanating from Washington, is so enormous that the Style Manual of the Government Printing Office simply lays down rules and forms.[4] A complete list is to be found in the United States Government Organization Manual. So many new civil government agencies have been

_____

[4] [Style Manual; rev. ed.; Jan. 1959, pp. 149-64.] The standard general work on abbreviations is Current Abbreviations, by George Earlie Shankle; New York, 1945.

set up, each with a long name and each name with an abbreviation, that no copyreader in the country could keep up with them. How many such monstrosities have been set afloat no one will ever know, for many of them, like the pews at the public teat that they designated, had their names changed frequently. No wonder the newspapers and press associations began dropping the periods, and making all other possible condensations. Thus the *W.A.A.C.* of 1942 became the *W.A.C.* of 1943 and then the *WAC* or *Wac*.[5] So early as 1939, in fact, the slaughter of periods had begun. The New Deal saviors of humanity had barely got started by then, but there were plenty of other troublesome abbreviations and the editors advocated taking the periods out of all of them, *e.g.*, *CIO, TVA, CCC, GOP* and even *AFL*. [The establishment of the United Nations has led to a further proliferation of abbreviations for its various administrative bodies, and some are widely known, such as *UNESCO* (United Nations Economic, Social and Cultural Organization) and *UNICEF* (United Nations International Children's Emergency Fund); many schools have diverted to Hallowe'en collections for *UNICEF* a great deal of the excess energy that used to be spent on window soaping, doorbell ringing and privy tipping.]

Nor are such abbreviations unknown outside the government, *e.g.*, *G.E.* (General Electric), *G.M.* (General Motors), *A.A.A.S.*, (American Association for the Advancement of Science), *L.P.* (long-playing record) and *M.L.A.* (Modern Language Association). The psychologists have their *I.Q.* (intelligence quotient), which the tender-minded gogues euphemize as *P.L.R.* (probable learning ratio), the theory being that (1) *intelligence* is a dirty word, and (2) the new gobbledygook will be less offensive. A great many abbreviations occur in the argot of various crafts and professions, *e.g.*, the common medical terms *G.Y.N.* (gynecology), *G.P.* (grateful patient or general practitioner) and *T.P.R.* (temperature, pulse, respiration),[6] and not a few of them are intended to be unintelligible to the outsider. Others of the same quasi-esoteric sort are in more or less general use, *e.g.*, *f.h.b.* (family hold back, *i.e.* with a guest present at table), *m.i.k.* (more in the kitchen)[7] and *P.D.* (plain drunk). [Public-school teachers flourish *kg.-p.* (kindergarten-primary), Episcopal clergy *A.-C.* (Anglo-Catholic), and almost every college or university has a few of its own, such as the late *O.M.P.* (Operations, Methods and Procedures) devised by the humanistic engineers of the University of Chicago.][8]

[5] This change was made by the War Department when the W.A.A.C. became an actual part of the Army, the word *Auxiliary* being dropped. [The dropping of periods is endorsed by the GPO Style Manual; rev. ed.; Jan. 1959, p. 162.]

[6] Hospital Talk, by Dorothy Barkley, *AS*, Vol. II, Apr. 1927, pp. 312–14.

[7] Semi-Secret Abbreviations, by Percy W. Long, *DN*, Vol. IV, Pt. III, 1915, pp. 245–6.

[8] [See also Some G.I. Alphabet Soup, by John Lancaster Riordan, *AS*, Vol. XXII, Apr. 1947, pp. 1008–14; and Parlez-Vous NATO?, *The New York Times Magazine*, Oct. 18, 1959, pp. 20, 22. The latter was based on NATO Handbook,

The advertising brethren are fertile inventors of abbreviations. They seem to have produced *I.X.L.* many years ago, and of late they have added *E.Z.* (for *easy:* part of the name of a brand of shoes), *Fits-U* (a brand of eyeglasses) and many other combinations of *U, e.g., Uneeda, U-Put-It-On* (a weather strip), *U-Rub-It-In* (an ointment) and *While-U-Wait*. [It is commonly suspected that bright young admen devised some of the abbreviations for the women's military organizations of World War II and then found a title to fit, *e.g.,* the Navy's *WAVES* (*W*omen *A*ppointed for *V*olunteer *E*mergency *S*ervice), the Coast Guard's *SPAR* (*S*emper *Par*atus —*A*lways *R*eady) and the Air Transport Command's *WASPS* (*W*omen's *A*uxiliary *S*ervice *P*ilots). Reporters anticipated the recognition of the *W*omen's *H*ome *O*rganized *R*eserves in *E*mergency *S*ervice, but the official proclamation never appeared.[9] Since World War II the same ingenuity has shown itself in the development of private philanthropic organizations, *e.g.,* the *C*ommittee on *A*merican *R*elief for *E*urope (*CARE*), the *A*merican *C*ommittee *to* *I*mprove *O*ur *N*eighborhoods (*ACTION*) and the *K*iyasoto *E*xperimental *E*ducational *P*roject (*KEEP*), an Episcopal missionary enterprise in Japan.]

The Navy meanwhile had developed its own system of making articulate words to designate various organizations and persons, *e.g., BuAer* (Bureau of Aeronautics), *BuOrd* (Bureau of Ordnance), *ComSubRon* (Commander Submarine Squadron), *ComAirSoPa* (Commander Aircraft South Pacific Force) and so on. [Before December 7, 1941, the Commander in Chief of the United States Fleet (Pacific Fleet) was designated *CinCUS*, naturally pronounced *sink us*, but after Pearl Harbor the new appointee was redesignated *ComInCh* (Commander in Chief.[1])]

The North Atlantic Treaty Organization; 1958, Appendix 6, p. 65. Some of the airlines use *PAWOB* for "Passenger Arrived *without* Baggage," as in "We just hate to have a *PAWOB* traveling on United." Caption on United Air Lines ad, *The New Yorker*, Apr. 27, 1963.]
[9] [See Rossell Hope Robbins, Acronyms and Abbreviations from Aviation, *AS*, Vol. XXVI, Feb. 1951, pp. 67–70.]
[1] [An Acronyms Dictionary, containing over 12,000 specimens, was published in Detroit in 1960. S. V. Baum has presented several reports in *AS, e.g.,* From *AWOL* to *VEEP:* the Growth and Specialization of the Acronym, Vol. XXX, May 1955, pp. 103–10; Feminine Characteristics of the Acronym, Vol. XXXI, Oct. 1956, pp. 224–5; Formal Dress for Initial Words, Vol. XXXII, Feb. 1957, pp. 73–5; The Acronym, Pure and Impure, Vol. XXXVII, Feb. 1962, pp. 48–50.]

I X

The Common Speech

1: OUTLINES OF ITS GRAMMAR [1]

My call for a comprehensive inductive grammar of the common speech of the United States, first made in a newspaper article in 1910, has never been answered by anyone learned in the tongues, though in the meantime philologists have given us searching studies of such esoteric Indian languages as Cuna, Chitamacha, Yuma and Klamath-Modoc, not to mention Eskimo.[2] There has even been an excellent grammar of Pennsylvania German.[3] But there have been some approaches to the business by the writers on regional dialects—for example, Vance Randolph[4] and Oma Stanley.[5] Also, there has been an oblique attempt upon the common speech by I. E. Clark, who sought his materials, not in the field, but in the pages of Ring Lardner.[6] Says Clark:

> The essence of Lardner's grammar is facility. His characters . . . do not distinguish between the forms for the nominative and accusative case of pronouns, the preterite and past participle of the verb, and the comparative and superlative of the adjective. . . . The environ-

---

[1] [The 1936 and 1948 versions of this chapter were appraised by Raven I. McDavid, Jr., in the *Ball State Teachers College Forum*, Vol. I, Spring 1960, pp. 39–42.]

[2] Most of these have appeared in *IJAL*. [A sketch of Eskimo was appended to An Introduction to Linguistic Structures: from Sound to Sentence in English, by A. A. Hill; New York, 1958.]

[3] A Simple Grammar of Pennsylvania Dutch, by J. William Frey; Clinton, S.C., 1942.

[4] The Grammar of the Ozark Dialect, *AS*, Vol. III, Oct. 1927, p. 1.

[5] The Speech of East Texas, *American Speech Reprints and Monographs*, No. 2; New York, 1937, p. 95.

[6] An Analysis of Ring Lardner's American Language, or, Who Learnt You Grammar, Bud? M.A. thesis (MS), U. of Texas, 1944. [The language of George Ade has been examined by Richard F. Bauerle, *AS*, Vol. XXXIII, Feb. 1958, pp. 77–9.]

ment of the average [American] during his early years did not provide all the niceties of cultured English. School teachers tried desperately to improve his grammar, but they were unskilled in psychology, and their method was unconvincing. . . . He accepted the language spoken by his family, and by the friends he made before he started school. It was simple, it had lost useless forms, it permitted use of the handiest word. The language of the English teachers, enforced by the psychology of the Department of Education, only confused him.

The American common speech, of course, is closely related grammatically to the vulgar dialects of the British Isles, and in many ways it is identical with them. In both one encounters the double negative, the use of the adjective as an adverb, the confusion of cases in the pronoun and of tenses in the verb and various other violations of the polite canon. But these similarities are accompanied by important differences. For one thing, the British dialects differ so greatly that some of them are mutually unintelligible. But a Boston taxi driver would encounter little difficulty in communicating in San Francisco, Chicago, New Orleans or Denver. For another thing, vulgar American shows the same tendency to ready change that characterizes the standard language, and is thus given to taking in new forms and abandoning old ones. Various observers have noted the disappearance of forms that were common only a decade ago, or their descent to the dialects, *e.g., sot* (for *sat*), *riz, driv, clomb, see'd* and *gin* (for *given*).[7] The English dialects have changed too, but apparently less than vulgar American, and the changes occurring in some of them have affected others hardly at all.

For many years the indefatigable schoolma'am has been trying to put down the American vulgate, but with very little success. At great pains she teaches her pupils the rules of what she conceives to be correct English, but the moment they get beyond reach of her constabulary ear they revert to the looser and more natural speech habits of home and work place. The schoolma'am's heroic struggles have got little aid from her professional superiors. They have provided her with a multitude of textbooks, most of them hopelessly pedantic, though others are sensible enough, and they have invented a wealth of teaching methods, mostly far more magical than scientific, but they have not thrown much light upon the psychological problem actually before her.

[7] See The Verbs of the Vulgate, by Robert J. Menner, *AS*, Vol. I, Jan. 1926, p. 239, and The Verbs of the Vulgate in Their Historical Relations, by Henry Alexander, *AS*, Vol. IV, Apr. 1929. [The present distribution of these verb forms is found in E. Bagby Atwood, A Survey of Verb Forms in the Eastern United States (Ann Arbor, 1953), and Virginia McDavid, Verb Forms in the North-Central States and Upper Midwest, diss. (microfilm), U. of Minnesota, 1956.]

That the grammar taught by these poor Holoferneses, male and female, is full of absurdities engendered by the medieval attempt to force English into the Procrustean bed of Latin was recognized by Noah Webster so long ago as 1789. "The most difficult task now to be performed by the advocates of pure English," he wrote in his "Dissertations on the English Language," [8] "is to restrain the influence of men learned in Greek and Latin, but ignorant of their own tongue." And then: "They seem not to consider that grammar is formed on language, and not language on grammar. Instead of examining to find out what the English language *is* they endeavor to show what it *ought to be* according to their rules." [9] Thomas Jefferson, with his invariable common sense, supported this on the plane of the vocabulary in a letter to John Adams in 1820:

> Dictionaries are but the depositories of words already legitimated by usage. Society is the workshop in which new ones are elaborated. When an individual uses a new word, if ill-formed, it is rejected in society; if well-formed, adopted, and after due time, laid up in the depository of dictionaries.

Unhappily, Webster's theory of the divine origin of language interfered with his attempt to set up a truly inductive grammar, and his doctrine of analogies gave considerable countenance to the pedants who sought to show what the language ought to be. These pedants had the floor unchallenged throughout the first half of the Nineteenth Century. Nothing was known at that time about the psychology of speech, and the contemporary European discoveries in linguistics did not penetrate to the Republic until after 1850, when they were brought home from Tübingen and Berlin by William Dwight Whitney. An Englishman, Robert Gordon Latham (1812–88), had proclaimed in the 40s that "in language whatever *is* is right," but he got no attention in this country, and so late as 1870 the American authority George P. Marsh [1] was misunderstanding and denouncing him, though constrained to admit that "the ignorance of grammarians" was "a frequent cause of the corruption of language."

The proliferation of public schools produced a heavy demand for textbooks of grammar, and nearly all were written by incompetents who simply followed the worst English models. "The larger part of grammatical instruction," says Rollo LaVerne Lyman, "remained a slavish verbal repetition of rules and a desperate struggle with complicated parsing formu-

---

[8] p. ix.
[9] p. 37. See also Early Application of Latin Grammar to English, by Sanford Brown Meech, *PMLA*, Dec. 1935, pp. 1012–32, and The Rules of Common School Grammars, by Charles C. Fries, *PMLA*, 1927, pp. 221–37.
[1] Lectures on the English Language: First Series; 4th ed.; New York, 1870, pp. 645–6.

lae."[2] Of course, some grammarians, even so early as the 1830s, saw the futility of this method of instruction, but the majority continued, as Lyman says, to favor "slavish memorizing, nothing more or less," and grammar remained a horror to schoolboys until the end of the Nineteenth Century. In 1870 Richard Grant White fluttered the pedagogical dovecotes by announcing the discovery that English really had no grammar at all,[3] but White was too pedantic to follow his own lead, and till his death in 1885 he devoted himself mainly to formulating canons of "correct" English which greatly aided the schoolma'am in afflicting her pupils.

The new philological learning was a long while taking root. The American Philological Association, which Whitney founded, was quickly engulfed by intransigent followers of Varro and Priscian, Posidonius and Apollonius Dyscolus, and the Sanskrit grammarians of the Fourth and Fifth Centuries B.C. The Modern Language Association, launched at the new Johns Hopkins in 1883, met a fate even more grisly, for the young college professors who flocked into it passed over the living language with a few sniffs and threw all their energies into flatulent studies of the influence of Lamb on Hazlitt, the changes made by Donne, Skelton and Cowper in the texts of forgotten poems, and suchlike pseudo-intellectual gymnastics. Not until the Linguistic Society followed in 1924 was there any organized attack upon language as it is, and even the Linguistic Society has given a great deal more attention to Hittite and other such fossil tongues than to the American spoken by 180,000,000-odd free, idealistic and more or less human Americans, including all the philologians themselves, at least when they are in their cups or otherwise off guard. On the level of the common, or dirt, pedagogues the notion that language should be studied objectively, like any other natural phenomenon, made even slower progress, and not until 1908 was any effort made to find out just what was in the common speech—in other words, to get together the makings of a purely descriptive and scientific grammar.[4] But in a little while the more intelligent inquirers —most of them *not* pedagogues, but philologians—began to question the validity of the rules inculcated by the schoolma'am, and to seek light in the speech habits of unquestionably cultured Americans.

One of the first investigators to follow this line of inquiry was Sterling

[2] English Grammar in American Schools before 1850; Washington, 1922, p. 140. The subject became a favorite soon after the Revolution. Lyman says that the most popular grammar book, that by Lindley Murray, sold more than a million copies in various editions before 1850. [Murray's work, of course, was essentially derivative. See E. Vorlat, The Sources of Lindley Murray's The English Grammar, *Leuwense Bijdragen*, Vol. XLVIII, 1959, pp. 108–25.]

[3] Words and Their Uses; New York, 1870, Ch. X.

[4] Unfortunately, as we will see later in this section, these investigators largely ignored the way the language actually worked and concentrated on "common errors," deviations from the way they assumed it *should* work.

Andrus Leonard, professor of English at the University of Wisconsin. In 1930 or thereabout he undertook to find out what was really good usage by asking a committee of linguists, teachers of speech, authors, editors and businessmen, 229 in number, to pronounce their judgment upon 230 usages, ranging all the way from forms endorsed even by purists to forms seldom encountered outside the talk of jockeys and policemen. His report[5] was influential in reorienting the traditional approach to English. It showed that at least 75% of the experts in linguistics approved *as regards, none-are, all dressed up, go slow, I don't know if, only* before the verb, *it is me, who are you looking for?, the reason was because, invite whoever you like, to loan, but what, I wish I was, everyone-they, providing* for *provided* and *awfully* as a general intensive, and that between 25% and 75% of them favored *proven, four first* [as in *the four first candidates to announce* (purists would say that only one could be *first*)], *gotten, either of these three, I can't seem, older than me, neither-are, these kind, most anybody, it is liable to snow, in search for, ain't I?, don't* in the singular, *sure* as an adverb, *like* for *as if, off of, due to* for *on account of, some, little ways* and *different than*. All these forms had been banned by the schoolbooks for years, and likewise by the innumerable books of "correct" English for adults. Two years after Leonard's study one of his students and successors at Wisconsin, Robert C. Pooley, supported its conclusions with examples from the historical dictionaries and the accepted *belles-lettres* of the language, and concluded with a recommendation that the books be given a drastic overhauling.[6] Three of his specific proposals were:

> Whenever traditional grammatical classification ignores or misrepresents current usage, it must be changed.
>
> When custom has established two forms or usages on approximately equal standing, both must be presented.
>
> When current established usage conflicts with traditional rules, the rules must be modified or discarded.

A little while afterward Walter Barnes, of New York University, re-examined the locutions covered by the Leonard study, especially those set down as "illiterate" or "disputable." In a number of cases his report raised a given word or phrase a grade or more. Thus *complected*, which appeared as "illiterate" in the Leonard study, became "disputable" in that of Barnes, *good and cold* was lifted from "disputable" to "established" and *data* in the singular all the way from "illiterate" to "established." Of the locutions marked "disputable" on the Leonard list, a special jury of 52 radio an-

[5] Current English Usage; Chicago, 1932.
[6] Grammar and Usage in Textbooks on English, *Educational Research Bulletin No. 14* of the University of Wisconsin, Madison, Aug. 1933.

nouncers, 29 writers and 40 business executives approved by a majority vote *to fix* in the sense of *to repair*, the *one-he* combination, *in back of* (often denounced by English purists as an abhorrent Americanism), *right* in the sense of *direct, I can't seem, dove* for *dived, going some, good and cold* and *to aggravate* in the sense of *to vex*.[7] Said the Barnes group in its summary:

> Certain self-appointed saviors of "English undefiled" have taken it upon themselves to put a stop to the evolution of the language, and to preserve it intact for future generations. They disregard the fact that it was far from a perfect tongue at the time from which their *status quo* begins.[8]

Between 1933 and 1937 Marckwardt and Fred G. Walcott found that a large percentage of the usages marked "disputable" by Leonard were to be found in English and American authors of high rank, and that many of the rest were recognized as allowable in colloquial speech. They unearthed *neither-are* from Johnson, Cowper, Southey and Ruskin, *like* as in "Do it *like* he tells you" from Southey and William Morris, *try and* from Milton and Coleridge, *only* before the verb from Dryden and Tennyson, *slow* as an adverb from Byron and Thackeray and *I wish I was* from Defoe, Swift, Fielding, Jane Austen, Byron, Marryat, Thackeray, Dickens, Thomas Hardy, George Meredith and Oscar Wilde. Their conclusion was:

> Grammar is seen to be not something final and static but merely the organized description or codification of the actual speech habits of educated men. If these habits change, grammar itself changes, and textbooks must follow suit.[9]

It is hard for grammarians, the archetypal pedagogues, to yield up their dogmatism, but in late years they have tended to do so. That tendency is not altogether new, for John Horne Tooke tried to clear away a lot of ancient grammatical rubbish in his "Diversions of Purley," the first volume of which was published in 1786, and some of his ideas were borrowed by Noah Webster in "A Philosophical and Practical Grammar of the English Language" in 1807, and by William B. Fowle in "The True English Gram-

---

[7] Studies in Current Colloquial Usage; New York, 1933. There is a bibliography of language tests in Pt. IV, pp. 3–4.

[8] Pt. II, p. 2.

[9] Facts about Current English Usage; New York, 1938. [In his American English (New York, 1958), pp. 184–5, Marckwardt suggests that the correctness bogey is responsible for an appalling number of taboo reactions and anxiety neuroses. How Correct Must Correct English Be?, by Norman Lewis, *Harper's Magazine*, Mar. 1949, pp. 68–74, is another follow-up of Leonard. It shows that academicians are most flexible in their judgments, the editors of women's magazines most rigid.]

mar" in 1827.[1] But not until comparatively recently have these more or less amateurish reformers got any substantial support from the professionals. The first break came when some of the latter began to turn their eyes from the written language to the spoken language, and to observe that what was true, grammatically, of writing was not always true of speech. The second came when others made a serious effort to find out what rules governed the speech of the vulgar, and to consider whether those rules were not quite as "good" as those that had long adorned the grammar books. The ensuing hot debate is still going on.[2]

The pioneer study of errors in the speech of a typical group of American school children was made by G. M. Wilson, superintendent of schools at Connersville, Ind., in 1908.[3] It was followed by a similar study of the speech of school children in Boise, Idaho, by C. S. Meek, during the years 1909–15,[4] and by a much more extensive investigation in the public schools of Kansas City, directed by W. W. Charters.[5] Many other local studies followed, and in 1930 one was begun on a national scale, directed by L. J. O'Rourke.[6] The result was the accumulation of a great deal of interesting (and often racy) information about the actual speechways of Americans, but the emphasis on recording errors distorted the perspective of all these investigators, and in any event most of the grammarians were reluctant to grant the implications of their studies. This was especially true of O'Rourke, whose somewhat timorous conclusions were criticized sharply, immediately after they were published, by Janet Rankin Aiken, of Columbia University:

> What the present writer wishes is that some competent scholar would take the O'Rourke tabulations and analyze them to show just where the English language stands today in respect to the wild flowers in its wood, the uncultivated usages which some of us find sweeter and more interesting than all the geraniums ever grown in pots. The

---

[1] Published in Boston. The subtitle was "an Attempt to form a Grammar of English not modelled upon those of the Latin, and Greek, and other Foreign Languages."

[2] [Serious students of the language now insist upon the distinction between *grammar*, the systematic description of the machinery of the language, and *usage*, the selection among alternative grammatical forms according to one's social background or the style in which he is writing or speaking. The distinction has been made by many writers, notably George P. Faust, *CE*, Vol. XIX, May 1958, p. 352.]

[3] Errors in the Language of Grade Pupils, *Educator-Journal*, Dec. 1909, pp. 178–80.

[4] Special Report of the Boise Public Schools, June 1915, pp. 29–35, republished in Sixteenth Yearbook of the National Society for the Study of Education, Pt. I, pp. 89–91.

[5] A Course of Study in Grammar Based upon the Grammatical Errors of School Children of Kansas City, Mo.; Columbia, Mo., 1915.

[6] Rebuilding the English-Usage Curriculum to Insure Greater Mastery of Essentials; Washington, 1934.

competent scholar will then tell of his findings, not in the weary, flat reportese of the average survey, but in an English which is itself worth imitating as a model of freshness and flexibility.[7]

Later studies have come into greater accord with Dr. Aiken's demands, notably the "American English Grammar," by Charles Carpenter Fries.[8] The material used consisted of letters from average Americans received by various departments of the federal government at Washington. Fries recognized the difficulty inherent in the fact that this material was all written, not spoken, but he used various ingenious devices to get rid of it as far as possible, and in his report he sought to separate his examples into three categories—Standard English, Common English and Vulgar English. His conclusions were conservative. He did not advocate wholesale abandonment of the traditional grammar, but called for a more intensive study of the language as it is, and advocated training pupils in that study. "Grammars with rules that were in part the rules of Latin grammar and in part the results of 'reason,' " he said, "did not and could not provide the tools of an effective language program. . . . To be really effective a program must prepare the pupil for independent growth, and the only possible means of accomplishing that end is to lead him to become an intelligent observer of language usage." This, if somewhat vague, at least turned its back upon the cocksure dogmatism of the old-time grammarians. It was not the long-awaited realistic grammar of the American common speech, but it brought that grammar a few inches nearer. [So did the grammatical data of the Linguistic Atlas.[9] So, too, did Fries's "The Structure of English," [1] in which he classified parts of speech and sentence types according to the distribution of words and phrases in a series of telephone conversations recorded in Ann Arbor. So, too, will a series of dissertations on the spoken language, most of them yet unpublished.[2]]

The movement to make the spoken language rather than the written language the object of grammatical study seems to have been launched in

[7] O'Rourke and Leonard, *AS*, Vol. IX, Dec. 1934, pp. 291–5.

[8] New York, 1940.

[9] [The Atlas findings have been summarized in E. Bagby Atwood, A Survey of Verb Forms in the Eastern United States, Ann Arbor, Mich., 1953; in Virginia McDavid, Verb Forms of the North-Central States and Upper Midwest, diss. (microfilm), U. of Minnesota, 1956; and in Raven I. McDavid, Jr., and Virginia McDavid, Grammatical Differences in the North-Central States, *AS*, Vol. XXXV, Feb. 1960, pp. 5–19. The Atlas evidence in these and other studies was utilized by Jean Malmstrom in A Study of the Validity of Textbook Statements about Certain Controversial Items in the Light of Evidence from the Linguistic Atlas, diss. (microfilm), U. of Minnesota, 1958. Mrs. Malmstrom reported on her findings in *EJ*, Vol. XLVIII, Apr. 1959, pp. 191–8.]

[1] New York, 1952.

[2] [The dissertation of Elizabeth Bowman, MS, University of Chicago, 1963, Sentence Patterns in English, is based on a ten-hour recording of the conversation of an upper-middle-class Midwestern family.]

this country by E. H. Sturtevant, though Henry Sweet preceded him in England.[3] "Whether we think of the history of human speech in general or of the linguistic experience of the individual speaker," Sturtevant wrote, "spoken language is the primary phenomenon, and writing is only a more or less imperfect reflection of it." [4] This lead was followed by various other writers on language, including the Englishman Harold E. Palmer [5] and the Dane Otto Jespersen, probably the most profound student of English of the early Twentieth Century.[6] Palmer's spoken English was "that variety which is generally used by educated people in the course of ordinary conversation or when writing letters to intimate friends." He went on:

> One of the most widely diffused of the many linguistic illusions current in the world is the belief that each language possesses a "pure" or "grammatical" form, a form which is intrinsically "correct," which is independent of usage, which exists, which has always existed, but which is now in danger of losing its existence. . . . [The purist] is generally perfectly unconscious of the forms of speech which he uses himself. He warns the unsuspecting foreigner against what he calls "vulgarisms," and says to him, "Don't ever use such vulgar forms as *don't* and *won't;* you won't hear educated people using them," or "Never use a preposition to finish a sentence with," or "Oh, I've got something else to tell you: don't say *I've got* instead of *I have*."

This movement against the traditional authoritarianism has not gone unchallenged. Some respectable philologians still believe that the teaching of orthodox grammar is still useful, and ought not to be abandoned until the reformers perfect a coherent and effective substitute. Tradition is also upheld by most of the authors of books on "correct" English, and by nearly all the sages who answer language questions in the newspapers. The schoolma'am clings to the same unhappy conservatism, and so does the college tutor who wrestles, in Freshman English, with students who come up from the high schools using *between you and I*. Says George O. Curme: "Our school grammarians . . . do not inform themselves upon the subjects they teach. They are helpless if the little antiquated school grammars do not give them information." [7] The hardest thing for these peewee pedants to understand is that language is never uniform—that different classes and

---

[3] [Sweet was the artist's model for Henry Higgins, the phonetician in Shaw's Pygmalion.]

[4] Linguistic Change; Chicago, 1917, p. 1.

[5] A Grammar of Spoken English on a Strictly Phonetic Basis; Cambridge (England), 1924.

[6] Essentials of English Grammar; New York, 1933.

[7] Are Our English Teachers Adequately Prepared for Their Work?, by George O. Curme, *PMLA*, Vol. XLVI, 1931, pp. 1415–26.

even different ages speak it differently. The American of a Harvard professor speaking *ex cathedra* is seldom the same as the American of a Boston bartender or a Mississippi evangelist. Let the daughter of a hog-sticker in the Omaha stockyards go home talking like the book and her ma will fan her fanny. "Substandard students," said Thomas A. Knott in 1934, "are not 'making mistakes.' They are simply talking or writing their own language." Knott suggested thinking of Standard English as a foreign language, and teaching it by the devices found effective in teaching French, German and Spanish.[8] But until this decade his proposal has seldom been consciously tried.[9]

In the General Explanations prefaced to the OED,[1] James A. H. Murray, the chief editor, undertook to show the interrelation of the various levels of English by means of a diagram. In the center he put "the common words of the language"; above this was placed the literary language, and underneath, colloquial speech, with various branches or offshoots running out from it. In 1927 Leonard and H. Y. Moffett substituted two intersecting circles for Murray's somewhat crude diagram. One circle was labeled "formal or literary" and the other "informal or colloquial." Where they overlapped there was a common area, perhaps amounting to one-third of each, to indicate the usages appearing in both. Outside the circles were places for the smaller and less important categories—archaic forms of the language, slang and argot, technical vocabularies, dialects and so on. They defined the four principal divisions as follows:

1. Formally correct English, appropriate chiefly for serious and important occasions . . . ; usually called "literary English."

2. Fully acceptable English for informal conversation, correspondence, and all other writing of well-bred ease . . . ; "standard, cultivated, colloquial English."

3. Commercial, foreign, scientific or other technical uses, limited in comprehensibility . . . ; "trade or technical English."

[8] Standard English and Incorrect English, *AS*, Vol. IX, Apr. 1934, p. 88.

[9] [It has been tried by Mrs. Ruth Golden in the Detroit public schools and by Mrs. San-ssu Lin at Claflin University, a Negro seminary in Orangeburg, S.C. The Detroit project, unfortunately, concentrates on what the teachers consider non-standard, without attempting to ascertain what are the differentiae between cultivated and uneducated speech, and which of these differentiae provide the greatest economic and social handicaps to the children (mostly Negroes) in slum areas. More realistic and systematic approaches have been undertaken by a team of New York educators, notably Samuel R. Levin, of Hunter College, and by a similar team in Chicago including, *inter alia*, William M. Austin and Alva L. Davis, of the Illinois Institute of Technology, and Robert Hess and Raven I. McDavid, Jr., of the University of Chicago.]

[1] Vol. I; Oxford, 1888, p. xvii.

4. Popular or illiterate speech, not used by persons who wish to pass as cultivated, save to represent uneducated speech, or to be jocose ... ; "naïf, popular, or uncultivated English." [2]

The authors make two important observations on this summary. First, the levels of English indicate status by reflecting environment and education. Second, "popular or illiterate speech is frequently just as clear and vigorous as more cultivated language." The former observation had been made long before by Ellis, Wyld and other English authorities. Its factual basis is largely responsible for the persistence with which the outworn rules of "correct" English are rammed into the bewildered young by school-ma'ams and the lesser varieties of college pedagogues. The overwhelming majority of such poor quacks come from the lower cultural levels, and take a fierce and perhaps pardonable pride in the linguistic arcanum they have acquired, for it testifies to their improvement in status. If they issued from a more secure and tolerant social class they would be less doctrinaire, but with the ten-cent store and the filling station barely escaped they are naturally eager to dig in. The easy way to improve their fitness would be to recruit them from better sources, but that would be as impossible, practically speaking, as trying to improve the race of charwomen by recruiting them from café society. *I have saw* and its analogues were probably introduced into the American vulgate by schoolma'ams over-eager to eradicate *I seen*. Their excess of zeal convinced their alarmed customers that *saw* was elegant and *seen* incurably abominable, so a substitution was made across the whole board.[3]

The second observation of Leonard and Moffett supports their first. They say:

> It is not correct ... to tell a boy who says "I didn't see no dog" that he has stated he did see a dog. His statement is clear and unequivocal. What we can tell him is that he has made a gross social *faux pas*, that he has said something which will definitely declass him. ... Ungrammatical expressions are very rarely unclear. In fact they are often clearer and more forceful than their cultivated equivalents.[4]

[2] Current Definition of Levels in English Usage, *EJ*, Vol. XVI, May 1927, p. 349. [The practical problem of usage indicators in dictionaries was surveyed by Daniel Cook at the 1963 meeting of the Midwest Modern Language Association.]

[3] This explanation was anticipated by Leonard Bloomfield in Literate and Il-

literate Speech, *AS*, Vol. II, July 1927, p. 436. See also Hypercorrect Forms in American English, by Robert J. Menner, *AS*, Vol. XII, Oct. 1937, pp. 167–78. For *hypercorrect*, Allen Walker Read would substitute the more accurate *hypersophic*.

[4] p. 348.

To this Robert A. Hall, Jr., of Cornell University, adds:

> In practical terms, if you say *it ain't me* instead of *it is not I*, or *I seen him* instead of *I saw him,* you will not be invited to tea again, or will not make a favorable impression on your department head and get the promotion you want. . . . [But] in itself, and apart from all considerations of social favor, one form of speech is just as good as another. *I seen him* has exactly the same meaning and is just as useful as *I saw him,* and there is of course no ethical "right" and "wrong" or "good" and "bad" involved. In many cases, however, certain forms are looked on with displeasure by certain people, often including those who are most influential. A complete description of the forms should, of course, include this fact; when we are telling others about the English language, for example, we need to describe the variation between *he did it* and *he done it,* and then to add: "If you say *he done it* some of your listeners will consider you beneath them in social status, and will be less inclined to favor you than if you said *he did it.*" . . . It should be added that the choice of forms to be favored or disfavored varies from one social stratum to another. It is just as bad a break to say *it is not I* among workmen (who will accuse you of "talking like a school teacher") as it is to say *it ain't me* among school teachers (who will accuse you of "talking like a workman").[5]

Carl G. F. Franzén, of Indiana University, concluded that "the only force which influences an individual to speak a better type of English than that to which he is accustomed is not the teacher in the classroom but the associates on the new level which he is trying to reach." [6] Robert C. Pooley stressed the fact, already noted, that a given individual frequently passes, under differing circumstances, from one level to another, and that sometimes his swing is very wide. The most illiterate speaker, he pointed out, is usually able, on occasion, to speak what passes for "good standard English," and even the most careful speaker occasionally descends to the lower levels. Of these levels Pooley distinguished six, to wit, the illiterate, the homely, the informal standard, the formal standard, the literary and the technical.[7]

---

[5] Language and Superstition, *French Review,* May 1944, p. 377. [At the Philadelphia meeting of the National Council of Teachers of English, J. J. Lamberts pointed out that a too obviously "correct" way of speaking may result in overcharges from such relatively uneducated but highly practical citizens as plumbers and garagemen. See *CE,* Vol. XXIV, Nov. 1962, p. 142.]

[6] A Technique for Determining Levels in English Usage, *EJ* (College Edition), Vol. XXIII, Jan. 1934, pp. 57–69. This study was followed by A Study of Levels of English Usage, by Mayme Berns, one of Franzén's students. It is still unpublished.

[7] The Levels of Language, *Educational Method,* Mar. 1937, pp. 289–98.

The second

often has a slightly quaint or old-fashioned cast to it and displays, in many of its specific forms, the survival of words and idioms once widely used but now dropped from standard speech. It is heard in rural homes (excluding foreign influences), in the shops and homes of small towns, and among the older natives of large cities. In fact, it is so universal that few people in the United States escape its influence entirely, including all but a small portion of school teachers.

Franzén and his associates examined current dialect stories and popular plays, and recorded locutions heard in railroad and bus stations, on the radio,[8] in the courts and from "after-dinner speakers, preachers, lecturers and politicians." They might have found even better grist for their mill in popular songs and the comic strips. Sigmund Spaeth has shown that "bad grammar" has been the tradition of the former for many years.[9] Paul Dresser, author of the immortal "Banks of the Wabash" and brother to Theodore Dreiser, the novelist, used the right pronoun in the title of his "Just Tell Them That You Saw Me," but in the text he indulged himself in "Remember I was once a girl like *she*." Old-timers will recall "Just Because She Made *Them* Goo-Goo Eyes," and the refrain of "Frankie and Johnnie": "He *done* her wrong." [1] "A song writer," says Spaeth, "would hardly dare to use *whom* in a sentence, even if he knew it was correct. Such things are just unsingable."

Rather curiously, the *sermo vulgus* was for long as diligently neglected by the professional writers of the country as by the philologians. There are foreshadowings of it in "The Biglow Papers," in "Huckleberry Finn" and in some of the frontier humor of the years before the Civil War, but the enormous dialect literature of the later Nineteenth Century left it almost untouched. Localisms in vocabulary and pronunciation were explored at length, but the general folk speech went virtually unobserved; it is not even in the fables of George Ade. The business of reporting it accurately

---

[8] In July 1946 a press agent disguised as an indignant schoolma'am got space in the newspapers by protesting against the Arkansas dialect forms used by Dizzy Dean, a former baseball player, *e.g., slud* as the preterite of *slide*.

[9] Stabilizing the Language Through Popular Songs, *The New Yorker*, July 7, 1934, pp. 32–6.

[1] A writer in *AS*, Vol. XVII, Oct. 1942, p. 181, says that in the Oxford Book of Light Verse this was changed to *did*. The first edition of Gray's famous elegy, published in 1751, had the title An Elegy *Wrote* in a Country Church Yard. [Some recent observations of merit: Karl W. Dykema, the Grammar of Spoken English: Its Relation to What Is Called English Grammar, *AS*, Vol. XXIV, Feb. 1949, pp. 43–8, and How Fast Is Standard English Changing?, *AS*, Vol. XXXI, May 1956, pp. 89–95; J. S. Kenyon, Cultural Levels and Functional Varieties of English, *CE*, Vol. X, Oct. 1949, pp. 31–6; A. J. Walker, What Language Shall We Teach?, *EJ*, Vol. XLII, Nov. 1953, pp. 431–6.]

had to wait for Ring Lardner, who began experimenting with it in 1908 or thereabout. In his tales of baseball players, pugilists, movie queens, song writers and other such dismal persons he set down common American with precision, and yet with enough imagination to make his work a contribution of genuine and permanent value to the national literature. In any story of his it is possible to unearth almost every grammatical peculiarity of the vulgar speech, and he resisted stoutly the temptation to lay it on too thick. Here are a few typical sentences from "The Busher's Honeymoon": [2]

> I and Florrie *was* married the day before yesterday, just *like* I told you we *was* going to be. . . . The sum of what I have *wrote* down is $29.40. . . . Allen told me I *should ought* to give the priest $5. . . . I never *seen* him before. . . . I didn't used to eat *no* lunch in the playing season except when I *knowed* I was not going to work. . . . I guess the meals *has* cost me all together about $1.50, and I have *eat* very little myself. . . . I was willing to tell her all about *them* two poor girls. . . . *They* must be *no* mistake about who is the boss in my house. Some men *lets* their *wife* run all over them. . . . Allen has *went* to a college foot-ball game. One of the reporters *give* him a pass. . . . He called up and said he *hadn't* only the one pass, but he was not hurting my feelings *none*. . . . The flat across the hall from this *here* one is for rent. . . . It will always be *ourn*. . . . Both *her* and you *is* welcome at my house. . . . I never *seen* so much wine *drank* in my life.

Here are verbs confused as to tense, pronouns confused as to case, double and even triple negatives, nouns and verbs disagreeing in number, *n* marking the possessive instead of *s*, *like* used in place of *as* and so on. Lardner's baseball player, though he has pen in hand and is thus very careful to write *would not* instead of *wouldn't* and *am not* instead of *ain't*, provides us with a comprehensive and highly instructive panorama of popular linguistic habits. The forms of the subjunctive have no existence, *shall* has almost disappeared, adjectives and adverbs are indistinguishable and the objective case in the pronoun is indicated only by word order. He uses the word that is simplest, the grammatical pattern that is handiest. This vulgar American is a very fluent and even garrulous fellow and he commonly pronounces his words distinctly, so that his grammatical felonies shine forth clearly. His vocabulary is much larger than his linguistic betters commonly assume. They labor under a tradition that the lowly manage to get through life with a few hundred or a few thousand words. That tradition apparently "originated with two English clergymen, one of whom stated that 'some

---

[2] *The Saturday Evening Post*, July 11, 1914. Reprinted in You Know Me, Al; Garden City, L.I., 1915.

of the laborers in his parish had not three hundred words in their vocabulary,' while the other, Archdeacon Farrar, said he 'once listened for a long time together to the conversation of three peasants who were gathering apples among the boughs of an orchard, and as far as I could conjecture, the whole number of words they used did not exceed a hundred.' " [3] Max Müller gave imprudent support to this nonsense, and it was later propagated by Wilhelm Wundt, the psychologist, by Barrett Wendell and by various other persons who should have known better. It still survives in handbooks of "correct" English, but there is no truth in it whatsoever. "The complete vocabulary of any full (not minimum or pidgin) language," says Robert A. Hall, Jr., "regardless of the cultural level of its speakers, is at least 20,000 to 25,000 words." [4] This is borne out by the anthropologist A. L. Kroeber, who has been able to find 27,000 words in the vocabulary of the Aztec Nahuatl and 20,000 in that of the Maya. [5]

It is not to be argued, of course, that any individual speaker of a language uses or even knows every word of it, but by the same token it must be borne in mind that no investigator, however competent and assiduous, can be expected to unearth them all. Indeed, it is impossible for even the most expert lexicographers to make complete reports. Noah Webster's first dictionary of 1806 listed 28,000 words, the largest vocabulary assembled up to that time, but when he undertook his larger dictionary of 1828 he increased the number to 70,000. His successors kept on discovering more and more words, until today Webster 1961 lists more than 450,000. [6] Meanwhile, the Century Dictionary, in its final form, listed 530,000; the Standard, 455,000; and the OED, without its Supplement, 414,825. These figures, of course, include combinations; Robert L. Ramsay has argued [7] that the total number of different words in English is actually "something like 250,000" and that "over 50,000 of these are obsolete." He says that the best German dictionary lists 71,750 simple words and 112,954 compounds, or 184,704 in all, and that the figures reported for other languages are: French, 93,032; Spanish, 70,683; Italian, 69,642; Latin, 51,686; ancient Greek, 96,438; and Anglo-Saxon, 41,142. But these vocabularies are far from complete, and nearly all dictionaries are based mainly on the written language alone. For Latin and Greek there is no other source.

---

[3] Margaret Morse Nice, in On the Size of Vocabularies, *AS*, Vol. II, Oct. 1926.

[4] Language and Superstition, *French Review*, May 1944, p. 378, *n*. 5.

[5] Extent of Personal Vocabularies and Cultural Control, by J. M. Gillette, *Scientific Monthly*, Nov. 1929, p. 453.

[6] [Its ostensible total is less than that of its 1934 predecessor, but it abandoned all words not found after 1755 except for those important in understanding major writers. In compensation, it offers a more detailed treatment of the words included, notably a larger number of illustrative citations.]

[7] Taking the Census of English Words, *AS*, Vol. VIII, Feb. 1933, pp. 36–41.

It is not easy to determine how many words a given man knows, and it is even harder to find out how many he uses. The method usually selected is to choose by some abitrary method one word on each page of a dictionary, determine how many of the words thus gathered the subject can define and then multiply the result by the number of pages in the dictionary. But this plan admits a large element of mere chance; moreover, it is limited by the limitations of the dictionary used. But in any case the vocabulary of a given person, when adequately tested, turns out to be much more extensive than a layman would guess. E. A. Kirkpatrick has estimated that the average child in the second grade at school knows 4,480 words; the average sixth-grader, 8,700; the ninth-grader, 13,400; and the high-school senior, 20,120.[8] E. H. Babbitt, writing in 1907, concluded that the vocabulary of the average American college sophomore, despite his superficial appearance of imbecility, runs to between 50,000 and 60,000 words, and that even non-college men and women, provided they read a few books, know between 25,000 and 35,000. F. M. Gerlach puts the average high-school student's vocabulary at 71,000 and the college student's at 85,000. Other inquirers offer more modest estimates, but none countenances the popular delusion that millions of people get along with vocabularies of a few thousand or even a few hundred words.

There is a plain fallacy in the frequent attempt to estimate an author's stock of words by counting those he uses in his writings. This has led to the notion that Shakespeare knew but 15,000 (some say 20,000), Milton but 8,000 [this based on his English poetry, excluding all his prose and all his writings in Italian, Latin and Greek, to say nothing of what must have been a well-spiced conversational vocabulary], and the translators of the Old Testament but 5,642. How far such nonsense can go was illustrated years ago by a floating newspaper paragraph reporting that there were but 600

---

[8] A Vocabulary Test, *Popular Science Monthly*, Feb. 1907. I take this and much of what follows from A Brief Outline of Vocabulary Measurement with a Summary of Some Methods Employed, *Word Study*, Feb. 1939, pp. 5–8. [Several recent studies, notably those by Mildred C. Templin (Minneapolis, 1957) and Ruth G. Strickland (Bloomington, Ind., 1962), indicated that eight-year-olds may have recognition vocabularies of 30,000 words and utilize very complicated sentence patterns. In Relations Between Ability and Social Status in a Midwestern Community. IV: Size of Vocabulary, *Journal of Educational Psychology*, Vol. XXXVIII, 1947, p. 437, Mary Jean Schulman and Robert J. Havighurst disclose that among a group of fourteen-year-olds the recognition vocabularies of working-class children ranged from 18,000 to 60,000 words and those of upper-class children from 35,000 to 57,000. Since the failure of the schools to recognize and utilize this foundation is perhaps the greatest weakness of American education, it is significant that Havighurst is the head of a commission appointed in 1963 to investigate the Chicago public schools. Significant also were the agonized brays with which the appointment was greeted by those whom a colleague (in Freudian accuracy) has described as "the entrenched *burroc-racy*."]

words in the vocabulary of Italian opera, and hinting that most singers knew no more. How hard it is to put down is shown by the following sentence in a 1944 issue of a putatively respectable literary review, written by a professional literatus of considerable pretensions: "The vocabulary of the average American business man, outside of profanity and pornography, is about a thousand words." [9] [And in 1948, in the same week in which Supplement II appeared, a professor of speech from Northwestern University proclaimed that many Ohio farmers commanded no more than 500 words.]

A good deal of this current balderdash about midget vocabularies is caused by confusion between words known and words used. The very nature of language puts a heavy burden upon a relatively small number of common words, and so tends to conceal the number and importance of those used only seldom. So long ago as 1925 Leonard P. Ayres made an investigation of the vocabulary of everyday correspondence which showed that 542 words constitute seven-eighths of the average letter, that 43 constitute one-half and that 9 constitute one-fourth.[1] The nine are *I, the, and, you, to, your, of, for* and *in*. Of these, the first three alone constitute an eighth.[2] But this really says nothing about vocabularies, for it must be manifest that all casual writing, like all casual talk, is made up very largely of a small group of common words.

2: THE VERB

"The most surprising fact about the illiterate level of speech," says Pooley,[3] "is its widespread uniformity. It is not merely a haphazard series of lapses from standard English, but is rather a distinct and national mode of speech, with a fairly regular grammar of its own." [The investigations of the Linguistic Atlas have modified these statements somewhat—many grammatical forms, like words and pronunciations, are regionally restricted, regardless of the social class in which they may be found [4]—but the kinds

---

[9] For a Literary Lend-Lease, by Struthers Burt, *Saturday Review of Literature*, Nov. 4, 1944, p. 6.

[1] The Spelling Vocabularies of Personal and Business Letters; New York, Feb. 13, 1925.

[2] In The Words and Sounds of Telephone Conversations, *Bell System Technical Journal*, Apr. 1930, pp. 290–324, N. R. French, C. W. Carter, Jr., and Walter Koenig, Jr., reported that the first nine recorded in telephone conversations are *I, you, the, a, on, to, that, it* and *is*. *And* is in tenth place, *of* in thir-

teenth, *in* in fourteenth, *for* in twentieth and *your* in ninety-third. [Reissued in June 1930 as Monograph B-491, *Bell Telephone System Technical Publications*, it was long out of print until Mrs. Edith C. Trager edited it in 1962, with addenda, for the Thompson Ramo Wooldridge Corp.]

[3] The Levels of Language, *Educational Method*, Mar. 1937, p. 291.

[4] [See, for example, the summary in Ch. IX of W. Nelson Francis, The Structure of American English; New York, 1958.]

of grammatical practices that characterize the vulgate are pretty much the same regardless of region.] Its chief grammatical peculiarities lie among the verbs and pronouns. The nouns in common use, in the main, are quite sound in form. The adjectives, too, are treated rather politely, and the adverbs, though commonly transformed into the forms of their corresponding adjectives, are not further mutilated. But the verbs and pronouns undergo changes which set off the common speech very sharply from both correct English and correct American. This is only natural, for it is among the verbs and pronouns that nearly all the remaining inflections in English are to be found, and so they must bear the chief pressure of the influences that have been warring upon every sort of inflection since the earliest days. The primordial Indo-European language had eight cases of the noun; in Old English they fell to four, with a moribund instrumental, largely identical with the dative, hanging in the air; in Middle English the dative and accusative began to decay; in Modern English the dative and accusative have disappeared altogether, save as ghosts to haunt grammarians. But we still have two plainly defined conjugations of the verb, and we still inflect it, in part, for number and person. And we yet retain an objective case of the pronoun, and inflect it for person, number and gender.

Robert J. Menner argues that any list of conjugations of the verbs of the vulgate should include a "liberal intersprinkling of normal principal parts, at least as alternates." [5] For most verbs, usage among the humble and sometimes even on higher levels is not fixed, and both the standard preterites and perfect participles and their vulgar variants are heard. All persons not downright illiterate reveal a distaste for certain forms, *e.g.*, *brung, druv* and *div*, and seldom employ them save in conscious attempts at waggishness. But all these verbs actually belong to the vulgate, though they may not be used invariably, and their grammatical and syntactical history and relations deserve a great deal more patient study than they have got so far. The same thing is true of the pronouns of common speech, and of all its other contents. The theory that it is somehow *infra dig* to investigate them is one that American linguistic scholarship no longer entertains, however much this concern distresses the purer brethren of the belletristic cloth.

Following are paradigms showing the principal parts of some of the more interesting verbs of the vulgate: [6]

---

[5] The Verbs of the Vulgate, *AS*, Vol. I, Jan. 1926, p. 232.

[6] [These forms are derived from E. Bagby Atwood, Verb Forms of the Eastern United States, and Virginia McDavid, Verb Forms in the North-Central States and Upper Midwest, previously cited. There are, of course, many verbs not sys-

tematically investigated as yet. For historical perspective, see the works of Wyld and Jespersen, and such studies as O. L. Abbott, The Preterit and Past Participle of Strong Verbs in Seventeenth-Century American English, *AS*, Vol. XXXII, Feb. 1957, pp. 31–42.]

PRESENT	PRETERITE	PERFECT PARTICIPLE
am, is, are	was, were	been
ask	ask, asked, ast	ask, asked, ast
begin	begin, began, begun	begin, begun
bite	bit	bit, bitten
blow	blew, blowed, blewd	blew, blowed, blown
boil	boiled, boilt	boiled, boilt
break	broke	broke, broken
bring	brought, brung, brang	brought, brung
burst	burst, bursted	burst, bursted
bust	busted, bust	busted, bust
buy	bought	bought, boughten
catch	caught, catched, ketched, kitched, cotch	caught, catched, ketched, kitched, cotch
climb	climed, clime, clim, clam, clammed, clom, clome, clum, cloom	climed, clime, clim, clam, clammed, clom, clome, clum, cloom
come	came, come	come, came
dive	dived, dove, div, duv	dived, dove, div, duv
do	did, done	done, did
drag	dragged, drug	dragged, drug
draw	drawed, drew	drawed, drawn
dream	dreamed, dreamt, dremp, drimpt, drimp	dreamed, dreamt, dremp, drimpt, drimp
drink	drank, drunk, drinked, drink	drank,[7] drunk, drinked, drink
drive	drove, driv, druv, drive, drived	driven, drove, driv, druv, droven, drived
drown	drowned, drownded	drowned, drownded
eat	ate, eat, et [8]	eaten, ate, eat, et
fetch	fetched, fotch	fetched, fotch
fight	fought, fit, fout	fought, fit, fout
fit	fit, fitted	fit, fitted
freeze	froze, freezed, frozed, frez, friz	frozen, froze, freezed, frozed, frez, friz
give	gave, give, gin	given, gave, give, gin
grow	grew, growed	grown, growed

[7] [See W. S. Avis, The Participle *Drank:* Standard American English?, *AS,* Vol. XXVIII, May 1953, pp. 106–11, and Harold B. Allen, On Accepting Participial *Drank, CE,* Vol. XVIII, Feb. 1957, pp. 283–5.]

[8] [According to Helen Rand Miller, *EJ,* Vol. XXXVII, Jan. 1948, p. 45, the preterite is always written *eat* and pronounced *et* in England. In the last decade, however, *ate* has supplanted *eat* as a spelling, though the pronunciation remains *et.*]

PRESENT	PRETERITE	PERFECT PARTICIPLE
hang	hung, hanged	hung, hanged
hear	heard, heerd	heard, heerd, heern
heat	heated, het	heated, het
help	helped, hope	helped, hope
kneel	kneeled, knelt	kneeled, knelt
knit	knit, knitted	knit, knitted
know	knew, knowed	known, knowed
learn	learned, learnt	learned, learnt
lie, lay	lay, laid, lied	lain, lay, laid, lied
may	might, mout	
plead	pled, pleaded	pled, pleaded
ride	rode, rid	ridden, rode, rid
ring	rang, rung	rung, rang
rise	rose, riz, rised, raised	risen, rose, riz, rised, raised
run	ran, run	run, ran
scare	scared, scairt	scared, scairt
see	saw, see, seed, seen	seen, saw, see, seed
shrink	shrunk, shrank, shrinked	shrunk, shrank, shrinked, shrunken
sit, set	sit, sat, sot, set	sit, sat, sot, set
spoil	spoiled, spoilt	spoiled, spoilt
steal	stole, stoled	stolen, stole, stoled
sweat	sweat, sweated	sweat, sweated
swell	swelled, swole, swoled, swollen, swell	swelled, swollen, swole, swullen, swoled, swell
swim	swam, swum, swim, swimmed, swom	swum, swam, swimmed, swim, swom
take	took, tuck, taken, takened, taked	taken, took, tuck, takened, taked
teach	taught, teached	taught, teached
tear	tore	tore, torn, tored
throw	threw, throwed, thrown	thrown, throwed
wake	woke, waked	woke, waked, woken
wear	wore	wore, worn
write	wrote, writ	written, wrote, writ

The movement among verbs in English is apparently away from the so-called strong or irregular conjugation, *i.e., sing, sang, sung,* and toward the weak or regular, *i.e., wish, wished, wished; mean, meant, meant.* Fries[9]

---

[9] *American English Grammar;* New York, 1940, p. 60.

observes that there were 312 strong verbs, including those unchanged for tense, in Old English, but that of the 195 which still survive at all, 129, or 65%, have gone over to the weak category. In recent years the old strong verbs have shown a marked tendency to take refuge in the vulgar speech. Chaucer used *clombe* as the preterite of *to climb* without challenge, but by Shakespeare's time *climbed* had begun to supplant it, and today *clomb, clum* and the like must be sought among the lowly. Strong verbs that have become weak since Middle English days include: *bow, beah, bowne; carve, carf, corven; delve, dalfe, dolven; glide, glod, glode; gnaw, gnew, gnawn; help, holp, holpen; melt, malt, molten; wash, wush, washen.*[1] This tendency began before the Norman Conquest, and was marked during the Middle English period. Chaucer used *growed* for *grew* in the prologue to "The Wife of Bath's Tale," and *rised* for *rose* and *smited* for *smote* are in John Purvey's edition of the Bible, c. 1385. Many of these transformations were afterwards abandoned in the standard idiom, but a large number survived, for example, *melted* for *malt* or *molt* as the preterite of *to melt*. Others showed themselves during the Early Modern period. This tendency went furthest, of course, in the vulgar speech, and it has been embalmed in the English dialects. *I knowed*, for example, is common to all of them. But during the Seventeenth Century there arose a contrary tendency—that is, toward strong conjugations. The vulgar speech of Ireland, which preserves many Seventeenth Century forms, shows it plainly. *Ped* for *paid, gother* for *gathered* and *ruz* for *raised* are still heard there.[2] Certain forms of the early American national period, now reduced to the estate of localisms, were also survivors of the Seventeenth Century, e.g., *wed* for *weeded, grez* for *greased*. [*Dove* for *dived*—standard in much of the country and expanding as a prestige form—probably dates from the same period.]

Although many observers have predicted that the strong conjugations would disappear altogether, they concede that popular speech tends to preserve many old preterites and participles. This partiality for the old is opposed, however, by the fact that the weak conjugations are easier to contrive and remember, and as a result there is a movement toward them on all levels. Sometimes it goes to the length of providing regular inflections for verbs that are historically invariable in all situations, e.g., *to slit* and *to cast*; sometimes it turns inflected verbs into invariable ones, e.g., *to sweat*; and in many more cases it transfers a past participle to the place of a preterite, e.g., *I taken*. In the latter event, as often happens, the admonitions of the schoolma'am sometimes have a greater effect than she intends, and the discarded preterite is often used as the participle, e.g., *I have took* and *I was*

---

[1] John Earle, The Philology of the English Tongue; 3rd ed.; Oxford, 1879, pp. 261–4.

[2] Joyce, p. 77.

broke. As the list earlier in this section shows, there are often competing forms, *e.g., I ate, I et* and *I eat,* all in the preterite. It would be hard to disentangle the conflicting tendencies visible here. Language, in fact, is very far from logical. Its development is determined, not by neat and obvious rules, but by a polyhedron of disparate and often sharply conflicting forces —the influence of the schoolma'am, imitation (often involving misunderstanding), the lazy desire for simplicity and ease, and sheer wantonness and imbecility. The tendency to take well-worn paths, paradoxically enough, seems to be responsible both for the transfer of verbs from the strong to the weak conjugation, and for the transfer of certain others from the weak to the strong. A verb in everyday use tends to pull less familiar verbs with it, whether it be strong or weak. Thus, *fed* as the preterite of *to feed* and *led* as the preterite of *to lead* eased the way in the American vulgate for *pled* as the preterite of *to plead;* and *rung* as plainly performed the same office for *brung,* and *drove* for *dove.* Contrariwise, the same combination of laziness and imitativeness worked toward the regularization of certain verbs that were historically irregular. One sees the antagonistic pull of the two influences in the case of verbs ending in *-ow.* The analogy of *knew* and *grew* suggests *snew* as the preterite of *to snow,* and it is sometimes encountered. But meanwhile *knew* and *grew* have been themselves succumbing to the greater regularity of *knowed* and *growed.* So *snew,* losing support, grows rare and is in palpable decay, but *knowed* and *growed* show great vigor, as do many of their analogues. The substitution of *heerd* for *heard* also presents a case of logic and convenience supporting analogy. The form is suggested by *feared, cheered, cleared,* etc., but its main advantage lies in the fact that it gets rid of a vowel change.

Some of the verbs of the vulgate show the end-products of other language movements that go back to an early period. There is, for example, the disappearance of the final *t* in such words as *slep* and *wep.* Most of these, in Old English, were strong verbs. The preterite of *to sleep (slǣpan),* for example, was *slēp,* and of *to weep* was *wēop.* But in the course of time both *to sleep* and *to weep* acquired weak preterite endings, the first becoming *slǣpte* and the second *wēpte,* [and the vowels of both were later shortened to that of *pep*]. Meanwhile the weak conjugation itself was changing. The prevailing Early Middle English suffix was *-de* or *-ede* (a sizable number of the latter going back to an Old English *-ode*), and the vowels were always pronounced. The wearing-down process that set in in the Twelfth Century disposed of the final *e,* but in certain words the other vowel survived for a good while, and we still observe it in such archaisms as *learnéd* and *belovéd.* Finally, however, it became silent in other preterites, and *loved* began to be pronounced (and often written) as a word of one syllable: *lov'd*.[3] After certain consonants this final *d* sound was changed into *t*, and such words as *pushed* and *clipped* became *pusht* and *clipt*. In other verbs, the *-t* (or *-te*) ending had come in long before, and their stem vowels had changed. Thus arose such forms as *slept*. In vulgar American another step is taken, and the *-t* is dropped. Thus, by a circuitous route, verbs originally strong, and for many centuries hovering between the two conjugations, have become strong again.

Helt is probably an example of change by false analogy. During the Thirteenth Century, according to Sweet,[4] "*d* was changed to *t* in the weak preterites of verbs [ending] in *rd, ld, nd*." Before that time the preterite of *sende* (*send*) had been *sende;* now it became *sente*. It survives in our modern *sent*, and the same process is also revealed in *built, lent* and *bent*. The popular speech, disregarding the fact that *to hold* is a strong verb, arrives at *helt* by imitation.[5] In *tole*, in place of *told*, the *d* is got rid of by assimilation with *l*. *Attackted* and *drownded* seem to be examples of an effort to dispose of harsh combinations by a contrary process. Both are old in English. *Attackted* is widespread in the United States, but Wright indicates [6] that it is confined to relatively few regional dialects in England, *e.g.*, those of Essex, Somerset, Devonshire and the town of Newcastle. In Warwickshire, he says, it "is used by the uneducated above the lowest class, such as small tradespeople." The DAE traces it to 1689 in American use, and John Witherspoon denounced it in 1781 as "a vulgarism in America only." [7] The corresponding noun, *attackt*, has been traced to 1706, when it appeared in the Virginia state papers. John Pickering, in 1816, said that *attackted* was then confined, in the American seaports, to "the most illiterate people," but that in the interior it was "sometimes heard among persons of a somewhat higher class." The analogous form *drownded* was used by Shaftesbury in his "Characteristics" (1711), and by Swift in his "Polite Conversation" (1738), but the DAE says that it is "now vulgar." Witherspoon listed it as "a vulgarism in England and America." [8] It seems to be in use in all parts of the country; so is *to drownd*, as in "He was scared of *drowndin'*." [9] Wentworth lists many other parallels, *e.g.*, *foalded, swoonded, tossted* and *ailded*, some of them confined to narrow areas or classes, *e.g.*, Appalachia or the Southern Negroes, but others in use in all parts of the country.

To the same general class, more or less, belong such reinforced verbs as

---

[3] The last stand of the distinct *-ed* was made in Addison's day. He was in favor of retaining it, and in *The Spectator* for Aug. 4, 1711, he protested against obliterating the syllable in the termination.

[4] A New English Grammar; Oxford, 1900, Pt. I, p. 380.

[5] The noun is often made *holt*, as in "I got a-*holt* of it."

[6] EDD, Vol. I, p. 90.

[7] *The Druid*, No. VI, May 16.

[8] *Ibid*.

[9] The Leatherwood God, by W. D. Howells; New York, 1916.

to loaden, to quieten and *to unloosen.* The OED shows that *to loose,* which is traced to *c.* 1225, had become *to loosen* in England by 1382, and *to unloosen* by *c.* 1450. The first has disappeared from the American common speech, and the third has pretty well displaced the second. In England *to unloosen* seems to be rare, but *to unloose* is preferred to *to loose* by respectable authorities.[1] *To loaden* is traced by the OED to a letter of Queen Elizabeth in 1568, and *to unloaden* to 1567. When *to quieten* first appeared in England, in 1828, it was denounced as "not English," but by 1852, the year of "Cranford," it was used by Mrs. Gaskell. Wentworth finds it in use in the Ozarks, Appalachia and Newfoundland, often with *down* following; and it probably occurs in most of the Republic. Other such forms recorded are *to shapen, to pinken, to safen, to thinnen* and *to smoothen.* Such inventions are suggested by the countless accepted words that follow the same plan. Thus *to thicken* produces *to thinnen, to unbend* produces *to unloose,* which becomes *to unloosen,* and so on.

The *p* sound in *drempt* follows a tendency that is also seen in such pronunciations as *warm(p)th, com(p)fort* and *some(p)thing,* and that has actually inserted a *p* in *Thompson* (*Tom's son*). The general movement toward regularization is well exhibited by the new verbs that come into the language constantly. Practically all of them show the weak conjugation, *e.g., to program.* Even when a compound has as its last member a verb ordinarily strong, it is often weak itself. Thus the preterite of *to joyride* is not *joyrode,* nor even *joyridden,* but *joyrided.* [And no baseball player ever *flew out* to end the inning; he always *flied out.*] *Bust,* from *burst,* is regular, and its usual preterite is *busted,* though *burst* is irregular and its preterite is the verb itself unchanged. The same tendency toward regularity is shown by the verbs of the *kneel* class; the preterite of *kneel* is often *kneeled,* though *knelt* is still more common, and even *feeled* instead of *felt,* as in "I *feeled* my way," can be heard. The confusion between *to lie* and *to lay* extends to the higher reaches of spoken American,[2] and so does that between *lend* and *loan.* In the vulgate, moreover, *leaned* becomes *lent,* as in "I *lent* on the counter." In the same way *to set* has almost superseded *to sit,* and the preterite and participle of the former, *set,* is often used in place of *sat,* [though the latter survives as both present and participle and freely alternates with *set,* sometimes even in the same sentence]. *To speed* and *to shoe* have become regular, not only because of the general tendency toward the weak conjugation but also for logical reasons. The prevalence of speed contests of various sorts, always to the intense interest of the proletariat, has brought such words as *speeder, speeding, speed mania, speed*

---

[1] For example, Jackdaw, a very popular writer on speech, in *John o' London's Weekly,* Mar. 25, 1938.

[2] [See, for example, the reports of E. Bagby Atwood and Virginia McDavid, previously cited.]

maniac and *speed limit* into daily use, and *speeded* harmonizes with them better than the irregular *sped*. The American's use of *to learn* for *to teach* is common to most of the English dialects. More peculiar to his speech, and possibly of German origin, is the use of *to leave* for *to let*, as in "Washington *left* them have it."[3]

In studying the American verb, it is necessary to remember always, as Menner reminds us, that it is in a state of transition. It is not uncommon to find corrupt forms side by side with orthodox forms, or even two corrupt forms [or (rarest) two orthodox forms] battling with each other. For *throw*, Lardner hears "if he had *throwed*"; *threw* is often used in that situation. Again, he uses "the rottenest I ever seen *gave*"; my own belief is that *give* is far more common. Other verbs show various other uncertainties and confusions. The preterite and participle of *to shake* may be either *shaken* or *shook* or *shuck*. The conjugation of *to win* is yet far from fixed. The correct English preterite, *won*, is still in use, but against this are arrayed *wan* and *winned*, and Lardner believed that the plain form of the present, *win*, would eventually oust all of them.

In certain strong verbs the substitution of the perfect participle for the preterite originated in a confusion between the singular and plural forms of the preterite, which were once distinct. When this distinction began to disappear, the plural preterite, usually with *u* for its vowel, was sometimes substituted for the singular form in *a*, and so the preterite and the perfect participle coalesced, for the latter was usually also in *u*. *Begun, clumb, rung, sung* and *swum* are examples.

The contrary substitution of the preterite for the perfect participle is old in English and there was a time indeed when even the best writers were apparently unconscious of its inelegance. Any play of Shakespeare's will show many such forms as "I have *wrote*," "I am *mistook*" and "He has *rode*." In several cases this confusion has survived. "I have *stood*," for example, is now perfectly correct English, but before 1560 the proper form was "I have *stonden*," or occasionally "I have *stonded*," or "I have *stand*."[4]

The substitution of the preterite for the perfect participle seems to be increasing of late. But a sense of its uncouthness appears to linger at the back of the proletarian mind, and sometimes it is embellished with an *en* suffix, and so brought into greater harmony with more orthodox forms of the participle. The quick ear of Lardner detects various coinages of the sort, among them *tooken*, as in "little Al might of *tooken* sick." *Hadden* is

---

[3] [This was not investigated by the LA, but is common in areas of heavy German settlement. A similar confusion between *bring* and *take* is found among the Scandinavians of Minnesota; a Duluth restaurant in 1949 invited its patrons: "*Bring* your leftovers home to your dog."]

[4] All three appear in the 1549 Book of Common Prayer.

also met with, as in "I would of *hadden*." But the majority of preterites used as participles remain unchanged. Lardner's baseball player never writes "I have *written*" or "I have *wroten*," but always "I have *wrote*." And in the same way he always writes "I have *did, ate, went, drank, rode, ran, saw, sang, woke* and *stole*."

In the American vulgate, says Menner, the auxiliary *have* is under heavy pressure in all situations, and promises to disappear. Because the weak-stressed forms are homonymous, it is sometimes written ignorantly as *of*, as in "She would *of* drove" and "I would *of* gave." Often in speech and sometimes in writing it is shaded to a sort of particle attached to the verb, as in "He *woulda* tole you," "Who *coulda* took it?" and "He *musta* been there." In going through this change it drags its surrogate, *of*, along, and so one encounters such forms as *kinda, sorta, coupla* and *outa*.[5] Finally, in its *of* incarnation, *have* is employed as a sort of auxiliary to itself, as in "if you had *of* went," "if it had *of* been hard" and "if I had *of* had."[6] The DAE traces the *-a* form to 1844 and marks it an Americanism, but it is actually old in unstudied English and is to be found in the Verney Letters of the Fifteenth, Sixteenth and Seventeenth Centuries.[7] The OED describes this reduction of the OE *habban* (Ger. *haben*) to *a* as the *ne plus ultra* of the wearing-down tendency among English words.

There is great need for a study of the history of such forms in American English, but so far the only attempt upon it was one by Henry Alexander in 1929.[8] He found no inflections of the verb that had not been recorded in England, but the fact is not of any significance, for American is itself an English dialect, and its vocabulary is largely made up of borrowings from its congeners But many forms have had histories in this country differing from their histories in England, and some that are used only in narrow areas there have come into almost universal use in the American common speech.

Even *I seen*, though it is traced to *c.* 1440 by the OED, and had a prototype in *sehen* nearly two centuries earlier, begins to take on a distinctively American color. It apparently did not gain its present wide vogue among the American underprivileged until the high tide of the Irish immigration in the 1840s. Witherspoon, in 1781,[9] denounced *I seed* and *I see* as preterites, but not *I seen*, and Pickering, in 1815,[1] and other early Nineteenth Century writers were content to echo Witherspoon. Wright ignores *I seen* in the

---

[5] There are many examples in The English of the Comic Cartoons, by Helen Trace Tysell, *AS*, Vol. X, Feb. 1935, p. 47.
[6] These examples are from Lardner's story A New Busher Breaks In, in You Know Me, Al, pp. 122 *ff.*

[7] Wyld, p. 166.
[8] The Verbs of the Vulgate in Their Historical Relations, *AS*, Vol. IV, Apr. 1929, pp. 307–15.
[9] *The Druid*, No. VI, May 23.
[1] Pickering, p. 171.

"English Dialect Grammar," though including *I see* and *I seed*, and in the "English Dialect Dictionary" makes *I seen* chiefly Irish. [The current English Dialect Survey, under Harold Orton, of Leeds, shows that *I seen* is common, though hardly dominant, in the English West Midlands, and elsewhere is only sporadic.[2]] Thornton's first American example is dated 1796, but after that he offers none until 1840. Menner believes that when *I seen* began to flourish in the American common speech it was "still in the perfect tense with the auxiliary syncopated," *i.e.*, "*I(ve) never seen* it," but that it soon "came to be regarded as a real preterite and extended to all the functions of the past tense."[3] Menner also believes that *I have saw* and *I have did* were probably launched and propagated by "the condemnation of *I seen* and *I done* by grammarians, teachers and family critics," as *between you and I* was prospered by the war on *it's me*.[4] His first example of *I have saw* is from Artemus Ward's "Scenes Outside the Fair-Ground" (*c.* 1862), and he says that "the grammarians of the early Nineteenth Century do not appear to include" it "in their 'exercises in false syntax,'" but it was frowned upon as a Pennsylvania provincialism in the eleventh edition of Samuel Kirkman's "English Grammar in Familiar Lectures" (1829).[5]

To bust might especially reward investigation. The OED Supplement finds it in Dickens's "Nicholas Nickleby," published in 1839, just before his first visit to America, but he may have borrowed it, for the DAE shows that it was in use in this country in 1806, and that by 1830 it was widespread. Bartlett says that when, in 1832, Henry Clay, the Whig candidate, was defeated for the presidency by Andrew Jackson, the following conundrum "went the rounds of the papers": "*Q.* Why is the Whig party like a sculptor? *A.* Because it takes Clay and makes a *bust*." The banks that blew up so copiously in 1837 did not *burst;* they *bust*. So with the boilers of the river steamers. *To bust out laughing, to bust a blood vessel* (or a *suspenders button*), *to go on a bust* (*i.e.*, a spree)[6] and the like became common phrases, and by 1845 *buster* was a popular designation for anything large or astounding and especially for a fat and hearty boy.[7] Not long afterward the last named became a nickname for such a boy, *e.g.*, *Buster Brown*, and survived in that capacity until our own time. *Bronco buster* has been traced to 1888, but it is no doubt much older. *Bust head*, meaning the cephalalgia following alcoholic indiscretion [or a kind of raw whiskey

---

[2] [W. Nelson Francis, Some Dialectal Verb Forms in England, *Orbis*, Vol. X, May 1961, pp. 1–14.]

[3] The Verbs of the Vulgate, *AS*, Vol. I, Jan. 1926.

[4] Hypercorrect Forms in American English, *AS*, Vol. XII, Oct. 1937, p. 173.

[5] Boston, 1829, p. 207.

[6] John S. Farmer, in his Americanisms Old and New, p. 108, says of this: "Now common in England, but of California origin."

[7] Partridge says that it originated in the United States before 1850 and was naturalized in England *c.* 1858.

capable of inducing it], is traced to 1857, and *bustinest*, synonym for *largest*, to 1851. "Pike's Peak or *bust*" was launched in 1858 and soon took on almost proverbial dignity. The Linguistic Atlas of New England [8] shows that *bust* and *busted* are widely prevalent in New England, and notes that *burst* and *bursted* "are felt as modern or refined." Berrey and Van den Bark, in the index to their "American Thesaurus of Slang," have nearly 200 entries for *to bust* and its derivatives, but only nine for *to burst*.

The subjunctive, which is disappearing from Standard American, is virtually extinct in the vulgar tongue. One rarely hears "if I *were* you," generally "if I *was* you." Such a sentence as "*Had* I wished her, I *had had* her" would be unintelligible to most Americans; even "I *had* rather" is forgotten. In the third person the *-s* is not dropped from the verb. One hears, not "if she *go*," but always "if she *goes*." "If he *be* the man" is never heard; it is always "if he *is*." In a few counter phrases, used now and then by the folk, the old form survives, *e.g.*, "*be* that as it may" and "far *be* it from me," but they carry an air of conscious sophistication. In ordinary talk the conjugation is *if I am, if I was* and *if I hadda been*. On higher levels, of course, the subjunctive shows more life, and there is ground for questioning the conclusion of various authorities that it is on its way out. But Thyra Jane Bevier has produced plenty of evidence [9] that it is by no means as often found in American writing as it was a few generations ago. "It was never actively alive in America," she concludes, "except about the period from 1855 to 1880."

On the other hand, in New England *be* as an indicative is still substituted for *am, is* and *are*, as in "I *be* going" and "*Be* he (or you) sick?" Pickering, in his Vocabulary of 1816, said that it was not then "so common as it was some years ago," and dismissed it as confined to "the interior towns or the vulgar," but the Linguistic Atlas of New England shows that it was still flourishing in the 1930s.[1] Some of the forms listed by the Atlas are: "I *be* what I *be*," "He says you *be* and I says you *ben't*," "I don't know as it *be*," "There you *be*," "They *be* good," "They *be* to Providence" and "You ain't going, *be* you?" Both *be* and *ben't* survive in the Southern and Eastern dialects of England, the chief sources of the New England dialects. In literary use *ic beo* (*i.e.*, *I be*) is traced to *c.* 1000, and *be* remained a formidable rival to *are* until the time of Shakespeare. *Be* is described by the OED as "an irregular and defective verb, the full conjugation of which in modern English is effected by a union of the surviving inflexions of three originally distinct and independent verbs, *viz.* (1) the original Aryan substantive verb with stem *es-* . . . , (2) the verb with stem *wes-* . . . , and (3) the stem *beu.*" The DAE traces *I be* in American use (in the negative

[8] Vol. III, Pt. II, Map 639.
[9] American Use of the Subjunctive, *AS*, Vol. VI, Feb. 1931.

[1] Vol. III, Pt. II, Map 677. [See also Atwood, before cited, p. 27, Fig. 21.]

form of *I been't*) to Cotton Mather's "Magnalia" (1702). Wentworth [and more recently the Linguistic Atlas] reports examples from various parts of the country, but the stronghold of *be* is and always has been New England.

In the vulgate the distinction between *shall* and *will*, preserved in Standard English but already breaking down in the most correct American, has been lost entirely. *Will* has displaced *shall* completely. This preference extends to the inflections of both. *Sha'n't* is very seldom heard, except in New England, and even there it is infrequent; almost always *won't* is used instead.[2]

Fries has shown [3] that the first serious effort to differentiate between *shall* and *will* was made by a grammarian named George Mason, whose "Grammaire Angloise," written in French, was published in 1622, though it was not until 1765 that a successor named William Ward brought the rules up to their present state of muddled refinement. But it was "only after the first quarter of the Nineteenth Century" that "the complete discussion of the rules for *shall* and *will* in independent-declarative statements, in interrogative sentences, and in subordinate clauses" became "a common feature of text-books of English grammar." These rules still survive [despite some attrition in the last three decades], but the schoolma'am has failed to implant them in her pupils, and they have never represented actual cultivated usage, British or American.

English observers often call attention to the fact that Americans neglect the distinction between *will* and *shall;* indeed, many Englishmen allege that only a Briton of superior capacity, schooled from birth in Oxford English, ever uses them properly. "The grammatical rules for [their] right use," said H. W. Fowler with prissy complacency in 1921, "are very elaborate, and anyone who studies them must see that a complete understanding of them cannot be expected from ordinary writers and speakers." [4] This same Fowler, in his "Dictionary of Modern English Usage" (1926), took nearly seven columns to expound them as he understood them, but his exposition was a great deal more learned than lucid, and most English schoolmasters probably prefer the easier device of teaching by an old and familiar example:

> I *shall* drown: nobody *will* save me.
> I *will* drown: nobody *shall* save me.

But the simplicity of this is deceptive, for like most of the other rules of grammar, those governing *will* and *shall* are subject to many exceptions. In

---

[2] See Atwood, before cited, p. 32.

[3] American English Grammar; New York, 1940, pp. 152–3. [See also On the Origin of the Grammarians' Rules for *Shall* and *Will*, by James R. Hulbert, *PMLA*, Vol. LXII, Dec. 1947, pp. 1178–87.]

[4] *Shall* and *Will, Should* and *Would* in the Newspapers of Today, *SPE Tract*, No. VI, 1921, p. 14.

the 1860s Richard Grant White said that "in New England . . . even the boys and girls playing on the commons" used the auxiliary verbs *will* and *shall* "correctly," which is to say, in accord with Southern English practice, and that "even in New York, New Jersey, and Ohio, in Virginia, Maryland and South Carolina fairly educated people of English stock" did the same.[5] But that was three generations ago, and it probably wasn't true even then. Today, only in the most painstaking and artificial varieties of American does a distinction between *will* and *shall* exist. No ordinary American would detect anything wrong in this sentence from the London *Times:* "We must reconcile what we *would* like to do with what we can do." Nor in this by W. B. Yeats: "The character who delights us may commit murder like Macbeth . . . and yet we *will* rejoice in every happiness that comes to him." Nor at the question: "*Will* you be at the Browns' this evening?" But the discriminating eyes of H. W. Fowler in "Modern English Usage" and of Fowler and his brother in "The King's English" reject all three. In Scotland and Ireland, as in the United States, *shall* is rare, and Northern English example may be partly responsible for American usage. As Leonard once pointed out,[6] "The whole mass of pronouncements about the matter in texts is of little moment now, since the future in English is most commonly expressed by neither *shall* nor *will*, but by the much commoner contraction '*ll*, and by the forms *is to go, about to go, is going to* and the whole range of auxiliary verbs which mean both past and future."

As for *should*, it is displaced by *ought to* (degenerated to *oughter* or *oughta* and sometimes *had oughta*) and [particularly in areas of Yankee settlement] in its negative form by the periphrastic *hadn't oughter*, as in "He *hadn't oughter* said that." Lardner gives various redundant combinations of *should* and *ought*, as in "I don't feel as if I *should ought to* leave" and "They *should not ought to of* had," but they are not as common as the simple *oughta* forms. [*Did ought, didn't ought,* not uncommon in England, are rare in the Republic.] In the main, *should* is avoided, sometimes at considerable pains. Often its place is taken by the more positive *don't*. Thus "I *don't* mind" is used instead of "I *shouldn't* mind."

The schoolma'am has begun to be wary of *shall* and *will*, for she finds the rules laid down for their use by the textbooks contradictory and unintelligible, and it is easy for a bright and wicked pupil to frame problems that leave her blushing and sweating. But she still makes a gallant effort to put down *ain't*, and if she has not succeeded, she has achieved the minor triumph of making most educated Americans, and the half-educated as

---

[5] Words and Their Uses; new ed.; New York, 1876, p. 264.

[6] *Shall* and *Will, AS,* Vol. IV, Aug. 1929, p. 498.

well, uneasy about using it. [*Ain't*, as we know it, probably developed from a predecessor *an't* which in turn arose from several sources: (*a*) the contraction of *am not* (perhaps through *amn't*);[7] (*b*) the contraction of *are not*, when *are* had lost the *r* and had the vowel of *hat* (as it still has in some unwashed parts of the South).[8] In the London area and its dependencies, *an't*, whatever its source, would have acquired the broad *a*, as in the London pronunciation of *aunt* and *can't*, and consequently the spelling *aren't*. In other areas *an't* would have developed the vowel of *paint*, best spelled as *ain't*. The history of *ain't* and its congeners is obscure, because until the rise of romantic realism in the Nineteenth Century, few writers bothered to note the forms of popular speech, and those who did usually confined their attention to low comedy.] *An't* is traced by the OED to 1706, but its first example of *ain't* is from Fanny Burney's "Evelina" (1778). *An't* was denounced by Witherspoon in 1781 as a vulgarism prevailing in both England and America, along with *can't*, *han't* (now *haven't* [or the rustic *hain't*]), *don't*, *shouldn't* and *wouldn't*, but he did not mention *ain't*. Nor did Pickering list it in his Vocabulary of 1816. In 1837, however, it was included by Sherwood among his Southern provincialisms, and defined as a substitute for both *is not* and *am not*. The DAE, whose first American example is dated 1779, defines it as a "contracted form of *airn't*, *are not*," and traces *air* for *are*, in American use, to 1777.[9] The DAE shows that *an't* was used in American for *are not* so early as 1723. There are logical objections to the use of *ain't* for *are not* and *is not*, but when used for *am not* it is certainly better than the clumsy English *aren't*.[1] Even Fowler says that "it is a pity that *ain't* for *am not*, being a natural contraction and supplying a real want, should shock us as though tarred with the same brush [as *ain't* for *isn't*]."[2]

Such forms as "He *ain't* there," "*Ain't* it the truth?," "You been there, *ain't* you?" and "I *ain't* heerd of it" are common. [*Hain't* is also heard, alongside *ain't*; in New England the rural purists sometimes use *hain't* only in place of *haven't*, *hasn't*, employing *ain't* alone as a substitute for *am not*, *isn't*, *aren't*, but in Appalachia and parts of the South the two forms may be used interchangeably Nevertheless, wherever it is used, *hain't* is considered much more old-fashioned or illiterate than *ain't*.[3]]

---

[7] A Modern English Grammar on Historical Principles, by Otto Jespersen; Pt. I: Sounds and Spellings; 3rd ed.; Heidelberg, 1922, p. 228.

[8] Harold H. Bender, The Origin of *Ain't*, *Word Study*, Mar. 1936, p. 3. A Grammar of the English Language, by George O. Curme; Vol. II: Parts of Speech and Accidence; Boston, 1935, p. 248.

[9] It still survives in Appalachia.

[1] Wallace Rice says in *Ain't*, *American Mercury*, Aug. 1927, p. 450, that "this Briticism began only with the present century."

[2] Dictionary of Modern English Usage; Oxford, 1926, p. 45.

[3] [This is particularly noticeable in the LA evidence from Kentucky.]

[Statistics on the use of *ain't* are hard to find. The schoolma'am's taboo has been so effective that even the barely literate avoid using it in writing and most of the half-educated shy away from it in speech, at least when they are on their guard. But, paradoxically, *ain't* for *am not* occurs freely in the intimate conversation of many of the old huntin' and shootin' families in England and their opposite numbers in such faded Sybarises as Charleston, S.C. In fact, a stranger in Charleston knows he is on his way to being accepted when scions of the old families drop their guard and say *ain't* in his presence.]

Mark Twain, in one of his philological moods, ventured the opinion that *got* is used more frequently in England than in the United States, as in "I haven't *got* any money," [4] but the weight of evidence is against him. All authorities agree, however, that *gotten* is one of the hallmarks of American speech. Says Curme: [5]

> The English colonists brought *gotten* along with them to their new American home. . . . It was good English.[6] But a great ocean lay between the English colonists and the mother country. English in England went on developing . . . and *gotten* became *got*, but in America *gotten* retained its original form. *Gotten* evidently belongs to the long list of American things.

Today *gotten* is so firmly lodged that in some parts of the South *got* has come to be considered improper in the past tense. But in the present it flourishes lushly in the form *gotta*, and in that form has almost obliterated *have*.

Another characteristic of vulgar American is the heavy use of *used to* as a general indicator of the past. It is always given the unvoiced *s* without a final *d*, and may be used also in the negative as in "He *use to didn't* like it." Wentworth and other scouts have found *use to could, would, was* and *wasn't* in all parts of the country, but especially in the South and South Midland.[7] *Use to could* was listed by Sherwood in the vocabulary accompanying his "Gazetteer of the State of Georgia" (1827), and in 1850 William C. Fowler put it among "ungrammatical expressions, disapproved by all," in his chapter on American dialects in "The English Language." [Today, however, *use to could* is in good standing in Southern familiar colloquial speech, and even *use to didn't* and *use to wasn't* are occasionally

---

[4] Concerning the American Language, in The Stolen White Elephant; Hartford, 1882, p. 269. [Cf. *Have Got* in Expressions of Possession and Obligation, by A. H. Marckwardt, *CE*, Vol. XVI, Feb. 1955, pp. 309–10.]

[5] *Gotten, AS*, Vol. II, Sept. 1927, pp. 495–6.
[6] The OED traces it to *c.* 1340, but marks it "now rare except in *ill-gotten*."
[7] [For *might could*, see Atwood, before cited, p. 35, Fig. 28.]

heard from educated Southerners. In eastern Kentucky, and perhaps elsewhere, *use to* is often reduced to a simple adverb to introduce a sentence, as "*Use to* everybody up here would make their own liquor." The development of *use to* in this construction is analogous to that of *maybe*, which started out as a verb phrase but is now in impeccable standing as a simple adverb.] Combinations of the *use to* type are numerous in the vulgar speech, *e.g.*, *gonna* and *gotta*. Meanwhile *have*—in the form *hafta*—promises to displace *must*. The American seldom says "I *must* go"; he almost invariably says "I *have to* go" or "I *have got to* go."

Another peculiarity of vulgar American speech that has interested philologians is the use of *done* as a perfective auxiliary, [chiefly though not exclusively in the South and South Midland]. Oma Stanley [8] recorded the following in East Texas: "He *done bought* a new hat," "He *done got* there" and "He *done did* it." Wentworth adds from other parts of the country: "I *done went* to town" and "The chores *done been done*." Robley Dunglison called the use of the auxiliary *done* "a prevalent vulgarism in the Southern States, . . . only heard amongst the lowest classes," and hazarded the guess that it "was probably obtained from Ireland." [9] Sherwood cited *done said it* and *done did it*, but without comment. The DAE offers no examples earlier than those of Sherwood. [Again, the form seems to have higher status in the South than the grammarians would concede. With the slightest trace of *v* before it, as in "I've *done* told you all I'm going to," it would go unnoticed in a colloquial situation almost anywhere in the late Confederacy, and one suspects that many a *v* disappears unremarked in rapid speech.]

In the negative a clear *not* is used only for special emphasis, as in "You will *not* do it!" In almost all other situations, it is reduced to *n't*, and sometimes this *n't*, in rapid utterance, shrinks to *n* or is dropped altogether. Says E. C. Hills:

> Usually before a consonant, and regularly before a dental, *not* becomes merely vocalic *n*, is in *I didn'(t)* do it," "We *couldn'(t)* stop," and "He *hasn'(t)* gone." With *can*, in rapid fluent speech uttered without self-consciousness, *not* before a consonant tends to disappear completely, so that "I *c'n* do it" is affirmative, while the negative form is "I *can'(t)* do it." . . . When they say "I *can'(t)* do it," or even "I *can'(t)* go tonight," without pronouncing the *t*, my friends regularly understand the expression to be negative. If one pronounces the *can* with emphasis and followed perhaps by a slight pause, "I *can* go tonight" is affirmative. In combination with the *y* of *you*, *nt* becomes *nch*

---

8. The Speech of East Texas, before cited, p. 98.

9 In his contributions to the *Virginia Literary Museum*, 1829.

as in "*Haven't you* seen it?" "*Didn't you* do it?" This change, however, does not occur before the initial *y* of a verb, as in "He *didn'(t)* yell," in which the *t* is usually not pronounced at all.[1]

Hills should have added that, for the speech of Baltimore and much of the rest of the Atlantic seaboard, when *can* is used in the negative it takes the *a* of its mother, *can't* (and also of *pan, stand,* etc.), not the shorter *a* of *ran,* etc. Thus there is a phonetic difference between affirmative *can* and negative *can,* though they must be written alike. The *nch* sound that Hills mentions has attracted the attention of the begetters of comic strips. They frequently use *can cha* for *can't you.* When *to do* is used in the negative, the form is usually *don't; doesn't* is seldom heard. Among Southerners this use rises to the level of cultured speech. When, during the Hoover Depression, a fresh effort to police the national speech habits was begun at Columbia University, the editor of the Petersburg, Va., *Progress-Index* replied as follows:

> One of the expressions listed in the indictment of the savants is *he don't,* a contraction, of course, of *he does not.* Here in Virginia many men of the highest education use the phrase habitually. Their ancestors have used it for many generations, and it might be argued with some reason that when the best blood and the best brains of Virginia use an expression for so long a time it becomes correct, regardless of the protests of the professional grammarians.[2]

According to Menner, the widespread use of the present for the preterite is relatively recent. "In almost all the comic writers of the first half of the [Nineteenth] Century," he says, *gin* and *give* are in rivalry as the preterites of *to give,* but in "Huckleberry Finn" *give* prevails. He suggests that its rise may be due to the fact that a number of common verbs showing the same vowel, *e.g., hit, quit* and *spit,* are unchanged in the preterite. Certainly it is a fact that such verbs are apparently rather more often put into the new historical present in the vulgate than those of any other class. Examples are *begin, sit* and *win.* But the other verbs seem to be going the same way, and the vulgar historical present of one of them, *sez* (*i.e., says*), appears to be older than *give.*

---

[1] *Not* in American English, *AS,* Vol. II, Sept. 1927. A similar study devoted to Southern speech and using oscillographic records, was published by James B. McMillan in *AS,* in Apr. 1939.

[2] Oct. 21, 1931. [See also An Example of Prescriptive Linguistic Change: *Don't* to *Doesn't,* by Karl W. Dykema, *EJ,* Vol. XXXVI, Sept. 1947, pp. 370–6, and *Don't,* by Kemp Malone, *EJ,* Vol. XXXIX, Feb. 1950, pp. 104–5. The most searching study of English verb phrases to date is The English Verb Auxiliaries, by W. Freeman Twaddell; Providence, R.I., 1960.]

3: THE PRONOUN

The following paradigm shows the usual inflections of the personal pronoun in the American vulgate: [3]

FIRST PERSON
Common Gender

		SINGULAR	PLURAL
Nominative		I	we
Possessive	*Conjoint*	my	our
	Absolute	mine	ours, ourn
Objective		me	us

SECOND PERSON
Common Gender

		SINGULAR	PLURAL
Nominative		you	yous, you-all, you, you-uns, mongst-ye
Possessive	*Conjoint*	your	your, you-all's, you-unses, mongst-ye's
	Absolute	yourn, yours	yourn, yours, you-all's, you-unses, mongst-ye's
Objective		you	you, yous, you-all, you-uns, mongst-ye

THIRD PERSON
Masculine Gender

		SINGULAR	PLURAL
Nominative		he	they
Possessive	*Conjoint*	his	their
	Absolute	his, hisn	theirs, theirn
Objective		him	them

Feminine Gender

		SINGULAR	PLURAL
Nominative		she	they
Possessive	*Conjoint*	her	their
	Absolute	hers, hern	theirs, theirn
Objective		her	them

---

[3] [This paradigm is based primarily on materials from the LA.]

Neuter Gender

Nominative		it	they
Possessive {	*Conjoint*	its	their
	Absolute	its	theirs, theirn
Objective		it	them

The only variations that these inflections show from Standard English are the frequent substitution of *n* for *s* as the distinguishing mark of the absolute form of the possessive, and the attempt to differentiate between the logical and the merely polite plurals in the second person. The use of *n* in place of *s* is not an American innovation. It is found in many of the dialects of England and is historically quite as sound as the use of *s*. In John Wycliffe's translation of the Bible (*c.* 1380) the first sentence of the Sermon on the Mount (Matthew v, 3) is made: "Blessed be the pore in spirit, for the kyngdam in hevenes is *heren*." Here *heren* represents, of course, not the modern *hers*, but *theirs*. In Old English the word was *heora*, and down to Chaucer's day a derivative of it, *here*, was still used in the possessive plural in London in place of the modern *their*, though *they* had already displaced *hīe* in the nominative.[4] But in John Purvey's revision of the Wycliffe Bible, made a few years later, *hern* actually occurs in II Kings VII, 6: "Restore thou to hire alle things that ben *hern*," and *hern* in this sense is traced by the OED to 1340. In Old English there had been no distinction between the conjoint and absolute forms of the possessive pronoun; the simple genitive sufficed for both uses. But with the decay of the language the surviving remnants began to be put to service somewhat recklessly, and there arose a genitive inflection of this genitive—a true double inflection. In the Northern dialects of English that inflection was made by simply adding *s*, the sign of the noun genitive. In the Southern dialects the old *n* declension was applied. Meanwhile, the original simple genitive also survived, and the literature of the Fourteenth Century shows the three forms flourishing side by side: *youre*, *youres* and *youren*. All of them are in Chaucer. *Ouren* is recorded from *c.* 1380 and *hysen* from *c.* 1410, but—like many everyday words—they are almost certainly older. The grammarians of the Seventeenth Century declared war on all these possessives, and they have been denounced in the grammar books ever since, but they survive in the popular speech. [In America they are commonest in Appalachia and other rural parts of the South and South Midland; in England, in the central Midlands.] Joseph Wright, in his "English Dialect Grammar," gives some curious double forms, analogous to *hisn*, *e.g.*, *hers'n* in Cheshire and

---

[4] Northern texts for *c.* 1300, *e.g.*, the Cursor Mundi, show *they*, *their* and *them*, while London texts for the same period have only *hīe* and its congeners.

mines in Yorkshire. David Humphreys, in 1815, and Adiel Sherwood, in 1827, listed *hern* and *hisn* as Americanisms, probably because they had no acquaintance with British dialects. Curme indicates that the somewhat analogous *thisn*, *thatn*, *thesen* and *thosen* are now mainly American, but shows that *whosen* occurs "in the south of England and in the Midlands." [5] Some interesting analogous specimens are:

> Whatever is *ourn* ain't *theirn*.
> I like *thisn* bettern *thatn*.
> Let him and her say what is *hisn* and *hern*.
> Everyone should have what is *theirn*.

The last of these reveals a defect in English that often afflicts writers and speakers on much higher levels, to wit, the lack of singular pronouns of common gender, so that the pronoun does not necessarily agree in number with its antecedent. When on September 17, 1918, Woodrow Wilson delivered a speech at a Red Cross potlatch in New York, he permitted himself to say "No man or woman can hesitate to give what *they have*," but when the time came to edit it for his "Selected Literary and Political Papers and Addresses" he changed it to "what *he or she has*." Mrs. Eleanor Roosevelt fell into the same trap in 1941, when she wrote in "My Day": "Someone told me last night that *they* . . ." Two examples occur in a single paragraph of an article by Associate Justice George B. Ethridge, of the Supreme Court of Mississippi: "We should keep it possible for anyone to correct *their* errors" and "No person can be happy in life if *they* . . ." [6] In the lower reaches of the language the plural is used with complete innocence, and such forms as "Everybody knows *their* way," "Somebody has gotten *theirs*," "Nobody could help *themselves*," "When a person has a corn *they* go to a chiropodist" [7] and "A person ought never take what ain't *theirn*" are common. Since 1858, when Charles Crozat Converse, the composer (1832–1918), tried to launch *thon* for *he or she* (and apparently also for *him or her*) and *thon's* for *his or her*, various ingenious persons have sought to fill this gap in English, but so far without success, even among spelling reformers; nor has there been any enthusiasm for the suggestion that English adopt the French indefinite pronoun *on*, which is identical in singular and plural. [8]

[5] A Grammar of the English Language; Vol. III: Syntax; Boston, 1931, p. 528.

[6] *Congressional Record*, Feb. 27, 1935, p. 47. [See also *Person . . . Their*, by Margaret M. Bryant, *CE*, Vol. XI, Mar. 1950, pp. 345–6.]

[7] A patient's letter in *Jour. AMA*, Mar. 25, 1939. [*The Hyde Park Herald* (Chicago) commented on Sept. 12, 1962: "But this treatment is no way to talk anyone into rehabilitating *their* property."]

[8] French *On*—English *One*, by George L. Trager, *Romanic Review*, 1931, pp. 311–17.

This *on*, in the Fifteenth Century, seems to have fostered the English pronoun *one* [to replace the Old English *man*, which had become indistinguishable from the common noun], but *one* continues to have so foreign and affected a smack that the plain people never use it, and even the high-toned seldom use it consistently, at least in this country. In England one occasionally encounters a sentence through which *ones* run like a string of pearls, but in the United States the second and succeeding ones are commonly changed to *he* or *his*. So long ago as 1921, when Harding used the *one-he* combination in his Inaugural Address, my shot in *The Nation* drew a barrage in its defense. It had previously appeared in a serious treatise on the national letters by a former editor of *The Atlantic Monthly*, edited by a posse of Yale professors and published by the University Press.[9]

The addition of *s* to *you* in the nominative and objective of the second-person plural exhibits no more than an effort to give clarity to the logical difference between the pure plural and the merely polite plural. Another device to the same end is the familiar dual, *you-two*, which also appears in the first and third persons, as in *we-two*, *us-two* and *them-two*. Others are the Southern *you-all* or *y'all*, the South Midland *you-uns* and the Delmarva *mongst-ye*, all of which simply mean *you* jointly as opposed to the *you* that means *thou*.[1] The substitution of the plural *you* for the singular *thou* began in England in the Thirteenth Century, and at the same time analogous substitutions occurred in the other Western European languages. In these languages the true singular survives alongside the debased plural, but English has dropped it, save for poetical and liturgical uses and in a few dialects. It had passed out of ordinary polite speech by Elizabeth I's day, and had acquired an air of the offensive, such as it has today, save between intimates or to children, in Germany. Thus at the trial of Sir Walter Raleigh in 1603, Sir Edward Coke, then Attorney General, displayed his animosity to Raleigh by addressing him as *thou*, and finally burst into the contemptuous "I *thou* thee, *thou* traitor!" And in "Twelfth Night" Sir Toby Belch urges Sir Andrew Aguecheek to provoke the disguised Viola to combat by *thouing* her.[2] In our own time, with *thou* passed out entirely, the confusion between *you* in the plural and *you* in the singular presents plain difficulties. The vulgate speaker sets up a distinction well

---

[9] The American Spirit in Literature, by Bliss Perry; New Haven, 1918, p. 117. [A defense of the indefinite *you*, which in speech often substitutes for *one*, entitled One Can Use an Indefinite *You* Occasionally, Can't You?, was published by Dora Jean Ashe in *CE*, Vol. XIV, Jan. 1953, pp. 216–19.]

[1] See Hans Kurath, A Word Geography of the Eastern United States; Ann Arbor, Mich., 1949, pp. 31, 40, 67; Figs. 30, 114.

[2] *Thou* was adopted by the Quakers, *c.* 1650, precisely because it had a connotation of humility. But *thee* soon replaced *thou* in their speech just as *you* had replaced the old nominative *ye* in standard English.

supported by logic and analogy: "I seen *yous*" is differentiated from "I seen *you*." And in the conjoint position "*yous* guys" is separated from "*you* liar."

The Southern *you-all* seems to be indigenous: there is no mention of it in Wright's "English Dialect Dictionary" or "English Dialect Grammar." What is more, it seems to be relatively recent. *You-all* struck a Northerner visiting Texas as "something fresh" so late as 1869, though he had apparently been in the South during the Civil War and was familiar with *you-uns*.[3] It was not listed by any of the early writers on Americanisms, and it is missing even from Bartlett's fourth and last edition of 1877. On the question of its origin there has never been any agreement. In 1907, C. Alphonso Smith, then head of the English Department at the University of North Carolina, sought to show, by quotations from Shakespeare and the King James Bible, that *you-all* went back in England to Elizabethan times,[4] but his quotations offered him very dubious support, for those that were metrical showed the accent falling on *all*, not on *you*.

Like any patriotic Southerner, Smith devoted a part of his paper to arguing that *you-all* is never used in the singular, and to that end he summoned Joel Chandler Harris and Thomas Nelson Page as witnesses. This is a cardinal article of faith in the South, and questioning it is almost as serious a *faux pas* as hinting that General Lee was an octoroon.[5] Nevertheless, it has been questioned with a considerable showing of evidence. Ninety-nine times out of a hundred, to be sure, *you-all* indicates a plural, implicit if not explicit, and thus means, when addressed to a single person, *you and your folks* or the like, but the hundredth time it is impossible to discover any such extension of meaning. In 1926, Miss Estelle Rees Morrison provoked an uproar by suggesting in *American Speech* that, when thus used in the singular, *you-all* was a pronoun of courtesy analogous to the German *Sie*, the Spanish *usted* and indeed the English *you* itself.[6] In May 1927, Lowry Axley, of Savannah, declared in the same journal that in an experience covering "all the States of the South," he had "never heard any person of any degree of education or station in life use the expression in addressing another as an individual." A correspondent signing himself G.B. and writing from New Orleans, offered Axley unqualified support,[7]

---

[3] South-western Slang, by Socrates Hyacinth, *Overland Monthly*, Aug. 1869, p. 131.

[4] *You All* as Used in the South, *Uncle Remus's Magazine*, July 1907.

[5] In Dixie Is Different, *Printers' Ink*, Sept. 28, 1945, D. C. Schnabel, of Shreveport, La., thus advised Northern advertisement writers: "And don't—don't—

don't have your copy character in the South saying *you-all* to one person (Hollywood please copy). It sounds as incongruous in the South as to say *they is*."

[6] *You All* and *We All*, *AS*, Vol. II, Dec. 1926, p. 133.

[7] *You-all*, *AS*, Vol. II, Aug. 1927, p. 476.

but Vance Randolph popped up with direct and unequivocal testimony that *you-all* was "used as singular in the Ozarks" and that he had "heard it daily for weeks at a time." [8]

This encouraged Miss Morrison, and in 1928 she pledged her word that she had heard it so used at Lynchburg, Va., and also in Missouri.[9] At the same time Miss Elsie Lomax offered indirect testimony to the use of *you-all* in the singular by showing that a plural form, *you-alls*, prevailed in Kentucky and Tennessee. Early in 1929 a witness from Kansas testified that he was "addressed as *you-all* twice in the singular in one day, at Lawrence," the seat of the state university.[1]

In the years following, various other depositions reporting *you-all* in the singular were printed in *American Speech*, but the Southerners stuck to their guns, and in 1944 they got sturdy support from Guy R. Vowles, a Northerner, who testified that, in nineteen years in the South, he had never heard *you-all* used in the singular. He added that he had often heard a second *all* added to *you-all*, as in "*Y'll all* well?," and cited support for it in the German "*Gehat es euch allen gut?*" [2] Oma Stanley says [3] that the white freemen of East Texas use *you-all* "only as a plural," express or understood, but that the blackamoors "may use it with singular meaning as a polite form." [The Linguistic Atlas finds the interrogative *who-all* fairly widespread in the South and adjacent territory. The interrogative *what-all* is even more widespread, and may be considered national.]

Vance Randolph, like many other observers in the Southern hill country, has noticed not only a second-person plural *you-uns* but also a first-person *we-uns*.[4] Other observers, as Wentworth notes, have reported *he-un*, *she-un*, *them-uns*, *this-un* and *that-un*. The use of *-un* is especially characteristic of Appalachian speech. The eastern slope of the mountains marks roughly the boundary between *you-uns* and *you-all*, and the Potomac River similarly marks off the territory of *you-all* from that of the Northern *yous*. But such boundaries are always very vague. In 1888, L. C. Catlett, of Gloucester Court-House, Va., protested in the *Century* [5] against the ascription of *we-uns* and *you-uns* to Tidewater Virginia speakers in some of the Civil War reminiscences then running in that magazine. He said: "I know all classes of people in Tidewater Virginia, the uneducated as well as the educated. I have never heard anyone say *we-uns* or *you-uns*." But

---

[8] The Grammar of the Ozark Dialect, *AS*, Vol. III, Oct. 1927, p. 5.

[9] *You-all* Again, *AS*, Vol. IV, Oct. 1928, pp. 54–5.

[1] More Testimony, *AS*, Vol. IV, Apr. 1929, p. 328.

[2] A Few Observations on Southern *You-all*, *AS*, Vol. XIX, Apr. 1944, pp. 146–7.

[3] The Speech of East Texas, pp. 98–9.

[4] The Grammar of the Ozark Dialect, *AS*, Vol. III, Oct. 1927, p. 6.

[5] Aug., pp. 477–8.

while this may have been true of Tidewater, it was certainly not true of the Virginia uplands, as a Pennsylvania soldier was soon testifying:

> At the surrender of General Lee's army . . . we were the last of the army to fall back to Petersburg, as our regiment . . . was detailed to act as provost-guard in Appomattox Court-House. As we were passing one of the houses on the outskirts of the town, a woman who was standing at the gate made use of the following expression: "It is no wonder *you-uns* whipped *we-uns*. I have been yer three days, and *you-uns* ain't all gone yet." [6]

Jespersen says that the pronouns in *-uns* are derived from Scottish dialect.[7] The DAE omits *we-uns*, but traces *you-uns* to 1810, when it was reported in Ohio by a lady traveler.[8] It was new to her, and "what it means," she said, "I don't know." With this solitary exception, neither *you-uns* nor *we-uns* was recorded by any observer of American speech before 1860.

"The pronoun of the second person singular" (to wit, *thou*), says Wright in "The English Dialect Grammar,"[9] "is in use in almost all the dialects of England to express familiarity or contempt, and also in times of strong emotion; it cannot be used to a superior without conveying the idea of impertinence. . . . In southern Scotland it has entirely disappeared from the spoken language and is only very occasionally heard in other parts of Scotland." In the United States it dropped out of use at a very early date, and no writer on American speech so much as mentions it. The more old-fashioned American Quakers still use the objective *thee* for the nominative *thou,* and the third-person singular verb with it, *e.g., Thee is* and *Is thee?* [The origin of this use of *thee* has been debated at length, but inconclusively.]

Of demonstrative pronouns, there are but two in Standard English, *this* and *that,* with their plural forms, *these* and *those.* To them vulgar American adds a third plural, *them,* which is also the personal pronoun of the third person, objective case.[1] In addition it has adopted certain adverbial pronouns, *this-here, these-here, that-there, those-there* and *them-there,* and set up inflections of the original demonstratives by analogy with *mine, hisn* and *yourn,* to wit, *thisn, thesen, thatn* and *thosen.* Some examples of everyday use:

---

[6] Notes on *We-uns* and *You-uns,* by George S. Scypes, *Century,* Oct. 1888, p. 799.

[7] A Modern English Grammar; Heidelberg, 1922, Pt. II, Vol. I, p. 262.

[8] A Journey to Ohio in 1810, by Margaret V. (Dwight) Bell; not published until 1920.

[9] p. 272.

[1] It occurs, of course, in other dialects of English, but by no means in all.

Them are the kind I like.
Them men all work here.
Who is *this-here* Smith I hear about?
These-here are mine.
That-there medicine ain't no good.
Those-there wops has all took to the woods.
I wisht I had one of *them-there* Fords.
I like *thesen* better'n *thosen*.

The demonstratives of the *thisn* group seem to be composition forms of *this-one*, *that-one*, etc., just as *none* is a composition form of *no one*. But they have been reinforced by the absolutes of the *hisn* group, for in their relation to the original demonstratives they play the part of just such absolutes and are never used conjointly. Thus one says, in American, "I take *thisn*" or "*Thisn* is mine," but one never says "I take *thisn* hat" or "*Thisn* dog is mine." In this conjoint situation plain *this* is always used, and the same rule applies to *these*, *those* and *that*. *Them*, being a newcomer among the demonstratives, seldom has an inflection in the absolute. One says, in American, both "*Them* are mine" and "*Them* collars are mine."

This-here, *these-here*, *those-there*, *that-there* and *them-there* are plainly combinations of pronouns and adverbs, and their function is to support the distinction between proximity, as embodied in *this* and *these*, and remoteness, as embodied in *that*, *those* and *them*. "*This-here* coat is mine" simply means "This coat *here* or this *present* coat is mine." [2] But the adverb promises to coalesce with the pronoun so completely as to obliterate all sense of its distinct existence, even as a false noun or adjective. As commonly pronounced, *this-here* becomes a single word, somewhat like *thish-yur*, and *these-here* becomes *these-yur*, and *that-there* and *them-there* become *that-ere* and *them-ere*. So far, *those-there*, a somewhat more elegant form, is pronounced more distinctly, but it, too, may succumb to composition in time. The adverb will then be a mere inflectional particle, like *one* in the absolutes of the *thisn* group. Wright says in "The English Dialect Grammar" [3] that in some of the English dialects *-here* has begun to take on the significance of proximity, not only in space but also in time, and that *-there* similarly connotes the past as well as distance. The same process has occurred in America.

Witherspoon, in 1781, listed *this-here* and *that-there* among vulgarisms prevailing in both England and America, and noted that they were used "very freely . . . by some merchants, whom I could name, in the English Parliament, whose wealth and not merit raised them to that dignity." This

---

[2] See Margaret Schlauch, The Gift of Tongues; New York, 1945, p. 147.   [3] p. 277.

use, he added, exposed them "to abundance of ridicule." [4] The OED traces *this-here* to *c.* 1460, but offers no example of *these-here* before the Nineteenth Century. It traces *that-there* to 1742.

Them, as a personal pronoun in the absolute, of course, is commonly pronounced *em*, as in "I seen *em*," and sometimes its vowel is almost lost. This *em* is not really a debased form of *them*, but the offspring of *hem*, which survived as the regular plural of the third person in the objective case down to the beginning of the Fifteenth Century. As a demonstrative in American, *them* is clearly pronounced: always "*them* men" and "*Them* are the kind I like." *Them*, in this situation, may be a descendant of the Old English *thæm* (those). The substitution of *them* for *these* or *those*, as in "*Them* are the kind I like," was denounced as a barbarism of the South and West by Adiel Sherwood in 1821, but it has survived gloriously in all parts of the country.

The relative pronouns are declined in the vulgate as follows:

Nominative who	which	what	that
Possessive { whose / whosen	whose / whosen		
Objective who	which	what	that

Two things will be noted: first, the disappearance of *whom* as the objective form of *who;* second, the appearance of an inflected form of *whose* in the absolute, by analogy with *mine, hisn* and *hern*. Although the schoolma'am continues the heroic task of trying to teach the difference between *who* and *whom, whom* is fast vanishing from Standard American; [5] in the vulgar language it is virtually extinct. Not only is *who* used instead in situations where good usage has begun to tolerate it; it is also used in such constructions as "the man *who* I saw" and "them *who* I trust in." Noah Webster denounced *whom* as useless and argued that common sense was on the side of "*Who* did he marry?" Krapp explains this use of *who* as based on a "general feeling" that "the word which precedes the verb is the subject word, or at least the subject form." [6]

Even in England, says the OED, and on the highest levels, *whom* is "no longer current in natural colloquial speech." When it is used on those levels in the United States it is frequently used incorrectly, as in "*Whom*

---

[4] *The Druid*, No. VI, May 16.
[5] S. A. Leonard, in Current English Usage, says that "*Who* are you looking for?" is "established."

[6] Modern English; New York, 1910, p. 300.

did you think he was?"[7] *Whom* was rejected as "effeminate" by Steadman's Emory University students,[8] and got as many adverse votes as
divine, dear and *gracious* (exclamations). Indeed, only *sweet, lovely* and
darling beat it. The Linguistic Atlas of New England shows that its use
there is pretty well confined to the auras of Harvard and Yale, and that
even so it is rare. In the common speech *that* is often substituted for both
who and *whom*, as in "He's the man *that* I seen." Menner has shown [9] that
that has also largely displaced *whose*, sometimes with a genitive pronoun to
help, as in "He's the fellow *that* I took his hat," and that *that* itself is suppressed by periphrasis, as in "She's the girl I've been trying to think of her
name," and "He was a man I never trusted his word." [1]

"The relative *whose*," says Menner, "is a rare word in popular speech.
One may listen to conversations for weeks without hearing it." [2] But
sometimes *whose* is used in place of the forbidding *whom*, especially
when a genitive sense is apprehended, *e.g.*, "Bless those *whose* it's our
duty to pray for." In the absolute, *whosen* is sometimes used, as in "If
it ain't hisn, then *whosen* is it?," obviously under the influence of the other
absolutes in *-n*. There is an analogous form of *which*, to wit, *whichn*,
resting heavily on *which one*. Thus "*Whichn* do you like?" and "I didn't
say *whichn*" are plainly variations of "*Which one* do you like?" and "I
didn't say *which one*." *That*, as we have seen, has a like form, *thatn*, but
never, of course, in the relative situation. "I like *thatn*" is familiar, but "The
one *thatn* I like" is never heard. So with *what*. *What* is sometimes substituted for *that*, as in "Them's the kind *what* I like." Joined to *but* it can also
take the place of *that* in other situations, as in "I don't know *but what* . . ."

The substitution of *who* for *whom* in the objective case is typical of a
general movement toward breaking down all case distinctions among the
pronouns, where they make their last stand in English and its dialects.
This movement is not peculiar to vulgar American, nor is it of recent
beginning. So long ago as the Fifteenth Century the old clear distinction
between *ye*, nominative, and *you*, objective, disappeared, and today the
latter is used in both cases. Phonetic similarity was responsible for this
confusion.[3] In modern spoken English, indeed, *you* often has a sound far
more like that of *ye* than like that of *you*, as, for example, in "How do *y'*
do?," and in American its vowel takes the neutral form of the *e* in the

---

[7] Horrible examples from *Liberty,
Redbook, Common Sense, The Commonweal* and an Associated Press dispatch are assembled by Dwight L. Bolinger in Whoming, *Words*, Sept. 1941,
p. 70.

[8] Affected and Effeminate Words, *AS*,
Vol. XIII, Feb. 1938, pp. 13–18.

[9] On *Who* and *Whom*, *AS*, Vol. V,
Feb. 1930, pp. 25–33.

[1] [All of these forms are copiously recorded in the LA.]

[2] Troublesome Relatives, *AS*, Vol. VI,
June 1931.

[3] Henry Sweet, A New English Grammar; Oxford, 1900, Pt. I, p. 339.

definite article, and the word becomes a sort of shortened *yeh*. But whenever emphasis is laid upon it, *you* becomes quite distinct, even in American. In "I mean *you*," for example, there is never any chance of mistaking it for *ye*. In Shakespeare's time the other personal pronouns of the objective case threatened to follow *you* into the nominative, and there was a compensatory movement of the nominative pronouns toward the objective.[4] Marlowe used "Is it *him* you seek?," " 'Tis *her* I esteem" and "Nor *thee* nor *them* shall want"; Fletcher used " 'Tis *her* I admire"; Shakespeare himself used "That's *me*." Contrariwise, Webster used "What difference is between the duke and *I?*" and Greene used "Nor earth nor heaven shall part my love and *I*." Among the Restoration dramatists,[5] Etheredge used " 'Tis *them*," "It may be *him*," "Let you and *I*" and "Nor is it *me*"; Matthew Prior, in a famous couplet, achieved this:

> *For thou art a girl as much brighter than* her
> *As he was a poet sublimer than* me.

This free exchange, in fact, continued until the Eighteenth Century was well advanced; there are examples of it in Addison. Moreover, it survived, on the colloquial level, even the furious attack that was then made upon it by grammarians, and to this day *It's me* is in good usage, and most authorities of any sense, if they do not actually defend it, at least condone it. On the level of the vulgate, it is firmly entrenched. The schoolma'am continues to inveigh against it, but her admonitions go unheeded. Similarly, *"us* fellas" is so far established that *"we* fellas" from the mouth of a truck driver would seem almost an affectation. So, too, is "*Me* and *her* are friends." So, again, are "*Him* and his wife" and "I knowed it was *her*."

Perhaps the best way to get at the principles underlying these changes is to examine first, not the cases of their occurrence, but the cases of their non-occurrence. Let us begin with the transfer of the objective form to the nominative in the subject relation. "*Me* and *her* was both late" is obviously sound American. But one never hears "*Me* was late" or "*Her* was late" or "*Us* was late" or "*Him* was late" or "*Them* was late." Again, one hears "*Us* girls was there" but never "*Us* was there." Yet again, one hears "*Her* and John was married" but never "*Her* was married." The distinction is immediately plain. It exactly parallels that between *her* and *hern*, *our* and *ourn*, *their* and *theirn*: the tendency, as Sweet says, is "to merge the distinction of nominative and objective in that of conjoint and absolute."[6]

[4] See, for example, T. R. Lounsbury, History of the English Language; rev. ed.; New York, 1894, pp. 274–5.

[5] See Krapp, Modern English; New York, 1910, pp. 288–9.

[6] A New English Grammar, Pt. I, p. 341. [On Sept. 28, 1962, in an Associated Press story about the civil strife in Yemen, the Chicago *Sun-Times* said: "Prince Hassan, *who* some Yemen sources call the rightful successor to the throne . . ."]

In the subject relation, the usual nominative form occurs only when it is in immediate contact with its verb. If it be separated from its verb by a conjunction or any other part of speech, even including another pronoun, the objective form occurs. Thus "*Me* went home" would strike even the most ignorant shopgirl as "bad grammar," but she would use "*me* and my friend went" or "*me* and *him*" or "*me* and *them*" without the slightest hesitation. What is more, if the separation be effected by a conjunction and another pronoun, the other pronoun also changes to the objective form, even though its contact with the verb may be immediate. Thus one hears "*Me* and *her* was there" and "*Her* and *him* kissed." Still more, this second pronoun commonly undergoes the same inflection even when the first member of the group is not another pronoun, but a noun. Thus one hears "John and *her* was married." To this rule there is but one exception, and that is in the case of the first-person pronoun, especially in the singular. "*Him* and *me* are friends" is heard often, but "*Him* and *I* are friends" is also heard. *I* resists the rule, at least partially, and may even do so when separated from the verb by another pronoun, itself in the objective form, as in "*I* and *him* were there."

In the predicate relation the pronouns respond to a more complex regulation. "I seen *he*" or "He kissed *she*" would seem as ridiculous to an ignorant American as to the Archbishop of Canterbury, and his instinct for simplicity and regularity naturally tends to make him reduce all similar expressions, or what seem to him to be similar expressions, to coincidence with the more seemly "I seen *him*." Some such unconscious logic has brought "It is *me*" to conversational respectability, even among rather careful speakers of English.

Of the expressions that Steadman's students considered affected, first place went to *limb*, but *It is I* was a good second, and ran ahead of *expectorate*.[7] The Linguistic Atlas of New England [8] shows that *It is me* prevails overwhelmingly in that region, even within the Boston area. Most of the informants who reported *It is I* confessed that their use of it was the product of belaboring by the schoolma'am. But not many of those consulted recalled the horrors of education so clearly. "If somebody knocked at my door and called '*It's I*,'" a New York schoolteacher told a writer for *The New York Times* in 1946,[9] "I'd faint." In late years *It is me* has even got support from eminent statesmen. When, just before Roosevelt II's inauguration day in 1933, the first New Deal martyr, Anton J. Cermak, was shot in Florida, he turned to Roosevelt and said, "I'm glad it was *me* instead of you," and when, in March 1946, Winston Churchill made a recorded

---

[7] Affected and Effeminate Words, *AS*, Vol. XIII, Feb. 1938, pp. 13–18.
[8] Vol. III, Pt. II, Map 603.

[9] The Way You Say It, by Doris Greenberg, *The New York Times Magazine*, Apr. 7.

speech at New Haven, he introduced himself by saying, "This is *me*, Winston Churchill." When, in 1926, the twenty-six linguists consulted by Sterling A. Leonard decided by a vote of 23 to 3 that *It is me* is sound English, and when, during the same year, the College Entrance Examination Board decided that nascent freshmen were free to use it, there was an uproar in academic circles but no noticeable jubilation among the plain people, for they had been using this form for centuries, with the support of many accepted authorities, including even Noah Webster.

But in compensation for the use of the objective form in the nominative position there occurs in vulgar American a use of the nominative form in the objective position, as in "She gave it to mother and *I*," "She took all of *we* children" and "Anything she has is O.K. for *I* and Florrie," all borrowed from Lardner. Wyld shows that *you and I* was thus used by English writers of the Seventeenth Century,[1] and Alexander produces examples from Pepys's Diary, including *between him and I*.[2] Menner believes that the form came in because *you* and *I* were "often felt to be grammatically indivisible," and because *you* "had come to be used for both nominative and accusative."[3] He says:

> Pronoun or noun plus *I* after preposition and verb . . . is coming to be the natural usage at certain speech levels. Yet when the first personal pronoun *precedes* another pronoun or noun it is not normally in the objective form in careless speech. I heard the following from one man calling to another from a porch:
> A. They invited *me and Jim*.
> B. (not having heard) What?
> A. (louder) They invited *Jim and I* to their party.
> This is natural syntax among people who are neither at the lowest speech level, where *me* and *him* and *her* are common as nominatives, nor at the highest, where family tradition or academic training makes the standard literary forms prevail.

I have even encountered *he* following a preposition in the headline of a great moral newspaper.[4] Mark Twain, a very reliable (if sometimes unconscious) witness to American speechways, used *between you and I* regularly until William Dean Howells took him in hand.[5]

What lies at the bottom of this counter trend seems to be a feeling somewhat resembling that which causes the use of the objective form before

[1] Wyld, p. 332.
[2] The Language of Pepys's Diary, *Queen's Quarterly*, Vol. LIII, No. 1, 1946.
[3] Hypercorrect English, *AS*, Vol. XII, Oct. 1937, pp. 176–7.
[4] Silva Says Killing Prompted by Insults at *He* and Buddy, Los Angeles *Examiner*, June 25, 1925, p. 2.
[5] For example, in a letter from New York to the *Alta Californian* (San Francisco), May 18, 1867.

the verb, but exactly contrary in its effects. That is, the nominative form is used when the pronoun is separated from its governing verb, whether by a noun, a noun phrase or another pronoun, as in "She gave it to mother and *I*," "She took all of *we* children" and "He paid her and *I*," respectively. But here one observes variations in both directions—that is, toward using the correct objective when the pronoun is detached from the verb, and toward using the nominative even when it directly follows the verb. "She gave it to mother and *me*," "She took all of *us* children" and "He paid her and *me*" would probably sound quite as correct, to a Knight of Pythias, as the forms just given. And at the other end are such forms as "I want you to meet *he* and *I*." However, the use of the nominative is most common with the pronoun of the first person, and particularly with its singular. Perhaps the most important force in establishing *between you and I* and its congeners is the carry-over of the pedagogical war upon *It is me*,[6] just as the attack on *I seen him* has prospered *I have saw*. "As such expressions," Sweet says,[7] "are still denounced by the grammars, many people try to avoid them in speech as well as in writing. The result of this reaction is that the *me* in such constructions as 'between John and *me*' and 'He saw John and *me*' sounds vulgar and ungrammatical, and is consequently corrected into *I*." Here the schoolma'am, seeking to impose an inelastic and illogical grammar upon a living speech, succeeds only in corrupting it still more.

Following *than* and *as* the American uses the objective form of the pronoun, as in "He is taller than *me*" and "such as *her*," save only when a verb follows the pronoun. He also uses it following *like*, with the same limitations. Thus he says "Do it like *him*," but "Do it like *he* does" and "She looks like *she* was sick." The rule seems to be that these words, followed by a pronoun only, are not adverbs, conjunctive or otherwise, but prepositions, which have the same power to put the pronoun into an oblique case that other prepositions have. Just as "the taller of *we*" would sound absurd to all of us, so "taller than *he*," to the unschooled American, sounds absurd. This feeling has a good deal of respectable support. "As *her*" was used by Swift, "than *me*" by Burke and "than *whom*" by Milton. The brothers Fowler show that, in some cases, "than *him*" is grammatically correct and logically necessary. For example, compare "I love you more than *him*" and "I love you more than *he*." The first means "I love you more than (I love) *him*"; the second, "I love you more than *he* (loves you)." In the first *him* is not compared with *I*, which is nominative, but with *you*, which is objective, and so it is properly objective also. But the American avoids such hair-splitting distinctions. He says "I love you better than *him*," but "I love you better than *he* does."

---

[6] The Irregularities of English, *SPE Tract*, No. XLVIII, 1937, pp. 286–91.

[7] A New English Grammar, Pt. I, p. 341.

The reflexive forms in the American vulgate plainly show that the spirit of the language regards *self*, not as an adjective, which it is historically, but as a noun. This confusion goes back to Old English days; it originated when both the adjectives and the nouns were losing their old inflections. Such forms as *Petrussylf* (*Peter's self*), *Cristsylf* (*Christ's self*) and *icsylf* (*I-self*) then came into use, and along with them came combinations of *self* and the genitive, still surviving in vulgar American in *hisself* and *theirselves* (or *theirself*). Down to the Sixteenth Century these forms remained in perfectly good usage. "Each for *hisself*" was written by Sir Philip Sidney, and is to be found in the dramatists of the time. How the dative pronoun got itself fastened upon *self* in the plural and the masculine singular of the third person is one of the mysteries of language, but *himself* and *themselves* are in favor today. But the American, as usual, inclines against these illogical exceptions to the rule set by *myself*, to say "He done it *hisself*" and "They know *theirselves*." Also, the emphatic *own* is often inserted between the pronoun and the noun, as in "Let every man save their *own* self." In general the American vulgate makes extensive use of the reflexive. It is constantly thrown in for good measure, as in "I overeat *myself*," and it is as constantly used separately, as in "*self* and wife."

In demotic American the pedantry which preserves such forms as *someone's else* is always disregarded; *someone else's* is invariably used, and few teachers now try to change it. I have heard "*Who else's* wife was there?" and "If it ain't hisn, then it ain't nobody here *else's*." Finally, among the uneducated Southern Negroes is a substitution of the simple personal pronoun for the genitive; examples are "He roll *he* eyeballs"[8] and "*Who* dog is it?" But this substitution is not encountered in the general vulgate.

4: THE NOUN

The only inflections of the noun remaining in English are those for number and for the genitive, and so it is in these two regions that the few variations to be found in vulgar American occur. The rule that, in forming the plurals of compound nouns or noun phrases, the *-s* shall be attached to the principal noun is commonly disregarded, and it goes at the end. Thus, "I have two *sons-in-law*" is never heard among the plain people; one always hears "I have two *son-in-laws*." So with the genitive: "*the boy next door's* bike" and "That umbrella is the *young lady I go with's*."[9]

[8] Curme, Parts of Speech and Accidence, before cited, p. 47.

[9] The history of such forms is recounted in The English Group Genitive, by Otto Jespersen, printed in his Chapters on English; London, 1918. [The occasional obeisance to the rule almost always creates a shock, *e.g.*, a headline in the University of Chicago *Maroon*, July 20, 1962: "Convict Cairo *Sitters*-In." Most lay newspapers would simply describe such persons as *sit-ins*.]

False singulars, made by back formation from nouns in -*s*, are numerous, e.g., *Chinee, Portugee, Japanee, trapee, specie, summon, tactic* and *measle;* nor are they confined to the untutored. *Statistic* has appeared in a solemn pronunciamento by a Catholic dignitary,[1] in an uplifting editorial in a literary weekly,[2] in a paper in a leading scientific journal,[3] in a report of a committee of the American Society of Newspaper Editors[4] and in the annual report of the Librarian of Congress,[5] [to say nothing of innumerable advertisements in which "Don't Be a *Statistic*" attempts (usually in vain) to dissuade the fools behind the steering wheels from slaughtering themselves and others]. The OED, which marks it "rare," presents only a few examples, the first of which, dated 1796, comes from an American book. Several correspondents have heard *len* (from *lens*) and even encountered it in print. *Pant* (from *pants*) has been found in various regions,[6] [as has the analogous *trouser;* both belong to the argot of men's tailors and clothing salesmen]. I have myself had the felicity to discover *homo sapien* in the Baltimore *Sun*.[7] When the English *innings* became *inning* in the United States is uncertain. *Innings* was used by Henry Chadwick in his pioneer treatise on baseball in 1868,[8] but the singular form had occurred in 1856. The OED says that in Great Britain the term is "always in the plural form *innings*, whether in singular or plural sense." It is traced as a cricket term to 1746. Noah Webster noted in 1789[9] that the Americans of that time mistook *chaise* (borrowed from the French about 1700) for a plural, and so developed a singular form *shay*, which the DAE traces to 1717. It did not appear in England until later.

Many obviously plural forms are used in the singular without change, e.g., *stockyards, gas works, woods, grounds, stairs* and (golf) *links*. [The Linguistic Atlas has found *ways* even among the illuminati, as in *a little ways down the road* and *a long ways to go*.] Louise Pound adds *suds*, as in a thick *suds*. Conversely, she has recorded *corp*, from *corpse*, and *appendic*, from *appendix*.[1] On at least one occasion a Texas congressman

---

[1] Catholics and Birth Control, by Monsignor John A. Ryan, *American Mercury*, Apr. 1944, p. 505.

[2] The Library's Customers, by J. T. W(interich?), *Saturday Review of Literature*, Dec. 22, 1945, p. 15.

[3] Heredity of the Agglutinogens M and N of Landsteiner and Levine, by Alexander S. Wiener, *Human Biology*, May 1935, p. 231.

[4] *Editor and Publisher*, Dec. 14, 1946, p. 78, col. 3.

[5] For the year ended June 30, 1945, p. 37.

[6] E.g., *AS*, Vol. I, May 1926, p. 460:

"There is a Kalamazoo *Pant* Company at Kalamazoo, manufacturers of Kazoo trousers."

[7] Advertisement of the McKay Foundation, Dec. 27, 1945, p. 9: "Some say it's fifty or a hundred million years since the first *homo sapien* roamed the plains and hunted in the hills."

[8] The Game of Baseball: How to Learn It, How to Play It, and How to Teach It; New York, p. 41.

[9] Dissertations on the English Language, p. 118.

[1] Some Plural-Singular Forms, *DN*, Vol. IV, Pt. I, 1913, pp. 48–50.

referred to a fellow member of the House as a "Knights of Columbus," [2] a usage not uncommon among the Catholic proletariat. *Intelligentsia*, in the singular, goes beyond the bounds of the vulgate.[3] *Incidence* is commonly misused for *incident*, as in "He told an *incidence*." Here *incidence* (or *incident*) seems to be regarded as a synonym, not for *happening*, but for *story*.

This confusion between singular and plural extends to many words ending in *-s*, *-ist*, *-ish*, *-ex* and even *-age*. John Gerard, writing in the latter part of the Sixteenth Century,[4] said "*radish* are eaten raw," and Cotton Mather, in his Diary for 1711, wrote "a number of people of both *sex*." The surname of Tom *Collins*, inventor of the drink of the same name, was converted into a plural in a rum advertisement in a liquor trade paper in 1944.[5] *Baptist*, pronounced *baptizz*, is not only in almost universal use as a plural among the folk of the "Are You Saved?" country; it also makes frequent appearances in print.[6] In the same region *cabbage* is a plural, as are *sausage* and *tourist*.[7] Will Rogers, a master of the common speech, made one out of *business*.[8]

Singulars, valid or false, are so far unrecorded for *spectacles*, *clothes*, *athletics*, *series* or *obsequies*, but wrestlers commonly speak of a *head* or *body scissor*. *Hoe* from *hose* is reported from the Ozarks;[9] *calv* from *calves* and *hoov* from *hooves* from Nebraska.[1] *Aborigine* from *aborigines*, described by the OED as "etymologically as indefensible as *serie* or *indice*," is traced in American use to 1858, though M. M. Mathews expresses doubt that it is an Americanism.[2] A. Smythe Palmer's "Folk Etymology"[3] points out that *Bible*, from the Latin *biblia*, is really a plural form, and that such forms as *the Book*, *the Good Book* and *the Book of Books* are incorrect. Palmer also reminds genealogists that the surname *Janeway* is from *Genoese* and used to be *Janeways* or *Januayes*, and that its present singular form is as questionable as *Chinee* or *Portugee*. Every high-school boy should be

---

[2] Mr. Blanton, *Congressional Record*, Apr. 3, 1935, p. 5103.

[3] Her World, by Lucile, San Francisco *News*, Apr. 1, 1924. [Louise Pound comments on *insignia* as singular and plural in *AS*, Vol. XXXI, May 1956, pp. 156–7.]

[4] The Herball, or General Historie of Plants; London, 1597. Quoted in *Encore*, Oct. 1943, p. 492.

[5] *Beverage Retailer Weekly*, Aug. 28, 1944, p. 9: "Thousands of Marimba *Collins* are being served and enjoyed every single day."

[6] Livermore (Ky.) *Times*, July 30, 1937, p. 1: "*Baptist* Hold Association." I am indebted here to Roger C. Hackett.

[7] *AS*, Vol. II, Jan. 1927, p. 217.

[8] Letters of a Self-Made Diplomat to His President; New York, 1926. Quoted in *Encore*, Apr. 1944, p. 395.

[9] More Words from the Ozarks, by Vance Randolph, *DN*, Vol. V, Pt. X, 1927, p. 425.

[1] Folk-Etymological Singulars, by Wilbur Gaffney, *AS*, Vol. III, Dec. 1927, p. 130.

[2] The New Element in American English, *AS*, Vol. X, Apr. 1945, p. 106. [W. S. Ramson reports it in Australian usage by 1850.]

[3] London, 1882, pp. 592–604.

aware that *pea* is a false singular from *pease*, but Palmer is on less familiar ground when he points out that the original form of *potato*, from the Haitian *batatas*, was *potatus*, *potados* or *potatoes* in both numbers, and that *sherry* is a false singular from *sherries* or *seres* (*Xeres* or *Jerez*, a town in Spain).

The disregard of number often appears when the noun is used as object. Lardner's "Some of the men has brung their *wife* along" is matched, in a popular magazine, by "Those book ethnologists . . . can't see what is before their *nose*." The common indicators of quantity often omit the plural sign in the vulgate. Especially when preceded by a numeral, such words as *mile, bushel, dozen, pound, pair, foot* and *year* frequently retain their singular form, [though the strength of the tendency varies from region to region and, within a given region, from word to word. Thus *two pound* is common in the South but rare in the areas of Yankee settlement, while *forty bushel* has the converse distribution.[4]]

Wentworth lists many double plurals in the common speech, especially in the South, *e.g.*, *oxens, womens, dices, currantses, lices, folkses, sheeps, childrens, geeses, hogses* and *jeanses*. He also turns up two triple plurals, *feetses* and *menses* (*mens*). Wright's "English Dialect Grammar" shows that such forms are very common in the English dialects, and that some of them preserve the old *-en* ending, *e.g.*, *geesen* and *micen*. [In New Jersey and Delmarva, the older informants for the Linguistic Atlas give, as the plural of *house*, *houzen* or *houzens*. In addition to *oxens* (and *one oxen* as a singular) the Atlas has turned up *oxes*, the unchanged plural *ox* and the subtraction plural *ock*.[5]]

5: THE ADJECTIVE

"In the dialects [of English]," says Wright, "the comparative suffix *-er* and the superlative *-est* are added to practically all adjectives, polysyllabic as well as monosyllabic. *More* and *most* are as a rule only used to supplement the regular comparisons, as *more beautifuller, more worst.*"[6] He adds *betterer, betterest, bestest, worser, worsest, morer* and *mostest*. Wyld, in his "History of Modern Colloquial English,"[7] recalls Shakespeare's *most unkindest cut of all*, and traces *badder, more better, more surer, more gladder, more larger, more greater, more stronger, more fresher, most best, most bitterest, most hardest* and *most nearest* to the Sixteenth and

---

[4] [The Plurals of Nouns of Measure in Spoken American English, by Raven I. McDavid, Jr., and Virginia McDavid, Fries Festschrift, ed. by A. H. Marckwardt; Ann Arbor, Mich., 1963.]

[5] [A report on these was given at the Dec. 1958 meeting of the Linguistic Society of America, New York.]
[6] EDG, p. 267.
[7] p. 326.

Seventeenth Centuries.[8] Jespersen notes that "the natural tendency in collo-quial speech is to use the superlative in speaking of two," and that "this is found very frequently in good authors." Russell Thomas assembles ex-amples from Malory, Pope, Boswell, Coleridge, Emerson, Melville and many others.[9]

In the American common speech, and even on higher levels, the com-parison of adjectives has thrown off linguistic prudery and returned to an Elizabethan abandon. The ascription of the military maxim "Git thar *fustest* with the *mostest* men" to the Confederate general Nathan Bedford Forrest (1821–77) is probably apocryphal, but *mostest* is in everyday use in his native wildwood. Adjectives not ordinarily subjected to the process are compared freely, *e.g.*, *onliest*, *fightinest*, *loviner*, *growed-uppest* and *tore-downdest*. All these are reported from the Ozarks by Randolph, and Wentworth and the Linguistic Atlas add other examples from other re-gions. On higher levels *disappearingest*, *getting-aroundest*, *most working-est*,[1] *he-est*, *thrillinger*, *superer*, *uniquer*, *uniquest* and *more ultra* have emanated from Hollywood and elsewhere. Charters reports *most prin-cipal*, and Randolph *Most Almighty God*.[2] I myself have heard *uniquer* and *more uniquer*, as in "I have never saw nothing *more uniquer*." I have also heard *more ultra*, *more worse*, *idealer*, *liver* (that is, more alive), *per-fectest* and *wellest*, as in "He was the *wellest* man you ever seen." [The preamble to the federal Constitution calls for "a *more perfect* union."] The fact that the comparative relates to two and the superlative to more than two is almost always forgotten by the average American. It is never "the *better* of the two," in the popular speech, but always "the *best* of the two." Contrariwise, however, "It ain't so *worse*" is in common use.

Adjectives are made much less rapidly in American than either sub-stantives or verbs. The only suffix that seems to be in general use for that purpose is -*y*, as in *tony*, *hefty*, *nutty*, *dinky*, *snappy*, etc.[3] The use of the adjectival prefix *super-* tends to be confined to the more sophisticated classes; the plain people seldom use it.[4]

E. C. Hills, in his study of the vocabulary of a two-year-old child, found that it contained but 23 descriptive adjectives, of which 6 were the names

---

[8] For the transition period immediately preceding, see Louise Pound's disserta-tion, The Comparison of Adjectives in English in the XV and the XVI Cen-tury; Heidelberg, 1901.
[9] The Use of the Superlative Degree for the Comparative, *EJ* (College Edi-tion), Vol. XXIV, Dec. 1935, pp. 821–9.
[1] *AS*, Vol. XII, Oct. 1937, p. 242.
[2] The Grammar of the Ozark Dialect,

AS, Vol. III, Oct. 1927, p. 8.
[3] See *Nifty*, *Hefty*, *Natty*, *Snappy*, by Klara H. Collitz, *AS*, Vol. III, Dec. 1927, and Observations on *Nifty*, *Hefty*, *Natty*, *Snappy*, by Henry J. Heck, *AS*, Vol. IV, Oct. 1928.
[4] See Vogue Affixes in Present-Day Word-Coinage, by Louise Pound, *DN*, Vol. V, Pt. I, 1918.

of colors, as against 59 verbs and 173 common nouns.[5] Moreover, most of the 23 minus 6 were adjectives of all work, such as *nasty, funny* and *nice.* Colloquial American uses the .same rubber stamps of speech. *Funny* connotes the whole range of the unusual; *hard* indicates every shade of difficulty; *nice* is everything satisfactory; *wonderful* is a superlative of almost limitless scope. The decay of *one* to *n*, as in *this'n*, is matched by a decay of *than* after comparatives. *Earlier than* is seldom if ever heard; composition reduces the two words to *earlier'n*. So with *better'n, faster'n, hotter'n, deader'n*, etc. Once I overheard the following dialogue: "I like a belt *more looser'n* this one is." "Well, then, why don't you *unloosen* it *more'n* you got it *unloosened?*"

Of late there has been a strong tendency, especially in the field of victualing, to omit the *-ed* ending from adjectives, following the example of *ice cream*, originally *iced cream.* Examples: *mash* potatoes, *hash*-brown potatoes, *whip* cream.[6] In Baltimore, in 1946, a sign advertised Frostie, "an *old-fashion* root-beer." It is seldom a *high-toned* man, but usually *high-tone.*[7]

6: THE ADVERB

All the adverbial endings in English, save *-ly*, have gradually fallen into decay; it is the only one used to form new adverbs, [except the revivified *-wise*, which is favored among the bright young writers of advertising copy]. At earlier stages of the language various other endings were used, and some of them survive in a few old words, though they are no longer employed in making new ones. The Old English endings were *-e* and *-lice.* The first was an *-e* ending to adjectives, whether ending in *-lic* or not. In Middle English the *-lice* changed to *-li* and *-ly.* Meanwhile, the *-e* ending, following the *-e* endings of the nouns, adjectives and verbs, ceased to be pronounced, and so it gradually fell away. Thus a good many adverbs came to be indistinguishable from their ancestral adjectives, *e.g., hard* in *to pull hard, loud* in *to speak loud* and *deep* in *to bury deep* (Old English *dēop-e*). Worse, not a few adverb forms became adjectives, *e.g., wide*, which was originally the Old English adjective *wid* (wide) with the ad-

---

[5] The Speech of a Child Two Years of Age, *DN*, Vol. IV, Pt. II, 1914.

[6] I am indebted here to Douglas Leechman, of the National Museum of Canada, Ottawa.

[7] The prevalence of incomplete comparatives in advertisements, *e.g.*, "a *better* department store" and "dresses for the *older* woman," is discussed in The Rise of the Incomplete Comparative, by Esther K. Sheldon, *AS*, Vol. XX, Oct. 1945, pp. 161–7. [Lynn G. Rumer, one of my students, commented wryly in a paper: "The value of *high tone* words has always been questionable to me."]

verbial ending *-e*, and *late*, which was originally the adjective *lǣt* (slow) with the same ending.[8]

The result of this movement toward identity in form was a confusion between the two classes of words, and from the time of Chaucer one finds innumerable instances of the use of the simple adjective as an adverb. "He will answer *trewe*" is in Sir Thomas More; "and *soft* unto himself he sayd" in Chaucer; "the singers sang *loud*" in the Authorized Version of the Bible (Nehemiah XII, 42); and "*indifferent* well" in Shakespeare. Even after the purists of the Eighteenth Century began their corrective work this confusion continued. Thus one finds "The people are *miserable* poor" in Hume; "How *unworthy* you treated mankind" in the *Spectator;* and "*wonderful* silly" in Joseph Butler. To this day the grammarians battle against the amalgamation, still without complete success. [They have been further handicapped by the example, if not the precept, of many public figures, especially in the entertainment world. When the rock-'n'-roll singer Elvis Presley, whose sub-equatorial gyrations won him the sobriquet "Elvis the Pelvis," achieved nation-wide notoriety in the 1950s with a ballad entitled "Love Me *Tender*," he must have been an incalculable influence toward the grammatical retardation of teen-agers of the Eisenhower Epoch.]

"In all the dialects [of English]," says Wright in his "English Dialect Grammar," [9] "it is common to use the adjective form for the adverbial, as in 'you might *easy* fall.'" This is certainly true of the American vulgate. *Sure* as adverb has become one of its chief hallmarks,[1] and *go slow*, often spelled *go slo*, has become official on road signs.[2] Both have been under fire, and the latter was denounced in *American Speech* in 1927,[3] but grammarians above the pedagogical level are in favor of it, and it is listed as soundly colloquial in accepted dictionaries. Mrs. Charles Archibald, in her unpublished study "The Doctrine of Correctness in English Usage in the Nineteenth Century," [4] shows that while adverbs shorn of the terminal *-ly* were countenanced by Noah Webster, it was not until the latter half of the century that the common run of grammarians made the discovery that

---

[8] [Conversely, some of the new adverbs in *-wise* are employed adjectivally, as in "*pairwise* constructions," which appears in Language Change and Linguistic Reconstruction, by Henry M. Hoenigswald; Chicago, 1960.]

[9] p. 299.

[1] Milton wrote "God *sure* esteems the growth and completing of one virtuous person," in the Areopagitica, 1644, but the form has always been rare in England, save as a conscious loan from American.

[2] *Slow* was thus used by Shakespeare, Byron and Thackeray. The OED traces it to *c.* 1500.

[3] Road Signs, by Ottilie Amend, Vol. II, Jan., pp. 191–2.

[4] A University of Wisconsin dissertation, quoted here by Mrs. Archibald's permission.

many of them were etymologically sound. One of the first to see the light was the Rev. Henry Alford, dean of Canterbury, who is chiefly remembered for his violent denunciation of Americans and the American language. Alford noted that most adjectives capable of use as adverbs "seem to be of one syllable," but so long as they qualified in that respect he had nothing against them, and cited *soft, sweet, plain, bright* and *wrong* with approbation.

In Lardner one finds "She drove *careless*," "She was dressed *neat*," "She was *awful* ugly" and "He loved her something *fierce*." On the level of the vulgate there is incapacity to distinguish any useful difference between adverb and adjective, and beneath it, perhaps, lies the similar incapacity to distinguish between the grammatical effect and the relations of the common verb of being and those of any other verb. If "It *is* bad" is correct, then why should "It *leaks* bad" be incorrect? It is just this disdain of philosophical reasons that is at the bottom of most of the phenomena visible in vulgar American, as in other languages during periods of inflectional decay. During the highly inflected stage of a language the parts of speech are sharply distinct, but when inflections fall off, the categories tend to merge. The ádverb, being at best the stepchild of grammar—as the old Latin grammarians used to say, *Omnis pars orationis migrat in adverbium*— is one of the chief victims of this anarchy. In his "Diversions of Purley," John Horne Tooke called it "the common sink and repository of all heterogeneous and unknown corruptions."

The use of *real* instead of *really* has been defended persuasively by Robert G. Pooley,[5] who says that its position "is considerably higher than that of *sure*," and that "it is constantly heard in the professional and social conversation of cultured people." Ramsay and Emberson say in their "Mark Twain Lexicon"[6] that Mark showed "a marked fondness for the old suffixless or flat adverbs, which are sometimes unjustly stigmatized as ungrammatical uses of the adjective." They cite *awful, bad, cruel, fair, good, loud, near* (as in "I mighty *near* stepped on a snake"), *real, square, sure* and *tight*, but have to add the hypersophic *illy*, which occurs in "The Gilded Age" and may have been the contribution of Charles Dudley Warner.

Where an obvious logical or lexical distinction has grown up between an adverb and its primary adjective, the unschooled American is very careful to give it its terminal *-ly*. For example, he seldom confuses *hard* and *hardly, scarce* and *scarcely, real* and *really*. These words convey different ideas. *Hard* means unyielding; *hardly* means barely. *Scarce* means present only

---

[5] *Real* and *Sure* as Adverbs, *AS*, Vol. VII, Feb. 1933, pp. 60–2. See also *Real, Adverb?*, by Leah Dennis, *Words*, Sept. 1935, pp. 9–10. [In baseball, switch hitters speak of their relative prowess batting *lefty* and *righty*.]

[6] *University of Missouri Studies*, Vol. XIII, No. 1, Jan. 1, 1938.

in small numbers; *scarcely* is substantially synonymous with *hardly*. *Real* means genuine; *really* is an assurance of veracity. So again with *late* and *lately*. Thus, an American says "I don't know, *scarcely*," not "I don't know, *scarce*"; "He died *lately*," not "He died *late*." But in nearly all such cases syntax is the preservative, not inflection. These adverbs seem to keep their tails largely because they are often put before verbs, as in "I *hardly* (or *scarcely*) know" and "I *really* mean it." Many other adverbs that take that position habitually are saved as well, *e.g.*, *generally, usually, surely, certainly*. But when they follow verbs they often succumb, as in "I'll do it *sure*," and when they appear in front of adjectives they usually succumb, too, as in "It was *sure* hot" and "I will write *real* soon." Practically all the adverbs made of adjectives in *-y* lose the terminal *-ly* [if they ever had it] and thus become identical with their adjectives. *Mightily* is never used; it is always *mighty*, as in "He hit him *mighty* hard." So with *filthy, dirty, nasty, lowly, naughty* and their cognates. One hears "He acted *dirty*," "He spoke *nasty*," "The child behaved *naughty*" and so on. Here even Standard English has had to make concessions to euphony. *Cleanlily* is seldom used; *cleanly* takes its place. E. L. Thorndike confirms this apparent taboo against adverbs in *-lily*, *e.g.*, *oilily* and *lordlily*: "Holy, lonely, lordly and other *-ly* adjectives in my records number over 3,000 occurrences without a single adverb in *-ly* formed from them."[7] And the use of *illy, muchly* and *thusly* is restricted to the half-educated or to conscious humor. A correspondent reports that Socialists and Communists frequently sign their letters *Yours comradely*, and that he has encountered *Yours friendly* at the end of a business letter.

All forms of American and all save the most precise forms of written English have abandoned the old inflections of *here, there* and *where*, to wit, *hither* and *hence, thither* and *thence, whither* and *whence*. For *hither* (*to here*) and its parallels even the preposition has been abandoned. One says, not "I came *to here*," but simply "I came *here*." For *hence*, however, *from here* is still used, and so with *from there* and *from where*.

The common American tendency to add *s* to such adverbs as *toward*, a survival of the old adverbial genitive in *-s*, is carried to full length in the vulgar language. One constantly hears not only *somewheres* and *forwards* but even *noways* and *anyways, where'bouts* and *here'bouts*. Here we have one more example of the movement toward uniformity and simplicity. As for the dropping of the *a* of *about* in *here'bouts* and *where'bouts*, it is supported by the analogous dropping of the *al* in *almost*, when the word precedes *all, anyone* or *everybody*. One seldom hears "*Almost anyone* can do that"; the common form is "*most anyone*."[8]

---

[7] Derivation Ratios, *Lg.*, Vol. XIX, Jan.–Mar. 1943, pp. 27–37.
[8] See Grammar and Usage in Text-books on English, by Robert C. Pooley; Madison, Wis., 1933, p. 136.

Withouten, both adverb and preposition, is found in Appalachia and parts of the coastal South. The OED traces it as an adverb to *c.* 1000, but indicates that it is obsolete in England. As a preposition, traced to *c.* 1175, it was used by Gower, Byron and Kipling. *Outen,* without *with-,* prevails in the common speech in much of the United States. Incidentally, it occurs no less than eight times in Longfellow's translation of Dante's "Divina Commedia." [9]

7: THE DOUBLE NEGATIVE

"Not a single good reason except the tyranny of usage," says John S. Kenyon, "can be given for not using two or more negatives to strengthen negation. It is wholly in accord with linguistic principle, being in the best of use in many other languages, as formerly in English, and is extremely effective, as in Chaucer's famous four-negative sentence.[1] It is still in full vigor in folk speech, where its great value keeps it alive; and it frequently occurs in disguise in cultivated use." [2] Noah Webster was of the same opinion, and said so in his "Philosophical and Practical Grammar" of 1807:

> The learned, with a view of philosophical correctness, have rejected the use of two negatives for one negation; but the . . . change has not reached the great mass of the people and probably never will reach them; it being nearly impossible, in my opinion, ever to change a usage which enters into the language of every cottage, every hour and almost every moment.

Like most other examples of "bad grammar" encountered in American, the compound negative is of great antiquity and was once quite respectable. In Old English the negative of the verb was formed by prefixing a particle, *ne.* Thus, *singan* (*to sing*) became *ne singan* (*not to sing*). In case the verb began with a vowel the *ne* was combined with the verb; where a verb began with an *h* or a *w* followed by a vowel, the *h* or *w* of the verb and the *e* of *ne* were both dropped, as in *næfth* (*has not*) from *ne-hæfth* (*not-has*) and *nolde* (*would not*) from *ne-wolde.*[3] But inasmuch as Old English was a fully inflected language, the inflections for the negative did not stop with the verbs; the indefinite article, the indefinite pronoun and

---

[9] I am indebted here to Frederic R. Gunsky, of San Francisco. He reports that it appears in Cantos I, III and XXIV of the Inferno, VI, XI, XVIII and XXVIII of the Purgatorio and XXIV of the Paradiso.

[1] He *nevere* yet *no* vileynye *ne* sayde
In all his lyf unto *no* maner wight.

[2] Ignorance Builds a Language, *American Scholar,* Autumn 1938, p. 477.

[3] [See Samuel R. Levin, Negative Contraction: an Old and Middle English Dialect Criterion, *JEGP,* Vol. LVII, July 1958, pp. 492–501; An Anglo-Frisian Morphological Correspondence, *Orbis,* Vol. IX, May 1960, pp. 73–8.]

even some of the nouns were also inflected, and survivors of those forms appear to this day in such words as *none* and *nothing*. Still more, it came to be the practice to reinforce *ne*, before a vowel, with *nā* (*not*) or *naht* (*nothing*), which later weakened respectively to *no* and *not*. As a result, there were fearful and wonderful combinations of negatives, some of them fully matching the best efforts of Lardner's baseball players.[4] "*Nan ne* dorste *nan* thing ascian," translated literally, becomes "*No* one dares *not* ask *nothing*." "Thæt hūs *nā ne* fēoll" becomes "The house did *not* fall *not*." As for the Middle English "He *never* hadde *nothing*," it has too modern and familiar a ring to need translating at all. Chaucer used the double negative with the utmost freedom, as Kenyon has indicated.

By the time of Shakespeare this license was already much restricted, but a good many double negatives are nevertheless to be found in his plays, and he was particularly shaky in the use of *nor*. In "Richard III" one finds "I never was *nor never* will be"; in "Measure for Measure," "Harp not on that *nor* do *not* banish treason"; and in "Romeo and Juliet," "I will *not* budge for *no* man's pleasure." Most of these have been expunged by ticklish editors, but the double negative continues to flourish, not only in the vulgar speech but also on higher levels. It is perfectly allowable in the Romance languages, and now and then some anarchistic English grammarian boldly defends and even advocates it. A long time ago a writer in the *London Review*[5] argued that its abandonment had worked "great injury to strength of expression." Obviously, "I *won't* take *nothing*" is stronger than either "I *will* take *nothing*" or "I *won't* take *anything*." And equally without doubt there is a picturesque charm, if not really any extra vigor, in the vulgar American "He *ain't* only got *but* one leg" and "*Ain't nobody* there," the latter, of course, being understood to mean "There is no one there." "I *wouldn't* be surprised if it *didn't* rain" is almost standard American.

Examples of multiple negation swarm in the records of American folk speech. Vance Randolph says[6] that in the Ozarks "the double negative, as in 'I *never* done *nothin'*,' is the rule rather than the exception. Often," he goes on, "*nohow* is added for greater emphasis, and we have a triple negative. Even the quadruple form, 'I *ain't never* done *nothin' nohow*,' is not at all uncommon. Occasionally one hears the quintuple, 'I *ain't never* done *no* dirt of *no* kind to *nobody*.' Such sentences as 'I *don't* want *but* one' are

---

[4] Henry Sweet, A New English Grammar, Pt. I, pp. 437–8.

[5] Oct. 1, 1864.

[6] The Grammar of the Ozark Dialect, *AS*, Vol. III, Oct. 1927, p. 8. [One must, however, take such statements with caution; as Fries has repeatedly pointed out, in the American English Grammar and elsewhere, the multiple negative has never appeared, at any time in the history of English, a majority of times in the situations where negation occurs. But since it is strange to speakers of the standard language, they remember when it is present, not when it is absent.]

used and defended even by educated Ozarkers." The free and irrational use of *but*, in fact, is almost universal in American English, especially in such forms as "I *haven't* any doubt *but that* (or *but what*)." In the common speech *ain't* is often combined with *nobody* to give a multiple negative a final polish, as in "*Ain't nobody never* been there" and "*Ain't nobody never* told me *nothing* about it." *Hardly* and *scarcely* are also used for this cosmetic effect, as in "I *don't* know *nothin' scarcely*," "He *hardly hadn't never* saw her" and "It *don't hardly* amount to *nothin'*." Some miscellaneous specimens:

> They *didn't none* of them go.
>
> I *ain't* seen *nobody* roun' here at *no* time.
>
> Once a child gets burnt once it *won't never* stick its hand in *no* fire *no* more.
>
> *Nobody ain't never* said *nothin'* about sendin' *no* flowers to *nobody*.[7]
>
> I *never* set *no* hens, *nor nothing* of the kind.
>
> *Nobody's never* wanted me.
>
> You *can't* get *nowhere neither*.

The last three are from the Linguistic Atlas of New England,[8] which presents massive evidence of the prevalence of double and triple negatives in the area it covers. It distinguishes six main divisions, as follows:

1. The subject and the verb are negated, as in "*Nobody hadn't* ought to."
2. The verb and the predicate noun or adjective are negated, as in "That *ain't nothin'*."
3. The verb and the object are negated, as in "I *ain't* done *nothin'*."
4. The verb and the adverb are negated, as in "I *couldn't* get *nowheres* near him."
5. The object and the adverb are negated, as in "She *never* done *no* hard work."
6. Triple negation, as in "'*Tain't no* place for *nobody*."

[And a Georgia informant for the Atlas produced the five-barreled "There *ain't nobody never* makes *no* pound cake *no* more."] To which may be added the title of a once-popular song: "I *Ain't Never* Done *Nothing* to *Nobody No* Time." And the contribution by Will Rogers: "*Neither don't* put anybody to work." [9] And the inquiry of a storekeeper in Washington County, Va.: "There *wouldn't* be *nothing* I *couldn't* show you, you *don't*

---

[7] I am indebted for this to K. L. Rankin.

[8] Vol. III, Pt. II, Map 718.

[9] *The New York Times*, Aug. 20, 1934.

think?" Says Carl Zeisberg, of Glenside, Pa., who supplied the last: "I think I know the reason for these complex negatives: their genesis lies in an innate consideration for the customer's wishes, an excessive timidity."

The *not-neither* combination, as in "I did *not* do it, *neither*," was in good usage until the end of the Eighteenth Century, and examples are to be found in Steele, Richardson, Burke and Cowper,[1] but for the past century it has been receding into the common speech, wherein it is still very much alive all over the United States. So with the *nor-not* combination, as in Shakespeare's *"Nor* do *not* saw the air."[2]

8: OTHER SYNTACTICAL PECULIARITIES

"Language begins," says A. H. Sayce, "with sentences, not with single words."[3] At a time of rapid development, the tendency to sacrifice the integrity of words to the needs of the complete sentence is especially marked. One finds it clearly in vulgar American. Already we have examined various assimilation and composition forms: *that'n, use to, woulda, them-ere* and so on. Many others are observable. *Off'n* or *offa* comes from *off of* or *off from* and shows a preposition decaying to a mere particle. One constantly hears "I bought it *off'n* John." *Sorta, coupla, outa* and their like follow in the footsteps of *woulda. Would've* and *should've* are widely used, often written *would of* and *should of*. The neutral *a*-particle also appears in other situations, especially before *way*, as in *that-a-way, this-a-way* and *atta-boy*.[4] It most often represents *of* or *have*, but sometimes it represents *to*, as in *oughta* and *gonta* or *gonna*. Some philologists believe that the appearance of such particles indicates that English, having shed most of its old inflections, is now entering upon a new inflected stage. "Form," says Curme,[5] "is now playing a greater rôle than in early Modern English. The simplification of our English, our most precious heritage, was carried a little too far in older English, and it was later found necessary to add more forms, and in the present interesting period of development still more are being created." A study of liaison in spoken American—*e.g.*, the

---

[1] For the first three, see the OED under *neither*, A3. For Cowper see his letter to William Unwin, Feb. 24, 1782.

[2] Hamlet, Act III, *c*. 1601.

[3] [This is the basic principle of generative grammar, the newest technological ramification of linguistic analysis, expounded with great diligence (though with something less than complete clarity) by Zellig Harris, Noam Chomsky, Robert Lees and others; it was continuously on display at the Ninth International Congress of Linguists, Cambridge, Mass., Aug. 27-31, 1962.]

[4] [*Off'n, sorta, this-a-way* and their congeners have been investigated in detail by the LA; findings for the first two (collected by Virginia McDavid) were utilized in Mrs. Malmstrom's dissertation, A Study of the Validity of Textbook Statements about Certain Controversial Items in the Light of Evidence from the Linguistic Atlas, U. of Minnesota, 1958.]

[5] Parts of Speech and Accidence, before cited, p. v.

use of *farzino* for *as far as I know*, noted by David Humphreys in his glossary of 1815—should throw some light upon this process, but that study still lags.[6]

Many of the forms that the grammatical pedants still rail against—the split infinitive; the use of *between, either* and *neither* with more than two [high-octane purists would restrict them to situations involving only two, since, for example, *between* literally and etymologically means "by two"]; the use of *than* after *different;* the use of *like* for *as*—are so firmly established in American, even in more or less elegant usage, that attempts to put them down are plainly hopeless, and the younger grammarians argue that the war upon them should be abandoned. So long ago as 1872 the peppery Fitzedward Hall demonstrated that *different than* had been used by Addison, Steele, Defoe, Richardson, Miss Burney, Coleridge, De Quincey, Thackeray and Newman, yet many current textbooks of "correct" English continue to denounce it. In September 1922, the novelist Meredith Nicholson joined in this *jehad* in a letter to the New York *Herald:*

> Within a few years the abominable phrase *different than* has spread through the country like a pestilence. In my own Indiana, where the wells of English undefiled are jealously guarded, the infection has awakened general alarm.

To which the New York *Sun,* a few days later, replied sensibly:

> The excellent tribe of grammarians, the precisians and all others who strive to be correct and correctors, have as much power to prohibit a single word or phrase as a gray squirrel has to put out Orion with a flicker of its tail.

The error of all such unhappy viewers with alarm is in assuming that there is enough magic in pedagogy to teach "correct" English to the plain people. There is, in fact, far too little; even the fearsome abracadabra of Teachers College, Columbia, will never suffice for the purpose. The plain people will always make their own language, and the best that grammarians can do is to follow after it, haltingly, and not often with much insight. Their lives would be more comfortable if they ceased to repine over it, and instead gave it some hard study. It is very amusing, and not a little instructive.

The split infinitive is still under fire from teachers and copyreaders, but most laymen would concede that it is preferable to the ambiguity of "He

---

[6] [Principally because the necessary recording apparatus and the basic linguistic theory were both lacking until recently. The new collaboration between linguists and psychiatrists is already revealing not only what kinds of liaison occur, but under what circumstances. Public presentation, however, is far off.]

failed completely to understand it." [7] Similarly, the terminal preposition, found in respectable usage from King Alfred's day, is gaining toleration on both sides of the Atlantic. When some editorial flunky attempted to remove them from a message written by Winston Churchill, he is said to have scribbled indignantly: "This is the kind of nonsense up with which I will not put." [8] *Good and* as an adverb and such verb forms as *try and* have gradually worked their way into polite usage; [9] others, *e.g.*, *like for*, are accepted in limited regions but not generally; [1] yet others, *e.g.*, *gone and done it*, are still definitely and apparently hopelessly vulgar. But there is no telling what will happen in language, and it is perfectly possible that the last class will one day gain acceptance, just as *It is me*, *like* as a conjunction, *to loan* for *to lend*, the use of the plural pronoun referring to *anyone*, *everyone*, etc., *somebody else's*, *gotten* as a participle, the *one-he* combination, the split infinitive, the terminal preposition, and a hundred other forms, all of them once damned from hell to high water by grammarians, have gained acceptance. In such matters there is simply no telling. Once, exploring the upper Midwest, I mislaid my shaving brush in a hotel room, and called in a chambermaid of unknown nationality to help me hunt for it. When I found it hidden behind the Gideon Bible and let go with a cry of triumph, she asked politely, *"Did* you *got* it?" This, by prevailing rules, was "bad" English. But why? And how long will it continue "bad"? I'd not like to answer too positively, for *did* is undoubtedly a sound preterite and *got* is equally a sound perfect participle.

[7] See G. O. Curme, The Split Infinitive, *AS*, Vol. II, May 1927, pp. 341–2. [A particularly dramatic example of the too-conscious avoidance of the split infinitive appears in Oscar Handlin's review of the twentieth anniversary edition of Gunnar Myrdal's An American Dilemma, in *The New York Times Book Review*, Apr. 21, 1963, p. 26: "the mood of a nation which wished honestly better to comprehend its own strengths and weaknesses."]

[8] [See Margaret M. Bryant, The End Preposition, *CE*, Vol. VIII, Jan. 1947, pp. 204–5.]

[9] *Good and*, by Steven T. Byington, *AS*, Vol. XIX, Oct. 1944, p. 229.

[1] *Like for*, by A. R. Dunlap, *AS*, Vol. XX, Feb. 1945, pp. 18–19.

X

Proper Names in America

On October 20, 1919, Mr. Mondell, of Wyoming, then the majority
leader, arose in the House of Representatives and called the attention of
the House to the presence in the gallery of a detachment of 27 soldiers,
"popularly known by the appropriate title and designation of Americans
All." A few moments later Mr. Tilson, of Connecticut, had the names of
these soldiers spread upon the record for the day. Here they are:

Pedro Arez	Frank Kristopoulos
Sylvester Balchunas	Johannes Lenferink
Arezio Aurechio	Fidel Martin
Jules Boutin	Attilio Marzi
Oasge Christiansen	Gurt Mistrioty
Kusti Franti	Michael Myatowych
Odilian Gosselin	Francisco Pungi
Walter Hucko	Joseph Rossignol
Argele Intili	Ichae Semos
Henry Jurk	Joe Shestak
David King	George Strong
John Klok	Hendrik Svennigsen
Norman Kerman	Fritz Wold
Eugene Kristiansen	

This was no unusual group of Americans, though it was deliberately
assembled to convince Congress of the existence of a "melting pot that
really melts." [The Army Register for 1960 lists among the generals on
active duty *Lemnitzer, Eddleman, Colglazier, Ruffner, Meloy, Trudeau,
Shambora, de Shazo, Van Houten, McNamara, Medaris, Hansen, Costello,*

Michaelis, Zwicker, Scheue, Dreyfus and *Palladino;* the Air Force counters with *Twining, LeMay, Norstad, O'Donnell, Eckert, Wetzel, Asensio, Disosway, Bergquist, Landry, Ruestow, Suarez, Luehman, Haugen, Funk* and *Spicer;* the Navy, not to be outdone, offers *Nimitz, Burke, Ingersoll, Goldthwait, Anderson, Pirie, Ekstrom, Kivette, Rickover, Smedberg, Sano, Hartman, Snackenberg, Solomons, Rodee, Younger* and *Donaho* among the admirals and *Shoup, Burger, Krulak, Larson, Salmon, Tschirgi, Kier, Buze, Vanryzin, Hochmuth* and *Kline* among the Marine Corps generals. The roll of the Eighty-seventh Congress provides *Burdick, Chavez, Dirksen, Dworshak, Fong, Goldwater, Gruening, Hartke, Hickenlooper, Hruska, Javits, Kefauver, Lausche, Magnusson, Monroney, Muskie, Neuberger* and *Pastore* in the Senate, and *Addabbo, Addonizio, Arends, Auchincloss, Battin, Beerman, Blatnik, Brademas, Cederberg, Chenoweth, Cohelan, Conte, Daddario, Dague, Derounian, Derwinski, Dominick, Durno, Farbstein, Feighan, Finnegan, Fine, Frelinghuysen, Friedel, Garmatz, Gialmo, Hagen, Harsha, Hébert, Herlong, Hiesland, Hoever, Hoffman, Hosmer, Hotzman, Ikard, Inouye, Jensen, Joelson, Johansen, Karsten, Keogh, Kirwan, Kluczynski, Kornegay, Kowalski, Kyl, Lesinski, Libonati, Machrowicz, Maillard, Monagan, Montoya, Mueller, Mumma, Nelsen, Norblad, Nygaard, O'Hara, O'Konski, Olsen, Ostertag, Pfost, Philbin, Pillion, Pirnie, Pucinski, Quie, Rabaut, Reuss, Riehlman, Roadebush, Rodino, Rooney, Rostenkowski, St. Germain, Santangelo, Saund, Scheebeli, Schweiker, Schwengel, Shadeberg, Siler, Teague, Tollefson, Vanik, VanPelt, VanZandt, Wallhauser, Widnal, Zablocki* and *Zelenko* in the House. The National Institute of Arts and Letters displays *Bogan, Cheever, Ciardi, Deutsch, Durant, Flanner, Guérard, Lafarge, Niebuhr, O'Hara, Perelman* and *Shapiro* among the literati; *Burchfield, DeMarco, Hopper, Levi, Levine, MacIver, Mestrovic, Rapuano, Rattner, Shahn, Stuempfig* and *Wyeth* among the painters and sculptors; and *Blitzstein, Brant, Fine, Piston, Toch* and *Weiss* among the musicians. Finally, a glance through "Who's Who in America" for 1960–1, limited to the *A*'s, quickly unearths, among others, *Aagaard, Aandahl, Abagnole, Abeles, Abrahams, Abramovitz, Abruzzo, Abt, Achilles, Adamec, Adank, Adelman, Adikes, Adler, Adriance, Ageton, Agnelli, Ahl, Ahlgren, Ahmanson, Ahrens, Aird, Alber, Albrand, Aldrin, Aleshire, Alexopoulos, Alinsky, Allee, Allerup, Alseuer, Alter, Althauser, Aly, Amara, Amdar, Amerman, Amsterdam, Andst, Andolsek, Andreae, Andreth, Angstman, Ankeny, Anoff, Anschuetz, Anslinger, Anthis, Anzalone, Aram, Archambault, Arend, Arensberg, Arentzen, Argento, Armacost, Arn, Arnaud, Arnow, Arons, Arpaia, Arraj, Aschaffenburg, Askren, Atkieski, Atyev, Auer, Ault, Aurelius, Ausmos, Aveyard, Axelrod, Aydelott* and *Azpeitia*—all "notable living men and women of the United States," and all native-born. The foreign-born include *Abrahamsen, Agha, Al-*

banese, Alfange, Alonso, Amateis, Andreoli, Anikeef, Applbaum, Arias, Arnon, Artzybasheff, Auerbach-Levy, Avakian and *Avshalamov.*]

Almost any other list of Americans, covering the whole country, would show as large a proportion of non-British surnames. Indeed, every telephone directory offers evidence that the American people have ceased to be "predominantly of British stock." [1] A touch of foreignness still lingers about millions of them, even in the country of their birth. Just as the Scotch and the Welsh have invaded England, elbowing out the actual English to make room for themselves, so the Irish, the Germans, the Italians, the Scandinavians and the Jews of Eastern Europe, and in some areas, the French, the Slavs and the hybrid-Spaniards, have elbowed out the descendants of the first colonists. Wherever the old stock comes into conflict with one of these new stocks, it tends to succumb. The Irish, in the big cities of the East, attained to a political hegemony before the first native-born generation of them had grown up, [though it was not till 1961 that one of their number became President].[2] The Germans, following the limestone belt of the Allegheny foothills, pre-empted the best lands east of the mountains before the Republic was born. And in our own time we have seen the Swedes and Norwegians shouldering the natives from the wheat lands of the Northwest, and the Italians driving the decadent New Englanders from their farms, and the Jews gobbling New York, and the Slavs getting a firm foothold in the mining regions and disputing with the Irish for Chicago, and the French Canadians penetrating New Hampshire and Vermont, and the Japanese and Portuguese overrunning Hawaii. The birth rate among all these foreign stocks is still greater than among the older stock, and the net increase remains considerable.

Smith remains the predominant surname in the United States, followed by *Johnson, Brown, Williams, Miller, Jones, Davis, Anderson, Wilson* and *Taylor* in order. All the first fifty names save *Cohen* are of British origin, but many of them, notably *Smith, Johnson* and *Miller*, conceal large numbers of non-British names that have been changed. The German name *Müller*, for example, has almost vanished from American directories: the umlaut either has been dropped, making it *Muller*, or is represented by *ue*, making it *Mueller*, or there has been a bold leap to *Miller*. Most of the dominating names are English, but there are several that suggest Scottish origins, *e.g., Johnston,*[3] or Welsh, *e.g., Jones, Lewis* and *Owens,* and at

---

[1] London *Nation*, Mar. 12, 1912.
[2] The great Irish famine, which launched the chief emigration to America, extended from 1845 to 1847. The Know-Nothing movement, which was chiefly aimed at the Irish, extended from 1852 to 1860.
[3] *Johnston* was originally territorial—

John's ton. Ton, tun, toun, toune and *tone* meant a farm, manor, parish or other well-defined piece of land. The founder of the *Johnston(e)* clan gave his name to lands in Annandale, Dumfriesshire, *c.* 1174. The name is frequently confused with *Jonson* or *Johnson.*

least one, *Burke*, is Irish. All other efforts that have been made to analyze the national onomatology have led to closely similar results. Of 2,474,502 officers and men of the Navy in World War II, 21,476, or one in every 115, were named *Smith*, and following came 15,045 *Johnsons* and 11,035 *Joneses*.[4] In the Army there were 54,180 *Smiths*, 41,580 *Johnsons*, 29,960 *Browns*, 28,140 *Williamses*, 25,720 *Joneses* and 25,620 *Millers*.[5] On the roll of the Veterans' Administration, in 1946, there were 13,000 *John Smiths*, and 8,000 of them had no middle initial.[6] On June 1, 1929, the American Council of Learned Societies' Committee on Linguistic and National Stocks in the Population of the United States issued a report showing the estimated numbers of persons in each 100,000 of population bearing the 250 most prevalent surnames. Its list shows a number of plainly non-British names, *e.g.*, *Meyer*, *Schultz*, *Cohen* and some of the forms in *-son* and *-sen*. A great many German and Jewish *Schmidts* must be concealed among the *Smiths* (1,132 per 100,000), but there is still room for 71 *Schmidts* per 100,000, or more than the number of *Armstrongs*, *Bradleys*, *Dixons*, *Elliotts* or *Fergusons*. As for *Cohen*, with 57 per 100,000, it outranks *Carpenter*, *Chapman*, *Dixon*, *Duncan*, *Fuller*, *Harper*, *Hopkins*, *Knight* and *Spencer*, and crowds *Grant*, *Hawkins*, *Perkins*, *Warren* and *Weaver*.[7] *Smith*, of course, is an occupational name, but in modern times the number of smiths in the population is certainly not enough to account for its dominance among surnames. The explanation lies in the fact that in the days when it was first used the term signified any craftsman employing a hammer, and hence included wood- and stone- as well as metal-workers.[8] *Smith* probably used to be an even more common surname than it is today. In 1876 a writer in *Galaxy* [9] said that one out of every 70 New Yorkers then bore it, and that the ratio had been one in 83 in 1825, but today the Manhattan telephone directory shows not much beyond one in 300. But elsewhere about one American in 100 is still a *Smith*. Thus it remains the leading surname in the United States, as it is in England, Scotland and Wales.[1] It is surpassed by *Cohen* in New York and by *Johnson* in Chicago,

[4] Washington dispatch in the Baltimore *Evening Sun*, Mar. 8, 1944.

[5] The Linguist Anthology; New York, 1945, p. 51.

[6] Associated Press dispatch from Washington, Feb. 23, 1946. The resultant confusion gave a headache of high amperage to General Omar N. Bradley, the administrator, and he smote his bloomin' lyre on the subject in a speech to the American Veterans of World War II.

[7] For much information in this chapter I am indebted to Howard F. Barker, one of the Committee's research associates and the foremost authority on American surnames.

[8] See the OED, Vol. X, Pt. I, p. 278.

[9] The Inconvenience of Being Named Smith, Apr., pp. 498–504. This article was signed John Smith but *Galaxy*'s index credited it to Col. Nicholas Smith.

[1] For the British ranking of names, see the *World* Almanac for 1914, p. 668. The report of the Registrar-General for Scotland for 1937, Edinburgh, 1938, pp. lvi-lvii, shows that the ten leading names in Scotland in 1860 were *Smith*, *Mac-Donald*, *Brown*, *Wilson*, *Thomson*, *Robertson*, *Campbell*, *Stewart*, *Anderson* and *Johnston*, and that in 1935 *Smith*, *Mac-Donald* and *Brown* still held the first three places.

but in both cases it is a close runner-up, and nearly everywhere else it is first.

Among the names that follow it there are differing arrangements in different places. For the United States as a whole, the order is *Smith, Johnson, Brown, Williams, Miller, Jones, Davis, Anderson, Wilson, Taylor, Thomas, Moore, White, Martin, Thompson, Jackson, Harris* and *Lewis*, with *Cohen* in forty-first place and *Burke* in forty-fifth, but in New York City *Cohen* is in first place, followed by *Smith, Brown, Miller, Johnson, Schwartz, Williams, Levine, Friedman* and *Davis*.[2] In Chicago, with *Johnson* in first place, those that follow are *Smith, Anderson, Brown, Miller, Williams, Jones, Jackson* and *Nelson*. In Philadelphia the order is *Smith, Brown, Miller, Williams, Johnson, Jones, Cohen, Davis, Wilson* and *Robinson*. In Boston it is *Smith, Sullivan, Murphy, Johnson, Brown, White, McCarthy, O'Brien, Miller* and *Anderson*. In Cincinnati it is *Smith, Miller, Jones, Johnson, Williams, Brown, Davis, Wilson, Meyer* and *Moore*. In New Orleans it is *Smith, Williams, Johnson, Jones, Brown, Jackson, Davis, Miller, Martin* and *Thomas*, with *LeBlanc* eleventh, *Landry* twelfth and *Boudreau(x)* seventeenth.[3] In San Francisco the order is *Smith, Johnson, Lee, Williams, Brown, Wong, Jones, Anderson, Miller* and *Davis*. The Social Security returns show that other common surnames tend to clump in distinct regions. Thus *Adams, Bailey* and *Jenkins* are most numerous in Ohio, Kentucky and Michigan, and *Moore* in Pennsylvania, Delaware and New Jersey. In Grand Rapids, Mich., in a region of heavy Dutch settlement, the first five names are *Smith, Johnson, Miller, Brown* and *Anderson*, but the sixth is the Dutch *DeVries*, and the eleventh is *Van Dyke*. [In Holland, Mich., a stronghold of Dutch Calvinism, Henry A. Ploegstra reports that the ten most frequent surnames are *DeVries, Van Dyke, Johnson, Smith, Mulder, DeJonge, Brower, Timmer, Dykstra* and *Bos*. In Lafayette, La., in the Acadian-French region, *Smith* is but fourteenth, preceded by

---

[2] [Standings vary sharply from borough to borough. In Brooklyn, *Schwartz* is third, followed by *Miller, Brown, Levine, Johnson, Friedman, Goldstein* and *Goldberg*. In the Bronx, *Schwartz* is again third, followed by *Miller, Brown, Rodriguez, Levine, Friedman, Goldstein* and *Williams*, with *Rivera* eleventh. In Manhattan the order is *Smith, Brown, Williams, Johnson, Cohen, Miller, Jones, Harris, Schwartz* and *White*, with *Lee* eleventh. In Queens it is *Smith, Cohen, Miller, Brown, Johnson, Schwartz, Williams, Friedman, Murphy* and *Kelly*. Staten Island has *Smith, Johnson, Brown, Murphy, Miller, Sullivan, Kelly, Jones,*

Williams and *Wilson*. In suburban Westchester the ranking is *Smith, Miller, Johnson, Brown, Murphy, Martin, Williams, Wilson* and *Kelly*, with *Cohen* eleventh. These calculations are all based on 1960–1 telephone directories, and probably underestimate not only the Spanish surnames but the traditional American ones borne by Negroes.]

[3] [The allegation that *Levy* is the second most common is probably only a pun on *levee*. A discussion of this problem, by Samuel R. Levin and Raven I. McDavid, Jr., is scheduled to appear in *Names*, Vol. XI, Fall 1963.]

Broussard, Hébert, Guidry, LeBlanc, Landry, Mouton, Trahan, Breaux, Comeaux, Boudreaux, Domingue, Bernard and *Duhon,* and closely pressed by *Dugas, Martin* and *Richard.*] Throughout Minnesota *Johnson* is so common that bearing it is a political asset, and some years ago a member of the clan became a formidable candidate for office by simply announcing his name: though he offered no platform and made no campaign he polled 44,029 votes out of 151,686 cast.[4]

In 1928, Howard F. Barker estimated [5] that there were about 66,250,000 persons in the country using English and Welsh names; of the number, 41,550,000 had got them by ancient inheritance, 7,500,000 were Negroes whose forebears had assumed them and 17,200,000 were whites who had adopted them themselves or got them from fathers or grandfathers who had adopted them. At the same time, of the 18,000,000 persons bearing Irish names, 15,750,000 had got them by inheritance, 1,300,000 were Negroes and 950,000 were whites who had got them by adoption, and of the 8,800,000 bearing Scottish names, 6,600,000 had them by inheritance, 1,200,000 were Negroes and 1,000,000 had them by adoption. Nor is this all. Only about a third of the bearers of English surnames derive them from English blood in the male line, though the ancestors of large numbers acquired such names in Scotland, Wales or Ireland. Counting in variants, about 35,000 native surnames are in use in England, but the number is less in the United States, for there has been a tendency here since the earliest days, save only in New England, to abandon unusual forms and spellings for commoner and more familiar ones. Thus *Leigh* and *Lea* have been largely absorbed by *Lee, Davies* by *Davis* [6] and *Smyth* and *Smythe* by *Smith. Baker, Carter* and *Moore,* no doubt because they are short and easy to remember, are relatively more frequent in this country than in England, and have probably engulfed various similar names, *e.g., More, Mohr* and *Muir. Parker* and *Hall* hold their own among us, maybe for much the same reasons.[7] Barker notes several general tendencies that seem to be peculiar to the United States. One wars upon final *e,* so that *Browne* and

[4] Believe It or Not, by R. L. Ripley, Buffalo *Evening News,* Aug. 25, 1936. [In Minneapolis the order of the first seventeen surnames is *Johnson, Anderson, Nelson, Peterson, Olson, Larson, Smith, Erickson, Carlson, Swanson, Miller, Thompson, Hanson, Williams, Brown, Hansen* and *Jansen;* in St. Paul it is *Johnson, Anderson, Peterson, Nelson, Olson, Smith, Miller, Carlson, Larson, Brown, Erickson, Swanson, Hanson, Thompson, Schmidt, Williams* and *Hansen.*]

[5] How We Got Our Surnames, *AS,* Vol. IV, Oct. 1928, and How the American Changes His Name, *American Mercury,* Sept. 1935.

[6] In the English Who's Who, in 1937, there were 98 *Davieses* and but 31 *Davises;* in the American Who's Who there were 163 *Davises* and but 14 *Davieses.* I am indebted here to Roger Howson, of New York.

[7] Hall, Parker, and Company, Surnames, by Howard F. Barker, *AS,* Vol. I, Aug. 1926, pp. 596–607.

Greene become *Brown* and *Green*. Another lops off the *-son* ending, so that *Harris* runs far ahead of *Harrison*. A third adds final *s* to various short names, so that *Hay* becomes *Hayes*, *Brook* becomes *Brooks* and *Stephen* becomes *Stevens*. A fourth converts such difficult endings as *-borough*, *-holme* and *-thwaite* into simple forms, *e.g.*, *-bury*, *-om* (as in *Newsom* from *Newsholme*) and *-white*. Many Americans of Scottish ancestry have dropped the *Mac* from their names, and many Irish families that came in as *Mc's* or *O's* have similarly abandoned the prefixes. Barker says that *Mack* and *Gill*, which are much more common in the United States than in Great Britain, "serve as substitutes or contractions for a host of 'hard' Irish names," such as *McGillicuddy*, *McIlhatton* and *McGeogheghan*. The Welsh form seen in *ap Lloyd*, *i.e.*, *son of Lloyd*, is almost unknown here. But in such vestigial forms as *Bowen*, *Powell*, *Price* and *Upjohn*, from *ap Owen*, *ap Howell*, *ap Rhys* and *ap John*, it flourishes.[8]

Changes in surnames go on in all countries, and at all times. They are effected largely by transliteration or translation. Thus the name *Taaffe*, familiar in Austrian history, had an Irish prototype, probably *Taft*. General *Demikof*, one of the Russian commanders at the battle of Zorndorf, in 1758, was a Swede born *Themicoud*, and no doubt the founder of the house in Sweden was a Frenchman. Edvard *Grieg*, the Norwegian composer, had a Scotch grandfather named *Greig*.[9] In *Bonaparte* the Italian *buon(o)* became the French *bon*. Many familiar English surnames are Anglicized forms of Norman-French names, *e.g.*, *Sidney* from *St. Denis*, *Bridgewater* from *Burgh de Walter*, *Sinclair* from *St. Clair* and *Seymour* from *St. Maure*. A large number of so-called Irish names are similarly the products of rough-and-ready transliterations of Gaelic patronymics, *e.g.*, *Findlay* from *Fionnlagh*, *Dermott* from *Diarmuid* and *McLane* from *Mac Illeathiain*. In the United States, with a language of peculiar vowel sounds and even consonant sounds struggling against a foreign invasion unmatched for strength and variety, such changes have been far more numerous than across the ocean, and the legal rule of *idem sonans* is of much wider utility than anywhere else in the world. If it were not for that rule there would be endless difficulties for the *Wises* whose grandfathers were *Weisses*, and the *Leonards* born *Leonhards*, *Leonhardts* or *Lehnerts* and the *Manneys* who descend and inherit from *Le Maines*.

"What changes names most," says Barker, "is the abrasion of common speech." They tend almost inevitably to be assimilated with more familiar names of like, or nearly like, sound, and folk etymology often helps the

---

[8] It is dealt with in A History of Surnames of the British Isles, by C. L'Estrange Ewen; New York, 1931, pp. 206–8, 255.

[9] Edvard *Grieg*, by David M. Johansen; New York, 1938, p. 11.

process along. Thus the German *Todenackers* have become the Pennsylvania *Toothachers*, and the Jewish *Jonases* have joined the tribe of *Jones*, and the Dutch *Wittenachts* have become the Kentucky *Whitenecks*. Major George *Armistead*, who defended Fort McHenry in 1814, when Francis Scott Key wrote "The Star-Spangled Banner," was the descendant of an *Armstädt* who came to Virginia from Hesse-Darmstadt. John *Morton*, one of the signers of the Declaration of Independence, had a Finnish grandfather named *Marttinen*. General George A. *Custer*, the Indian fighter, was the great-grandson of one *Köster*, a Hessian soldier paroled after Burgoyne's surrender. General J. J. *Pershing* was the descendant of a German named Friedrich *Pfoersching*, who immigrated to Pennsylvania in 1749; the name was at first debased to *Pershin*, but in 1838 the final *g* was restored.[1] General W. S. *Rosecrans*, who lost the battle of Chickamauga, was a *Rosenkrantz*. General James *Longstreet* was the descendant of one Dirck Stuffels *Langestraet* who came to New Amsterdam in 1657. Herbert C. *Hoover* is the great-great-great-grandson of Andreas *Huber*, a German who settled in Lancaster County, Pa., in 1740. Edmund Burke *Fairfield*, once chancellor of the University of Nebraska, had a French forefather named *Beauchamp*. And the ancestors and kinsmen of Dwight D. *Eisenhower* have rendered the surname in various shapes.

Such changes have been almost innumerable in the United States; every work upon American genealogy is full of examples. The first foreign names to undergo the process were Dutch and French. Some of the wealthier and more resolute Dutch, dug in up the Hudson, resisted with great pertinacity, and in consequence a number of their names survive to this day, along with some of their money—*e.g.*, *Van Rensselaer*, *Stuyvesant*, *Ten Eyck* and *Schuyler*. But the lesser folk were helpless, and in a little while most of the *Kuipers* were *Coopers* and nearly all the *Haerlens* were *Harlands*. The carnage of names closely resembling English forms, *e.g.*, *Smid*, *Visscher*, *Jong* and *Prins*, must have been great indeed: it is still great among the later Dutch of Michigan.

Despite the grandiose social pretensions of some of their descendants, not many of the Dutch settlers of New Amsterdam were of gentle blood. The *Van* in the names of so many of them is not to be confused with the German *von*, which connotes the *Adelstand*.[2] In the United States some of the persons of Dutch descent have sought to enhance their status by writing the *Van* of their names as *van*, but the rest take it lightly, and many of them amalgamate it with other particles or with the stem or with both, *e.g.*,

[1] See The German Element in The United States, by A. B. Faust; New York, 1900, Vol. II, pp. 183–4.

[2] This is true, of course, only when it is written with a small *v*. The capitalized *Von* is no more significant than the Dutch *Van*.

Vanderbilt, Vandenberg, Vandergrift and *Vandervelde*. Many other families have dropped the *Van* altogether, notably the *Roosevelts*, who were originally *Van Roosevelts*.

Among the French in New England there were similar transmogrifications, and *Petit* changed to *Poteet, Guizot* to *Gossett, Gervaise* to *Jarvis, Bayle* to *Bailey* and *Fontaine* to *Fountain*. [In later years a *Beauchemin* has become *MacAdam*.[3]]

But it was the German immigration that provoked the first really wholesale slaughter. The Germans were represented in the colonies of John Smith in Virginia, of the Dutch in New York and of the Swedes on the Delaware, but the first whole shipload of them to arrive landed in 1683. After that they came in increasing numbers, chiefly to Pennsylvania, and by the middle of the Eighteenth Century they or their children made up a third of the population of the colony. But the Quakers and so-called Scotch-Irish had been ahead of them, and when their names were enrolled, as the laws of the time required, the enrolling officials made a dreadful mess of the business. Nearly all the newcomers spoke rustic dialects of German and many of them were illiterate, so the difficulty of enrolling their true surnames, in numerous cases, amounted to an impossibility. There were, for example, the frequent names in *bach*, including *Bach* alone. The German *ch* sound did not daunt the Celtic jobholders, for it existed in their own speech, but in that speech it was often spelled *gh*, as in *MacLaughlin, Dougherty* and *McCullough*, so it was turned into *gh* on the record, and there thus arose the innumerable *Baughs, Baughmans, Harbaughs, Ebaughs* (*Ebach* or *Ibach*) and the like.

At the start these names were probably pronounced more or less correctly, but before long they acquired spelling pronunciations, and at present the *baugh* in them is usually *baw*, though in some instances it stops at the halfway point of *bock*. In other names the *ch* was changed to *k* forthwith, so that *Bloch* became *Block, Hoch* became *Hoke* and *Koch* became *Cook* or *Coke*. In yet others it was changed to an *i* sound, so that *Albrecht* became *Albright*, or in spelling to *x*, so that *Trechsler* became *Trexler*. And in still others the guttural *g* was lost, so that *Hollweg* became *Holloway*. The umlaut met the same fate: *Grün* was changed to *Green, Sänger* to *Sanger* or *Singer, Glück* to *Gluck* or *Glick, Wärner* to *Warner, Löwe* to *Lowe, Brühl* to *Brill, Stäheli* to *Staley, Düring* to *Deering* and *Schnäbele* to *Snabely, Snavely* or *Snively*.[4] In many other cases there were changes in

---

[3] [The last was in the Department of Romance Languages of Brown University; for this information I am indebted to his former colleague and my close personal friend, William B. S. Smith. See also Further Mutations of French-Canadian Proper Names, by Robert E. Pike, *AS*, Vol. XXXI, May 1956, p. 153.]

[4] Pennsylvania German Pioneers: a Publication of the Original Lists of Ar-

spelling to preserve vowel sounds differently represented in German and English. Thus *Blum* was changed to *Bloom*, and *Reuss* to *Royce*. Among other changes, many a *Johannes Kuntz* of the ship lists became a *John Coons* in the interior, and many a *Pfeffer* a *Pepper*, and *Lang* (as the best compromise possible) *Long*. Other changes were *Bowers* for *Bauer*, *Rockefeller* for *Roggenfelder*,[5] *Swope* for *Schwab* and *Young* for *Jung*.

The American tendency to add *s* to short British names, as in the cases of *Hayes* and *Brooks*, extended to names originally German, and there are examples in *Ames* from *Oehm*, *Richards* from *Reichardt*, *Bowers* from *Bauer* and *Sowers* from *Sauer*. Sometimes the original German spellings are preserved, even when the pronunciation has changed. Thus a man always called *Smith* still writes his name *Schmidt*, and one called *Bryan* writes it *Broihahn*. Even in Pennsylvania, some members of a family have altered their names and others left them unchanged. Many of the *Schwarzes* are now *Swartzes* and others are *Blacks*.[6] In Maryland there are *Kaelbers* who have become *Calvert*,[7] but others remain *Kaelber*.

The foreign vowels are always under hard pressure. Thus the German *oe* disappears and *Loeb* is changed to *Lobe* or *Laib*, *Oehler* to *Ohler*, *Loeser* to *Leser*, *Schoen* to *Schon* or *Shane*. Similarly the umlauted *ü* disappears, as in the name of Whittier's Maud *Muller* and that of the banking firm *Kuhn*, Loeb and Company.[8] The *k* in German words beginning with *kn* tends to disappear; *Knoebel* is often pronounced *Noble*, [though a South Carolina branch of the family made it three syllables, *Kuh-nee'-b'l*]. In the same way the German *sch* shrinks to *s*; *Schneider* becomes *Snyder* and *Schluter* becomes *Sluter*. If a German or other foreigner in America clings to the original spelling of his name he must expect to hear it mispronounced. Frederick Henry *Koch* (1877–1944), professor of dramatic literature at the University of North Carolina and founder of the folk-play movement, was always called *Kosh*, rhyming with *bosh*. *Roth* quickly becomes *Rawth*; *Frémont*, losing both accent and the French *e*, becomes

---

rivals in the Port of Philadelphia from 1727 to 1808, edited by W. J. Hinke, 3 vols., Norristown, Pa., 1934. [See also Alfred Senn, Notes on Swiss Personal Names, *Names*, Vol. X, Sept. 1962, pp. 149–58, and Elmer L. Reed, The Amish System of Nomenclature, *Historical Review of Berks County*, Vol. XXVII, Winter 1961–2, pp. 21–5.]

[5] The researches of Stephen Kekulé von Stradonitz showed that the original American *Rockefeller* was a German *Roggenfelder* (rye-fielder) from the lower Rhine.

[6] Hanover (Pa.) *Sun*, Aug. 16, 1942:

"One hundred and four were present . . . when the annual *Swartz-Black* reunion was held."

[7] Death notice in the Baltimore *Sun*, Oct. 23, 1942.

[8] There was a wholesale change of German names in England during World War I. King George V led by changing the family name from *Wettin* to *Windsor* by proclamation on July 17, 1917. At the same time the *Tecks*, Queen Mary's family, changed their name to *Cambridge*, and the *Battenbergs* became *Mountbattens*.

Freemont; Blum begins to rhyme with *dumb; Mann* rhymes with *van;* the first syllable of *Werner* with *turn;* the first of *Wagner* with *nag. Berg* loses its German *e* sound and becomes identical with the *berg* of *iceberg.* In *König* the German vowel succumbs to a long *o,* and the hard *g* becomes *k;* the common pronunciation is *Cone-ik,* [though some Midwesterners prefer *Cane-ig*]. In *Anheuser* the *eu* changes to *ow* or *ei.* The final *e,* important in German, is nearly always silenced. *Dohme* rhymes with *foam; Kühne* becomes *Keen.* Any unusual German name is bound to be mispronounced and misspelled. Mr. F. C. *Fiechter,* Jr., a lawyer of Philadelphia, has amused himself by collecting such distortions of his surname, *e.g.,* as *Fletcher, Flechter, Feichter, Feighter, Frechter, Fichter, Fietcher* and *Fiescher.*[9] Even German names that have become well known, *e.g., Schurz, Mayer* and *Steinmetz,* are seldom pronounced correctly.

In addition to the transliterations there are constant translations of foreign proper names. A great many such translations are under everyday observation. *Pfund* becomes *Pound; Becker, Baker; Schumacher, Shoemaker; Weiss, White; Kurtz, Short; Weber, Weaver; Vogelgesang, Birdsong;* and so on. Partial translations are also encountered, *e.g., Studebaker* from *Studebecker,* and *Reindollar* from *Rheinthaler,* and radical shortenings, *e.g., Kirk* from *Kirkeslager,* and *Castle* (somewhat fantastically) from *Katzenellenbogen.* "Whenever William Penn could translate a German name into a corresponding English one," says an early chronicler,[1] "he did so in issuing patents for land in Pennsylvania; thus the respectable *Carpenter* family in Lancaster are the descendants of a *Zimmerman.*" But *Zimmerman* is still a more common name in Pennsylvania than *Carpenter.*

It would be possible to compile an enormous catalogue of Americans of mark who have borne names originally German. Some of these have already been mentioned. George *Westinghouse,* the inventor of the air brake, was the descendant of a Westphalian named *Wistinghausen.*[2] Owen *Wister's Ur-Grossvater* was a *Wüster.* The evangelist Billy *Sunday* was the son of a Union soldier originally named *Sonntag.* Buffalo Bill *Cody's* actual surname was *Kothe* or *Köthe.*[3] Dr. Frederick A. *Cook,* the Arctic explorer, was the son of a German *Koch.* The William *Rittenhouse* who was the first American papermaker and grandfather of the first American

[9] Private communication, Nov. 20, 1941.

[1] Milledulcia: A Thousand Pleasant Things from *Notes & Queries;* New York, 1857, p. 34. I am indebted here to Huntington Cairns.

[2] George *Westinghouse,* by Albert B. Faust, *American-German Review,* Aug. 1945, p. 6.

[3] Cousin of Buffalo Bill Dies Here at Age of 94, Baltimore *Sun,* Mar. 23, 1936. [For similar transmogrifications north of the border, see The Anglicization of German Family Names in Western Canada, by Robert Somerville Graham, *AS,* Vol. XXX, Dec. 1955, pp. 260–4.]

astronomer arrived in Pennsylvania by way of Holland as William *Ritting-huysen*, originally the German Wilhelm *Rittershausen*, [and Robert *Hiller*, of the German Department at the University of Nebraska, had a father with the *Adelstandisch* surname of *von Hochberg*].

Where the early Germans encountered forerunners who were not British, they often changed their names to accommodate non-English speechways, *e.g.*, French. On the so-called German Coast of Louisiana, settled in the Eighteenth Century, many of their surnames were thus Gallicized almost beyond recognition. *Buchwalter* became *Bouchevaldre*, *Wagensbach* became *Vacquensbac* and *Huber* became *Houbre, Houver* and *Uhre*.[4] The same process has been recorded in France itself, and also in Spain, Italy and the Slavic lands. The Germans have made the balance even by Germanizing many non-German names at home and also in their settlements in this country. To balance a German *Lesch* family which became *Lech, Laiche, Lesc, Leichert* and *Lecheux* in Louisiana, there was a French *Lecher* family in Pennsylvania which became *Lesher*, and a French *Lessecq* family which became *Lessig*.[5] An old tale tells of a Scotsman named *Ferguson* who, on settling among Germans in western New York, suffered the change of his name to *Feuerstein*, and then, on moving to an English-speaking settlement, had to submit to its translation into *Flint*. One of his grandsons, on immigrating to Louisiana, became *Pierre à Fusil*, and a son of this grandson, on returning to civilization, became Peter *Gun*.[6]

The same processes show themselves in the changes undergone by the names of the newer immigrants. The Hollanders in Michigan often have to submit to translations of their surnames. Thus *Hoogsteen* becomes *Highstone; Zwartefoote, Blackfoot; Koning, King; Nieuwhuis, Newhouse;* and *Christiaanse, Christians*.[7] Similarly the Greek *Triantafyllou* (signifying *rose*) is often turned into *Rose, Mylonas* becomes *Miller* and *Giannopoulos* (the descendant of *Giannis*, or *Ioannis*) becomes *Johnson*. The Greek surnames are often very long, and in American they have to be shortened. Thus, "*Pappadakis, Pappachristides* and *Pappadimitracoupoulos*," said Sotirios S. Lontos, editor of *Atlantis*, the Greek daily of New York, "become *Pappas* by taking a portion of the front part of the name, while *Panagiotopoulos, Constantinopoulos* and *Gerasimopoulos* change into

[4] The Settlement of the German Coast of Louisiana and the Creoles of German Descent, by J. Hanno Deiler, *German American Annals*, July and Aug. 1909, pp. 194–7.

[5] Pennsylvania English, by George W. Hibbitt, *AS*, Vol. XIV, Feb. 1939, p. 43.

[6] *Ladies' Repository* (Cincinnati), Nov. 1861, p. 691. Another version, recorded by Olaf Sölmund in Namen Wandern,

New York *Staats-Zeitung*, in 1940, makes the original name of the Scotsman *Freyerstone*.

[7] For these Dutch examples I am indebted to President John J. Hiemenga and Prof. Henry J. G. Van Andel, of Calvin College, Grand Rapids, Mich., to Prof. B. K. Kuiper, of the same city, and to Dr. Paul de Kruif.

Poulos by adopting only the tail end. So the *Pappases* and *Pouloses* have naturally become the *Smiths* and *Browns* of American Greeks, although these names are fairly uncommon in their native land." [8] But *Pappas* itself is sometimes sacrificed. Thus *Pappageorgiou* is shaved down to *Georgiou*, and *Pappapolychronopoulos* becomes *Chronos*, with *Poulos* following *Pappas* into the discard.[9] Other Greek names are changed to bring them into harmony with American analogues. Thus *Christides* becomes *Christie*, *Nikolaou* becomes *Nicholas* and *Georgiou* becomes *George*. Occasionally the process is reversed. In 1941 a Chicago Greek who had been known as *Harris* petitioned one of the local courts to let him go back to *Haralampopoulos*. He kept a store, he explained, in a Greek neighborhood, and *Haralampopoulos* was easier to most of his customers than *Harris*.[1] But it is far more common for a Greek to try to get rid of his long name and substitute something shorter.

The Slavic immigrants to America brought with them names even more difficult to American tongues than those of the Greeks, and they had to make changes following all the usual patterns. Among the Czechs these include more or less crude transliterations, *e.g.*, of *Zděný* into *Stenny*, *Hřebec* into *Hurbick*, and *Červiček* into *Servisk*; translations, *e.g.*, of *Kovář* into *Smith*, *Mlynář* into *Miller* and *Zelený* into *Green*; and efforts to bring untranslatable names into harmony with English names of similar sound, *e.g.*, *Máca* becomes *Macy*, *Mošnička* becomes *Mason* and *Vališ* becomes *Wallace*. Some of the Czech immigrants, put down as Austrians in the earlier immigration returns, settled among Germans, and in consequence not a few of them adopted German names, often by translation. Thus *Krejčí* (tailor) became *Schneider*, *Dvořák* (courtier) became *Hoffman* and *Švec* (shoemaker) became *Schumacher*.[2] Some of the Czechs also changed their names to Irish forms. Thus *Prujín* became *Brian* and then *O'Brien*, and *Otřáska* became *O'Tracy*. Even when a Czech clings to the original form of his name, he must bear with its mutilation at the hands of his neighbors. Such forms as *Hořčička*, *Trpaslík* and *Uprchl*, says Monsignor J. B. Dudek, the leading authority on the Czech language in America, "are, while they last, the despair of rural editors and printers, of postmasters, small-town bankers, county clerks, justices of the peace and other officials." The Czech accents disappear almost at once, and the values of the Czech letters are quickly changed.[3]

Among the Poles, as among the Czechs, the older immigrants regard

[8] American Greek, *AS*, Vol. I, Mar. 1926, p. 308.
[9] I am indebted here to T. D. Curculakis, of Athens.
[1] United Press dispatch from Chicago, July 8, 1941.
[2] A similar translation of Slavic names has probably gone on in the German areas of Pennsylvania, though I can find no record of it.
[3] Monsignor J. B. Dudek, Czech Surnames in America, *American Mercury*, Nov. 1925.

abandonment of the native surnames with aversion. Many of them resist stoutly the changes forced upon them by the fact that Polish accents are unintelligible to most Americans and many Polish sounds are unpronounce-able. Thus the names of *Krzyzanowski*,[4] *Kosciuszko, Szybczyński, Korzyb-ski* and *Mikolajezyk* still survive in American reference books and even in newspaper dispatches, though it is highly unlikely that more than one non-Polish-American in ten thousand can pronounce them. But many more Polish names have been simplified, *e.g., Siminowicz* to *Simmons, Zmudzin-ski* to *Zmuday* and *Gwzcarczyszyn* to *Guscas*. Others have been translated into English, *e.g., Smith* for *Kowalczyk, Hopson* and then *Hobson* for *Chmielewski* (*chmiel* = hops) and *Gardner* for *Ogrodowski*, or transliter-ated as *Jaroscz* into *Jerris*, or abandoned altogether for common British names, *e.g., Wawrzynski* for *Stone, Chrzanowski* for *Dunlap*[5] and *Kedjer-ski* for *Kent*.[6] Sometimes a poor Pole abandons his surname and elevates a given name to its place. The example of *Josef Konrad Korzienowski* will be recalled; he became *Joseph Conrad* in England, and made the name one that will be long remembered. Sometimes the old name is retained as a middle name as when Anthony *Mierzejewski* became *Anthony Mierzejew-ski Mackey*. And not infrequently the new name chosen is not English, but Irish or German, *e.g., Micsza* to *McShea, Golebiewski* to *Kress* and *Smial-kowski* to *Schultz*.[7]

Louis *Adamic* has described the changes of name among his countrymen, the Slovenes. His own name, originally *Adamič, i.e., Adamson* or *Little Adam*, presented an accented consonant that Americans could not fathom, and a stress, *Ah-dáh-mitch*, that they could not be expected to follow. He finally decided on *Adamic*, without the accent.[8]

The Slovaks in America rejoice when they happen to bear surnames which fall in with American speechways, *e.g., Kuban, Toman, Urban* and *Polak* or *Polack*.[9] Those with more difficult names sometimes find it so hard to teach Americans how to pronounce them that they are abandoned altogether.

All the Slavs differentiate between the masculine and feminine forms of surnames. Thus the son of the famous actress Helena *Modjeska* became Ralph *Modjeski*, and as such attained to fame of his own as an engineer. But in this country the feminine form disappears.[1]

[4] A general officer in the Civil War and the first governor of Alaska. His descend-ants retain the name unchanged.

[5] I am indebted for these examples to Charles C. Arensberg, of the Pittsburgh bar. They come from the records of the Alleghany County Court of Common Pleas.

[6] Death notice, *The New York Times*,

Mar. 20, 1946. I am indebted for this to Alexander Kadison.

[7] Baltimore *Sun*, Jan. 28, 1936.

[8] What's Your Name?, pp. 11-13.

[9] The Americanization of Slovak Sur-names, by Ivan J. Kramoris, *Slovak Re-view*, Autumn 1946, pp. 67-73.

[1] I am indebted here to Emil Revyuk, of the Ukrainian daily *Svoboda*, of Jersey

The American Lithuanians, who are Balto-Slavs and thus bridge the geographical gap between the Slavs and the Teutonic peoples, are fortunate in that their surnames, taking one with another, are considerably more amenable to American speech habits than those, say, of the Poles; they are thus under less pressure to change them. Such names as *Klypa*, *Surgailis*, *Grigonis*, *Varnas* and *Zadeikis* may seem a bit strange to an American who encounters them for the first time, but they do not really alarm him. There are, however, other Lithuanian names that do, especially in their written form, and their bearers are thus constrained to change them. One of the commonest changes is made by substituting English consonants for the Lithuanian consonants, so that *Sŭekevičius*, for example, becomes *Sukevicius* and *Valančiunas* becomes *Valanciunas*. This, of course, involves a change in pronunciation, but it is sometimes only slight. Other names are changed by omitting the original endings, *e.g.*, *-aitis*, *-onis* and *-unas*, which are authentically Lithuanian, and *-evicius*, *-avicius*, *-auska* and *-inskas*, which are Polish. Thus *Norkaitis* becomes *Norkat*, *Šalinskas* becomes *Shalins* and *Bertasius* becomes *Bertash* or *Bartash*. Finally, there are the usual bold leaps to English names, sometimes related and sometimes not, *e.g.*, *Alksninis* to *Andrews*, *Tamošitis* to *Thomas* and *Bogdžiunas* to *Borden*.[2] As in Slavic, surnames are inflected for gender, so the wife of a man named *Vabalas* is Mrs. *Vabalienė*. Moreover, there is a special inflection to distinguish unmarried women, so that the daughter of this couple is Miss *Vabalaitė*. At home in Lithuania "it would be unthinkable and utterly ridiculous" to speak of *Mrs.* or *Miss Vabalas*, but in America these old inflections have broken down, and the masculine form is used "regardless of the sex of the person referred to."[3]

The Gypsies, who originated in northern India but came to the United States by way of Europe, sometimes bear Slavic names, or *nav romanes*, which they use among themselves, but, especially in their dealings with Americans, these are usually converted in this country into what they call *nav gajikanes*, or Gentile names. Thus *Ivan Stefanovitch* becomes *John Stevenson*, and all the *MiXails* become *Mitchells*. *Joe Adams*, long celebrated as King of the Gypsies, was originally *Ioano Adamovič*. Gypsy names are often patronymics. *Giorgi* the son of *Tsino* becomes *O Giorgi de Tisako*, and *Mary* the daughter of *John* becomes *Mary John*. Such grotesque forms as *Millie Mike* and *Rosie Pete* are not uncommon among the

---

City. [The most systematic study of what happens to Slavic surnames in the New World is R. B. A. Klymasz, A Classified Dictionary of Slavic Surname Changes in Canada, *Onomastica* No. 22, Winnipeg, 1961.]

[2] I am indebted here to the kindness of Dr. Alfred Senn, of the University of Pennsylvania, the foremost American authority on Lithuanian.

[3] Lithuanian Surnames, by Alfred Senn, *American Slavic and East European Review*, Aug. 1945, pp. 127-37.

women.[4] In England most of the Gypsies have taken British surnames. Many of these are translations or transliterations. Thus *Taylor* comes from *Chokamengro*, a tailor; *Lee* from *Purum*, a leek; *Lovel* from *Kamlo* or *Kamescro*, a lover; and *Smith* from *Petulengro*, a blacksmith. Some of these names are also common among the Gypsies in the United States, notably *Lee*.[5]

The Scandinavians have had to make almost as many changes in their surnames as the Slavs. "A number of characteristic Swedish sounds, particularly *ö* and *sj*," says Roy W. Swanson,[6] "are almost impossible to the Anglo-Saxon vocal organs. Thus *Sjögren* . . . is variously written *Shogren, Schugren, Segren* or *Seagren*." Very few Swedish-Americans have the courage and patience to insist upon the retention of the Swedish diacritical marks: *å*, pronounced like the English *o* in *more; ä*, which has the sound of *a* in *sad*, and *ö*, which is identical to the German *ö* in *böse*. Transliteration produces *Monson* from *Månson, Backman* from *Bäckman* and *Turnvall* from *Törnwall*—all of them approximations. Certain combinations of letters in Swedish, *e.g., bj, hj, ki* and *lilj*, quickly succumb to Americanization. Thus one *Esbjörn* enrolled in the Federal Army during the Civil War as *Esbyorn* and was mustered out as *Osborn*.

The Swedish *lj* is often got rid of by bold devices, as when *Ljung* (signifying heather) is turned into *Young, Ljungdahl* into *Youngdahl* and so on. In addition, *-qvist* and *-kvist* become *-quist* or *-quest; -gren* (a bough) becomes *green* or *grain*, as in *Holmgrain* and *Younggreen; -blad* (a leaf) becomes *blade*, as in *Cedarblade;* and *bo-* (an inhabitant) is turned into *bow*, as in *Bowman* from *Boman*. Direct translations are also frequent, *e.g.*, of *Nygren* into *Newbranch, Sjöstrand* into *Seashore* and *Högfelt* into *Highfield*. Sometimes the spelling of a name is changed to preserve the Swedish pronunciation, as when *Ros* becomes *Roos, Strid* becomes *Streed* and *Andrén* becomes *Andreen*. Nearly all these changes are in what the Swedes call *borgerliganamn, i.e.*, names of the plain people. The *prästnamn* (priest names), all of which end with either *-us* or *-ander*, are changed less often, partly because their bearers are very proud of them, and partly because they usually present less difficulty to Americans. The *adelsnamn* (aristocratic names) are cherished even more jealously, but they are naturally not numerous. Many well-known Swedish-Americans bear changed names. Thus Charles A. *Lindbergh*'s family name was originally *Månsson*,[7] and that of Professor C. H. *Seashore*, of the University of Iowa, was *Sjöstrand*. The orthodox Swedish spelling calls for two *s*'s in such names as *Svensson*,

---

[4] Gypsy Fires in America, by Irving Brown; New York, 1924, p. 20.

[5] The Gypsies, by Charles G. Leland; 4th ed.; Boston, 1886, pp. 304-7.

[6] The Swedish Surname in America, AS, Vol. III, Aug. 1928.

[7] Days in Sweden, by James W. Lane, The Commonweal, Sept. 9, 1931.

Jonsson and *Olsson*, but one of them is usually dropped in America. In the names ending in *-ander*, e.g., *Lekander*, *Kilander* and *Bolander*, the accent is shifted from the second syllable, where it lies in Sweden, to the first.[8] Many of the early Swedish immigrants really had no surnames, in our sense of the word, only simple patronymics. The custom of using true surnames did not become general among the Swedish peasantry until the earliest part of the Nineteenth Century. Before that the son of *Johann Gustafsson*, on being baptized with his grandfather's given name, became *Gustaf Johansson*, and *his* son in turn, named *Johann* after his grandfather, became *Johann Gustafsson*. When these patronymics began to be made permanent a difficulty arose, for a daughter who, in the past, would have been *Anna Gustafsdotter*,[9] became *Anna Gustafsson*, which set the yokels to tittering. In time they got used to it, and many an *Anna Gustafsson* is to be found in both Sweden and America, but the incongruity set them to hunting for other surnames. The Swedish government helped the process along by circulating the suggestion that various common nouns be combined in euphonious forms, and the result was a great proliferation of names in *alm* (elm), *kvist* (twig), *lund* (grove), *strand* (shore), *sten* (stone), *dal* (valley), *berg* (mountain), *ek* (oak) and *gren* (branch).

The Norwegians and Danes have also made changes in their names. The Norwegian immigrants who began to swarm into the Midwest toward the middle of the Nineteenth Century brought with them a system of nomenclature that was even more vague and unstable than that of the Swedes. They came chiefly from the remoter farming areas of their country, and most of them had no surnames at all, but only patronymics. *Ole* the son of *Lars* was *Ole Larsen*, and *Johannes* the son of *Ole* was *Johannes Olessen* or *Olesen*. If any further identification was needed it was supplied by appending the name of the family farm, for all farms in Norway had names. But this farm name was hardly a surname in our sense, for if a given *Lars* or *Ole* moved from the paternal farm to another, whether as its new owner or tenant, or as the husband of its heiress, or simply as a hired hand, he sometimes took the name of the latter. Usually, however, he did not use this farm name save for official purposes; in everyday life he was simply *Ole Olesen*. This simple system sufficed in the isolated communities of rural Norway, but when immigrants from all parts of the country were thrown together in America it caused hopeless confusion.

Many of these immigrants then recalled the names of their home farms

---

[8] I am indebted here to John A. Stahlberg, of Plentywood, Mont.

[9] This practice still survives in Iceland, and it survived in the Shetland Islands, which were settled by Scandinavians, until the middle of the Eighteenth Century, e.g., *Margaret Nicholsdaughter* was the sister of *John Nicholson*. See A Shetland Merchant's Day-Book in 1762, by William Sandson; Lerwick, 1934.

and began to use them as surnames, but others simply froze their patronymics as surnames for their children, so that the son of *Lars Olesen* was not *Nils Larsen*, as at home, but *Nils Olesen*. But this did not disperse the confusion, for the number of Norwegian given names was limited, and it was not uncommon for *Olesens* or *Larsens* of a dozen different parts of Norway to be gathered in one American village. To this day the Norwegian-Americans have a great many more names in *-sen* and *-son* than any other group, but the number is much less than it used to be. Gradually the suffix *-sen* was changed to *-son* to bring it into accord with American speechways, and for the same reason the redundant *s* was deleted. Thus *Johannessen* became *Johnson*, *Andersen* became *Anderson*, *Peterssen* became *Peterson* and so on.[1]

The Norwegian-Americans, in adopting settled surnames, did not confine themselves to those suggested by logical associations. If their traditional farm names were those of remote and meager farms, connoting poverty to their fellow Norsemen, they collared better ones, connoting opulence. Certain names became fashionable, and others went below the salt. A name in *-hof* stood at the head of the list, and was followed, in order of prestige, by names in *-boer, -vin, -heimr, -saetr, -land, -stadir* and *-rud*. Of names other than those of farms, *-skiold* (shield) and *-hjelm* (helmet) hinted at nobility, and a Latin suffix at learning. "Very few trade names were used," says Marjorie Kimmerle,[2] "because every Norwegian looked upon himself as being principally a farmer."[3] Often two or more sons of the same father chose different names, and the result was a disorder that still afflicts Norwegian-American genealogists.

More unhappily, many of these names were written in official Norwegian, which was basically Danish, but pronounced in the fashion of one or another of the Norwegian dialects, so that a given man had a name in two forms, and not infrequently Americans could not master either. In consequence, there was the usual wholesale change to American equivalents, real or fancied, so that *Praestegaard* became *Prescott;* *Asbjørnsen,*

---

[1] I am indebted here and for most of what follows to the doctoral dissertation of Marjorie M. Kimmerle, a study of the names in the church records of two Norwegian Lutheran congregations in Dane County, Wis. It was summarized in Norwegian-American Surnames, *Norwegian-American Studies and Records* (Northfield, Minn.), Vol. XII, 1941, pp. 1–32. Miss Kimmerle has since published Norwegian-American Surnames in Transition, *AS*, Vol. XVII, Oct. 1942, pp. 158–65. [She served valiantly as director of the Linguistic Atlas of the Rocky Mountain States from 1950 till her death Feb. 9, 1963.]

[2] Norwegian-American Surnames, before cited, p. 17.

[3] The reference here, of course, is to rural Norway. In the larger towns the merchants began to take surnames in the Fifteenth Century, chiefly influenced by German example. The names of the nobles and of the learned were also imitations of German usage. The clergy did not use family names until the Seventeenth Century.

Aspenwall; and *Kjaerret, Cherrie* or *Cherry.* Long names were ruthlessly shortened, *e.g., Halsteingaardbakken* to *Bakken,* and *Magnusholmen* to *Magnus.* Some of the Norwegian vowel sounds were changed considerably. The *a* in *Hagen, Hanson, Fladen* and the like, corresponding to the English *a* in *art,* became the *a* of *band* or *cat,* save where it was supported by *h,* as in *Dahl.* The *u* in *Gunderson* and *Munson* became the American *u* of *grunt.* The *ø* suffered various mutations, mainly into the *u* of *curt* or the *o* of *cod.* The *d,* often silent in the common pronunciations of Norwegian names, was usually sounded, as in *Gunderson* and the names in *-stad* and *-rud.* The Norwegian *th,* pronounced *t,* became the American *th,* as in *Thorstad.* But on the whole the changes have been fewer among the Norwegians than among the Swedes.

The Finns, who are neither Slavs nor Teutons, but Finno-Ugrians and hence allied linguistically to the Hungarians, have plenty of surnames that are quite easy for Americans and call for no change, *e.g., Hakala, Irkonen, Kesti* and *Talvio,* but there are also others that pop the Yankee eye even when they do not strain the Yankee larynx, *e.g., Sillanpää, Tuomikoski, Wuorijäri, Vuolijoki* and *Määrälä,* and these are changed, most frequently in the large cities.[4] Names are simplified by dropping their prefixes, *e.g., Niemi* from *Syrjäniemi, Saari* from *Pyöriasaari, Koski* from *Kalliokoski* and *Maki* (often spelled *Mackey* or reduced to *Mack*) from *Kaunismäki* and many other names in *-mäki* (Finn. hill); by dropping their suffixes, *e.g., Niemi* from *Nieminen, Kallio* from *Kalliokoski* and *Maki* from *Mäkelä, Mäkitalo* and their cognates; by dropping both prefix and suffix, *e.g., Kane* from *Nykänen;* by more or less crude transliteration, *e.g., Marlowe* from *Määrälä, Jervey* from *Järvi* and *Perry* from *Piira;* by translation, either of the whole name or of a part, *e.g., Sandhill* from *Hietemäki* (Finn. *hiekka,* sand; *mäki,* hill), *Rose* from *Ruusu, Stone* from *Kiviniemi* (Finn. *kivi,* stone), *Churchill* from *Kirkkomäki* and *Smith* from *Seppänen* (Finn. *seppä,* blacksmith); and by the bold assumption of unrelated but popular British names, *e.g., Harrison* for *Pirilä, Daniels* for *Puhakka* and *Kelley* for *Karikanta.* The long cultural dependence of Finland upon Sweden introduced many Swedish and other Scandinavian surnames, and many Finns brought them to the United States. Among these names "the most common were *Anderson, Abrahamson, Erickson, Gustafson, Hendrickson, Jacobson, Johnson, Larson, Michelson* and *Peterson,*" with *Johnson* the commonest by far. Most of them have been retained.[5] Not infrequently a Finn makes

---

[4] Finnish Surnames in America, by John Ilmari Kolehmainen, *AS,* Vol. XIV, Feb. 1939, pp. 33–8. [More recent studies, as yet unpublished, have been made by Donald Larmouth and Miss Leena Rintala.]

[5] [Those bearing Scandinavian names are usually bilingual in Finnish and Swedish and are properly called *Finlanders* to distinguish them from the *Finns* proper, among whom bilingualism is less common. I am indebted here to Holgar Nygard.]

a surname for himself by adding -*son* to his father's given name. Thus the son of *Jaakko* becomes *Jackson* and the son of *Antti* becomes *Anderson*. The fact that the Finnish *p* has a sound somewhere between the English *p* and *b* and the Finnish *t* a sound somewhere between the English *t* and *d* is responsible for other changes. Thus when a Finn named *Pelto* gives his name, it may be written down *Beldo*, and like the German *Schneiders* who became *Snyders* he may decide to retain the "American" form.

The Italians, in the early days of their immigration to the United States, changed their names with some frequency, but as they became established this process was halted.[6] *Jim Flynn*, the only man who ever knocked out Jack Dempsey, was *Andrea Chiariglione*. *Henry Woodhouse*, a gentleman once prominent in aeronautical affairs, came to the United States from Italy as Mario Terenzio *Enrico Casalegno;* his new surname was simply a translation of his old one. Other such translations are fairly common, *e.g.*, *Little* for *Piccolo*, *White* for *Bianco*, *Pope* for *Pape*, *Miller* for *Molinari* and *Church* for *Chiesa*. Those Italian names that present no difficulties in American are commonly retained intact, though usually with some changes in pronunciation, *e.g.*, *La Guardia, Marcantonio, Russo, Papini, Valentino* and *Serra*, but others have to yield. Sometimes vowels are dropped, so that *Olivieri* becomes *Oliver* and *Bonifazio* becomes *Boniface;* sometimes the final vowel is changed to an American equivalent, as when *Conte* becomes *Contey;* sometimes Italian consonant sounds are saved by changes in spelling, as when *Amici* becomes *Ameche, Cecco* becomes *Checko* and *Sciortino* becomes *Shortino*. And it is not uncommon for Italian names to acquire the favorite American *s* as a suffix, as when *Alberti* becomes *Alberts; De Clemente, Clements;* and *Landi, Landis*.[7] Finally, there are the bold changes to purely British forms, as when *Canadeo* becomes *Kennedy; Marino, Manning; Rosellini* or *Rubba, Russell;* and *Scaccia, Scott*. There is an Italian *Galloway* in New York whose name was originally *Gallo*. The early Italians ran to Irish names for two reasons. The first was that they came into contact with the Irish in the Catholic churches, and not infrequently married Irish girls. The other was that most of the politicians and prize fighters of their admiration were Irishmen. Moreover, those who entered the prize ring themselves soon found out that Irish names drew larger houses. Some Italians discard the frequent prefixes to their names, *e.g.*, *di, de, della, la, li* or *lo*, when they kiss the flag, but not many; oftener the particle is incorporated, as when *La Rocca* becomes *Larocca* and *Di Matteo, Dimatteo*. Names ending in *e* tend to lose it, at least in pronuncia-

---

[6] The changes have been studied by Joseph G. Fucilla, in *Our Italian Surnames;* Evanston, Ill., 1949.

[7] Says Dr. Vincenzo Campora in Hammonton Notes, *Columbus* (New York), Sept. 1945, p. 7: "Hammonton was . . . founded by Charles K. *Landis*, a Philadelphia gentleman whose original name in the Seventeenth Century was *Landi*, changed to *Landis* when the family immigrated to America from Italy."

tion, like the analagous German names. The surname of Al *Capone* is commonly pronounced to rhyme with *zone*, and its bearer apparently preferred it so. The Italian *a* is quickly Americanized, so that the first syllable of *Sacco* rhymes with *back*, and the first of *Vanzetti* with *can*. Now and then an Italian-American, having worn an American-sounding name for some years, reverts to his original Italian name—usually as a matter of national pride, but sometimes only because Americans seem to be getting used to Italian surnames and finding many of them less difficult than aforetime.

Of the names of Latin immigrants, those of the Spanish have fared the best in this country. Most Americans are familiar with such Spanish surnames as *Gómez, González, López, Rodríguez* and *García* and pronounce them at least as accurately as the plain people of Latin America, who commonly follow Andalusian speechways and so neglect the *th* sound of the Castilian terminal *z*. Very few of the Cubans and Mexicans who have come to the United States have changed their names—probably because they usually settle in regions where Spanish is the second language. There have been few translations, and even fewer attempts at transliteration.[8] The Portuguese are less fortunate, perhaps because they are always surrounded by a population which can't fathom their language. In southeastern Massachusetts and also in Hawaii many common Portuguese surnames undergo radical changes in spelling and pronunciation, *e.g.*, *Marks* for *Marques*, *Perry* for *Perreira* or *Pereida* and *Rogers* for *Rodrigues*.[9] Sometimes a name is translated, as when *Silva* becomes *Wood* or *Forest*, and *Reis*, *King*.[1] Many Spanish names in *-ez* have corresponding Portuguese forms in *-es;* most Americans insist on regarding the latter as Spanish, and pronouncing them as they think Spanish should be pronounced. Neither the Spanish nor the Portuguese in the United States maintain the system of surnames prevailing in their homelands, especially among the upper classes. In Spain a son's full name consists of his given name, the surname of his father and the surname of his mother, the last two connected by *y* (and); thus: *Juan Espinosa y Pelayo*, which may be abbreviated on occasion to *Juan Espinosa y P.*, or *Juan Espinosa P.* or even plain *Juan Espinosa*. A daughter's name follows the same plan, but when she marries she drops her mother's

[8] Hugh Morrison, of New York, who has a wide acquaintance among Mexican-Americans, says that he knows of but two who bear "American" names. One of them, born *Pérez*, is now *Peters;* the other, a full-blooded Indian, is *Jim Anderson*.
[9] I borrow most of these from Personal Names in Hawaii, by John E. Reinecke,

AS, Vol. XV, Dec. 1940, p. 350.
[1] I am indebted here to G. A. Meek, of Oakland, Cal. Charles J. Lovell tells me that *Silva* also often becomes *Smith*. In New Bedford, Mass., *Silva* is the commonest surname, followed by *Smith*, which conceals many *Silvás*. *Perry* is third.

surname and substitutes that of her husband, preceded by *de*.[2] The Portuguese combine the paternal and maternal surnames in the same way, but with *de* in place of *y*, *e.g.*, *Manoel Silva de Dias*. But in America they commonly use their mothers' surnames as middle names, as many Americans do, *e.g.*, *Manoel Dias Silva*.

Changes in other Latin names are more frequent. The long Romanian patronymics are quickly shortened in this country, and many of the difficult shorter ones are supplanted by translated or transliterated forms, *e.g.*, *Miller* for *Morariu*, *Jones* for *Ionescu* and *Stanley* or *Stanton* for *Stănilă*.[3] But of all the Latin surnames, the French seem to fare the worst. The spread of American dominion over the Mississippi Valley and the later invasion of New England by French Canadians has produced a carnage—*White* for *Le Blanc*, *Woods* for *Dubois*, *Drinkwater* for *Boileau*, *Larch* for *L'Archevêque*, *Larraby* for *La Rivière* and so on.[4] A small colony of Hollanders, including Flemings of French name, settled in Boyle County, Ky., in the Nineteenth Century, and in a little while all its *Badeaus* were *Beddows*, its *LaRues* were plain *Rues* and its *Des Champses* were *Scomps*.[5] In the late Eighteenth Century the Spanish were in control of the Mississippi from 1763 to 1800 and kept the public records. Thus the names of many French traders and settlers were changed to accord with Spanish notions. In this way *Chouteau* became *Chotau* and *Choto* (and was later transformed by the invading Americans into *Shoto*). In 1939, J. M. Carrière reported [6] that the following spellings had come in during "the last generation or two" in a settlement of French origin in the foothills of the Missouri Ozarks: *Rulo* for *Rouleau*, *Courteway* for *Courtois*, *Pashia*, for *Pagé*, *Partney* for *Parthenais*, *Degonia* for *Degagné* and *Osia* and *O'Shea* for *Augier*. The early French system of surnames was strange enough to make for confusion,[7] and that confusion was increased as the years passed, both along the Mississippi and along the northern border, by the frequent modification of spellings and pronunciations. These changes in spelling, in the course of time, as Carrière says, tended "to conform to primitive phonetic patterns based upon English orthography," so that *Archambault* became *Shambo* or

[2] *Amigos* (Chicago), Oct. 1941.

[3] I am indebted here to George Stanculescu, of the *American Roumanian News* (Cleveland).

[4] See La Langue française au Canada, by Louvigny de Montigny, Ottawa, 1916, p. 146, and Name Tragedies, by C. P. Mason, *AS*, Vol. XIV, Apr. 1929, p. 329.

[5] A Tragedy of Surnames, by Fayette Dunlap, *DN*, Vol. IV, Pt. II, 1913.

[6] Creole Dialect of Missouri, *AS*, Vol. XIV, Apr., p. 119, *n.* 29.

[7] It is described by John Francis McDermott in French Surnames in the Mississippi Valley, *AS*, Vol. IX, Feb. 1934, pp. 28–30. There were patronymics, *dit* names referring to some personal characteristic or item of personal history, and names borrowed from estates. The latter did not always descend to sons, who not infrequently acquired estates and names of their own.

Shampoo; Bon Coeur, Bunker; Choquette, Shackway; Renaud, Reno; Aubert, Obear; Bourgeois, Bushway; Blancpied, Blumpy; Rossignol, Russel.

Many Americans who have retained the French spelling of their names have been forced to suffer changes in the pronunciation. Among those of the Charleston, S.C., region *Huger* is pronounced *You-gée; Legaré, Le-grée; Gaillard, Guilyard,* with the accent on the first syllable; *Gourdin, Guddine,* rhyming with *divine; de Saussure, Déssosore,* or *-so; Girardeau, Jírrardo;*[8] and *Des Portes, Déssports.* The tendency of the accent to go forward will be noted.

Other groups change their names in the same ways. When a Hungarian's name is *Feleky, Bartus, Simko* or *Yartin* his neighbors are able to pronounce it more or less correctly, but if it is *Mészöly, Skalička, Eötvös, Gyongyosy* or *Csüry* he has to change either the pronunciation or the spelling, and sometimes he changes both.[9] Surnames analogous to the English *St. John* are often translated, *e.g., Szentgyörgyi* becomes *Saint George,* and *Szentpétery* becomes *Saint Peter.* Sometimes other names are translated, *e.g., Papp* into *Priest, Kovács* into *Smith, Mészáros* into *Butcher, Kerekes* into *Wheeler* and *Szabó* into *Taylor;* and sometimes they are transliterated, *e.g., Kállay* into *Kelly, Szüle* into *Sewell* and *Makláry* into *McCleary.* When names are retained they are frequently changed in spelling. Thus *Köszegy* becomes *Koesegi* and *Kiss* becomes *Kish.* The Hungarians, like the Chinese, always put the surname first, and sometimes this custom is kept up after their names have been Americanized. Thus *Charley Braun* is *Braun Charley,* and *Ilona Nagy,* wife of *Péter Kiss,* is either *Kiss Péterné Nagy Ilona* or *Kissné Nagy Ilona.* But most Hungarians adopt the usual American order.

The Arabic-speaking Syrians in the United States occasionally bear surnames that fit into the American pattern easily enough, *e.g., Kassab, Barsa* and *Katibah,* but more often they have to make changes. Sometimes it is sufficient to substitute new spellings, *e.g., Arbeeli* for *'Arbīli, Mallouk* for *Mallūk, Mouakad* for *Mu'aqqad* and *Arout* for *'Ayrūt,* but more frequently there are more substantial changes, *e.g., Sleyman* for *Sulaymān, Jacobs* for *Yaqūb, Bourjaily* for *Abu-Rujayli, Abbott* for *'Abbūd* and *McKaba* for *Muqabba'ah.*[1] *Al-Khuri,* a common Syrian name, becomes *Khoury, Courey*

---

[8] But the name of the Mississippi River town in Missouri is pronounced *Jirrárdo.*

[9] I take most of these from the Magyar in America, by D. A. Souders; New York, 1922. [In 1962, according to an undated United Press story, *Geza E. Szentgyoergyvoelgyi,* of Pittsburgh, an architect, petitioned the courts for permission to change his name to *Andrew G. Valley,* on the ground that the length

of his name made it difficult for him to obtain employment in his profession. Data processing machines, now greatly in vogue in American offices for statements, checks and the like, often find such long names indigestible.]

[1] I take these examples from Arabic-Speaking Americans, by H. I. Katibah and Farhat Ziadeh; New York, 1946.

or *Corey*. The Syrian *Haddad*, though it presents no phonological difficulties, is commonly translated into *Smith*, and *Ashshi* into *Cook*. The most distinguished of Armenian-Americans, William *Saroyan*, born in Fresno, Cal., has been able to keep his family name, but only at the expense of accepting the accent on *roy*, where it does not belong in Armenian.[2] Many of his *Landsleute* have been less fortunate. Sometimes their names are translated, *e.g.*, *Tertzagian* into *Taylor*, *Ohanesian* or *Hovanesian* into *Johnson* and *Hatzakordzian* into *Baker;* sometimes they are crudely transliterated, *e.g.*, *Jamgotvhian* into *Jameson* and *Melkonian* into *Malcolm;* sometimes they are abbreviated, *e.g.*, *Bozoian* into *Bozo*, *Karageozian* into *Kara* and *Mooradian* into *Moore;* and sometimes they are subjected to even more brutal processes, as when *Kizirboghosian* becomes *Curzon* and *Khachadoorian* becomes *Hatch*.[3] Fresno once had a citizen named *Paul Paul* whose original name was *Boghos Boghossian*. Many Armenians arrived in the United States bearing names imposed upon them by their Turkish overlords. These, in some cases, have been turned into true Armenian names, as when *Chilingirian* became *Darbinian*, both meaning *Smith*.[4]

But of all the immigrant peoples in the United States, the Jews seem to be the most willing to change their names. This willingness did not originate in the Republic; they brought it with them.[5] In the Russian Pale from which so many of them came the eldest son of a family was exempt from military service, and in consequence the custom arose of younger sons bribing the 100% Russian officials to change their surnames, thus enabling them to pass as the eldest sons of mythical families.[6] It was also common for Jews who got on in the world to exchange their distinctively Jewish and usually commonplace names for new ones sounding more Russian and more elegant. In a story by Sholom Aleichem there is a character named *Peshach Pessi* who adopts the sonorous *Platon Pantolonovich Lokshentopov*. His wife becomes *Pantomina*, and one of his cousins takes the style and appellation of *Fanfaron Faaronovich Yomtovson*. Many of the principal recent figures in Russian history, bearing Russian names, came into the world with Jewish ones. *Lev Davidovich Trotsky*, for example,

---

[2] Mr. Saroyan tells me that family tradition makes the original form of the name *Sarou Khan*, meaning blond lord, but the present form has been in use for generations.

[3] I am indebted here to R. Darbinian, of *Hairenik* (Boston), and to Dr. K. A. Sarafian, of La Verne College, University of Southern California.

[4] I am indebted here to Richard Badlian, of Boston; private communication, Sept. 28, 1936.

[5] [See Rufinus Intacitus, De Nominibus, Scripta Minora; Bologna, 1569, p. 409 b-c. There is scholarly dispute as to whether this Rufinus is to be identified with Tyrannius Rufinus, transmitter of the works of Origen.]

[6] I am indebted here to David Otis, of Brooklyn.

was born *Bronstein,* and the diplomat *Maxim Maximovich Litvinov* was born *Finkelstein.*[7] In all other countries where name changing is, legally speaking, relatively facile, Jews assume names borrowed from the local onomasticon. In England there are thousands of *Mosses* who were originally *Moseses, Brahams* who were *Abrahamses,* and *Montagues, Taylors, Gordons, Davises, Phillipses, Lewises* and *Lees* who have no blood kinship to those ancient tribes.[8] In France there has been a similar assumption of protective coloration in names, but it has been limited by statutes forbidding changes without legal permission by persons holding professional licenses from the state—for example, for the practice of medicine. In the United States, the first native-born generation tend to shrink from all the disadvantages that go with their foreignness and their Jewishness,[9] and seek to avoid making it unnecessarily noticeable.[1] At the height of the immigration from Eastern Europe even the members of the first generation moved rapidly in that direction. Possibly half the Jews of New York now sport new names. They follow all the patterns other newcomers use, and have added one of their own, *i.e.,* the prettification of their traditional names, whereby the names in *Rosen-* become *Rose* or *Ross.* Like the Germans whose names they so often bear, they seek refuge in translations more or less literal. Thus *Blumenthal* is changed to *Bloomingdale* and *Schlachtfeld* to *Warfield. Stolar,* which is a Yiddish word borrowed from the Russian, signifying a carpenter, is changed to *Carpenter. Lichtman* and *Lichtenstein* become *Chandler. Meilach,* which is Hebrew for *king,* becomes *King,* and so does *Meilachson. Sher* is changed into *Sherman, Moiseyev* into *Macy* or *Mason* and *Jacobson, Jacobovitch* and *Jacobovsky* into *Jackson.* This last change proceeds by way of a transient change to *Jake* or *Jack* as a nickname. *Jacob* is always abbreviated to one or the other among the Russian and Polish Jews.

It has thus become impossible in America to recognize Jews by their names. There are not only multitudes of *Smiths, Browns* and *Joneses*

[7] The name changing among the comrades was not due wholly to a desire to get rid of Jewish names; another, and stronger, purpose was to throw off the police. Jews and non-Jews alike adopted aliases. *Nikolai Lenin* was that of a man originally *Vladimir Ilyitch Ulianov,* and *Joseph Vissarionovitch Stalin* that of *Iosiph Djagashvilli, Djugashvilli* or *Dzhugashville.*

[8] Howard F. Barker notes in Surnames in *-is, AS,* Vol. II, Apr. 1927, p. 317, that *Davis, Harris, Lewis* and *Morris* are also very popular among American Jews. [See also German-Jewish Names in America, by Rudolph Glanz, *Jewish Social Studies,* Vol. XXIII, July 1961, pp. 143–69.]

[9] Jewishness, on occasion, is a heavy burden, for there is always more or less anti-Semitism afloat. Its causes remain to be investigated. The reasons for it that Jews commonly accept are almost as dubious as those advanced by anti-Semites.

[1] See The Jews, by Maurice Fishberg; New York, 1911, especially pp. 485 *ff.* Also, Reaction to Personal Names, by Dr. C. P. Oberndorf, *Psychoanalytic Review,* Vol. V, No. 1, Jan. 1918.

among them, but also many *Adamses, Lincolns, Jeffersons* and *Harrisons,* and even *Vanderbilts, Schuylers,*[2] *Cabots* and *Lowells.* [The Commission on Church and State of the Central Conference of American Rabbis (1959) lists a *Brooks,* a *Cooper* and a *Gilbert;* its Committee on Contemporary History includes a *Conrad,* a *Lyons* and a *Martin.* The officers and national committees of the Zeta Beta Tau, a fraternity of otherwise *Kultur-*conscious Jewish college men, include *Allen, Baron, Barr, Davis, Evans, Fisher, Gage, Gibbs, Graham, Harris, Kramer, Lee, London, Paley, Parker, Pierson, Robinson, Sharpe, Stone* and *Wagner.*[3]] A roll of Boston Jews who have written books offers *Taylor, Lyons, Millin, Davis, White* and *Burroughs.*[4]

The spelling of Jewish names is frequently changed, even when their pronunciation is but little modified. *Schlessinger* has changed to *Slessinger* or *Slazenger,* and *Labovitz* to *Laboris, Labouisse* and even *La Borwits.* The spelling of the *-heimer* names is often changed to *-himer,* that of the *-heim* names to *-hym* and that of the *-baum* names to *-bem* or even *-bum.*

Many of the changes in Jewish surnames are effected by degrees. Thus *Goldstein* first becomes *Goldstone,* then *Golston,* and finally *Golson.* Sometimes these successive changes have method in them, as is indicated by the following tale from Dr. Pepys's Diary in the *Journal of the American Medical Association* written by Dr. Morris Fishbein, himself a Jew:

> Today in ye clinic a tale told of Dr. *Levy* who hath had his name changed to *Sullivan.* A month after he cometh again to ye court, this time wishing to become *Kilpatrick.* On request for ye reason, he telleth ye court that ye patients continually ask of him, "What was your name *before?*" If granted ye change, he shall then tell them "*Sullivan.*" [5]

The Jews make these changes with extraordinary facility, not only because they desire to get rid of the two handicaps of foreignness and Jewishness at one clip, but because those surnames, in many cases, are relatively recent, and hence do not radiate old associations and family pride. It was not until 1782 that the Jews of Austria were compelled to assume surnames, and not until 1812 and 1813 that those of Prussia and Bavaria, respectively,

---

[2] [There may be unconscious irony in the assumption of *Schuyler,* since it is possible that the New York *Schuylers* were originally Sephardic Jews who fled to Holland in the Sixteenth Century to avoid the blessings of the Spanish Inquisition.]

[3] [*Zeta Beta Tau Quarterly,* Autumn 1960.]

[4] Long List of Books Written by Boston Jews, by Fanny Goldstein, Boston

Evening Globe, May 23, 1934.

[5] [Such changes are not uncommon in Irish history. If I may inject a personal note, genealogists allege that the *Mc-Davids* were originally *DeBurghs* and subsequently *Burkes,* but assumed the patronymic after a brush with Sassenach law. I am sometimes asked if it is a Jewish conversion name, an inquiry which leads me to suspect that it is so used.]

had to follow. This compulsion was resisted by large numbers, and the harassed officials punished them by giving them names of a grandiose or otherwise ridiculous character, *e.g.*, *Armenfreund* (friend of the poor), *Ochsenschwanz* (ox tail), *Wanzenknicker* (louse cracker), *Eselkopf* (ass's head) and *Saumagen* (sow's paunch). Not infrequently a Jew was blackmailed by being threatened with a name that was obscene or otherwise ruinous,[6] but those who paid handsomely were permitted to choose names gratifying to their sometimes florid fancy, [characteristic, to be sure, of the whole Romantic Movement in Germany]. This last fact accounts for the large number of surnames in *Gold-*, *Fein-* (fine) and *-blum* (flower) among the German Jews. Among the Sephardic or Spanish Jews, surnames are rarely changed, even in America: the *Cardozos*, *daSilvas*, *Fonsecas*, *deCassereses* and *Solis Cohens* are as proud of their ancient names as the *Percys* or *Salm-Salms*. But the Ashkenazim (German, Polish and Russian Jews) have no such reason for clinging to the names clapped on them.

Many familiar Jewish names are translations of Hebrew given names into German, Russian or some other language of the Diaspora.[7] Thus *Naftali* (defined in Genesis XLIX, 21, as "a hind let loose") became *Hirsch* (deer) in German, and from *Hirsch* flowed a number of other names, *e.g.*, *Herz*, *Herzl* and *Herzler*. Similarly, *Jehuda* or *Judah* (defined in Genesis XLIX, 9, as "a lion's whelp") became *Löwe* (lion) and produced *Loew*, *Loeb* and *Leon*; *Schalom* (peace) was turned into *Frieden* (Ger. peace) and produced *Fried* and *Friedman*; and *Simcha* (joy) became *Freude* (Ger. joy) and produced *Freud*, *Freudman* and various other derivatives. The formation of surnames by the addition of some form of *-son* to a father's given name was as common among the Jews as among Christians. In German *-sohn* was used, and in the Slavic languages *-ice*, *-ovice* or *-ovitch*. Many surnames were also made by the additions of diminutives to given names, *e.g.*, *-ig*, *-ich*, *-el*, *-la*, *-lein*, *-ing* and *-ung*. Many Russian, Polish and Romanian Jews assumed such Germanized Jewish names at the time of the first big immigration to America from Eastern Europe. The German Jews were here before them, and had won to a respected position, and it seemed good policy to seek the shelter of that position.

The assumption by Jews of well-known non-Jewish names is sometimes protested by the bearers of the latter. Indeed, even Jews of the older stock have been known to object, as happened when a Philadelphia dentist

---

[6] C. L'Estrange Ewen, in A History of Surnames of the British Isles, New York, 1931, pp. 213 ff., tells of two Jews who compared notes after visiting the police office. One had drawn an excellent name, *Weisheit* (wisdom) but the other had been labeled *Schweisshund* (bloodhound). "Why *Schweisshund?*" demanded Weisheit. "Didn't you pay enough?" "Gott und die Welt," replied Schweisshund, "I have given half of my wealth to buy that *w* alone." The Jews have a vast repertory of such stories.

[7] See Die deutschen Familiennamen, by Albert Heintze; 2nd ed.; Halle, 1903, pp. 66–8.

named *Isaac Solomon Cohen* began subscribing himself *I. Solis Cohen*, the name of an ancient and honored Jewish medical family of that city. Again, there was an uproar from the Cabots of Boston when, in 1923, a Russian Jew named *Kabotchnick*,[8] denized there, gave notice that he had shortened his name to *Cabot*. But such objections, when they are taken into court, seldom profit the plaintiff, for under American law a man has a right to change his name at will, though it is common for a would-be changeling of any means to ask the countenance of a court of record, that there may be no trouble thereafter about voting rights and the conveyance of property.[9] The Solis Cohens were advised that restraining Dr. Cohen was impossible under Pennsylvania law, and they did not go to court. The Cabots went and lost.

Once a new name has been recognized, whether by judicial approval or by common consent, it becomes as much the bearer's possession as his original name, and may be used and defended in all situations in which the latter may be used and defended. This was decided in 1923 by Judge Learned Hand, then a federal district judge in New York, in the case of *Goldwyn Pictures Corporation* v. *Samuel Goldwyn*. Born *Gelbfisch* and *Goldfish* in his pupal stage, Goldwyn had risen to fame and wealth as a movie magnate. But he lost control of the Goldwyn Pictures Corporation to others, and when, in 1923, he resumed making pictures and launched a screen version of "Potash and Perlmutter" on Broadway, the corporation got a temporary injunction ordering him to credit the production on his billing to *S. G. Inc.* On the hearing of an application to make the injunction permanent, Judge Hand vacated it, with the provision, accepted by Goldwyn, that he should add "not connected with Goldwyn Pictures Corporation" to all his public announcements.[1]

The marriage, death and other personal notices in the newspapers frequently record changes in Jewish surnames: *Burstein* to *Burr*, *Loewenthal* to *Lowell*, *Ginsborg* to *Gilbert*, *Markowitz* to *Marlowe*, *Katzenstein* to *Kaye*, *Finkelstein* to *Flint* and to *Fenton*, *Isaac* to *Ives*, *Leberstein* to *Livingstone*, *Wasserschweig* to *Vassar-Smith*,[2] *Schmetterling* to *Smith* and *Goldberg* to *Gould* and *Coburn*.[3]

Changes are frequently made in Jewish names that are not abandoned

---

[8] United Press dispatch from Boston, Aug. 16, 1923.

[9] In England the law is substantially the same as in the United States, but it is customary for a man seeking to change his name to do so by applying for a royal license, which may be obtained as a matter of course by paying a large fee, or by advertising his intention in the newspapers and filing a deed poll with the clerk of the Supreme Court.

[1] The case is reported in *Variety*, Oct. 25, 1923, p. 19.

[2] Court Circular, London *Times*, Sept. 20, 1945.

[3] The last from The How and Why of Name-Changing, by Helen P. Wulbern, *American Mercury*, June 1947, p. 719. The article also cites the law in New York on the subject.

altogether. *Cohen*, which is the commonest of such surnames in the United States,[4] is to be encountered as *Cohn, Cone, Cowan, Cahan, Cohan, Coen*,[5] *Kohn, Kohen* and the like, [to say nothing of such prettifications as *Cain*]. *Cohen* is a Hebrew word, signifying, originally, a prince or priest, but later a priest only. By Jewish tradition the name and the office are restricted to descendants of Aaron, but that tradition, like many others, has long since lost force.[6] [At the turn of the century the number of *Cohens* multiplied enormously, as ordinary Israelites assumed the name in the hope of upgrading themselves socially.[7]] The Sephardic Jews pronounce the word *Ko-hén;* the German Jews make it *Koh'n,* in one syllable; the Polish Jews make the first syllable rhyme with *now;* and the Russian Jews prefer *Káy-hun*.[8]

Levy is another Jewish surname that has many permutations. It is derived from the name of the Levites, the tribe assigned the care of the Ark and Tabernacle, and later of the Temple. From *Lewi*, the original Hebrew designation, have sprung *Levi, Levy, Lewy, Levey, Levin, Levine, Levitan, Levinsohn, Lewisohn, Lewis, Levanne, Lever* and a host of other forms, including *Halevy* (Hebrew *ha,* the). *Lév-vee*, with the accent on the first syllable, probably comes closer to the original Hebrew pronunciation than either *Lée-vee* or *Lée-vigh*. The Sephardic Jews use *Láy-fee*. A number of American *Levys* have changed their name to *Lee*,[9] and one family has chosen *Leeds*. Another name with many variations, especially in spelling, is *Ginsberg, e.g., Ginzberg, Ginsburgh, Gainsburg* and *Ginsborough*.[1] Many other familiar Jewish names are similarly transmogrified. *Goldberg* becomes *Goldhill* or *Goldsborough; Schapiro* or *Shapiro* becomes *Schapira, Shapero, Chapereau, Chapiro* or the terminal *Rowe*. Many of the German-Jewish names in *-berg, -thal, -feld, -mann* and so on have both elements translated, so that *Rosenberg*, for example, becomes *Rosehill*,

[4] Samuel H. Abramson shows in *Abramson Blames the Goldbergs, Canadian Jewish Chronicle*, Mar. 20, 1942, that it also leads in Canada, followed by *Greenberg, Freedman* or *Friedman, Katz, Levy, Goldberg, Rosenberg, Bernstein* and *Abramson*.

[5] *Cohan(e)* and *Coen* are Irish names, and occasionally an Irish *Cohen* appears.

[6] [But apparently the prerogatives and liabilities have been restored in Israel. According to *The New York Times*, Apr. 9, 1962, the Hadassah-Hebrew University Medical Center in Jerusalem is out of bounds for the priestly clan of *Kohainim*, ostensive descendants of Aaron, by virtue of Leviticus xxi, which forbids them to enter a building where a corpse lies.]

[7] [Here I am indebted to Dr. Jerome Kavka.]

[8] Here I am indebted to Dr. Solomon Solis Cohen, of Philadelphia; private communication, May 7, 1937.

[9] *Lee* is also a favorite with other immigrant groups. It is adopted in place of difficult German names, *e.g., Liebknecht* and *Lietsche;* common Jewish names other than *Levy, e.g., Leon;* and the Chinese *Li* and Scandinavian *Lie*.

[1] Which recalls the *Ginzberg* in Anita Loos's But Gentlemen Marry Brunettes (1928), who, following the example of the *Battenbergs* (now *Mountbattens*), changed his name to *Mountginz*.

Wassermann becomes *Waterman* and *Schwarzmann* becomes *Blackman*.

Not a few Jewish names of German origin present phonological difficulties to the average American, and thus suffer changes in pronunciation
like those undergone by the names of German and other non-Jewish immigrants. All the *Strauses* and *Strausses* who mention the pronunciation of
their names in "Who's Who in America" give the *au* the sound of *ou* in
out, but there seems to be a tendency to *Straws*, especially in the South.
Even when it is not *Straws* it has the American *s* sound at the start, not
the German *sh* sound. Several *Goldsteins* in "Who's Who" ordain that the
-*stein* of their name be pronounced *steen*, but Albert *Einstein*, the physicist, stuck to *stine*. This *steen* pronunciation seems to prevail only when
-*stein* is terminal. In such names as *Feinstein* and *Weinstein* one often hears
-*een* in the final syllable, but never in the first. Nor does it appear in *Wein-
berg, Klein, Fein, Steinbeck, Brandeis, Eichelberger, Eisenhower, Eis-
ner, Dreiser* and the like, some of them Jewish and some not, nor in
simple *Stein*, nor in numerous Jewish names in -*heim* and -*heimer*. In
names in *Braun-* and *Blau-* the German *au* is often pronounced *aw*, so
that *Braunstein* becomes *Brawnsteen* and *Blaustein* becomes *Blawsteen*.
Something of the sort also happens in the case of the terminal -*baum*,
which becomes *bawm*, as in *Barenbawm* for *Barenbaum*. Many early
German-Jewish immigrants, like the German *goyim*, changed the spelling
of their names in order to preserve the pronunciation, as *Gorfein* to *Gorfine*
and *Klein* to *Kline*.[2] In innumerable cases, however, this was inconvenient
or impossible, so the Jews, like other immigrants, had to submit to the
mispronunciation of their names. Thus *Sachs* became *Sax* and has remained
so, and *Katz*[3] came to be identical in sound with *cats*, and *Adler* acquired
a flat American *a*. In the common speech of New York, the element -*berger*
or -*burger* changes to -*boiger*, sometimes with a soft *g*. Of late *Lehman* has
almost ceased to be *Layman*, becoming *Leeman*.[4] *Meier* is often *Meer*, *Bache*
is *Baysh* or *Baytch*, *Shapiro* is sometimes *Shap-yro*, and *Baruch* is *Ber-
óok*, with the accent on the last syllable.

The Chinese in the United States have only about sixty different family
names, of which *Chan, Wong* and *Lee* (*Li*) are the most often encountered.[5] The Chinese seldom change their surnames, which are really clan
names, but representing them in English presents many difficulties, so that

---

[2] But I have heard even *Gorfine* turned
into *Gorfeen*, and likewise *Durstine* into
Dursteen.

[3] Rabbi Jacob Tarlau, of Flushing, L.I.
(private communication, Apr. 30, 1937),
tells me that *Katz* has nothing to do
with the identical German word signifying a cat. It is a characteristic Hebrew abbreviation of two words, *kohen*

tzedek, and indicates that the man bearing it is a descendant of Aaron, and
hence a priest.

[4] As Herbert H. *Lehman*, former governor of New York. [But Winfred *Lehmann*, Germanicist of the University of
Texas, makes his name *Lay-man*.]

[5] Chinatown Inside Out, by Leong
Gor Lum; New York, 1936, p. 55.

there are many variants. One name appears as *Lok, Look* and *Luke,* and another as *Hiu, Heu* and *Hew.*[6] To compound the difficulty, the same ideograph represents different pronunciations in different parts of China, so that a Northern man named *Tsur* may be called *Chow* in the South and *Jo* elsewhere.[7] But though surnames are almost always retained, the Chinese usually adopt American given names. Also, they often change the order of their names, for at home the surname goes first, as with the Hungarians, and this causes misunderstanding and confusion among Western strangers. So *Lee Loy,* in order to avoid being called Mr. *Loy,* becomes *Loy Lee.*[8] Japanese personal names, like American ones, have the surnames last. Since most of them are easily pronounceable, there is no motive for changing.

The surnames of the American Indians are in a state of apparently hopeless confusion. Some of them have adopted names wholly American, *e.g., Philip Marshall, George Williams* and *Alfred B. Richards*;[9] others have hitched their native surnames to American given names, *e.g., Moses Bull Bear, Charles Little Dog* and *Fred Cut Grass;* yet others have retained their native names unchanged. This last category, alas, is small and seems to be vanishing. The original Redskins bore nothing properly describable as fixed surnames, and even their given names were frequently changed.

When Indians began to come in from the warpath and settle on reservations, this chaos gave great difficulty to the Indian agents. In 1903 the Indian Bureau employed Charles A. Eastman to overhaul the surnames of the Sioux[1] and various others were put to work among other tribes. Whenever a child entering school or an adult entering a government hospital lacked a name in the American fashion, one was supplied. If there was already a native name it was commonly translated, which explains the origin of such surnames as *Little Cloud, Fast Horse* and *Lone Wolf.* The surnames that survive mainly related to personal characteristics, *e.g., Black Eye* and *Yellow Boy,*[2] or were suggested by a fancied likeness to some bird or animal, *e.g., Red Owl, Flying Hawk* and *Crazy Horse,* or some feature of the landscape, *e.g., Howling Water, High Pine* or *Red Cedar.*[3]

---

[6] Personal Names in Hawaii, by John E. Reinecke, *AS*, Vol. XV, Dec. 1940, p. 347.

[7] Inside Asia, by John Gunther; New York, 1939, p. 158. Other examples are *Oong, Wong* and *Wen, Chang* and *Jong, Feng* and *Fung.*

[8] *Dong Kingman,* the San Francisco water-colorist, is commonly called *Kingman,* but his surname is actually *Dong.*

[9] These appear on a petition to Congress in 1946 (*Congressional Record,* July 19, p. A4506) by the Oglala Sioux of the Pine Ridge Reservation.

[1] Eastman, himself a Sioux, was born in 1858. He became a homeopathic doctor and held various posts in the Indian Service.

[2] See Indian Personal Names from the Nebraska and Dakota Regions, by Margaret Cannell, *AS*, Vol. X, Oct. 1935, pp. 184–7.

[3] On July 17, 1937, the United Press correspondent at Watonga, Okla., reported the marriage of Emma *Standing Elk,* described as a "pretty 18-year-old Montana Cheyenne Princess," to Horace *Howling Water.* Among the spectators

It is not surprising that many of these surnames should be opprobrious: the same is true of many Indian tribal names.[4] In the Indian tongues they tend to be jawbreakers, and the early white colonists found them difficult. William Nelson lists the following monstrosities from the early days: *Abozaweramud* (1681), *Kekroppamont* (1677) and *Rawautoaqwaywoaky* (1709).[5] Sometimes these names embodied syllables which passed on from father to son, to become primeval equivalents of surnames, *e.g.*, *baq* (bone), *ik* (pepper), *kok* (tortoise), *may* (tobacco), *pek* (stone), *seb* (clay), *yat* (fly), *gwuq* (seven) and *sam* (snot).[6]

The surnames of American Negroes have been studied by Howard F. Barker,[7] Newbell Niles Puckett[8] and Lorenzo D. Turner.[9] Barker estimates that of the ten-million-odd Negroes living on the American mainland in 1924, 7,500,000 bore English or Welsh surnames, 1,300,000 Irish names, and 1,200,000 Scottish names, with a small minority bearing Dutch, German, Spanish, French or Jewish names.[1] It is commonly assumed that the surnames of Afro-Americans are those of their masters in slavery times, but this is seldom the case. The name of Samuel *Hairston*, the largest American slaveowner in 1861, is very rare among colored folk, and those of other large slaveowners, *e.g.*, *Hampton*, *Pinckney* and *Rutledge*, are anything but common. The favorite is *Johnson*, which accounts for no less than 190 Negroes in every 10,000. Next in order come *Brown*, *Smith*, *Jones*, *Williams*, *Jackson*, *Davis*, *Harris*, *Robinson* and *Thomas*. It may be that the popularity of John *Brown* of Osawatomie put his surname in second place, and the fame of George *Washington* apparently accounts for the fact that *Washington* is far commoner among Negroes than among whites,[2] but how

---

at the ringside were Jane *Walking Coyote*, Louise *Long Bear*, Eva *Old Crow*, Rose *Shoulder Blade* and James *Night Walker*. I am indebted here to Dr. Claude M. Simpson, Jr., of the University of Wisconsin.

[4] American Indian Tribal Names, by Maurice G. Smith, *AS*, Vol. V, Feb. 1930, pp. 114–17.

[5] Indian Words, Personal Names and Place-Names in New Jersey, *American Anthropologist*, Vol. IV, Jan.–Mar. 1902, pp. 183 ff.

[6] Notes on the Kekchi Language, by Robert Burkitt, *American Anthropologist*, Vol. IV, July–Sept. 1902, pp. 441 ff.

[7] The Family Names of American Negroes, *AS*, Vol. XIV, Oct. 1939, pp. 163–74, and How We Got Our Surnames, *AS*, Vol. XIII, Oct. 1938, pp. 48–53.

[8] Names of American Negro Slaves, in Studies in the Science of Society Presented to Albert Galloway Keller; New Haven, 1937, pp. 471–94.

[9] [Africanisms in the Gullah Dialect; Chicago, 1949.]

[1] The *Amsterdam News* reported on Feb. 1, 1944, p. 2–A, that a Negro Coast Guardsman named George Jack *Goldstein*, a native of New York City, was visiting in Harlem. [At West Virginia State College, one of the administrative officers is *Newman Goldston*, a West Virginia Negro.]

[2] Booker T. Washington says in Up from Slavery, New York, 1900, pp. 34–5, that his slave mother called him *Booker Taliaferro* but that he grew up knowing only *Booker*. When he went to school and discovered that surnames were necessary, he added *Washington*. Later, informed of the *Taliaferro*, he made it his middle name and reduced it to its initial.

are we to account for *Johnson?* It can hardly be a patronymic, for relatively few slaves had the given name *John,* and Andrew *Johnson* was certainly not its eponym, for it stood in first place, and among free Negroes, so early as 1830.[3]

The fact is that freed slaves probably adopted the names of overseers as often as they took those of masters, and in even more cases chose names that were simply common where they lived and thus seemed regular and proper and suitable to their station in life. Very few of them named themselves after Abraham *Lincoln,* and even fewer after *Garrison, Grant* and *Sherman.* Their favorite among all their liberators was General O. O. *Howard,* head of the Freedmen's Bureau from 1865 to 1874. Barker says that more than one-third of all the *Howards* in the United States are now colored. Unusual surnames are rare among Negroes, though, as is the case with whites, they are relatively frequent among persons of distinction, *e.g., Du Bois, Chesnutt, Bunche, Douglass, Hastie, Schuyler, Robeson, Garvey, Bethune* and *Carver.*

The earliest known list of English surnames comes from the Pipe Roll of 1159–60, where they were borne by 94% of the persons listed. Of these names, 5% indicated racial extraction, 35% were geographical, 19% were occupational, 21% showed descent and 14% remained unidentifiable.[4] The first Irish names are recorded in documents nearly three centuries older than the Pipe Rolls, and many of them are still common, *e.g., O'Connor, O'Donnell, O'Neill* and *O'Brien.*[5] Since the dawn of the Irish Literary Renaissance, *c.* 1890, there has been a fashion among Irish politicians and literati for reviving the ancient Gaelic forms of both surnames and given names, and as a result such forbidding examples as *O Tuathail (O'Toole), Omarchadha (Murphy)* and *O Muircheartaigh (Moriarty)* now spot the Irish newspapers, but in America this romantic affectation has found very few imitators.[6] The public records of Scotland, with few exceptions, do not go back beyond 1300, and as a result the study of Scottish surnames, many of them common in America, is full of difficulties.[7]

Many familiar Scottish names are not Gaelic in origin, but Norman, English, Flemish, Danish or Irish. *Carlisle,* for example, comes from the name of the town in England, *Bruce* is a French territorial name and *Macaulay* is from the Norse. There is little assurance that in a Scot's ar-

---

[3] Barker, lately cited, p. 168.

[4] C. L'Estrange Ewen, A History of Surnames of the British Isles; New York, 1931.

[5] Irish Names and Surnames, by Patrick Woulfe; Dublin, 1923, pp. xvi–xix. Ireland, says Woulfe, "was the first country after the fall of the Western Empire to adopt hereditary surnames."

[6] Many examples are in Woulfe's Irish Names and Surnames, pp. 55–161.

[7] The best available work is George F. Black, The Surnames of Scotland: Their Origin, Meaning and History; New York, 1946.

teries runs the blood of the clan to which he apparently belongs. The plain people of early days simply took the names of the bloodletters whose banners they followed, and not infrequently they changed their names as they switched clans. In the early Seventeenth Century, so many ruffians enrolled themselves as *MacGregors* that an act was passed on April 3, 1603, abolishing that surname altogether, and making its use a capital offense. In 1661 the law was suspended by Charles II, but in 1693, after the Mac-Gregors took to the bush again, it was re-enacted. The bearers of the name continued to cling to it, and during the Eighteenth Century many of them brought it to America.[8] Most of their descendants are probably no more related to the King Giric who is said to have founded the clan, *c.* 900, nor even to that later chief who boasted that wherever he sat was the head of the table, than Booker T. *Washington* was related to George. [It is one of the commonest surnames among the Manitoulin Island, Ontario, band of Ojibwas; but the genes of the original *Rob Roy MacGregor* who brought it there are pretty well diluted.] Other famous Scottish names attracted recruits in the same wholesale manner, notably *Stewart, Campbell* and *MacDonald.* Thousands of the proscribed *MacGregors* became *Mac-Donalds,* and to this day *MacDonald* is the most common of all surnames in Scotland, next to *Smith.* Even in the United States it ranks above such familiar English names as *Barnes, Ellis, Ford, Graham* and *James. Campbell* outranks *Mitchell, Turner, Cook* and *Lee. Stewart* in its various forms is ahead of *Ward, Rogers* and *Edwards* and on a par with *Parker* and *Morris.*

The popular history of onomatology is largely given over to discussions of strange and unearthly surnames. Their collection was begun by William Camden, who listed some interesting specimens in his "Remains Concerning Britain," first published in 1605,[9] *e.g., Bigot, Devil, Pentacost, Calf, Hoof, Loophole* and *Gallows.* The bibliography in the United States apparently began with N. I. Bowditch's "Suffolk Surnames." [1] The Suffolk of the title was the Massachusetts county, but Bowditch also included names from other parts of the country. Some of his prize specimens were *Ague, Darkies, Dudgeon, Gotobed, Lighthead, Oxx, Strachatinstry, Ugly* and *Wedlock.* Edward Duffield Ingraham, a Philadelphia lawyer, followed in 1873 with "Singular Surnames," the materials for which came chiefly from

[8] The act was finally repealed in 1784. By 1863, according to the Annual Report of the Registrar-General of Scotland, there were 10,000 of them again at large on the old soil.

[9] This book was made up in part of selections from his Britannia, published in Latin in 1586 but not translated into English until 1610.

[1] Boston, 1857; revised and enlarged edition, 1858. [In Common American Surnames and Their Relationship to Eminence, *Names*, Vol. X, Mar. 1962, pp. 38–44, Elsdon C. Smith points out that such names as *Smith* and *Johnson* consistently appear in Who's Who in America and other such rosters of fame less frequently than in the population as a whole.]

the Philadelphia newspapers of the 20s, 30s, 40s and 50s. He listed, among others, *Allchin, Bitsh, Christmas, Glue, Oyster, Toad, Whisker* and *Yeast*. The collection of such monstrosities still goes on, and the newspapers frequently report the discovery of one hitherto unwept, unhonored and unsung. Frank Sullivan, an eager collector of such delicacies, gives the place of honor in his cabinet to the Misses Dagmar *Sewer* and Mary Lou *Wham*. [A Benjamin *Wham* currently practices law in Chicago.] Some time ago one of the large life-insurance companies printed a list designed to show "the colorful variety of appellations which policy-holders bear." From it I take the following:

Harry B. *Ill*	Chintz *Royalty*	Memory D. *Orange*
E. J. *Cheesewright*	Barnum B. *Bobo*	Oscar R. *Apathy*
Robert *Redheffer*	John *Bilious*	Alphonse *Forgetto*
Julia C. *Barefoot*	James A. *Masculine*	Henry *Kicklighter*
Sello *Bibo*	Ansen B. *Outhouse*	William *Dollarhide*
G. H. *Upthegrove*	Christian *Girl*	Emil E. *Buttermilk*

Miss Mary C. Oursler, formerly administrative assistant in the Census Bureau, is authority for the statement that 30% of the heads of families in three of the thirteen original states in 1790, when the first census was taken, bore "names appearing as parts of speech in everyday conversation," *e.g.*, *Dumb, Looney, Gushing, Soup, Vinegar, Waffle, Grog, Grapevine, Petticoat, Hornbuckle* and *Turnipseed*.[2] Many of these have succumbed to the ribald humors of the populace, but a liberal sufficiency remains. When such names are combined with the weird given names that will be considered in the next section the effect is often startling, *e.g.*, *Uffie Grunt, Sunny Piazzi, Ima Hogg* and *Byzantine Botts*.[3] A learned man in Canada tells me of a pretty immigrant girl who came to school in Manitoba bearing the name of Helen *Zahss*, and was much upset when the first roll call produced titters. England can still boast, to match, such specimens as *Caitiff, Foulfish, Killer, Makehate, Burnup, Goodbeer, Kisser, Venus, Shakelady, Sucksmith, Pitchfork, Gumboil, Handsomely* and *Cutmutton*.[4]

The literature dealing with English, Scotch, Welsh and Irish surnames is enormous,[5] but there is little in print about their permutations in the United States. Hyphenated names are rare; they began to appear on the

[2] She Could Answer, How Old is Ann?, by Katherine Scarborough, Baltimore *Sun*, Apr. 18, 1943.

[3] Surnames in the Blue Ridge of Virginia, by Miriam Sizer, *AS*, Vol. XII, Dec. 1937, p. 269. [My sister, Mrs. L. L. Barrett, once unearthed *Cosey Hussey* (male) among the clients of the North Carolina Hospital Saving Association.]

[4] See Charles Wareing Bardsley, Dictionary of English and Welsh Surnames;

Ernest Weekley, The Romance of Names; J. J. Kneen, The Personal Names of the Isle of Man; Ernest Weekley, Surnames; Mark Antony Lower, English Surnames.

[5] [The latest compilation is Personal Names: a Bibliography, by Elsdon C. Smith; New York, 1952. Mr. Smith is also the founding father of the American Name Society and author of The Story of Our Names; New York, 1950.]

wave of Anglomania that followed the Civil War, but the ribaldry of the vulgar quickly discouraged them.[6] They survive, generally speaking, only among grass widows and female singers and elocutionists. But to compensate for abandoning the hyphenated surnames, American nomenclature has developed the intrusion of second capitals into names, *e.g., GaNun, Ken-More* and *VisKocil.* Names that are really two names, separated by a space and not hyphenated, are occasionally encountered, *e.g., Bel Geddes*[7] and *Ben Ami,* but the early American custom of hitching territorial or occupational appendices to surnames, *e.g., Charles Carroll of Carrollton, John Randolph of Roanoke* and *Charles Carroll the Barrister,* seems to have passed out.

A few of the older English surnames have undergone modification in America, *e.g., Venables,* which has lost its final *s.* There has also been a tendency to abandon *Griffiths* for *Griffith.*[8] And where spellings have remained unchanged, pronunciations have been modified, especially in the South.[9] *Callowhill,* in Virginia, is sometimes pronounced *Carroll; Norsworthy, Nazary; Farinholt, Fernall;* and *Drewry, Droit.* To match such prodigies the English themselves have *Crippiny* for *Crespigny, Marshbanks* for *Marjoribanks, Beecham* for *Beauchamp, Chumly* for *Cholmondeley,* and *Trosley* for *Trotterscliffe.* In general, there is a tendency in America to throw the accents back, *i.e.,* in such names as *Gerard, Doran, Burnett* and *Maurice.* In England the first syllable is commonly accented; in the United States, the second. This difference is often to be noticed in Irish names. "An Irishman," says Ernest Boyd, the Irish critic, "says *Wáddell, Móran, Bérnard, Púrcell, Máhony,* etc., but Americans and Irish-Americans stress the last syllable, as in *Morán,* or the penult, as in *Mahóny.*" The Welsh custom of spelling certain names in *F* with two small *f*'s, *e.g., ffinch* and *ffoulkes,* has been imitated in England, but rarely in America. The Chicago telephone directory lists only one *ffoulkes* and three *ffrenches,* and neither appears in "Who's Who in America."

"Almost every discarded fashion of spelling," says John Earle in "The Philology of the English Tongue,"[1] "lives on somewhere in proper names." The early scribes and notaries played hob with them, as Anders Orbeck

---

[6] They arose in England through the custom of requiring an heir by the female line to adopt the family name on inheriting the family property. Formerly the heir dropped his own surname; but about a hundred years ago heirs in like case began to join the two names by hyphenation, and such names are now very common in England.

[7] The name of Norman *Bel Geddes,* the stage designer, was so entered in the Manhattan telephone book for Winter-

Spring 1946, though he gives his father's name as *Geddes* in Who's Who in America, 1946–7.

[8] According to Howard F. Barker, Surnames in *-is, AS,* Vol. II, Apr. 1927, p. 318, "the defection from *Griffiths* dates far back."

[9] See Word-Book of Virginia Folk-Speech, by B. W. Green; Richmond, 1899.

[1] 3rd ed.; Oxford, 1879, p. 158.

shows for colonial America in his "Early New England Pronunciation," [2] and many of the variants they propagated survive to this day, *e.g.*, *Millar-Millard, Farrar-Farrow, Buckminster-Buckmaster* and *Haywood-Heyward.* In the census returns for 1790 *Kennedy* and *McLaughlin* were spelled in thirty-two different ways, and *Campbell* in twenty-seven. *Shakespeare's* name, in his day, was spelled in eighty-three.[3] George *Washington's* forefather, Laurence, was registered at Oxford as *Wasshington* in 1567; *Jefferson* was once *Jeffreson* and *Giffersonne; Adams* is interchangeable with *Addams, Adamson* and *Addamson; Jackson,* in its day, has been *Jakson, Jacson, Jackeson, Jakeson* and *Jaxon;* and *Lincoln* has gone through the forms of *Linccolne, Lyncoln, Lincon* and *Linkhorn.*[4] On Cape Cod *Mayo* and *Mayhew* are forms of the same name,[5] and so are *Harding* and *Hardin; Shelley* and *Sherley; Crow* and *Crowell; Burge, Birge* and *Burgass.* Any American with an uncommon name is bound to find it grossly misspelled in his correspondence. Thad *Eure,* formerly Secretary of State of North Carolina, was addressed by his constituents as *Ure, Euri, Ewar, Uue, Euria, Aure, Yuer, Erra, Eura* and *Eyre,*[6] and Wilberforce *Eames,* the bibliographer, cherished a collection of envelopes directed to *Anies, Bames, Earres, Gaines, Rames, Trames, Wames,* etc.[7]

But it is in pronunciation rather than in spelling that surnames suffer their greatest mutations. Americans tend to favor spelling pronunciations, so that *Crowninshield,* which is *Crunchell* in England, is given the full value of all its syllables here, and *Heyward* is seldom *Howard,* and *Powell* is never *Po-ell,* and *St. John* is only rarely *Sin-jun.* But this tendency is not universal, and in the older parts of the country it meets with many checks. B. W. Green, in his "Word-Book of Virginia Folk-Speech," [8] lists a number of curious pronunciations in Tidewater Virginia, *e.g., Umsted* for *Armistead, Barnet* for *Bernard, Boler* for *Boulware, Granger* for *Crenshaw, Gouge* for *Gooch, Horton* for *Hawthorne, Murray* for *Maury, Partrick* for *Patrick, Tolliver* for *Taliaferro* and *Darby* for *Enroughty.*

---

[2] Ann Arbor, Mich., 1927, pp. 11–13. See also Krapp, Vol. I, pp. 201–5.

[3] *Shakespeare's* Name and Origin, by Johannes Hoops, in Studies for William A. Read; University, La., 1940, pp. 67–87. It contains references to other discussions. [According to M. M. Mathews, A Survey of English Dictionaries, Oxford, 1933, p. 42: "Thomas Fuller was told that the name *Villiers* is spelled fourteen different ways in the family records. The name of *Shakespeare's* father appears in sixteen different spellings. The family name *Mainwaring* is said to have been spelled in one hundred and thirty-one different ways."]

[4] I take most of these variants from Bardsley's Dictionary of English and Welsh Surnames; London, 1901.

[5] I am indebted here, and for what follows, to Gustavus Swift Paine, of Southbury, Conn. In England, *Mayhew,* in the past, has been written *Maheu, Mayeu, Mayowe, Mayhoe* and even *Matthew.*

[6] *The New Yorker,* Jan. 6, 1940.

[7] What's in a Name?, *Bulletin of the New York Public Library,* Nov. 1942, pp. 957–8.

[8] Richmond, 1899, pp. 13–16.

The last two have attracted much attention from students of names. Whether *Taliaferro* was originally French or Italian is disputed. The French theory connects it with a Norman minstrel named *Taillefer*, who came to England with William the Conqueror and died gallantly at Hastings. The Italian theory, which was supported by Thomas Jefferson and Chancellor George Wythe, connects it with a Venetian musician named Bartolomeo *Taliaferro*, who immigrated to England in Elizabethan times. Whatever the fact, there are still plenty of *Tallifers*, *Telefers* and *Tollivers* in England, and the American family has produced many men of distinction. No less than five are in "Who's Who in America" for 1960–1, four noting that they pronounce the name *Tól-i-ver*. This change seems to go back to an early date in England, but the actress Mabel *Taliaferro*, born in New York in 1887, used *Tal-ya-fér-ro*. Whether *Taliaferro* was her family name or only a stage name I do not know.[9]

There are *Enroughtys* in Virginia who pronounce their name *En-ruff-ty* and others who pronounce it *Darby*. How this confusion arose has been thus described by F. W. Sydnor:

> The records [of Henrico County] show one *Darby Enroughty* to have been living near Four-Mile Creek[1] in 1690. He had a son named *John* and one named *Darby*. Later there were two *John Enroughtys* living in the same locality, cousins, . . . and it became necessary to distinguish between the two *Johns*. *John Enroughty*, the son of *John*, was known by his Christian name, but *John*, the son of *Darby Enroughty*, was designated *John Enroughty the son of Darby*, *John Enroughty of Darby*, and at least once as *John Darby*. The *Enroughtys* of Henrico and those known as *Darby* (real name *Enroughty*) are all descendants of *Darby Enroughty*. Those bearing the name *Enroughty* are the descendants of his son *John*, and those bearing the name of *Darby* are the descendants of his son *Darby*.[2]

This reveals the falsity of the theory that the *Darby-Enroughtys* are really *Enroughtys* who pronounce the name *Darby*. They actually bear two names—*Enroughty* in writing and *Darby* in speech.

In England the pronunciation of many surnames differs in different places, and as a result the authorities do not agree. Very often, indeed, the same authority gives two or more forms. Thus *Devereux*, which is an old Irish

---

[9] There is a considerable literature on the name and genealogy of the family, *e.g.*, The *Taliaferro* Family, by John Bailey Calvert Nicklin, *Tyler's Quarterly Historical and Genealogical Magazine*, Vol. VII, pp. 12–28; The *Taliaferro* Family, by William Buckner McGroarty, the same, pp. 179–82, and The *Taliaferro* Family, by the same, *William and Mary Quarterly Historical Magazine*, Vol. IV, pp. 191–9.

[1] Four-Mile Creek was apparently a branch of the James River, near Richmond.

[2] Richmond *News-Leader*, May 16, 1930.

name derived from France, is pronounced *Déveroo* and *Déveroox* (*de* as in *devil*), *Dévveruh* (with the neutral vowel at the end) and *Dévverecks*. *Gell* takes both the hard and the soft *g*, *Heygate* is both *Haygait* and *Haygit*, *Lisle* is both *Lile* and *Leel* and *Onions* is both *Unnions* and *Onighons*. In parts of Scotland, *Cunningham* is pronounced *Kinnicum*,[3] and in Lord *Byron*'s day he was usually called *Birron* by his intimates.[4] Similar aberrations, of course, are also frequently encountered in the United States. Some of those prevailing in Virginia have been listed; in New Hampshire *Pierce* is pronounced *Purse*, and Franklin of that ilk (1804–69), fourteenth President of the United States, was so called by his friends, one of whom, Nathaniel *Hathorne*, changed the spelling of his own name to *Hawthorne* to bring it into accord with his notion of its euphonious pronunciation.

[American surnames have been greatly stabilized during the Twentieth Century.[5] This has partly been due to increasing literacy, both of the public at large and of the keepers of vital statistics, but perhaps more to the large number of occasions on which names must be publicly recorded —for the draft, for ration books in wartime, for Social Security and private pension plans, for automobile registration and driver's licenses, for life insurance and for the income tax. As the standard of living improves, more and more people acquire some form of public identification. What is more, vital statistics themselves are more comprehensive than they used to be: the official registration of births, a casual matter half a century ago even in large communities, is now universal. Once a person is identified by a particular rendering of his surname, he is inclined to stick to it.]

2: GIVEN NAMES [6]

John, which was the most popular given name in the United States at the time of Simon Newton's survey in 1920, remains the favorite given name

---

[3] See W. E. Henley's note in The Letters of Robert Louis Stevenson; New York, 1923, Vol. II, p. 305.

[4] Memoirs of My Times, Including Personal Reminiscences of Eminent Men, by George Hodder, London, 1870, reprinted in Personal Reminiscences of Barham, Harness and Hodder, by Richard Henry Stoddard; New York, 1875, p. 321.

[5] [Barker noted this in a private communication to HLM, but the process has been accelerated and emphasized in the last two decades. According to You're on This List, by R. M. Yoder, *The Saturday Evening Post*, Aug. 9, 1958, pp.

37, 83–4, there are approximately 1,100,000 surnames on the U.S. census rolls. Of these 685,532 are shared by nine persons or less; among the loners are the exotic Demetra *Xixi* and the prosaic Thomas *Dayburn*. There are 330 named *Jesus* and 15 named *God*.]

[6] In this section a few passages are lifted from Notes on American Given-Names, a paper I contributed to Bookman's Holiday, a *Festschrift* in honor of Harry Miller Lydenberg; New York, 1943. I am indebted for permission to use them to Deoch Fulton, of the New York Public Library Press.

for males among Americans today, as it has been among people of British stock since the Norman Conquest. Following it comes *William*, and following *William* come *Charles, James, George, Robert, Thomas, Henry, Joseph* and *Edward*. [Among females, *Mary* is more than twice as popular as the second-ranking *Elizabeth*, with *Barbara* and *Dorothy* a close third and fourth, respectively; following *Dorothy* come *Helen, Margaret, Ruth, Virginia, Jean* and *Frances*.[7]] In one American family of German origin it was customary to name every son *John*. The eight or ten in a given generation were distinguished by their middle names, which ranged from *Adam* to *Thomas*. The roster of the first Common Council of London, held in 1347, showed 34 *Johns*, 17 *Williams*, 15 *Thomases*, 10 *Richards* and 8 *Roberts* in a total enrollment of 133.[8] In the interval there have been passing fashions for other given names, but not one of them has forced its way into the top bracket. That, of course, is not saying that *John*'s frequency continues to be absolute as well as relative. On the contrary, it is slowly losing ground in the United States, along with all the other ancient saints' names.[9] Saints' names are still, however, almost unchallenged on the continent of Europe, for in the Catholic areas Canon 761 of the Canon Law ordains that such a name must be given to every child at baptism, and even in such Protestant areas as Prussia, Denmark and Sweden they are still dominant.[1]

Canon 761 is also followed, of course, by Catholics in the United States, if not by parents then at least by priests. If a mother or father insists upon giving a child some non-canonical name, the priest is required to add a saint's name, and the saint's name goes on the records of the parish. There has been some murmuring against Canon 761 among American Catholics in recent years, especially in the Midwest, for it works against the fanciful names that are in vogue there.

Not a few of the common saints' names are of heathen origin—*e.g.*, the Greek *George*, the Latin *Paul* and the Germanic *Charles*—but all that the

---

[7] [Eldson C. Smith, The Story of Our Names; New York, 1950. The pioneer survey of American male given names was made by Simon Newton in 1920.]

[8] *N or M*, London *Times Literary Supplement*, Mar. 30, 1946, p. 151. But in the Domesday Book of *c.* 1086 there had been 68 *Williams*, 48 *Roberts* and 28 *Walters* to but 10 *Johns*.

[9] It seems to be resented by some of its bearers on the ground that it is too common.

[1] In France, during the Revolution, an effort was made to abolish, or, at all events, to limit the use of saints' names, but nearly all Frenchmen of today bear them. [In a Reuters dispatch from Rennes, published in *The New York Times* of June 3, 1962, it was reported that authorities had told the le Goarnic family of the Brittany village of Kertelg-en-Moelan-sur-Mer that their five children "do not exist in the eyes of the law" because they have unusual Celtic names —*Kaiwenn, Gwendall, Diwezha, Sklerijen* and *Adraboran*. Only names figuring in "different calendars" or those of well-known historical personages are acceptable.]

Canon Law now demands is that saints on the Calendar or prophets of an earlier day once bore them. Thus, in an official list of permissible baptismal names published in 1935 by authority of Patrick Cardinal Hayes, then Archbishop of New York,[2] both *Adolf* and *Benito* appear. *Adolf* was the name of an Osnabrück saint of the Thirteenth Century, remembered for his devotion to the poor, and *Benito* is an accepted form, in Italy, of the name of *Benedictus* (signifying blessed), the great founder of Western monasticism who passes in England and the United States as *Benedict*.

The official list sanctions some far from dignified distortions of prophets' and saints' names, *e.g.*, *Abe*, *Aggie*, *Alick*, *Andy* and *Atty* (from *Attracta*, the name of an Irish saint of the Fifth Century), to go no further than the *A*'s. It also permits *Dolores*, which is not a given name at all, but comes from one of the titles of the Virgin Mary—*Mater Dolorosa* (Sorrowful Mother). *Virginia*, which is likewise permitted, gets in by the same route. Such American favorites as *Homer*, *Horace* and *Ulysses* are banned, for they are the names of invincible heathens, but *Caesar* is admitted on the ground that there was a saintly Archbishop of Arles of that name in the Sixth Century, and *Virgil* because it was borne by an Irish missionary saint. Even in Italy there is some encroachment of non-canonical names. Consider Cardinal *Amleto* Giovanni Cicognani, Secretary of State under two popes. His Eminence is not only a high Roman dignitary; he is also a former professor of Canon Law and the author of a standard treatise on the subject; yet the first of his two given names is the Italian form of the old Danish *Amleth* or *Hamleth*, the appellation of a probably fabulous heathen prince of the Second Century who has been immortalized by Shakespeare as *Hamlet*.

Toward the end of the Sixteenth Century the English Puritans staged the first revolt against saints' names. They were opposed to honoring any of those on the Roman calendar who had lived since Apostolic times,[3] and so turned to the Old Testament for names for their children. *Abraham*, *Moses*, *Joshua* and their like began to have a vogue,[4] though they had been permissible names to Catholics all the while. The more extreme Puritans made names of various pious hopes and admonitions, *e.g.*, *Fear-not*, *Increase*, *Fly-fornication* and *Praise-God*,[5] and many of these, along with the Old Testament names, were brought to America by immigrants to

---

[2] Baptismal and Confirmation Names, by Edward F. Smith; New York, 1935.

[3] John Knox's Calvinist Book of Discipline, their favorite guide to conduct, said: "Let persuasions be used that names that do not savor of either paganism or popery be given to children at their baptism, but principally those whereof there are examples in the Scriptures." [See The Geneva Bible on Names for Children, by DeWitt T. Starnes, *Names*, Vol. X, Mar. 1962, pp. 53-7.]

[4] The more earnest Puritans unearthed some really formidable specimens, *e.g.*, *Zerubbabel*, *Zaphenathpaneah* and *Mahershalalhashbaz*. See In the Driftway, *The Nation*, Feb. 7, 1923, p. 150.

[5] Ecclesiastical History of Great Britain, by Jeremy Collier; London, 1708-14.

New England. Most such inventions were soon abandoned, but a number survived into the Eighteenth Century, *e.g.*, *Increase* and *Preserved*, and a few are occasionally encountered even today. The Old Testament names that preceded and accompanied them are now more popular in the South than in New England, though even in the South they are going out. There was a revolt against them at the time New England Puritanism began to fade into Unitarianism, for *Noah* Webster disliked his given name [6] and refused to let it be given to any of his male descendants. The Puritan names for girls, *e.g.*, *Grace*, *Hope* and *Faith*, were nearly all permissible to Catholics, for they had been borne by female martyrs in the early days of Christianity, but the Puritans gave them a new lease on life.[7]

The chief competition that saints' names encounter in the Republic today comes from the use of surnames as given names and the wholesale invention of entirely new and unprecedented names in the Bible country of the South and Southwest. Many names of the former sort, *e.g.*, *Howard*, *Douglas*, *Clifford* and *Russell*, are now in wide esteem in both England and the United States, but they did not appear in England until the latter part of the Sixteenth Century. The first mention of them seems to be in William Camden's "Remains Concerning Britain," first published in 1605.[8] Camden noted that their use was then a novelty, that it was purely English, to be encountered "nowhere else in Christendom." He gave twelve current examples, to wit, *Pickering*, *Worton*, *Grevil*, *Varney*, *Bassingburne*, *Gawdy*, *Calthorp*, *Parker*, *Pecsal*, *Brocas*, *Fitz-Raulf* and *Chamberlain*. Of these only *Parker* ever attained any marked popularity, and it has been swamped in recent years by *Cecil*, *Spencer*, *Seymour*, *Dudley*, *Desmond* and *Stanley*, among others. At the start, according to Camden, the use of surnames as given names was confined to "worshipful ancient families," but it soon spread to lower and lower strata, and by the middle of the Seventeenth Century *Percy*, *Howard*, *Sidney* and *Cecil* had become common given names in England.

In America the favorite English names were soon reinforced by American additions, *e.g.*, *Chauncey* (originally *Chauncy*, and often pronounced *Chancey*), *Dwight*, *Bradford* and *Winthrop*, and by the time of the Revolution the custom of naming children after conspicuous persons, not relatives, was already sufficiently noticeable to be remarked in the newspapers.

From the outset John *Hancock* proved a prime favorite on baptismal occasions. . . . He was president of the First Continental Congress

---

[6] Warfel, p. 329.

[7] [The Eighty-seventh Congress, elected in 1960, boasts such Old Testament names as *Benjamin*, *Caleb*, *Hiram* and *Jacob* in the Senate, and *Abner*, *Abraham*, *Adam*, *Jacob*, *Joel* and *Noah* in the House, with the Norse pantheon represented by an *Odin* and a *Thor*, and the Caliphate of Islam by an *Omar*.]

[8] My quotations are from the reprint of the 7th ed. of 1674, in the Library of Old Authors; London, 1870, pp. 56–7.

(and later of the Second), and therefore personified the united colonial effort. Before 1774 drew to an end his namesakes were recorded in Providence, R.I., and Marblehead, Mass.[9]

But the outbreak of actual war offered stiff competition to *Hancock*'s popularity, and thereafter the favorite name for male babies was *Washington*. The first upon whom it was bestowed seems to have been the infant son of Colonel John Robinson, of Dorchester, Mass., who was christened toward the end of July 1775. The first real hero of the Revolution, Joseph *Warren*, killed at Bunker Hill, was scarcely in his grave before babies were being named after him, and by the next year thousands were being baptized *Franklin, Jefferson, Otis* and *Adams*, to be followed in due course by *Hamilton, Lincoln, Lafayette, Jackson, Lee* and so on, leading down to the *Grover Cleveland, George Dewey, Theodore Roosevelt* and *Franklin Delano* of our own era.[1] [Among the thirty-four Presidents of the United States up to 1961, four had surnames as given names and eight had them as middle names. Of the latter, three dropped their given names and used their middle names. The Eighty-seventh Congress lists senators christened *Bourke, Clairbourne, Clifford, Clinton, Estes, Everett, Lister, Morris, Prescott, Russell, Strom, Styles, Vance* and *Winston*, and representatives endowed with *Armistead, Blaine, Bradford, Brent, Burr, Carleton, Carlton, Durward, Elford, Gardner, Harley, Hastings, Lindley, Mendel, Neal, Overton, Perkins, Porter, Vaughan, Watkins* and *Wright*, besides the more common *Allen, Barry, Bruce, Byron, Carroll, Cecil, Cleveland, Dale, Elliott, Elmer, Glenn, Harlan, Harris, Howard, Irving, Jackson, Jeffery, Leslie, Lester, Milton, Morgan, Otis, Ross, Seymour, Sidney, Stuart, Vernon, Wallace, Wayne* and *Willard*.]

The long survival of names taken over during the Revolutionary period is shown by the cases of *Warren* Harding and *Franklin* Roosevelt. Rather curiously, the most popular nomenclature relic of that time in vogue today, not excepting *Washington*, is *Elmer*, derived from the name of two heroes so far forgotten that it does not appear in any of the ordinary reference books.[2] *Elmer* is encountered from end to end of the United

[9] Arthur M. Schlesinger, Patriotism Names the Baby, *New England Quarterly*, Dec. 1941, pp. 611–18.

[1] For the permutations of *Lafayette*, see *AS*, Vol. XVI, Dec. 1941, p. 312, Vol. XVII, Dec. 1942, p. 225, and Vol. XXI, Apr. 1946, p. 1955. This last reports the recent death of *DeMarkous Lafayette* Traylor, Jr., of Farmville, Va., *aet.* 79. See What's in a Name?, by Joyce G. Agnew, *The New York Times Magazine*, Nov. 5, 1944, p. 38. After the Civil War many admirers of *Stonewall Jackson* named their sons, not *Jackson*, but *Stonewall*. Such names usually date their bearers.

[2] Of it the New York *Herald Tribune* said in 1935 (In Defense of *Elmer*, editorial, Jan. 18):

The brothers Ebenezer and Jonathan *Elmer*, of Cumberland County,

States, but it seems to be most popular in the Midwest, where it was once a common greeting name for strangers. *Waldo*, though it is not unknown elsewhere, is a specialty of New England: it seems to have come in as a surname, but its early history is obscure.[3] In the same way *Truman* is mainly found in the Pennsylvania-German country and its colonies, *Clay* in Kentucky, *Randolph* in Virginia and *Pinckney* in South Carolina. The names of the Protestant heroes *Luther*, *Calvin* and *Wesley* have become so common that they are often borrowed by immigrants of non-British stock, usually in an attempt to Americanize names they have brought with them, *e.g.*, *Wesley* for the Czech *Václav*. All three are sometimes borne by Catholics, though Canon 761 forbids them, just as it forbids *Jupiter*, *Mohammed* and *Satan*,[4] [and in 1960 a *Calvin Cohen* was domiciled in Chicago].

Though the English invented the use of surnames as given names, they make less frequent and less bold additions to it than we do, despite such cases as *Rudyard* Kipling, *Hartley* Coleridge, *Hallam* Tennyson and *Aldous* Huxley. Where they run ahead of us is in the multiplication of given names, sometimes all of them saints' names but usually a mixture of saints' names and family names. Those of the Duke of Windsor are *Edward Albert Christian George Andrew Patrick David*. The American custom of giving a boy his mother's surname as a middle name originated in England, but is now far more widespread in this country; possibly three out of four eldest sons, in American families of any pretensions, bear their mothers' surnames, either as first names or as middle names. Many girls are similarly named, and in the South, at least, some are given surnames as their first names. Thus *Barrett* Snodgrass or *Powell* Smith may be female and lovely. Mrs. George E. Pickett, the second wife of the general, was baptized *LaSalle* and called *Sally*. Sometimes a Southern girl is actually called *George*, *Frank* or *Charles*, after her father.

The English eschew the American custom whereby a woman, at marriage, drops her baptismal middle name and substitutes her maiden surname.

New Jersey, . . . were Revolutionary pamphleteers, organizers of Revolutionary militia, surgeons and officers in command of troops throughout the Revolution, members of Congress and fierce debaters of a hundred stirring issues of their times, enjoying a fame and popularity that is easier to understand than their present oblivion. The name *Elmer* therefore has such an honorable genealogy that it is time for America's countless *Elmers* to know it and stand up for it.

[3] It is of German origin, and Reclams Namenbuch, Leipzig, 1938, says that it is a shortened form of *Walderich*, the root of which is *walten*, meaning to rule or sway. See also Jack and Jill, by Ernest Weekley; London, 1939, p. 45.

[4] *Luther* stands in 104th place on the Newton list. It is thus above *Mark*, *Vincent* and *Christian*, and far above *Washington*.

This custom was launched before the Civil War.[5] After Harriet Elizabeth Beecher, the sister of Henry Ward Beecher, married the Rev. Calvin E. Stowe in 1836, she thus dropped the *Elizabeth* in her name and substituted *Beecher*. Said an English commentator in 1867, apparently forgetting (or unaware) that Mrs. Stowe no longer used *Elizabeth:*

> It is not a bad plan for girls to have only one name, so that they may retain their maiden surname after their marriage, as that honoured lady, Mrs. Harriet *Beecher* Stowe, has done.[6]

But this English commendation of Mrs. Stowe's example has not been followed by imitation. Nor does an English grass widow, on getting rid of her husband *John*, cease, in the American fashion, to be Mrs. *John* Smith and become Mrs. *Jones* Smith, the *Jones* being her maiden surname. The American custom of representing a middle name by its simple initial, though it is not altogether unknown in Britain, is not common, and such a form as George *B.* Shaw would strike most Englishmen as odd.

Camden says that second given names were "rare in England" in his time, *c.* 1605, though common in the Catholic countries. James I had been christened *Charles James* and his son was *Henry Frederick*, but it was not until his other son, later Charles I, married *Henrietta Maria* of France in 1625 that they came into any popularity. Even so, they were confined for a long while to the gentry. In America they were adopted only slowly. The first graduate of Harvard to have one is said to have been *Anmi Ruhamah* Corlet, who set up as a schoolmaster at Plymouth, Mass., in 1672.[7]

Of all the remembered worthies of the early days only *John Quincy* Adams, *Robert Treat* Paine and the two Virginia Lees, *Richard Henry* and *Francis Lightfoot*, had middle names,[8] and of the first seventeen Presidents only *John Quincy* Adams, *William Henry* Harrison and *James Knox* Polk. They were more numerous among the literati, *e.g.*, James *Fenimore* Cooper, *Nathaniel Parker* Willis and *Francis Scott* Key, but so late as 1859 they were still rare enough for a writer in *Harper's Magazine* to be arguing that they should be bestowed more frequently.[9]

---

[5] The anonymous author of Our Given Names, *Putnam's Monthly*, Jan. 1855, p. 59, said that it originated among the Quakers.

[6] *Happy Hours*, reprinted in *Every Saturday* (Boston), June 8, 1867, p. 716.

[7] Gustavus Swift Paine, of Southbury, Conn., who has made an extensive study of nomenclature on Cape Cod, tells me that middle names were not in general use there until late in the Eighteenth Century.

[8] *John Paul* Jones was originally *John Paul*; he added the *Jones* for reasons still undetermined.

[9] Editor's Table, Dec. 1859, p. 122. [In England, apparently, the number of given names varies directly with social status. An article on this theme in *Crossbow*, by one Ronald Hall, was reported by Drew Middleton in *The New York Times*, July 4, 1960.]

In late years there have been three curious tendencies in the naming of American children: (*a*) the growing popularity of nicknames as given names, (*b*) the bestowal of mere initials on boys instead of names and (*c*) the fashion for inventing new and unprecedented names for girls, often of an unearthly and supercolossal character. All three tendencies are most marked among the evangelical tribesmen of the South and Southwest. The late Texan who served as Speaker of the House of Representatives, officially the third in rank among all American statesmen, described himself in the Congressional Directory as *Sam*—not as *Samuel*, but as plain *Sam*— and under his eye, when an appropriation bill was on its passage and all hands crowded up to vote, were another *Sam*, an *Al*, an *Arch*, two *Bens*, a *Billy*, two *Bobs*, a *Chet*, a *Clem*, a *Dan*, a *Dave*, two *Dons*, an *Ed*, two *Freds*, a *Gracie*, a *Harry*, a *Jack*, a *Jamie*, a *Jim*, two *Joes*, a *Ken*, a *Pat*, three *Toms* and a *Walt*, while the more sedate Senate boasted a *Sam*, a *Joe*, a *Pat* and two *Mikes*. Nor were all these bob-tailed brethren Southerners; some came from the upper Midwest and the Pacific coast, and several actually emanated from Pennsylvania, New Jersey and New York. The Newton survey of American given names puts *Harry* in thirteenth place, with 1,112 occurrences in every 100,000 individuals, and *Fred* in twenty-seventh, with 509. The English *Hal* is seldom used in this country; here the usual diminutives for *Henry* are *Harry*, *Hank* and *Hen*. *Ted*, in England, is the diminutive for *Edward;* here it is used for *Theodore*, especially in the form of *Teddy*. [But Senator *Edward* Kennedy is known to his intimates as *Ted* or *Teddy*.]

It is in the South, however, that such stable names are most frequently conferred upon he-babies at the sacrament of baptism. [The Register of the Oklahoma State University for 1960–1 yields a *Bill*, two *Bobbys*, a *Danny*, two *Dons*, three *Jacks*, seven *Jerrys*, a *Jim*, a *Jimmy Pete*, a *Joe*, three *Larrys*, a *Max*, a *Ned* and a *Phil* among the students listed upon a single page, and an *Alec*, a *Ben*, a *Bill*, a *Buck*, a *Cliff*, a *Don*, an *Eddie*, four *Freds*, five *Harrys*, six *Jacks*, two *Jims*, three *Joes*, a *Larry*, two *Maxes*, a *Pete*, a *Sam* and a *Tom* on the faculty, which also boasts a music professor with the soul-stirring name of *Cyclone Covey*.] In the Southern highlands, says Josiah Combs,[1] diminutives are very widely used, and "any highlander is lucky if he escapes with his original first-name." The same might be said of most parts of the country. Combs gives some examples: *Ad* for *Adam*, *Cece* for *Cecil*, *Gid* for *Gideon*, *Rance* for *Ransom* and *Zach* for *Zachariah*, and, among girls' names, *Barb* for *Barbara*, *Tildy* for *Matilda* and *Tish* for *Letitia*. He might have added a great many more,

---

[1] Language of the Southern Highlanders, *PMLA*, Vol. XLVI, No. 4, 1931, p. 1313. [See also Patterns of Child-Naming in Tennessee during the Depression Years, by George Grise, *Southern Folklore*, Vol. XXIII, Sept. 1959, pp. 150–4.]

e.g., Lafe or *Fate* for *Lafayette, Wash* for *Washington, Jeff* for *Jefferson, Gussie* for *Augusta* and so on.

The custom of giving boys simple initials instead of given names is not quite new, but it seems to have been growing rapidly of late, especially in the South. The middle initial of former President Harry S. Truman, according to the Associated Press,

> is just an initial—it has no name significance. It represents a compromise by his parents. One of his grandfathers had the first-name of *Solomon;* the other, *Shippe.* Not wanting to play favorites, the President's parents decided on the *S.*[2]

Mr. Truman was born in 1884, when the custom under discussion was in its cradle days, but he had forerunners. One of them may have been U. S. Grant, for Captain Charles King says: "Grant was never formally baptized until late in life, and then, by his own choice, as *Ulysses S.* He would not take the full [middle] name of *Simpson* [the surname of his mother], but elected to be baptized as he had been so long and well known to the Nation."[3] In the generation between Grant's and Truman's there were a number of conspicuous Americans bearing initials as given names, *e.g., W J* (no periods) *McGee,* the anthropologist (1853–1912), and *D-Cady* Herrick, candidate for the governorship of New York in 1904 (1846–1926). Also, there have been others among Mr. Truman's contemporaries, *e.g.,* Ferris *J* Stephens, curator of the Babylonian collection at Yale; *J* Milton Cowan, chairman of the Cornell Division of Modern Languages, who signs himself *J M; DR* Scott, of the University of Missouri;[4] and Mrs. *Bj* Kidd, secretary of the Advertising Federation of America and a well-known writer of and on advertising.[5]

The craze for afflicting girl babies with bizarre and unheard-of given names is relatively recent and is principally manifest in the South and

---

[2] Dispatch from Washington, Apr. 12, 1945.

[3] The True Ulysses S. Grant, 1915. There is considerable confusion regarding Grant's given names. Mr. Lloyd Lewis, his biographer, refused on advice of counsel to choose between discordant stories.

[4] Scott writes: "My father's name was *David Rowland* Scott. I was given his two initials as a given-name. The problem of translating it into written language was left to me. The form I use was not a matter of positive choice but rather the result of unwillingness to use any other form." [There is no truth in the rumor, common among linguists who served under Cowan during World War II when he was Director of the National Intensive Language Program, that the *J* really signifies *Jehovah.* Arjay Miller, new president of the Ford Motor Company, was named "for the initials of his father, *Rawley John.* It is, says Miller, 'a compromise junior.'" *Time,* Apr. 19, 1963, p. 104.]

[5] *Editor and Publisher,* Feb. 1., 1947, p. 17: "Christened *Elizabeth Jane,* she grew up as *Betty Jane.* In the business world she signed inter-office correspondence *BJK,* and from that achieved the pen-name of *Bj.*"

the rural Midwest, but it appeared sporadically in the North before the Civil War, and the swarming of the underprivileged before and during World War II carried it to the Pacific coast. In a list of "the most usual names" of American women, published in an 1814 edition of Webster's Spelling-Book, the 69 names given included such old favorites as *Ann, Helen, Jane* and *Mary*, along with such Puritan survivals as *Abigail, Priscilla* and *Temperance*, but the utmost advance of fancy forms was represented by *Clarissa, Huldah* and *Susannah*, none of them novel. In 1834, however, Longworth's Directory listed *Aletta, Blandina, Coritha, Dovinda, Elima, Hilah, Keturah, Parnethia* and *Zina*.[6] In a little while there were contemporary Connecticut records of *Minuleta, Typhosa, Irista, Zeriah* and *Wealthena*—all of them worthy of the best efforts of an Oklahoma mother today.[7] Other name lists of the 1840–60 period show *Rodintha, Sula, Delvina, Auria, Calina, Milma*,[8] *Isaphene, Levantia* and *Philena*.[9] After the Civil War there was a great access of romanticism in all departments of American life, and the naming of infants marched shoulder to shoulder with the crocheting of tidies and the jigsaw adornment of suburban villas. The new fashion was short-lived in the Northeast, but it went into the Southwest and West with the immigration of the post-Civil War period, and there it began to flourish. Before 1900 it was apparently only a feeble growth, for lists of frontier women born before 1890 show only a few of the more grotesque names, though such diminutives as *Lovie, Dolly, Hattie* and *Nellie* are numerous.[1] It has not gained much headway in the large cities east of the Mississippi, but some of them, *e.g.*, Chicago, Detroit and Baltimore, acquired large colonies of Okie and Linthead females bearing its stigmata during World War II. With its center in Oklahoma,[2] the

---

[6] I am indebted for this to Joseph M. Carrière, of the University of Virginia.

[7] For this I am indebted to Lockwood Barr, of New York, author of a history of clockmaking in Bristol, Conn.

[8] These were unearthed from New Hampshire records by Paul St. Gaudens.

[9] The last three were found at the Ontario Female Seminary, Canandaigua, N.Y., in 1841 by an English traveler, J. S. Buckingham. I am indebted here to Charles J. Lovell. [On May 19, 1963, *Midwest Magazine* (Sunday Supplement to the Chicago *Sun-Times*) mentioned *Dympna* Lavin among a group of English-born nurses now working in Chicago. *The New York Times* of the same date reported the nuptials of *Perdita* Plowden, an Englishwoman. It is evident that the influence of the classics is far from dead in English onomastics.]

[1] Many examples are to be found in Belles and Beaux of 40 Years Ago, by J. Marvin Hunter, *Frontier Times* (Bandera, Tex.), Mar. 1944, pp. 269–73.

[2] [Several notable studies: Thomas Pyles, Onomastic Individualism in Oklahoma, *AS*, Vol. XXII, Dec. 1947, pp. 256–64, and Bible Belt Onomastics, or Some Curiosities of Anti-Paedobaptist Nomenclature, *Names*, Vol. VII, June 1959, pp. 84–110; Thomas L. Crowell, Opinions on Onomastic Individualism, *AS*, Vol. XXIII, Oct.–Dec. 1948, pp. 265–72; George Grise, Patterns of Child-Naming in Tennessee During the Depression Years, *Southern Folklore*, Vol. XXIII, Sept. 1959, pp. 150–4. Perhaps here should be cited What Not to Name the Baby, by Roger Price and Leonard Stern; Chicago, 1960.]

current epidemic now has fastnesses in Texas and the Deep South, and there are outposts stretching all the way from upstate New York to the Los Angeles region of California.

In the lush onomastic efflorescence of the Southwest there are certain patterns and tendencies. Many of these names are more or less plausible and euphonious modifications of common male names, usually by the addition of suffixes generally thought of as feminine, *e.g.*, *Philelle*, *Ulyssia*, *Lloydine*, *Alexanderene*, *Oscaretta*, *Alburtis*. Others are diminutives of male names, often given a feminine flavor by combining them with accepted women's names, *e.g.*, *Bennie Mae*, *Jimmie Lou*, *Mary Jo*. Yet others are surnames converted into given names, *e.g.*, *Beverly*, *Sidney*, *Shirley*, *Dabney*, *Powell*, *Shelby*. And still others are geographical names —sometimes used unchanged, *e.g.*, *Manila*, *Maryland*, *Sonora*, *Elba*, and sometimes modified to please a whimsical fancy, *e.g.*, *Texana*, *Denva*, *Okla*, *Venazualia*.

All these processes have roots in the past. The ancient German man's name *Albert* produced a St. *Alberta* in the Third Century. So with *Julia*, which comes down from Roman times and was borne by a saint of the same era. So, again, with *Philippa*, *Theodora*, *Henrietta*, *Caroline* and many another. So, even, with *Sophia*, which was originally one of the Names of Jesus, and hence masculine, though it was transferred to women in Apostolic times and has been accepted by Holy Church ever since.[3] *Mary Jo* and the like may be traced to the day before surnames, when it was common to distinguish between two women of the same name by appending their fathers' given names. The custom of giving surnames as given names to girls apparently came in simultaneously with the custom of using such names for boys. *Douglas* was thus adopted in England shortly before Camden's time, and Henry Howard, Earl of Northampton (1540–1614), had a daughter of that name who was the subject of a poem by Spenser.[4] This use of surnames as given names for girls had always been commonest in the South, where it marks the gentry rather than the plain people. But in recent years it has flourished lushly among the lowly of Oklahoma.

Another large class of non-canonical girls' names is produced by adorning old names with new and mellifluous terminations, *e.g.*, *Carrine*, *Marcellette*, *Olgalene*, or by making collision forms of two or more, *e.g.*, *Gracella*, *Mariedythe*, *Abbieann*. With it goes a long series of novel abbreviations, *e.g.*, *Affie*, *Berthie*, *Osbie*, and another and longer of rococo spellings, *e.g.*, *Cylvia*, *Wroberta*, *Scharlott*, *Phaye*. Such spellings were

---

[3] Camden, in his Remains Concerning Britain, says that it was frowned upon by "some godly men" of his time, *c.* 1600, as too pretentious, and hence "irreligious."

[4] *PMLA*, Vol. XLIII, Sept. 1928, p. 645.

once fashionable in the great Babylons of the East, with *Edythe, Kathryn* and *Sadye* as familiar examples, but in late years they have passed out there. In the Dust Bowl and its colonies, however, they continue to flourish, and some of them are of a great boldness, *e.g., Feby (Phoebe), Gladdis, Rhey* and *Qay*. In some cases their forms suggest mere illiteracy, as *Cloteel, Milderd* and *Roxaner*,[5] but much more common is a highly self-conscious artfulness, also visible in the lavish misuse of particles, capitals, apostrophes and other such alarms and delights to the eye and psyche, *e.g., ClarEtta, De'An, Je Nanne, DeDonda, Lo Venia, McNara* and *La Lahoma*.[6] In such forms as *Garguerite, Maomi, Orene* and *Omelia*, old names are turned into new ones by the simple device of changing the initial letters. It may be ingenuity that operates here, or only ignorance.

A large residue defies analysis and even classification. Its masterpieces show a determination to achieve something unmatched and unimagined, at whatever cost to tradition and decorum. It is as if the ambitious mother of a newly hatched darling wrote all the elements of all the ancient girls' names upon slips of paper, added slips bearing syllables filched from the terminology of all the arts and sciences, heaved the whole into an electric mixer, and then arranged the seethed contents two by two or three by three. On what other theory is one to arrive at the genesis of *Flouzelle, Ulestine, Wheirmelda* and *Moonean*? They bear no apparent relation to the ordinary nomenclature of the language, but seem to be altogether synthetic. The woman who achieves so shining a novelty not only marks off her little darling from all other little darlings within ear- or rumor-shot; she also establishes herself in her community as a salient social reformer and forward-looker and is quickly rewarded with the envy and imitation of other mothers. In the heat of this creative urge, alas, she sometimes contrives something that may wring snickers from city slickers, *e.g., Faucette, Phalla* or *Coita*,[7] but her friends and admirers are unaware of any cryptic meaning or suggestion, and so is she herself. The woman next door who can fetch up nothing better than *Echo, Kiwanis* or *Apple* is plainly of an inferior order.

Most such inventions come from mothers in the lower-income brackets, but by no means all. Some of the most extraordinary specimens are taken, not from the police news in the Bible Belt newspapers, but from rosters of college students and the elegant gossip of the society columns. Indeed, the

---

[5] There are other examples in Feminine Names, *AS*, Vol. I, Nov. 1925, p. 130. [A lady named *Jone* was mentioned in the Miami *Herald*, May 1, 1963.]

[6] The incomparable *Shir Lee* falls under three headings. It is a surname, it is a doublet of the *Betty Jo* class and it involves an orthographical novelty.

[7] All borne by actual girls, mainly in Oklahoma. Names in *Merd-* are numerous, *e.g., Merdena, Merdelle* and *Merdis*.

impulse to make strange names for their daughters sometimes seizes upon women on the highest cultural levels, and not a few female Americans of considerable dignity bear them. A lady professor in California was named *Eschscholtzia*—in honor of the California poppy, or perhaps of the Russian naturalist who was its eponym. *Irita*, the charming given name of a charming woman, formerly editor of the New York *Herald Tribune*'s "Books," was concocted, by her account, "with no excuse except that it pleased my parents' fancy." [8] *Tallulah*, the name of a very successful actress, is geographical and has been borne by ladies of her family, the Bankheads of Alabama, for several generations. The four daughters of the late Owen Cattell, one of the editors of *Science*, are *Coryl*, *Roma*, *Quinta* and *Jayjay*.[9] Miss M. *Burneice* Larson, director of the Medical Bureau in Chicago, finds her name so spelled because her mother objected to the way that *Bernice* was pronounced by the Cornish miners of the Michigan copper country where she was born, to wit, *Búrniss*, and determined to do something about it.[1]

In the Cumberland Mountains of Tennessee an inquirer unearthed *Olsie*, *Coba*, *Bleba*, *Onza*, *Otella* and *Latrina*.[2] In the same vicinity lived a girl named *Trailing Arbutus Vines*. Another investigator, in the Blue Ridge of Virginia, found girls named *Needa*, *Zannis*, *Avaline* and *Weeda* (the last possibly a corruption of *Ouida*).[3] Bold combinations of common given names are frequent, *e.g.*, *Lucybelle*, *Floramay* and *Sallyrose*. Dr. Louise Pound has unearthed *Olouise* (from *Olive* and *Louise*), *Lunette* (*Luna* + *Nettie*), *Adrielle* (*Adrienna* + *Belle*), *Birdene* (*Birdie* + *Pauline*), *Bethene* (*Elizabeth* + *Christine*), *Olabelle* (*Ola* + *Isabel*) and *Armina* (*Ardelia* + *Wilhelmina*).[4] Even surnames and men's given names are employed in these feminine blends, as in *Romiette* (*Romeo* + *Juliette*), *Adnelle* (*Addison* + *Nellie*) and *Adelloyd* (*Addie* + *Lloyd*). The common feminine endings are often used to make entirely new names, some of them very florid in fancy: *Darlene*, *Eneatha*, *Arzareta*, *Burtyce*, *Colice*, *Icel*, *Twila* and *Vola*. The regions of onomatological new growth, of course, are predominantly Protestant.

Strange given names are common among lady professors and among librarians. One named *Ullainee* is reported from Illinois, and others named *Vannelda*, *Zola Mae*, *Azaleen* and *Mirth* have been found below the Potomac. Still another lady of the craft, *Tommie* by name, is said to have

---

[8] Wild Names I Have Met, by Alfred H. Holt; n.p., n.d., p. 17.
[9] See his obituary notice in *The New York Times*, Mar. 28, 1940.
[1] I am indebted here to the courtesy of Miss Larson herself.
[2] Christian Names in the Cumberlands, by James A. Still, *AS*, Vol. V, Apr. 1930.
[3] Christian Names in the Blue Ridge of Virginia, by Miriam M. Sizer, *AS*, Vol. VIII, Apr. 1933.
[4] Stunts in Language, *EJ*, Vol. IX, Feb. 1920, p. 92; Blends, *Anglistische Forschungen*, Heft. XLII, p. 16.

once suffered the embarrassment of being booked to share a room with a he-colleague at a professional convention. [To match this, *Alva* Lee Davis, now professor of English linguistics at the Illinois Institute of Technology and probably the American most knowledgeable about teaching English to speakers of other languages, was once invited to a reunion of the Women's Army Corps. He declined, regretfully, at the suggestion of his wife.[5]] In Canada there was a female public official whose given names were the simple initials *O.P.*

The invention and adoption of such names must have begun long ago. Sydney Smith gave the name *Saba* to his eldest daughter, born *c.* 1800, in an effort to find something striking enough to divert attention from *Smith*.[6] General Richard S. Ewell's wife had the name *Lizinka*.[7] Cornelius Vanderbilt II, in 1869, married, as his second wife, a lady of Mobile, Ala., named *Frank* Crawford. *Lamiza* has come to its fifth generation in the Breckenridge family, and has been borrowed outside.[8]

The fashion for artificial names may be spreading, for they have begun to be listed in the handbooks for puzzled parents got out by enterprising parents. In one of these books I find *Arvia, Sidra, Thadine* and *Xylia*,[9] and in another *Gelda, Marette, Xanthe* and *Zella*.[1] But even in the heart of the Swell Names Zone the older girls' names have not yet gone wholly underground. In a list of recent graduates of the Capitol City High School of Oklahoma City, despite the throng of *Frenas, Phillie Joes, Narasonas* and *Twylas*, are yet two *Katherines* and *Helens*, three *Margarets* and *Dorothys*, four *Ruths*, nine *Marys* and no less than seventeen *Bettys*. These old names have been facing the competition of successive waves of newer ones for centuries, but they still hold out. There are recurrent crazes for naming girls after the heroines of novels and movies and the stars of stage and screen, but they do not last. The old names go into disuse for a while, and then come back triumphantly. "The only thing that has kept girls' names from collapsing into sheer frivolity or worse," wrote a Canadian observer in 1935, "has been the astonishing recrudescence of *Ann* and *Jane*." [2] Both have flourished, with occasional short eclipses, since the Fourteenth Cen-

---

[5] [Personal communication from Mr. and Mrs. Davis.]

[6] A Memoir of the Rev. Sydney Smith by His Daughter, Lady Holland; London, 1855, II.

[7] This was a Russian loan; she was born in St. Petersburg while her father was American minister there.

[8] Mrs. Breckenridge Lambert, of St. Louis, tells me that family legend makes it of Indian origin

[9] What Shall We Name the Baby?, ed. by Winthrop Ames; New York, 1935.

[1] Naming Your Baby, by Elsdon C. Smith; New York, 1943. [More recent handbooks include Baby Name Booklet, Roslyn Heights, N.Y., 1960; A New Treasury of Names for the Baby, by Dorothy Burton, Englewood Cliffs, N.J., 1961; Names for Every Child, by Christine Campbell Thompson, London, 1961; and Chs. 3–5 in The Catholic Baby Book, by John and Ellen Springer, New York, 1961.]

[2] Improper Nouns, by J. H. Simpson, Toronto *Saturday Night*, Mar. 16, 1935.

tury. So have *Amy, Beatrice, Blanche, Mary, Philippa, Helen, Emma, Katherine* and *Sibyl*.

Two fashions in boys' names have been mentioned—that for diminutives and that for mere initials. A third of almost equal oddity converts *Junior* from an indicator following the surname into a middle name, *e.g.*, John *Junior* Jones. In a list of 88 students, male and female, graduated from the Marshall (Mo.) High School in the class of 1946, are no less than three boys thus named, and in a roster of Army recruits from the same town are two more. One of the Marshall *Juniors* applied to the local circuit court in 1946 for permission to drop his middle name on the ground that it had "caused him difficulty and confusion." [3] Even when the adjective is in its proper place it is common for an American boy to be called *Junior* by his family and friends, to distinguish him from his father. In writing, *Jr.* is in most frequent use in the United States, but in England *Jun.* seems to be preferred.

The use of *2nd, 3rd*, etc., is marked as an Americanism by the DAE and traced to 1804. At the start *2nd* seemed to have been only a substitute for *Jr.*, but now it often indicates, not the son, but the grandson or nephew of the first bearer of the name; [when *2nd* is assumed by the son, it often indicates that the father is distinguished and recently deceased]. The use of the Roman numerals *II, III*, etc., came much later. It is frowned upon in England as an invasion of royal prerogative, and also by the American Army and Navy, which use only *2d, 3d*, etc., in their lists.[4] There was a time when *Sr.* was encountered almost as frequently as *Jr.*, but it seems to be passing out: the old man now evades admitting his age by using his name unadorned.

The masculine given names of the Bible Belt are not quite so fanciful as the feminine names, but nevertheless they often depart widely from the accepted standards of the cities. American statesmen named *Hoke, Ollie, Finis* and *Champ* (a shortening of *Beauchamp*, pronounced to rhyme with *lamp*) will be recalled. From the Cumberlands of Tennessee come *Oder, Oarly, Osie, Cam* and *Mord*. Sometimes the pet names of infancy persist, as in the cases of young men named *Pee Wee, Poke, Cap, Babe* and *Hoss*. Kentucky had a *Cap* R. Carden (*b.* 1866) in the Seventy-fourth Congress.

That the invention of new and unearthly boys' names lags behind the fancy that has enriched and glorified the repertoire of girls' names is probably explicable on the ground that fathers ordinarily have more to say about the naming of their sons than about the naming of their daughters,

---

[3] Marshall *Democrat-News*, June 19. I am indebted here to Dr. W. L. Carter.
[4] But Commodore Allen George Quynn, U.S.N., reports in Who's Who in America that his son is *Allen George VIII*. I am indebted here to Alexander Kadison.

and oppose masculine Toryism to feminine advanced thinking. Yet nearly all the categories of girls' names that we have examined are represented, though the specimens as a whole are a good deal less rich. In not a few cases, indeed, girls' names also reappear as boys' names—a phenomenon certainly not new in the world, as the bisexual use of *Evelyn* in England and *Maria* in Latin Europe testifies. It is not uncommon in Oklahoma for a male *Dixie* or *Marion* or *LaVerne* or even *Beryl* to espouse a lady of the same given name, and in 1941 R. L. Ripley unearthed an *Ora* Jones married to an *Ora* Jones.[5] Manuel Prenner has published a study of the names most frequently found in both sexes, *e.g.*, *Beverly, Carmen, Carol, Cecil, Cleo, Darryl, Fay, Gail, Hope, Jean, Lee, Leslie, Lynn, Merle, Ray, Sidney, Vaughn* and *Vivian*. To this list Oklahoma adds *Delores, Dorotha, Laurel* and *Osie*.[6]

Odd spellings seem to be almost as numerous among boys' names as among those of girls, but whether they are produced by a deficiency in orthographic science or by a sophisticated artfulness is hard to determine. The former may account for *Amel* (*Emil*), *Byard, Hilry, Malcum, Markus* and *Virgle*, but the latter is probably responsible for *Benjiman, Eligh, Frederique, Johnathon, Lesley* and *Seymore*. Such bizarre spellings as *DeLaine, Del Ray, LaFerry, LeMon* and *LuReign*, so common among girls' names, seem to be relatively rare. So are the combinations and collision forms, *e.g., Jamanuel, Jimmie Lee* and *Joela*. But the making of new names by changing letters in old ones, *e.g., Arlando, Garl, Terbert, Bearl* and *Urxula*, is more frequent. As we have seen, diminutives are often bestowed at baptism and some of them show novelty, *e.g., Chan, Clint, Orv* and *Ulys*, and equally popular are the pet names, *Bo, Chick, Doc, Monk* and *Rowdy*. Names of literal significance, *e.g., Comma, Moose* and *Vital*, are often encountered, but those suggesting medical matters, *e.g., Cardia, Toxie* and *Voyd*, are not as numerous as among girls. Nor are common given names with fancy suffixes, *e.g., Carolle* and *Claudere*, nor geographical names, *e.g., Denver, California* and *Nevada*.[7] But the deficit is made up for by titles, *e.g., Colonel, Commodore, Count, Earl, Gov, Speaker;* by the popularity of well-worn

---

[5] *Ora* Jones Married *Ora* Jones, by Manuel Prenner, *AS*, Vol. XVII, Apr. 1942, pp. 84–8, and Dec. 1942, p. 282.

[6] One of the attorneys for Jahveh, at the trial of Scopes at Dayton, Tenn., in 1925, bore the name of *Sue*, though his he-ness was manifest. In 1941, according to Prenner, *Case and Comment*, the lawyers' magazine, unearthed male barristers named *Clare, Velma, Shirley* and *Gail*. In the Seventy-ninth Congress there were two members of the House named *Clare*, one male and one female. See

Bulletin on *Hon.*, by H. L. Mencken, *AS*, Vol. XXI, Apr. 1946, p. 81. [*Gwin* J. Kolb, chairman of the English Department at the University of Chicago, reports receiving communications to *Mrs.* and *Miss*, as well as some unidentified as to sex, while he was associate editor of *Modern Philology*.]

[7] Captain *California* C. McMillan, of the Coast Guard, retired in 1938 after 36 years' service, and died in San Francisco, Dec. 4, 1946.

surnames, especially *Clay, Wayne, Dwight, Dallas, Preston* and *Harlan;*[8] and by the surviving if diminishing vogue, throughout rural America, for names borrowed from the heroes of classical history and legend. Oklahoma has borne *Ovid, Solon, Euclid, Virgil, Apollo* and even *Deo*. And *Homer* flourishes from Bangor to San Diego.

Nothing here is really new. Paul St. Gaudens has unearthed *Sterling* and *Urian* from the Killingly, Conn., records of 1725–40; *Irastus, Delor* and *Ozno* from New Hampshire records of 1850–70; *Aldace, Erdix, Royal, Volney, Nomus* and *Sardis* from the rolls of Kimball Union Academy at Meriden, N.H., 1834–48; and *Noble, Leroy, Earl, Lysander, Euclid, Romaine, Hector* and *Dolph* from various New England account books of 1850–60. The fame of Ralph *Waldo* Emerson (1803–82) after his Phi Beta Kappa oration at Harvard in 1837 started a vogue for his middle name. William *Tecumseh* Sherman, born in 1813, was not the first American to bear an Indian name,[9] nor was *Kenesaw Mountain* Landis, born in 1866, the first to be named for a battle.[1] Geographical names began to be used as given names in the period of expansion into the West. *Wisconsin Illinois* and *Arizona Dakota* were two North Carolina brothers,[2] and *Lewes Delaware* was a Washington physician. In Connecticut, a generation or two ago, there was a politico surnamed *Bill* whose given names were *Kansas Nebraska*. He had brothers named *Lecompton Constitution* and *Emancipation Proclamation*,[3] and sisters named *Louisiana Purchase* and *Missouri Compromise*. Long before their time Governor William H. Gist, of South Carolina, named a son *States Rights*. This *States Rights* was graduated from the Harvard Law School in 1852, joined the Confederate Army in 1861, rose to be a brigadier general, and was killed at the battle of Franklin, Tenn., November 30, 1864.

The austere pages of "Who's Who in America" are adorned with many strange names, *e.g., Champion, Erdis, Balpha, Doel, Ival, Tubal* and *Cola*, though they are naturally less numerous than among the sturdy yeomen of Oklahoma and Texas. [There are congressmen (1961) named *Silvio, Roman, Dante, Ancher* and *Oren*.] The newspapers are constantly turning up

---

[8] On June 29, 1940, the United Press reported from Springville, Utah, that a filling station there had both a *Taylor Burt* and a *Burt Taylor* on its faculty.

[9] Lloyd Lewis says in Sherman, Fighting Prophet, New York, 1932, p. 517, that Sherman was christened *Tecumseh*, but that *William* was later prefixed at the suggestion of his foster father, Thomas Ewing.

[1] Sherman was defeated by Joseph E. Johnston at Kenesaw Mountain, near Marietta, Ga., June 27, 1864. Dr. *Malvern Hill* Price, a Washington physician, maybe preceded Landis, for Malvern Hill was fought on July 1, 1862. I am indebted here to Dr. John B. Nicols, of Washington.

[2] I am indebted here to Thomas E. Street, of Enfield, N.C.

[3] I am indebted here to Mrs. L. B. Bailey, of South Freeport, Me.

given names of a fantastic improbability. In 1944 *E Pluribus Unum* Husted was found in Oklahoma City, though he was a native of Quincy, Ill.[4] In 1936 *Willie ⅜* Smith was unearthed in rural Georgia.[5] In 1901 *Loyal Lodge No. 296 Knights of Pythias Ponca City Oklahoma Territory* Smith was baptized at Ponca City. [In 1949 *John Hodge Opera House Centennial Gargling Oil Samuel J. Tilden* Ten Brink was interviewed for the Linguistic Atlas in upstate New York.] The late Cap Anson, manager of the Chicago baseball club, was baptized *Adrian Constantine*, because his mother was born at *Adrian*, Mich., and his father at *Constantine* in the same state.[6] For a long time the chaplain of the United States Senate was the Rev. Ze Barney T. Phillips; the Public Printer had to have a character specially cut to print his name.[7] A well-known American writer, of Spanish ancestry, is *Emjo* Basshe. His given names were originally *Emmanuel Jode Abarbanel*.[8] Thornton reprints a paragraph from the *Congressional Globe* of June 13, 1854, alleging that in 1846, during the row over the Oregon boundary, when "Fifty-four forty or fight" was a political slogan, many "canal-boats, and even some of the babies . . . were christened *54° 40′*."

In many minor ways there are differences in nomenclatural usage between England and the United States. The English, especially of the upper classes, frequently give a boy three or more given names, but it is most unusual in the United States. *Michael* is now fashionable in England, but here it is bestowed only rarely. Many aristocratic English given names, *e.g.*, *Reginald, Algernon, Percy, Wilfred* and *Cecil*, are commonly looked upon as sissified in the United States, and any boy who bears one of them is likely to have to defend it with his fists.[9] Only one *Percival*, so far as I know, has ever appeared in "Who's Who in America."

Every Southern town boasts a Negro denizen who is exhibited to stran-

---

[4] Oklahoma City *Oklahoman*, Aug. 8, 1944.

[5] I am indebted here to Leonard G. Pardue, of Jacksonville, Fla.

[6] On the Side, by E. V. Durling, Baltimore *News-Post*, July 13, 1945. Anson, says Durling, "thanked the Lord his mother had not been born in Ypsilanti and his father in Kalamazoo."

[7] Dr. Phillips's given name is the surname of some of his father's relatives; the Ze Barney family, once well known in Chautauqua County, N.Y., is now extinct there.

[8] Private communication, July 22, 1935. [In Common American Surnames and Their Relation to Eminence, *Names*, Vol. X, Mar. 1962, pp. 43–4, Elsdon C. Smith reports: "Two psychologists, Albert Ellis and Robert M. Beechley, have discovered that boys with peculiar first names are more likely to be emotionally disturbed than boys with popular forenames."]

[9] In *Claude* and *Percy*, *AS*, Vol. III, Apr. 1928, Howard F. Barker quotes the following from an unidentified issue of the *Christian Science Monitor* (Boston): "Captain Claude S. Cochrane, commander of the *Bear* and associated with its later adventures, will leave his old ship and go North in command of the Bering Sea patrol-force. . . . It is said by those who know that he is the only man afloat in the Coast Guard who could afford to admit to the name of *Claude*."

gers as *Seaboard Airline Railway* Jackson, *Way Down upon the Swanee River* Johnson, *Are You Ready for the Judgment Day* Brown or *Sunday Night Supper* Jones, but most such grotesque names are invented by sportive whites and accepted only to gain their attention and favor. All the students who have investigated Afro-American onomastics in a scientific spirit have found such monstrosities to be few and far between, and when a particularly amazing specimen is reported the news of it usually comes at second or third hand. The nomenclature of the educated portion of them is indistinguishable from that of the whites. Here are the given names of the clergy mentioned on the church page of a single issue of the Pittsburgh *Courier: Frederick, John, Talmadge, James, Allen, Miles, Louis, Arthur, Wilbur, George, Claude.* Even in the South, Negro parents have, for the most part, kept to standard names. In 1930, Urban T. Holmes, of the University of North Carolina, found that 542 of 722 Negro school children in a typical mill town of that state bore ancient and commonplace names on the order of *Mary* and *Margaret, James* and *William,* that 136 boasted such fancier but nonetheless familiar names as *Clarissa* and *Eugenia, Elbert* and *Gordon,* and that only 44 were adorned with such inventions as *Orcellia* and *Margorilla, Sandas* and *Venton.*[1] In 1938, of 22,105 colored college students—12,220 females and 9,885 males—Newbell N. Puckett, of Western Reserve University, found "unusual" names borne by 15.3% of the females and 8.4% of the males. Of the Negro given names in "Who's Who in Negro America," including those of parents, spouses and children, he found a "rate of unusualness," for the two sexes together, of 7.6% among individuals born before 1870, one of 9.8% among those born between 1870 and 1900 and one of 15.6% among those born since the latter year. Inasmuch as his criterion of "unusualness," whatever it was, was applied alike in all three periods, it is safe to accept his conclusion that "the rate of unusualness with the females appears to be on the increase." The same applies to students in two colored colleges—one in South Carolina and the other in Arkansas. At the former he found 10.3% of "unusualness" before 1901, and 17.5% in 1935. At the latter the rate was 14.6% from 1900 to 1919, 22.4% from 1920 to 1929 and 35.6% in 1935.[2]

Here the effect of the circumambient white *Kultur* is well displayed. Lists of Southern colored students indicate that the density of fancy names, as among the white population, runs in inverse proportion to the degree of

---

[1] A Study in Negro Onomastics, *AS,* Vol. V, Aug. 1930, pp. 463–7.

[2] Negro Names, *Journal of Negro History,* Vol. XXIII, Jan. 1938, pp. 35–48. In Names of American Negro Slaves, to be noticed presently, Puckett found that the order of frequency in names among Negro college students of today runs *James, William, John, Robert, Charles, George, Edward, Joseph, Thomas, Henry, Samuel* and *Walter* for the men, and *Mary, Annie, Ruth, Helen, Dorothy, Thelma, Louise, Alice, Katherine, Elizabeth, Lillian* and *Ethel* for the women.

local civilization. In the 1940s, the North Carolina College for Negroes at Durham, a high-toned seminary, sported less than a dozen fancy names among nearly 600, and at Tuskegee Institute in 1946–7, among students of a decidedly ambitious and superior class, with relatively cultured home backgrounds, the ordinary given names ran to at least 90%. There were some eyebrow-lifting *Arrenwinthas*, *Berneths* and *LaFauns*, but they would be outnumbered at least six to one by the *Fledareas*, *Jessoises*, *Merhizes* and *Oyonnas* in any comparable white list from Oklahoma, Arkansas or the Baptist areas of Louisiana and Texas.

On the lowest social level the study of Negro given names is impeded by the fact that the sacrament of baptism is delayed among the majority of blacks until they are sturdy enough to stand a violent ducking, by which time they have often become known to their friends by pet names or nicknames, and are disinclined to change them. As a result, when they depart from the standard, Negroes sometimes go even further than their fellow Methodists and Baptists of the dominant race. Medical men making a malaria survey of Northampton County, N.C., staggered back to civilization with the news that they had found male Afro-Americans named *Handbag* Johnson, *Squirrel* Bowes, *Prophet* Ransom, *Bootjack* Webb and *Solicitor* Ransom, and females named *Alimenta*, *Iodine*, *Zooa*, *Negolia*, *Abolena*, *Arginta* and *Dozine*.[3] Three of the sisters of Joe Louis, the pugilist, are *Eammarell*, *Eulalia* and *Vunies*.

Many of the double names in vogue among the dark-blanket Christians of the South are the product of piety, for the uneducated Negro is almost as religious as the white Cracker. Examples are *King Solomon*, *Queen Esther*, *Holy Moses* and *Virgin Mary*.[4] Once in a while these combinations run to formidable length, recalling the worst imbecilities of the Puritans, e.g., *I Will Arise and Go Unto My Father*,[5] *Jesus Christ and Him Crucified*, *Matthew Mark Luke John Acts of the Apostles*. Some of the pious names show a considerable shakiness in Bible scholarship, e.g., *Deuteronomy*, *Ecclesiastes*, *Judas Iscariot*, *Ananias*, *Verily*, *Balaam*, *Cain*, *Herod*, *Archangel* and *Onan*. I have even heard of a colored boy baptized *Jehovah*.[6]

There are also cognate prodigies in the secular field, e.g., *Pictorial Review*,[7] *Quo Vadis*, *Lake Erie*, and, when a romantic colored mother decides to shoot the works, *Christine Nancy Luanna Jane Rio Miranda Mary Jane*, *George Washington Thomas Jefferson Andrew Jackson*, *Georgia May*

---

[3] See the *American Mercury*, Mar. 1927, p. 303.
[4] Some Curious Negro Names, by Arthur Palmer Hudson, *Southern Folklore Quarterly*, Vol. II, Dec. 1938, pp. 179–93.

[5] *Willie* for short.
[6] Found by Mrs. Louise B. Ellison, of Charleston, S.C.
[7] Called *Torial* for short. Reported from Greensburg, Pa., by Miss Lenora Lund.

Virginia Dare Martha Annie Louise,[8] *Mary Beatrice Love Divine Ceeno Tatrice Belle Carolina*[9] or (a mixed example) *Daisy Bell Rise Up and Tell the Glory of Emanuel.*[1] Other secular names showing the same talent for absurdity are *Delirious, Anonymous, Neuralgia, Sterilize, Sal Hepatica, Morphine, Castor Oil, Ether, Constipation,*[2] *Castile, Jingo, Vaseline* and *LaUrine.* The name *Positive Wasserman* Johnson, sometime of Evanston, Ill., probably represents the indelicate humor of a medical student. The young brethren who deliver colored mothers in the vicinity of the Johns Hopkins Hospital in Baltimore sometimes induce the mothers to give their babies grandiose physiological and pathological names, but these are commonly expunged later on by watchful social workers and colored pastors. *Placenta, Granuloma* and *Gonadia,* however, seem to have survived in a few cases. [Medical humor probably explains the names of the colored female twins, *Roseola* and *Variola,* born on James Island, S.C., in 1936.]

Puckett finds that the earliest slaves usually had commonplace English or Spanish given names, with *John* and *Mary* in the lead.[3] His first example of what later came to be regarded as a characteristically Negro name, *Sambo,* is found in Maryland in 1692. During the Eighteenth Century *Cuffy, Cudjo, Mungo* and *Quashie* appeared, and the prevailing classical influence showed itself in such names as *Caesar, Cato, Hannibal* and *Ulysses.* But the old names held their own, as they did among the whites, with *John* in the lead for men, followed by *Henry, George, Sam, Jim, Jack, Tom, Charles, Peter, Joe, Bob* and *William,* and *Mary* in the lead for women, followed by *Maria, Nancy, Lucy, Sarah, Harriet, Hannah, Eliza, Martha, Jane, Amy* and *Ann.* By the beginning of the Nineteenth Century, Negro nomenclature began to take on the patterns it shows today. After Emancipation it was assimilated by the given-name patterns and fashions of the whites, though perhaps with a larger admixture of downright ridiculous names and a lesser admixture of mere fancy names. Says Puckett:

---

[8] Reported by Durward King, of Leaksville, N.C.

[9] Reported from Bladen County, N.C., by Worth B. Baldwin, of Laurinburg.

[1] I am indebted for this to A. Wilson Dods, of Fredonia, N.Y.

[2] The last five are from Some Curious Negro Names, by Arthur Palmer Hudson, before cited.

[3] Names of American Negro Slaves, in Studies in the Science of Society Presented to Albert Galloway Keller; New Haven, 1937, pp. 471–94. [An earlier study by Miss Blanche Britt Armfield, of Concord, N.C., has not been published.

More recent studies: Hennig Cohen, Slave Names in Colonial South Carolina, *AS,* Vol. XXVII, May 1952, pp. 102–7; George Walton Williams, Slave Names in Ante-Bellum South Carolina, *AS,* Vol. XXXIII, Dec. 1958, pp. 294–5; Cecil D. Eby, Jr., Classical Names among Southern Negro Slaves, *AS,* Vol. XXXVI, May 1961, pp. 140–1. There is also a discussion of classical names for slaves in Norman E. Eliason, Tarheel Talk, Chapel Hill, N.C., 1956, pp. 177–8. These last discussants point out that not only slaves but mules as well were given classical names.]

With freedom . . . *Romeo* Jones signed his name *Romey O.* Jones, and *Pericles* Smith became *Perry Clees* Smith. A boy who had always been known as *Polly's Jim,* having learned to read the New Testament, became Mr. *Apollos James.* . . . *Corinthia Marigold Wilkinson Ball Wemyss Alexander Jones Mitchell* owed her collection of names to the fact that she had been owned successively by half a dozen families and after Emancipation took the names of them all.

The American Negroes have generally dropped the names they brought with them from Africa, and also the Indian names they picked up in the New World. The single exception is the Gullah country along the South Carolina and Georgia coasts, including the offshore islands. Most of the 6,000 African words that survive in Gullah are personal names. "In some families on the Sea Islands," writes Lorenzo Turner,[4] "the names of all the children are African. Many have no English names, though in most cases the African words in use are mere nicknames. Very few of the Gullahs of today know the meaning of these names; they use them because their parents and grandparents did so." Some of Turner's examples, with their languages of origin and original meanings, are:

Abeshe (Yoruba): worthless.
Agali (Wolof): welcome.
Alamisa (Bambara): born on Thursday.
Alovizo (Jeji): inflamed fingers or toes.
Anika (Vai): very beautiful.
Asigbe (Ewe): market day.
Bambula (Kongo): to transfer by witchcraft.
Ishi (Kimbundu): the ground.
Lainde (Fula): a forest.
Maungau (Kongo): a hill.
Randa (Wolof): a thicket.
Sanko (Mende): one of triplets.
Simung (Mandinka): time to eat.
Sina (Mende): a female twin.
Sukuta (Mandinka): night is arriving.
Tiwauni (Yoruba): it is yours.
Winiwini (Jeji): delicate.

Many of these relate to personal characteristics, or to the place or circumstances of birth. The Gullahs also carry this habit of name-making

[4] Private communication, June 5, 1944. [See also his Africanisms in the Gullah Dialect; Chicago, 1949.]

into English. "In addition to the names of the months and days," Turner says, "the following are typical: *Blossom* (born when the flowers were in bloom), *Wind, Hail, Storm, Freeze, Morning, Cotton* (born in cotton-picking time), *Easter* and *Harvest*."

The Mormons, in their early days, extracted a roster of names for their male offspring from the Book of Mormon, and to this day some of them are still called *Nephi, Mahonri, Lehi, Laman* and *Moroni;* also the custom survives among them of naming the seventh son of a seventh son *Doctor*.[5] Other curious names, chiefly loans from afar, *e.g., Luana* and *Aloha*, testify to the fact that every pious Mormon must go on a missionary journey in his youth. But all these names are falling into disuse. [Among the Youngs in the 1960 Salt Lake City telephone directory are a *Brigham*, a *Bud*, a *Douglas*, an *Erla*, two *Gaylens*, a *Horst*, a *Ladoyle*, two *Lorenzos*, two *Parleys*, a *Raymond*, a *Spencer* and a *Waldo*, but not a single *Nephi* or *Moroni*.] The young saints of today bear the same fancy appellations that prevail among other Bible searchers, *e.g., Filna, WaNeta, Janell* and *Myldreth* for girls; *Legene, Rondell, La Mar* and *Wildis* for boys, and *LaVon* and *LaVerne* for both sexes.[6] Indeed, it is possible that this murrain of made-up names was launched upon the country by the Saints, for as long ago as the 1836–44 era their prophet and martyr, Joseph Smith, had wives named *Presindia, Zina, Delcena* and *Almera*.[7]

The non-British American's willingness to anglicize his patronymic is far exceeded by his eagerness to give "American" baptismal names to his children. The favorite given names of the old country almost disappear in the first native-born generation. The Irish immigrants who flocked in after the famine of 1845–7 bearing such names as *Patrick, Terence* and *Dennis* named their American-born sons *John, George, William* and *James*. Today, even the most politically conscious Irish-Americans seldom succumb to that fashion for Gaelic given names which now prevails in the Republic of Ireland. An occasional boy is named *Padraic* (*Patrick*) or *Seumas* (*James*), but when this is done a concession is commonly made to American speech habits by giving *Padraic* three syllables instead of two and by making *Seumas Seemas* or *Sumas* instead of *Shamus*.[8]

Among the first German immigrants to America such characteristic given names as *Johann, Hans, Franz, Conrad, Caspar, Gottfried, Andreas, Ludwig, Otto, Herman, August, Anton* and *Dietrich* were very common,[9]

[5] I am indebted here to J. F. Hill, of Salinas, Cal.

[6] I am indebted here to Mrs. George Lucas, of Ogden, Utah.

[7] No Man Knows My History, by Fawn M. Brodie; New York, 1945, pp. 335–6.

[8] Here I am indebted to Ernest Boyd.

[9] A Collection of Upwards of 30,000 Names of German, Swiss, Dutch, French and Other Immigrants to Pennsylvania from 1727 to 1776, by I. Daniel Rupp; 2nd ed.; Philadelphia, 1927. [They too have their nicknames. See Nicknames

but with the flight of the years most of them have been transformed into their British equivalents—as *Franz* and *Ludwig* into *Frank* and *Lewis*—or abandoned altogether. The former process was facilitated by the fact that not a few were already identical with British names in spelling, though usually not in pronunciation, *e.g.*, *Robert* and *Arnold*. The one brilliant exception to this obliteration is *Carl*, which is now quite as common in the United States as it ever was in Germany. German influence may have helped to popularize certain girls' names, *e.g.*, *Anna*, *Emma*, *Gertrude*, *Ida* and *Irma*, but it certainly did not suffice to naturalize *Kunigunde*, *Waldburgia*, *Irmingard* and *Sieglinde*. The Scandinavians in the Northwest have added *Helma*, *Karen* [1] and *Ingeborg* to the American repertoire, especially in that region, but for every name they have thus managed to preserve they have lost dozens. So with their boys' names, *e.g.*, *Olaf*, *Axel*, *Nils*, *Knut;* of the whole lot only *Erik*, spelled *Eric*, seems to have been adopted by Americans.

Nils Flaten, of St. Olaf College, Northfield, Minn., found that of the 702 students enrolled there in 1937-8, nearly all of Norwegian ancestry, only 42 bore genuinely Norwegian given names. [2] *Anders*, *Fritjof*, *Halvor*, *Leif*, *Nils* and *Thorvald* each appeared but once, even among males whose parents were both Norwegians; among those with but one Norwegian parent they were lacking altogether. Among the girls *Astrid*, *Ragna*, *Sigrid*, and *Solveig* likewise appeared but once, and again only in children of pure Norwegian stock. The favorite boys' names were *Arthur*, *Clifford*, *Clarence*, *Donald*, *Gordon*, *Harold* (from *Harald*), *Kenneth*, *Lloyd*, *Norman*, *Orville*, *Paul*, *Robert*, *Thomas* and *William*. The favorite girls' names were *Helen*, *Margaret*, *Ruth*, *Dorothy*, *Marion*, *Lois*, *Mary*, *Mildred*, *Elaine*, *Esther*, *Charlotte*, *Eunice*, *Irene* and *June*. Fancy names of the Dust Bowl sort were numerous, *e.g.*, *Brunell*, *Daryl*, *Durwood*, *Erliss*, *Glendor*, *Judean*, *Kermon*, *Murley*, *Selmer* and *Theos* among the males, and *Alette*, *Ardis*, *Edellyn*, *Erdine*, *Ferne*, *Juella*, *La Vaughn*, *La Verne*, *Marolyn*, *Monne Fay*, *Ninnie*, *Norena* and *Selpha* among the females. When the early Norwegian immigrants sent their American-born children to the public schools it was not uncommon for the schoolma'ams to give them American names. Thus *Knut* Larson became *Kenneth* and *Nils* Olson became *Nelson;* *Hjalmar* became *Elmer* or *Henry*, and *Sven* became *Stephen*. Some of these children kept both names through life, one for family and *Landsleute* and the other

---

Among the Amish, by Maurice A. Mook, *Mennonite Life*, Vol. XVI, July 1961, pp. 129-31, and Nicknames Among the Mennonites from Russia, by Mrs. Herbert R. Smith, p. 132 of the same issue.]

[1] In 1947, Clifford R. Adams, of Pennsylvania State College, reported that *Karen* was the favorite of the co-eds there assembled, followed by *Dianne*, *Catherine*, *Linda*, *Ellen*, *Barbara*, *Gail*, *Carol*, *Margot* and *Kathleen* in order.

[2] Flaten's report has not been published, but I have had access to it by his courtesy.

"to serve when dealing with Yankee neighbors." [On a higher level, of the 43 *Olsens, Olsons* and *Olssons* in the 1960–1 "Who's Who in America" are a *Carl Augustus,* a *Herluf Vagn,* a *Leif Ericson,* a *Sigurd Ferdinand,* a *Nils* and a *Sture,* but the remainder are indistinguishable from other Americans outside the Bible Belt.]

The willingness of Jews to change their surnames is more than matched by their willingness to adopt non-Jewish given names. This process is anything but new, for the Jewish exiles brought back many names from the Babylonian Captivity, and Moses himself apparently bore an Egyptian name.[3] Other names were borrowed from the other great nations of antiquity, *e.g., Feivl* and *Kalman,* from the Greek *Phoebus* and *Kelonymos.*[4] From medieval times onward borrowing and adaptation have gone on in all countries. Thus *Abraham* has been transformed in Russia into *Abrasha,* in France into *Armand,* in Germany into *Armin,* in Austria into *Adolf,* in England into *Bram* and in the United States into *Albert, Arthur* and *Alvin.*[5] In the same way *Isaac,* an ancient Hebrew name meaning to laugh, has become *Ignatz* in Galicia, *Isidor* in France and Germany and *Irving, Irwin, Edward* and even *Edmund* in the United States,[6] and *Samuel* has been supplanted by *Sidney, Stanley, Sylvan, Seymour, Sanford* and *Salwyn* or *Selwyn,* some of which also do duty as substitutes for *Solomon.* Even the sacred name of *Moses* has given way in Russia to *Misha,* in France and Italy to *Moïse*[7] or *Maurice,* in Germany to *Moritz* and in the United States to *Morris, Morton, Mortimer, Marcus, Marvin, Melvin, Martin, Milton, Murray* and even *Malcolm.*

It will be noted that in nearly all these cases the initial letter is preserved. Roback says that often the original Jewish name survives "underneath and complementary to the protective Gentile name" and "it is this original name that is pronounced over them, following a whispered conference between rabbi and relatives, just before the last remains are gathered to their fathers." In many cases the widespread adoption of Gentile names by Jews has led to their abandonment by Gentiles. It probably had something to do with the gradual disappearance of certain Old Testament names, *e.g., Abraham, Isaac* and *Moses,* in mid-Nineteenth Century America. In not a few cases the Jews have adopted names of distinctively Christian character, *e.g.,* the Yiddish *Nitul,* which is related to *Natalie,* meaning a child born at

---

[3] Its source seems to lie in the Egyptian *mes* or *messu,* a son or child.

[4] *Sarah* to *Sylvia* to *Shirley,* by A. A. Roback, *Commentary,* Sept. 1946, p. 272.

[5] Roback predicts that "the next phase will be *Aldrich.*"

[6] "Next in line," says Roback, "are *Eugene, Evan* and heaven knows what."

He adds: "*Irving* came into vogue some sixty years ago. Lately, it has fallen from grace—for the obvious reason that too many Jews bear it."

[7] I am indebted here to *Moïse* K. Cohen, of New York. *Moïse* is common among the Jews of Louisiana, and in South Carolina it is a surname.

Christmas. *Dolores*, taken from *Mater Dolorosa*, one of the names of the Virgin Mary, offers another example. In the same way *Alexander* and *Julius* were borrowed from the heathen centuries ago.

Of late the Jews have taken to naming their sons *John, Thomas, Mark, James* and *Paul*, not to mention *Kenneth, Clifton, Lionel, Tracy* and *Vernon*.[8] Roback reports that of the four presidents of the leading Jewish theological seminaries of the United States in 1946, three were named *Stephen, Louis* and *Julian*. Another distinguished rabbi has the name *Beryl*,[9] a late president of the Central Conference of American Rabbis was *Edward* and a rabbi who got into the *Congressional Record* with an Armistice Day address in 1945 was *Norman*.[1] The changes that have gone on during the past century and a half are well shown by the family trees of the American Guggenheim family.[2] The founder was *Simon*, born in 1792, and his wife was *Rachel*. Their son was *Meyer* and their oldest grandson was *Isaac*. Among their other grandsons were *Daniel, Solomon* and *Benjamin*, but interspersed among them were *Murry, Robert* and *William*. In the fourth generation the *Stammhalter* was *Robert*. After that the male line began to languish, but meanwhile there were many daughters, and among them were *Lucille, Natalie, Diana, Margaret, Joan, Beulah, Edyth, Helen, Marguerite, Eleanor* and *Gertrude*. Some of these daughters (not counting those who married goyim) had children or grandchildren named *Jean, Jack, Roger, Norman, Betty, Gene, Janet, Terrence, Gwendolyn, Harold, Willard, Timothy* and *Mary Ann*. Thus Jewish given names are being rapidly assimilated to the general American stock, including the stock of fancy names. *Shirley* is now probably more common among Jewish girls than among Christians.

The Sephardic or Spanish Jews—the first to come to America in any numbers—seem to cling to their traditional given names much more firmly than the Ashkenazim, *e.g., Benjamin, Elias, Abraham, David, Emmanuel, Nathaniel, Solomon, Nathan, Isaac, Miriam, Rachel* and *Rebecca*,[3] but even the Sephardim have begun to weaken, and there are individuals of their proud clan in New York named *Ernest, William, Robert, Harold, Edgar* and *John*.[4] The German Jews who came in after 1848 were considerably less faithful to the ancestral names, most of which have been gradually disappearing. The most recently arrived Polish and Russian Jews have gone the fastest and furthest. Even the most old-fashioned of them changed

[8] Earl and Samuel G. Wiener, in On Naming the Boy, *Zeta Beta Tau Quarterly*, Dec. 1926, call such names as the last five baronial.

[9] *Bloch's Book Bulletin*, Jan.-Feb. 1945, p. 18.

[1] Nov. 16, p. A5291.

[2] The Guggenheims: The Making of an American Dynasty, by Harvey O'Connor; New York, 1937.

[3] I am indebted here to Benjamin De Casseres.

[4] De Casseres himself admitted to having two female cousins named *Lulu*.

Yosel to *Joseph* and *Moishe* or *Motel* to *Morris* as soon as they began to find their way about, and presently their sons burst forth as *Sidney*, *Irving* and *Milton*. Their grandsons are *John*, *Charles*, *Harold*, *James*, *Edward*, *Thomas* and even *Mark*, *Luke* and *Matthew*, and their daughters are *Mary*, *Jane*, *Elizabeth*, *Alice* and *Edith*. In the Midwest, prompted by Scandinavian examples, there are Jewish *Huldas*, *Karens* and *Helgas*. [In the Manhattan telephone directory (Winter, 1960–1) are Cohens male named *Allen*, *Archie*, *Arthur*, *Bert*, *Carl*, *Charles*, *Cornelius*, *Donald*, *Edgar*, *Edward*, *Edwin*, *Elliot*, *Ellis*, *Ernest*, *Frank*, *Frederic*, *George*, *Godfrey*, *Harry*,[5] *Harvey*, *Haskell*, *Henry*, *Herbert*, *Howard*, *Irving*, *Jack*, *Jerome*, *Jules*, *Kenneth*, *Lawrence*, *Lee*, *Lester*, *Malcolm*, *Mark*, *Martin*, *Marvin*, *Maximilian*, *Maxwell*, *Michael*, *Mitchell*, *Mortimer*, *Morton*, *Murray*, *Norman*, *Oscar*, *Paul*, *Philip*, *Ralph*, *Sidney*, *Victor*, *Wilfrid* and *William*, and Cohens female named *Alma*, *Angele*, *Annette*, *Arline*, *Bessie*, *Betty*, *Beverly*, *Charlotte*, *Dorothy*, *Elizabeth*, *Emily*, *Estelle*, *Ethel*, *Florence*, *Gertrude*, *Helen*, *Irene*, *Izena*, *Jennie*, *Josephine*, *Lucille*, *Mae*, *Mary*, *Myra*, *Rae*, *Regina*, *Rose*, *Sophie*, *Sue* and *Sylvia*. There are but four *Moses* Cohens and five *Moes*, but there are eight *Lawrences*, twenty *Herberts* and twenty-nine *Henrys*. Among the ladies there is not a single *Rachel* and only two *Miriams* and three *Rebeccas*, and the two surviving *Sarahs* are overborne by eight *Sadies*, two *Sadyes* and one *Sara*.]

Any other list of Jewish names would show a similar disappearance of the older forms. [The *Zeta Beta Tau Quarterly* (Autumn 1960) reveals the following given names among Jews who are otherwise extremely conscious of their Jewishness: *John*, *Paul*, *James*, *Philip*, *Jerome*, *Lawrence*, *Leo*, *Stephen*, *Martin*, *Mark*, *George*, *Robert*, *Harold*, *Ronald*, *Richard*, *Edwin*, *Reginald*, *Arthur*, *Walter*, *Stanley*, *Murray*, *Lee*, *Barry*, *Leslie*, *Irving*, *Howard* and *Adolph*.] In an earlier issue of the same magazine is a somewhat spoofish article on current Jewish given names.[6] The authors divide them into three classes, the Biblical, the mercantile and the baronial. "Examples of the first group," they say, "though not entirely extinct, have about lapsed into disuse." The mercantile names "are those of children who are bound to succeed in the world of affairs."

> We find possessors of these names in operators of the cloak and suit industry. . . . Generally, the bearer of a mercantile name, *viz.*, *Julius*, *Max*, *Emanuel*, *Gus* or *Nathan*, is a representative constituent of our most conservative and substantial citizenry. His business continues successfully through two or more generations. He passes important mo-

---

[5] [The most numerous, with 67 entries.]

[6] On Naming the Boy, by Earl and Samuel G. Wiener, *Zeta Beta Tau Quarterly*, Dec. 1926, p. 7.

tions at the B'nai B'rith Conventions and at the Conventions of the National Clothiers Association. Horatio Alger's Julius the Street Boy was probably of Jewish extraction, for his exploits exemplify a protagonist of this type.

The authors divide their baronial group into four subgroups—English family names, *e.g.*, *Sydney*, *Melvin* and *Murray;* names taken from the map of England, *e.g.*, *Chester*, *Ely* and *Hastings;* aromatic French names, *e.g.*, *Lucien*, *Jacques* and *Armand;* and surnames of popular heroes, *e.g.*, *Lincoln*, *Sherman* and *Lee*. "The eldest son," they say, "is *Abraham;* then in order follow *Hyman*, *Julius*, *Sydney*, *Leonard*, and finally the élite *Llewelyn*."

The impact of Hitler made the American Jews acutely self-conscious, and from 1933 onward there was some tendency to go back to Jewish names.[7] But it did not proceed very far. Among the refugees in Palestine, however, it went to great lengths and is still in progress in the Israeli republic.[8] In the 1930s the *Palestine Gazette* was full of notices of changes of name registered with the Commissioner for Migration and Statistics, *e.g.*, *Leopold* to *Bezalel*, *Bernhard* to *Dov*, *Kurt* to *Yoel* or *Amnon*, *Franz* to *Yehiel*, *Frida* to *Tsipora* and *Sylvia* to *Shifrah*.[9]

The Latin immigrants to the United States have had even less difficulty with their given names than with their surnames, and have thus changed them more rarely than the Jews. The Spanish *José*, *Juan*, *Francisco*, *Manuel*, *Pedro*, *Tomás* and *Antonio* have fared pretty well in this country, and in the regions where there is a relatively large Spanish-speaking population they are even pronounced more or less correctly. Occasionally, along the border, *Francisco* becomes *Frank*, *José* becomes *Joe* and *Pedro* becomes *Pete*, but *Juan* seldom if ever changes his name to *John*. *Jesús* (*hay-soos*, with the accent on the second syllable) often sticks to his name, but occasionally he is constrained to change to *José* or *Joe* in order to allay the horror and check the ribaldry of 100% Americans. *Angel* may add an *o* for the same reason, and thus become an Italianate *Angelo*.[1] In the Southwest many American girls have been given Spanish names, *e.g.*, *Dolores*, *Juanita*, *Anita* and *Constancia*, and some of these have got into wide circulation, but in compensation the Mexican girls have taken to American

---

[7] Marcus Rosenblum, of New York, tells me of a Jewish woman who had changed her own name of *Sarah* to *Karen* at the age of sixteen, but named her daughters *Drazia* and *Avram*.

[8] Says William B. Ziff, in The Rape of Palestine, New York, 1938, p. 189: "In Palestine, when a Jew changes his

name, which is frequent, he selects the most Jewish one he can find."

[9] I am indebted here to G. Agronsky, of the *Palestine Post* (Jerusalem).

[1] I am indebted here to Hugh Morrison, who says that this addition of *o* occurs in other cases.

names, *e.g., Margaret, Edna, Lulu* and *Lucile*.[2] In theory, at least, every Mexican girl of pious parents is christened *María*, with the addition of one of the titles of the Virgin Mary—*e.g., María de los Dolores, María del Rosario, María del Pilar*—but in practice the *María* is commonly dropped, and *Dolores, Rosario* or *Pilar* is used alone.[3]

The Portuguese in Massachusetts and Hawaii have a few given names for boys that are very hard-worked, *e.g., José, João, Manoel, Antonio* and *Francisco*, usually Americanized to *Joseph, John, Manuel, Antone* (or *Tony*) and *Frank*.[4] Other frequent changes are from *Maria* to *Mary*, from *Rafael* to *Ralph*, from *Inês* to *Agnes*, from *Amelia* to *Emma* and from *Isabel* to *Lizzie, Betty* or *Elizabeth*.[5] In recent years the Portuguese-Americans have begun to bestow purely British names upon both boys and girls, and in a little while we may expect Portuguese *Elmers* and *Douglases, Doryses* and *LaVaughans*. Among the Romanians, *Ioan* becomes *John, Marin* becomes *Martin* or *Marian, Dănilă* and *Dumitrue* become *Daniel* or *Dan, Florea* becomes *Frank, Catiline* becomes *Katie* and *Lina*, rather curiously, becomes *Helen*.[6]

The Italian given names fare pretty well in the United States. Most Americans call any strange Italian *Joe* or *John*, but it does not outrage them to discover that his real name is *Antonio, Bartolomeo, Niccolo* or *Vincenzo. Giuseppe, Giacomo* and *Giovanni*, being harder for them, are commonly changed to *Joseph, Jack* and *John*. In the second generation almost every *Vincenzo* becomes a *Vincent*, every *Riccardo* a *Richard* and every *Tomaso* a *Thomas*, but the influence of the priests keeps the Italians, like the Mexicans, from venturing into gaudy nomenclature. The charming Italian names for women, *e.g., Antonietta, Bianca, Costanza* and *Letizia*, show signs of surviving in America: they are sometimes, though still rarely, borrowed by Americans of the older stocks.

The Finns willingly abandon their native given names. Most of the children born in this country are given American names, and even among their elders *Kalle* and *Kaarlo* are commonly changed to *Charley* or *Charles, Matti* to *Matthew, Jaakko* to *Jack, Maija* to *Mary* and *Elli* to *Ellen*. Sometimes a *Kalle*, on changing his name to *Charley*, finds the combination of sounds impossible, and must make shift with *Sali*.

It is the Slavs whose given names suffer most sadly in the Republic.

---

[2] I am indebted here to Marvin Hunter, of the *Frontier Times* (Bandera, Tex.).

[3] I am indebted here to L. Clark Keating, of Minneapolis.

[4] Personal Names in Hawaii, by John E. Reinecke, *AS*, Vol. XV, Dec. 1940, p. 350.

[5] I am indebted here to Peter L. Silvera, of *Jornal Portugues* (Oakland, Cal.), to João R. Rocha, of *O Independente*

(New Bedford, Mass.), and to Charles J. Lovell. Mr. Lovell's investigations show that among the *Sylvas*, a numerous Portuguese-American tribe, the four names *Manuel, Joseph, John* and *Antone* account for 47.3% of all males.

[6] I am indebted here to George Stanculescu, of the *American Roumanian News* (Cleveland).

The Slavic *Jan* like the Scandinavian *Karen* has gained some popularity among the Americans, male and female, in the Fancy Names Belt,[7] but the Slavs themselves show a strong tendency to adopt American names. Whatever his own wishes may be, every Pole named *Stanislaw* must resign himself to being called *Stanley*, and every *Sztefan* to *Steve*. In the same way *Czeslaw* is changed to *Chester* and *Kazimierz* to *Casey*, and, among women's names, *Mieczyslawa* to *Mildred* and *Bronislawa* to *Bertha*. In 1940 a Detroit Pole, bearing the easy given name of *Antoni*, applied to the local probate judge for permission to change it to *Clinton*. The reason was that some of his American friends called him *Tony*, some *Anton* and some *Anthony*, to his confusion and embarrassment. But he did not propose to change his surname, so *Antoni Przybysz* became *Clinton Przybysz*.[8] The Russian *Mikhail* becomes *Mike* and his cousin *Grisha* joins the Polish *Grzegdrz* as *Harry*. All *Ivans*, of course, quickly become *Johns*. Among the Ukrainians nearly every *Wasil* (a popular name in the Ukraine) becomes *William*, though *Basil* would be a better equivalent. In the case of *Hryhory* (*Gregory*) transliteration beats translation, and it becomes *Harry*. Other common changes are from *Volodymyr* (the Russian *Vladimir*) to *Walter*, from *Andrey* (*Andrew*) to *Albert*, from *Bohdan* to *Daniel* and from the lovely *Nadia* to the banal *Hope*.[9] When Czech given names show any resemblance to American names, as *Jan*, *Petr*, *Tomáš*, *Antonín* and *Marie*, they are quickly displaced by the American names.[1] In other cases they are translated, as when *Vavrinec* becomes *Lawrence* and *Bohdanka* becomes *Dorothy*. In yet other cases there are arbitrary changes to unrelated American names, as when *Václav*, which means crowned with a wreath, becomes *James* or *William*, and *Vojtěch*, which means the leader of an army, becomes *William* or *Albert*.

Monsignor Dudek reports some curious efforts to take American given names into American-Czech:

> *Džán* and *Dzım* have attained recognition in print as Bohemian versions of *John* and *Jim;* there are also the diminutives, *Džaník* (*Johnnie*) and *Džimík* (*Jimmie*).[2] *Gladyška* is American-Bohemian for *Gladys*, which, as far as I know, does not exist in Czech proper.

[7] The pronunciation is changed to make it rhyme with *fan*. [And I know of one upper-class Chicago Negro family with a daughter named *Nikita*. The name here seems to lack political implications.]

[8] *Newsweek*, Jan. 15, 1940. [In Kup's Column, the Chicago *Sun-Times*, Sept. 28, 1962, Irving Kupcinet reported: "New Traffic Court judge will be Casimir (*Casey*) Cwiklinski."]

[9] I am indebted here to Emil Revyuk, of *Svoboda*, the Ukrainian daily of Jersey City, and to Vladimir Geeza, of *New Life* (Olyphant, Pa.).

[1] Monsignor J. B. Dudek, The Americanization of Czech Given-Names, *AS*, Vol. I, Oct. 1925.

[2] In the same way the Lithuanians in America have developed *Dzióvas* for *Joe*. See Einiges aus der Sprache der Amerika-Litauer, by Alfred Senn, *Sudi Baltici* (Rome), Vol. II, 1932, p. 47.

Chauncey, says Monsignor Dudek, is one American given name from which Czech-American boys are safe, for it suggests the Czech word *cunce*, a suckling pig. The girls are likewise protected against *Mabel*, for most Czechs know sufficient German to think of the German word *Möbel*, which means furniture. "But fond Bohemian-American mammas," he concludes, "have tried everything from *Abalina* to *Zymole* on female infants, and *Kenneth*, *Chilson*, *Luther*, *Dewey*, *Woodrow*, *Calvin*, etc., have been bestowed upon the sons of families clinging to surnames like *Kubíček*, *Ševčík*, *Borecký*, *Pospsíšil*, *Veverka* and *Vrba*." The Slovak *Jaroslav* is frequently changed to *Jerry*, and *Miloslav* to *Milo*, and *Kenneth*, *Lee*, *Wayne*, *Deane*, *Anita* and *Gail* are growing in popularity.[3] Some of the Slovak girls have even adopted *Karen*.

The Greek given names go the same route. They are not changed, says Sotirios S. Lontos, "in a haphazard way, but more or less in accordance with established standards."

> [If a Greek's] first name is *Panagiotis* he is advised that henceforth he will be called *Pete*. *Demetrios* becomes *Jim*. . . . *Haralampos* [is changed to] *Harry*, . . . and *Christos* into *Crist*. . . . If he is called *Athanasios* he can select either *Athan* or *Nathan* or *Tom* for his new name. *Demosthenes* is usually abbreviated into *Demos*. That was too plebeian a name, however, for a certain proprietor of an aristocratic candy shop, who very effectively gave his name the noble form of *De Moss*. Finally, while anybody called *Michael* may retain this name for American usage, among his countrymen here he will be known as *Mackis*, which is the Greek form of *Mike*.[4]

Greek given names are so often changed in America that in 1943 the Greek War Relief Association found it necessary to issue a list of twenty-six of the more frequent ones, showing their original forms, the usual American equivalents and the true English translations or transliterations.[5] *Konstantinos*, it revealed, is commonly turned into *Gus* or *Frank*, *Vasilos* into *William* or *Bill*, *Ilias* into *Louie* and *Anestis* into *Ernest*.

Among the Armenians there has been a wholesale change of native given names into more or less equivalent American forms, *e.g.*, *Hovsep* into *Joseph*, *Sumpad* into *Sam*, *Vart* into *Rose* and *Hrant*, *Harutyoun* and *Hriar* into *Harry*.[6] The State College at Fresno, Cal., has boasted girls with

---

[3] The Americanization of Slovak Surnames, *Slovak Review*, Autumn 1946, p. 70.

[4] American Greek, *AS*, Vol. I, Mar. 1926.

[5] I am indebted here to J. H. Young, then of the Association Headquarters in New York.

[6] I am indebted here to William Saroyan, the Armenian-American dramatist and story writer, and to Richard Badlian, of Boston.

Armenian surnames named *Bernice, Isabel, Margaret, Betty, Dorothe, Dorthea, Roxie, Grace, Blanche, Doris, Aurora* and *Mary Jane*, and boys named *Milton, Luther, Karl, Martin, Jacques, Harold, Albert, Ralph, Ray* and *Vaughn.* The Arabic-speaking immigrants, mainly Syrians, frequently change the spelling of their names to make them less difficult for Americans, and sometimes drop them altogether. *Mahmūd* is changed to *Mike, Dāwūd* to *David* and *Abu* to *George.* A painter of Lebanese descent, originally *Fuʾād Sāba*, is now *Clifford Saber,* and various Arabic artistes have the names *Julia, Selma, Elvira* and *Lucile.* But there are plenty of Arabic names that fit into English speechways without serious change, and these tend to be preserved, *e.g., Aziz, Habib, Salīm, Gibran, Salom, Fadwa, Khalil* and *Farhat.*[7] The Hungarians change *Ferenz* to *Frank* or *Frederick, István* to *Stephen, Mihály* to *Michael, János* to *John, Mór* to *Maurus* or *Maurice, József* to *Joseph, Géza* to *George* and *Elémer* to *Elmer,* but some of their other names, *e.g., Árpád, Béla, Lajos* and *Imre,* seem to be surviving.

The Chinese in America commonly keep their surnames but abandon their given names for American given names, and at the same time shift their surnames from first position to last, so that *Lu Chi-hsin,* for example, becomes *David Lu.*[8] Some of the names adopted have a curious smack. Among the Chinese laundrymen of Baltimore *Tom, Bennie, Harry, Willie* and *Charlie* are common, and there is at least one *Wesley* and one *Lear.*[9] And in lists of Chinese intellectuals are *Daniel, Pearl, Jane, Rose, Jimmy, Eric* and *William.*[1] On higher levels more pretentious names are taken. A late Chinese ambassador to the United States, educated in this country, was Dr. Vi-Kyuin *Wellington* Koo; one of his successors was Dr. Sao-ke *Alfred* Sze. Most such Chinese use their original Chinese names at home; the American given names are commonly for use abroad only.

The Japanese, like the Chinese, seldom change their surnames, and until the rise of the first American-born generation were similarly tenacious of their given names, but of late many of them have begun to adopt American given names. In Fresno State College, already cited for Armenian names, have been boys with Japanese surnames named *George, James, Hugh, Ben* and *Don* and girls named *Ruth, Olive, Ethel* and *Enid.* Of 400 *Matsus* listed in the Hawaii directory for 1934–5 only 1.2% had American given names alone, and only 12.2% American names plus the initials that almost always stand for Japanese names,[2] but these percentages have

[7] All of these names are from Arabic-Speaking Americans, by H. I. Katibah and Farhat Ziadeh; New York, 1946.

[8] *Parade,* Apr. 14, 1946, p. 18.

[9] 13 Fines Assessed on Trash Counts, Baltimore *Evening Sun,* Jan. 4, 1946, p. 29.

[1] Chinese in the United States Today, by Rose Hum Lee, *Survey Graphic,* Oct. 1942, p. 419. On Feb. 18, 1946, *Donaldine Lew,* a Chinese soprano, sang at the Hotel Ambassador in New York.

[2] As in *Samuel I.* Hayakawa, semanticist.

greatly increased since Pearl Harbor. Even in 1934–5 the Japanese teachers in the public schools, a highly Americanized class, showed 56% American given names. The Japanese do not run to nicknames and are chary of using given names save in the family.

Many native Hawaiian given names, *e.g., Leilani, Iwalani, Maunaloa* and *Leimoni,* continue to flourish in the islands, and even carry prestige, especially among mixed-bloods. A child of such mixed-bloods, even if it bears an American first name, is usually also outfitted with a Hawaiian middle name, and such middle names are sometimes of formidable length, *e.g., Kekoalauliionapalihauliuliokekoolau,* meaning "the fine-leaved kao tree on the beautiful green ridges of the Koolau Mountains." So long a name, of course, has to be abbreviated for everyday use. Some of the mixed-bloods, especially those having Filipino blood, have a liking for curious double names, *e.g., Dorothy Dot* and *Moses Moke.*[3] Others have "tasteless names reminiscent of those found in Southern directories," *e.g., Luckie, Buddy, Sonny, Sweetheart* and *Loving.*

The American Indians, as they take on the ways of the white man, commonly abandon their native names, at least outside the tribal circle. Among the graduates of the Carlisle Indian School[4] I find a Chippewa named *Francis Coleman,* a Seneca named *Mary J. Greene,* a Gros Ventre named *Jefferson Smith* and a Sioux named *Inez Brown.* Sometimes the tribal names are retained as surnames, either translated or not, *e.g., Standing Bear, Yellow Robe, Lone Wolf, White Thunder, Owl Wahneeta, Wauskakamick, Nauwagesic, Weshinawatok, Yukkanatche, Ironroad* and *Whitetree,* but such forms are greatly outnumbered by commonplace English names, *e.g., Jackson, Brown, Johnson, Smith* and *Walker,* and by names borrowed from the Spanish, *e.g., Martinez, Rodriguez* and *Ruiz,* and from various white immigrant languages, *e.g., Leider, Snyder, McDonald, Hogan, Peazzoni, Lundquist* and *DeGrasse.* On the reservations, the tribal names are in wider use, but even there they are often translated.

3: PLACE NAMES

"There is no part of the world," said Robert Louis Stevenson,[5] "where nomenclature is so rich, poetical, humorous and picturesque as the United States of America. All times, races and languages have brought their contribution. *Pekin* is in the same state with *Euclid,* with *Bellefontaine,* and with *Sandusky.* The names of the states themselves form a chorus of sweet

---

[3] Additional Notes on Personal Names in Hawaii, by John E. Reinecke, *AS,* Vol. XVIII, Feb. 1943, pp. 69–70.
[4] Names of Graduates of the Carlisle Indian School, 1889–1913; Carlisle, Pa., 1914.
[5] In Across the Plains; New York, 1892.

and most romantic vocables: *Delaware, Ohio, Indiana, Florida, Dakota, Iowa, Wyoming, Minnesota* and the *Carolinas:* there are few poems with a nobler music for the ear: a songful, tuneful land." A glance at the United States Official Postal Guide [6] quite bears out this encomium. The map of the country is besprinkled with place names from at least half a hundred languages, living and dead, and among them one finds examples of the most daring and charming fancy. There are Spanish, French and Indian names as melodious and charming as running water; there are names out of the histories and mythologies of all the great races of man; there are names grotesque and names almost sublime. "*Mississippi!*" rhapsodized Walt Whitman; "the word winds with chutes—it rolls a stream three thousand miles long. . . . *Monongahela;* it rolls with venison richness upon the palate."

American place names fall into eight general classes: (*a*) those embodying personal names, chiefly the surnames of pioneers or of national heroes; (*b*) those transferred from other and older places, either in the Eastern states or in Europe; (*c*) Indian names; (*d*) Dutch, Spanish, French, German and Scandinavian names; (*e*) Biblical and mythological names; (*f*) descriptive names; (*g*) names suggested by local flora, fauna or geology; (*h*) purely fanciful names.

The need for a comprehensive treatise on American place names, sufficiently well informed to content specialists in the subject and yet written with enough sense of the picturesque to please the general reader, was met in 1945 by the appearance of George R. Stewart's "Names on the Land"; [a second edition, in 1958, added chapters on Alaska and Hawaii as well as scholarly notes]. It begins with a discussion of the lovely names that the early Spaniards bestowed upon the coasts and rivers of their discovery, and proceeds to the banal and unimaginative town names of the New England Puritans, to those borrowed from the French, Dutch and later immigrants, to those carried westward by the first flights of pioneers and to those issuing from the exuberant fancy of the same. It does not linger long over Indian names, though they are always the first to attract the attention of a foreigner glancing at a map of the United States, but perhaps this is not illogical, for Indian place names were in a state of chaos among the Indians themselves, and to this day the meaning of large numbers of them is in dispute or quite unintelligible.

Consider *Allegheny*. "The name," says a leading authority on Pennsylvania names, "has been a battleground for the Indian etymologists; no less than six different explanations are current." [7] Two other examples are *Penobscot* and *Milwaukee*. The meaning of the former has been debated

---

[6] Issued annually, with monthly supplements.
[7] Pennsylvania Place-Names, by A. Howry Espenshade; State College, Pa., 1925, p. 120.

for years, but with no result save the agreement that it somehow relates to water falling over rocks.[8] The latter is said by some authorities to be derived from an Indian word, *milioke* or *miloaki*, meaning good earth, and by others from *mahnah-wauk-seepe*, meaning a council ground near a river; yet others favor *man-a-waukee*, meaning a place where the Indians harvested a medicinal root called *man-wau*. A French map of 1648 made it *Meleke;* Father Louis Hennepin, the Franciscan missionary and explorer, spelled it *Melleoke* in 1679. The first post office established on the site of the present city was called *Melwakee*, but that was soon changed to *Milwaukie*, which has been perpetuated in the name of a town in Oregon.[9]

Great confusion prevails especially among the Indian names of the Eastern seaboard, for at the time they were adopted but little was known about the Indian languages,[1] and since the study thereof has been tackled by competent linguists, the number of persons speaking them has greatly diminished, and in many cases fallen to zero. The Indians themselves often forgot the meaning of their names for hills, meadows and streams: they became simply arbitrary words, like many of our own proper nouns. Moreover, one tribe frequently borrowed a name from another using a different language, and had no more idea of its significance than we have today. Thus the Hurons got the name *Susquehanna*, meaning a muddy river, from the Delawares, and presently transformed it into a meaningless word which went into French as *Andastoei* and then into English as *Conestoga*, and in English became the name of a branch of the Susquehanna, of a town on that branch and of a heavy wagon first built in the vicinity.[2] A crude folk etymology often transformed Indian names into forms that seemed (and still seem) to be of English origin. *Crow Wing*, a village in Minnesota, was originally *Kakakiwing*, a Chippewa term meaning "at the place of the raven." The first two syllables were approximately translated as *crow*, but *wing* was mistaken for the English word. *Port Tobacco* in Maryland, originally *Pentapang* or *Pootuppag*, was transmuted into its present form

---

[8] There is a good discussion of it in Indian Place-Names of the Penobscot Valley and the Maine Coast, by Fannie Hardy Eckstrom; Orono, Me., 1941, pp. 1–2.

[9] The etymology of the name is discussed at length in A History of the Origin of the Place Names in Nine Northwestern States; Chicago, 1908, pp. 102–3. [For the general problem, see M. S. Beeler, On Etymologizing Indian Place-Names, *Names,* Vol. V, Dec. 1957, pp. 237–40.]

[1] "The main problem of American place-name study," said the distinguished German philologian Max Förster, of Munich, in *AS*, Vol. XIV, Oct. 1939, "seems to me the investigation of American names of Indian origin. . . . There is only one drawback: that the scientific study of Indian languages and dialects is hardly advanced enough to form a safe basis." [See Madison S. Beeler, On Etymologizing Indian Place-Names, *Names,* Vol. V, Dec. 1957, pp. 237–40.]

[2] Sixth Report of the United States Geographic Board; Washington, 1933, pp. 13–14. There was an inn called the *Conestoga Waggon* in Philadelphia in 1750.

when the early colonists began loading tobacco in an adjacent arm of the Potomac. The *Rockaways* on Long Island were originally *Reckawackes* and seem to have got into English by way of Dutch; and *Tia Juana* (California), which seems to be Spanish for *Aunt Jane*, is actually an Indian term, *tiwana*, meaning "by the sea." [3] Other sufferers are *Potowanmeac*, reduced to *Potomac*, and *Unéaukara*, which became *Niagara*. But the charm of thousands of Indian names remained, and today they are responsible for much of the characteristic color of American geographical nomenclature. Such names as *Tallahassee, Chicago, Kennebec, Patuxent* and *Kalamazoo* give a barbaric brilliancy to the American map. No fewer than twenty-seven of the states have names borrowed from the aborigines, and the same thing is true of large numbers of towns and counties. The second city of the country bears one, and so do the largest American river, the the most important military decision ever reached on American soil. [4] "In a list of 1,885 lakes and ponds of the United States," says Louis N. Feipel, [5] "285 are still found to have Indian names; and more than a thousand rivers and streams have names derived from Indian words." Walt Whitman was so earnestly in favor of these Indian names that he proposed substituting them for all other place names, even the oldest and most hallowed. "California," he said in "An American Primer," "is sown thick with the names of all the little and big saints. Chase them away and substitute aboriginal names. . . . Among names to be revolutionized: that of the city of *Baltimore*. . . . The name of *Niagara* should be substituted for the *St. Lawrence*. Among places that stand in need of fresh, appropriate names are the great cities of *St. Louis, New Orleans, St. Paul.*" But eloquent argument has also been offered on the other side, chiefly on the ground that Indian names are often hard to pronounce and even harder to spell. There are still towns in Maine called *Anasagunticook, Mattawamkeag, Oquossoc* and *Wytopitlock*, and lakes called *Unsuntabunt* and *Mattagomonsis*. But many Indian names began to disappear in colonial days. Thus the early Virginians changed the name of the *Powhatan* to the *James*, and the first settlers in New York changed the name of *Horicon* to *Lake George*. In the same way the present name of the *White* Mountains displaced *Agiochook;* and *New Amsterdam* (1626), and later *New York* (1664), displaced *Manhattan*, which survived, however, as the name of an island, and was revived in 1898 as the name of a borough. In our own time *Mount Rainier* has displaced *Tacoma* (or *Tahoma*).

When an Indian name is borne by a place of any importance, such as

---

[3] Spanish and Indian Place Names of California, by Nellie Van de Grift Sanchez; San Francisco, 1914, p. 47.

[4] Saratoga.
[5] American Place-Names, *AS*, Vol. I, Nov. 1925, p. 79.

Milwaukee, its spelling and pronunciation tend to become fixed, but there is seldom any agreement about the names of smaller places. The Board on Geographic Names has spent a great deal of time and energy settling such differences. A small lake in New Hampshire was known by no less than 132 different spellings; of these the Board chose *Winnepesaukee,* but soon afterward found reason to change to *Winnipesaukee.* The familiar *Mohawk* appears in the literature of the early frontier in 142 spellings, all coming down, apparently, from an Iroquois word *maqua* or *mahaqua,* meaning a bear. Even *Seneca* has been spelled in 110 ways, and *Oneida* in 103. Some of the Indian names that survive in remote places are very formidable, *e.g.,* *Quohquinapassakessamanagnog* [6] and *Chargoggagaugmanchaugagoggchau-bunagungamaugg.* [7]

Worse, the original meanings of many turn out to be opprobrious or obscene. The Indians often had several or even many names for the same place, and some of them were far from flattering. In other instances they had no names at all, for what was huge, obvious and inescapable seemed to them to be hardly worth naming. When a white colonist pressed them for a name, they sometimes gave him the worst one current, and in the latter case they replied with the aboriginal equivalent of "That is a river" or "Go to hell!" [8] The most reliable opinion today is to the effect that *Chicago,* as the sportive Indians imparted it to the first whites, meant "the place of strong smells," or *Skunktown.* [9] At different times in the past it has been spelled in twenty-three different ways.

The early English settlers were dull dogs, and very few of the names they bestowed upon the land showed any imagination. The Pilgrim Fathers could think of nothing better than *Plymouth Rock* to call the place of their landing, and their opposite numbers in Virginia, though they succumbed to a few lovely Indian names, displaced many others with such banalities as *James, York, Charles, Henry, Williamsburg* and *Richmond.*

The settlement of the continent, once the Eastern coast ranges were crossed, proceeded with unparalleled speed, and so the naming of the new rivers, lakes, peaks and valleys, and of the new towns and districts, strained the inventiveness of the pioneers. The result is the vast duplication of names that shows itself in the Postal Guide. No less than eighteen imitative *Bostons*

---

[6] The name of a brook in New Hampshire. The Board on Geographic Names abolished it in 1916 and ordered that it be called *Beaver.*

[7] This monster is reported in Connecticut Past and Present, by Odell Shepard; New York, 1939, p. 100. It is the name of a lake commonly called *Webster.*

[8] This process is well described in The Aleut Language, by Richard Henry Geoghegan; Washington, 1944, p. 87.

[9] See Great Skunk Theory Stands Up, Chicago *Tribune,* Sept. 12, 1939. Charles F. Hockett derives it immediately from a Fox word meaning wild onion, in turn derived from the word for skunk. [See Reactions to Indian Place Names, *AS,* Vol. XXV, 1950.]

and *New Bostons* still appear, and there are nineteen *Bristols,* twenty-eight *Newports* and twenty-two *Londons* and *New Londons.*[1] Argonauts starting out from an older settlement on the coast would take its name with them, and so we find *Philadelphias* in Illinois, Mississippi, Missouri and Tennessee, *Richmonds* in Iowa, Kansas and nine other Western states and *Princetons* in fifteen. Even when a new name was hit upon it seems to have been hit upon simultaneously by scores of scattered bands of settlers; thus we find the whole land bespattered with *Washingtons, Lafayettes, Jeffersons* and *Jacksons,* and with names suggested by common and obvious natural objects, *e.g., Bear Creek* and *Buffalo.*

More than 600 post offices bear the prefix *New,* ranging from *New Albany* to *New Windsor.* Others bear such prefixes as *West, North* and *South,* or various distinguishing affixes, *e.g., Bostonia, Pittsburg Landing, Yorktown* and *Hartford City.* Eastern county names are often applied to Western towns, and Eastern town names to Western rivers and mountains. *Cambria,* the name of a county but not of a post office in Pennsylvania, is a town in seven Western states. *Baltimore* is the name of a glacier in Alaska, and *Princeton* is the name of a peak in Colorado. In the same way the names of the more easterly states often reappear, *e.g.,* in *Mount Ohio,* Col., *Delaware,* Okla., and *Virginia City,* Nev. The tendency to name small American towns after the great capitals of antiquity has fallen into abeyance, though sixteen *Athenses*[2] still remain, and there are yet many *Carthages, Uticas, Spartas, Syracuses, Romes, Alexandrias, Ninevehs* and *Troys.*[3] The fourth city of the nation, *Philadelphia,* got its name from the ancient stronghold of Philadelphus of Pergamon.

The classical place names which engaud the map of central New York, *e.g., Troy, Utica, Ithaca* and *Syracuse,* have often been credited to Simeon DeWitt, surveyor general of the state from 1784 to 1834. But they appear to have been chosen by the Commissioners of the Land Office, at a meeting held in New York City on July 3, 1790,[4] at which DeWitt was not present. Yet the names bestowed at that meeting, though they included many personal names, *e.g., Brutus, Cicero, Romulus* and *Pompey,* did *not* include such place names as *Troy, Utica* and *Syracuse.* Whatever the actual provenance of the latter, and in spite of the ridicule which the wits of the

---

[1] [See David Lindsey, Ohio's Western Reserve: the Story of Its Place Names, Cleveland, 1955, and New England Origins of Western Reserve Place Names, *AS,* Vol. XXX, Dec. 1955, pp. 243–55.]

[2] [Often with the vowel of *faith* as in New York and Illinois, and *New Athens,* Ohio; *Athens,* Ohio, however, has the vowel of *path.*]

[3] See Classical Place-Names in America,

by Evan T. Sage, *AS,* Vol. IV, Apr. 1929, pp. 261–71. [There are also 139 place names, in forty states, from the Moslem world. See Eastern Names in the Western World, *Aramco World,* Aug. 1959, pp. 6–8.]

[4] The Classic Nomenclature of Western New York, by Victor H. Palsits, *Magazine of History,* May 1911, pp. 246–9.

time heaped upon them,[5] they appealed to the American imagination, and were presently imitated upon a large scale in the new West. So late as 1929 there were still 2,200 on the American map, and they were to be found in every one of the then forty-eight states.

There were similar wholesale bestowals of place names in later years. The Post Office was active in naming new communities, sometimes by deciding between rival contenders and at other times by inventing names of its own, and the Geological Survey and later the Forest Service commonly determined the names of newly surveyed lakes, streams, mountains and valleys. However, there has been a falling off of the craze for classical names. In partial compensation, the more recent immigrants have brought with them the names of the capitals and the great cities of their fatherlands. Thus the American map bristles with *Berlins*, *Bremens*, *Warsaws* and *Leipzigs*, and also show *Stockholms*, *Venices*, *Belgrades* and *Christianias*. In contrast, literary names are sporadic. The Postal Guide shows two *Ben Hurs*, five *St. Elmos* and ten *Ivanhoes*, but only one *Middlemarch*.

The vicissitudes of American Indian place names have been recounted. Other non-English place names have been subjected to the same barbarization. The *Low Freight*, a stream in Arkansas, was originally the French *L'Eau Froid;* the *Ambrosia* in Indiana was the French *Embaras; Gramercy* Park in New York City was the Dutch *Kromme Zee* (crooked lake); *Baraboo* in Wisconsin was the French *Baribault; Waco* in Texas was the Spanish *Hueco;* and so on.[6] Numerous bastard names have been formed by outfitting non-English stems with English indicators, *e.g.*, *Romeroville*, *Glenrico*, *Point Loma*, *Ninaview*[7] and *Pass aux Huitres*,[8] and the process is still in full blast, especially in the naming of new resorts and suburbs, *e.g.*, *Buena Park* and *Mount Alta*. Non-English names are naturally most prevalent in the areas in which the languages from which they come have been most spoken, *e.g.*, Spanish in the Southwest, German in Pennsylvania,[9] Dutch in New York, French in Louisiana[1] and along the Canadian border and Scandinavian in Minnesota.[2] But some of them have wandered far. In

[5] For example, Fitz-Greene Halleck and Joseph Rodman Drake in one of their Croaker Papers in the New York *Evening Post*, June 17, 1819.

[6] The process was witnessed on a large scale in France during the two world wars. *Ypres* became *Wipers, Isigny* became *Easy Knee,* and *Bricquebec* became *Bricabrac.* See Some Folk Etymologies for Place Names, by J. W. Aston, *JAF*, Apr.–June 1944, pp. 139–40.

[7] A Dictionary of Spanish Terms in English, by Harold W. Bentley; New York, 1932, p. 17.

[8] Language Mixture in American Place Names, by Mamie Meredith, *AS*, Vol. V, Feb. 1930, p. 224.

[9] Der deutschamerikanische Farmer, by J. T. Och; Cincinnati, 1913, pp. 228–35.

[1] French Names in Our Geography, by Henry G. Bayer, *Romanic Review*, July–Sept. 1930, pp. 195–203.

[2] Roy W. Swanson, in Scandinavian Place-Names in the American Danelaw, *Swedish-American Historical Bulletin*, Aug. 1929, p. 8, says that he has counted more than 400 in that state.

most cases they were brought by immigrants, but returned soldiers also had something to do with it—for example, after the Mexican War.

A good many of the Dutch place names in the vicinity of New York have become greatly corrupted. *Brooklyn* was originally *Breuckelen; Wallabout* was *Waale Bobbt. Hell Gate* is a crude translation of the Dutch *Helle-Gat.* During the early Nineteenth Century the more delicate New Yorkers transformed the term into *Hurlgate*, but the change was vigorously opposed by Washington Irving, and *Hell Gate* was revived. The Dutch *hoek* was early respelled *hook*, and as such is found in various place names, *e.g., Kinderhook*, Sandy *Hook*, Corlaers's *Hook* and *Hook* Mountain. The Dutch *kill*, meaning creek or channel, is in *Kill* van Kull, *Peekskill, Catskill* and *Schuylkill. Dorp* (village) is in New *Dorp. Kloof* (valley, ravine) survives, in the Catskills, in Kaatersill *Clove*, North *Clove* and *Clove* Valley. *Bosch* (now *bush*), *wijk* (anglicized as *wick* or *wyck*) and *vlei* (usually *vly* or *fly*) are also occasionally encountered. The first means a wood, the second a district and the third a marsh. Very familiar Dutch place names are *Harlem, Staten, Flushing* (from *Vlissingen*), *Cortlandt, Nassau, Coenties, Spuyten Duyvel, Yonkers, Barnegat* and *Bowery* (from *bouwerij*, a farmstead).

The French place names have suffered even more severely than the Dutch. Few persons would recognize *Smackover*, the name of a small town in Arkansas, as French; yet in its original form it was *Chemin Couvert.* Schele de Vere, in 1871, recorded the degeneration of the name to *Smack Cover;* the Post Office, always eager to shorten and simplify names, has since made one word of it. In the same way *Bob Ruly*, a Michigan name, descends from *Bois Brulé; Glazypool*, the name of an Arkansas mountain, from *Glaise à Paul; Loose* Creek, in Missouri, from *L'Ours;* and *Picketwire*, in Arkansas, from *Purgatoire.*

No less than 2,000 American cities and towns have Spanish names, and thousands more are borne by rivers, mountains, valleys and other geographical entities.[3] There are more than 400 cities and towns of Spanish name in California alone. They are numerous all over the rest of the trans-Mississippi region, and curiously enough, are even rather common in the East. The Mexican War was responsible for many of the Eastern examples, but others, *e.g., Alhambra* and *Eldorado*, seem to reveal nothing more than a fondness for mellifluous names. The map of California is studded with lovely specimens: *Santa Margarita, Alamogordo, Tierra Amarilla, Las Palomas, San Patricio* and so on. Unfortunately, they are intermingled with horrifying Anglo-Saxon inventions, *e.g., Oakhurst, Drytown, Susanville, Uno* and *Ono*, including harsh bastard forms, *e.g., Sierraville, Hermosa Beach* and

---

[3] See Bentley, above cited, p 17.

Casitas Springs. Many names originally Spanish have been translated, *e.g.*, *Rio de las Plumas* into *Feather* River, or mauled by crude attempts to turn them into something more "American," *e.g.*, *Elsinore* in place of *El Señor*. Probably a fifth of the Spanish place names in California are the names of saints. The names of the Jewish patriarchs and those of the holy places of Palestine are seldom, if ever, encountered: the Christianity of the early Spaniards seems to have concerned itself with the New Testament far more than with the Old, and with Catholic doctrine even more than with the New Testament. There are no *Canaans* or rivers *Jordan* in the Southwest, but *Concepcions*, *Sacramentos* and *Trinidads* are not hard to find.

The Americans who ousted the Spaniards were intimately familiar with both books of the Bible, and one finds copious proof of it on the map. In the United States as a whole, there are no less than eleven *Beulahs*, nine *Canaans*, eleven *Jordans* and twenty-one *Sharons*. *Adam* is sponsor for a town in West Virginia and an island in the Chesapeake, and *Eve* for a village in Kentucky. There are five post offices named *Aaron*, two named *Abraham*, two named *Job* and a town and a lake named *Moses*. Most of the *St. Pauls* and *St. Josephs* of the country were inherited from the French, but the two *St. Patricks* show a later influence. Eight *Wesleys* and *Wesleyvilles*, eight *Asburys* and twelve names embodying *Luther* indicate the general theological trend of the plain people. There are four *Trinitys*, to say nothing of the inherited *Trinidads*. And in Arkansas and New York there are *Sodoms*.

Of all classes of place names, those derived from personal names are the most numerous. Some consist of surnames standing alone, as *Washington*, *Cleveland*, *Bismarck*, *Lafayette*, *Taylor* and *Randolph;* others consist of surnames in combination with various old and new *Grundwörter*, as *Pittsburgh*, *Knoxville*, *Bailey's Switch*, *Hagerstown*, *Franklinton*, *Dodge City*, *Fort Riley*, *Wayne Junction* and *McKeesport;* and yet others are contrived of given names, either alone or in combination, as *Louisville*, *Johnstown*, *Charlotte*, *Williamsburg* and *Marysville*. All our great cities are surrounded by grotesque *Bensonhursts*, *Bryn Joneses*, *Smithvales* and *Krauswoods*. The number of towns in the United States bearing women's given names is enormous. There are eleven post offices called *Charlotte*, ten *Adas* and no less than nineteen *Almas*. [Most of these places are small, but there is a *Charlotte* with over 200,000 population, an *Elizabeth* with nearly 110,000, an *Elmira* with 46,000 and an *Augusta* with more than 70,000. The importance of a city, of course, has nothing to do with the merits of its eponym. *Houston* is fittingly named for the military hero of the Texas War of Liberation, but its rival, *Dallas*, commemorates an obscure Pennsylvania dignitary who happened to be Vice-President under Polk at the time of the Mexican War.] There are seventeen *Roosevelts*, six *Codys* and six

Barnums, but no *Shakespeare;* [Canada, however, provides a *Shakespeare* in Ontario, a village near *Stratford* on the river *Avon*]. *Washington*, of course, is the most popular of American place names. But among names of post offices it is hard pushed by *Clinton, Centerville, Liberty, Canton, Greenville, Marion* and *Madison*, and even by *Springfield, Warren* and *Bismarck*. Washington Irving, in 1839,[4] charged that "the persons employed by government to survey and lay out townships" in his day were largely responsible for the embalming of politicians' cognomens as place names. But most such names as *Tubbsville* and *Pottsylvania* were actually invented and bestowed by Tubbses or Pottses who happened to have land in the vicinity, or by their local admirers or parasites.

Names wholly or partly descriptive are very numerous throughout the country, and among their *Grundwörter* are terms highly characteristic of American and almost unknown to the English vocabulary. *Bald Knob* would puzzle an Englishman, but the name is so common in the United States that the Geographic Board had to take measures against it. Others of that sort are *Council Bluffs, Patapsco Neck, Delaware Water Gap*,[5] *Walden Pond, Key West, Bull Run, Portage, French Lick, Jones Gulch, Watkins Gully, Cedar Bayou, Keams Canyon, Poker Flat, Parker Notch, Sucker Branch, Frazier's Bottom* and *Eagle Pass*. There are thirty-five post offices embodying the word *prairie*, several of them, *e.g.*, *Prairie du Chien*, Wis., inherited from the French. There are seven *Divides*, eight *Buttes*, eight town names embodying the word *burnt*, innumerable names embodying *grove, barren, plain, fork, cove* and *ferry* and a great swarm of *Cold Springs, Coldwaters, Summits, Middletowns* and *Highlands*. The flora and fauna of the land are enormously represented. There are twenty-two *Buffalos* besides the city in New York, and scores of *Buffalo Creeks, Ridges, Springs* and *Wallows*. The *Elks* are still more numerous, and there are dozens of towns, mountains, lakes, creeks and country districts named after the *beaver, marten, coyote, moose* and *otter*, and as many more named after such characteristic flora as the *pawpaw*, the *sycamore*, the *cottonwood*, the *locust* and the *sunflower*. There is an *Alligator* in Mississippi, a *Crawfish* in Kentucky, and a *Rat Lake* on the Canadian border of Minnesota. The endless search for mineral wealth has besprinkled the map with such names as *Bromide, Oil City, Anthracite, Chrome, Chloride, Coal Run, Goldfield, Telluride, Leadville* and *Cement*.

The hearty Philistines who swarmed over the Alleghenies and then over the Rockies were often content to give their new settlements names brought from the East or fashioned of familiar materials. But the rough

---

[4] In the *Knickerbocker Magazine*.
[5] *Gap* occurs in England, but it is very rare. There is a Goring *Gap* between the Chiltern Hills and the Berkshire Downs, on the railway from London to Oxford.

humor of the country also showed itself in the invention of extravagant and often highly felicitous place names. This was the period which saw the founding of such surrealist communities as *Hog Eye, Gourd Neck, Black Ankle, Lick Skillet* and *Nip and Tuck*, Tex.;[6] *Bowlegs*, Okla.; *Bugtussle*, Tex.;[7] *Braggadocia*, Mo.; *Big Arm*, Mont.; and *Defeated*, Tenn.

The popularity of such grotesque names in the new West seems to have been first noted by James Hall (1793–1868).[8] But it was after the plains and the Rockies were crossed that the pioneers really spit on their hands and showed what they could do. Many of their inventions have become part of the romantic tradition of the Pacific coast and have thus taken on a kind of improbability, but *Humbug Flat, Jackass Gulch, Gouge Eye, Red Dog, Lousy Level, Gomorrah, Shirt Tail* and *Hangtown* were very real.[9]

In the years since then, many of these names have vanished with the ghost towns they adorned. With the growth of population and the rise of the civic spirit, many others have been replaced by more seemly or elegant coinages. *Catfish* Creek, in Wisconsin, is now the *Yakara* River; the *Bulldog* Mountains, in Arizona, have become the *Harosomas*. Nearly all the old *Boozevilles, Jackass Flats, Undershirt Hills, Razzle-Dazzles, Jump-Offs, Poker Citys* and *Skunktowns* have yielded to the growth of delicacy, but *Tombstone* still stands in Arizona, and the Geographic Board gave its imprimatur to the *Horsethief* Trail in Colorado, to *Burning Bear* in the same state and to *Pig Eye* Lake in Minnesota. Various other survivors of a more lively and innocent day linger on the map: *Hot Coffee*, Miss.; *Dollarville*, Mich.; *Oven Fork*, Ky.; *Social Circle*, Ga.; *Sleepy Eye*, Minn.; *Bubble*, Ark.; *Gizzard*, Tenn.; *Rough-and-Ready*, Cal.; *Non-Intervention*, Va.; *Noodle*, Tex.; *Vinegar Bend*, Ala.; *Matrimony*, N.C.; *Oblong*, Ill.; *Stock Yards*, Neb.; *Stout*, Iowa; and so on. West Virginia, the wildest of the Eastern states, is full of such place names: *Affinity, Bias, Big Chimney, Bulltown, Caress, Cinderella, Cowhide, Czar, Halcyon, Jingo, Left Hand, Raven's Eye, Six, Skull Run, Three Churches, Uneeda, Wide Mouth, War Eagle* and *Stumptown*. There are plenty of lovely specimens in regions that were also frontier in their days, *e.g.*, the famous cluster in Lancaster

---

[6] These Texas specimens are from Southwestern Slang, by Socrates Hyacinth, *Overland Monthly*, Aug. 1869.

[7] For the last two I am indebted to Capt. Morris U. Lively, of Norman, Okla.

[8] Letters from the West, Containing Sketches of Scenery, Manners and Customs, and Anecdotes Connected with the First Settlements of the Western Sections of the United States; London, 1828. See John T. Flanagan, An Early Discussion of Place Names, *AS*, Vol. XIV, Apr. 1939, pp. 157–9, and his James Hall, Frontiersman. Hall was a Philadelphian who went down the Ohio by keelboat in 1820, settled on what was then the frontier, became a judge in Illinois and finally engaged in banking in Cincinnati.

[9] California Gold-Rush English, by Marian Hamilton, *AS*, Vol. VII, Aug. 1932, p. 425.

County, Pa.: *Bird in Hand, Bareville, Blue Ball, Mount Joy, Intercourse* and *Paradise*.[1] New Jersey has a *Dolphin*, a *Straws* and a *Wall*. Maryland and Ohio each has a *Blue Ball* to match Pennsylvania's. Maryland also has a *Basket*, a *Bald Friar*, a *Fiery Siding*, an *Issue*, a *Number Nine* and a *T.B.*, supported by some even more charming names for regions and neighborhoods, *e.g.*, *Dame's Quarter, My Lady's Manor* and *Soldier's Delight*.[2]

Many American place names are purely arbitrary coinages; the synthetic place name seems to be indigenous to the United States. Characteristic examples are *Texarkana* (*Texas + Arkansas + Louisiana*),[3] *Penn Yan*, N.Y. (*Pennsylvania + Yankee*, to commemorate the two major groups of early settlers), *Wascott* (*W. A. Scott*), *Paragould* (*W. J. Paramore* and Jay *Gould*), *Carasaljo* (*Carrie + Sallie + Josephine*) and *Asco* (*Atlantic Smokeless Coal Company*). Of the first class there are many examples along the borders of the states, *e.g.*, *Kenova* (*Kentucky + Ohio + West Virginia*),[4] *Calexico* (*California + Mexico*), *Mardela* and *Delmar* (*Maryland + Delaware*).[5] The lower part of the peninsula separating Chesapeake Bay from the Atlantic is known locally as *Delmarva*, a blend of *Delaware, Maryland* and *Virginia*. A part of the area is in each of the three states.

All the other varieties of blend names show numerous examples. Hamill Kenny reports *Ameagle* (*American Eagle Colliery*), *Champwood* (*Champ Clark + Woodrow Wilson*), *Cumbo* (*Cumberland Valley Railroad + Baltimore & Ohio Railroad*) and *Gamoca* (*Gauley + Moley + Campbell*) from West Virginia;[6] and Dorothy J. Hughes reports *Alkabo* (*alkali + gumbo*) and *Seroco* (a memorial of the fact that the first piece of mail

[1] Some of these got their names from old inn signs, as did *Broad Axe* in Montgomery County and *Compass* and *White Horse* in Chester. But the origin of *Intercourse* is mysterious, and A. Howry Espenshade does not discuss it in his Pennsylvania Place-Names; State College, Pa., 1925. The village, which is near Lancaster, does a roaring trade in postcards with passing motorists. Some Western geographical names of an indelicate nature are listed in Nomina Abitera, by W. L. McAtee; Washington, 1945, pp. 3–4.

[2] [Such information is a godsend to weary columnists and city editors, *e.g.*, Thanks to Readers, *Polecat Hollow* is in the Same Orbit as *Mars*, by P. W. Porter, Cleveland *Plain Dealer*, May 3, 1958.]

[3] The Name *Texarkana*, by M. E. Melton, *AS*, Vol. II, Nov. 1926, p. 113.

[4] *AS*, Vol. VIII, Dec. 1933, p. 80. See

also Towns on State Borders Go by Interesting Names, an Associated Press story by Francis J. Kelly, picked up in the Omaha *World-Herald*, Aug. 16, 1953, and in the Austin (Tex.) *Statesman*, Aug. 27.

[5] Louise Pound, Blends, *Anglistische Forschungen*, Heft. XLII, 1914, p. 10. There are twelve *Delmars* in the United States, most of them probably from the Spanish *del mar*, "by the sea," as Donald L. Cherry, of Watsonville, Cal., suggested. But the one in Iowa, says Miss Pound, was "made by using the names [*i.e.*, the initials of the names] of six women who accompanied an excursion that opened the railroad from Clinton, Iowa."

[6] The Synthetic Place Name in West Virginia, *AS*, Vol. XV, Feb. 1940, pp. 39–44. See also his West Virginia Place Names; Piedmont, W. Va., 1945, pp. 57–8.

reaching the village post office was a *Sears Roebuck* catalogue) from North Dakota.[7] Some other curious specimens are *Benld* in Illinois, a blend of *Benjamin L. Dorsey; Westkan* in Kansas, from *West Kansas; Miloma* in Minnesota, a blend of *Milwaukee* and *Omaha*, not formed directly from the names of the two cities, but from those of the *Chicago, Milwaukee & St. Paul* and the *Chicago, Minneapolis & Omaha* railroads; *Pacoman*, N.C., derived from the name of *E. H. Coapman*, a former vice-president of the Southern Railway; *Marenisco*, Mich., named after *Mary Relief Niles Scott; Gerled*, Iowa, a blend of *Germanic* and *Ledyard*, the names of two nearby townships; *Biltmore*, N.C., the last syllable of *Vanderbilt* plus the Gaelic *more*, signifying great; *Ardenwald*, Ore., from *Arden Rockwood*, with the last syllable translated into German; *Ti*, Okla., made up of the initials of *Indian Territory* reversed; *Pawn*, Ore., of the initials of *Poole, Aberley, Worthington* and *Nolen*;[8] *E. T. City*, Utah, named for *E. T. Benson*, "an early miller and Mormon official"; and *Veyo*, in the same state, "coined from the words *verdure* and *youth* by a group of Mormon Beehive Girls."[9]

Another American invention is the addition of *Courthouse* or *Court House* to the name of a county town. Such forms are most prevalent in Virginia, but they are also to be found in New Jersey and North Carolina.[1] The low amperage of patriotic passion during World War II saved twelve of the thirteen *Berlins* in the United States from rechristening. The one casualty was *Berlin*, Ala., which became *Sardis*.[2] [Despite the tensions of the Cold War, there has been no movement to alter the name of *Moscow*, Idaho.]

The new state of Michigan, admitted to the Union on January 26, 1837, sought to stem the tides of nomenclatomania then running by enacting a law forbidding calling a town "after any other place or after any man without first obtaining the consent of the Legislature." "The consequence is," said a writer in the Providence *Journal* later in 1837,[3]

> that Michigan is destitute of *London, Paris* and *Amsterdam*. Unlike her sister States, she boasts neither *Thebes, Palmyra, Carthage* or *Troy*.

Alas, the law turned out to be as unenforceable as Prohibition, and at present Michigan has a *London*, a *Paris*, a *Palmyra*, a *Troy*, an *Athens*, a

---

[7] Coined Town-Names of North Dakota, *AS*, Vol. XIV, Dec. 1939, p. 315.

[8] The last four are from George R. Stewart, Names on the Land, previously cited, p. 363.

[9] The last two come from Origins of Utah Place Names; 3rd ed.; Salt Lake City, 1940.

[1] They are discussed by Stewart in Some American Place-Name Problems, *AS*, Vol. XIX, Dec. 1944, pp. 289–92.

[2] *American Notes and Queries*, Vol. VI, Jan. 1946, p. 155.

[3] The precise date I do not know; the article was reprinted in the New York *Mirror*, Oct. 21. I am indebted here to Joseph M. Carrière.

Sparta, a *Moscow*, a *Franklin* and a *Washington*, to say nothing of a *Rome*, a *Dublin*, an *Oxford*, a *Turin*, a *Sans Souci*, a *Topaz*, a *Payment*, a *Hell*, a *Paradise*,[4] an *Eden*, a *Zion* and a *Dice*. It was not, in fact, until more than half a century afterward that any effective effort was undertaken to bring U.S. place names under official regulation. On September 4, 1890, President Benjamin Harrison appointed a United States Board on Geographic Names. The authority of the Board, at the start, was confined to settling disputes regarding place names which arose in the departments, but on January 23, 1906, President Theodore Roosevelt widened its scope by charging it with "the duty of determining, changing and fixing" all such names "within the United States and insular possessions," and a little later its name was shortened to United States Geographic Board.

Unfortunately, it was treated parsimoniously by an otherwise lavish government. Down to 1917 it had no appropriation of its own, but fed its members out of the salaries they got from the various departments, and down to 1929 it had no paid secretary.[5] On April 17, 1934, as an incident of the departmental reorganization then in progress, it was abolished, its functions were transferred to the Interior Department and it there reappeared as the United States Board on Geographical Names. For some time it seems to have escaped the notice of the idealists then fashioning a new world, but after Pearl Harbor it began to move into high gear. During the war years it naturally gave most of its attention to foreign place names. The place names of the United States were rather neglected, and nearly all decisions about them dealt with the names of mountains, rivers, etc., not of inhabited places.

With the end of World War II, the Board returned to its home grounds, and since then—as the Board on Geographic Names—it has been carrying on the work of getting something approaching order into the American map, [though most of its energies have been absorbed by the problems of the Cold War and the torrent of new names released by the emergent nationalities of Asia and Africa [6]]. It seems determined to knock all apostrophes out of the national place names, even at the cost of logic. Thus the county in Maryland which was *St. Mary's* for centuries is now *St. Marys* and the

---

4 [These are worked hard by desperate city editors. A typical winter story (often with pictures): *Hell* Freezes Over; A summer one: *Paradise* Ten Degrees Hotter than *Hell*. In May 1962, it was announced over the radio that there will soon be a state highway to *Paradise*, but that you will still have to go to *Hell* on a country road.]

5 Its first report, issued Dec. 31, 1890, was published at the cost of the Smith-sonian; its second, May 25, 1891, at that of the Coast and Geodetic Survey; and its third, Aug. 1, 1891, at that of the Lighthouse Board.

6 [The enterprise involves close co-operation among theoretical linguists, onomasticians, translators and geographers, and for obvious reasons much of it cannot be publicly discussed in times of international crisis.]

county which used to be *Prince George's* is now *Prince Georges*. In various foreign names, *e.g.*, that of *St. John's*, the capital of Newfoundland, the Board has been constrained to retain the apostrophe, but not within the continental limits of the United States.[7] Accents appear to be similarly doomed. What was once *San José*, Cal., is now plain *San Jose*. So with *Wilkes-Barre*, Pa., once *-Barré*. So with *Coeur d'Alêne*, Idaho. The Board also advocates simplified spelling and has changed *centre* to *center* in many town names.

The Board has proceeded to the shortening and simplification of names by various other devices. It deleted such suffixes as *town, city, mills, junction, station, center, grove, crossroads* and *courthouse*. It shortened *burgh* to *burg*[8] and *borough* to *boro;* and it sometimes combined separate and highly discrete words. The last habit often produced grotesque forms, *e.g.*, *Newberlin, Fallentimber, Bluehill* and *Threetops*. It apparently cherished a hope of eventually regularizing the spelling of *Allegany*. This is now *Allegany* for the Maryland county, the Pennsylvania township and the New York and Oregon towns, *Alleghany* for the Colorado town and the Virginia county and springs and *Allegheny* for the mountains, the Pittsburgh borough and the Pennsylvania county, college and river. The Board inclined to *Allegheny* for all, [but unsuccessfully so far]. Other Indian names gave it constant concern. Its struggles to set up *Chemquasabamticook* as the name of a Maine lake in place of *Chemquasabamtic* and *Chemquassabamticook*, and *Chatahospee* as the name of an Alabama creek in place of *Chattahospee, Hoolethlocco, Hoolethloces, Hoolethloco* and *Hootethlocco*, were worthy of its learning and authority.

The Board has played ducks and drakes with some of the most picturesque names on the national map. It decided against *Portage des Flacons* and in favor of *Burro Canyon*, against *Cañones y Ylas de la Cruz* and in favor of the barbarous *Cruz Island*. The name of the *De Grasse* River it changed to *Grass, De Laux* to the intolerable *D'lo*. It steadily amalgamated French and Spanish articles with their nouns, thus achieving such barbarous forms as *Duchesne, Degroff* and *Eldorado*. But its policy was fortunately so inconsistent that a number of fine old names escaped. Thus, it decided in favor of *De Soto, La Crosse* and *La Moure*. Its decisions were often unintelligible. Why *Laporte*, Pa., and *La Porte*, Ind. and Iowa; *Lagrange*, Ind., and *La Grange*, Ky.? Here it would seem to have yielded a great deal more than was necessary to local usage.

But in one respect, at least, it is conservative. It rarely gives countenance

---

[7] One of the few exceptions is *Martha's Vineyard*, where the pressure of local opinion kept the apostrophe.

[8] But not in *Pittsburgh*, where local opinion kept the *h*.

to such clumsy collision forms as *Jonespoint*,[9] *Annarbor*, *Limesprings*, *Burroak*, *Wallawalla* and *Coscob*, [though in compensation it has ordained the *Pee Dee* River in South Carolina, over the protests of local historians who recall its derivation from the *Peedee* Indians, a once formidable but now extinct Eastern Siouan tribe [1]]. Also it frowns upon the false delicacy that wars upon picturesque old names. In its earlier incarnation it consented to changing the name of *Dishwater Pond* in New Hampshire to *Mirror Lake*, but it kept *Cow Creek* on the Chesapeake, *Ironjaw Lake*, Mich., and *Cat Island*, Mass. In general, however, it tries to follow local desires, and when a village or natural object has a name which arouses mirth it usually gives its imprimatur to a change. Thus it consented to turning *Muskrattown*, Md., into *Little Georgetown*, *Bug Lake*, Minn., into *Herriman* Lake, and *Great Gut*, Va., into *Houseboat Creek*. In most such cases it finds support for its decision in local history or legend. In the matter of foreign names it has favored using native forms of the names of towns, *e.g.*, *Firenze*, *'s Gravenhage* and *München*, on outgoing mail in order to facilitate ultimate delivery, but the usual English forms for the names of countries, *e.g.*, *Germany*, *Greece* and *Switzerland*, to facilitate sorting in the American post office. It apparently looks forward to the day when the ordinary English names for foreign cities, *e.g.*, *Florence*, *The Hague*, *Naples*, *Vienna* and *Munich*, will disappear altogether, but that day is not yet,[2] [and meanwhile its employees use these despised forms in oral intra-office communication].

The American weakness for spelling pronunciations shows itself in the case of geographical names. Richard Grant White [3] recorded an increasing tendency to give full value to the unstressed syllables of such borrowed English names as *Worcester* and *Warwick*. In *Worcester* County, Md., the name is usually pronounced *Wooster*, but on the western shore of the

---

[9] A landing on the Hudson River. The Board prefers *Jones Point*. [One of the pressures hardest to combat is that of large corporations who buy up Southern textile mills and their company villages, and then change the names of the latter, as *Tucapau*, a local Indian name in Spartanburg County, S.C., was deleted in favor of *Startex*, the engulfing corporation. Since the residents of such communities have no voice in their government, protests are futile. One may comment wryly on the similarity to the fate of place names behind the Iron Curtain: *e.g.*, *Tsaritsyn* became *Stalingrad* and as such became a synonym for Russian heroism during World War II, but has since become *Volgagrad*.]

[1] [In comparing the results of protests, one must reckon with the relative literacy of Massachusetts, Pennsylvania and South Carolina.]

[2] [Here, Americans seem less sure of themselves than the English, who naturalize foreign place names as rapidly as possible.] The American press associations, on Apr. 8, 1944, decided to use native forms in their foreign correspondence in all save 78 cases. These exceptions include *Moscow* instead of *Moskva*, *Athens* instead of *Athenai* and *Limerick* instead of *Luimmeach*. A full list is in *Editor and Publisher*, Apr. 15, 1944.

[3] Every-Day English, p. 100.

state one hears *Worcest'r*. *Norwich* is another such name; one hears *Norwitch* quite as often as *Norrich*. *Greenwich* as the name of a Connecticut town is pronounced *Grennidge* as in England, but as the name of a San Francisco street it is *Green-witch*. *Thames* as the name of a Connecticut river is pronounced as spelled, but is *Temz* in England. *Houston* as the name of the Texas city is *Hyewston*, but as the name of a New York City street it is *Howston*. There is frequently a considerable difference between the pronunciation of a name by natives of a place and its pronunciation by those who are familiar with it only in print. *Baltimore* offers an example. The natives always drop the medial *i* and so reduce the name to two syllables; in addition, they substitute a neutral vowel, very short, for the *o*. The name thus becomes *Baltm'r*. *Maryland*, at home, is always *Mare-l'nd*. *Anne Arundel*, the name of a county in the state, is *Ann'ran'l*. *Calvert* County, also in Maryland, is given a broad *a*, but in *Calvert* Street, Baltimore, it is flat. *Staunton*, Va., the birthplace of Woodrow Wilson, is *Stanton* to its people, but *Taunton*, Mass., has an *au* sound. The local pronunciation of *Illinois* is *Illinoy*. *St. Louis*, to the people of the city, is *St. Lewis*, but *Louisville*, to its denizens, is *Louie-ville*. *Des Moines*, locally, is *Daymoin*, but *Dee-moin* is also heard; the two *s*'s are always silent. *Terre Haute* is *Terra-Hote* or *-Hut*. *New Orleans* is *New Or-lins*, with a heavy accent on the *Or-*, but when *New* is omitted and *Orleans* is used as an adjective modifying a following noun, it becomes *Or-leens*, with the accent on the second syllable. *Coeur d'Alene* is *Kur-da-lane*, with the accent on the *lane*, and the vowel of *kur* lying between that of *cur* and that of *poor*.[4] *Cairo*, Ill., is always *Care-o* locally, never *Ky-ro*. The name of *Taos*, N. Mex., is pronounced to rhyme with *house*. *Laramie*, Wyo., is often reduced to two syllables locally, and pronounced *Lormie* or *Lahrmie*. *Beatrice*, Neb., is accented on the second syllable. *Wichita* is *Witch-i-taw*. The first syllable of *Akron* rhymes with *jack*, not with *jake*. *Spokane* is *Spo-can*, not *Spo-cane*. *Bonne Terre*, an old town near St. Louis, is *Bonnie-tar*. *Lafayette*, a frequent town name, is *Laugh-y-et*. *Havre de Grace* is pronounced *Haver de Grass*, with two flat *a*'s. *Versailles*, Ind. and Ky., is *Versáles*. In northern Michigan the pronunciation of *Sault* in *Sault Ste. Marie* is commonly more or less correct; the Minneapolis, St. Paul and *Sault* Ste. Marie Railroad is called the *Soo*, and there is a *Soo* Canal. This may be due to Canadian example, or to some confusion between *Sault* and *Sioux*. It is a great point in San Francisco to pronounce the name of *Kearny* Street *Karny*, and that of *Sutter* with the vowel of *put;* doing so proves that one is an old-timer.[5]

---

[4] I am indebted here to Marshall Ballard, of the New Orleans *Item*, and to H. F. Kretchman, of the Coeur d'Alene *Press*.

[5] Private communication from Miss Miriam Allen de Ford, of San Francisco.

The Spanish place names of California offer difficulties to natives and strangers alike. The name of the Indian village that originally occupied the site of the city of *Los Angeles* was *Yang-na;* the Spaniards, in 1769, changed this to *El Pueblo de Nuestra Señora la Reina de Los Angeles* (The Town of Our Lady, Queen of Angels). Many other California towns have shortened their Spanish names in the same way. What is now *Ventura* was formerly *San Buena Ventura, San Jose* was *San José de Guadelupe* and *Santa Clara* was *Santa Clara de Asís. Santa Fe,* in New Mexico, was originally the *Villa Real de Santa Fé de San Francisco.* Some of the Spanish place names in the Southwest have been further shortened for daily use. *Frisco* for *San Francisco* is frowned upon locally, but is used elsewhere. *San Bernardino* is *San Berna'dino, San B'rdino, San B'rdoo* or *B'rdoo; San Pedro* is *Pedro* and *Santa Monica* is *Santa Mon.*[6] In New Mexico and Arizona, where the Spanish-speaking population is relatively large, the Spanish pronunciation is preserved, but in the adjoining states it is fast succumbing to Americanization. The name of the *Raton* Pass, separating New Mexico from Colorado, is pronounced *Rah-ton* in New Mexico, but *Ra-toon* in Colorado. Similarly, *Costilla,* a border town, is *Koas-tee-yah* in New Mexico and *Kostil-la* in Colorado. *San Luis,* in Colorado, is *San Loo-is* and *Saguache* is *Sigh-watch.*[7] Even the name of the state is often *Color-ray-do.* The Spanish *a* appears to be doomed, and the *o* and *i* are going with it. The value of *ñ* has been preserved only by changing it to *ny,* as in *canyon.* The Scottish *ch* sound, when it appears in such words as *Loch,* is always converted into *ck.*

The Board on Geographic Names rarely concerns itself with the pronunciation of place names, and when other governmental agencies venture to do so it is seldom to much edification. The legislature of Arkansas decided solemnly in 1881 that the name of the state "should be pronounced in three syllables, with the final *s* silent, the *a* in each syllable with the Italian sound, and the accent on the first and last syllables,"[8] but it will be noted that the *a*'s in the second and third syllables, as one now hears them in *Árkansaw,* are actually anything but Italianate. Moreover, the name of the *Arkansas* River is the *Arkánsas* along its course through Kansas and so is the name of *Arkansas City,* which is in Kansas just over the Oklahoma line. "The *Árkansaw* Traveler," the national hymn of the state, is always, however, *Árkansaw,* and evidence assembled by the DAE shows that the Indians who infested the region in the early days were called *Ar-*

---

[6] I am indebted here to Dr. Joseph M. Prendergast, of Burlingame, Cal.

[7] Spanish Place-Names in Colorado, by Eleanor L. Ritchie, *AS,* Vol. X, Apr. 1935, and Some Spanish Place-Names of Colorado, by George L. Trager, *AS,* Oct. 1935. See also Arizona Place-Names,

by W. C. Barnes; Tucson, 1935.

[8] This joint resolution was approved Mar. 15, 1881. It is given in full in The Basis of Correctness in the Pronunciation of Place-Names, by Allen Walker Read, *AS,* Vol. VIII, Feb. 1933, pp. 42–3.

kansaws so early as 1772, and that Congress so spelled the name in 1819. Indeed, there are Arkansawyers who argue spitefully that *Kansas* itself should be *Kansaw*.[9] Meanwhile, *Arkansaw* for the state has been accepted by the British Broadcasting Corporation, though it makes the Kansas town *Arkánsas City*.[1] The *Arkánsas* pronunciation, so abhorrent to all patriotic citizens of the state, may have arisen by assimilation with that of *Kansas,* and perhaps it was helped on by the Eastern schoolma'ams who once tried to substitute *Gloucéster* for *Gloster* and *Worcéster* for *Wooster*. Similarly, the presence of an *a* instead of an *i* at the end of *Missouri, Cincinnati, Miami,* etc., is possibly the end product of a schoolma'amish war upon an early tendency to turn every terminal *a* into *y, e.g., Indiany, Uticy, Susquehanny, sody, opery, asthmy, balony*.[2] [However, George Pace, of the University of Missouri, argues plausibly that the neutral *-a* pronunciation, much as it recently may owe to schoolma'amish intervention, is a relic of an early diphthongal pronunciation, when the final syllable of *Missouri* was homonymous with *rye*.[3]]

The pronunciation of *Missouri* has been under debate for many years and has produced a large literature, some of it marked by anything but scholarly calm.[4] Allen Walker Read has published a characteristically comprehensive review of the whole matter.[5] In that review he rejects the theory that the *-a* ending represents a fastidious effort to get rid of the apparent vulgarism of the *-y* ending.[6] Instead, he seeks an explanation in the disinclination of the carnivora of a proud and once bloodthirsty state to let it pass under a name which suggests a diminutive. But he overlooks the unchallenged presence of the same diminutive in *Mississippi,* one of the least infantile names on the American map, and in the names or pet names of such testosteronic towns as *Boise,* Idaho; *Tulsy,* Okla.;[7] *Hickory,* N.C.;

---

[9] Charles J. Lovell tells me that The Ohio and Mississippi Pilot, Pittsburgh, 1820, p. 132, says: "The name *Kanzaw* is applied to the country watered by the river *Kansas,* which should be pronounced *Kanzaw*." See the Pronunciation of *Arkansas,* by Robert T. Hill, *Science,* Aug. 26, 1887, pp. 107–8.

[1] Broadcast English, VI, by A. Lloyd James; London, 1937, p. 22.

[2] Harold Wentworth, in his American Dialect Dictionary, New York, 1944, pp. 722–3, prints about 200 examples.

[3] [Linguistic Geography and Names Ending in ⟨i⟩, *AS,* Vol. XXXV, Oct. 1960, pp. 175–87.]

[4] Franz Boas says in Geographical Names of the Kwakiutl Indians, New York, 1934, p. 20, that *Missouri* is derived from an Indian term *m'nisose,* meaning roily water.

[5] Pronunciation of the Word *Missouri, AS,* Vol. VIII, Dec. 1933, pp. 22–36. See also The Word *Missouri, Missouri Historical Review,* Oct. 1939, pp. 87–93.

[6] See E. H. Sturtevant, Linguistic Change, Chicago, 1917, pp. 79–80; G. P. Krapp, The Pronunciation of Standard English in America, New York, 1919, pp. 80–1; J. S. Kenyon, American Pronunciation, 9th ed., Ann Arbor, Mich., 1945, pp. 168–9.

[7] The use of the diminutive in this case is justified historically, for *Tulsa* was named after an Osage chief named *Tulsey.* I am indebted here to Capt. Morris U. Lively, of Norman, Okla.

and *Corpus Christi*, Tex. The early authorities show that *Missouri*, not *Mizzoura*, was first in the field, and that it apparently remained in favor until the Civil War era. At that time a craze for elegance seized the nascent intelligentsia of the state, and the *-a* ending was urged upon the plain people with such fervor that the overwhelming majority of them adopted it and have continued to use it to this day. But in the early 90s or thereabout a new wave of pedagogues launched a counterattack in behalf of the *-i* ending, and a bitter battle was soon joined. The gogues might have had some chance of success if they had been content to argue only for the *-i* ending; unhappily, they also tried to unvoice the two z's in the middle of the name, and so convert the manly Roman sound of *buzz* and *whizz* into the puny Phoenician cheep of *kiss* and *bliss*. This was a fatal blunder, for even those Missouri sophisticates who were willing to accept *-i* revolted against *-ss-* in disgust and indignation. Today even the dictionaries and encyclopedias, usually at least a generation behind-hand, prefer the *-zz-* to the *-ss-*, and most of them have also surrendered to the *-a* ending.

Three other conspicuous American place names whose pronunciation has kicked up controversy are *Iowa*, *Los Angeles* and *San Antonio*. *Ioway* seems to be preferred by the plain people of the state, and the name so appears in the state song, but the Geographical Board long ago declared for *I-o-wa*, and it is supported not only by the majority of outsiders but also by a formidable faction within the state. There is even a body of opinion in favor of putting the accent on the second syllable, but it is apparently feeble. The controversy over the pronunciation of *Los Angeles* has been going on for years,[8] and will probably never end. Even Frank H. Vizetelly, usually so sure of himself, could not decide between *Los Anggeles*, with the *o* as in *go*, and *Los Anjuhliz*, with the *o* as in *not*.[9] Webster 1934 gives both *Los Anggeles* and *Los Anjeles*, and Kenyon and Knott give half a dozen pronunciations without deciding among them, and record despairingly that "a resident phonetician says: 'The only one I've never heard is *Los Angheles.*' "[1] The controversy over *San Antonio* has to do with the question whether the people there ever call the town *Santóne*. The late Maury Maverick, its best-known citizen, averred that they do not. "The average person," he reported, "says *Santónyo*, although the well-informed generally say *San An-tón-i-o*. The Mexicans, of whom there are some

---

[8] [There is now some semi-official sanction for *Lahs Ánjuhluss*, recommended by a special committee in 1952 and accepted by Mayor Fletcher Bowron. See *Los Angeles: A Noble Fight Nobly Lost*, by David Stein, *Names*, Vol. I, Jan. 1953, pp. 35–8. Webster's Seventh New Collegiate Dictionary, Springfield, Mass., does not offer this, but recommends *Laws Ánjuhluss* and *Laws Ang(guh)luss*.]

[9] A Desk Book of 25,000 Words Frequently Mispronounced; New York, 1917, p. 561.

[1] A Pronouncing Dictionary of American English; Springfield, Mass., 1944, p. 260.

90,000 in San Antonio, pronounce the word with a broad *a* and sound every syllable."[2] But other observers insist that *Santóne* is in common use.

So long ago as 1803 Noah Webster advocated following local usage in the pronunciation of place names.[3] "The true pronunciation of the name of a place," he said, "is that which prevails in and near the place." But he defended and indeed advocated changes in Indian names to bring them in accord with "the genius of our language, which is accommodated to a civilized people." This is the line taken by Allen Walker Read in his excellent review of the subject.[4] He concludes that it should be determined "simply by impartial observation of selected speakers in the locality of the places named." Even this rule, of course, cannot be followed slavishly, for sometimes there is a sharp difference of opinion, even among natives, as to the true pronunciation of a given name, and more often an accepted local form is challenged by another prevailing somewhere else, or even generally. We have just seen examples in the cases of *Arkansas, Los Angeles* and *Iowa*. Another is provided by *Chicago*, which is *Chicawgo* in the city itself but *Chicahgo* in the rest of the country.

Read raises the question as to what is to be done about a name which, while designating the same place or object, differs in pronunciation in two regions, *e.g.*, that of the *Arkansas* River. Is it, he asks, "to change its name for different parts of its course?" Well, why not? If the people of Kansas prefer *Arkánsas* for that part of the river within their boundaries, then it *is* the *Arkánsas* there, but it becomes the *Árkansaw* as the border is crossed. The name of *Beaufort* is pronounced differently in the two Carolinas—and both forms are "correct." The best pronouncing dictionary of American place names, that of Alfred H. Holt, first published in 1938,[5] avoids all vain speculations as to how names *ought* to be pronounced, and is content to record accurately how they *are* pronounced. Holt's authority is always local, and he is careful to find out if there are variations on different cultural levels.

The study of place names is comparatively recent in the United States. Washington Irving printed some observations upon them in the *Knickerbocker Magazine* in 1839 and Henry R. Schoolcraft discussed the Indian names of New York before the New-York Historical Society in 1844, but it was not until 1861 that a separate work upon the subject appeared, a pamphlet of thirty-two pages by a surgeon named Usher Parsons, entitled "Indian Names of Place in Rhode-Island."[6] Parsons's interest was mainly

---

[2] Private communication, Mar. 21, 1935.
[3] The American Spelling-Book; revised impression; Brattleborough, Vt., 1814, p. v.

[4] The Basis of Correctness in the Pronunciation of Place-Names, *AS*, Vol. VIII, Feb. 1933, pp. 42–6.
[5] American Place Names, New York.
[6] Providence, 1861.

in the Indian names in use in the state "when civilization commenced" and his stated purpose was to provide a supply "for the convenience of those who may hereafter wish to apply them to their country villas, factories or institutions," but within those limits he made a good job of it, and it was more than thirty years before a better study of Rhode Island place names appeared. In 1870 James Hammond Trumbull followed with a work which remains one of the classics on the subject,[7] and by the 80s Henry Gannett had begun an investigation which was to result in gazetteers and "geographical dictionaries" of Connecticut, Massachusetts, New Jersey, Rhode Island, Kansas, Utah, Texas, Delaware, Maryland, Virginia, West Virginia, Colorado and the Indian Territory, and an omnibus volume entitled "The Origin of Certain Place Names in the United States."[8] It was this book which set the study of American place names on its feet.[9]

The French names of Canada resemble the Spanish names of the Southwest in that they are frequently very long, *e.g.*, *Coeur-Très-Pur de la Bienheureuse Vierge Marie de Plaisance*, but usually, though not always, it is

---

[7] The Composition of Indian Geographical Names, Illustrated from the Algonkin Languages; Hartford, 1870.

[8] Washington, 1902; 2nd ed.; 1905. A volume of 334 pages, listing nearly 9,000 names.

[9] Unfortunately, that study is still to be organized on a national scale, and in consequence the work done so far is spotty and incoordinate. In some states, *e.g.*, Oregon, Arizona, South Dakota, California and Missouri, the record is substantially complete, and in others, *e.g.*, Pennsylvania, Nebraska, Minnesota, Wyoming and West Virginia, admirable progress has been made, but in yet others, *e.g.*, Maryland and New Jersey, there is hardly a beginning. In 1927 Robert L. Ramsay undertook a systematic effort to investigate the nomenclature of Missouri. The material accumulated by 1945, covering all the 114 counties of the state, was entered upon three sets of cards, one of which was deposited with the Board on Geographic Names in Washington. At the beginning of the enterprise Ramsay published an Introduction to a Survey of Missouri Place-Names, which amounted to a treatise upon the whole technic of place-name research and remains the best American handbook on the subject. Meanwhile Lewis A. McArthur, a Portland businessman, had been carrying on an inquiry into the place names of Oregon, and in 1928 there appeared the first edition of his Oregon Geographic Names; a second edition was published by the Oregon Historical Society in 1944. It is not based upon local tradition alone, but represents a diligent and thorough examination of all the available records.

The literature of the subject is extensive, but a large part of it is concealed in pamphlets and papers published locally, and hence difficult of access. A bibliography listing 195 titles was presented to the Modern Language Association in 1938 by Harold W. Bentley and M. Robert Snyder, and in 1948 Richard B. Sealock, librarian of the Gary, Ind., Public Library, and Pauline A. Seely, of the Los Angeles County Public Library, published a Bibliography of Place Name Literature: United States, Canada, Alaska and Newfoundland. [Supplementary bibliographies, by the same authors, appear at intervals in *Names*, the journal of the American Name Society. With the establishment of this society in 1952, as Stewart remarks (Names on the Land, 2nd ed., p. 433), "for the first time the name scholars of America have begun to attain the position that their European counterparts have occupied for a century."]

the last element that is used for everyday purposes, not the first or a middle one. Some of the combinations of French and English are not without humor, *e.g.*, *Notre-Dame de L'Assomption de MacNider* and *Saint-Henri des Tanneries*. Canada has had a Geographic Board like our own since 1897, and there is another for Quebec alone, where the great majority of place names are French, and a Nomenclature Board for Newfoundland. The first has endeavored to preserve locally accepted name forms whenever possible, but is required by law to follow forms "found in the statutes, proclamations, orders in council or other official acts of a Province" establishing districts or communities. Also it has been considerably harassed by demands from Quebec that all the *k*'s in place names be changed to *c*'s, on the ground that, in French, *k* is used only in foreign loans.[1] The Board has got rid of the offending *k* in many Indian names by approving the substitution of French names, *e.g.*, *Dufresnoy* for *Kajakani-kamak*, but it survives defiantly in many others, *e.g.*, *Kakekekwaki*.

Canada, like the United States, is afflicted by the heavy duplication of names. There are thirty-seven *Blanche* Rivers in Quebec alone. The picturesque names translated from the Indian languages by the pioneers, or invented by their own fancy, are under fire and many have been changed. *Rat Portage* is *Kenora*, and *Pile o' Bones* Creek is *Regina*. But *Medicine Hat* and *Moosejaw* happily survive.

The Geographic Board has published a number of valuable monographs on the place names of various parts of Canada, *e.g.*, Manitoba, Prince Edward Island and the Thousand Islands. There is also a considerable literature on the subject by private inquirers. The origin of *Canada* has long engaged geographers, and many fantastic etymologies have been offered, but the predominance of opinion today seems to favor its derivation from an Iroquois word, *kanata*, which is defined as meaning *ville, village, amas de cabànes, bourgade, bourg, group de tentes, campement de plusieurs*. The Indian guides of the early explorers called out *kanata* every time they passed a village on the St. Lawrence, and the explorers mistook the word for the name of the country.[2]

With the settlement of America, such ancient English terms as *moor, heath, dell, fell, fen, weald* and *combe* disappeared from the vocabulary, and in place of them there arose a large stock of novelties, *e.g.*, *branch, run, fork, bluff, hollow, bottom, lick, neck, gap, notch, divide, knob* and *flat*. A few of these, to be sure, were known in England, but they were not

---

[1] *Le Petit Journal* (Montreal), Nov. 22, 1931.

[2] [See also Marius Barbeau, Legend and History in the Oldest Geographical Names of the St. Lawrence, *Inland Seas*, Vol. XVII, Summer 1961, pp. 105–13.]

E. R. Seary is engaged in a monumental study, The Toponymy of the Island of Newfoundland. Two large volumes have been published in preliminary form, but the work is far from complete.]

common there, whereas in the new land they became words of every day. As the settlements extended, terms were borrowed from the French, *e.g., rapids, prairie* and *butte;* from the Dutch, *e.g., hook* and *kill;* [3] and from the Spanish, *e.g., canyon, mesa* and *sierra.*[4] Rather curiously, no Indian term seems to have been taken in,[5] save only *bayou,* which came from the Choctaw *bayuk* through the French. Many of these terms are confined to relatively small areas. Those from the Dutch are scarcely to be found outside southeastern New York and northern New Jersey, and many from the Spanish are understood only in the Southwest, *e.g., arroyo* and *vega. Butte* and *coulee,* which are from the French, are pretty well limited to the West [though *coulee* in southern Louisiana denotes a small fresh-water stream, which is a *branch* elsewhere in the South], and *run* is rare south of Virginia,[6] just as *pond* for a natural body of water is rare outside New England. *Gulch,* which is of uncertain origin, is commonly thought of as Western today, but the DAE's first example, dated 1835, is from Newfoundland. *Notch* is used in New England for what is commonly called a *gap* south of New York. *Creek,* which is mainly applied to an arm of the sea in England, has the same sense along the Atlantic tidewater, but elsewhere it usually means a small fresh-water stream. *Swamp* is unknown in England save as an exoticism, and so are *barrens, bad lands* and *bluff.*

How many place names are there in the United States? Allen Walker Read, in a paper read before the American Dialect Society at Indianapolis, December 30, 1941, ventured to guess "well over a million," and in view of the fact that Ramsay and his associates have unearthed 32,324 in Missouri alone, this estimate seems quite reasonable. In addition, there are many thousands of obsolete names, recoverable from old maps and records.

---

[3] Other examples are in Dutch Place-Names in Eastern New York, by A. E. H. Swaen, *AS,* Vol. V, June 1930, p. 400, and Dialectal Evidence in the Place-Names of Eastern New York, by Edward E. Hale, *AS,* Vol. V, Feb. 1930, pp. 154-67.

[4] Others are in Geographical Terms from the Spanish, by Mary Austin, *AS,* Vol. VIII, Oct. 1933, pp. 7-10.

[5] Says J. D. Whitney in Names and Places, Cambridge, 1888, p. 77: "A considerable number of Indian words form all or part of various proper names, and have thus become quite familiar to us, as, for instance, *sipi, minne, squam, kitchi* and many others, but no one of these words has been generalized so as to have become applicable to any class or form of scenic description."

[6] [Hans Kurath, A Word Geography of the Eastern United States, Ann Arbor, Mich., 1949, pp. 13, 32, 40, 61, Figs. 18, 93; see also L. Dudley Stamp, A Glossary of Geographical Terms, London, 1961; George R. Stewart, *Leah, Woods* and Deforestation as an Influence on Place-Names, *Names,* Vol. X, Mar. 1962, pp. 11-20; E. Wallace McMullen, Jr., English Topographic Terms in Florida, 1563-1874, Gainesville, Fla., 1953; H. F. Raup, Names of Ohio's Streams, *Names,* Vol. V, Sept. 1957, pp. 162-8; D. B. Sands, The Nature of the Generics in Island, Ledge and Rock Names of the Maine Coast, *Names,* Vol. VII, Dec. 1959, pp. 193-202; Wilbur Zelinsky, Some Problems in the Distribution of Generic Terms in the Place-Names of the Northeastern United States, *Annals of the Association of American Geographers,* Dec. 1955, pp. 319-49.]

[Stewart estimates that these alone might amount to a million, with probably three million place names in current use.[7]] Thus the field of place-name study is immense, with room in it for an army corps of investigators.

4: OTHER PROPER NAMES

The literature dealing with other American proper names is extensive, and deals, *inter alia*, with apartment houses, cemeteries, churches, warships, merchant ships, newspapers, express trains, eating houses, streets, telephone exchanges, quilts and domestic animals. To the casual observer, names are chosen arbitrarily and even irrationally, but in some cases well-defined systems are followed, planned carefully to avoid or get rid of difficulties. "Such a locality as *at the corner of Avenue H and Twenty-third Street*," says W. W. Crane, "is about as distinctly American as Algonkian and Iriquois names like *Mississippi* and *Saratoga*."[8] Rudyard Kipling gave testimony to the strangeness with which the number names, the phrase *the corner of*, the word *block* and the custom of omitting *street* fell upon the ear of a Britisher two generations ago.[9] He quotes with amazement directions given to him on his arrival in San Francisco from India: "Go six *blocks* north to [the] *corner of Geary and Markey* [*Market?*]; then walk around till you strike [the] *corner of Sutter and Sixteenth*."[1] The English almost always add the word *street* (or *road* or *place* or *avenue*) when speaking of a thoroughfare: such a phrase as *Oxford and New Bond* would strike them as incongruous.[2] The American custom of numbering and lettering streets is usually ascribed by English writers to sheer poverty of invention, but of late some of them have borne witness to its convenience.

The English often give one street more than one name. Thus, *Oxford Street*, in London, becomes the *Bayswater Road, High Street, Holland Park Avenue, Goldhawk Road* and finally the *Oxford Road* to the westward, and *High Holborn, Holborn Viaduct, Newgate Street, Cheapside, the Poultry, Cornhill* and *Leadenhall Street* to the eastward. *The Strand*, in the same way, becomes *Fleet Street, Ludgate Hill* and *Cannon Street*. But the American system of numbering and lettering streets shows some signs of increasing acceptance. There is a *First Avenue* in Queen's Park, London, and parallel to it are *Second, Third, Fourth, Fifth* and *Sixth* ave-

---

[7] [Names on the Land; 2nd ed.; 1958, p. 444.]

[8] Our Street Names, *Lippincott's Magazine*, Aug. 1897, p. 264.

[9] American Notes; New York, 1891, Ch. I.

[1] Here Kipling made two errors. The *the* would never be omitted before *corner*, and Sutter and Sixteenth streets do not meet.

[2] But I am reminded, by Mrs. Pieter Juiliter, of Scotia, N.Y., that "true Oxonians always speak of *the Broad, the High, the Turl* and *the Corn* instead of *Broad Street, High Street, Turl Street* and *Cornmarket Street*." The article, however, is always used; it is never used in the United States.

nues—small streets leading northward from the Harrow Road, just east of Kensal Green Cemetery. There is also a *First* Street in Chelsea—a very modest thoroughfare near Lennox Gardens and not far from the Brompton Oratory.[3]

The numbering and lettering of streets was apparently invented by Major Pierre-Charles L'Enfant in 1791, when he laid out the plan of Washington. In the older American cities the downtown streets still usually have names surviving from colonial days, and some of them were borrowed originally from London, *e.g., Cheapside, Cornhill* and *Broadway*.[4] In the United States such pretentious designations as *avenue, boulevard, drive* and *speedway* are used much more freely than in England. *Boulevard,* in some American cities, has of late taken on the meaning of a highway for through traffic, on entering which all vehicles must first halt; [it also is used to designate the center strip, now often *median,* of a divided street or highway, and in the Minneapolis area it designates the grass strip between the sidewalk and the curb, elsewhere called a *tree lawn* or a *parking strip.* In many cities, notably Chicago, Cleveland, Detroit and Los Angeles, high-speed through streets are called *expressways* or *freeways*.] In England such a highway is commonly called an *arterial road.* Every American town of any airs has a *Great White Way;* in the Midwest, rows of fine shade trees have been cut down to make room for them. *Avenue* is used in England, but, according to Horwill, it is "usually reserved for a road bordered by trees"; [in the South, it is still used for the tree-bordered drive into a plantation]. In America the word was formerly used to designate a thoroughfare in the suburbs, not built up like a street, but laid out for future building, and hence not a road. In Baltimore of the late Nineteenth Century *Charles Street* became *Charles Street Avenue* at the old city boundary, and the *Charles Street Avenue Road* a bit further out. At Towanda, Pa., there is a *Plank Road Street.* Many American towns now have *plazas,* which are quite unknown in England, and nearly all have *City Hall parks, squares* or *places.* The principal street of a small town in the United States is still *Main Street,* having survived the derogatory implications of Sinclair Lewis's novel of that name. In England, *Main Street* is usually *the High Street,* not forgetting the article, but in Scotland there are many *Main Streets.* [In Ohio, *High Street,* without the article, is the Main Street of Columbus, and of several smaller towns to the north, on the highway to Toledo.] The newer suburbs of American cities are full of *lanes, terraces,*

---

[3] See the chapter on London Street-Names in Adjectives—and Other Words, by Ernest Weekley; London, 1930. A brief bibliography is appended.

[4] I am informed by Miss Miriam Allen de Ford that *Broadway Street* appears on some street signs in San Francisco, and also in San Diego. This suggests that *Broadway* is recent on the Pacific coast.

roads and *ways*, but the English *circus, crescent, walk, passage* and *garden* are seldom encountered. *Alley* survives in a few of the older cities, but *row, court* and *yard* are virtually extinct. These English names for thoroughfares, like the American *boulevard* and *avenue*, have lost most of their original significance.

The pronunciation of street names in the United States shows the same freedom that marks the pronunciation of place names. The old Dutch names of New York City are sadly mangled by the present inhabitants of the town; *e.g., Desbrosses*, which was *de Broose* in Dutch, is now *Desbrossez*. Spanish names are often corrupted in the same way in the Southwest, and French names in the Great Lakes region and in Louisiana and thereabout. In New Orleans *Bourbon* has become *Bur-bun, Dauphine* is *Daw-fin, Foucher* is *Foosh'r, Enghien* is *En-gine, Chartres* is *Charters* and *Felicity* (originally *Félicité*) is *Fill-a-city*. The names of the Muses, bestowed upon certain of the city streets, are now pronounced *You-terp, Mel-po-mean* and so on. *Bons Enfants*, apparently too difficult for the present inhabitants, has been translated into *Good Children*.[5]

The first New York telephone directory, issued in 1878, did not show any exchanges at all, but only the names of subscribers, then 241 in number.[6] A subscriber who wanted to talk to another simply asked for him by name and address. But as the number of subscribers increased this method broke down, and it was necessary to give each subscriber a number, and a little later the numbers had to be apportioned to exchanges, each with a name. The first chosen were familiar neighborhood names, *e.g., Gramercy, Chelsea, Murray Hill* and *Madison Square*, but soon these ran out, and the telephone engineers had to discover or invent new ones. Every new name had to differ clearly from every name already in use, and in addition had to be "easy to read, easy to hear, and easy to remember."

Thus the number of such names, whether borrowed or invented, was anything but unlimited. In fact, long experiment showed that there were only about 240. When 200 had been put to use it became necessary to devise a new plan. In December 1930, numbers were added to the exchange

---

[5] [The street generics *corso* and *rue* are reported from Nebraska City, Neb., by G. Thomas Fairclough, *AS*, Vol. XXXIV, Feb. 1959, pp. 70–1. See also H. L. Mencken, American Street Names, *AS*, Vol. XXIII, Apr. 1948, pp. 81–8. The problems of street numbering in Edmonton, Alberta, where the center of town is *100th St.* (running north and south) and *100th Ave.* (running east and west), are noted in *The New York* *Times*, Aug. 30, 1962. Some of the patterns of street naming in Minneapolis have been analyzed by Mrs. Barbara Epstein, of the University of Chicago, in a paper yet unpublished. Changing fashions in street names are discussed by Audrey R. Duckert, *Names*, Vol. X, Sept. 1962, pp. 206–8.]

[6] Pitt F. Carl, Jr., in *Word Study*, Oct. 1941, pp. 6–7.

names, so that *Plaza*, for example, was divided into *Plaza 1*, *Plaza 2* and so on. Inasmuch as the usual four-digit number had to follow, this gave every subscriber a number of five digits, but telephone users soon got used to them. They greatly facilitated the introduction of dial telephones, for the addition of numbers multiplied every existing exchange by ten. [But even this multiplication does not cope with the foreseeable load; and in 1960 the Bell System announced plans to convert all telephone numbers to simple seven-digit numerals and to abolish exchange names altogether. Conversion to the new system—*All Number Calling* or simply *ANC*—is already under way.[7]]

The names of American suburbs often engage the national wits. The garden-city movement, launched by an Englishman, Sir Ebenezer Howard, in 1898, was quickly imitated in this country, and with it came a new popularity for names suggesting feudal estates, *e.g., Cecil Manor, Bryn Jenkins* and *Smithdale*. The developers of suburbs in low, marshy places have a great liking for adding *heights* to their names.

Apartment-house names show a rich efflorescence in the United States. In New York City, in 1945, of the 5,500 apartment houses listed in the Polk directories of the five boroughs, about a fourth had names.[8] This proportion was probably much higher at an earlier time, for it is now fashionable to live in a house, however huge, that shows only a street address. The names follow a few banal patterns. Between a quarter and a third include the generics *Arms* or *Court*, and many of the rest include *Hall, Manor, Towers, Gardens, Terrace, House, Chambers, Plaza* or *Gables*. Sometimes two designations are combined, as in *Chelsea Court Tower*.[9] The non-generic parts of the names come mainly from five sources—adjacent streets and localities, personal names, historical or romantic associations, "natural features of the landscape" and a sheer exuberance of fancy. Of the first class, *Kingsbridge Vanity Court* (in the Kingsbridge section of Brooklyn) and *Parkside Arms* (on Parkside Avenue) offer examples; of the second, *Florence Towers* and the *Bertha;* of the third, *Caledonia, Cinderella Hall* and *Mona Lisa;* of the fourth, *Ocean Towers, Hillcrest* and *Superview;* and of the fifth *Shergold, Dalmac* and *Empec Court*. The names based on per-

---

[7] [*ANC, Time*, May 11, 1962, pp. 49–50. The inevitable Anti-Digit-Dialing League was reported forming on the West Coast in *The New York Times*, June 24. A more detailed account is The New Numbers Game, by Fred J. Cook, *The New York Times Magazine*, Sept. 23, 1962, pp. 31 *ff.*]

[8] Arthur Minton, Apartment-House Names, *AS*, Vol. XX, Oct. 1945, pp. 165–77. [In *Names*, Vol. IX, Mar. 1961, pp. 8–36, Minton discussed the Names of Real-Estate Developments.]

[9] "For the most part," says Minton, "these generic elements are obviously derived from English usage—*Arms*, for example, from English inn names, and *Court, Hall* and *Manor* from names of English dwellings and estates . . . —for connotations of prestige and security."

sonal names show some lush incongruities, *e.g.*, *Kaplan Court*, *Leibman Manor* and *Hochroth Arms*.[1] But the strongest visible tendency is toward British-sounding names, and there are many examples in *-leigh* and *moor*.

The names of American hotels show measurably less yielding to Anglomania, though in New York there are still some evidences of it, *e.g.*, *Berkshire*, *Cornish Arms*, *Gladstone*, *Piccadilly*, *Prince George* and *Sussex*. American hotels are often named after the owners or managers, *e.g.*, *Astor* (New York), *Parker* (Boston), *Willard* (Washington), *Rennert* (Baltimore), *Hollenden* (Cleveland), *Palmer* (Chicago) and *Delevan* (Albany). When a new hotel in some large city makes a conspicuous success, it is common for its name to be borrowed in smaller places: there are *Plazas*, *Astors* and *Ritzes* all over the hinterland. [The rise of chain hotels has meant the proliferating of *Hiltons* and *Sheratons*, sometimes hyphenated with older names, as the *Sheraton-Blackstone* in Chicago, and sometimes supplanting the old names altogether, as the *Conrad Hilton* in Chicago and the *Statler Hilton* in New York, once known as the *Stevens* and the *Pennsylvania*, respectively.] Up to 1900 or thereabout many an American hotel used *House* after its name, but that fashion has gone out, and when *House* now appears in the United States it is usually applied to an apartment house or an office building, in imitation of English usage.

The English fashion for giving names to individual dwelling houses has never got lodgment in this country, save in the case of country residences with more or less extensive grounds,[2] but the cottages in summer colonies are often given names, sometimes puns or satirical misspellings. In 1944, Mrs. Edith Morgan King classified them as follows:[3]

1. Names of the owners in reverse, *e.g.*, *Nitsua* (Austin) and *Notluf Farm* (Fulton).

2. Conjugal combinations, *e.g.*, *Virma* (Virginia-Martin) and *Witso* (William-Sophia).

3. Whimsies and puns, *e.g.*, *Suitsme*, *Biltover*, *Rope's End*, *Upson Downs* and *Holme Run*.

4. Bogus Indian names, *e.g.*, *Wa-a-wa*, *Waywayanda* and *Caplunk*.

Tourist camps, now more often *motor courts*, *motels* or *motor hotels*, often bear names of the same sort. The revival of *inn* as a punning substitute for *in* in some of these names—*e.g.*, *Dew Drop Inn*—restores a word

---

[1] In Venice, Cal., there is (or was) a *Finklestein Arms* and a *Burkeshire Arms*. *The New Yorker* (Mar. 9, 1946, p. 18) reports a *Venus Arms*, and *AS* (Feb. 1946, p. 75) a *Magdalene Arms*, both in Brooklyn.

[2] See Tidewater Virginians Name Their Homes, by P. Burwell Rogers, *AS*, Vol. XXXIV, Dec. 1959, pp. 251–7.

[3] No Namee, *The New Yorker*, Aug. 16, 1944, pp. 55–7. See also Naming the Bungalow, by Ida M. Mellen, *AS*, Vol. II, Mar. 1927, p. 269. [The use of *camp* for a summer cottage is discussed by Margaret M. Bryant in *AS*, Vol. XXII, Dec. 1947, p. 298, and by Thomas A. Kirby, *AS*, Vol. XXIII, Oct.–Dec. 1948, p. 184.]

that threatened to be lost to the American language. Before the Revolution inns were relatively rare in the colonies save in the larger towns, but with the movement into the wilderness after the Treaty of Paris they multiplied enormously. They all bore names and their signs commonly showed images of the persons, animals or objects after which they were named. As towns grew up about the more prosperous ones, their names were commonly transferred thereto, and that was the origin of some curious town names noted in Section 3 of this chapter, *e.g.*, *King of Prussia* and *Red Lion* in Pennsylvania, and *Bishop's Head* and *Cross Keys* in Maryland.[4]

A florid fancy is also visible in names of eating houses catering to the migratory trade. Marguerite Cooke Goodner has classified the names of more than 4,000 such establishments in fifteen Texas towns.[5] Banal attempts at humor show in *Do Drive Inn*, *Dine-a-Mite*, *Kool Kave*, *Just-a-Bite* and *Goodie Goodie*. About "thirty-four per cent carried the names of the owners in some form," *e.g.*, *Berry's Thrifty Corner*, *Carroll's Eat Shop*, *Jimmie's Tamale House* and *Irene's Bar and Café*. First names were most popular, as promoting "a bond of friendship and understanding." "Men who are forced to eat day after day in commercial eating-houses," Miss Goodner said, "are apt to seek the friendly establishment where they can call their host by his first name."

In the early days of the railroad it was common to give names to loco-motives, but it is no longer general. But names for fast trains seem likely to go on; indeed, the introduction of streamliners promoted their inven-titon.[6] Some of them are merely gaudy, but others have no little charm, *e.g.*, the *Lark*, a night train between Los Angeles and San Francisco, arriving in the morning, the *Humming Bird*, Cincinnati to New Orleans, of the Louisville & Nashville and the *Southern Belle* of the Kansas City Southern. Among noteworthy trains are the *Chief* of the Atchison, Topeka & Santa Fe (now reinforced by a streamlined *Super-Chief*, a *San Francisco Chief* and a *Texas Chief*), the *North Coast Limited* of the Northern Pacific, the *Empire Builder* of the Great Northern, the *Golden State Limited* of the

---

[4] [*Inn* now seems to designate an establishment catering primarily to the automobilist or to the traveler by air. Some of them, as the *Hilton Inns* (operated by the Hilton Hotel Corporation), are extremely plush. *House* is also used as a designation for such establishments.]

[5] Her report, a thesis at Southern Methodist University, was summarized in The Names of Texas Eateries, Baltimore *Evening Sun*, editorial page, Feb. 8, 1940. [In The Neighborhood Tavern and the Cocktail Lounge, *American Journal of Sociology*, Vol. LXII, May 1957, David

Gottleib emphasizes one of Miss Goodner's arguments: that a "familiar name" is calculated to draw the working-class custom. Among saloons catering to that class in the Chicago area, the combination of names of husband and wife is especially popular.]

[6] Charles Angoff, The Railroads at Bay, *American Mercury*, Jan. 1928, p. 89. [See also Named Passenger Trains Operated on the Railroads of the United States, Canada, and Mexico; Washington, 1948. The number, alas, has declined alarmingly in the last decade.]

Southern Pacific, the various *Hiawathas* of the Chicago & Milwaukee, the *Champions* of the Atlantic Coast Line, the *Capitol Limited* of the Baltimore & Ohio, the *Rocky Mountain Rocket* (and others of the *Rocket* family) of the Rock Island, the various *Zephyrs* of the Burlington, the *F.F.V.* (first families of Virginia) of the Chesapeake & Ohio, the *Twentieth Century Limited* [7] and *Empire State Express* of the New York Central, the *Silver Meteor* of the Seaboard Air Line and the decorously named Washington-New York expresses of the Pennsylvania—the *Federal*, the *Congressional*, the *Legislator*, the *Representative*, the *Executive*, the *Embassy* and the *President*, with the *Patriot* thrown in to stir the heart. The Pennsylvania has a *Mount Vernon* and an *Arlington*, the New Haven a *Nathan Hale*, the Chesapeake & Ohio a *George Washington* and the Norfolk & Western a *Pocahontas*. *Express train* is not an Americanism, for the English were using it in 1841, whereas it is not traced beyond 1849 in this country. But *limited*, traced to 1879, probably is, and *cannonball*, traced to 1888, undoubtedly is.

The first Pullman [8] cars bore numbers, and then letters, but the letters soon ran out and the numbers conflicted with those of other railroad cars. The first to have a name was the *Pioneer*, which started out as *Car A*. It was hastily completed in 1865 for use in the train which bore Abraham Lincoln's body on its long and eventful trip from Washington to Springfield, Ill. It cost $20,000 and was the first car built from top to bottom by George M. Pullman: its predecessors had all been converted day coaches. When the Pullman Company took over the remains of the Wagner Company, in 1899, it was found that about 300 of the Wagner cars bore names duplicated by Pullmans. Richmond Dean, a Pullman vice-president, got rid of this difficulty by visiting the Chicago Public Library and searching ancient history. The resulting rash of classical names for the Wagner cars astonished and enchanted the country.

In 1943 the Pullman Company issued a revised list of its cars, and in 1944 a supplement followed. [9] In general the list revealed only a feeble fancy. Whenever the company's onomasticians hit upon a name that suggested a whole series, they worked it for all it was worth. Thus when one of them thought of calling a car after a Scotch *glen* there ensued a long row of names in *Glen*, including such painfully un-Scotch forms as *Glen Beach*, *Glen Hollow* and *Glen Rio*. With the transfer of operations of Pull-

---

[7] [The Greatest Train in the World, by Lucius Beebe, *The New York Times Magazine*, June 10, 1962, pp. 30, 52, 55, and his book *20th Century Limited*, New York, 1962.]

[8] [Many of the new lightweight cars are now made by the Budd Company, but *Pullman* promises to remain a popular synonym for *sleeper*, regardless of the maker.]

[9] List of Standard, Private and Tourist Cars, No. 34, Chicago, Oct. 1, 1943; and Supplement No. 1 to List of Cars No. 34, Chicago, Dec. 15, 1944. [Henry Ploegstra is undertaking an analysis of the practices of selected railroads.]

man cars from the Pullman Company to the railroads, and with the rise of the new streamliners, the custom has arisen of identifying the cars with famous men, with particular railroads or with the country through which they travel. [The *Crescent Limited*, of the Southern Railway, has cars named after Southern patriots, such as *Lucius Quintus Cincinnatus Lamar*.. Many of the Burlington sleepers begin with the word *Silver;* many on the Great Northern are named after various glaciers, and those on the *Panama Limited* of the Illinois Central are named after cities en route. Some of the streamlined all-coach trains have named cars; for example, those on the *Southerner*, of the Southern Railway, were named after the various Southern states.[1]]

In the heyday of canals all the boats had names and some of them were alarming, *e.g.*, *Bluddy Pirate*, *Bridge-Smasher* and *Larger Bier* (lager beer).[2] Most such boats, now barges, have only numbers today, but the naming of larger craft goes on, and during World War II put considerable strain upon the onomastic engineers and poets of the Maritime Commission. Liberty ships (EC-2s) were named for deceased American heroes and for "merchant seamen who lost their lives in the service." The first 34 Victory ships were named for the United Nations, with *Victory* appended; the next 218 were named for American towns and small cities, also with *Victory* added, *e.g.*, *Luray Victory;* the remainder were named after American colleges and universities, *e.g.*, *Tuskegee Victory*. Of standard-type cargo vessels, C-1s were named after capes, C-2s after clipper ships, C-3s after birds, fishes and animals prefixed by *Sea* and C-4s after the same prefixed by *Marine*.[3]

The Navy follows a system of naming its ships that goes back to an act of Congress of 1819, providing that "all ships of the first class . . . shall be called after the States of the Union, those of the second after the rivers, and those of the third after the principal cities and towns." As new types of ships have come in it has had to seek new kinds of names for them. The schedules followed during World War II included the following:

Battleships

All were named for states.

Aircraft Carriers

For battles, historic American ships and persons identified with the development of aviation.

---

[1] [For a long time the Jim Crow car of the *Southerner* was *Mississippi;* the car is now desegregated, like all interstate transportation.]

[2] These were names of boats on the Morris Canal. I take them from Among the Nail-Makers, *Harper's Magazine*, July 1860, p. 149.

[3] I am indebted here to Robert W. Horton, of the Commission's division of information.

Cruisers

For American cities, the capitals of American territories and possessions, and those territories and possessions themselves. [One exception, the *Canberra*, commemorates the Australian cruiser of that name, sunk in the Solomons campaign while serving with American forces.]

Destroyers

For deceased persons identified with the Navy and Marine Corps.

Destroyer Escorts

For "personnel of the Navy, Marine Corps and Coast Guard killed by enemy action in World War II."

Submarines

After "fish and denizens of the deep." [The new submarines carrying Polaris missiles are named after national heroes of the first rank, e.g., *George Washington, Patrick Henry, Robert E. Lee.*[4]]

Minelayers

After monitors formerly on the Navy list.

Minesweepers

After birds.[5]

Ammunition Ships

After volcanoes and with terms "suggestive of fire and explosives."

Provision Storeships

After astronomical bodies.

Cargo Ships

After astronomical bodies or "counties in the United States."

Surveying Ships

After astronomers and mathematicians.

Amphibious Force Flagships

After mountains in the United States or in its territories and possessions.

Hospital Ships

With "synonyms for kindness" or "other logical and euphonious words."

---

[4] [Besides the *Robert E. Lee*, the roster includes another Confederate, *Stonewall Jackson*, a Frenchman, *Lafayette*, a German, *Von Steuben*, and an Indian, *Tecumseh*.]

[5] In the two last cases it is provided that "logical and euphonious words" may be substituted.

Tankers

After the Indian names of rivers.

Transports fitted for evacuating wounded

After deceased surgeons general of the Navy.

Salvage Ships

"Names descriptive of their functions."

Submarine Tenders

"Names of pioneers in submarine development; characters in mythology."

Ocean Tugs

Names of Indian tribes.

Seaplane Tenders

Names of straits, bays and inlets in the United States and its possessions.

Landing Ships

Names of places of historical interest.

Net Tenders and Harbor Tugs

Names of trees, or of Indian chiefs, "and other noted Indians."

[The Navy buff's bible, *Jane's Fighting Ships*, issued annually, lists in connection with the British Navy the number of times a given ship name has appeared on the Navy list. Some of these names have a record of service covering four centuries.] The revolutionary *Dreadnought* of 1904, with its turbine engines, its speed of 21 knots, its ten 12-inch guns and its displacement of 17,000 tons was the eighth since 1573; the new atomic-powered submarine is the ninth. The English follow no set system for the naming of their warships, but they have a liking for saucy names calculated to scare the foe, *e.g.*, *Furious, Invincible, Victory, Conqueror, Devastation, Shark, Tiger*, even *Hyena*.[6] The Japanese, in their heyday, apparently preferred more romantic ones, *e.g.*, *Siranui* (Phosphorescent Foam), *Natusio* (Summer Tide), *Urakeze* (Wind in the Bay) and *Kasumi* (Mist of Flowers).[7]

All naval ships are given nicknames by their crews, and some of those in use in the American Navy are picturesque and amusing. During World

---

[6] These names were noted during the Eighteenth Century by Francis Grose, author of A Classical Dictionary of the Vulgar Tongue. In a posthumous collection of essays called The Olio, London, 1792 (2nd ed., 1796), he called them "boastful" and warned that the hazards of war might make them ridiculous.

[7] I take these from First Snow of the Season, *The New Yorker*, Jan. 17, 1942.

War II the cruiser *Salt Lake City* was the *Swayback Maru;* the *Missouri, Misery* or *Old Mo* or the *Mighty Mo;* the *Brooklyn,* the *Teakettle;* the *Boise,* the *Reluctant Dragon;* the *South Dakota, Battleship X;* the *Franklin, Big Ben;* and the *Pope, Honest John.*[8]

One of the curious byways of homicidal nomenclature takes us into the names of battles, and history shows that the contesting peoples often call the same one by different names. *Waterloo* is *Belle Alliance* to the French and even to the Germans, who fought with the English, and the battle which Grant called *Pittsburg Landing* became *Shiloh* to the Confederates and is now *Shiloh* to most other Americans. These differences were discussed by the Confederate General D. H. Hill in one of *Century Magazine's* "Battles and Leaders of the Civil War" series: [9]

> So many battlefields of the Civil War bear double names that we cannot believe that duplication has been accidental. It is the unusual which impresses. The troops of the North came mainly from cities, towns, and villages, and were, therefore, impressed by some natural object near the scene of the conflict and named the battle from it. The soldiers of the South were chiefly from the country, and were, therefore, impressed by some artificial object near the field of action. . . . Thus, the first passage of arms is called the battle of *Bull Run* at the North —the name of a little stream. At the South it takes the name of *Manassas,* from a railroad station. . . . Stone's defeat is the battle of *Ball's Bluff* with the Federals, and the battle of *Leesburg* with the Confederates. . . . Rosecrans called his first great fight with Bragg the battle of *Stone River,* while Bragg named it after *Murfreesboro,* a village. . . . The Union soldiers called the bloody battle three days after South Mountain from the little stream *Antietam,* and the Southern troops named it after the village of *Sharpsburg.*

The first study of church names ever undertaken in the United States was published in 1891 by two anonymous laymen of Rhode Island—pious Episcopalians who confined their inquiry to their own communion.[1] Of 3,918 Episcopal churches then in operation in the United States, all save 54 of this number bore the names of saints, or higher personages in the heavenly hierarchy, or of salient events, objects or doctrines, *e.g., Ascension, Atonement, Mount Calvary, Incarnation* and *Advent.* Not less than

---

[8] See Sailor Nicknames for Fighting Ships, *U. S. Naval Institute Proceedings,* Jan. 1946, p. 83.

[9] The Battle of *South Mountain,* or *Boonsboro', Century Magazine,* May 1886, p. 137.

[1] On the Dedications of American Churches: An Enquiry into the Naming of Churches in the United States, Some Account of English Dedications, and Suggestions for Future Dedications in the American Church; Cambridge, Mass., 1891.

385 were dedicated to *St. Paul*—18 more than were dedicated to *Christ*. The latter, however, were reinforced by 67 churches called *Good Shepherd*, 38 called *Redeemer*, 26 called *Our Saviour*, 21 called *Messiah* and perhaps a score more of similar names. *St. John* followed *St. Paul* with 366 churches, and then came *Trinity* with 354, *Grace* with 279, *St. James* with 178, *St. Luke* with 142, *St. Mark* with 136 and *St. Peter* with 122. There were only 97 dedicated to *St. Mary* and three to *St. Mary the Virgin*. Of the 54 which lacked pious names, nearly all were in Virginia and Maryland. In both states it was the custom, in colonial days, to name churches, not after saints, but after the communities in which they were built, and those old names have survived. Some of the curious church names unearthed by this inquiry were *House of Prayer*, *Gloria Dei*, *Reconciliation*, *Bread of Life*, *Holy Fellowship*, *Regeneration*, *St. Ansgarius*, *Saint Esprit* (French for *Holy Ghost*) and *St. Mary Magdalene*. An appended survey of British churches turned up, in England, *Charles King the Martyr*, *SS. Cyricus and Julieta*, *St. Gaffo*, *SS. Gluvias and Budoke*, *St. Peter Port*, *St. Ursula and the Eleven Thousand Virgins*, and *St. Delta*, and, in Wales, *St. Cwfig*, *SS. Dyunog, Iddog and Menw*, *St. Llanwddog*, *St. Wrthwl* and *St. Ynghednoddle*. The English are much less shy of Mariolatry than American Episcopalians; so they have 2,453 churches named *St. Mary the Blessed Virgin*, and perhaps a hundred more showing *Mary* in other combinations.[2]

Very few Episcopal churches are named after the persons who built them, but this was a common custom in the early days, when the founder was usually promoted to sainthood later on if his church turned out well.[3] The Methodists, Baptists, Presbyterians and other such non-conformists still honor founders in this way, and sometimes a process not unlike canonization follows, [as with the *Duke Memorial* Methodist Church, in Durham, N.C.[4]]. They use actual saints' names sparingly, but name many churches after streets or neighborhoods, or numerically. All the Christian Science dispensaries are numbered, and in citadels of the faith like Los Angeles they

---

[2] See also Names of Churches, *Current Religious Thought*, Nov. 1945, p. 6, and Church Dedications of the Oxford Diocese, by K. E. Kirk; Oxford, 1946.

[3] "It was not until 1170 that the Roman Church reserved to herself the right to canonize; and only about 250 years ago that the regulations were laid down for substantially the present Roman procedure." On the Dedications of American Churches, pp. 30-1. [The names of churches in the Roman Catholic archdiocese of Chicago have been studied by Br. David Fleming, S.M. Store-front churches in Chicago are briefly surveyed by James B. Stronks, *Names*, Vol. X, Sept. 1962, pp. 203-4. See also Naming Protestant Churches in America, by P. Burwell Rogers, *Names*, Vol. XI, Mar. 1963, pp. 44-51.]

[4] [The *Robert E. Lee Memorial* Episcopal Church, Lexington, Va., is more to the point, for Lee is venerated by pious Southerners above most of the official saints in the calendar.]

go into high figures. Catholic churches usually have saints' names, though such forms as *Corpus Christi, Immaculate Conception* and *Sacred Heart of Jesus* are common. They are never called after streets, neighborhoods or founders.

The tendency to seek mellifluous euphemisms for such terms as *cemetery, churchyard, burial ground* and *graveyard* long ago influenced the naming of cemeteries, and there are many *Heavenly Rests, Memory Groves* and *Sweet Homes* throughout the country. Many cemeteries bear the names of the local communities, as *Corn Cob, Red Bone, Toe Nail, Jumpertown, Yellow Leaf, Pickle, Turtleskin* and *Cistern Hill*, all from Mississippi.[5] To the bucolic regions of the country also belong the traditional names of quilts,[6] e.g., *Turkey Tracks, Star in a Mist, Widower's Choice, Spider Web, Grandmother's Fan, So Mote It Be, Rob Peter and Pay Paul, Hearts and Gizzards* and *Steps to the Altar.*

"There remains one stronghold," says Willis Thornton,[7] "where the romance of name is undimmed: it is the turf." In support he offered some mellifluous specimens from the roll of American thoroughbreds, e.g., *Summer Sigh, Dream of Allah* and *Ethereal Blue*, and also a few on the sportive side, *Spot Cash* and *Jealous Woman*. But the naming of colts headed for the big tracks is rigidly regulated by the Jockey Club, so that the fancy of breeders and owners is seriously hobbled:

1. Names are limited to fourteen letters, and are to consist of not more than three words; space, punctuation marks, etc., to count as letters.

2. Names of living persons are not eligible unless their written permission to use their names is filed with the Jockey Club.

3. Names of stallions whose daughters are in the stud are not eligible.

4. Names of famous horses are not eligible.

5. Names whose spelling or pronunciation is similar to names in use are not eligible.

6. Names of famous or notorious people are not eligible.

7. Trade names, etc., or names claimed for advertising purposes are not eligible.[8]

[5] Cemetery Names Give State Distinction, Jackson *News*, Mar. 5, 1939, p. 24. Miss Lila M. Herring, of the State Bureau of Vital Statistics at Jackson, has been gathering specimens. Acknowledgments are also due to Miss Anabel Power, of the State Department of Public Welfare, Jackson, and to Karl Kastrup, of Rockford, Ill.

[6] Vance Randolph and Isabel Spradley, Quilt Names in the Ozarks, *AS*, Vol.

VIII, Feb. 1933, pp. 33–6; Carrie A. Hall and Rose G. Kretsinger, The Romance of the Patchwork Quilt in America; Caldwell, Idaho, 1935.

[7] O Tempora, O Nomina!, *AS*, Vol. I, July 1926, pp. 529–60. [See also Naming the Nags, by Louise M. Ackerman, *Names*, Vol. I, Dec. 1953, pp. 262–5.]

[8] I am indebted here to Marshall Cassidy, of the Jockey Club.

Race horses commonly have stable names to go with their registered names, so that one appearing on the register as a *Whirlwind* or *Cleopatra* may be *Jack* or *Molly* to his or her intimates. The same is true of blooded dogs. In the studbooks of their breeds they often bear names that approximate genealogies, but at home even the proudest champion is usually only *Butch* or *Lassie* or *Pooh*. Of 116,000 dogs entered in a radio contest in 1939, 1,400 were named *Prince*, 1,200 *Queenie*, 1,000 *Spot*, 500 *Rover* and 30 each *Rags*, *Towser*, *Muggsie* and *Fido*.[9] *Fido*, once a favorite, has sunk into the shadows, and *Rover* has since been yielding to *Butch*,[1] which was apparently introduced by a popular comic strip, along with *Sandy*. Other color names are also in vogue, *e.g.*, *Whitie*, *Red*, *Buff* and *Blackie*, and the two world wars gave a lift to *Colonel*, *Major*, *Captain* and *General*.[2] Dogs of German origin are often called *Fritz* or *Heinie*, and many Irish terriers are *Tim*, *Terry* or *Mickey*. Other names now favored are *Mitzie*, *Rex*, *Dixie* and *Danny*.[3] Dorothy Parker once had a dachshund named *Robinson*, and several vicious hounds have been named *Mencken*.

"Editors of early newspapers in America," said Cedric Larson,[4] "delighted to give their organs pretentious names. Patriotism was exuberant . . . and the tyrannies of Europe were real." The result was a great spate of such titles as *Vox Populi*, *Freeman* and *Genius of Liberty*. That fashion abated when the movement into the West began, and was succeeded by one for homelier and more picturesque names, often humorous, *e.g.*, *Hustler*, *Tomahawk*, *Plain Dealer* and *Bazoo*. Walt Whitman, in "Slang in America," recalled some curious Western examples: the Tombstone *Epitaph* in Arizona, the Fairplay *Flume* in Colorado (it still exists), the Ouray *Solid Muldoon* in the same state and the *Jimplecute* in Texas; and Farmer, in his "Americanisms Old and New," added a *Rustler*, a *Cyclone*, a *Prairie Dog*, a *Cowboy*, a *Knuckle* and a *Lucifer*. Nearly all of these yielded to the ideas of elegance which came in after the Civil War. Most American newspapers, in the smaller towns as in the big cities, now have extremely decorous names. The favorite is *News*, which was borne by 375 of the 3,000-odd dailies of 1936, and it was followed in order by *Times*, *Journal*, *Herald*, *Tribune*, *Press* (including *Free Press*), *Star*, *Record* (or *Recorder*), *Demo-*

[9] Capt. William Lewis (Will) Judy, Care of the Dog; Chicago, 1940; 2nd ed., 1943, p. 19.

[1] *Rover* Gives Way to *Butch* as Dog's Tag, New York *Daily News*, Sept. 18, 1946.

[2] I am indebted here to Frank E. Bechman, of Battle Creek, Mich.

[3] I am indebted here to Miss Alice Rosenthal, of *Dog News*. [See also One Thousand and One Names for Pets; Tujunga, Cal., 1952.]

[4] American Newspaper Titles, *AS*, Vol. XII, Feb. 1937, pp. 10–18. [Some recent reports on the subject: Nebraska Newspaper Names, by Elizabeth Grone, *AS*, Vol. XXIV, Oct. 1949, pp. 194–200; The Names of Negro Newspapers, by Armistead Scott Pride, *AS*, Vol. XXIX, May 1954, pp. 114–18; Names and Newspapers, by Kenneth Kraft, *Christian Science Monitor*, Feb. 3, 1950, p. 15; Southern Newspaper Names, by James P. Jones, *Names*, Vol. X, June 1962, pp. 115–26.]

crat, Gazette, Post, Courier, Sun, Leader and *Republican* (or *Republic*).

Of the old racy names few survive, *e.g.*, the *Rustler-Herald* of King City, Cal., and the *Searchlight and Republic* of Culbertson, Mont. Among the college papers a more picturesque nomenclature remains: the *Diamondback* at the University of Maryland, the *Polygraph* at the Billings (Mont.) Polytechnic Institute and the *Sour Owl* at the University of Kansas. The papers published by soldiers during World War II often had amusing names.[5] They included a *White Falcon* in Iceland, a *Kodiak Bear* on Kodiak Island, a *Fever Sheet* at the Carlisle (Pa.) Army Hospital, a *Jungle Cat* in Panama, a *Horned Toad* at Las Vegas, Nev., and a *Midnight Sun* in Alaska.[6]

As everyone knows, the right of Americans to be so called is frequently challenged, especially in Latin America, but so far no plausible substitute has been devised, though many have been proposed, *e.g.*, *Unisians, Unitedstatesians, Columbards.*[7] There are also frequent debates over the designation to be applied to the inhabitants of various states and cities.[8] The people of Alabama commonly call themselves *Alabamians*, and those of Indiana call themselves *Indianians*, but in both states there are minorities which object to the redundant *i*.[9] In Oklahoma *Oklahoman* has the weight of enlightened opinion behind it, but *Oklahomian* is often heard. In Idaho the English faculty of the state university favors *Idahovan*, but *Idahoan* is more common. A citizen of Arkansas is an *Arkansawyer*, one of New Jersey a *Jerseyman* (now more often a *Jerseyite* or *New Jerseyite*) and one of Michigan a *Michigander*. In New Orleans, *Orleánian*, with the accent on the *an*, is preferred by the elegant, but the vast majority of citizens say *Orléenian*, with the accent on the *leen*. George R. Stewart has attempted to determine the principles underlying the formation of such designations:[1]

---

[5] [The best study of them is by H. Harrison Jenkins, *AS*, Vol. XXVI, Oct. 1951, pp. 185–9, based on a collection of more than a thousand such names. There were 400 such papers in 1942, 3,269 in 1945, 1,300 in 1947; since no definitive list exists, an exhaustive study is impossible.]

[6] For the names of American colleges see American College Names, by Harold B. Allen, *Words*, Mar. 1937, pp. 70–2; Apr., pp. 86–8; and May, pp. 110–12. For the nicknames of football elevens see *AS*, Vol. XII, Apr. 1937, pp. 158–9.

[7] The Baffling Designation *American*, by R. S. Boggs, *AS*, Vol. XXIV, Dec. 1949, pp. 312–13.

[8] [See H. L. Mencken, Names for Americans, *AS*, Vol. XXII, Dec. 1947,

pp. 241–56; What the People of American Towns Call Themselves, *AS*, Vol. XXIII, Oct.–Dec. 1948, pp. 161–84. The Style Manual of the Government Printing Office, rev. ed., Jan. 1959, p. 68, has a list of putatively official designations for the inhabitants of states.]

[9] See Dunn and *Indianan*, by Jacob P. Dunn, Indianapolis *News*, Aug. 11, 1922. But local preference for *Alabamian* and *Floridian* is reported in *AS*, Vol. XXII, Dec. 1947, p. 247.

[1] Larousse's Grand Dictionnaire Universel prints (under *noms*) a list of the designations of persons living in all the principal towns of France, but no American lexicographer has attempted this for the United States.

1. If the name of the town ends in *-ia*, the name of the citizen is formed by adding *n*, *e.g.*, *Philadelphian*.

2. If it ends in *-on*, *-ian* is added, *e.g.*, *Bostonian*, *Tucsonian*.

3. If it ends in *-i*, *-an* is added, *e.g.*, *Miamian*.

4. If it ends in *-y*, the *y* is changed to *i* and *-an* is added, *e.g.*, *Albanian*, *Kansas Citian*.

5. If it ends in *-o*, *-an* is added, *e.g.*, *Chicagoan*, *El Pasoan*.

6. If it ends in a sounded *-e*, or in *-ie* or *-ee*, *-an* is added, *e.g.*, *Muskogeean*, *Albuquerquean*, *Poughkeepsian*.

7. If it ends in *-a*, not preceded by *i*, the common rule is to add *-n*, *e.g.*, *Topekan*.

8. If it ends in *-olis*, the change is to *-olitan*, *e.g.*, *Annapolitan*.

9. If it ends with a consonant or with a silent *-e*, *-ite* or *-er* is added, *e.g.*, *Brooklynite*, *Boiseite*, *New Yorker*, *Pittsburgher*.

But there are exceptions. In California the Spanish names ending in *-o* do not take *-an* but change the *o* to *a* and add *-n*, *e.g.*, *San Franciscan*. Even those not ending in *-o* tend to take *-an*, *e.g.*, *Santa Cruzan* and *Montereyan*. A Buffalo man is not a *Buffaloan* but a *Buffalonian*, and by the same token a Toronto man is a *Torontonian*. A Quincy, Ill., man is not a *Quincian* but a *Quincyan*. The hideous suffix *-ite* seems to be gaining. A citizen of Akron, Ohio, used to be an *Akronian*, but is now an *Akronite*. In Moscow, Idaho, the intelligentsia of the state university prefer *Moscovite*, with *Moscovian* a second choice, but the Moscow *Star-Mirror* prefers *Moscowite*, and so do the people of the town.[2] A citizen of Raleigh, N.C. (pronounced *Rolly*), should be a *Raleighan* by Stewart's rule, but he is actually a *Raleighite*, though a citizen of Berkeley, Cal., remains a *Berkeleyan*. The names ending in *-k* and *-t* usually take *-er*, *e.g.*, *Yorker*, *Davenporter*, but in Passaic, N.J., *Passaicite* is preferred, and in Frederick, Md., the proper form is *Fredericktonian*. In the few American towns whose names end with the French *-ge*, *-an* is added, *e.g.*, *Baton Rougean*. Those in *-ville* drop the final *e* and add *-ian*, *e.g.*, *Louisvillian*. In Los Angeles the correct form is *Angeleño* (*An-juh-lee-nyo*), but it is not yet in universal use. In Taos, N. Mex., *Taoseño* is used, with *Taoseña* for a female, and the tilde is carefully preserved. *Taosian* and *Taosite* are sometimes used by tourists and the indigenous vulgar, but "the Spanish form is used even by the Lions and the Chamber of Commerce."[3] The people of Cambridge, Mass., borrowing from those of the English university town, call themselves *Can-*

[2] *Moscowite* or *Moscovian?*, Moscow *Star-Mirror*, Apr. 22, 1935. I am indebted here to Louis A. Boas, of the *Star-Mirror*.

[3] Private communication from Spud Johnson, of the Taos *Valley News*, June 15, 1935.

tabrigians, and those of Saugus, Mass., call themselves *Saugonians*. A citizen of Schenectady, N.Y., is ordinarily a *Schenectadian*, but often says that he is a *Dorpian*, from the ancient Dutch designation of the town—the *Dorp*, or the *Old Dorp*. A man of Lancaster, Pa., is a *Lancastrian*. A man of Hagerstown, Md., is not a *Hagerstownite*, but a *Hagerstowner* or (occasionally) *Hagerstonian*. A *Montrealer*, if French, is *un Montréalais*, and if female *une Montréalaise*. A *Quebecer*, if French, is a *Québecois*. In the towns bearing classical or pseudo-classical names the inhabitants wear extremely majestic labels, *e.g.*, *Trojan*, *Carthaginian* (Carthage, Mo.), *Phoenician* (Phoenix, Ariz.), *Florentine* (Florence, Ala.), *Roman*, *Athenian*, *Spartan*, but a citizen of Columbus, Ohio, is a *Columbusite* not a *Columbian*. The names of certain American towns are so refractory that no special designations for their citizens have ever arisen: La Crosse, Wis.; Oshkosh, Wis.; Little Rock, Ark.; and Independence, Mo. Some of the states are in the same position, *e.g.*, Massachusetts and Connecticut. A rough popular humor often supplies opprobrious forms. Thus the people of Chicago (or some of them) have been called *Chicagorillas*, those of Baltimore *Baltimorons*,[4] those of Omaha *Omahogs*, those of Louisville *Louisvillains* and those of the state of Maine *Maniacs*.

All the states have nicknames, some often as well known as the actual state names, *e.g.*, *Hoosier* (Indiana), *Old Dominion* (Virginia) and *Lone Star* (Texas). The eldest seems to be *Old Dominion;* it is not traced beyond 1778, but an earlier form, *Ancient Dominion*, goes back to the end of the Seventeenth Century. *Ancient Dominion*, however, was not a nickname but a formal legal designation, arising when Charles II, on ascending the English throne, quartered the arms of the Virginia colony upon his royal shield, along with those of his other dominions, England, Scotland, Ireland and (in theory) France. Charles granted Virginia a new seal, with the motto *En dat Virginia quintam*, and it continued in use until October 1779, when it was supplanted by the present seal, with the new motto, *Sic semper tyrannis*. Both quartering and motto were graceful acknowledgments of the fact that Virginia was the first British possession to recognize the restored monarch. Two other once-familiar nicknames for the state, the *Cavalier State* and the *Mother of Presidents*, have lost vogue in recent years, the first because historians have demonstrated that many of the early settlers were not cavaliers at all, and the second because though Virginia supplied the Republic with seven of its first dozen Presidents, it has hatched

---

[4] *Chicagorilla* is the invention of Walter Winchell. *Baltimoron* was coined by Harry C. Black, of the Baltimore *Evening Sun*, and first appeared in that paper, Feb. 15, 1922. [See also Some Opprobrious Nicknames, by H. L. Mencken, *AS*, Vol. XXIV, Feb. 1949, pp. 25-30.]

only Woodrow Wilson since the death of Zachary Taylor in 1850. The state has also been called the *Mother of States*, an allusion to the fact that a number of the new states west of the Blue Ridge were carved out of its soil and settled by its people. But this name was not applied to Virginia until 1855, whereas it had been given to Connecticut seventeen years earlier.

So long ago as December 2, 1784, George Washington referred to New York as "the seat of Empire," but the term *Empire State* did not come into general use until the census of 1820 showed that the state had gone ahead of Virginia in population. After the opening of the Erie Canal in 1825, New York City acquired a commercial and financial pre-eminence that it has not lost since. At this time, and for that reason, the state was dubbed the *Gateway to the West*, but the sobriquet is now forgotten. But *Empire State* goes on in full glory, and is in frequent use. The *Empire State Express*, of the New York Central System, has been running since October 26, 1891, and for many years was the fastest long-run train in the United States.[5] The *Empire State Building* at Fifth Avenue and Thirty-fourth Street, the highest structure on earth—1,287 feet, including its 102 stories and spire— was opened on May 1, 1931.

Another of the older state nicknames is that of Pennsylvania, the *Keystone State*. The DA's first example is dated 1803, when Howard Jenkins's *Pennsylvania* described it "as the *keystone* of the federal arch," but two other etymologies are to be found in George E. Shankle's "American Nicknames."[6] At one time or another it has also been called the *Coal State*, the *Oil State* and the *Steel State*, but these obvious names are seldom heard to- day. *Quaker State* is sometimes used, but not nearly so often as *Quaker City* for Philadelphia. The DA traces the latter to 1836, but it must be older. *Bay State*, for Massachusetts, is traced to 1789, and *Old Bay State* to 1838. Both refer to the colony of Massachusetts Bay, founded in 1628. *Old Colony*, traced by the DAE to 1798, refers to the earlier Plymouth settle- ment. Vermont has never been described as anything save the *Green Mountain State*, which the DAE traces only to 1838, though *Green Moun- tain Boy*, to designate an inhabitant, goes back to 1772, a year after the militia so called was organized to protect the present territory of the state against forays from New York. The adjoining New Hampshire is usually

---

[5] It made a record of 112.5 miles an hour west of Batavia, N.Y., so long ago as May 10, 1893, drawn by the famous locomotive 999. Its first trip in stream- lined, stainless-steel equipment was made on Dec. 7, 1941.

[6] New York, 1937, p. 410. It is one of the best reference books ever published, and deserves to be in every library. It is heavily documented, and shows few omissions. I am indebted to it for much of what follows. For permission to quote it I owe thanks both to him and to his publishers, the H. W. Wilson Company. [A second edition appeared in 1955.]

called the *Granite State*, which the DAE traces to 1830. It has also been called the *White Mountain State*, the *Mother of Rivers* and the *Switzerland of America*. These nicknames, however, have not had much vogue.

Connecticut is commonly called the *Wooden Nutmeg State* or *Nutmeg State* in facetious remembrance of the early days when the peddlers it sent out into the back country were sharp traders and devised a thousand ways to rook the settlers. One of these schemes, according to legend, was to sell them nutmegs made of wood. At the start *Land of Wooden Nutmegs* seems to have been applied to the whole of New England, but it soon became confined to Connecticut, which took an early lead in manufacturing. At other times the state has been called the *Constitution State*, the *Blue Law State*, the *Brownstone State*, the *Freestone State* and the *Land of Steady Habits*. *Constitution State* refers to the fact that the Fundamental Orders drawn up by Thomas Hooker at Hartford in 1639[7] were the first formal constitution written on American soil. *Blue Law State*, traced to 1839 but no doubt older, refers to the Blue Laws allegedly in force in Connecticut in colonial days. *Freestone State* was the only nickname attributed to Connecticut in an article headed "Names and Nick-names of the Several States," published in *Brother Jonathan* on August 12, 1843.[8]

Rhode Island, the smallest of the states in area, is now usually called *Little Rhody*, but the DAE's earliest example is dated no further back than 1851. In *Warrock's Almanac* for 1847 the nickname given to it is the *Plantation State*, an obvious reference to its official name—the *State of Rhode Island and Providence Plantations*. It has also been called the *Lively Experiment*, in commemoration of a phrase in its original charter of 1663: ". . . to hold forth a *lively experiment*, that a most flourishing civil state may stand and best be maintained . . . with a full liberty in religious concernment."[9] A list of state nicknames that used to be published annually in the *World* Almanac gave New Jersey four of them—*Mosquito State, Garden State, Jersey Blue State* and *New Spain*—but now *Garden State* is the only one that remains. It seems to be relatively recent, for in 1863 the Washington (D.C.) *Daily Morning Chronicle* gave it to Illinois; Schele de Vere, in 1871, said that Kansas was then the *Garden State;* and J. H. Beadle, in "Western Wilds and the Men Who Redeem Them" (1883), gave the name to Minnesota.

In the 80s and 90s New Jersey was known almost universally as the

---

[7] Hooker (*c.* 1586–1647) was an English Puritan clergyman who was driven to Holland by Laud, then Bishop of London, and in 1633 proceeded to New England. He became pastor of a flourishing congregation at Cambridge, and a man of mark in the community. In 1636 he and his people migrated to the Connecti-cut Valley. In 1643 he had a hand in organizing the United Colonies of New England, the remote progenitor of the United States.

[8] p. 441.

[9] I am indebted here to Bradford F. Swan, of the Providence *Journal*.

Mosquito State, mainly because of the swarms of the insects that beset New York City from the Jersey marshes, but after the Spanish-American War they began to abate.[1] These Jersey mosquitoes were frequent themes of the comic artists of the years before 1900, and were represented as having snouts resembling bulldozers or flame throwers. *Clam State,* listed by Shankle, refers to the clam fisheries of the Delaware Bay and the Atlantic seacoast, and is still occasionally heard. Another nickname he lists, *Switzerland of America,* shared with four other states, must seem grotesque to travelers across the melancholy flats which lead to the Jersey coast resorts, but it is justified by some fine scenery along the western border.

Maryland has had half a dozen or more nicknames since colonial times, but only *Old Line State* and *Terrapin State* have any remaining vitality today. Both are under formidable competition from *Maryland Free State,* which was invented in 1923 by Hamilton Owens, then editor of the Baltimore *Evening Sun.*[2] It appealed greatly to Marylanders, for it was a convenient crystallization of a body of ideas, all favorable to personal liberty, that had been traditional in their state since colonial days, and had been revived and revivified by the *Evening Sun* after its establishment in 1910. *Maryland Free State* was taken up by other editors throughout the nation, and soon spread the idea that Maryland was a sanctuary from the oppressive legislation and official usurpation that beset the country in general and most of the other states in particular. This idea was given powerful reinforcement in 1938, when President Franklin D. Roosevelt came into the state in an effort to purge the United States Senate of one of the Maryland senators, Millard E. Tydings, then an active opponent of the New Deal. The result was that Tydings was re-elected by an overwhelming majority, [a precedent unhappily not followed in 1950, when Red-hunting carpetbaggers, led by Senator McCarthy, of Wisconsin, conned the Maryland voters into getting rid of Tydings, who had continued to maintain the integrity of his office against outside pressures, however patriotic in name].

Maryland Free State was suggested by *Irish Free State* (*Saorstat Eireann*),[3] which was apparently suggested in turn by *Orange Free State.*[4] It has overshadowed all the old nicknames of the state, including *Old Line*

---

[1] On Mar. 24, 1930, the state librarian, Charles R. Bacon, was writing to Shankle that "a considerable number of other states have fully as many, if not more." [Cognoscenti consider the Alaska mosquitoes the most ferocious known.]

[2] See The Sunpapers of Baltimore, by Gerald W. Johnson, Frank R. Kent, H. L. Mencken and Hamilton Owens; New York, 1937, p. 389.

[3] Proclaimed on Dec. 6, 1922, after a struggle with England that had gone on

off and on since 1171. Under the new constitution of Dec. 29, 1937, the name was changed to *Eire*.

[4] The *Orange Free State* declared its independence on Feb. 23, 1854. It was annexed to England on May 24, 1900, and became the *Orange River Colony*. [Later it joined the *Union of South Africa*, which became the *Republic of South Africa* and left the (British) Commonwealth in 1961.]

State and *Terrapin State*. The former is generally assumed to recall the Maryland Line in the Continental Army, described by a historian as "among the finest bodies of troops in the Army." The DAE's earliest citation is dated 1871, but the designation is much older. *Terrapin State* is a melancholy memorial to the state's former glory. Other names that have been applied to Maryland are *Monumental State* and *Oyster State*. The first was an extension of *Monumental City*, still often used of Baltimore; it was listed by *Brother Jonathan* in 1843. The second, like *Terrapin State*, recalls a faded and now half-forgotten pride, for the Chesapeake oyster has been deteriorating steadily for sixty years, and is now seldom encountered in its former state of perfection.

Delaware, which lies cheek by jowl with Maryland, is usually called the *Blue Hen State*. [Various rationalizations have been offered, but the DA states, "The reason for the association of this term with Delaware and its citizens is not clear."] The DAE traces *blue hen's chicken* for a "fiery, quick-tempered person" to 1830, and *Blue Hen State* to 1840. Delaware has also been called the *Diamond State*,[5] *New Sweden* and *Uncle Sam's Pocket Handkerchief*. The DAE says that the first was suggested by the small size of the state, as the third unquestionably was. *Diamond State* is traced to 1869, but *Uncle Sam's Pocket Handkerchief* is not listed. *New Sweden* is simply a translation of *Nye Sverige*, the name of the original settlement of Swedes on Christiana Creek, founded in 1638.

The two Carolinas have been called variously, but *Tarheel State* for North Carolina and *Palmetto State* for South Carolina seem likely to prevail. Of the origin of the former the *Overland Monthly* gave the following account in 1869:

> A brigade of North Carolinians . . . failed to hold a certain hill, and were laughed at by the Mississippians for having forgotten to tar their heels that morning. Hence originated the cant name.

There are several more flattering versions of the origin of the nickname, but all of these suggest that North Carolinians were known as *Tarheels* before the Confederate War, or, at all events, that some notion of tar was associated with them. The DA offers evidence that they were called *Tarboilers* so early as 1845, and that their state was the *Turpentine State* by 1850, and *Tar and Turpentine State* six years earlier. No one, so far, has unearthed an example of *Tarheel* older than the Civil War, but a more diligent investigation might produce many. At the start, it appears, the term was regarded as opprobrious, but that is certainly not true today,[6] [any

---

[5] One of the races run at the Wilmington track is the *Diamond State Stakes*.

[6] It is supposed to have been amelio-

rated by Governor Zebulon Vance, one of the greater state heroes, when he addressed as "fellow *Tar Heels*" North

more than the English resent Napoleon's sneer that "the English never know when they are beaten" [7]. The newspaper of the students at the University of North Carolina has been *The Tarheel* since 1892, and when, in 1922, the state bankers launched a monthly organ at Raleigh it was given the name of *Tarheel Banker*. The other common nickname for North Carolina is *Old North State;* it arose naturally out of the geography and history of the state, and the DA traces it to 1839. *Land of the Sky* is applied to the beautiful mountain country in the far western part of the state; eastern North Carolina is far closer to the bottom of the Atlantic than to the sky. [As a counter to the grandiose pretensions of their neighbors, North Carolinians often refer to their state as the *Valley of Humility between Two Mountains of Conceit*—Virginia and South Carolina.]

The palmetto, a variety of fan palm, has been associated with South Carolina since colonial days, though it also grows in other states. *Palmetto State* appeared in 1843. During the turmoils preceding the Civil War *palmetto* was used in various terms associated with the Nullification and Secession movements—*e.g., palmetto speech* (1840), *palmetto cockade* (1846) and *palmetto banner* (1860)—and at the outbreak of the war the *palmetto flag* was the shining symbol of the Confederacy. The prevailing American belief in those days was that the South Carolinians were an especially bellicose folk, so the state was sometimes called the *Gamecock State* at that time, [a name, incidentally, honoring its Revolutionary hero General Thomas Sumter, whose personal nickname was the *Gamecock*. The football team of the state university is still known as the *Gamecocks*.] The state has also been called the *Rice State*, the *Swamp State*, the *Sand-Lapper State* and the *Iodine State*, [the last a short-lived public relations coinage of *c.* 1930, in an effort to promote the sale of presumably iodine-rich South Carolina produce in the Goiter Belt of the Great Lakes region]. Between the Revolution and the Civil War those living on the low-lying coastal plain were often called *Ricebirds* by the people of higher regions. During the years before the Civil War the inhabitants of sandy regions throughout the South were often called *Sand-lappers*. *Sand-hiller* was a variant. *Clay-hiller* and *Clay-eater* belonged to both Carolinas, as well as other parts of the late Confederacy, and designated

> a miserable set of people . . . who subsist chiefly on turpentine whiskey and appease their craving for more substantial food by filling their stomachs with a kind of aluminous earth which abounds everywhere.

Carolina troops in the Army of Northern Virginia. This story was published in a speech in 1915 by Major William A. Graham, a North Carolina veteran of the Confederate Army.

[7] [Listed in A Dictionary of International Slurs, by A. A. Roback; Cambridge, Mass., 1944.]

This gives them a yellowish-drab-colored complexion, with dull eyes and faces whose idiotic expression is only varied by a dull despair or a devilish malignity. They are looked down upon by the Negroes with a contempt that they return with a hearty hatred.[8]

Most of them were dissuaded from this diet by the Public Health Service doctors and nurses who began purging them of hookworms in the early days of the present century, but the breed is far from extinct.

Georgia was listed as the *Pine State* in 1843, but by 1872 Schele de Vere was calling it the *Cracker State*. *Cracker* as a designation for a low-down Southern white man is traced to 1766,[9] and from the start it seems to have been felt that such persons were especially numerous in Georgia. The term was used in the sense of a boaster by Alexander Barclay in "The Shyp of Folys" in 1509, and by Shakespeare in "King John" in 1595, and in this sense it seems to have been suggested by a verb common to all the Germanic languages.[1] The DA accepts this etymology, but another school holds that many of the early *Crackers* were teamsters, and got their name from their loud and incessant cracking of their whips. *Crackers*, of course, are by no means confined to Georgia; they are to be found in all the states south of the Potomac and Ohio.[2] There was a time when Georgians bitterly resented *Cracker State*, but of late they have become more philosophical.

At various times in the past Georgia has suffered even more opprobrious nicknames, *e.g.*, *Buzzard State*, and also basked in some very flattering ones, *e.g.*, *Empire State of the South*. The DAE traces *Buzzard* for Georgian to 1845. *Empire State of the South* is traced by the DA to 1855. It has been disputed by Texas, but is well deserved by Georgia, which is the largest state east of the Mississippi. *Goober State*, yet another nickname for Georgia, comes from a common Southern name for the peanut. Georgia is a heavy producer of peanuts, and the hams of its peanut-fed hogs are highly esteemed by connoisseurs. Before the Civil War era *Goober-grabber* was a common nickname for a backwoods Georgian, but it was also applied to Alabamians, and the simple *Goober* was a nickname for North Carolinians. [*Peach State*, which appears on Georgia license plates, is an anachronism, for Spartanburg County, S.C., normally ships more peaches than the entire state of Georgia.]

After the Thirteen Original States it is more convenient to proceed

---

[8] Thornton's definition, on the authority of a mysterious Ida May.

[9] [According to *AS*, Vol. XXXIV, May 1959, pp. 126–7, this was in a letter of June 17, 1766, from Gavin Cochrane to the Earl of Dartmouth.]

[1] *Cf.* the German *krachen* and the American *wisecrack* and *wisecracker*.

[2] Kentucky was reported as the *Corn-cracker State* in Letters from the United States, Cuba and Canada, by the Hon. Amelia M. Murray; New York, 1856, p. 324. I am indebted for this to Joseph M. Carrière.

alphabetically, beginning with Alabama. It has been called the *Cotton State* and *Cotton Plantation State* because of its central position in the cotton-growing area east of the Mississippi, now in sad decay. *Cotton States* is a generic name for the whole group, traced to 1844, with *Cottondom* (1856), *Cotton Belt* (1871), *Cotton Country* (1871) and *Cottonia* (1862) as variants. *Lizard State* derives from an early nickname for the Alabamians, probably opprobrious, first recorded in 1845. *Yellow-Hammer State* is more flattering, for the yellow-hammer (*Colaptes auratus*) is a beautiful variety of woodpecker. But a more prosaic explanation is that during the Civil War the home-dyed uniforms of the Alabama troops had a yellowish tinge.[3]

[Alaska has no official or generally accepted nickname. According to Ernest Gruening, former Territorial Governor and now United States senator, "the most widely accepted designation . . . is the *Last Frontier*. Alaska is also known as the *49th State* and the *Great Land*. Some of the other suggestions were the *Sourdough State* and the *North Star State*. There is also *Up Over*, presumably in contrast to New Zealand and Australia, often called *Down Under*." [4] *North Star State*, incidentally, is also claimed by Minnesota.

[Arizona, the forty-eighth state admitted to the Union, was appropriately the *Baby State* from its admission in 1912 until the admission of Alaska in 1959.] There is, however, nothing infantile about its *Kultur;* it was settled by the Spaniards in 1580, and its Indian civilization goes back to a remote antiquity. It has also been known as the *Apache State*, the *Aztec State*, the *Sand Hill State*, the *Grand Canyon State*, the *Sunset State* and the *Valentine State*—the last because it was admitted on St. Valentine's Day, and the others for obvious reasons.

In 1923 the Arkansas legislature, prodded by the visionaries of the Arkansas Advancement Association, passed an act designating *Wonder State* as its nickname,[5] but in the past it was the *Bear State*, the *Hot Water State*, the *Bowie State* and the *Toothpick State*. Bartlett recorded *Bear State* so early as 1848; California and Missouri, in those days, pretended to the same nickname, and there are bears on their state seals to this day. *Hot Water State*, of course, refers to the springs at Hot Springs and elsewhere. Both *Bowie State* and *Toothpick State* recall the Bowie knife, the favorite weapon of the hardy blood-letters who wrested the Southwest from the Mexican, the Indian, the bear, the catamount and all lesser fauna. It was commonly made by grinding a flat, broad file, nine or ten inches

---

[3] Both *Lizard State* and *Yellow-Hammer State*, with possible explanations of the latter, are cited by Shankle.

[4] [Personal communication, June 14, 1961.]

[5] There is a weekly *Wonder State Herald* in Kensett, Ark., population 889.

long, to a fine point, sharpening both edges to razor keenness and fitting a guard between blade and handle. It was really invented by Rezin Pleasant Bowie (1793–1841), at some indefinite time before 1827. Its popularity, however, was due to Rezin's more illustrious brother James, later killed in the Alamo, who used it with great effect in 1827 in a famous mass duel at Natchez.[6] How the Bowie knife came to be associated with Arkansas is not known, for the Bowies operated in Louisiana and Texas. But the DA shows that it was identified as an *Arkansas toothpick* in "Crockett's Almanac" for 1837, printed at Nashville in 1836. The legend was that the Arkansawyers of the time used it not only for murder but also for fighting wild animals, butchering cattle, cutting up their victuals and picking their teeth.

California was called the *Gold State* by the Hon. Amelia M. Murray in her "Letters from the United States, Cuba and Canada" (1856),[7] but by 1867 this had become the *Golden State*. It has, in late years, got much more glory and money out of its oil wells, orchards, vineyards, truck farms, aircraft factories and movie lots than it has out of its gold mines, but the glamour of 1849 survives, probably helped by the suggestion in that most romantic of geographical names, *Golden Gate*. In 1846 *El Dorado*[8] came into use as a nickname for California, but it was by no means new, and had been applied previously to various other regions promising fabulous riches. Schele de Vere adds *Bear State*, also claimed by Arkansas, and explains that the California bear is a grizzly.

Colorado is usually called the *Centennial State*, for it was admitted to the Union in 1876. The DAE's first example of the term is dated 1878. It was also called the *Silver State*, but this designation was disputed by Nevada so long ago as 1871. It has also been called the *Switzerland of America*, which is challenged by Maine, New Hampshire, New Jersey and West Virginia, and the *Treasure State*, which is disputed by Montana.

The most common designations for Florida are *Everglade State* and *Peninsula State*. The DAE traces *Everglade State* only to 1893, and omits *Peninsula State;* the DA traces the latter to 1866, and omits the former. The boosters who swarm in Florida have made diligent efforts to devise a nickname connecting it with the Fountain of Eternal Youth which Juan Ponce de León vainly sought there in 1513 and 1521. As a result of their

---

[6] The most plausible account of the Bowie knife is in the Bowie Brothers and Their Famous Knife, by Matilda Elanor Bowie Moore, a daughter of Rezin P. Bowie, *Frontier Times* (Bandera, Tex.), Feb. 1942, pp. 199–205. Mrs. Moore was long dead in 1942, but she had prepared a history of the Bowies during her lifetime, and this was sent to the *Frontier Times* by her granddaughter, Mrs. Bessie Bird Moore Bryant. See also Bowie Knife, by E. E. Ericson, *AS*, Vol. XII, Feb. 1937, pp. 77–9.

[7] I am indebted for this to Joseph M. Carrière.

[8] *Dorado* is Spanish for golden or gilt.

efforts *Sunshine State*—also claimed by New Mexico—appears on Florida license plates.[9] [Hawaii, the latest state admitted (1959), prefers the designation *Aloha State*, commemorating a traditional Polynesian greeting. Its boosters call it the *Paradise of the Pacific. Crossroads of the Pacific* is also heard, both for the islands and for the principal city of Honolulu.]

Idaho prefers to be called the *Gem of the Mountains,* or the *Gem State,* but *Little Ida* has also been recorded.[1] The first is allegedly a translation of *Idaho.* Illinois has had many nicknames in the past, *e.g., Garden of the West* and *Corn State,* but *Prairie State* [2] and *Sucker State* are the only ones surviving. The DA traces *Sucker* for an Illinoisian to 1834. *Sucker* may be derived from the name of a fresh-water fish of the genus *Catostomus,* related to the catfish and plentiful in Western rivers. This fish swam up the rivers in the spring and returned in the autumn. When the lead mines at Galena, in the far northern part of the state, were opened in the 1820s, they were manned largely by itinerants from the southward, who came up the river with the fish and returned with them.[3] By the 1830s *sucker* had become a common term in the Western country for a gull or easy mark, and it has since got into almost universal American use. [The DA adds: "Perhaps the best, and certainly the simplest, explanation is that many of the first settlers of Illinois were the dupes of land speculators."] The DA traces *Prairie State* for Illinois to 1842. It had been in use before that, in the plural, as a general designation for all the states in the plains area, from Indiana in the east to Kansas in the west. A writer in the *Atlantic Monthly* for March 1867, quoted by the DAE, even included Missouri, Wisconsin and Minnesota. *Egypt* has long been the common designation for the region of deep black soil in the southern part of Illinois, surrounding Cairo, where the Ohio River enters the Mississippi. Thornton says maliciously that the name was applied to it "with reference to the supposed intellectual darkness of the inhabitants." [4]

---

[9] [See Florida: Land of Epithets, by Lalia Phipps Boone, *Southern Folklore Quarterly,* Vol. XXII, June 1958, pp. 86–92.]

[1] A Book of Nicknames, by John Goff; Louisville, 1892, p. 13; quoted by Shankle.

[2] The old battleship *Illinois* was stripped of guns and machinery and as the *Prairie State* served as a receiving ship in World War II.

[3] Thornton gives this on the authority of Charles Fenno Hoffman, A Winter in the Far West; London, 1835, Vol. I, p. 207 *n.* It was also published in New York the same year as A Winter in the West.

[4] [The best explanation is given by Grace Partridge Smith, They Call it Egypt, *Names,* Vol. II, Mar. 1954, pp. 51–4. After *Cairo* had been founded at the confluence of the Ohio and Mississippi, and *Thebes* and *Karnak* followed, the region developed its name. The popular explanation that there were good crops in southern Illinois one year but poor ones in the north, so that it was necessary to "go down into Egypt to buy corn," is shown by Herbert Halpert to be an explanation after the fact, also shared by various communities named *Egypt* or *New Egypt* as far apart as New Hampshire and Texas. *Midwest Folklore,* Vol. IV, Fall 1954, pp. 165–8. In an article entitled Trouble

Indiana is the *Hoosier State*, and seems to have no other nickname. The DA's first example of *Hoosier* is dated 1826. Its etymology has been much disputed. Thornton, in his "American Glossary," called attention to the fact that *whoosher* was defined in a dictionary of 1659 as "a rocker, a stiller, a luller, a dandler of children asleep," but there was obviously no connection between this *whoosher* and *Hoosier*. The earlier American etymologists all sought to connect the term with some idea of ruffianism, and in the Southern uplands it is still applied to backwoodsmen in general, not only to Indianans. [In South Carolina and Georgia the cruder poor whites are referred to as *country hoosiers* or *mountain hoosiers*, and a child whose table manners fall short of parental standards is said to *eat like a hoosier*.] Beyond North America, the most reliable etymology connects it with *hoozer*, a Cumberland dialect term applied to "anything unusually large." In any event, all authorities seem to be agreed that *Hoosier*, at the start, did not signify an Indianan particularly, but any rough fellow of what was then the Wild West. In Indiana, however, the term apparently became restricted to a resident of the state at an early date. The term *Hoosier*, as Charles Fenno Hoffman remarked, "like that of *Yankee* or *Buckeye*, [was] first applied contemptuously, but has now become a sobriquet that bears nothing invidious, to the ear even of an Indianan." [5]

Iowa is universally the *Hawkeye State*, and is so called in the subtitle of the state guide brought out by the Federal Writers' Project.[6] The DA traces the nickname to 1859, and *Hawkeye* as a designation for an Iowan to 1839, but both dates are probably too late. The name is variously derived: in the Encyclopedia Americana from that of "a great Indian chief, the terror of the early settlers"; in the New International from "J[ames] G[ardiner] Edwards, familiarly known as *Old Hawkeye*, editor of the Burlington *Patriot*, now the *Hawkeye and Patriot*." Its probable source is the nickname *Hawkeye*, under which Natty Bumppo, the hero of James Fenimore Cooper's "Leatherstocking Tales," figures in "The Last of the Mohicans" (1826). Natty was everything that the pioneer of those days fancied himself to be—brave, resourceful and honorable. According to a "Commercial and Statistical Review of the City of Burlington," [7] the name was added to the title of Edwards's paper at the suggestion of his wife. Mrs. Edwards, like her husband, was a romantic person, probably a diligent reader of Cooper.

---

in *Little Egypt, The New York Times*, July 24, 1962, Paul M. Angle, director of the Chicago Historical Society, is reported as considering most likely the derivation from the delta-like character of the region and the Egyptian place names.]

[5] A Winter in the Far West; London, 1835, Vol. I, p. 223.
[6] Iowa: a Guide to the *Hawkeye State*; New York, 1938.
[7] Burlington, 1882, p. 63.

Shankle lists no less than ten nicknames for Kansas—the *Battleground of Freedom*, the *Central State*, the *Cyclone State*, the *Garden State*, the *Garden of the West*, the *Grasshopper State*, the *Jayhawker State*, the *Navel of the Nation*, the *Squatter State* and the *Sunflower State*. *Battleground of Freedom* seems to have passed out with the Civil War; it referred to the sanguinary combats between Abolitionists and slavery men which had reddened the soil of the Territory. *Garden State* is challenged by New Jersey and *Garden of the West* by Illinois, and neither has ever had much vogue. *Squatter State*, listed by Schele de Vere, is long obsolete, for no one remembers, three generations after the Civil War, the once explosive issue of *squatter sovereignty*.[8] *Cyclone State* and *Grasshopper State* refer to two of the many calamitous acts of God from which Bleeding Kansas has suffered; to them *Dust Bowl State* might be added. The DAE traces *Grasshopper State* to 1890, but does not list *Cyclone State*.[9] *Sunflower State*, dating from 1888, seems to be favored in Kansas itself, for the sunflower is the state flower. It has, however, a formidable rival in *Jayhawk* or *Jayhawker State*. The latter is traced by the DAE no further than 1885, but *Jayhawker* for a Kansan goes back to 1875, and in the wider sense of a fighting Abolitionist to 1858.[1]

Kentucky has been the *Blue Grass State* since the Civil War era, and is the heir to a much larger *Blue Grass region* that includes middle Tennessee and once extended into Ohio, Indiana, Virginia and Pennsylvania. The DA's first example of *Blue Grass State* as applied specifically to Kentucky comes from the Chicago *Weekly News*, 1886, but it is probably considerably older. In the years immediately following the Revolution, Kentucky was often called the *Dark and Bloody Ground*, supposedly a translation of the Indian phrase from which its name was derived. *Dark and Bloody Ground* alluded, not to battles between Indians and the first white settlers, but to contests between Northern and Southern tribes of Indians, but by 1839, as the DAE shows, it had come to be accepted as a reference to "the slaughter of white pioneers." Kentucky has also been called the *Hemp*

---

[8] *Squatter* is an Americanism, traced to 1788, when it was used by James Madison. [It has migrated to Australia, according to W. S. Ramson, and has been upgraded to designate large landowners who usurp grazing rights on vast territories; hence the term *squattocracy*.] *Squatter sovereignty* meant the right of settlers in the Western lands to make their own laws. It is traced to 1854; *squatter law* to 1857.

[9] *Cyclone* was proposed in 1848 by an English nautical writer named Piddington, but *cyclone cellar* is an American-ism, traced to 1887.

[1] According to Kirke Mecham, secretary of the Kansas State Historical Society, the name "was at first applied to both sides. Jennison's regiment of Free-State men, as well as Quantrill's raiders, were at one time called *Jayhawkers*. The name finally stuck to the anti-slavery side and eventually to all the people of Kansas." *The Mythical Jayhawk*; Topeka, 1944, p. 2. *Cf.* Nebraska Pioneer English, by Melvin Van den Bark, *AS*, Vol. VIII, Dec. 1933, p. 50.

State, the *Rock-Ribbed State* and the *Tobacco State*, but without much frequency. The first of these honored, not its busy and accomplished hangmen, but its large crops of hemp. Surprisingly the state has acquired no appellation calling up the speed of its race horses, the traditional beauty of its women or its Bourbon whiskey. The DAE's first citation of *Bourbon* whiskey is dated 1850, but with the name already preceded by *good old*.

Pelican State for Louisiana goes back to 1859, and seems destined to outlive all rivals. The pelican has appeared on the state seal since before the Civil War, and a committee of the State Convention of 1861, appointed to prepare a new state flag and seal, resolved to keep it there on the ground that it had "long been the cherished emblem of Louisiana." The pelican was chosen originally because it is plentiful along the Gulf coast of the state. Schele de Vere, in 1872, listed *Creole State* as an alternative nickname for Louisiana, "on account of the large number of its inhabitants who are descendants of the original French and Spanish settlers." This designation was borne proudly so long as it was generally understood that a *Creole* was a Caucasian,[2] but when ignorant Northerners began assuming that the term connoted African blood it passed out of favor. The DAE traces it to 1792, and shows that it began to be applied especially to the people of New Orleans by 1807.

Maine is the *Pine Tree State*, and a pine tree appears upon its seal. The DAE's first use of the term is from *Harper's Magazine* for March 1860, but it appears in Bartlett's second edition of 1859 and must be older. On the *Brother Jonathan* list of 1843, Maine is called the *Lumber State*. The saying "As Maine goes, so goes the country" was first heard in the national campaign of 1888 but is now obsolete. Otherwise, Maine has led the country on but one occasion—when, in 1858, it passed a Prohibition law which paved the way for the Eighteenth Amendment of 1919.

Michigan is the *Wolverine State*, but it has also been called the *Lady of the Lakes*, the *Lake State* and, in recent years, the *Auto State*. *Wolverine State* is traced to 1846, when it appeared in the *Knickerbocker Magazine*. The DA's first example of *Wolverine*, for an inhabitant, is dated 1834. Why the name of this voracious creature should have been given to the people of Michigan is still a matter for speculation. The early fur-trade inventories offer no evidence that "the *wolverine* ever lived or was trapped in our Michigan southern peninsula," and during the 30s of the last century, when the people of the Territory became *Wolverines*, it had no northern peninsula. Nevertheless, the nickname was already current at that time, for Charles Fenno Hoffman told of meeting a typical *Wolverine* at

---

[2] See Ch. VI, Sec. 9. See also *Creole and Cajan*, by William A. Read, *AS*, Vol. I, June 1926, p. 483; and *Creole and West Indies*, by E. C. Hills, *AS*, Vol. II, Mar. 1927, pp. 293–4.

"Prairie Ronde, Kalamazoo Co., M.T." This specimen he described as "a sturdy yeoman-like fellow whose white capot, Indian moccasins and red sash proclaimed, while he boasted a three years' residence, the genuine *Wolverine*, or naturalized Michiganian." [3] *Lake State* for Michigan early collided with *Lake States*, which began to be applied generally to all the states bordering upon the Great Lakes so early as 1845.

Minnesota chooses to be called the *North Star State*, though the DA's earliest citation is dated 1909, and has the motto *L'Étoile du Nord* on its seal. [But popularly it is the *Gopher State*, dating from 1880, and the football representatives of its state university are known as the *Golden Gophers*.] *Gopher State* was also claimed, *c.* 1845, by Arkansas. Shankle also lists *Bread Basket of the Nation*, the *Bread and Butter State*, the *Cream Pitcher of the Nation*, the *Playground of the Nation* and the *Wheat State*, but all of these reflect the passion of boosters rather than *vox populi*.

Schele de Vere, in 1872, reported that Mississippi was the *Mudcat State*, after "a large catfish abounding in the swamps and the mud of the rivers," but this designation seems to be obsolescent. The nickname of choice is now *Magnolia State*. It has rivals, according to Shankle, in *Bayou State*, *Eagle State*, *Border-Eagle State*, *Groundhog State* and *Mud-Waddler State*. The DAE traces *Bayou State* to 1867, but overlooks *Eagle State*. The latter is said to have been suggested, like *Border-Eagle State* (traced by Lovell to 1846), by the fact that there is an eagle on the state seal. But there are also eagles on the seals of nine other states. [In 1928 an objective survey by the *American Mercury* recognized Mississippi as the "worst American State," but this was a description and not a nickname.]

Missouri in former days was the *Iron Mountain State*, the *Bullion State*, the *Lead State*, the *Ozark State*, the *Puke State* and the *Pennsylvania of the West*, but now is known universally as the *Show Me State*. This designation seems to have been given nation-wide currency by a speech made in 1899 or thereabout by Willard D. Vandiver,[4] then a congressman from Missouri, in Philadelphia at a dinner of the Five O'Clock Club. Vandiver, who was in Philadelphia on public business, had not expected to be invited and had thus brought no dress clothes. He and another impromptu guest, Congressman John A. T. Hull, of Iowa, decided to go in their ordinary

---

[3] [A scholarly discussion is *Wolverine* and *Michigander*, by Albert H. Marckwardt, *Michigan Alumnus Quarterly Review*, Vol. LVIII, Spring 1952, pp. 203–8. In Words and Phrases in American Politics: *Michigander*, *AS*, Vol. XXIX, Feb. 1954, pp. 21–7, Hans Sperber suggests that *Michigander* was originally a personal nickname of Lewis Cass, Territorial and later state governor, from his ungainly appearance.]

[4] Vandiver (1854–1932) was a pedagogue turned politician. He served in Congress from 1897 to 1905. His later years were mainly devoted to the insurance business, though he was assistant United States treasurer at St. Louis from 1913 to 1920.

clothes, but at the last minute Hull somewhere found a dress suit, and thereby greatly embarrassed Vandiver, who was the only diner without one. When the time came for speeches, Hull delivered an eloquent eulogy of Philadelphia, and the toastmaster then called upon Vandiver. Let him tell his own story:

> I made a rough-and-tumble speech, saying the meanest things I could think of about the old Quaker town . . . and then, turning to Hull, followed up with a roast something like this:
>
> "His talk about your hospitality is all bunk; he wants another feed. He tells you that the tailors, finding he was here without a dress suit, made one for him in fifteen minutes. I have a different explanation. . . . He stole mine, and that's why you see him with one on and me without any. This story from Iowa doesn't go with me. I'm from Missouri, and you'll have to show me."

Vandiver did not claim the invention of the phrase; all he apparently intended to suggest was that his apt use of it before an Eastern audience served to spread it. But its origin plainly goes beyond Vandiver; there are Missouri antiquarians who seek to run it back to pioneer days.

Missourians are probably fond of *Show Me State* because it has mercifully obliterated *Puke State*, which seems to have prevailed for years. The origin of *Puke* to designate a Missourian is not known, but it is traced to 1835. A humane theory, apparently favored in the state, is that it is simply a misprint for *Pike*, the name of a Missouri county bordering on the Mississippi. There is another Pike County across the river in Illinois, and in the early days the two were grouped together as the habitat of a singularly backward type of yokel. In 1849 a good many such yokels flocked to California, and there they were known as *Pike Countians*, a term which ultimately embraced any newcomer of rustic aspect, whatever his origin.[5] But Missourians were called *Pukes* before this, and it is unlikely that the term began as a corruption of *Pike*. *Bullion State* is traced by the DAE to 1848, and is thought to have been suggested by *Old Bullion*, the sobriquet of Thomas Hart Benton (1782–1858), senator from Missouri from 1821 to 1853 and a conspicuous advocate of a metallic currency.

Montana, in its earlier days, was the *Bonanza State* (1893) and the *Stub-Toe State* (1890), the first referring to its mineral riches and the second to its precipitous slopes, but it is now, because of its mining and smelting industry, the *Treasure State*. Nebraska was listed by the *World* Almanac, in 1922, as the *Antelope State* and the *Black Water State;* by formal act of the

---

[5] In a prefatory note to Huckleberry Finn, New York, 1884, Mark Twain lists among the dialects used "the ordinary Pike-County dialect, and four modified varieties of this last."

1895 legislature, it is the *Tree Planters State*, and by its license plates the *Beef State*. The New International Encyclopedia made it the *Black Water State* in 1916, "from the dark color of its rivers," with *Tree Planter State* (in the singular) as an alternative. Shankle adds *Bugeating State* and *Corn Huskers' State*. The DAE lists only *Tree Planters State*, but notes that *Bug-eater*, as a nickname for a Nebraskan, goes back to 1872, and quotes *American Notes and Queries* (1888) to the effect that it was used derisively "by travelers on account of the poverty-stricken appearance of many parts of the state." *Cornhuskers* was at first applied to the University of Nebraska football eleven, and was only later extended to the state and its general population.

Nevada prefers to be called the *Battle-Born State*, to recall the fact that it was admitted to the Union during the Civil War, but it is usually called the *Sagebrush State* or the *Silver State*,[6] with many votes, since the rise of Reno and Las Vegas, for the *Divorce State*. *Sagebrush State* has been challenged by Wyoming and *Silver State* by Colorado.

New Mexico glories in the plausible appellation of the *Sunshine State* (cited from 1926), but it has also been called the *Spanish State*, the *Cactus State*, the *Land of the Cactus*, the *Land of the Montezumas*, the *Land of the Delight Makers*, the *Land of Heart's Desire*, the *Land of Opportunity* and the *Land of Enchantment*, the last five being the inventions of boosters. Which brings us to North Dakota, the *Sioux State*, with *Flickertail State*, *Great Central State* and *Land of the Dakotas* lurking in the background. The Sioux Indians roved the wilds which are now North Dakota, and were hostile when the first white settlers appeared. In 1851 they were induced to cede some of their land to the invaders, but it was a long while before they became reconciled to the boons of civilization. *Flickertail State* comes from the popular name of *Citellus richardsonii*, a ground squirrel which, according to a local authority cited by Shankle, is found in North Dakota only.

Ohio, the first of the Midwestern states to be admitted to the Union (1803), is the *Buckeye State*, after the tree of that name, and has thus been recorded since 1835. During the first years of the Nineteenth Century it was often called the *Yankee State*, since many of its settlers came from New England, but that designation was abandoned long ago. For a time some of its boosters, having Grant, Hayes, Garfield, Benjamin Harrison, McKinley, Taft and Harding in mind, claimed for it the nickname *Mother of Presidents*, once borne by Virginia. *Buckeye* is derived from the name of a native horse chestnut (*Aesculus glabra*), so called, according to Schele de

---

[6] This is used in the subtitle of the State Guide brought out by the Federal Writers' Project. Charles J. Lovell traces the name to 1851. In The Background to Mark Twain's Vocabulary, *AS*, Vol. XXII, Apr. 1947, p. 96, he traces *Silverland* to 1863.

Vere, because of "the resemblance its fruit bears to a deer's eye." The term was first used for the tree in 1763, but when and why it came to be applied to the people of Ohio is not known.

Oklahoma is the *Sooner State*, from the term used to designate the early settlers who sneaked across the border before the land was thrown open to white settlement. When the proclamation of President Benjamin Harrison opened it as of noon of April 22, 1889, about 20,000 progenitors of the later *Okies* were gathered along the border, hoping to find Utopia. Unhappily, many of them discovered, when they came to likely-looking tracts, that there were claimants there ahead of them, and many of these succeeded in holding their claims. They were called *sooners*, and in a little while the term began to be applied to all the citizens of the state. By 1892 it had been extended to any one of "that numerous class of . . . people who insist upon crossing bridges before they come to them."

Oregon is the *Beaver State* officially, but has been known as the *Sunset State*, the *Webfoot State* and the *Hard-Case State*. *Sunset State* was once disputed by Arizona, but now seems to be in the public domain. *Hard-Case State* had reference to the evil characters who flocked into the Oregon country in the early days: their descendants are now austere Rotarians and Shriners. *Hard case*, to designate such a character, is run back to 1836. *Webfoot State* is traced by the DA to 1866, and *Webfoot*, for a citizen of the state, by Charles J. Lovell to 1853. It was suggested by the copious rainfall between the Cascade Range and the Pacific Ocean. Around Astoria, the first settlement in the valley of the Columbia, it is 77.2 inches a year, as compared to 42.87 inches in New York City and 33.5 inches in Chicago. [The official plural of *Webfoot*, incidentally, is *Webfoots*.[7]]

South Dakota, which was joined to North Dakota until 1889, is the *Coyote State*. In its first days it was known variously as the *Blizzard State*, the *Artesian State*, the *Sunshine State* and the *Land of Plenty*, but *Sunshine State* has been taken over by New Mexico, and the others have passed out. In 1898 the *Monthly South Dakotan* of Mitchell was predicting that *Coyote* as a designation for a citizen of the state would "probably last." The name comes, of course, from that of the prairie wolf (*Canis latrans*), borrowed by the Spaniards from a Nahuatl Indian word, *coyotl*.

Tennessee prefers to be the *Volunteer State*,[8] but after the Scopes trial at Dayton in 1925 it was called the *Monkey State* with painful frequency, and was a long time living down that derisive designation. The effort to repeal natural selection by law made the state ridiculous throughout the world, and its civilized minority suffered severely. *Volunteer State* goes back to

---

[7] [This information was supplied by Leo C. Dean, of the Salem *Capital Press*.]
[8] It appears in the subtitle of the guide to the state brought out by the Federal Writers' Project under the sponsorship of the State Department of Conservation.

1847, when Governor Aaron V. Brown issued a call for three regiments to serve in the Mexican War—and 30,000 men responded. At various times Tennessee has also been known as the *Big Bend State*, the *Hog and Hominy State* and the *Lion's Den*. The last-named, listed by *Brother Jonathan* in 1843, perhaps arose from the fact that the border ruffians of the early days were sometimes called *lions of the West*, or simply *lions*. *Hog and Hominy State* refers to the favorite diet of the Tennessee yeomanry—a diet popular throughout the Bible Belt. *Hog and hominy* means, colloquially, fatback and any preparation of corn meal; [9] the term is traced by the DA to 1776. This combination is deficient in vitamins, and those who feed upon it often suffer from pellagra. *Big Bend State* refers to the various bends in the Tennessee River, especially the one at Chattanooga.

Texas, as everyone knows, is the *Lone Star State*—the device on the flag of the Texas Republic (1836–45), and the device on the state flag and seal today. Attempts have been made at various times to substitute *Banner State*, *Jumbo State*, *Blizzard State* and *Beef State*, but in vain. [A portrait in *The New Yorker* (1961) labeled it the *Super-American State* or *Super America*, in recognition of the way in which Texans exaggerate American stereotypes.[1]] An important part of Texas is the *Panhandle*, which runs up between Oklahoma and New Mexico in the northwest. The term, suggested by the handle of a frying pan, is traced by the DA to 1856, and was applied to the Texas *Panhandle* so long ago as 1873.

Utah calls itself the *Beehive State*, and sports on its seal "a conical beehive with a swarm of bees round it, emblematical of the industry of the people," [2] but the *Mormon State* is far more popular, and seems likely to stick. The state, which did not enter the Union until 1896, delayed by the long battle over polygamy, has also been called the *Deseret State*, the *Salt Lake State*, the *Land of the Mormons* and the *Land of the Saints*. *Deseret*, the original name which the Mormons gave the state, is borrowed from a word in the Book of Mormon [3] signifying a honeybee and appearing in a passage describing the wanderings of the prophet Jared and his brother and their families in search of the Promised Land. Reaching the Valley of Nimrod, they pastured their flocks, turned loose edible fowl, stocked the streams with fish, liberated swarms of bees and planted "seeds of every kind." Washington is both the *Evergreen State* and the *Chinook State*, with the latter, traced to 1890, apparently the more in use. *Chinook* is the name of a local tribe of Indians, once numerous at the mouth of the Columbia River.

---

[9] [In South Carolina I was taught that *hominy* designated what the less fortunate called *grits*; *hog and hominy* would be a breakfast or supper involving this preparation and ham or sausage.]

[1] [John V. Bainbridge, The Super-American State; later published in book form as the Super Americans; New York, 1961.]

[2] Political Americanisms, by Charles Ledyard Norton, New York, 1890, p. 64.

[3] Ether II, 3.

They gave their name to a trade language that was in common use along the coast for more than a century.[4] The DA traces *Evergreen State* to 1905. It refers to the state's immense stretches of conifer forest.

West Virginia, one of the five contending *Switzerlands of America*, is now more generally known as the *Mountain State* or the *Panhandle State*, the former because a large part of its area is in the Allegheny chain, and the second because of the panhandle which juts up between Pennsylvania and Ohio and is in places less than ten miles wide, though it includes the metropolitan area of Wheeling and Moundsville, the seat of the state penitentiary.[5] The people of the state often speak of it proudly as *West by God Virginia*.[6] Wisconsin is the *Badger State*, and its people are *Badgers*. The appellation seems to have arisen, like *Sucker* for Illinoisian and *Puke* for Missourian, at the Galena, Ill., lead mines in the 1830s. These mines were near the place where Illinois, Iowa and Wisconsin meet, and many Wisconsin pioneers were occasionally employed in them. There were no houses, and they commonly lived in caves in the hillsides that resembled badger burrows. Hence they were called *Badgers*, and the nickname stuck when they returned home. Wyoming is the *Equality* or *Suffrage State*, so called because its Territorial Legislature made the first grant of the suffrage to women voters in 1869.

As we have seen, inhabitants are often known by the nicknames of their states, *e.g.*, *Hoosiers, Tarheels, Buckeyes, Crackers* (Georgia). In other cases separate nicknames have arisen, *e.g.*, *Colonels* (Kentucky). In the early days most of the designations in vogue were ribald, *e.g.*, *Whelps* (Tennessee), *Beetheads* (Texas), *Leatherheads* (Pennsylvania), *Foxes* (Maine), *Tadpoles* (Mississippi), *Muskrats* (Delaware), *Clam-catchers* (New Jersey), *Crawthumpers* (Maryland).[7] Many cities also have generally recognized nicknames, *e.g.*, the *Hub* (Boston), the *Windy City* (Chicago), and nearly every small place of any pretensions has tried to launch one for itself, usually embodying *Queen* or *Wonder*.[8]

---

[4] See Ch. IV, Sec. 3.

[5] [West Virginians speak of two *panhandles*—the *Northern Panhandle*, here described, and the *Eastern Panhandle*, a narrowing wedge between Pennsylvania and Virginia.]

[6] [In anticipation of its centennial in 1963, a number of dissident boosters and publicists have been agitating to change the name of the state to *Lincoln*, but with little effect. *Kanawha* has also been proposed.]

[7] In Slang in America (part of November Boughs, 1888) Walt Whitman printed a list largely identical with the foregoing; apparently he borrowed it from an anonymous newspaper article reprinted in the *Broadway Journal* for May 3, 1845. See Nicknames of the States: a Note on Walt Whitman, by John Howard Birss, *AS*, Vol. VII, June 1932, p. 389. [In addition to the references on nicknames cited in this section, one might examine David Shulman, Nicknames of States and Their Inhabitants, *AS*, Vol. XXVII, Oct. 1952, pp. 183-5.]

[8] [See Nicknames of American Cities, Towns and Villages, Past and Present, by G. L. Alexander; New York, 1951.]

Another field that awaits scientific exploration is that of the joke towns—
Podunk, Squeedunk, Goose Hill, Hard-Scrabble and so on. Almost every
large American city is provided with such a neighbor, and mention of it on
the local stage arouses instant mirth. For many years *Hoboken* was the
joke town of New York, but won its way to metropolitan envy and respect during Prohibition. "The humorous connotation of certain Indian
names," said George Philip Krapp, "has always been felt, and names like
Hohokus, Hoboken, Kalamazoo,[9] *Keokuk, Oshkosh, Skaneateles,* names of
real places, have acquired more than local significance, as though they
were grotesque creations of fancy. There is, however, no postoffice named
Podunk. . . . Just how this word came to be used as a designation for any
small, out-of-the-way place is not known. It is an Indian word by origin,
the name of a brook in Connecticut and a pond in Massachusetts. There is
also a *Potunk* on Long Island." [1] But within a decade E. A. Plimpton discovered a veritable *Podunk* in Massachusetts not far from Worcester.[2]
Skunk Center, Cottonwood Crossing and *Hayseed Center* are favorite
imaginary towns in Nebraska; *Sagebrush Center* reigns in Wyoming,
Rabbit Ridge in Kansas and *Pumpkin Hollow* in the state of Washington.
For Missouri, Charles E. Bess reports *Gobbler's Knob, Possum Hollow,
Hog Heaven, Slabtown, Hog-Eye, Skintown, Bugtown* and *Puckey-
Huddle.*[3]

---

[9] [A favorite story in Michigan concerns the outlander who asks, "What's
the real name of this town that everybody calls *Kalamazoo*?"]

[1] Krapp, Vol. I, p. 176. [See also "Gag"
Towns, by Louise Pound, *AS*, Vol.
XXVI, May 1951, p. 137.]

[2] See the Locus of *Podunk*, by Louise
Pound, *AS*, Vol. IX, Feb. 1934, p. 80.
[See also Postscripts to The American
Language: The *Podunk* Mystery, *The
New Yorker*, Sept. 25, 1948.]

[3] *Podunk* in Southeast Missouri, *AS*,
Vol. X, Feb. 1935, p. 80.

XI

American Slang

1: THE NATURE OF SLANG

Slang is defined by the Oxford Dictionary as "language of a highly colloquial type, considered as below the level of standard educated speech, and consisting either of new words or of current words employed in some special sense." The essence of slang is that it is of general dispersion, but still stands outside the accepted canon of the language. It is, says George H. McKnight,[1] "a form of colloquial speech created in a spirit of defiance and aiming at freshness and novelty. . . . Its figures are consciously far-fetched and are intentionally drawn from the most ignoble of sources. Closely akin to profanity in its spirit, its aim is to shock."

What chiefly lies behind it is simply a kind of linguistic exuberance, an excess of word-making energy. But there is also something else. The best slang is not only ingenious and amusing; it also embodies a kind of social criticism. It not only provides new names for a series of everyday concepts, some new and some old; it also says something about them.[2] "Words which produce the slang effect," observes Frank K. Sechrist,[3] "arouses associations which are incongruous or incompatible with those of customary thinking." Everyone, including even the metaphysician in his study and the eremite in his cell, has a large vocabulary of slang, but the vocabulary of the vulgar is likely to be larger, in proportion to the total vocabulary, than that of the cultured, and it is harder-worked.

[Current investigation shows that even nuns in cloisters have developed

---

[1] English Words and Their Background; New York, 1923, p. 43.
[2] See American Slang, the London Times (editorial), May 11, 1931; and What Is Slang? by H. F. Reeves, AS,

Vol. I, Jan. 1926.
[3] The Psychology of Unconventional Language, Pedagogical Seminary, Dec. 1913, p. 443.

their own slang (amusing, but of course genteel) and that Trappist monks, for whom silence is the rule, have introduced slang among themselves. In a collection of some 1,000 entries of sign language (much of it undoubtedly very ancient) used by Trappists, there are some which express attitudes and concepts which are more or less taboo and are not used in the presence of the Bishop.]

Slang originates in the effort of ingenious individuals to make the language more pungent and picturesque—to increase the store of terse and striking words, to widen the boundaries of metaphor, and to provide a vocabulary for new shades of difference in meaning. As Jespersen has pointed out,[4] this is also the aim of poets (as, indeed, it is of prose writers), but they are restrained by consideration of taste and decorum, and also, not infrequently, by historical or logical considerations. The maker of slang is under no such limitations: he is free to confect his neologism by any process that can be grasped by his customers, and out of any materials available, whether native or foreign.

The origin of the word *slang* is unknown. Ernest Weekley, in his "Etymological Dictionary of Modern English" (1921), suggests that it may have some relation to the verb *to sling*, and cites two Norwegian dialect words, based upon the cognate verb *slenge* or *slengje*, that appear to be its brothers: *slengjeord*, a neologism, and *slengjenamn*, a nickname. But he is not sure, so he adds the note that "some regard it as an argotic perversion of the French *langue*, language." A German philologian, O. Ritter, believes that it may be derived, not from *langue*, but from *language* itself, most probably by a combination of blending and shortening, as in *thieve(s' lang)-uage, beggar(s' lang)uage* and so on.[5]

When it first appeared in English, about the middle of the Eighteenth Century, it was employed as a synonym of *cant*, and so designated "the special vocabulary used by any set of persons of a low or disreputable character"; and half a century later it began to be used interchangeably with *argot*, which means the vocabulary special to any group, trade or profession. But during the past fifty years the three terms have tended to be more or less clearly distinguished.

The boundaries separating true slang from cant and argot are wavering and not easily defined, and there is a constant movement of words and phrases from one category to another. When, in 1785, Captain Francis Grose published the first edition of his "Classical Dictionary of the Vulgar

---

[4] Language: Its Nature, Development and Origin; London, 1922, p. 300.
[5] *Archiv für das Studium der neueren Sprachen*, Vol. CXVI, 1906. I am indebted for the reference to Concerning the Etymology of *Slang*, by Fr. Klaeber, *AS*, Vol. I, Apr. 1926. The process is not unfamiliar in English: *tawdry*, from *Saint Audrey*, offers an example.

Tongue," the word *slang* itself seems to have been confined mainly to the argot of criminals and vagabonds, but today it appears unchallenged in all dictionaries.

As everyone knows, most slang terms have relatively short lives, and nothing seems more stale than one that has passed out, *e.g., skiddoo, snake's hips, nerts, attaboy* and *I don't think,* but now and then one survives for years and even for centuries, without either going into eclipse on the one hand or being elevated to standard speech on the other. *To bamboozle* is still below the salt and would hardly be used by a bishop in warning against Satan, but it is more than two hundred years old and was listed as slang by Richard Steele in the *Tatler* in 1710. *Gas* (talk) has been traced to 1847, *kibosh* to 1836, *lip* (impudence) to 1821, *sap* to 1815, *cheese it* to 1811, *to chisel* to 1808, *racket* to 1785, *hush money* to 1709, *to knock off* (to quit) to 1662, *tick* (credit) to 1661, *grub* to 1659, *to cotton to* to 1605, *bat* (a loose woman) to 1612, *to plant* (to hide) to 1610, *brass* (impudence) to 1594, *duds* (clothes) to 1567 and *to blow* (to boast) to c. 1400: all remain in use today and all continue to be slang.[6] *Booze* has never got into Standard English, but it was used as slang as early as the Fourteenth Century.

It would be hard to figure out precisely what makes one slang term survive for years and another perish quickly and miserably, but some of the elements which may shape the process are discernible. One of them is the degree to which a neologism fills a genuine need. It may do so by providing a pungent name, nearly always metaphorical, for an object or concept that is new to the generality of people, *e.g., ghost writer* and *caterpillar* (running gear), or it may do so by supplying a more succinct or more picturesque designation for something already familiar in terms more commonplace, *e.g., bellhop, sorehead, rubberneck* and *kill-joy.* Many of the best slang terms are simple compounds, as the examples I have just given show; others are bold tropes, *e.g., bull* (a policeman), *to squeal, masher, cold feet, yellow* (cowardly), *baloney, applesauce* and *chick* (from *chicken,* a girl); yet others are the products of a delirious delight in language making, *e.g., fantods, heebie-jeebies, nifty, whoopee, hubba-hubba, to burp* and *oomph.* When a novelty is obvious it seldom lasts very long, *e.g., shellacked* for drunk, *skirt* for woman, *peach* for a beautiful girl, and when its humor is strained it dies as quickly, like *movie cathedral, lounge lizard, third-termite* and the frequent inventions of the Broadway school. Moreover, its longevity seems to run in obverse proportion to its first success, so that overnight crazes like *yes, we have no bananas* and *goo-goo*

---

[6] I take these from Modern Slang, by   pp. 293–7.
J. Louis Kuethe, *AS,* Vol. XI, Dec. 1936,

eyes are soon done for, whereas novelties of slower growth, *e.g., booze, to goose* and *gimcrack* last a long, long while. This auto-intoxication seems to cut short the silly phrases of negation that come and go, *e.g., sez you, oh yeah, I don't think* and the numerous catch phrases that have little if any precise meaning but simply delight the moron by letting him show that he knows the latest.

Slang tends to multiply terms for the same concept: its chief aim seems to be to say something new, not necessarily something good. Thus there is a constant succession of novel synonyms for *girl, head, money, drunk, yes, good, bad* and other such words of everyday usage. Slang terms relating to the head always have a derogatory significance, and many of them hint at idiocy. In 1928 Mamie Meredith listed some of those then current, *e.g., bean, coco* and *nut,* along with the fashionable derivatives, *e.g., bonehead, pinhead* and *mutt* (from *muttonhead*), but many of these are now obsolete. On the other hand, the French word *tête* has been a sound word for head for many centuries, but its origin was in *testa,* meaning a pot, exactly analogous to our *block, nut* and *bean.* The vast vogue of *sheik* (pronounced *sheek,* not *shike*) for a predatory male will be recalled by the middle-aged; it is now as extinct as *masher.*[7] The late George Ade, in 1935, attempted a list of substitutes for such words as *girl, married, idiot, begone* and *drunk,* arranging them in categories of "old," "later" and "latest."[8] Most of the terms he entered under the last heading are now almost forgotten, *e.g., cutie, babe, eyeful, pip* and *wow* for a pretty girl. William Feather, searching "The American Thesaurus of Slang," by Lester V. Berrey and Melvin Van den Bark,[9] found that it listed 52 synonyms for *wife,* and that there was "not an affectionate reference in the lot."[1] Indeed, this attitude is characteristic of all slang, which commonly represents no more than the effort of some smartie to voice his derision, not infrequently for some person, object or idea obviously above his own lowly thought and station. The wit of Broadway, now the source of much American slang, is thus essentially opprobrious, and many of its brighter words and sayings may be readily reduced to "Oh, you son of a bitch."

[Today we know that much if not most slang is argot which emerges from or is discarded from the subcultures of the professional criminal on many levels and in many different specialties. The "wit of Broadway," while still the immediate source of much slang, always was—and still is—

---

[7] Sinclair Lewis, in Cass Timberlane, New York, 1945, pp. 323-4, listed some of the terms then in use for "the sort of male once described with relish as an agreeable scoundrel," *e.g., lug, jerk, louse, stinker, twirp, rat, crumb, goon* and *wolf.* Most of them soon passed out.

[8] A Check-Up on Slang in America, Baltimore *Sun* (and other papers), Sept. 8, 1935.

[9] New York, 1942.

[1] *William Feather Magazine,* Oct. 1943, p. 19.

closely attuned to the underworld for new and salty terms. For example, Damon Runyon studied the fringes of criminal cultures closely, Wilson Mizner spent many years as a professional grifter before he became a writer and went right on writing just the way he talked, and S. J. Perelman has long been a discerning observer of the criminal world and its idiom. Nowadays there are many other channels which also pipe words from criminal subcultures into the speech and writing of the dominant culture— TV, movies, newspaper columnists, jazz musicians, teen-age pseudo-hoodlums, a few novelists and short-story writers and, certainly not to be overlooked, a growing body of trained sociologists and linguists who are bringing carefully documented, firsthand studies of underworld speech and behavior into professional literature. The contempt in which the criminal subcultures hold the dominant culture accounts for much of the element of derision mentioned above. Invention of slang words by the literati of the dominant culture appears to be meager; most of them, it seems, are borrowed from underworld sources.]

It is from this quarter that most American slang comes, a large part of it invented by gag writers, newspaper columnists and press agents, and the rest borrowed from the vocabularies of criminals, prostitutes and the lower orders of showfolk. There was a time when it was chiefly propagated by vaudeville performers, but now that vaudeville is in eclipse the torch has been taken over by the harlequins of movie, radio and television. A good deal of this slang comes close to being obscene, *e.g.*, the *hot mamma* of a few years ago, the *jerk* of yesterday and the Yiddish loans, like *schmoo*, that come and go,[2] but their literal meanings are soon lost, and they are presently on the tongues of multitudes of college students and even school children. [Currently this trend seems to be burgeoning. A recent survey among teen-agers in Louisville, Ky., turned up some 1,800 slang terms, with a heavy representation of near obscene *double-entendre*, of which modern teen-agers are very much aware.] It would certainly be absurd, however, to argue that slang is wholly, or even predominantly, vulgar and debased, or to dismiss its inventions lightly. It is, in fact, the most powerful of all the stimulants that keep language alive and growing, and some of the most pungent and valuable words and phrases in English, and especially in American English, have arisen out of its bilge. J. Y. P. Greig, the Scots professor, was quite right when he described *rubberneck* as "one of the best words ever coined."[3] It may be homely, but it is nevertheless superb, and whoever invented it, if he could be discovered, would be worthy not only of a Harvard LL.D. but also of the thanks of both Rotary and Con-

[2] Some American Idioms from the Yiddish, by Julius G. Rothenberg, *AS*, Vol. XVII, Feb. 1943, pp. 43–8.

[3] Breaking Priscian's Head; New York, 1929, p. 83.

gress, half a bushel of medals and thirty days as the husband of Miss America. *Stooge* is another masterpiece, though it has many competitors, and *yes man* is yet another. Others are *fan, piker,*[4] *stag party,*[5] *stunt,*[6] *to debunk, to hike,*[7] *O.K.,*[8] *racketeer,*[9] *nut* (a half-wit), *boom,*[1] *boost,*[2] *phony, highbrow, tightwad, strong arm, loan shark, hard-boiled, he-man, nuts, getaway, square shooter, fifty-fifty, double-cross, kicker* and the almost innumerable verb phrases, *e.g., to get together, to stop over, to eat crow, to saw wood, to bawl out* and *to play possum.*

Americans seem to be vastly more adept at making new slang than Englishmen, just as they are more adept at making more seemly neologisms. There was a time when this was not true, and most of the slang that American purists frowned upon was of English origin,[3] but after the War of 1812 and the beginning of the great movement into the West, Americans began to roll their own, and for years past the flow has been in the other direction. Not only the movies and television but also American comic strips have flooded England with the latest confections of the Broadway and Hollywood neologists, and the fecund American keyhole columnists have been widely imitated. The London correspondent of the Baltimore *Sun* reported in 1937, "Britons are gradually growing reconciled to the Americanization of their language."[4] Many of them, indeed, go further: they declare that they like it. "American slang," wrote Horace Annesley Vachell, in 1935 or thereabout, "is not a tyranny, but a beneficent autocracy. . . . English slang at its best has to curtsey to American slang, and at its worst it is *toppingly* the worst in the world." Even the

---

[4] The DAE's first example is dated 1869, when *piker* meant a yokel from Pike County, Mo., then the common symbol of everything poverty-stricken and uncouth.

[5] Traced by the DAE to 1856 and marked an Americanism. Partridge says that the English adopted it *c.* 1870.

[6] The DAE's first example comes from a word list in *DN,* Vol. I, Pt. VIII, 1895, p. 400, but I recall hearing it before that.

[7] Listed by Francis Grose in the second edition of his Classical Dictionary of the Vulgar Tongue; London, 1788.

[8] The history of this most successful of all American slang terms is given by Allen Walker Read, The Evidence on *O.K., Saturday Review of Literature,* July 19, 1941, pp. 3–11. [Subsequent brilliant research by Read definitely settles the question of origin, in The First Stage in the History of *O.K., AS,* Vol. XXXVIII, Feb. 1963, and The Second

Stage in the History of *O.K., AS,* Vol. XXXVIII, May 1963, to say nothing of other articles on specific details of the tradition.]

[9] *Racket* is old, but *racketeer* was a product of Prohibition.

[1] The noun (*log boom*) is traced by the DAE to 1676 and marked an Americanism. The earliest example of the verb in the sense of to whoop it up is dated 1873.

[2] *Boost* the noun has not been found before 1825 but the verb is in the glossary attached to David Humphreys's The Yankey in England, 1815. It is defined therein as to raise up, lift up or exalt.

[3] To this day, in fact, many slang terms of English origin continue in everyday American use, *e.g., horse laugh, soft soap, cold shoulder* and *lady killer.*

[4] English Potpourri, by Paul W. Ward, Aug. 1.

Manchester *Guardian* and the London *Times* have praised the neologisms
that the invasion brings in. The *Guardian*, in 1932, spoke editorially of "its
Elizabethan vigor and its sometimes more than Elizabethan capacity for
uncouth inventiveness" [5] and in 1937 of its "rich wit and expressive metaphor," [6] and the *Times*, so long ago as 1931, granted "the variety of the
sources, the ingenuity of the adaptation, and the lively vigor of these hard-
hitting words." [7]

I once described Maurice H. Weseen's "Dictionary of American Slang"
(1934) as "extremely slipshod and even ridiculous." [It has been supplanted since by the superb "Dictionary of American Slang" by Harold
Wentworth and Stuart Flexner.[8]] Also, there has appeared an excellent
bibliography of slang, cant and argot by W. J. Burke.[9] In England the
indefatigable Eric Partridge has followed his "Slang Today and Yesterday" [1] and his annotated edition of Francis Grose's "Classical Dictionary
of the Vulgar Tongue" [2] with a large "Dictionary of Slang and Unconventional English" [3] [and a "Dictionary of the Underworld" (1950)], and
William Matthews has published "Cockney Past and Present." [4] In Australia Sidney J. Baker has brought out "A Popular Dictionary of Australian Slang" [5] (which has many resemblances to American) and a large
and valuable work on Australian English in general.[6] Meanwhile, *American Speech* occasionally publishes useful papers on this or that aspect of
American slang, and there is frequent (if seldom illuminating) discussion of the theme in the newspapers.[7]

The common slang of the United States, as I have noted, is a catchall
for the inventions of various quite different classes of wits, though most
of them have the common quality of being more or less disreputable. A
neologism coined by a smart Harlem wisecracker today may be raging
in all the fashionable finishing schools tomorrow, and there is a constant
infiltration from the argots of rackets. We owe common words and
phrases, for example, to the circus folks, *e.g.*, *guy*, *ballyhoo*, *three-ring*
and *to shoot the chutes;* many more to the hoboes, *e.g.*, *jungle*, *handout*,

---

[5] Still More American Language, Aug.
19.

[6] American Slang, June 28.

[7] American Slang, May 11.

[8] [New York, 1960.]

[9] The Literature of Slang; New York,
1939.

[1] 2nd ed., London, 1935.

[2] London, 1931.

[3] New York, 1937; 2nd ed., rev. and
enlarged, 1938. It includes the numerous
Americanisms that have become naturalized in England.

[4] London, 1938.

[5] Melbourne, 1941; 2nd ed., 1943.

[6] The Australian Language; Sydney,
1945. Baker has also published Australian
Pronunciation, Sydney, 1947, and New
Zealand Slang, Christchurch, 1940; and
Arnold Wall has done New Zealand
English, Christchurch, 1938.

[7] Burke's The Literature of Slang,
which ran serially in the *Bulletin of the
New York Public Library* in 1936-8, is
close to complete down to the latter
year.

panhandler and probably *hobo* itself; and yet more to downright criminals, *e.g.*, *cop* (for policeman), *third degree, to gyp, to bump off, to take
for a ride, to shake down, to hijack* and *once-over*. We have borrowed *by
a head, to scratch* and *to tout* from the race tracks; *nineteenth hole, to
stymie* and *birdie* from the golf links; *yen, take it main, hop-up, hit the
pipe* and *to needle* from the drug addicts; and *understudy, barnstormer,
star, angel, box office, to ring down the curtain on* and *full house* from
the stage. In addition, large numbers of terms that belong to argot or
cant are understood and occasionally used by Americans, though they
have not yet entered (and perhaps never will enter) the common slang
of the country.

2: CANT AND ARGOT

The cant of modern criminals, still somewhat international in nature,
began to be formulated in western Europe in the early Fifteenth Century,
when roving bands of a strange, dark race of petty thieves appeared from
the mysterious East and were presently intermingled with the native
tramps, beggars, parasite friars and other fly-by-night rogues. These newcomers, at the start, were assumed to be Egyptians, which explains our
English name of *Gypsies* for them, but later studies of their history and
language have demonstrated that they actually came from northwestern
India. They were in Germany by 1414, in Italy by 1422, in France by
1427 and in England by the early 1500s. Two of the largest classes of
indigenous vagabonds that they encountered were those of the begging
friars and the displaced Jews. Both of these borrowed words and phrases
from them and in turn reinforced their language with homemade inventions, and by the end of the Fifteenth Century there had developed
in Germany a rogues' jargon that was based on German, but included
many Hebrew and Gypsy terms. Some of these survive to the present
day, even in the United States, *e.g.*, *pal* from the Gypsy[8] and *ganov*
[*ganef*] from the Hebrew.

The first writings in and on this jargon were done in Germany, and
the earliest of them that have been preserved seem to have been based
upon reports of a series of criminal trials at Basel in Switzerland, prepared by John Knebel, one of the clergy of the cathedral there.[9] This was

[8] Everett DeBaun, of Philadelphia, calls
my attention to other apparent loans
from Romany speech, *e.g.*, *benny*, an
overcoat (Rom. *bengree*, a waistcoat);
can, a jail or privy (Rom. *caen*, to
stink); *to cop*, to steal, and maybe also
cop or *copper*, a policeman (Rom. *cappi*,
booty, gain); *cush*, money (Rom. *cushti*,
good); *shiv*, a knife (Rom. *chiv*, a
blade); and *stir*, prison (Rom. *staripen*,
a prison).

[9] Knebel's MS. is still preserved in the
university library at Basel. It was printed
for the first time in *Taschenbuch für*

in 1475, but it was not until 1512 or thereabout that Knebel's material got into print. It then appeared at Augsburg in the once-famous "Liber Vagatorum," which ran through many editions during the ensuing half-century, including one edited at Wittenberg in 1528 by Martin Luther. All the Englishmen who wrote about thieves' cant during the Sixteenth Century seem to have made use of it, but there was no English translation until 1860, when John Camden Hotten brought out one in London under the title "The Book of Vagabonds and Beggars, with a Vocabulary of Their Language." [1] Hotten, in his introduction, put the chief blame for the growth of vagabondage in the later Middle Ages, not on the coming of the Gypsies, but on "the begging system of the friars." [The monasteries were dissolved in 1539.]

But the German authority, Schreiber,[2] laid more stress upon the influence of the Gypsies, thus:

> The beggars of Germany rejoiced in a Golden Age which extended through nearly two centuries, from the invasions of the Turks until after the conclusion of the Swedish war (1450 to 1650). During this long period it was frequently the case that begging was practiced less from necessity than for pleasure—indeed, it was pursued like a regular calling. . . . Mendicancy became a distinct institution, was divided into various branches, and was provided with a language of its own. Besides the frequent wars, it was the Gypsies—appearing in Germany at the beginning of the Fifteenth Century—who contributed most of this state of things.

"Liber Vagatorum" lists the twenty-nine principal varieties of German rogues of the time, and provides a glossary of their *Rotwelsch*, or cant.

The earliest English references to the subject are in Robert Copland's "The Hye Way to the Spittell Hous" (1517), a dialogue in verse between the author and the porter at the door of St. Bartholomew's Hospital, London. Burke says in "The Literature of Slang" that this book was probably not actually published until *c.* 1535. Copland was a printer who once worked for Wynken de Worde and maybe also for William Caxton. "The porter in 'The Hye Way to the Spittell Hous,' " says Burke, "talks the language of rogues, and there are passages entirely in cant." But Copland's

---

[1] *Geschichte und Alterthum in Süd-Deutschland*, by Heinrich Schreiber; Freiburg, Switz., 1839. Records of the trials were also made by Hieronymus Wilhelm Ebner, and his MS. is also preserved at Basel. It was printed in Exercitationes Iuris Universi, by Johann Heumann; Altdorf, 1749.

[1] The text of Liber Vagatorum, with Luther's prefaces, is in the *Weimarisches Jahrbuch für deutsche Sprache, Litteratur und Kunst* for 1856, Vol. IV, pp. 65–101.

[2] *Taschenbuch für Geschichte und Alterthum*, before mentioned.

source does not appear to have been "Liber Vagatorum"; he borrowed, rather, from a French translation of Sebastian Brant's "Das Narrenschiff," a somewhat earlier work which also included some thieves' jargon but was not a formal treatise on the subject. Brant's book was given over chiefly to the follies of the upper and middle classes; what he added about rogues and vagabonds seems to have been derived from the same Basel records that have been mentioned as the possible sources of "Liber Vagatorum." Alexander Barclay's "The Ship of Fools," first printed in 1509, was a very free rendering of "Das Narrenschiff," with most of Brant's classical pedantry omitted and many additions of purely English material. Like its original, it had an enormous success, and is still pored over by the learned.

Copland's "Hye Way to the Spittell Hous" was followed by many other books embodying specimens of English criminal cant, and among their authors were such remembered writers as Thomas Dekker and Robert Greene, but the first formal glossary did not appear until nearly two centuries later. This was "A New Dictionary of the Terms Ancient and Modern of the Canting Crew, in its Several Tribes of Gipsies, Beggars, Thieves, Cheats, Etc.," published in London in 1698. Its author concealed himself behind the initials B.E., and has never been identified. Says Burke, his "is perhaps the most important dictionary of slang ever printed, since it had such an influence upon later compilations."

The vocabulary runs to 176 double-column pages, with a preface of six pages. In that preface the author confines himself mainly to discussing the origin of Gypsies and beggars. In England, says B.E.,

> it may be observed that the first statute which makes provision for
> the parish poor is no older than Queen Elizabeth, from which it may
> be fairly collected that they entered with us upon the dissolution of
> the abbeys, as with them abroad upon the delivery of the slaves.[3]

B.E.'s glossary shows a number of terms that are still more or less in vogue, many of them appearing in the Berrey and Van den Bark "American Thesaurus of Slang."

After the publication of this dictionary by B.E. there was an interval of nearly a century before England saw another work of importance in the same field. Then, in 1785, came the first edition of Captain Francis Grose's "Classical Dictionary of the Vulgar Tongue," the foundation of every treatise on thieves' cant and likewise on ordinary slang that has been done since. There was a second edition in 1788, and a third in 1796, five years after the author's death. In 1811 there was a fourth, brought out under the title "Lexicon Balatronicum" by Hewson Clarke, a literary hack of the

---

[3] The first English poor law was passed in 1601.

time,[4] and in 1823 there was a fifth, with the original title restored and Pierce Egan serving as editor.[5] Finally, there is the reprint issued in 1931, edited by Eric Partridge and limited to 550 copies. This reprint is based on the third edition of 1796, which seems to have embodied corrections and additions prepared by Grose himself. Partridge adds a brief biography of the author, and enriches the dictionary itself with a large number of glosses, some of them very valuable.

Grose was the son of a Swiss jeweler who came to England early in the Eighteenth Century, set up business in London and acquired a moderate fortune. He was married and had seven children, one of whom rose to be deputy governor of New South Wales, but he was a gay dog and put in a large part of his leisure investigating the night life of London. He also made a number of exploratory tours of the British Isles, and on one of them had a meeting with Robert Burns in Scotland which developed into a close friendship. Burns wrote two poems about him, in one of which, "On Captain Grose's Peregrinations Through Scotland," occur the famous lines:

> *A chiel's amang ye, taking notes,*
> *And, faith, he'll prent it.*

This couplet has been taken over by journalists as referring to their mystery, but it actually alludes to Grose's antiquarian researches. Egan says that his nocturnal tours of the London underworld were made in company with a retainer named Batch, and goes on:

> Batch and his master used frequently to start at midnight from the King's Arms in Holborn in search of adventures. The back slums of St. Giles's were explored again and again, and the captain and Batch made themselves as affable and jolly as the rest of the motley crew among the beggars, cadgers, thieves, etc., who at that time infested the Holy Land [*i.e.*, St. Giles's]. It was from these nocturnal sallies and the slang expressions which continually assailed his ears, that Grose was first induced to compile "A Classical Dictionary of the Vulgar Tongue."

However, the fact is that Grose's dictionary leaned heavily upon the before-mentioned "New Dictionary" of B.E., though neither Egan nor Partridge calls attention to it.[6] But it is not to be gainsaid that he added a

---

[4] His additions were not numerous, but some of them have survived, *e.g.*, *bang-up*.

[5] Egan (1772–1849) is chiefly remembered (and collected) today because George and Robert Cruikshank illustrated his Life in London, 1821. There are interesting notes on him in the London *Times Literary Supplement*, Aug. 7 and 21, 1943.

[6] In all probability this influence may have been exerted through A Collection

great deal of new matter of his own and got rid of many of B.E.'s nonce words and literary affectations, so that his dictionary came much closer to the actual vulgar speech than its predecessor. And if he mined B.E., then all his successors have mined Grose; indeed, his dictionary remained the best thing of its sort until Partridge began to investigate English slang during World War I. With Partridge's glosses his book still makes excellent reading. In his first edition of 1785 there were about 3,000 entries, and in his third of 1796 the number had grown to nearly 4,000.

Many of the terms listed by Grose have survived to our day. Some still belong to slang or the lower levels of colloquial speech, *e.g., cow juice, to crook the elbow, duds, grub, hush money, leery, to lush, pigheaded, sky parlor, spliced* (married), *to touch* (borrow) and *uncle* (pawnbroker), but others have climbed to more respectable standing, *e.g., crocodile tears, of easy virtue, elbow room, fogy, foul-mouthed, to fuss, gingerbread* (decoration), *greenhorn,*[7] *humbug, lopsided, mum, pin money, pug nose, sandwich,*[8] *tidy* and *white lie.*

Grose borrowed his account of the origin of cant from William Harrison's "Description of England" prefaced to Raphael Holinshed's famous "Chronicles of England, Scotland and Ireland," published in two volumes in 1577–8. Said Harrison:

> It is not yet fifty years sith this trade [of beggars] began, but how it hath prospered sithens that time it is easy to judge, for they are now supposed, of one sex and another, to amount unto above ten thousand persons, as I have heard reported; moreover, in counterfeiting the Egyptian rogues they have devised a language among themselves, which they name canting, . . . a speech compact thirty years since of English and a great number of words of their own devising, without all order or reason, and yet such it is as none but themselves are able to understand. The first deviser thereof was hanged by the neck, as a just reward no doubt for his deserts and a common end to all of that profession. A gentleman, Mr. Thomas Harman, of late hath taken great pains to search out the secret practices of this ungracious rabble, and among other things he setteth down and prescribed twenty-two sorts of them.

The book by Harman, here mentioned by Harrison, was entitled "A Caveat or Warening for Commen Cursetors Vulgarely Called Vaga-

---

of the Canting Words and Terms Both Ancient and Modern Used by Beggars, Gypsies, Cheats, House-Breakers, Shop-Lifters, Footpads, Highwaymen, &c., appended to Nathan Bailey's Universal Etymological Dictionary, 3rd ed., Lon-

don, 1737, for Bailey also borrowed from B.E.

[7] B.E., 1698, lists *greenhead*, "a very raw novice, or unexperienc'd fellow."

[8] The OED traces *sandwich* to 1762, but it was still rather slangy in 1785.

bondes." It was published in London in 1567, and not a few of the terms it listed survived in B.E.'s "New Dictionary" of 1698 and even into Grose. Not much is known about Harman save that he was a country gentleman and apparently interested in police matters. He indicated that the region in which he lived was hard beset, in his time, by troops of wandering rogues, and he describes their depredations at length. At the end of his book there is a brief vocabulary of "the leud, lousey language of these lewtering luskes and lasy lorrels." Harman apparently picked up some of these from the fugitive literature of the time, but the rest seem to have come out of his own observation.[9]

As I have noted, many works dealing with rogues and vagabonds and recording more or less of their cant appeared in England during the Seventeenth Century and more followed in the Eighteenth. There is a bibliography of them in Burke and they are discussed in "The Development of Cant Lexicography in England, 1566–1765," by Gertrude E. Noyes.[1]

The literature of criminals' cant since Grose has been voluminous, but on the whole it was of small value until recent years. Godfrey Irwin's "American Tramp and Underworld Slang," brought out in 1931, was mainly devoted to the argot of tramps, but within its limits it was well done.[2] [Meanwhile there is the much more authentic "Dictionary of American Underworld Lingo," by Goldin, O'Leary and Lipsius,[3] and another dictionary, currently listing about 10,000 terms, is being compiled by Frank Prewitt and Francis K. Schaeffer in a California prison.] At about the same time David W. Maurer, of the University of Louisville, began to interest himself in the subject, and has since become the chief American authority upon it. He has two important qualifications for his task: he is a man trained in scholarly and especially linguistic method, and he has an extraordinary capacity for gaining the confidence of criminals. He has published a book upon the techniques and speech of the confidence men who constitute the gentry of the underworld[4] and papers in the learned journals and elsewhere upon the argots of various lesser groups, ranging from forgers and safecrackers to drug peddlers and prostitutes. [His books "Whiz Mob"[5] and "Narcotics and Narcotic Addiction"[6] explore the re-

---

[9] Harman's list was reprinted in full in The Oldest Rogues' Dictionary, *Encore*, Sept. 1942, pp. 343–5.

[1] Studies in Philology (Chapel Hill, N.C.), Vol. XXXVIII, 1941, pp. 462–72.

[2] It is significant that Irwin had to go to England to find a publisher. There he got aid from Eric Partridge. His material was accumulated during "more than twenty years' experience as a tramp

on the railroads and roads of the United States, Canada, Mexico and Central America, and on tramp steamers in Central American waters."

[3] [New York, 1950.]

[4] The Big Con; [3rd ed.; New York, 1963].

[5] [*PADS*, No. 24, 1955.]

[6] [2nd ed.; Springfield, Ill., 1962.]

lation of language to human behavior within the subcultures of the thief and the drug addict.] A century ago the cant of American criminals was still largely dependent upon that of their English colleagues, stretching back for centuries, but though it still shows marks of that influence [7] it is now predominantly on its own. Its chief characteristics, says Maurer, are "its machine-gun staccato, its hard timbre, its rather grim humor, its vivid imagery, and its remarkable compactness." [8] It differs considerably, of course, from specialty to specialty, but within a given specialty "it appears to be well standardized from coast to coast and from the Gulf into Canada." [Subsequently three geographical dialect areas have been tentatively identified—East Coast, Midwest and West Coast.] It shows the cosmopolitan quality of all American speech, and includes loans from Yiddish, Spanish, German, French, Chinese and even Hindustani. Like slang in general, it is the product, not of the common run of ordinary lawbreakers or amateur criminals, but of the well-established criminal subcultures; it tends to increase in picturesqueness as one goes up the scale of professional rank and dignity. Says Maurer:

Why do criminals speak a lingo? There are several reasons, perhaps the most widely accepted of which is that they must have a secret language in order to conceal their plans from their victims or from the police. In some instances it is undoubtedly used for this purpose— for instance, *flat-jointers, three-card monte men,* and other *short-con workers* [9] sometimes use it to confuse or deceive their victims. But most professional criminals do not so use it. They speak argot only among themselves, . . . for using it in public would mark them as underworld characters whether or not they were understood. . . . There is a very strong sense of camaraderie among them, a highly developed

---

[7] For example, in the survival of rhyming slang. An account of the argot of American criminals of the 1900 era is in The Lingo of the Good People, by David W. Maurer, *AS,* Vol. X, Feb. 1935, pp. 10–23. A great deal of it is now obsolete.

[8] The Argot of the Underworld, *AS,* Vol. VII, Dec. 1931, pp. 99–118.

[9] *Short-con workers* operate on a modest scale, and are usually content with whatever money the victim has on him at the time he is rooked. They seldom employ the *send*—that is, they seldom send him home for more. [*Short-con* argots have been studied by Maurer in The Argot of the Three-Shell Game, *AS,* Vol. XXII, Oct. 1947, and The Argot of the Faro Bank, *AS,* Vol.

XVIII, Feb. 1943. Many additional examples of it occur in his The Argot of the Dice Gambler, included in Scarne on Dice, by Clayton Rawson and John Scarne, Harrisburg, Pa., 1945; in his The Argot of the Racetrack, *PADS,* No. 16, 1951; and in his The Argot of the Professional Dice Gambler, *The Annals of the American Academy of Political and Social Science,* Vol. 269, May 1950. Most *short-con* games are connected with professional gambling, which has argots so voluminous that they cannot be treated in this work, and which have, in turn, vastly enriched American slang. An excellent survey of gambling, with much argot included, is John Scarne's classic book, Scarne's Complete Guide to Gambling; New York, 1961.]

group-solidarity. . . . A common language helps to bind these groups together and gives expression to the strong fraternal spirit. . . . Professional crime is nothing more than a way of living and working within a great variety of parasitic sub-cultures; hence it is only natural that many of the same factors which operate in the dominant culture and among legitimate craftsmen should affect criminal speech.[1]

The vast upsurge of crime brought in by Prohibition made all Americans familiar with a large number of criminal words and phrases, and many of these, as I have noted, have entered into the everyday speech of the country. How much of the argot of the Volsteadian racketeers was the product of their own fancy and how much was thrust upon them by outside admirers, *e.g.*, newspaper reporters and movie writers, is not easily determined, but Maurer has cited some examples from the latter, including even such apparently characteristic terms as *big shot*. He says [2] that actual members of the *mob* called the brass hats of the profession *wheels* (in the plural). But *trigger man*, *torpedo*, *gorilla*, *pineapple* (bomb), *whiskers* (a federal agent: a reference to Uncle Sam), *hot* (a stolen object or a criminal pursued by the law), *on the lam*, *to snatch* (to kidnap), *moll* and *racket*, whatever their provenance, were indigenous to the subcultures using them. The gentlemen of the *big con*, *i.e.*, swindlers who specialize in rooking persons of means, constitute the aristocracy of the underworld, and hold aloof from all lesser criminals. They are, taking one with another, of superior intelligence, and not many of them ever land in prison. Their lingo thus shows a considerable elegance and also some humor, *e.g.*, *apple*, *savage* or *Mr. Bates* for a victim; *big store*, the bogus gambling house or brokerage office to which *apples* are lured; *coarse ones*, large bills; *earwigger*, one who tries to eavesdrop; *excess baggage*, a member of a mob who fails to pull his weight in the boat; *to fit the mitt*, to bribe an official; *Joe Hep*, a victim who tumbles (or thinks he does) to what is happening; *larceny*, the itch for illicit money that lures a victim on: "He has *larceny* in his heart"; *to light a rag*, to run away; *to play the C*, to operate a confidence game; *to sting*, to swindle; *sucker word*, a term not used by professionals,[3] and *yellow*, a telegram. The craft is now called the *grift*, not the *graft*;[4] and is characterized by its lack of violence.

At the opposite pole from practitioners of the *big con* are the brutal

---

[1] The Big Con, before cited, pp. 270-1.
[2] Private communication, Apr. 7, 1940. The anonymous author of The Capone I Knew, *True Detective*, June 1947, p. 80, says that *syndicate*, used by Al to describe his mob, was "picked up from the newspaper stories about him."

[3] I take all these from Maurer.
[4] The glossary in The Big Con is also in The Argot of Confidence Men, *AS*, Vol. XV, Apr. 1940, pp. 113-23, and Confidence Games, by Carlton Brown, *Life*, Aug. 12, 1946, pp. 45-52.

fellows who follow the *heavy rackets, i.e.,* those involving violence. They include some types of burglars, safe blowers (yeggs), hijackers, kidnapers, automobile thieves, window smashers, mail robbers, payroll grabbers, bank stick-up men and so on. They had their heyday during the thirteen delirious years of Prohibition, and there was a revival of their art, made much of by the newspapers, following World War II, but on the whole they seem to be declining in prosperity, and the new methods of thief-taking organized by the Federal Bureau of Investigation have landed large numbers of them in prison. They range in professional dignity from the *jug-heavies* or *bank burglars,* who stand at the top, to the mere hoodlums, many of them young neophytes, at the bottom. Among the cant terms of the *jug-heavies* are *bug,* a burglar alarm; *to case,* to spy out; *cutter,* a prosecuting attorney; *dinah* or *noise,* dynamite; *double,* a false key; *forty,* O.K.; *gopher,* an iron safe; *hack,* a watchman; *soup* or *pete,* nitroglycerine; *stiffs,* negotiable securities; *swamped,* surprised and surrounded; and *V,* a safe. Maurer says [5] that there are some regional differences in *jug-heavy* speech; *e.g.,* a bank is a *jug* everywhere but sometimes a *jay* in the Midwest or a *tomb* in the East. [While big-time safecracking disappeared with another generation of experts—new federal laws, improved safes and changes in business practice also had a bearing on the decline of the racket —a large number of smaller safes are still cracked by a younger generation, some of them *turned out* by old-time experts in prisons. Banks today are seldom blown, but occasionally some *mob shoots a jug* for a good *score.* The use of *stew* is declining, modern *heavy gees* preferring to use a *stick, ripper* or *can opener* on laminated safes, or specially made tools *to punch the box* or *to pull the combo.* Safes weighing up to half a ton are often trucked away to be opened elsewhere. Present-day *mechanics* are usually expert machinists capable of making such tools as the four-pronged electric vibrator to line up safe-lock tumblers, and possessed of sufficient knowledge of electronics to bypass new alarm systems. Newly invented fiberglass safes which cannot be blown or punched are now literally shaken to pieces by the expert application of precision electronic vibration.] The automobile thieves who once ranged in large and well-organized gangs also had an argot of their own, *e.g., doghouse,* a small garage; *bent one* or *kinky,* a stolen car, and *consent job,* a car stolen with the connivance of an owner eager for the insurance,[6] and so did the hijackers who arose during Prohibition and flourished in the aftermath of World War II, *e.g.,*

---

[5] The Lingo of the *Jug-Heavy, Writer's Digest,* Oct. 1931, pp. 27–9.
[6] I Wonder Who's Driving Her Now, by William G. Shepherd, *Journal of American Insurance,* Feb. 1929, pp. 5–8

(reprinted in *AS,* Vol. V, Feb. 1930, pp. 236–7); Hot Shorts, by T. J. Courtney, *The Saturday Evening Post,* Nov. 30, 1935, pp. 12–13, 72–4.

baloney, an automobile tire; *box*, a truck trailer; *to carry the mail*, to drive fast; *crate*, a truck; *dark horse*, a watchman; *girl scout* or *hairpin*, a female associate; *in creeper*, in low gear; *on the I.C.*, on the lookout; *powder wagon* or *blast furnace*, a sawed-off shotgun; *red eye*, a stop signal; *stick*, a crowbar; *toby*, a highway; *traveler*, a hijacker; and *whistler*, a police car.[7] The stick-up men who specialize in robbing pedestrians often operate in pairs. One clasps the victim around the neck from behind and chokes him while the other goes through his pockets. This is often done very violently and sometimes the victim is badly hurt. It is called *mugging* in New York, but *yoking* in most other places.[8]

Forgers (*penmen*), counterfeiters (*designers*) and other such intellectuals have a certain standing in the underworld and even pickpockets are respected more or less as the masters of a difficult art, but they do not rank with the princes of the *big con* nor even with the more daring heroes of the *heavy rackets*. Among forgers, says Maurer,[9] there is a "sharp division of labor." The men who produce forged checks (*makers, designers, scratchers* or *connections*) are usually wholesalers who supply the actual *passers*, but do not tackle the public. The former, like their allies, the counterfeiters, often operate in safety for years on end, but the latter are frequently taken. The *passer* is also called a *paperhanger*, but the colleague who works off counterfeit money is a *paper pusher, pusher* or *shover*. A forged check is *paper, scrip* or a *stiff*, and when it is a cashier's check it is a *jug stiff* or *cert*. *Bouncer* and *rubber check*, both in common use among laymen, do not seem to be in the professional vocabulary. The *paperhanger* does most of his *spread* on Saturday, after the banks close; in consequence he is usually broke by Friday, and he thus calls a dismal countenance a *Friday face*. To him a store detective is a *shamus, Mr. Fakus* or *Oscar*, a warrant for his arrest is a *sticker*, a credit manager is a *credie* or a *Joe Goss*, a checkbook is a *damper pad* and the confidence talk which precedes his passing of a bad check is the *business*. Among pickpockets the act of picking a pocket is called the *beat*, the *sting* or a *come-off*, a watch (seldom taken nowadays) is a *toy, thimble, turnip, kettle* or *super*,[1] a policeman is a *buttons, fuzz* or *shamus*, a victim is a *chump, mark, yap* or *hoosier*, the member of a mob who does the actual stealing is a *claw, wire* or *tool*, his assistants are *stalls*, a wallet is a *poke, leather, hide* or *okus*,[2] an empty wal-

---

[7] Hijacker's Argot, Chicago *Tribune*, Jan. 22, 1939.

[8] *Yoking* Means Just That, Baltimore *Evening Sun*, July 16, 1946, p. 32. Ordinarily, *to mugg* means to photograph, especially for the rogues' gallery.

[9] The Argot of Forgery, *AS*, Vol. XVI, Dec. 1941, pp. 243-50.

[1] Says Maurer in *AS*, Vol. XVI, Apr. 1941, p. 154: "Modern thieves call a stolen watch a *super* (or *super and slang* if the chain accompanies it), . . . not realizing that the word is really *souper*, a pun on the older form, *kettle*."

[2] In Along the Main Stem, *True Detective*, Mar. 1942, p. 73, a writer sign-

let is a *cold poke, dead skin* or *bloomer*, a ring is a *hoop*, paper money is *rag* or *soft* and an overcoat is a *tog*. All pickpockets are *guns, cannons* or *whiz*, and a lady of the profession is a *gun moll*.[3] *Dip* for a practitioner is now obsolete in America, though it is still used by lay writers upon crime waves and seems to survive in England.[4] Shoplifters, or *boosters,* have some resemblance to pickpockets, but they are much less daring. Many of them are women, and most of the women are amateurs. The professionals often carry a *booster box,* which is a box resembling an ordinary shopper's parcel, but with a trap door for receiving the loot.[5] [Some professional women are highly expert, and can *fork* any object up to the size of a portable TV set—that is, clamp it between the thighs and walk away flat-footed and undetected. All of the good ones know how to make and use *booster bloomers* for concealing large numbers of smaller articles beneath a full skirt.]

A large part of the vocabulary of the rum-running mobs of Prohibition days passed into the general speech, *e.g.,* the real McCoy,[6] *to take for a ride,*[7] *torpedo, triggerman, bathtub gin,*[8] *alky, to muscle in, to cut* (to dilute), *hideout, jake* (all right), *to needle* (to add alcohol), *piece* (a share), *tommy gun* and *hijacker,*[9] and some of them seem likely to stick, along with the Yiddish loans that these public servants also made familiar,

---

ing himself The Fly Kid suggested that *okus* (or *hokus*) may have issued from *poke* by way of *hocus-pocus. Hocuspocus* itself has long been a headache to etymologists. The OED inclines to the theory that it came from the pseudo-Latin patter and assumed name of a juggler during the reign of King James I, but Weekley believes that it may have arisen as a blasphemous perversion of the sacramental blessing, *hoc est corpus (filii).* It has analogues in Norwegian, Swedish and German.

[3] I am indebted here to Everett De-Baun. He tells me that *gun* and *cannon* have nothing to do with artillery. The former is derived from the Yiddish *ganov,* a thief, and *cannon* is simply a more elegant form. During the Golden Age of the Dillingers the newspapers took to calling a racketeer's girl a *gun moll,* but this was an error. [A *gun moll* is simply a female pickpocket, professional.]

[4] In the Argot of the Underworld, by James P. Burke, *American Mercury,* Dec. 1930, pp. 454–8, *catholic* is given as another name for a pickpocket, but without any attempt at an etymology.

[5] I am indebted here to Victor T. Reno, of Los Angeles. See Slick Fingers, by Ralph L. Woods, *Forum,* Dec. 1939, pp. 273–7.

[6] The origin of this term has been much debated and is still unsettled.

[7] Herbert Asbury says in Gem of the Prairie, New York, 1940, p. 327, that this lovely euphemism was coined by Hymie Weiss, one of the four ranking dignitaries of Chicago gangdom, the others being Johnny Torrio, Al Capone and Dion O'Banion.

[8] Like *big shot,* this one was probably invented by some smart newspaper reporter and imposed upon the racket. Fred Hamann tells me that on the revival of bootlegging during World War II it became *blitz water, bang water* or *ceiling buster.*

[9] Said H. K. Croessman in the *American Mercury,* June 1926, pp. 241–2: "The first time I heard *hijacker* was from the lips of an Oklahoman. He explained it as coming from the command customary in hold-ups: 'Stick 'em up high, Jack,' or, more simply, 'Up high, Jack.'"

e.g., kosher (reliable), *meshuga* (crazy) and *to yentze* (to cheat). The assorted ruffians who adorned the same glorious era made every American schoolboy aware of the meaning of *to rub out, mob, to scram,*[1] *G man,*[2] *canary,*[3] *to put the heat on, gat,*[4] *on the lam,*[5]—or else, *gangster, racketeer*[6] and *public enemy.*[7]

[Although the Mafia has long been deep in the rackets, it is only in recent years that it has been recognized. In fact, the term *Mafia* is such a taboo within the Sicilian subculture that many people are unaware—or pretend to be unaware—of its existence, and the organization itself is tightly closed to outsiders. Some terms from the argot are working out, however, among them *capo*, a high-ranking member of the *Mafiosi*, who are also known as *dons, mustachios* or *mustaches* (even though they may be clean-shaven) because the first-generation Mafiosi all wore handle-bar mustaches; *fratuzzi*, the neighborhood folks (little brothers), whom the Mafiosi exploit, though they are supposed to protect them; *ricottari*, the apprentice hoodlums who hope to become Mafiosi someday; *pezzinorante*, the skilled executioners who set up and carry out official (and never solved) murders; *lupara* (literally, *bitch-wolf*), the shot gun loaded with slugs, which is a preferred murder weapon since the slugs are not identifiable ballistically; and *omertà*, the very strict code of the Mafia.]

"One might expect prison slang," says Maurer, "to be a composite of the various specialized argots, but while some bona fide argot crops out in it, it is, on the whole, a separate institutional lingo which differs somewhat from prison to prison." He goes on:

---

[1] The first appearance of *to scram* in print seems to have been in Walter Winchell's column, Your Broadway and Mine, Oct. 4, 1928. See *Scram*—a Swell Five-Letter Word, by V. Royce West, *AS*, Vol. XII, Oct. 1937, pp. 195–202. Partridge says that it reached England via the movies by 1930. Its etymology remains mysterious.

[2] In A Couple of Cops, *The Commonweal*, Jan. 31, 1936, p. 373, Roger Shaw says that the celebrated Machine-Gun Kelly complained of the deadly efficiency of the *G men* when he was captured at Memphis, Tenn., Sept. 26, 1933, and that "newspapers, fictioneers and the movies took it up." It is from *government man*. [Dr. A. C. Russell, the federal agent who arrested Kelly and guarded him in Memphis, is skeptical of this story, and expressed surprise that the prisoner had held a press conference following his arrest.]

[3] One who *sings, i.e.,* confesses to the police.

[4] Apparently from *Gatling gun*. But Booth, before cited, derives it from *catting up*, meaning to rob itinerant workers at pistol point.

[5] Says Peter Tamony in Origin of Words: *Lam*, San Francisco *News-Letter and Wasp*, Apr. 9, 1939, p. 5: "Its origin should be apparent to anyone who runs over several colloquial phrases for leave-taking, such as *to beat it, to hit the trail.* . . . The allusion in *lam* is to *beat. Beat it* is old English, meaning to leave."

[6] *Racket*, in the current sense of an anti-social enterprise, appeared in A New and Comprehensive Vocabulary of the Flash Language: London, 1812. But *racketeer* is American.

[7] *Public enemy*, usually followed by a numeral, is said to have been coined by the Hon. Homer S. Cummings, LL.D., Attorney General of the United States, 1933–9. The original *Public Enemy No. 1* was John Dillinger, killed by FBI men in Chicago, July 22, 1934.

Relatively few successful professionals *do* much *time*, and when they do they tend to hold themselves somewhat apart from the general run of prisoners. They count upon their strong political connections to secure preferment and often associate with the prison administration on intimate terms. The great bulk of prison populations is composed of amateurs or failures; hence the fallacious belief among some psychologists and criminologists that criminals are subnormal in intelligence. Thorough-going and successful professionals are usually superior in intelligence and have nothing about them to suggest the popular conception of a criminal. If you mixed a hundred of them with an equal number of business and professional men all the statistics of a Hooton or a Lombroso would never set them apart.[8]

But the residuum actually behind the bars is of generally low mentality [9] and in consequence the lingo of the average prison, save insofar as it is reinforced by the inventions of the aloof minority or by contributions from outside, shows little imagination. Its basis, says James Hargan, is "a variety of Anglo-Saxon terms dealing mainly with the sexual and simpler life processes, which have survived the centuries in defiance of the dictionary's refusal to receive them." [1] A large part of it, adds Hargan, shows a "euphemistic, often humorous understatement" by which the prisoner "softens an otherwise too unpleasant reality into something bearable," *e.g., kimono,* a coffin; *dance hall,* the death house; *sleeping time,* a short sentence; *mouse,* a spy or informer; and *bird cage,* a cell. The animal appetites naturally take a major place in his thinking, and much of his humor, such as it is, is devoted to flings at his always monotonous and usually tasteless fare.

This vocabulary has its local variations, but most of it seems to be in general use in American prisons, for the same malefactors move from one to another. A large part of it is identical with the table talk of soldiers and sailors. Milk is *chalk;* macaroni, *dago;* eggs, *cacklers, cackleberries* or *shells,* or, if fried, *red eyes;* potatoes, *spuds;* onions, *stinkers* or *tear gas;* butter, *grease;* catsup, *red lead;* soup, *water;* bread, *duffer* or *punk;* sugar, *sand* or *dirt;* roast beef, *shoe sole, leather* or *young horse;* veal, lamb or mutton, *goat meat;* coffee, *gargle, suds* or *black soup;* sausage, *beagle, dog* or *balloon;* tea, *dishwater;* sauerkraut, *shrubbery* or *hay;* a meatloaf, *mystery* or *rubber heels;* biscuits, *cat heads* or *humpers;* bread and gravy, *poultice;* tapioca, *fish eyes* or *cats' eyes;* and a sandwich, *duki* (from *duke,*

---

[8] Private communication, Apr. 7, 1940.

[9] A survey of all the male inmates of the state prisons of New York showed that 80.2% of them were of less than normal intelligence. My authority here is Dr. H. Curtis Wood, Jr. Dr. James Asa Shield, psychiatrist to the Virginia State Penitentiary at Richmond, reports that among 749 white prisoners examined there in 1935 only 21 showed a mental age of 14 years or over, and that among colored prisoners there were but two.

[1] The Psychology of Prison Language, *Journal of Abnormal and Social Psychology,* Vol. XXXVIII, Oct.–Dec. 1935, pp. 359–65.

the hand). Meat as a whole is *pig* and food in general is *swag, garbage, scoff, chow, chuck* or *peelings*. A waiter is a *soup jockey*. The prison functionaries all have derisive names. The head warden is the *big noise*, the *ball of fire* or *the Man;* the guards are *shields, screws, hooligans, roaches, hacks, slave drivers* or *herders;* the chaplain is a *frocker, goody, psalmer, buck* (if a Catholic priest), *Bible-back* or *the Church;* the doctor is a *croaker, cutemup, sawbones, pill punk, iodine, salts* or *pills;* the barber is a *scraper, chin polisher* or *butcher*.

A new prisoner is a *fish;* a letter smuggled out of prison is a *kite;* a crime is a *trick* or *caper;* a cell, when not a *bird cage*, is a *drum;* a drug addict is a *junker, junkie, hype, whang, hophead* or *snowbird*. A prisoner who goes *stir-crazy* is said to be *on his top, conky, footch, guzzly, beered, loco, blogo, buggy, woody* or *meshuga* (from *meshuggah*). To die is *to go down* or *to slam off*. To escape is *to gut, to mouse, to have the measles, to take* (or *cop*) *a mope, to hang it, to be on the bush, to lam the joint, to go over the wall, to get a bush bond* (or *parole*) or *to crush out*. To finish a sentence is *to get up*. A sentence is a *trick, knock, rap, hitch, bit, stretch* or *jolt*. If short it is *sleeping time*, if for one year it is a *boffo*, if for two a *deuce*, if for five a *five-specker* or *V*, if for twenty a *double sawbuck*, if for life the *book*, the *icebox* or *all*. The prison is the *big house*, the *college* or the *joint*. A pardon or commutation is a *lifeboat*. An arrest is a *fall*, a man is a *gee*, a bed is a *kip*, and the prison morgue is the *greenhouse*. Many euphemisms are in use. At Sing Sing, for example, the death house is *Box Z*, the section for insane convicts is *Box A* and the place where dead inmates are buried is *Box 25*. Not a few of the terms reported smell of the lamp, and certainly did not emanate from the common run of prisoners, *e.g., last mile* for the march to the gallows or electric chair, *Cupid's itch* for venereal disease, *pussy bandit* for a rapist, *gospel fowl* for chicken, *sleigh bells* for silver and *toad hides* for paper money.[2]

---

[2] I am indebted here to Clinton A. Sanders, Joseph W. Blackwell, Jr., Samuel Meyer and the editors of the *San Quentin News*. I have also made use of *My San Quentin Years*, by James B. Holohan, published serially in the Los Angeles *Times*, in 1936; Prison Slang, by Clinton T. Duffy, San Quentin, n.d.; Can Cant, by J. Louis Kuethe, Baltimore *Evening Sun*, Dec. 9, 1932 (republished as Prison Parlance, *American Mercury*, Feb. 1934, pp. 25–8); English Behind the Walls, by William H. Hine, *Better Speech*, Dec. 1939, pp. 19–20 (sent to me by Fred Hamann); Convicts' Jargon, by George Milburn, *AS*, Vol. VI, Aug. 1931, pp. 436–42; Prison Phraseology, by Bruce Airey, Montgomery, Ala., 1943; A Prison Dictionary (Expurgated), by Hi Simons, *AS*, Vol. VIII, Oct. 1933, pp. 22–3; Underworld and Prison Slang, by Noel Ersine, Upland, Ind., 1935; Prison Lingo, by Herbert Yenne, *AS*, Vol. II, Mar. 1927, pp. 280–2; More Crook Words, by Paul Robert Beath, *AS*, Vol. VI, Dec. 1930, pp. 131–4; Hipped to the Tip, by Jack Schuyler, *Current History*, Nov. 7, 1940, pp. 21–2; An Analysis of Prison Jargon, by V. Erle Leichty, *Papers of the Michigan Academy of Sciences, Arts and Letters*, Vol. XXX, 1945, pp. 589–600, and the glossaries in Almanac for New Yorkers, 1939, p. 125; Farewell, Mr. Gangster, by Her-

Between the world of professional criminals and that of honest folk there is a half-world of part-time, in-and-out malefactors, and to it belongs the army of hoboes, beggars, prostitutes, drug addicts and so on. Most juvenile delinquents are part of it and remain so, for not many of them can ever hope to be promoted from neighborhood gangs to touring mobs. At the bottom of the pile are the poor wretches, mainly aging, who find road life increasingly insupportable, and so gravitate dismally toward the big cities, to become beggars and *mission stiffs*.

It will be recalled that the first investigation of underworld speech in the Fifteenth and Sixteenth Centuries had to do with the talk of such vagrants rather than with the cant of more daring criminals. That speech still excites the interest of the curious, and there is a large literature upon it.[3] In part it is made up of borrowings from criminal cant, in part of loans from the argot of railroad men and in part of what seems to be original inventions. Many of its terms are familiar to most Americans, *e.g.*, *jungles* (usually plural), the camp of vagabonds outside a city, sometimes occupied for years, [to which the modern *asphalt jungle* is related]; *blind*, the front of a baggage car, directly behind the engine tender; *flop*, a place to sleep (*flop house*, a cheap lodging house); *mulligan*, a stew made in the jungles of any food the assembled hoboes can beg, borrow or steal; *slave market*, an employment agency; *main stem* or *drag*, the main street of a town; *crummy*, lousy; *to mooch*, to beg; *handout*, food begged at a house door; *to panhandle*; *to ride the rods*; *hoosegow*, a jail; *bughouse*, crazy; *barrelhouse*, a low saloon; *to pound the ties*; and *to rustle a meal*.

Among the more esoteric terms recorded in the literature are *to go gooseberrying*, to rob clothes lines (*gooseberries*); *filling station*, a small town (once a *tank town* or *whistle stop*); *bindle*, the hobo's roll of clothes and bedding (if he carries one he is a *bindle stiff*); *scissors bill*, a law-abiding citizen; *rattler*, a freight car; *red ball*, a fast freight; *stash*, a hiding place; *clown*, a rustic policeman; *gay cat*, a newcomer to the road; *jungle buzzard*, one who partakes of a meal in a jungle without contributing anything to it; *skid road* (often *skid row*), a city street frequented by hoboes; *tourist* or *snowfly*, a tramp who goes South in winter to escape the cold weather; *lump* or *poke-out*, a handout (if unwrapped it is a *bald lump*); *locust* or *sap*, a policeman's stick; *to be fanned*, to be awakened by having it applied to the soles of one's feet; *gandy dancer*, a section hand; *hairpin*, a housewife; *pie card*, a union card used as credentials in begging; *shark*, an employment agent; *man catcher*, an employer seeking workers;

bert Corey, New York, 1936; The Professional Thief, ed. by Edwin H. Sutherland, Chicago, 1937; Crime as a Business, by J. C. R. MacDonald, Palo Alto, Cal., 1939; [and Statesville Names: A Prison Vocabulary, by Nathan Kantrowitz and Joanne Kantrowitz (in manuscript)].

[3] Many titles are listed in Burke's bibliography.

stew bum, a drunkard; *sit-down*, a meal in a house; *hump*, a mountain; *tin cow*, canned milk; *Peoria*, soup;[4] *drag*, a train; *reefer*, a refrigerator car; *shack*, a brakeman; *to put it down*, to get off a train; and *to carry the banner*, to walk the streets all night lacking money for lodging.

The *bums* who congregate in cities and live by panhandling have special names to designate men whose appeals to charity are helped by various disabilities, real or imaginary. Those who exhibit sores, usually made with acid, are *blisters;* those who throw their bones out of joint are *throw-outs* or *toss-outs*, those who cough dismally are *ghosts* and those who squat in front of churches or other public buildings and pretend to be helpless are *floppers*.[5] Cripples in general are *crips*. Those who repair umbrellas at street corners are *mush fakers* (an umbrella is a *mush*).[6] Those who make and sell objects of wire, *e.g.*, coat hangers, are *qually workers*. Those who gaze longingly into restaurants or bakeshops while they gnaw at prop bread crusts are *nibblers*. Those who dig into garbage cans are *divers*. Those who pretend to have fainted from hunger are *flickers*. Those with hard-luck stories are *weepers*. Those who practice minor con games are *dingoes*.[7] Those who pick up cigar and cigarette butts are *snipe hunters*. Homosexuals are common among hoboes, and have a vocabulary of their own. They are called *wolves* or *jockers* and the boys accompanying them are *guntzels*, *gazoonies*, *punks*, *lambs* or *prushuns*.[8] There are generally recognized hobo nicknames for most towns and many railroads. Chicago is *the Village*, Cincinnati is *Death Valley*, Richmond, Va., is *Grantsville*, Pittsburgh is *Cinders* or *the Burg*, Spokane, Wash., is *the Spokes*, Walla Walla, Wash., is *the Wallows*, Kalamazoo, Mich., is *the Zoo*, Columbus, Ohio, is *Louse Town*, Little Rock, Ark., is *the Rock*, Joliet, Ill., is *Jolly*, Salt Lake City is *the Lake*, Toledo is *T.O.*, Butte, Mont., is *Brass*, Kansas City is *K.C.*, Cleveland is *Yap Town*, Minneapolis is *Minnie*, Washington is *the Cap*, Terre Haute, Ind., is *the Hut* and New York is simply *the City*.[9]

The origin of *hobo* is apparently unknown. The DAE's first example of the word comes from one of the magazine articles of Josiah Flynt, and is dated 1891. It came into wide use soon afterward.[1] *Tramp* has been traced

---

[4] Said to be not from the town name, but from *puree*.

[5] I take all these names of specialists from Sister of the Road, by Ben L. Reitman; New York, 1937, pp. 300–1.

[6] From *mushroom*. Partridge traces it to 1821 in England.

[7] I am indebted here to The Beggars Are Coming, by Meyer Berger, *The New Yorker*, Mar. 11, 1939.

[8] See The Language of Homosexuality,

by G. Legman, in Sex Variants, by P. W. Henry; New York, 1941, Vol. II, pp. 1149–79.

[9] I take these from David W. Maurer's Underworld Place-Names, *AS*, Vol. XV, Oct. 1940, pp. 340–2, and More Underworld Place-Names, *AS*, Vol. XVII, Feb. 1942, pp. 75–6.

[1] Charles J. Lovell, who had found examples earlier than the DAE's first, suggests that the word may be from the

in England to 1664, but it was not in general use in the United States until the 1880s. *Bum*, which is usually assumed to be derived from the German *Bummler*, of the same meaning, first came into use in San Francisco, in the form of *bummer*, c. 1870.

Also hanging about the outskirts of the professional criminals are the drug addicts, the prostitutes and the disorderly children (not a few of them with well-to-do and even rich parents) who hope for entrance into one or another of the other three groups. There is nothing inherently criminal about taking drugs, and in many cases it is not even anti-social, but the laws against it have made those who do so partners of the racketeers who supply them, just as Prohibition made even the most moderate boozer a partner of Al Capone. Moreover, small-time criminals themselves often become addicts, and all drug sellers are criminals, so the relation between crime and addiction is close. The language of the vice and trade has been reported by David W. Maurer,[2] James A. Donovan, Jr.,[3] Victor Folke Nelson,[4] Milton Mezzrow[5] and Meyer Berger:[6] it varies according to the drug used, but has many general terms, some of them borrowed from the vocabulary of criminals. Maurer says that "it changes rapidly, for as soon as a word is generally known outside the fraternity it dies and another is coined to take its place." [The following illustrate the more stable aspects of the argot: a wholesaler is a *big man*, a retailer is a *peddler* or *connection* (not infrequently he is also an *ice-tong doctor*, i.e., an abortionist), a beginning addict is a *joy popper* or *student*, a finished addict is a *gowster* or *junker* and is said to have a *monkey on his back*, non-addicts are *square Johns* or *do-right people*, an addict well supplied is *on the mojo* and is said to be *in high*, a standard dose is a *ration, check, desk, bindle, block, card, cube, cap* or *piece*, a half size is a *bird's eye*, to adulterate is *to shave* and an adulterated piece is a *short piece*, a dose injected hypodermically is a *shot, pop, bang, jolt, fix-up* or *geezer*, a needle is a *spike, gun, joint, nail, luer* or *artillery*, and a federal narcotics agent is *whiskers, gazer, uncle* or a *headache man*. Opium is *tar, mud, black stuff, gum* or *hop*, morphine is *white stuff, Racehorse Charlie, sugar, white nurse* or *sweet stuff*, cocaine is *snow, happy dust, C* or *heaven dust*, and marijuana

Chinese or some Indian language. He says that it apparently originated in the Seattle-Tacoma area.

[2] "Junker Lingo," By-Product of Underworld Argot, *AS*, Vol. VIII, Apr. 1933, pp. 27–8; The Argot of the Underworld Narcotic Addict, *AS*, Vol. XI, Apr. 1936, pp. 116–27, and Oct. 1938, pp. 179–92; Narcotic Argot, *AS*, Vol. XI, Oct. 1936, p. 222; Speech of the Narcotic Underworld, *American Mer*cury, Feb. 1946, pp. 225–9, and Marijuana Addicts and Their Lingo, *American Mercury*, Nov. 1946, pp. 571–5.

[3] Jargon of Marihuana Addicts, *AS*, Vol. XV, Oct. 1940, pp. 336–7.

[4] Addenda to "Junker Lingo," *AS*, Vol. VIII, Oct. 1933, pp. 33–4.

[5] Really the Blues; New York, 1946.

[6] Tea for a Viper, *The New Yorker*, Mar. 12, 1938, pp. 47–50.

is *muggles, Mary Warner, mezz, Indian hay, loco weed, Mary Jane, mooter, love weed, bambalacha, Mohasky, fu, mootah, grass, tea* or *blue sage*.]

Opium smoking, says Maurer, is going out, largely because the drug is bulky and smoking it calls for prepared quarters and a somewhat elaborate apparatus. [Also, smoking opium is now rare on the market and the cost of a moderate opium habit is at least $150 a day. A few die-hards still smoke, but most have gone to the needle.] Many of the terms used by smokers are of Chinese origin, *e.g., yen*, the craving; *yen-pok* or *fun* (pronounced *foon*), the prepared pill; *yen-shee-kwoi*, an unsophisticated smoker; *toy*, the box in which opium is kept; *yen-shee* or *gee-yen*, unburned gum; *suey-pow*, a sponge for cleaning the pipe; *yen-shee-gow*, a scraper for the same purpose; and *hop* with its derivative, *hophead*. In English the pipe is a *stem, saxophone, gong, gonger, dream stick, joy stick* or *bamboo*. An addict smoking is said to be *hitting* (or *beating*) *the gong, kicking the gonger, kicking the gong around* or *laying the hip*, the preparation of the opium is called *cooking* (or *rolling*) *a pill*, an addict is a *cookie* and one who cooks it for others is a *chef*. A marijuana smoker is a *viper, tea man* or *reefing man*, a cigarette is a *reefer*,[7] *stick, killer, goof butt, giggle smoke, gyve* or *twist*, smoking is *viping* or *sending*, a place devoted to *sending* is a *pad* and a peddler is a *pusher*. A smoker is *high* when contentment creeps over him and *down* on the morning after. The stump of a cigarette is a *roach*, whiskey is *shake up* and the jukebox or phonograph usually present in a *pad* is a *piccolo*. In the days when cocaine was a popular tipple a devotee was a *cokie, snowbird snifter* or *Charlie Coke*, to inhale the drug, often called *Bernice*, was *to go on a sleigh ride* or *to go coasting* and [today] a mixture of cocaine and morphine [or heroin and morphine] is a *whizz-bang* or *speed ball*. The vocabulary of addicts differs somewhat from place to place. Maurer recorded that in Chicago (1938) they called themselves *ads, junk hogs, jabbers, knockers* and *smeckers*, terms now generally current everywhere, and Sanders tells me that prisoners in the Virginia State Prison (1942) had a long list of local names for various mild narcotics and sedatives, *e.g., cement*, codeine; *ping-pong*, pantopon; *yellow jacket*, nembutal; *green hornet*, sodium pentobarbital; and *blue devil*, sodium amytal. Most of these were suggested by the colors of the capsules. Elsewhere a sodium pento-

---

[7] Hugh Morrison calls my attention to the fact that *reefer* is probably derived from the Mexican Spanish *grifa* or *grifo*, which is defined in Francisco J. Santamaría's Diccionario General de Americanismos, Mexico City, 1942, as meaning "la persona intoxicada de drogas como la marihuana, la morfina o la co-caína." The result was *reefa*, whence *reefer*, though Maurer says that among American addicts *greefo* survives as the name of the dried drug, which is also *muggles, bo-bo bush* or *potiguaya*. [*Reefer*, as well as *stick* and *joint*, always refers to a rolled cigarette.]

barbital capsule is a *goof ball*. [These terms are also now generally used.]

Maurer says that prostitutes are so stupid and so little group-conscious that they have never developed "the technical vocabulary which characterizes all other criminal groups." [8] Nevertheless, there are trade terms that prevail widely among them, and some are of considerable antiquity, e.g., *landlady* or *madam*, the keeper of a brothel; *boarder*, an inmate; *hustler*, a street walker; *friend*, a pimp; *hooker*, an old prostitute; *dark meat*, a colored prostitute; *stable*, a group of women under the control of one padrone; *cathouse*, *crib* or *sporting house*, a brothel; *call house*, one with no internes, which sends for *call girls* on demand; *to sit for company*, to be on the staff of a brothel; *to be busy*, to be engaged professionally; and *professor*, a house musician. A *creep joint* or *panel house* is one in which patrons are robbed, and a *roller* or *lush worker* is a girl who robs them. During World War II many patriotic young girls, some of them in their early teens, devoted themselves to entertaining soldiers and sailors on leave. They were usually called *V-girls*. Women who frequent taverns or night clubs, getting a percentage on the drinks they induce male patrons to buy, are *taxi drinkers*, *mixers*, *percentage girls*, *B-girls* or *sitters*.[9] *Crib*, a very low form of brothel, and *cat wagon*, a car used by touring prostitutes, seem to be obsolete, or nearly so.

[The old-time parlor house is now practically extinct, and the newer *broad rackets* have their own argot, much of it coined, one suspects, by the pimps who control the business. Also, higher-priced girls ($50 to $100 is common) are of a different mentality and are technically more adept at *turning a trick*. Representative terms include *one-way girl*, *two-way girl* and *three-way girl*, for girls with various specialties; *jack roller* (West Coast) or *lush roller* (Middle West), for one skilled at *rolling* drunks; *straight date*, a customer with old-fashioned tastes; *sil*, a prostitute's female lover (freely chosen lesbianism is frequently encountered); *she stoops to conquer*, a French girl or *blower* (a fellatrix); a *trip around the world*, a tongue bath administered by a girl; *turquoise*, a girl who is expert at pederasty; a woman's anus is a *leather*, *roulette wheel* or *keister*. A pimp is a *box coat* (also *jelly bean*, *sweet back*, *p.i.*, *barber*, *bludger*, *b.f.*, *bung*, *kite*, *bung kite*, *buzzard*, *calf*, *custom-made man*, *he-madam*, *man*, *mack*, *McGimp*, *fish and shrimp*, *lover*, *Latin lover* and many others). Most girls want and have a pimp, primarily a parasite or kept man who supplies her love life; the more durable pimps may have a *stable* of two to

---

[8] Prostitutes' and Criminals' Argots, *American Journal of Sociology*, Vol. XXXIII, Jan. 1939, p. 546.

[9] Peter Tamony says in the San Francisco *News-Letter and Wasp*, Feb. 24, 1939, that in that city they are called

B-girls, and derives the term from *to buzz* or *to put the bee on*, both meaning to wheedle money. [*B-girls* had appeared in Chicago by the summer of 1939, and in New Orleans by Dec. 1939, if not much earlier.]

four girls, sometimes unknown to one another. A newly emerging phenomenon is the *bull bitch* or *butch pimp*, a lesbian who has one or more girls and services them like a man; *butch pimps* are *drivers*, and are said to keep the girls working better than male pimps. A girl temporarily without a pimp is an *orphan*, but one who rejects all pimps is an *outlaw* and is likely to be beaten up by any pimp who finds out about her. With the passing of the brothel or *house*, the *madam* is no more, though former *madams* are often found in other rackets. A *king bung* or *maggot* is a "white slaver" or a big-time procurer who breaks girls in for the racket; a *Greek* is an ex-pug or a tough hoodlum who manhandles a girl while she is being broken in. *Creepers* or *panel workers* are girls who specialize in robbing customers. Today the higher-priced girls are often connected with burlesque or work in strip-bars, and consider themselves "actresses" in that they also participate in the sex shows now popular with conventioneers; such a show is known as a *circus, gazupi, trick-a-track, exhibition, trip to the Red Sea, dig* or *show;* some customers pay extra to bring their own movie cameras. A *gentleman of the press* is an uncouth customer who manipulates himself under a folded newspaper while attending a sex show.

[The juvenile delinquents have now definitely established themselves as part of the semi-professional and even professional rackets. First, because most state and federal laws protect the juvenile, even to the extent of prohibiting the publication of his name in newspapers, many juveniles are used in the rackets—from narcotics peddling to moonshining—in various ways which protect the older mob members. These boys and girls pass into adulthood with some regret, for with age their immunity vanishes. But most of them go on into adult professional crime with a tremendous advantage—extensive experience with good operators plus the total absence of a criminal record. This type can be observed in considerable numbers around Clark and Division streets in Chicago, but that is only an example, for they thrive in most large cities.

[Those, on the other hand, who do not work for or with established mobs often create their own rackets—ranging from extortion to murder—and organize their own groups, which differ considerably from those of the professional criminal subcultures. These youngsters try to emulate the professional without the benefit of his experience and counsel. They can be observed in profusion on the Lower East Side of Manhattan, but, like the first type, they tend to appear in most major cities. The New York juvenile gangs have gone out of control and are now the center of extensive study financed by local, state, federal and foundation funds. Neither of these two types are to be confused with the youngsters who, in great numbers, rebel against adult dominance and get into a certain amount of trouble, usually minor.

[The juvenile delinquent has enriched the language with a number of terms, among which are *turf*, the territory ruled by one gang; *to sound* or *to sound off*, to provoke a rival gang to violence by means of insults; *war councilor*, a gang leader or a known fighter with much prestige; *rumble*, a battle, often prearranged, in which lethal weapons are used; *D.A. haircut* (often euphemized to *ducktail*), for a particularly distinctive hair style; *piece*, a real pistol as contrasted with a *zip gun*, a homemade single-shot contraption; *to declare a talk*, to negotiate differences with a rival gang; *cool*, a term of wide application, but chiefly referring to restraint in manner or dress; *to turn (someone) on*, to initiate a newcomer to a certain racket; *to gang-shag* or *line up on*, for a number of boys to have intercourse consecutively with the same girl, with or without her consent; *fall-in*, a mass appearance or entrance, especially on rival *turf*, to create an impression of power; *hustle*, a racket which one *pushes* to get his *bread*, often pimping by the boys, prostitution by the girls.

[Because narcotic addiction is almost universal among juvenile criminals, they not only have developed their own argot in this area but have played hob with the established argot long in use by adult criminal addicts.

[An example of an area from which some slang is newly emerging (largely via the whodunits and TV crime shows) is law enforcement on local, state, and federal levels. Even the CIA now reportedly uses an argot (*e.g., dubok*, a drop, from the Russian for oak tree, and *treff*, a clandestine meeting place, from the German *treffen*) from which some terms appear to be filtering into underworld usage. Modern enforcement agencies, staffed by trained men, are rather recent departures from tradition; historically, police were recruited from the criminal subcultures (set a thief to catch a thief), and there is still some of this, but it is passing. The stool pigeon, however, is still the keystone of police work. We might say that police have long constituted a kind of synthetic subculture serving as a buffer between the dominant culture and highly organized criminal subcultures, an arrangement helpful to both groups. There is always an undercurrent of crime in any police department despite improving administration, police protection is sold to the right people (usually only professional criminals), and recently in such cities as Denver and Chicago the police actually reverted to type and became professional burglars.

[A study now in progress shows a widespread lingo or argot in use on many levels of enforcement (more than 1,500 entries to date). It is a strange amalgam of technical jargon, codes used for communication between mobile units (*10-68*, transmission not clear; *10-10*, subject to call; *10-16*, have prisoner; etc.), abbreviations and codes for various offenses (*DAAW/OOP*, driving away car without owner's permission), a good deal of discarded criminal argot, or argot used in a sense not used by professional criminals, along with a little which is current, and slang or argot which naturally evolves in this kind of work. It has been observed that most policemen know little if any bona fide criminal argot, although occasionally a specialized detective will be very well versed in it. However, there is usually a difference between the way such detectives use argot and the way criminals in corresponding specialties use it, even though both know many of the same words. For example, tapes made from the speech of Danny Campion, a really great whizz-dick in New York City, were recognized immediately for what they were—a detective talking—when heard by professional thieves.

[A few of the terms not commonly known to outsiders are: *dry snitch*, to give a detective information without seeming to do so; *crested hen*, a butch lesbian; *diaper-rashed punk*, a juvenile hoodlum; *ear loft*, a useful rumor or information; *easter egg*, a car easily identified because of its color; *skunk wagon*, a black-and-white patrol car; *feel for*, to check by radio; *flip*, for a criminal to turn informer; *Settling Sam*, a prosecutor who will take any kind of sentence on a guilty plea rather than go to trial; *sneaking deacon*, a married policeman who cheats on his wife; *stick daddy*, a cop who likes the ladies and vice versa; *cop-out room*, a room at headquarters or in a jail where deals are made with the prosecutor, suspects confer with their attorneys or where the third degree is sometimes administered (when it is used for defendant-attorney conferences, it is often *bugged*); *panty thief*, a pervert who robs clotheslines, hotel rooms or homes for fetishes; *hummer*, any kind of charge placed against a suspect so that he can be held although there is insufficient evidence to hold him on the charge for which he is really wanted; *highway mopery, attempting a creep*, etc., fictitious crimes for which suspects are arrested for investigation.

[The rivalry between various departments and divisions of enforcement is reflected by such terms as *bear tracker*, a plain-clothes man; *possum sheriff*, a game warden; *short-pants division*, juvenile court and its officers; *pussy posse*, the vice squad; *FIB*, the FBI; *Dickless Tracy*, a policewoman.

[Some of the terms from criminal argots used in senses not known to criminals, or not so used by them, are *bumper*, a stall in a pickpocket team (also sometimes the *wire*, though detectives usually use *wire* to mean any pickpocket, *wire* or not); *cloud* or *fog*, the stall to whom the wallet is sometimes passed; *crust*, a *big-con* man; *spieler*, the inside man for the *big-con*; *hard-ass*, to break open a safe by punching, ripping or methods other than by drilling, pulling the combination, or explosives; *bunco game*, a *big-con* game; *heavy man*, one transporting narcotics. It is interesting that professionals often recognize plain-clothes men, police *plants* or undercover men by these and many other off-center uses of argot terms.

Some criminals have said that they deliberately plant these terms, and some terms have been encountered being used as bona fide argot by very competent police officers. Joe Furey once said that years ago he planted *spieler* (in a special sense) on Herb Graham, a famous federal officer, and Graham has been heard defending it vigorously as genuine *big-con* argot.]

The line separating the criminal argots from ordinary slang is hard to draw, and in certain areas the two are mixed. Consider, for example, the language of showfolks. At the top it is highly respectable, and some of it is of considerable antiquity, but on the lower levels, as with traveling carnivals, it coalesces with that of hoboes, Gypsies and thieves. Similarly, the transient slang of jitterbugs and other incandescent youngsters is connected through that of jazz musicians with that of drug addicts. All showfolks who work under canvas say that they are *on the show* or *with it*, not *in it*, just as pickpockets say they are *on the cannon* and yeggs that they are *on the heavy*, and there are many circus and carnival terms that are identical with criminal terms, *e.g.*, *grift*, an illicit or half-illicit means of getting money; *benny*, an overcoat; *shill*, one hired to entice customers; *cheaters*, spectacles; *mouthpiece*, a lawyer; *to lam*, to depart hastily; *hoosier*, a yokel; *home guard*, those who do not travel; *leather*, a pocketbook; *moniker*, a person's name or nickname; *office*, a signal; and the various names for money, ranging from *ace* for a $1 bill to *grand* for $1,000. This lingo has been studied by David W. Maurer,[1] George Milburn,[2] Percy W. White,[3] E. P. Conkle,[4] A. J. Liebling,[5] Marcus H. Boulware,[6] Joe Laurie, Jr.,[7] and Charles Wolverton.[8]

[Carnival workers, and especially *strong-joint* or *flat-joint* operators, have a more or less secret argot called *ceazarney* or *alfalfa*, which is based on phonetic distortion and cannot be reproduced in print without resort to a complex phonemic rendering. It is one of the few argots which are spoken with a deliberate attempt to deceive or to conceal meaning.]

The language of the showfolks proper is picturesque and often amusing. "Few occupations," says Maurer, "have so colorful a technical vocabulary." A clown is a *paleface*, a *whiteface* or *Joey*, a tattooed man is a *picture gallery*, a bareback rider is a *rosinback*, a contortionist is a *frog*, *bender* or

[1] Carnival Cant; a Glossary of Circus and Carnival Slang, *AS*, Vol. VI, June 1931, pp. 327–37.

[2] Circus Words, *American Mercury*, Nov. 1931, pp. 351–4.

[3] A Circus List, *AS*, Vol. I, Feb. 1926, pp. 282–3; More About the Language of the Lot, *AS*, Vol. III, June 1928, pp. 413–15.

[4] Carnival Slang, *AS*, Vol. III, Feb. 1928, pp. 253–4.

[5] Masters of the Midway, *The New Yorker*, Aug. 12, 1939, pp. 21–5.

[6] Circus Slang, Pittsburgh *Courier*, Mar. 20 and 27, 1943.

[7] Lefty's Notebook, *Variety*, Apr. 7, 1943.

[8] Mysteries of the Carnival Language, *American Mercury*, June 1936, pp. 227–31.

Limber Jim, a freak or snake charmer is a *geek* and all performers are *kinkers*. The owner of the show is the *governor* or *gaffer*, the head electrician is *shanty*,[9] a musician is a *windjammer*, a palmist is a *mitt reader*, a phrenologist is a *bump reader*, the stake drivers are the *hammer gang*, those who load and unload the show are *razorbacks*, elephant handlers are *bull men* or *bull hookers*, the barker outside a side show is the *spieler*, his talk is the *opening* or *ballyhoo*, a bouncer is a *pretty boy*, a newcomer to the show is a *first-of-May* or *Johnny-come-lately* and the august master of ceremonies is the *equestrian director*.[1]

Any elephant, male or female, is a *bull*, a zebra is a *convict*, a hippopotamus is a *hip*, a leopard is a *spot* and a tiger is a *stripe*, but any feline is a *cat*. All tents save the *cookhouse* and the *clown alley* are *tops*, and all concessions are *joints*—the *juice joint* (refreshment stand), *mug joint* (photograph gallery), *grab joint* (eating stand), *mitt joint* (fortune teller's tent), *sinker joint* (doughnut stand), *grease joint* (hamburger stand) and so on. All animal cages are *dens*, the show ground is the *lot*, a side show is an *annex* or *kid show*, the program is the *Bible*, the dressing tent is the *pad room*, the clowns' quarters are *clown alley*, the latrine is a *donniker*, the space behind the big top is the *backyard*, the cheap goods sold by concessionaires are *slum*, *junk*, *garbage* or *schlock*, the powder used to make lemonade is *flookum*, the diner or club car on the train is the *privilege car*, a Ferris wheel is a *hoister*, a merry-go-round is a *jenny*, the last performance of the season is the *blow-off*, the trip to winter quarters is the *home run*, the South is *down yonder* and the show itself is the *opery*. The traveling showmen have borrowed many terms from the stage, *e.g.*, *props*, *stand*, *paper* (posters), *dark* (closed), *B.O.* (box office) and *at liberty* (out of work), and others, as I have noted, from the argot of criminals. An outsider is a *clem* or *gilly*, and Milburn says that the old cry of "Hey-rube!," raised when local rowdies attacked a show, is now supplanted by "Clem!" [The large traveling circuses are now almost a thing of the past, though Ringling as of 1960 has reactivated the circus train, and the smaller shows no longer carry the *grifters* as they once did.]

Traveling shows and fairs are still followed by some minor enterprisers —operators of gambling devices, sellers of quack medicine, street peddlers and so on. Some of these are tolerated and others simply exercise their inalienable right to flock along. The street peddlers, who call themselves *pitchmen*, frequently undertake independent tours, and not a few of them have covered the whole country. Their trade journal is *Billboard* (Cincinnati), which also caters to all other outdoor showmen, and every week they contribute to it what they call *pipes*, *i.e.*, news reports from the field,

---

[9] Apparently from *chandelier*.

[1] "*Ringmaster*," says Milburn, "is un-known to circus parlance."

describing business conditions and telling of the movements of pitchmen. There are *high* pitchmen and *low*, the former addressing their customers from automobiles or platforms, and the latter operating from the ground level, with their goods displayed on or in a suitcase (*keister*) set upon a tripod (*tripes*). The contents of the *keister* are the *flash*, the audience is the *tip*, to sell is *to turn*, listeners who fade away without buying are *mooches* and are said *to blow*, those who buy are *monkeys*, *chumps* or *naturals*, when business is bad it is *larry*, to hand out merchandise is *to duke*, and confederates, if they are used, are *boosters*, *lumpers*, *sticks* or *shills*. Money is *gelt*, *take*, *kale*, *scratch* or *geetus*. *To cut up pipes* or *jackpots* is to gossip or boast. An indoor stand is a *jam pitch*.

The various specialists have their own names. One who sells fruit or vegetable squeezers is a *juice worker*, one who takes subscriptions is a *paper man*, *leaf worker*, *name gatherer* or *sheet worker*, one who sells medicines (now usually vitamins) is a *med worker* and one who deals in horoscopes is a *scope worker*. Plated ware is *floozum*, metal polish is *flookum*, knives are *shivs*, cement is *gummy*, spot removers or other cleaners are *rads* (from *eradicator*), watches are *blocks*, billfolds are *pokes*, ball-points are *ink sticks*, spectacles are *googs*, corn cures are *corn punk*, handkerchiefs are *wipes* and flower bulbs are *horn nuts*. Household articles in general are *gadgets*, and any sort of electrical device is a *coil*. To disperse an audience is *to slough the tip*. To break sales resistance is *to turn the tip*.[2] One of the gifts of pitchmen to the general vocabulary seems to be *phony* or *phoney*, the origin of which still engages lexicographers.[3]

The fakers who hire stores and stage auction sales of phony jewelry, silverware and other such gimcrackery constitute a variety of pitchmen, somewhat below the salt. Their sales are known in the trade as *grind* auctions. Their business, of course, calls for more capital than the ordinary pitchman can command, but otherwise they follow his methods pretty closely, especially those he uses in a *jam pitch*. A study of their argot, by Fred Witman, was published in *American Speech* in 1928,[4] and the racket is still very much alive.

---

[2] I am indebted here to William J. Sachs (Bill Baker), who conducted the Pipes for Pitchmen department in *Billboard*. The English pitchmen, who call themselves *grafters*, have a quite different vocabulary. Many of its terms are in The Grafters' Corner, by Semi-Detached (Arthur Pearson), *World's Fair*, Jan. 17, 1942, and some are reprinted in *Billboard*, June 26, 1943, pp. 59–60.

[3] In The Origin of *Phoney*, *AS*, Vol. XII, Apr. 1937, pp. 108–10, Peter Tam-

ony offers strong evidence that it came originally from *fawney*, [from Gaelic *fáinne*, a ring], traced in England to 1781, but the dictionaries continue to mark it "origin uncertain." See Ch. V, Sec. 2, above.

[4] Jewelry Auction Jargon, June, pp. 375–6. [See also The Life and Lingo of Big Show Novelty Vendors, by Albert Hunter Roemer, M.A. thesis, Western Reserve U., 1955.]

The stage in its various forms shares with the newspapers, radio and television the burden of disseminating neologisms in the Republic, and its chief organ, *Variety*, has probably set afloat more of them than any other single agency. But in addition to their services in this cultural field, stagefolks also use many peculiar terms of their own. Some of them go back to the days of Shakespeare, but most, of course, are more recent, and there is a constant birth of new ones. The first effort that I am aware of to compile an American glossary was made by the highly respectable but stage-struck Brander Matthews in 1917.[5] In the following list[6] I have omitted terms whose meaning is known to everyone, *e.g.*, *star, box office, ingénue, one-night stand, angel, hand, S.R.O., properties, understudy, tryout* and *free list.*

Backing. Scenery hung behind doors, windows and other openings in the set.

Blow up, or dry up, or balloon, *v.* To forget one's lines.

Borders. Short curtains or strips of scenery (foliage, etc.) behind the top of the proscenium arch and across the top of the stage; also lights along the sides thereof.

Dog. An audience outside New York. To try out a play on the road is *to try it on the dog.*

Dressing. Filling a house with pass holders likely to applaud.

George Spelvin. A name used on playbills for a minor actor in a walk-on role, or to conceal the fact that an actor whose real name is given in one role is doubling in another.

---

[5] In an article in *Billboard*, Dec. 22, pp. 8–9. It was reprinted as The Vocabulary of the Show Business in his Principles of Playmaking; New York, 1919, pp. 251–64.

[6] In compiling it I have made use of Trouper Talk, by Gretchen Lee, *AS*, Vol. I, Oct. 1925, pp. 36–7; Stage Terms, by Percy W. White, *AS*, Vol. II, May 1926, pp. 436–7; Theatrical Lingo, by Ottille Amend, *AS*, Vol. III, Oct. 1927, pp. 21–3; Jewels from a Box-Office: The Language of Show Business, by Arnold Moss, *AS*, Vol. XI, Oct. 1936, pp. 219–22; Speech of the Theatre, by W. P. Daggett, *QJS Ed.*, Vol. IX, Apr. 1923, pp. 154–62; Show Talk and Stage Slang, by Joseph Arnold, *Bookman*, June 1929, pp. 33–64; A Glossary of Stage Terms and Parlance, in A Handbook for the Amateur Actor, by Van H. Cartmell, New York, 1936, pp. 85–98; A Stageland Dictionary, by Walter J. Kingsley and Loney Haskell, *The New York Times*, Oct. 14, 1923, sec. 8, p. 4; Broadway Glossary, in So You Want to Go into the Theatre?, by Shepard Traube, Boston, 1936, pp. 243–7; and Theatrical Workers' Slang and Jargon, in Lexicon of Trade Jargon, Vol. III, comp. by the Federal Writers' Project in New York. The argot of the English stage is in A Dictionary of Stage Terms, in Theatre and Stage, edited by Harold Downs, London, 1934, pp. 91–104; English Theatrical Terms and Their American Equivalents, by Henry J. Heck, *AS*, Vol. V, Aug. 1930, p. 468, and English Show Slang, *Billboard*, Dec. 18, 1915, p. 193. It is also discussed in *Notes and Queries*, Oct. 24 and Nov. 21, 1942. A bibliography of books and articles on both American and English theatrical argot is in Burke's Literature of Slang, pp. 119–120.

Ghost. The company treasurer. The *ghost* is said to *walk* on payday.

Open cold, *v*. To present a play in New York without a tryout elsewhere.

Pop. The traditional nickname for the stage doorkeeper.

Side. A page in the typescript of an actor's speeches, given to him to memorize.

Thinking part. A part including no spoken lines.

Turkey. A failure.

Vaudeville, in its heyday, had a rich argot of its own, some of which survives in the general vocabulary of the stage.[7] Many of its terms, like those given in the preceding vocabulary, are now more or less obsolete, for vaudeville has decayed sadly. At the same time the minstrel show has disappeared. Meanwhile, the argot of burlesque, which was once virtually identical with that of vaudeville, has had to be enlarged to take in the vocabulary of strip tease. The latter was listed by H. M. Alexander in his "Strip Tease" in 1938.[8] From his list, and with the help of other authorities, I have put together the following:

Boston version. A show purged of its worst indecencies.

Bump, *v*. To thrust the hips forward.

Bust developer. A performer who croons offstage while the strip-teaser is at work.

Catching the bumps. One of the jobs of the drummer in the orchestra.

Flannel mouth, or stooge. A *straight man* who acts as *feeder* to the comedian.

Flash. The sudden exposure at the end of an act, presumably of the entire carcass.

Gadget. A G-string.

Grind, *v*. To revolve the backside.

Panel. A strip-teaser's diaphanous draperies.

Quiver, *v*. To rotate or oscillate the breasts.

Slinger, or peeler, or shucker, or stripper. A strip-teaser.

Third banana. A comedian who submits to assault by another comedian.

---

[7] Many of its terms are listed in Stage Terms, by Percy W. White, *AS*, Vol. I, May 1926, pp. 436–7, and in Vol. III (Theatrical Workers' Slang and Jargon) of the Federal Writers' Project Lexicon of Trade Jargon. [See also Walter P. Bowman and Robert H. Ball, Theatre Language; New York, 1961.]

[8] New York, pp. 120–3.

Trailer. The strip-teaser's exhibitionary strut before beginning to take off her clothes.

Wham. A strip tease in which the teaser removes virtually all her clothes.

Before the days of the strip tease the women of burlesque were largely of Brünnhildian build, as indeed were the chorus girls of musical comedy before 1900. They were called *hill horses* or *beef trusts*, the last a reference to Billy Watson's famous "Beef Trust" company, the billing of which announced that it offered "two tons of women." When less massive girls began to appear they were called *ponies*. But *hill horse* disappeared from memory with the old-time horsecars, and was supplanted by *big horse*. In the 1900 era there was a distinction between a *chorus girl* and a *show girl* or *clothes horse*. The former simply hoofed and sang in the ensembles; the latter was a more pretentious performer who wore expensive costumes and sometimes had a few lines. In recent years there has appeared the *swing girl*, who, when shows play seven nights a week, relieves other girls on their nights off. Chorus girls apparently speak the argot of whatever branch of the theater they happen to adorn, but they also have some terms of their own. In 1943 Earl Wilson, then saloon editor of the New York *Evening Post* and a recognized expert on Broadway lexicography, was reporting that those then laboring in the night clubs were using *to fluff off* to signify getting rid of an unwelcome admirer, *falsies* for the pads which converted them from perfect 32s to perfect 34s [9] and "Don't give me that *jive*" or "Don't give me that *routine*" as a set reply to honeyed advances.[1] From time to time afterward he added other terms, *e.g.*, *square* or *creep* for a stupid and tiresome person,[2] *body* for any man, *to give him the B.R.U.* (from *brushoff*) for to get rid of him, *to smoke up* for to smarten up, *fractured* for under the influence of alcohol and *sex appeal* for the aforesaid *falsies*. The ladies of the more decorous ballet, whether Russian or operatic, also have a trade language, made up chiefly of technical terms,[3] but so far as I have been able to discover there is no special lingo of opera proper.

There remain the theater auxiliaries—for example, the box-office crew and the corps of stagehands. The vocabulary of the former was printed in

[9] In the pre-strip-tease age such a pad was called a *heart*.

[1] It Happened Last Night, Oct. 6, 1941.

[2] Borrowed from the jive vocabulary. Wilson reported in the *Evening Post*, Sept. 28, 1945, that when he appealed to Toots Shor, a Broadway savant, for precise definitions of *square* and *creep* he was told: "A *square* don't know from nothin' and a *creep* is worse'n a *jerk*."

[3] It is to be found in The Ballet-Lover's Pocket-Book, by Kay Ambrose, New York, 1945, and The Borzoi Book of Ballet, by Grace Robert, New York, 1946, pp. 351–62.

The New York Times in 1935,[4] and that of the latter in *American Speech* in 1928.[5]

The argot of the movie lots shows a good many loans from that of the theater, but it has also produced some picturesque novelties of its own, chiefly having to do with the technical process of picture making. Most of the following specimens, assembled from various sources,[6] were scrutinized and revised by Miss Anita Loos and the late Edgar Selwyn, to whose friendly aid I am much indebted.

While the movies have popularized *yes-man* (a sycophant),[7] Hollywood did not invent *preview*, meaning the showing of a picture, before its first public performance, at a special performance for movie critics and other privileged persons. The identical verb is traced by the OED to 1607. The noun, however, seems to be an Americanism, for the OED's two examples, one dated 1882 and the other 1899, and both antedating the movies, come from American publications, where we also find *sneak preview*, which emphasizes the privilege of attending. It has been borrowed by the English, and is now used in senses having nothing to do with motion pic-

---

[4] The Strange Vernacular of the Box-Office, Oct. 30. See also The Forty Thieves, by Maurice Zolotow, *Reader's Digest*, Jan. 1944, pp. 91–4.

[5] American Stage-Hand Language, by J. Harris Gable, Vol. IV, Oct., pp. 67–70.

[6] There is a bibliography of glossaries of motion-picture terms in Burke's Literature of Slang, pp. 121–2. Not listed there are Neologisms of the Film Industry, by P. R. Beath, *AS*, Vol. VIII, Apr. 1933, pp. 73–4; Logomachia, by Cecil B. De Mille, *Words*, Oct. 1936, p. 6; Strange Lingo of the Movies, *Popular Mechanics*, May 1937, pp. 722–6; Glossary of Movie Terms, by James Hogan, North American Newspaper Alliance syndicated article, June 5, 1938; The Playwright in Paradise, by Edmund Wilson, *New Republic*, Apr. 26, 1939; Movie Talk, by Philip H. Bailey, *Minicam*, June 1939, pp. 115–18; Hollywood Slang, *Woman's Home Companion*, Aug. 1940, p. 8; Pill? Skull Doily? It's Movie Talk, by Virginia Oakey, Richmond (Va.) *News-Leader*, Apr. 1943, pp. 155–6.

[7] In Origin of Words: *Yes, Man*, San Francisco *News-Letter and Wasp*, June 30, 1939, p. 10, Peter Tamony says that *yes-man* was invented by T. A. (Tad)

Dorgan, the cartoonist, in 1913. It appeared first in a cartoon entitled Giving the First Edition the Once-Over, showing the editor and his assistants looking over an edition fresh from the press. The assistants are praising it, and are labeled *yes-men*. "The extension of the term to indicate assistant directors in motion-picture organizations," says Mr. Tamony, "was natural. The early 1920s saw the industry rapidly developing to the stupendous, colossal, flamboyant mystery it now is, and the many who strove for fame and fortune did it with hats in hand." In a short while the late Wilson Mizner was calling Hollywood "the land where nobody noes," and *Variety* nominated one of the assistants of Darryl Zanuck, the producer, for the dignity of *super-yes-man*. Mr. Tamony calls attention to the fact that *yes-men* were known in the Eighteenth Century as *amens*, which appeared in the third edition of Grose's Classical Dictionary of the Vulgar Tongue, 1796. The term is defined thus: "He said *yes* and *amen* to everything; he agreed to everything." For Dorgan see Tad Dorgan Is Dead, by W. L. Werner, *AS*, Vol. IV, Aug. 1929, p. 430. Werner does not list *yes-men* among Dorgan's coinages.

tures, as it is in America. The austere *Literary Supplement* of the London *Times* uses *preview*, for example, as a heading on advance notices of new books. *Release*, in the sense of a new picture just delivered, or about to be delivered, to exhibitors, was apparently borrowed by Hollywood from the jargon of newspaper offices. It arose in the latter when public dignitaries began sending out advance copies of their speeches marked *For release* at such-and-such a time. This legend was presently used by press agents for a similar purpose, and a document so marked came to be known as a *release*. According to Eric Berger, writing in *Coronet*,[8] *photoplay* was invented by Edgar Strakosch in 1912. The early motion-picture producers disliked *movie*, which had begun to displace *biograph*, *kinetoscope*, *kinetograph*[9] and *cinematograph*,[1] and in 1912 the Essanay Company offered the princely prize of $25 for something more elegant. The money went to *photoplay*, sent in by Strakosch. The term gained a considerable popularity, and became the name of one of the earliest and most influential magazines for movie fans, edited from 1914 to 1932 by James R. Quirk, but *movie* nevertheless survived.

A term which often puzzles movie fans is *Oscar*, the name of a gold statuette awarded each year for various sorts of professional achievement by the Academy of Motion Picture Arts and Sciences, the Hollywood opposite number to the American Academy of Arts and Letters. For the following account of the origin of the word I am indebted to Edgar Selwyn:

> Donald Gledhill, secretary of the Academy, and his wife were in Gledhill's office and fell to discussing the impending arrival of a relative called Uncle Oscar. A newspaper man was waiting in an outer office. While this conversation was going on a jeweler arrived with a sample statue. At first glance Gledhill mistook him for the missing relative and said to Mrs. Gledhill, "Here's Oscar now." The newspaper man, thinking he referred to the statue, wrote in his column the next day: "The gold Academy awards are referred to as *Oscars* by Academy officials." This was lifted by other newspaper men all over

[8] New Models in Words, Nov. 1940, pp. 28–9.

[9] Both *kinetoscope* and *kinetograph* were used by Thomas A. Edison to designate his original motion-picture machine of 1893.

[1] *Movie* is not listed in the DAE, but the OED Supplement marks it an Americanism and traces it to 1913. The DA has no citation before 1913, but cites Terry Ramsaye, who says in Movie Jargon, *AS*, Vol. I, Apr. 1926, p. 357, that it really goes back to 1906–7. *Movie parlor* came in on its heels, along with *movie actor*, *movie show*, etc. When sound pictures were first heard of they were called *speakies*, but in 1926, when their production was begun on a commercial scale by Warner Brothers, they became *talkies*. The Australians call March of Time reconstructions of history *thinkies*. No short name for colored pictures is in general use, [unless we accept *in Technicolor*].

the country, and in a little while the awards were being called *Oscars* everywhere.[2]

Many terms associated with the movies are the product of press agents,[3] *e.g.*, *wampas*, a female aspirant to stardom; *cobra*, a girl powerfully aphrodisiacal; *starlet, sex appeal, oomph, glamour girl* and the magnificent *super-colossal*. Some of the other terms emanating from Hollywood wits have their points, *e.g.*, *to go Hollywood*, meaning, when applied to an actor, to succumb to a suffocating sense of his own importance, and when applied to a movie writer or other intellectual, to abandon the habits and ideas of civilization and embrace the levantine life of the richer movie folks; *casting couch* for the divan in a casting director's office; *tear bucket* for an elderly actress playing heart-broken mothers; *finger wringer* for a star given to emoting; *baddie* for an actor playing villains; *cliff-hanger* for a serial melodrama; *sobbie* or *weepie* for a picture running to sadness; and *bump man* for a performer who undertakes dangerous stunts. *Variety* uses *flesh* to designate live players who appear in moviehouses.

The queer jargon called *jive*, which emerged in the early 1940s, was an amalgam of Negro slang from Harlem and the argots of drug addicts and the pettier sort of criminals, with occasional additions from the Broadway gossip columns and the high-school campus. It seems to have been current at the start among jazz musicians, many of them Negroes and perhaps more of them addicts, and its chief users were always youthful devotees of the more delirious type of dancing, *i.e.*, the so-called *jitterbugs*. It actually arose in the honky-tonks and tingle-tangles of the pre-jazz era, and many of its current names for musical instruments go back to that era or even beyond, *e.g.*, *bull fiddle* or *doghouse* for a double bass; *groan box* or *box of teeth* for an accordion; *slip horn, slush pump, gas pipe, syringe* or *push pipe* for a trombone; *thermometer* for an oboe; *iron horn, plumbing, squeeze horn* or *piston* for a trumpet; *pretzel* or *peck horn* for a French horn; *licorice stick, wop stick, gob stick, blackstick* or *agony pipe* for a

---

[2] The term has also come into use outside movie circles, always to designate some symbol of merit. See Among the New Words, by I. Willis Russell, *AS*, Vol. XIX, Dec. 1944, p. 306. *Baltimore & Ohio Magazine*, Nov. 1945, p. 9: Our Annual Report Wins *Oscar* (a bronze trophy offered by the *Financial World*). *Editor and Publisher*, Apr. 5, 1947, p. 7: Promotion *Oscars* Awarded to 6 Newspapers (bronze plaques). There are also derivative *Edgars, Gertrudes* [and *Emmys*], the first named for *Edgar* Allan Poe, going to writers and producers of whodunits, and *Ger-* trudes to writers of Pocket Books which sell 1,000,000 copies, [while *Emmys* are awarded to television shows of alleged merit]. See *American Notes and Queries*, Vol. VII, Apr. 26, 1947, p. 24.

[3] *Variety* calls press agents *flacks*, a World War II term for antiaircraft fire. It was borrowed from the German *flak*, an abbreviation of *Fliegerabwehrkanone*, an antiaircraft cannon. Agents of extraordinary virulence are *blast artists*. They call themselves *publicists, public relations counsel* or *publicity engineers*. See Ch. VI, Sec. 7.

clarinet; *foghorn, fishhorn* or *gobble pipe* for a saxophone; *box, moth box* or *88* for a piano; *scratch box* for a violin; *chin bass* for a viola; *gitter, gitbox* or *belly fiddle* for a guitar; *grunt iron* for a tuba; *god box* for an organ; *woodpile* for a xylophone; and *skin* or *suitcase* for a drum. [Currently any instrument is an *ax*.] So with the names for performers, *e.g., skin tickler, skin beater, hide beater* or *brave boy* for a drummer; *squeaker* for a violinist; *sliver sucker* for a clarinetist; *whanger, plunker boy* or *plink-plonker* for a guitarist; *monkey hurdler* for an organist; *gabriel* for a trumpeter; and *brass officer* for a cornetist. Any performer on a brass wind instrument is a *lip splitter*.

The jazz band is a variable quantity, and may run from four or five men to what almost amounts to a symphony orchestra. Jazz itself is divided into two halves, the *sweet* kind and the *hot* kind or *jive* and *swing*, of which *boogie-woogie* is a subspecies. [*Sweet* jazz is usually played *straight* or according to the score, while *hot* jazz is played with plenty of leeway for improvisation.] [4] A performer who sticks to the printed notes is a *paperman*, and if he ever undertakes conventional music is a *commercial, salon man, long underwear* or *longhair*. An adept at *hot jazz* is a *cat*, and if he excels at arousing the libido of the fans (who are also, by courtesy, *cats*) he is said to *send* or *give* or *ride* or *go to town* or to be *in the groove*, and becomes a *solid sender* or *gate*. The test of his skill is his proficiency at adorning the music with *ad lib*, ornaments called *licks, riffs, get-offs* or *take-offs*. The wilder they are the better. When swing performers meet to *lick* and *riff* for their own entertainment, they are said to hold a *jam session, clambake* or *barrelhouse*. Music that is banal or stale is *corny*. *Boogie-woogie* accentuates a monotonous bass, usually of eight notes to a measure.[5] A woman singer is a *canary* or *chirp*. Any wind performer is a *Joe blow*. Tuning up is *licking the chops*. High trumpet notes are *Armstrongs*.[6] Notes are *spots*. Rests are *layouts*. To emphasize the rhythm is to *beat it out*. To be out of a job is to be *cooling*. Jazz in Negroid style is *gut-bucket*. To

[4] The structure of jazz is discussed learnedly in So This Is Jazz, by Henry Osborne Osgood, New York, 1926, and by the same author in The Anatomy of Jazz, *American Mercury*, Apr. 1926, pp. 385–95. Its history is recounted in Reflections on the History of Jazz, by S. I. Hayakawa, a lecture delivered before the Arts Club of Chicago, Mar. 17, 1945, and later printed as a pamphlet by the author. See also Is Jazz Music?, by Winthrop Parkhurst, *American Mercury*, Oct. 1943, pp. 403–9.

[5] It is discussed learnedly, and with approbation, in *Étude*, the trade journal of American music teachers, Dec. 1943, p. 757, and by Nicholas Slonimsky in Jazz, Swing and *Boogie-Woogie, Christian Science Monitor*, May 20, 1944. Slonimsky says that it was launched by Meade Lewis and Albert Ammons, Negro pianists, at Carnegie Hall, New York, Dec. 23, 1938.

[6] From Louis *Armstrong*, alias Satchelmouth, alias Satchmo, a famous colored trumpet player. For his triumphs see Hot Jazz Jargon, by E. J. Nicholas and W. L. Werner, *Vanity Fair*, Nov. 1935, p. 38, and *Jazz*, by Robert Coffin; New York, 1946.

keep good time is to *ride*. The jazz bands have changed much of the conventional Italian terminology of music. Music played *dolce* is said to be *schmalz* (German for lard), *scherzo* is *medium bounce*, a grace note is a *rip*, the final chord is a *button*, a drop in pitch on a sustained note is a *bend* and a *glissando* is a *smear* or *slurp*.

The vocabulary of the jazz addict is largely identical with that of the jazz performer. He himself is a *hepcat, alligator* or *rugcutter*. To him those who dislike swing music are *tin ears*, and are said to be *icky*. A dance is a *rat race* or *cement mixer;* anything excellent is *killer-diller, murder* or *Dracula;* a girl is a *chick, witch, drape, mouse, spook* or *bree;* face powder is *dazzle dust;* a shot of Coca-Cola is a *fizz;* a blind date is a *grab bag;* a hamburger is *ground horse;* a kiss is a *honey cooler;* money is *moola;* a sandwich is a *slab;* to sit down is to *swoon;* to dance wildly is to *get whacky;* an aggressive girl is a *vulture* or *wolverine;* a fat girl is a *five-by-five;* and a person disliked is a *specimen, herkle, prune, corpse, droop, fumb, gleep, cold cut, apple* or *sloop.*[7] When he encounters swing that really lifts him he says that he has been *sent down to the very bricks,* an experience comparable to suffering demoniacal possession or dying in the electric chair. This slang of the adolescent burgeons quickly, and just as quickly becomes as passé as a yearling egg. [Much of this jive lingo, modernized and intermingled with pseudo-intellectualisms, appears today in the patois of the beatnik.]

[*Beatnik* is said to have been coined by Herb Caen, a San Francisco newspaperman, in 1958, but one suspects antecedents in, and perhaps indebtedness to, Al Capp. *Beat,* in the sense of frustrated, has long been in the language, but the Beat Generation probably acquired it from the Negro *hipster* along with many other attitudes and cultural accouterments. However, the *beats,* both Negro and white, have given the *hipster* borrowings a mystic depth which is supposed to make up in inner intensity for any lack of communication, for to the *beat* any attempt at coherence is a sure indication of emotional death. Syntax is the sign of the *square,* whose world they have repudiated. *Beats* extend their introvert horizons largely by *digging,* by which they mean picking over their own psychic junkpiles in order to salvage some bits of emotional experience unattainable by *squares,* and one becomes truly *hip* only by *digging.* Once *digging* (and

---

[7] I take most of these from Jabberwocky and Jive, by Nancy Pepper; New York, 1943. See also The New Cab Calloway's Hepster's Dictionary, New York, 1938; new editions, 1939 and 1944 (said by *Variety,* June 22, 1938, to have been written by Ned Williams, a press agent); Hepcats' Jive Dictionary, by Lou Shelly, Derby, Conn., 1945, and Really the Blues, by Milton "Mezz" Mezzrow and Bernard Wolfe, New York, 1946, pp. 371-80. The last is extremely interesting and also authoritative, for Mezzrow has functioned successfully as both jazz musician and marijuana peddler.

other mystic experiences) has produced, one is ready to *go*, that is, to *flip*, which may be either *up* or *down* on either side of the manic-depressive cycle, and most *cats* consider it necessary to probe the mystic depths with the assistance of wine, a *joint of pot* or perchance a *roach* or two salvaged in a *tea pad*, heroin via the *main line* by means of the needle, *peyote* buttons and large infusions of invigorating jazz music—most of which are indulged in as continuously as money provided by the *chick* permits, but in any event indulged in with friends as part of the *Saturday night kicks*. The *beat makes it* in friendship or in love largely by *swinging*, a subtle exchange of the very rhythms of internal being. A *cool cat*—and all aspire to this temperature—is one who knows he has stumbled on the basic truths and eternal verities and is always well organized within, cautious but not fearful, reserved, inarticulate, and much of the time *stoned* on wine, *pot* (marijuana, from the Mexican Spanish *potiguaya*), heroin or an overdose of Zen Buddhism. Allen Ginsberg calls the beats "angel-headed *hipsters* burning for the ancient heavenly connection," but that *connection* is all too often a *cat* in *shades* who has a few *decks* or *caps* of *horse* stashed in the fly of his pants. This synthetic subculture has produced some literature (Ginsberg, Kerouac, Brossard and others) and their behavior has been analyzed by John Ciardi, Norman Mailer, John Cellon Holmes, David McReynolds and Ned Polsky, to mention a few. Most likely vocabulary survivals are *man, hip* (not new but durable; I published it in 1940 and ran it back as far as the 1890s), the widely applicable suffix *-'sville* as in *Square'sville, cool, flip, swing* or *swing with it* and *pad*.]

In view of the background of latter-day jive it is not surprising to find that some of its principal terms were originally of indecent significance. *Jazz* itself is one of them. Efforts have been made to derive it from the names of various Negro performers of years ago, but the plain fact is that *to jazz* has long had the meaning in American folk speech of to engage in sexual intercourse, and is so defined by many lexicographers, *e.g.*, Godfrey Irwin,[8] Allen Walker Read,[9] Berrey and Van den Bark,[1] Maurice H. Weseen[2] and "Justinian."[3] According to Clay Smith, an old-time traveling performer and song writer,[4] the transfer of the accompanying noun to the orgiastic music it now denominates occurred in the bawdy honky-tonks of the Western mining towns *c.* 1890. "If the truth were known about the origin of the word," he says, "it would never be mentioned in polite society." [Peter Tamony has done the soundest work so far on this word and its origin, with excellent documentation, in "Jazz: The Word,

---

[8] American Tramp and Underworld Slang, before cited, p. 109.

[9] Lexical Evidence from Folk Epigraphy in Western North America; Paris, 1935, p. 62.

[1] p. 342.

[2] p. 22.

[3] America Sexualis; Chicago, 1939.

[4] Where Is *Jazz* Leading America?, *Étude*, Sept. 1924, p. 395.

and Its Extension to Music." [5]] The first New York *jazz band* appeared in February 1917,[6] and by August 20 of the same year one was billed at the Holborn Empire in London. Three months later there was one playing at the Casino de Paris.

The decorous DAE does not list *jazz*, but the OED Supplement, while avoiding the original meaning of the term, shows that the musical meaning was well understood in England by 1918, and that *to jazz up* in the sense of to liven or brighten, was in vogue by 1920. [The DA cites *jazz* from 1917.] The DAE traces *ragtime*, the predecessor of *jazz*, to 1897, but it must be considerably older. The first *blues* were written by W. C. Handy, of Memphis, in 1911, [though the term is much older in folk speech, where it also has a strong sexual significance]. Some of the other terms of *jazz* addicts come from sources almost as blushful as that of *jazz* itself, *e.g., jitterbug, cat, jerk, hot, to blow one's top, I ain't coming* and *juke*.[7] Lorenzo D. Turner, the chief American authority on African loan words in Negro American, says that *juke* is a corruption of a Wolof term, *dzug* or *dzog*, meaning to lead a disorderly life, to misconduct oneself,[8] and that *juke house*, among the Negroes of the Southeast, means a house of ill repute. *Cat*, according to the OED, has been in use as a synonym for harlot since *c.* 1400. *Boogie-woogie*, according to Zora Neal Hurston, had the original significance, in the South, of secondary syphilis.[9] *Jitterbug*, according to Tamony, is a fan "whose reaction to swing is always physical." [1] The rest scarcely need glosses.[2]

---

[5] [*JAZZ 1: A Quarterly of American Music,* Oct. 1958, pp. 39–42. See also Tamony's Is Jive Linguistic Jabberwocky? in *JAZZ 3*, Summer 1959, pp. 235–9. According to Raven I. McDavid, Sr., of Greenville, S.C., the announcement, in 1919, of the first *jazz band* to play in Columbia, where he was then serving in the state legislature, inspired feelings of terror among the local Baptists such as what might have been aroused by a personal appearance of Yahweh. Until that time *jazz* had never been heard in the Palmetto State except as a verb meaning to copulate.]

[6] Slonimsky, before cited.

[7] The obscene significance of many words commonly found in *blues* texts, *e.g., jelly roll, shortnin' bread* and *easy rider*, was noted by Guy B. Johnson in Double Meaning in the Popular Negro Blues, *Journal of Abnormal and Social Psychology,* Vol. XXX, Apr.–June 1927, pp. 12–20.

[8] West African Survivals in the Vocabulary of Gullah, a paper read at the Dec. 1938 meeting of the American Dialect Society in New York. See *Dzug, Dzog, Dzuga, Jook, Juke,* by Will McGuire, *Time,* Jan. 29, 1940, p. 8.

[9] Story in Harlem Slang, *American Mercury,* July 1942, p. 84.

[1] *Jitterbug,* San Francisco *News-Letter and Wasp,* Mar. 3, 1939.

[2] "The association of marihuana with *hot jazz*," says *Time,* July 19, 1943, p. 56, "is no accident. The drug's power to slow the sense of time gives an improvisor the illusion that he has all the time in the world to conceive his next phrases. . . . Among *hot jazz* players there are few (except the confirmed lushes) who do not occasionally smoke." "Most addicts," adds Maurer in Marihuana Addicts and Their Lingo, *American Mercury,* Nov. 1946, p. 573, "want swing music while they are on a jag. . . . [Certain popular songs] reflect, in a very thinly disguised manner, the close relation of drug-aroused sexual desire to swing music."

[Currently the more advanced *jive* is found in profusion among Negro *cats*. A *blue farouq* is a real *dap swinger* who is *down with* jazz and its *jive*. A *prophet* plays (or *digs*) jazz with religious fervor. A *skrouk* is anything or anyone who is *insane* or wonderful; *skrouk* is a synthetic word with a pseudo-Near Eastern flavor and, like *blue farouq* and *prophet*, reflects the strong preoccupation with Islam which many *cats* now affect. (The spelling of both *farouq* and *skrouk* is speculative.) A *whirl daddy* is a *nutty wig* who *jives* expertly, *digs* jazz, dresses *dap* and probably has a *stone marten* or *chick* who almost always *brings it on home to Jerome*. Much of the *jive* of the *groovy cats* revolves around jazz, as a few examples will indicate.

[*Funk* is that *low-down*, deeply rhythmic quality which is the earmark of all good jazz. It also designates *progressive bop* containing a strong *blues* element which marks its Negro origin. A *funky* musician like Nat Adderley knows how to bring out *funk* and is called a *funkster*. *Funkosity* is a far-out brand of *funk* and a *funkie* is a devotee of *funk*. This is one of many terms with a derogatory or even obscene meaning used by *hipsters* in an adulatory sense, thus expressing their disdain for the taboos of *cubeular* society. A *gutty* or *guts* style of playing directs the rhythmic pulsations toward the solar plexus; the musician, like Erroll Garner, who *blows* some *guts* piano may make audible visceral grunts to help him keep just behind the beat: a *gutty* style is replete with a *blue tonality* and a *back beat*. *Fours* are a series of four-bar runs used by jazz soloists to make paralinguistic comments on what a previous soloist has just "said." For example, a drummer may do a take-off on a trombonist's phrase, or a trumpeter may satirize the pianist; on the *side* "Cherokee" Art Blakey and Clifford Brown demonstrate repartee in *fours*. The *flatted fifth* is a departure from "square" techniques in that the *flatted fifth* gets the emphasis, especially in *bop*, as illustrated by Miles Davis in the recording "Weird-O." *Hard bop* is *hard* because it hits you in the belly, and *hard boppers* are musicians who are expert at hitting you there—like Art Blakey and his Messengers. *Cool jazz* is mostly favored by white musicians today and is not popular with the Negro *cats* who are *cool*, though at least three Negro musicians (Miles Davis, Paul Quinichette and Lester Young) play *cool jazz* with plenty of *funk*.

[Sex and drugs are the main side interests of the true *cool cats*, and their drug lingo follows the general pattern. Several original sex-linked terms may be noted, however. Many *cats* have a *hustle* which they *push*— either a *chick on the blocks* (prostitute) or drugs. A *cat* who *hits on* or *sounds on* a chick is trying to seduce her. One who is *cock-strong* has been deprived of sex, and this is the source of much ridicule; sex, it is believed, depletes physical strength and hence many *cats* affect languorous movements, even to a limp handshake, in order to avoid being classed as *cock-strong*. *Trim* is sexual intercourse enjoyed by *bedding down*. A *cat* in hot pursuit of a *chick* or *fox* is said to *have his nose wide open*. A *chick's* clitoris is *the little man in the boat* or, among *butch lesbians* who are spectacularly endowed, a *spare tongue*. Sexual prowess spawns sexual legend, and among the celebrated heroes thereof we might note John the Conqueroo, a legendary *natural man* from Kansas City who, since Bo Diddley immortalized him on the *platter* "I'm a MAN," is often believed to be a real personage. There is also the evanescent Oolong Joe, the Grind-Boy, whose talents are catalogued, in retrospect so to speak, on the *side* "So Long, Oolong." *Jive talk* varies considerably from city to city, but manifests a surprising uniformity for an idiom that is almost exclusively spoken, not written.]

The American underworld is much less given than that of England to the banalities of what is called rhyming slang, e.g., *twist and twirl* for girl; *bowl of chalk* for talk; *bang and biff* for syphilis (*syph*); *by the peck* for neck; and *fleas and ants* for pants. Maurer, from whom I take these examples,[3] says that such forms are vastly more prevalent on the Pacific coast than in the East, but that the common belief that they are introduced there from Australia is erroneous. The Australians use them to some extent, but mainly only as loans from England. "There is a tendency," says Maurer, "to clip one term and allow it to carry the meaning, even though it no longer rhymes, as *twist*, a girl, from *twist and twirl*." Not a few such words and phrases were picked up in England by American soldiers during World War II, but they seem unlikely to survive. In 1943 many of them were used in a movie called "Mr. Lucky," but they apparently puzzled and displeased the American fans. They are most used today by the lower varieties of underworld denizens, and seem to be more prevalent in prison than outside, though a few, e.g., *twist*, have some currency and have been adopted by the *hepcats*. [In 1960 Julian Franklyn added to his sound studies of Cockney life a valuable "Dictionary of Rhyming Slang."[4]]

Campus slang,[5] once a chief source of popular neologisms, has been swamped in recent years by those welling up from the underworld, and

[3] "Australian" Rhyming Argot in the American Underworld (with Sidney J. Baker), *AS*, Vol. XIX, Oct. 1944, pp. 183–95; Rhyming Underworld Slang, *American Mercury*, Oct. 1946, pp. 473–9.

[4] [London, 1960.]

[5] Many reports on the campus vocabulary, new and old, are listed by Burke, pp. 130–5. The best recent work on campus slang in England is Public School Slang, by Morris Marples; London, 1940. The German authority is Deutsche Studentensprache, by F. Klug; Strassburg, 1895. For Scandinavia there is Skolpojks ock Studentslang, by R. Berg, *Svenska Låndmalen*, No. 8, 1900.

the grove of Academe borrows more from the barbarians than it offers them.· What passed for collegiate speech formerly had a considerable vogue in the movies, but in 1943 a war correspondent in Hollywood was reporting that it had "suddenly and unaccountably gone into a slump."[6] I should add that he said in the same dispatch that the slang of the jitterbugs was also beginning to lose ground. This last may have been a bit premature, for jive in its various forms is still going strong.

In the days of the Federal Writers' Project in New York it planned a "Lexicon of Trade Jargon" that promised to be very useful, but when the project blew up the manuscript was still incomplete, and since then it has reposed, unpublished, in the Library of Congress.[7] One must regret that it was never finished, for the argots of the trades contain many picturesque terms,[8] and the orthodox dictionaries of slang give them only the most cursory notice. Inasmuch as an adequate account of them would fill a volume several times as large as the present one, we can only glance at some characteristic specimens. The argot of railroad men may well come first, for it is extraordinarily extensive, has provided the common vocabulary with many familiar phrases—*e.g.*, *to jump the track* and *asleep at the switch*—and in part descends from the much older argots of coaching and the sailing ships.

In its terms for various functionaries and objects it is largely derisory. A locomotive engineer is a *hogger, hog head, hog jockey, hog mauler,*[9] *grunt* or *eagle-eye;* a fireman is an *ash cat, ash eater, blackie, diamond cracker, bake head, tallow pot, fire boy, bell ringer, dust raiser, soda jerker, coal heaver* or *smoke;* a conductor is a *big ox, big O, skipper, brains, boss, captain, drum, grabber* (passenger service) or *king* (freight); a brakeman is a *shack, hind hook, club winder* or *groundhog* (freight) or a *thin skin, baby lifter* or *dude wrangler* (passenger); a section hand is a *donkey, gandy dancer, jerry, snipe* or *terrier;* the foreman of a section gang is a *king snipe;* a flagman is a *bookkeeper;* a switchman is a *yard goose;* a yardmaster is a *ringmaster, dinger* or *bull goose;* a stationmaster is an *ornament;* a trainmaster is a *master mind;* a master mechanic is a *master maniac;* a train dispatcher is a *detainer* or *delayer;* a car re-

---

[6] Hollywood, by Robin Coons, in various papers of Oct. 16.

[7] For a while it seemed to be lost altogether, and not until after a long search did I find it in the Library, and borrow it through the courtesy of Dr. Luther H. Evans, then chief assistant librarian.

[8] "The American skilled craftsman," said Ernest A. Dewey in *Labor Today*, Sept. 1941, p. 19, "speaks two languages —his native tongue and the language of his trade. Sometimes humorous, always odd to the uninitiated ear, are the strange terms, titles and phrases he applies to the tools, processes and machinery he uses in his work. Over a period of years these technical and derisive terms have developed into a craft language as distinctive to his trade as the skill in his practised hands."

[9] From *hog*, one of the names for a steam freight locomotive.

pairer is a *cherry picker, tonk* or *car knocker;* an engine wiper is a *dishwasher;* a roundhouse machinist is a *chambermaid, nut splitter, -buster* or *-cracker,* or *kettle mender;* a boilermaker is an *iron skull;* a repairer of air brakes is an *air monkey;* a railroad policeman is an *egg;* a clerk is a *paperweight* or *shiny pants;* a Pullman porter is a *bedbug;* an official is a *brass collar* or *main pin;* a new employee is a *Casey;* one who is unpopular is a *scissorbill* or *scissor;* and one who is solicitous for the company's interest is a *stockholder.* A locomotive is a *hog, pig, mill, calliope, smoker, jack* or *pot* or (if small) a *coffeepot, kettle, peanut roaster* or *dinky;* a caboose is a *bouncer, shack, chariot, bedhouse, crib, cage, cracker box, crumb box, crummy, louse cage, doghouse, glory wagon, go-cart, monkey wagon, palace, pavilion, shelter house, buggy, hack, van, parlor, way car, shanty, hearse, library, saloon, cook shack, clown wagon* or *zoo;* [1] a refrigerator car is a *reefer, reef* or *freezer;* a tank car is a *can* or *oiler;* a cattle car is a *cow cage* or *cow crate;* a sleeping car is a *snoozer;* a locomotive tender is a *tank;* passenger cars are *cushions;* and a private car is a *drone cage.* [2] [With the demise of steam and the institution of diesels, the lingo is changing also.]

Pullman porters, cooks and waiters have an argot of their own, *e.g., alarm clock,* a passenger who snores loudly; *battleship,* an old-fashioned Pullman with sixteen sections and no private rooms; *to buck the bronco,* to sit up all night because no berths are vacant; *eye drops,* cinders; *to go upstairs,* to carry food from the diner to the day coaches; *nailer,* a railroad detective; *rubber-tired,* said of a crack express train; *snake,* a cheap tipper; *tin can,* a buffet car; and *turtle,* a dishwasher. [3] Trolley crews, in the days of their glory, had their jargon, too, *e.g., boat* for a trolley car, *horse* for a motorman, *poorbox* for a fare box, *stick* for a trolley pole and *Sunday* for any day of light traffic, [4] but it has faded out with their art

---

[1] On the Pennsylvania Railroad a caboose is known officially as a *cabin car.*

[2] I take most of the above and those following from A Glossary of Railroad Terms, by W. F. Cottrell and H. C. Montgomery, *AS,* Vol. XVIII, Oct. 1943, pp. 161–70, but have also borrowed from Lingo of the Rails, by Freeman H. Hubbard, *Railroad Magazine,* Apr. 1940, pp. 32–55; Railroad Avenue by the same, New York, 1945; Highball, by Lucius Beebe, New York, 1945; Glossary of Railroad Slang, *Photography,* Jan. 1946, p. 149; The Railroader, by W. F. Cottrell, Palo Alto, Cal., 1940, pp. 118–39; The Engineer Explains It, by Frank Shippy, *The Saturday Evening Post,* Apr. 15, 1939, p. 26; Lingo of the Line, *Tracks,* June 1945, pp. 28–31; Rail-

road Stuff, by Stephen J. Lynch, *Writer's Digest,* Apr. 1942, pp. 30–2; Railroaders Have a Word for It, by Doris McFerran, *American Mercury,* June 1942, pp. 739–42; and The Rails Have a Word for It, by Lyman Anson and Clifford Funkhouser, *The Saturday Evening Post,* June 13, 1942, p. 27. Earlier sources are listed in Burke, p. 110. I am also indebted to Paul F. Laning, Phil Hamilton, James F. Rabbitt, Phil Stong, Fred Hamann, J. H. Fountain and Henry B. Brainerd.

[3] I take these from the Lexicon of Trade Jargon, before cited.

[4] These come from the same Lexicon of Trade Jargon. The trolley car gave us *to slip one's trolley.*

and mystery. So has that of the telegraphers, and for the same reason,[5] though some of it is preserved by radio operators. In the Golden Age of the craft its aristocrats were the newspaper telegraphers, who not only had to be fast and accurate at the Morse Code but also had to master the Phillips Code, which changed almost from day to day.[6] The old-time operators all suffered from *glass arm*, a variety of writers' cramp, but it was cured for the senders when someone invented the *bug*, a semi-automatic key which worked sideways instead of up and down, and for the receivers on the advent of the *mill, i.e.,* the typewriter, [and later the *teletypewriter*]. An unskilled operator was a *lid, ham, bum* or *plug*. To send a message at high speed was to *paste* the receiving operator, who was said to be *burnt up* or to *go under the table*. A wire to a remote place was a *monkey wire*. At the end of his shift or of the day's or night's work the sender sent *30*.[7] His ordinary symbol of personal greeting to a colleague was *73*.[8] The modern automatic sending machine is an *iron horse*, the receiver is a *printer* and the girls who paste its tape messages on delivery forms are *paperhangers*. Messenger boys and linemen also have their jargon. To the former a delivery to a distant address is a *breezer* and they themselves are *trotters*, though they seldom go on foot. To the latter a pole is a *stick*, cross arms are *toothpicks*, an insulator is a *bottle*, digging tools are *knives and forks*, climbing spurs are *hooks*, a cant hook is a *log wrench* or *mooley cow*, a safety belt is a *scared strap*, a transformer is a *pot*, to fall from a pole is to *burn the stick*, and an inexperienced workman is a *grunt*.[9]

---

[5] Said R. E. L. Russell in Twilight Falling on Men of Morse, Baltimore *Sunday Sun*, Aug. 22, 1943: "Little new blood is coming into the trade, for it has long been slowly dying." I am indebted to Mr. Russell, an old newspaper colleague and a famous telegrapher in his day, for help with what follows.

[6] It was launched by Walter P. Phillips, of the Associated Press, in 1876. Every word or phrase in daily newspaper use was abbreviated, *e.g., gb*, Great Britain; *ik*, instantly killed; *td*, Treasury Department; *ac*, and company; *ancm*, announcement; *elcud*, electrocuted; *fapid*, filed a petition in bankruptcy; *hur*, House of Representatives; *pips*, Philippines; *twm*, tomorrow morning; and *scotus*, Supreme Court of the United States. In the 1925 edition of the Phillips Code there were 2,500 such abbreviations, and a new one was added whenever a new personality or idea began to appear in the news. Carl A. Nelson, of the *Telegraphy and Tele-*

phone Age, tells me that at the start the operators took down the code words as received, and newspaper editors had to write in their meaning, but that after the typewriter came in operators did the expanding. The code has now been adapted for use with the teletype. See Phillips Code Today, *Telegraph and Telephone Age*, Apr. 1939.

[7] Its origin is discussed in *American Notes and Queries*, Vol. I, July 1941, p. 58, and Jan. 1942, p. 156; in *Editor and Publisher*, May 4, 1940, p. 36, and in the Chicago *Tribune*, Jan. 13, 1940, p. 10, Jan. 15, p. 10, and Jan. 16, p. 10.

[8] *73*: Origin of the Symbol, Chicago *Tribune*, May 3, 1941, p. 12. See also Lingo of the Telegraph Operators, by Minnie Swan Mitchell, *AS*, Vol. XII, Apr. 1937, pp. 154-5, and Some Telegraphers' Terms, by Hervey Brackbill, *AS*, Vol. IV, Apr. 1929, pp. 287-90.

[9] Lineman's English, by Charles P. Loomis, *AS*, Vol. I, Sept. 1926, pp. 659-60, and The Lingo of Railroad Linemen,

Many of these are also used by telephone and power linemen, but both of the latter have some terms of their own. To the telephone men insulation on a wire is *bark*, a pole dipped in creosote is a *black jack* or *black diamond*, a transformer is a *kettle* or *stove*, a service truck is a *loop wagon*, a safety belt is a *crupper*, a cross arm is a *slat*, a lineman is a *stump jumper* or *hiker* or *Joe Hooks*, a foreman is a *gaffer* or *brains*, a power lineman is a *hot monkey*, the company is *Maw Bell*, to get an electric shock is to be *bit* or *burned* and to be electrocuted is to be *crossed up*. A lineman's helper or other workman who never leaves the ground is a *goofer, gopher,*[1] *groundhog, grunt, click* or *squeak*. The cry of warning when anything drops from a pole is *Headache!*[2] Two terms in use by all electricians, *juice* and *live wire*, long since entered the general vocabulary.

With the movement of communications toward radio and of transport toward gasoline there appeared some new and pungent argots, *e.g.,* those of the truckmen and taxi drivers. Not a few terms of the former are borrowed from older crafts, *e.g., bull o' the woods*, a company supervisor, from the lumbermen, and *reefer*, a refrigerator, and *highballing*, running at high speed, from the railroad men. Of the more original words and phrases of the truckmen we have:[3]

Balloon, or load of wind. A light, bulky cargo.
Bareback, or bobtail. A tractor without a trailer.
Dog. A motor vehicle inspector.

---

by D. V. Snapp, *AS*, Vol. XIII, Feb. 1938, pp. 70–1.
[1] *Go f'r this* or *go f'r that.*
[2] These come from The Vernacular of the Lineman, by Don Wolverton, *Southern Telephone News*, June 1930, pp. 13–14; Telephone Shop Talk, by Edna L. Waldo, *Writer's Digest*, May 1927, pp. 407–9; Telephone Workers' Jargon, by Jean Dickinson, *AS*, Vol. XVI, Apr. 1941, p. 156; and Lexicon of Trade Jargon. I am also indebted to Edwin R. Austin, Fred Hamann, Edward L. Bernays and J. Earle Miller.
[3] Most of these come from Truck Drivers' Lingo, *Commercial Car Journal*, Mar. 1938, pp. 18–19. Additions are from the Lexicon of Trade Jargon, and from Taxi-Cab Language, *Christian Science Monitor*, May 27, 1940, p. 14; Truck Drivers Have a Word for It, by Doris McFerran, *American Mercury*, Apr. 1941, pp. 459–62; Knights of the Line, by James H. Street, New York *World-Telegram*, Apr. 8, 9 and 10, 1937; and

Truck Driver Lingo, by Bernard H. Porter, *AS*, Vol. XVII, Apr. 1942, pp. 102–5. I am also indebted to Robert J. Icks, of Stevens Point, Wis. The drivers of moving vans use some of these terms, but have many others of their own, *e.g., bagger*, a flight of stairs (*three-bagger*: three flights); *chowder*, small miscellaneous articles; *climber*, a house without an elevator; *doll's house*, a penthouse; *fiddle*, a grand piano; *heel*, the heavier end of a large piece of furniture; *lap*, a round trip from van to apartment; *mountain climber*, a moving man; *mousetrap*, a house or apartment with narrow doors; *sweetheart* or *honey*, an object so large that it must be taken through a window with block and tackle; *Tammany Hall*, a poorly furnished home; and *washboard*, a small piano. I take these from the Lexicon of Trade Jargon; Moving Words, New York *Evening Journal*, Sept. 29, 1936; and Farmer's Market, by Fred Beck, Los Angeles *Times*, Jan. 5, 1946.

Gypsy. An independent truckman, usually with but one truck.

Hack hand, juice jockey, spinner, or tooler. A driver.

Jesse James. A police magistrate.

Kidney buster. A hard-riding truck.

Load of postholes. No cargo.

Soft-coal burner. A diesel truck.

Sweatshop. A bullet-proof cab with bad ventilation.

The lingo of taxi and bus drivers differs a bit from city to city, but some of its terms seem to run through the country. The lingo of deep-sea sailors (including whalers and fisherman) has produced so large and so accessible a literature [4] that there is no need to deal with it here. Many of its terms have got into the common speech and are familiar to everyone, *e.g., aboveboard, three sheets in the wind, Davy Jones' locker, on the beach, bilge* (buncombe), *to pipe down, to be taken aback, plain* (originally *plane*) *sailing, shipshape, half-seas over, to give a wide berth to, to run afoul of, to keel over* and *to stand by.*[5] Coastwise, lake and river mariners base their talk upon the lingo of the deep sea, but the pseudonym of Samuel L. Clemens is a sufficient reminder that they also have some terms of their own.[6] The argot of canalboatmen is now almost forgotten, but in its day it showed some picturesque terms, mainly borrowed from the speech of the yokels along the way.[7] The men who load and unload ships are still a large and rambunctious fraternity, and their talk bristles with words and phrases unintelligible to the outsider,[8] as does that of the men who build and service ships.[9]

The automobile and the plane have both brought in large vocabularies

---

[4] Nearly all of it in English before 1939 is listed in Burke, pp. 105–8.

[5] Many more are listed in Sea Language Comes Ashore, by Joanna Carver Colcord; New York, 1945.

[6] The calls of the leadsmen on the Mississippi in its palmy days were in feet up to nine feet and in fathoms after that. *Mark twain* was two fathoms, or 12 feet. *Half twain* was two fathoms and a half, or 15 feet. On May 20, 1941, Albert K. Dawson, of the American Express Company, issued an interview with Captain Tom Greene, of the *Gordon C. Greene,* saying that these calls were then still in use on the Mississippi and its tributaries.

[7] Erie Canal Colloquial Expressions, by Jason Almus Russell, *AS,* Vol. VI, Dec. 1930, pp. 97–100; Some Quotations Supplementing the DAE, by Elliott V. K.

Dobbie, *AS,* Vol. XXI, Dec. 1946, pp. 305–7; Snubbin' Thro' Jersey, by F. Hopkinson Smith and J. B. Millet, *Century Magazine,* Aug. 1887, pp. 483–96.

[8] Its more seemly vocabulary is listed in A Port Dictionary of Technical Terms, published by the American Association of Port Authorities; New Orleans, 1940. See also Port Terminal Operation, by Eugene H. Lederer, New York, 1943; and Longshoreman's Lingo, by John Alfred Knoetgen, *Encore,* Sept.-Oct. 1944, pp. 336–8, and the Lexicon of Trade Jargon.

[9] See Shipyard Terms of the Northwest, 1944 Style, by Hal Babbitt, *AS,* Vol. XIX, Oct. 1944, pp. 230–2; Navy Yard Talk, by Jack G. Arbolino, *AS,* Vol. XVII, Dec. 1942, pp. 279–80; and the Lexicon of Trade Jargon.

of new terms. Many of those introduced by the former have got into the common speech, *e.g., to park, back-seat driver, road hog, to step on the gas, garage, detour, filling station, gas, chauffeur, streamlined, joyride, hit-and-run, jaywalker, fender, speed cop, traffic light, motel* (formerly *tourist camp*), *safety zone* and *to thumb a ride,* the meanings of which are generally known, but there are others that remain the private property of the men working in the automobile plants and of those who sell or repair cars. [Likewise, the present-day *hot-rodders* have developed an extensive technical vocabulary which is working out into general usage, mostly on the level of slang.]

Jalopy is defined by the New Practical Standard Dictionary (1946) as a "decrepit automobile or airplane" and marked "origin obscure." Whether it arose among the airmen or the automobile dealers I do not know, nor am I sure about the spelling, for it has appeared variously as *jalopy, jallopy, jaloppy, jollopy, jaloopy, jalupie* and *julappi.* Wentworth says that it was in oral use *c.* 1925, but his first printed example is dated 1934. The Winston Dictionary says that it was used by sports writers in 1924, in the form *julappi.*[1] [While still a durable term, it is yielding to numerous recent synonyms from the teen-age group.]

The argot of aviators has been compiled in a workmanlike manner by Fred Hamann.[2] "Aviation," he says, "is less than half a century old, yet no other industry has originated a language as rich in slang, argot, colloquialisms and colorful terms." Many of them are already familiar to everyone, *e.g., to zoom, to bail out, on the beam, to fly blind, air pocket, blimp, low* (or *high*) *ceiling, to hedge-hop, to nose-dive* and *tail spin.* The airmen, like the railroad men, use many derisory terms in speaking of themselves and their apparatus, *e.g., truck driver, chauffeur* or *throttle jockey* for a pilot; *paddlefoot, blisterfoot, ground-gripper* or *dust eater* for a member of the ground crew; *clerk* or *pencil pusher* for a navigator; *stooge* or *kid* for a co-pilot; *barrel* or *can* for an engine cylinder; *pants slapper, blower, windmill, butter paddle, club* or *fan* for a propeller and *hut, greenhouse* or *pulpit* for a cockpit. Not a few of these terms show *Galgenhumor, e.g., meat wagon* for an ambulance, *first man down* for a flyer in trouble whose parachute doesn't open and *funeral glide* for a landing out of control. Some are also more or less indecent, *e.g., joy stick* for the pilot's control stick and *condom* for a wind cone. The airmen have borrowed heavily from the argot of sailors, *e.g., to trim ship, logbook,*

---

[1] Current English Forum, *CE,* Vol. IV, Apr. 1943, p. 439. [Professor Lomas Barrett, a specialist in Latin-American Spanish at Washington and Lee University, passes the information on to the editors that *jalopy* comes from a Spanish dialect word meaning "wreck," though he does not supply the Spanish word.]

[2] Air Words; Seattle, 1946.

tail wind and *rigger* (applied to a parachute repairer), and also from that of railroad men, *e.g.*, *hoghead* (the manager of an airport); that of lumbermen, *e.g.*, *haywire;* that of actors, *e.g.*, *barnstormer;* that of automobile drivers, *e.g.*, *crate, flivver* and *hot* (fast); and that of hoboes, *e.g.*, *hump* (a mountain). The workers in airplane plants use many of these terms also, and their vocabulary is otherwise full of the terms in common use in all metalworking plants, but they also have some that I have not found elsewhere, *e.g.*, *blue ox*, a bombsight; *bones*, the skeleton of an airplane fuselage (body); *Buck Rogers*, a rivet gun; *bug chaser*, an inspector; *sewing machine*, an automatic riveter or welder; *squawk*, an inspection; and *fisterris* and *kajody*, any indefinite object.[3]

[The significant changes taking place in the slang of aviation can be clearly seen by comparing Thomas A. Dickinson's "The Aeronautical Dictionary" (1945) with Woodford A. Heflin's "The United States Air Force Dictionary" (1956) and his later "Aerospace Glossary." One interesting effect of Heflin's work is that large blocks of graphic air-force slang have been shifted bodily into standard American English after they have been officially adopted as technical terminology by the Air Force. A few of the new terms are *scream downhill*, to dive a plane; *green run*, the initial run made in a new plane or with a new engine; *eggs*, bombs (an old term, still in very active use but not listed); *modoc*, a would-be pilot; *ghost*, an unwanted echo on a radar screen; *above*, radio communication indicating a plane above you; *bandits above*, which now tends to replace the longer and more cumbersome series of communications used to locate enemy planes, for jet combat takes place at very high speed; *drop it!*, meaning do not attack, or cease attacking; *scramble*, to get off the ground fully prepared for combat; *flameout*, a jet-engine failure; *blast*, to take off; *bingo*, short of fuel or down to a minimum; *brain bucket*, a crash helmet; *auger in*, to crash.]

Radio is even younger than the airplane, but its impact upon American life has been terrific, and so long ago as 1937 a writer on its vocabulary was calling it the *fifth estate*.[4] That vocabulary is now large, but much of it is of very recent date. The word *radio* itself did not come into general use in the United States until *c.* 1920, and the English still seem to prefer *wireless*. Until the death of the Hon. Alfred E. Smith on October 4, 1944, there lingered some doubt among American fans as to whether the word should be pronounced *ray-dio* or *rad-dio*, and the learned still disagree about the conjugation of *to broadcast*. Many of the terms in use

---

[3] There are many lexicons of air argot, but Hamann's, before cited, is the best. The earlier literature is listed by Burke, p. 109. An Encyclopedic Aviation Dictionary, by Charles A. Zweng, Los Angeles, 1944, defines mainly technical terms.

[4] The Fifth Estate Vocabulary, by Julian T. Bentley, *AS*, Vol. XII, Apr. 1937, pp. 100–2.

in the studios are loans from the stage, *e.g.,* *to ad lib*, *bit* (a small part), *blue* (indecent), *cue*, *to double*, *flack* (a press agent), *gag*, *grip* (a stage carpenter), *emcee*, *props* and *turkey*, and others come from the argot of the movie lots or the jazz bands, *e.g.,* *canary*, *continuity*, *corny*, *88*, *flesh peddler* (a talent agent), *groan box*, *longhair*, *schmalz*, *script* and *who-dunit*.[5]

The meaning of many radio terms is now familiar to every American, *e.g.,* *web*, *sponsor*, *sustaining program*, *soap opera*, *to dial*, *plug*, *platter*, *on the air*, *commercial*, *network*, *canned music* and *static*. Television, sometimes called *video*, has introduced its own, *e.g.,* *blizzard head*, a blonde; *flag* or *gobo*, a screen to shade the camera; *ghost*, an unwanted secondary image; *gismo* or *gizmo*, any contrivance which yet lacks a name; *hot light*, a concentrated light; *inky*, an incandescent light; *gilding*, performers' make-up; *womp*, a sudden flare-up of light on the receiving screen; *noise*, spots or a pattern on the picture; *model*, to move gracefully before the camera, as in a fashion show; *roll it*, the cue to start work; and *stretch*, to stall for time.[6]

[Radio slang has changed little in recent years, owing to its eclipse by television, but there are a few new terms, including *sleeper*, a record that hangs fire and then becomes popular; *bust out*, said of a record that sells heavily; *session*, the recording of a piece of music for sale; *dub session*, a preliminary demonstration tape made to determine whether or not a *session* should be held. The fine old term *payola* has vanished under FCC censure, but the practice continues to some extent. A promoter may ask, "Does he *swing on it?*" or "Is he *on the take?*" to find

---

[5] See Radio Alphabet: A Glossary of Radio Terms, ed. by Gilbert Seldes, Paul Hollister and a dozen others and published by the Columbia Broadcasting System in 1946. The early authorities are listed in Burke, p. 122. Other works worth consulting are Wireline Webster, issued by the Mutual Broadcasting System, June 1945; Glossary of Commercial Terms, by J. J. Weed, in *Variety* Radio Directory, 1937–8, New York, 1937, pp. 353–8; Some Radio Terms, by John S. Carlile, *Fortune*, May 1938, p. 54; Radio Vocabulary, by S. Stephenson Smith, *QJS*, Vol. XXXVIII, Feb. 1942, pp. 1–7; Radio Jargon, by William White, *Words*, Dec. 1941, pp. 97–101; A Study of the Vocabulary of Radio, by Donald E. Hargis, *Speech Monographs*, XII, 1945, pp. 77–87; Dictionary of Radio Terms, Chicago, 1940; Radio Slanguage, by K. W. Strong, *Better English*, Mar. 1940, pp. 118–19; and Radio Has a Word

for It, by Doris McFerran, *American Mercury*, Nov. 1941, pp. 578–81. The gestures used in radio studios (speaking, of course, is forbidden) are illustrated in Radio Alphabet, above cited, and described in Lexicon of Trade Jargon, Vol. III.

[6] These come from Television Talk, issued by the National Broadcasting Company in 1946. See also The Words, *The New Yorker*, Dec. 3, 1938, p. 20. The vocabulary of radar is in Radar Nomenclature, *AS*, Vol. X, Dec. 1945, pp. 309–10; Radar Language, *Newsweek*, Sept. 10, 1945, p. 92; and Radar, issued by the British Information Services, New York, 1945. That of amateur radio operators, or *hams*, is in Ham Slang, by R. D. Bass, *Words*, Dec. 1938, pp. 138–9, and Jan. 1939, pp. 10–12; and Ham Lingo, by Marion Fry, *AS*, Vol. V, Oct. 1929, pp. 45–9.

out if a disc jockey will take money for promoting a record or, as the disc jockeys say, *swing for bread*. Most of the lively talk of radio stems from colorful *D.J.'s*, who often borrow from the *cool cats*.

[In television we might note *mark it* and *strike it*, directions to stage hands to chalk out the position for scenery and then rub out the mark for the next set—a phrase used by Steve Allen in the title of his autobiography to suggest the ephemeral nature of the TV show. There are the director's *ready to take!* or *ready to take, one, stand by two*, and *take!* as directions to the camera men; *take!* indicates that camera one is on the air while camera two is ready to operate as needed. *Roll!* tells the engineer to turn on the projector, and *roll the film!* means that in three seconds the film *cuts in*. From the movies TV has adopted *pan*, to swing the camera horizontally, and *tilt*, to move it vertically. The *board* is the control room where shows (both *live* and *taped*) are monitored and edited to go on the air. *Dolly in!* and *dolly out!* mean to move the boom toward or away from the subject, while *truck!* directs the camera man to move the camera, tripod, etc., to any desired position. There is also a system of hand signals to indicate time and speed, and a continuous interchange of salty language between the control room and the camera men and boom men (doubtless an antidote for the honeyed suavity of the announcers), but this is difficult to study since it is carried on in whispers over a closed communication system. There is not much new in TV lingo, largely because new language burgeons in this area with new equipment and new techniques. These have not changed basically, in most local TV stations, in the past fifteen years, but as video tape, color TV and other as yet unpublicized wonders become generally used, new slang (or, more probably, technical jargon) may spread with them.]

Every other trade, profession, sport and hobby has its argot, and it would be impossible to give specimens of all of them. Even such strange folk as aquarium attendants, apple pickers, dog breeders, philatelists and social workers talk among themselves in terms unintelligible to the outsider. The best I can do here is to list those which I know have been studied, in alphabetical order: Advertising Agents, Aquarists, Apple Pickers, Architects, Bakers, Barbers, Bartenders, Baseball Players, Beauticians, Booksellers, Brewery Workers, Cannery Workers, Carpenters, Cattlemen, Chautauquans,[7] Clergymen, Cock Fighters,[8] Corset Makers, Crapshooters.

---

[7] The itinerant chautauqua is now extinct, though the Mother Church, established in 1874 at Chautauqua, N.Y., still exists. Many of the old-time chautauquans have become radio crooners or public jobholders.

[8] [Though cock fighting is illegal, there exists a wide underground frater-

Dairymen, Department-Store Salespeople, Distillery Workers, Dog Breeders, Farmers, Firemen, Fishermen, Food Dispensers, Furniture Workers, Garbage Men, Garment Workers, Glassblowers, Glaziers, Golfers, Hospital Attendants, Hotel Workers, House Painters, House Wreckers, Installment-House Salesmen, Laundrymen, Leather Workers, Loggers, Machinists, Miners (Coal), Miners (Metal), Oilfield Workers, Packinghouse Workers, Photographers, Plasterers, Plumbers and Steamfitters, Post-Office Workers, Potters, Pugilists, Race-Track Followers, Rubber Workers.

Sandhogs, Sheepmen, Shoe Clerks, Shoemakers, Soda Jerkers, Steel Workers, Stockbrokers, Stonecutters, Structural Iron Workers, Tanners, Textile Workers, Tobacco Growers, Union Men in General.

World War II, though it threw off an enormous number of what, to newspaper lexicographers, appeared to be neologisms, actually produced few that were really new, and not many of them have stuck. [Probably the largest number were new technical terms which never reached the general public.] Some of the most familiar, *e.g.*, *foxhole*, *brass hat*, *M.P.*[9] and *black market*, were legacies from World War I, and others went back to earlier wars, including the Civil War, *e.g.*, *dog tag*, *K.P.*, *a.w.o.l.*, *hike*, *pup tent*, *gook*,[1] *belly robber*, *to bust* (to reduce in rank), *commando* (South African War).[2] What differentiated World War II from all others in history, aside from the curious fact that it produced no popular hero and no song, was the enormous number of newspaper correspondents who followed its operations, and the even greater number of press agents who served its *brass*. Many of these literati were aspirants to the ermine of Walter Winchell, and as a result they adorned the daily history of the war with multitudinous bright inventions, but the actual soldier, like his predecessors of the past, limited his slang to a series of derisive names for the things he had to do and endure, and to the ancient stock of profanity and obscenity. All the more observant and intelligent veterans that I have consulted tell me that a few four-letter words were put to excessively heavy service. One of them, beginning with *f*, became an almost universal verb, and with *-ing* added, a universal adjective; another, beginning with *s*, ran a close second to it. The former penetrated to the highest levels, and was the essence of one of the few really good coinages of the war, to wit, *snafu*, meaning, according to Colonel Elbridge Colby, the leading authority on Army

---

nity of *cockers*, and *cocking mains* are still widely attended throughout the entire United States.]

[9] Called a *red cap* by the English.

[1] Probably a derivative of *goo-goo* and *gu-gu*, early military names for a Filipino.

[2] The Word *Commando*, by Elliott V. K. Dobbie, *AS*, Vol. XIX, Apr. 1944, pp. 81–90.

speech, "the confusion that comes from sudden changes in orders." [3] Colby says that it is an abbreviation of "situation normal, all *foozled* up," and other lexicographers have substituted *fouled* for *foozled*, but the word really in mind was something else again.[4] Nor were the two taboo terms mentioned the only ones in constant use. The verb in the last clause of I Samuel xxv, 22, also had a heavy play [5] and so did the ancient Germanic word for backside.[6] Nor were their lesser analogues forgotten.[7]

The precise provenance of most of the terms that issued from the war is dark and disputed. Where, how and at whose hands *GI* came into use is not known. Colby, before cited, says that in World War I, and perhaps before, the initials stood for *galvanized iron*, as in *GI* (ash)*can* and *GI bucket*, but that they were transferred early in World War II to *general issue*, as in *GI soap*, *GI haircut* and *GI food*. [Actually the transfer took place in the 1920s.] All such things were disesteemed by

---

[3] Army Talk; 2nd ed., Princeton, N.J., 1943, p. 230.

[4] *Snafu* (pronounced as a word) produced a numerous progeny, *e.g.*, *susfu*, situation unchanged: still *fu; fubar, fu* beyond all recognition; *janfu*, joint Army and Navy *fu;* and *tarfu*, things are really *fu;* but Jeffrey A. Fleece says in Words in -*fu, AS*, Vol. XXI, Feb. 1946, pp. 70–2, that none of them ever "really became part of Army language." Morroe Berger, in Army Language, *AS*, Vol. XX, Dec. 1945, p. 262, adds *G.F.U.*, a soldier who never does anything correctly; *F.O.*, to avoid work; and various others. In *F.O.*, *off* takes the place of the usual *up*.

[5] It came originally from the French, and the OED says that it got into English as a euphemism. It is to be found in nearly all the standard writers before the Eighteenth Century.

[6] Pronounced *arse* in England, but *ass* in this country. It has cognates in all the Germanic languages. It lies defectively hidden in *BAM*, the Navy name for a lady marine, *i.e., Broad-assed marine*. During the war a naval officer of rank and fancy suggested that *leatherteat* be substituted, but this stroke of genius was frowned upon by the High Command. The lady marines were known officially as the *Women's Reserve of the Marine Corps*. Their heroic record is given in the *Congressional Record*, Dec. 18, 1945, pp. A6042–43. That of their comrades-in-arms, the *WAVES* of the Navy proper, is in the same, Feb. 11, 1946, p. A685. That of the *SPARS*, who fought with

the Coast Guard, is in the same, Jan. 25, 1946, pp. A237–38. *SPARS* was coined by the commander of the outfit, Captain Dorothy G. Stratton. She got it from the Coast Guard motto, *Semper paratus*, Always ready.

[7] Says Frederick Elkin in the Soldier's Language, *American Journal of Sociology*, Vol. XLI, Mar. 1946, pp. 414–22: "Such terms, used by themselves or in combination phrases, are in almost every sentence a soldier says." Elkin adds that "this constant and crude use of obscenity" often shocks recruits, but that "with constant exposure the shock lessens," and "eventually, to a greater or lesser degree, practically all soldiers adopt it. . . . Violating the taboos of language gives feelings of courage and freedom, . . . strength and virility." In the same issue of the same journal, p. 411, Henry Elkin (not the same writer), says: "By pronouncing those 'dirty words,' which he never dared to utter in the presence of Mom or his old-maid schoolteachers, the GI symbolically throws off the shackles of the matriarchy in which he grew up." Testimony to their prevalence in the Army is to be found in many other discussions of soldiers' argot, *e.g.*, Warriors' Slang, by Robert L. Wheeler, Providence (R.I.) *Sunday Journal*, Feb. 4, 1945, Section VI, p. 1; American Army Speech in the European Theatre, by Joseph W. Bishop, Jr., *AS*, Vol. XXI, Dec. 1946, pp. 241–52; and War and the Language, by David W. Maurer, *The New Republic*, Vol. CXIII, Dec. 27, 1945.

the soldier, mainly because they were purely utilitarian and hence unattractive, so he presently began to transfer the letters, metaphorically, to other things that he didn't admire, *e.g.,* *GI hop* or *struggle*, a dance at an Army post; *GI girl*, a female brought in to dance wih him; *GI war*, maneuvers; *GI sky pilot*, a chaplain; *GI lemonade*, water; and so on. These terms soon appeared numerously in *Yank,* the soldiers' newspaper, and *GI Joe,* for the soldier himself, and *GI Jane* for his female comrade-in-arms, followed inevitably. But the *Joe* part was disliked,[8] and soon *GI Joe* became plain *GI.* The latter also had some vogue as an adjective standing alone, as in "Are they very *GI* around here?," always expressing distaste, but it did not last for long. Neither did *GI kraut,* listed in 1945 as in use in the Army of the Occupation to designate a former private in the German Army.[9]

It was official fiat which substituted the euphemistic *selectee* for the somewhat harsh *draftee* of World War I. The former first appeared in the Selective Training and Service Act of 1940, along with *trainee. Trainee* didn't have much prosperity, but *selectee* was in almost universal use and still is. *Evacuee,* which raged among the English, though it was violently denounced by their purists,[1] never made any progress in this country, probably because the only American citizens actually evacuated were the heathen Japanese of the Pacific coast. Once the war was over *displaced person,* usually abbreviated to *DP,* came into use on both sides of the water.[2] *Stateside,* in the sense of relating to or in the direction of the United States —in other words, *back home*—impinged upon the national consciousness during World War II. The introduction of the *pin-up girl* has been claimed by Walter Thornton,[3] but he apparently did not invent the term.[4] *Mae West* for an inflatable life preserver used by aviators and later for a tank

---

[8] A writer in the Baltimore *Evening Sun*—*GI and Other Army Terms,* editorial page, Mar. 14, 1945—reported that it was resented as much as the English *Sammy* had been resented in World War I. Said Wheeler, before cited: "The *GI* doesn't mind being called a *GI* or a *Joe* by other soldiers . . . but there are standard four-letter words for what he thinks about being tagged *GI Joe* by, say, a guy like me." Westbrook Pegler predicted in his column, Jan. 17, 1945, that *GI* would soon fade, but the *GI Bill of Rights* apparently gave it a new lease of life.

[9] By James F. Bender, in *Thirty Thousand New Words, The New York Times Magazine,* Dec. 2, p. 22. The favorite of American headline writers was the innocuous *Nazi,* which almost completely displaced *kraut, jerry, heinie* and the *hun* of World War I.

[1] War Words in England, by H. L. Mencken, *AS,* Vol. XXI, Apr. 1946, p. 140.

[2] Among the New Words, by I. Willis Russell, *AS,* Vol. XXI, Apr. 1946, p. 140.

[3] *Pin-up Girl, American Notes and Queries,* Vol. VI, July 1946, pp. 55–6. He says that "at the outset of World War II" he offered General Powell, then in command at Fort Dix, a collection of 5,000 photographs typifying "not the usual glamorous, show-girl type, but the girl back home, wholesome, sweet and vivacious."

[4] M. D. C. says in *American Notes and Queries,* Vol. V, Oct. 1945, p. 108, that it was first used in *Yank,* Apr. 30, 1943. "Prior to that date," he adds, "*Yank* had been fumbling for a tag-line with such commonplaces as *dream-girl.*"

with two turrets, came from the English,[5] as did the German *blitz* and its derivatives, and *blackout*. When *blitz* began to work its way into English use, at the beginning of the war, there were many violent protests from chauvinists,[6] but by 1940 it had been fully accepted, along with *ersatz* and *flak*.[7]

The English invented *blackout* in 1939,[8] but it did not cross the ocean until after Pearl Harbor. *Task force* had to wait until the resumption of the offensive in the Pacific; it is apparently American, but who coined it I do not know. *V-day*, *VE-day*, *VJ-day* and *V-mail* also appear to be of American origin, though the terms in *-day* may have been suggested by the German *der Tag*, one of the chief proofs of German wickedness in World War I.[9] *Black market*, of course, was a legacy from that war, and was possibly borrowed from the German *Schwarzmarkt*, which preceded it. *Lend-lease* was coined by some anonymous Washington onomatologist at the time the thing itself was invented, before Pearl Harbor. The enormous number of abbreviations in use during the war, *e.g.*, *WAC*, *Pfc.*, *AMGOT*,[1] *SHEAF*, *ETO* and *Seabee*[2] began to fade the moment hostilities ended, along with the even more numerous abbreviations designating sectors of the home front, but some of them will no doubt be revived when the bugles blow again. The device of calling a military enterprise *Operation* this-or-that shows some sign of enduring. The fate of *to liberate* I do not venture to predict. It signifies to loot and had a large vogue in the Army of Occupation in Germany, *c.* 1946, but the sentence of fifteen years at hard labor imposed upon the master liberator, Colonel Jack W. Durant, on Apr. 30,

---

[5] Said Fred Backhouse in Pre-War *Mae West*, *Newsweek*, Sept. 4, 1944: "[It] was thought up by an unknown Royal Air Force man before the war and was in common usage when I joined the slang-loving body in 1940. . . . From being slang it moved up into official documents. . . . The *Mae West* is a bulky canvas and rubber affair, and when worn gives you a bust measurement like that attributed to the actress."

[6] War Words in England, before cited, p. 7.

[7] On June 19, 1941, the Edinburgh *Evening Dispatch* headed an editorial *Blitz* Comes to Stay, and said: "After all, the word does express something that is not adequately expressed by any English word. And it has doubled its hold by becoming adjective and verb as well as noun." *AS*, Vol. XV, Feb. 1940, p. 110, shows that it had come into use in the United States in 1939.

[8] Global Darkness, *American Notes and Queries*, Vol. II, Oct. 1942, pp. 99–100.

[9] In Among the New Words, *AS*, Vol. XXI, Apr. 1946, p. 145, I. Willis Russell traces *V-day* to Mar. 16, 1942, *VE-day* to Sept. 18, 1944, and *VJ-day* to the same day. See also Russell's paper in *AS*, Vol. XXI, Oct. 1946, pp. 220–2.

[1] *Amgot* (soon shortened to *AMG*) seems to have been an English invention. In *AMGOT* (editorial), July 19, 1943, the London *Daily Sketch* described it as "a new word" and said: "It stands for the *Allied Military Government of Occupied Territory*, which is headed by Major-General Lord Rennell."

[2] From *CB*, construction battalion. The New Practical Standard Dictionary says that the *seabees* were "given this name in 1942, soon after they were inaugurated to handle all construction for the Navy in combat zones abroad, such as air bases and landing places."

1947, gave it a setback. It has an American smack, but there is evidence that it was actually borrowed from the English.[3] *Quisling* and its verb, *to quisling* or *to quisle*, are also English loans.

Jeep seems to be authentically American, but the history of the word is almost as obscure as the history of the car itself. The latter, [though not yet named *jeep*], was apparently first projected by Captain (later Colonel) R. G. Howie, then in command of the Seventh Tank Company at Fort Snelling, Minn., in 1932. In the developments which followed, various other persons had some hand, and also different manufacturers, *e.g.*, the Willys-Overland Motors of Toledo, the American Bantam Car Company of Butler, Pa., and the Minneapolis-Moline Power Implement Company. Indeed, there were so many fingers in the pie that after the *jeep* was adopted by the Army and became a vast success, conflicting claims of interest produced a controversy before the Federal Trade Commission,[4] and it dragged on wearily. The first batch of seventy *jeeps* was produced by the Bantam Car Company in 1940, and delivered to the Army Quartermaster Depot at Holabird, Md., on September 23 of that year.[5] The fact that the code symbol of Ford on Army cars was *GP* has led to the surmise that the word *jeep* was born there and then,[6] but there is no evidence for it. Nor is there any evidence that the word came from the same letters in the sense of *general purpose*, for the first *jeeps* were not called, officially, *general purpose cars*, but *half-ton four-by-four command-reconnaissance cars*.[7] It seems to be much more probable that the name was borrowed from that of a character in E. C. Segar's comic strip, "Popeye the Sailor," which also gave the language *goon*. Eugene the *Jeep* appeared in Segar's drawings on Mar. 16, 1936,[8] but who first applied *jeep* to the new Army car is not known.

The fact is that, at that time, *jeep* was in the air, and many other contrivances were so called, *e.g.*, the Link Trainer for aviators. Colby says that it was also applied to a recruit, to ill-fitting hats and coats and to various other objects.[9] At one time an autogyro was a *jumping jeep*, and the barracks where recruits were quartered was a *jeep town*. In 1938 Jerome

---

[3] Let's Be Honest Again, *Tit-Bits* (London), Dec. 14, 1945: "In the services *scrounging* (or *liberating*, in the current slang) is not generally frowned upon."

[4] Docket No. 4959, May 6, 1943. More details are given in Hail to the *Jeep*, by A. Wode Wells; New York, 1946. See also Whose *Jeep?*, *Tide*, Feb. 15, 1944, pp. 21–2.

[5] *PM* reported, Mar. 28, 1944, that the sole survivor of this first batch, affectionately called *Gramps*, was deposited in the Smithsonian Institution a short while before. I take this from *American Notes and Queries*, Vol. IV, Apr. 1944, p. 12.

[6] J. K. Layton in *Life*, Aug. 10, 1942, p. 6.

[7] Colby, before cited, p. 116.

[8] I am indebted here to Mr. Ward Greene, of the King Features Syndicate, and to A Word-Creator, by Jeffrey A. Fleece, *AS*, Vol. XVIII, Feb. 1943, pp. 68–9.

[9] *Jeep*, by P. Burwell Rogers, *American Notes and Queries*, Vol. III, Mar. 1944, p. 189.

Barry reported that *jeep* was then in use among soda jerkers to designate a slow and incompetent colleague,[1] and in 1940 a writer in the Baltimore *Evening Sun* said that it was used among automobile finance men for "one who rides with the adjuster in order to drive back the cars repossessed."[2] The English, during World War II, used it for a radio operator and also for a member of the Royal Canadian Naval Volunteer Reserve.[3] In the sense of a bantam car it once had many rivals, *e.g., blitz buggy, baby buggy, bug, gnat tank, scout car, leaping Lena, puddle jumper, jeepers-creepers, midget, midgie, quad* and plain *bantam car. Peep* was invented to differentiate the half-ton car from a quarter-ton model.[4] *Jeep* quickly passed into most of the European languages. "No Frenchman, Belgian, Dutchman, Luxemburger, Dane, Norwegian or German, and very few Poles or Russians," says Bishop, before cited, "is ignorant of *OK, GI* or *jeep*."[5]

The English apparently preferred the *European War* as a designation for the conflict of 1914–18, but in the United States it came to be known as the *World War*, and when another round began in 1939 it naturally became *World War II*. But there were poets who groped for something less prosaic, and one of them was President Franklin D. Roosevelt. So late as the spring of 1942 he was calling for suggestions, and many flowed in. The Hon. Thomas E. Dewey proposed the *War for Survival*, Mrs. Anne M. Rosenberg *Freedom's War*, Dr. William Lyon Phelps the *War of Liberty*, the Hon. Henry H. Curran the *Necessary War* and Jack Dempsey the *Fight to Live*. The Hon. Emil Schram, president of the New York Stock Exchange, put his hopes into the *Last World War*, and other less eminent persons contributed the *War to Save Humanity*, the *Fight for Right*, the *War to Save Civilization*, the *War of the Ages*, the *People's War*, the *Survival War*, the *War of World Freedom*, the *War Against Tyrants*, the *Hitler War* and the *World Order War*. There were even cynics who proposed the *Crazy War*, the *War of Illusions*, the *Meddler's War*, the *Roosevelt War*, the *Devil's War* and *Hell*. How and by whom the votes were counted I do not know, but when the uproar was over it was announced that *World War II* had won by a large plurality. Soon after Pearl Harbor, in fact, the Army and Navy had adopted *World War II*, and by the middle of 1942 it was appearing in the *Congressional Record*. By

---

[1] The Jerk, *The Saturday Evening Post*, July 16. I take these from *AS*, Vol. XIII, Oct. 1938, p. 235.

[2] What Happens When the Finance Adjuster Steps In, editorial page, Oct. 8.

[3] Service Slang, by J. L. Hunt and A. G. Pringle; London, 1943, p. 41.

[4] *Jeep*, by Richard Gordon McClosky, *American Notes and Queries*, Vol. III, Dec. 1943, pp. 136–7.

[5] But Maurice Hindus reported in a Moscow dispatch in the New York *Herald Tribune*, Mar. 28, 1944, that the Russians used *Willys*. So did *Tide*, Feb. 15, 1944, p. 22.

the end of that year it had obliterated all the other proposed names, and prophets were already beginning to talk hopefully of *World War III*.

Ernest K. Lindley and Forrest Davis say in "How War Came" [6] that *United Nations* was coined by President Roosevelt. This was during Winston Churchill's visit to Washington at the end of December 1941. He was a guest at the White House, and he and Roosevelt discussed the choice of a name for the new alliance. One morning, lying in bed, Roosevelt thought of *United Nations*, and at once sought Churchill, who was in his bath. "How about *United Nations*?" he called through the door. "That," replied Churchill, "should do it." And so it was.

---

[6] New York, 1942.

XII

The Future of the Language

1: THE SPREAD OF ENGLISH

The English tongue is of small reach,
stretching no further than this island
of ours, nay not there over all.

This was written in 1582. The writer was Richard Mulcaster, headmaster of the Merchant Taylors' School, teacher of prosody to Edmund Spenser, and one of the earliest of English grammarians. At the time he wrote, English was spoken by between four and five millions of people, and stood fifth among the European languages, with French, German, Italian and Spanish ahead of it in that order, and Russian following. Two hundred years later Italian had dropped behind but Russian had gone ahead, so that English was still in fifth place. But by the end of the Eighteenth Century it had forced its way into first place. Today, it is still there.

It is not only the first—and in large part, the only—language of one of the world's two strongest powers and of several of the second rank; it is also the second language of large and populous regions beyond their bounds. Its teaching is obligatory in the secondary schools of countries as diverse as Germany and Argentina, Turkey and Denmark, Portugal and Japan. No ship captain can trade upon the oceans without some knowledge of it; [1] it is the common tongue of all the great ports, and likewise of all the maritime Bad Lands, from the South Sea Islands to the West Coast of Africa and the Persian Gulf. [2] Every language of the free world that still

---

[1] [It has also become the international language of aviation, according to a report in *The New York Times*, Feb. 9, 1958. By international convention, all cockpit-tower communication (at least in the free world) is in English except when plane and tower are of the same nationality.]

[2] Cosmopolitan Conversation, by Herbert Newhard Shenton; New York, 1933, p. 315.

resists its advance—for example, Spanish and Portuguese in Latin America, Italian and French in the Levant, Japanese and Hindi in Asia—has made large concessions. Everywhere in Latin America, Spanish has taken in many English and American words.[3] Japanese has gone even further. Professor Sanki Ichikawa, of the University of Tokyo, reports that in a few months' reading of Japanese newspapers and magazines he encountered 1,400 English words,[4] and Dr. Sawbay Arakawa lists nearly 5,000 in his "Japanized English." [5] [The American occupation following World War II and the still later Japanese-American alliance have greatly accelerated a process already well under way by 1930.

[Before the rise of the Communists to power in China, Chinese seemed destined to go the way of Japanese. Its stock of English loan words had been greatly reinforced since the revolution of 1911, and it was fashionable to display them. On Formosa, where American ships and planes prop up the Nationalist government of Chiang Kai-shek, the trend still continues; on the mainland, however, it has probably been arrested by the open hostility of the Chinese Communists to all things American.]

How many people speak English today? It is hard to answer with any precision, but an approximation is nevertheless possible. First, let us list those to whom English is their native tongue. They run to about 170,000,000 in the continental United States, to 45,000,000 in the United Kingdom, to 10,000,000 in Canada, 10,000,000 in Australia, 4,000,000 in Ireland, 3,000,000 in South Africa and probably 3,000,000 in the rest of the British Commonwealth.[6] Now add the people who, though born to some other language, live in English-speaking communities and speak English themselves in their daily business, and whose children are being brought up to

---

[3] See The American Language in Mexico, by H. E. McKinistry, *American Mercury*, Mar. 1930.

[4] English Influence on Japanese; Tokyo, 1928, p. 165.

[5] 4th ed.; Tokyo, 1930.

[6] [According to Sir David Eccles, formerly British Minister of Education, as reported in *Time*, June 22, 1962, p. 33, English is the mother tongue of 250 million and the second language of 250 million others. It has long been the language of world commerce, and is rapidly becoming "the accepted language of development and aid in all continents." Even Communist-bloc engineers on foreign aid missions accept English as the *lingua franca*; more than 50% of all Soviet school children take an intensive eleven-year English course.

["English," said Eccles, "is now so far from being the suspect channel of Anglo-American culture and propaganda that it is accepted as the medium of rebellion and anti-colonialism." Britain's government, he said, is under continuous pressure from new nations in Africa and Asia that need help in setting up English courses in their schools. The greatest demand comes not from governments but from private individuals, "simply because English is now the language of good jobs. Young people know that to get on in a scientific age they must know English."

[In the *Saturday Review*, Oct. 4, 1952, p. 15, W. L. Werner says that estimates of speakers of English run as high as a billion. This probably involves very liberal estimates of what constitutes a "speaker."]

it—say 10,000,000 for the United States, 2,000,000 for Canada, 1,000,000 for the United Kingdom and Ireland and 2,000,000 for the rest of the world—and you have a grand total of 260,000,000. Obviously, no other European language is the everyday tongue of more people. [Russian has gained enormously in the last generation, by natural increase in population, as a second language among the minorities of the Soviet Union and in the other Communist nations and by aggressive teaching programs in the neutral nations. However, it is still apparently behind English.] Spanish is spoken by more than 140,000,000, but that is little more than half the total of English. German is spoken by 70,000,000 in the two Germanys, by perhaps 8,000,000 in Austria, by a scant 4,000,000 in German Switzerland and by perhaps 5,000,000 elsewhere. This makes 87,000,000. French and Portuguese and Italian are the runners-up, and the rest of the European languages are nowhere. In Asia, Chinese is ostensibly the native tongue of more than 600,000,000 people, but it is split into so many mutually unintelligible varieties that it must be thought of less as a language than as a group of languages. [North Chinese, formerly known as Mandarin, claims 450,000,000; but even within North Chinese the dialect variations are great. The increasingly aggressive role of the Chinese Communists in world affairs, especially in Asia, suggests a greater role for their language in world affairs—it is already one of the official tongues of the United Nations—but that role is now only dimly foreshadowed. The status of Hindu-Urdu, the official language of India and Pakistan (with different alphabets in the two nations), is much like that of North Chinese.[7]]

Thus English has had a favored position for some time. Moreover, it promises to retain this position despite the formidable competition of Russian. There was a time when French was the acknowledged second language of Christendom, but it is now studied as an accomplishment far

---

[7] [In Languages Now Spoken by Over a Million Speakers, by Charles F. and Florence M. Vogelin, *Anthropological Linguistics*, Vol. III, No. 8, Nov. 1961, the twenty leading languages, out of 134 listed, are as follows:

1.	Mandarin Chinese	460,000,000
2.	English	250,000,000
3.	Spanish	140,000,000
4.	Russian	130,000,000
5.	German	100,000,000
6.	Japanese	95,000,000
7.	Arabic	80,000,000
8.	Bengali	75,000,000
9.	Portuguese	75,000,000
10.	Urdu	75,000,000
11.	French	65,000,000
12.	Hindi	65,000,000
13.	Italian	55,000,000
14.	Wu (Shanghai)	50,000,000
15.	Min (Fukien)	46,000,000
16.	Cantonese	46,000,000
17.	Javanese	45,000,000
18.	Telugu	37,000,000
19.	Punjabi	36,000,000
20.	Ukrainian	35,000,000

Other observers, notably William M. Austin, of the Illinois Institute of Technology, question some of the details, including the accuracy of specific figures and the justification of separating Russian and Ukrainian or Urdu and Hindi. The general picture, however, remains the same.]

more often than as a utility. [In the Soviet Union it has lost the prestige it had in Czarist Russia, when it was the everyday tongue of the elite for polite conversation.] In our own high schools and colleges French is retained in the curriculum, but hardly 5% of the students ever acquire any facility at speaking it, or even at reading it. In the schools of Germany, Scandinavia and Japan, however, English is taught with relentless earnestness, and a great deal of it sticks. Indeed, even the French begin to learn it.

How far it has thus gone as a second language I do not know, but a few facts and figures taken at random may throw some light on the question. In February 1929, the Stockholm newspaper *Nya Dagligt Allehanda* undertook to find out what proportion of the population of Stockholm had acquired it. It was discovered that every fourth person had enough of the language for all ordinary purposes, and that 65% of all the foreign business of Sweden was carried on in English. In writing to German correspondents the Swedish firms used German, but for all other foreign correspondence they used English. The place thus held by English was formerly held by German and French; the change has come since 1900. In Norway, Denmark and Finland there has been a similar movement. Its position in Portugal is the same, with no minorities to challenge it.[8] In Turkey, before 1923, the second language was French, but since the proclamation of the Republic "the tendency has entirely changed. . . . The Ministry of Public Instruction has introduced English as a regular part of the school routine in all the secondary schools throughout the country." All this, in 1929, on the authority of Herbert M. Thompson, professor of English at the Galata Saray Lycée, "the Eton of Turkey." [Since World War II, the intimate relationship between the United States and Turkey—particularly between the armed forces of the two nations—has increased Turkish interest in English, and several distinguished American linguists have served as consultants to the program of making every Turkish officer, at least, familiar with American English.]

But perhaps the largest advances of English have been made in Latin America. A century ago, the second language in all these nations, insofar as they had a second language, was French. But the impact of the Spanish-American War forced French to share its hegemony. The Latin Americans may still prefer French on cultural counts, but they turn to English for the hard reasons of every day. This movement is naturally most marked in the areas that have come under direct American influence—above all, in Puerto Rico [9]—but it is also visible everywhere below the Rio Grande.

---

[8] English in Portugal, by J. Da Providéncia Costa and S. George West, London *Times Literary Supplement*, Feb. 28, 1935, p. 124.

[9] For this I am indebted to Dr. José Padín, commissioner of education for Puerto Rico. He says: "On the whole I should say that about 400,000 people out

In the Philippines, a survey of tenant rice farmers' families, made so long ago as 1921–2, showed that 34% of the children were literate in English, as against only 2% literate in Spanish. Among the older people twice as many were literate in English as in Spanish. Under the Constitution of the Philippine Commonwealth, Art. XIII, Sec. 3, "the Legislative Assembly shall take steps toward the development and adoption of a common national language based on one of the existing native languages." [Tagalog was chosen, but it is not yet used by the generality of Filipinos. Meanwhile, among the commonalty, the native variety of Philippine English—hardly recognizable as English to British or Americans, but English nonetheless— is a living language, and the Ministry of Education is active in promoting the study of the American variety, an enterprise in which it has the co-operation of several major American universities and foundations. In the neutral nations of Asia and the Middle East, the teaching of English goes hand in hand with the teaching of American technology, and at the Uganda Conference of December 1960, American linguists participated in plans for extending the teaching of English in the emerging nations of Africa.[1] The extent and success of these programs, with their terrifying potentiali-ties for the survival or extinction of the United States as a nation, is limited only by the unwillingness of the humanities-dominated English depart-ments of our universities to support the training of teachers, since this would mean dirtying their hands with the practical business of education. But fortunately other agencies, including the despised educationists, are responding to this apparently insatiable demand.]

English has made steady inroads upon French as the language of diplo-macy and of other international intercourse, and upon German as the language of science. In the latter case, Russian is beginning to offer compe-tition, and in the former, French still offers sturdy resistance. [Neverthe-less, in the United Nations not only English but Chinese, Russian and Spanish are recognized as official languages.] Perhaps the turn of the tide came with the Versailles Conference of 1919, where the two representatives

---

of a total population of 1,600,000 speak and read English, and, in a lesser degree, write it." See also his English in Puerto Rico; San Juan, 1935. [The population of the island has increased enormously since 1935, but the proportion of speak-ers of English has likewise grown.]

[1] [See Yaoundé Conference on Teach-ing Second European Language in Africa, *Linguistic Reporter*, Vol. IV, No. 1, Feb. 1962, pp. 1–2. Fulbright programs in linguistics and the teaching of English were outlined by Trusten W. Russell in the *ACLS Newsletter*, Nov. 1961, pp. 8–12. In English without Frontiers, *The New York Times Magazine*, Dec. 4, 1955, pp. 17, 19, Edward T. Cornelius, Jr., describes the operation of Bi-National English Language Centers in 26 coun-tries. A special issue (June 1958) of *Lan-guage Learning* is devoted to a report on a conference on linguistics and the teach-ing of English as a foreign language, held at the University of Michigan, July 28–30, 1957.]

of the English-speaking countries, Wilson and Lloyd George, had no French, whereas the French spokesman, Clemenceau, spoke English fluently—with a strong American accent. Thus English became the language of negotiation, and it has been heard round council tables with increasing frequency ever since.

All over the Far East, English has been a *lingua franca* since the Eighteenth Century, at first in the barbarous guise of Pidgin English, but of late in increasingly seemly forms, often with an American admixture. In Japan it is the language of business. In India and Pakistan, it not only competes with Hindu-Urdu in business, but is often the language of politics. Those Indians who know it, says Sir John A. R. Marriott,[2] "are the only persons who are politically conscious. Indian nationalism is almost entirely the product of English education; the medium of all political discussion is necessarily English." It is, adds R. C. Goffin,[3] "the readiest means of obtaining (*a*) employment under the government; (*b*) employment in commercial houses of any standing, whether Indian or foreign; (*c*) command of the real *lingua franca* of the country—for Hindustani is of very little use [in the south]; (*d*) knowledge of Western ideas, both ancient and modern. . . . English in other ways has shown itself a useful instrument for a country setting out to learn the habits of democracy. It is most convenient for the politician, for example, to be able to employ a language with only one word (instead of three or even four) for *you*. . . . There is no country today where a foreign language has been so thoroughly domesticated as has English in India." [The Indian Congress Party had hoped to replace English by Hindi within a few years of independence. But they now recognize that for generations to come it will be the medium through which their countrymen acquire the science and technology of the modern world.[4] And the experience of India is being repeated as each of the former British colonies becomes an independent nation. Paradoxically, the liquidation of the British colonial empire seems destined to bring a wider dissemination of the English language.[5]]

It has become a platitude that one may go almost anywhere with no other

---

[2] The English in India; London, 1932, p. 18.

[3] Some Notes on Indian English, *SPE Tract*, No. XLI, 1934, p. 22.

[4] [In 1961 it was formally decided that English should continue as an official tongue in India. See English Spoken Here, by Dana Adams Schmidt, *The New York Times Magazine*, Oct. 15, 1961, pp. 131, 136. However, the problems of language-usage in India are related to many other things, as Paul Friedrich points out in Language and Culture in India, *Daedalus*, Summer 1962, pp. 543–59. Protests against the continuing use of English in India were reported in *The New York Times*, Apr. 14, 1963.]

[5] [According to Ernest K. Lindley, *Newsweek*, July 4, 1955, English was the official language of the neutralist conference of African and Asian nations at Bandung, Indonesia; it is the only language in which most Asian countries can communicate with one another.]

linguistic equipment, and get along almost as well as in large areas of New York City. My own experience may be cited for whatever it is worth. I visited, between the two wars, sixteen countries in Europe, five in Africa, three in Asia and three in Latin America, besides a large miscellany of islands, but I don't remember ever encountering a situation that English could not resolve. I heard it spoken with reasonable fluency in a Moroccan bazaar, in an Albanian fishing port and on the streets of Istanbul. In part, of course, its spread has been due to the extraordinary dispersion of the English-speaking peoples. They have been the greatest travelers of modern times, and the most adventurous merchants and the most assiduous colonists. Moreover, they have been, on the whole, poor linguists, and so they have dragged their language with them, and forced it upon the human race. Wherever it has met with serious competition, as with French in Canada, with Spanish along our southwestern border and with Dutch in South Africa, they have compromised with its local rival only reluctantly. If English is the language of the sea, it is largely because there are more English ships on the sea than any other kind, and English ship captains refuse to learn what they think of as the barbaric gibberishes of Hamburg, Rio and Marseilles.

But there is more to the matter than this. English, brought to close quarters with formidable rivals, has won very often, not by mere force of numbers and intransigence, but by the weight of its intrinsic merit. "In riches, good sense and terse convenience (*Reichstum, Vernunft und gedrängter Fuge*)," said Jacob Grimm nearly a century ago,[6] "no other of the living languages may be put beside it." To which the eminent Otto Jespersen adds: "It seems to me positively and expressively masculine. It is the language of a grown-up man, and has very little childish or feminine about it."[7] Jespersen then goes on to explain the origin and nature of this "masculine" air: it is grounded chiefly upon clarity, directness and force.

Jespersen then proceeds to consider certain peculiarities of English morphology and syntax, and to point out the simplicity and forcefulness of the everyday English vocabulary. The grammatical baldness of the language, he argues (against the old tradition in philology), is one of the chief sources of its vigor.

The prevalence of very short words in English, and the syntactical law which enables it to dispense with the definite article in many constructions "where other languages think it indispensable, *e.g.*, 'life is short,' 'dinner is ready' "—these are further marks of vigor and clarity, according to Jes-

---

[6] Über den Ursprung der Sprache, a lecture delivered before the Berlin Academy of Sciences, Jan. 9, 1851. Reprinted in Auswahl aus den kleineren Schriften; Berlin, 1871.
[7] Growth and Structure of the English Language; 3rd ed.; Leipzig, 1919, p. 2.

persen. " 'First come, first served,' " he says, "is much more vigorous than the French 'Premier venu, premier moulu,' or 'Le premier venu engrène,' the German 'Wer zuerst kommt, mahlt zuerst,' and especially than the Danish 'Den der kommer først til mølle, far først malet.' " Again, there is the superior logical sense of English—the arrangement of words according to their meaning. "In English," says Jespersen, "an auxiliary verb does not stand far from its main verb, and a negative will be found in the immediate neighborhood of the word it negatives, generally the verb (auxiliary). An adjective nearly always stands before its noun; the only really important exception is where there are qualifications added to it which draw it after the noun so that the whole complex serves the purpose of a relative clause." In English, the subject almost invariably precedes the verb and the object follows after. Once Jespersen had his pupils determine the percentage of sentences in various authors in which this order was observed. They found that even in English poetry it was seldom violated; the percentage of observances in Tennyson's poetry ran to 88. But in the poetry of Holger Drachmann, the Dane, it fell to 61, in Anatole France's prose to 66, in Gabriele D'Annunzio to 49 and in the poetry of Goethe to 30. All these things make English clearer and more logical than other tongues. It is, says Jespersen, "a methodical, energetic, business-like and sober language, that does not care much for finery and elegance, but does care for logical consistency and is opposed to any attempt to narrow life by police regulations and strict rules either of grammar or of lexicon." [Even when we concede the effects of Jespersen's personal bias, and of the illusion of inevitable progress which he inherited from the Nineteenth Century, we must still recognize the facts on which his opinions are based.]

Several years ago Walter Kirkconnell undertook to count the number of syllables needed to translate the Gospel of Mark into forty Indo-European languages, ranging from Persian and Hindi to English and French.[8] He found that, of all of them, English was the most economical, for it took but 29,000 syllables to do the job, whereas the average for all the Teutonic languages was 32,650, that for the Slavic group 36,500, that for the Romance group 40,200 and that for the Indo-Iranian group (Bengali, Persian, Sanskrit, etc.) 43,100. It is commonly believed that French is a terse language, and compared with its cousins, Italian and Spanish, it actually is, but compared with English it is garrulous, for it takes 36,000 syllables to say what English says in 29,000. "If it had not been for the great number of long foreign, especially Latin, words," says Jespersen, "English would have approached the state of such monosyllabic languages as Chinese."

For these and other reasons English strikes most foreigners as an ex-

---

[8] Linguistic Laconism, *AJP*, Vol. XLVIII, 1927, p. 34.

traordinarily succinct, straightforward and simple tongue—in some of its aspects, in fact, almost as a kind of baby talk. When they proceed from trying to speak it to trying to read and write it they are painfully undeceived, for its spelling is as irrational as that of French, but so long as they are content to tackle it *viva voce* they find it loose and comfortable, and at the same time very precise. The Russian, coming into it burdened with his six cases, his three genders, his palatalized consonants and his complicated pronouns, luxuriates in a language which has only two cases, no grammatical gender, a set of consonants which (save only *r*) maintain their integrity in the face of any imaginable rush of vowels, and an outfit of pronouns so simple that one of them suffices to address the President of the United States or a child in arms, a lovely female creature *in camera* or the vast hordes of television and radio. And the German, the Scandinavian, the Italian and the Frenchman, though the change for them is measurably less sharp, nevertheless find it gratifying too. Only the Spaniard brings with him a language comparable to English for clarity, and even the Spaniard is afflicted with grammatical gender.

The huge English vocabulary is likely to make the foreigner uneasy, but he soon finds that nine-tenths of it lies safely buried in the dictionaries, and is never drawn upon for everyday use. That the language may be spoken intelligibly with even less than 1,000 words has been argued by C. K. Ogden, the English psychologist. Ogden believes that 850 are sufficient for all ordinary purposes, and he has devised a form of simplified English, called by him Basic (from *B*ritish *A*merican *S*cientific *I*nternational *C*ommercial), which uses no more. Of this number, 600 are nouns, 100 are adjectives, 100 are "adjectival opposites," 30 are verbs and the rest are particles, etc. Two hundred of the nouns consist of the names of common objects, *e.g., bottle, brick, ear, potato* and *umbrella;* the rest are the names of familiar groups and concepts, *e.g., people, music, crime, loss* and *weather*. No noun is admitted (save for the names of a few common objects) "which can't be defined in not more than ten other words." The reduction of verbs to 30 is effected by taking advantage of one of the prime characteristics of English (and especially of American)—its capacity for getting an infinity of meanings out of a single verb by combining it with simple modifiers. Consider, for example, the difference (in American) between *to get, to get going, to get by, to get on, to get onto, to get off, to get ahead of, to get wise, to get religion* and *to get over*. The fundamental verbs of Basic are ten in number—*come, go, put, take, give, get, make, keep, let* and *do*. "Every time," says Ogden (writing in Basic), "you put together the name of one of these ten simple acts (all of which are free to go in almost any direction) with the name of one of the twenty directions or positions in space, you are making a verb" [—and, point out his critics, creating a new lexical unit whose meaning is unpredictable from the meanings of its parts, and therefore a greater problem to the stranger than an undisguised new word might be]. In addition to its 850 words, of course, Basic is free to take in international words that are universally understood, *e.g.*, *coffee*, *engineer*, *tobacco*, *police* and *biology*, and to add words specially pertinent to the matter in hand, *e.g.*, *chloride* and *platinum* in a treatise on chemistry. It is interesting to note that of the fifty international words listed by Ogden, no less than seven are Americanisms, new or old, *viz.*, *cocktail*, *jazz*, *radio*, *phonograph*, *telegram*, *telephone* and *tobacco*, and that one more, *check*, is listed in American spelling.[9]

Whether Basic will make any progress remains to be seen. It has been criticized on various grounds. For one thing, its vocabulary shows some serious omissions—for example, the numerals—and for another its dependence upon verb phrases may confuse rather than help the foreigner, whose difficulties with prepositions are notorious;[1] [also, the superficial simplicity of its vocabulary conceals a multitude of homonyms with lexical and semantic pitfalls]. Spelling is still a cruel difficulty to a foreigner. But Ogden waves this difficulty away. For one thing, he argues that his list of 850 words, being made up mainly of the commonest coins of speech, avoids most spelling problems; for another, he believes that the very eccentricity of the spelling of some of the rest will help the foreigner to remember them. Every schoolboy, as we all know, seizes upon such bizarre forms as *through*, *straight* and *island* with fascinated eagerness, and not infrequently he masters them before he masters such phonetically spelled words as *first*, *tomorrow* and *engineer*. In my own youth, far away in the dark backward and abysm of time, the glory of every young American was *phthisic*, with the English proper name, *Cholmondeley*, a close second. Ogden proposes to let the foreigners attempting Basic share the joy of hunting down such basilisks. For the rest he leaves the snarls of English spelling to the judgments of a just God, and the natural tendency of all things Anglo-Saxon to move toward an ultimate perfection. Unluckily, his Basic now has a number of competitors on its own ground,[2] and it must also meet the competition of the so-called universal languages. Some of these languages, notably Esperanto and Novial, show a great ingenuity, and all have enthusiastic customers who believe that they are about to be adopted generally. There are also persons who hold that some

---

[9] The literature of Basic is already extensive. The most comprehensive textbook is The System of Basic English, by C. K. Ogden; New York, 1934.

[1] [Some of the differences between English and American usage are mentioned at the end of Sec. 2, of Ch. VI. Publication of the regional and social variations in American, as recorded by the Linguistic Atlas, is still to come.]

[2] Some of these rivals are examined critically in English as the International Language, by Janet Rankin Aiken, *AS*, Vol. IX, Apr. 1934. In 1935 Dr. Aiken put forward a rival to Basic under the name of Little English. It has a vocabulary of 800 words, or 50 less than Basic.

such language is bound to come in soon or late, though remaining doubtful about all those proposed so far.

But this is only a hope, and no man now born will ever see it realized. The trouble with all the "universal" languages, [leaving out their parochial devotion to the Latinate vocabulary and their blithe unconcern with all the languages of Asia and Africa], is that the juices of life are simply not in them. They are the creations of scholars drowning in murky oceans of dead prefixes and suffixes, and so they fail to meet the needs of a highly human world. People do not yearn for a generalized articulateness; what they want is the capacity to communicate with definite other people.[3] To that end even Basic, for all its deficiencies, is better than any conceivable Esperanto, for it at least springs from a living speech, and behind that speech are some 260,000,000 men and women, many of them amusing and some of them wise. The larger the gang, the larger the numbers of both classes. English forges ahead of all its competitors, whether natural or unnatural, simply because it is already spoken by so many educated, or at least technically competent, people. A few years ago, Dr. Knut Sanstedt, general secretary to the Northern Peace Union, sent a circular to a number of representative European publicists, asking them "what language, dead or living or artificial" they preferred for international communications. Not one of these publicists was a native or resident of the British Isles, yet out of fifty-nine who replied thirty voted for English. Of the six Swedes, all preferred it; of the seven Norwegians, five; of the five Hollanders, four. Among the whole fifty-nine, only one man voted for Esperanto.[4]

2: ENGLISH OR AMERICAN?

But as English spreads over the world, will it be able to maintain its present form?[5] Probably not. But why should it? The notion that any-

---

[3] The most persuasive argument that I am aware of against the feasibility of setting up an artificial language is to be found in Interlanguage, by T. C. Macaulay, *SPE Tract*, No. XXXIV, 1930. [In Breaking Down Babel, *Aramco World*, May 1956, pp. 10–13, it is pointed out what linguistic scientists have been observing for a generation, that the so-called "international languages" disregard all the linguistic stocks of Asia, and generally the Slavic languages as well. They are commonly built around the vocabularies of a limited group of Western European languages, chiefly Romance, and are just as ethnocentrically biased as those languages themselves—without

leading to everyday communication with a community of living speakers. In English—Tomorrow's International Language, *EJ*, Vol. XLV, Oct. 1956, pp. 395–9, Ruth S. Bentley and Sheldon Grebstein point out that in 1950 only .007% of the world's people were using Esperanto.]

[4] Anglic: A New Agreed Simplified English Spelling, by R. E. Zachrisson; Uppsala, Sweden, 1931, p. 7.

[5] [In his comments on the future of English, *Time*, June 22, 1962, p. 33, Sir David Eccles, then Britain's Minister of Education, spoke in Eighteenth Century terms about the necessity for "preserving common meanings and standards of pu-

thing is gained by fixing a language is cherished only by pedants. Every successful effort at standardization, as Ernest Weekley has well said, results in nothing better than emasculation.[6] "Stability in language is synonymous with *rigor mortis*." It is the very anarchy of English, adds Claude de Crespigny, that has made it the dominant language of the world today.[7] In its early forms it was a highly inflected tongue—indeed, it was more inflected than modern German, and almost as much so as Russian. The West Saxon dialect, for example, in the days before the Norman Conquest, had grammatical gender, and in addition the noun was inflected for number and for case, and there were five cases in all. Moreover, there were two quite different declensions, the strong and the weak, so that the total number of inflections was immense. The same ending, of course, was commonly used more than once, but that fact only added to the difficulties of the language. The impact of the Conquest knocked this elaborate grammatical structure—already weakening—into a cocked hat. The upper classes spoke French, and so the populace had English at its mercy. It quickly wore down the vowels of the endings to a neutral *e*, reduced the importance of their consonants by moving the stress forward to the root, and finally lopped off many inflections *in toto*. By the time of Chaucer (1340?–1400) English was moving rapidly toward its present form. It had already come to depend heavily upon word position for expressing meanings, and meanwhile the influence of French, which had been official from 1066 to 1362, had left it full of new words and made its vocabulary hybrid. To this day, indeed, in its vocabulary the likeness of English to French, Italian and Spanish is often more marked than its likeness to German. Once its East Midland dialect had been given pre-eminence over all other dialects by the importance of the city of London, it began to develop rapidly, and in the time of Shakespeare it enjoyed an extraordinarily lush and vigorous growth. New words were taken in from all the other languages of Europe and from many of those of Africa and Asia, other

---

rity for the English language," and warned against the dangers of fission of the English-speaking world. However, a better scholar and more astute observer, Randolph Quirk, professor of the English Language, University College, London, and one of the most perceptive students of the language anywhere, had previously spoken to the contrary. In American English and English English, *The New York Times Magazine*, Dec. 2, 1956, pp. 132–40, he had emphasized that the similarities are far greater than the differences, and that we can expect a confluence of the two streams in the future. The position of English in the future is also discussed perceptively by Quirk in The Study of the Mother Tongue: An Inaugural Lecture Delivered at University College, London, 1961, and in The Use of English (in collaboration with A. C. Gimson and Jeremy Warburg), London, 1962. This last is not only illuminating but an enjoyable book to read.]

[6] English as She Will Be Spoke, *Atlantic Monthly*, May 1932. The quotation following is from the English Language, by the same author; New York, 1929, p. 9.

[7] Esperanto, *AS*, Vol. I, Sept. 1926.

new words in large number were made of its own materials and almost everything that remained of the old inflections was sloughed off. Thus it gradually took on a singularly simple and flexible form, and passed ahead of the languages that were more rigidly bound by rule.

I think I have offered sufficient evidence that the American of today is much more honestly English, in any sense that Shakespeare would have understood, than the so-called Standard English of England. It still shows all the characteristics that marked the common tongue in the days of Elizabeth I, and it continues to resist stoutly the policing that ironed out Standard English in the Seventeenth and Eighteenth Centuries. Standard English must always strike an American as a bit stilted and precious. Its vocabulary is less abundant than his own, it has lost to an appreciable extent its old capacity for bold metaphor and in pronunciation and spelling it seems to him to be extremely uncomfortable and not a little ridiculous. When he hears a speech in its Oxford (or Public School) form he must be a Bostonian to avoid open mirth. He believes, on very plausible grounds, that American is better on all counts—clearer, more rational and, above all, more charming. And he holds not illogically that there is no reason under the sun why a dialect spoken almost uniformly by nearly 180,000,000 people should yield anything to the dialect of a small minority in a nation of 50,000,000. He sees that wherever American and this dialect come into fair competition—as in Canada, for example, or in the Far East—American tends to prevail,[8] and that even in England many of its reforms and innovations are making steady headway, so he concludes that it will probably prevail everywhere hereafter. "When two-thirds of the people who use a certain language," says one of his spokesmen,[9] "decide to call it a *freight train* instead of a *goods train* they are 'right'; and the first is correct English and the second a dialect."

Nor is the American, in entertaining such notions, without English support. The absurdities of Standard English are denounced by every English philologian, and by a great many other Englishmen. Those who accept it without cavil are simply persons who are unfamiliar with any other form of the language; the Irishman, the Scotsman, the Canadian and the Australian laugh at it along with the American—and with the Englishman who has lived in the United States. H. W. Seaman, a Norwich man who had spent ten years on American and Canadian newspapers and was in practice, when he wrote, as a journalist in London, says:

---

[8] Its influence upon the English of Australia and of South Africa is already marked. [Americanisms, according to W. S. Ramson, have been infiltrating Australian English for more than a century; he devotes a section to them in his dissertation An Historical Study of the Australian Vocabulary, U. of Sydney, 1962.]

[9] William McAlpine, *New Republic*, June 26, 1929.

We are as sick and tired of this so-called English as you Americans are. It has far less right to be called Standard English speech than Yorkshire or any other country dialect has—or than any American dialect. It is as alien to us as it is to you. True, some of my neighbors have acquired it—for social or other reasons—but then some of the Saxon peasants took pains to acquire Norman French, which also was imposed upon them from above.[1]

Seaman describes with humor his attempts as a schoolboy to shed his native Norwich English and to acquire the prissy fashionable dialect that passes as Standard. He managed to do so, and is thus able today to palaver on equal terms with "an English public-school boy, an Oxford man, a clergyman of the Establishment, an announcer of the British Broadcasting Company, or a West End actor," but he confesses that it still strikes him, as it strikes an American, as having "a mauve, Episcopalian and ephebian ring." And he quotes George Bernard Shaw:

The English have no respect for their language. . . . It is impossible for an Englishman to open his mouth without making some other Englishman hate or despise him. . . . An honest and natural slum dialect is more tolerable than the attempt of a phonetically untaught person to imitate the vulgar dialect of the golf club.

Basil de Sélincourt, author of "Pomona, or The Future of English," and J. Y. T. Greig, author of "Breaking Priscian's Head," both hope that some form of English denizened in England may eventually become the universal form of the language, but both are plainly upset by fears that American will prevail. "Right and wrong in such a matter," says de Sélincourt, "can be decided only by the event. However it be, the United States, obviously, is now the scene of the severest ordeals, the vividest excitements of our language. . . . The contrasting and competitive use of their one language by the English and Americans gives it a new occasion for the exercise of its old and noble faculty of compromise. In a period of promise and renewal, it was beginning to grow old; the Americans are young. . . . Its strong constitution will assimilate tonics as fast as friends can supply them, and take no serious harm. Changes are certainly in store for it." Mr. Greig is rather less sanguine about the prospects of compromise between English and American. "It is possible," he says gloomily, "that in fifty or a hundred years . . . American and not English will be the chief foreign language taught in the schools of Asia and the European Continent. Some Americans look forward to this without misgiving, nay, with exultation; and I for one would rather have it fall

[1] The Awful English of England, *American Mercury*, Sept. 1933, p. 73.

out than see perpetuated and extended that silliest and dwabliest of all the English dialects, Public-School Standard."

The defects of English, whether in its American or its British form, are almost too obvious to need rehearsal. One of the worst is that the two great branches of the language differ not only in vocabulary but also in pronunciation. Thus the foreigner must make his choice, and though in most cases he is probably unconscious of it, he nevertheless makes it. The East Indian, when he learns English at all, almost always learns something approximating Oxford English, but the Latin American is very apt to learn American, and American is what the immigrant returning to Sweden or Yugoslavia, Israel or Syria, Italy or Finland, certainly takes home with him. In Russia, American has begun to challenge English, and in Japan and elsewhere in the Far East the two dialects are in bitter competition, with American apparently prevailing. This competition, which has been going on in Europe since World War I, presents a serious problem to foreign teachers of the language.

Unluckily, neither of the great dialects of English may be described as anything approaching a perfect language. Within the limits of both there are still innumerable obscurities, contradictions and irrationalities. Those in spelling are especially exasperating. "But spelling," says Krapp,[2]

> would be only a beginning of the general house-cleaning for which our precious heritage of English speech as we know it today provides a profitable opportunity. The language is burdened with quantities of useless lumber, which from the point of view of common sense and reason might just as well be burned on the rubbish heap. . . . Why should we permit an exceptional plural *feet* or *teeth* when we possess a perfectly good way of making plurals by adding *s?* And why should verbs like *write* have two past forms, *wrote* and *written*, when most verbs of the language get along quite satisfactorily with only one?

There is yet another difficulty, and a very serious one. Of it Janet Rankin Aiken says:

> This difficulty is idiom—idiom observable in a large part of what we say and write, but centering particularly in verb and preposition. It has been calculated[3] that including all phrase constructions there are well over a hundred different forms for even a simple, regular verb like *call*, besides extra or lacking forms for irregular verbs like *speak, be,* and *set.* Each of these verb forms has several uses, some

---

[2] The Future of English, in The Knowledge of English; New York, 1927, p. 537.

[3] By Dr. Aiken herself in A New Plan of English Grammar; New York, 1933, Ch. XIX.

as high as a dozen or more, to express permission, ability, interrogation, negation, generalization, expectation, duration, inception, and a bewildering number of other ideas. Native speakers of English have difficulty with verb constructions; how much more so the foreign student of the language! [4]

Finally there are the snarls of sentence order—naturally numerous in an analytical language. Says Dr. Aiken:

Each of the sentence-types—declarative, interrogative, imperative, and exclamatory—has its own normal order, but there are many exceptional orders as well. In certain constructions the verb may or must come before the subject, and frequently the complement comes before the subject, or the subject is embedded in the verb phrase. All these orders, both normal and exceptional, must somehow be mastered before the student can be said to use English properly.

As we have seen in Chapter VIII, efforts to remedy the irrationalities of English spelling have been under way for many years, but so far without much success. The improvement of English in other respects must await a revolutionist who will do for it what Mark Twain tried to do for German in "The Awful German Language"—but with much less dependence upon logic. "If English is to be a continuously progressive creation," said Krapp,[5] "then it must escape from the tyranny of the reason. . . . Suppose the children of this generation and of the next were permitted to cultivate expressiveness instead of fineness of speech, were praised and promoted for doing something interesting, not for doing something correct and proper. If this should happen, as indeed it is already beginning to happen, the English language and literature would undergo such a renascence as they have never known." Meanwhile, despite its multitudinous defects, English goes on. I began this chapter with the pessimistic realism of Richard Mulcaster, 1582. I close it with the florid vision of Samuel Daniel, only seventeen years later:

> And who in time knows whither we may vent
>   The treasure of our tongue? To what strange shores
> This gain of our best glory shall be sent,
>   T' enrich unknowing nations with our stores?
> What worlds in th' yet unformed Occident
> May come refin'd with th' accents that are ours? [6]

---

[4] English as the International Language, *AS*, Vol. IX, Apr. 1934, p. 104.
[5] The Future of English, above cited, p. 543.

[6] Musophilus, 1599. Musophilus is a dialogue between a courtier and a poet, in which the latter defends the worldly value of literary learning.

LIST OF WORDS AND PHRASES

NOTE: For nouns with irregular plurals, both the singular and plural are listed, and for irregular verbs, both the infinitive and the preterite or participle. Infinitives are indicated by *to*.

hunky, 371, 372; -dory, 121, 175; 265
hunting, 286; -grounds, 119
hur, 748 *n*
Hurbick, 584
hurd, 433
Hurlgate, 121 *n*, 649
hurrah, 460
hurricane, 274
hurry, 416, 416 *n*
hurry, to, 244
hurry up, to, 244
huse, 496
hush money, 704, 713
huskiburger, 257
husking bee, 158
hussy, 360
hustle, 729, 744
hustle, to, 269
hustler, 727
Hustler, 679
hut, 751
Hut, 724
Hutterian Brethren, 298
hutzpa, 262 *n*
Huxley, 615
hw, 445
hyar, 460
Hydramatic, 248
hydrant, 284
hyena, 675
Hyewston, 658
hygiologist, 227
-hym, 597
Hyman, 637
hymnfest, 256
hymnster, 223
hype, 722
hypercorrect, 519 *n*
hypersophic, 519 *n*
hypocrite, 444
hysen, 544
hysterical, 444

I

i, 431, 433, 438, 463, 468, 474, 479, 479 *n*, 484, 580, 658, 660, 681
i, final, 660, 661
i, long, 426, 463
i, redundant, 680
i, short, 426, 430, 438, 468, 474
i, Spanish, 659
I, 462, 463, 525, 525 *n*, 543, 553, 554, 555, 556
-ia, 681

-ian, 681
I ain't coming, 743
I am, 478
Ibach, 580
I be, 536
Ibuya, 218
-ic, 249
I can't seem, 513, 514
ic bee, 536
I.C.C., 506
ice, 222, 281, 463; -attendant, 345; -berg, 582; -box, 155, 722; -breaker, 155; -man, 155; -pick, 155; -wagon, 155; -water, 199
ice-, 154
-ice, 598
icecapade, 222
ice cream, 155, 281, 281 *n*, 562; -cone, 279 *n*; -freezer, 155; -saloon, 155; -soda, 155, 207 *n*, 270, 270 *n*
iced cream, 155, 562
iced tea, 155
iced water, 199
Icel, 622
ice-tong doctor, 725
-ich, 598
-ician, 227, 343
icky, 741
Icsylf, 557
Ida, 633
Idaho, 691
Idahoan, 680
Idahovan, 680
ídea, 417
idealer, 561
idear, 442
identification tag, 281
identity disk, 281
idiot, 705
idolatries, 358
I don't know if, 513
I don't think, 704, 705
-ie, 230, 681
iffy, 249
if I am, 536
-ific, 249
if I hadda been, 536
if I was, 536
if I were you, 536
-ify, 156, 236, 241
if you'll excuse the expression, 263
-ig, 598
Ignatz, 634
I have, 517
I is, 478

-ij, 219
I judge, 303
ik, 603, 748 *n*
Ikard, 573
Ike, 188, 211
iland, 490
ile, 438
Ilias, 640
ill, 70, 140, 287; -gotten, 540 *n*
Ill, 606
illicit relations, 366
Illinois, 658, 691 *n*
Illinoy, 658
illy, 17, 564, 565
Ilona Nagy, 594
im-, 486
-im, 262
Ima Hogg, 606
imkeeled, 19
Immaculate Conception, 678
immediately, 298
immigrant, 51, 52, 53
immigrate, to, 53, 134
immigration, 21, 53
imminent, 9
immunity bath, 182
impend, to, 10
imperialism, 184
implementation, 334
important, 433
imprescriptible, 134
improve, to, 8, 48, 51
impurities, 358
Imre, 641
in, 54, 290, 393 *n*, 525, 525 *n*, 670
in-, 241, 241 *n*
-in, 443, 486
in, to, 240
in a hellish hurry, 393
in a street, 295, 295 *n*
inaugural address, 183
inaugural ball, 183
inaugurate, to, 78 *n*, 183
inauguration ball, 183
in back of, 289, 514
in bad, 247
inbred, 417
Inc., 293
in cahoots, 155
Incarnation, 676
incidence, 559
incident, 7, 559
income engineer, 348
incommunicado, 191, 263
incomplete, to, 241
incompleted, 241
incorporated, 293

INDEX

NOTE: Reference works and scholarly publications—such as *American Speech, Dialect Notes,* and the "Dictionary of Americanisms"—are not listed for ordinary articles, but only where their editorial policies or their scope is mentioned in the text or notes. No attempt has been made to index topics listed in the Table of Contents.

A Note about the Author

H. L. Mencken was born in Baltimore in 1880 and died there in 1956. Educated privately and at Baltimore Polytechnic, he began his long career as journalist, critic and philologist on the Baltimore *Morning Herald* in 1899. In 1906 he joined the staff of the Baltimore *Sun*, thus beginning an association with the *Sun* papers which lasted until a few years before his death. He was co-editor of the *Smart Set* with George Jean Nathan from 1908 to 1923, and with Nathan he founded the *American Mercury*, of which he was sole editor from 1925 to 1933.

A Note about the Editor

Raven I. McDavid, Jr., professor of English at the University of Chicago, is a passionate admirer of Mencken's work and a distinguished linguist in his own right. The two men corresponded regularly from 1938 until Mencken suffered a stroke in 1948, and met on several occasions. McDavid provided HLM with much valuable data, especially on questions of pronunciation and dialect.

Born in Greenville, S.C., in 1911, Raven McDavid received his B.A. degree from Furman University in 1931, and his M.A. and Ph.D. degrees from Duke University in 1933 and 1935. Before taking up his present post at the University of Chicago, he taught at the University of Michigan's Linguistic Institute, at Western Reserve University and at the University of Illinois. Since 1941, he has spent thousands of hours as a field investigator for *The Linguistic Atlas of the United States and Canada*, has served as a technical assistant to several dictionary publishers and has published more than 150 technical articles and reviews, including several written jointly with his wife, who is also a linguist. His own books include *The Structure of American English* (1958), with W. Nelson Francis, and *The Pronunciation of English in the Atlantic States* (1961), with Hans Kurath.

A Note on the Type

THE TEXT of this book was set on the Linotype in
JANSON, a recutting made direct from type cast from
matrices long thought to have been made by the Dutchman Anton Janson, who was a practicing type founder
in Leipzig during the years 1668–87. However, it has
been conclusively demonstrated that these types are actually the work of Nicholas Kis (1650–1702), a Hungarian, who most probably learned his trade from the
master Dutch type founder Dirk Voskens. The type is
an excellent example of the influential and sturdy Dutch
types that prevailed in England up to the time William
Caslon developed his own incomparable designs from
these Dutch faces.

The book was printed and bound by
R. R. Donnelley and Sons Company, Crawfordsville, Indiana.

Typography based on the original design by
W. A. DWIGGINS.